10

New York Painting and Sculpture: 1940–1970

New York Painting and Sculpture: 1940-1970

BY HENRY GELDZAHLER

Curator of Contemporary Arts,
The Metropolitan Museum of Art

Foreword by Thomas P. F. Hoving

Director, The Metropolitan Museum of Art

E. P. Dutton & Co., Inc.   New York

in association with The Metropolitan Museum of Art

To the memory of two museum men:
James J. Rorimer
and René d'Harnoncourt

First Edition

No part of this publication may be reproduced or transmitted in any form or by any means, electronic
or mechanical, including photocopy, recording, or any information storage and retrieval system now
known or to be invented, without permission in writing from the publishers, except by a reviewer who
wishes to quote brief passages in connection with a review written for inclusion in a magazine, newspaper, or broadcast.

Published simultaneously in Canada by Clarke, Irwin & Company Limited, Toronto and Vancouver.

Library of Congress Catalog Card Number: 71–87179

Contents

Acknowledgments

A generous grant from the Xerox Corporation helped make this exhibition possible.

Without the help of Kay Bearman, Consultant to this exhibition, and without the encouragement of George Trescher, Secretary to the Museum's Centennial, this exhibition and its book would not have materialized.

I would like to thank Christopher Scott and Allen Rosenbaum for assistance with the introduction, Stuart Silver for his flexible ideas about installation, and Clifford La Fontaine for his maquettes.

I am grateful to Walter Hopps for securing and installing the Joseph Cornells.

Conversations with Philip Leider, Clement Greenberg, Michael Fried, John J. McKendry, and many of the lenders to the exhibition have been of great help and interest.

I would also like to mention the following people for their special cooperation in supplying material for this publication: Barbara Adler, Elita Agee, Martha Baer, Leslie Feely, Manuel E. Gonzalez, Bruce Jones, Alkis Klonaridis, Phyllis Lester, Cintra Lofting, Linda Loving, Margaret McConnell, Audrey McCowin, April McMenamin, Eric Pollitzer, Jane Salzfass, David Spangler, Jock Truman, Diane Waldman, Joan Washburn, David White, David Whitney, and Barbara Wool.

The members of my office staff worked unstintingly: Kay Bearman provided the catalogue information and the biographies; Jacquelyn Serwer the bibliography; and James Wood, Assistant Curator of the Department, has been responsible for overseeing the countless details of shipping and insurance. Karen Asakawa has been a valuable secretary.

Finally, I would like to thank Thomas P. F. Hoving and the Trustees of the Metropolitan Museum for their confidence; and the artists in the exhibition and their families for their generosity and encouragement.

Private Collectors

Harry N. Abrams Family Collection, New York
Josef Albers, New Haven, Connecticut
Mr. and Mrs. Harry W. Anderson, Atherton, California
Mr. and Mrs. Lester Francis Avnet, New York
Mr. and Mrs. E. A. Bergman, Chicago, Illinois
Mr. and Mrs. Jacob Berman, Sherman Oaks, California
Mr. and Mrs. Donald Blinken, New York
Irving Blum, Los Angeles, California
Jason Ferus Blum, Los Angeles, California
Peter Brant, New York
Mrs. Abner Brenner, Washington, D.C.
Dr. and Mrs. Bernard Brodsky, New York
Leonard M. Brown, Springfield, Massachusetts
Carter Burden, New York
Edward Carey, New York
Mr. and Mrs. Leo Castelli, New York
Mr. and Mrs. Louis D. Cohen, Great Neck, New York
Joseph Cornell, Flushing, New York
Mrs. Stuart Davis, New York
Jaime C. del Amo, Madrid, Spain
Mr. and Mrs. Edward L. Diehl, Cambridge, Massachusetts
Mrs. Elise C. Dixon, Scottsdale, Arizona
Mrs. Marcel Duchamp, New York
Mrs. Julius Epstein, Northfield, Illinois
Estate of Hans Hofmann
Estate of Franz Kline
Estate of David Smith
Mr. and Mrs. Richard L. Feigen, New York
Morton Feldman, New York
Helen Frankenthaler, New York
Mr. and Mrs. Allan Frumkin, New York
Mr. and Mrs. Victor W. Ganz, New York
Mr. and Mrs. Maurice Geller, New York
Mr. and Mrs. Milton A. Gordon, New York
Adolph Gottlieb, New York
Mrs. Esther Gottlieb, New York
Mr. and Mrs. Clement Greenberg, New York
Mrs. Albert M. Greenfield, Sr., Philadelphia, Pennsylvania
Robert Halff, Beverly Hills, California

Joseph H. Hazen, New York
Mr. and Mrs. Ben Heller, New York
Dr. and Mrs. Charles Hendrickson, Newport Beach, California
Joseph H. Hirshhorn Collection
Joseph H. Hirshhorn Foundation
Mr. and Mrs. Richard Hokin, New York
Mr. and Mrs. Norman Ives, Woodbridge, Connecticut
Mrs. Martha K. Jackson, New York
Jasper Johns, New York
Carl W. Johnson, Beverly Hills, California
Philip Johnson, New Canaan, Connecticut
Mrs. Julie Judd, New York
Dr. and Mrs. Ernest Kafka, New York
The Kleiner Foundation
Mr. J. Patrick Lannan, Palm Beach, Florida
The Lannan Foundation
Mr. and Mrs. Julien Levy, Bridgewater, Connecticut
The Albert A. List Family Collection
Mrs. H. Gates Lloyd, Haverford, Pennsylvania
Miss Lois Long, New York
Dr. Peter Ludwig, Cologne, Germany
Lewis Manilow, Chicago, Illinois
Dr. and Mrs. Edward Massie, St. Louis, Missouri
Mr. and Mrs. Robert B. Mayer, Winnetka, Illinois
Richard Meier, New York
Mr. and Mrs. David Mirvish, Toronto, Canada
Robert Motherwell, New York
Mr. and Mrs. Morton Neumann, Chicago, Illinois
S. I. Newhouse, Jr., New York
Mrs. Albert H. Newman, Chicago, Illinois
Mrs. Annalee Newman, New York
Mr. and Mrs. Kenneth Noland, New York
Mrs. Claes Oldenburg, New York
Jules Olitski, New York
Mr. and Mrs. David I. Orr, New York
Mr. and Mrs. Stephen D. Paine, Boston, Massachusetts
Dott. Giuseppe Panza di Buomo, Milan, Italy
Mrs. Betty Parsons, New York
Mrs. Barbara Reis Poe, New York
Alan Power, London, England
Mr. and Mrs. John Powers, Aspen, Colorado
Robert Rauschenberg, New York
Miss Anna Reinhardt, New York
Mrs. Rita Reinhardt, New York
Mr. and Mrs. Bernard J. Reis, New York

Dustin Rice, New York
Robert Rosenblum, New York
Mr. and Mrs. Robert A. Rowan, Pasadena, California
Lawrence Rubin, New York
William S. Rubin, New York
Steve Schapiro, New York
Mr. and Mrs. Eugene M. Schwartz, New York
Mr. and Mrs. Robert C. Scull, New York
Mr. and Mrs. Stanley K. Sheinbaum, Santa Barbara, California
Mr. and Mrs. Robert E. Simon, Jr., New York
Mr. and Mrs. Joseph Slifka, New York
Mr. and Mrs. Sonnabend, Paris, France
Mrs. Doris Starrels, Los Angeles, California
Frank Stella, New York
Mr. and Mrs. Robert A. M. Stern, New York
Mr. and Mrs. Frank M. Titelman, Altoona, Pennsylvania
Mr. and Mrs. Burton Tremaine, Meriden, Connecticut
Miss Ondine Vaughn, New York
Samuel Wagstaff, Jr., Detroit, Michigan
Mrs. Eleanor Ward, New York
Andy Warhol, New York
Albert F. Weis, Savannah, Georgia
William M. White, Jr., New York
David Whitney, New York
Donald Windham, New York
Mr. and Mrs. Lewis V. Winter, New York
The Woodward Foundation of Washington, D.C.
Mr. and Mrs. C. B. Wright, Seattle, Washington
and, in addition, several lenders who prefer to remain anonymous

Museums
Albright-Knox Art Gallery, Buffalo, New York
Allen Memorial Art Museum, Oberlin College, Oberlin, Ohio
Art Gallery of Ontario, Toronto, Canada
The Art Institute of Chicago, Chicago, Illinois
The Baltimore Museum of Art, Baltimore, Maryland
The Brooklyn Museum, Brooklyn, New York
California State College, Long Beach, California
The Cleveland Museum of Art, Cleveland, Ohio
The Connecticut Bank and Trust Company, Hartford, Connecticut
Dallas Museum of Fine Arts, Dallas, Texas
Isaac Delgado Museum of Art, New Orleans, Louisiana
The Detroit Institute of Arts, Detroit, Michigan
Everson Museum of Art, Syracuse, New York
The Solomon R. Guggenheim Museum, New York

The Israel Museum, Jerusalem, Israel
Los Angeles County Museum of Art, Los Angeles, California
Fondation Maeght, Saint Paul, France
Munson-Williams-Proctor Institute, Utica, New York
Museum of Art, Carnegie Institute, Pittsburgh, Pennsylvania
The Museum of Contemporary Art, Nagaoka, Japan
The Museum of Modern Art, New York
The National Gallery of Canada, Ottawa, Canada
Pasadena Art Museum, Pasadena, California
The San Francisco Museum of Art, San Francisco, California
Seattle-First National Bank, Seattle, Washington
University Art Museum, Berkeley, California
Victoria & Albert Museum, London, England
Wadsworth Atheneum, Hartford, Connecticut
The Walker Art Center, Minneapolis, Minnesota
Wallraf-Richartz Museum, Cologne, Germany
The Whitney Museum of American Art, New York
Yale University Art Gallery, New Haven, Connecticut

Art Galleries
Richard Bellamy, New York
Grace Borgenicht Gallery, New York
Leo Castelli Gallery, New York
Cordier & Ekstrom, Inc., New York
The Downtown Gallery, New York
Dwan Gallery, New York
Fischbach Gallery, New York
Noah Goldowsky, New York
Sidney Janis Gallery, New York
Tirca Karlis Gallery, Provincetown, Massachusetts
M. Knoedler & Company, Inc., New York
Gordon Locksley Gallery, Minneapolis, Minnesota
Lo Giudice Gallery, Chicago, Illinois
Marlborough-Gerson Gallery, New York
The David Mirvish Gallery, Toronto, Canada
Betty Parsons Gallery, New York
Perls Galleries, New York

The Metropolitan Museum of Art has been called "the most extraordinary visual encyclopedia in the Western Hemisphere." And that is what it is— stuffed with treasures, splendid with the myriad designs of all facets of art history. The treasures of the Metropolitan reach as far back in time as we can see, into all the places of the world where man has been turning his visual experience into concrete form. Man continues to bring forth visual treasures today. He will never stop.

An encyclopedia like the Metropolitan Museum is therefore never complete. It has a constant growth process and is continually being reedited and refined. Whole volumes are being added to the encyclopedia, for the Metropolitan is, for those who know it, not one museum but eighteen encompassing a span of fifty centuries of creativity.

One of the newest volumes, the most recent museum within the Metropolitan, is the Department of Contemporary Arts, instituted barely two years ago and given the duties of collecting, preserving, and exhibiting not only paintings and sculpture, but drawings, prints, furniture, period rooms, and decorative arts of the twentieth century. This department has even recently been granted the additional charge of presenting one-man shows of living artists. This was an extremely important decision by the Museum's Board of Trustees because it puts us on our mettle not to become purely academic and safe, and it ensures a continuing vitality by forcing us to keep our doors open to any style of painting and sculpture of any period that presents artistic excellence.

This extraordinary exhibition, "New York Painting and Sculpture: 1940–1970," consists of 408 works of art by forty-three gifted creators loaned from museums and private collections around the world. It is a landmark for the new Department of Contemporary Arts, being its first major effort to investigate that moment fully and deeply in a way that has never been done before. Many of these works come back to New York for the first time since they were created. The unique nature of this historical view of the New York School—the first ever undertaken on this scale—makes it imperative that this exhibition appear during our Centennial year. It is also the first exhibition of a distinguished series that will be held in a five-year period starting with the Centennial year. Through this series the Museum will attempt to illuminate for its visitors some of the key moments of five millennia of the visual arts.

"New York Painting and Sculpture: 1940–1970" has been a difficult and creative endeavor. It has been difficult because we have not had the luxury of looking back over a long period of time. The works of art of 1940–1970 are around us in profusion. Most of the artists who worked in the period are still alive and vocal. The show is creative in the curatorial sense because one man, Henry Geldzahler, endowed with a formidable visual talent has chosen 408 paintings, sculptures, and drawings of the highest character, each the most important statement in a particular moment of an artist's career. The choices have been made from literally thousands of possibilities.

Although it is conceivable that no two people would have picked anywhere near the same works of art from the New York School, 1940–1970, it is highly unlikely. Quality in any period, if it is sought after with diligence and determination, is sure to come out. Anyone who sees this show will be convinced, I believe, that the highest quality of this exciting time has been fully captured.

The exhibition, the book, and the program of lectures and concerts relating to the exhibition have been made possible through a generous grant from the Xerox Corporation. It is particularly appropriate that Xerox chose to underwrite "New York Painting and Sculpture: 1940–1970"; the corporation's own growth and success parallels exactly the period that this exhibition celebrates, and the graphic image of Xerox has always reflected the best in contemporary design. Through its generosity and enthusiasm, Xerox sets an example for other United States corporations to follow as enlightened patrons of the arts.

I know that Arthur A. Houghton, Jr., President, and Roswell L. Gilpatric, Chairman of the 100th Anniversary Committee, join me in thanking Xerox and the 165 lenders to the exhibition. Without the generosity of collectors and museums as far away as Japan and Israel, it would not have been possible to build such a comprehensive exhibition. John Macrae III and Cyril Nelson of E. P. Dutton & Co. have contributed enormously to the preparation of this book.

Finally, I want to thank Henry Geldzahler and the members of his staff of the Department of Contemporary Arts and Stuart Silver and the members of his staff of the Department of Exhibition Design for conceiving and executing the exhibition and its installation as the opening event of the Museum's Centennial celebration.

Thomas P. F. Hoving
Director

July, 1969

New York Painting and Sculpture: 1940–1970

New York Painting and Sculpture: 1940–1970

Almost thirty years have passed since Arshile Gorky and Jackson Pollock announced in their painting that a new era was breaking in American art. The augury was correct. By reason of its own achievement and the clear and indisputable effect it has had throughout the world, the art of the New York School stands as the most recent in the grand succession of modern movements from Impressionism through Cubism and Surrealism.

Much has been said about the achievement of the New York School in the past several decades. National pride and international acclaim recognize that something magnificent has happened. On the occasion of its Centennial, The Metropolitan Museum of Art celebrates this achievement with the exhibition "New York Painting and Sculpture: 1940–1970." For the first time, admirers of modern art will be able to see in this book, which is an extension of the Museum's exhibition, paintings and sculptures in large numbers by the major figures who have produced the vital sequence of moments that make the New York School the historical successor to the School of Paris, the two generations of artists who have so successfully perpetuated the vitality and innovative energy that is the hallmark of any major movement.

The limitation to New York art in this exhibition is not parochial. The term "New York art," in fact, includes most of the significant American art produced in the past three decades. The School of Paris was an umbrella that covered Russia as well as Spain. Regardless of where a work is made, unless it is primitive, anachronistic, or truly eccentric, it becomes associated with the center of its day, the city whose style it reflects. Thus we unblushingly include Morris Louis and Kenneth Noland, the acknowledged leaders of what Washington likes to call its School of Color Painters, because their exhibiting history, the sources of their art, and their most cogent influence have all been located in New York.

The fact that New York has followed Paris as the dominant center of world art does not preclude the possibility of another, even several other cities, being the loci for important art. It seems clear at this writing, as it has been for a decade, that London and Los Angeles provide the two most fertile alternatives to New York.

The New York School includes Americans born in Armenia (Arshile Gorky), Holland (Willem de Kooning), Germany (Josef Albers and Hans Hofmann), Russia (Mark Rothko), and Sweden (Claes Oldenburg), as well as three men who grew up in California (Jackson Pollock, Philip Guston, and Robert Motherwell), a Texan (Robert Rauschenberg), and a Georgian

15

(Jasper Johns). Except for Albers and Hofmann, who spent their formative years in Europe, all those named came as young men to paint or sculpt in New York.

Artists, both American and foreign, have looked to New York for much the same reasons that have always caused ambitious artists to gravitate toward contemporary cultural centers. The climate of discussion, theory, and technical advance at the center offers the opportunity for learning, testing, and growing. The teachers and schools are here, as are the accomplished artists whom they want to emulate and measure themselves against. Economic factors make New York (Paris, London, or Los Angeles) a center as well. The connoisseurs, collectors, critics, and commissioners are here, as are the art dealers, architects, and the private foundations that grant awards to artists. And perhaps most important of all, the museums and continuing gallery exhibitions that make possible the dialogue out of which significant art is produced are present in New York to an unprecedented degree.

New York stands for a style of life to the artist, a reference point, and a base of operations. Even if he is in no way associated with New York, except as one of the places he exhibits (one thinks of Mark Tobey, Sam Francis, Richard Diebenkorn, Larry Bell, and Robert Irwin, all West Coast artists), he makes the occasional talismanic visit to the city, most often simply to see what is happening. Artists of fully mature and personal styles, while their work remains largely untouched by the new, often are curious to see it just the same, for while they are passionately committed to their vision and expression, they are also disinterestedly committed to and fascinated by all art.

It is quite possible to produce great mainstream art at a distance from the center. But this is only possible (except in the rare case of the primitive) after the artist has first steeped himself in the continuous and evolving traditions which can only be absorbed in the sophisticated centers. Later, it is possible to move away, as did Georgia O'Keeffe to New Mexico and David Smith to Bolton's Landing, and continue to produce art in touch with the vital forces of the day. It is during the period of development, of formation of outlook and style, that the immediate contact with the sources of energy is necessary. These, in time, came to be built into the fiber and character of the artist, and he can, when mature, move wherever he will and carry his interiorized contemporary world with him.

Thus the true school for the young artist, once he has gained the confidence and passionate certainty to know that he wants to be a painter or a sculptor, is the ferment and activity of the center, its multiplicity of styles and its complex traditions. Over and over again in repeated studio visits over the past ten years and in many days spent in viewing students' work in provincial art schools, I have found that nothing can replace the firsthand knowledge of the

16

great works on view in New York's museums and the turmoil that follows the exhibition of new work by contemporaries and older colleagues.

In 1929, when in the face of the Metropolitan Museum's conservatism the founders of The Museum of Modern Art had the excellent idea of making advanced European art available to an American public that had been tantalized and scandalized sixteen years earlier by the Armory show, they moved with courage and energy into an educational project of great importance. History records that the job was done superbly. In fact, the Modern's educational program helped make it possible for a generation of New York-based painters and sculptors to inherit the European Modernist tradition.

In his article, "Arshile Gorky, Surrealism, and the New American Painting" (reprinted in this book), William Rubin provides a specific example of the American painter's dependence on firsthand knowledge of works of art in New York's public collections. Professor Rubin posits Gorky's knowledge of a specific Miró, the *Dutch Interior* of 1928, "a picture that was constantly on view in the permanent collection of The Museum of Modern Art and was probably a major influence on Gorky's *Garden in Sochi*," and then goes on to say that it was in the 1941 Miró retrospective held at the museum that "Gorky could observe in detail Miró's conversion from Cubism to Surrealism."

In the forties and early fifties The Museum of Modern Art and The Solomon R. Guggenheim Museum, with its excellent collection of nonobjective art, were among the daily meeting places and discussion centers for the serious artist and student who had to come to grips with Cubism and its aftermath if they were to paint in the Modernist tradition. Two factors, in addition to The Museum of Modern Art's persuasive permanent collection of modern European art, are generally recognized as having helped make New York a major international center for painting and sculpture after 1940. One was the Works Progress Administration; the other was the presence of European artists in New York during the years of World War II. W.P.A., with its various programs, was designed by the Roosevelt Administration during the years of the Depression to assist artists in surviving an economic catastrophe that had cut to virtually nothing private support of the arts. The W.P.A. programs gave artists a sense of community, shared problems, and styles of life. Out of this grew friendships and alliances, discussion groups, and several short-lived schools. W.P.A., with its resemblance to an artists' union, provided a common ground for the largely isolated American painter and sculptor. Discussions became fruitful and engaging; they developed from the artists' position in society to artists' rights, to questioning Marxism as the answer, to considerations of style, to admiration of and resistance to Picasso's overwhelming presence. Eventually, a key institution in the development of an artistic community in New York, The Club, was to be the issue and heir of the sense of shared involvement engendered

17

during the difficult years of the Depression, alleviated in some measure by the W.P.A. Among the artists who participated in the program were Jackson Pollock, Willem de Kooning, Burgoyne Diller, Arshile Gorky, Stuart Davis, and David Smith. Something of the mood of the period is revealed in David Smith's memoir:

Our hangouts were Stewart's Cafeteria 7th Ave. near 14 St close to [Stuart] Davis' studio and school and 5¢ coffee was much closer to our standards but on occasion we went to the Dutchman's, McSorley's and Romany Marie's. We followed Romany Marie from 8 St where Gorky once gave a chalk talk on Cubism, to several locations. Her place came closer to being a continental cafe with its varied types of professionals than any other place I knew. It was in Marie's where we once formed a group, [John] Graham, Edgar Levy, Resnikoff, de Kooning, Gorky and myself with Davis being asked to join. This was short lived. We never exhibited and we lasted in union about 30 days. Our only action was to notify the Whitney Museum that we were a group and would only exhibit in the 1935 abstract show if we were all asked. Some of us were, some exhibited, some didn't and that ended our group. But we were all what was then termed abstractionists.[1]

Another factor that liberated the American artist was the transfer of much of the School of Paris's energy to New York through the emigration of several of Europe's most advanced and admired artists. Léger and Mondrian and a sizable contingent of Surrealists—Marcel Duchamp, Matta, Max Ernst, Marc Chagall, Yves Tanguy, Salvador Dali, André Masson, and André Breton—spent the war years in New York and continued to produce important work here. There was something sacrosanct about the presence of these figures in New York, for they made flesh of legend and of recent art history. Mondrian and Léger, especially, continued to develop along lines that were consistent and continuous with their European work but which yet took cognizance of New York as their environment; Mondrian's *Broadway Boogie Woogie* and *Victory Boogie Woogie* are great American works by a European. The American artist, looking at the new and radical art by the Europeans executed in New York, no longer felt it was necessary to go abroad to become an artist, an American prejudice since the days of John Singleton Copley and Benjamin West. Jackson Pollock put the matter succinctly in his answer to a question put to him by an interviewer in 1944:

I accept the fact that the important painting of the last hundred years was done in France. American painters have generally missed the point of modern painting from beginning to end. (The only American master who interests me is Ryder.) Thus the fact that good European moderns are now here is very important, for they bring with them an understanding of the problems of modern painting. I am particularly impressed with their idea

[1] *David Smith by David Smith* (New York: Holt, Rinehart & Winston, 1968), p. 35.

of the source of art being the unconscious. The idea interests me more than these specific painters do, for the two artists I admire most, Picasso and Miró, are still abroad.[2]

It became clear that great international painting could be executed in New York, that there was nothing talismanic about Paris. American painters understood that artists make art wherever they are, once they have absorbed those elements of tradition they find personally useful.

The familiarity of the young American abstractionists with each other's work in the thirties and forties, fostered in part by the W.P.A.'s role as an artists' union, and gained through studio visits, informal discussions, and group shows in both galleries and museums, created a new resonance and a new level of ambition. Dependence on European models, illustrated by Miró's influence on Gorky and Pollock's frank avowal, constituted invaluable apprenticeships without which they would never have attained the independent mastery that made them the forerunners of the new American painting. These historical examples indicate that future practitioners and supporters of new art must have an opportunity to see what has been so far achieved so that they may come to terms with it and find unique ways to contribute to its perpetuation. One of the reasons French art weakened so considerably after World War II was that the key paintings and sculptures of the first half of the century were not on view in Paris. Thus, in showing the work of the New York School, we do more than honor the artists and do justice to history. That their work is on view, even relatively briefly, helps to ensure the continuation of the tradition.

New York's museums have served our artists and public well by collecting and exhibiting the key works of the Modernist tradition as it evolved in Europe between 1870 and 1940. The Metropolitan Museum's collection of Impressionist and Post-Impressionist pictures, the Modern's unparalleled history of the modern period (illustrated by originals), and the Guggenheim Museum's largely non-Parisian (Russian, Dutch, German) range of nonobjective art, form a more significant collection than that of any city in Europe. Each of these museums and The Whitney Museum of American Art have shown an awareness of the new American art as it has developed, but now, with three decades of clear historical achievement by the New York School, we must meet our responsibility to the continuing process out of which new art develops by showing the best recent art and by presenting it in conjunction with the older and more established work.

At the Metropolitan Museum there have never been funds allocated specifically for the purchase of European modern art. With the limited money

[2] Jackson Pollock, Interview (formulated by Pollock with the help of Howard Putzel), *Arts and Architecture*, Vol. 61 (February, 1944), p. 14. Francis V. O'Connor, *Jackson Pollock* (New York: The Museum of Modern Art, 1967), p. 32.

Henry Geldzahler

available, the European Paintings Department has concentrated its energies in fields less well covered in New York than the modern. The most continuous and coherent modern collection at the Metropolitan is of American painting. The reasons for this are twofold and equally important in the history of the collection. The first was the establishment of the George A. Hearn Fund (1906) and the Arthur H. Hearn Fund (1911) that were specifically earmarked for the purchase of American painting (not sculpture). The second was the magnificent Alfred Stieglitz Bequest, made in 1949, coincidentally the year that pressure by New York artists led to the founding of the Department of American Painting and Sculpture. The Stieglitz Bequest gave us an impressive collection of works by American artists who were first exhibited in Stieglitz's galleries, such as Marsden Hartley, Arthur Dove, John Marin, and Georgia O'Keeffe, together with fascinating minor works by Matisse, Picasso, Brancusi, Severini, and other European artists Stieglitz introduced into America.

With the aid of the Hearn Funds, Robert Beverly Hale, the curator of the new department, was able to make such major purchases as Pollock's *Autumn Rhythm* (illustrated page 270), and Gorky's *Water of the Flowery Mill* (illustrated page 76), both in the current exhibition. The pressure on the part of the artists that caused the creation of the department coincided quite naturally with the growth in importance of our native art. It is thus ironic but understandable that as pressure mounted to expend the Hearn Funds, the rise in prices made these funds inadequate for their purpose. Rumor persisted into the sixties that the fabulous Hearn Funds lay idle. If they did, it was so that the money could accumulate long enough to make an important purchase. When major American paintings cost eight hundred or a thousand dollars, it was possible to make many significant acquisitions with the funds' income each year. Today the income cannot purchase the tenth part of a major Pollock. Recently, accumulated income has made it possible to purchase three major paintings in the exhibition, Morris Louis's *Alpha-Pi* (illustrated page 91), Ad Reinhardt's *Red Painting* (illustrated page 102), and Barnett Newman's *Concord* (illustrated page 94), which he exhibited at his first one-man show at the Betty Parsons Gallery in 1950.

While the Metropolitan Museum has not had an extensive collection of contemporary New York art to draw upon, it was often, through the fifties and sixties, the one place in New York where several galleries were consistently devoted to the permanent exhibition of the new American painting. With the founding of the Department of Contemporary Arts in 1967 the Museum, under its new director Thomas P. F. Hoving, further committed itself to collecting and exhibiting American and international painting, sculpture, and the decorative arts of the twentieth century. In three exhibitions mounted in the past two years—James Rosenquist's mammoth *F-111*, a small show of large works

20

by Morris Louis, Kenneth Noland, and the English sculptor Anthony Caro, and five new sculptures by Jules Olitski—the Museum discovered that its size and flexibility, particularly during the current period of renovation, provided a unique opportunity to exhibit new work that has often in recent years grown in size and originality of concept beyond the normal confines of the commercial gallery.

New York's specialized museums have been so locked into complex and far-reaching exhibition schedules, which commit their time and space as much as three years into the future, that they have often been unable to serve the needs of the present. In spite of its concentration of artistic activity, New York does not provide an adequate exhibition hall, spacious, flexible, and available at fairly short notice to survey developments as they occur.

The Jewish Museum performed this essential function when it presented valuable mid-career retrospectives of the work of Helen Frankenthaler (1960), Robert Rauschenberg (1963), Jasper Johns (1964), and Kenneth Noland (1965), as well as the important sculpture exhibition called "Primary Structures" (1966), which revealed the strengths and some of the emptiness of the new Minimal sculpture. But it is clear that The Jewish Museum, with several roles to play in the community and with space that is not really adequate to the task, cannot fulfill the need for timely exhibitions all by itself.

The Metropolitan Museum's Centennial celebration has created the opportunity to see the shape of our recent tradition.

We point with optimism to increased museum attendance figures as an indication of a more interested public, and while this may be true, we should remember that statistics do not make a cultural renaissance. In the past century the increasing privacy of the artist's vocabulary and the decreasing regard for public reaction has attenuated the public for contemporary art to an alert and interested few attuned to the closest scrutiny of formal and philosophical developments that escape the inexperienced. At first, advanced art has meaning only to a small but passionate audience made up of artists and their immediate coterie. But no matter how many or how few people come through each year, the museum must continue to make the best works in the collection available to the public. It must continue to acquire and borrow the finest works of art and to present them intelligently to the real audience, to those of the newly immense public who linger and look.

Nonetheless, as a result of the heroic program of art education which began with the founding of The Museum of Modern Art and has been extended to the art departments of our schools and colleges, newspapers, periodicals, and television, advanced art is gradually being made accessible and comprehensible to the general public. But even though much of the public is unaware of the

21

presuppositions that make modern art fully comprehensible, this does not exclude the possibility of response or enthusiasm. It is only a matter of time before important changes and breakthroughs become clearer, especially as key paintings and sculptures continue to make their way into public collections. We must remember that the Impressionist paintings, which are perhaps the most universally appreciated works of art in the Metropolitan's collection, originally outraged a public goaded by hostile critics.

The second floor galleries of the Museum, usually devoted to the permanent collection of European paintings, are ideal for showing American art of the past three decades (it is in these galleries that "New York Painting and Sculpture: 1940–1970" is being housed). The juxtaposition of grand and intimate spaces provides a setting for works of art of every scale. Contrary to prevalent opinion, paintings by such artists as Jackson Pollock and Morris Louis demand the same natural light in which we are accustomed to seeing Rembrandt and Monet. The original Museum of Modern Art building of 1939 (by Edward Durell Stone and Philip L. Goodwin) and Frank Lloyd Wright's Guggenheim Museum were conceived in the thirties for easel pictures. In both buildings the natural lighting in the architects' original plans has been eliminated for reasons of expansion and taste. At the Modern, the window wall facing 53rd Street has been covered by false interior walls to increase hanging space. At the Guggenheim, Wright's combination clerestory and skylighting was eliminated when James Johnson Sweeney cantilevered paintings off the wall rather than hanging them close to the wall as was intended, necessitating a supplementary artificial lighting system.

In 1947, in his application to the John Simon Guggenheim Foundation, Jackson Pollock heralded an end to the historical situation for which these museums were designed in a prophetic statement:

I intend to paint large movable pictures which will function between the easel and mural
. . . I believe the easel picture to be a dying form, and the tendency of modern feeling is toward the wall picture or mural. I believe the time is not yet ripe for a full transition from easel to mural. The pictures I contemplate painting would constitute a halfway state, and an attempt to point out the direction of the future without arriving there completely.[3]

(By 1949 and 1950 Pollock and Barnett Newman were painting their huge, mural-sized pictures.) Philip Johnson's addition to the Modern (1962–64) and Marcel Breuer's new Whitney Museum (1966) accommodate the new large paintings and sculptures. Because of the insistence on artificial lighting in both buildings and the lack of truly generous space at the Modern, it is the Metropolitan that will serve best (until a modern museum is built with a grand,

[3] Francis V. O'Connor, *Jackson Pollock* (New York: The Museum of Modern Art, 1967), pp. 39–40.

rhythmic procession of skylight galleries) as the place in New York in which to see our own monumentally scaled art.

There are other than physical advantages to exhibiting contemporary art at the Metropolitan. The extent to which even the most radical Modern Art is continuous with and dependent upon tradition can be revealed as never before when that new art is exhibited alongside the art of the past. The isolation of Modern Art at the other museums creates an essentially artificial separation between contemporary art and the art of the past. Specialists in Modern Art too easily fall into the trap of measuring contemporary art only against itself, rather than the art of the past, the ultimate test of quality. De Kooning has said it gives him particular joy to see his work (*Easter Monday,* in the Metropolitan's permanent collection) hanging forty feet from the Rembrandts against which he must finally measure himself.

Robert Rosenblum, in his cogent article, "The Abstract Sublime," (reprinted in this book) has suggested revealing and enriching analogies between painting of the Romantic movement and the work of Jackson Pollock, Mark Rothko, Clyfford Still, and Barnett Newman. Clyfford Still is seen as an analogue to the British Romantic painter James Ward; Mark Rothko is compared to Caspar David Friedrich and Joseph Turner; and Jackson Pollock is also viewed in terms of Turner. Barnett Newman may be understood as well to participate in the Sublime, but without a specific predecessor. Such comparisons with the past are not intended to sanction or justify the achievement of these contemporaries; they enlarge our vision and enrich our experience of their work. Rosenblum's thesis demonstrates that these works breathe naturally in the history of art. The way is open to other telling analogies linking our artists with other ideas and epochs, links across history that Henri Focillon saw as families of ideas.

As curator, my guiding principles in deciding which artists to include in the exhibition "New York Painting and Sculpture: 1940–1970" have been the extent to which their work has commanded critical attention or significantly deflected the course of recent art. These "deflectors," as they may be called, are those artists who have been crucial in redirecting the history of painting and sculpture in the past three decades. My aim has been to choose works of quality and stature by those artists who have posited the major problems and solutions of our immediate tradition.

George Kubler in his stunning essay *The Shape of Time,* a work that makes Kubler a natural heir to his teacher, Henri Focillon, writes:

Every important work of art can be regarded both as a historical event and as a hard-won solution to some problem . . . The important clue is that any solution points to the existence of some problem to which there have been other solutions, and that other solutions to this

23

same problem will most likely be invented to follow the one now in view. As the solutions accumulate, the problem alters. The chain of solutions nevertheless discloses the problem.[4]

The innovative artist in his grasp of a new possibility inevitably alters the problem and therefore deflects the tradition through his solution. The current exhibition was conceived as an accumulation of thirty years of solutions to a constantly changing set of problems—problems and solutions that make up a vital tradition.

Forty-three artists are represented in this giant exhibition. Not even at the height of the High Renaissance, Impressionism, or Cubism has anything like this number of artists finally seemed crucial to the development of the art of their time. Arshile Gorky, Jackson Pollock, and David Smith today look like the giants of their epoch, and a safer and more classical show could have been mounted devoted to their work alone. But we are celebrating a fortunate era of plentitude, and it is this sense of plentitude I hope to re-create in the current exhibition.

At a later time, one might well look back to reconsider and reevaluate, to see different clusters and configurations of artists and movements. Many artists of quality have not been included in the exhibition. One thinks of the American Surrealism of William Baziotes and Theodore Stamos; the Abstract Expressionism of Richard Poussette-Dart, James Brooks, Jack Tworkov, Conrad Marca-Relli, Joan Mitchell, and Al Leslie; the abstractions of Rollin Crampton, Robert Goodenough, Jack Youngerman, Cy Twombly, Ray Parker, Al Held, and Friedel Dzubas; the Abstract-Expressionist sculpture of Herbert Ferber, Seymour Lipton, Theodore Roszak, Raoul Hague, and Reuben Nakian; the figuration of Larry Rivers and Alex Katz; and the full Pop Art of Tom Wesselmann, Jim Dine, Marisol, and Robert Indiana. All these artists will be remembered and collected and, like the art in the exhibition, will be reevaluated by each successive generation of artists, critics, museum men, collectors, and the general public in that process in which the history of taste merges indistinctly with the history of art.

"New York Painting and Sculpture: 1940–1970" has been limited to artists whose distinctive styles emerged and were viewed before 1965 in galleries, group shows, and museums. This by no means indicates a lack of interest in subsequent developments. But the making of reputations and the discovery of new talent is not the role of the Metropolitan. Three young artists, Edward Avedisian, Walter Darby Bannard, and the Californian, Ron Davis, for example, have each grown rapidly in accomplishment and stature, but the record of their achievement is not yet clear and they are not included in the current exhibition.

[4] George Kubler, *The Shape of Time* (New Haven: Yale University Press, 1962), p. 33.

It has been the Whitney Museum's function, especially during the fifties and sixties when so much varied work was on view every year in New York's many galleries, to recapitulate the season, impartially, in the mammoth Annuals devoted in alternate years to sculpture and painting. While the Whitney emphasized perhaps too much the provincial and regional aspects of American art, it provided a forum in the thirties and forties for our internationally minded abstract artists before they had an audience to support them. (The Whitney Museum held a show of American abstract art in 1935.) It was at the Whitney Museum, when it was on Eighth Street, that I saw the Arshile Gorky Retrospective in 1951, which convinced me of the emotional power in contemporary abstract art.

From its founding, the Whitney has had a sense of responsibility and fairness to all the styles that at any moment make up the totality of contemporary art. This sense of fairness has always made the annual exhibitions of painting and sculpture at the Whitney anthologies rather than attempts to define styles and emphasize quality. For many of us growing up in New York, the Whitney Annual was always a much-anticipated event, for it allowed us to see in one large exhibition much of the best that was being produced along with the most stagnant, least provocative art imaginable. Thus the viewer was thrown into the healthful turmoil of doing what some consider the museum's job—of deciding, comparing, rejecting, and accepting until he felt, often after several visits to the same Annual, that he was able to find his own way to what constituted quality in contemporary American art.

"New York Painting and Sculpture: 1940–1970" is not a general inventory of the past three decades but an evaluation, a sorting out of major themes and figures. This exhibition represents my view of the historic impulse that produced such continued excitement and high achievement in the past three decades.

The Museum of Modern Art's program is to illustrate art history, applying historical methodology into and through the twentieth century up to the most recent movement which can be dealt with historically, Abstract Expressionism. The Museum of Modern Art was founded in the nineteen twenties to take up the slack left by the Metropolitan Museum whose coverage of the history of art ended with the Impressionists. Alfred Barr and his staff put together the world's finest collection of painting and sculpture of the period from 1870 to 1940, which from one point of view may be seen as a discrete historical entity entitled "The Modern Period." In two exhibitions in 1936, "Cubism and Abstract Art" and "Fantastic Art, Dada and Surrealism," and in the accompanying catalogues, Alfred Barr formulated the sequence of movements and pinpointed the great works of the twentieth century up to that time, setting the

25

standard for subsequent scholars. With "The New American Painting and Sculpture: The First Generation," held in the summer of 1969, William Rubin assembled an exhibition consistent with the policy established by Alfred Barr.

The Museum of Modern Art deals with history as a continually closing system up to the point where there is sufficient data and perspective to tell the story convincingly. Collecting paintings at the Metropolitan in the past century has been geared to the values of the connoisseur-collector rather than to those of the systematic historian. Thus, while the result of what might be termed a century of the leisurely accumulation of works of art has led to a persuasive survey of the history of art, the collection was not formed systematically. This informality makes it possible to bring together works of art from the standpoint of both the historian and the connoisseur.

The current exhibition has been planned in a similarly open spirit. There is a danger that in acceding to the demands of historical processing, we may fail to do justice to the present. Far from closing the books on the Abstract Expressionists, we celebrate the continuing vitality of the New York School. Several of the artists in the exhibition, well known for successful work in an earlier manner, are currently extending their visions and reputations into the present with some of their best work; Robert Motherwell's new "Open" series of 1968 and 1969 will be seen in retrospect as essential to a clear understanding of his achievement as are the well-known Spanish Elegies (three works from his new series are in the current exhibition); Adolph Gottlieb has turned to sculpture for the first time (the two pieces shown here are his first sculptures to be seen publicly in New York); and Barnett Newman has opened new vistas with his recent paintings in triangular format, which relate to his sculptures, *Here I* and *Here III* (both illustrated page 244). Among the younger men, Kenneth Noland's new horizontal stripe paintings and Jules Olitski's low-lying sprayed aluminum sculptures are as subtle and as full of implications for the future as anything in the art of the past decade. Invariably, artists want to feature their most recent work. It is understandable that as they change and develop they naturally feel closest to their most recent styles.

New work by established artists is judged, praised, or faulted with even greater rigor than that of the fledgling. There are no safe reputations in Modern Art. The same dialogue that leads so productively to the constant renewal of tradition makes of each new departure an adventure and a dare. The art of the past seems more orderly; critics and historians have marshaled the facts for us, and our sense of quality is aided by perspective. It is possible to clarify the art of a past, closed historical period. New work is judged qualitatively almost as if it were discontinuous with everything done before. While the critical process in which the new art is dissected, in which rules change as fast as new problems and solutions are set, is exhilarating and rigorous it is also seemingly chaotic and shapeless except to the few who are continually in touch and in sympathy with it.

The art historian and critic, Michael Fried, extends the historical approach beyond Abstract Expressionism to an analysis of the achievements of Morris Louis, Kenneth Noland, Jules Olitski, the English sculptor Anthony Caro, and Frank Stella, and deals convincingly with the sources and achievements of these artists, who continue the Modernist tradition in abstract art (see his essay, "Shape as Form: Frank Stella's New Paintings," reprinted in this book). Pollock and Newman are seen not only as great artists in their own time but as problem setters whose new ideas enriched the possibilities in abstraction. Louis, Noland, Olitski, Caro, and Stella can then be seen as taking the hint, providing solutions to some of the questions raised by the older generation.

Clement Greenberg, whose writings both Rubin and Fried acknowledge, and whose essay is also included in this book, has been the most acutely perceptive observer of and commentator on American painting and sculpture during the years covered by the current exhibition. His greatness has been not only in recognizing the achievement of Pollock and Gorky in the early forties, Newman, Rothko, and Still in the fifties, and Louis, Noland, and Olitski in the late fifties and sixties, but also in locating them in terms both of their uniqueness and their place in a tradition that Greenberg, more than anyone else, has revealed as a continually vital one.

While the process by which journalists come to terms with the art of the past decade has accelerated, many continue to be hostile to most recent art on first consideration. Time and again they lament the choice of artists representing the United States at Venice, São Paulo, or the international world's fairs, never suggesting alternate artists, who would, in their opinion, better represent our culture abroad. We miss the fierce and positive dialogue of the European journalists. In this country one must turn to the art magazines, which presuppose a greater degree of sophistication and commitment than do the dailies and Sunday supplements.

During the period covered by the current exhibition, four art magazines have served as forums in the presentation and interpretation of the new art, thus making it available to a much wider audience than could frequent the studios, galleries, and clubs whose exclusive concern was the new art. *Art News*, under Thomas B. Hess since the mid-forties, has consistently covered the art world, often with relish (Abstract Expressionism), sometimes with disdain (Pop Art), but always fully and with copious illustrations. *Arts Magazine*, under Hilton Kramer in the fifties and early sixties, devoted extensive coverage to the new art with Donald Judd as a regular contributor. James Fitzsimmons' Swiss-based *Art International* has covered both European and American art since

27

The latest entry into the field, *Artforum,* was founded in California in the early sixties and moved to New York in June, 1967, to observe the scene better in the person of its editor Philip Leider. No clearer record of these decades exists or is likely to exist than the issues of these magazines. Not only are the major figures treated often and in depth, but there is also much to learn about the context in which their art was produced, about fellow artists who struck off in other directions, often personal and eccentric, but fruitful nonetheless. Critical positions are stated with passion and vigor, artists' statements abound, and the rise and fall of minor reputations alongside the constant rise of the major ones make fascinating reading.

Making one's way intelligently through the maze of art produced in our time has been complicated unnecessarily by journalistic simplifications, attempts on the part of the various media to make sense of the new on a popular level. An example of a phrase coined by a journalist in the effort to encapsulate the art of the mid-sixties in New York was the nonsensical and unhistorical impression fostered by *Time* magazine that Op Art followed Pop Art. This is cute, memorable, and untrue. Duchamp, Albers, Max Bill, and Vasarely, among many others, were producing art in the twenties, thirties, and forties, one element of which was a concern with optical effects, as everyone conversant with these developments knows, and as anyone can learn from a casual perusal of the art periodicals of the period.

The mass media with their concern for immediacy and emphasis on the current moment make it imperative that we recall the simple historical truth that it is the total career, not merely the novel moments that matter. Bonnard developed the elements of his style in the 1890s and went on to paint beautiful pictures until his death in 1947. His style changed somewhat over the years, but the changes were gradual and internal, and they had nothing to do with fashion or with contemporary movements (Cubism, then Surrealism) which seemed at the time to be the only styles in which a vital artist could work. When we organize a Bonnard show today, it is not only that first innovative decade of the 1890s we consider, but also the total evolution of a style that encompassed fifty years.

I well remember in the late 1950s being shocked to hear painters, who believed in the primacy of de Kooning's position and who admired him, wondering aloud whether next year's show would repeat his success, whether he could consolidate his lead not by painting a beautiful show but by changing in an unexpected and unpredictable way. Pollock and Kline were also under this kind of pressure, which is cruel and destructive even for the strongest character. Fortunately, the younger generation has had the example of the successful Abstract Expressionists before them and are much less vulnerable than were the artists in the fifties, the first to sit on this particular griddle.

It was not until the nineteenth century that a regular, professional art critic became necessary to interpret current painting to the public. The artist of the Renaissance, the Baroque, and the eighteenth century painted for an educated, enlightened, and enfranchised class of art connoisseurs, the aristocracy and the church hierarchy of the period before the French Revolution. His audience was clearly defined and there was a shared body of knowledge, literary and artistic, that patron and artist took for granted. Thus if a myth were referred to in a painting, or more likely, if a painting were commissioned to illustrate a favorite, personally meaningful myth, no educated viewer found it incomprehensible; at times a complicated literary painting might be an elegant visual puzzle, but there was a correct answer and it could be worked out. With the loss of a literary apparatus we have the beginnings of Modernism which Clement Greenberg defines as ". . . the use of the characteristic methods of a discipline to criticize the discipline itself, not in order to subvert it, but in order to entrench it more firmly in its area of competence."[5] Artistic problems become the subject of art. It is then not surprising that the media and the journalists jumped at the chance to write about Pop Art and Minimal Sculpture, for both these styles are theatrical. The cooler art of Newman, Rothko, Louis, and Noland is undeniably more difficult for the critic who, by his very nature, is reduced to words. An art that is antiexpressionistic and nongeometric, that makes no references to nature or literature and is comprehensible only in the context of Modernist art, is tremendously difficult to write about. This very difficulty may well have contributed to its greater staying power. It has been allowed to remain visual; the impact is still in the works themselves, whereas art that has news value must necessarily run the risk of becoming, in time, stale news.

It seemed for a while that the gallery system, with its biennial exhibitions of each artist's work, was implicated with the media in applying the false urgency of Hollywood to the fine arts. Certain galleries were open to criticism for playing to an audience overeager to spot trends, rising reputations, and falls from favor. It appeared to many that new shows by even the most established artists were conceived more in response to the demands of fashion than art. Before the galleries were discovered by the media, several major artists, David Smith, Barnett Newman, and Clyfford Still, among others, had broken ties with their dealers and started to sell their work privately to individuals and to museums. By breaking away from galleries, these artists freed themselves of confining relationships and commissions often as high as fifty percent. During the sixties the gallery system in itself came to be pictured as sordid and commercial, at best a necessary evil. The idea has grown among a group of radical younger

[5] Clement Greenberg, "Modernist Painting," *Arts Yearbook 4* (1961), p. 103.

men that the system is parasitic and overcommitted to established styles in painting and sculpture. In addition, contemporary art has continued to grow in scale and conception defying the physical limits of the conventional gallery, which, in a sense, reproduces the intimacy of the home. Some new art, such as Frank Stella's forty-foot paintings and Mark di Suvero's huge constructed sculptures, too big for galleries, looks better and can be better viewed in the studio, warehouse, museum, or exhibition hall than in the commercial gallery.

However, looking back over the exhibiting history of the postwar period, it is clear that the art dealers performed an invaluable service in supporting artists and in making art available. In the last twenty years younger artists in search of the inspiration and challenge necessary to their development have had to shift their attention away from the museums to the only place where new and advanced art has been systematically exhibited, the commercial art galleries. The galleries play more than an amusing social role in the history of the period, they have served as school, forum, and news transmitter to the community interested in the complex course art has taken. The dealer who is alert to quality, who has committed himself early and clearly to the new art, has risked ego, prestige, and money, and must finally be considered a minor cultural hero.

In 1942 the gallery became the focal point for the artists and their immediate coterie, which comprised their total audience at the time, when Peggy Guggenheim, encouraged by the presence of the Surrealists in New York, among them her husband Max Ernst, opened her gallery called Art of This Century. She gave one-man shows to Jackson Pollock (1943, 1945, 1947), Hans Hofmann (1944), Robert Motherwell (1944), and Mark Rothko (1945), as well as to such Europeans as Jean Helion, Hans Arp, Max Ernst, Alberto Giacometti, and Theo Van Doesburg, exhibiting the work of these Americans in the more sophisticated context of European art. After the war Art of This Century was closed and Peggy Guggenheim moved to Venice.

The postwar New York market for European Modernist art and the growing challenge of New York's own artists led to the opening of two more galleries in the forties, those of Samuel Kootz in 1945 and Sidney Janis in 1948. Kootz's first triumph was in bringing back recent Picassos from liberated France to an American audience that had been deprived during the war years of the work of an artist they regarded as a hero. By the late forties Kootz was also exhibiting William Baziotes, Robert Motherwell, Hans Hofmann, David Hare, and Adolph Gottlieb. Janis opened with a stable dominated by European Cubists and Surrealists including Léger, Kandinsky, Delaunay, Mondrian, and Henri Rousseau, all of whom were given one-man shows. Collectors whose eyes had been trained by The Museum of Modern Art bought works that later ended up there as gifts or on loan, as did Mr. Janis's own collection. Janis's original list of Europeans was gradually complemented by the addition of a number of American artists who had proved themselves in previous gallery exhibitions; first Josef Albers in 1949, followed by Pollock in 1952, de Kooning and Arshile Gorky in 1953, Rothko in 1955, Philip Guston and Franz Kline in 1956, and Motherwell in 1957. Janis has continued to change with the times. In the sixties, after putting together the first show of Pop Art, which he called, in the French manner, The New Realism, he has shown the work of Claes Oldenburg, George Segal, Jim Dine, and Marisol, as well as such abstractionists as Ellsworth Kelly and Richard Anuszkiewicz. Two other dealers who also contributed to the density and richness of exhibition life in New York in the 1950s were Charles Egan who showed Jack Tworkov, Reuben Nakian, Kline, Guston, Joseph Cornell, and Robert Rauschenberg, all between 1952 and 1955, and Eleanor Ward whose Stable Gallery exhibited Conrad Marca-Relli, Joan Mitchell, Cy Twombly, Larry Rivers, John Graham, Myron Stout, Isamu Noguchi, Joseph Cornell, and James Brooks in the fifties, and Richard Stankiewicz, Andy Warhol, and Robert Indiana in the sixties.

Betty Parsons' first gallery, the Wakefield, was in a bookstore. She opened in 1940 and showed Walter Murch (1941), Alfonso Ossorio (1941, 1943), Joseph Cornell (1942), Saul Steinberg (1943), Constantine Nivola (1943), Theodore Stamos (1943), and Adolph Gottlieb (1944). Between 1944 and 1946, as director of the Mortimer Brandt Gallery, she gave one-man shows to John Graham, Theodore Stamos, Hedda Sterne, Alfonso Ossorio, Hans Hofmann, Mark Rothko, and Ad Reinhardt. In her continuing capacity as director of the Betty Parsons Gallery she has been responsible for presenting the committed art public with some of its most memorable moments, among them Pollock's 1948 exhibition in which he showed pictures such as *Cathedral* (illustrated page 269), a painting that announced his most radically innovative period (Pollock had shows at Parsons in 1948, 1949, 1950, and 1951). She was also responsible for Barnett Newman's two one-man shows of 1950 (which included *Concord* [illustrated page 94] and *Covenant* [illustrated page 239]) and 1951, which introduced a powerful new voice into contemporary art. (He was not to show again in New York until his French and Company exhibit in 1958.) With Rothko, Still, and Reinhardt, Newman offered a viable alternative to the full-blown painterly abstraction that seemed to typify the style of the fifties. The austerity of Newman's work, his refusal to employ tired devices in even their most elemental form, gave him an extremely limited audience through the fifties (Clement Greenberg, Betty Parsons, Tony Smith, and some fellow artists), until another generation of painters, Louis, Noland, and Stella among them, referred to him in their work. His vertical stripe, or "zip" as he prefers to call it, denies both Cubism and geometry, two of the staple props of abstract

31

art before him. Betty Parsons also showed Clyfford Still (1947, 1950, 1951), Ad Reinhardt (twelve times between 1946 and 1965), Bradley Walker Tomlin (1950, 1953), Robert Rauschenberg (1951), and Ellsworth Kelly (five times between 1956 and 1963). The Betty Parsons Gallery continues to provide a forum for both older and younger artists.

Leo Castelli opened his gallery in 1957 with a group show made up largely of European masters, but which included de Kooning, Pollock, and David Smith, thus indicating the possibility of a drift toward the Americans in whom Castelli had been interested since the forties. In 1957–58 Castelli showed Marisol, Jasper Johns, Robert Rauschenberg, and Friedel Dzubas, in 1958–59 Esteban Vicente and Gabriel Kohn, and in 1959–60 he represented Frank Stella, Cy Twombly, John Chamberlain, Lee Bontecou, and Jack Tworkov in group and one-man shows. Since then he has added James Rosenquist, Andy Warhol, Roy Lichtenstein, Larry Poons, Donald Judd, and, most recently, Dan Flavin. Like Janis, Castelli runs a gallery that reflects the growth and change of the American scene.

André Emmerich through the sixties showed the work of Morris Louis, Kenneth Noland, Helen Frankenthaler, and Jules Olitski. (Olitski's history demonstrates the complexity of many artists' gallery associations. Before showing with Emmerich he had been with Iolas, French and Company, and Poindexter. He is now represented by the Lawrence Rubin Gallery.) Two "blue chip" galleries currently represent many of the original generation of the New York School. The Pollock Estate, the David Smith Estate, the Kline Estate, Rothko, Guston, Motherwell, and Gottlieb exhibit at Marlborough-Gerson, while M. Knoedler and Company handles Newman, de Kooning, and the Gorky Estate.

One of the most fascinating galleries of the sixties was Richard Bellamy's Green Gallery. Its greatest strength was in Bellamy's constant search for new talent, a search not enough dealers are willing to undertake. Bellamy made countless tours of studios and subsequently exhibited for the first time James Rosenquist, Larry Poons, Lucas Samaras, Robert Morris, and Donald Judd and gave the first uptown shows to Tom Wesselmann, Claes Oldenburg, and Dan Flavin, the first sculpture show to George Segal, and the first American show to the British painter Richard Smith. He accomplished all this in about five years. The Green Gallery worked, in effect, as a talent scout for the larger and more established dealers. Today, former Green Gallery artists show at Sidney Janis, Leo Castelli, The Pace Gallery, and Richard Feigen. Bellamy has become a private dealer.

The 1964 and 1966 Venice Biennales and the 1965 São Paulo Bienal were the occasions for attacks on the art dealers because nearly all the artists chosen to represent the United States came from four galleries: Leo Castelli, André

32

Emmerich, Sidney Janis, and The Pace Gallery. (Alan Solomon was United States Commissioner in 1964 at Venice; he showed Louis, Noland, Rauschenberg, Johns, Stella, Chamberlain, Oldenburg, and Dine. Walter Hopps chose the artists for the 1965 São Paulo Bienal: Barnett Newman, Larry Poons, Donald Judd, Frank Stella, Larry Bell, Billy Al Bengston, and Robert Irwin. In 1966 I chose Helen Frankenthaler, Jules Olitski, Ellsworth Kelly, and Roy Lichtenstein to represent the United States at the Venice Biennale.) This should have been in no way surprising. In the past hundred years in which advanced art and the gallery system have coexisted there has never been more than a handful of galleries at any one time prepared to show the best, most innovative work of the moment. With the Impressionists and the Post-Impressionists the galleries were Durand Ruel, Bernheim Jeune, and Wildenstein; Kahnweiler was, at first, almost the exclusive dealer for the Cubists; the Abstract Expressionists, as we have seen, were launched by Peggy Guggenheim, then by Charles Egan, Betty Parsons, Samuel Kootz, and Sidney Janis. It is clearly more important to represent the United States at these international exhibitions and world's fairs by the best being done than to be concerned with an equitable distribution among dealers.

While the total self-interest of New York's real-estate industry, for example, is contributing to the destruction of the city, this same self-interest in the economics of the art world may finally benefit the public. A work of art often makes its way from the privacy of the artist's studio, through the gallery, to the collector, and finally to the museum. The general public is excluded from purchasing and living with much of the best art being produced in our society, for it is in short supply in relation to the number of potential owners, and because it is expensive. Ironically enough, these very factors, scarcity and price, inevitably help speed paintings and sculptures into museums and other public situations where they become available to the widest possible audience. Our tax laws make it sensible for the wealthy to give works of art to museums, and our social structure makes it attractive to be associated with a museum. These tax laws are a major factor in the rapidly increasing number of museums in the United States and in the continuing expansion of existing institutions. While works of art are sometimes bought cheap and sold dear, or are accumulated in the drive toward upward social mobility, there are also many collectors who love art, and are willing to share it with others.

We need not turn to ancient times to find knotty problems of precedence, dating, and sequence in art. The years 1948–50 in New York provide them in abundance. Future historians will inherit the task of unraveling the intricacies of these years. What is clear is that Gorky and Pollock opened the way for a generation of abstract artists. Gorky pushed the European biomorphic tradition beyond the influence of Picasso, Miró, and Matta. Pollock's mastery of the controlled accident, his ability to project his style with both gesture and exactitude on a broad, allover surface created a new level of expectation that served as an inspiration to the artists who followed. These steps in large part made it possible to shed the Surrealist preconceptions of small format and multiple elements that were, before 1948, the hallmarks of American abstraction.

David Smith's career spanned three decades, from the Picasso–Gonzalez inspired thirties to the close relationship with the new American abstraction in the sixties, specifically with the work of Kenneth Noland. Smith subsumed and surpassed his sources, as did Gorky, to create a body of work that stands indisputably with the best sculpture of the modern period. The late and glorious "Cubi" and planar pieces in stainless steel, such as *Becca* (illustrated page 107) and "Untitled" (illustrated page 312), have buffered surfaces reminiscent of the activated plane of Pollock's allover painting. The painted pieces of his last years (with endless changes of color in the attempt to get it "right") comment upon and learn from the color painting of the sixties.

His love of materials, the joy with which he contemplated and then extended their possibilities, shines through in his writing:

Steel . . . can be stainless, painted, lacquered, waxed, processed and electroplated with molybdenum. It can be cast. Steel has mural possibilities which have never been used. It has high tensile strength, pinnions can support masses, soft steel can bend cold, both with and across its grain, yet have a tensile strength of 30,000 lbs. to one square inch. It can be drawn, cupped, spun and forged. It can be cut and patterned by acetylene gas and oxygen and welded both electrically and by the acetylene oxygen process. It can be chiseled, ground, filed and polished. It can be welded the seams ground down leaving no evidence. The welds can possess greater strength than the parent metal. It can be formed with various metals by welding, brazing and soldering. Metals fall naturally to my use and [are] useful to my concept.[6]

Language for Smith was another joyous material.

In the mid- and late fifties it looked to many as if de Kooning would dominate painting for a significant time to come. A group of small galleries sprang up on East Tenth Street devoted to artists later called Second Generation Abstract Expressionists; much of their work derived its impulse and borrowed some of its energy from de Kooning's manner in the mid-fifties, the wide, slashing abstractions that look tame and lovely now, but seemed raw and angry then. It was to artists such as Alfred Leslie, Michael Goldberg, Grace Hartigan, and Norman Bluhm that Sam Hunter referred when he wrote in 1958:

[6] *David Smith by David Smith* (New York: Holt, Rinehart & Winston, 1968), p. 53.

There is no single figure who has exerted greater influence on American painting over the past decade [than de Kooning]; he is directly responsible for the general physiognomy of much of the painting of the rising generation.[7]

While de Kooning's personal contribution has been great, the line he fathered, as it turns out, was not the fertile one. De Kooning himself retired from the scene to East Hampton to work almost exclusively on the "Women," a unifying theme in his work since the late thirties.

There was a richer vein to be explored in the implications suggested by the works of Newman, Rothko, Reinhardt, and Diller, which were to engage the cooler sensibilities of the younger abstractionists such as Stella, Judd, Morris, Poons, and Flavin. And in the late fifties another alternative to Abstract Expressionism emerged—first around the Reuben Gallery on the Lower East Side, then uptown at the Green Gallery, Castelli, and the Stable—the Happenings and the new painting and sculpture with recognizable subject matter derived from contemporary mass culture, which came to be known as Pop Art.

The imagery of Pop Art can be seen as the new American landscape. Landscape painting has always selected, idealized, and described man's environment. The subject of landscape has shifted from nature to urban life in the twentieth century, and Pop Art, in its development since 1960, has used the close-up technique of film on the artifacts and data of contemporary communication, making billboards, comic strips, packaging, picture magazines, and advertising the legitimate subjects of an art that is peculiarly American and of our decade.

No movement in the history of American art was named and received more quickly. A year after it hit the galleries and magazines, I had an air conditioner installed in my apartment. An Andy Warhol painting of six Marilyn Monroes was leaning against a wall. "What's that, Pop Art?" the air-conditioner man asked. Can you imagine someone in a similar situation in 1950, asking of a Jackson Pollock, "What's that, Abstract Expressionism?" For one thing, Pop Art was literally named before it began (Lawrence Alloway coined the phrase for certain English painters in the late 1950s), while the art of Pollock, Kline, and de Kooning was called Action Painting, New York School Painting, and still other names before it settled down as Abstract Expressionism.

Pop Art was radical and came as a surprise, yet somehow the American public was responsive to it. This, of course, became clear only after the fact. Nobody could have predicted it. There were critics in the fifties crying for a return to the figure, for a "new humanism." What they were hoping for was something comfortable and recognizable, a resuscitation of the art of the past veiled in the flaying brushstrokes of Abstract Expressionism. When they got their new figuration, it was not the tortured humanism of the postnuclear world

[7] Sam Hunter, "The United States," *Art Since 1945* (New York: Harry N. Abrams, 1958), p. 284.

35

for which they were longing but an art based on billboards, comic strips, and advertising. These critics cried "foul," and they cried it hard and long. Adolph Gottlieb has written, "Certain people always say we should go back to nature. I notice they never say we should go forward to nature. It seems to me they are more concerned that we should go back, than about nature." [8]

The situation in painting in New York in the late fifties offered the possibility of a return to representational art that would be both contemporary and meaningful. After two decades of tremendous energy and inventiveness in abstract painting, the reintroduction of recognizable content (objects, landscape, and figure) appeared at first *retardataire* and beside the point. The best and most mature artists at the time had created personal and distinct abstract manners and images. These men left little room for the younger artist dissatisfied with the choice between the manner of de Kooning and, let us say, Philip Guston.

Robert Rauschenberg pointed a way out of this dilemma by the mid-fifties by incorporating real objects in his work. Instead of representing a goat—that is, attempting to translate a goat into a two-dimensional painted image, Rauschenberg included the goat itself (stuffed, but only slightly less a goat for that). There was ample precedent for Rauschenberg's gesture, in kind if not in degree. His point of departure was collage, by then an eminently respectable Cubist technique, incorporating bits and pieces of reality such as newspaper and rope in works of art, a technique that Rauschenberg logically extended. Kurt Schwitters set the most specific precedent for Rauschenberg, as did Marcel Duchamp for Jasper Johns.

Younger than Rauschenberg, Jasper Johns, forms, with him, the bridge between Abstract Expressionism and Pop Art. Rauschenberg incorporated real objects and photographs in his work, imbedded in a matrix of brushed and spilled paint that was clearly Abstract Expressionist. Johns created images of objects that we know to be two-dimensional, flags, maps, numbers, and targets. The integrity of these objects in his work made it possible for the Pop artists to separate them from Johns's painterly style that was characteristic of the fifties. The Pop artists of the sixties (Warhol, Rosenquist, Oldenburg, Lichtenstein) seized upon the recognizable image and dropped the painterly style of the previous decade.

Just as Surrealism retreated from the almost frightening formal innovations and implications of Cubism (and its aftermath) to new subject matter (Freudianism and the interpretation of dreams), so Pop Art coming some fifteen years after another formal explosion, Abstract Expressionism, stepped back to legitimize another subject, the imagery of advertising and the mass media. Of course, there had been precursors in the history of art for both Surrealism and Pop Art. In the case of Pop, Duchamp, Schwitters, Gerald Murphy, Léger, and Stuart

[8] "The Ides of Art," *The Tiger's Eye*, Vol. 1, no. 2. (December, 1947), p. 43.

Davis may be cited. But the exclusive concern with comic strips, billboards, television commercials, and newspaper advertising in the fine arts of painting and sculpture was new in American art in 1959 and 1960. Both Surrealism and Pop Art were, to some extent, respites from problems of form; both returned to representation, distorted and dreamlike in the case of Surrealism, outsized and commercial in Pop Art.

Pop Art is seen by some to be radically different from the post-Abstract-Expressionist painting of the sixties by Noland, Stella, Kelly, and Frankenthaler. But art of any given period shares certain stylistic presuppositions no matter how varied it may seem in its time. The abstract painting of Olitski, Noland, and Frankenthaler and the Pop paintings of Lichtenstein, Warhol, and Rosenquist will come in time to look typical of the 1960s in New York. All have been concerned with the large canvas, the simple, flat, close-up image of the movie screen, all have used the new brilliant plastic colors. The aesthetic permission to project immense Pop images derives in part from these artists' awareness of the most advanced abstract art.

The tradition of American abstract painting and sculpture of the past three decades is still very much alive, both in the continuing work of the established masters and in the younger men who emerge every few years, making clear the ongoing vitality of abstract art. It seems today that Pop Art was an episode, an interesting one that has left its mark on the decade, and will continue to affect the future, but not a major modern movement which continues to spawn new artists. In fact, just about everything new and original in Pop Art was stated by a few artists in the first years of its existence. Since then no artists of first importance have been recruited and no second generation has come along. There is a strong possibility that the second generation of potential Pop artists has been fed directly into television and advertising, thus repaying art's debt to the media. Just as Surrealism continues to haunt Modernist art, cropping up as an influence in unexpected places, for example, New York painting of the 1940s, so Pop Art may well find its converts and adherents in unexpected future corners and pockets of major art.

Donald Judd, Robert Morris, and Dan Flavin are both the leading theoreticians of Minimal Sculpture and its most accomplished practitioners. Tony Smith, an architect whose involvement with the New American Painting dates from the late forties (he was among the first to realize the implications in the work of both Pollock and Newman), brings a richer and longer experience to his sculpture, making it more resonant and, conversely, less purely Minimal. This new sculpture of the sixties shares several of its presuppositions with the paintings of Burgoyne Diller, Ad Reinhardt, and Frank Stella; all chose to eliminate from their work the roughness of surface and eccentric evidences of

37

personality they associated with previous art. The Minimal sculptors strive for anonymity of craftsmanship, a clear projection of simple formal relationships, and a suppression of "signature."

The Minimal sculptors prefer to use common industrial material and processes, much as the Pop artists use common images and commercial techniques. Aluminum, fiberglas, and sheets of colored transparent plastic are their typical materials, materials which are familiar enough, but not in the context of sculpture. Dan Flavin uses light, first incandescent, now fluorescent, to create memorable icons with a minimum of construction and a minimum of compositional effects characteristic of the movement. Minimal Sculpture relies, for the most part, on three-dimensional geometric forms such as the cube; it avoids figurative references—it never stands on two legs—it hangs from the wall, leans in a corner, or sits foursquare on the floor. While the Pop artists still most often do their own work, these new sculptors are not sentimental about the artist's hand or touch. In fact, many of their pieces are fabricated industrially. Minimal Sculpture is the most recent movement in American art with a coherent body of work and a sizable critical literature.

This has been a brief recapitulation of what I consider to be the importance of the New York School as seen both in this book and in the exhibition it accompanies. We hope that by emphasizing aspects of the exhibiting history of the new American painting and sculpture in the past three decades we may call attention to New York's continuing responsibility to the arts that so enrich it. New York must provide an opportunity to see recent art in much the same way that Cubism and Surrealism are visible at The Museum of Modern Art. The achievement of the New York School merits such a permanent base. Rather than devoting an inordinate amount of time to an accelerated schedule of theme shows and retrospectives, museum directors and their staffs, when concentrating on modern art, might do better to expend their greatest efforts on providing gallery after gallery of important recent works by major artists so that our students, foreign and out-of-town visitors, New York's own passionate audience for art and, most importantly, practicing artists can always have before them a collection of challenging contemporary art of the highest quality and relevance. In this way we may hope to avoid the unfortunate situation of the past three decades in which the new art has not been consistently visible. This goal might be achieved through the cooperation of four museums, the Modern, Guggenheim, Whitney, and Metropolitan, or it might be the additive result of four separate but dovetailing programs. It is a goal eminently worth the best efforts of all concerned with New York art.

HENRY GELDZAHLER

Catalogue of the Exhibition

JOSEF ALBERS

1. *Growing.* 1940. Oil on masonite. 15″ x 17¾″.
   The Collection of The San Francisco Museum of Art, San Francisco, California.
   Gift of Mrs. Charlotte Mack. (p. 113)

2. *Vice Versa C. ca.* 1943. Oil on masonite. 16¼″ x 31½″.
   Collection of the artist. (Not illustrated.)

3. *Indicating Solids.* 1949. Oil on masonite. 26″ x 25¾″.
   Collection of the artist. (p. 114)

4. *Transformations of a Scheme Series: No. 10.* 1950.
   Machine-engraved in laminated formica. 17″ x 22½″.
   Collection of the artist. (p. 114)

5. *Homage to the Square Series: New Gate.* 1951. Oil on masonite.
   24″ x 24″. Collection of the artist. (p. 115)

6. *Transformations of a Scheme Series: No. 26.* 1952.
   Machine-engraved in laminated formica. 17″ x 22½″.
   Collection of the artist. (p. 116)

7. *Homage to the Square Series: In Wide Light.* 1953. Oil on masonite.
   18″ x 18″. Collection of the artist. (p. 117)

8. *Homage to the Square Series: With Aura.* 1959. Oil on masonite.
   18″ x 18″. Collection of the artist. (Not illustrated.)

9. *Biconjugate Series: Red Orange Wall.* 1959. Oil on masonite.
   24″ x 34½″. Collection of the artist. (p. 117)

10. *Biconjugate Series: Chalk-Green Facade.* 1960. Oil on masonite.
    28″ x 40½″. Collection of the artist. (p. 118)

11. *Homage to the Square Series: Lone Light.* 1960. Oil on masonite.
    18″ x 18″. Collection of the artist. (Not illustrated.)

12. *Late Thought.* 1964. Oil on board. 48″ x 48″.
    The Woodward Foundation of Washington, D.C. (p. 65).

13. *Homage to the Square Series: Despite Mist* (diptych). 1967 and 1968.
    Oil on masonite. 40″ x 80″. Collection of the artist. (Not illustrated.)

MILTON AVERY

14. *Gaspé—Pink Sky.* 1940. Oil on canvas. 40″ x 50″.
    Collection of Mr. and Mrs. Maurice Geller, New York. (p. 119)

15. *Mother and Child.* 1944. Oil on canvas. 40″ x 30″.
    Tirca Karlis Gallery, Provincetown, Massachusetts. (p. 119)

16. *Sail.* 1958. Oil on canvas. 72″ x 50″.
    Grace Borgenicht Gallery, New York. (p. 120)

17. *Sunset Sea.* 1958. Oil on canvas. 49½″ x 73½″.
    The David Mirvish Gallery, Toronto, Canada. (p. 120)

18. *Speedboat's Wake.* 1959. Oil on canvas. 55″ x 73″.
    The David Mirvish Gallery, Toronto, Canada. (p. 66)

ALEXANDER CALDER

19. *Little Spider. ca.* 1940. Painted sheet metal and steel wire and rods.
    55″ x 50″. Perls Galleries, New York. (p. 121)

20. *Mobile.* 1963. Sheet steel. 27′.
    The Connecticut Bank and Trust Company, Hartford, Connecticut. (p. 122)

21. *The Pregnant Whale.* 1963. Steel plate painted. 9′6″ x 8′10″ x 7′2″.
    Collection of Mrs. Julius Epstein, Northfield, Illinois. (p. 67)

22. *Four Planes Écartés.* 1967. Painted sheet steel. *ca.* 10′6″ (high).
    Perls Galleries, New York. (p. 123)

23. *Six Planes Écartés.* 1967. Painted sheet steel. *ca.* 10′6″ (high).
    Perls Galleries, New York. (p. 123)

JOHN CHAMBERLAIN

24. *Fantail.* 1961. Painted steel. 70″ x 75″ x 60″.
    Collection of Jasper Johns, New York. (p. 124)

25. *Velvet White.* 1962. Welded steel. 83″ x 57″ x 48″.
    The Albert A. List Family Collection, New York. (p. 125)

26. *Dolores James.* 1962. Welded auto metal. 76″ x 97″ x 39″.
    Leo Castelli Gallery, New York. (p. 68)

JOSEPH CORNELL

27. *Taglioni's Jewel Casket.* 1940. Wooden box containing glass ice cubes, jewelry, etc.
    4¾″ x 11⅞″ x 8¼″. The Museum of Modern Art, New York.
    Gift of James Thrall Soby, 1953. (Not illustrated.)

28. *L'Égypte de Mlle. Cléo de Mérode; cours élémentaire d'histoire
    naturelle.* 1940. Wood, glass, cork, and miscellaneous materials. 4¾″ x 10¾″ x 7¼″.
    Collection of Mr. and Mrs. Richard L. Feigen, New York. (p. 126)

29. *Medici Slot Machine.* 1942. Construction. 15½″ x 12″ x 4⅜″.
    Collection of Mr. and Mrs. Bernard J. Reis, New York. (p. 126)

30. *A Pantry Ballet (for Jacques Offenbach).* Summer, 1942.
    Wood, paper, plastic, metal, glass, etc. 10½″ x 18″ x 6″.
    Collection of Mr. and Mrs. Richard L. Feigen, New York. (p. 127)

31. *Habitat Group for a Shooting Gallery.* 1943. Wood cabinet containing colored cut-
    out of parrots, printed cards, and papers, etc., behind shattered glass.
    15½″ x 11⅛″ x 4¼″. Collection of Irving Blum, Los Angeles, California. (p. 69)

32. *Pharmacy.* 1943. Wooden box with glass bottles. 15¼″ x 12″ x 3″.
    Collection of Mrs. Marcel Duchamp, New York. (p. 127)

33. *Paolo and Francesca.* 1943–48. Box construction. 14¾″ x 11⅜″ x 3¹³⁄₁₆″.
    Collection of Mr. and Mrs. Richard L. Feigen, New York. (Not illustrated.)

34. *American Rabbit.* 1945–46. Box construction. 11⅜″ x 15½″ x 3¹³⁄₁₆″.
    Collection of Mr. and Mrs. Jacob Berman, Sherman Oaks,
    California. (Not illustrated.)

35. *Multiple Cubes.* 1946–48. Construction. 14″ x 10⅜″ x 2¼″.
    Collection of Mr. and Mrs. E. A. Bergman, Chicago, Illinois. (Not illustrated.)

36. *Soap Bubble Set.* 1948. Black box construction. 15³⁄₁₆″ x 20⅜″ x 3¹³⁄₁₆″.
Collection of Mrs. Doris Starrels, Los Angeles, California.
(Not illustrated.)

37. *Cockatoo: "Keepsake Parakeet."* 1949–53. Construction in wood.
20¼″ x 12″ x 5″. Collection of Donald Windham, New York. (p. 128)

38. *Observatory.* 1950. Construction. 18″ x 11⅞″ x 5½″.
Collection of Mr. and Mrs. E. A. Bergman, Chicago, Illinois. (Not illustrated.)

39. *Grand Hotel Semiramis.* 1950. Construction of wood, glass, and diverse materials.
18″ x 12″ x 4″. Collection of Mr. and Mrs. Allan Frumkin, New York. (p. 128)

40. *Hotel (Night Sky). ca.* 1952. Wood box construction with glass face. 16½″ x 10″ x 6″.
Collection of Irving Blum, Los Angeles, California. (Not illustrated.)

41. *Medici Princess. ca.* 1952. Wood, glass, and diverse materials. 14½″ x 11″ x 5″.
Collection of Jean Frumkin, New York. (Not illustrated.)

42. *Hotel du Nord. ca.* 1953. Construction in wood, glass, and paper.
19″ x 13¼″. The Whitney Museum of American Art, New York. (p. 129)

43. *Grand Hotel de L'Observatoire.* 1954. Blue box construction.
18⁵⁄₁₆″ x 12⁵⁄₁₆″ x 3¹³⁄₁₆″. Collection of the artist. (Not illustrated.)

44. *Blériot.* 1956. Box containing painted wooden trapeze supported by
rusted steel spring. 18½″ x 11¼″ x 4¾″. Collection of Mr. and Mrs. E. A. Bergman,
Chicago, Illinois. (Not illustrated.)

45. *Hotel de L'Étoile. ca.* 1956–57. Painted wood construction.
18½″ x 14″ x 7½″. Collection of Mrs. Eleanor Ward, New York. (p. 129)

46. *Apollinaris.* (n.d.) Blue box construction. 19″ x 11¹⁄₁₆″ x 4⅝″.
Collection of the artist. (Not illustrated.)

47. *Grand Hotel de L'Univers.* (n.d.). Blue box construction. 19″ x 12⅝″ x 4¾″.
Anonymous loan courtesy of The Pasadena Art Museum, Pasadena, California.
(Not illustrated.)

48. *Hotel du Nord (Little Durer).* (n.d.). Box construction. 18″ x 12¼″ x 4″.
The Pasadena Art Museum, Funds donated by Mr. William Janss and the
Storrier-Stearns Fund. (Not illustrated.)

STUART DAVIS

49. *Hot Stillscape in Six Colors.* 1940. Oil on canvas. 36″ x 45″.
Courtesy of The Downtown Gallery, New York. (p. 70)

50. *New York Under Gaslight.* 1941. Oil on canvas. 32″ x 45″.
The Israel Museum, Jerusalem, gift of Mrs. Rebecca Shulman, New York.
(Not illustrated.)

51. *Owh! In San Paõ.* 1951. Oil on canvas. 52¼″ x 41¾″.
The Whitney Museum of American Art, New York. (p. 130)

52. *Colonial Cubism.* 1954. Oil on canvas. 45″ x 60″.
Collection of The Walker Art Center, Minneapolis, Minnesota. (p. 131)

53. *Pochade.* 1958. Oil on canvas. 60″ x 52″.
Courtesy of The Downtown Gallery, New York. (p. 131)

54. *Switchsky's Syntax.* 1961–64. Tempera on canvas. 42″ x 56″.
Courtesy of Mrs. Stuart Davis, New York. (p. 132)

WILLEM DE KOONING

55. *Seated Woman. ca.* 1940. Oil and charcoal on composition board. 54″ x 36″. Collection of Mrs. Albert M. Greenfield, Sr., Philadelphia, Pennsylvania. (p. 133)

56. *Queen of Hearts.* 1943–46. Oil and charcoal on composition board. 46″ x 27½″. Joseph H. Hirshhorn Foundation. (p. 134)

57. *Pink Lady. ca.* 1944. Oil and charcoal on masonite composition board. 48¼″ x 35¼″. Collection of Mr. and Mrs. Stanley K. Sheinbaum, Santa Barbara, California. (p. 135)

58. *The Marshes. ca.* 1945. Charcoal and oil on composition board. 32″ x 23⅞″. University Art Museum, Berkeley, California. Gift of Julian J. and Joachim Jean Aberbach, New York. (p. 136)

59. *Light in August. ca.* 1946. Oil and enamel on paper, mounted on canvas. 55″ x 44½″. Collection of Elise C. Dixon, Scottsdale, Arizona. (p. 137)

60. *Bill-Lee's Delight. ca.* 1946. Oil on paper. 27½″ x 34¼″. Collection of Mr. and Mrs. Lee V. Eastman, New York. (p. 71)

61. *Untitled.* 1948. Oil on paper, mounted on masonite. 24″ x 36″. Collection of Mr. and Mrs. Stephen D. Paine, Boston, Massachusetts. (p. 138)

62. *Night Square.* 1950–51. Oil on masonite. 30″ x 40″. Collection of Mrs. Martha K. Jackson, New York. (Not illustrated.)

63. *Police Gazette.* 1954–55. Oil on canvas. 43¼″ x 50¼″. Collection of Mr. and Mrs. Robert C. Scull, New York. (p. 138)

64. *Easter Monday.* 1955–56. Oil and newspaper transfer on canvas. 96″ x 74″. The Metropolitan Museum of Art, New York, Rogers Fund, 1956. (p. 139)

65. *Spike's Folly I.* 1959. Oil on canvas. 79″ x 68½″. Collection of Mr. and Mrs. Robert C. Scull, New York. (p. 140)

66. *Door to the River.* 1960. Oil on canvas. 80″ x 70″. The Whitney Museum of American Art, New York. Gift of the Friends of The Whitney Museum of American Art and purchase. (p. 141)

BURGOYNE DILLER

67. *First Theme.* 1962. Oil on canvas. 72″ x 72″. The Art Institute of Chicago, Wilson L. Mead Fund Income. (p. 142)

68. *No. 33, First Theme.* 1962. Oil on canvas. 32″ x 32″. Collection of Mr. and Mrs. Richard Hokin, New York. (p. 72)

69. *No. 5, Third Theme.* 1963. Oil on canvas. 42″ x 42″. The Diller Estate, Courtesy of Noah Goldowsky and Richard Bellamy, New York. (p. 143)

70. *No. 10, First Theme.* 1963–64. Oil on canvas. 72″ x 72″. The Diller Estate, Courtesy of Noah Goldowsky and Richard Bellamy, New York. (p. 144)

71. *No. 9, First Theme.* 1963–64. Oil on canvas. 72″ x 72″. Albright-Knox Art Gallery, Buffalo, New York, Gift of Seymour H. Knox. (p. 144)

MARK DI SUVERO

72. *Hankchampion*. 1960. Wood and chain construction. 6′ x 10′.
Collection of Mr. and Mrs. Robert C. Scull, New York. (p. 145)

73. *Tom*. 1961. Wood and steel. 8′ x 10′ x 10′.
Lo Giudice Gallery, Chicago, Illinois, and Richard Bellamy, New York. (p. 146)

74. *Mohican*. 1967. Steel and wood, 15′ x 9′ x 30′.
Collection of Mr. Lewis Manilow, Chicago, Illinois. (p. 73)

DAN FLAVIN

75. *the nominal three (to William of Ockham)*. 1963. Cool white fluorescent
light. 8′ (high). The National Gallery of Canada, Ottawa, Canada. (p. 74)

76. untitled. 1965. A set of seven cubes. White baked enamel on steel with
cool white fluorescent light. Size determined by length of fixture.
Dwan Gallery, New York. (Illustrated by drawing page 147.)

77. untitled. 1966. Cool white fluorescent light. 8′ (high).
Collection of Mr. and Mrs. Robert A. M. Stern, New York. (p. 147)

78. untitled. 1966. Cool white fluorescent light. *ca.* 8′ x 8′.
Collection of Irving Blum, Los Angeles, California. (p. 148)

HELEN FRANKENTHALER

79. *Abstract Landscape*. 1951. Oil on canvas. 69″ x 71⅞″.
Collection of the artist. (p. 149)

80. *Other Generations*. 1957. Oil on canvas. 70″ x 70″.
Collection of the artist. (p. 149)

81. *Europa*. 1957. Oil on canvas. 70½″ x 54″.
Collection of the artist. (p. 150)

82. *Yellow Caterpillar*. 1961. Oil on canvas. 90″ x 120″.
Private collection, New York. (p. 75)

83. *The Moors*. 1962. Acrylic on canvas. 107″ x 47″.
Collection of William S. Rubin, New York. (p. 151)

84. *Blue Atmosphere*. 1963. Acrylic on canvas. 117½″ x 70″.
Collection of the artist. (p. 152)

85. *Orange Shapes in Frame*. 1964. Acrylic on canvas. 93″ x 74″.
Collection of Mr. and Mrs. Robert B. Mayer, Winnetka, Illinois. (p. 153)

86. *One O'Clock*. 1966. Acrylic paint on canvas. 93¾″ x 75¾″.
Collection of Albert F. Weis, Savannah, Georgia. (p. 154)

87. *Gamut*. 1968. Acrylic on canvas. 11′2″ x 93″.
Collection of the artist. (p. 155)

ARSHILE GORKY

88. *Garden in Sochi*. 1940–41. Oil on canvas. 25″ x 29″
Private collection, courtesy of M. Knoedler & Company, Inc., New York. (p. 156)

89. *The Pirate I*. 1942. Oil on canvas. 29¼″ x 40⅛″.
Collection of Mr. and Mrs. Julien Levy, Bridgewater, Connecticut. (p. 158)

90. *The Pirate II.* 1943. Oil on canvas. 30″ x 36″.
Collection of Mr. and Mrs. Julien Levy, Bridgewater, Connecticut. (p. 158)

91. *Water of the Flowery Mill.* 1944. Oil on canvas. 42¼″ x 48¾″.
The Metropolitan Museum of Art, New York, George A. Hearn Fund, 1956. (p. 76)

92. *The Unattainable.* 1945. Oil on canvas. 41⅛″ x 29¼″.
The Baltimore Museum of Art, Baltimore, Maryland, Friends of Art Fund. (p. 159)

93. *The Plough and the Song.* 1947. Oil on burlap. 52⅛″ x 64¼″.
Collection of Mr. and Mrs. Milton A. Gordon, New York. (p. 160)

94. *The Plough and the Song.* 1947. Oil on canvas. 50¾″ x 62¾″.
Allen Memorial Art Museum, Oberlin College, Oberlin, Ohio. (p. 160)

95. *The Betrothal, II.* 1947. Oil on canvas. 50¾″ x 38″.
The Whitney Museum of American Art, New York. (p. 161)

96. *The Limit.* 1947. Oil on paper over burlap. 50¾″ x 62½″.
Private collection, courtesy of M. Knoedler & Company, Inc., New York. (p. 162)

97. *Dark Green Painting. ca.* 1948. Oil on canvas. 43¾″ x 56″.
Collection of Mrs. H. Gates Lloyd, Haverford, Pennsylvania. (p. 163)

ADOLPH GOTTLIEB

98. *Masquerade.* 1945. Oil and egg tempera on canvas. 36″ x 24″.
Collection of Mrs. Esther Gottlieb, New York. (p. 164)

99. *Recurrent Apparition.* 1946. Oil on canvas. 36″ x 54″.
Collection of Mrs. Esther Gottlieb, New York. (p. 165)

100. *Oracle.* 1947–48. Oil on canvas. 60″ x 44″.
The Albert A. List Family Collection, New York. (Not illustrated.)

101. *Dream.* 1948. Oil on canvas. 20″ x 24″.
Isaac Delgado Museum of Art, New Orleans, Louisiana,
Gift of William Edward Campbell, 1951. (p. 165)

102. *Thrust.* 1959. Oil on canvas. 108″ x 90″.
The Metropolitan Museum of Art, New York, George A. Hearn Fund, 1959. (p. 166)

103. *Aureole.* 1959. Oil on canvas. 108″ x 90″.
Collection of Mrs. Esther Gottlieb, New York. (p. 167)

104. *Una.* 1959. Oil on canvas. 108″ x 90″.
Collection of the artist. (p. 77)

105. *Sign.* 1962. Oil on canvas. 90″ x 84″.
Collection of the artist. (p. 168)

106. *Red, Blue, Yellow.* 1966. Oil on canvas. 84″ x 90″.
Collection of William S. Rubin, New York. (p. 169)

107. *Petaloid.* 1967. Cor-Ten steel. 96″ x 96″ x 48″.
Collection of Mrs. Esther Gottlieb, New York. (p. 169)

108. *Wall.* 1969. Painted aluminum. 7½′ x 4½′ x 11′.
Collection of the artist. (Illustrated by model page 78.)

PHILIP GUSTON

109. *To B. W. T.* 1952. Oil on canvas. 48″ x 51″.
Collection of Mr. Leonard M. Brown, Springfield, Massachusetts. (p. 170)

110. *Painting.* 1952. Oil on canvas. 50¾" x 48".
Collection of Mrs. Albert H. Newman, Chicago, Illinois. (p. 79)

111. *Attar.* 1953. Oil on canvas. 48½" x 46".
Collection of Morton Feldman, New York. (Not illustrated.)

112. *Zone.* 1954. Oil on canvas. 46" x 48⅛".
Collection of Mr. and Mrs. Ben Heller, New York. (p. 171)

113. Untitled. 1954. Oil on canvas. 51" x 48¾".
Collection of Mr. and Mrs. C. B. Wright, Seattle, Washington. (p. 171)

114. *For M.* 1955. Oil on canvas. 76¼" x 72".
Private collection, Los Angeles, California. (p. 172)

115. *Cythera.* 1957. Oil on canvas. 72" x 64".
Collection of Mr. and Mrs. Donald Blinken, New York. (p. 173)

HANS HOFMANN

116. *In the Wake of the Hurricane.* 1960. Oil on canvas. 72¼" x 60".
University Art Museum, Berkeley, California, Gift of the artist. (p. 174)

117. *Summer Night's Bliss.* 1961. Oil on canvas. 84" x 78".
The Baltimore Museum of Art, Baltimore, Maryland, Gift of the artist. (p. 175)

118. *Agrigento.* 1961. Oil on canvas. 84¼" x 72".
University Art Museum, Berkeley, California, Gift of the artist. (p. 176)

119. *Memoria in Aeterne.* 1962. Oil on canvas. 84" x 72⅛".
The Museum of Modern Art, New York, Gift of the artist, 1963. (p. 177)

120. *Veluti in Speculum.* 1962. Oil on canvas. 85¼" x 73½".
The Metropolitan Museum of Art, Gift of Mr. and Mrs. Richard Rodgers and the Francis Lathrop Fund, 1963. (p. 80)

121. *Gloriamundi.* 1963. Oil on canvas. 60⅛" x 52".
University Art Museum, Berkeley, California, Gift of the artist. (p. 178)

122. *Song of a Nightingale.* 1964. Oil on canvas. 7' x 6'.
Collection of Mr. and Mrs. Eugene M. Schwartz, New York. (p. 179)

123. *In Sober Ecstasy.* 1965. Oil on canvas. 73½" x 61½".
Collection of Mr. and Mrs. David Mirvish, Toronto, Canada. (p. 180)

124. *Little Cherry* (Renata Series No. 1). 1965. Oil on canvas. 84" x 78".
Estate of Hans Hofmann. (p. 181)

125. *Lust and Delight* (Renata Series No. 2). 1965. Oil on canvas. 84" x 60".
Estate of Hans Hofmann. (p. 181)

EDWARD HOPPER

126. *Gas.* 1940. Oil on canvas. 26¼" x 40¼".
The Museum of Modern Art, New York, Mrs. Simon Guggenheim Fund, 1943. (p. 182)

127. *First Row, Orchestra.* 1951. Oil on canvas. 31" x 40".
Joseph H. Hirshhorn Foundation. (p. 183)

128. *Office in a Small City.* 1953. Oil on canvas. 28" x 40".
The Metropolitan Museum of Art, New York, George A. Hearn Fund, 1953. (p. 184)

129. *Western Motel.* 1957. Oil on canvas. 30¼" x 50⅛".
Yale University Art Gallery, Bequest of Stephen Carlton Clark, B.A., 1903. (p. 82)

130. *Green Target.* 1955. Encaustic on newspaper on canvas. 60″ x 60″.
The Museum of Modern Art, New York, Richard S. Zeisler Fund, 1958. (p. 184)

131. *White Flag.* 1955. Encaustic and collage on canvas. 72″ x 144″.
Collection of the artist. (p. 185)

132. *Three Flags.* 1958. Encaustic on canvas. 30⅞″ x 45½″.
Collection of Mr. and Mrs. Burton Tremaine, Meriden, Connecticut. (p. 185)

133. *Device Circle.* 1959. Encaustic and collage on canvas. 40″ x 40″.
Collection of Mr. and Mrs. Burton Tremaine, Meriden, Connecticut. (p. 186)

134. *Jubilee.* 1959. Oil on canvas. 60″ x 44″.
Collection of Robert Rauschenberg, New York. (p. 187)

135. *False Start.* 1959. Oil on canvas. 67¼″ x 54″.
Collection of Mr. and Mrs. Robert C. Scull, New York. (p. 188)

136. *Painting with Two Balls.* 1960. Encaustic and collage on canvas with
objects. 65″ x 54″ (three panels). Collection of the artist. (p. 83)

137. *Studio.* 1964. Oil on canvas. 73½″ x 145½″.
The Whitney Museum of American Art, New York, Gift of the Friends of The
Whitney Museum of American Art and purchase. (p. 188)

138. *Double White Map.* 1965. Encaustic and collage on canvas. 90″ x 70″.
Collection of Mr. and Mrs. Robert C. Scull, New York. (p. 189)

139. *Screen Piece.* 1967. Oil on canvas. 72″ x 50″.
Collection of David Whitney, New York. (p. 190)

140. *Screen Piece 2.* 1968. Oil on canvas. 72″ x 50″.
Collection of Mr. and Mrs. Victor W. Ganz, New York. (p. 191)

141. *Flag (64 stars).* 1955. Pencil on paper. 7″ x 9″.
Collection of the artist. (Not illustrated.)

142. *Target with Four Faces.* 1955. Pencil on paper. 8½″ x 7¼″.
Collection of the artist. (Not illustrated.)

143. *Green Flag.* 1956. Pencil and crayon on canvas. 7″ x 9″.
Collection of Lois Long, New York. (Not illustrated.)

144. *Flag on Orange Field.* 1957. Day-Glo, watercolor, chalk, pencil on paper.
10½″ x 7¾″. Collection of the artist. (Not illustrated.)

145. *Alphabets.* 1957. Pencil and pasted index tabs. 13¾″ x 9¾″.
Collection of Robert Rosenblum, New York. (Not illustrated.)

146. *Light Bulb.* 1958. Pencil and graphite wash. 6½″ x 8¾″.
Collection of Andy Warhol, New York. (Not illustrated.)

147. *Flag.* 1958. Pencil and graphite wash on paper. 7½″ x 10⅜″.
Collection of Leo Castelli, New York. (p. 192)

148. *Tennyson.* 1958. Ink on paper. 14¾″ x 9¾″.
Collection of the artist. (Not illustrated.)

149. *Study for Painting with a Ball.* 1958. Conté on paper. 15″ x 14½″.
Collection of the artist. (p. 192)

150. *Three Flags.* 1959. Pencil on paper. 14½″ x 23½″.
Collection of the Victoria & Albert Museum, London, England. (Not illustrated.)

151. *Study for Painting with Two Balls.* 1960. Charcoal on paper.
19½″ x 15½″. Joseph H. Hirshhorn Collection. (p. 193)

152. *Numbers.* 1960. Pencil on paper. Ten drawings matted separately.
2¾″ x 2¼″ each. Collection of Edward Carey, New York. (p. 194)

153. *Device Circle.* 1960. Pencil on paper. 15″ x 14½″.
Collection of Mr. and Mrs. Ben Heller, New York. (p. 194)

154. *Two Flags.* 1960. Graphite wash on paper. 26″ x 19″.
Collection of the artist. (Not illustrated.)

155. *Out the Window.* 1960. Charcoal and pastel. 34½″ x 28½″.
Collection of Dr. and Mrs. Bernard Brodsky, New York. (Not illustrated.)

156. *0 through 9.* 1960. Charcoal on paper. 29″ x 23″.
Collection of the artist. (Not illustrated.)

157. *Gray Alphabets.* 1960. Graphite wash on paper. 32″ x 23½″.
Collection of Mr. and Mrs. Leo Castelli, New York. (Not illustrated.)

158. *Numbers.* 1960. Charcoal on paper. 9½″ x 7½″.
Collection of the artist. (Not illustrated.)

159. *Jubilee.* 1960. Graphite wash. 28″ x 21″.
Collection of Mr. and Mrs. Lester Francis Avnet, New York. (Not illustrated.)

160. *Floral Design.* 1961. Watercolor on paper and collage. 20¼″ x 10½″.
Collection of the artist. (Not illustrated.)

161. *0 through 9.* 1961. Charcoal and pastel on paper. 54″ x 45″.
Collection of Mr. and Mrs. Robert C. Scull, New York. (p. 195)

162. *Study for Skin I.* 1962. Charcoal on paper. 22″ x 34″.
Collection of the artist. (p. 196)

163. *Study for Skin II.* 1962. Charcoal on paper. 22″ x 34″.
Collection of the artist. (p. 196)

164. *Study for Skin III.* 1962. Charcoal on paper. 22″ x 34″.
Collection of the artist. (p. 196)

165. *Study for Skin IV.* 1962. Charcoal on paper. 22″ x 34″.
Collection of the artist. (p. 196)

166. *Diver.* 1963. Charcoal, pastel, paper on canvas. 86½″ x 71″.
Collection of Mr. and Mrs. Victor W. Ganz, New York. (p. 197)

167. *Map.* 1965. Graphite wash on paper. 13¼″ x 20½″.
Collection of the artist. (Not illustrated.)

168. *Study for Flags.* 1965. Watercolor. 29″ x 21¼″.
Collection of the artist. (Not illustrated.)

169. *Studies for 0–9 lithographs.* 1969. Watercolor. Ten watercolors, each 2¼″ x 2″.
Collection of Jason Ferus Blum, Los Angeles, California. (Not illustrated.)

DONALD JUDD

170. Untitled. 1963. Painted wood and aluminum. 48″ x 83″ x 48″.
Collection of Julie Judd, New York. (p. 84)

171. Untitled. 1965. Perforated steel. 8″ x 120″ x 66″.
Leo Castelli Gallery, New York. (p. 198)

172. Untitled. 1969. Stainless steel and plexiglas.
Six units, each 34″ x 34″ x 34″. Leo Castelli Gallery, New York. (p. 198)

173. Untitled. 1969. Aluminum. 5′ x 7′ x 12′ approximately.
Leo Castelli Gallery. New York. (Not illustrated.)

ELLSWORTH KELLY

174. *White Relief with Blue.* 1950. Oil on wood. 45″ x 17½″.
Private collection, New York. (p. 199)

175. *Blue Red Green.* 1962–63. Oil on canvas. 91″ x 82″.
The Metropolitan Museum of Art, New York, Arthur H. Hearn Fund, 1963. (p. 200)

176. *3 Panels: Red, Yellow, Blue.* 1963. Acrylic on canvas. 90″ x 90″.
Fondation Maeght, Saint Paul, France. (p. 200)

177. *Orange White.* 1964. Oil on canvas. 122″ x 96″.
Courtesy of Sidney Janis Gallery, New York. (p. 201)

178. *Red Blue Green Yellow.* 1965. Oil on canvas. 86″ x 53½″.
Collection of Mr. and Mrs. Robert B. Mayer, Winnetka, Illinois. (p. 85)

179. *2 Panels: White Dark Blue.* 1968. Oil on canvas. 96″ x 144″.
Courtesy of Sidney Janis Gallery, New York. (p. 202)

180. *13 Panels: Spectrum V.* 1969. Oil on canvas. 84″ x 443″.
Courtesy of Sidney Janis Gallery, New York. (Not illustrated.)

181. *White Ring.* 1963. Epoxy on aluminum. 70″ x 72″ x 12″.
Private collection, New York. (p. 202)

182. *Blue White Angle.* 1966. Epoxy on aluminum. 72″ x 36″ x 72″.
Private collection, New York. (p. 86)

183. *Green.* 1968. Painted aluminum. 21″ x 105″ x 112″.
Collection of The Walker Art Center, Minneapolis, Minnesota. (p. 203)

184. Untitled. 1968. Painted aluminum. 100½″ x 146½″ x 38⅜″.
Collection of William S. Rubin, New York. (p. 204)

185. *Black White.* 1968. Painted aluminum. 100½″ x 146½″ x 38⅜″.
Courtesy of Sidney Janis Gallery, New York. (p. 205)

186. *Rubber Tree.* 1958. Pencil on paper. 29″ x 23″.
Private collection, New York. (Not illustrated.)

187. *Tulip.* 1958. Pencil on paper. 29″ x 23″.
Private collection, New York. (p. 206)

188. *Mango.* 1959. Pencil on paper. 28½ x 22½″.
Private collection, New York. (Not illustrated.)

189. *Avocado.* 1960. Pencil on paper. 28½″ x 22½″.
Private collection, New York. (Not illustrated.)

190. *Sweet Pea.* 1960. Pencil on paper. 22½″ x 28½″.
Private collection, New York. (Not illustrated.)

191. *Lily.* 1960. Ink on paper. 28½″ x 22½″.
Private collection, New York. (Not illustrated.)

192. *Wild Grape.* 1960. Pencil on paper, 28½ ″x 45″.
Private collection, New York. (Not illustrated.)

193. *Brier*. 1960. Pencil on paper, 28½″ x 22½″.
Private collection, New York. (Not illustrated.)

194. *Brier*. 1960. Pencil on paper. 28½″ x 22½″.
Private collection, New York. (Not illustrated.)

195. *Grass*. 1961. Pencil on paper. 28½″ x 22½″.
Private collection, New York. (p. 206)

196. *Wild Grape*. 1961. Ink on paper. 22½″ x 28½″.
Private collection, New York. (Not illustrated.)

197. *Castor Bean*. 1961. Ink on paper, 22½ x 28½″.
Private collection, New York. (p. 206)

198. *Philodendron*. 1963. Ink on paper, 28½″ x 22½″.
Private collection, New York. (Not illustrated.)

199. *Oak*. 1964. Pencil on paper. 28½″ x 22½″.
Private collection, New York. (p. 207)

200. *Lemon Branch*. 1964. Pencil on paper. 28½″ x 22½″.
Private collection, New York. (Not illustrated.)

201. *Catalpa*. 1964. Pencil on paper. 28½″ x 45″.
Private collection, New York. (Not illustrated.)

202. *Chrysanthemum*. 1965. Pencil on paper. 28½″ x 22½″.
Private collection, New York. (Not illustrated.)

203. *Leaves*. 1965. Pencil on paper. 29″ x 23″.
Private collection, New York. (Not illustrated.)

204. *Oranges*. 1966. Pencil on paper. 22½″ x 28½″.
Private collection, New York. (Not illustrated.)

205. *Magnolia*. 1966. Pencil on paper. 29″ x 23″.
Private collection, New York. (p. 207)

206. *Woodland Plant*. 1967. Pencil on paper. 29″ x 23″.
Private collection, New York. (Not illustrated.)

207. *Avocado*. 1967. Pencil on paper. 29″ x 23″.
Private collection, New York. (Not illustrated.)

208. *Oak*. 1967. Pencil on paper. 22″ x 30″.
Private collection, New York. (Not illustrated.)

209. *Avocado*. 1967. Pencil on paper. 29″ x 23″.
Private collection, New York. (p. 207)

210. *Woodland Plant*. 1967. Pencil on paper. 30″ x 22″.
Private collection, New York. (Not illustrated.)

211. *Ghinko*. 1967. Pencil on paper. 29″ x 23″.
Private collection, New York. (Not illustrated.)

212. *Avocado*. 1967. Pencil on paper. 30″ x 22″.
Private collection, New York. (Not illustrated.)

213. *Cyclamen*. 1967. Pencil on paper, 29″ x 23″.
Private collection, New York. (Not illustrated.)

214. *Chrysanthemum*. 1967. Pencil on paper. 30″ x 22″.
Private collection, New York. (p. 208)

215. *Water Lily*. 1968. Pencil on paper. 29″ x 23″.
Private collection, New York. (p. 208)

FRANZ KLINE

216. *Nijinsky.* 1949. Oil on canvas. 33″ x 28″.
Collection of Mr. and Mrs. David I. Orr, New York. (p. 209)

217. *Wotan.* 1950. Oil on canvas. 55⅛″ x 79¼″.
Collection of Mr. and Mrs. Robert C. Scull, New York. (p. 210)

218. *Horizontals Two.* 1952. Oil on canvas. 77″ x 100″.
Estate of Franz Kline. Courtesy of Marlborough-Gerson Gallery, New York. (p. 210)

219. *Figure Eight.* 1952. Oil on canvas. 80½″ x 63½″.
Collection of William S. Rubin, New York. (p. 211)

220. Untitled. 1953–54. Oil on canvas. 57¼″ x 82″.
Collection of Robert H. Halff and Carl W. Johnson, Beverly Hills, California. (p. 212)

221. Untitled. 1954. Oil on canvas. 43″ x 36″.
Collection of Mr. and Mrs. David I. Orr, New York. (p. 212)

222. *White Forms.* 1955. Oil on canvas. 74″ x 50″.
Collection of Philip Johnson, New Canaan, Connecticut. (p. 213)

223. *Blue Center.* 1958. Oil on canvas. 36″ x 40″.
Collection of Mr. and Mrs. Robert C. Scull, New York. (p. 87)

224. *Orange and Black Wall.* 1959. Oil on canvas. 66½″ x 144″.
Collection of Mr. and Mrs. Robert C. Scull, New York. (p. 214)

225. *Riverbed.* 1961. Oil on canvas. 78⅞″ x 109¼″.
Collection of William M. White, Jr., New York. (p. 214)

GABE KOHN

226. *Acrotère.* 1960. Laminated wood. 35¼″ x 31″ x 22¼″.
The Museum of Modern Art, New York, Given anonymously, 1963. (p. 88)

227. *Long Beach Contract.* 1965. Laminated redwood. 10′ x 7′.
California State College, Long Beach, California. (p. 215)

ROY LICHTENSTEIN

228. *I Can See the Whole Room.* . . . 1961. Oil on canvas. 48″ x 48″.
Collection of Mr. and Mrs. Burton Tremaine, Meriden, Connecticut. (p. 216)

229. *The Engagement Ring.* 1961. Oil on canvas. 67¾″ x 79½″.
Collection of Mr. and Mrs. Robert A. Rowan, Pasadena, California. (p. 89)

230. *Live Ammo.* 1962. Oil on canvas. 68″ x 92″ (two panels).
Collection of Mr. and Mrs. Morton Neumann, Chicago, Illinois. (p. 217)

231. *Sussex.* 1964. Oil and magna on canvas. 36″ x 68″.
Collection of Robert Rosenblum, New York. (p. 217)

232. *Big Painting #6.* 1965. Oil and magna on canvas. 92½″ x 129″.
Collection of Mr. and Mrs. Robert C. Scull, New York. (p. 218)

233. *Haystacks.* 1968. Oil and magna on canvas. 18″ x 24″.
Private collection, New York. (p. 219)

234. *Haystacks.* 1969. Oil and magna on canvas. 16″ x 24″.
Private collection, New York. (Not illustrated.)

235. *Haystacks.* 1969. Oil and magna on canvas. 16″ x 24″.
Private collection, New York. (p. 219)

236. *Rouen Cathedral (seen at five different times of day) III.* 1969.
Oil and magna on canvas. 63″ x 42″. (#1 of five paintings in set.)
Private collection, New York. (p. 220)

237. *Rouen Cathedral (seen at five different times of day) III.* 1969.
Oil and magna on canvas. 63″ x 42″. (#2 of five paintings in set.)
Private collection, New York. (Not illustrated.)

238. *Rouen Cathedral (seen at five different times of day) III.* 1969.
Oil and magna on canvas. 63″ x 42″. (#3 of five paintings in set.)
Private collection, New York. (p. 221)

MORRIS LOUIS

239. *Iris.* 1954. Acrylic on canvas. 80″ x 106″.
Collection of Mr. and Mrs. Eugene M. Schwartz, New York. (p. 90)

240. *Saraband.* 1959. Acrylic on canvas. 100½″ x 149″.
The Solomon R. Guggenheim Museum, New York. (p. 222)

241. *Terranean.* 1959. Acrylic resin paint on canvas. 90½″ x 146″.
Collection of Mr. and Mrs. Kenneth Noland, New York. (p. 223)

242. *While.* 1959. Acrylic on canvas. 96½″ x 136⅜″.
Harry N. Abrams Family Collection, New York. (p. 224)

243. *Aleph.* 1960. Magna acrylic on canvas. 105″ x 92¾″.
Collection of Jaime C. del Amo, Madrid, Spain. (p. 225)

244. *Alpha-Pi.* 1961. Acrylic on canvas. 102½″ x 177″.
The Metropolitan Museum of Art, New York, Arthur H. Hearn Fund, 1967. (p. 91)

245. *Alpha-Delta.* 1961. Acrylic on canvas. 8′8″ x 20′.
Everson Museum of Art, Syracuse, New York. (p. 225)

246. *Moving In.* 1961. Magna acrylic on canvas. 87½″ x 41½″.
Private collection. New York. (p. 226)

247. *Hot Half.* 1962. Acrylic resin on canvas. 63″ x 63″.
Collection of Mrs. Abner Brenner, Washington, D.C. (p. 227)

ROBERT MORRIS

248. Untitled. 1964. Painted plywood. 6′6″ x 9 .
Collection of Dott. Giuseppe Panza di Buomo, Milan, Italy.
Courtesy of Leo Castelli Gallery, New York. (p. 228)

249. Untitled. 1965. Aluminum construction. 6′ x 11′7″ x 3″.
Collection of Mr. and Mrs. Robert C. Scull, New York. (p. 92)

250. Untitled. 1966. Steel mesh. 31″ x 106″ x 106″.
Lent by The Kleiner Foundation, Beverly Hills, California.
Courtesy of Los Angeles County Museum of Art, Los Angeles, California. (p. 228)

251. Untitled. 1967–68. Felt. 180″ x 72″ x 1″.
The Detroit Institute of Arts, Gift of the Friends of Modern Art. (p. 229)

252. Untitled. 1968. Translucent fiberglas. Nine units, each 48″ x 24″ x 24″.
Collection of Philip Johnson, New Canaan, Connecticut. (p. 230)

ROBERT MOTHERWELL

253. *The Little Spanish Prison.* 1941–44. Oil on canvas. 27⅛″ x 17″.
Collection of the artist. (p. 231)

254. *Mallarmé's Swan.* 1944. Collage using gouache, crayon, and paper on cardboard.
43½″ x 35½″. Contemporary Collection of The Cleveland Museum of Art, Cleveland, Ohio. (p. 93)

255. *Homely Protestant.* 1948. Oil on composition board. 96″ x 48″.
Collection of Helen Frankenthaler, New York. (p. 232)

256. *Elegy to the Spanish Republic, 70.* 1961. Oil on canvas. 69″ x 114″.
The Metropolitan Museum of Art, New York, Anonymous gift, 1965. (p. 233)

257. *Africa.* 1965. Acrylic on canvas. 80″ x 225″.
The Baltimore Museum of Art, Baltimore, Maryland, Gift of the artist. (p. 233)

258. *Beige Figuration No. 3.* 1967. Collage (paper). 30″ x 22″.
Collection of the artist. (p. 234)

259. *"Open" No. 14: In Ochre with Charcoal Line.* 1968.
Polymer paint and charcoal on canvas. 114″ x 69″.
Collection of the artist. (p. 235)

260. *"Open" No. 17: In Ultramarine with Charcoal Line.* 1968.
Polymer paint and charcoal on canvas. 100″ x 197″.
Collection of the artist. (p. 236)

261. *"Open" No. 31B: In Raw Sienna.* 1968. Charcoal on blotting paper.
17″ x 37½″. Collection of the artist. (p. 236)

BARNETT NEWMAN

262. *Pagan Void.* 1946. Oil on canvas. 33″ x 38″.
Collection of Mrs. Annalee Newman, New York. (p. 237)

263. *The Euclidian Abyss.* 1946–47. Oil and crayon on fabric. 28″ x 22″.
Collection of Mr. and Mrs. Burton Tremaine, Meriden, Connecticut. (p. 237)

264. *Concord.* 1949. Oil on canvas. 89¾″ x 53⅝″.
The Metropolitan Museum of Art, New York, George A. Hearn Fund, 1968. (p. 94)

265. *Onement III.* 1949. Oil on canvas. 72″ x 34″.
Collection of Mr. and Mrs. Joseph Slifka, New York. (p. 238)

266. *Covenant.* 1949. Oil on canvas. 48″ x 60″.
Joseph H. Hirshhorn Collection. (p. 239)

267. *Prometheus Bound.* 1952. Oil on canvas. 131¾″ x 50″.
Collection of William S. Rubin, New York. (p. 240)

268. *Shining Forth (for George).* 1961. Oil on canvas. 9½′ x 14½′.
Collection of Mrs. Annalee Newman, New York. (p. 241)

269. *Who's Afraid of Red, Yellow, Blue I.* 1966. Oil on canvas. 60″ x 50″.
Collection of S. I. Newhouse, Jr., New York. (p. 242)

270. *Anna's Light.* 1968. Acrylic on canvas. 9′ x 20′.
M. Knoedler & Company, Inc., New York. (p. 243)

271. *Jericho.* 1968–69. Acrylic on canvas. 9′6″ x 9′6″.
M. Knoedler & Company, Inc., New York. (p. 243)

272. *Here I (to Marcia).* 1950. Bronze. 8′ x 26″ x 27″.
    Collection of Mrs. Annalee Newman, New York. (p. 244)

273. *Here III.* 1966. Stainless steel and Cor-Ten steel.
    10′5″ x 23½″ x 18½″. M. Knoedler & Company, Inc., New York. (p. 244)

274. *Broken Obelisk.* 1967. Cor-Ten steel. 26′ x 10½′ x 10½′.
    M. Knoedler & Company, Inc., New York. (p. 245)

ISAMU NOGUCHI

275. *The Cry.* 1959. Balsa wood with steel base. 84″ x 30″ x 18″.
    The Solomon R. Guggenheim Museum, New York. (p. 246)

276. *Life of a Cube.* 1962. Black granite. 21″ x 21″ x 21″.
    Cordier & Ekstrom, Inc., New York. (p. 247)

277. *Sky Frame.* 1966. Rose Aurora Portuguese marble. 22″ x 28″ x 8¼″.
    Cordier & Ekstrom, Inc., New York. (p. 247)

278. *White Sun.* 1966. White Italian Saravezza marble. 28½″ (diameter).
    Cordier & Ekstrom, Inc., New York. (p. 95)

279. *Euripides.* 1966. White Italian Altissimo marble. Two pieces, 45″ and
    90″ (high). Cordier & Ekstrom, Inc., New York. (p. 248)

KENNETH NOLAND

280. *Teton Noir.* 1961. Acrylic on canvas. 81″ x 81″.
    Collection of Carter Burden, New York. (p. 249)

281. *Mach II.* 1964. Acrylic resin on canvas. 9′ x 17′. Collection of
    Kimiko and John Powers, Aspen, Colorado. (p. 250)

282. *17th Stage.* 1964. Acrylic on canvas. 8′ x 7′.
    Collection of Mr. and Mrs. Eugene M. Schwartz, New York. (p. 251)

283. *Bend Sinister.* 1964. Acrylic on canvas. 98″ x 161¾″.
    Joseph H. Hirshhorn Collection. (p. 252)

284. *Embrown.* 1964. Acrylic on canvas. 96″ x 145″.
    Collection of Mr. and Mrs. David Mirvish, Toronto, Canada. (p. 252)

285. *Trans-Median.* 1968. Acrylic on canvas. 7½′ x 7½′.
    Collection of Mr. and Mrs. David Mirvish, Toronto, Canada. (p. 253)

286. *Trans-Median II.* 1968. Acrylic emulsion on canvas. 90½″ x 160″.
    Collection of Lawrence Rubin, New York. (p. 96)

287. *Dawn-Dusk.* 1968. Water-miscible acrylic on cotton duck. 30½″ x
    141½″. Collection of Mr. and Mrs. Clement Greenberg, New York. (p. 254)

288. *Via Lime.* 1968–69. Acrylic emulsion on canvas. 90½″ x 240″.
    Collection of Ondine Vaughn and Steve Schapiro, New York. (p. 254)

CLAES OLDENBURG

289. *7-up.* 1961. Enamel on plaster. 50⅛″ x 37⅜″ x 6¼″.
    Collection of Mr. and Mrs. Burton Tremaine, Meriden, Connecticut. (p. 255)

290. *Strong Arm.* 1961. Enamel on plaster. 43⅜″ x 32⅜″ x 5½″.
    Collection of Mr. and Mrs. Burton Tremaine, Meriden, Connecticut. (p. 256)

291. *Soft Typewriter.* 1963. Vinyl, kapok, cloth, and plexiglas.
9″ x 27½″ x 26″. Collection of Alan Power, London, England. (p. 257)

292. *Ironing Board with Shirt and Iron.* 1964. Wood, cloth, vinyl, nylon, and hydrostone.
80″ x 67½″ x 24″. Collection of Mr. and Mrs. Sonnabend, Paris, France. (p. 257)

293. *Tub (hard model).* 1966. Corrugated paper, wood, enamel.
80″ x 32½″ x 28″. Collection of Mrs. Claes Oldenburg, New York. (p. 258)

294. *Giant Pool Balls.* 1967. Sixteen plexiglas balls, 24″ each, wood rack,
120″ x 120″ x 108″. Courtesy of Sidney Janis Gallery, New York. (p. 97)

JULES OLITSKI

295. *Ten O'Clock.* 1959. Paint, spackle, polymer emulsion on panel.
36″ x 36″. Collection of the artist. (p. 259)

296. *Bathsheba.* 1959. Oil on canvas. 78″ x 70″.
Collection of J. Patrick Lannan, Palm Beach, Florida. (p. 260)

297. *Ritual of L.* 1959. Paint, spackle, polymer emulsion on canvas.
6′ x 7′. Collection of the artist. (p. 261)

298. *Commissar Demikovsky.* 1965. Acrylic on canvas. 8′ x 7′.
Collection of Mr. and Mrs. Eugene M. Schwartz, New York. (p. 262)

299. *Thigh Smoke.* 1966. Acrylic on canvas. 167″ x 92½″.
Seattle–First National Bank Collection, Seattle, Washington. (p. 263)

300. *Disarmed.* 1968. Acrylic on canvas. 9′10″ x 16′.
Collection of Mr. and Mrs. Eugene M. Schwartz, New York. (p. 98)

301. *Green Volya.* 1969. Acrylic emulsion on canvas. 9′9″ x 17′5″.
Collection of Lawrence Rubin, New York. (p. 264)

302. *Warehouse Light.* 1969. Acrylic on canvas. 118″ x 174″.
Collection of Lawrence Rubin, New York. (p. 265)

303. *Twelve Nights.* 1968. Aluminum and acrylic, air drying lacquer.
9′ x 16½′ x 12′. Collection of the artist. (p. 265)

JACKSON POLLOCK

304. *Male and Female.* 1942. Oil on canvas. 73¼″ x 49″.
Collection of Mrs. H. Gates Lloyd, Haverford, Pennsylvania. (p. 266)

305. *Moon Woman Cuts the Circle.* 1943. Oil on canvas. 43″ x 41″.
Courtesy of Marlborough-Gerson Gallery, New York. (p. 267)

306. *Night Ceremony.* 1944. Oil and enamel on canvas. 72″ x 43⅛″.
Collection of Mrs. Barbara Reis Poe, New York. (p. 268)

307. *Cathedral.* 1947. Duco and aluminum paint on canvas. 71½″ x 35¹⁄₁₆″.
Dallas Museum of Fine Arts, Gift of Mr. and Mrs. Bernard J. Reis. (p. 269)

308. *Lucifer.* 1947. Oil, enamel, and aluminum paint on canvas.
41″ x 8′9½″. Collection of Joseph H. Hazen, New York. (p. 270)

309. *Mural.* 1950. Oil, enamel, and aluminum paint on canvas, mounted on
wood. 6′ x 8′. Collection of William S. Rubin, New York. (p. 99)

310. *Autumn Rhythm.* 1950. Oil on canvas. 105″ x 207″.
The Metropolitan Museum of Art, New York, Estate of Jackson Pollock,
George A. Hearn Fund, 1957. (p. 270)

311. *Portrait and a Dream.* 1953. Enamel on canvas. 58⅛″ x 134¼″.
Dallas Museum of Fine Arts, Gift of Mr. and Mrs. Algur H. Meadows and
the Meadows Foundation, Inc. (p. 271)

312. *The Deep.* 1953. Oil and duco on canvas. 86¾″ x 51⅛″.
Collection of Samuel Wagstaff, Jr., Detroit, Michigan. (p. 272)

LARRY POONS

313. *Double Speed.* 1962–63. Acrylic and fabric dye on canvas. 72″ x 144″.
Collection of Frank Stella, New York. (p. 273)

314. *Enforcer.* 1963. Liquitex and fabric spray on canvas. 80″ x 80″.
Collection of Mr. and Mrs. Robert C. Scull, New York. (p. 273)

315. *Mary Queen of Scots.* 1965. Acrylic on canvas. 12′ x 90″.
Collection of Mr. and Mrs. Robert C. Scull, New York. (p. 274)

316. *Rosewood.* 1966. Acrylic on canvas. 120″ x 160″.
Collection of William S. Rubin, New York. (p. 275)

317. *Brown Sound.* 1968. Acrylic on canvas. 96″ x 125″.
The Woodward Foundation of Washington, D.C. (p. 100)

318. *Night Journey.* 1968. Acrylic on canvas. 108″ x 124″.
Collection of Carter Burden, New York. (p. 276)

319. *Doge's Palace.* 1969. Acrylic on canvas. 112″ x 17′10″.
Collection of Lawrence Rubin, New York. (p. 277)

ROBERT RAUSCHENBERG

320. *Bed.* 1955. Combine painting. 74″ x 31″.
Collection of Mr. and Mrs. Leo Castelli, New York. (p. 101)

321. *Rebus.* 1955. Combine painting. 96″ x 144″.
Collection of Mr. and Mrs. Victor W. Ganz, New York. (p. 278)

322. *Odalisk.* 1955–58. Construction. 81″ x 25″ x 25″.
Collection of Mr. and Mrs. Victor W. Ganz, New York. (p. 279)

323. *Factum I.* 1957. Combine painting. 62″ x 35½″.
Collection of Dott. Giuseppe Panza di Buomo, Milan, Italy. (p. 280)

324. *Factum II.* 1957. Oil and collage on canvas. 61½″ x 35½″.
Collection of Mr. and Mrs. Morton Neumann, Chicago, Illinois. (p. 281)

325. *Third Time Painting.* 1961. Oil on canvas with clock. 84″ x 60″.
Harry N. Abrams Family Collection, New York. (p. 282)

326. *Tracer.* 1964. Oil on canvas with silkscreen. 84″ x 60″.
Collection of Mr. and Mrs. Frank M. Titelman, Altoona, Pennsylvania. (p. 283)

AD REINHARDT

327. *Yellow Painting.* 1949. Oil on canvas. 40″ x 60″.
Collection of Anna Reinhardt, New York. (p. 284)

328. *Abstract Painting Grey.* 1950. Oil on canvas. 30″ x 40″.
Collection of Rita Reinhardt, New York. (p. 284)

329. *White.* 1950. Oil on canvas. 80″ x 36″.
Collection of Rita Reinhardt, New York. (p. 285)

330. *Red Painting.* 1952. Oil on canvas. 60″ x 82″.
Courtesy of Marlborough-Gerson Gallery, New York. (p. 102)

331. *Red Painting.* 1952. Oil on canvas. 6½′ x 12′.
The Metropolitan Museum of Art, New York, Arthur H. Hearn Fund, 1968. (p. 286)

332. *Abstract Painting.* 1956–60. Oil on canvas. 108″ x 40″.
Courtesy of Marlborough-Gerson Gallery, New York. (p. 287)

333. *Abstract Painting.* 1959. Oil on canvas. 108″ x 40″.
Courtesy of Marlborough-Gerson Gallery, New York. (p. 288)

334. *Abstract Painting.* 1964. Oil on canvas. 60″ x 60″.
Courtesy of Marlborough-Gerson Gallery, New York. (p. 103)

335. *Black Quadruptych.* 1966. Oil on canvas. 120″ x 120″.
Courtesy of Marlborough-Gerson Gallery, New York. (Not illustrated.)

JAMES ROSENQUIST

336. *The Lines Were Deeply Etched on the Map of Her Face.* 1961–62.
Oil on canvas. 66″ x 78″. Collection of Mr. and Mrs. Robert C. Scull,
New York. (p. 104)

337. *Four Young Revolutionaries.* 1962. Glass, wood, and oil paint. 24″ x 32″.
Collection of Mr. and Mrs. Lewis V. Winter, New York. (p. 289)

338. Untitled. 1962. Oil on canvas. 84″ x 72″.
Collection of Mr. and Mrs. Robert A. Rowan, Pasadena, California. (p. 290)

339. *Silver Skies.* 1962. Oil on canvas. 78″ x 16½″.
Collection of Mr. and Mrs. Robert C. Scull, New York. (p. 291)

340. *Early in the Morning.* 1963. Oil on canvas. 95″ x 56″.
Collection of Mr. and Mrs. Robert C. Scull, New York. (p. 292)

341. *Nomad.* 1963. Oil on canvas, plastic paint, wood. 84″ x 210″.
Albright-Knox Art Gallery, Buffalo, New York, Gift of Seymour H. Knox. (p. 293)

342. *Growth Plan.* 1966. Oil on canvas. 70″ x 140″ (2 panels).
Museum of Contemporary Art, Nagaoka, Japan. (p. 293)

343. *Tumbleweed.* 1963–66. Chromed barbed wire and neon. 54″ x 60″ x 60″ approximately. Leo Castelli Gallery, New York. (p. 294)

MARK ROTHKO

344. Untitled. 1946. Watercolor. 38¾″ x 25½″.
Collection of Mr. and Mrs. Donald Blinken, New York. (p. 295)

345. *Vessels of Magic.* 1946–47. Watercolor. 38¾″ x 25¾″.
The Brooklyn Museum, New York. (p. 296)

346. *Fantasy.* 1947. Watercolor. 25½″ x 39½″.
Collection of Mr. and Mrs. Donald Blinken, New York. (p. 297)

347. *No. 26.* 1947. Oil on canvas. 34″ x 45¼″.
Collection of Mrs. Betty Parsons, New York. (p. 297)

348. *Black, Pink and Yellow over Orange.* 1951–52. Oil on canvas.
116″ x 92¼″. Collection of William S. Rubin, New York. (p. 298)

349. *No. 10.* 1952. Oil on canvas. 81½″ x 42½″.
Collection of Mr. and Mrs. C. B. Wright, Seattle, Washington. (p. 299)

350. *No. 8.* 1952. Oil on canvas. 80½″ x 68″.
Collection of Mr. and Mrs. Burton Tremaine, Meriden, Connecticut. (p. 300)

351. *Brown, Black and Blue.* 1958. Oil on canvas. 5′9″ x 5′.
Collection of Dr. and Mrs. Edward Massie, St. Louis, Missouri. (p. 301)

352. *Reds, No. 16.* 1960. Oil on canvas. 102″ x 119½″.
Collection of Mr. and Mrs. Robert C. Scull, New York. (p. 105)

353. *Number 207 (Red Over Dark Blue on Dark Gray).* 1961. Oil on canvas.
92¾″ x 81⅛″. University Art Museum, Berkeley, California. Acquired from the
artist. (p. 302)

GEORGE SEGAL

354. *The Gas Station.* 1963. Plaster and mixed media. 8′6″ x 24′ x 4′.
The National Gallery of Canada, Ottawa, Canada. (p. 106)

DAVID SMITH

355. *False Peace Specter.* 1945. Bronze and steel painted blue.
21½″ x 27¼″ x 10¾″. Private collection. (Not illustrated.)

356. *Billiard Player II.* 1945. Steel. 16¾″ x 17⅞″ x 6⅝″.
Collection of Mr. and Mrs. Louis D. Cohen, Great Neck, New York.
(Not illustrated.)

357. *Deserted Garden Landscape.* 1946. Steel, bronze. 11¾″ x 10⅛″ x 4¾″.
Collection of Mr. and Mrs. Harry W. Anderson, Atherton, California. (p. 303)

358. *Puritan Landscape.* 1946. Steel, bronze, cast iron, nickel.
28¼″ x 15″ x 10″. Collection of Peter Brant, New York. (p. 304)

359. *Australia.* 1951. Painted steel. 97½″ x 107⅞″ x 16⅛″ (including base).
Collection of William S. Rubin, New York. (p. 305)

360. *Forging No. 4.* 1955. Steel. 90⅝″ x 8½″ x 8¼″. Estate of David Smith.
Courtesy of Marlborough-Gerson Gallery, New York. (Not illustrated.)

361. *Forging No. 10.* 1955. Steel. 70½″ x 11″ x 12″.
Estate of David Smith. Courtesy of Marlborough-Gerson Gallery,
New York. (Not illustrated.)

362. *Forging No. 11.* 1955. Steel. 8⅝″ x 8½″ x 7⅞″.
Estate of David Smith. Courtesy of Marlborough-Gerson Gallery,
New York. (Not illustrated.)

363. *Albany III.* 1959. Painted steel. 26½″ x 19¼″ x 13⅛″.
Estate of David Smith. Courtesy of Marlborough-Gerson Gallery,
New York. (Not illustrated.)

364. *Albany XII.* 1961. Welded steel painted black. 30″ x 14½″ x 21½″.
Collection of Mr. and Mrs. Stephen D. Paine, Boston, Massachusetts. (p. 305)

365. *2 Circles IV.* 1962. Painted steel. 124″ x 60″ x 28½″.
Estate of David Smith. Courtesy of Marlborough-Gerson Gallery, New York. (p. 306)

366. *Primo Piano III.* 1962. Painted steel. 124″ x 145″ x 18″.
Courtesy of Marlborough-Gerson Gallery, New York. (p. 307)

367. *Voltri VI.* 1962. Steel. 103″ x 102¾″ x 25½″.
Private collection, New York. (p. 307)

368. *Voltri XIII.* 1962. Steel. 64⅛″ x 103¾″ x 26″.
University Art Museum, Berkeley, California, Gift of Mr. and Mrs. Eugene E. Trefethen, Jr., Piedmont, California. (p. 308)

369. *Voltri XIX.* 1962. Welded and shaped iron and found objects. 55″ x 45″ x 50″.
Collection of Mr. and Mrs. Stephen D. Paine, Boston, Massachusetts. (p. 308)

370. Untitled. 1962–63. Stainless steel. 96¼″ x 63″ x 26″.
Art Gallery of Ontario, Purchase with assistance from the Women's Committee Fund, 1968. (p. 309)

371. *Voltron XII.* 1963. Steel. 95³⁄₁₆″ x 18″.
Collection of Anne and Robert Simon, Jr., New York. (Not illustrated.)

372. *Wagon II.* 1964. Forged iron. 84″ x 112″ x 45″.
Estate of David Smith. Courtesy of Marlborough-Gerson Gallery, New York. (p. 310)

373. *Cubi XXIV.* 1964. Stainless steel. 114¼″ x 83½″.
Museum of Art, Carnegie Institute, Pittsburgh, Pennsylvania, Howard Heinz Endowment Purchase Fund. (p. 311)

374. Untitled. 1965. Stainless steel. 102½″ x 120″ x 31¼″.
Estate of David Smith. Courtesy of Marlborough-Gerson Gallery, New York. (p. 312)

375. *Cubi XXV.* 1965. Stainless steel. 119¼″ x 120¾″ x 31¼″.
Estate of David Smith. Courtesy of Marlborough-Gerson Gallery, New York. (p. 313)

376. *Becca.* 1965. Stainless steel. 116″ x 120¼″ x 31½″.
Estate of David Smith. Courtesy of Marlborough-Gerson Gallery, New York. (p. 107)

TONY SMITH

377. *Die.* 1962. Steel. 6′ x 6′ x 6′.
Collection of Samuel Wagstaff, Jr., Detroit, Michigan. (p. 108)

378. *Black Box.* 1962. Steel. 22½″ x 33″ x 25″.
Collection of Mr. and Mrs. Norman Ives, Woodbridge, Connecticut. (p. 314)

379. *Free Ride.* 1962. Steel. (#2 of an edition of three.) 6′8″ x 6′8″ x 6′8″.
Courtesy of Fischbach Gallery, New York. (p. 314)

FRANK STELLA

380. *Zambesi.* 1959. Enamel on canvas. 90″ x 78″.
Collection of Lawrence Rubin, New York. (p. 315)

381. *Nunca Pasa Nada.* 1964. Metallic powder in acrylic emulsion on canvas. 9′ x 18′ approximately. The Lannan Foundation. (p. 316)

382. *Valparaiso (flesh and green).* 1964. Metallic paint on canvas. 84″ x 144″. Collection of the artist. (p. 316)

383. *Ossippee I.* 1966. Fluorescent alkyd and epoxy paint on canvas. 95″ x 138″. Collection of Dr. and Mrs. Ernest Kafka, New York. (p. 317)

384. *Union IV.* 1966. Fluorescent alkyd and epoxy paint on canvas. 103″ x 174″. Collection of Richard Meier, New York. (p. 318)

385. *Sangre de Cristo.* 1967. Metallic powder in polymer emulsion. 10′ x 42′. Collection of Dr. and Mrs. Charles Hendrickson, Newport Beach, California. (p. 319)

386. *Hagmatana II.* 1967. Acrylic on canvas. 10′ x 15′.
Collection of Mr. and Mrs. Eugene M. Schwartz, New York. (p. 320)

387. *Sinjerli Variation IV.* 1968. Fluorescent acrylic on canvas. 120″ (diameter).
Collection of Mr. and Mrs. David Mirvish, Toronto, Canada. (p. 109)

388. *Ctesiphon III.* 1968. Fluorescent acrylic on canvas. 10′ x 20′.
Wallraf-Richartz Museum, Köln, Germany, Sammlung Ludwig. (p. 320)

CLYFFORD STILL

389. *Painting 1948-D.* 1948. Oil on canvas. 93⅛″ x 79⅝″.
Collection of William S. Rubin, New York. (p. 321)

390. *No. 5.* 1951. Oil on canvas. 55″ x 46″.
Wadsworth Atheneum, Hartford, Connecticut, (p. 322)

391. *Painting.* 1951. Oil on canvas. 93¼″ x 75¾″.
The Detroit Institute of Arts, W. Hawkins Ferry Fund. (p. 323)

392. *1957-D No. 1.* 1957. Oil on canvas. 113″ x 159″.
Albright-Knox Art Gallery, Buffalo, New York, Gift of Seymour H. Knox. (p. 110)

393. *Painting.* 1958. Oil on canvas. 113¾″ x 159½″.
Collection of J. Patrick Lannan, Palm Beach, Florida. (p. 324)

BRADLEY WALKER TOMLIN

394. *All Souls' Night.* 1948. Oil on canvas. 42½″ x 64″.
Betty Parsons Gallery, New York. (p. 325)

395. *Tension by Moonlight.* 1948. Oil on canvas. 32″ x 44″.
Betty Parsons Gallery, New York. (p. 326)

396. *Number 3.* 1948. Oil on canvas. 40″ x 50⅛″.
The Museum of Modern Art, New York, Fractional gift of John E.
Hutchins in memory of Frances E. Marder Hutchins, 1960. (p. 327)

397. *Number 4.* 1949. Oil on canvas. 43″ x 61″. Collection of
Mr. and Mrs. Edward L. Diehl, Cambridge, Massachusetts. (Not illustrated.)

398. *Number 10-A.* 1949. Oil on canvas. 46″ x 31″.
Collection of Dustin Rice, New York. (p. 111)

399. *Number 11.* 1949. Oil on canvas. 44⅛″ x 29″.
Munson-Williams-Proctor Institute, Utica, New York, Edward W. Root Bequest.
(p. 328)

400. *Number 9: In Memory of Gertrude Stein.* 1950. Oil on canvas.
49″ x 8′6¼″. The Museum of Modern Art, New York,
Gift of Mrs. John D. Rockefeller, III, 1955. (p. 329)

401. *Number 5.* 1952. Oil on canvas. 79″ x 45″.
Collection of Mrs. Betty Parsons, New York. (p. 330)

ANDY WARHOL

402. *Dick Tracy.* 1960. Casein on canvas. 70⅛″ x 52¼″.
Gordon Locksley Gallery, Minneapolis, Minnesota. (p. 331)

403. *Campbell's Soup Cans.* 1961–62. Oil on canvas. 32 panels, each 20″ x 16″
Collection of Irving Blum, Los Angeles, California. (pp. 332–33)

404. *Do It Yourself.* 1962. Liquitex on canvas. 72″ x 54″.
Collection of Kimiko and John Powers, Aspen, Colorado. (p. 334)

405. *Marilyn Monroe Diptych.* 1962. Oil on canvas. 82″ x 114″.
Collection of Mr. and Mrs. Burton Tremaine, Meriden, Connecticut. (p. 335)

406. *Ethel Scull 36 times.* 1963. Silkscreen media on canvas. 12′ x 8′4″.
Collection of Mr. and Mrs. Robert C. Scull, New York. (p. 112)

407. *Orange Disaster.* 1963. Oil on canvas. 106″ x 82″.
Harry N. Abrams Family Collection, New York. (p. 336)

408. *Brillo Box.* 1964. Silkscreen ink on wood. 17″ x 17″ x 17″.
Leo Castelli Gallery, New York. (p. 337)

Reproductions in Color
Reproductions in Black and White

Josef Albers:
Late Thought. 1964. Oil on board. 48″ x 48″.
The Woodward Foundation of Washington, D.C.

Milton Avery:
Speedboat's Wake. 1959. Oil on canvas. 55″ x 73″.
The David Mirvish Gallery, Toronto, Canada.

Alexander Calder:
The Pregnant Whale. 1963. Steel plate painted. 9′6″ x 8′10″ x 7′2″.
Collection of Mrs. Julius Epstein, Northfield, Illinois.

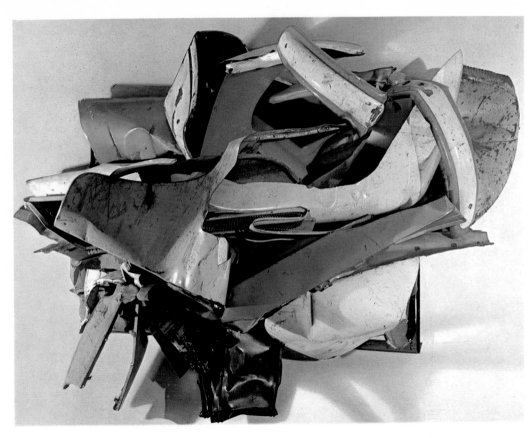

John Chamberlain:
Dolores James. 1962. Welded auto metal. 76″ x 97″ x 39″.
Leo Castelli Gallery, New York.

Joseph Cornell:
Habitat Group for a Shooting Gallery. 1943.
Wood cabinet containing colored cutouts of parrots,
printed cards, and papers, etc. behind shattered glass.
15½″ x 11⅛″ x 4¼″.
Collection of Irving Blum, Los Angeles, California.

Stuart Davis:
Hot Stillscape in Six Colors. 1940. Oil on canvas. 36″ x 45″.
Courtesy of The Downtown Gallery, New York.

Willem de Kooning:
Bill-Lee's Delight. ca. 1946. Oil on paper. 27½″ x 34¼″.
Collection of Mr. and Mrs. Lee V. Eastman, New York.

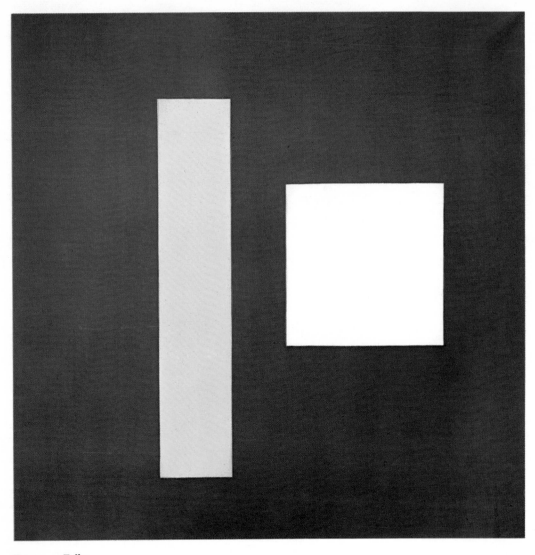

Burgoyne Diller:
No. 33, First Theme. 1962. Oil on canvas. 32″ x 32″.
Collection of Mr. and Mrs. Richard Hokin, New York.

Mark di Suvero:
Mohican. 1967. Steel and wood. 15′ x 9′ x 30′.
Collection of Mr. Lewis Manilow, Chicago, Illinois.

Dan Flavin:
the nominal three (to William of Ockham). 1963.
Cool white fluorescent light. 8′ (high).
The National Gallery of Canada, Ottawa, Canada.

Helen Frankenthaler:
Yellow Caterpillar. 1961. Oil on canvas. 90″ x 120″.
Private collection, New York.

Arshile Gorky:
Water of the Flowery Mill. 1944. Oil on canvas. 42¼″ x 48¾″.
The Metropolitan Museum of Art, New York, George A. Hearn Fund, 1956.

Adolph Gottlieb:
Una. 1959. Oil on canvas. 108″ x 90″.
Collection of the artist.

Adolph Gottlieb:
Wall (maquette). 1968. Painted steel.
27½" x 40½" x 24½" (one-third size of projected sculpture).
Collection of the artist.

Philip Guston:
Painting. 1952. Oil on canvas. 50¾″ x 48″.
Collection of Mrs. Albert H. Newman, Chicago, Illinois.

Hans Hofmann: *Veluti in Speculum.* 1962.
Oil on canvas. 85¼″ x 73½″.
The Metropolitan Museum of Art, New York,
Gift of Mr. and Mrs. Richard Rodgers
and the Francis Lathrop Fund, 1963.

Hans Hofmann
Lust and Delight (Renata Series No. 2).
1965. Oil on canvas. 84″ x 60″.
Estate of Hans Hofmann.

Edward Hopper:
Western Motel. 1957. Oil on canvas. 30¼″ x 50⅛″.
Yale University Art Gallery, Bequest of Stephen Carlton Clark, B.A., 1903.

Jasper Johns:
Painting with Two Balls. 1960. Encaustic and collage on canvas with objects. 65″ x 54″
(three panels). Collection of the artist.

Donald Judd:
Untitled. 1963. Painted wood and aluminum. 48″ x 83″ x 48″.
Collection of Julie Judd, New York.

Ellsworth Kelly:
Red Blue Green Yellow. 1965. Oil on canvas. 86″ x 53½″.
Collection of Mr. and Mrs. Robert B. Mayer, Winnetka, Illinois.

Franz Kline:
Blue Center. 1958. Oil on canvas. 36″ x 40″.
Collection of Mr. and Mrs. Robert C. Scull, New York.

Ellsworth Kelly:
Blue White Angle. 1966. Epoxy on aluminum. 72″ x 36″ x 72″.
Private collection, New York.

Gabe Kohn:
Acrotere. 1960. Laminated wood. 35¼″ x 31″ x 22¼″.
The Museum of Modern Art, New York, Given anonymously, 1963.

Roy Lichtenstein:
The Engagement Ring. 1961. Oil on canvas. 67¾″ x 79½″.
Collection of Mr. and Mrs. Robert A. Rowan, Pasadena, California.

Morris Louis:
Iris. 1954. Acrylic on canvas. 80″ x 106″.
Collection of Mr. and Mrs. Eugene M. Schwartz, New York.

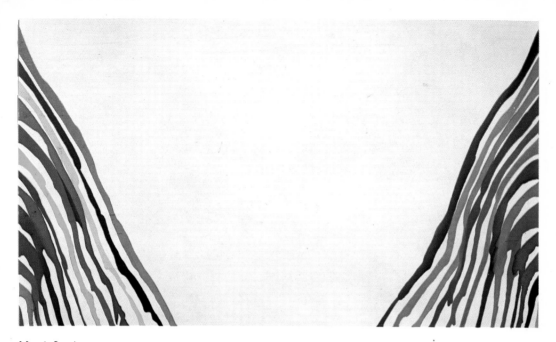

Morris Louis:
Alpha-Pi. 1961. Acrylic on canvas. 102½″ x 177″.
The Metropolitan Museum of Art, New York, Arthur H. Hearn Fund, 1967.

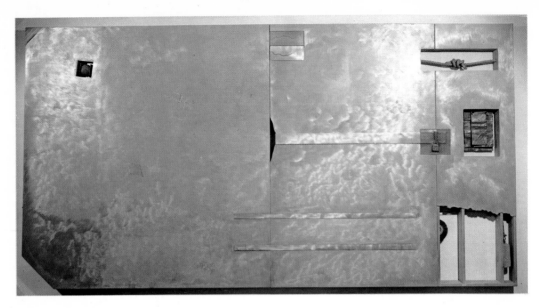

Robert Morris:
Untitled. 1965. Aluminum construction. 6′ x 11′7″ x 3″.
Collection of Mr. and Mrs. Robert C. Scull, New York.

Robert Motherwell:
Mallarmé's Swan. 1944. Collage using gouache, crayon, and paper on
cardboard. 43½″ x 35½″.
Contemporary Collection of The Cleveland Museum of Art, Cleveland, Ohio.

Isamu Noguchi:
White Sun. 1966. White Italian Saravezza marble. 28½″ (diameter).
Cordier & Ekstrom, Inc., New York.

Barnett Newman:
Concord. 1949. Oil on canvas. 89¾″ x 53⅝″.
The Metropolitan Museum of Art, New York, George A. Hearn Fund, 1968.

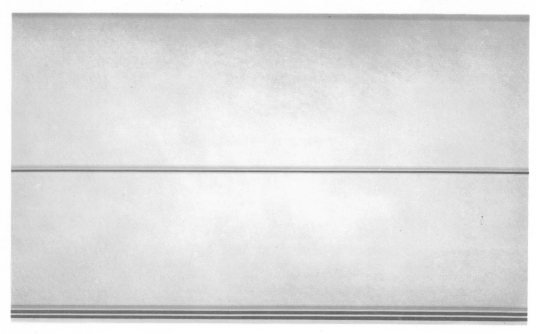

Kenneth Noland:
Trans-Median II. 1968. Acrylic emulsion on canvas. 90½″ x 160″.
Collection of Lawrence Rubin, New York.

Claes Oldenburg:
Giant Pool Balls. 1967. Sixteen plexiglas balls 24″ each, wood rack.
120″ x 120″ x 108″.
Courtesy of Sidney Janis Gallery, New York.

Jules Olitski:
Disarmed. 1968. Acrylic on canvas. 9'10" x 16'.
Collection of Mr. and Mrs. Eugene M. Schwartz, New York.

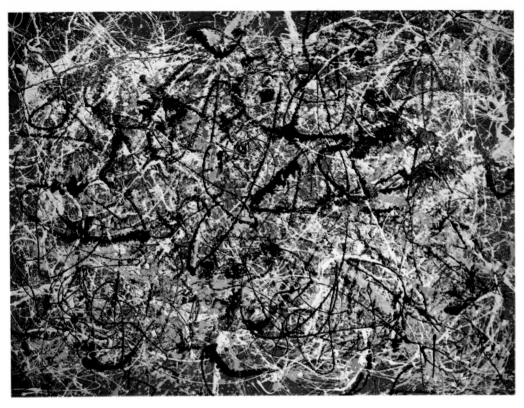

Jackson Pollock:
Mural. 1950. Oil, enamel, and aluminum paint on canvas, mounted on wood.
6′ x 8′. Collection of William S. Rubin, New York.

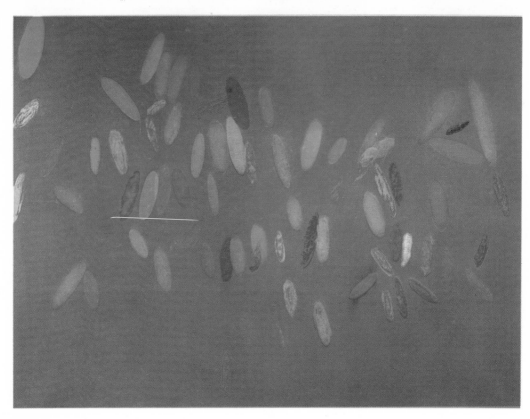

Larry Poons:
Brown Sound. 1968. Acrylic on canvas. 96″ x 125″.
The Woodward Foundation of Washington, D.C.

Robert Rauschenberg:
Bed. 1955. Combine painting. 74″ x 31″.
Collection of Mr. and Mrs. Leo Castelli,
New York.

Ad Reinhardt:
Red Painting. 1952. Oil on canvas. 60″ x 82″.
Courtesy of Marlborough-Gerson Gallery, New York.

Ad Reinhardt:
Abstract Painting. 1964. Oil on canvas. 60″ x 60″.
Courtesy of Marlborough-Gerson Gallery, New York.

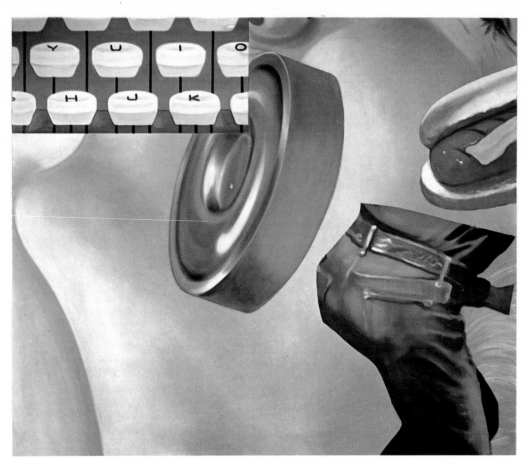

James Rosenquist:
The Lines Were Deeply Etched on the Map of Her Face. 1961–62.
Oil on canvas. 66″ x 78″.
Collection of Mr. and Mrs. Robert C. Scull, New York.

Mark Rothko:
Reds, No. 16. 1960. Oil on canvas. 102″ x 119½″.
Collection of Mr. and Mrs. Robert C. Scull, New York.

George Segal:
The Gas Station. 1964. Plaster and mixed media. 8′6″ x 24′ x 4′.
The National Gallery of Canada, Ottawa, Canada.

David Smith:
Becca. 1965. Stainless steel. 116″ x 120¼″ x 31½″.
Estate of David Smith. Courtesy of Marlborough-Gerson Gallery, New York.

Frank Stella:
Sinjerli Variation IV. 1968. Fluorescent acrylic on canvas. 120″ (diameter).
Collection of Mr. and Mrs. David Mirvish, Toronto, Canada.

Tony Smith:
Die. 1962. Steel. 6′ x 6′ x 6′.
Collection of Samuel Wagstaff, Jr., Detroit, Michigan.

109

Clyfford Still:
1957-D no. 1. 1957. Oil on canvas. 113″ x 159″.
Albright-Knox Art Gallery, Buffalo, New York, Gift of Seymour H. Knox.

Bradley Walker Tomlin:
Number 10-A. 1949. Oil on canvas. 46″ x 31″.
Collection of Dustin Rice, New York.

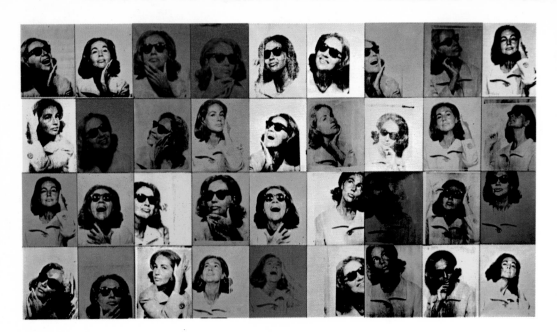

Andy Warhol:
Ethel Scull 36 Times. 1963. Silkscreen media on canvas. 12′ x 8′4″.
Collection of Mr. and Mrs. Robert C. Scull, New York.

Josef Albers:
Growing. 1940. Oil on masonite. 15″ x 17¾″.
The Collection of The San Francisco Museum of Art, San Francisco, California,
Gift of Mrs. Charlotte Mack.

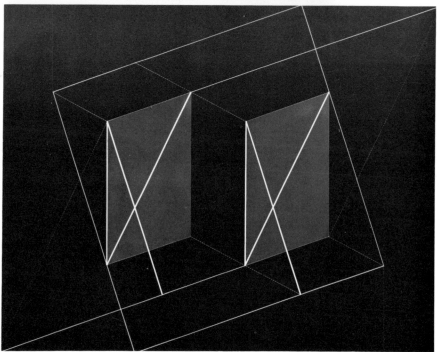

LEFT, ABOVE. Josef Albers:
Indicating Solids. 1949. Oil on masonite. 26″ x 25¾″.
Collection of the artist.

LEFT, BELOW. Josef Albers:
Transformations of a Scheme Series: No. 10. 1950.
Machine-engraved in laminated formica. 17″ x 22½″.
Collection of the artist.

ABOVE. Josef Albers:
Homage to the Square Series: New Gate. 1951.
Oil on masonite. 24″ x 24″. Collection of the artist.

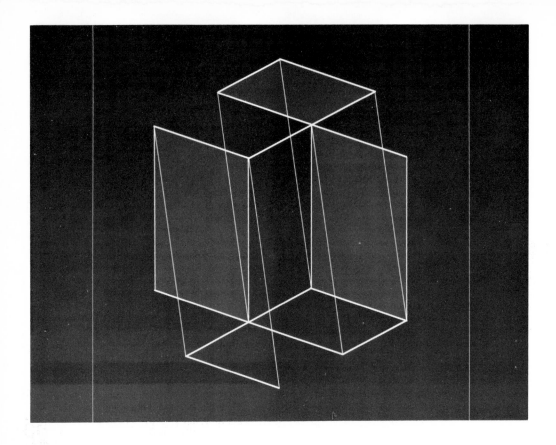

ABOVE. Josef Albers:
Transformations of a Scheme Series: No. 26. 1952.
Machine-engraved in laminated formica. 17″ x 22½″.
Collection of the artist.

RIGHT, ABOVE. Josef Albers:
Homage to the Square Series: In Wide Light. 1953.
Oil on masonite. 18″ x 18″. Collection of the artist.

RIGHT, BELOW. Josef Albers:
Biconjugate Series: Red Orange Wall. 1959.
Oil on masonite. 24″ x 34½″. Collection of the artist.

117

ABOVE. Josef Albers:
Biconjugate Series: Chalk-Green Facade. 1960.
Oil on masonite. 28″ x 40½″. Collection of the artist.

RIGHT, ABOVE. Milton Avery:
Gaspé—Pink Sky. 1940. Oil on canvas. 40″ x 50″.
Collection of Mr. and Mrs. Maurice Geller, New York.

RIGHT, BELOW. Milton Avery:
Mother and Child. 1944. Oil on canvas. 40″ x 30″.
Tirca Karlis Gallery, Provincetown, Massachusetts.

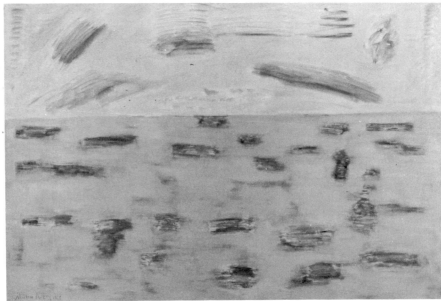

LEFT, ABOVE. Milton Avery:
Sail. 1958. Oil on canvas. 72″ x 50″.
Grace Borgenicht Gallery, New York.

LEFT, BELOW. Milton Avery:
Sunset Sea. 1958. Oil on canvas. 49½″ x 73½″.
The David Mirvish Gallery, Toronto, Canada.

ABOVE. Alexander Calder:
Little Spider. ca. 1940. Painted sheet metal and steel wire and rods.
55″ x 50″. Perls Galleries, New York.

ABOVE. Alexander Calder:
Mobile. 1963. Sheet steel. 27′.
The Connecticut Bank and Trust Company, Hartford, Connecticut.

RIGHT, ABOVE. Alexander Calder:
Four Planes Écartés. 1967. Painted sheet steel. *ca.* 10′6″ (high).
Perls Galleries, New York.

RIGHT, BELOW. Alexander Calder:
Six Planes Écartés. 1967. Painted sheet steel. *ca.* 10′6″ (high).
Perls Galleries, New York.

John Chamberlain:
Fantail. 1961. Painted steel. 70″ x 75″ x 60″.
Collection of Jasper Johns, New York.

John Chamberlain:
Velvet White. 1962. Welded steel. 83″ x 57″ x 48″.
The Albert A. List Family Collection, New York.

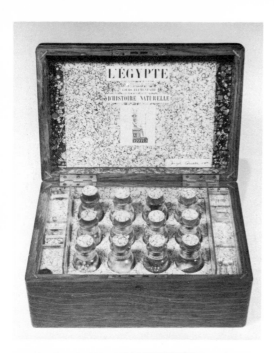

Joseph Cornell:
L'Egypte de Mlle. Cléo de Mérode; cours élémentaire d'histoire naturelle.
1940. Wood, glass, cork, and miscellaneous materials. 4¾″ x 10¾″ x 7¼″.
Collection of Mr. and Mrs. Richard L. Feigen, New York.

Joseph Cornell:
Medici Slot Machine. 1942. Construction. 15½″ x 12″ x 4⅜″.
Collection of Mr. and Mrs. Bernard J. Reis, New York.

Joseph Cornell:
A Pantry Ballet (for Jacques Offenbach).
Summer, 1942.
Wood, paper, plastic, metal, glass, etc.
10½″ x 18″ x 6″.
Collection of Mr. and Mrs. Richard L.
Feigen, New York.

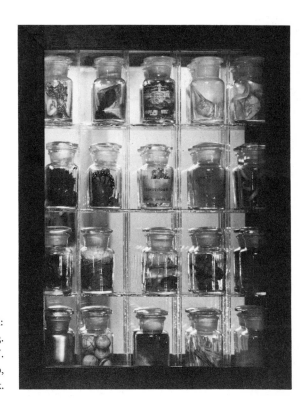

Joseph Cornell:
Pharmacy. 1943.
Wooden box with glass bottles. 15¼″ x 12″ x 3″.
Collection of Mrs. Marcel Duchamp,
New York.

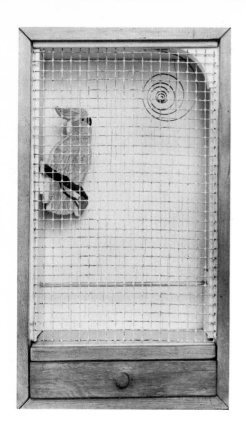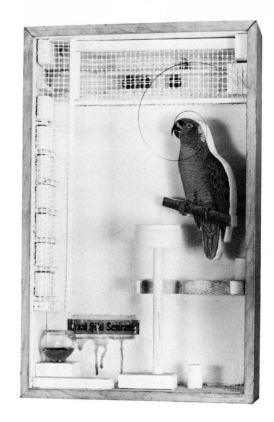

LEFT. Joseph Cornell:
Cockatoo: "Keepsake Parakeet." 1949–53. Construction in wood.
20¼″ x 12″ x 5″. Collection of Donald Windham, New York.

RIGHT. Joseph Cornell:
Grand Hotel Semiramis. 1950. Construction of wood, glass, and diverse
materials. 18″ x 12″ x 4″. Collection of Mr. and Mrs. Allan Frumkin, New York.

LEFT. Joseph Cornell:
Hotel du Nord. ca. 1953. Construction in wood, glass, and paper.
19″ x 13¼″. The Whitney Museum of American Art, New York.

RIGHT. Joseph Cornell:
Hotel de L'Étoile. ca. 1956–57. Painted wood construction.
18½″ x 14″ x 7½″. Collection of Mrs. Eleanor Ward, New York.

ABOVE. Stuart Davis:
Owh! In San Paõ. 1951. Oil on canvas. 52¼″ x 41¾″.
The Whitney Museum of American Art, New York.

RIGHT, ABOVE. Stuart Davis:
Colonial Cubism. 1954. Oil on canvas. 45″ x 60″.
Collection of The Walker Art Center, Minneapolis, Minnesota.

RIGHT, BELOW. Stuart Davis:
Pochade. 1958. Oil on canvas. 60″ x 52″.
Courtesy of The Downtown Gallery, New York.

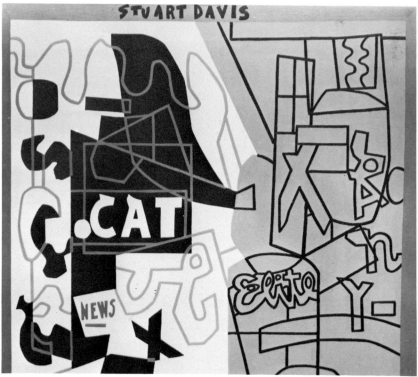

Stuart Davis:
Switchsky's Syntax. 1961–64. Tempera on canvas. 42″ x 56″.
Courtesy of Mrs. Stuart Davis, New York.

Willem de Kooning:
Seated Woman. ca. 1940. Oil and charcoal on composition board.
54″ x 36″. Collection of Mrs. Albert M. Greenfield, Sr., Philadelphia, Pennsylvania.

Willem de Kooning:
Queen of Hearts. 1943–46. Oil and charcoal on composition board.
46″ x 27½″. Joseph H. Hirshhorn Foundation.

Willem de Kooning:
Pink Lady. ca. 1944. Oil and charcoal on masonite composition board.
48¼″ x 35¼″.
Collection of Mr. and Mrs. Stanley K. Sheinbaum, Santa Barbara, California.

Willem de Kooning:
The Marshes. ca. 1945. Charcoal and oil on composition board.
32″ x 23⅞″. University Art Museum, Berkeley, California,
Gift of Julian J. and Joachim Jean Aberbach, New York.

Willem de Kooning:
Light in August. ca. 1946. Oil and enamel on paper, mounted on canvas.
55″ x 44½″. Collection of Elise C. Dixon, Scottsdale, Arizona.

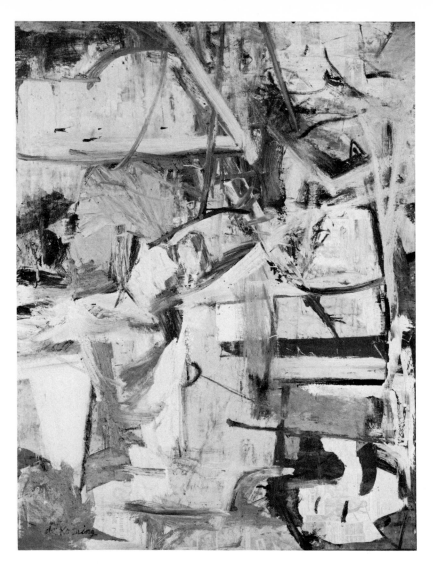

LEFT, ABOVE. Willem de Kooning:
Untitled. 1948. Oil on paper, mounted on masonite. 24" x 36".
Collection of Mr. and Mrs. Stephen D. Paine, Boston, Massachusetts.

LEFT, BELOW. Willem de Kooning:
Police Gazette. 1954–55. Oil on canvas. 43¼" x 50¼".
Collection of Mr. and Mrs. Robert C. Scull, New York.

ABOVE. Willem de Kooning:
Easter Monday. 1955–56. Oil and newspaper transfer on canvas.
96" x 74". The Metropolitan Museum of Art, New York, Rogers Fund, 1956.

Willem de Kooning:
Spike's Folly I. 1959. Oil on canvas. 79″ x 68½″.
Collection of Mr. and Mrs. Robert C. Scull, New York.

Willem de Kooning:
Door to the River. 1960. Oil on canvas. 80″ x 70″.
The Whitney Museum of American Art, New York, Gift of the Friends of The
Whitney Museum of American Art and purchase.

Burgoyne Diller:
First Theme. 1962. Oil on canvas. 72″ x 72″.
The Art Institute of Chicago, Wilson L. Mead Fund Income.

Burgoyne Diller:
No. 5, Third Theme. 1963. Oil on canvas. 42″ x 42″.
The Diller Estate, Courtesy of Noah Goldowsky and Richard Bellamy, New York.

LEFT, ABOVE. Burgoyne Diller:
No. 10, First Theme. 1963–64. Oil on canvas. 72″ x 72″.
The Diller Estate, Courtesy of Noah Goldowsky and Richard Bellamy, New York.

LEFT, BELOW. Burgoyne Diller:
No. 9, First Theme. 1963–64. Oil on canvas. 72″ x 72″.
Albright–Knox Art Gallery, Buffalo, New York, Gift of Seymour H. Knox.

ABOVE. Mark di Suvero:
Hankchampion. 1960. Wood and chain construction. 6′ x 10′.
Collection of Mr. and Mrs. Robert C. Scull, New York.

ABOVE. Mark di Suvero:
Tom. 1961. Wood and steel. 8′ x 10′ x 10′.
Lo Giudice Gallery, Chicago, Illinois, and Richard Bellamy, New York.

RIGHT, ABOVE. Dan Flavin:
untitled. 1965. (Drawing for.)
A set of seven cubes. White baked enamel on steel with cool white
fluorescent light. Size determined by length of fixture. Dwan Gallery, New York.

RIGHT, BELOW. Dan Flavin:
untitled. 1966. Cool white fluorescent light. 8′ (high).
Collection of Mr. and Mrs. Robert A. M. Stern, New York.

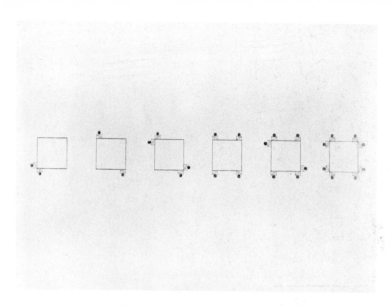

ABOVE. Dan Flavin:
untitled. 1966. Cool white fluorescent light. *ca.* 8′ x 8′.
Collection of Irving Blum, Los Angeles, California.

RIGHT, ABOVE. Helen Frankenthaler:
Abstract Landscape. 1951. Oil on canvas. 69″ x 71⅞″.
Collection of the artist.

RIGHT, BELOW. Helen Frankenthaler:
Other Generations. 1957. Oil on canvas. 70″ x 70″.
Collection of the artist.

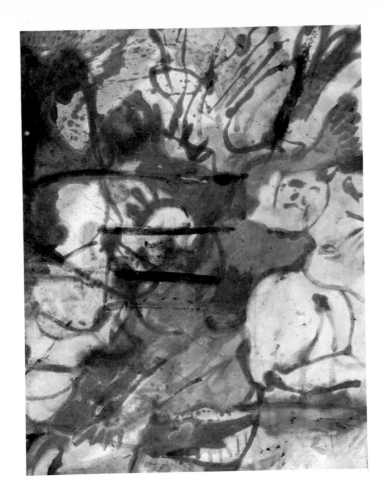

ABOVE. Helen Frankenthaler:
Europa. 1957. Oil on canvas. 70½″ x 54″.
Collection of the artist.

RIGHT. Helen Frankenthaler:
The Moors. 1962. Acrylic on canvas. 107″ x 47″.
Collection of William S. Rubin, New York.

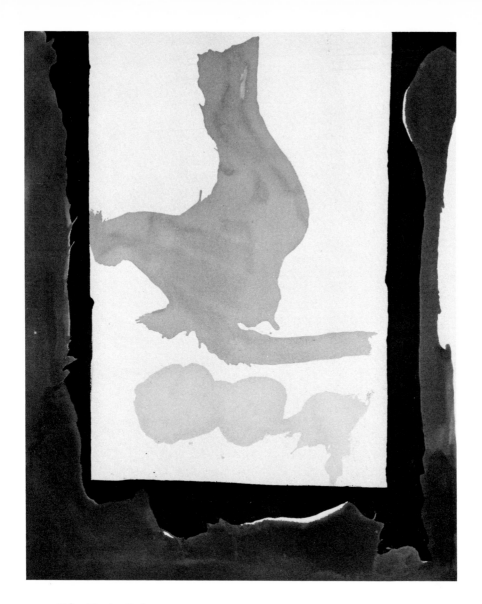

LEFT. Helen Frankenthaler:
Blue Atmosphere. 1963. Acrylic on canvas. 117½″ x 70″.
Collection of the artist.

ABOVE. Helen Frankenthaler:
Orange Shapes in Frame. 1964. Acrylic on canvas. 93″ x 74″.
Collection of Mr. and Mrs. Robert B. Mayer, Winnetka, Illinois.

Helen Frankenthaler:
One O'Clock. 1966. Acrylic paint on canvas. 93¾" x 75¾".
Collection of Albert F. Weis, Savannah, Georgia.

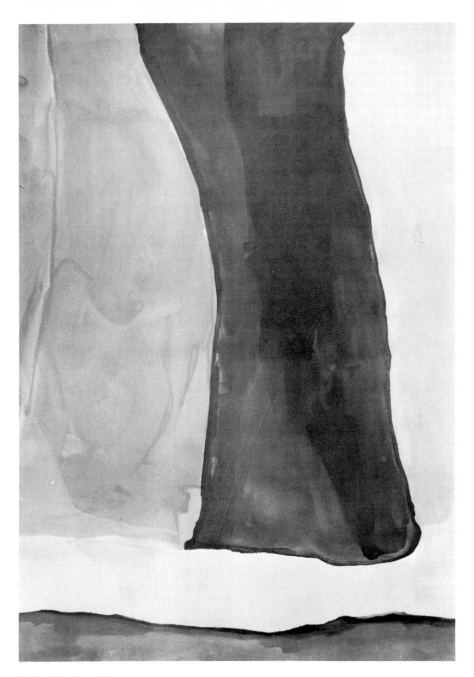

Helen Frankenthaler:
Gamut. 1968. Acrylic on canvas. 11′2″ x 93″.
Collection of the artist.

Arshile Gorky:
Garden in Sochi. 1940–41. Oil on canvas. 25″ x 29″.
Private collection, Courtesy of M. Knoedler & Company, Inc., New York.

Arshile Gorky:
Garden in Sochi. ca. 1943. Oil on canvas. 31″ x 39″.
The Museum of Modern Art, New York, Purchase, 1969. (Not in exhibition.)

LEFT, ABOVE. Arshile Gorky:
The Pirate I. 1942. Oil on canvas. 29¼″ x 40⅛″.
Collection of Mr. and Mrs. Julien Levy, Bridgewater, Connecticut.

LEFT, BELOW. Arshile Gorky:
The Pirate II. 1943. Oil on canvas. 30″ x 36″.
Collection of Mr. and Mrs. Julien Levy, Bridgewater, Connecticut.

ABOVE. Arshile Gorky:
The Unattainable. 1945. Oil on canvas. 41⅛″ x 29¼″.
The Baltimore Museum of Art, Baltimore, Maryland, Friends of Art Fund.

LEFT, ABOVE. Arshile Gorky:
The Plough and the Song. 1947. Oil on burlap. 52⅛″ x 64¼″.
Collection of Mr. and Mrs. Milton A. Gordon, New York.

LEFT, BELOW. Arshile Gorky:
The Plough and the Song. 1947. Oil on canvas. 50¾″ x 62¾″.
Allen Memorial Art Museum, Oberlin College, Oberlin, Ohio.

ABOVE. Arshile Gorky:
The Betrothal II. 1947. Oil on canvas. 50¾″ x 38″.
The Whitney Museum of American Art, New York.

Arshile Gorky:
The Limit. 1947. Oil on paper over burlap. 50¾″ x 62½″.
Private collection, Courtesy of M. Knoedler & Company, Inc., New York.

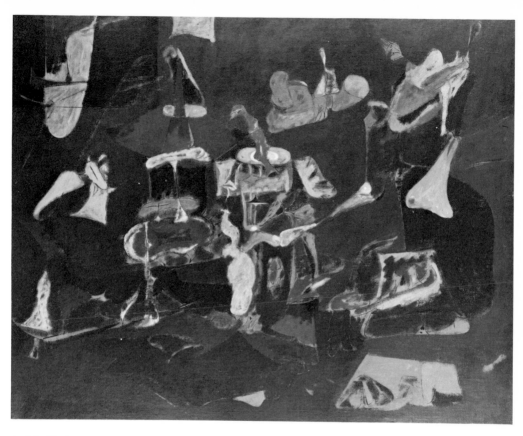

Arshile Gorky:
Dark Green Painting. ca. 1948. Oil on canvas. 43¾″ x 56″.
Collection of Mrs. H. Gates Lloyd, Haverford, Pennsylvania.

ABOVE. Adolph Gottlieb:
Masquerade. 1945. Oil and egg tempera on canvas. 36″ x 24″.
Collection of Mrs. Esther Gottlieb, New York.

RIGHT, ABOVE. Adolph Gottlieb:
Recurrent Apparition. 1946. Oil on canvas. 36″ x 54″.
Collection of Mrs. Esther Gottlieb, New York.

RIGHT, BELOW. Adolph Gottlieb:
Dream. 1948. Oil on canvas. 20″ x 24″.
Isaac Delgado Museum of Art, New Orleans, Louisiana,
Gift of William Edward Campbell, 1951.

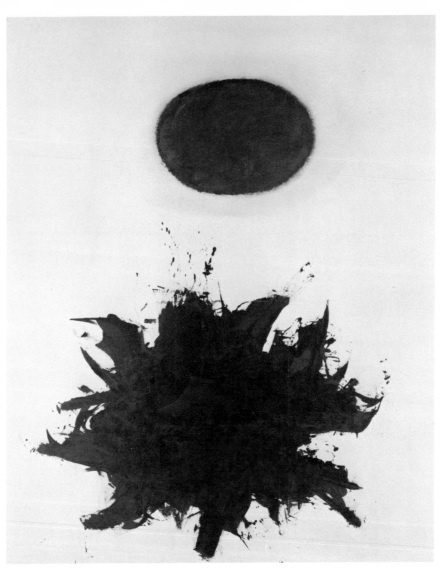

Adolph Gottlieb:
Thrust. 1959. Oil on canvas. 108″ x 90″.
The Metropolitan Museum of Art, New York, George A. Hearn Fund, 1959.

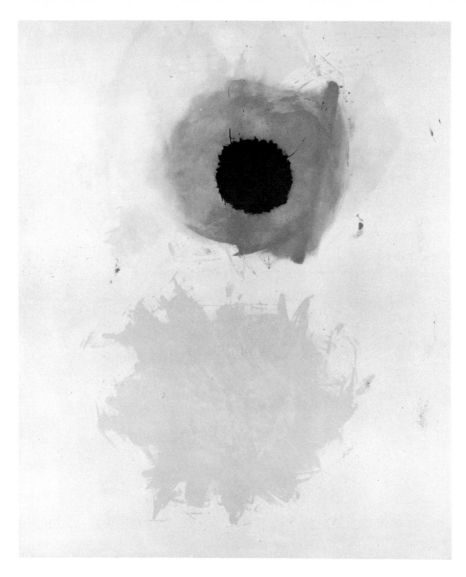

Adolph Gottlieb:
Aureole. 1959. Oil on canvas. 108″ x 90″.
Collection of Mrs. Esther Gottlieb, New York.

ABOVE. Adolph Gottlieb:
Sign. 1962. Oil on canvas. 90″ x 84″.
Collection of the artist.

RIGHT, ABOVE. Adolph Gottlieb:
Red, Blue, Yellow. 1966. Oil on canvas. 84″ x 90″.
Collection of William S. Rubin, New York.

RIGHT, BELOW. Adolph Gottlieb:
Petaloid. 1967. Cor-Ten steel. 96″ x 96″ x 48″.
Collection of Mrs. Esther Gottlieb, New York.

ABOVE. Philip Guston:
To B. W. T. 1952. Oil on canvas. 48″ x 51″.
Collection of Leonard M. Brown, Springfield, Massachusetts.

RIGHT, ABOVE. Philip Guston:
Zone. 1954. Oil on canvas. 46″ x 48⅛″.
Collection of Mr. and Mrs. Ben Heller, New York.

RIGHT, BELOW. Philip Guston:
Untitled. 1954. Oil on canvas. 51″ x 48¾″.
Collection of Mr. and Mrs. C. B. Wright, Seattle, Washington.

Philip Guston:
For M. 1955. Oil on canvas. 76¼″ x 72″.
Private collection, Los Angeles, California.

Philip Guston:
Cythera. 1957. Oil on canvas. 72″ x 64″.
Collection of Mr. and Mrs. Donald Blinken, New York.

Hans Hofmann:
In the Wake of the Hurricane. 1960. Oil on canvas. 72¼″ x 60″.
University Art Museum, Berkeley, California,
Gift of the artist.

Hans Hofmann:
Summer Night's Bliss. 1961. Oil on canvas. 84″ x 78″.
The Baltimore Museum of Art, Baltimore, Maryland, Gift of the artist.

Hans Hofmann:
Agrigento. 1961. Oil on canvas. 84¼″ x 72″.
University Art Museum, Berkeley, California,
Gift of the artist.

Hans Hofmann:
Memoria in Aeterne. 1962. Oil on canvas. 84″ x 72⅛″.
The Museum of Modern Art, New York, Gift of the artist, 1963.

Hans Hofmann:
Gloriamundi. 1963. Oil on canvas. 60⅛″ x 52″.
University Art Museum, Berkeley, California,
Gift of the artist.

Hans Hofmann:
Song of a Nightingale. 1964. Oil on canvas. 7′ x 6′.
Collection of Mr. and Mrs. Eugene M. Schwartz, New York.

Hans Hofmann:
In Sober Ecstasy. 1965. Oil on canvas. 73½″ x 61½″.
Collection of Mr. and Mrs. David Mirvish, Toronto, Canada.

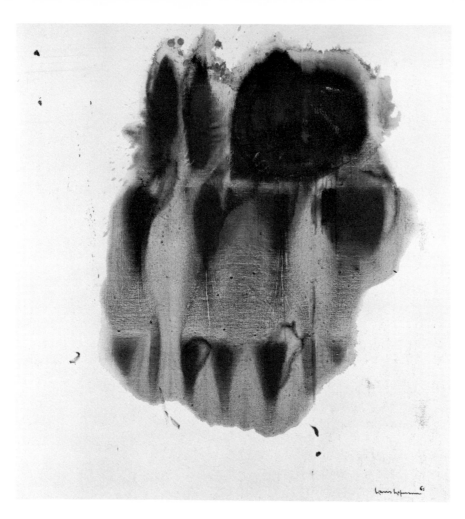

Hans Hofmann:
Little Cherry (Renata Series No. 1). 1965. Oil on canvas.
84″ x 78″. Estate of Hans Hofmann.

ABOVE. Edward Hopper:
Gas. 1940. Oil on canvas. 26¼″ x 40¼″.
The Museum of Modern Art, New York, Mrs. Simon Guggenheim Fund, 1943.

RIGHT, ABOVE. Edward Hopper:
First Row Orchestra. 1951. Oil on canvas. 31″ x 40″.
Joseph H. Hirshhorn Foundation.

RIGHT, BELOW. Edward Hopper:
Office in a Small City. 1953. Oil on canvas. 28″ x 40″.
The Metropolitan Museum of Art, New York, George A. Hearn Fund, 1953.

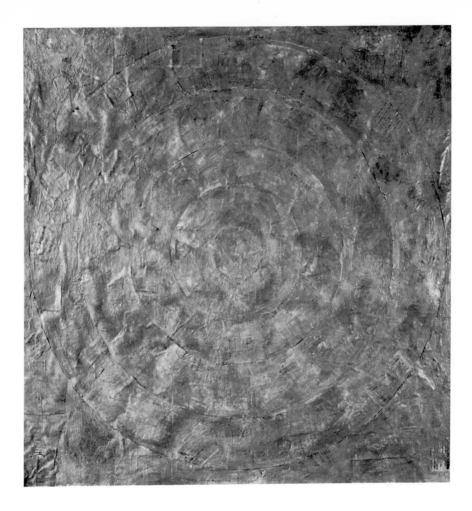

ABOVE. Jasper Johns:
Green Target. 1955. Encaustic on newspaper on canvas. 60″ x 60″.
The Museum of Modern Art, New York, Richard S. Zeisler Fund, 1958.

RIGHT, ABOVE. Jasper Johns:
White Flag. 1955. Encaustic and collage on canvas. 72″ x 144″.
Collection of the artist.

RIGHT, BELOW. Jasper Johns:
Three Flags. 1958. Encaustic on canvas. 30⅞″ x 45½″.
Collection of Mr. and Mrs. Burton Tremaine, Meriden, Connecticut.

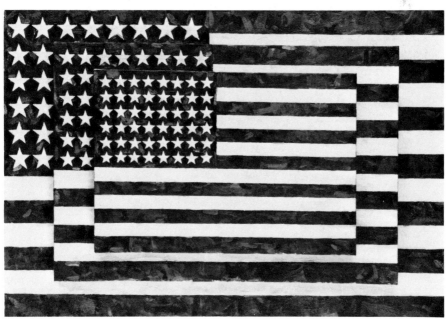

Jasper Johns:
Device Circle. 1959. Encaustic and collage on canvas. 40″ x 40″.
Collection of Mr. and Mrs. Burton Tremaine, Meriden, Connecticut.

Jasper Johns:
Jubilee. 1959. Oil on canvas. 60″ x 44″.
Collection of Robert Rauschenberg, New York.

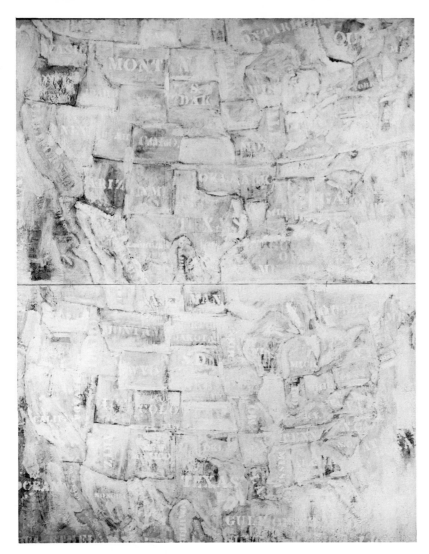

LEFT, ABOVE. Jasper Johns:
False Start. 1959. Oil on canvas. 67¼" x 54".
Collection of Mr. and Mrs. Robert C. Scull, New York.

LEFT, BELOW. Jasper Johns:
Studio. 1964. Oil on canvas. 73½" x 145½".
The Whitney Museum of American Art, New York, Gift of the Friends
of The Whitney Museum of American Art and purchase.

ABOVE. Jasper Johns:
Double White Map. 1965. Encaustic and collage on canvas. 90" x 70".
Collection of Mr. and Mrs. Robert C. Scull, New York.

189

Jasper Johns:
Screen Piece. 1967. Oil on canvas. 72″ x 50″.
Collection of David Whitney, New York.

Jasper Johns:
Screen Piece 2. 1968. Oil on canvas. 72″ x 50″.
Collection of Mr. and Mrs. Victor W. Ganz, New York.

191

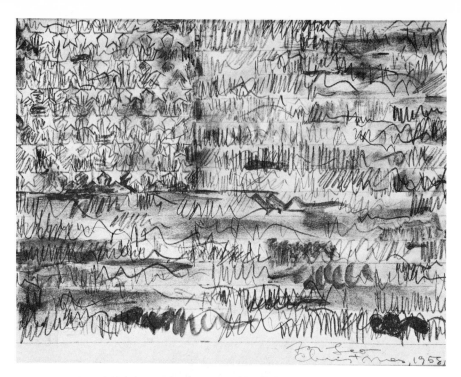

LEFT, ABOVE. Jasper Johns:
Flag. 1958. Pencil and graphite wash on paper. 7½″ x 10⅜″.
Collection of Leo Castelli, New York.

LEFT, BELOW. Jasper Johns:
Study for Painting with a Ball. 1958. Conté on paper. 15″ x 14½″.
Collection of the artist.

ABOVE. Jasper Johns:
Study for Painting with Two Balls. 1960. Charcoal on paper.
19½″ x 15½″. Joseph H. Hirshhorn Collection.

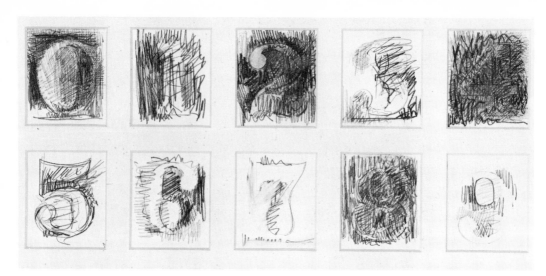

ABOVE. Jasper Johns:
Numbers. 1960. Pencil on paper; ten drawings each matted
separately. 2¾″ x 2¼″ each. Collection of Edward Carey, New York.

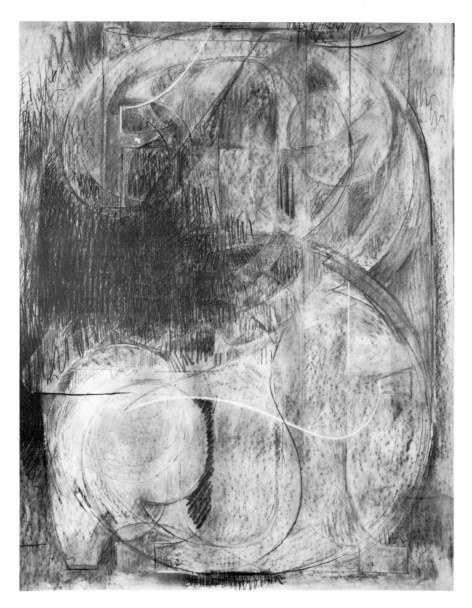

LEFT. Jasper Johns:
Device Circle. 1960. Pencil on paper. 15″ x 14½″.
Collection of Mr. and Mrs. Ben Heller, New York.

ABOVE. Jasper Johns:
0 through 9. 1961. Charcoal and pastel on paper. 54″ x 45″.
Collection of Mr. and Mrs. Robert C. Scull, New York.

195

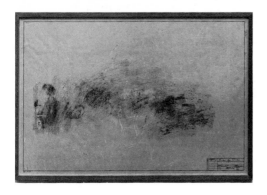

Jasper Johns:
Study for Skin I. 1962. Charcoal on paper. 22″ x 34″.
Study for Skin II. 1962. Charcoal on paper. 22″ x 34″.
Study for Skin III. 1962. Charcoal on paper. 22″ x 34″.
Study for Skin IV. 1962. Charcoal on paper. 22″ x 34″.
Collection of the artist.

Jasper Johns:
Diver. 1963. Charcoal, pastel, paper on canvas. 86½″ x 71″.
Collection of Mr. and Mrs. Victor W. Ganz, New York.

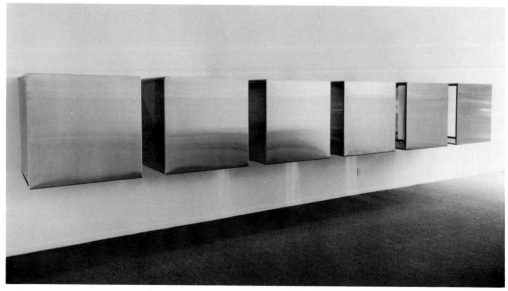

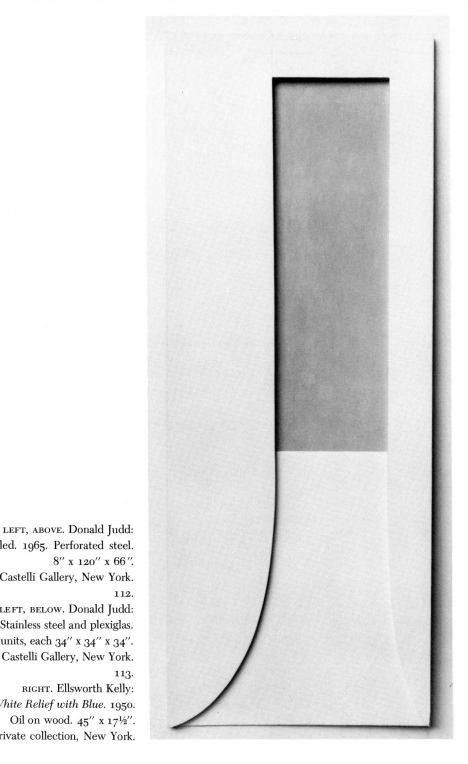

LEFT, ABOVE. Donald Judd:
Untitled. 1965. Perforated steel.
8″ x 120″ x 66″.
Leo Castelli Gallery, New York.
112.
LEFT, BELOW. Donald Judd:
Untitled. 1969. Stainless steel and plexiglas.
Six units, each 34″ x 34″ x 34″.
Leo Castelli Gallery, New York.
113.
RIGHT. Ellsworth Kelly:
White Relief with Blue. 1950.
Oil on wood. 45″ x 17½″.
Private collection, New York.

LEFT, ABOVE. Ellsworth Kelly:
Blue Red Green. 1962–63. Oil on canvas. 91″ x 82″.
The Metropolitan Museum of Art, Arthur H. Hearn Fund, 1963.

LEFT, BELOW. Ellsworth Kelly:
3 Panels: Red, Yellow, Blue. 1963. Acrylic on canvas. 90″ x 90″.
Fondation Maeght, Saint Paul, France.

ABOVE. Ellsworth Kelly:
Orange White. 1964. Oil on canvas. 122″ x 96″.
Courtesy of Sidney Janis Gallery, New York.

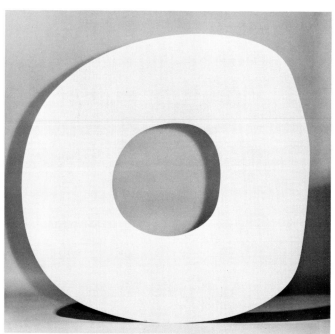

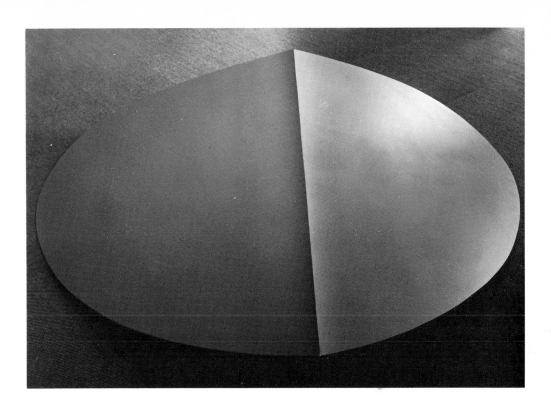

LEFT, ABOVE. Ellsworth Kelly:
2 Panels: White Dark Blue. 1968. Oil on canvas. 96″ x 144″.
Courtesy of Sidney Janis Gallery, New York.

LEFT, BELOW. Ellsworth Kelly:
White Ring. 1963. Epoxy on aluminum. 70″ x 72″ x 12″.
Private collection, New York.

ABOVE. Ellsworth Kelly:
Green. 1968. Painted aluminum. 21″ x 105″ x 112″.
Collection of The Walker Art Center, Minneapolis, Minnesota.

Ellsworth Kelly:
Untitled. 1968. Painted aluminum. 100½" x 146½" x 38⅜".
Collection of William S. Rubin, New York.

Ellsworth Kelly:
Black White. 1968. Painted aluminum. 100½″ x 146½″ x 38⅜″.
Courtesy of Sidney Janis Gallery, New York.

Ellsworth Kelly:
Tulip. 1958. Pencil on paper.
29″ x 23″.
Private collection, New York.

Ellsworth Kelly:
Grass. 1961. Pencil on paper.
28½″ x 22½″.
Private collection, New York.

Ellsworth Kelly:
Castor Bean. 1961. Ink on paper.
22½″ x 28½″.
Private collection, New York.

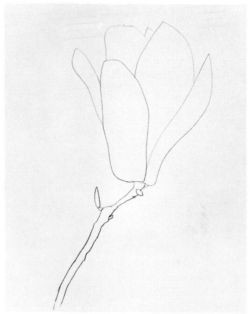

Ellsworth Kelly:
Oak. 1964. Pencil on paper.
28½″ x 22½″.
Private collection, New York.

Ellsworth Kelly:
Magnolia. 1966. Pencil on paper.
29″ x 23″.
Private collection, New York.

Ellsworth Kelly:
Avocado. 1967. Pencil on paper.
29″ x 23″.
Private collection, New York.

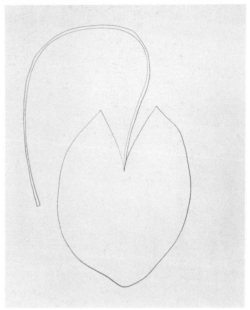

Ellsworth Kelly:
Chrysanthemum. 1967. Pencil on paper.
30″ x 22″.
Private collection, New York.

Ellsworth Kelly:
Water Lily. 1968. Pencil on paper.
29″ x 23″.
Private collection, New York.

Franz Kline:
Nijinsky. 1949. Oil on canvas. 33″ x 28″.
Collection of Mr. and Mrs. David I. Orr, New York.

LEFT, ABOVE. Franz Kline:
Wotan. 1950. Oil on canvas. 55⅛″ x 79¼″.
Collection of Mr. and Mrs. Robert C. Scull, New York.

LEFT, BELOW. Franz Kline:
Horizontals Two. 1952. Oil on canvas. 77″ x 100″.
Estate of Franz Kline, Courtesy of Marlborough-Gerson Gallery, New York.

ABOVE. Franz Kline:
Figure Eight. 1952. Oil on canvas. 80½″ x 63½″.
Collection of William S. Rubin, New York.

LEFT, ABOVE. Franz Kline:
Untitled. 1953–54. Oil on canvas. 57¼″ x 82″.
Collection of Robert H. Halff and Carl W. Johnson, Beverly Hills, California.

LEFT, BELOW. Franz Kline:
Untitled. 1954. Oil on canvas. 43″ x 36″.
Collection of Mr. and Mrs. David I. Orr, New York.

ABOVE. Franz Kline:
White Forms. 1955. Oil on canvas. 74″ x 50″.
Collection of Philip Johnson, New Canaan, Connecticut.

LEFT, ABOVE. Franz Kline:
Orange and Black Wall. 1959. Oil on canvas. 66½″ x 144″.
Collection of Mr. and Mrs. Robert C. Scull, New York.

LEFT, BELOW. Franz Kline:
Riverbed. 1961. Oil on canvas. 78⅞″ x 109¼″.
Collection of William M. White, Jr., New York.

ABOVE. Gabe Kohn:
Long Beach Contract. 1965. Laminated redwood. 10′ x 7′.
California State College, Long Beach, California.

ABOVE. Roy Lichtenstein:
I Can See the Whole Room. . . . 1961. Oil on canvas. 48″ x 48″.
Collection of Mr. and Mrs. Burton Tremaine, Meriden, Connecticut.

RIGHT, ABOVE. Roy Lichtenstein:
Live Ammo. 1962. Oil on canvas. 68″ x 92″ (two panels).
Collection of Mr. and Mrs. Morton Neumann, Chicago, Illinois.

RIGHT, BELOW. Roy Lichtenstein:
Sussex. 1964. Oil and magna on canvas. 36″ x 68″.
Collection of Robert Rosenblum, New York.

ABOVE. Roy Lichtenstein:
Big Painting #6. 1965. Oil and magna on canvas. 92½″ x 129″.
Collection of Mr. and Mrs. Robert C. Scull, New York.

RIGHT, ABOVE. Roy Lichtenstein:
Haystacks. 1968. Oil and magna on canvas. 18″ x 24″.
Private collection, New York.

RIGHT, BELOW. Roy Lichtenstein:
Haystacks. 1969. Oil and magna on canvas. 16″ x 24″.
Private collection, New York.

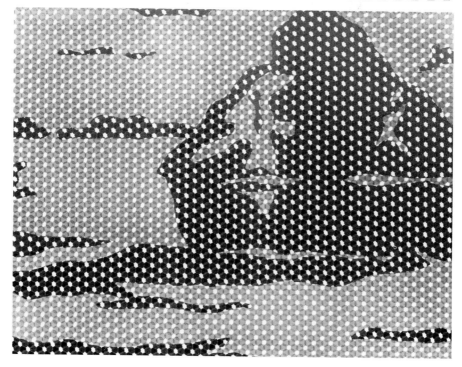

Roy Lichtenstein:
Rouen Cathedral (seen at five different times of day), III. 1969.
Oil and magna on canvas. 63″ x 42″. (#1 of five paintings in set.)
Private collection, New York.

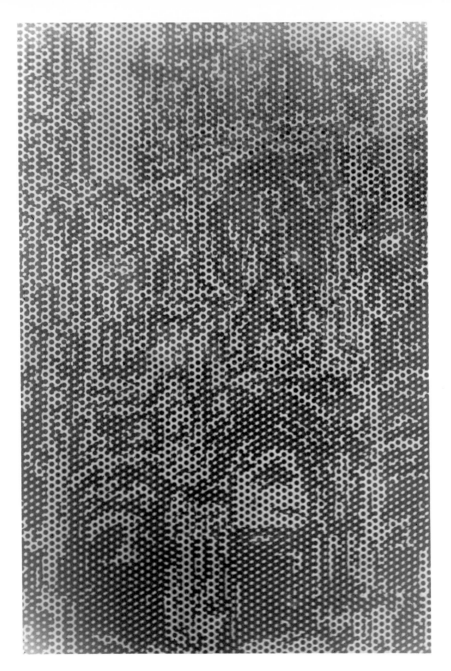

Roy Lichtenstein:
Rouen Cathedral (seen at five different times of day), III. 1969.
Oil and magna on canvas. 63″ x 42″. (#3 of five paintings in set.)
Private collection, New York.

Morris Louis:
Saraband. 1959. Acrylic on canvas. 100½" x 149".
The Solomon R. Guggenheim Museum, New York.

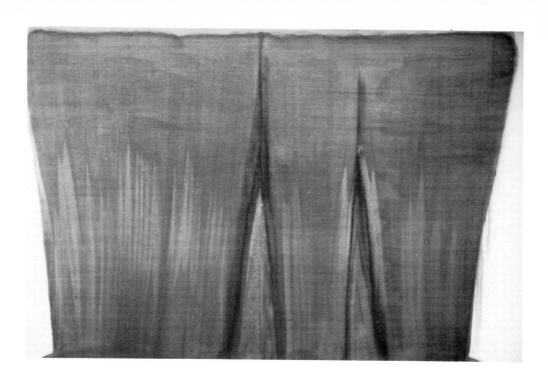

Morris Louis:
Terranean. 1959. Acrylic resin paint on canvas. 90½″ x 146″.
Collection of Mr. and Mrs. Kenneth Noland, New York.

ABOVE. Morris Louis:
While. 1959. Acrylic on canvas. 96½″ x 136⅜″.
Harry N. Abrams Family Collection, New York.

RIGHT, ABOVE. Morris Louis:
Aleph. 1960. Magna acrylic on canvas. 105″ x 92¾″.
Collection of Jaime C. del Amo, Madrid, Spain.

RIGHT, BELOW. Morris Louis:
Alpha-Delta. 1961. Acrylic on canvas. 8′8″ x 20′.
Everson Museum of Art, Syracuse, New York.

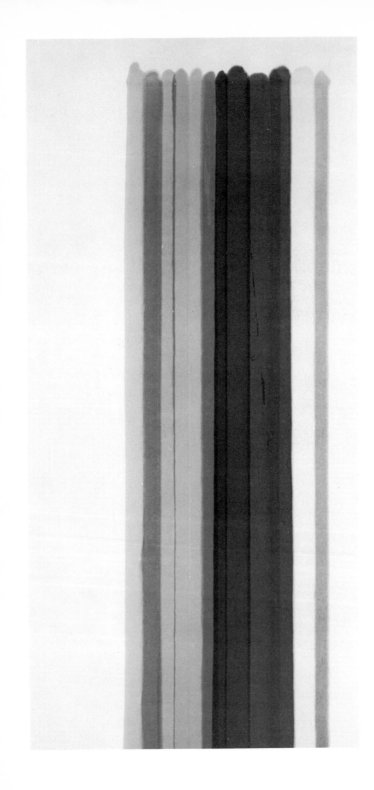

LEFT. Morris Louis:
Moving In. 1961. Magna acrylic on canvas. 87½″ x 41½″.
Private collection, New York.

ABOVE. Morris Louis:
Hot Half. 1962. Acrylic resin on canvas. 63″ x 63″.
Collection of Mrs. Abner Brenner, Washington, D.C.

LEFT, ABOVE. Robert Morris:
Untitled. 1964. Painted plywood. 6'6" x 9'.
Collection Dott. Giuseppe Panza di Buomo, Milan, Italy,
Courtesy of Leo Castelli Gallery, New York.

LEFT, BELOW. Robert Morris:
Untitled. 1966. Steel mesh. 31" x 106" x 106".
Lent by The Kleiner Foundation, Beverly Hills, Courtesy of
Los Angeles County Museum of Art, Los Angeles, California.

ABOVE. Robert Morris:
Untitled. 1967–68. Felt. 180" x 72" x 1".
The Detroit Institute of Arts, Gift of The Friends of Modern Art.

Robert Morris:
Untitled. 1968. Translucent fiberglas. Nine units, each 48″ x 24″ x 24″.
Collection of Philip Johnson, New Canaan, Connecticut.

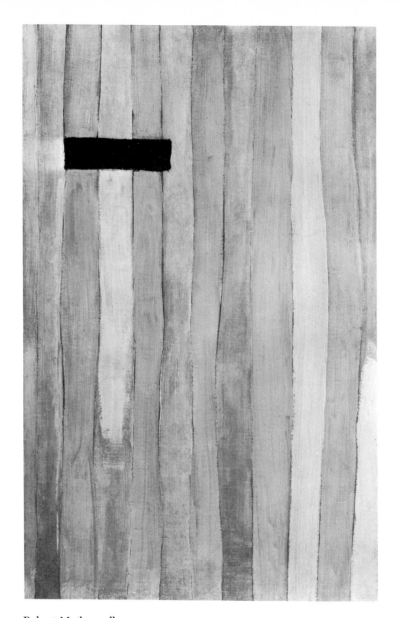

Robert Motherwell:
The Little Spanish Prison. 1941–44. Oil on canvas. 27⅛" x 17".
Collection of the artist.

LEFT. Robert Motherwell:
Homely Protestant. 1948. Oil on composition board. 96″ x 48″.
Collection of Helen Frankenthaler, New York.

ABOVE. Robert Motherwell:
Elegy to the Spanish Republic, 70. 1961. Oil on canvas. 69″ x 114″.
The Metropolitan Museum of Art, Anonymous gift, 1965.

BELOW. Robert Motherwell:
Africa. 1965. Acrylic on canvas. 80″ x 225″.
The Baltimore Museum of Art, Baltimore, Maryland, Gift of the artist.

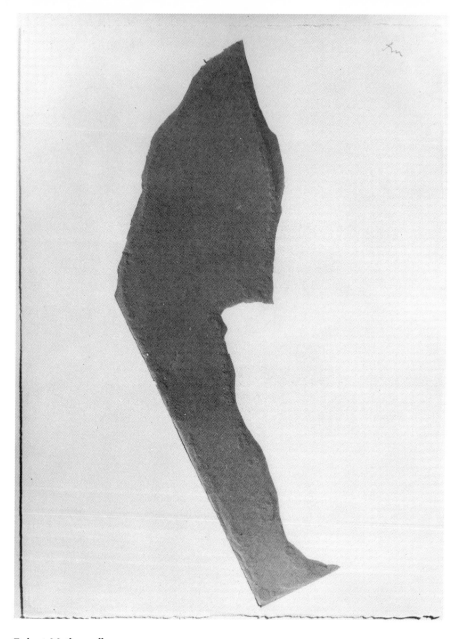

Robert Motherwell:
Beige Figuration No. 3. 1967. Collage (paper). 30″ x 22″.
Collection of the artist.

Robert Motherwell:
"Open" No. 14: In Ochre with Charcoal Line. 1968.
Polymer paint and charcoal on canvas. 114" x 69".
Collection of the artist.

Robert Motherwell:
"Open" No. 17: In Ultramarine with Charcoal Line. 1968.
Polymer paint and charcoal on canvas. 100″ x 197″.
Collection of the artist.

Robert Motherwell:
"Open" No. 31B: In Raw Sienna. 1968. Charcoal on blotting paper.
17″ x 37½″. Collection of the artist.

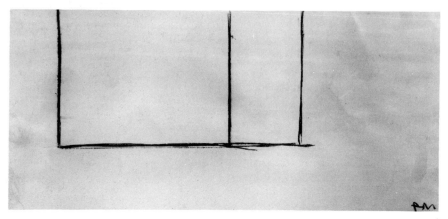

Barnett Newman:
Pagan Void. 1946. Oil on canvas.
33″ x 38″.
Collection of Mrs. Annalee Newman,
New York.

Barnett Newman:
The Euclidian Abyss. 1946–47.
Oil and crayon on fabric. 28″ x 22″.
Collection of Mr. and Mrs. Burton
Tremaine, Meriden, Connecticut.

LEFT. Barnett Newman:
Onement III. 1949. Oil on canvas. 72″ x 34″.
Collection of Mr. and Mrs. Joseph Slifka, New York.

ABOVE. Barnett Newman:
Covenant. 1949. Oil on canvas. 48″ x 60″. Joseph H. Hirshhorn Collection.

Barnett Newman:
Prometheus Bound. 1952.
Oil on canvas. 131¾" x 50".
Collection of William S. Rubin,
New York.

Barnett Newman:
Shining Forth (for George). 1961. Oil on canvas. 9½′ x 14½′.
Collection of Mrs. Annalee Newman, New York.

ABOVE. Barnett Newman:
Who's Afraid of Red, Yellow, Blue I. 1966. Oil on canvas. 60″ x 50″.
Collection of S. I. Newhouse, Jr., New York.

RIGHT, ABOVE. Barnett Newman:
Anna's Light. 1968. Acrylic on canvas. 9′ x 20′.
M. Knoedler & Company, Inc., New York.

RIGHT, BELOW. Barnett Newman:
Jericho. 1968–69. Acrylic on canvas. 9′ 6″ x 9′ 6″.
M. Knoedler & Company, Inc., New York.

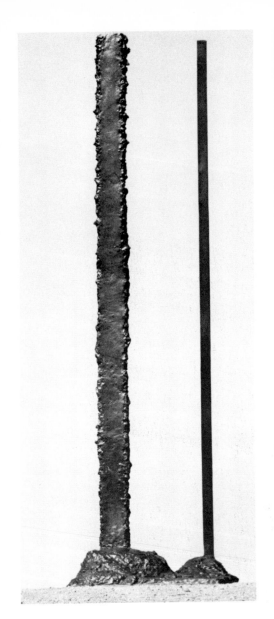

LEFT. Barnett Newman:
Here I (to Marcia). 1950. Bronze. 8' x 26" x 27".
Collection of Mrs. Annalee Newman, New York.

RIGHT. Barnett Newman:
Here III. 1966. Stainless steel and Cor-Ten steel. 10' 5" x 23½" x 18½".
M. Knoedler & Company, Inc., New York.

Barnett Newman:
Broken Obelisk. 1967. Cor-Ten steel. 26′ x 10½′ x 10½′.
M. Knoedler & Company, Inc., New York.

Isamu Noguchi:
The Cry. 1959.
Balsa wood with steel base.
84″ x 30″ x 18″.
The Solomon R. Guggenheim Museum,
New York.

Isamu Noguchi:
Life of a Cube. 1962.
Black granite.
21″ x 21″ x 21″.
Cordier & Ekstrom, Inc.,
New York.

Isamu Noguchi:
Sky Frame. 1966.
Rose Aurora Portuguese Marble.
22″ x 28″ x 8¼″.
Cordier & Ekstrom,
Inc., New York.

Isamu Noguchi:
Euripides. 1966. White Italian Altissimo marble.
Two pieces, 45″ and 90″ (high).
Cordier & Ekstrom, Inc., New York.

Kenneth Noland:
Teton Noir. 1961. Acrylic on canvas. 81″ x 81″.
Collection of Carter Burden, New York.

Kenneth Noland:
Mach II. 1964. Acrylic resin on canvas. 9′ x 17′.
Collection of Kimiko and John Powers, Aspen, Colorado.

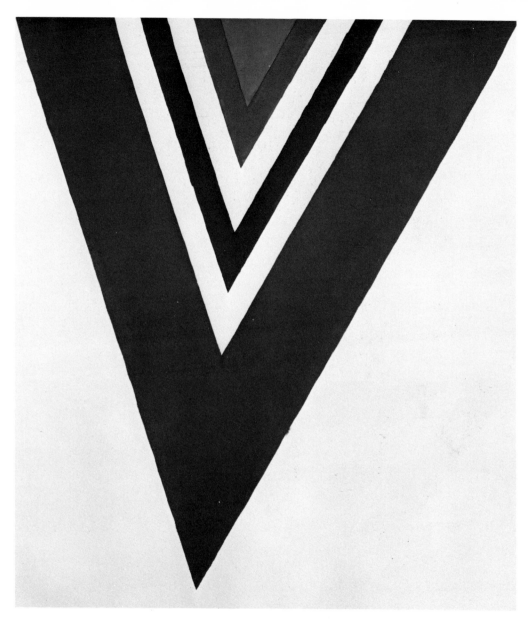

Kenneth Noland:
17th Stage. 1964. Acrylic on canvas. 8' x 7'.
Collection of Mr. and Mrs. Eugene M. Schwartz, New York.

LEFT, ABOVE. Kenneth Noland:
Bend Sinister. 1964. Acrylic on canvas. 98″ x 161¾″.
Joseph H. Hirshhorn Collection.

LEFT, BELOW. Kenneth Noland:
Embrown. 1964. Acrylic on canvas. 96″ x 145″.
Collection of Mr. and Mrs. David Mirvish, Toronto, Canada.

ABOVE. Kenneth Noland:
Trans-Median. 1968. Acrylic on canvas. 7½′ x 7½′.
Collection of Mr. and Mrs. David Mirvish, Toronto, Canada.

Kenneth Noland:
Dawn-Dusk. 1968. Water-miscible acrylic on cotton duck. 30½″ x 141½″.
Collection of Mr. and Mrs. Clement Greenberg, New York.

Kenneth Noland:
Via Lime. 1968–69. Acrylic emulsion on canvas. 90½″ x 240″.
Collection of Ondine Vaughn and Steve Schapiro, New York.

Claes Oldenburg:
7-up. 1961. Enamel on plaster. 50⅛″ x 37⅜″ x 6¼″
Collection of Mr. and Mrs. Burton Tremaine, Meriden, Connecticut.

ABOVE. Claes Oldenburg:
Strong Arm. 1961. Enamel on plaster. 43⅜″ x 32⅜″ x 5½″.
Collection of Mr. and Mrs. Burton Tremaine, Meriden, Connecticut.

RIGHT, ABOVE. Claes Oldenburg:
Soft Typewriter. 1963. Vinyl, kapok, cloth, and plexiglas. 9″ x 27½″ x 26″.
Collection of Alan Power, London, England.

RIGHT, BELOW. Claes Oldenburg:
Ironing Board with Shirt and Iron. 1964. Wood, cloth, vinyl, nylon, and hydrostone.
80″ x 67½″ x 24″. Collection of Mr. and Mrs. Sonnabend, Paris, France.

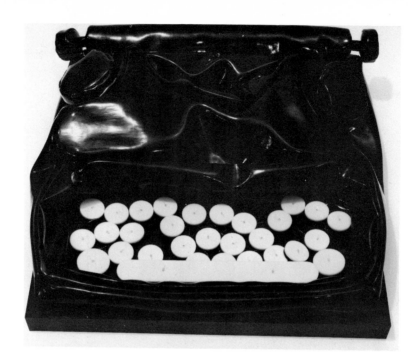

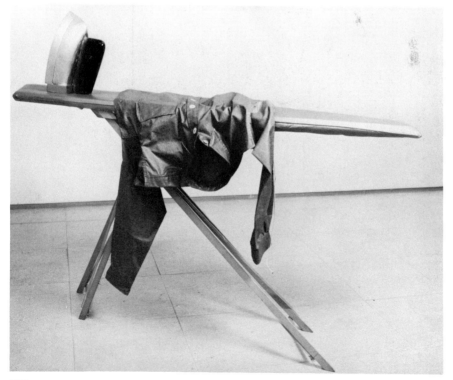

LEFT. Claes Oldenburg:
Tub (hard model). 1966. Corrugated paper, wood, enamel.
80″ x 32½″ x 28″. Collection of Mrs. Claes Oldenburg, New York.

ABOVE. Jules Olitski:
Ten O'Clock. 1959. Paint, spackle, polymer emulsion on panel.
36″ x 36″. Collection of the artist.

Jules Olitski:
Bathsheba. 1959. Oil on canvas. 78″ x 70″.
Collection of J. Patrick Lannan, Palm Beach, Florida.
198.

Jules Olitski:
Ritual of L. 1959. Paint, spackle, polymer emulsion on canvas.
6′ x 7′. Collection of the artist.

ABOVE. Jules Olitski:
Commissar Demikovsky. 1965. Acrylic on canvas: 8′ x 7′.
Collection of Mr. and Mrs. Eugene M. Schwartz, New York.

RIGHT. Jules Olitski:
Thigh Smoke. 1966. Acrylic on canvas. 167″ x 92½″.
Seattle–First National Bank Collection, Seattle, Washington.

ABOVE. Jules Olitski:
Green Volya. 1969. Acrylic emulsion on canvas. 9′ 9″ x 17′ 5″.
Collection of Lawrence Rubin, New York.

RIGHT, ABOVE. Jules Olitski:
Warehouse Light. 1969. Acrylic on canvas. 118″ x 174″.
Collection of Lawrence Rubin, New York.

RIGHT, BELOW. Jules Olitski:
Twelve Nights. 1968. Aluminum and acrylic, air drying lacquer. 9′ x 16½′ x 12′.
Collection of the artist.

265

LEFT. Jackson Pollock:
Male and Female. 1942. Oil on canvas. 73¼″ x 49″.
Collection of Mrs. H. Gates Lloyd, Haverford, Pennsylvania.

ABOVE. Jackson Pollock:
Moon Woman Cuts the Circle. 1943. Oil on canvas. 43″ x 41″.
Courtesy of Marlborough-Gerson Gallery, New York.

267

LEFT. Jackson Pollock:
Night Ceremony. 1944.
Oil and enamel on canvas.
72″ x 43⅛″.
Collection of Mrs. Barbara
Reis Poe, New York.

RIGHT. Jackson Pollock:
Cathedral. 1947.
Duco and aluminum paint on canvas.
71½″ x 35¹⁄₁₆″.
Dallas Museum of Fine Arts,
Gift of Mr. and Mrs.
Bernard J. Reis.

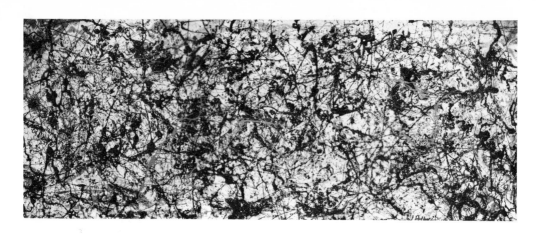

Jackson Pollock:
Lucifer. 1947. Oil, enamel, and aluminum paint on canvas.
41″ x 8′ x 9½″. Collection of Joseph H. Hazen, New York.

Jackson Pollock:
Autumn Rhythm. 1950. Oil on canvas. 105″ x 207″.
The Metropolitan Museum of Art, New York,
Estate of Jackson Pollock, George A. Hearn Fund, 1957.

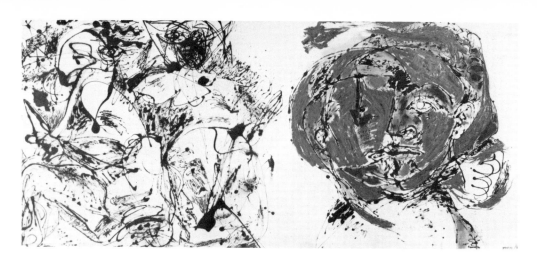

Jackson Pollock:
Portrait and a Dream. 1953. Enamel on canvas. 58⅛″ x 134¼″.
Dallas Museum of Fine Arts, Gift of Mr. and Mrs. Algur H. Meadows
and the Meadows Foundation, Inc.

ABOVE. Jackson Pollock:
The Deep. 1953. Oil and duco on canvas. 86¾″ x 51⅛″.
Collection of Samuel Wagstaff, Jr., Detroit, Michigan.

RIGHT, ABOVE. Larry Poons:
Double Speed. 1962–63. Acrylic and fabric dye on canvas.
72″ x 144″. Collection of Frank Stella, New York.

RIGHT, BELOW. Larry Poons:
Enforcer. 1963. Liquitex and fabric spray on canvas. 80″ x 80″.
Collection of Mr. and Mrs. Robert C. Scull, New York.

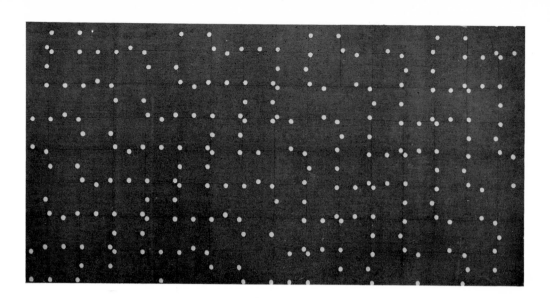

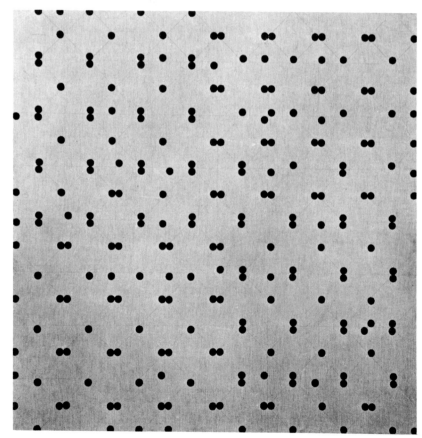

LEFT. Larry Poons:
Mary Queen of Scots. 1965. Acrylic on canvas. 12′ x 90″.
Collection of Mr. and Mrs. Robert C. Scull, New York.

ABOVE. Larry Poons:
Rosewood. 1966. Acrylic on canvas. 120″ x 160″.
Collection of William S. Rubin, New York.

Larry Poons:
Night Journey. 1968. Acrylic on canvas. 108″ x 124″.
Collection of Carter Burden, New York.

Larry Poons:
Doge's Palace. 1969. Acrylic on canvas. 112″ x 17′ 10″.
Collection of Lawrence Rubin, New York.

Robert Rauschenberg:
Rebus. 1955. Combine painting. 96″ x 144″.
Collection of Mr. and Mrs. Victor W. Ganz, New York.

Robert Rauschenberg:
Odalisk. 1955–58. Construction.
81″ x 25″ x 25″.
Collection of Mr. and Mrs.
Victor W. Ganz, New York.

Robert Rauschenberg:
Factum I. 1957. Combine painting. 62″ x 35½″.
Collection of Dott. Giuseppe Panza di Buomo, Milan, Italy.

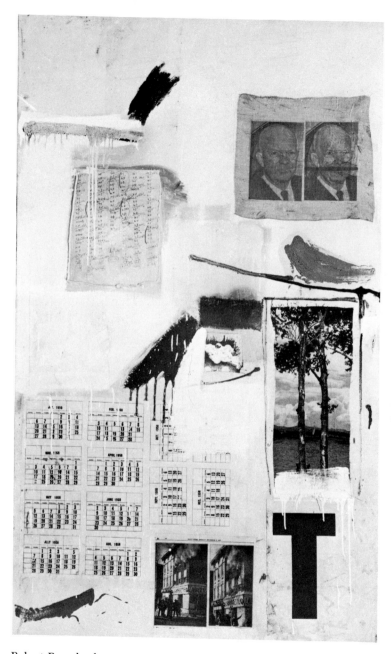

Robert Rauschenberg:
Factum II. 1957. Oil and collage on canvas. 61½″ x 35½″.
Collection of Mr. and Mrs. Morton Neumann, Chicago, Illinois.

Robert Rauschenberg:
Third Time Painting. 1961. Oil on canvas with clock. 84″ x 60″.
Harry N. Abrams Family Collection, New York.

Robert Rauschenberg:
Tracer. 1964. Oil on canvas with silkscreen. 84″ x 60″.
Collection of Mr. and Mrs. Frank M. Titelman, Altoona, Pennsylvania.

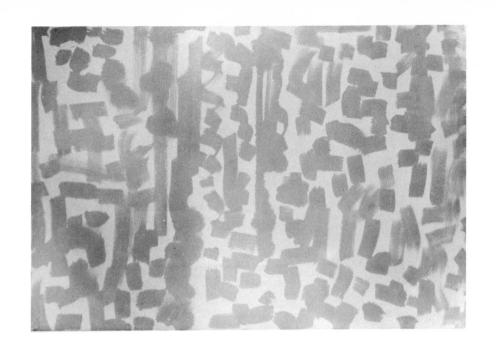

LEFT, ABOVE. Ad Reinhardt:
Yellow Painting. 1949.
Oil on canvas. 40″ x 60″.
Collection of Anna Reinhardt,
New York.

LEFT, BELOW. Ad Reinhardt:
Abstract Painting Grey.
1950. Oil on canvas. 30″ x 40″.
Collection of Rita Reinhardt,
New York.

RIGHT. Ad Reinhardt:
White. 1950. Oil on canvas.
80″ x 36″.
Collection of Rita Reinhardt,
New York.

Ad Reinhardt:
Red Painting. 1952. Oil on canvas. 6½′ x 12′.
The Metropolitan Museum of Art, New York, Arthur H. Hearn Fund, 1968.

Ad Reinhardt:
Abstract Painting. 1956–60.
Oil on canvas. 108″ x 40″.
Courtesy of Marlborough-Gerson
Gallery, New York.

Ad Reinhardt:
Abstract Painting. 1959.
Oil on canvas. 108″ x 40″.
Courtesy of Marlborough-Gerson
Gallery, New York.

288

James Rosenquist:
Four Young Revolutionaries. 1962. Glass, wood, and oil paint.
24″ x 32″. Collection of Mr. and Mrs. Lewis V. Winter, New York.

James Rosenquist:
Untitled. 1962. Oil on canvas. 84″ x 72″.
Collection of Mr. and Mrs. Robert A. Rowan, Pasadena, California.

James Rosenquist:
Silver Skies. 1962. Oil on canvas. 78″ x 16½″.
Collection of Mr. and Mrs. Robert C. Scull, New York.

James Rosenquist:
Early in the Morning. 1963. Oil on canvas. 95″ x 56″.
Collection of Mr. and Mrs. Robert C. Scull, New York.

James Rosenquist:
Nomad. 1963. Oil on canvas, plastic paint, wood. 84″ x 210″.
Albright-Knox Art Gallery, Buffalo, New York, Gift of Seymour H. Knox.

James Rosenquist:
Growth Plan. 1966. Oil on canvas. 70″ x 140″ (2 panels).
Museum of Contemporary Art, Nagaoka, Japan.

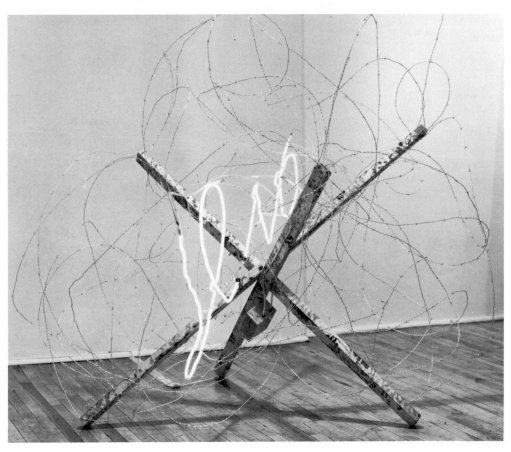

James Rosenquist:
Tumbleweed. 1963–66. Chromed barbed wire and neon.
54″ x 60″ x 60″ approximately. Leo Castelli Gallery, New York.

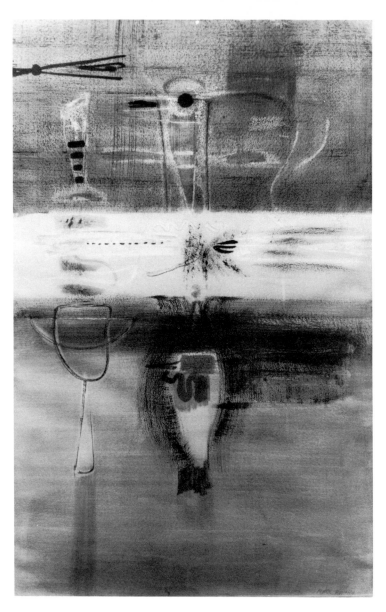

Mark Rothko:
Untitled. 1946. Watercolor. 38¾″ x 25½″.
Collection of Mr. and Mrs. Donald Blinken, New York.

ABOVE. Mark Rothko:
Vessels of Magic. 1946–47. Watercolor. 38¾″ x 25¾″.
The Brooklyn Museum, New York.

RIGHT, ABOVE. Mark Rothko:
Fantasy. 1947. Watercolor. 25½″ x 39½″.
Collection of Mr. and Mrs. Donald Blinken, New York.

RIGHT, BELOW. Mark Rothko:
No. 26. 1947. Oil on canvas. 34″ x 45¼″.
Collection of Mrs. Betty Parsons, New York.

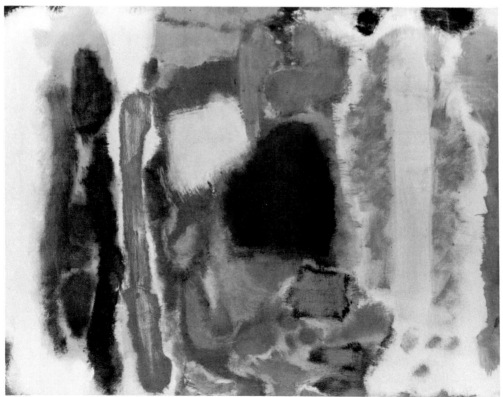

Mark Rothko:
Black, Pink, and Yellow over Orange. 1951–52. Oil on canvas.
116″ x 92¼″. Collection of William S. Rubin, New York.

Mark Rothko:
No. 10. 1952. Oil on canvas. 81½″ x 42½″.
Collection of Mr. and Mrs. C. B. Wright, Seattle, Washington.

Mark Rothko:
No. 8. 1952. Oil on canvas. 80½″ x 68″.
Collection of Mr. and Mrs. Burton Tremaine, Meriden, Connecticut.

Mark Rothko:
Brown, Black, and Blue. 1958. Oil on canvas. 5′9″ x 5′.
Collection of Dr. and Mrs. Edward Massie, St. Louis, Missouri.

Mark Rothko:
Number 207 (Red Over Dark Blue on Dark Gray). 1961.
Oil on canvas. 92¾″ x 81⅛″.
University Art Museum, Berkeley, California,
Acquired from the artist.

David Smith:
Deserted Garden Landscape. 1946. Steel, bronze. 11¾″ x 10⅛″ x 4¾″
Collection of Mr. and Mrs. Harry W. Anderson, Atherton, California.

David Smith:
Puritan Landscape. 1946. Steel, bronze, cast iron, nickel.
28¼" x 15" x 10"
Collection of Peter Brant, New York.

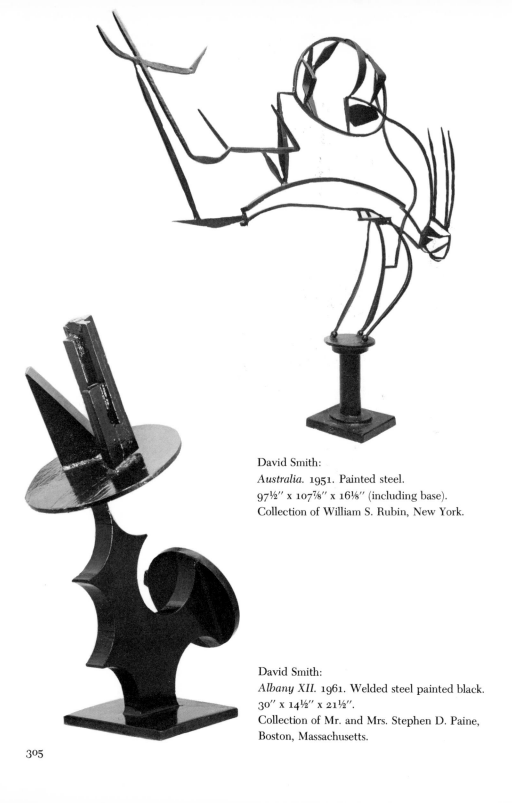

David Smith:
Australia. 1951. Painted steel.
97½″ x 107⅞″ x 16⅛″ (including base).
Collection of William S. Rubin, New York.

David Smith:
Albany XII. 1961. Welded steel painted black.
30″ x 14½″ x 21½″.
Collection of Mr. and Mrs. Stephen D. Paine,
Boston, Massachusetts.

ABOVE. David Smith:
2 Circles IV. 1962. Painted steel. 124″ x 60″ x 28½″.
Estate of David Smith, Courtesy of Marlborough-Gerson Gallery, New York.

RIGHT, ABOVE. David Smith:
Primo Piano III. 1962. Painted steel. 124″ x 145″ x 18″.
Courtesy of Marlborough-Gerson Gallery, New York.

RIGHT, BELOW. David Smith:
Voltri VI. 1962. Steel. 103″ x 102¾″ x 25½″.
Private collection, New York.

LEFT, ABOVE. David Smith:
Voltri XIII. 1962. Steel. 64⅛″ x 103¾″ x 26 ″.
University Art Museum, Berkeley, California.
Gift of Mr. and Mrs. Eugene E. Trefethen, Jr., Piedmont, California.

LEFT, BELOW. David Smith:
Voltri XIX. 1962. Welded and shaped iron and found objects. 55″ x 45″ x 50″.
Collection of Mr. and Mrs. Stephen D. Paine, Boston, Massachusetts.

ABOVE. David Smith:
Untitled. 1962–63. Stainless steel. 96¼″ x 63″ x 26″.
Art Gallery of Ontario, Purchase with assistance from the Women's Committee Fund, 1968.

David Smith:
Wagon II. 1964. Forged iron. 84″ x 112″ x 45″. Estate of David Smith, Courtesy of
Marlborough-Gerson Gallery, New York.

David Smith:
Cubi XXIV. 1964. Stainless steel. 114¼″ x 83½″.
Museum of Art, Carnegie Institute, Pittsburgh, Pennsylvania,
Howard Heinz Endowment Purchase Fund.

David Smith:
Untitled. 1965. Stainless steel, 102½″ x 120″ x 31¼″.
Estate of David Smith, Courtesy of Marlborough-Gerson Gallery, New York.

David Smith:
Cubi XXV. 1965. Stainless steel. 119¼″ x 120¾″ x 31¼″.
Estate of David Smith, Courtesy of Marlborough-Gerson Gallery, New York.

Tony Smith:
Black Box. 1962. Steel.
22½″ x 33″ x 25″.
Collection of Mr. and Mrs. Norman Ives,
Woodbridge, Connecticut.

Tony Smith:
Free Ride. 1962. Steel.
(#2 of an edition of three.)
6′ 8″ x 6′ 8″ x 6′ 8″.
Courtesy of Fischbach Gallery, New York.

Frank Stella:
Zambesi. 1959. Enamel on canvas. 90″ x 78″.
Collection of Lawrence Rubin, New York.

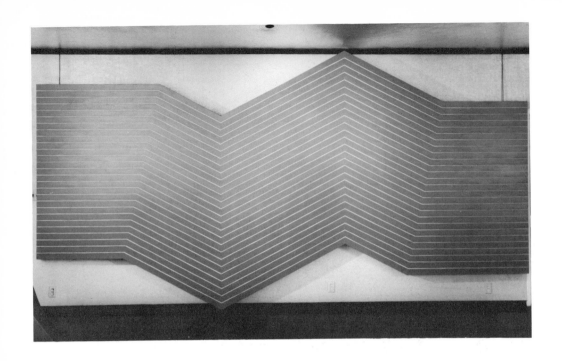

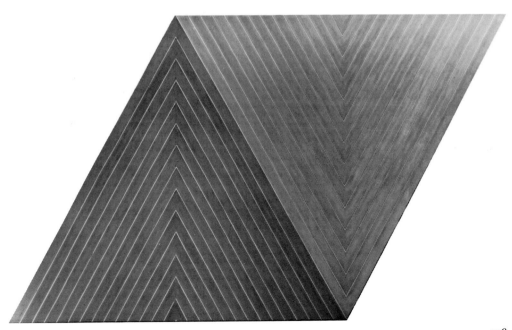

316

LEFT, ABOVE. Frank Stella:
Nunca Pasa Nada. 1964. Metallic powder in acrylic emulsion on canvas.
9′ x 18′ approximately. The Lannan Foundation.

LEFT, BELOW. Frank Stella:
Valparaiso (flesh and green). 1964. Metallic paint on canvas.
84″ x 144″. Collection of the artist.

ABOVE. Frank Stella:
Ossippee I. 1966. Fluorescent alkyd and epoxy paint on canvas.
95″ x 138″. Collection of Dr. and Mrs. Ernest Kafka, New York.

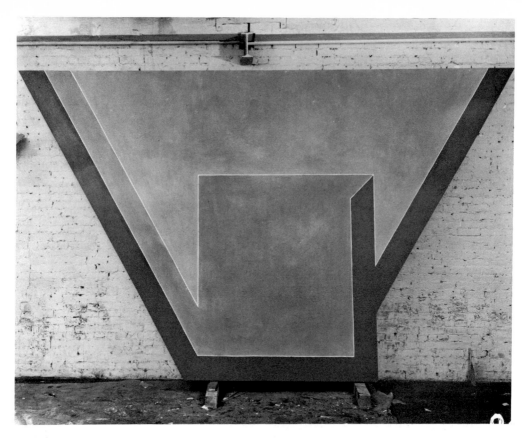

Frank Stella:
Union IV. 1966. Fluorescent alkyd and epoxy paint on canvas.
103″ x 174″. Collection of Richard Meier, New York.

Frank Stella:
Sangre de Cristo. 1967. Metallic powder in polymer emulsion.
10′ x 42′. Collection of Dr. and Mrs. Charles Hendrickson, Newport Beach, California.

LEFT, ABOVE. Frank Stella:
Hagmatana II. 1967. Acrylic on canvas. 10′ x 15′.
Collection of Mr. and Mrs. Eugene M. Schwartz, New York.

LEFT, BELOW. Frank Stella:
Ctesiphon III. 1968. Fluorescent acrylic on canvas. 10′ x 20′.
Wallraf-Richartz Museum, Köln, Germany, Sammlung Ludwig.

ABOVE. Clyfford Still:
Painting 1948-D. 1948. Oil on canvas. 93⅛″ x 79⅝″.
Collection of William S. Rubin, New York.

Clyfford Still:
No. 5. 1951. Oil on canvas. 55″ x 46″.
Wadsworth Atheneum, Hartford, Connecticut.

Clyfford Still:
Painting. 1951. Oil on canvas. 93¼″ x 75¾″.
The Detroit Institute of Arts, W. Hawkins Ferry Fund.

Clyfford Still:
Painting. 1958. Oil on canvas. 113¾″ x 159½″.
Collection of J. Patrick Lannan, Palm Beach, Florida.

Bradley Walker Tomlin:
All Souls' Night. 1948. Oil on canvas. 42½" x 64".
Betty Parsons Gallery, New York.

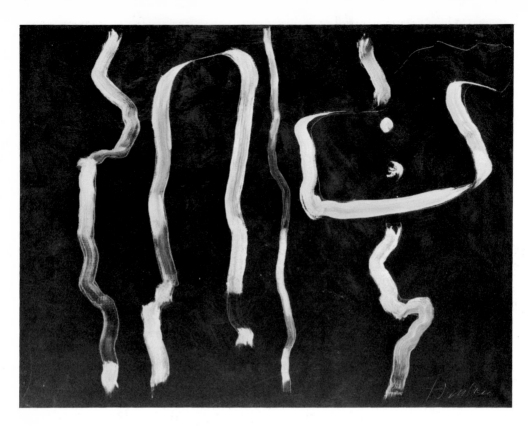

Bradley Walker Tomlin:
Tension by Moonlight. 1948. Oil on canvas. 32″ x 44″.
Betty Parsons Gallery, New York.

Bradley Walker Tomlin:
Number 3. 1948. Oil on canvas. 40″ x 50⅛″.
The Museum of Modern Art, New York, Fractional gift of
John E. Hutchins in memory of Frances E. Marder Hutchins, 1960.

Bradley Walker Tomlin:
Number 11. 1949. Oil on canvas. 44⅛″ x 29″.
Munson-Williams-Proctor Institute, Utica, New York.
Edward W. Root Bequest.

Bradley Walker Tomlin:
Number 9: In Memory of Gertrude Stein. 1950. Oil on canvas. 49″ x 8′ 6¼″.
The Museum of Modern Art, New York, Gift of Mrs. John D. Rockefeller, III, 1955.

330

LEFT. Bradley Walker Tomlin:
Number 5. 1952. Oil on canvas. 79″ x 45″.
Collection of Mrs. Betty Parsons, New York.

ABOVE. Andy Warhol:
Dick Tracy. 1960. Casein on canvas. 70⅛″ x 52¼″.
Gordon Locksley Gallery, Minneapolis, Minnesota.

Andy Warhol:
Campbell's Soup Cans. 1961–62. Oil on canvas.
Thirty-two panels, each 20″ x 16″.
Collection of Irving Blum, Los Angeles, California.

Andy Warhol:
Do It Yourself. 1962. Liquitex on canvas. 72″ x 54″.
Collection of Kimiko and John Powers, Aspen, Colorado.

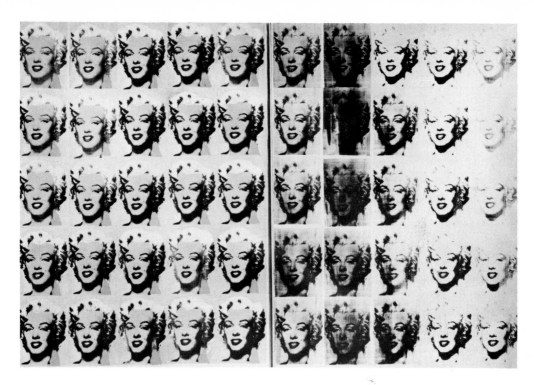

Andy Warhol:
Marilyn Monroe Diptych. 1962. Oil on canvas. 82″ x 114″.
Collection of Mr. and Mrs. Burton Tremaine, Meriden, Connecticut.

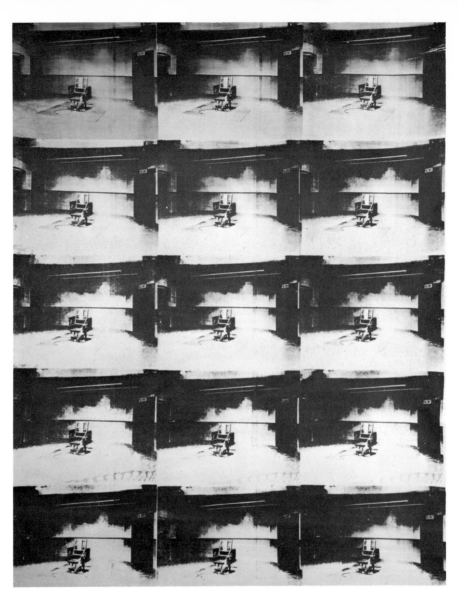

Andy Warhol:
Orange Disaster. 1963. Oil on canvas. 106″ x 82″.
Harry N. Abrams Family Collection, New York.

Andy Warhol:
Brillo Box. 1964. Silkscreen ink on wood. 17″ x 17″ x 17″.
Leo Castelli Gallery, New York.

Contemporary Criticism

The American Action Painters*

By Harold Rosenberg

"J'ai fait des gestes blanc parmi les solitudes."
—APOLLINAIRE

"The American will is easily satisfied
in its efforts to realize itself in knowing itself."
—WALLACE STEVENS

What makes any definition of a movement in art dubious is that it never fits the deepest artists in the movement—certainly not as well as, if successful, it does the others. Yet without the definition something essential in those best is bound to be missed. The attempt to define is like a game in which you cannot possibly reach the goal from the starting point but can only close in on it by picking up each time from where the last play landed.

Modern Art? Or an Art of the Modern?

Since the War every twentieth-century style in painting is being brought to profusion in the United States: thousands of "abstract" painters—crowded teaching courses in Modern Art—a scattering of new heroes—ambitions stimulated by new galleries, mass exhibitions, reproductions in popular magazines, festivals, appropriations.

Is this the usual catching up of America with European art forms? Or is something new being created? . . . For the question of novelty, a definition would seem indispensable.

Some people deny that there is anything original in the recent American painting. Whatever is being done here now, they claim, was done thirty years ago in Paris. You can trace this painter's boxes of symbols to Kandinsky, that one's moony shapes to Miró or even back to Cézanne.

Quantitatively, it is true that most of the symphonies in blue and red rectangles, the wandering pelvises and birdbills, the line constructions and plane suspensions, the virginal dissections of flat areas that crowd the art shows are accretions to the "School of Paris" brought into being by the fact that the mode of production of modern masterpieces has now been all too clearly rationalized. There are styles in the present displays that the painter could have acquired by putting a square inch of a Soutine or a Bonnard under a microscope. . . . All this is training based on a new conception of what art is, rather than original work demonstrating what art is about to become.

° Reprinted from *Art News*, Vol. 51, No. 5 (September, 1952).

of this wide practicing of the immediate past, however, the ⸻ of some painters has separated itself from the rest by a consciousness of a function for painting different from that of the earlier "abstractionists," both the Europeans themselves and the Americans who joined them in the years of the Great Vanguard.

This new painting does not constitute a School. To form a School in modern times not only is a new painting consciousness needed but a consciousness of that consciousness—and even an insistence on certain formulas. A School is the result of the linkage of practice with terminology—different paintings are affected by the same words. In the American vanguard the words, as we shall see, belong not to the art but to the individual artists. What they think in common is represented only by what they do separately.

Getting Inside the Canvas

At a certain moment the canvas began to appear to one American painter after another as an arena in which to act—rather than as a space in which to reproduce, re-design, analyze, or "express" an object, actual or imagined. What was to go on the canvas was not a picture but an event.

The painter no longer approached his easel with an image in his mind; he went up to it with material in his hand to do something to that other piece of material in front of him. The image would be the result of this encounter.

It is pointless to argue that Rembrandt or Michelangelo worked in the same way. You don't get Lucrece with a dagger out of staining a piece of cloth or spontaneously putting forms into motion upon it. She had to exist someplace else before she got on the canvas, and the paint was Rembrandt's means for bringing her here. Now, everything must have been in the tubes, in the painter's muscles, and in the cream-colored sea into which he dives. If Lucrece should come out she will be among us for the first time—a surprise. To the painter, she *must* be a surprise. In this mood there is no point in an act if you already know what it contains.

"B. is not modern," one of the leaders of this mode said to me the other day. "He works from sketches. That makes him Renaissance."

Here the principle, and the difference from the old painting, is made into a formula. A sketch is the preliminary form of an image the *mind* is trying to grasp. To work from sketches arouses the suspicion that the artist still regards the canvas as a place where the mind records its contents—rather than itself the "mind" through which the painter thinks by changing a surface with paint.

If a painting is an action, the sketch is one action, the painting that follows it another. The second cannot be "better" or more complete than the first. There is just as much significance in their difference as in their similarity.

Of course, the painter who spoke had no right to assume that the other had the old mental conception of a sketch. There is no reason why an act cannot be prolonged from a piece of paper to a canvas. Or repeated on another scale and with more control. A sketch can have the function of a skirmish.

Call this painting "abstract" or "Expressionist" or "Abstract-Expressionist," what counts is its special motive for extinguishing the object, which is not the same as in other abstract or Expressionist phases of modern art.

The New American Painting is not "pure art," since the extrusion of the object was not for the sake of the aesthetic. The apples weren't brushed off the table in order to make room for perfect relations of space and color. They had to go so that nothing would get in the way of the act of painting. In this gesturing with materials the aesthetic, too, has been subordinated. Form, color, composition, drawing, are auxiliaries, any one of which—or practically all, as has been attempted, logically, with unpainted canvases—can be dispensed with. What matters always is the revelation contained in the act. It is to be taken for granted that in the final effect, the image, whatever be or be not in it, will be a *tension*.

Dramas of as if

A painting that is an act is inseparable from the biography of the artist. The painting itself is a "moment" in the adulterated mixture of his life—whether "moment" means, in one case, the actual minutes taken up with spotting the canvas or, in another, the entire duration of a lucid drama conducted in sign language. The act-painting is of the same metaphysical substance as the artist's existence. The new painting has broken down every distinction between art and life.

It follows that anything is relevant to it. Anything that has to do with action—psychology, philosophy, history, mythology, hero worship. Anything but art criticism. The painter gets away from Art through his act of painting; the critic can't get away from it. The critic who goes on judging in terms of schools, styles, form, as if the painter were still concerned with producing a certain kind of object (the work of art), instead of living on the canvas, is bound to seem a stranger.

Some painters take advantage of this stranger. Having insisted that their painting is an act, they then claim admiration for the act as art. This turns the act back toward the aesthetic in a petty circle. If the picture is an act, it cannot be justified *as an act of genius* in a field whose whole measuring apparatus has been sent to the devil. Its value must be found apart from art. Otherwise the "act" gets to be "making a painting" at sufficient speed to meet an exhibition date.

Art—relation of the painting to the works of the past, rightness of color, texture, balance, etc.—comes back into painting by way of psychology. As Stevens says of poetry, "it is a process of the personality of the poet." But the psychology is the psychology of creation. Not that of the so-called psychological criticism that wants to "read" a painting for clues to the artist's sexual preferences or debilities. The work, the act, translates the psychologically given into the intentional, into a "world"—and thus transcends it.

With traditional aesthetic references discarded as irrelevant, what gives the canvas its meaning is not psychological data but *role*, the way the artist organizes his emotional and intellectual energy as if he were in a living situation. The interest lies on the kind of act taking place in the four-sided arena, a dramatic interest.

Criticism must begin by recognizing in the painting the assumptions inherent in its mode of creation. Since the painter has become an actor, the spectator has to think in a vocabulary of action: its inception, duration, direction—psychic state, concentration and relaxation of the will, passivity, alert waiting. He must become a connoisseur of the gradations among the automatic, the spontaneous, the evoked.

"It's Not That, It's Not That, It's Not That"

With a few important exceptions, most of the artists of this vanguard found their way to their present work by being cut in two. Their type is not a young painter but a reborn one. The man may be over forty, the painter around seven. The diagonal of a grand crisis separates him from his personal and artistic past.

Many of the painters were "Marxists" (W.P.A. unions, artists' congresses)—they had been trying to paint Society. Others had been trying to paint Art (Cubism, Post-Impressionism)—it amounts to the same thing.

The big moment came when it was decided to paint. . . . Just *To Paint*. The gesture on the canvas was a gesture of liberation, from Value—political, aesthetic, moral.

If the war and the decline of radicalism in America had anything to do with this sudden impatience, there is no evidence of it. About the effects of large issues upon their emotions, Americans tend to be either reticent or unconscious. The French artist thinks of himself as a battleground of history; here one hears only of private Dark Nights. Yet it is strange how many segregated individuals came to a dead stop within the past ten years and abandoned, even physically destroyed, the work they had been doing. A far-off watcher, unable to realize that these events were taking place in silence, might have assumed they were being directed by a single voice.

At its center the movement was away from rather than toward. The Great Works of the Past and the Good Life of the Future became equally nil.

The refusal of Value did not take the form of condemnation or defiance of

344

society, as it did after World War I. It was diffident. The lone artist did not want the world to be different, he wanted his canvas to be a world. Liberation from the object meant liberation from the "nature," society, and art already there. It was a movement to leave behind the self that wished to choose its future and to nullify its promissory notes to the past.

With the American, heir of the pioneer and the immigrant, the foundering of Art and Society was not experienced as a loss. On the contrary, the end of Art marked the beginning of an optimism regarding himself as an artist.

The American vanguard painter took to the white expanse of the canvas as Melville's Ishmael took to the sea.

On the one hand, a desperate recognition of moral and intellectual exhaustion; on the other, the exhilaration of an adventure over depths in which he might find reflected the true image of his identity.

Painting could now be reduced to that equipment which the artist needed for an activity that would be an alternative to both utility and idleness. Guided by visual and somatic memories of paintings he had seen or made—memories which he did his best to keep from intruding into his consciousness—he gesticulated upon the canvas and watched for what each novelty would declare him and his art to be.

Based on the phenomenon of conversion the new movement is, with the majority of the painters, essentially a religious movement. In every case, however, the conversion has been experienced in secular terms. The result has been the creation of private myths.

The tension of the private myth is the content of every painting of this vanguard. The act on the canvas springs from an attempt to resurrect the saving moment in his "story" when the painter first felt himself released from Value— myth of past self-recognition. Or it attempts to initiate a new moment in which the painter will realize his total personality—myth of future self-recognition.

Some formulate their myths verbally and connect individual works with their episodes. With others, usually deeper, the painting itself is the exclusive formulation, it is a Sign.

The revolution against the given, in the self and in the world, which since Hegel has provided European vanguard art with theories of a New Reality, has re-entered America in the form of personal revolts. Art as action rests on the enormous assumption that the artist accepts as real only that which he is in the process of creating. "Except the soul has divested itself of the love of created things . . ." The artist works in a condition of open possibility, risking, to follow Kierkegaard, the anguish of the aesthetic, which accompanies possibility lacking in reality. To maintain the force to refrain from settling anything, he must exercise in himself a constant No.

345

Apocalypse and Wallpaper

The most comfortable intercourse with the void is mysticism, especially a mysticism that avoids ritualizing itself.

Philosophy is not popular among American painters. For most, thinking consists of the various arguments that TO PAINT is something different from, say, to write or criticize: a mystique of the particular activity. Lacking verbal flexibility, the painters speak of what they are doing in a jargon still involved in the metaphysics of *things*: "My painting is not Art; it's an Is." "It's not a picture of a thing; it's the thing itself." "It doesn't reproduce Nature; it is Nature." "The painter doesn't think; he knows." Etc., etc. "Art is not, not not not not . . ." As against this, a few reply, art today is the same as it always has been.

Language has not accustomed itself to a situation in which the act itself is the "object." Along with the philosophy of TO PAINT appear bits of Vedanta and popular pantheism.

In terms of American tradition, the new painters stand somewhere between Christian Science and Whitman's "gangs of cosmos." That is, between a discipline of vagueness by which one protects oneself from disturbance while keeping one's eyes open for benefits; and the discipline of the Open Road of risk that leads to the farther side of the object and the outer spaces of the consciousness.

What made Whitman's mysticism serious was that he directed his "cosmic 'I'" toward a Pike's-Peak-or-Bust of morality and politics. He wanted the ineffable in *all* behavior—he wanted it *to win the streets.*

The test of any of the new paintings is its seriousness—and the test of its seriousness is the degree to which the act on the canvas is an extension of the artist's total effort to make over his experience.

A good painting in this mode leaves no doubt concerning its reality as an action and its relation to a transforming process in the artist. The canvas has "talked back" to the artist not to quiet him with Sibylline murmurs or to stun him with Dionysian outcries but to provoke him into a dramatic dialogue. Each stroke had to be a decision and was answered by a new question. By its very nature, action painting is painting in the medium of difficulties.

Weak mysticism, the "Christian Science" side of the new movement, tends in the opposite direction, toward *easy* painting—never so many unearned masterpieces! Works of this sort lack the dialectical tension of a genuine act, associated with risk and will. When a tube of paint is squeezed by the Absolute, the result can only be a Success. The painter need keeps himself on hand solely to collect the benefits of an endless series of strokes of luck. His gesture completes itself without arousing either an opposing movement within itself or his own desire to make the act more fully his own. Satisfied with wonders that remain safely inside the canvas, the artist accepts the permanence of the com-

The American Action Painters

monplace and decorates it with his own daily annihilation. The result is an apocalyptic wallpaper.

The cosmic "I" that turns up to paint pictures but shudders and departs the moment there is a knock on the studio door brings to the artist a megalomania that is the opposite of revolutionary. The tremors produced by a few expanses of tone or by the juxtaposition of colors and shapes purposely brought to the verge of bad taste in the manner of Park Avenue shop windows are sufficient cataclysms in many of these happy overthrows of Art. The mystical dissociation of painting as an ineffable event has made it common to mistake for an act the mere sensation of having acted—or of having been acted upon. Since there is nothing to be "communicated," a unique signature comes to seem the equivalent of a new plastic language. In a single stroke the painter exists as a Somebody—at least on a wall. That this Somebody is not he seems beside the point.

Once the difficulties that belong to a real act have been evaded by mysticism, the artist's experience of transformation is at an end. In that case what is left? Or to put it differently: What is a painting that is not an object nor the representation of an object nor the analysis or impression of it nor whatever else a painting has ever been—and that has also ceased to be the emblem of a personal struggle? It is the painter himself changed into a ghost inhabiting The Art World. Here the common phrase, "I have bought an O" (rather than a painting by O) becomes literally true. The man who started to remake himself has made himself into a commodity with a trademark.

Milieu: The Busy No-Audience

We said that the new painting calls for a new kind of criticism, one that would distinguish the specific qualities of each artist's act.

Unhappily for an art whose value depends on the authenticity of its mysteries, the new movement appeared at the same moment that Modern Art *en masse* "arrived" in America: Modern architecture, not only for sophisticated homes, but for corporations, municipalities, synagogues; Modern furniture and crockery in mail-order catalogues; Modern vacuum cleaners, can openers; beer ad "mobiles"—along with reproductions and articles on advanced painting in big-circulation magazines. *Enigmas for everybody.* Art in America today is not only nouveau, it's news.

The new painting came into being fastened to Modern Art and without intellectual allies—in literature everything had found its niche.

From this isolated liaison it has derived certain superstitions comparable to those of a wife with a famous husband. Superiorities, supremacies even, are taken for granted. It is boasted that modern painting in America is not only original but an "advance" in world art (at the same time that one says "to hell with world art").

Everyone knows that the label Modern Art no longer has any relation to the words that compose it. To be Modern Art a work need not be either modern or art; it need not even be a work. A three-thousand-year-old mask from the South Pacific qualifies as Modern and a piece of wood found on a beach becomes Art.

When they find this out, some people grow extremely enthusiastic, even, oddly enough, proud of themselves; others become infuriated.

These reactions suggest what Modern Art actually is. It is not a certain kind of art object. It is not even a style. It has nothing to do either with the period when a thing was made or with the intention of the maker. It is something that someone has had the power to designate as psychologically, aesthetically, or ideologically relevant to our epoch. The question of the driftwood is: *Who found it?*

Modern Art in America represents a revolution of taste—and serves to identify power of the caste conducting that revolution. Responses to Modern Art are primarily responses to claims to social leadership. For this reason Modern Art is periodically attacked as snobbish, Red, immoral, etc., by established interests in society, politics, the church. Comedy of a revolution that restricts itself to weapons of taste—and which at the same time addresses itself to the masses: Modern-design fabrics in bargain basements, Modern interiors for office girls living alone, Modern milk bottles.

Modern Art is educational, not with regard to art but with regard to life. You cannot explain Mondrian's painting to people who don't know anything about Vermeer, but you can easily explain the social importance of admiring Mondrian and forgetting about Vermeer.

Through Modern Art the expanding caste of professional enlighteners of the masses—designers, architects, decorators, fashion people, exhibition directors—informs the populace that a supreme Value has emerged in our time, the Value of the NEW, and that there are persons and things that embody that Value. This Value is a completely fluid one. As we have seen, Modern Art does not have to be actually new; it only has to be new to *somebody*—to the last lady who found out about the driftwood—and to win neophytes is the chief interest of the caste.

Since the only thing that counts for Modern Art is that a work shall be *new*, and since the question of its newness is determined not by analysis but by social power and pedagogy, the vanguard painter functions in a milieu utterly indifferent to the content of his work.

Unlike the art of nineteenth-century America, advanced paintings today are not bought by the middle class. Nor are they by the populace. Considering the degree to which it is publicized and feted, vanguard painting is hardly bought at all. It is *used* in its totality as material for educational and profit-

348

making enterprises: color reproductions, design adaptations, human-interest stories. Despite the fact that more people see and hear about works of art than ever before, the vanguard artist has an audience of nobody. An interested individual here and there, but no audience. He creates in an environment not of people but of functions. His paintings are employed not wanted. The public for whose edification he is periodically trotted out accepts the choices made for it as phenomena of The Age of Queer Things.

An action is not a matter of taste.

You don't let taste decide the firing of a pistol or the building of a maze.

As the Marquis de Sade understood, even experiments in sensation, if deliberately repeated, presuppose a morality.

To see in the explosion of shrapnel over No Man's Land only the opening of a flower of flame, Marinetti had to erase the moral premises of the act of destruction—as Molotov did explicitly when he said that Fascism is a matter of taste. Both M's were, of course, speaking the driftwood language of the Modern Art International.

Limited to the aesthetics, the taste bureaucracies of Modern Art cannot grasp the human experience involved in the new action paintings. One work is equivalent to another on the basis of resemblances of surface, and the movement as a whole a modish addition to twentieth-century picture making. Examples in every style are packed side by side in annuals and in the heads of newspaper reviewers like canned meats in a chain store—all standard brands.

To counteract the obtuseness, venality, and aimlessness of the Art World, American vanguard art needs a genuine audience—not just a market. It needs understanding—not just publicity.

In our form of society, audience and understanding for advanced painting have been produced, both here and abroad, first of all by the tiny circle of poets, musicians, theoreticians, men of letters, who have sensed in their own work the presence of the new creative principle.

So far, the silence of American literature on the new painting all but amounts to a scandal.

Harold Rosenberg

349

The Abstract Sublime*

By Robert Rosenblum

**How Some of the Most Heretical Concepts of Modern
American Abstract Painting Relate
to the Visionary Nature-painting of a Century Ago**

"It's like a religious experience!" With such words, a pilgrim I met in Buffalo
last winter attempted to describe his unfamiliar sensations before the awesome
phenomenon created by seventy-two Clyfford Stills at the Albright Art Gallery. A century and a half ago, the Irish Romantic poet, Thomas Moore, also
made a pilgrimage to the Buffalo area, except that his goal was Niagara Falls.
His experience, as recorded in a letter to his mother, July 24, 1804, similarly
beggared prosaic response:

I felt as if approaching the very residence of the Deity; the tears started into my eyes; and
I remained, for moments after we had lost sight of the scene, in that delicious absorption
which pious euthusiasm alone can produce. We arrived at the New Ladder and descended
to the bottom. Here all its awful sublimities rushed full upon me . . . My whole heart and
soul ascended towards the Divinity in a swell of devout admiration, which I never before
experienced. Oh! bring the atheist here, and he cannot return an atheist! I pity the man
who can coldly sit down to write a description of these ineffable wonders: much more do
I pity him who can submit them to the admeasurement of gallons and yards . . . We must
have new combinations of language to describe the Fall of Niagara.

Moore's bafflement before a unique spectacle, his need to abandon measur-
able reason for mystical empathy, are the very ingredients of the mid-twentieth-
century spectator's "religious experience" before the work of Still. During the
Romantic Movement, Moore's response to Niagara would have been called an
experience of the "Sublime," an aesthetic category that suddenly acquires
fresh relevance in the face of the most astonishing summits of pictorial heresy
attained in America in the last fifteen years.

Originating with Longinus, the Sublime was fervently explored in the later
eighteenth and early nineteenth centuries and recurs constantly in the aesthetics of such writers as Burke, Reynolds, Kant, Diderot, and Delacroix. For them
and for their contemporaries, the Sublime provided a flexible semantic container for the murky new Romantic experiences of awe, terror, boundlessness,
and divinity that began to rupture the decorous confines of earlier aesthetic
systems. As imprecise and irrational as the feelings it tried to name, the Sublime
could be extended to art as well as to nature. One of its major expressions, in
fact, was the painting of sublime landscapes.

° Reprinted from *Art News*, Vol. 59, No. 10 (February, 1961).

A case in point is the dwarfing immensity of Gordale Scar, a natural wonder of Yorkshire and a goal of many Romantic tourists. Re-created on canvas between 1811 and 1815 by the British painter James Ward (1769–1855), *Gordale Scar* [Fig. 1] is meant to stun the spectator into an experience of the Sublime that may well be unparalleled in painting until a work like Clyfford Still's *1957-D* [Fig. 2]. In the words of Edmund Burke, whose *Philosophical Enquiry into the Origin of Our Ideas of the Sublime and the Beautiful* (1757) was the most influential analysis of such feelings, "Greatness of dimension is a powerful cause of the sublime." Indeed, in both the Ward and the Still, the spectator is first awed by the sheer magnitude of the sight before him. (Ward's canvas is 131 by 166 inches; Still's, 113 by 159 inches.) At the same time, his breath is held by the dizzy drop to the pit of an abyss; and then, shuddering like Moore at the bottom of Niagara, he can only look up with what senses are left him and gasp before something akin to divinity.

Lest the dumbfounding size of these paintings prove insufficient to paralyze the spectator's traditional habits of seeing and thinking, both Ward and Still insist on a comparably bewildering structure. In the Ward, the chasms and cascades, whose vertiginous heights transform the ox, deer, and cattle into Lilliputian toys, are spread out into unpredictable patterns of jagged silhouettes. No laws of man or man-made beauty can account for these God-made shapes; their mysterious, dark formations (echoing Burke's belief that obscurity is another cause of the Sublime) lie outside the intelligible boundaries of aesthetic law. In the Still, Ward's limestone cliffs have been translated into an abstract geology, but the effects are substantially the same. We move physically across such a picture like a visitor touring the Grand Canyon or journeying to the center of the earth. Suddenly, a wall of black rock is split by a searing crevice of light, or a stalactite threatens the approach to a precipice. No less than caverns and waterfalls, Still's paintings seem the product of eons of change; and their flaking surfaces, parched like bark or slate, almost promise that this natural process will continue, as unsusceptible to human order as the immeasurable patterns of ocean, sky, earth, or water. And not the least awesome thing about Still's work is the paradox that the more elemental and monolithic its vocabulary becomes, the more complex and mysterious are its effects. As the Romantics discovered, all the sublimity of God can be found in the simplest natural phenomena, whether a blade of grass or an expanse of sky.

In his *Critique of Judgment* (1790), Kant tells us that whereas "the Beautiful in nature is connected with the form of the object, which consists in having boundaries, the Sublime is to be found in a formless object, so far as in it, or by occasion of it, *boundlessness* is represented" (I, Book 2, §23). Indeed, such a breathtaking confrontation with a boundlessness in which we also experience an equally powerful totality is a motif that continually links the painters of

351

1. James Ward: *Gordale Scar*. 1811–15. Oil on canvas. 131″ x 166″.
The Tate Gallery, London.

2. Clyfford Still: *1957-D No. 1*. 1957. Oil on canvas. 113″ x 159″.
The Albright–Knox Art Gallery, Buffalo, New York, Gift of Seymour H. Knox.

the Romantic Sublime with a group of recent American painters who seek out what might be called the "Abstract Sublime." In the context of two sea meditations by two great Romantic painters, Caspar David Friedrich's *Monk by the Sea* of about 1809 [Fig. 3] and Joseph Mallord William Turner's *Evening Star* [Fig. 4], Mark Rothko's *Light, Earth and Blue* of 1954 [Fig. 5] reveals affinities of vision and feeling. Replacing the abrasive, ragged fissures of Ward's and Still's real and abstract gorges with a no less numbing phenomenon of light and void, Rothko, like Friedrich and Turner, places us on the threshold of those shapeless infinities discussed by the aestheticians of the Sublime. The tiny monk in the Friedrich and the fisher in the Turner establish, like the cattle in *Gordale Scar*, a poignant contrast between the infinite vastness of a pantheistic God and the infinite smallness of His creatures. In the abstract language of Rothko, such literal detail—a bridge of empathy between the real spectator and the presentation of a transcendental landscape—is no longer necessary; we ourselves are the monk before the sea, standing silently and contemplatively before these huge and soundless pictures as if we were looking at a sunset or a moonlit night. Like the mystic trinity of sky, water, and earth that, in the Friedrich and Turner, appears to emanate from one unseen source, the floating, horizontal tiers of veiled light in the Rothko seem to conceal a total, remote presence that we can only intuit and never fully grasp. These infinite, glowing voids carry us beyond reason to the Sublime; we can only submit to them in an act of faith and let ourselves be absorbed into their radiant depths.

If the Sublime can be attained by saturating such limitless expanses with a luminous, hushed stillness, it can also be reached inversely by filling this void with a teeming, unleashed power. Turner's art, for one, presents both of these sublime extremes. In his *Snowstorm* of 1842 [Fig. 7], the infinities are dynamic rather than static, and the most extravagant of nature's phenomena are sought out as metaphors for this experience of cosmic energy. Steam, wind, water, snow, and fire spin wildly around the pitiful work of man—the ghost of a boat— in vortical rhythms that suck one into a sublime whirlpool before reason can intervene. And if the immeasurable spaces and incalculable energies of such a Turner evoke the elemental power of creation, other works of the period grapple even more literally with these primordial forces. Turner's contemporary, John Martin (1779–1854), dedicated his erratic life to the pursuit of an art which, in the words of the *Edinburgh Review* (1829), "awakes a sense of awe and sublimity, beneath which the mind seems overpowered." Of the cataclysmic themes that alone satisfied him, *The Creation*, an engraving of 1831 [Fig. 8], is characteristically sublime. With Turner, it aims at nothing short of God's full power, upheaving rock, sky, cloud, sun, moon, stars, and sea in the primal act. With its torrential description of molten paths of energy, it locates us once more on a near-hysterical brink of sublime chaos.

353

3. Caspar David Friedrich: *Monk by the Sea. ca.* 1809. Oil on canvas. 43″ x 67″.
Berlin, Palace collections.

4. J. M. W. Turner: *The Evening Star.* Oil on canvas. 36¼″ x 48¼″.
The National Gallery, London.

5. Mark Rothko: *Light, Earth and Blue.* 1954. Oil on canvas.
75¾″ x 67″. Collection of Lady D'Avigdor Goldsmid, London.

6. Barnett Newman: *Vir Heroicus Sublimis.* 1950–51. Oil on canvas.
96″ x 114½″. Collection of Ben Heller, New York.

7. J. M. W. Turner: *Snowstorm: Steamboat Off a Harbour's Mouth*. 1842.
Oil on canvas. 35½″ high. The National Gallery, London.

8. John Martin: *The Creation*. 1831. Engraving.

9. Jackson Pollock: *Number 1*. 1948. Oil on canvas. 68″ x 104″.
The Museum of Modern Art, New York.

That brink is again reached when we stand before a *perpetuum mobile* of
Jackson Pollock, whose gyrating labyrinths re-create in the metaphorical language of abstraction the superhuman turbulence depicted more literally in
Turner and Martin. In *Number 1, 1948* [Fig. 9], we are as immediately plunged
into divine fury as we are drenched in Turner's sea; in neither case can our
minds provide systems of navigation. Again, sheer magnitude can help produce
the Sublime. Here, the very size of the Pollock—68 by 104 inches—permits
no pause before the engulfing; we are almost physically lost in this boundless
web of inexhaustible energy. To be sure, Pollock's generally abstract vocabulary allows multiple readings of its mood and imagery, although occasional
titles (*Full Fathom Five, Ocean Greyness, The Deep, Greyed Rainbow*) may
indicate a more explicit region of nature. But whether achieved by the most
blinding of blizzards or the most gentle of winds and rains, Pollock invariably
evokes the sublime mysteries of nature's untamable forces. Like the awesome
vistas of telescope and microscope, his pictures leave us dazzled before the
imponderables of galaxy and atom.

The fourth master of the Abstract Sublime, Barnett Newman, explores a
realm of sublimity so perilous that it defies comparison with even the most
357

Robert Rosenblum

adventurous Romantic explorations into sublime nature. Yet it is worth noting that in the 1940s Newman, like Still, Rothko, and Pollock, painted pictures with more literal references to an elemental nature; and that more recently, he has spoken of a strong desire to visit the tundra, so that he might have the sensation of being surrounded by four horizons in a total surrender to spatial infinity. In abstract terms, at least, some of his paintings of the 1950s already approached this sublime goal. In its all-embracing width (114½ inches), Newman's *Vir Heroicus Sublimis* [Fig. 6] puts us before a void as terrifying, if exhilarating, as the arctic emptiness of the tundra; and in its passionate reduction of pictorial means to a single hue (warm red) and a single kind of structural division (vertical) for some 144 square feet, it likewise achieves a simplicity as heroic and sublime as the protagonist of its title. Yet again, as with Still, Rothko, and Pollock, such a rudimentary vocabulary creates bafflingly complex results. Thus the single hue is varied by an extremely wide range of light values; and these unexpected mutations occur at intervals that thoroughly elude any rational system. Like the other three masters of the Abstract Sublime, Newman bravely abandons the securities of familiar pictorial geometries in favor of the risks of untested pictorial intuitions; and like them, he produces awesomely simple mysteries that evoke the primeval moment of creation. His very titles (*Onement, The Beginning, Pagan Void, Death of Euclid, Adam, Day One*) attest to this sublime intention. Indeed, a quartet of the largest canvases by Newman, Still, Rothko, and Pollock might well be interpreted as a post-World-War-II myth of Genesis. During the Romantic era, the sublimities of nature gave proof of the divine; today, such supernatural experiences are conveyed through the abstract medium of paint alone. What used to be pantheism has now become a kind of "paint-theism."

Much has been written about how these four masters of the Abstract Sublime have rejected the Cubist tradition and replaced its geometric vocabulary and intellectual structure with a new kind of space created by flattened, spreading expanses of light, color, and plane. Yet it should not be overlooked that this denial of the Cubist tradition is not only determined by formal needs, but also by emotional ones that, in the anxieties of the atomic age, suddenly seem to correspond with a Romantic tradition of the irrational and the awesome as well as with a Romantic vocabulary of boundless energies and limitless spaces. The line from the Romantic Sublime to the Abstract Sublime is broken and devious, for its tradition is more one of erratic, private feeling than submission to objective disciplines. If certain vestiges of sublime landscape painting linger into the later nineteenth century in the popularized panoramic travelogues of Americans like Bierstadt and Church (with whom Dore Ashton has compared Still), the tradition was generally suppressed by the international domination of the French tradition, with its familiar values of reason, intellect,

358

and objectivity. At times, the countervalues of the Northern Romantic tradition have been partially reasserted (with a strong admixture of French pictorial discipline) by such masters as van Gogh, Ryder, Marc, Klee, Feininger, Mondrian; but its most spectacular manifestations—the sublimities of British and German Romantic landscape—have only been resurrected after 1945 in America, where the authority of Parisian painting has been challenged to an unprecedented degree. In its heroic search for a private myth to embody the sublime power of the supernatural, the art of Still, Rothko, Pollock, and Newman should remind us once more that the disturbing heritage of the Romantics has not yet been exhausted.

Robert Rosenblum

After Abstract Expressionism*

By Clement Greenberg

Twenty-odd years ago all the ambitious young painters I knew in New York saw abstract art as the only way out. Rightly or wrongly, they could perceive no other way in which to go in order to say something personal, therefore new, therefore worth saying. Representational art confronted their ambition with too many occupied positions. But it was not so much representation *per se* that cramped them; rather it was illusion, the illusion of the three-dimensional. Schematic representation survived in the art of Matisse and Picasso (as today in Dubuffet's) and in that of Léger, Braque, Klee, and Miró, but nevertheless their art was felt to be virtually abstract. It was from these artists, in fact, along with Mondrian, that the young painters I am speaking of got their most important lessons in abstraction.

In those years serious abstract art seemed inseparable from the canons of Synthetic Cubism, which meant cleanly marked contours, closed and more or less regular shapes, and flat color. It may not have been necessary to observe these canons literally, but it did seem necessary to keep oriented to them. By the end of the 1930s this orientation began to be a constricting one. Despite the growing appreciation of Klee (whose influence freed at least Tobey, Ralph Rosenborg, and even Loren MacIver), and though the early abstract paintings of Kandinsky were beginning to be admired in New York, most of the young artists I have in mind continued to believe that the only way to real style in abstract art lay through trued and faired, silhouetted and flattened forms. Any other way seemed an evasion or, at best, too idiosyncratic for more than one artist to take at a time.

This was pretty much the plight of abstract art in New York up into the early 1940s—and I say "plight" advisedly. Good abstract art was being produced in New York at that time: not only by Stuart Davis, but also by Bolotowsky, Cavallon, Diller, Ferren, Glarner, Balcomb and Gertrude Green, George L. K. Morris, and a few others, all of whom adhered to "closed" Cubism. Some of Gorky's work of that period looks more independent now than it used to, and de Kooning was then doing what I think remain his supreme paintings, unshown though they were. Nevertheless, the sense of how confining closed Cubism had become betrayed itself in the feeling that Stuart Davis had to be surpassed rather than emulated. This was unfair, but in retrospect I can see why it was necessary. As good as he was—and still is—Davis remained a provincial artist, and there was a feeling abroad, however dim, that provincial-

* Originally published in *Art International*, Vol. VI, No. 8 (October, 1962); somewhat revised in 1969.

ism was what had most to be overcome. At the same time it seemed harder than ever to paint one's way out of provincialism, out of tutelage to Paris.

The cramping hold of Synthetic Cubism, as felt in the early 1940s, helps explain why Baziotes' Surrealist-influenced pictures of 1942 came as a breath of fresh air. Daring to hint at illusionist space, they somehow—unlike Matta's paintings of that time—got away with it. They did not strike me, for one, as taking the easy way out—at least not altogether. The real break-out came, however, with Pollock's and Hofmann's first one-man shows in New York, in October 1943 and March 1944 respectively. There I saw abstract pictures that were painterly (*malerisch*) in what impressed me as being for the first time a full-blown way. Kandinsky's abstract paintings of 1910–18 looked almost clean-shaven by comparison, and Klee like a tidy miniaturist: neither had been so loose or open, or extravagant, in his use of mauled paint. The only precedent lay in representational painting, and that neither Pollock nor Hofmann was completely abstract in these first shows of theirs had its significance.

Then it was like a general thaw. In 1943 and 1944 Gorky, too, became much more painterly, under the influence of landscape subjects and the early abstract Kandinsky. Several students and former students of Hofmann began to do abstract pictures under Bonnard's or Rouault's influence. De Kooning, whose abandonment of closed, if not exactly Synthetic, Cubism dates from around 1946, was in another few years accepting the influence of Soutine. In 1947 and 1948 the more conscious passage to Abstract Expressionism of such artists as Tworkov, Guston, Brooks, even of Tomlin in a sense, was a passage, precisely, to loose and painterly handling.

"Painterly" was not the word used, but what was really meant, as I see it, when Robert Coates called the new open abstract art in New York "Abstract Expressionism." Though a reaction against the tightness of Synthetic Cubism, it used the same vocabulary at first. Looser paint-handling, combined with what remained an essentially Cubist sense of design, drawing, layout, was what artists as different as Gorky and Pollock had in common during the mid-1940s. If the term "Abstract Expressionist" means anything verifiable, it means painterliness: loose, rapid handling, or the look of it; masses that blot and fuse instead of shapes that stay distinct; large, conspicuous rhythms; broken color; uneven saturations or densities of paint; exhibited brush, knife, finger, or rag marks—in short, a constellation of physical features like those defined by Wölfflin when he extracted his notion of the *Malerische* from Baroque art. As we can now see, the displacing of the "linear" and quasi-geometrical as the dominant mode in New York (and Parisian) abstract art after 1943 offers another instance of that cyclical alternation of non-painterly, or linear, and painterly which has marked the evolution of Western art since the sixteenth century.

361

Painterly abstraction has tended to be less flat, or less taut in its flatness, than the "closed" or linear abstraction which preceded it. Above all, it contains many more velleities towards illusion. And I mean here illusion as distinct from representation or illustration; I mean the illusion of three-dimensional space with or without the bodying-forth of three-dimensional entities. The Kandinskys of 1910–18, so like landscapes, had already revealed this, and Abstract Expressionism again revealed, and continued to reveal, it. This should not have been surprising. The painterly in Western art had started out almost four hundred years ago as a means, first and foremost, to a heightened illusion of three-dimensional space; and in the course of painting and time uneven saturations of paint and color, and broken or blurred outlines, had come to evoke a bodily sense of space in depth almost as immediately and automatically as shading did, and more readily than perspective lines could. Three-dimensional space in the abstract and near-abstract painting of the 1920s and 1930s had been a matter mainly of "diagram" and association; in the painterly 1940s and 1950s it became again something closer to *trompe-l'oeil* illusion, atmospheric illusion. Not that it became *deeper*—not at all—but it did become more tangible as it were, more a thing of immediate perception and less a construct of "reading."

In June 1948 *Partisan Review* published a communication from George L. K. Morris in which he took me to task for, among other things, preferring what he called "behind-the-frame" painting. In my rejoinder I said that Mr. Morris had succumbed to the kind of dogmatism which held that in a given period one species of art must be the supreme one. All the same, his dogmatism did not take away from the acuteness of his "behind-the-frame" characterization, especially in its implications, as I only later came to recognize. Hofmann's and Pollock's and Gorky's pictures did stay further behind their frames than Mondrian's or than Picasso's post-1913 pictures did. This in itself said nothing about relative aesthetic value, and Mr. Morris was altogether wrong in inferring that it did. But he had a real point in his insinuation that painterly abstraction was headed backwards in terms of the evolution of style—even if going backwards in the literal sense of these terms was, at the time, almost the only way in which to go forwards in terms of major quality: that is, the only way in which to *maintain* major quality, not necessarily to *improve* on it.

Later, as the 1950s wore on, a good deal in Abstract Expressionist painting began fairly to cry out for a more coherent illusion of three-dimensional space; and to the extent that it did this it cried for representation, since such coherence can, as a rule, be created only through the tangible representation of three-dimensional objects. It was quite logical therefore that when painterly abstraction in New York finally crystallized into a set manner, it did so in a series of outspokenly representational works, namely de Kooning's "Women"

362

pictures of 1952–55. This manner, as returned to abstract art by de Kooning himself and by the countless artists he has influenced, I call "homeless representation." By this I mean a plastic and descriptive painterliness that is applied to abstract ends but continues to suggest representational ones. In itself "homeless representation" is neither good nor bad, and maybe some of the best results of Abstract Expressionism earlier on were got by flirting with representation. Badness becomes endemic to a manner only when the latter hardens into mannerism. This happened with "homeless representation" in the mid-1950s, in de Kooning's and Guston's art, in the post-1953 art of Kline, and in the art of the many imitators of these painters. It is on the basis of actual results that I find fault with "homeless representation," not because of any *parti pris*. It's because what were merely its logical contradictions have turned into artistic ones too.

Something similar has happened with the two main tendencies of the European version of painterly abstraction (which likewise emerged during the war). In Europe too painterly abstraction presses towards the three-dimensional. But if one tendency leans, like our "homeless representation," towards the three-dimensionality of illusion, the other leans towards the literal, actual three-dimensionality of piled-on paint, and for its part could be called "furtive bas-relief." The latter tendency does happen to be more closely involved with representation than the former—even if it is largely schematic representation—because it started with Dubuffet and Fautrier, and came to a head—though not at all to an extreme—in the art of de Staël's last years. (By "schematic" representation I mean representation that depends mostly on linear handling or placing, without bodying forth what is represented through shading or atmospheric effects—i.e. without illusion.) Curiously enough, the other tendency in European painterly abstraction, the one closer to our "homeless representation," got its start from the very abstract works of Hartung and Mathieu, as well as from Wols, all three of whom are linear before they are anything else. (I do not profess to be able to explain the pictorial logic at work here, but I do think that one clue lies in the extent to which "furtive bas-relief," while employing the linear together with the protuberances and indentations of thick paint-matter for representation, is able at the same time to rely for pictorial unity on the kind of coherence provided automatically by literal, bodily, *real* three-dimensionality. There is, on the other hand, the more strictly pictorial kind of coherence that is automatically produced by the illusion of deep space— at least by now. I say "by now" because, after four-hundred-odd years of illusionist pictorial art, the devices of illusion tend to have a built-in unity and coherence.)

In Europe too painterly abstraction has degenerated into an affair largely of mannerisms, whether those of "homeless representation" or those of "furtive

363

bas-relief." There too a vast quantity of bad abstract painting is relieved, within the orbit of the mannerisms, only by felicitous minor art. For our Johns and Diebenkorn, Europe has its Tápies and Sugai to show. This placing may be unfair to Diebenkorn, however, whose case is so exemplary that it is worth pausing over.

Diebenkorn's development has been what one might say that of Abstract Expressionism should have been. Earlier on he was the only *abstract* painter, as far as I know, to do anything substantially independent with de Kooning's touch (and it makes no difference that he did it with some help from Rothko's design). More recently, he has let the logic of that touch carry him back—with Matisse's help—to representational art, and one might say that this consistency of logic is partly responsible for his becoming at least as good a representational as he was an abstract painter. That de Kooning's touch remains as unmistakable as before in Diebenkorn's art does not take away anything from the success of the change. Uneven densities of paint, as produced by smearing, swiping, scrubbing, and scumbling, had in de Kooning's own hands created gradations of light and dark like those of conventional shading; though these were kept from actually modeling back into deep space by the declamatory abruptness with which they were juxtaposed, deep space is nevertheless increasingly suggested in almost everything de Kooning has done lately. By letting this suggestion become a forthright statement, Diebenkorn (along with another Californian, Elmer Bischoff) has in effect found a home for de Kooning's touch where it can fulfill itself more truthfully, and by the same token less pretentiously, than it has been able to so far in de Kooning's own art.

There are other painters, mainly in New York, who have begun to put de Kooning's manner to the uses of outright representational art, but until now their success has been less consistent or less significant. Jasper Johns should not be classed among these, however much he, too, takes from de Kooning, and however representational his art is. His case is another exemplary one; he brings de Kooning's influence to a head so to speak by suspending it vividly between abstraction and representation. The motifs of Johns's paintings and bas-reliefs, as William Rubin pointed out in *Art International* a few years ago, are always two-dimensional to start with, being taken from a repertory of man-made signs and images not too different in kind from that on which Picasso and Braque drew for the stenciled and affixed elements of their 1911–13 Cubism. Unlike them, Johns is interested in the literary irony that results from *representing* flat and artificial configurations which in actuality can be *reproduced;* yet the abiding significance of his art, as distinct from its journalistic one, lies mostly in the area of the formal or plastic. Just as the vivid possibility of deep space in photographs of signs or house-fronts, or in Harnett's and Peto's paintings of pin-up boards, sets off the native flatness of the objects

364

shown, so the painterly paintedness of a Johns picture sets off, and is set off by, the ineluctable flatness of his number, letter, target, flag, and map images.

By means of this "dialectic" the arrival of Abstract Expressionism at representation, homeless and not homeless, is declared and spelled out. The original flatness of the picture surface, with a few outlines stenciled on it, is shown as sufficing to represent all that a picture by Johns really does represent. The covering of paint itself, with its de Kooningesque play of lights and darks, is shown as being completely superfluous to this end. Everything that usually serves representation and illusion is left to serve nothing but itself, that is abstraction; while everything that usually connotes the abstract or the decorative—flatness, bare outlines, all-over or symmetrical design—is put to the service of representation. And the more explicit this contradiction is made, the more effective in every sense the picture tends to be. When the image is too obscured the paint covering is liable to become less pointedly superfluous; conversely, when the image is left too prominent the whole picture is liable to dwindle to a mere image—an image on the order of Johns's sculptures, which, even when their bronze surfaces are left unpainted, amount to nothing more than what they really are: cast reproductions of man-made objects that, as far as three-dimensional art is concerned, could never be anything other than merely reproducible. The effect of a Johns painting is also weakened, often, when it is done in bright instead of neutral colors like black and gray, for the latter, being the shading colors *par excellence,* are just those that become the most exhibitedly and poignantly superfluous when applied to images of flatness.

I do not mean to imply that the effectiveness of Johns's paintings depends on a mere device. There is far more to them than that; otherwise I would not get the kind of effect from his art that I do. But the fact that as much of his art can be explained as has been explained here without the exertion of any particular powers of insight would indicate a certain narrowness. Johns sings the swan song of "homeless representation," and like most swan songs, it carries only a limited distance.

Echoes of Analytical Cubism and of its transition to Synthetic Cubism are not found in Johns alone among Abstract Expressionists, early and late (and Johns remains a kind of Abstract Expressionist even while pointing the way to Pop Art). Far from it. The whole evolution of Abstract Expressionism could, in fact, be described as the *de*volution from a Synthetic to an Analytical kind of abstract Cubism. By 1911 original Analytical Cubism had itself arrived at "homeless representation": a way of depicting objects in planar segments kept parallel to the picture plane that ended up by effacing the objects themselves, leaving only the illusion of the kind of space in which they were possible, along with a weaker illusion of the surfaces—the planar segments—that once clothed

365

them. In the all-over Pollocks and in the de Koonings of the last seven or eight years, analogous planar segments are analogously deployed (smaller in Pollock, larger in de Kooning), with the principal difference from Analytical Cubism lying in the articulation or jointing of the segments, which is no longer governed, as it still was in Braque and Picasso, by a model in nature. Yet, as I've already said more or less, de Kooning's large-ish facet-planes seem to grope for such a model—and off and on actually find it. Nor does the indeterminate space created by Pollock's webs and blotches always function as "abstract" space; it can also function as illusion. Whereas Analytical Cubism had arrived at the brink of outright abstraction by pursuing both art and nature, Abstract Expressionism returned to the verge of nature by pursuing, apparently, art alone. In several of his black and white pictures of 1951 Pollock actually signaled this return; de Kooning, in his "Women," which marked his real transition from Synthetic to Analytical Cubism, did more than signal it.

Meanwhile another kind of return was being made, though not under the auspices of Abstract Expressionism as defined so far. Abstract Expressionism was not, and is not, just painterly abstraction. Like all momentous tendencies in art, it exceeded any verbal or phenomenal definition of itself, making room for a variety of "deviations" and even "contradictions." Analytical Cubism, besides being a case of homeless representation, had embodied a synthesis of painterly and non-painterly. Synthetic Cubism and Mondrian had dissolved this synthesis in favor of the non-painterly, and Abstract Expressionism, as we have just seen, reacted violently in the opposite direction. But just before 1950 something like a new synthesis of painterly and non-painterly began to emerge in New York abstract art, as if to complete its inverted recapitulation of the original evolution of Cubism.

Actually, most of the New York painters first called Abstract Expressionists have not been painterly in a consistent or committed way. This is true even of Hofmann: the best things he has done in recent years—and they are among the best things he has ever done—move towards a personal synthesis in which the painterly is fused with the linear at the same time that Fauvism is married to Cubism. Kline turned painterly only after 1953, to the cost of his quality, as is negatively confirmed by the improvement his art showed whenever he reverted, as he did frequently in the last two years or so of his life, to his former sharp-edged manner. Motherwell has been painterly off and on, and several of his masterpieces of the late 1940s were quite so, but most of his successful pictures still tend towards the non-painterly. Gottlieb too wavers between the painterly and the non-painterly, and has done superb things in both manners.

Yet I feel that Gottlieb's wavering has the effect somehow of making him disloyal to his greatest gift, which is for color. In this respect he might have done well to take a hint from the example of three other New York painters

366

who stand somewhat apart within Abstract Expressionism. I mean Newman, Rothko, and Still, who have renounced painterliness, or at least the kind associated with Abstract Expressionism, for the sake, precisely, of a vision keyed to the primacy of color.

Like so much of painterly art before it, Abstract Expressionism has worked in the end to reduce color's role. Unequal densities of paint become, as I have said, so many differences of light and dark, and these deprive color of both its purity and fullness. And though openness is supposed to be another quintessentially painterly aim, the slapdash application of paint ends by crowding the picture surface into a compact jumble—a jumble that, as we see it in de Kooning and his followers, is another version of academically Cubist compactness. Still, Newman, and Rothko turn away from the painterliness of Abstract Expressionism as though to save the objects of painterliness—color and openness—from painterliness itself. But rather than effecting a synthesis of painterly and non-painterly, their art could be said to transcend the differences between the two. A transcending, not a reconciliation—the latter belonged to Analytical Cubism, as it now belongs to Hofmann. These three painters take their lead from Impressionism as well as Cubism; and the fact that Impressionism was an epitome of painterly handling seems to have given an artist like Newman all the more insight into the whole question of painterly versus non-painterly as it affected abstract art.

Clyfford Still, who is one of the great innovators of Modernist art, is the leader and pioneer of this group with respect to the insistence on color. Setting himself against the immemorial emphasis on light-and-dark contrasts, he asserted color's capacity to act through the contrasts of pure hue more or less independently of value differences. Late Impressionism furnished the precedent here, and as with the later Monet, the suppression of light-and-dark contrasts made for a new kind of openness, a new expansiveness. The picture no longer divided itself into shapes, but rather into zones and areas and fields of color. This was the essential, but it was left to Newman and Rothko to drive this home. If Still's largest paintings, and especially those in which width exceeds height, fail so often to realize the grand openness they promise, it is not only because he will choose a surface too large for what he has to say; it is also because too many of his smaller color areas will fail to function as *areas*, and will remain merely patches—patches whose rustic-Gothic complications of outline interfere with and halt the flow of color-space.

With Newman and Rothko, temperaments that might strike one as natively far more painterly than Still's administer themselves copious antidotes in the form of the rectilinear. The latter is kept ambiguous, however; Rothko fuzzes all his dividing edges; Newman will insert a smudged edge as foil to his ruled

367

ones. Like Still, they both make a show of studiedness, as if to demonstrate their rejection of the mannerisms that have become inseparable by now from rapid brush or knife handling. Newman's occasional blurred edge, and the torn but exact one left by Still's knife, are there as though to advertise both their awareness and their repudiation of the plausible effects of spontaneity (*unconsideredness* would be the better word here perhaps). Still continues to invest in textures, and the tactile irregularities of his surfaces, with their contrasts of matt and shiny, paint coat and priming, contribute to the force of his art. But by eschewing tactility, and detail in drawing, Newman and Rothko reach what I find to be a more positive openness and more pungent effects of color. The rectilinear is "open" by definition as it were: it calls the least attention to drawing and design, gets least in the way of color-space. A thin paint surface likewise gets least in the way of color-space, simply by excluding tactile associations. (Here both Rothko and Newman seem to have taken their lead from Milton Avery, who took his from Matisse.) At the same time color is given more autonomy by being relieved of its localizing and denotative functions. It no longer specifies or *fills in* an area or plane, but speaks for itself by more or less dissolving definiteness of shape and distance. To this end—as Still was the first to show—it has to be warm color, or cool color infused with warmth. It also has to be uniform color, with only the subtlest variations of value if any at all; and it has, furthermore, to be spread over an absolutely, not relatively, large area. Size guarantees the purity as well as the intensity of hue needed to suggest indeterminate space: more blue being simply bluer than less blue. This too is why the picture has to be confined to but a few colors. Here again, Still pointed the way, the vision of the two- or three-color painting (as E. C. Goossen calls it) being his in the first place (whatever help towards it he may have got from the Miró of 1925–30).

It remains, however, that Newman and Rothko stand or fall by color more conspicuously than Still does. The right color in the right place can more readily redeem—at least in seeming—errors of spatial proportioning or configuration in their art. Similarly, the particular color key appears to decide everything in Monet's large "Lily Pad" pictures. But the converse is equally true: the right proportioning of spatial quantities of shapes can overcome the most refractory color or color relations. (It cannot be emphasized enough that art is entirely a matter of relativities and adjustments.)

The ultimate effect achieved in the art of all three of these painters has to be described as one of more than chromatic intensity. It is rather an effect of almost literal openness that embraces and absorbs color in the act of being created by it. Openness—and not only in pictorial art—is the quality that seems most to exhilarate the attuned eye of this time. Facile explanations suggest themselves here which I leave the reader to explore for himself. Let it suffice that I think that the new openness in Newman's Rothko's, and Still's painting shows the way to what I would risk saying is the only direction for high pictorial art in the near future.

That direction is also pointed to by their repudiation of virtuosity in execution or handling. Elsewhere I have written of the kind of self-critical process that I believe provides the infralogic of Modernist art ("Modernist Painting" in *Arts Yearbook 4*, 1961). The aim of the self-criticism, which is entirely empirical and not at all an affair of theory, is to determine the irreducible working essence of art and of the separate arts. Under the testing of this process more and more of the conventions of the art of painting have shown themselves to be dispensable, unessential. It has been established by now, it would seem, that the irreducibility of pictorial art consists in but two constitutive conventions or norms: flatness and the delimitation of flatness. In other words, the observance of merely these two norms is enough to create an object which can be experienced as a picture: thus a stretched or tacked-up canvas already exists as a picture—though not necessarily as a *successful one*. (The paradoxical outcome of this reduction has been not to contract, but actually to expand the possibilities of the pictorial. Much more lends itself now to being experienced pictorially or in meaningful relation to the pictorial: all sorts of large and small visual incidents and items that used to belong wholly to the realm of the aesthetically meaningless.)

As it looks to me, Newman, Rothko, and Still have swung the self-criticism of Modernist painting in a new direction by dint simply of continuing it far enough in its original one. The question now asked in their art is no longer what constitutes art, or the art of painting, as such, but what constitutes *good* art as such. What is the ultimate source of value or quality in art? And the worked-out answer appears to be: not skill, training, or anything else having to do with execution or performance, but conception alone. Culture or taste may be a necessary condition of conception, but the latter is alone decisive. Conception can be called invention, inspiration, or even intuition (which last is what it was called by Croce, who did anticipate theoretically what practice has just now discovered and confirmed for itself). On the other hand, it is true that skill used to be a vessel of inspiration and do some of the work of conception, but that was when the best pictorial art was, by and large, the most naturalistic. Skill, dexterity, is now revealed as no longer capable of generating quality because it has become too generalized, too accessible, and by the same token too patterned.

Inspiration, conception, alone belongs altogether to the individual; everything else can be acquired by anyone now. Inspiration or conception remains the only factor in the creation of a successful work that cannot be copied or imitated. It was left to artists like Mondrian and Newman to make this explicit (and it is really the only thing that Mondrian and Newman have in common). Newman's pictures look easy to copy, and maybe they are. But they are far from easy to conceive or invent, and their quality lies almost entirely in their conception. This should be self-evident, but even if it were not the frustrated efforts of Newman's imitators would reveal it. The onlooker who says his child could paint a Newman may be right, but Newman would have to be there to tell the child *exactly* what to do. The *exact* choices of medium, color, size, shape, and proportion—including the size and shape of the support—are what determine the success of the result, and these choices have to depend solely on inspiration (just as they did for Mondrian, despite much nonsense to the contrary). Like Rothko and Still, Newman happens to be a conventionally skilled artist—need I say it? But if he uses his skill, it is to suppress the evidence of it. And the suppression is part of the triumph of his art; next to it, most other contemporary painting begins to look fussy.

Because of this, the admiration of some of the strongest among the newer or younger American abstract artists goes out to Newman particularly. His rejection of virtuosity (of prestigious handwriting *à la* de Kooning, for instance) confirms them in what they themselves long to renounce, as it also confirms them in what they dare. It confirms painters like Louis and Noland all the more, precisely because they have not been directly influenced by Newman (or, for that matter, by Still or Rothko either). They may pursue a related vision of color and openness, but they do so all the more resolutely because it is not a derived vision. Not only do Louis and Noland *not* make two- or three-color pictures; they have also been more influenced in aim and means by Pollock than by anyone else. This takes nothing away from Newman, Rothko, or Still, and I stress the point only to clear up misconceptions circulated by journalists and curators. The fact that, so far, the direct influence of these three painters has been a crushing one—with Sam Francis being the only younger artist yet able to realize himself under it—may attest to the very power of their art.

The crux of the matter of the aftermath of Abstract Expressionism has, in any case, little to do with influence as such. Where artists divide in the last resort is where safe taste leaves off. This is as true in what begins to look like the aftermath of Abstract Expressionism as it ever was. Those who follow Newman, Rothko, or Still, individually or collectively, have become as safe by now in their taste as they would be following de Kooning, Gorky, or Kline. (I have the impression, anyhow, that some of the painters who have chosen to do the first instead of the second have been motivated more by *mere* frustration than by dissatisfaction or impatience with the going versions of Abstract Expressionism on Tenth Street.)

Nor do those other artists in this country who have gone in for "neo-Dada," or construction-collage, or ironic comments on the banalities of the industrial environment escape the jurisdiction of good safe taste—*they* almost least of all. (Johns is the sole exception.) For all the novel objects they represent or insert in their works, not one of these artists has taken a chance with color or design that the Cubists or the Abstract Expressionists did not take before them. (What happens when a real chance is taken with color can be seen from the shocked distaste that the "pure" painting of Jules Olitski provokes among New York artists.) Nor has any one of them, whether he harpoons stuffed whales to plane surfaces or fills watercloset bowls with diamonds, yet ventured to arrange these things outside the directional lines of the "all-over" Cubist grid. The results in every case have a conventional, Cubist prettiness that hardly entitles them to be discussed under the heading "After Abstract Expressionism." The same applies to those painters whose contribution lies in depicting plucked chickens instead of dead pheasants, or coffee cans and pieces of pastry instead of flowers in vases. Not that I do not find the clear and straightforward academic handling of their pictures refreshing and even intriguing after the turgidities of Abstract Expressionism; yet this effect is only momentary, since novelty, as distinct from originality, has no staying power.

Arshile Gorky, Surrealism, and the New American Painting*

By William Rubin

As critics and historians have brought into focus their views of painting in America during and just after World War II, a consensus has emerged regarding the quality of Arshile Gorky's art. Today no serious critic remains untouched by the beauty of his paintings; and if few would concede him the stature of Jackson Pollock, let alone that of Matisse, none would deny him a place among the masters of twentieth-century painting. However, this unanimity as to the quality of Gorky's art is in marked contrast to the divergence of opinion on the nature of his style and its historical position during the critical decade of the 1940s, or, more specifically, his possible role either as the last Surrealist or as a pioneer of the New American Painting.

The Surrealists themselves treat Gorky as a significant ornament of their movement, and he was, indeed, the last important painter accepted into their circle. His work attracted the attention of André Breton in 1943; two years later, when he exhibited at the Surrealist-oriented Julien Levy Gallery, he was considered a full-fledged member of the Surrealist group. The concluding section of Breton's 1945 edition of *Surrealism and Painting* is devoted to Gorky; he is also the last Surrealist to be dealt with in the quite different histories of Surrealist painting recently published by Patrick Waldberg and Marcel Jean. Painter-critic Robert Motherwell asserts that there is nothing in Gorky's work that cannot be understood within the context of Surrealism.

But there is also a considerable body of opinion that views Gorky as a pioneer of the New American Painting. His inclusion in the exhibition of that title, which The Museum of Modern Art circulated through Europe a few years ago, is symptomatic in this regard, as was the earlier (1950) exhibition of his work at the American Pavilion of the Venice Biennial along with Pollock and de Kooning. In a recent monograph Harold Rosenberg minimizes Gorky's relation to Surrealism and speaks of him as "a typical hero of Abstract Expressionism."

It is the coincidence in Gorky's art of elements usually associated with either Surrealism or recent American abstraction (far fewer of the latter, I believe) that provokes the divergence of opinion, and this dualism itself stems, to a large extent, from Gorky's unique historical position in a decade that saw both the end of Surrealism and the rise of the New American Painting. To view Gorky simply as the last Surrealist is to overlook certain qualities that differentiate his painting from that of all other Surrealists, qualities that are in fact contrary to

*Reprinted from *Art International*, Vol. VII, No. 3 (February, 1963). Portions of this article were delivered as a lecture at The Museum of Modern Art in connection with the Retrospective Exhibition of Gorky's work held there from December 19, 1962, through February 12, 1963.

the theory and practice of Surrealism. Yet to conceive of him primarily as a pioneer of the New American Painting necessitates gerrymandering one's image of his art so as to suppress not only its morphology, but its particular poetic sensibility and psychological disposition as well. Sufficient time has now elapsed for art historians to approach the decade of the forties, and the problem of Gorky's place in it, independently of the *partis pris*, both geographical and personal, which have converted much recent criticism of this period into polemic.

A proper assessment of Gorky's relationship to Surrealism requires that we reconsider certain aspects of that as yet imperfectly understood movement. The interwar period of the 1920s and 1930s, which Surrealism dominated, was clearly, it seems to me, a parenthetical phase of the great continuing revolution in style that had begun with Manet and the Impressionists. This revolution had reached a climax in the years immediately preceding the First World War, by which time the Cubists, Kandinsky, Delaunay, Mondrian, and others were producing non-figurative paintings or their approximations. The euphoria of those adventurous years—so movingly reflected in the tone of Apollinaire's *Cubist Painters*—was abruptly ended by the outbreak of the war.

In contrast to the galvanic speed with which the various "isms" followed one after the other from 1860 to 1914, the period from Sarajevo to Munich saw the rise of only two major avant-garde movements: Dada and Surrealism.[1] To be sure, most of the masters who had matured between 1905 and 1914 remained active, though frequently with less rewarding results, and more than one of the young painters who rallied around André Breton during Surrealism's pioneer years of the mid-twenties shared his view that Matisse was "an old lion, discouraged and discouraging."[2] Ludicrous as this sounds today, we must remember that Breton spoke at a time when the further development of "pure painting"—such as Mondrian, Kandinsky, and Delaunay had wrought from Fauvism and Cubism—no longer seemed possible *or even desirable*. The new art, or anti-art, of the Dada and Surrealist generations differed strikingly in its premises and character from that which had preceded it. For the first time the continuity of the plastic evolution, in which the generations of the first fifty years of Modern Painting were merged, was broken, to be resumed only with the advent of post-World War II abstraction.

The most salient aspect of the consecutive and interrelated movements called Dada and Surrealism, when we contrast them with Impressionism, Fauvism, and Cubism, is that neither of them emerged primarily from the evolution of art; rather, both began as broader revolutions in philosophical, literary, psychological, and political values. If, in other disciplines, Dada and Surrealism

[1] I consider the *Neue Sachlichkeit*, the Abstraction-Creation group, and the various Neoclassic reactions of secondary importance, *as movements*, to the history of painting.

[2] In fairness to Breton we must concede that the early and middle twenties constituted a relatively dry period in the work of such painters as Matisse, Bonnard, Picasso, and Kandinsky.

William Rubin

were truly radical and progressive, their posture led, paradoxically, to an attitude toward painting which—in terms of the history of art—turned out to be radical but reactionary. Though the apparent "new look" of the bulk of Dada and Surrealist art seemed to verify the avant-garde stance of the movements as a whole, this new look (which, like much of the pseudo-Dada of today, was not so new as it looked) not only argued the denial of many premises essential to earlier Modern Art, but, indeed, was only made possible by this denial. Thus, when Tzara called for an art "once again under the domination of man," and when Breton insisted that painting was only a window and all that mattered was "what it looks out upon," both were reacting against the advanced abstraction that had dominated the years of their youth. In the face of the crisis of World War I, such art seemed to them too hermetic, too incapable of direct and specific communication.

Their position, though infinitely more sophisticated, had something in common with that of the recent so-called New Humanist critics, who, in their turn, have reacted against history's next major advance in the direction of "pure painting," the American avant-garde in the late forties and fifties. For painting to be meaningful to Breton, it had to have subject matter in the Old Master sense and hence an iconography. But unlike the New Humanist critics, Breton was able to distinguish between a subject and a motif; Matisse's pot of flowers was as unacceptable to him as Delaunay's colored disks, in fact even more so, since to his mind it added a disturbingly trivial aspect to the picture. Breton had understood advanced abstraction as an assertion of the non-viability of the familiar subject matter of the phenomenological world and concluded that the artist would now have to replace such objective imagery with one drawn from the realm of his own psychology. This could be projected either through illusion (the "hand-painted dream photographs" of Dali and Magritte) or through allusion (the evocation of the artist's inner world by means of ambiguous signs, as in Miró, Arp, and Masson).

The Surrealist movement, which Breton's First Manifesto of 1924 formalized, continued for the next twenty years as the main embodiment of the avant-garde, a phenomenon unparalleled in the history of modern painting. Not that other movements have failed to last that long; some have lasted even longer, Impressionism for example. But in those cases, newer movements or individuals intervened at diminishing intervals to usurp the leadership of the avant-garde. This failed to happen, however, in the case of Surrealism. After 1929—by which time the most crucial work of Ernst, Miró, Masson, Tanguy, Arp, Magritte, and Dali had all been realized—Surrealism suffered a decade of relative dryness and indecision. And when, on the eve of the Second World War, the movement began to be revitalized, it still found itself unchallenged, if only by default, in its position as the avant-garde. The crises attendant upon the war—and particularly the flight of Breton, Ernst, Masson, Dali, Tanguy, Matta, and others to the Americas—seemed to have a quickening effect. Between 1938 and 1942 a number of young painters joined the Surrealist circle, though only two of them, Matta and Lam, were artists of consequence. This late flowering in exile was brought to a conclusion by the celebration of Gorky as a Surrealist in the last year of the war, the end of which was the signal for the hasty repatriation of the Surrealist exiles to France.

The vacuum left by the departure of the Surrealists from America—most were gone by 1947—was quickly filled by a group of American painters, many of whom had had contacts with the Surrealists and had exhibited with them in Peggy Guggenheim's gallery, Art of This Century. The end of the decade saw these artists established as painters of great force and originality, and by then Gorky's art was being looked at in a new context: not in terms of what had gone before, but of what had come after.

In attempting to bring into focus the historical picture of the remarkable transition that characterized the decade of the 1940s, we might start with the year 1947. If we accept Willem de Kooning's generous statement that it was "Jackson Pollock [who] broke the ice," the breakthrough surely dates from the winter of 1946–47, when Pollock first articulated his canvases with "all-over" webs of poured paint. Pollock had painted some beautiful pictures in the early forties, but, unlike his later work, they are not "world historical" in the Hegelian sense; despite their originality, they do not possess his full identity, containing perhaps too much of Picasso, Miró, and Masson, to allow this. De Kooning, Still, Motherwell, and Rothko, among others, also painted fine pictures in the early forties, but again, it was only during the period 1947–50 that they realized their more personal styles and painted what in some cases remain their best pictures.

The major influence on these American painters in the early forties was Picasso, but the most omnipresent and pervasive, though in generalized form, was Surrealism, mostly Miró, secondarily Masson and Matta, and marginally Ernst and Arp (the illusionistic side of Surrealist painting, as exemplified by Dali and Magritte, had no influence at all on these artists). But transcending the works of the Surrealist painters were certain Surrealist ideas relating picture-making to unconscious impulses and fantasies through the methods of automatism; these ideas—never fully realized in Surrealist painting itself—were very much in the air in the early and middle forties. Gorky was by no means the first to come in contact with them; as early as 1940 Motherwell was exploring ideas like these in discussions with Matta, with whom he was then quite friendly, and the former soon brought them to the attention of Pollock. Within a few years such diverse painters as Still, Rothko, Gottlieb, Baziotes, and Newman were working in a manner that might well be termed quasi-Surrealist (what the

375

French call *surrèalisant*). None were members of the Surrealist group (although Motherwell and Baziotes were shown in a major Surrealist exhibition), but the morphology of their work, its Freudianized mythological symbolism, and the flirtation with automatism, all seemed related to Surrealism. These were just the qualities (with the exception of automatism) that tended to be purged by the end of the decade.

The year 1947, which signaled the ripening of the New American Painting, also heralded the definite end of Surrealism. We know that historical movements do not instantly crystallize or dissolve and that periodicity always involves a set of abstractions. Nevertheless, there are significant events that clarify history by summarizing lengthy processes in their own brief moments. If the inception of Pollock's drip style was one such event, another was the International Exhibition of Surrealism held in Paris in 1947. Whereas the earlier and more lively exhibition that had been installed in the Reid Mansion on Fifth Avenue in 1942 had an air of "work in progress," the one in Paris was clearly a postmortem. Only one first-rate painter—Gorky—had been added to the roster in the interim, among a mass of mediocrities, and despite the title of the exhibition—Surrealism in 1947—not one good picture in the show was executed after 1945.[3]

The years 1942 through 1946 embrace the crucial period in which the conclusions of 1947 were being prepared. This, it seems to me, is essential to the understanding of Gorky's historical role; for his career as an independent painter, *and his alone*, spans exactly this critical period, Despite some vagueness and possible misrepresentation in the dates of his paintings through 1942, there is no question that he was working in his personal style by the end of that year, that he was creating masterpieces by the following year, and that he continued to produce them, if somewhat erratically, through 1947, the year before his death by suicide. Gorky's peculiar historical position sustains the impression that his style is hybrid and identifies him as what we may truly call a *transitional* painter. The idea that he is thus a link between the European tradition and present-day American abstraction finds favor with many critics, but Harold Rosenberg rightly cautions that

the "link" idea slips when it is applied to suggest that Gorky is nothing more than a transition to a body of painting more "advanced" and more "authentically American." . . . Those to whom Gorky represents a link to something newer and better should be reminded that in art, as elsewhere, a chain is nothing *but* links, and there is no particular virtue in being the one at the end.

[3] Unwilling to accept the fact that Surrealism has run its course, André Breton continues to stage Surrealist exhibitions, but the new work shown is generally abysmally bad, and when, rarely, it is not— as, for example, the Jasper Johns that figured prominently in the Surrealist International—it has had little to do with Surrealism.

We can sympathize with Rosenberg's reaction to the general tendency to confuse novelty and quality, to attribute to the word "advanced" the implications it would have if we were talking about technological progress. But the word "newer," which Rosenberg paired with the word "better," need not go down the drain with it, for American painting after Gorky is manifestly newer, and it is new in ways that differentiate it collectively from Gorky.

In any case, Rosenberg's image of art history as a chain with "nothing but links," that is, as a series of transitions, is as inadequate a critique of Gorky's position as it is of the general problem of periodicity. For Gorky is a transitional painter in the sense that very few painters in history have been. Cézanne, for example, synthesized much from Impressionism, and in its turn Cubism assimilated a great deal from Cézanne, but this does not make Cézanne a transitional painter. Moreover, the components of Cézanne's mature style do not have the hybrid character of Gorky's, neither does he occupy the peculiar position in history that was Gorky's. But even if we accept Rosenberg's metaphor, it should be pointed out that it is quite a different matter for a painter to be located in the middle of a link than precisely at the point at which it interlocks with the next one.

The nature of Gorky's unique and ambiguous relationship to Surrealism was unalterably conditioned by his earlier apprenticeship to pre-Surrealist European abstraction. This began in the late twenties with some very handsome pictures in the style of Cézanne, whom Gorky, significantly, considered the greatest painter of all time, and continued into the early and middle thirties with paraphrases of Picasso in both his Neoclassic and Synthetic Cubist phases. Subsequent influences—Miró, Masson, and Matta—were all drawn from Surrealism, except for Kandinsky, whose work became important for Gorky in 1943 and 1944.

Two things have consistently struck critics about the Cézannesque and Picassoid pictures: first, the frankness and lack of embarrassment with which Gorky imitated these masters; second, the surprisingly excellent quality of the results, given this fact of imitation. For Gorky, who never had any formal art-school education, the recapitulation of various stages of European painting was not simply a series of identifications, subsequently rejected, which allowed him to discover who he was by discovering who he was not; it was a series of lessons about the possibilities of painting. These possibilities were to remain part of his vocabulary long after the vehicles of their assimilation had disappeared.

Harold Rosenberg has advanced the theory that Gorky's work in the twenties and thirties was premised on *the deliberate rejection of originality*. If this is so, then his rejection of originality at the very time when Dada and Surrealism had consciously made it a goal of avant-garde painting constituted a kind of originality in reverse.

377

From the time of the Impressionists until the First World War neither artists nor critics placed a premium on originality *for its own sake*. Manet had set the tone with the statement that he "presumed neither to overthrow earlier painting nor to make it new," but "merely tried to be himself and not someone else." In the work of those pioneer generations, originality seemed a natural by-product—though by no means an inevitable concomitant—of making communicative, moving paintings. Bonnard, for example, was a painter with great prestige on the eve of World War I, despite the fact that his form of late Impressionism was much less "advanced" than the avant-garde art of the previous decade. The greatness of his painting was in no way diminished by the fact that its premises were hardly revolutionary.

It was with the Dada and Surrealist generations of the interwar period (and *not* recently in America, as some believe) that the situation changed. For the first time, originality—which was to become indistinguishable from novelty—was itself a goal. "Before all else," said Picabia, "we wanted to make something new. Something that nobody had ever seen before." Precisely at that moment the quality of avant-garde painting fell off. Genuine aesthetic invention gave way in large measure to an illusory originality in which the novelty depended on an increasing load of extra-plastic, often frankly literary, effects.

A not unrelated notion of originality held sway in America at that time; many painters believed that they could create a new and peculiarly American art by drawing their subjects from the "American Scene." This was not really very different from the run-of-the-mill Dada and Surrealist work being produced abroad, which, insofar as it *illustrated* the political, psychological, and literary ideas in vogue in the twenties and thirties, might well have been called the art of the "European Scene." But while the Europeans of the interwar generations incorporated elements of advanced painting into their description of the European Scene, the "American Scene" painters demonstrated their provincialism by the academic, art-school formulas they continued to employ.

There was, however, during the thirties, a small group of Americans, which included Gorky, de Kooning, Gottlieb, Rothko, and Pollock, who resisted the chauvinism of the painters of the "American Scene" and embraced the essentially international, pre-Surrealist tradition of modern painting. None was more resolute in this position than Gorky; in his commitment to Cézanne and Picasso he was much closer to the fountainhead of modern art than the painters of his own generation in Paris. This is what Meyer Schapiro was alluding to when he said that Gorky "belonged then to the School of Paris more surely than many painters living in France." An inveterate museum-goer, his attachment to the art in museums, rather than to the "scene" outside them (taken literally or figuratively) not only distinguished him from most of his European and American coevals, but *set him apart fundamentally from Surrealism* even

378

when he later accepted much from it and was in turn accepted into its circles.

The first and still fragmentary traces of Surrealist influence in Gorky's art date from the middle and late thirties, when they were assimilated into the Picassoid type of Cubism he was imitating. We see the mark of early Surrealists Miró and Masson in a group of pictures that begin around 1935, such as *Image in Xhorkom* and *Enigmatic Combat*. The general organization of the picture surface here is Cubist; the touch, pigment texture, and contouring are still Picasso's; but the biomorphic forms, particularly in the *Image in Xhorkom*, belong to Surrealism and especially to Miró. These organic forms, which later became a pictorial and design cliché known as "free form," are particularly endowed with a power to evoke the subjective world of psychosexual associations; they are common to almost all Surrealist painting, from illusionists like Dali and Tanguy to more abstract painters like Miró and Masson.

Gorky's assimilation of Surrealist biomorphism into the context of firmly brushed, heavily impastoed Synthetic Cubism had already been anticipated by Picasso in such paintings as the *Girl Before the Mirror*. In this picture, which was shown at Valentine Dudensing's gallery in 1936 (four years after its execution) and which became part of the permanent collection of The Museum of Modern Art in 1938, Gorky had the model for the synthesis he was now to explore. In fact, we can see the specific influence of this painting in Gorky's *Enigmatic Combat*, which probably dates from 1936. As Harold Rosenberg has pointed out, some general aspects of design[4] as well as the title of the picture derive from a series of "Combats" painted by Masson from 1932 to 1935 and exhibited then in New York by Pierre Matisse. But the facture here is nevertheless Picasso's, and the circular "breast" on the lower left and the head on the lower right are quite clearly quotations from the *Girl Before the Mirror*, while the "liver" shape just left of center derives from Picasso's earlier *Artist and Model*. It was as if the dislocations of Masson's "Combats" had helped Gorky to break up the integrity of figuration still obtaining in Picasso's *Girl Before the Mirror*, leaving the elements strewn about the surface.

That it was possible for Gorky to synthesize Miró and Masson into his Cub-

[4] The relationship to Masson, particularly in the closing of the composition at the top, is evident only if we view the picture as it is reproduced here, which is upside down in relation to the way it is hung in The Museum of Modern Art exhibition. The Museum of Modern Art followed the practice of the San Francisco Museum, which owns the picture; the monograph by Schwabacher reproduces the picture in the same way. Rosenberg, in his monograph, turns the picture the other way, rightly, I believe. Good arguments can be made for both possibilities. However, Gorky saw the picture in California during his Retrospective there and presumably approved the way it was hung. At my suggestion, The Museum of Modern Art removed the present backing from the picture, uncovering the original labels. These indicate that the picture runs from top to bottom as reproduced here, suggesting that it was turned bottom end up by accident when the new backing was added. In any event, at this stage in his development, Gorky was given to turning his pictures bottom end up while working on them, which may account for the fact that one derives satisfaction from viewing this painting either way.

Arshile Gorky: *Image in Xhorkom. ca.* 1936.
Oil on canvas. 32⅞″ x 43″.
Collection of Maro Gorky and Natasha Gorky.

Arshile Gorky: *Still Life with Skull.*
ca. 1925. Oil on canvas. 33″ x 26″.
Estate of Arshile Gorky.
Courtesy of M. Knoedler & Co., Inc.,
New York, Paris, London.

Pablo Picasso: *Girl Before the Mirror.*
March, 1932. Oil on canvas. 63¾″ x 51¼″.
Collection of The Museum of Modern Art,
New York;
Gift of Mrs. Simon Guggenheim.

Arshile Gorky: *Enigmatic Combat. ca.* 1936.
Oil on canvas. 35¾″ x 48″.
Collection of The San Francisco Museum of Art,
Gift of Jeanne Reynal.

ism, whereas to do the same with Surrealists like Dali and Tanguy would have been unthinkable, makes sense if we recall that Miró and Masson alone among the Surrealists had earlier been convinced Cubists. While their organic forms strayed far from the morphology of Cubism, they rarely sacrificed the taste for shallow (as opposed to deep) space and for disposing the composition comfortably inside the frame, which they had learned during their Cubist apprenticeship.

Gorky's metamorphosis from an imitative painter, albeit an extraordinary one, into an independent painter began around 1940 and extended through 1942. This transformation, which took place under the sign of Surrealism in general and Miró in particular, can be traced in three pictures entitled *Garden in Sochi*. These three, the most important of at least six on the same theme, are something of a puzzle with respect to their specific dating and even to their sequence, and yet, it is only with the resolution of this problem that the history of Gorky's transformation can be clarified. The one quite certain date we have is 1941, that of the largest version, acquired by The Museum of Modern Art before Gorky's death. A smaller, more tightly painted, Miróesque version is dated 1940 by William Seitz in the catalogue-monograph for the museum exhibition; Schwabacher and Rosenberg have dated it between 1938 and 1941. A third version, loosely painted and not quite so small, has been dated "around 1941" in all publications. Since the historical problem involved here resists solution on the basis of the documentation we possess, we are forced to fall back mainly on the internal evidence of style in determining the order and dating; in my opinion, there is sufficient such evidence to warrant a far more specific account of this transitional series than now exists.

The image itself—the iconography, if you will—is common to all three versions. *Garden in Sochi* (Sochi is a Russian Black Sea resort) is the title Gorky gave to a vision actually derived from recollections of his father's farm on the shores of Lake Van in Armenia, where he grew up. In 1941 he recorded the following memories:

My father had a little garden with a few apple trees which had retired from bearing fruit. There was a patch of ground constantly in shade where grew incalculable amounts of wild carrots, and porcupines had made their nests. There was a blue rock half buried in the black earth with a few patches of moss placed here and there like fallen clouds. But from where came all the shadows in constant battle like the lancers in Paolo Uccello's painting? This garden was identified as the Garden of Wish Fulfillment, and I had often seen my mother and other village women opening their bosoms and taking their soft pendent breasts in their hands to rub them on the rock. Above all this stood an enormous tree completely bleached by the sun, the rain, the cold, and deprived of leaves. This was the Holy Tree. I myself don't know why this tree was holy, but I have witnessed many people, whoever passed by, who would voluntarily tear off a strip from their clothing and tie it to the tree.

André Masson: *Tormented Woman,*
from the series *Combats et Massacres.*
1933. Oil.

RIGHT, ABOVE. Arshile Gorky: *Garden in Sochi.* Oil
on canvas. 44¼″ x 62¼″. Collection of The Museum of Modern Art, New York, Purchase Fund
and gift of Wolfgang S. Schwabacher. (Painted in
1941 and previously considered Number III in the
series. I propose that it is Number 1.)

RIGHT, CENTER. Arshile Gorky: *Garden in Sochi.*
Oil on canvas. 25″ x 29″. Estate of Arshile Gorky.
Courtesy of M. Knoedler & Co., Inc., New York,
Paris, London. (Previously dated 1938–41 by
Schwabacher and 1940 by Seitz, this picture has
been considered Number 1 of the series. I propose
that it is Number II and was painted in 1941.)

RIGHT, BELOW. Arshile Gorky: *Garden in Sochi.*
Oil on canvas. 31″ x 39¾″. Estate of Arshile
Gorky. Courtesy of M. Knoedler & Co., Inc., New
York, Paris, London. (Previously dated "around
1941" and considered Number II of the series. I
propose that it is Number III and was painted late
in 1943.)

Thus, through many years of the same act, like a veritable parade of banners under the pressure of the wind all these personal inscriptions of signatures, very softly to my innocent ear used to give echo to the sh-h-h-sh-h of silver leaves of the poplars.

It would be idle to try to decipher literally the various *Gardens in Sochi* on the basis of this description, for the process of abstraction and the cross-fertilization of images from different sources produced hybrids that defy such limited readings. However, we can speculate as to whether the large vertical in the top center is not the trunk of the Holy Tree, with strips of tattered cloth waving around it in the breeze and a bird flying past on the right. Ethel Schwabacher, Gorky's friend and biographer, sees the shape of a crouching animal, probably one of Gorky's porcupines, on the lower right and, with more certainty, the blue rock and black earth on the lower left. This textual analysis, however, provides no clue to the image's most prominent form, occupying the center of all three versions, one that has been referred to variously as a boot, a shoe, and a slipper. (William Seitz observes that pointed slippers, birds, and similar paraphernalia can be found in Armenian manuscripts from Gorky's native region of Lake Van.) Whatever its original source, this is among the first of certain persistent shapes, indefinable but charged with evocative power, that illuminate Gorky's fantasy-world and endow his biomorphism with a specifically personal character.[5]

The three versions of *Garden in Sochi* show Gorky disengaging himself from the picture-making attitudes of Picasso's Cubism in favor of conceptions closer to Surrealism. The process involved a substitution of landscape for still life and a transformation of abstraction springing from immediate confrontation of the subject, that is, from visual perception, into a more subjective imagery pervaded with memories and fantasies. The temporal and geographical distance from the subject (his father's garden as against his studio props) permitted the aesthetic to fuse myriad associations from different levels of psychic experience into a hybrid image. The resultant type of ambiguity, a poetic device rendered possible by abstraction, is fundamental to the art of Miró, Arp, and the best of Masson and Matta; it contrasts with the more literal paradoxes of the "double image" exploited by Dali and Matta.

In this triad of *Gardens in Sochi* the Miróesque version is the pivotal picture. Contrary to the impressions given by Gorky's commentators, it is his *only* finished picture that may be called an imitation of Miró in something of the sense that most of his pictures of the twenties and thirties are imitations

[5] The flat and colorful Miróesque version of *Garden in Sochi* makes clearest the way in which all these recollections may have been merged (as in Gorky's description) with associations to the decorative patterns of Paolo Uccello's paintings. Long a favorite of Gorky's, Uccello held a special interest for the Surrealists, he was the only Old Master mentioned by Breton (in the First Manifesto) as a precursor of Surrealism. The Surrealist poet René Crevel wrote the earliest monograph devoted to him.

383

of Cézanne and Picasso. But even here there is much in the way Gorky scallops his forms for which there is no precedent in Miró, and the meandering contouring, almost oriental in its melismatic fluidity, anticipates the later very personal character of Gorky's line.

That Gorky should have used Miró to propel himself out of Cubism into imaginative, Surrealist biomorphism is logical; he was, in fact, reenacting the same transformation that had taken place in Miró's development during the early twenties. From 1919 (when he first visited Paris) through 1922, Miró had been occupied primarily with still-life and figure paintings realized in his own particularly decorative and schematized brand of Cubism; with *The Tilled Field* of 1923–24 his work moved toward fantasy, taking on interest for Breton and the Surrealists, whose acquaintance he had made shortly before. The overall schema of *The Tilled Field* is still obviously Cubist, as are many of the motifs, from the furrows to the printed newspaper letters. But strange things have happened: For example, a lizard wearing a dunce cap reads a newspaper, while a tree sprouts a giant eye and ear. Miró in Paris, like Gorky in New York, was weaving fantasies about the distant landscape of his youth.

Miró's disavowal of the rational world of Cubism in favor of synthesizing subjective, poetic images had its plastic counterpart in the introduction of curvilinear organic forms. This biomorphism soon triumphed completely in his art, as is demonstrated by his *Dutch Interior* of 1928, a picture that was constantly on view in the permanent collection of The Museum of Modern Art, and was probably a major influence on Gorky's *Garden in Sochi*.

It may be, however, that the unique affinity to Miró in the latter picture was catalyzed by a very particular event: the first Retrospective Exhibition of Miró in New York, held at The Museum of Modern Art in 1941. There Gorky could observe in detail Miró's conversion from Cubism to Surrealism. Among the pictures included were *The Tilled Field*, and one other which I believe may have left a particular impress on the *Garden in Sochi, The Still Life with Old Shoe* of 1937. (Apart from the shoe form—differently located in Gorky, to be sure— this painting also contains a strong vertical device in the top center around which the other forms cluster.) I do not insist on this possibility, though the synthesis of ideas from different Miró pictures is perfectly consistent with Gorky's methodology. But if the Miró Retrospective was a causal factor in the creation of the Miróesque version of *Garden in Sochi*, we would possess a new *terminus ante quem* for the execution of the picture, a date no earlier than 1941. I prefer this new date on internal stylistic evidence alone, and suggest that the painting is roughly contemporaneous with the version in The Museum of Modern Art and probably somewhat later in view of its thinner, less opaque paint film.

Where I really part company with previous Gorky critics is in the sequence

Joan Miró: *The Tilled Field*. 1932–4.
Oil on canvas. 26″ x 37″.
Collection of Mr. and Mrs. Henry Clifford,
Radnor, Pennsylvania.

Joan Miró: *Dutch Interior*. 1928.
36⅛″ x 28¾″.
Collection of The Museum of Modern Art,
New York, Mrs. Simon Guggenheim Fund.

Joan Miró: *Still Life with Old Shoe*. 1937.
Oil on canvas. 32″ x 46″.
Collection of James Thrall Soby,
New Canaan, Connecticut.

Matta: *Psychological Morphology*. 1939.
Oil on canvas. 28″ x 36″.

of the two other versions. As we have seen, one of these, the green-ground version in The Museum of Modern Art collection, is definitely dated 1941. Schwabacher places the other—which I will call the painterly version—"around 1941," a dating concurred in by Seitz, who believes this picture precedes the museum's painting, which he considers the concluding and "most fully synthesized" version of the trio. I cannot accept this order and still make sense out of Gorky's development, for, as I see it, the painterly version (and I use this term in the sense of Wölfflin's *malerisch*) contains most of the elements of Gorky's mature style and is a more personal, if somewhat less imposing, picture than the one in The Museum of Modern Art.[6] While all three pictures contain Gorky's characteristic form language, the museum's version is realized with an opaque surface, a carry-over from his earlier Synthetic Cubist manner, even to the foreign substances—the Cubists had used sand and coffee grounds —mixed into the pigment to give it a raised, slightly abrasive look. Moreover, the Synthetic Cubist flatness is reinforced by the way the green ground is often applied *over* the figure elements, cutting into them and giving them the appearance of "reserve" shapes; this ambiguous overlapping of figure and ground entirely thwarts any tendency to read them three-dimensionally.

In contrast to such early characteristics evident in the museum's picture, the painterly version of *Garden in Sochi* displays some features as yet unseen in Gorky but common to his art *after 1942*. One of these is the suggestion of a shallow, slightly atmospheric space created by patchwork modeling, and the inherent illusionism of a loose, painterly style (much of this is lost in reproduction). Another is the advanced and exquisite draftsmanship. His fluent line, here taut or slightly brittle, there lyrical, is completely independent of the color patches whose contours it had previously delineated; these have retreated back from the line in a manner we see nowhere else in Gorky's art prior to 1943. Finally, the transparency and refinement of the surface, the delicacy of touch as compared with the other two versions, belong to Gorky's maturity.

These facts point inescapably to a later date for this picture: not 1941, but toward the end of 1943 in all probability, though 1946–47 is not impossible. (Gorky's style during the intervening years, 1944–45, rule out ascribing it to that period.) This would place the painting well after *The Pirate I* executed late in 1942, the first and most tentative of the loose, painterly canvases of Gorky's mature years[7] and one for which we have a sure date.[8] There the handling

---

[6] A small pendant to the series, known as *Garden in Sochi Motif*, is dated April, 1942. It is unthinkable that such an advanced picture as the painterly version of *Garden in Sochi* could antedate this.

[7] Certain pictures loosely dated in the late twenties and thirties, among them *The Artist and His Mother* (Whitney Museum) and a *Self-Portrait*, contain a number of soft painterly passages that adumbrate the touch and texture of Gorky's mature painting. It has been suggested that these passages are overpaintings done late in Gorky's life, but this seems to me unlikely.

[8] "Sure" to the extent that we can accept Gorky's own inscription. Elaine de Kooning has noted that Gorky was not above predating his pictures. *Art News*, V (January, 1951).

is much less assured than in the painterly version of *Garden in Sochi,* the drawing is uncertain, and the bipolarization of line and color-patch is in an incipient state. *Pirate I* and its mate *The Pirate II,* executed early in 1943, are the really exploratory pictures of the end of Gorky's transition, in which, with the help of Kandinsky, he was able to go beyond Picasso and Miró into his own loosely articulated, diaphanous world. What I regard as the last of the *Garden in Sochi* pictures unquestionably presupposes their existence.

It was during the crucial transitional moment in his art defined by the two versions of the *The Pirate* that Gorky turned to nature, not to imitate her but to stimulate inspiration. Some weeks in the Connecticut countryside in the summer of 1942 were followed a year later by a stay at the Virginia farm of his wife's father. The drawings made during these and the following summers served as the bases of paintings executed during the winters between. William Seitz relates how the conjunction of a new and happy marriage, the prospect of a family, and "the return to the bucolic environment he looked back to so nostalgically" seemed to realize the promise of the Garden of Wish Fulfillment.

Taking a worshiper's delight in the sun, Gorky produced some of [his] most original and sophisticated drawings. . . . he drew the life he saw "in the grass." But Gorky, as he once remarked, "never put a face on an image." While he scrutinized the botanical and biological organisms at close range, another vision was directed inward and backward, bringing into focus passages from the works of artists he admired, moments of past emotional experience or points of pain, fear or sexual desire. All these diverse levels and kinds of images joined in his mind the phenomena before him.

What Gorky had in fact done was to re-create the landscape as a theatre in which to project his own psychological drama. In so doing he was following in the footsteps of both Kandinsky and Matta (in this period the latter was one of Gorky's closest friends). Between 1938 and 1942 Matta had made a series of ambiguous biomorphic landscape pictures, which he called *Psychological Morphologies,* or *Inscapes,* whose hybrid forms were intended to dissolve the distinction between the subjective and objective, the mind and the senses, the painter and the world around him. The veiled identification of the human body with the landscape (*The Earth Is a Man* is a significant title) was expressed through ambiguous shapes that were meant to connote both while denoting neither. Though Matta provided the more immediate model for Gorky's "psychological landscapes," the latter surpass Matta's *Inscapes* in their range of feeling and in their poetry, to say nothing of their greater richness as paintings. This is partly due to the fact that Gorky was able to create a personal form of biomorphism that was less literal, less specific in its evocation, and hence more universal than even Miró's.

William Rubin

Arshile Gorky: *The Pirate I.* 1942.
Oil on canvas. 29¼" x 40⅛".
Collection of Mr. and Mrs. Julien Levy,
Bridgewater, Connecticut.

Matta: *Landscape.* 1940.
Pencil and crayon drawing.
Courtesy of Robert Elkon Gallery,
New York.

Arshile Gorky: *Landscape.* 1943.
Pencil and crayon drawing.
Collection of Walter Bareiss.

It is in Gorky's pencil and wax crayon drawings of 1943 that Matta's influence is most evident: he provided Gorky with a model of a more disjointed, loosely articulated surface than can be found even in the *Improvisations* of Kandinsky, whose influence was soon to become dominant. In comparing these Gorky drawings with Matta's work in the same media in previous years, we find common to both of them networks of lines that spread tenuously across the surface, completely obviating, through radiating patterns and other shorthand schemata of spatial notation, the flatness to which Gorky had previously subscribed. Here and there, too, in this implicitly deep space both artists summarily model little biomorphic animals or personages.

Kandinsky and Matta also furnished general precedents for the adoption of a painterly style, which emerges in Gorky's work at the end of 1942. However, with the exception of a few of Gorky's pictures from the winter of 1944–45, Matta's influence in this respect is clearly secondary, despite his more immediate presence in Gorky's world as both friend and painter. Matta had worked in a painterly manner from 1938, when he softened up the sculpturesque landscape of Tanguy, to 1944, when his semiautomatic veils, or washes, began to give way to harder, skeletonic forms that prophesied the later cybernetic monsters. To the extent that his style was abstract, his paintings represented a significant break with the flat, linear abstraction of Synthetic Cubist inspiration, which had dominated the thirties, particularly among the American abstract painters who constituted the avant-garde in New York. Matta's paintings pointed the way to a more informal, spontaneous, and lyrical abstraction, in which three-dimensional, illusionist space was again proposed as viable.

But despite the looseness of his painterly fabric—the paint was often applied with rags and allowed to drip or coagulate—an innate commitment to illustration tended to transform Matta's pigment into an illusion of something other than itself. At its most transparent, it suggested vaporous gases, and as it coagulated, it resembled molten rock and crystalline jewels. This was another form of the telluric fairyland of Surrealism, the inspiration of which reaches back through Max Ernst's decalcomania landscapes to the Byzantinism of Gustave Moreau.

Matta, like all Surrealist painters except Miró and Masson, had an inbred disdain for paint. Dali, Magritte, and Tanguy expressed this by the suppression of pigment inherent in their academic manner. Max Ernst and Matta preferred to exacerbate the medium by dripping, blotting, and rubbing it in a way that strained rather than explored its possibilities. Nothing could have been further from Gorky's taste. All his life Gorky nurtured a love for paint as an exquisite substance that had to be courted, cajoled, and tenderly assisted to its fullest blossoming. It is this remarkably refined sensibility to paint quality that invests the mature Gorky with a beauty that led Clement Greenberg to consider him

389

"in many ways . . . a better handler of brush and paint than anyone he was radically influenced by, including Picasso and Miró."

When, during the winter of 1942–43, Gorky went over into his loose, painterly manner, he did not resort to the paraphernalia of deep space as had Matta (though he employed it for some drawings), preferring only hints of modeling and atmospheric effects. His narrow frontal space, ultimately derived from the Cézannesque illusion of bas-relief taken over by Analytic Cubism, did not retreat from the picture plane to deep vanishing points, but was measured by half-modeled forms that seemed to project toward the spectator from a back

Matta: *Les grands transparents.*
1942.
Pencil and wax crayon drawing.
Collection of the artist.

Arshile Gorky: *Drawing.*
Pencil and wax crayon.
18½″ x 24½″.
Collection of
Mr. and Mrs. Stephen Hahn,
New York.

Wassily Kandinsky: *Sunday*. 1911.
Oil on canvas. 42⅜″ x 37⅜″.
Collection of Städtische Galerie, München,
Gabriele Münter Foundation.

Arshile Gorky: *Waterfall*.
Estate of Arshile Gorky.
Courtesy of M. Knoedler & Co., Inc.,
New York, Paris, London.

plane, which effectively closed the space. This was similar to the shallow
space—also inspired by landscape painting—that we find in the Kandinskys of
1910 to 1914, and partially explains the affinity of such Gorky pictures as
Waterfall with Kandinskys like *Sunday*.

The synthesis, in an entirely personal form, of the painterly language inspired
by Kandinsky, the biomorphism of Miró, and the automatist Surreal "Inscape"
of Matta was reached early in 1944 with one of Gorky's most stunning canvases, *The Liver Is the Cock's Comb*. Though confused and overcrowded in
spots, and lacking the distilled perfection of later works like *The Diary of a
Seducer* and *Agony*, *The Liver Is the Cock's Comb* contains some remarkable
passages and recommends itself by its ambitiousness. The great plumes of color,
probably inspired by Kandinskys on the order of *Black Lines* (1913), are
potently seductive even though as a group their registration does not finally
cohere. The general design, which subsequently was to be a favorite of Gorky's,
involves a clustering of the slightly modeled forms above and below an implied
horizontal that bisects the surface. These clusters thin out and disappear as
391

Arshile Gorky: *The Liver Is the Cock's Comb.* 1944. Oil on canvas. 72″ x 98″.
Collection of The Albright–Knox Art Gallery, Buffalo, New York, Gift of Seymour H. Knox.

Wassily Kandinsky: *Black Lines, No. 189.*
1913. Oil on canvas. 51¼″ x 51⅜″.
Collection of The
Solomon R. Guggenheim Museum, New York.

Kyle Morris: Untitled. 1959. 48″ x 72″.
Courtesy of The Kootz Gallery, New York.

we move to the top or the bottom of the field, where the ground color, which seems somewhat deeper in space than the plumes, shows through.[9]

The poetry of *The Liver Is the Cock's Comb* is more comprehensive, but also more self-conscious, than that of the *Gardens in Sochi,* and this must certainly be attributed to Gorky's close contacts with the Surrealists. One has only to compare the awkward but straightforward recollections of the Garden of Wish Fulfillment quoted earlier with the pretentious text with which he "describes" *The Liver Is the Cock's Comb:* "The song of a cardinal, liver, mirrors that have not caught reflection, the aggressively heraldic branches, the saliva of the hungry man whose face is painted with white chalk." As with the Surrealists, neither Gorky's title nor his description should be taken literally. One critic, misled by the title, interpreted the picture as "the successfully deceptive dismemberment of a rooster."

Another aspect of Surrealism synthesized in *The Liver Is the Cock's Comb* is the erotic, a concern already quite clear in the drawings of 1943 and one that later formed, as Ethel Schwabacher has observed, the core of his myth. Surrealism was the first movement in art to make sexuality central, a perfectly understandable development in view of its general commitment to Freud. Each painter handled the theme consistently with the character of his art as a whole. In Miró, for example, sex is always playful and whimsical; in Dali it is associated with voyeurism and impotence. But the two artists who gave the erotic the crucial role of catalyst to the imagination are Masson and Matta. Both understood the sexual paroxysm as the moment of the fusion of contraries: the conscious and unconscious, mind and body, the self and the "other";[10] and, hence, the moment of the liberation of the imagination. In Masson, sex has a robust quality that galvanizes the automatism of the methodology and binds all sorts of hybrid themes with its energy; in Matta, on the other hand, it developed in time an exceedingly aggressive and self-conscious character. In *The Liver Is the Cock's Comb* male and female genitalia (center left of the picture) are the only literal forms to emerge from the otherwise ambiguous context of shapes. But the sumptuous affirmation of the sexual in this picture was to give way to a context of nervous tension, suffering, and masochism in *The Diary of a Seducer* and, more notably, *Agony.*

It was during the winter of 1945–46 that Gorky's interest in spontaneousness carried him beyond the *Improvisations* of Kandinsky to the technique of automatism. This essay brought him nearer to Surrealism than he had yet been—or

---

[9] It is this design idea, combined with forms of a Motherwell-like profile realized in a de Kooning-esque manner, that we see in some paintings by Kyle Morris, one of the few American painters still influenced by Gorky.

[10] In the First Surrealist Manifesto, Breton had identified "Surreality" as an "absolute reality" achieved by the "resolution of the two states—in appearance so contradictory—of the dream and (consciously perceived) reality."

was ever to be afterward—and marks precisely the time of his greatest personal closeness to Breton and to Matta. Such pictures as *The Leaf of the Artichoke Is an Owl* and *One Year the Milkweed* were executed with a spontaneity far greater than anything we find in Kandinsky. The rapid drawing, the loose brushwork that encouraged spilling and dripping of the liquid paint, departed from Matta's automatism of 1938–42 and went beyond it. It was only natural that Breton should have encouraged Gorky in this excursion; in the First Surrealist Manifesto he had defined Surrealism primarily in terms of automatism.[11]

[11] *"Surrealism,* n.m. Pure psychic automatism by which one seeks to express, be it verbally, in writing, or in any other manner, the real workings of the mind. Dictated by the unconscious, in the absence of any control exercised by reason, and free from aesthetic or moral preoccupations."

Arshile Gorky:
The Diary of a Seducer. 1945.
Oil on canvas. 50″ x 62″.
Collection of
Mr. and Mrs. William A. M. Burden,
New York.

BELOW. Arshile Gorky:
Study for Agony. 1946–7.
Pencil, wax crayon, and wash.
22″ x 30″. Estate of Arshile Gorky.
Courtesy of M. Knoedler & Co., Inc.,
New York.

BELOW, LEFT. Arshile Gorky:
Agony. 1947.
Oil on canvas. 47″ x 50½″.
Collection of The Museum of Modern Art,
New York, A. Conger Goodyear Fund.

Julien Levy, Gorky's dealer at the time, writes that "automatism was a re-demption" for Gorky, an emotional "liberation." Surrealism, he continues, had "made Gorky dig himself deep into his work . . . bring himself to the surface," so that "his most secret doodling could become central."

Pierre Naville used the last phrase of this definition to support his contention that Surrealist art involved a contradiction in terms. The "Naville Crisis" divided Surrealists briefly during the mid-twenties but was resolved by the *de facto* presence of works by Ernst, Miró, and Masson of generally Surrealist nature. Breton converted this into *de jure* recognition with short essays on these and other painters in *Le Revolution surréaliste*, which later appeared together as a book, *Le Surréalisme et la peinture*.

Needless to say, automatism in artmaking was no longer "pure," since to some degree there was a conscious organization of the picture surface.

Arshile Gorky:
The Leaf of the Artichoke Is an Owl.
1944. Oil on canvas. 24″ x 36″.
Collection of Mrs. Ethel K. Schwabacher,
New York.

Arshile Gorky:
One Year the Milkweed. 1944.
Oil on canvas. 37″ x 47″.
Estate of Arshile Gorky.
Courtesy of M. Knoedler & Co., Inc.,
New York.

But there is an essential difference between Gorky's automatism and that of the Surrealists, and it was to this that Breton alluded when he singled out Gorky as the "only Surrealist" who kept "in direct contact with nature, placing himself *before her* to paint." (Not that the pictures in question had been inspired by drawings made from nature.) This fundamental distinction between Surrealist techniques and those of abstract painting is made clear in a memorable exchange that took place in the 1930s between Matisse and Masson (who was then spending a few weeks as Matisse's guest in Grasse). Masson was explaining his manner of working:

"I begin without an image or plan in mind, but just draw or paint rapidly according to my impulses. Gradually, in the marks I make, I see suggestions of figures or objects. I encourage these to emerge, trying to bring out their implications even as I now consciously try to give order to the composition."

"That's curious," Matisse replied, "with me it's just the reverse. I always start with something—a chair, a table—but as the work proceeds, I become less conscious of it. By the end I am hardly aware of the subject with which I started."

Even when it appears most abstract, Surrealist art is thus moving, to use Breton's phrase, *in favor of the subject.* Although automatist Massons, such as the sand painting illustrated here, appear less figurative and hence apparently more abstract than Matisse's pictures (despite the "figure" emerging in the Masson), the image evolves in a manner that tends to clarify a subject and is thus opposite to the abstracting process of Matisse (or Picasso, or Kandinsky). And while the employment of one or another of these contrary approaches neither assures nor precludes quality, it nevertheless leaves a particular imprint on the expressive character of the work.

The methodological divergence revealed in the Matisse-Masson conversation holds, with some modifications, for the difference between Gorky's and Matta's automatism. Matta began by unpremeditatedly spreading washes of color (usually with rags) and then "provoked" the image, which became more particularized, more illustrative, as he proceeded. In contrast, the drawings that constituted Gorky's starting points are more illustrative than the paintings that derive from them. This is perfectly understandable, given the fact that Gorky began his drawings from nature, that is, in direct contact with his motif; as these were transformed into paintings, the elements became less literal, more abstract. Gorky's painterliness does not—like Matta's—harden or dissolve into illusion, but constantly affirms—even when it is most airy—its own material character as pigment resting on the surface of a canvas. In this sense it is related more to European abstract painting (and the extension of that art in the New American Painting) than to Surrealism.

Curiously enough, Breton's observation that Gorky worked from nature did not restrain him from formally identifying Gorky as a Surrealist, even though,

396

André Masson:
Painting. 1927.
Oil and sand on canvas.

as he noted, this was true of no other Surrealist painter. This inconsistency is sharpened by my recollection of a conversation in which Breton explained that Picasso was never really a Surrealist, notwithstanding his many fantasy pictures and his participation in the activities of the Surrealist group, "because he always started with something he saw, something in nature, whereas the Surrealist always starts with his imagination."

Despite the beauty of a few of these automatist Gorkys, *One Year the Milkweed* in particular, most of them are confused and overcomplicated (*How My Mother's Embroidered Apron Unfolds in My Life,* for example). Others, like *The Unattainable,* contain excessively suave drawing that degenerates into emotionally shallow linear figure skating. By the end of 1945, however, Gorky returned to his more personal style, with a new delicacy and transparency in the backgrounds (not unrelated to Baziotes) for which his automatist wash pictures were very likely responsible. By then he had been an independent painter for three years, though during that time he had still found it necessary to explore the ideas of others. Now he had literally experienced everything, and he was ready to produce his most individual works. One of them, *The Diary of a Seducer,* executed late in 1945, is probably his masterpiece. The most sorrowful aspect of the studio fire of January, 1946, was that the greater number of the twenty-seven pictures destroyed (as well as numerous drawings) came from this most perfect moment of his art.

In 1947, the tragedies that were to lead to Gorky's suicide the following year—the fire, cancer, sexual impotence, a broken neck—were taking their toll, and his work reflects this. Already for a year his biomorphism had been marked

397

by extremes of pathos and aggression. The new profiles of his shapes suggested emotions that were being exacerbated, literally drawn out almost beyond the point of endurance. In the center right of *Betrothal II* (see detail) is one of these new biomorphic shapes. Its contour is pinched together and drawn upward in a more and more fragile line—like a nerve that is being stretched tight—until, just before it snaps, it is resolved into another plane. The four corners of this plane are in turn tortuously pulled outward so that its sides appear scalloped, a painful distortion that is set off boldly by the more regular rectangular plane on which it is superimposed. Precedent for this type of transmutation of the entire contour of a plane into an independent line may be found in Mirós like *Fratellini* (1926). But there the drawing is relaxed; Miró's line never attains the tautness and ductility of Gorky's.

In the drawings of 1946 and 1947 cruel and monstrous personages, of the type that had entered Matta's art in 1945, manifested themselves through a kind of hard and summary modeling that Gorky had never used before. But, as we observe in comparing the drawing for *Agony* with the finished work, these specters were rendered less descriptive when converted into painting, where the gentle, though deeply poignant, touch dissolved them into the surface design.

With the pictures of 1947 Gorky's contribution to modern painting ends. The few canvases of the last tormented months of his life are understandably overwrought and add nothing.

The year of *Agony* (1947) was, as we have seen, the year when Pollock "broke the ice"; from then until the end of the decade a large number of New York painters were to integrate moving and highly original styles of their own. Nobody, and least of all Gorky in view of his attachment to European art and culture, could have, in 1947, grasped the full extent of the native movement that was emerging. But Gorky had been particularly close to at least one major painter of that movement, Willem de Kooning, and it was through him that a few aspects of Gorky's art found their way into the New American Painting. In his works of the early forties de Kooning had created a highly personal amalgam out of elements of Miró and Picasso, and such pictures as *Pink Angels* (*ca.* 1945), with its distant organic forms laced together by a tangle of angular and mordant lines, show his extraordinary draftsmanship already fully developed. In 1948 his language of forms was temporarily inflected by Gorky's biomorphism. *Painting* of that year (Museum of Modern Art) develops a cluster of such forms slightly in front of the vestiges of a rectilinear ground, like a still life seen against architecture. It is in such black paintings of 1948 and 1949 that Gorky is painted into de Kooning's pictures. But he is painted right out again; and in the process his symbolic forms are reduced to signs and finally to marks.

Gorky had discovered himself by building upon his sources; de Kooning

398

The Bethrothal II. (detail).

Arshile Gorky: *The Bethrothal II.* 1947.
Oil on canvas. 50¾″ x 38″.
Collection of The Whitney Museum of
American Art, New York.

Joan Miró: *Fratellini.* 1927.
Oil on canvas. 51¾″ x 38″.
Collection of
Mr. and Mrs. Harry Lewis Winston,
Birmingham, Michigan.

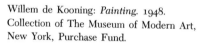

Willem de Kooning: *Painting.* 1948.
Collection of The Museum of Modern Art,
New York, Purchase Fund.

399

affirmed himself by annihilating them. Even in *Painting*, the Gorkyesque bio-morphism is rendered with an Expressionist roughness and directness that has no antecedent in Gorky or, for that matter, anywhere in the European tradition, including Van Gogh and the 1910–14 Kandinsky. De Kooning smothered Gorky's morphology in a rude painterliness—scumbled, dry-brushed, blotted—which was to become the characteristic manner of most New York Painting for a decade; in pictures like *Night Square* the biomorphism is so flayed and torn open as to be virtually unrecognizable. In making Gorky's morphology his own, de Kooning obliterated it, and with it went the tradition of *peinture-poésie* which variants of that morphology had served from the time of the early Arp reliefs through Miró to Matta and Gorky.

It can be said for Gorky that his was one of the first truly painterly styles to emerge after World War I. And since Abstract Expressionism, "if it means anything, means painterliness," as Clement Greenberg has observed, then Gorky is one of the godfathers of the new abstraction. But Gorky was painterly (i.e., *malerisch*) in the manner of earlier European painting, even as he expanded this manner, while de Kooning was painterly in a new and prophetic way. There was a bludgeoning forthrightness to the passion of the de Kooning manner; Gorky's exquisite anguish always retained that emotional fragility tinged with masochism, which had been the common denominator of the Symbolist-Surrealist tradition.[12]

To the limited extent that Gorky was to influence subsequent American painting, de Kooning was the primary channel. As a matter of fact, the Gorky component in de Kooning's morphology is sometimes more manifest in the work of de Kooning's followers, like Marca-Relli, than it is in his own. In charting the relationship of Gorky's painting to that of the younger generation, the case of Joan Mitchell is perhaps the most illustrative. Her paintings of around 1950 are an amalgam of Kandinsky and Gorky, though larger, blander, and more vigorously executed than the work of either. In the course of the fifties these sources were assimilated into a de Kooningesque manner, within which she soon found her own profile (contrary to the development of the majority of Tenth-Street painters who, in recapitulating a similar progression, remained mere imitators). It was clear that one could operate more freely and more personally in the *manner* of de Kooning than in the *morphology* of Gorky, the adoption of which (like that of the "drip" Pollock) led to an appearance of slavish imitation. The few painters who committed themselves to that morphology, like Seong Moy, whose painting drew momentary critical attention just after 1950, soon found themselves its prisoners. Even today allusions to Gorky are difficult to assimilate. In the work of Hassel Smith, for example, the morphology is Gorky's, while the manner is de Kooning's, and it is the Gorky that is obtrusive.

[12] How many times had supplice been rhymed with delice in such poetry!

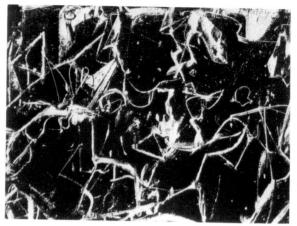

Willem de Kooning: *Night Square.* 1948.
Oil on masonite. 30″ x 40″.
Collection of Mrs. Martha Jackson,
New York.

Conrad Marca-Relli. *Battle Theme.* 1957.
Oil and collage. 52″ x 60″.
Courtesy of The Kootz Gallery, New York.

Joan Mitchell: *Abstraction.* 1950. Oil on canvas.
Collection of the Vassar College Art Museum.

Joan Mitchell: *Harbour December.* 1956.
Oil on canvas. 80″ x 80″.
Courtesy of The Stable Gallery, New York.

Hassel Smith: *Number 6, 1960.*
Oil on canvas. 68″ x 69½″.
Collection of the Washington University Gallery of Art,
St. Louis, Missouri.

Seong Moy: *The King and His Paramour.*
1950. Oil.

The mere fact that Gorky had no immediate followers among younger American painters is no measure of his quality or his historical position, for the same is true of Pollock (contrary to popular misconceptions). The styles of these painters resisted transformation and assimilation, whereas de Kooning's did not. But there the similarity ends, for Pollock's style shared, as Gorky's did not,[13] certain broader characteristics with the styles of such painters as de Kooning, Kline, Rothko, Still, Motherwell, and Newman. None of these characteristics (which include handling of scale, drawing, chiaroscuro and color, touch, and impasto) were common to all these painters, but every one of those generally identified as "the first generation" of the New York School shared some of them with a few others. Clyfford Still, for example, relates to Rothko and Newman as a "color painter," and to de Kooning, Pollock, and Kline in the impastoed character of his surface. As one went from room to room in The Museum of Modern Art's New American Painting exhibition, it was interesting to see how, for all their differences of style, some underlying identity ran through the works of these artists. With the partial exception of Baziotes, only Gorky's paintings seemed out of place, despite their beauty, or perhaps because of their very nature. One felt that if Gorky was indeed a Janus figure facing backward to the European tradition and forward to the New American Painting, then only the eyes that looked back were in focus.

[13] Only with Baziotes can we find any extensive affinities, and his case rather proves the point, for unlike that of the rest of that generation, his style has remained essentially within the character of the middle forties.

Shape as Form: Frank Stella's New Paintings*
By Michael Fried

The craving for simplicity. People would like to say: "What really matters is only the colors." You say this mostly because you wish it to be the case. If your explanation is complicated, it is disagreeable, especially if you don't have strong feelings about the thing itself.
—WITTGENSTEIN

I

Frank Stella's new paintings investigate the viability of shape as such. By *shape as such* I mean not merely the silhouette of the support (which I shall call literal shape), not merely that of the outlines of elements in a given picture (which I shall call depicted shape), but shape as a medium within which choices about both literal and depicted shapes are made, and made mutually responsive. And by the viability of shape, I mean its power to hold, to stamp itself out, and in— as verisimilitude and narrative and symbolism used to impress themselves— compelling conviction. Stella's undertaking in these paintings is therapeutic: to restore shape to health, at least temporarily, though of course its implied "sickness" is simply the other face of the unprecedented importance shape has assumed in the finest Modernist painting of the past several years—most notably, in the work of Kenneth Noland and Jules Olitski. It is only in their work that shape as such can be said to have become capable of holding, or stamping itself out, or compelling conviction—as well as, so to speak, capable of failing to do so. These are powers or potentialities—not to say responsibilities—which shape never until now possessed, and which have been conferred upon it by the development of Modernist painting itself. In this sense shape has become something different from what it was in traditional painting or, for that matter, in Modernist painting until recently. It has become, one might say, an object of conviction, whereas before it was merely . . . a kind of object. Stella's new pictures are a response to the recognition that shape itself may be lost to the art of painting as a resource able to compel conviction, precisely because—as never before—it is being called upon to do just that.

The way in which this has come about is, in the fullest sense of the word, dialectical, and I shall not try to do justice to its enormous complexity in these rough notes. An adequate account of the developments leading up to Stella's new paintings would, however, deal with the following:

1. *The emergence of a new, exclusively visual mode of illusionism in the work of Pollock, Newman, and Louis.* No single issue has been as continuously

* Somewhat revised version of an article first published in *Artforum*, Vol. V, No. 3 (November, 1966).

fundamental to the development of Modernist painting as the need to acknowledge the literal character of the picture-support. Above all, this has tended
to mean acknowledging its flatness or two-dimensionality. There is a sense in
which a new illusionism was implicit in this development all along. As Clement
Greenberg has remarked:

The flatness toward which Modernist painting orients itself can never be an utter flatness.
The heightened sensitivity of the picture plane may no longer permit sculptural illusion, or
trompe-l'oeil, but it does and must permit optical illusion. The first mark on a surface
destroys its virtual flatness, and the configurations of a Mondrian still suggest a kind of
illusion of a kind of third dimension. Only now it is a strictly pictorial, strictly optical third
dimension.[1]

But the universal power of any mark to suggest something like depth belongs
not so much to the art of painting as to the eye itself; it is, one might say, not
something that has had to be established so much as something—a perceptual
limitation—that cannot be escaped,[2] whereas the dissolution of traditional
drawing in Pollock's work, the reliance on large and generally rather warm
expanses of barely fluctuating color in Newman's, and the staining of thinned
(acrylic) pigment into mostly unsized canvas in Louis' were instrumental in
the creation of a depth or space accessible to eyesight alone which, so to speak,
specifically belongs to the art of painting.[3]

    2. *The neutralizing of the flatness of the picture-support by the new, exclu-
sively optical illusionism.* In the work of Pollock and Newman, but even more
in that of Louis, Noland, and Olitski, the new illusionism both subsumes and
dissolves the picture-surface—opening it, as Greenberg has said, from the
rear[4]—while simultaneously preserving its integrity. More accurately, it is
the *flatness* of the picture-surface, and not that surface itself, that is dissolved,
or at least neutralized, by the illusion in question. The literalness of the picture-
surface is not denied; but one's experience of that literalness is an experience
of the properties of different pigments, of foreign substances applied to the sur-

   [1] "Modernist Painting," *The New Art: A Critical Anthology*, ed. Gregory Battcock (New York: E. P.
Dutton, 1966), p. 107.
   [2] Mondrian, in his paintings of the 1920s and after, often seems to be attempting to combat just this
minimal illusionism. Sometimes, for example, he stops his black lines short of the framing-edge, thereby emphasizing their paintedness, i.e., the fact that they are marks on a flat surface. In other paintings
he takes the more radical step of *continuing* the black lines and even the blocks of color *past* the edge
onto the sides of the canvas (which appears to have been meant to be exhibited with its sides visible).
The result is that one tends to see these paintings as solid *slabs*, which helps to counteract—though it
cannot efface—their minimal illusionism.
   [3] For discussions of these developments see Greenberg's essay "Louis and Noland," *Art International*, IV:5, pp. 26–29, and my *Three American Painters* (Cambridge: Harvard University Press,
1965). The latter also discusses in some detail the emergence of what I have called "deductive structure," a development I adumbrate here.
   [4] Greenberg says this of Noland's paintings in his "Louis and Noland," p. 28.

face of the painting, of the weave of the canvas, above all of color—but not, or not in particular, of the flatness of the support. (One could say that here the literalness of the picture-surface is not an aspect of the literalness of the support.) Not that literalness here is experienced as competing in any way with the illusionistic presence of the painting as a whole; on the contrary, one somehow *constitutes* the other. And in fact there is no distinction one can make between attending to the surface of the painting and to the illusion it generates: to be gripped by one is to be held, and moved, by the other.

3. *The discovery shortly before 1960 of a new mode of pictorial structure based on the shape, rather than the flatness, of the support.* With the dissolution or neutralizing of the flatness of the support by the new optical illusionism, the shape of the support—including its proportions and exact dimensions—came to assume a more active, more explicit importance than ever before. The crucial figures in this development are Frank Stella and Kenneth Noland. In Stella's aluminum stripe paintings of 1960, for example, 2½-inch-wide stripes begin at the framing-edge and reiterate the shape of that edge until the entire picture is filled; moreover, by actually shaping each picture—the canvases are rectangles with shallow (one-stripe deep) notches at two corners or along the sides or both—Stella was able to make the fact that the literal shape determines the structure of the entire painting completely perspicuous. That is, in each painting the stripes appear to have been generated by the framing-edge and, starting there, to have taken possession of the rest of the canvas, as though the whole painting self-evidently followed from, not merely the shape of the support, but its actual physical limits. Noland, on the other hand, cannot be said to have come into contact with the physical limits of the support until his first chevron paintings of 1962. His initial breakthrough to major achievement in the late 1950s came when he began to locate the center of concentric or radiating motifs at the exact center of square canvases. This related depicted shape to literal shape through a shared focus of symmetry. Whether or not Noland recognized that *this* was the significance of centering his rings and armatures of color is less important than that he experienced the centering itself as a discovery: a constraint in whose necessity he could believe, and in submission to which his magnificent gifts as a colorist were liberated. His shift to chevron motifs a few years later was, I believe, inspired in part by the need to achieve a more active or explicit relation between depicted and literal shape than the use of concentric rings, none of which actually made contact with the framing-edge, allowed. Within a few months Noland discovered that suspending his chevrons from the upper corners of the support (the bottom edge of the lowest chevron running into each corner) empowered him, first, to prize loose the point of the bottommost chevron from the midpoint of the bottom framing-edge, and second, to pull all the chevrons away from the central axis of the

405

painting—besides enabling him to work with rectangular formats other than the square. In these paintings—the asymmetrical chevrons of 1964—the exact dimensions of the support become important in this sense: that if the edge of the bottommost chevron did not *exactly* intersect the upper corners of the canvas, the relation of *all* the chevrons—that is, of depicted shape—to the shape of the support became acutely problematic and the ability of the painting as a whole to compel conviction was called into question. Since that time, apparently in an attempt to make depicted shape relate more generally to the shape of the support in its entirety, Noland too has shaped his pictures. (His recent work includes a number of narrow diamond-shaped pictures that I will discuss further on.) It cannot be emphasized too strongly, however, that Noland's chief concern throughout his career has been with color—or rather, with feeling *through* color—and not with structure: which makes the role that structural decisions and alterations have played in his development all the more significant. This is not to say that Noland's colorism has had to maintain itself in the teeth of his forced involvement with structural concerns. On the contrary, it is precisely his deep and impassioned commitment to making color yield major painting that has compelled him to discover structures in which the shape of the support is acknowledged lucidly and explicitly enough to compel conviction.

    4. The primacy of literal over depicted shape. In both Noland's and Stella's (stripe) paintings the burden of acknowledging the shape of the support is borne by the depicted shape, or perhaps more accurately, by the relation between it and the literal shape—a relation that declares the primacy of the latter. And in general the development of Modernist painting during the past six years can be described as having involved the progressive assumption by literal shape of a greater—that is, more active, more explicit—importance than ever before, and the consequent subordination of depicted shape. It is as though depicted shape has become less and less capable of venturing on its own, of pursuing its own ends; as though unless, in a given painting, depicted shape manages to participate in—by helping to establish—the authority of the shape of the support, conviction is aborted and the painting fails. In this sense depicted shape may be said to have become dependent upon literal shape—and indeed unable to make itself felt as shape except by acknowledging that dependence.

II

    Let this stand as the general background of concerns from which Stella's new paintings emerge. A fuller delineation of their immediate context is still required, however, if the concentrated and radical exploration of shape which they undertake is meaningfully to be described.

    Although Noland has found it necessary to develop structures in which the shape of the support plays a determining role, his continuing ambition to liberate feeling through color has made him reluctant to call attention to the physical limits of the support—the way, for example, Stella's stripe paintings call attention to them. In the latter, Stella identifies the shape of a given picture with its framing-edge, thereby assimilating the first to the second. Noland, on the other hand, is anxious to keep this from happening; or rather, the same concerns that, in effect, compel him to acknowledge the shape of the support also compel him to try to keep our awareness of its physical limits to an absolute minimum. Above all Noland is anxious to keep us from experiencing the shape of his paintings as *edge*, hence as something literal and nonillusive; and in order to make sure this does not happen, he tries to keep us from experiencing the shape at all. It is as though, for Noland, to experience the shape of a painting is inescapably to experience the painting itself as something literal, as a kind of object; and this would compromise its presence as visual illusion. And in general the shapes of his paintings are never experienced as acutely as the limits of and boundaries between the depicted elements within them.

That Noland's paintings avoid calling attention to their physical limits does not mean that those limits are not still there—and there to be felt. What *put* them there to be felt is the acknowledgment of literal shape that the paintings themselves make—and which, as it were, exerts upon the edge a kind of pressure, or inquisition, from which it cannot escape. If Noland's paintings offered some alternative to our experiencing their shapes as an aspect of their literalness —either by positively identifying literal shape with illusion, or by repudiating it altogether—their efficacy as illusion or presence would not be, as I sometimes find them to be, threatened by, or at, the edges. (The suggested alternatives are those explored in Olitski's spray paintings and Stella's new pictures respectively.) This is not to deny that throughout Noland's masterful paintings of the past several years the literal shape of the support is made to seem the *outcome,* or *result,* of the depicted shapes—rather than, as in Stella's stripe paintings, the other way around. But the fact remains that a painting by Noland cannot be said to *hold* as shape—it cannot be said to need to either—but merely to *have* one, like any solid object in the world. Or rather, it is as though the shape were *itself* a kind of object in the world—an object that has been prized loose from the illusionistic presence of the painting by its very importance to the structure of that painting. One is made to feel, that is, that in these paintings the distinction between depicted and literal shape marks a difference, not simply between two kinds of *shape*—each, so to speak, conceived of as a pictorial entity—but between two utterly distinct and different kinds of entities. The first of these, depicted shape, is powerless to make itself felt except by acknowledging the primacy of the other, while that other—literal shape—does not *hold* as shape. It *is* a shape, but what this suddenly seems to mean is only that it is an object in
407

the world—an object whose relevance to our experience of the painting is not clear.

The fact that in some of his recent paintings Noland has not been content simply to minimize the shape of the support, but has instead begun actively to subvert it, suggests that his previous paintings may have come to seem problematic to him for the sorts of reasons I have been discussing. For example, his last show at the Emmerich Gallery included four 8-by-2-foot diamond-shaped paintings in each of which four relatively broad bands of color run parallel to one or the other pair of sides, thereby acknowledging the shape of the support. At the same time, however, the extreme attenuation of these pictures makes them unable to contain within the limits of the support their own extraordinary presences as color and illusion. In the grip of the sheerly visual illusion generated by the interaction of the colored bands, the acute-angled corners of the supports appear to vibrate and shimmer, to erode both from within and without, to become even more attenuated and needle-like than they are, while the obtuse-angled corners tend to round off, to appear dull or blunt. The result is that the physical limits of the supports are overrun, indeed all but dissolved, by the painting's illusionistic presences. At the same time an effect like that of simultaneous contrast between the colored bands makes them appear to overlap one another physically, like shingles. So that, while the physical limits of the support are assaulted by illusion, the (depicted) boundaries between the bands are the more acutely felt—as if absorbing the literalness or objecthood given up by the support. Moreover, because some sort of progressive sequence (e.g., of value) among the bands appears to be required for the illusionistic overlapping I have just described, one's actual experience, or sensation, of these paintings is *directional*. One is aware, that is, of being held and moved by a progression or sequence—a resource until now foreign to Modernist painting—and this further intensifies the assault these paintings make on their own static, literal shapes. In several other paintings in the same show—long horizontal rectangles with a few parallel bands of color, again arranged progressively, running their entire lengths—Noland achieved an equal subversion by somewhat simpler means: the rectangles are too long, and proportionally too narrow, to be experienced as discrete shapes. Instead, confronted head on, they seem to extend almost beyond the limits of our field of vision, to become nothing but extension, to *end up* only being rectangular; approached from the side (their length makes this inviting) what is striking is not their rectangularity but the speed with which that rectangle—or rather, the speed with which the colored bands—appears to diminish in perspective recession.[5] Here, again, although

[5] That Noland's long horizontal paintings make their own shapes ungraspable in this way was observed by Rosalind Krauss in her article "Allusion and Illusion in Donald Judd," *Artforum*, IV:9, p. 26. In the same issue Mrs. Krauss discusses Stella's new paintings, pp. 47–49.

Kenneth Noland: *Up Cadmium*. 1966. Acrylic paint on canvas. 6′ x 18′.
Photograph courtesy of André Emmerich Gallery, New York.

the relation of depicted to literal shape within each painting acknowledges in the simplest possible way the primacy of the latter, the actual limits of the support do not quite manage to constitute a single, definite shape, while the boundaries between the colored bands seem almost tactile or *stepped* by comparison.

I have argued elsewhere that the desire to oppose the kind of structure at work in Noland's and Stella's paintings provided much of the motivation behind Jules Olitski's first spray paintings of 1965.[6] These pictures are completely devoid of depicted shape, and in fact represent what is almost certainly the most radical and thoroughgoing attempt in the history of Modernism to make major art out of nothing but color. At the same time, no paintings have ever depended so completely or so nakedly for their success on the shape (and in particular the proportions) of their supports, experienced, one might say, in relation both to nothing particular within each painting and to everything it contains.[7] It is, I think, true of these paintings—and of no others—that they succeed as paintings just so far as they succeed, or hold, or stamp themselves out, as shapes. And in fact no shapes, depicted or literal, have ever stamped themselves out more compellingly or more feelingly. In the sense in which I have been using the word, it is not true to say that these paintings *acknowledge* the shape of the support; but their relative quality depends even more intimately upon it. (In this respect they differ sharply from Noland's paintings, whose success or failure as art does not depend on their efficacy as shapes.) So that while they were made in opposition to a mode of pictorial organization which established the primacy of literal over depicted shape, in these paintings literal shape's assumption of

[6] In my essay "Jules Olitski's New Paintings," *Artforum*, IV:3, pp. 36–40.

[7] In his brief remarks on Olitski's work, published in the catalogue to the United States pavilion at the last Biennale, Clement Greenberg wrote, "The degree to which the success of Olitski's paintings depends on proportion of height to width in their enclosing shapes is, I feel, unprecedented." Greenberg goes on to note the relative superiority of the pictures with tall, narrow formats.

authority has become not merely relative but absolute: as though it alone were capable of performing the office of shape, of being felt as shape.

The very success of Olitski's paintings as shapes lays bare the conditions that make this success possible—conditions it is hard to imagine any paintings but Olitski's being able to fulfill. It is, to begin with, clearly central to their potency as shapes that they are wholly devoid of depicted shape; but it is also clear that two paintings equally devoid of depicted shape may succeed unequally as shapes—and, therewith, as works of art. Moreover, virtually all the best early spray paintings belong to a single format—the narrow vertical rectangle—and the more any painting departs from this format toward the horizontal or square the more likely it is to fail. This is connected with the fact that when the early spray paintings fail—relatively speaking—we tend to see the framing-edge as marking the limits of a spatial *container*, and the sprayed canvas itself as something like *background* in traditional painting. The narrow vertical format somehow keeps this from happening: not by denying the illusion but, so to speak, by making it self-sufficient, a presence, like that of a human figure, instead of a void waiting to be filled. In the best narrow vertical paintings the framing-edge does not appear to contain the illusion; on the contrary, it is the illusion that contains the limits of the support. So that whereas the relatively square paintings can often be seen as receptacles which may happen to be empty but which could be filled, could contain objects, the best of the narrow vertical pictures *already contain* their object, namely, the edges of the painting, its outermost and tactile limits. (In this connection it is significant that, in the paintings in question, all relatively well-defined bursts of color and variations in value are restricted to the vicinity of the edges and corners of the canvas.) One might say that whereas in traditional painting the illusion of a tactile space commences at the inside of the framing-edge, in the best early spray paintings the illusion of something like depth or space accessible to eyesight alone ends at the outside of that edge. And that whereas traditional illusionism begins at the surface of the canvas, the strictly visual mode of illusionism of the Olitskis in question ends there.

In recent paintings, such as those exhibited at the Biennale [of 1966], Olitski has taken to masking out all but thin bands around two or three sides of the sprayed canvas, spraying some more and then removing the masking. The result is a clear difference between the previously masked and unmasked areas, a difference that can be subtle or blatant, and can vary enormously from place to place along the boundary between the bands and the rest of the picture which they partly frame. Further, this internal "frame" is not strictly parallel to the edges of the canvas; sometimes its long vertical component is inflected slightly away from the perpendicular. Both these developments can be understood, at least in part, as undermining or mitigating the absoluteness of the primacy

Jules Olitski: *Prinkep.* 1966.
Acrylic paint on canvas. 94″ x 48″.
Photograph courtesy of
André Emmerich Gallery, New York.

which literal shape assumes in his first spray paintings. To begin with, the partial internal "frame" amounts to something like depicted shape; and this in itself means that the quality of individual paintings no longer solely depends on the almost unanalyzable relation between the sprayed canvas and the shape of the support that apparently governs the success or failure of the first spray paintings. But because the boundary between the framing bands and the rest of the painting consists of the same pictorial stuff—the same sprayed color— as the areas it delimits, the role of the internal "frame" as a kind of middle term between the shape of the support and the rest of the painting is far more complex than that played by depicted shape in Noland's paintings or Stella's stripe paintings. To be sure, the internal "frame"—or, more accurately, the boundary between the "framing"-bands and the rest of the painting—relates structurally to the shape of the support. But it also establishes an extraordinary, and indeed unprecedented, continuity *across* that boundary. This enables the paintings in question both to contain depicted shape, or something like it, and yet be seen as pictorially seamless and integral—like the early spray paintings. Moreover, the fact that the long vertical component of the internal "frame"— or the vertical boundary between that "frame" and the rest of the picture—is

411

sometimes inflected away from the perpendicular further reduces the perspicuity of literal shape's primacy at the same time that it acknowledges, or is made possible by, this primacy. That is, in these paintings the primacy of literal shape is such that even a slight departure from verticality within the painting makes itself felt with an intensity of expression I, for one, find astonishing. But it is precisely the strength of this primacy that enables the paintings in question both to tolerate the departure and to move us by it. The very acuteness, even poignancy, of our experience of what is, after all, an extremely slight inflection, acknowledges the strength, and more than that, the *depth*, of the norm from which that inflection departed—in this case, the shape of the support. But the fact remains that what we actually feel, and are inexplicably moved by, is the inflection from the norm rather than the norm itself. All these differences between his early and later spray paintings have enabled Olitski to realize his ambitions across a considerably wider range of formats. And if it is true, as I believe it is, that none of the later spray paintings (none that I have seen at any rate) stamps itself out as shape quite as powerfully as the best of the early ones, part of what these differences have meant is that the quality of a given picture no longer depends entirely on its success or failure as shape.

There is, then, a sense in which the conflict between a sheerly visual or optical mode of illusionism and the literal character of the support is central both to Noland's and Olitski's paintings. In Olitski's pictures—at any rate, the early spray pictures—the conflict is naked and direct. It is, for example, felt in the threat that the illusion will seem almost to come detached from the framing-edge, to leave the literal shape hanging on the wall and situate itself indefinitely further back. This is not to say that when this does *not* happen the illusion is properly described as *attached* to the edge of the support. Rather, the physical limits of the support mark, or declare, or simply *are,* the limits of the illusion itself. We become aware of the conflict in question only when, in relatively less successful paintings, illusion and literal shape actually part company—despite the fact that when this happens, the illusion can no longer be described as sheerly visual, any more than background in traditional painting can be characterized in these terms. In Noland's paintings, on the other hand, opticality and the physical limits of the support are not juxtaposed against one another as in Olitski's paintings. Instead, it is the structure of his paintings—the relation between depicted and literal shape in them—that *brings* the two into conflict with one another. This is what makes the fact that his paintings do not stamp themselves out as shapes feel like a failure or refusal to do so—a failure or refusal that, especially in the light of Olitski's spray paintings, leaves the literalness, or *objecthood,* of the limits of the support there to be felt. I said earlier that Noland himself seems to have become increasingly troubled by this, and in his recent narrow diamond and long horizontal rectangle paintings appears to have tried to subvert their shapes. But it should be remarked that this does not resolve the conflict between opticality and the literal character of the support that, I have claimed, is central to both Noland's and Olitski's work; if anything, it intensifies it.

III

It is only in the presence of this conflict that the question of whether or not a given painting holds or stamps itself out as shape makes full sense—or rather, only here that the issue of "the viability of shape as such" characterizes a specific stage in resolving, or unfolding, problems of acknowledgment, literalness, and illusion which, as I said at the beginning of these notes, have been among the issues of Modernism from its beginning. In Stella's stripe paintings, for example, the reiteration by the stripes of the irregular shapes of the support makes the dependence of depicted on literal shape far more explicit than Noland's paintings ever allow it to seem. But if one asks whether Stella's paintings hold better or make themselves felt more acutely as shapes than Noland's paintings, the answer, I think, is not just that they do not, but that the whole issue of holding or failing to hold is much less relevant to them. That is, because they are not illusive in anything like the way Noland's and Olitski's paintings are, there is nothing for them to hold as shapes *against*.[8]

I must emphasize that in defining this conflict between visual illusionism and literal shape in Noland's and Olitski's paintings I have not meant to imply an adverse criticism either of the quality of their best paintings or of the general level of their respective achievements. This is worth stressing precisely because there are certain younger artists to whose sensibilities all conflict between the literal character of the support and illusion of any kind is intolerable, and for whom, accordingly, the future of art lies in the creation of works that, more than anything else, are *wholly literal*—in this respect *going beyond* painting. It should be evident that what I think of as literalist sensibility is itself a product, or by-product, of the development of Modernist painting itself—more accurately, by the increasingly explicit acknowledgment of the literal character of the support that has been central to that development. But it ought also to be observed that the literalness isolated and hypostatized in the work of artists like Donald Judd and Larry Bell is by no means the *same* literalness as that acknowl-

[8] The aluminum paintings of 1960 are an exception to this. Although not illusionistic, they can, I think, be said to hold as shape—chiefly by virtue of the fact that their supports depart from the rectangular only by a few shallow notches at the corners and sides. As a result the paintings are seen as restrained or held back by these notches by completing the rectangles they all but occupy. This gives the shapes of these paintings something to hold against—i.e., the pressure from within each painting toward the rectangle it almost is—and, in effect, makes the question of whether or nor they make themselves felt as shapes a real one.

413

edged by advanced painting throughout the past century: it is not the literalness *of the support*. Moreover, hypostatization is not acknowledgment. The continuing problem of *how* to acknowledge the literal character of the support—of *what counts* as that acknowledgment—has been at least as crucial to the development of Modernist painting as the fact of its literalness; and this problem has been eliminated, not solved, by the artists in question. Their pieces cannot be said to acknowledge literalness; they simply *are literal*. And it is hard to see how literalness as such, divorced from the conventions which, from Manet to Noland, Olitski and Stella, have *given* literalness value and have *made* it a bearer of conviction, can be experienced as a *source* of both of these—and what is more, one powerful enough to generate new conventions, a new art.[9]

Because Frank Stella's stripe paintings, especially those executed in metallic paint, represent the most unequivocal and conflictless acknowledgment of literal shape in the history of Modernism, they have been crucial to the literalist view I have just adumbrated, both because they are seen as extreme instances of a putative development within Modernist painting—i.e., the increasingly explicit acknowledgment of literalness per se—and because they help to make that development visible, or arguable, in the first place. They are among the last paintings that literalists like Judd are able to endorse more or less without reservation: largely because the ambition to go beyond them—to pursue their apparent implications—was instrumental in the abandonment of painting altogether by these same artists.

In Stella's new paintings, however, the relation between depicted and literal

---

[9] Judd, almost certainly the foremost ideologist of the literalist position, has claimed—in "Specific Objects," *Arts Yearbook*, No. 8 (1965)—that "a work needs only to be interesting." It is hard to know exactly what this means, because some work, such as Noland's, Olitski's, and Stella's paintings, is *more* than just interesting. It is, I want to say, *good*—more accurately, good *painting*. And in fact—despite the proliferation of work that is neither painting nor sculpture, and despite the pervasiveness of the facile notion that the arts in our time are at last heading toward synthesis—what Modernism has come increasingly to mean is that, more than ever, *value* or *quality* can persuasively be predicated of work that lies only *within*, not *between*, the individual arts. (Though it has also come to mean that that work must challenge, in characteristic ways, what we are prepared to *count* as belonging more than trivially to the art in question.) The circularity of this state of affairs will be repugnant to many, and it is certainly harrowing, but I do not think that it is self-condemning. The crucial question, after all, is not so much whether anything artistically valuable lies outside the circle, as whether a meaningful concept of artistic value or a significant experience of it can reside anywhere but in its coils.

My own impulse is to say that interest is basic to art—but not to either *making* or *judging* it. And if it is objected that what we ought to try to do is enjoy art rather than judge it, I would simply say that that may have been possible once but isn't anymore. This, however, is not to *contrast* enjoyment with judging—it is rather to insist that there is no *real* enjoyment, or no enjoyment of what is *really there*, apart from judging. One can still enjoy Olitski's paintings simply as color, if one wants, but that is not to enjoy them, or be moved by them, or see them as *paintings*. And this means that there is an important sense in which one is not seeing them *at all*. But to experience painting as painting is inescapably to engage with the question of quality. This, too, is the work of Modernism, and if one does not like it one ought to face the fact that what one does not like is painting, or at least what painting has become.

414

shape seems nowhere near as straightforward in its declaration of the latter as in the stripe paintings—or, for that matter, in Noland's work. Rather, there is a new and even somewhat startling freedom both in the variety of shapes used in a given picture and in their disposition relative to one another and to the support. This is not to say that the shape of the support is either ignored or denied. On the contrary, it is very clearly taken into account; but the way in which this is accomplished does not affirm the dependence of depicted on literal shape so much as it establishes an unprecented *continuity* between them. In *Moultonboro III*, for example, the shape of the support is an irregular polygon formed by superimposing a triangle and a square, the first apparently having come slanting down from the upper right to wedge itself deeply into the second. (In *Chocorua III* a triangle is superimposed on a rectangle; the same is true of *Tuftonboro III* except that the rectangle is missing its upper right corner; while in *Conway III* a parallelogram is superimposed on another, this time more horizontal, rectangle. These are the only formats among the eleven Stella has used for his new paintings that have been arrived at by superimposition, pure and simple.[10]) The triangle itself comprises two elements—an eight-inch-wide light yellow band around its perimeter and the smaller triangle, in Day-Glo yellow, bounded by that band—both of which seem to be acknowledging, by repeating, the shape of the support. For that reason it is almost startling to realize that only a relatively small segment of the triangle coincides with, is part of, the shape of the support. Most of the triangle lies wholly inside the picture and, in the terms proposed at the outset, exists only as depicted shape. Even more surprising, however, is the fact that realizing this does not in itself undermine the triangle's efficacy as shape. It is as though that segment which coincides with the literal shape of the painting somehow implies the rest of the triangle—the merely depicted portion of it—strongly enough for the latter to succeed as shape despite its failure to relate self-evidently to any other segment of the framing-edge. But it would, I think, be just as true to one's experience of *Moultonboro III* to claim that what enables the relatively small segment of the triangle that coincides with the shape of the support to make itself felt as shape is what might be called the implicative power, in this context, of the merely depicted portion of the triangle. The yellow triangular band and the Day-Glo triangle within it are, after all, what make that segment intelligible: without them, and without another largely internal shape—the blue Z-form in which the triangular band (and hence the triangle as a whole) rests—the upper-right-hand segment of the support would not be part of a triangle but would belong instead to the literal shape of the painting perceived in its entirety as an

---

[10] Stella made four paintings in each of the eleven formats. There are, then, eleven subseries within which not only the shape of the support but the configurations on the surface of the canvas are identical.

Frank Stella: *Moultonboro III.* 1966.
110″ x 120″.
(The media for all the paintings,
unless otherwise noted,
is fluorescent alkyd and epoxy
paint on canvas.)
Collection of Carter Burden, New York.
Photograph courtesy of
Leo Castelli Gallery, New York.

Frank Stella: *Chocorua III.* 1967.
120″ x 128″.
Collection of Leo Castelli Gallery, New York.

Frank Stella: *Tuftonboro III.* 1966.
100½″ x 109″.
Collection of Leo Castelli Gallery, New York.

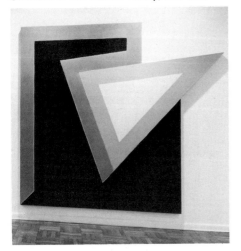

Frank Stella: *Conway III.* 1966.
80″ x 122″.
Collection of Leo Castelli Gallery, New York.

416

irregular seven-sided polygon, whereas in the painting as it stands roughly the opposite is the case. The beholder is, in effect, compelled *not* to experience the literal shape in its entirety—as a single entity—but rather to perceive it segment by segment, each of which is felt to belong to one or another of the smaller shapes that constitute the painting as a whole.

This last point is important. For one thing it indicates a crucial difference between Stella's new paintings on the one hand and Noland's and Olitski's pictures, as well as Stella's own previous work, on the other. In this respect Noland's paintings in general are closer to Olitski's spray pictures than to Stella's new work, despite the fact that—unlike Olitski—both he and Stella work with nonrectangular supports and discrete areas of color. It also suggests that, confronted by Stella's new paintings, the distinction between depicted and literal shape becomes nugatory. It is as though in a painting like *Moulton-boro III* there *is no* literal shape and, therefore, no depicted shape either; more accurately, because none of the shapes that we experience in that painting is wholly literal, there is none that we are tempted to call merely depicted. There *are* shapes that lie entirely inside the picture limits—that do not make contact with those limits—just as there are others that partly coincide with the edge of the support. But neither enjoys precedence over the other—in particular, neither sponsors nor guarantees the other's efficacy as shape—any more than either the depicted or the literal limits of a shape that partly coincides with the edge of the support is experienced as more fundamental to that shape's efficacy than the other. Both types of shape succeed or fail on exactly the same grounds—grounds that do not concern the relation of a given shape to the shape of the support seen in its entirety. Each, one might say, is implicated in the other's failure and strengthened by the other's success. But the failure and success of individual shapes cannot be understood in terms of the distinction between depicted and literal shape with which I have been working until now.

The relation between depicted and literal shape that holds in the stripe paintings no longer holds in these, not because the relation has been altered or defied but because the distinction is defeated by the paintings themselves. Nothing, apparently, is more central to their conception than the desire to establish all shapes on an equal footing—to make pictures that comprise nothing but individual shapes, each of which is felt to stand or fall without reference, or appeal, to a single master shape, the support seen as a single entity. In fact, because in most of the new pictures the physical limits of the support are not perceived as constituting a single shape, there is even a sense in which—despite the nonrectangularity of their supports—the pictures in question are *not shaped:* if being shaped implies having an *enclosing* shape, the term is less applicable to Stella's nonrectangular pictures than, for example, to Olitski's rectangular ones. (In this same sense the physical limits of the support can be

417

said not to constitute a *framing* edge.) It should be remarked, however, that Stella could not have made paintings of which this is true except by using irregular supports—that is, by avoiding not only the rectangle but geometrically regular figures of any kind—in order to prevent the eye from instantly perceiving the shape of the support as a single entity. Moreover, the fact that in perhaps the three most successful subseries of the new paintings—the *Union, Effingham,* and *Wolfeboro* pictures—Stella has not used regular geometric shapes at all seems to me to have something to do with their success. In certain other of the new paintings, the eye pounces on a shape of this kind and only then takes in the rest of the painting. When this happens, the rest of the painting is put under enormous pressure by the geometrically regular shape to match its own sheer perspicuousness—which, inevitably, it cannot do. In other words, regularity of shape seems to be enough in itself to disturb the parity among shapes on which the success of Stella's new pictures seems largely to depend. In *Moultonboro III*—as in the *Chocorua* and *Tuftonboro* paintings mentioned earlier—the desire for parity manifests itself in the implied juxtaposition of two equally regular and hence equally perspicuous shapes (i.e., a triangle and a rectangle). But in each painting the two shapes compete for one's attention, almost as though they were juxtaposed to one another within a larger conventional painting—with the result that one tends to pull back, to distance the pictures in question and, as it were, to surround each of them with an imaginary rectangular frame large enough to contain the painting and some space around it besides, whereas in the *Union, Effingham,* and *Wolfeboro* paintings there is no competition for one's attention. None of the elements they comprise is in any way perspicuous, or even particularly interesting in itself; one does not, so to speak, *recognize* any of them—except perhaps the trapezoid at the bottom of *Wolfeboro* (and then, as we shall see, it is an open question what one recognizes it *as*). And far from being inclined to distance or frame these pictures, I for one feel strongly that—more than any pictures I have ever seen—they ought not to be framed at all.

Moreover, the fact that the physical limits of the support do not make themselves felt as a single entity but, in effect, belong segment by segment to individual shapes the remainder of whose limits do not coincide with those of the support implies a strong and, I think, unprecedented continuity between the "outside" of a given painting (its physical limits) and its "inside" (everything else). The eight-inch-wide colored bands deployed throughout the new paintings are a kind of paradigm for this continuity. In general one such band begins by running along at least one side of the support—in *Union III* the same band runs along four or five sides—until, at some point or other, it encounters another shape whose "merely" depicted portion it follows into the heart of the canvas, taking the beholder with it. That is, a particular stretch of the edge

418

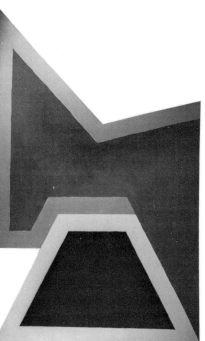

Frank Stella: *Effingham III*. 1966.
128″ x 132″.
Collection of Ferus Gallery, Los Angeles.
Photograph courtesy of
Leo Castelli Gallery, New York.

Frank Stella: *Wolfeboro III*. 1966.
160″ x 100″.
Collection of Ferus Gallery, Los Angeles.
Photograph courtesy of
Leo Castelli Gallery, New York.

of the painting is, in effect, first isolated from the rest of that edge—the band, as it were, broadens and usurps the office of the edge—and is then carried into the interior of the painting. The result is both that the paintings are infused with an extraordinary and compelling directionality, and that one is made to feel that the important difference in them is not between "inside" and "outside" but between *open* and *closed*. The side or sides along which the bands run are experienced as closed (or closed *off*) while the others are felt as open—and when, as in *Union III* and *Effingham III*, the open side or sides are at the top of the painting, the effect can be one of an astonishing vertical acceleration, or soaring, or release. There is, one might say, no more "outside" or "inside" to the best of Stella's new paintings than to the individual shapes they comprise; and to the extent that a given shape can be said to have an "outside" and "inside" the relation between the two is closer to that, say, between the edge of a tabletop and the rest of that tabletop than to the relation between the edge of a Noland or an Olitski or even a Stella stripe painting and the rest of that painting. This is not to say that Stella's new pictures are *nothing more* than objects. Unlike Judd's constructions, for example, or Bell's glass boxes, they

419

Michael Fried

do not isolate and hypostatize literalness as such. At the same time, however, literalness in them is no longer experienced as the exclusive property of the support. Rather, it is suffused more generally and, as it were, more *deeply* throughout them. It is as though literalness in these pictures does not belong to the support *at all* except by coincidence—specifically, the coincidence between the limits of the individual shapes that constitute a given painting and the physical limits of the support; as though, that is, one's experience of literalness is above all an experience of the literalness of the *individual shapes themselves.* Though of course what I have just called their literalness is identical with their success as shapes—and *that,* while not a direct function of the literalness of the support, is at any rate inconceivable apart from that literalness.

The dissociation of literalness from the support that I have just tried to describe is intimately related to another aspect of Stella's new paintings, namely, their extraordinary, and sheerly visual, illusiveness. This is not to say that, in a given picture, each shape seems to lie in a definite or specifiable depth relation to every other. On the contrary, nothing is more fundamental to the nature of the new paintings' illusiveness than the extreme ambiguity, indeterminacy, and multivalence of the relations that appear to obtain among the individual shapes, as well as between those shapes and the surface of the picture (or, at any rate, the *plane* of that surface). In *Moultonboro III*, for example, although one is not made to feel that the light yellow triangular band stands in any single or definite spatial relation to the turquoise blue Z-shaped band into which it fits, one nevertheless experiences their juxtaposition somewhat as though both were objects in the world, not simply or even chiefly shapes on a flat surface— objects, moreover, whose relation to one another, and indeed whose actual character, are ineluctably ambiguous. This is most salient in the case of the Z-shaped turquoise band, largely because—or so it seems—its top and bottom segments are not parallel to one another. (The first, running as it does along the upper edge of the square, is horizontal, while the second, flush with the lowest side of the triangle, slants from the lower left toward the upper right.) That is, one tends to see the bottom segment, or the bottom two segments, as though somewhat from above and in perspective—while at the same time one is not given enough data to locate them in a definite spatial context, in relation either to contiguous shapes or to some ground plane. Moreover, because the top segment of the Z-form runs across the upper edge of the square and is therefore horizontal, one tends to experience that segment as frontal. But this would mean that the Z-form is not only irregular in two dimensions but bent or warped in three—though it is not at all clear which segment or segments are bent or warped and which, if any, are to be taken as normative. The beveled ends of the Z-form, each parallel to nothing else in the painting, compound the ambiguity by implying that the respective planes of both the bottom and top

420

segments are warped away from, or are oblique to, that of the picture-surface—though, of course, they might *not* be. (Almost all the bands in Stella's new paintings are beveled in this way—a factor that adds immeasurably to the illusionistic power, and general complexity, of the paintings in question. In fact its absence from *Conway III* is partly responsible for the relatively flat and conventional appearance of that picture.) The result is that the Z-form is seen as participating in a wide range of equally ambiguous and indeterminate spatial situations—more accurately, an entire gamut of such situations each of which is simultaneously not merely compatible with but continuous with or transparent to every other. But it is not just the situations in which the Z-form finds itself or the relationships into which it enters that continually escape one but—more than anything else—its "real" shape. (Similarly, when one "recognizes" the shape at the bottom of *Wolfeboro III*, does one recognize it as a trapezoid—its configuration on the surface of the canvas—or as a rectangle seen in perspective?) It is as though across the entire gamut of illusionistic possibilities the "real" Z-form—flat or warped, regular or irregular, partly or wholly parallel or oblique to the picture-surface—lies somewhere out there, beyond the painting, waiting to be known. There is, of course, a "real" Z-form on the surface of the canvas. But the configuration on that surface of the individual shapes that constitute a given picture is no more definitive in this regard than their possible configurations in illusionistic space: above all because, as I have claimed, literalness in these paintings is primarily experienced as the property, not of the support, but of the shapes themselves. All this makes Stella's new paintings as radically illusive and intractably ambiguous as any in the history of Modernism. Radically illusive in that what is rendered illusive in them is nothing less than literalness itself; and intractably ambiguous in that the shapes they comprise are experienced as embracing an entire gamut of existential possibilities—including their juxtaposition on the surface of the canvas—each of which is simultaneously continuous with every other, and none of which is sufficiently privileged to make one feel that it, at any rate, is really *there*. There is, one might say, no *it* at all.

Stella's new paintings, then, depart from his stripe paintings in two general respects—first, by not acknowledging literal shape, and second, by resorting to illusion—both of which ought to make them unpalatable to literalist sensibility. And indeed I want to suggest that it is one of the most significant facts about his new pictures that Stella seeks in them to repudiate—not literalist taste or sensibility exactly—but the literalist implications which, in the grip of a particular conception of the nature of Modernist painting, his stripe paintings appear to carry. This is not to claim that his new pictures are chiefly a response to the drawing of those implications by others—Judd, for example. Rather, I am suggesting that it was in *his own* unwillingness, even inability, to pursue

421

beyond painting what were *to him as well*—if not indeed before anyone—
his stripe paintings' apparent implications in that direction that Stella discovered both the depth of his commitment to the enterprise of painting, and
the irreconcilability with that commitment of what may be called a reductionist
conception of the nature of that enterprise.[11] At the same time it is hard not
to see their relation to Noland's and Olitski's paintings as issuing, at least in
part, from a dissatisfaction, or anyway an uneasiness, with their work that—
to my mind, at any rate—has much in common with that which literalist sensibility appears to feel. Moreover, it is tempting to regard this in turn as evidence in favor of the suggestion that the impulse behind the work of literalists
like Judd and Bell is anything but alien to Stella. Because if it is true that, unlike
Noland and Olitski, Stella has actually *felt* a reductionist conception of his
undertaking urge toward the isolation and hypostatization of literalness, it
would be surprising if there were not at least some agreement between his response to painting other than his own and the literalist attitude toward that
same painting. And in fact Stella's new paintings can, I believe, be seen as
responding critically to the same aspect of Noland's and Olitski's paintings
that, I suggested earlier, literalist taste finds unacceptable, though here again
the differences between Stella and the literalists lie deeper than their apparent
agreement. From a literalist point of view the aspect in question is experienced
as a conflict between pictorial illusion of any kind on the one hand and literalness as such on the other; this conflict is unacceptable because it compromises
the latter; and its elimination entails making works of art (or putative works of
art) that are nothing but literal—works in which illusion, to the extent that it
may be said to exist at all, is itself literal. Whereas Stella's new paintings, by

---

[11] I take a reductionist conception of Modernist painting to mean this: that painting roughly since
Manet is seen as a kind of cognitive enterprise in which a certain quality (e.g., literalness), set of norms
(e.g., flatness and the delimiting of flatness) or core of problems (e.g., how to acknowledge the literal
character of the support) is progressively revealed as constituting the *essence* of painting—and, by
implication, of having done so all along. This seems to me gravely mistaken, not on the grounds that
Modernist painting is *not* a cognitive enterprise, but because it radically misconstrues the *kind* of
cognitive enterprise Modernist painting is. What the Modernist painter can be said to discover in his
work—what can be said to be revealed to him in it—is not the irreducible essence of *all* painting,
but rather that which, at the present moment in painting's history, is capable of convincing him that
it can stand comparison with the painting of both the Modernist and pre-Modernist past whose quality
seems to him beyond question. (In this sense one might say that Modernist painting discovers the
essence of all painting to be *quality*.) The object of his enterprise is therefore *both* knowledge and
conviction—knowledge *through*, or better still, *in*, conviction. And this knowledge is simultaneously
knowledge of *painting* (i.e., what it must be in order to elicit conviction) and of *himself* (i.e., what
he finds himself convinced by)—apprehended not as two distinct entities, but in a single, inextricable
fruition. It should be clear that the conception of Modernist painting that I have just adumbrated is
not only anti-reductionist, but anti-positivist; in this respect I believe it has significant affinities with
the persuasive account of the enterprise of science put forward by Thomas S. Kuhn in *The Structure
of Scientific Revolutions* (Chicago: University of Chicago Press, 1962). The further exploration of
these affinities would, I am sure, prove rewarding. But a footnote is not the best place to begin.

making literalness illusive, not only come to grips with but actually resolve what I characterized earlier as the conflict in Noland's and Olitski's paintings between a particular kind of pictorial illusionism—i.e., addressed to eyesight alone—and the literal character of the support. And by so doing they unmake —at least in the event and for the moment—the distinction between shape as a fundamental property of objects and shape as an entity belonging to painting alone that emerges for the first time in Noland's and Olitski's paintings.

IV

In closing I want merely to touch on another aspect of Stella's new paintings—namely, what seems to me their intimate and profoundly significant relation to the finest Modernist *sculpture* of the recent past. (I am thinking chiefly of the work of English sculptor Anthony Caro.) Almost any of the remarks and observations I have made about the new pictures could, I think, lead to an obvious comparison with Caro's sculptures: what, for example, do pieces like *Bennington* and *Yellow Swing* do if not make literalness illusive? Moreover, the relation between Stella and contemporary sculpture is far from superficial or coincidental. Rather, it has to do with the problematic character

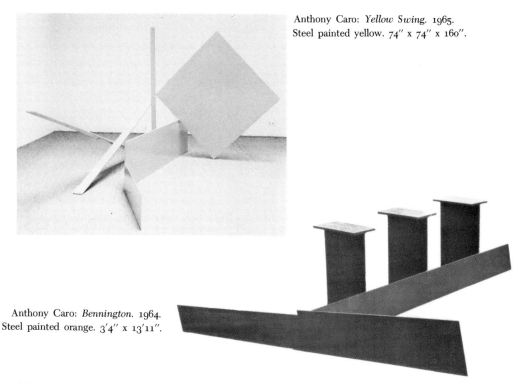

Anthony Caro: *Yellow Swing*. 1965.
Steel painted yellow. 74″ x 74″ x 160″.

Anthony Caro: *Bennington*. 1964.
Steel painted orange. 3′4″ x 13′11″.

423

of shape in the most advanced painting of our time—even, I want to say, with the nature of shape itself, with what shape is. In any case, I am suggesting that one result of the development within Modernist painting discussed in these notes is that for the first time since the late eighteenth century sculpure is in a position to inspire painting; and that in Stella's recent paintings this has actually begun to happen. At the same time, however, painting is in a position not simply to be inspired by advanced sculpture, but in certain respects fundamental to that sculpture actually to have an advantage—though not of quality—over it. I will mention three: (1) The intractable ambiguity of the visual illusionism in Stella's new pictures goes beyond advanced sculpture in the direction of the opticality and illusiveness—of seeming a kind of mirage—that, as Greenberg was the first to remark, is basic to it.[12] Because sculpture is literal it can, in the end, be *known;* whereas the shapes that constitute Stella's new paintings, and the new paintings as experienced wholes, cannot. (2) The fact, or the convention, that paintings hang on a wall means that Stella's new paintings *begin off the ground;* whereas advanced sculpture—which, as Greenberg has again remarked, is illusively weightless—has to begin at ground level and literally *climb* to whatever height it reaches. This "advantage" is perhaps most strikingly evident in *Effingham III,* largely because that painting as a whole is most like a *ground* plan. *Union III,* as well, profits from it immensely. And in general Stella can float or suspend elements as though without visible means of support. (3) There is no *general* difficulty about the use of color in Stella's paintings; but the problem of color in contemporary sculpture is in important respects acute. And by this I mean not simply the propriety of *applied* color but the fact that all sculpture—like all solid, opaque objects—*is* colored, or *has* color, or anyway has *surface.* It is as though, finally, the opticality toward which advanced sculpture aspires brings one up short, not against its literalness exactly, but against the fact that when we perceive a solid object eyesight makes contact with no more than its surface (and then only part of that). That is to say, advanced sculpture, such as Caro's, makes this fact a disturbing one, and in effect thrusts it into our awareness. It makes us *note* it, whereas painting, one wants to say, in comparison with sculpture, is all *surface.*[13] (Which is not at all the same as saying that it is done on a flat and *very thin* surface; an element of equal thinness in a Caro is experienced as solid.) Stella's paintings, by the very closeness of their relation to advanced sculpture, make this difference more salient than it has ever been.

[12] See "The New Sculpture," *Art and Culture* (Boston, 1961), p. 144. I also want to call attention to Greenberg's essay on the sculpture of Anthony Caro in *Arts Yearbook,* No. 8 (1965). The relevance to Stella's paintings of many of Greenberg's observations about Caro's work seems to me striking.

[13] See Thompson Clarke's essay, "Seeing Surfaces and Physical Objects," in *Philosophy in America,* ed. Max Black (London, 1966). The fact that eyesight touches only the surface of solid objects, and then only part of that surface, has traditionally played an important role in philosophical skepticism.

Postscript

I wrote this essay in August and September, 1966. It was the first of four essays written between then and April, 1967, the last of which, "Art and Objecthood," builds explicitly on conclusions reached in "Shape as Form." In readying these pages for republication here, I have made various changes for the sake of clarity and form. However, I have let the argument stand as it was— not because I believe it to be correct in all particulars (for example, I would not now characterize Stella's undertaking as "therapeutic"; and Noland's paintings of 1965–66 are not seen to receive justice), but because if I had tried to fix everything that now seems to me to need fixing I would have ended up writing a new essay.

In closing I want to thank Stanley Cavell who read this essay in manuscript and made suggestions that I have used. I have also put to use remarks and observations made in my presence by Noland, Olitski, and Stella.

—Michael Fried
July, 1969

Biographical Data

JOSEF ALBERS

Born in Bottrop, Germany, 1888
Came to the United States, 1933
Lives in New Haven, Connecticut

Selected one-man exhibitions:
1936 New Art Circle, J. B. Neumann, New York City
1938 New Art Circle, J. B. Neumann
     Artists Gallery, New York City
1940 The San Francisco Museum of Art, San Francisco, California
1942 The Baltimore Museum of Art, Baltimore, Maryland
     Museum of New Mexico, Santa Fe, New Mexico
1944 Mint Museum of Art, Charlotte, North Carolina
1947 California Palace of the Legion of Honor, San Francisco, California
1949 Cincinnati Art Museum, Cincinnati, Ohio
     Museum of Fine Arts, Richmond, Virginia
     Yale University Art Gallery, New Haven, Connecticut
1950 J. B. Speed Art Museum, Louisville, Kentucky
1951 Contemporary Art Society, Sydney, Australia
1953 Wadsworth Atheneum, Hartford, Connecticut
     The San Francisco Museum of Art
1954 Honolulu Academy of Arts, Honolulu, Hawaii
1955 Hayden Gallery, Massachusetts Institute of Technology, Cambridge, Massachusetts
1956 Kunsthaus, Zurich, Switzerland
     Yale University Art Gallery
1957 Museum der Stadt Ulm, Ulm, Germany
     Karl-Ernst-Osthaus-Museum, Hagen, Germany
1958 Kunstverein, Münster, Germany
     Kunstverein, Freiburg, Germany
1959 Landesmuseum, Münster, Germany
     Museum am Ostwall, Dortmund, Germany
1961 Stedelijk Museum, Amsterdam, The Netherlands
1963 Mint Museum of Art
     Kunsthaus, Hamburg, Germany
     Museum Folkwang, Essen, Germany
1965 Dallas Museum of Fine Arts, Dallas, Texas
     The San Francisco Museum of Art
1965–67 The Museum of Modern Art, New York City (circulated in the United States, South America, and Mexico)
Sidney Janis Gallery, New York City, 1949, 1952, 1955, 1958, 1959, 1961, 1963, 1964, 1968

MILTON AVERY

Born in Altmar, New York, 1893
Died in New York City, 1965

Selected one-man exhibitions:
1928 Opportunity Gallery, New York City
1932 Gallery, 144 West 13th Street, New York City
1935 Valentine Gallery, New York City

429

1936 Valentine Gallery
1938 Valentine Gallery
1943 Phillips Gallery, Washington, D.C.
1944 Phillips Gallery
     Arts Club of Chicago, Chicago, Illinois
1946 Colorado Springs Fine Arts Center, Colorado Springs, Colorado
1947 Portland Art Museum, Portland, Oregon
1952 The Baltimore Museum of Art, Baltimore, Maryland
     Institute of Contemporary Art, Boston, Massachusetts
     Joe and Emily Lowe Gallery, Coral Gables, Florida
     Phillips Gallery
     Wadsworth Atheneum, Hartford, Connecticut
1956 Mills College, Oakland, California
     Houston Museum of Fine Arts, Houston, Texas
     Santa Barbara Museum of Art, Santa Barbara, California
     Art Gallery, University of Nebraska, Lincoln, Nebraska
1959 Art Alliance, Philadelphia, Pennsylvania
1960 The Whitney Museum of American Art, New York City (circulated in the United States)
1965–66 The Museum of Modern Art, New York City (circulated in the United States)
1966 Arkansas Art Center, Little Rock, Arkansas
     Art Gallery, University of Nebraska
1969 National Collection of Fine Arts, Smithsonian Institution, Washington, D.C.
Grace Borgenicht Gallery, New York City, 1951, 1952, 1954, 1956, 1957, 1958, 1959, 1960, 1963, 1964, 1968

ALEXANDER CALDER

Born in Philadelphia, Pennsylvania, 1898
Lives in Roxbury, Connecticut, and Saché, France

Selected one-man exhibitions:
1928 Weyhe Gallery, New York City
1934 Pierre Matisse Gallery, New York City
1938 George Walter Vincent Smith Art Museum, Springfield, Massachusetts
1940 Willard Gallery, New York City
1943 The Museum of Modern Art, New York City
1944 Buchholz Gallery, New York City (first of several)
1946 Galerie Louis Carré, Paris, France
1948 Ministry of Education, Rio de Janeiro, Brazil
     Museum of Art, São Paulo, Brazil
1949 Museum of Fine Arts, Richmond, Virginia
1950 Galerie Maeght, Paris, France (first of several)
     Hayden Gallery, Massachusetts Institute of Technology, Cambridge, Massachusetts
1953 The Walker Art Center, Minneapolis, Minnesota
1955 Museo de Arte, Caracas, Venezuela
1956 Perls Galleries, New York City (first of several)
     Galleria dell'Obelisco, Rome, Italy
     Galerie Weill, Paris, France
1959 Museu de Arte Moderno, Rio de Janeiro, Brazil
1962 Tate Gallery, London, England
     Musée des Beaux-Arts, Rennes, France

1964–65 The Solomon R. Guggenheim Museum, New York City
Milwaukee Art Center, Milwaukee, Wisconsin
Washington University Art Gallery, St. Louis, Missouri
Des Moines Art Center, Des Moines, Iowa
The National Gallery of Canada, Ottawa, Canada
Musée National d'Art Moderne, Paris, France
1967 Akademie der Kunst, Berlin, Germany
1968 Musée des Augustins, Toulouse, France
1969 Fondation Maeght, Saint Paul, France

JOHN CHAMBERLAIN

Born in Rochester, Indiana, 1927
Lives in New York City

One-man exhibitions:
1957 Wells Street Gallery, Chicago, Illinois
1958 Davida Gallery, Chicago, Illinois
1960 Martha Jackson Gallery, New York City
1962 Leo Castelli Gallery, New York City
Dilexi Gallery, Los Angeles, California
1964 Galerie Ileana Sonnabend, Paris, France
Pace Gallery, Boston, Massachusetts
Leo Castelli Gallery
1965 Leo Castelli Gallery
1966 Dwan Gallery, Los Angeles, California
1967 The Cleveland Museum of Art, Cleveland, Ohio
1968 Leo Castelli Gallery
Contemporary Arts Center, Cincinnati, Ohio
1969 Leo Castelli Warehouse, New York City

JOSEPH CORNELL

Born in Nyack, New York, 1903
Lives in Flushing, New York

One-man exhibitions:
1939 Julien Levy Gallery, New York City
1940 Julien Levy Gallery
1942 Wakefield Gallery, New York City
1946 Hugo Gallery, New York City
1948 Copley Galleries, Beverly Hills, California
1949 Egan Gallery, New York City
1950 Egan Gallery
1953 Egan Gallery
Allan Frumkin Gallery, Chicago, Illinois
1955 Stable Gallery, New York City
1956 Wittenborn, New York City
1957 Stable Gallery

431

1959 Bennington College, Bennington, Vermont
1962 Ferus Gallery, Los Angeles, California
1963 New York University Art Collection, Loeb Student Center, New York City
1965 The J. L. Hudson Gallery, Detroit, Michigan
1966 Robert Schoelkopf Gallery, New York City
1967 Pasadena Art Museum, Pasadena, California
The Solomon R. Guggenheim Museum, New York City

STUART DAVIS

Born in Philadelphia, Pennsylvania, 1894
Died in New York City, 1964

Selected one-man exhibitions:
1917 Sheridan Square Gallery, New York City
1918 Ardsley Gallery, Brooklyn, New York
1925 Newark Museum, Newark, New Jersey
1929 Whitney Studio Galleries, New York City
1941 Cincinnati Modern Art Society, Cincinnati, Ohio
Indiana University, Bloomington, Indiana
1945 The Museum of Modern Art, New York City
1946 The Baltimore Museum of Art, Baltimore, Maryland
1952 American Pavilion, XXVI Biennale, Venice, Italy
1957 The Walker Art Center, Minneapolis, Minnesota
Des Moines Art Center, Des Moines, Iowa
The San Francisco Museum of Art, San Francisco, California
The Whitney Museum of American Art, New York City
1965 National Collection of Fine Arts, Smithsonian Institution, Washington, D.C.
The Art Institute of Chicago, Chicago, Illinois
The Whitney Museum of American Art
Art Galleries of the University of California, Los Angeles, California
The Downtown Gallery, New York City, 1927, 1932, 1943, 1946, 1952, 1954, 1956, 1958, 1960, 1962,
1963

WILLEM DE KOONING

Born in Rotterdam, The Netherlands, 1904
Came to the United States, 1926
Lives in The Springs, Long Island

Selected one-man exhibitions:
1948 Egan Gallery, New York City
1951 Egan Gallery
1953 Sidney Janis Gallery, New York City
School of the Museum of Fine Arts, Boston, Massachusetts
Workshop Art Center, Washington, D.C.
1955 Martha Jackson Gallery, New York City
1956 Sidney Janis Gallery
1959 Sidney Janis Gallery
1961 Paul Kantor Gallery, Beverly Hills, California
1962 Sidney Janis Gallery
Alan Stone Gallery, New York City (with Barnett Newman)

1964 James Goodman Gallery, Buffalo, New York
     Alan Stone Gallery
1965 Smith College, Northampton, Massachusetts
1967 M. Knoedler & Company, Inc., New York City
1968 M. Knoedler & Cie., Inc., Paris, France
1968–69 Stedelijk Museum, Amsterdam, The Netherlands
     Tate Gallery, London, England
     The Museum of Modern Art, New York City
     The Art Institute of Chicago, Chicago, Illinois
     Los Angeles County Museum of Art, Los Angeles, California
1969 M. Knoedler & Company, Inc.

BURGOYNE DILLER

Born in New York City, 1906
Died in New York City, 1965

Selected one-man exhibitions:
1933 Contemporary Arts Gallery, New York City
1946 Pinacotheca Gallery, New York City
1949 Pinacotheca Gallery
1951 Rose Fried Gallery, New York City
1961 Galerie Chalette, New York City
1962 Galerie Chalette
1963 Galerie Chalette
1964 Galerie Chalette
1966 New Jersey State Museum, Trenton, New Jersey
1968 Noah Goldowsky Gallery, New York City
     Los Angeles County Museum of Art, Los Angeles, California

MARK DI SUVERO

Born in Shanghai, China, 1933
Came to the United States, 1941
Lives in New York City

One-man exhibitions:
1960 Green Gallery, New York City
1965 Dwan Gallery, Los Angeles, California
1966 Park Place Gallery, New York City
1968 Lo Giudice Gallery, Chicago, Illinois

DAN FLAVIN

Born in New York City, 1933
Lives in Cold Spring, New York

One-man exhibitions:
1961 Judson Gallery, New York City
1964 Kaymar Gallery, New York City
     Green Gallery, New York City
1965 Ohio State University, Columbus, Ohio

433

1966 Galerie Rudolf Zwirner, Cologne, Germany
Nicholas Wilder Gallery, Los Angeles, California
1967 Kornblee Gallery, New York City
1968 Museum of Contemporary Art, Chicago, Illinois
Galleria Sperone, Turin, Italy
Galerie Heiner Friedrich, Munich, Germany
1969 Konrad Fischer Gallery, Düsseldorf, Germany
Irving Blum Gallery, Los Angeles, California
The National Gallery of Canada, Ottawa, Canada

HELEN FRANKENTHALER

Born in New York City, 1928
Lives in New York City

One-man exhibitions:
1951–58 Tibor de Nagy Gallery, New York City
1959 André Emmerich Gallery, New York City
1960 The Jewish Museum, New York City
André Emmerich Gallery
1961 Everett Ellin Gallery, Los Angeles, California
André Emmerich Gallery
Galerie Lawrence, Paris, France
1962 André Emmerich Gallery
Bennington College, Bennington, Vermont
Galleria dell'Ariete, Milan, Italy
1963 André Emmerich Gallery
Galerie Lawrence
1964 Kasmin Ltd., London, England
1965 André Emmerich Gallery
The David Mirvish Gallery, Toronto, Canada
1966 André Emmerich Gallery
1968 André Emmerich Gallery
1969 The Whitney Museum of American Art, New York City
Whitechapel Gallery, London, England

ARSHILE GORKY

Born in Khorkom Vari Haiyotz, Armenia, 1904
Came to the United States, 1920
Died in Sherman, Connecticut, 1948

Selected one-man exhibitions:
1934 Mellon Galleries, Philadelphia, Pennsylvania
1938 Boyer Galleries, New York City
1941 The San Francisco Museum of Art, San Francisco, California
1945 Julien Levy Gallery, New York City
1946 Julien Levy Gallery
1947 Julien Levy Gallery
1948 Julien Levy Gallery
1951 The Whitney Museum of American Art, New York City
The Walker Art Center, Minneapolis, Minnesota
The San Francisco Museum of Art

1952 The Art Museum, Princeton University, Princeton, New Jersey
1962 The Museum of Modern Art, New York City
      Washington Gallery of Modern Art, Washington, D.C.

ADOLPH GOTTLIEB

Born in New York City, 1903
Lives in New York City

One-man exhibitions:
1930 Dudensing Galleries, New York City
1934 Uptown Gallery, New York City
      Theodore A. Kohn & Son, New York City
1940 Artists Gallery, New York City
1942 Artists Gallery
1944 Wakefield Gallery, New York City
1945 Gallery 67, New York City
      Nierendorf Galleries, New York City
1947 Kootz Gallery, New York City
      Kootz Gallery
1949 Jacques Seligmann Galleries, New York City
1950 Kootz Gallery
1951 Kootz Gallery
1952 Kootz Gallery
1953 Kootz Gallery
      Area Arts, San Francisco, California
1954 Kootz Gallery
      Bennington College, Bennington, Vermont
      Lawrence Art Museum, Williams College, Williamstown, Massachusetts
      Kootz Gallery, Provincetown, Massachusetts
1957 Martha Jackson Gallery, New York City
      HCE Gallery, Provincetown, Massachusetts
      The Jewish Museum, New York City
1958 André Emmerich Gallery, New York City
1959 André Emmerich Gallery
      Galerie Rive Droite, Paris, France
      Institute of Contemporary Arts, London, England
      Paul Kantor Gallery, Beverly Hills, California
1960 French and Company, New York City
      Sidney Janis Gallery, New York City
1961 Galleria dell'Ariete, Milan, Italy
      Galerie Handschin, Basel, Switzerland
1962 Sidney Janis Gallery
1963 The Walker Art Center, Minneapolis, Minnesota,
      American Section of VII Bienal de São Paulo, São Paulo, Brazil
1964 Marlborough-Gerson Gallery, New York City
1966 Marlborough-Gerson Gallery
      Hayden Gallery, Massachusetts Institute of Technology, Cambridge, Massachusetts
1967 Arts Club of Chicago, Chicago, Illinois
1968 The Whitney Museum of American Art, New York City
      The Solomon R. Guggenheim Museum, New York City
      The Corcoran Gallery of Art, Washington, D.C.
      Rose Art Museum, Brandeis University, Waltham, Massachusetts

PHILIP GUSTON

Born in Montreal, Canada, 1913
Came to the United States, 1919
Lives in Woodstock, New York

One-man exhibitions:
1944 University of Iowa, Iowa City, Iowa
1945 Midtown Galleries, New York City
1947 School of the Museum of Fine Arts, Boston, Massachusetts
     Munson-Williams-Proctor Institute, Utica, New York
1950 University of Minnesota, Minneapolis, Minnesota
1952 Peridot Gallery, New York City
1953 Egan Gallery, New York City
1956 Sidney Janis Gallery, New York City
1958 Sidney Janis Gallery
1959 V Bienal, São Paulo, Brazil
1960 XXX Biennale, Venice, Italy
     Sidney Janis Gallery
1961 Sidney Janis Gallery
1962 The Solomon R. Guggenheim Museum, New York City
     Stedelijk Museum, Amsterdam, The Netherlands
     Musée des Beaux-Arts, Brussels, Belgium
1963 Whitechapel Gallery, London, England
     Los Angeles County Museum of Art, Los Angeles, California
1966 The Jewish Museum, New York City

HANS HOFMANN

Born in Weissenburg, Bavaria, Germany, 1880
Came to the United States, 1933
Died in New York City, 1966

Selected one-man exhibitions:
1931 California Palace of the Legion of Honor, San Francisco, California
1941 Isaac Delgado Museum of Art, New Orleans, Louisiana
1944 Art of This Century, New York City
     Arts Club of Chicago, Chicago, Illinois
1946 Mortimer Brandt Gallery, New York City
1947 Betty Parsons Gallery, New York City
1948 Addison Gallery of American Art, Andover, Massachusetts
1949 Galerie Maeght, Paris, France
1954 The Baltimore Museum of Art, Baltimore, Maryland
1955 Bennington College, Bennington, Vermont
1956 Art Alliance, Philadelphia, Pennsylvania
     Rutgers University, New Brunswick, New Jersey
1957 The Whitney Museum of American Art, New York City
1958 Des Moines Art Center, Des Moines, Iowa
     The San Francisco Museum of Art, San Francisco, California
     Art Galleries of the University of California, Los Angeles, California
     Seattle Art Museum, Seattle, Washington
     The Walker Art Center, Minneapolis, Minnesota
     Munson-Williams-Proctor Institute, Utica, New York
     The Baltimore Museum of Art

1962 Frankische Galerie am Marientor, Nuremberg, Germany
Kölnischer Kunstverein, Cologne, Germany
Kongresshalle, Berlin, Germany
1963 Santa Barbara Museum of Art, Santa Barbara, California
The Museum of Modern Art, New York City
1964 Worth Ryder Art Gallery, University of California, Berkeley, California
1966 Stanford Art Museum, Stanford University, Stanford, California
1969 Everson Museum of Art, Syracuse, New York
Between 1947 and 1966 he showed annually or biannually with Kootz Gallery, New York City

EDWARD HOPPER

Born in Nyack, New York, 1882
Died in New York City, 1967

Selected one-man exhibitions:
1933 The Museum of Modern Art, New York City
1934 Arts Club of Chicago, Chicago, Illinois
1937 Carnegie Institute, Pittsburgh, Pennsylvania
1950 The Whitney Museum of American Art, New York City
Museum of Fine Arts, Boston, Massachusetts
The Detroit Institute of Arts, Detroit, Michigan
1959 Rhode Island School of Design, Providence, Rhode Island
1960 Wadsworth Atheneum, Hartford, Connecticut
1962 Philadelphia Museum of Art, Philadelphia, Pennsylvania
Worcester Art Museum, Worcester, Massachusetts
1963 University of Arizona Art Gallery, Tucson, Arizona
1964 Munson-Williams-Proctor Institute, Utica, New York
The Whitney Museum of American Art
1965 The Art Institute of Chicago, Chicago, Illinois
The Detroit Institute of Arts
City Art Museum of St. Louis, St. Louis, Missouri

JASPER JOHNS

Born in Augusta, Georgia, 1930
Lives in New York City

One-man exhibitions:
1958 Leo Castelli Gallery, New York City
1959 Galleria d'Arte del Naviglio, Milan, Italy
Galerie Rive Droite, Paris, France
1960 Tweed Gallery, Minneapolis, Minnesota
Columbia Museum of Art, Columbia, South Carolina
Leo Castelli Gallery
1961 Galerie Rive Droite
Leo Castelli Gallery
1962 Galerie Ileana Sonnabend, Paris, France
Everett Ellin Gallery, Los Angeles, California
1963 Leo Castelli Gallery
1964 Whitechapel Gallery, London, England
The Jewish Museum, New York City
1965 Pasadena Art Museum, Pasadena, California

437

1965 Ashmolean Museum, Oxford, England
American Embassy, London, England
Minami Gallery, Tokyo, Japan
1966 Leo Castelli Gallery
National Collection of Fine Arts, Smithsonian Institution, Washington, D.C. (drawings)
1968 Leo Castelli Gallery
The Museum of Modern Art, New York City (circulating exhibition, lithographs)
Galerie Buren, Stockholm, Sweden
1969 Castelli-Whitney, New York City
David Whitney Gallery, New York City
Castelli Graphics, New York City

DONALD JUDD

Born in Excelsior Springs, Missouri, 1928
Lives in New York City

One-man exhibitions:
1964 Green Gallery, New York City
1966 Leo Castelli Gallery, New York City
1968 The Whitney Museum of American Art, New York City
Irving Blum Gallery, Los Angeles, California
1969 Leo Castelli Gallery
Galerie Ileana Sonnabend, Paris, France
Galerie Rudolf Zwirner, Cologne, Germany

ELLSWORTH KELLY

Born in Newburgh, New York, 1923
Lives in New York City

One-man exhibitions:
1951 Galerie Arnaud, Paris, France
1956 Betty Parsons Gallery, New York City
1957 Betty Parsons Gallery
1958 Galerie Maeght, Paris, France
1959 Betty Parsons Gallery
1961 Betty Parsons Gallery
1962 Tooth Gallery, London, England
1963 Betty Parsons Gallery
Gallery of Modern Art, Washington, D.C.
1964 Galerie Maeght
Institute of Contemporary Art, Boston, Massachusetts
1965 Sidney Janis Gallery, New York City
Ferus Gallery, Los Angeles, California
Galerie Maeght
Knull International, Düsseldorf, Germany
1967 Sidney Janis Gallery
Irving Blum Gallery, Los Angeles, California
1968 Sidney Janis Gallery
Irving Blum Gallery

438

FRANZ KLINE

Born in Wilkes-Barre, Pennsylvania, 1910
Died in New York City, 1962

Selected one-man exhibitions:
1950 Egan Gallery, New York City
1951 Egan Gallery
1952 Margaret Brown Gallery, Boston, Massachusetts
1954 Institute of Design, Chicago, Illinois
     Allan Frumkin Gallery, Chicago, Illinois
     Egan Gallery
1956 Sidney Janis Gallery, New York City
1958 Galleria La Tartaruga, Rome, Italy
     Galleria d'Arte del Naviglio, Milan, Italy
     Sidney Janis Gallery
1960 Sidney Janis Gallery
1961 Sidney Janis Gallery
     Collector's Gallery, New York City
     New Arts Gallery, Atlanta, Georgia
     Arts Club of Chicago, Chicago, Illinois
1962 Gallery of Modern Art, Washington, D.C.
     Rose Art Museum, Brandeis University, Waltham, Massachusetts
     The Baltimore Museum of Art, Baltimore, Maryland
1968 The Whitney Museum of American Art, New York City
1969 Dallas Museum of Fine Arts, Dallas, Texas
     The San Francisco Museum of Art, San Francisco, California
     Museum of Contemporary Art, Chicago, Illinois

GABE KOHN

Born in Philadelphia, Pennsylvania, 1910
Lives in Los Angeles, California

Selected one-man exhibitions:
1948 Atelier Mannuci, Rome, Italy
1950 Galleria dello Zodiaco, Rome, Italy
1958 Tanager Gallery, New York City
1959 Leo Castelli Gallery, New York City
1961 Otto Gerson Gallery, New York City
1963 David Stuart Galleries, Los Angeles, California
     La Jolla Museum of Art, La Jolla, California
1966 David Stuart Galleries

ROY LICHTENSTEIN

Born in New York City, 1923
Lives in New York City

One-man exhibitions:
1951 Carlebach Gallery, New York City
1952 John Heller Gallery, New York City
1953 John Heller Gallery

439

1954 John Heller Gallery
1957 John Heller Gallery
1962 Leo Castelli Gallery, New York City
1963 Ferus Gallery, Los Angeles, California
     Galerie Ileana Sonnabend, Paris, France
     Leo Castelli Gallery
1964 Il Punto, Turin, Italy
     Leo Castelli Gallery
     Ferus Gallery
1965 Galerie Ileana Sonnabend
     Leo Castelli Gallery
1966 The Cleveland Museum of Art, Cleveland, Ohio
1967 Pasadena Art Museum, Pasadena, California
     The Walker Art Center, Minneapolis, Minnesota
     Leo Castelli Galley
     Contemporary Arts Center, Cincinnati, Ohio
     Stedelijk Museum, Amsterdam, The Netherlands
1968 Tate Gallery, London, England
     Kunsthalle, Bern, Switzerland
     Kestner-Gesellschaft, Hannover, Germany
     Irving Blum Gallery, Los Angeles, California
1969 Irving Blum Gallery

MORRIS LOUIS

Born in Baltimore, Maryland, 1912
Died in Washington, D.C., 1962

One-man exhibitions:
1957 Martha Jackson Gallery, New York City
1959 French and Company, New York City
1960 French and Company
     Institute of Contemporary Arts, London, England
     Galleria dell'Ariete, Milan, Italy
     Galerie Lawrence, Paris, France
     Bennington College, Bennington, Vermont
1961 Galerie Neufville, Paris, France
     André Emmerich Gallery, New York City
1962 Galerie Schmela, Düsseldorf, Germany
     Galerie Müller, Stuttgart, Germany
     Galerie Lawrence
     André Emmerich Gallery
1963 Kasmin Ltd., London, England
     The Solomon R. Guggenheim Museum, New York City
1964 Galerie Renée Ziegler, Zurich, Switzerland
     André Emmerich Gallery
1965 Staatliche Kunsthalle, Baden, Germany
     André Emmerich Gallery
1966 Washington Gallery of Modern Art, Washington, D.C.
     André Emmerich Gallery
1967 The Cleveland Museum of Art, Cleveland, Ohio
     Seattle Art Museum, Seattle, Washington
     Los Angeles County Museum of Art, Los Angeles, California
     Museum of Fine Arts, Boston, Massachusetts

1967 City Art Museum of St. Louis, St. Louis, Missouri
   André Emmerich Gallery
1968 André Emmerich Gallery
1969 André Emmerich Gallery
   Lawrence Rubin Gallery, New York City

ROBERT MORRIS

Born in Kansas City, Missouri, 1931
Lives in New York City

One-man exhibitions:
1957 Dilexi Gallery, San Francisco, California
1958 Dilexi Gallery
1963 Green Gallery, New York City
1964 Galerie Schmela, Düsseldorf, Germany
   Green Gallery
1965 Green Gallery
1966 Dwan Gallery, Los Angeles, California
1967 Leo Castelli Gallery, New York City
1968 Stedelijk van Abbemuseum, Eindhoven, The Netherlands
   Galerie Ileana Sonnabend, Paris, France (spring)
   Galerie Ileana Sonnabend (fall)
   Leo Castelli Gallery
1969 Leo Castelli Gallery
   Galleria Enzo Sperone, Turin, Italy
   Irving Blum Gallery, Los Angeles, California

ROBERT MOTHERWELL

Born in Aberdeen, Washington, 1915
Lives in New York City

Selected one-man exhibitions:
1944 Art of This Century, New York City
1946 Kootz Gallery, New York City
   The San Francisco Museum of Art, San Francisco, California
   Arts Club of Chicago, Chicago, Illinois
1949 Kootz Gallery
1952 Kootz Gallery
1953 Allen Memorial Art Museum, Oberlin College, Oberlin, Ohio
1957 Sidney Janis Gallery, New York City
1959 Bennington College, Bennington, Vermont
   Sidney Janis Gallery
1961 Sidney Janis Gallery
   Galerie Berggruen, Paris, France
1962 Pasadena Art Museum, Pasadena, California
   Galleria Odyssia, Rome, Italy
   Galerie del Spiegel, Cologne, Germany
1963 Smith College, Northampton, Massachusetts
   Hayden Gallery, Massachusetts Institute of Technology, Cambridge, Massachusetts
1965 Phillips Gallery, Washington, D.C.
   The Museum of Modern Art, New York City

441

1966 Contemporary Art Museum, Houston, Texas
     The Baltimore Museum of Art, Baltimore, Maryland
     Stedelijk Museum, Amsterdam, The Netherlands
     Whitechapel Gallery, London, England
     Volkswang Museum, Essen, Germany
     Civic Museum, Turin, Italy
1967 The San Francisco Museum of Art
1968 The Whitney Museum of American Art, New York City
1969 Marlborough-Gerson Gallery, New York City
     Virginia Museum of Art, Richmond, Virginia
     Marlborough Galleria d'Arte, Rome, Italy

BARNETT NEWMAN

Born in New York City, 1905
Lives in New York City

One-man exhibitions:
1950 Betty Parsons Gallery, New York City
1951 Betty Parsons Gallery
1958 Bennington College, Bennington, Vermont
1959 French and Company, New York City
1962 Alan Stone Gallery, New York City (with Willem de Kooning)
1965 Nicholas Wilder Gallery, Los Angeles, California
1966 The Solomon R. Guggenheim Museum, New York City
1969 M. Knoedler & Company, Inc., New York City

ISAMU NOGUCHI

Born in Los Angeles, California, 1904
Lives in Long Island City, New York

One-man exhibitions:
1929 Eugene Schoen Gallery, New York City
1930 Marie Sterner Gallery, New York City
     Harvard Society for Contemporary Art, Cambridge, Massachusetts
     Arts Club of Chicago, Chicago, Illinois
1931 Albright Art Gallery, Buffalo, New York
     Rochester Memorial Art Gallery, Rochester, New York
     Becker Gallery, New York City
1932 Becker Gallery
     Demotte Gallery, New York City
     Reinhardt Galleries, New York City
1933 Mellon Galleries, Philadelphia, Pennsylvania
1934 Honolulu Academy of Arts, Honolulu, Hawaii
     Sidney Burney Gallery, London, England
     Western Association of Art Museum Directors touring show
1935 Marie Harriman Gallery, New York City
1939 Honolulu Academy of Arts
1942 The San Francisco Museum of Art, San Francisco, California
1948 Egan Gallery, New York City
1951 Mitsukoshi Department Store, Tokyo, Japan
1952 Kamakura Modern Museum, Kamakura, Japan

1953 Stable Gallery, New York City
1955 Stable Gallery
1959 Stable Gallery
1961 Daniel Cordier & Michel Warren Galleries, New York City
Fort Worth Art Center, Fort Worth, Texas
1963 Cordier & Ekstrom, Inc., New York City
1964 Claude Bernard Gallery, Paris, France
1965 Cordier & Ekstrom, Inc.
1967 Cordier & Ekstrom, Inc.
1968 The Whitney Museum of American Art, New York City
Cordier & Ekstrom, Inc.

KENNETH NOLAND

Born in Asheville, North Carolina, 1924
Lives in New York City

One-man exhibitions:
1956 Tibor de Nagy Gallery, New York City
1958 Tibor de Nagy Gallery
1959 French and Company, New York City
1960 Galleria dell'Ariete, Milan, Italy
André Emmerich Gallery, New York City
Galerie Lawrence, Paris, France
1961 Bennington College, Bennington, Vermont
Galerie Neufville, Paris, France
André Emmerich Gallery
1962 Galerie Schmela, Düsseldorf, Germany
Galerie Charles Lienhard, Zurich, Switzerland
André Emmerich Gallery
1963 Galerie Lawrence
Kasmin Ltd., London, England
André Emmerich Gallery
1964 Galerie Schmela
The Jewish Museum, New York City
1965 Kasmin Ltd.
The David Mirvish Gallery, Toronto, Canada
1966 André Emmerich Gallery
1967 André Emmerich Gallery
1968 The David Mirvish Gallery
Kasmin Ltd.
1969 Lawrence Rubin Gallery, New York City

CLAES OLDENBURG

Born in Stockholm, Sweden, 1929
Came to the United States, 1936
Lives in New York City

One-man exhibitions:
1959 Judson Gallery, New York City
1960 Reuben Gallery, New York City
1961 The Store, New York City (sponsored by Green Gallery)

443

1962 Green Gallery, New York City
1963 Dwan Gallery, Los Angeles, California
1964 Sidney Janis Gallery, New York City
      Pace Gallery, Boston, Massachusetts
1966 Sidney Janis Gallery
      Galerie Ileana Sonnabend, Paris, France
      Robert Fraser Gallery, London, England
      Moderna Museet, Stockholm, Sweden
1967 Sidney Janis Gallery
1969 The Museum of Modern Art, New York City

JULES OLITSKI

Born in Gomel, Russia, 1922
Came to the United States, 1924
Lives in New York City

One-man exhibitions:
1950 Galerie Huit, Paris, France
1958 Iolas Gallery, New York City
1959 French and Company, New York City
1960 French and Company
1961 Poindexter Gallery, New York City
1962 Poindexter Gallery
1963 Poindexter Gallery
      Bennington College, Bennington, Vermont
      Galleria d'Arte, Santa Croce, Florence, Italy
      Galleria Travestere di Topazia Alianta, Rome, Italy
      Toninelli Arte Moderna, Milan, Italy
1964 Poindexter Gallery
      Richard Gray Gallery, Chicago, Illinois
      Galerie Lawrence, Paris, France
      Kasmin Ltd., London, England
      The David Mirvish Gallery, Toronto, Canada
1965 Poindexter Gallery
      Kasmin Ltd.
      The David Mirvish Gallery
1966 Kasmin Ltd.
      The David Mirvish Gallery
      Nicholas Wilder Gallery, Los Angeles, California
      André Emmerich Gallery, New York City
1967 The Corcoran Gallery of Art, Washington, D.C.
      Pasadena Art Museum, Pasadena, California
      The San Francisco Museum of Art, San Francisco, California
      André Emmerich Gallery
1968 Kasmin Ltd.
      Nicholas Wilder Gallery, Los Angeles, California
      André Emmerich Gallery
      Institute of Contemporary Art, University of Pennsylvania, Philadelphia, Pennsylvania
      Hayden Gallery, Massachusetts Institute of Technology, Cambridge, Massachusetts
1969 The Metropolitan Museum of Art, New York City

JACKSON POLLOCK

Born in Cody, Wyoming, 1912
Died in Easthampton, Long Island, 1956

Selected one-man exhibitions:
1943 Art of This Century, New York City
1945 Arts Club of Chicago, Chicago, Illinois
  Art of This Century
  The San Francisco Museum of Art, San Francisco, California
1946 Art of This Century
1947 Art of This Century
1948 Betty Parsons Gallery, New York City
1949 Betty Parsons Gallery (Jan.–Feb. and Nov.–Dec.)
1950 Museo Correr, Venice, Italy
  Galleria d'Arte del Naviglio, Milan, Italy
  Betty Parsons Gallery
1951 Hilltop Theatre Art Room, Lutherville, Maryland
  Betty Parsons Gallery
1952 Studio Paul Facchetti, Paris, France
  Sidney Janis Gallery, New York City
  Bennington College, Bennington, Vermont
  Lawrence Art Museum, Williams College, Williamstown, Massachusetts
1954 Sidney Janis Gallery
1955 Sidney Janis Gallery
1956–57 The Museum of Modern Art, New York City
1967 The Museum of Modern Art

LARRY POONS

Born in Tokyo, Japan, 1937
Came to the United States, 1938
Lives in New York City

One-man exhibitions:
1963 Green Gallery, New York City
1964 Green Gallery
1965 Green Gallery
1967 Leo Castelli Gallery, New York City
1968 Kasmin Ltd., London, England
  Leo Castelli Gallery

ROBERT RAUSCHENBERG

Born in Port Arthur, Texas, 1925
Lives in New York City

One-man exhibitions:
1951 Betty Parsons Gallery, New York City
1953 Stable Gallery, New York City
  Galleria d'Arte Contemporanea, Florence, Italy
  Galleria del Obelisco, Rome, Italy

445

1955 Egan Gallery, New York City
1958 Leo Castelli Gallery, New York City
1959 Galleria La Tartaruga, Rome, Italy
     Galerie 22, Düsseldorf, Germany
     Leo Castelli Gallery
1960 Leo Castelli Gallery
1961 Galerie Daniel Cordier, Paris, France
     Galleria dell'Ariete, Milan, Italy
     Leo Castelli Gallery
1962 Dwan Gallery, Los Angeles, California
1963 Galerie Ileana Sonnabend, Paris, France
     The Jewish Museum, New York City
     Leo Castelli Gallery
1964 Whitechapel Gallery, London, England
     Galerie Ileana Sonnabend
     Arte Moderna, Turin, Italy
1965 Amerika House, Berlin, Germany
     Contemporary Arts Society, Houston, Texas
     The Walker Art Center, Minneapolis, Minnesota
     Moderna Museet, Stockholm, Sweden
     Leo Castelli Gallery
1966 The Museum of Modern Art, New York City
1967 Leo Castelli Gallery
     Douglas Gallery, Vancouver, British Columbia, Canada
1968 Stedelijk Museum, Amsterdam, The Netherlands
     Peale House, Pennsylvania Academy of the Fine Arts, Philadelphia, Pennsylvania
     Kolnischer Kunstverein, Cologne, Germany
     Musée d'Arte Moderne de la Ville de Paris, Paris, France
     The Museum of Modern Art
     Leo Castelli Gallery
1969 Leo Castelli Gallery
     Fort Worth Art Center, Fort Worth, Texas

AD REINHARDT

Born in Buffalo, New York, 1913
Died in New York City, 1967

One-man exhibitions:
1943 Columbia University, New York City
1944 Artists Gallery, New York City
1946 Art School Gallery, Brooklyn Museum, Brooklyn, New York
     Mortimer Brandt Gallery, New York City
1960 Galerie Iris Clert, Paris, France
1964 Dwan Gallery, Los Angeles, California
     Galerie Iris Clert
     I.C.A. Gallery, London, England
1965 Graham Gallery, New York City
     Stable Gallery, New York City
1967 The Jewish Museum, New York City
Betty Parsons Gallery, New York City—1946, 1947, 1948, 1949, 1950, 1951, 1952, 1953, 1955, 1956,
     1959, 1960, 1965

JAMES ROSENQUIST

Born in Grand Forks, North Dakota, 1933
Lives in Easthampton, Long Island

One-man exhibitions:
1962 Green Gallery, New York City
1963 Green Gallery
1964 Green Gallery
 Dwan Gallery, Los Angeles, California
1965 Arte Moderna, Turin, Italy
 Galerie Ileana Sonnabend, Paris, France
 Leo Castelli Gallery, New York City
1966 Leo Castelli Gallery
 Moderna Museet, Stockholm, Sweden
 Stedelijk Museum, Amsterdam, The Netherlands
 Kunsthalle, Bern, Switzerland
 Louisiana Museum, Humlebaek, Denmark
 Baden-Baden Museum, Baden-Baden, Germany
1968 National Gallery of Canada, Ottawa, Canada
 Galerie Ileana Sonnabend
1969 Leo Castelli Gallery

MARK ROTHKO

Born in Dvinska, Russia, 1903
Came to the United States, 1913
Lives in New York City

One-man exhibitions:
1933 Art Museum, Portland, Oregon
 Contemporary Arts Gallery, New York City
1945 Art of This Century, New York City
1946 Museum of Art, Santa Barbara, California
 Betty Parsons Gallery, New York City
1947 Betty Parsons Gallery
1948 Betty Parsons Gallery
1949 Betty Parsons Gallery
1950 Betty Parsons Gallery
1951 Betty Parsons Gallery
1954 Rhode Island School of Design, Providence, Rhode Island
 The Art Institute of Chicago, Chicago, Illinois
1955 Sidney Janis Gallery, New York City
1957 Contemporary Arts Museum, Houston, Texas
1958 Sidney Janis Gallery
1960 Phillips Gallery, Washington, D.C.
1961 The Museum of Modern Art, New York City
 Whitechapel Gallery, London, England
 Stedelijk Museum, Amsterdam, The Netherlands
1962 Palais des Beaux-Arts, Brussels, Belgium
 Kunsthalle, Basel, Switzerland
1962–63 Museum of Modern Art, Paris, France
1963 The Solomon R. Guggenheim Museum, New York City
1964 Marlborough Fine Art Ltd., London, England

447

GEORGE SEGAL

Born in New York City, 1924
Lives in South Brunswick, New Jersey

One-man exhibitions:
1956 Hansa Gallery, New York City
1957 Hansa Gallery
1958 Hansa Gallery
       Rutgers University, New Brunswick, New Jersey
1959 Hansa Gallery
1960 Green Gallery, New York City
1962 Green Gallery
1963 Galerie Ileana Sonnabend, Paris, France
       Gallery Schmela, Düsseldorf, Germany
       Douglass College, New Brunswick, New Jersey
1964 Green Gallery
1965 Sidney Janis Gallery, New York City
1967 Sidney Janis Gallery
1968 Museum of Contemporary Art, Chicago, Illinois
       Sidney Janis Gallery
1969 Galerie Darthea Speyer, Paris, France

DAVID SMITH

Born in Decatur, Indiana, 1906
Died near Bennington, Vermont, 1965

Selected one-man exhibitions:
1939 Skidmore College, Saratoga Springs, New York
1941 Kalamazoo Institute of Art, Kalamazoo, Michigan
       St. Paul Gallery and School of Art, St. Paul, Minnesota
       University of Minnesota, Minneapolis, Minnesota
       Sculptor's Guild, Outdoor Exhibition, New York City
1942 The Walker Art Center, Minneapolis, Minnesota
1943 Skidmore College
       The Walker Art Center
1946 Skidmore College
1947 Munson-Williams-Proctor Institute, Utica, New York
1951 Bennington College, Bennington, Vermont
1952 Bennington College
       Deerfield Academy, Deerfield, Massachusetts
       Lawrence Art Museum, Williams College, Williamstown, Massachusetts
       The Walker Art Center
1954 Cincinnati Art Museum, Cincinnati, Ohio
       The San Francisco Museum of Art, San Francisco, California
1957 The Museum of Modern Art, New York City
1959 French and Company, New York City
       New Gallery, Bennington College
1960 French and Company
       Everett Ellin Gallery, Los Angeles, California

1961 Carnegie Institute, Pittsburgh, Pennsylvania
1961–63 The Museum of Modern Art (circulated in the United States—sculptures)
1963 The Museum of Modern Art (circulated in the United States and Canada—drawings)
1964 Institute of Contemporary Art, University of Pennsylvania, Philadelphia, Pennsylvania
1965 Los Angeles County Museum of Art, Los Angeles, California
1966 The Museum of Modern Art (circulated in Europe—retrospective)
Fogg Art Museum, Harvard University, Cambridge, Massachusetts
1967 Washington Gallery of Modern Art, Washington, D.C.
1969 The Solomon R. Guggenheim Museum, New York City
Dallas Museum of Fine Arts, Dallas, Texas
The Corcoran Gallery of Art, Washington, D.C.

TONY SMITH

Born in South Orange, New Jersey, 1912
Lives in South Orange, New Jersey

One-man exhibitions:
1966 Wadsworth Atheneum, Hartford, Connecticut
1967 Institute of Contemporary Art, University of Pennsylvania, Philadelphia, Pennsylvania
Bryant Park, New York City
The Walker Art Center, Minneapolis, Minnesota
Galerie Müller, Stuttgart, Germany
1968 Galerie Renée Ziegler, Zurich, Switzerland
Fischbach Gallery, New York City
University of Southern Illinois, Carbondale, Illinois
1969 Donald Morris Gallery, Detroit, Michigan
The Museum of Modern Art, New York City (circulating exhibition)
University of Hawaii, Honolulu, Hawaii

FRANK STELLA

Born in Malden, Massachusetts, 1936
Lives in New York City

One-man exhibitions:
1960 Leo Castelli Gallery, New York City
1961 Galerie Lawrence, Paris, France
1962 Leo Castelli Gallery
1963 Ferus Gallery, Los Angeles, California
1964 Leo Castelli Gallery
Galerie Lawrence
Kasmin Ltd., London, England
1965 Ferus Gallery
1966 Leo Castelli Gallery
The David Mirvish Gallery, Toronto, Canada
Pasadena Art Museum, Pasadena, California
Kasmin Ltd.
1967 Seattle Art Museum, Seattle, Washington
Galerie Bischofberger, Zurich, Switzerland

1967 Douglas Gallery, Vancouver, British Columbia, Canada
Leo Castelli Gallery
1968 Washington Gallery of Modern Art, Washington, D.C.
The David Mirvish Gallery
Irving Blum Gallery, Los Angeles, California
Bennington College, Bennington, Vermont
Kasmin, Ltd.
1969 University of Puerto Rico, Mayagüez, Puerto Rico
Rose Art Museum, Brandeis University, Waltham, Massachusetts

CLYFFORD STILL

Born in Grandin, North Dakota, 1904
Lives in Westminster, Maryland

One-man exhibitions:
1943 The San Francisco Museum of Art, San Francisco, California
1946 Art of This Century, New York City
1947 Betty Parsons Gallery, New York City
California Palace of the Legion of Honor, San Francisco, California
1950 Betty Parsons Gallery
Metart Gallery, San Francisco, California
1951 Betty Parsons Gallery
1959 Albright-Knox Art Gallery, Buffalo, New York
1963 Institute of Contemporary Art, University of Pennsylvania, Philadelphia, Pennsylvania
1966 Albright-Knox Art Gallery

BRADLEY WALKER TOMLIN

Born in Syracuse, New York, 1899
Died in New York City, 1953

One-man exhibitions:
1922 Skaneateles and Cazenovia, New York
1923 Anderson Galleries, New York City
1926 Montross Gallery, New York City
1927 Montross Gallery
1931 Frank K. M. Rehn Galleries, New York City
1944 Frank K. M. Rehn Galleries
1950 Betty Parsons Gallery, New York City
1953 Betty Parsons Gallery
1955 Phillips Gallery, Washington, D.C.
1957–58 The Whitney Museum of American Art, New York City
North Carolina Museum of Art, Raleigh, North Carolina
Colorado Springs Fine Arts Center, Colorado Springs, Colorado
Art Galleries of the University of California, Los Angeles, California
Pasadena Art Museum, Pasadena, California
Fine Arts Gallery of San Diego, San Diego, California
The San Francisco Museum of Art, San Francisco, California
Munson-Williams-Proctor Institute, Utica, New York

ANDY WARHOL

Born in Philadelphia, Pennsylvania, 1930
Lives in New York City

One-man exhibitions:

1962 Ferus Gallery, Los Angeles, California
     Stable Gallery, New York City

1963 Ferus Gallery

1964 Galerie Ileana Sonnabend, Paris, France
     Stable Gallery
     Leo Castelli Gallery, New York City

1965 Morris International Gallery, Toronto, Canada
     Galerie Ileana Sonnabend
     Gian Enzo Sperone Arte Moderna, Turin, Italy
     Galleria Rubbers, Buenos Aires, Argentina
     Institute of Contemporary Art, University of Pennsylvania, Philadelphia, Pennsylvania
     Galerie Buren, Stockholm, Sweden

1966 Leo Castelli Gallery
     Institute of Contemporary Art, Boston, Massachusetts
     Galerie Hans R. Nuendorf, Hamburg, Germany

1967 Galerie Ileana Sonnabend
     Galerie Rudolf Zwirner, Cologne, Germany

1968 Moderna Museet, Stockholm, Sweden
     Rowan Gallery, London, England

1969 Castelli-Whitney, New York City

Selected Bibliography

Selected Bibliography

(The reader should note that the entries are listed in chronological order.)

JOSEF ALBERS

On Albers:

Thwaites, J., and Thwaites, M. "Albers and De Monda at the Katherine Kuh Gallery," *Magazine of Art*, vol. 30 (November, 1937), 682–683.

"Abstractionist Albers' Glass Pictures," *Baltimore Museum News*, vol. 5 (December, 1942), 1.

de Kooning, Elaine. "Albers Paints a Picture," *Art News*, vol. 49 (November, 1950), 40–43.

Bill, Max. *Josef Albers, Fritz Glarner, Friedrich Vordemberge-Gildewart.* Zurich: Kunsthaus, 1956.

Charlot, J. "Nature and the Art of Josef Albers," *College Art Journal*, vol. 15, no. 3 (1956), 190–196.

Hamilton, G. H. *Josef Albers.* New Haven: Yale University Art Gallery, 1956.

Loew, M. "Albers, Impersonalization in Perfect Form," *Art News*, vol. 55 (April, 1956), 28–29.

Catalogue on Albers. Articles on Albers by Arp, W. Grohmann, F. Roh. Paris: Denise René Galerie, 1957.

Grohmann, Will. "Zum 70 Geburtstag von Josef Albers," *Frankfurter Allgemeine Zeitung* (March 19, 1958). Also in *Yale University Art Bulletin*, 1958.

Bill, Max. "Josef Albers," *Werk*, Switzerland (April, 1958).

Tillim, Sidney. "What Happened to Geometry? An Inquiry into Geometrical Painting in America," *Arts*, vol. 33 (June, 1959), 38–44.

Hopkins, Henry. "Josef Albers," *Artforum*, vol. 2 (February, 1964), 26–27.

Josef Albers: The American Years. Washington, D.C.: Washington Gallery of Modern Art, 1965.

Coplans, J. "Albers as a Printmaker," *Art News*, vol. 63 (February, 1965), 51.

Josef Albers: White Line Squares. Los Angeles: Los Angeles County Museum of Art, 1966.

Gomringer, Eugen. *Josef Albers.* New York: Wittenborn, 1968.

By Albers:

"Interview," *Art Digest*, vol. 19 (January, 1945), 15.

"On Art and Expression," "On Enunciation," "On Articulation," "Seeing Art," *Yale Literary Magazine*, New Haven, 1960.

Bucher, François. *Despite Straight Lines.* Contains explanatory text by Albers. New Haven: Yale University Press, 1961.

"The Color in My Painting," *Josef Albers.* Raleigh: North Carolina Museum of Art, 1962.

Interaction of Color. Explanatory text by Albers. New Haven: Yale University Press, 1963.

Statements in *Josef Albers: Homage to the Square.* New York: The Museum of Modern Art, Under Auspices of the International Council, 1964.

"Op Art and/or Perceptual Effects," *Yale Scientific Magazine* (November, 1965).

Statements in *Josef Albers: White Line Squares.* Los Angeles: Los Angeles County Museum of Art, 1966.

MILTON AVERY

On Avery:

Frost, Rosamund. "American Fauve," *Art News*, vol. 41 (December 15, 1942), 28.

Farber, M. "Chaim Gross, Milton Avery, and William Steig," *Magazine of Art*, vol. 36 (January, 1943), 10–15.

"Two Averys Grow; Exhibition at the Durand-Ruel Galleries; Theme, Growth, and Development of the Painter's Daughter," *Art Digest*, vol. 21 (February 15, 1946), 23.

Wight, Frederick S. *Milton Avery.* Baltimore: The Baltimore Museum of Art, 1952.

Greenberg, Clement. "Milton Avery," *Arts Magazine*, vol. 32 (December, 1957), 40–45.

Guest, B. "Avery and Gatch: Lonely Americans," *Art News*, vol. 59 (March, 1960), 42–45.

Kramer, Hilton. *Milton Avery: Paintings, 1930-1960*. New York: Thomas Yoseloff, 1962.

Judd, Don. "Exhibition at Borgenicht Gallery," *Arts Magazine*, vol. 38 (December, 1963), 61.

Milton Avery. Lincoln, Nebraska: Shelton Memorial Art Gallery, 1966.

Milton Avery 1893-1965. San Francisco: Reece Palley Gallery, 1968. (Contains essay by James Mellow and statements by Gottlieb and Rothko.)

Ashton, Dore. "Milton Avery: A Painter's Painter at Borgenicht," *Arts Magazine*, vol. 42 (May, 1968), 34–35.

ALEXANDER CALDER

On Calder:

Sweeney, J. J. *Mobiles by Calder*. Chicago: Arts Club of Chicago, 1935.

――――. "Alexander Calder," *Axis*, vol. 1, no. 3 (July, 1935), 19–21.

Buffet-Picabia, Gabrielle. "Sandy Calder, Forgeron Lunaire," *Cahiers d'Art*, vol. 20–21 (1946), 324–333.

Sartre, Jean-Paul. *Alexander Calder: Mobiles, Stabiles, Constellations*. Paris: Louis Carré Galerie, 1946.

Soby, James Thrall. "Three Humorists: Klee, Miró, Calder," *Contemporary Painters*. New York: The Museum of Modern Art, 1948. Pp. 99–103.

Masson, André. "L'Atelier de Calder," *Cahiers d'Art*, vol. 24, no. 2 (1949).

"Calder," *Derrière le Miroir*, Paris, no. 31 (July, 1950).

Sweeney, J. J. *Alexander Calder*. New York: The Museum of Modern Art, 1951.

Sylvester, David. "Mobiles and Stabiles by Alexander Calder," *Art News and Review*, vol. 2, no. 26 (January 27, 1951), 4.

XXVI Biennale di Venezia, Venice, 1952, 371–378. Introduction by J. J. Sweeney.

Banham, Rayner. *"Eppur si mouve,"* *Art*, London, vol. 1, no. 7 (February 17, 1955), 4.

Calder. Basel: Kunsthalle, 1957.

Alexander Calder. Amsterdam: Stedelijk Museum, 1959.

Derrière le Miroir, Paris, no. 113 (1959). Issue devoted to Calder.

Restany, Pierre. "L'Autre Calder," *Art International*, vol. 3, nos. 5–6 (1959), 46–47.

Sweeney, J. J. *Alexander Calder*. London: The Arts Council of Great Britain, 1962.

Rickey, George. "Calder in London," *Arts Magazine*, vol. 36 (September, 1962), 22–27.

Agam. Y. "Calder en Pleine Nature," *XXᵉ Siècle* (December, 1962), 79–82 (Eng. trans.).

Derrière le Miroir, Paris, no. 141 (November, 1963). Issue devoted to Calder.

Alexander Calder: A Retrospective Exhibition. New York: The Solomon R. Guggenheim Museum, 1964. Introduction by Thomas Messer.

Anderson, Wayne V. "Calder at the Guggenheim," *Artforum*, vol. 3 (March, 1965), 37–41.

Arnason, H. H. *Alexander Calder*. Princeton: Van Nostrand, 1966.

Calder. Saint Paul, France: Fondation Maeght, 1969.

By Calder:

Statement in *Mobiles by Calder*. Andover, Mass.: Addison Gallery of American Art, 1943.

"The Ides of Art: 14 Sculptors Write," *The Tiger's Eye*, vol. 1, no. 4 (June 15, 1948), 74.

Giedion-Welker, Carola. *Contemporary Sculpture*. New York: Wittenborn, 1960. Pp. 92, 204–209, 212, 326.

Calder, An Autobiography with Pictures. New York: Pantheon, 1966.

JOHN CHAMBERLAIN

On Chamberlain:

Judd, D. "Exhibition at Castelli Gallery," *Arts Magazine*, vol. 38 (September, 1961), 71.

Creeley, Robert. "John Chamberlain," *Recent American Sculpture*. New York: The Jewish Museum, 1964. Pp. 17–18.

Judd, Donald. "Chamberlain: Another View," *Art International*, vol. 7, no. 10 (January, 1964), 38–39.

Rose, Barbara. "How to Look at Chamberlain's Sculpture," *Art International*, vol. 7, no. 10 (January, 1964), 38–39.

Lippard, Lucy. "New York Letter," *Art International*, vol. 9, no. 3 (April, 1965), 53.

Judd, Donald. "John Chamberlain," *7 Sculptors*. Philadelphia: Institute of Contemporary Art, University of Pennsylvania, 1966. Pp. 7–9.

JOSEPH CORNELL

On Cornell:

Tyler, Parker. *Exhibition of Objects by Joseph Cornell*. New York: Julien Levy Gallery, 1939.

Motherwell, Robert. "Preface to a Joseph Cornell Exhibition," A Statement on Cornell for a Proposed Catalogue for a Joseph Cornell Exhibition held at The Walker Art Center, Minneapolis, 1953. Unpublished.

Goosen, E. C. "The Plastic Poetry of Joseph Cornell," *Art International*, vol. 3, no. 10 (1959–60), 37–40.

Goldwater, Robert. "Joseph Cornell," *Dictionary of Modern Sculpture*, ed. Robert Maillard. New York: Tudor Publishing Co., 1960. Pp. 64–65.

Seitz, William. *Art of Assemblage*. New York: The Museum of Modern Art, 1961. Pp. 68–71, 72, 73, 85, 86.

Coplans, John. "Notes on the Nature of Joseph Cornell," *Artforum*, vol. 1 (February, 1963), 27–29.

Ashton, Dore. "New York Letter," *Das Kunstwerk*, Baden-Baden, vol. 16, no. 10 (April, 1963), 32.

Hopps, Walter. "Boxes," *Art International*, vol. 8, no. 2 (March, 1964), 38–41.

Waldman, Diane. "Cornell: The Compass of Boxing," *Art News*, vol. 64 (March, 1965), 42–45, 49–50.

Johnson, Ellen H. "Arcadia Enclosed: The Boxes of Joseph Cornell," *Arts Magazine*, vol. 39 (September–October, 1965), 35–37.

Hess, Thomas B. "Eccentric Propositions," *Art News Annual*, vol. 33 (1966), 9–27.

Joseph Cornell. Pasadena: Pasadena Art Museum, 1966. Introduction by Fairfield Porter.

Porter, Fairfield. "Joseph Cornell," *Art and Literature*, no. 8 (Spring, 1966), 120–130.

Waldman, Diane. *Joseph Cornell*. New York: The Solomon R. Guggenheim Museum, 1967.

Samaras, L. "Cornell's Size," *Arts Magazine*, vol. 41 (May, 1967), 45–47.

Rosenberg, Harold. "Object Poems," *The New Yorker* (June 3, 1967), 112, 114–118.

Ashbery, John. "Cornell: The Cube Root of Dreams." *Art News*, vol. 66 (Summer, 1967), 56–59.

STUART DAVIS

On Davis:

Gorky, Arshele. "Stuart Davis," *Creative Art*, vol. 9 (September, 1931), 12–17.

Jewell, Edward Alden. "Stuart Davis Offers a Penetrating Survey of the American Scene," *The New York Times* (May 10, 1932), 19.

Coates, Robert M. "Davis, Hartley and the River Seine," *The New Yorker*, vol. 18 (February 13, 1943), 58.

Wolf, Ben. "Stuart Davis: 30 Years of Evolution," *Art Digest*, vol. 20 (November 1, 1945), 10, 34.

457

Greenberg, Clement. "Art," *The Nation*, vol. 161 (November 17, 1945), 533–534.

Wight, Frederick S. "Stuart Davis," *Art Digest*, vol. 27 (May 15, 1953), 13, 23.

Stuart Davis. Minneapolis: The Walker Art Center, 1957.

de Kooning, Elaine. "Stuart Davis: True to Life," *Art News*, vol. 56 (April, 1957), 40–42, 54–55.

Woodruff, Hale A. "Stuart Davis, American Modern," *School Arts*, vol. 57 (October, 1957), 36–37.

Goosen, E. C. *Stuart Davis*. New York: George Braziller, 1959.

Blesh, Rudi. *Stuart Davis*. New York: Grove Press, 1960.

Stuart Davis Memorial Exhibition. Washington, D.C.: Smithsonian Institution, National Collection of Fine Arts, 1965.

By Davis:

"Self-Interview," *Creative Art*, vol. 9 (September, 1931), 208–211.

Introduction, *Abstract Painting in America*. New York: The Whitney Museum of American Art, 1935. Reprinted in *Art of Today*, vol. 6, no. 3 (April, 1935), 9–10; reprinted in part in Homer St. Gaudens, *The American Artist and His Times*. New York: Dodd, Mead, 1941. Pp. 224–225.

"Paintings by Salvadore Dali, Julien Levy Gallery," *Art Front*, vol. 1, no. 2 (January, 1935), 7.

"The New York American Scene in Art," *Art Front*, vol. 1, no. 3 (February, 1935), 6. Reprinted in part and with comment in *Art Digest*, vol. 9, no. 11 (March 1, 1935), 4, 21. Thomas Benton replies in *Art Digest*, vol. 9, no. 12 (March 12, 1935), 20–21, 25; reprinted in *Art Front*, vol. 1, no. 4 (April, 1935), 4, 8.

"American Artists and the American Dream," *New York World Telegram* (May 4, 1935), 14.

"Art at the Fair," *The Nation*, vol. 149 (July 22, 1939), 112.

"Abstraction," *The New York Times* (August 20, 1939), sec. 9, p. 7.

"Art and the Masses," *Art Digest*, vol. 14 (October 1, 1939), 13, 34.

"Abstract Art in the American Scene," *Parnassus*, vol. 13 (March, 1941), 100–103.

"Arshile Gorky in the 1930's: A Personal Recollection," *Magazine of Art*, vol. 44 (February, 1951), 56–58.

"What Abstract Art Means to Me," *Museum of Modern Art Bulletin*, vol. 18 (Spring, 1951), 14–15.

"Place of Painting in Contemporary Culture," *Art News*, vol. 56 (June, 1957), 29–30.

Statement in *Second Loan Exhibition*. New York: The Whitney Museum of American Art, 1959.

"Artists on Art and Reality, on Their Work and Values," *Daedalus*, vol. 89 (1960), 118–120.

WILLEM DE KOONING

On de Kooning:

"Spotlight on de Kooning," *Art News*, vol. 47 (April, 1948), 33.

Venice XXV Biennale, Catalogo, 1950, pp. 383–386.

de Kooning Retrospective. Boston: Boston Museum School, 1953. Foreword by Clement Greenberg.

Hess, Thomas B. "de Kooning Paints a Picture: *Woman*," *Art News*, vol. 52 (March, 1953), 30–33, 64–67.

Fitzsimmons, J. "Review of Exhibition at Sidney Janis Gallery with Comments on 'de Kooning Paints a Picture: *Woman*,' by T. B. Hess," *Arts and Architecture*, vol. 70 (May, 1953), 4.

Steinberg, L. "de Kooning Shows Recent Painting in Woman Series at Janis Gallery," *Arts Magazine*, vol. 30 (November, 1955), 46–47.

Hess, Thomas. *Willem de Kooning*. New York: George Braziller, 1959.

Janis, Harriet, and Blesh, Rudi. *De Kooning*. New York: Grove Press, 1960.

Recent Painting by Willem de Kooning. New York: Sidney Janis Gallery, 1962. Introduction by T. B. Hess.

Hess, Thomas B. "Willem de Kooning," *Art News*, vol. 61 (March, 1962), 40–51, 60–61.

Porter, F. "Class Content in American Abstract Painting," *Art News*, vol. 61 (April, 1962), 26–28.

Fried, Michael. "New York Letter," *Art International*, vol. 6, no. 10 (December 20, 1962), 54–55, 57.

Denby, Edwin. "My Friend, de Kooning," *Art News Annual*, no. 29 (1964), 82–99.

Kozloff, Max. "The Impact of de Kooning," *Arts Yearbook*, no. 7 (1964), 77–88.

Rosenberg, Harold. "de Kooning," *The Anxious Object: Art Today and Its Audience*. New York: Horizon Press, 1964.

Within the Easel Convention: Sources of Abstract Expressionism. Cambridge, Mass.: Fogg Art Museum, 1964. Text on de Kooning by Rosalind Krauss.

Ashton, Dore, *Willem de Kooning*. Northampton, Mass.: Smith College Museum of Art, 1965.

Hess, Thomas B. "de Kooning's New Women," *Art News*, vol. 64 (March, 1965), 36–38, 63–65.

Kozloff, Max. "The Critical Reception of Abstract Expressionism," *Arts Magazine*, vol. 40 (December, 1965), 27–32.

Hess, Thomas B. *De Kooning: Recent Painting*. New York: Walter and Co., 1967.

————. *Willem de Kooning*. Amsterdam: Stedelijk Museum, 1968.

Krauss, Rosalind. "The New de Koonings," *Artforum*, vol. 6 (January, 1968), 44–47.

Hess, Thomas B. *Willem de Kooning*. New York: The Museum of Modern Art, 1969.

Bannard, Walter Darby. "Willem de Kooning's Retrospective at the Museum of Modern Art," *Artforum*, vol. 7 (April, 1969), 42–49.

By de Kooning:

Letter to the Editor (on Arshile Gorky), *Art News*, vol. 47 (January, 1949), 6. (Reprinted in *New American Painting*. New York: The Museum of Modern Art, 1958–59).

"Renaissance and Order," *Transformation*, vol. 1, no. 2 (1951), 85–87. (Reprinted in *Willem de Kooning*. Northampton, Mass.: Smith College Museum of Art, 1965.)

"Is Today's Artist with or Against the Past?" *Art News*, vol. 57 (Summer, 1958), 27, 56.

Sylvester, David. "de Kooning's Women," *Ramparts*, vol. 7, no. 11 (April, 1969), 20–24.

BURGOYNE DILLER

On Diller:

Ashton, Dore. "Exhibition Rose Fried Gallery," *Art Digest*, vol. 26 (November 15, 1951), 20.

de Kooning, Elaine. "Diller Paints a Picture: *Third Theme, 1946–1952*," *Art News*, vol. 51 (January, 1953), 26–29.

Tillim, Sidney. "What Happened to Geometry? An Inquiry into Geometrical Painting in America," *Arts Magazine*, vol. 33 (June, 1959), 38–44.

Campbell, Lawrence. "The Rule that Measures Emotion," *Art News*, vol. 60 (May, 1961), 34–35, 56–58.

Sandler, Irving H. "New York Letter," *Quadrum*, no. 14 (1963), 116.

Judd, Donald. "Exhibition at the Chalette Gallery," *Arts Magazine*, vol. 37 (January, 1963), 52.

Ashton, Dore. "Exhibition at Chalette Gallery," *Studio*, vol. 165 (March, 1963), 118.

Burgoyne Diller: 1906–1965. Trenton, N.J.: State Museum, 1966. (Contains a reprint of Campbell's 1961 article.)

Campbell, Lawrence. "Diller: The Ruling Passion," *Art News*, vol. 6 (October, 1968), 36–37.

MARK DI SUVERO

On Di Suvero:

Judd, Don. "Exhibition at the Green Gallery," *Arts Magazine*, vol. 35 (October, 1960), 60.

Geist, S. "New Sculptor: Mark di Suvero," *Arts Magazine*, vol. 35 (December, 1960), 40–43. Discussion, vol. 35 (March, 1961), 7.

Johnston, Jill. "Mark di Suvero," *Recent American Sculpture*. New York: The Jewish Museum, 1964.

Judd, Don. "Exhibition at 79 Park Place Gallery," *Arts Magazine*, vol. 38 (February, 1964), 23.

Kozloff, Max. "Further Adventures in American Sculpture," *Arts Magazine*, vol. 39 (February, 1965), 30.

Rosenstein, H. "Di Suvero: The Pressures of Reality," *Art News*, vol. 65 (February, 1967), 36–39.

Kozloff, Max. "Mark di Suvero," *Artforum*, vol. 5 (Summer, 1967), 41–46.

By Di Suvero:

McShine, Kynaston. Moderator for "New Sculpture," Symposium on Primary Structures Held at The Jewish Museum, New York, May 3, 1966, with Barbara Rose, Robert Morris, Don Judd, Mark di Suvero.

DAN FLAVIN

On Flavin:

Judd, Donald. "Black, White and Gray," *Arts Magazine*, vol. 38 (March, 1964), 38.

_____. "New York Exhibition: In the Galleries, Dan Flavin," *Arts Magazine*, vol. 38 (April, 1964), 31.

Johnston, Jill. "Reviews and Previews: Dan Flavin," *Art News*, vol. 63 (January, 1965), 13.

Kozloff, Max. "Further Adventures of American Sculpture," *Arts Magazine*, vol. 39 (February, 1965), 26.

Lippard, Lucy R. "New York Letter: Off Color," *Art International*, vol. 10 (April 20, 1966), 73–75.

_____. "Rejective Art," *Art International*, vol. 10 (October 20, 1966), 33–36.

Piene, N. R. "Light Art," *Art in America*, vol. 55, no. 3 (May, 1967), 38.

By Flavin:

"The Artists Say," *Art News*, vol. 4 (Summer, 1965), 72.

Statement in Barbara Rose, "ABC Art," *Art in America* (October, 1965), 68.

"'. . . In Daylight or Cool White,' An Autobiographical Sketch," *Artforum*, vol. 4 (December, 1965), 20–24.

"Some Remarks," *Artforum*, vol. 5 (December, 1966), 27–29.

Portfolio: 4 Sculptors, Recent Works and Statements by Four Young Americans," *Perspecta*, no. 11 (1967), 44.

Statement in *American Sculpture of the Sixties*. Los Angeles: Los Angeles County Museum of Art, 1967. P. 45.

"Some Other Comments . . . ," *Artforum*, vol. 6 (December, 1967), 20–25.

HELEN FRANKENTHALER

On Frankenthaler:

Coates, Robert M. "The Art Galleries," *The New Yorker*, vol. 27 (November 24, 1951), 89–91.

_____. "The Art Galleries," *The New Yorker*, vol. 33 (March 9, 1957), 80, 83–84.

Rudikoff, Sonya. "Helen Frankenthaler's Painting," in B. H. Friedman, ed. *School of New York: Some Younger Artists*. New York: Grove Press, 1959.

O'Hara, Frank. *Helen Frankenthaler*. New York: The Jewish Museum, 1960.

Goosen, E. C. "Helen Frankenthaler," *Art International*, vol. 5 (October 20, 1961), 76–79.

Ashbery, John. "Paris Notes," *Art International*, vol. 5 (November 20, 1961), 48–50.

Judd, Don. "In the Galleries," *Arts Magazine*, vol. 36 (January, 1962), 38–39.

Fried, Michael. "New York Letter," *Art International*, vol. 7 (April 25, 1963), 54–56.

_____. "New York Letter," *Art International*, vol. 7 (May 25, 1963), 69–72.

Kozloff, Max. "Art and the New York Avant-Garde," *Partisan Review*, vol. 31 (Fall, 1964), 535–554.

Berkson, William. "Poet of the Surface," *Arts Magazine*, vol. 39 (May–June, 1965), 44–50.

Ashton, Dore. "Helen Frankenthaler," *Studio,* vol. 170 (August, 1965), 52–55.

Baro, Gene. "The Achievement of Helen Frankenthaler," *Art International,* vol. 11, no. 7 (September 20, 1967), 33–38.

Goosen, E. C. *Helen Frankenthaler.* New York: The Whitney Museum of American Art, 1969.

Rosenstein, Harris. "The Colorful Gesture," *Art News,* vol. 68 (March, 1969), 29–31, 68.

Rose, Barbara. "Painting Within the Tradition, the Career of Helen Frankenthaler," *Artforum,* vol. 7 (April, 1969), 28–33.

By Frankenthaler

"New Talent in the U.S.," With Note by the Artist, *Art in America,* vol. 45 (March, 1957), 28–29.

"Discussion: Is There a New Academy?" *Art News,* vol. 58 (June, 1959), 34.

Quotations from an Interview for the B.B.C., London, by David Sylvester, 1962, in *Helen Frankenthaler.* Bennington, Vt.: Bennington College, 1962.

Geldzahler, Henry. "An Interview with Helen Frankenthaler," *Artforum,* vol. 4 (October, 1965), 36–38.

Cyr, Donald J. "A Conversation with Helen Frankenthaler," *School Arts,* vol. 67 (April, 1968), 30–32.

Transcript of a Tape-Recorded Interview by Barbara Rose (August, 1968). Archives of American Art.

ARSHILE GORKY

On Gorky:

An Exhibition of Work by 46 Painters and Sculptors under 35 Years of Age, ed. Dorothy C. Miller. New York: The Museum of Modern Art, 1930.

Kiesler, Frederick J. "Murals Without Walls: Relating to Gorky's Newark Project," *Art Front,* vol. 2 (December, 1936), 10–11.

Sweeney, J. J. "Five American Painters," *Harper's Bazaar* (April, 1944), 122, 124.

Greenberg, Clement. "Art: Arshile Gorky," *The Nation,* vol. 160 (March 24, 1945), 342–343; vol. 162 (May 4, 1946), 552–553; vol. 166 (March 6, 1948), 384–385; vol. 167 (December 11, 1948), 676.

————. "Art Chronicle," *Partisan Review,* vol. 15 (March, 1948), 369; vol. 17 (May–June, 1950), 512–513; vol. 22 (Spring, 1955), 179–196.

Crowley, Malcolm. "Arshile Gorky—A Note from a Friend," *New York Herald Tribune* (September 5, 1948), sec. 6, p. 3.

de Kooning, Willem. Letter to the Editor, *Art News,* vol. 47 (January, 1949), 6.

Barr, Alfred H., Jr. "Gorky, de Kooning, Pollock," *Art News,* vol. 49 (Summer, 1950), 22, 60.

Schwabacher, Ethel. *Arshile Gorky Memorial Exhibition.* New York: The Whitney Museum of American Art, 1951.

de Kooning, Elaine. "Gorky: Painter of His Own Legend," *Art News,* vol. 49 (January, 1951), 38–41, 63–66.

Davis, Stuart. "Arshile Gorky in the 1930's," *Magazine of Art,* vol. 44 (February, 1951), 56–58.

Goodenough, Robert. "Arshile Gorky," *Art News,* vol. 49 (February, 1951), 46.

Goodrich, Lloyd. "Notes on Eight Works by Arshile Gorky," *Magazine of Art,* vol. 44 (February, 1951), 59–61.

Arshile Gorky. Princeton: Princeton University Art Museum, 1952.

Seitz, William C. "A Gorky Exhibit," *Daily Princetonian,* vol. 76 (October 14, 1952), 2.

Fitzsimmons, James. "The Late Gorky," *Art Digest,* vol. 27 (May 1, 1953), 16.

Seitz, William. "Arshile Gorky's *The Plough and the Song,*" Oberlin College, *Allen Memorial Art Museum Bulletin,* vol. 12, no. 1 (1954), 4–15.

Porter, Fairfield. "Arshile Gorky," *Art News,* vol. 53 (April, 1954), 53.

Schwabacher, Ethel. *Arshile Gorky.* New York: Macmillan, 1957.

Shapiro, Meyer. "Gorky: The Creative Influence," *Art News,* vol. 56 (September, 1957), 28–31, 52.

Ashton, Dore. "Art: Gorky and Contemporary American Painting," *Art and Architecture,* vol. 75 (January, 1958), 6.

Rosenblum, Robert. "Arshile Gorky," *Arts Magazine,* vol. 32 (January, 1958), 30–33.

Rosenberg, Harold. *Gorky.* New York: Horizon Press, 1962.

Seitz, William. *Arshile Gorky: Paintings, Drawings, Studies.* New York: The Museum of Modern Art, 1962.

Rieff, R. "Late Works of Arshile Gorky," *Art Journal,* vol. 22 (Spring, 1963), 148–152.

Rubin, William. "Arshile Gorky, Surrealism, and the New American Painting," *Art International,* vol. 7, no. 2 (February 25, 1963), 27–38.

Roberts, K. "Major Retrospective Exhibition at the Tate," *Burlington Magazine,* vol. 107 (May, 1965), 270–271.

Mooradian, K. "Unknown Gorky," *Art News,* vol. 66 (September, 1967), 52–53.

Levy, Julien. *Arshile Gorky.* New York: Harry N. Abrams, 1968.

By Gorky:

Johnson, Malcolm. "Interview," *New York Sun* (August 22, 1941).

Statement about *Garden in Sochi,* Collections Archives, The Museum of Modern Art, June, 1942 (at request of Dorothy Miller).

"The WPA Murals at the Newark Airport" (included in H. Rosenberg, *Gorky.* New York: Horizon Press, 1962).

ADOLPH GOTTLIEB

On Gottlieb:

Newman, Barnett. *Adolph Gottlieb.* New York: Wakefield Gallery, 1944.

Frost, Rosamund. "Adolph Gottlieb," *Art News,* vol. 43 (February 15, 1944), 23.

Greenberg, Clement. "Art: Adolph Gottlieb," *The Nation,* vol. 165 (December 6, 1947), 629–630.

Kootz, Samuel M. *Adolph Gottlieb.* New York: Kootz Gallery, 1952.

Fitzsimmons, James. "Adolph Gottlieb," *Everyday Art Quarterly,* no. 25 (1953), 1–4.

Greenberg, Clement. *Adolph Gottlieb.* Bennington, Vt.: Bennington College, Williams College, 1954.

Rosenblum, Robert. "Adolph Gottlieb: New Murals," *Art Digest,* vol. 28 (April 15, 1954), 11.

Greenberg, Clement. *Adolph Gottlieb.* New York: The Jewish Museum, 1957.

Rubin, William. "Adolph Gottlieb," *Art International,* vol. 3, nos. 3–4 (1959), 34–37.

Sandler, Irving H. "Adolph Gottlieb," *Art News,* vol. 57 (February, 1959), 10.

Alloway, Lawrence. "Sign and Surface: Notes on Black and White Painting in New York," *Quadrum,* no. 9 (1960), 49–62.

Judd, Don. "Adolph Gottlieb," *Arts Magazine,* vol. 35 (December, 1960), 52–53.

Fried, Michael. "New York Letter," *Art International,* vol. 6 (October 25, 1962), 75–76.

Friedman, Martin. *Adolph Gottlieb.* Minneapolis: The Walker Art Center, 1963.

Rosenstein, Harris. "Gottlieb at the Summit," *Art News,* vol. 65 (April, 1966), 42–43.

Doty, Robert, and Waldman, Diane. *Adolph Gottlieb.* New York: The Whitney Museum of American Art, The Solomon R. Guggenheim Museum, 1968.

Waldman, D. "Gottlieb: Signs and Suns," *Art News,* vol. 66 (February, 1968), 26–29.

Ashton, Dore. "Adolph Gottlieb at the Guggenheim and Whitney Museums," *Studio,* vol. 175 (April, 1968), 201–202.

Hudson, Andrew. "Adolph Gottlieb's Paintings at the Whitney," *Art International,* vol. 12, no. 4 (April 20, 1968), 24–28.

By Gottlieb:

Gottlieb, Adolph, and Rothko, Mark, in "The Realism of Art: A New Platform: Globalism Pops into View," by Edward Alden Jewell. *The New York Times* (June 13, 1943), 9.

Letter to the Editor, *The New York Times* (June 13, 1943), sec. 2, p. 9 (with Rothko and Newman).

"The Portrait and the Modern Artist," mimeographed script of broadcast by Gottlieb and Rothko on "Art in New York," H. Stix, Director, WNYC, New York (October 13, 1943).

Statement in "The Ides of Art," *The Tiger's Eye*, vol. 1, no. 2 (December, 1947), 43.

"Unintelligibility," 1948 mimeographed script of talk given in forum: The Artist Speaks, The Museum of Modern Art, New York, May 5, 1948.

"My Painting," *Arts and Architecture*, vol. 68 (September, 1951), 21.

"The Artist and the Public," *Art in America*, vol. 42, no. 4 (December, 1954), 266–271.

"Artist and Society: A Brief Case History," *College Art Journal*, vol. 14 (Winter, 1955), 96–101.

"Adolph Gottlieb: An Interview with David Sylvester," *Living Arts*, no. 2 (1963), 2–10.

"Postcards from Adolph Gottlieb," *Location*, vol. 1 (Summer, 1964), 19–26.

"Jackson Pollock: An Artists' Symposium," *Art News*, vol. 66 (April, 1967), 31.

PHILIP GUSTON

On Guston:

Janson, H. W. "Philip Guston," *Magazine of Art*, vol. 40, no. 2 (February, 1947), 54–58.

Ashton, Dore. "Art: The Age of Lyricism," *Arts and Architecture*, vol. 73, no. 3 (March, 1956), 14–15, 43–44.

Creeley, Robert. "Philip Guston: A Note," *Black Mountain Review*, Black Mountain, N.C. (Spring, 1956).

Steinberg, Leo. "Fritz Glarner and Philip Guston Among '12 Americans' at the Museum of Modern Art," *Arts Magazine*, vol. 30 (June, 1956), 42–45.

Sandler, Irving. "Guston: A Long Voyage Home," *Art News*, vol. 58 (December, 1959), 36–39, 64–65.

Ashton, Dore. *Philip Guston*. New York: Grove Press, 1960.

Arnason, H. H. *Philip Guston*. New York: The Solomon R. Guggenheim Museum, 1962.

Hunter, Sam. "Philip Guston," *Art International*, vol. 6, no. 4 (May, 1962), 62–67.

O'Hara, Frank. "Growth and Guston," *Art News*, vol. 61 (May, 1962), 31–33.

Ashton, Dore. "Philip Guston," *Aujourd'hui*, vol. 6 (June, 1962), 28–29.

Alloway, Lawrence. "Notes on Guston," *Art Journal*, vol. 22, no. 1 (Fall, 1962), 8–11.

Sylvester, David. "London," *New Statesman*, vol. 65, no. 1666 (February 15, 1963), 247–248.

Feldman, Morton. "Philip Guston: The Last Painter," *Art News Annual*, no. 31 (1965), 97–100.

Berkson, Bill. "Dialogue with Philip Guston," *Art and Literature*, no. 7 (Winter, 1965), 56–59.

Philip Guston: Recent Paintings and Drawings. New York: The Jewish Museum, 1966. Introduction by Sam Hunter.

Berkson, W. "Philip Guston: A New Emphasis," *Arts Magazine*, vol. 40 (February, 1966), 15–18.

Ashton, Dore. "Exhibition at the Jewish Museum," *Arts and Architecture*, vol. 83 (April, 1966), 7.

By Guston:

Statement in *It Is*, no. 1 (Spring, 1958), 44.

Recorded Interview with H. H. Arnason in *Philip Guston*. New York: The Solomon R. Guggenheim Museum, 1962.

Statements (translated) in *Philip Guston*. Amsterdam: Stedelijk Museum, 1962.

Interview with David Sylvester, B.B.C., 1963 (typescript).

"Piero della Francesca: The Impossibility of Painting," *Art News*, vol. 64 (May, 1965), 38–39.

"Philip Guston's Object: A Dialogue with Harold Rosenberg," *Philip Guston: Recent Paintings and Drawings*. New York: The Jewish Museum, 1966.

HANS HOFMANN

On Hofmann

Matter, Mercedes. "Hans Hofmann," *Arts and Architecture*, vol. 63 (May, 1946), 26–28, 48.

de Kooning, Elaine. "Hans Hofmann Paints a Picture," *Art News*, vol. 48 (February, 1950), 38–41, 58–59.

Fitzsimmons, James. "Hans Hofmann," *Everyday Art Quarterly*, no. 28 (1953), 23–26.

Greenberg, Clement. *Hans Hofmann: A Retrospective Exhibition*. Bennington, Vt.: Bennington College, 1955.

Sawyer, Kenneth B. "Largely Hans Hofmann," *Baltimore Museum of Art News*, vol. 18, no. 3 (February, 1955), pp. 9–12.

Kaprow, Allan. "Hans Hofmann." New Brunswick, N.J.: Rutgers University, 1956.

Wight, Frederick S. *Hans Hofmann*. Berkeley: University of California Press, 1957. Published on the occasion of the Hofmann Retrospective at The Whitney Museum of American Art and the Art Galleries of the University of California.

Greenberg, Clement. "Hofmann's Early Abstract Paintings," *Hans Hofmann*. New York: Kootz Gallery, 1959

_____. *Hofmann*. Paris: Georges Fall, 1961.

Hunter, Sam. *Hans Hofmann*. New York: Harry N. Abrams, 1963 (reprints of five texts by the artist).

Seitz, William, *Hans Hofmann*. New York: The Museum of Modern Art, 1963.

Fried, Michael. "New York Letter," *Art International*, vol. 1, no. 1 (April, 1963), 54–55.

Judd, Don. "Hofmann," *Arts*, vol. 37, no. 7 (April, 1963), 55.

Bultman, Fritz. "The Achievement of Hans Hofmann," *Art News*, vol. 62 (September, 1963), 43–45, 54–55.

Rosenberg, Harold. "Hans Hofmann and the Stability of the New," *The New Yorker*, vol. 39 (November 2, 1963), 100, 103–105, 108–110.

Fried, Michael. "New York Letter," *Art International*, vol. 7, no. 9 (December, 1963), 66.

Hans Hofmann. New York: Kootz Gallery, 1964.

Loran, Erle. *Hans Hofmann*. Berkeley: University of California Press, 1964.

Rosenberg, Harold. "Homage to Hans Hofmann," *Art News*, vol. 65 (January, 1967), 49.

Kootz, Sam. "Credibility of Color: Hans Hofmann, An Area of Optimism," *Arts Magazine*, vol. 41 (February, 1967), 37–39.

Bannard, Walter Darby. "Hofmann's Rectangles," *Artforum*, vol. 7 (Summer, 1969), 38–41.

By Hofmann:

"Painting and Culture," *Fortnightly*, Campbell, Calif., vol. 1, no. 1 (September 11, 1931), 5–7.

"On the Aims of Art," *Fortnightly*, Campbell, Calif. vol. 1, no. 13 (February 26, 1932), 7–11.

Statement in *Hans Hofmann*. New York: Art of This Century, 1944.

Search for the Real and Other Essays. Andover, Mass.: Addison Gallery of American Art, 1948. Republished by the M.I.T. Press, 1967.

"The Resurrection of the Plastic Art," *Hans Hofmann*. New York: Kootz Gallery, 1954.

"The Color Problem in Pure Painting: Its Creative Origin," *Hans Hofmann*. New York: Kootz Gallery, 1955. (Reprinted in *Hans Hofmann Retrospective Exhibition Catalogue*. Berkeley: University of California Press, 1957; and in San Hunter, *Hans Hofmann*. New York: Harry N. Abrams, 1963.)

Statement in *It Is*, no. 3 (Winter–Spring, 1959), 10.

Statement in *Hans Hofmann*. New York: Kootz Gallery, 1960.

"Hans Hofmann on Art," *Art Journal*, vol. 22, no. 3 (Spring, 1963), 180, 182.

EDWARD HOPPER

On Hopper:

Goodrich, Lloyd. "The Paintings of Edward Hopper," *The Arts*, vol. 11 (March, 1927), 134–138.

du Bois, Guy Pène. "The American Paintings of Edward Hopper," *Creative Art*, vol. 8 (March, 1931), 187–191.

Crowninshield, Frank. "A Series of American Artists, No. 3—Edward Hopper," *Vanity Fair*, vol. 38 (June, 1932), 11, 30.

Edward Hopper Retrospective. New York: The Museum of Modern Art, 1933. Articles by Alfred H. Barr, Jr., and Charles Burchfield.

Paintings, Watercolors and Etchings by Edward Hopper. Pittsburgh: Carnegie Institute, 1937.

Robert Henri and Five of His Pupils. New York: Century Association, 1946.

Brown, Milton. "The Early Realism of Hopper and Burchfield," *College Art Journal,* vol. 7 (Autumn, 1947), 3–11.

Goodrich, Lloyd. *Edward Hopper Retrospective Exhibition.* New York: The Whitney Museum of American Art, 1950.

Burchfield, Charles. "Hopper: Career of Silent Poetry," *Art News,* vol. 49 (March, 1950), 14–17.

Richardson, E. P. "Three American Painters: Sheeler, Hopper, Burchfield," *Perspectives U.S.A.,* vol. 16 (Summer, 1956), 111–119.

Tyler, Parker. "Hopper/Pollock," *Art News Annual,* no. 26 (1957), 86–107.

Geldzahler, Henry. "Edward Hopper," *Metropolitan Museum Bulletin,* vol. 21 (November, 1962), 113–117.

A Retrospective of Oils and Watercolors by Edward Hopper. Tucson: University of Arizona, 1963.

Goodrich, Lloyd. *Edward Hopper.* New York: The Whitney Museum of American Art, 1964.

Tillim, Sidney. "Edward Hopper and the Provincial Principle," *Arts Magazine,* vol. 39 (November, 1964), 24–31.

Edward Hopper. São Paulo IX, United States of America, 1967. Statements by B. O'Doherty, J. T. Soby, John Canaday; Essays by Lloyd Goodrich and William C. Seitz. Published by the Smithsonian Institution, Washington, D.C.

By Hopper:

Statement in *Edward Hopper.* New York: The Museum of Modern Art, 1933.

"Edward Hopper Objects" (Letter to Nathaniel Pousette-Dart), *The Art of Today,* vol. 6 (February, 1935), 11.

JASPER JOHNS

On Johns:

Heller, Ben. "Jasper Johns," *School of New York: Some Younger Painters,* ed. by B. H. Friedman. New York: Grove Press, 1959. Pp. 30–35.

16 Americans. New York: The Museum of Modern Art, 1959.

Restany, Pierre. "Jasper Johns and the Metaphysic of the Commonplace," *Cimaise,* Serie 8, no. 3 (September, 1961), 90–97.

Janis, Harriet, and Blesh, Rudi. *Collage.* Philadelphia: Chilton Co., 1962.

Jasper Johns Retrospective. Los Angeles: Everett Ellin Gallery, 1962.

Rosenblum, Robert. "Les Œuvres Recentes de Jasper Johns," *XXe Siècle,* ns. 24, Supp. 19–20 (February, 1962).

Gottlieb, Carla. "The Pregnant Woman, The Flag, The Eye: Three New Themes in Twentieth Century Art," *The Journal of Aesthetics and Art Criticism* (Winter, 1962), 117–187.

Tono, Yoshiaki. "Jasper Johns, or the Metaphysics of Vulgarity," *Mizue,* Tokyo, no. 685 (April, 1962), 24–40.

Steinberg, Leo. *Jasper Johns.* New York: Wittenborn, 1963.

Fried, Michael. "New York Letter," *Art International,* vol. 7, no. 2 (February 25, 1963), 60–62.

Swenson, G. R. "Reviews and Previews: Jasper Johns," *Art News,* vol. 61 (February, 1963), 11–12.

Judd, Don. "Six Painters and the Object at the Guggenheim," *Arts Magazine,* vol. 37 (May, 1963), 108.

Jasper Johns. New York: The Jewish Museum, 1964. Essays by Alan Solomon and John Cage.

Porter, Fairfield. "The Education of Jasper Johns," *Art News,* vol. 62 (February, 1964), 44–45, 61–62.

Rosenberg, Harold. "Jasper Johns; Things the Mind Already Knows," *Vogue,* vol. 143, no. 3 (February, 1964), 74.

Tillim, Sidney. "Ten Years of Jasper Johns," *Arts Magazine,* vol. 38 (April, 1964), 22–26.

Selected Bibliography

Ashbery, John. "Brooms and Prisms," *Art News*, vol. 65 (March, 1966), 58–59.
Kozloff, Max. "Jasper Johns: Colors, Maps, Devices," *Artforum*, vol. 6 (November, 1967), 26–31.
———— *Jasper Johns.* New York: Harry N. Abrams, 1969.

By Johns:

Statement in *16 Americans.* New York: The Museum of Modern Art, 1959. P. 22.
"Duchamp," *Scrap* (December 23, 1960).
Interview with Walter Hopps, *Artforum*, vol. 3 (March, 1965), 32–36.

DONALD JUDD

On Judd:

Hopps, Walter. "Donald Judd," United States of America, An Exhibition Organized by the Pasadena Art Museum for the VIII Bienal de São Paulo, Brazil, 1965.
Rose, Barbara. "Donald Judd," in U.S. Section VIII, São Paulo Bienal, 1965, *Artforum*, vol. 3 (June, 1965), 30–32.
Rose, Barbara. "ABC Art," *Art in America*, vol. 53 (October–November, 1965), 58–69.
Friedman, Martin. "Donald Judd," *Eight Sculptors: The Ambiguous Image.* Minneapolis: The Walker Art Center, 1966.
McShine, Kynaston. Introduction, *Primary Structures.* New York: The Jewish Museum, 1966.
Krauss, Rosalind. "Allusion and Illusion in Donald Judd," *Artforum*, vol. 4 (May, 1966), 24–26.
Bochner, M. "Primary Structures," *Arts Magazine*, vol. 40 (June, 1966), 32–35.
Rose, Barbara. *A New Aesthetic.* Washington: Washington Gallery of Modern Art, 1967. Pp. 8–20, 43–49.
Fried, Michael. "Art and Objecthood," *Artforum*, vol. 5 (June, 1967), 12–23.
Agee, William C. *Don Judd.* New York: The Whitney Museum of American Art, 1968.

By Judd:

Regular Reviewer for *Arts Magazine*, 1959–1965.
"Specific Objects," *Contemporary Sculpture, Arts Yearbook 8* (1965), 74–82.
Glaser, Bruce, moderator; Lucy Lippard, ed. "Questions to Stella and Judd," *Art News*, vol. 65 (September, 1966), 55–61.

ELLSWORTH KELLY

On Kelly:

Goosen, E. C. "Ellsworth Kelly," *Derrière le Miroir,* no. 110 (1958).
Tillim, S. "Profiles: Ellsworth Kelly," *Arts Yearbook 3* (1959), 148–155.
———— "Exhibition at Betty Parsons," *Arts Magazine*, vol. 34 (October, 1959), 48–50.
Alloway, Lawrence. "Heraldry and Sculpture," *Art International*, vol. 6, no. 3 (April, 1962), 52–53.
Rubin, William. "Ellsworth Kelly: The Big Form," *Art News*, vol. 62 (November, 1963), 32–35.
Fried, Michael. "New York Letter," *Art International*, vol. 7, no. 9 (Christmas–New Year, 1963–64), 54–55.
Ashton, Dore. "Exhibition at Janis Gallery," *Studio*, vol. 170 (July, 1965), 40–42.
"4 Drawings of 1965," *Artforum*, vol. 4 (February, 1966), 40–41.
Rose, Barbara. "Ellsworth Kelly as Sculptor," *Artforum*, vol. 5 (Summer, 1967), 51–55.
"*Spectrum II*, 1966–1967, A Painting by E. Kelly, American, Born 1923," *St. Louis Museum Bulletin*, vol. 3 (November, 1967), 4–5.

Waldman, D. "Kelly Color, New Show at Janis," *Art News*, vol. 67 (October, 1968), 40–41.

Coplans, John. "The Earlier Work of Ellsworth Kelly," *Artforum*, vol. 7 (Summer, 1969), 48–55.

By Kelly:

Geldzahler, Henry. "Kelly," Interview with Ellsworth Kelly, *Art International*, vol. 8, no. 1 (February 15, 1964), 47–48.

FRANZ KLINE

On Kline:

Hess, Thomas B. "Miracle at Schenby Park," *Art News*, vol. 51 (November, 1952), 28–30, 66–67.

Goodenough, Robert. "Kline Paints a Picture," *Art News*, vol. 51 (December, 1952), 36–39, 63–64.

Ashton, Dore. "Art," *Arts and Architecture*, vol. 73 (April, 1956), 3, 10–12; vol. 75 (July, 1958), 10, 31–33; vol. 76 (March, 1959), 8, 28–29.

Sawyer, Kenneth B. "Franz Kline," Venice XXX Biennale, United States Section, 1960, pp. 314–316.

Kline. New York: Sidney Janis Gallery, 1960, 1961, 1963.

Ashton, Dore. "Franz Kline," *Cimaise*, vol. 8 (May–June, 1961), 70–83.

de Kooning, Elaine. *Franz Kline Memorial Exhibition.* Washington: Washington Gallery of Modern Art, 1962.

Goldwater, Robert. "Art Chronicle: Masters of the New," *Partisan Review*, vol. 29 (Summer, 1962), 416–420.

Langsner, Jules. "Kline," *Artforum*, vol. 1 (July, 1962), 4–5.

de Kooning, Elaine. "Franz Kline: Painter of His Own Life," *Art News*, vol. 61 (November, 1962), 28–31, 64–69.

Franz Kline. Amsterdam: Stedelijk Museum, 1963. Introduction by Frank O'Hara.

Langsner, Jules. "Franz Kline Calligraphy and Information Theory," *Art International*, vol. 7, no. 3 (March, 1963), 25–29.

O'Hara, Frank, *Franz Kline.* London: Whitechapel Gallery, 1964.

Robbins, Daniel and Eugenia. "Franz Kline: Rough Impulsive Gesture," *Studio*, vol. 167 (May, 1964), 186–189.

Pavia, Philip. "Polemic on One-Eye Formats," *Art News*, vol. 65 (December, 1966), 28–31, 62–64.

Dawson, Fielding. *An Emotional Memoir of Franz Kline.* New York: Pantheon Books, 1967.

Franz Kline. New York: Marlborough-Gerson Gallery, 1967. (Introduction by Robert Goldwater.)

Gordon, John. *Franz Kline: 1910–1962.* New York: The Whitney Museum of American Art, 1968.

By Kline:

O'Hara, Frank. "Franz Kline Talking," *Evergreen Review*, vol. 2 (Autumn, 1958), 58–68.

"Franz Kline, 1910–1962: An Interview with David Sylvester," *Living Arts*, no. 1 (1963), 2–13.

GABRIEL KOHN

On Kohn:

Petersen, Valerie. "Gabriel Kohn Makes a Sculpture," *Art News*, vol. 60 (October, 1961), 48–51, 66–67.

"Gabriel Kohn," *Art News*, vol. 61 (January, 1963), 39, 49.

Tillim, Sidney. "Month in Review: Gabe Kohn," *Arts Magazine*, vol. 37 (February, 1963), 43–44.

Rose, Barbara. "New York Notes," *Art International*, vol. 7, no. 2 (February 25, 1963), 77–78.

Coplans, J. "Sculptors Meet at Long Beach," *Art News*, vol. 64 (December, 1965), 52, 61.

Wilson, W. "Four Defectors to L.A.," *Art in America*, vol. 56 (March, 1968), 102.

ROY LICHTENSTEIN

On Lichtenstein:

Swenson, G. R. "New American Sign Painters," *Art News,* vol. 61 (September, 1962), 44–47.

Tillim, Sidney. "Roy Lichtenstein and the Hudson River School at Mi Chou," *Arts Magazine,* vol. 37 (October, 1962), 55–56.

Rosenblum, Robert. "Roy Lichtenstein and the Realist Revolt," *Metro,* 8 (April, 1963), 38–46.

Loran, Erle. "Cézanne and Lichtenstein: Problem of Transformation," *Artforum,* vol. 2 (September, 1963), 34–35.

Judd, Don. "Exhibition at Castelli Gallery," *Arts Magazine,* vol. 38 (November, 1963), 32–33.

Kozloff, Max. "Art: Dissimulated Pop," *The Nation,* vol. 199 (November 30, 1964), 418.

Lichtenstein. Rome: Fantazaria, 1966. (Contains Alan Solomon, "Conversation with Lichtenstein"; Maurizio Calvesi, "Lichtenstein: A Global Painter"; Alberto Boatto, "The Comic Strip Under the Microscope"; Filiberta Menna, "The Organized Perception of Lichtenstein"; Max Kozloff, "Dissimulated Pop"; Ellen H. Johnson, "Lichtenstein and the Printed Image"; Robert Rosenblum, "Lichtenstein at the XXXIII Venice Biennale.")

Fry, Edward F. "Roy Lichtenstein's Recent Landscapes," *Art and Literature,* Lausanne, no. 8 (Spring, 1966), 111–119.

Beeren, Wim. *Roy Lichtenstein.* Amsterdam: Stedelijk Museum, 1967.

Coplans, John. *Roy Lichtenstein.* Pasadena: Pasadena Art Museum, 1967.

Alloway, Lawrence. "Roy Lichtenstein's Period Style: From the Thirties to the Sixties and Back," *Arts Magazine,* vol. 42 (September, 1967), 24–29.

Waldman, D. "Remarkable Commonplace," *Art News,* vol. 66 (October, 1967), 28–31.

Hamilton, R., and Alloway, L. "Roy Lichtenstein," *Studio,* vol. 175 (January, 1968), 20–31.

Baro, Gene. "Roy Lichtenstein: Technique as Style," *Art International,* vol. 12, no. 9 (November 20, 1968), 35–39.

Boime, Albert. "Roy Lichtenstein and the Comic Strip," *Art Journal,* vol. 28 (Winter, 1968–69), 155–159.

By Lichtenstein:

Coplans, John. Interview, *Artforum,* vol 2 (October, 1963), 31. (Reprinted in *Roy Lichtenstein.* Amsterdam: Stedelijk Museum, 1967.)

Swenson, Gene. "What Is Pop Art?" Interview, *Art News,* vol. 62 (November, 1963), 25, 62–63.

Glaser, B. "Lichtenstein, Oldenburg, Warhol: A Discussion," *Artforum,* vol. 4 (February, 1966), 20–24.

Coplans, John. "Talking with Roy Lichtenstein," *Artforum,* vol. 4 (May, 1967), 34–40.

MORRIS LOUIS

On Louis:

Berkowitz, Leon. "Statement on the Artist," *Morris Louis.* Washington, D.C.: Workshop Art Center, 1953.

Greenberg, Clement. Note, in Gallery Announcement, Emerging Talent. New York: Kootz Gallery, 1954.

Tapié de Céylèran, Michel. Introduction to Catalogue: *Morris Louis.* New York: Martha Jackson Gallery, 1957.

Sawin, Martica. "Morris Louis," *Arts Magazine,* vol. 33 (May, 1959), 58–59.

Greenberg, Clement. "Louis and Noland," *Art International,* vol. 4, no. 5 (May 25, 1960), 26–29.

Alloway, Lawrence. Introduction, *Morris Louis: 1912–1962.* New York: The Solomon R. Guggenheim Museum, 1963.

Greenberg, Clement. Introduction, in *Three New American Painters: Louis, Noland, Olitski*. Regina, Canada: Normal McKenzie Art Gallery, 1963. (Reprinted in *Canadian Art*, vol. 20 [May, 1963], 172–175 and excerpts reprinted in *Morris Louis*. London: Kasmin Ltd., 1963.)

Rosenblum, Robert. Note in *Towards a New Abstraction*. New York: The Solomon R. Guggenheim Museum, 1963.

Fried, Michael. "Some Notes on Morris Louis," *Arts Magazine*, vol. 38 (November, 1963), 22–27.

Rosenblum, Robert. "Morris Louis at the Guggenheim Museum," *Art International*, vol. 7, no. 9 (December 5, 1963), 24–27.

Fried, Michael. "The Confounding of Confusion," *Arts Yearbook*, no. 7 (1964), 36–45.

Tillim, Sidney. "Exhibition at Emmerich Gallery," *Arts Magazine*, vol. 39 (December, 1964), 66–67.

Robbins, Daniel. "Morris Louis at the Juncture of Two Traditions," *Quadrum*, no. 18 (1965), 41–54.

Rosenblum, Robert. Introduction, *Morris Louis*. Amsterdam: Stedelijk Museum, 1965.

Solomon, Alan. Introduction, *Morris Louis*. London: Whitechapel Gallery, 1965.

Greenberg, Clement. Letter to the Editor, *Art International*, vol. 9, no. 4 (May, 1965), 66.

Fried, Michael. *Morris Louis: 1912–1962*. Boston: Boston Museum of Fine Arts, 1967.

———. "The Achievement of Morris Louis," *Artforum*, vol. 5 (February, 1967), 34–40.

Goldin, A. "Morris Louis Thinking the Unwordable," *Art News*, vol. 67 (April, 1968), 48–49.

"Kenneth Noland, Morris Louis and Anthony Caro at the Metropolitan Museum," *Arts Magazine*, vol. 42 (Summer, 1968), 56.

Fried, Michael. *Morris Louis*. New York: Harry N. Abrams, 1969.

ROBERT MORRIS

On Morris:

Judd, Don. "Black, White and Gray," *Arts Magazine*, vol. 38 (March, 1964), 36–38.

———. "Exhibition at the Green Gallery," *Arts Magazine*, vol. 39 (February, 1965), 54.

Kozloff, Max. "Further Adventures in American Sculpture," *Arts Magazine*, vol. 39 (February, 1965), 27.

Rose, Barbara. "Looking at American Sculpture," *Artforum*, vol. 3 (February, 1965), 29–36.

———. "ABC Art," *Art in America*, vol. 53 (October–November, 1965), 58–69.

Friedman, Martin. *Eight Sculptors: The Ambiguous Image*. Minneapolis: The Walker Art Center, 1966. Pp. 18, 20–21.

Antin, David. "Art and Information. 1: Grey Paint, Robert Morris," *Art News*, vol. 65 (April, 1966), 22–24, 56–58.

Ranier, Y. "Don't Give the Game Away," *Arts Magazine*, vol. 41 (April, 1967), 44.

Battcock, Gregory. "Robert Morris: New Sculptures at Castelli," *Arts Magazine*, vol. 42 (May, 1968), 30–31.

Müller, Gregoire. "Robert Morris Presents Anti-Form," *Arts Magazine*, vol. 43 (February, 1969), 29–30.

By Morris:

"Notes on Dance," *Tulane Drama Review*, vol. 10 (Winter, 1965), 179–186.

"Notes on Sculpture," *Artforum*, vol. 4 (February, 1966), 42–44; Part II, vol. 5 (October, 1966), 20–23; Part III, vol. 5 (Summer, 1967), 24–29; Part IV, vol. 7 (April, 1969), 50–54.

McShine, Kynaston, moderator. "The New Sculpture," Symposium on Primary Structures Held at The Jewish Museum, New York, May 3, 1966, with Barbara Rose, Robert Morris, Don Judd, Mark di Suvero.

"Anti-Form," *Artforum*, vol. 6 (April, 1968), 33–35.

ROBERT MOTHERWELL

On Motherwell:

Greenberg, Clement. "Art," *The Nation*, vol. 159 (November 11, 1944), 598–599; vol. 164 (May 31, 1947), 664–665; vol. 166 (May 29, 1948), 612–614.

Kees, W. "Robert Motherwell," *Magazine of Art*, vol. 4 (March, 1948), 86–88.

Fitzsimmons, James. "Robert Motherwell," *Design Quarterly*, no. 29 (1954), 18–22.

Goosen, Eugene C. *Robert Motherwell: First Retrospective Exhibition.* Bennington, Vt.: Bennington College, 1959.

————. "Robert Motherwell and the Seriousness of Subject," *Art International*, vol. 3, nos. 1–2 (1959), 33–35, 38, 51.

Robert Motherwell: A Retrospective Exhibition. Pasadena: Pasadena Art Museum, 1962. Texts by T. W. Leavitt, Frank O'Hara, Sam Hunter.

"Exhibition at the Sidney Janis Gallery," *Art News*, vol. 61 (January, 1963). Reply by E. Vicente, vol. 61 (February, 1963), 6; Rejoinder by Motherwell, vol. 62 (March, 1963), 6.

Tillim, Sidney. "Exhibition at the Sidney Janis Gallery," *Arts Magazine*, vol. 37 (January, 1963), 40–42.

Ashton, Dore. "Motherwell Loves and Believes," *Studio*, vol. 165 (March, 1963), 116–117.

————. "Robert Motherwell: Passion and Transfiguration," *Studio*, vol. 167 (March, 1964), 100–105.

O'Hara, Frank. *Robert Motherwell.* New York: The Museum of Modern Art, 1965.

Robert Motherwell. Northampton, Mass.: Smith College Museum of Art, 1965 (Preface by the artist).

Edgar, N. "Satisfactions of Robert Motherwell," *Art News*, vol. 64 (October, 1965), 38–41. Reply by Motherwell, vol. 6 (December, 1965), 6.

O'Hara, Frank. "Robert Motherwell at the Museum of Modern Art," *Art in America*, vol. 53, no. 5 (October–November, 1965), 80–81.

Tillim, Sidney. "Motherwell: The Echo of Protest," *Artforum*, vol. 4 (December, 1965), 34–36.

Robertson, B. "From a Notebook on Robert Motherwell," *Studio*, vol. 171 (March, 1966), 89–93.

Banham, R. "Motherwell Retrospective at Whitechapel," *Architectural Review*, vol. 140 (July, 1966), 59–60.

Krauss, Rosalind. "Robert Motherwell's New Paintings," *Artforum*, vol. 7 (May, 1969), 26–28.

Arnason, H. H. "Motherwell and the Window," *Art News*, vol. 68 (Summer, 1969), 48–52.

By Motherwell:

"Painter's Objects," *Partisan Review*, vol. 11 (Winter, 1944), 93–97.

"The Modern Painter's World," *Dyn*, vol. 1, no. 6 (November, 1944), 9–14.

Editorial Statement in *Possibilities*, vol. 1, no. 1 (Winter, 1947–48), 1.

Statement in *Robert Motherwell: Collages 1943–1949.* New York: Kootz Gallery, 1949.

Modern Artists in America. New York: Wittenborn, Schultz, 1951 (co-editor with Ad Reinhardt).

The School of New York. Beverly Hills: Frank Perls Gallery, 1951.

"The Rise and Continuity of Abstract Art," *Arts and Architecture*, vol. 68 (September, 1951), 20–21, 41. (Lecture at the Fogg Art Museum, Cambridge, Mass.)

"Painting as Existence," *Metro*, 7 (1962), 94–97. Interview with David Sylvester, Recorded and Broadcast over B.B.C. (October 23, 1960).

Kozloff, Max. "Interview with Robert Motherwell," *Artforum*, vol. 4 (September, 1965), 33–37.

"David Smith: A Major American Sculptor; A Personal Appreciation," *Studio*, vol. 172 (August, 1966), 65–68.

BARNETT NEWMAN

On Newman:

Greenberg, Clement, "Art," *The Nation*, vol. 165 (December 6, 1947), 629–630.

Hess, Thomas B. "Newman," *Art News*, vol. 49 (March, 1950), 48.

_____. "Newman," *Art News*, vol. 50 (Summer, 1951), 47.

Greenberg, Clement. *Barnett Newman: First Retrospective Exhibition*. Bennington, Vt.: Bennington College, 1958.

_____. *Barnett Newman: A Selection, 1946–1952*. New York: French and Co., 1959 (reprinted from Bennington Catalogue, 1958).

Goosen, E. C. "The Philosophic Line of Barnett Newman," *Art News*, vol. 57 (Summer, 1958), 30–31, 62–63.

Crehan, Hubert. "Barnett Newman," *Art News*, vol. 58 (April, 1959), 12.

Ashton, Dore. "Art," *Arts and Architecture*, vol. 76 (May, 1959), 6, 7.

Hess, Thomas B. "Willem de Kooning and Barnett Newman," *Art News*, vol. 61 (December, 1962), 12.

Tillim, Sidney. "Paintings by William de Kooning and Barnett Newman at the Allan Stone Gallery," *Arts Magazine*, vol. 37 (December, 1962), 38–40.

Fried, Michael. "New York Letter," *Art International*, vol. 6, no. 10 (December 20, 1962), 54–57.

Rosenberg, Harold. "Barnett Newman: A Man of Controversy and Spiritual Grandeur," *Vogue*, vol. 141 (February 1, 1963), 134–135, 163, 166 (reprinted in *The Anxious Object*. New York: Horizon Press, 1964, pp. 169–174).

Alloway, Lawrence. "Barnett Newman," *Artforum*, vol. 3 (June, 1965), 20–22.

_____. *Stations of the Cross*. New York: The Solomon R. Guggenheim Museum, 1966.

Calas, Nicolas. "Subject Matter in the Work of Barnett Newman," *Arts Magazine*, vol. 42 (November, 1967), 38–40. (Reprinted in Calas, *Art in the Age of Risk*. New York: E. P. Dutton, 1968.)

Hess, Thomas B. *Barnett Newman*. New York: Walker and Co., 1969. (On occasion of Knoedler exhibition.)

Rosenberg, Harold. "The Art World: Icon Maker," *The New Yorker*, vol. 45 (April 19, 1969), 136, 138, 140, 142.

By Newman:

Adolph Gottlieb. New York: Wakefield Gallery, 1944.

Pre-Columbian Stone Sculpture. New York: Betty Parsons Gallery, 1944.

North West Coast Indian Painting. New York: Betty Parsons Gallery, 1946.

The Ideographic Picture. New York: Betty Parsons Gallery, 1947.

"The First Man Was an Artist," *The Tiger's Eye*, vol. 1 (October, 1947), 57–60.

"The Object and the Image," *The Tiger's Eye*, vol. 1, no. 3 (March, 1948), 111.

"The Sublime Is Now," *The Tiger's Eye*, vol. 1, no. 6 (December 15, 1948), 51–53.

Letter to the Editor, *Art News*, vol. 60 (May, 1961), 6 (first reply to Panofsky).

Letter to the Editor, *Art News*, vol. 60 (September, 1961), 6 (second reply to Panofsky).

18 Cantos 1963–64. Preface to a volume of lithographs by Barnett Newman. West Islip, N.Y.: 1964.

Statement in São Paulo Bienal VIII, São Paulo, Brazil: 1965.

"The Fourteen Stations of the Cross," *Art News*, vol. 65 (May, 1966), 26–28.

Letter to the Editor, *Art International*, vol. 11, no. 7 (September, 1967), 51 (first reply to Motherwell). Refers to Interview with Motherwell by Sidney Simon called "Concerning the Beginnings of the New York School," *Art International*, vol. 11, no. 6 (Summer, 1967), 20–23.

Letter to the Editor, *Art International*, vol. 11 (November, 1967), 24, 27 (second reply to Motherwell). Answers letter from Motherwell in the October, 1965, issue, p. 38.

"For Impassioned Criticism," *Art News*, vol. 67 (Summer, 1968), 26. *Discussion*, vol. 67 (September, 1968), 6.

ISAMU NOGUCHI

On Noguchi:

Levy, Julien. "Isamu Noguchi," *Creative Art*, vol. 12 (January, 1933), 29–35.

Hess, Thomas B. "Isamu Noguchi, '46," *Art News*, vol. 45 (September, 1946), 34–38, 47, 50–51.

Greenberg, Clement. "Art: Isamu Noguchi," *The Nation,* vol. 168 (March 19, 1949), 341–342.

Frankfurter, Alfred. "The Controversial Noguchi Sets for Lear," *Art News,* vol. 54 (December, 1955), 42–43.

Page, Addison Franklin. "Isamu Noguchi: The Evolution of a Style," *Art in America,* vol. 44 (Winter, 1956–57), 24–26, 64–66.

Ashton, Dore. "Isamu Noguchi," *Arts and Architecture,* vol. 46 (August, 1959), 14–15; vol. 80 (June, 1963), 6–7.

Raynor, Vivien. "In the Galleries: Isamu Noguchi," *Arts Magazine,* vol. 35 (September, 1961), 36–37.

Michelson, Annette. *Isamu Noguchi.* Paris: Galerie Claude Bernard, 1964 (text in English and French).

Jacobs, J. "Projects for Playgrounds, *Art in America,* vol. 55 (November, 1967), 44–47.

Gordon, John. *Isamu Noguchi.* New York: The Whitney Museum of American Art, 1968.

Edgar, N. "Noguchi, Master of Ceremony," *Art News,* vol. 67 (April, 1968), 50–52.

By Noguchi:

"Meanings in Modern Sculpture," *Art News,* vol. 48 (March, 1949), 12–15.

"Towards a Reintegration of the Arts," *College Art Journal,* vol. 9, no. 1 (Autumn, 1949), 59–60.

A Sculptor's World. New York: Harper and Row, 1968.

"Artist Speaks: Isamu Noguchi," *Art in America,* vol. 56 (March, 1968), 28–31.

KENNETH NOLAND

On Noland:

Greenberg, Clement. "Louis and Noland," *Art International,* vol. 4, no. 5 (May 25, 1960), 26–29.

Ashbery, John. "Paris Notes," *Art International,* vol. 5, nos. 5–6 (June–August, 1961), 42, 92.

Kenneth Noland. Zurich: Galerie Charles Lunhard AG, 1962. Introduction by E. C. Goosen.

Judd, Don. "Exhibition at Emmerich Gallery," *Arts Magazine,* vol. 36 (September, 1962), 49.

Greenberg, Clement. "After Abstract Expressionism," *Art International,* vol. 6 (October 25, 1962), 24–32.

———. Introduction, *Three New American Painters: Louis, Noland, Olitski.* Regina, Canada: Norman McKenzie Art Gallery, 1963. (Reprinted in *Canadian Art,* vol. 20 [May, 1963], 172–175.)

Fried, Michael. "New York Letter," *Art International,* vol. 7, no. 5 (May, 1963), 69–70.

Judd, Donald. "In the Galleries," *Arts Magazine,* vol. 37 (September, 1963), 53–54.

Solomon, Alan. XXXII International Biennial Exhibition of Art, Venice, 1964, United States of America, New York: The Jewish Museum, 1964.

Rose, Barbara. "Kenneth Noland," *Art International,* vol. 8, nos. 5–6 (Summer, 1964), 58–61.

Geldzahler, Henry. "Recent American Painting," *Cimaise,* nos. 69–70 (July–October, 1964), 42–47.

Fried, Michael. *Kenneth Noland.* New York: The Jewish Museum, 1965.

———. *Three American Painters* (Noland, Olitski, Stella). Cambridge, Mass.: Fogg Art Museum, 1965.

Nordland, Gerald. *The Washington Color Painters.* Washington: Washington Gallery of Modern Art, 1965.

Cone, Jane Harrison. "On Color in Kenneth Noland's Painting," *Art International,* vol. 9, no. 5 (June, 1965), 36–38.

———. "Kenneth Noland's New Paintings," *Artforum,* vol. 6 (November, 1967), 36–41.

Fried, Michael. "Recent Work by Kenneth Noland," *Artforum,* vol. 7 (Summer, 1969), 36–37.

By Noland:

Letter to the Editor, *Art News,* vol. 61 (November, 1962), 6 (on Louis).

CLAES OLDENBURG

On Oldenburg:

Tillim, Sidney. "Claes Oldenburg's 'The Store,'" *Arts Magazine*, vol. 36 (February, 1962), 35–37.

Kozloff, Max. "Art: New Works by Oldenburg," *The Nation*, vol. 198, no. 18 (April 27, 1964), 445–446.

Restany, Pierre. "Une Personalité Charnière de l'Art Americain: Claes Oldenburg Premieres Œuvres," *Metro*, 9 (April, 1965), 20–26.

Geldzahler, Henry. "Happenings: Theatre by Painters," *Hudson Review*, vol. 18, no. 4 (Winter, 1965–66), 581–586.

Claes Oldenburg: Skulpturer och Teckningar. Stockholm: Moderna Museet, 1966.

Rosenstein, Harris. "Climbing Mt. Oldenburg," *Art News*, vol. 64 (February, 1966), 21–25, 56.

Ashton, Dore. "Exhibition at the Sidney Janis Gallery," *Studio*, vol. 171 (May, 1966), 204–205.

Berkson, William. "In the Galleries: Claes Oldenburg," *Arts Magazine*, vol. 40 (May, 1966), 57–58.

Baro, Gene. "Claes Oldenburg or the Things of This World," *Art International*, vol. 10 (November 20, 1966), 40–43, 45–49.

Melville, R. "Exhibition at the Robert Frazer Gallery," *Architectural Review*, vol. 141 (February, 1967), 141–142.

"Take a Cigarette Butt and Make It Heroic: Projects for Colossal Civic Monuments in Capital Cities," *Art News*, vol. 66 (May, 1967), 30–31.

Rose, Barbara. "Claes Oldenburg's Soft Machines," *Artforum*, vol. 5 (Summer, 1967), 30–35.

———. *Claes Oldenburg.* New York: The Museum of Modern Art, 1969.

By Oldenburg:

"Environments, Situations, Spaces." New York: Martha Jackson Gallery, 1961.

"From the Studio Notes by Claes Oldenburg," *New Work by Oldenburg.* New York: Sidney Janis Gallery, 1966.

Injun and Other Histories. New York: Something Else Press, 1966.

Statements in *Claes Oldenburg: Sculpturer och Techningar.* Stockholm: Moderna Museet, 1966.

Store Days. New York: Something Else Press, 1967.

JULES OLITSKI

On Olitski:

Greenburg, Clement. Introduction. *Three New American Painters: Louis, Noland, Olitski.* Regina, Canada: Norman McKenzie Art Gallery, 1963. (Reprinted in *Canadian Art*, vol. 20 [May, 1963], 172–175.)

Rose, Barbara. "New York Letter," *Art International*, vol. 7, no. 4 (April 25, 1963), 57, 58.

Kozloff, Max. "Frankenthaler and Olitski," *The Nation* (April, 1965), 374.

Fried, Michael. "Jules Olitski's New Paintings," *Artforum*, vol. 4 (November, 1965), 36–40.

———. *Three American Painters* (Noland, Olitski, Stella). Cambridge, Mass.: Fogg Art Museum, 1966.

Lord, Barry. *Frankenthaler, Noland, Olitski.* New Brunswick, Canada: New Brunswick Museum, 1966.

Fried, Michael. *Jules Olitski: Paintings, 1963–1967.* Washington, D.C.: The Corcoran Gallery of Art, 1967.

———. "Olitski and Shape," *Artforum*, vol. 5 (January, 1967), 20–21.

Champa, K. S. "Olitski: Nothing But Color," *Art News*, vol. 66 (May, 1967), 36–38, 74–76.

Krauss, Rosalind. *Jules Olitski: Recent Paintings.* Philadelphia: Institute of Contemporary Art, University of Pennsylvania, 1968.

Hudson, Andrew. "On Jules Olitski's Painting and Some Changes of View," *Art International*, vol. 12, no. 1 (January, 1968), 31–36.

Moffett, Kenworth. "The Sculpture of Jules Olitski," *Metropolitan Museum of Art Bulletin*, vol. 27 (April, 1969), 366–371. (Reprinted and revised in *Artforum*, vol. 7 [April, 1969], 55–58.)

By Olitski:

"Olitski on Color," *Artforum*, vol. 5 (January, 1967), 20. (Slightly revised and expanded version of Olitski's catalogue statement in Venice Biennale Catalogue, 1966.)

"On Sculpture," *Metropolitan Museum of Art Bulletin*, vol. 27 (April, 1969), 366. (Reprinted in *Artforum*, vol. 7 [April, 1969], 59.)

JACKSON POLLOCK

On Pollock:

Sweeney, J. J. *Jackson Pollock*. New York: Art of This Century, 1943.

Greenberg, Clement. "Art: Jackson Pollock," *The Nation*, vol. 157 (November 27, 1943), 621; vol. 160 (April 7, 1945), 397; vol. 162 (April 13, 1946), 445; vol. 164 (February 1, 1947), 137, 139; vol. 166 (January 24, 1948), 107–108; vol. 168 (February 19, 1949), 221.

"Jackson Pollock: Is He the Greatest Living Artist in the United States?" *Life*, vol. 27 (August 8, 1949), 42–45.

Tyler, Parker. "Jackson Pollock: The Infinite Labyrinth," *Magazine of Art*, vol. 43 (March, 1950), 92–93.

Ossorio, Alfonso. *Jackson Pollock*. New York: Betty Parsons Gallery, 1951.

Goodenough, Robert. "Pollock Paints a Picture," *Art News*, vol. 50 (May, 1951), 38–41.

Greenberg, Clement. Preface, *Retrospective Exhibition of Jackson Pollock*. Bennington, Vt.: Bennington College, 1952.

———. "Jackson Pollock's New Style," *Harper's Magazine*, vol. 85 (February, 1952), 174–175.

Friedman, B. H. "Profile: Jackson Pollock," *Art in America*, vol. 43 (December, 1955), 49.

Steinberg, L. "Fifteen Years of Work Shown at the Sidney Janis Gallery," *Arts Magazine*, vol. 30 (December, 1955), 43–44.

Hunter, Sam. "Jackson Pollock: The Maze and the Minotaur," *New World Writing*. New York: New American Library, 1956.

Shapiro, Meyer. "The Younger American Painters of Today," *The Listener* (January 26, 1956), 146.

Hess, Thomas B. "Jackson Pollock, 1912–1956," *Art News*, vol. 55 (September, 1956), 44–45.

Greenberg, Clement. "Jackson Pollock," *Evergreen Review*, vol. 1 (1957).

Tillim, Sidney. "Jackson Pollock: A Critical Evaluation," *College Art Journal*, vol. 16, no. 3 (Spring, 1957), 242–243.

Kaprow, Allan. "The Legacy of Jackson Pollock," *Art News*, vol. 57 (October, 1958), 24–26.

Alloway, Lawrence. "The Art of Jackson Pollock: 1912–1956," *The Listener*, vol. 60 (November 27, 1958), 888.

Kramer, Hilton. "Jackson Pollock and Nicholas de Staël, Two Painters and Their Myths," *Arts Yearbook*, no. 3 (1959), 53–60.

O'Hara, Frank. "Jackson Pollock, 1912–1956," in Peter Selz, *New Images of Man*. New York: The Museum of Modern Art, 1959. Pp. 123–128.

———. *Jackson Pollock*. New York: George Braziller, 1959.

Rubin, William. "Notes on Masson and Pollock," *Arts Magazine*, vol. 34 (November, 1959), 36–43; Correction: vol. 34 (December, 1959), 9.

Guggenheim, Peggy. "Art of This Century," in *Confessions of an Art Addict*. New York: Macmillan, 1960.

Robertson, Bryan. *Jackson Pollock*. New York: Harry N. Abrams, 1960.

Alloway, Lawrence. *Jackson Pollock: Paintings, Drawings and Watercolors from the Collection of Lee Krasner Pollock.* London: Marlborough Fine Art Ltd., 1961.

Tillim, Sidney. "Retrospective at the Marlborough-Gerson Gallery," *Arts Magazine,* vol. 38 (March, 1964), 55–56.

Fried, Michael. "New York Letter," *Art International,* vol. 8 (April, 1964), 57–58.

O'Connor, Francis V. "The Genesis of Jackson Pollock: 1912–1943." Unpublished Ph.D. dissertation, The Johns Hopkins University, Baltimore, 1965.

Fried, Michael. "Jackson Pollock," *Artforum,* vol. 4 (September, 1965), 14–17.

O'Connor, Francis V. *Jackson Pollock.* New York: The Museum of Modern Art, 1967.

Rubin, William. "Jackson Pollock and the Modern Tradition," *Artforum,* vol. 5 (February, 1967), 14–22; (March, 1967), 28–37; (April, 1967), 18–31; (May, 1967), 28–33. (April and May issues contain correspondence between Rubin and Rosenberg.)

"Jackson Pollock: An Artists' Symposium, Part I," *Art News,* vol. 66 (April, 1967), 29. (Statements by James Brooks, Elaine de Kooning, Adolph Gottlieb, Al Held, Allan Kaprow, Alex Katz, Robert Motherwell, Barnett Newman, Philip Pavia, Larry Rivers.)

Judd, Don. "Jackson Pollock," *Arts Magazine,* vol. 41 (April, 1967), 32–35.

"Jackson Pollock: An Artists' Symposium," Part II, *Art News,* vol. 66 (May, 1967), 27. (Statements by Al Brunelle, Jane Freilicher, David Lee, Joan Mitchell, Kenneth Noland, David Novros, Claes Oldenburg, George Segal.) Editorial on Symposium by T. B. Hess, vol. 66 (April, 1967), 27; Rejoinder by W. Rubin, vol. 66 (May, 1967), 6.

O'Connor, Francis V. "The Genesis of Jackson Pollock," *Artforum,* vol. 5 (May, 1967), 16–23.

Rosenberg, Harold. "The Mythic Act," *The New Yorker,* vol. 43 (May 6, 1967), 162, 164, 167–171.

By Pollock:

"Jackson Pollock Answers to a Questionnaire," *Arts and Architecture,* vol. 61 (February, 1944), 14.

"My Paintings," *Possibilities,* vol. 1 (Winter, 1947–48), 78–83.

Excerpts from an Interview. Taped by William Wright, The Springs, Long Island, 1950. *Art in America,* vol. 53 (August–September, 1965), 111; reprinted in Francis V. O'Connor, *Jackson Pollock.* New York: The Museum of Modern Art, 1967. Pp. 79–81.

Narration for the film, *Jackson Pollock,* made by Hans Namuth and Paul Falkenberg, 1951. Typescript in Library of The Museum of Modern Art, New York.

LARRY POONS

On Poons:

Tillim, Sidney. "Larry Poons: The Dotted Line," *Arts Magazine,* vol. 39 (February, 1965), 16–21.

Johnson, Ellen H. "Three Young Americans: Hinman, Poons and Williams," *Oberlin College Bulletin* (Spring, 1965), 83–100.

Kozloff, Max. "Larry Poons," *Artforum,* vol. 3 (April, 1965), 26–29.

Fry, E. F. "Poons: A Clean and Balanced World?" *Art News,* vol. 65 (February, 1967), 34–35.

Lippard, Lucy R. "Larry Poons: The Illusion of Disorder," *Art International,* vol. 11 (April 20, 1967), 22–26.

Champa, Kermit S. "New Paintings by Larry Poons," *Artforum,* vol. 6 (Summer, 1968), 39–42.

ROBERT RAUSCHENBERG

On Rauschenberg:

"Exhibition at the Stable," *Arts and Architecture,* vol. 70 (October, 1953), 33–34.

Meyers, David. "Robert Rauschenberg," in B. H. Friedman, ed., *School of New York: Some Younger Artists.* New York: Grove Press, 1959.

The United States Representation at Venice Biennale of The Museum of Modern Art, 1959. Introduction by Sam Hunter, published by Minneapolis Institute of Arts.

Ashton, Dore. "Rauschenberg's Thirty-Four Illustrations for Dante's Inferno," *Metro,* vol. 2 (1961), 51–62.

Cage, John. "On Robert Rauschenberg, Artist and His Work," *Metro,* vol. 2 (1961), 36–51.

Rauschenberg. Paris: Galerie Ileana Sonnabend, 1963. (Text by Lawrence Alloway, John Cage, Françoise Choay, Gillo Dorfles, Alain Jouffroy, André Parinaud, Michel Ragon.)

Solomon, Alan. *Robert Rauschenberg.* New York: The Jewish Museum, 1963.

Swenson, G. R. "Rauschenberg Paints a Picture," *Art News,* vol. 62 (April, 1963), 44–47.

Robert Rauschenberg. London: Whitechapel Gallery, 1964. (Articles by John Cage, Henry Geldzahler, Max Kozloff, Bryan Robertson.)

Swanson, Dean. *Robert Rauschenberg.* Minneapolis: The Walker Art Center, 1965.

Tomkins, Calvin. *The Bride and the Bachelors.* New York: Viking, 1965.

Johnson, E. H. "Image Duplicators: Lichtenstein, Rauschenberg, Warhol," *Canadian Art,* vol. 23 (January, 1966), 12–19.

Forge, Andrew. *Robert Rauschenberg.* Amsterdam: Stedelijk Museum, 1968.

————. *Robert Rauschenberg.* New York: Harry N. Abrams. To be published.

By Rauschenberg:

"The Artist Speaks: Robert Rauschenberg," *Art in America,* vol. 54, no. 3 (May–June, 1966), 84.

AD REINHARDT

On Reinhardt:

"Reinhardt," *Arts and Architecture,* vol. 64 (January, 1947), 20, 27.

Hess, Thomas B. "Reinhardt: The Position and Perils of Purity," *Art News,* vol. 52 (December, 1953), 26–27.

de Kooning, Elaine. "Pure Paints a Picture," *Art News,* vol. 56 (Summer, 1957), 57, 86–87.

Tillim, Sidney. "What Happened to Geometry? An Inquiry into Geometrical Painting in America," *Arts Magazine,* vol. 33 (June, 1959), 38–44.

Ad Reinhardt: 25 Years of Abstract Painting. New York: Betty Parsons Gallery, 1960.

Kramer, Hilton. "Art," *The Nation,* vol. 196 (June 22, 1963), 533–534.

Colt, Priscilla. "Notes on Ad Reinhardt," *Art International,* vol. 8, no. 8 (October, 1964), 32–34.

Lippard, Lucy R. *Ad Reinhardt.* New York: The Jewish Museum, 1966.

Michelson, Annette. "Ad Reinhardt or the Artist as Artist," *Harper's Bazaar* (November, 1966), 176.

Rose, Barbara. "Reinhardt," *Vogue,* vol. 148 (November 1, 1966), 183.

McShine, Kynaston. "More than Black," *Arts Magazine,* vol. 41 (December, 1966), 49–50.

Sandler, Irving. "The Purist Backlash," *Arts Magazine,* (December, 1966), 40–47.

Ashton, Dore. "Notes on Reinhardt's Exhibition," *Arts and Architecture,* vol. 83 (January, 1967), 4–5.

By Reinhardt:

"Stuart Davis," *New Masses* (November 27, 1945), 15.

"Open Letter to Roland L. Redmond, President of the Metropolitan Museum of Art, Protesting the American Painting Exhibition There," *Art News,* vol. 49 (Summer, 1950), 15.

Modern Artists in America. New York: Wittenborn, Schultz, 1951. (Co-editor with Robert Motherwell.)

"Twelve Rules for a New Academy," *Art News,* vol. 56 (May, 1957), 37–38, 56. (Reprinted in *Ad Reinhardt: 25 Years of Abstract Painting.* New York: Betty Parsons Gallery, 1960.)

"44 Titles for Articles for Artists Under 45," *It Is,* no. 1 (Spring, 1958), 22–23.

"25 Lines of Words on Art," *It Is,* no. 1 (Spring, 1958), 42.

"Is Today's Artist With or Against the Past?" *Art News*, vol. 57 (Summer, 1958), 26–28, 56–58.

Sandler, Irving. "In the Art Galleries: Interview with Ad Reinhardt," *New York Post* (August 12, 1962), 12.

"Art as Art," *Art International*, vol. 6, no. 10 (December, 1962), 36–37.

"The Next Revolution in Art," *Art News*, vol. 62 (February, 1964), 48–49.

"The Next Revolution in Art: Art as Art Dogma," Part II, *Art International*, vol. 8, no. 2 (March, 1964), 57–58.

"Reinhardt Paints a Picture" (Auto-Interview), *Art News*, vol. 64 (March, 1965), 39–41, 66.

"Art vs. History" (Book Review of George Kubler's *The Shape of Time*), *Art News*, vol. 64 (January, 1966), 19, 61–62.

Glaser, Bruce. Interview with Ad Reinhardt, *Art International*, vol. 10, no. 10 (December, 1966), 18–21.

Kallick, P. Interview with Ad Reinhardt, *Studio*, vol. 174 (December, 1967), 269–273.

JAMES ROSENQUIST

On Rosenquist:

Seckler, Dorothy G. "Folklore of the Banal," *Art in America*, vol. 50, no. 4 (Winter, 1962), 56–61.

Lippard, Lucy. "James Rosenquist: Aspects of a Multiple Art," *Artforum*, vol. 4 (December, 1965), 41–44.

Irwin, D. "Pop Art and Surrealism," *Studio*, vol. 171 (May, 1966), 191.

"Les Images sans Passion de Rosenquist," *Aujourd'hui*, vol. 10 (January, 1967), 142–143.

James Rosenquist. Ottawa: National Gallery of Canada, 1968.

Geldzahler, Henry. "James Rosenquist's *F-111*," *Metropolitan Museum of Art Bulletin*, vol. 26 (March, 1968), 177–281.

By Rosenquist:

Statement in *Art in America*, vol. 51, no. 3 (1963), 48.

"What Is Pop Art?" Interview with G. R. Swenson, *Art News*, vol. 62 (February, 1964), 40–43.

Swenson, G. R. "The *F-111*: An Interview with James Rosenquist," *Partisan Review*, vol. 32 (Fall, 1965), 589–601.

MARK ROTHKO

On Rothko:

Collier, Oskar. "Mark Rothko," *Iconograph* (Fall, 1947), 40–44.

MacAgy, Douglas. "Mark Rothko," *Magazine of Art*, vol. 42 (January, 1949), 20–21.

Mark Rothko, Houston: Contemporary Arts Museum, 1957. Preface by Elaine de Kooning (reprinted in *Art News Annual*, 1957–58).

de Kooning, Elaine. "Two Americans in Action: Kline and Rothko," *Art News Annual*, vol. 27, Part II (1958), 86–97, 174–179.

Hunter, Sam. "Mark Rothko." New York: The Museum of Modern Art, Stati Uniti d'America, XXIX Biennale, Venice, 1958.

Ashton, Dore. "Art: Mark Rothko," *Arts and Architecture*, vol. 74, no. 8 (April, 1958), 8, 29, 32.

Butor, Michel. "Les Mosquées de New York ou l'Art de Mark Rothko," *Revue-Critique Editions de Minuit*, no. 173 (1961), 843–860.

Mark Rothko. London: Whitechapel Gallery, 1961. Preface by Bryan Robertson.

Selz, Peter. *Mark Rothko*. New York: The Museum of Modern Art, 1961.

Goosen, E. C. "Rothko: The Omnibus Image," *Art News,* vol. 59 (January, 1961), 38–40, 60–61.

Goldwater, Robert. "Reflections on the Rothko Exhibit," *Arts Magazine,* vol. 35 (March, 1961), 42–45.

Sandler, I. "New York Letter: Rothko," *Art International,* vol. 2 (March, 1961), 40–41.

Kozloff, Max. "Mark Rothko's New Retrospective," *Art Journal,* vol. 20 (Spring, 1961), 148–149.

Harrison, Jane. "Rothko," *Arts Review,* vol. 13 (October 21–November 4, 1961), 2, 18.

Alloway, Lawrence. "Notes on Rothko," *Art International,* vol. 6, nos. 5–6 (Summer, 1962), 90–94.

Fried, Michael. "New York Letter," *Art International,* vol. 7 (May 25, 1963), 70–72.

Judd, Don. "Mark Rothko," *Arts Magazine,* vol. 37 (September, 1963), 57–58.

"Recent Acquisitions," *St. Louis Museum Bulletin,* no. 2 (May, 1966), 2–3.

By Rothko:

Letter to the Editor, *The New York Times,* June 13, 1943. Quoted in Rudi Blesh, *Modern Art USA.* New York: Alfred A. Knopf, 1956. Pp. 226–227. Also in Thomas B. Hess, *Abstract Painting: Background and American Phase.* New York: Viking, 1951. P. 145.

"The Romantics Were Prompted," *Possibilities,* vol. 1, no. 1 (Winter, 1947–48), 84–86.

Ashton, Dore. "Art: Lecture by Rothko," *The New York Times* (October 31, 1958), p. 26, col. 2. Lecture from the Pratt Institute.

GEORGE SEGAL

On Segal:

Judd, Don. "Exhibition at the Green Gallery," *Arts Magazine,* vol. 36 (September, 1962), 55.

Segal. Paris: Galerie Ileana Sonnabend, 1963. (Introductory essays by Michel Courtouis and Allan Kaprow.)

Van der Marck, Jan. "George Segal," *Ten American Sculptors.* Organized by The Walker Art Center, Minneapolis, for United States Section of the VII Bienal de São Paulo, Brazil, 1963.

Geldzahler, Henry. "George Segal," *Recent American Sculpture.* New York: The Jewish Museum, 1964. (Reprinted in *Quadrum,* no. 19 [1965], 115–116.)

Solomon, Alan. *Amerikanst Pop-Konst.* Stockholm: Moderna Museet, 1964.

Kaprow, Allan. "Segal's Vital Mummies," *Art News,* vol. 62 (February, 1964), 30–33, 65.

Pincus-Witten, Robert. "George Segal as Realist," *Artforum,* vol. 5 (Summer, 1967), 84–87.

Tuchman, Phyllis. "George Segal," *Art International,* vol. 12, no. 7 (September 29, 1968), 51–53.

Perreault, John. "Plaster Caste," *Art News,* vol. 67 (November, 1968), 54–55, 75, 76.

By Segal:

Geldzahler, Henry. An Interview with George Segal, *Artforum,* vol. 3 (November, 1964), 26–29. (Reprinted in *Quadrum,* no. 19 [1965], 118–126.)

DAVID SMITH

On Smith:

Greenberg, Clement. "Art," *The Nation,* vol. 156 (January 23, 1943), 140–141; vol. 162 (January 26, 1946), 109–110; vol. 164 (April 19, 1947), 459–460.

Valentier, W. R. "Sculpture by David Smith," *Arts and Architecture,* vol. 65 (August, 1948), 22–23, 52.

Motherwell, Robert. "For David Smith," Foreword in *David Smith.* New York: Willard Gallery, 1950. Pp. 1–3.

de Kooning, Elaine. "David Smith Makes a Sculpture: Cathedral," *Art News*, vol. 50 (September, 1951), 38–41, 50–51.

Goosen, E. C. "David Smith," *Arts*, vol. 30 (March, 1956), 23–27.

Greenberg, Clement. "David Smith," *Art in America*, vol. 44, no. 5 (Winter, 1956–57), 30–33, 66. (Reprinted in *Art in America*, vol. 51, no. 4 [August, 1963], 112–117.)

Hunter, Sam. "David Smith" (with catalogue and bibliography), *Museum of Modern Art Bulletin*, vol. 25, no. 2 (1957), 3–36.

Porter, Fairfield. "David Smith: Steel into Sculpture," *Art News*, vol. 56 (September, 1957), 40–43, 54–55.

Kramer, Hilton. "Month in Review: Exhibition of Sculptures and Drawings at the Museum of Modern Art and Other Galleries," *Arts Magazine*, vol. 32 (October, 1957), 48–51.

———. "The Sculpture of David Smith," *Arts Magazine*, vol. 34 (February, 1960), 22–43. (Special David Smith issue.)

O'Hara, Frank. "David Smith: The Color of Steel," *Art News*, vol. 60 (December, 1961), 32–34, 69–70.

Rubin, William. "David Smith," *Art International*, vol. 7, no. 9 (December 5, 1963), 48–59.

Carandente, Giovanni. *Voltron*. Philadelphia: Institute of Contemporary Art, University of Pennsylvania, 1964.

Greenberg, Clement. *David Smith's New Sculpture*. Philadelphia: Institute of Contemporary Art, University of Pennsylvania, 1964. (Reprinted in *Art International*, vol. 8, no. 4 [May, 1964], 35–37.)

Judd, Don. "David Smith," *Arts Magazine*, vol. 39 (December, 1964), 62.

Baro, Gene. "Contemporary Sculpture: David Smith, 1906–1965," *Arts Yearbook*, no. 8 (1965), 100–105.

Motherwell, Robert. "David Smith: A Major American Sculptor," *Vogue*, vol. 145 (February 1, 1965), 134–139, 190–191. (Revised version in *Studio*, vol. 172 [August, 1966], 65–68.)

David Smith: A Retrospective Exhibition. Cambridge, Mass.: Fogg Art Museum, 1966. (Introduction by Jane Harrison Cone.)

Krauss, Rosalind. Introduction, *David Smith: Eight Early Works, 1935–1938*. New York: Marlborough-Gerson Gallery, 1967.

Cone, Jane Harrison. "David Smith," *Artforum*, vol. 5 (Summer, 1967), 72–78.

Krauss, Rosalind. Introduction, *David Smith, Small Sculptures of the Mid-Forties*. New York: Marlborough-Gerson Gallery, 1968.

Bannard, Darby Walter. "Cubism, Abstract Expressionism, David Smith," *Artforum*, vol. 6 (April, 1968), 22–32.

Fry, Edward. *David Smith*. New York: The Solomon R. Guggenheim Museum, 1969.

Kramer, Hilton. "A Critic Calls David Smith: Greatest of All American Artists," *The New York Times Magazine*, (February 16, 1969), 40–42, 44, 46, 49–52, 54, 59–60, 62.

Krauss, Rosalind. "The Essential David Smith," Part I, *Artforum*, vol. 7 (February, 1969), 43–49: Part II, vol. 7 (April, 1969), 34–41.

By Smith:

"David Smith," *The New Sculpture: A Symposium*. New York: The Museum of Modern Art, 1952. (Transcript in MOMA Library.)

"Hudson River Landscape," *Bennington Magazine*, vol. 3 (Spring, 1952), 16–17.

"Thoughts on Sculpture," *College Art Journal*, vol. 13, no. 2 (Winter, 1954), 96–100.

"Second Thoughts on Sculpture," *College Art Journal*, vol. 13, no. 3 (Spring, 1954), 203–207.

"Gonzalez: First Master of the Torch," *Art News*, vol. 54 (February, 1956), 34–37, 64–65.

"Sculpture and Architecture," *Arts Magazine*, vol. 31 (May, 1957), 20.

"The Secret Letter" (an interview with David Smith by Thomas B. Hess), June, 1964, in *David Smith*. New York: Marlborough-Gerson Gallery, 1964.

"David Smith Interviewed by David Sylvester," *Living Arts*, no. 3 (April, 1964), 4–13.

David Smith by David Smith, ed. by Cleve Gray. New York: Holt, Rinehart and Winston, 1968.

TONY SMITH

On Smith:

Judd, D. "Black, White and Gray," *Arts Magazine*, vol. 38 (March, 1964), 36–38.

Tony Smith: Two Exhibitions of Sculpture. Hartford, Conn.: Wadsworth Atheneum, 1966.

Burton, S. "Old Master at the New Frontier," *Art News*, vol. 65 (December, 1966), 52–55.

Baro, Gene. "Tony Smith: Toward Speculation in Pure Form," *Art International*, vol. 11, no. 6 (Summer, 1967), 27–30.

Lippard, Lucy R. "Tony Smith: The Ineluctable Modality of the Visible," *Art International*, vol. 11, no. 6 (Summer, 1967), 24–26.

Robbins, C. "New York: Public Sculpture in Public Places," *Arts Magazine*, vol. 41 (Summer, 1967), 50–51.

Chandler, John N. "Tony Smith and Sol Lewitt; Mutations and Permutations," *Art International*, vol. 12, no. 7 (September 20, 1968), 16–19.

By Smith:

"Remarks on Modules," *Tony Smith: Two Exhibitions of Sculpture.* Hartford, Conn.: Wadsworth Atheneum, 1966.

Wagstaff, Samuel, Jr. "Talking to Tony Smith," *Artforum*, vol. 5 (December, 1966), 14–19.

FRANK STELLA

On Stella:

"Three Young Americans," Oberlin College, *Allen Memorial Art Museum Bulletin*, vol. 17 (Fall, (1959), 18–19.

Judd, Donald. "Exhibition at Castelli Gallery," *Arts Magazine*, vol. 36 (September, 1962), 51.

Ashton, Dore. "Exhibition at the Castelli Gallery," *Das Kunstwerk*, Baden-Baden, vol. 16 (November –December, 1962), 69.

———. "Exhibition at the Leo Castelli Gallery," *Studio*, vol. 165 (February, 1963), 67.

Fried, Michael. *Three American Painters* (Noland, Olitski, Stella). Cambridge, Mass.: Fogg Art Museum, 1965.

Judd, Donald. "The Shaped Canvas," *Arts Magazine*, vol. 39 (February, 1965), 56.

Rosenblum, Robert. "Frank Stella," *Artforum*, vol. 3 (March, 1965), 20–27.

Kozloff, Max. "Art," *The Nation*, vol. 202 (March 28, 1966), 270–272.

Fried, Michael. *Frank Stella.* Pasadena: Pasadena Art Museum, 1966

Ashton, Dore. "Exhibition at Castelli Gallery," *Arts and Architecture*, vol. 83 (May, 1966), 5.

———. "New York at the Castelli Gallery," *Studio*, vol. 171 (May, 1966), 205.

Krauss, Rosalind. "Frank Stella, Castelli Gallery," *Artforum*, vol. 4 (May, 1966), 47–49.

Fried, Michael. "Shape as Form: Frank Stella's New Paintings," *Artforum*, vol. 5 (November, 1966), 18–27. (Reprinted from Pasadena Catalogue, 1966).

Cone, Jane Harrison. "Frank Stella's New Paintings," *Artforum*, vol. 6 (November, 1967), 34.

Kramer, Hilton. "Frank Stella: What You See Is What You See," *The New York Times*, sec. 2 (December 10, 1967), 39.

By Stella:

"Questions to Stella and Judd," B. Glaser, *Art News*, vol. 65 (September, 1966), 55–61.

CLYFFORD STILL

On Still:

Krasne, Belle. "Still's Non-Objective Cartography," *Art Digest*, vol. 24 (May 1, 1950), 22, 23.

Loran, Erle. "Art News from San Francisco . . . Clyfford Still," *Art News*, vol. 49 (October, 1950), 58–59.

Fitzsimmons, James. "Clyfford Still," *Art Digest*, vol. 25 (February 1, 1951), 17–18.

Paintings of Clyfford Still. Buffalo: Buffalo Fine Arts Academy and Albright Art Gallery, 1959.

Crehan, Hubert. "Clyfford Still: Black Angel in Buffalo," *Art News*, vol. 58 (December, 1959), 32, 58–60.

Goosen, E. C. "Painting as Confrontation: Clyfford Still," *Art International*, vol. 4 (1960), 39–43.

Sharpless, Ti-Grace. *Clyfford Still*. Philadelphia: Institute of Contemporary Art, University of Pennsylvania, 1963.

Kozloff, Max. "Art: Clyfford Still," *The Nation*, vol. 198 (January 6, 1964), 39–40.

Clyfford Still: Thirty-Three Paintings in the Albright-Knox Art Gallery. Buffalo: Albright-Knox Art Gallery, 1966. Introduction by Ti-Grace Sharpless.

By Still:

"Comment," *Albright-Knox Gallery Notes*, vol. 23, no. 2 (Summer, 1960).

Statements in *Clyfford Still*. Philadelphia: Institute of Contemporary Art, University of Pennsylvania, 1963. Pp. 9–10.

"An Open Letter to an Art Critic," *Artforum*, vol. 2 (December, 1963), 32.

Letter to the Editor, *Artforum*, vol. 2 (February, 1964), 2.

BRADLEY WALKER TOMLIN

On Tomlin:

Hess, Thomas B. "Bradley Walker Tomlin," *Art News*, vol. 49 (May, 1950), 52.

Krasne, Belle. "Of Time and Tomlin," *Art Digest*, vol. 24 (June 1, 1950), 18.

Baur, John I. H. *Bradley Walker Tomlin*. New York: The Whitney Museum of American Art, 1957.

Ashbery, John. "Tomlin: The Pleasures of Color," *Art News*, vol. 56 (October, 1957), 28–29, 54.

Sawin, Martica. "Bradley Walker Tomlin," *Arts Magazine*, vol. 32 (November, 1957), 22–25.

Ashton, Dore. "Art," *Arts and Architecture*, vol. 74 (December, 1957), 32–33.

Doty, B. "Trends and Traditions: Recent Acquisitions," *Albright-Knox Gallery Notes*, vol. 27 (Spring, 1964), 16–17.

By Tomlin:

Foreword, *Frank London*. Woodstock: Woodstock Art Association, 1948. Pp. 2–3.

Foreword, *Judson Smith Retrospective Exhibition*. Woodstock: Woodstock Art Association, 1952. Pp. 2–3.

ANDY WARHOL

On Warhol:

Fried, Michael. "New York Letter," *Art International*, vol. 6, no. 10 (December 20, 1962), 57.

Warhol. Paris: Galerie Ileana Sonnabend, 1964. Contains articles by John Ashbery, Alain Jouffroy, and Jean-Jacques Lebel.

Geldzahler, Henry. "Andy Warhol," *Art International*, vol. 8, no. 3 (April, 1964), 34–35.

Green, Samuel Adams. *Andy Warhol*. Philadelphia: Institute of Contemporary Art, University of Pennsylvania, 1965.

Solomon, Alan. *Andy Warhol*. Boston: I.C.A. Gallery, 1966.

Johnson, Ellen H. "Image Duplicators: Lichtenstein, Rauschenberg, Warhol," *Canadian Art*, vol. 23 (January, 1966), 12–19.

Antin, D. "Warhol: The Silver Tenement," *Art News*, vol. 65 (Summer, 1966), 47–49.

Andy Warhol. Stockholm: Moderna Museet, 1967–68.

By Warhol:

Andy Warhol's Index Book. New York: Random House, 1967.

GENERAL

Books:

Janis, Sidney. *Abstract and Surrealist Art in America.* New York: Reynal and Hitchcock, 1944.

Hess, Thomas B. *Abstract Painting: Background and American Phase.* New York: Viking Press, 1951.

Motherwell, Robert, and Reinhardt, Ad, eds. *Modern Artists in America.* New York: Wittenborn, Schultz, 1951.

Seitz, William. "Abstract Expressionist Painting in America." Princeton University, 1955. (Unpublished Ph.D. dissertation.)

Blesh, Rudi. *Modern Art USA.* New York: Alfred A. Knopf, 1956.

Rodman, Selden. *Conversations with Artists.* New York: Devin-Adair, 1957. Includes interviews with Calder, de Kooning, Gottlieb, Hopper, Kline, Pollock, Reinhardt, Rothko, D. Smith.

Hunter, Sam. "The United States," *Art Since 1945.* New York: Harry N. Abrams, 1958.

———. *Modern American Painting and Sculpture.* New York: Dell, 1959.

Greenberg, Clement. *Art and Culture.* Boston: Beacon Press, 1961.

Ashton, Dore. *The Unknown Shore: A View of Contemporary Art.* Boston: Little, Brown and Co., 1962.

Kuh, Katherine. *The Artist's Voice.* New York: Harper and Row, 1962. Includes interviews with Albers, Calder, Davis, Hofmann, Hopper, Kline, Noguchi, D. Smith.

Rosenberg, Harold. *The Anxious Object: Art Today and Its Audience.* New York: Horizon Press, 1964. Includes chapters on de Kooning, Gorky, Hofmann, Newman, and Johns.

Geldzahler, Henry. *American Painting of the Twentieth Century.* New York: The Metropolitan Museum of Art, 1965.

Rublowsky, John. *Pop Art.* New York: Basic Books, Inc., 1965. Includes sections on Lichtenstein, Oldenburg, Rosenquist, and Warhol.

Battcock, Gregory, ed. *The New Art.* New York: E. P. Dutton, 1966.

Lippard, Lucy. *Pop Art.* New York: Frederick A. Praeger, 1966.

Art Criticism of the Sixties. New York: October House, 1967. Symposium at the Poses Institute of Fine Arts, Brandeis University, Waltham, Mass. Participants included Michael Fried, Max Kozloff, Barbara Rose, Sidney Tillim.

Rose, Barbara. *American Art Since 1900.* New York: Frederick A. Praeger, 1967.

Battcock, Gregory, ed. *Minimal Art.* New York: E. P. Dutton, 1968.

Rose, Barbara. *Readings in American Art Since 1900.* New York: Frederick A. Praeger, 1968.

Cavell, Stanley. *Must We Mean What We Say?* New York: Charles Scribner's Sons, 1969.

Exhibition Catalogues:

Fourteen Americans. New York: The Museum of Modern Art, 1946. Includes Gorky, Motherwell, Noguchi.

40 American Painters: 1940–1950. Minneapolis: University of Minnesota, The University Gallery, Department of Art, 1951. Includes Davis, Gottlieb, Guston, Hofmann, Hopper, Motherwell, Pollock, Reinhardt, Rothko, Tomlin. Contains statements by the artists.

Contemporary American Painting and Sculpture. Urbana: University of Illinois, 1948, 1949, 1950, 1951, 1952, 1953, 1955, 1957, 1959, 1961, 1963, 1965, 1967.
1948 includes Gottlieb, Guston, Hofmann, Hopper, Tomlin.
1949 includes Guston, Hofmann, Motherwell, Pollock, Tomlin.
1950 includes Avery, Davis, Gottlieb, Hofmann, Motherwell, Pollock, Rothko.
1951 includes Avery, Gottlieb, Hofmann, Motherwell, Pollock, Rothko, Tomlin.
1952 includes Avery, Davis, de Kooning, Gottlieb, Hofmann, Motherwell, Reinhardt.
1953 includes Albers, Davis, Gottlieb, Hofmann, Motherwell, Pollock, D. Smith.
1955 includes Albers, Avery, Davis, Gottlieb, Hofmann, Motherwell.
1957 includes Avery, Davis, Hofmann.

1959 includes Avery, Calder, Davis, Frankenthaler, Hofmann, Rauschenberg.

1961 includes Avery, Davis, Hofmann.

1963 includes Avery, Davis, Gottlieb, Hofmann, Kelly.

1965 includes Guston, Hofmann, Lichenstein, Motherwell.

15 Americans. New York: The Museum of Modern Art, 1952. Includes Pollock, Rothko, Still, Tomlin.

Younger American Painters. New York: The Solomon R. Guggenheim Museum, 1954. Includes de Kooning, Gottlieb, Guston, Kline, Motherwell, and Pollock.

The New Decade: 35 American Painters and Sculptors. New York: The Whitney Museum of American Art, 1955. Includes de Kooning, Gottlieb, Kline, Motherwell, Pollock, Reinhardt, Tomlin.

12 Americans. New York: The Museum of Modern Art, 1956. Includes Guston, Kline.

The New American Painting as Shown in Eight European Countries. New York: The Museum of Modern Art, International Council, 1958–59. Includes de Kooning, Gorky, Gottlieb, Guston, Kline, Motherwell, Newman, Pollock, Rothko, Still, Tomlin. Eight countries: Basel, Switzerland; Milan, Italy; Madrid, Spain; Berlin, Germany; Amsterdam, The Netherlands; Brussels, Belgium; Paris, France; London, England.

Sixteen Americans. New York: The Museum of Modern Art, 1959. Includes Johns, Kelly, Rauschenberg, Stella.

Arnason, H. H. *American Abstract Expressionists and Imagists.* New York: The Solomon R. Guggenheim Museum, 1961. Includes Albers, de Kooning, Frankenthaler, Gorky, Gottlieb, Guston, Hofmann, Johns, Kelly, Kline, Louis, Motherwell, Newman, Noland, Pollock, Rauschenberg, Reinhardt, Rothko, Stella, Still, Tomlin.

Seitz, William. *Art of Assemblage.* New York: The Museum of Modern Art, 1961. Includes Chamberlain, Cornell, de Kooning, Johns, Motherwell, Rauschenberg.

4 Amerikanare. Stockholm: Moderna Museet, 1962. Includes Johns, Rauschenberg.

Geometric Abstraction in America. New York: The Whitney Museum of American Art, 1962. Includes Albers, Calder, Davis, Diller, Gorky, Hofmann, Kelly, Noland, Reinhardt, D. Smith, Stella.

Americans 1963. New York: The Museum of Modern Art, 1963. Includes Kohn, Oldenburg, Reinhardt, and Rosenquist.

Toward a New Abstraction. New York: The Jewish Museum, 1963. Includes Kelly, Louis, Noland, Stella.

Amerikanst Pop-Konst. Stockholm: Moderna Museet, 1964. Includes Lichtenstein, Oldenburg, Segal, Warhol.

The New York School: The First Generation. Los Angeles: Los Angeles County Museum of Art, 1965. Includes de Kooning, Gorky, Gottlieb, Guston, Hofmann, Kline, Motherwell, Newman, Pollock, Reinhardt, Rothko, Still, Tomlin.

Alloway, Lawrence. *Systemic Painting.* New York: The Solomon R. Guggenheim Museum, 1966. Includes Kelly, Noland, Poons, and Stella.

McShine, Kynaston. *Primary Structures.* New York: The Jewish Museum, 1966. Includes Flavin, Judd, Morris, T. Smith.

Two Decades of American Painting. New York: The Museum of Modern Art, International Council, 1966. Exhibition traveled to Japan, India, Australia. Includes Albers, de Kooning, Frankenthaler, Gorky, Gottlieb, Guston, Hofmann, Johns, Kelly, Kline, Lichtenstein, Louis, Motherwell, Newman, Noland, Pollock, Poons, Rauschenberg, Reinhardt, Rosenquist, Rothko, Stella, Still, Tomlin, Warhol.

American Sculpture of the Sixties. Los Angeles: Los Angeles County Museum of Art, 1967. Includes Chamberlain, Cornell, Di Suvero, Flavin, Judd, Kelly, Kohn, Morris, Noguchi, Oldenburg, Rauschenberg, Segal, D. Smith, T. Smith.

14 Sculptors: The Industrial Edge. Minneapolis: The Walker Art Center, 1969. Includes Judd, Kelly, and Morris. Articles are by Barbara Rose, Christopher Finch, and Martin Friedman.

Russell, John and Gablik, Suzi. *Pop Art Redefined.* London, Thames and Hudson, 1969.

Solomon, Alan. *New York: The Second Breakthrough, 1959–1964.* Irvine: University of California at Irvine Art Gallery, 1969. Includes Johns, Lichtenstein, Louis, Noland, Oldenburg, Rauschenberg, Rosenquist, Stella, Warhol.

Photography Credits for Color Plates

Lee Boltin: 78
Dan Budnik: 107
Richard Nickel: 67, 73, 79, 85
M. Noguchi: 95
Eric Pollitzer: 68, 70, 71, 72, 75, 77, 83, 84, 86, 87, 88, 90, 91, 92, 94, 96, 97, 98, 99, 102, 103, 104, 105, 108, 109, 111, 112
Walter J. Russell: 74
Lois Steen: 66
F. J. Thomas: 69, 89
Malcolm Varon: 81
Courtesy Albright-Knox Art Gallery: 110
Courtesy Leo Castelli Gallery: 101
Courtesy The Cleveland Museum of Art: 93
Courtesy The Metropolitan Museum of Art: 76, 80
Courtesy The National Gallery of Canada, Ottawa: 106
Courtesy The Woodward Foundation: 65, 100
Courtesy Yale University Art Gallery: 82

Photography Credits for Black and White Illustrations

Oliver Baker: 217, 330
Lee Boltin: 169
Barbara Brown: 146
Rudolph Burckhardt: 124, 125, 145, 149 (top and bottom), 150, 152, 154, 155, 167, 185 (top), 187, 188 (top and bottom), 190, 191, 192 (top and bottom), 193, 194 (top and bottom), 196, 197, 198 (top), 217 (top and bottom), 218, 225, 228 (top), 230, 250, 251, 255, 256, 273 (top and bottom), 275, 276, 278, 279, 280, 281, 282, 283, 289, 291, 293 (bottom), 305 (top), 317, 318, 337
Barney Burstein: 138 (top), 308 (bottom)
Joe Cameron: 320 (top)
Ron Chamberlain: 137, 174, 176, 178, 302, 308 (top)
Geoffrey Clements: 126 (top), 127 (top), 129 (left), 130, 134, 161, 170, 171 (top), 199, 200 (bottom), 201, 202 (top and bottom), 206 (top left, top right, bottom), 207 (top left, top right, bottom), 208 (left and right), 213, 226, 246, 257 (top), 297 (bottom), 325, 326
Hollis Frampton: 294
Frank Lerner: 254 (bottom)
Robert E. Mates: 126 (bottom), 127 (bottom), 128 (left and right), 305 (bottom)
Ron Miyashiro: 228 (bottom)
O. E. Nelson: 120 (top), 169 (top), 235, 236 (top)
Richard Nickel: 153
M. Noguchi: 248
Eric Pollitzer: 119 (top), 132, 138 (bottom), 140, 151, 165 (top), 168, 173, 179, 189, 195, 209, 210 (top and bottom), 212 (bottom), 214 (top and bottom), 219 (top and bottom), 220, 221, 234, 236 (bottom), 239, 241, 247 (top and bottom), 254, 259, 260, 261, 262, 264, 265 (top), 274, 277, 284 (top and bottom), 285, 286, 287, 288, 292, 293 (top), 295, 297 (top), 298, 315, 316 (top and bottom), 320 (bottom), 321, 324
A. E. Princehorn: 160 (bottom)
Robert A. Propper: 306, 307 (top), 313
Nathan Rabin: 258
Walter K. Rosenblum: 135
Walter J. Russell: 147 (top), 240
Savage Studio: 301
John D. Schiff: 129, 143, 144 (top and bottom), 336
Lois Steen: 120 (bottom), 180, 252 (bottom), 253
Gregg Sterling: 123 (top and bottom)
Adolph Studly: 267
Joseph Szaszfai, Yale Art Gallery: 114 (top and bottom), 115, 116, 117 (top and bottom), 118
Frank J. Thomas Photography: 172, 290
Charles Uht: 249
Malcolm Varon: 181
Alfred J. Wyatt: 163, 266

485

Credit is also due the following museums, galleries, and institutions whose assistance provided photographs of works not necessarily within their domain at the time of this printing.

Harry N. Abrams, Inc.: 158 (top and bottom), 160 (top), 162
Albright-Knox Art Gallery: 319
Arts Magazine: 252 (top)
Irving Blum Gallery: 198 (bottom), 334
Leo Castelli Gallery: 185 (bottom), 186
André Emmerich Gallery: 223, 225 (top), 226, 227
Fischbach Gallery: 314 (top)
John Gibson Gallery: 146
The Solomon R. Guggenheim Museum: 126 (bottom), 127 (bottom), 128 (left and right)
Sidney Janis Gallery: 202 (top), 211, 257 (top), 258
M. Knoedler & Co., Inc.: 237 (top), 238, 240, 241, 242, 244 (left)
Kornblee Gallery: 147 (bottom)
Marlborough-Gerson Gallery: 235, 236 (top), 267, 273, 303, 304, 307 (bottom), 309
The Museum of Modern Art, New York: 133, 136, 231, 232, 268
Pasadena Art Museum: 172
Seattle Art Museum: 171 (bottom), 299

Otherwise it is understood that photographs were provided by those museums and galleries, etc., that are also credited with ownership of the works.

Index

DATE DUE

BY H. S. EDE

SAVAGE

MESSIAH

GAUDIER · BRZESKA

NEW YORK · THE LITERARY GUILD · 1931

PREFACE

I HAVE personally met very few of the people mentioned in this book, and any remarks about them in no way denote my own feeling, but entirely those of Henri Gaudier and Sophie Brzeska.

My authority for what I have written has mostly been a Diary kept by Miss Brzeska, whose statements I have checked both with letters from Henri Gaudier and by conversations with people who knew them both. Where it has been possible, I have used Miss Brzeska's own words, putting them between quotation marks; but usually the Diary is too diffuse, and too personal to Miss Brzeska, to allow of a direct translation.

All Henri Gaudier's letters were written in French, with the exception of two early letters to Miss Brzeska, pages *20* and *37*, and the rough draft of one to Middleton Murry, page *141*, and these are printed in their original language. In translating the letters I have occasionally left out passages which are mere repetitions, or of no general interest.

Several works by Henri Gaudier-Brzeska, and Miss Brzeska's papers, passed at her death to the Treasury. These were purchased by Mr. McKnight Kauffer, from whom I in turn obtained them.

H. S. EDE

CONTENTS

THE PLATES

CHAPTER I
THE MEETING

SOPHIE SUZANNE BRZESKA and Henri Gaudier met for the first time at the St. Geneviève Library in Paris during the early part of 1910. It was the strange meeting of two people with violent temperaments, widely different in age and experience, utterly unsuited to each other, and yet destined to live together for the next five years, and in the end to die violently as they had lived, the one on the battle-field, the other in a madhouse.

Miss Brzeska, a highly-strung Polish woman, already thirty-eight years old, was working, or fancied she was working, at German: she was interested in languages and in the literature of different countries, but owing to her hate of the Germans she had not studied their language before. She was small, flat-chested, with a pointed chin, thin lips, tilted nose, sensitive nostrils and high cheek-bones, which rose up to meet the large eyelids sheltering strange tired eyes, eyes that often stared big and vacant, and then of a sudden melted into roguish intimacy. Her movements were rapid, abrupt, and angular; her student's paraphernalia, which she set about her on the table with neurotic precision, were extensive, and often attracted the attention of the young men who sat and worked at the same table, and to whom her eccentricities and seeming independence were the cause of much speculation: a speculation not to be wondered at, since she was a woman who was bodily ill and mentally diseased, whose life had been a succession of continual emotional crises; of terrors, intuitions of evil, forebodings of madness, outbursts of rage, meditations of suicide and intimations of her own greatness. She was extremely poor and absolutely alone, without a friend to speak to; she had come to Paris, a few months before, with the firm intention of killing

herself to escape from the fine torment of life into those vast spaces
of rest and forgetfulness which she believed to be the reward of
death; but life in Paris, with its keen student energy, and the
thought that if she were buried her body would be eaten by worms,
had weakened her resolve, and she was again making frantic efforts
to conquer her depression.

Sitting by her, in the Library, was a young boy who often looked
at her furtively, almost timidly. He was about eighteen, with dark,
finely-chiselled features and sparkling eyes, and his attentions occupied much of Miss Brzeska's thought; he was an artist, she supposed, since he was studying anatomy; he looked poor and tired,
indefinably gentle and yet somehow alert and cruel, like a panther.
This incongruity fascinated her, for it had much in common with
her own swift outbursts. She wondered why he looked at her with
such interest: he was so young and she—she might be his mother.
Why had she never had a child, she whose experience of life was so
vast? She could have protected and helped a son, studied the growth
of his ideas, and found satisfaction in his turning to her for support;
such were the thoughts she noted in her Diary as she watched Henri
Gaudier, and as she felt his young presence near her. She even wondered if he might love her; but no, that was impossible: love did
not exist, she had been too often mistaken to fall a prey to that deception.

In order to break the monotony of her daily life she was prepared
to do anything, even to give up her eternal search for an experience
in which love and friendship would be united, and just to give herself quite wantonly, asking for nothing but to be possessed by the

deep-reaching abandon of physical love. But it was quite clear to her that it must not be with Henri Gaudier. Such an action could only bring her shame and remorse; she wished to revenge herself on men, but to break into his life would be like torturing a baby. She wanted to be happy, to laugh and to be free, to forget her grinding pain. She would like to smile at Henri, take his hand, no more. They might be companions and help each other; but then her heart cried out to her that she was old, in the autumn of her life, and that she could never play so austere a part, for she would need to be strong enough for two, since he was so young, and young people were so easily excited. Besides, she felt that he was far too good for her, she needed someone cast in a rougher mould.

She chose a Russian, largely built, a pale-faced man with small, penetrating eyes, and she threw him a significant look which he smilingly received; he seemed to set no barrier between them, and already, as she looked at him across the table, she felt herself in his arms. But Miss Brzeska's temperament was not of the kind which made her able to give herself easily; she was spirited and proud, so she drew back again into herself, and hid behind her provocative air of listless gaiety.

At the end of a couple of weeks she no longer wanted to abandon herself to this Russian: her immediate excitement was allayed, and she felt that perhaps after all she would find somewhere a real friend. She continued, however, to play with the Russian, who after making many vain attempts to come to an understanding with her, to meet her when she came to or from the Library, would decide to give her up, but then returned to the attack only to disappear again beaten. She did not care for him, but the game amused her, though her conscientious nature began to give her serious pangs of regret; what right had she to make the poor fellow suffer? The other students at the table followed the flirtation with great interest, and some of them gave her encouraging looks, hoping that they too might be drawn in, but on their own account, thinking themselves more able to gain a victory than their fellow-student.

Henri Gaudier was the most assiduous of these. He always managed to sit by her side, putting his books quite close to hers. This often upset her plans with the Russian, but she had never the heart to look at him severely. One day she asked him to show her his book of drawings, which he did with evident pleasure, trying to draw her into conversation; later he waited for her at the exit, and they walked a little way together. He evidently wanted to talk to her, and she allowed her interest to ripen for this young life, which thought only of Art and the big work it would accomplish. One night Sophie let him walk with her as far as the door of her hotel. He complained of his loneliness and of his desire to know someone who would understand him and encourage him in his ambitions. Sophie was immediately touched to the finest fibre of her nature; spontaneously she replied: 'I am too old for you really, but I will be a mother to you, if you agree.' Henri said he would be enchanted, he had wanted to know her for so long, he thought her beautiful, and she pleased him. Sophie looked at him with surprise; no one had ever felt like that about her before, and at home since her childhood she had always been spoken of as ugly. Henri explained that that was because people did not see true beauty, the beauty which lay in the heart and in the expression. What was more, he loved her concentrated energy and was intrigued by its changefulness; at times she would be completely absorbed by her work, and then she would stare at the ceiling with eyes full of tragedy.

'Sometimes you look as if all the devils in hell possessed you—for instance, when you look at the Russian.'

'Aren't you then frightened of me,' said Sophie, 'seeing how wicked I can be?'

'On the contrary, I hate those mincing beauties whose expressions never change—they are no more than mummies.'

So for a long time they walked and talked in the Rue Cujas, hours filled for them with breathless excitement; what did it matter what they said, since to be talking at all meant that they were no longer lonely, and before they separated they arranged that on the next day they would visit the Louvre together.

MISS BRZESKA

CHAPTER II
MISS BRZESKA

SOPHIE BRZESKA was born in a large house in the heart of the country, not far from Cracow. Her father, a solicitor, had, according to her own report, only two interests—wasting his inheritance, and entertaining women of all stations in life, provided they were young; and so long as he was left quietly to this occupation he was a pleasant enough man to live with, but it kept him much from home.

Mrs. Brzeska, on the other hand, was always at home. She gave birth to nine children, of whom Sophie was the only girl. Her parents were constantly irritated and humiliated by this, and kept telling her that she was a useless encumbrance who would remain on their hands and give them no return.

During her early childhood she was alone with her mother, who was continually pregnant, often bearing still-born children; Sophie watched the funerals of four of these. There were young brothers growing up entirely neglected by their mother, who read and studied all day without any system, and they naturally joined in their parents' abuse of Sophie. Mr. Brzeski shut his eyes to all the disharmony in his family so long as his own pleasures, which were the cause of many objectionable scandals in the house, were not interfered with.

Sophie tried, when she was sixteen, to escape from the miseries of her home; she wished to work, and already felt a desire to write; but her parents told her that there was no money for so stupid a person, and that the only thing she could do was to find a rich man as stupid as herself, and persuade him to marry her.

The only subject of conversation on her account seemed to be of arranging such a marriage, and after several attempts, an elderly Jew was found who consented to become engaged to her, much against her wishes. She even thought of escaping from her troubles by suicide, only the fear of her mother forced her to accept the Jew's proposal. Happily the Jew expected a dowry with her, and this in-furiated Mr. Brzeski, who felt that anyone of such obscure origin should think it a sufficient honour to be given his daughter; so the engagement fell through with insults on both sides.

During the next four years there were three incidents which might have led to marriage, the first two with men as little to Sophie's taste as the Jew. The third was a young man, of shockingly poor physique, but universally spoken of as a decent fellow. He had a rich mother who wished him to make a brilliant marriage, but who for a time countenanced his attachment to Sophie. One day Mrs. Brzeska made a dreadful scene with him over a game of cards, and without consulting Sophie's feelings turned him out of the house. His own mother was in her turn furious, and made him promise never to see Sophie again; but he wrote to tell her that he would always love her, and that they must trust in the future. Then came Mr. Brzeski's bankruptcy, and a little later, his death.

Miss Brzeska, who suffered much from gastric catarrh, had saved a little money out of her dress allowance, and, driven from the house by her mother's ill-treatment, went to study in Cracow. From there she moved to Paris, where she worked for a time as a nursemaid, but was made miserable by the gibes of her fellow-servants. Then she obtained a succession of posts, often only for a fortnight at a time, until her health entirely broke down. She was obliged to take a short rest, after which she found a position with a family who were going to Philadelphia. There was a little boy of ten years old and a girl of sixteen. Sophie became deeply attached to the boy, but after a few weeks he died, leaving only his sister for her to take care of. This girl kept asking for indecent stories, and because Sophie did not tell her any, she complained to her mother that Sophie was dull. The mother told Miss Brzeska that she must try to entertain her pupil better; so in fear of losing her job, and because the child was already more worldly-wise than she, Sophie invented scandals about Parisian actresses, much to the delight of her pupil. One day the mother and father overheard their talk, and Miss Brzeska was dismissed.

She now went to live in a French 'Home' in New York, kept by nuns. From that time on there came more and more detestable children and impossible parents, and each year she became more painfully nervous. Her whole aim was now to get back to her own country, particularly as she had heard from her cousins that her young man was still faithful to her. She must economize, make money; but she must make it honestly. Many a time, from fathers in whose families she worked, she might have earned in a week, had she been amiable and complying, more than she could otherwise do in four years; but she had a profound belief in the sacredness of love.

In the meantime she longed for human affection, and felt so much the need to forget herself in her love for someone else that she began to fall in love with other women. In this she met with nothing but disaster. For all her affection and her generosity she got only deception and abuse. Miss Brzeska felt at this time that she had reached the acme of suffering, that life could hold no bigger trials for her; and it was only want of money that prevented her from returning to Poland, which she now felt to be her only escape.

Little by little she saved enough for her return, and then heard from her eldest brother that he wanted to come to New York. She was fond of him, for he was sensitive and delicate, and she pitied his being under the maternal roof. She sent him enough money for his journey, and so gave up her own chance of returning. For five months her brother could find no kind of work, and finally had to accept a post as kitchen boy in a large hotel. He began to accuse Sophie of having persuaded him to come to America, and finally he refused to see her. To add to her troubles, she was out of employ ment herself; so when suddenly a chance offered of getting to Paris, she accepted it with alacrity.

She had planned to stay in Paris, and make a position for herself, in preference to returning home; for she was now thirty-six years old, and feared that the man who had promised to wait for her might think her too old and too battered by the life she had been forced to lead. However, in Paris she could get no work, and thus was compelled to return to her mother's house, where another severe blow to her pride awaited her. She had an uncle, aged seventy, of whom she was tremendously fond; she had always treated him as a father, and felt him to be her one stay in life. She found that on the death of his wife he had persuaded a shameless cousin to come and live with him; and although there was no need of arguments to accomplish her seduction, he told her that Sophie, the refined and correct Sophie, had been his mistress, and that in order to avoid a scandal he had sent her to Paris. This discovery so shattered Miss Brzeska that she felt its effects for the rest of her life.

Her family ridiculed her for having only saved a thousand francs during all her years in America, and they laughed at her ideas of virtue. She then heard that her friend had become engaged to an heiress, and she wrote to him imploring him not to ruin his life, saying that she was prepared to wait for him as long as it was necessary: he replied, coldly polite, that he loved and respected his fiancée.

By such blows Sophie was turned sceptical, and believed that she no longer desired the love of men. To deaden her distress she forced herself into a life of dissipation. Her health soon broke down and she went to Baden for a cure.

It was here that she met Monsieur M., a rich manufacturer aged fifty-three, with whom she had her most serious love affair. Now was her chance to show her relations that when she chose she could make a good marriage; but again she was caught. Monsieur M. proved to be amusing, intelligent, a lover of nature and full of kindness, understanding quickly all the pent-up troubles of her heart; and before she knew where she was, she was passionately in love with him. He assured her of his love for her, and she believed him, her nature needed so intensely to believe him; but he did not ask her to marry him.

Their friendship lasted for over a year. During this time Monsieur M. encouraged her and to a great extent used her, but never gave her the complete satisfaction for which she craved. Ultimately, after a dreadful scene which nearly ended in the death of both, he told her that he had a son, and that he had promised always to remain free in case the boy's mother wished to marry him—that he adored his son, and that his one ambition was to make him a home.

Poor Sophie, she who was so famished for love, who had guarded herself so carefully until she felt that she had found someone who was worthy of her love, who wanted love to be eternal, how was she now distressed! She felt her senses leaving her, and for some time she was on the verge of madness. She wrote to Monsieur M., imploring him to kill her if she went mad; and he replied that she had upset his nerves for nothing, that she had better go to the country to cure her hysteria, and that he was quite willing to pay. After heart-rending scenes she returned in despair to her home. Her allusions to madness had decided Monsieur M. to have no more to do with her, and he left her numberless letters unanswered.

At home she would lie for hours on a sofa wondering how best she could kill herself. A fat aunt, who was there, occasionally indulged in vulgar pity. 'Poor girl—you evidently want something—it's a pity, all the same, that you did not marry that old man your mother found for you—he was certainly stupid, but he seemed to have a kind nature.' Then Sophie would stamp and shriek with rage, flinging invective and injury upon her aunt, while her mother would stand by smiling. 'You see what a toad she is—what a scorpion; didn't I tell you? But you would never believe it. You can see for yourself now.'

It was less than two months after this that Miss Brzeska saw Henri Gaudier for the first time in the St. Geneviève Library.

CHAPTER III
HENRI GAUDIER

WHEN HENRI visited the Louvre with Miss Brzeska he was very attentive to her, explaining everything most vividly. He enjoyed so much being able to enlarge on his ideas to his enthusiastic companion, for he had never met anyone before who cared to listen to him. He was particularly attracted by the sculpture, and endeared himself to Sophie by taking off his hat in front of the Samothrace Victory.

Henri was very poor, his clothes were torn and dirty and his shoes full of holes, but Sophie felt proud to be with him, although usually she would have been much put out by such things; for several years she had not followed the fashions, but she had always been scrupulously clean in herself and her linen.

Slowly but surely he entrenched himself deeply in Sophie's heart; he gave her his diary, in which he complained of being 'without love and without friends', and he told her that he was fully satisfied with her motherly love.

She herself was in a seventh heaven: it was, I think, the happiest time in her life, perhaps also in Henri's. Once or twice a week she would go to his tiny room at 14 Rue Bernard Palissy and he would draw her portrait while she told him of her ambition to be a writer, and read him several of the short stories she had written. Henri used to talk to her in English, and they learnt together Shakespeare's sonnets and discussed the literature of many nations; for Sophie was widely read, and they were both intensely keen on searching into the manifestations of human development. Many were the delicious moments which they passed together, he with his head on her shoulder or she resting on his; the solace of kisses was not allowed, but

19

their spirits were united in a radiant joy. They had their own troubles to talk about, and they discovered that they were both suffering from the same ills. Miss Brzeska had been a short time before to a specialist, thinking she had caught some disease in the hotel where she was living, and the doctor had told her that her state was one of nervous prostration due to lack of food and over-anxiety. Henri was in just the same position: his weakness was extreme, his hands were always moist, his cheeks hollow. For some time he would not confess to being short of money, and when he did, it was with the greatest difficulty that Sophie persuaded him to accept a few francs. Often she would buy food and come to share it with him in his room. Once when she had to keep to her bed, he bought her a fine rose. 'But I won't leave it,' he wrote,[1] 'lest the old mufflers at your hotel give a false meaning, and profane the idea I have and which you share. Anyhow, I shall not have bought it for nothing, and I enclose some of the petals—you won't get this letter before to-morrow, which is a great pity. I am sure you would have much more pleasure in reading it to-night. Good-night, with love. Syn.'

In a letter to Dr. Uhlemayr, with whom Gaudier had lived at Nuremberg during part of the previous year, he tells of his meeting with Sophie Brzeska:

Paris
18th June 1910

I have such a lot of things to tell you, but things quite different from those I have already talked about—I refer to the effect of love

---

[1] This letter is written in English.

on one's working power. Would you believe it, I am in Love! I see that you already picture me with some 'backfisch' strolling in the 'Boul Mich', or whispering sweet nothings in secluded corners around the Pantheon. You are wrong; the woman I love is thirty years old[1]—you smile—I love her with a purely ideal love, it is a flow of sensation which you must feel, since words are too coarse a medium to convey it. She is Polish—Brzeska is her name. I met her in the Library where I go to work each evening. I've done several sketches of her, and thus we got to know each other. She is a poet, and her ideas on the family, society, and Western civilization are the same as ours; she has an entirely independent nature, is an anarchist—simply and naturally, has a beauty à la Baudelaire—and might have stepped out of *Fleurs du Mal*. She is lithe and simple, with a feline carriage and enigmatic face, the fine character of which reflects her most intimate thought—planes combining in the most surprising manner, impressions of age and of youth in alarming contrast. In a word, we are both as mad as hatters. Would you believe it, last Sunday we talked from eight in the morning until three in the afternoon without noticing how the time had passed. I told her of my ideas about Art for Art's sake, and she explained hers on the basis of a society founded on motherhood undertaken freely and with open eyes. We parted about four o'clock, and I came home and at once set to work. I was so thrilled that I did a great bust that evening to give her next morning, as she had asked me for a bit of sculpture. Since then I have been like a man bewitched, and I would work like a machine, only that I have forced myself, with

[1] Miss Brzeska was thirty-nine.

some success, to be reasonable. All the same, I am happy, and I only hope that the fever of work which possesses me won't as suddenly leave me. I am also very pleased to know this Pole, particularly because she is a Slav and I know nothing about Slavs. She is going to teach me her language so that I may steep myself in the Slavonic spirit. I hope that I shall profit as much by it as I have by meeting with German culture, and that it may open for me the great gateway of the East. You mustn't be annoyed with me for telling you all this, since it is only natural that men and women should love each other, and that the nearness of one should cause happiness in the other.

I don't know what my fellowcountrymen must think of me, for in the Latin Quarter I know only Russians and Germans— there is one who looks very like you and another who takes opium, he's a very interesting subject; he wished to hypnotize me the other day, but couldn't.

I begin to understand the Greek and pagan antiquity, which I now prefer to the Gothic. For a long time I have been obsessed by Ruskin and the English; now I have finished with them, as with Christian philosophy, that hysterical egoism which contemplates the material sufferings of a material body and says: 'I have no wish to be crucified. I thank you, Christ, for having suffered in my stead, to save me from Hell where my body would have burned eternally.' This now seems to me only a repugnant sadism, and I much prefer the pantheistic idea. What pleases me most of all is the Buddhist philosophy, with its 'Nirvana' as the highest form of thought. . . .

Henri had arrived in Paris from Germany in October 1909; he was eighteen years old, and became an enthusiastic admirer of Puvis de Chavannes, Rodin, and Whistler's 'Portrait of his Mother'.

Through the help of Monsieur Simonet, a professor at the Sorbonne, he obtained the work of translating books and letters in a bookshop;[1] this occupied the whole of his day, while his evenings were spent in studying anatomy and his Sundays in drawing. His letters to Dr. Uhlemayr, written during these first few months of his stay in Paris before he met Miss Brzeska, show clearly the nature of his life and interests, and parts of them are worth quoting:

Paris
October 1909

(To Dr. Uhlemayr)

Now that I have definitely begun to live I find myself more and more convinced that civilization with its trappings and artificialities is not so good as nature. By nature I mean a natural culture—the kind you and I used to discuss in the forest of St. Gebald. But that was no more than a dream, and the present reality seems the sadder for it. Ten hours of each day I have to do translations and letters in a book-shop, which you will agree is a pretty poor look-out; the rest of the time I work for my own pleasure—I am trying to perfect my drawing, and hope to succeed. I've made immense strides since I was with you, but how small they seem beside those I must still make! Every evening I work in the St. Geneviève Library—crowds

[1] Mr. Ezra Pound says this was the Libraire Collins. *Gaudier-Brzeska*, by Ezra Pound, p. 43.

of foreign students fill the place, and at the table where I usually sit they are all 'Slavs' and Germans. . . .

His evenings in the St. Geneviève Library were mostly occupied in studying anatomy. The reproduced page shows the characteristically methodical care with which he approaches this subject.

> *Paris, 14 Rue Bernard Palissy*
> *1st January 1910*

(To Dr. Uhlemayr)

We shall never see a greater sculptor than Rodin, who exhausted himself in efforts to outvie Phidias, and did outvie him in his 'Penseur', which reaches heights he can never surpass. Rodin is for France what Michelangelo was for Florence, he will have imitators but never rivals. . . . It is fatal, for these men by their monstrous personality bleed a nation to death and leave others only the alternatives of imitation or veneration. . . .

> *Paris*
> *5th March 1910*

(To Dr. Uhlemayr)

I have been, during this last week, the stage of a great battle. One of my friends has a little house and garden in the country, and I often go there for Sunday. Last Sunday I dug in the garden all day long, and a happier man than I could not have been found. My friend, who had to go to town on some business, left me alone in his house. I started to dream and to think, and so the battle began, and these are the opposing forces. On one side happiness and nature, repre-

MAJOR SMYTHIES

sented by the simple life of the fields, and on the other the sadness and artificiality of business and town life. The pleasure of the fields is clouded by bad weather, by danger to the harvest; but, in spite of this, happiness remains, no less truly. The misery of the office, though tempered by art, is the enemy of pleasure. The two main things: nature, a superhuman and beautiful creation, and the town, human and ugly—these will always keep their peculiar character-istics.

The exigencies of life compel man to obtain money. A com-mercial life provides this, but I cannot face it, and since art doesn't bring money, I am inclined to abandon this life of a middleman robber which repels me, and will do all that I can to learn some handicraft which will dispose of the idea that to produce nothing during the day is to waste my time.

But I have decided nothing, the town and the fields sit opposite each other—and if I have a trade, I shall still need art. Only a coun-try life can give me pleasure, and I have begun to feel that farming is one of the most lovely of the fine arts. But since I am an anarchist in my soul and a friend of great solitude, if I wish to have done with it once for all—I should go to Canada, there they will give me land and I shall be free and happy.

If this were all life would be easy, but my principles are to a cer-tain extent in opposition. I am the friend of the producer, of the worker; I support him against his masters. Would it not be a horrid cowardice, a profound egoism, to go to the colonies instead of fight-ing at the side of my fellows? Land—Canada, these are my per-sonal happiness. In trade, suffering, art, the town, the battle, I seek a collective happiness. I uphold the creative spirit of mankind, maintain it and make it triumph over the middle-class man who seems to deny its existence. If I abandon the workman, I take sides with the fat-bellied, flabby-faced plutocrat—a hideous idea. All the same, it is rather beauty than a selfish satisfaction which attracts me to nature—and there I come round again, and can arrive at no decision. One thing I can absolutely decide, it is the only thing I can cut off at once, namely, to give up business for some craft. I am going to learn the technique of sculpture in wood for cabinet-making. I shall give next month to this, and it is with this I hope to earn my daily bread, and not by fleecing the masses. When I face the beauty of nature, I am no longer sensitive to art, but in the town I appreciate its myriad benefits—the more I go into the woods and the fields the more distrustful I become of art and wish all civilization to the devil; the more I wander about amidst filth and sweat the better I understand art and love it; the desire for it becomes my crying need. . . .

Paris
24th May 1910

(To Dr. Uhlemayr)

I have taken a great decision—I am not going to do any more colour work, but shall restrict myself entirely to the plastic. I have never been able to see colour detached from form, and this year, after doing a few studies in painting I noticed that the drawing and the modelling were all I had been concerned with. I have put by the brushes and tubes and have snatched the chisel and the boaster —two simple instruments which so admirably second the most wonderful of modelling tools, the human thumb. This and clay is all that I now need, with charcoal or red chalk and paper. Painting is too complicated with its oils and its pigments, and is too easily destroyed. What is more, I love the sense of creation, the ample voluptuousness of kneading the material and bringing forth life, a joy which I never found in painting; for, as you have seen, I don't know how to manipulate colour, and as I've always said, I'm not a painter, but a sculptor. It may surprise you that I can be content with confining myself to this one branch of art, leaving all others untouched. Yet sculpture is the art of expressing the reality of ideas in the most palpable form. It makes plain, even to the eyes of fools, the power of the human mind to conceive ideas, and demonstrates in cold lucidity all that is fervent, ideal and everlasting in the soul of man.

You will have noticed that civilizations begin with sculpture and end with it. Painting, music, letters, are later refinements. . . . For my part I see quite clearly that I don't wish to wield the brush any longer, it's too monotonous and one cannot feel the material near enough, paint sticks well to the hairs of the brush and sings on the canvas, one appreciates its fertile texture; but the sensuous enjoyment is far greater with the clay slipping through your hands; when you feel how plastic it is, how thick, how well bound together, and when you see it constantly bringing forth.

I am now right in the midst of Bohemia, a queer mystic group, but happy enough; there are days when you have nothing to eat, but life is so full of the unexpected that I love it as much as I used to detest the stupid and regular life of trade. . . .

.　　.　　.　　.　　.　　.

Henri's boyhood had been lived at St. Jean de Braye, near Or⁄
leans, where he was born on October 4, 1891. His father was a car⁄
penter, a clever workman interested in what he was doing, and it
was from him that Henri first learnt his love of materials. There was
a family tradition that one of his ancestors had worked on the ca⁄
thedral at Chartres, and Henri was very proud of this legend.[1] He
was a very sensitive child, delicate and frail⁄looking, but beneath
all this lay a deep assurance and strength of will.

His father used always to encourage him to defend hotly what
seemed to him to be right until the contrary was irrefutably proved;
and as he grew in intelligence his disputes with his father became
more and more intense. Already at the age of fourteen he had be⁄
come the master in argument, and when he was older he would
often tell how his father 'a essayé de me battre, mais je lui ai donné
de tels coups de pieds qu'il n'a pu réussir'.[2]

At six years old he began trying to draw the things which inter⁄
ested him, and it is curious that already these should have been in⁄
sects and the lovely patterns of which they are composed. He used to
tear up all his drawings, and when his father protested he would say:
'I have done them, and that is sufficient; if I kept them I should be
tempted to do them again, and that would be worthless.' This was

[1] Once in 1913 when he was to visit Miss Brzeska in the country, and was to
pass as her brother, she asked him not to mention his Chartres ancestor, as she was
considered by her landlady to be of gentle birth.

[2] This is a Beauceron proverb, not to be taken literally; but Gaudier sometimes
amused himself by using it for his story, and watching the effect on his audience,
who were generally horrified; and so the legend arose that his nature was so
violent that he used to kick his father.

his attitude all through his life; he always counted on fresh inspiration, and never surrounded himself with the past as a support to the present.

At his school in St. Jean de Braye he did very well, and at the age of twelve he went to Orleans, where he won at fifteen a scholarship which took him to London for two months. This visit, in 1906, was his first experience of travelling; it gave him a decided pull over his school companions, and at the beginning of 1908 he won a second scholarship, this time of 3000 francs, to be spent on studying business methods abroad. His parents were very anxious that he should take to business. Some friends of theirs at St. Jean de Braye had a son who was already launched in Paris, and it was hoped that Henri might be able to join him; but Henri could never bring himself to show any zeal for a financial life, though for the next two years he still fluttered around the idea.

He went from Orleans to University College, Bristol, where he lived with Mr. Smith, one of the professors; and from this time on he was engrossed by his desire to draw. Already he felt that an artistic future lay before him, and he signed and dated all his drawings with meticulous care. His first sketch-book begins with a page of heraldic design, circling the name of Henri Gaudier; he saw his name repeated through the ages, it stood for the glory and honour which would be his; and this feeling was with him still in 1914, when he dreamt he had a studio with his name written up in letters of gold over the door. His continued interest in animals and flowers shows itself in this sketch-book, which he took with him on a holiday in Devon and Somerset, but of his swift certainty of line there was as yet no trace whatever. He holds his pencil with a bourgeois closeness, and it is astonishing how commonplace several of his drawings are. Two illustrations for *Omar Khayyám*, done about this time, are almost shocking in their lack of taste, and yet even in these there is no disguising his ability to convey with his pen a visual impression. He had become a square-shouldered young man, with short hair parted in the middle, and wore an upright collar, a small made-up bow tie, and clothes suited to a man of thirty.

By August of 1908 he was back in Bristol, and had begun a series of highly-finished architectural drawings; and in these, particularly in the signing of his name, the easy flow of his pen first shows itself. After a short visit to London in September he concentrated on copying the antique in the Bristol Museum.

Towards the end of 1908 he was placed in the firm of Fifoot, Ching & Co., coal contractors in Cardiff, where he lived at No. 29 Claude Road. Mr. Ching writes of him in 1928: 'He was one of several students who came to us, and whilst he excellently fulfilled the duties allotted to him, one could easily notice that his mind was not altogether in his work. Art undoubtedly occupied the greater part of it, and in his spare moments he was everlastingly, pencil or pen in hand, sketching some little incident that appealed to him. During his lunch hours he periodically walked across to the Docks, and brought back with him a small sketch of, perhaps, the bow of a boat, or the elevation of a crane or tip, all of which showed genius. I encouraged him in this work because I felt that commerce was not his forte, and that he would be bound to leave it at the first possible chance. . . . In character he was somewhat Bohemian, and just a little casual, which was natural, but he was the kind of boy that one would have expected, if necessary, to have lived in a garret while he got on with his life's work as he felt it to be, and therefore you can imagine how disappointed I was when I heard nothing more of him [until you wrote] after he left our employ.'

Not only did he sketch at the Docks, but he made the most elab-orately finished drawings of birds, which he studied in the Museum, or in Victoria Park, Canton.

On the 15th of April 1909, he left England for Nuremberg via Holland, where he went to stay with Dr. Uhlemayr; in his first letter to his mother and father he speaks of his arrival.

9 Schlüsselfelderstrasse, Nürnberg
20th April 1909

Dear Parents,

Here I am at last, after three days of continuous travelling, and not a bit tired. Dr. Uhlemayr and his wife are very nice people, and are a pleasant change after Cardiff. I sent cards to Henriette and to Renée [1] from Brussels, Cologne, and Frankfort, I wonder if they got them. Nuremberg seems to me to be a very lovely town, but I like England better than Germany, and if ever the English go to war with the Germans, I shall be on their side and will be delighted every time these 'pointed helmets' get the worst of it. Everything seems to be moving that way, and only last month, when Mr. Hal-

[1] Henri's sisters.

dane said that the country was in danger, in less than fifteen days they had more volunteers than they wanted. All the same, perhaps I'm not very just towards the Germans, although they do deserve a big defeating to the tune of 'Rule, Britannia, Britannia, rule the waves'.

Dr. Uhlemayr speaks French very well, which is a great comfort, for I can speak hardly any German yet; but soon I will.

H. Gaudier.

Dr. Uhlemayr and his family were amongst Gaudier's first sitters, and he did several sketches of the Doctor with his violin, and one of the violin alone, which is curiously sensitive, and very reminiscent of Dürer, as is also the idea of an inscription; and it is characteristic of Henri's mind that the titles of all his sketches done at this time are in German script, a small instance of his thoroughness in acquiring knowledge: he always liked to know about everything, and by the time he was twenty-one was extremely well-informed. He would instantly pretend to full acquaintance with things quite new to him, and it was this kind of 'boastfulness', as Miss Brzeska used afterwards to call it, which in 1911 prompted his reply to Epstein. He was introduced to him at an Exhibition, and Epstein asked him if he cut direct in stone. Gaudier, who had never yet worked in stone, replied, 'Most certainly'; upon which Epstein said that he would visit him on the following Sunday. Gaudier rushed off, got three small blocks of stone, worked furiously all night, and had three original works lying casually in his studio by the time Epstein arrived.

Gaudier's sketches in Nuremberg and its environs are still of an architectural nature, but not so minutely expressed as those he did in Bristol—there is in them an obvious desire to be paint-ing.

One day a Zeppelin came over Nuremberg, and Henri describes it to his father in a letter:

9–3 Schlüsselfelderstrasse, Nürnberg
31st May 1909

Dear Father,

'Herr Doctor, Herr Gaudier, Der Graf Zeppelin mit seinem Luftschiff!' Thus we were interrupted yesterday, bang in the mid-dle of our lunch, by Marie. In the twinkling of an eye we snatched up the glasses, which mercifully were near at hand, and with one leap we were out on the balcony. There the most wonderful spectacle awaited us.

This balloon, floating in space, like the frieze and metopes of the Parthenon, defies exact reproduction or description. Picture an enor-mous long polygonal-shaped mass of a startling whiteness sailing two thousand feet above us. The propellers, murmuring like in-numerable bees, made the canvas shiver along its rigid structure. The aerostat tacked about against the north wind, but unlike sea ships, which tack on a horizontal plane, it tilted itself upwards. It was all so full of life, vibrating with so joyous a sound and so har-moniously lovely in its setting that one could scarcely believe it a man-invented thing, but thought it some strange animal come from the higher regions of the air, prompted to look at us by contempt or curiosity. With the help of glasses I counted fifteen people in the front gondola and five in the back one; the last mechanics, no doubt. It had come from Friedrichshaven to the Alps, and so had done two hundred and twenty-five kilometres when we saw it here, and it went like the wind—only a few seconds and it was gone. We put on our shoes and rushed downstairs, where we joined a great throng of people, half-dressed, who also hoped to see the Zeppelin a little longer. At last we caught it again just in time to see it sail over the mountains, a truly lovely sight. Its white, which had been so alive and gay, had changed to a mist, blue and airy, on which the elegant forms of its framework were delicately shadowed, the colour of light blue violets, so simple that it was one with the mountains over which it hung—and then it vanished in the air.

A memory remained, already faded; was it towards Bayreuth and Bamberg that it was going, on its course towards the north? I don't know yet, but, with Dr. Uhlemayr, we hope it will come back. It was so beautiful; not pretty, but beautiful, agreeing with the laws of Greek art and with nature, and what fun if only it would take us for a trip!

The children, Gunther and Walter, were delighted, and Walter, the younger one, aged five, hasn't ceased to look for it. After it had gone, he came to find me on the verandah, and said so sweetly, 'Mr. Gaudierlé, you must fly to catch the Zeppelin, to ask it to come back—I want to see it again'. 'But Walterlé, I can't, I haven't any wings.'—'Ach! You are a naughty Mr. Gaudier!'

We walked yesterday through the woods, which remind me very much of the forests around Orleans, to a fortified church at Gratshof, where a venerable 'pasteur' was preaching. His hair and his long beard were pure white, his face beautiful and austere, and so religious a calm enfolded the peasants who were met there that it would have made a wonderful subject for a painting.

My German is getting on quite well, and I am very friendly with the people of the house. I frequently discuss art and civilization with the Doctor; 'Kultur' they call it here. He is a good and simple man, son of a mountain peasant; was born in 1871, while his father was at the war, leaving twelve sons and daughters at home. His father-in-law got a bullet in his left arm at Bazeilles, and has never been able to use it since, so you see that the war wasn't all rose-coloured to the Germans either.

I kiss all the family—my love to you. H. G.

Ezra Pound says that after he left Nuremberg he went to Munich, where he was employed on the manufacture of faked Rembrandts.[1]

Gaudier's stay in Munich made a great artistic impression on him; he started two large series of drawings relating to Munich life, and worked so hard (amongst other things he was learning Russian) that he began to have serious trouble with his eyes. He then returned to Paris, which, as we have seen, became the stage of his revolt against business life, and his new-found friendship with Miss Brzeska must have contributed very considerably to his ever-growing discontent with a life so little suited to his nature. To have someone to whom he could open his heart, someone who encouraged his strong desire to devote himself to Art, gave him the extra confidence which he

[1] *Gaudier-Brzeska*, by Ezra Pound, p. 49.

required; and he threw up an irksome job which he had taken with the firm of Goerz, after leaving the bookshop where he had been placed on his first arrival in Paris, and, as is described in the following letter to his parents, accepted temporary work of a more congenial kind.

22nd June 1910

Dear Parents,

I have just seen Mr. Maurice—it seems that you are anxious about me, and you think that I have run away abroad. I am safe and sound in Paris, and hope to be here for some time yet. I've only changed my job. I went away from Goerz without giving notice because they would have made me stay fifteen extra days. I have now got a job as a draughtsman for materials and carpets. I work ten hours a day and get sixty centimes an hour [five shillings a day at that time], I believe, I haven't been told yet, and even if I only get two francs a day I am relatively happier, and I can no longer think why I was such an ass as ever to go in for trade. I know that you will be annoyed by this, but do for goodness' sake get it into your heads that I am an artist and that nothing else holds any interest for me. At figures I am an absolute nincompoop, and in a commercial life one must be interested in figures and in money. I shall stay here long enough to learn the tricks of the trade, and then I think I shall go and work in Poland or in Russia. Please don't write me nasty letters about this. With all the will in the world I cannot conscientiously do any kind of work, other than that of a sculptor of wood. Apart from this job I work very hard at my modelling; the drawing here doesn't require any intellectual energy, and when I get home I am still fresh and keen. I am free on Saturday afternoons and Sundays, which is excellent.

Love to all.   H. Gaudier.

In the meantime, Henri's and Sophie's health, far from getting better, got worse, and Sophie went into the country to Royon. Henri was not very assiduous with his textile firm, and often left it to wander the streets, to observe people, to visit museums. He did odd jobs here and there, and for some time earned a few francs a day as a servant in someone's studio, but as these francs mostly went in the purchase of prints and engravings, he soon became seriously ill for want of food. He wrote to tell Sophie that he would come to her on foot, that his nose had taken to bleeding and that he was utterly run down. Sophie was afraid to encourage him; she had so often before been deceived in her affections, and felt that closer familiarity might breed contempt between them. Apart from this, her own savings were so small, and her health so poor, that she could not contemplate looking after him at her expense.

His mother and father, who had a comfortable house by the Loire, were trying to persuade him to come to them, but he was stubborn. He writes to Sophie,[1] 'I told them I would not go, I would rather stay in the hospital than receive help from anybody whatsoever. I shall go and see them on Sunday week and let them understand I am going to stop a week, but I will not. I am quite decided not to give way. When I am with them they will try to get me into commerce again, and I would rather die than go again typewriting and

[1] Gaudier writes this letter in English.

making parcels—don't you think so? They seem to do it for love, but I cannot believe it. Anyhow, the matter is over, and I am in Paris, and will remain here, since you tell me not to go to you. I shall rather fight with the "harakiri" than to be stirred a foot out of my doors.'

Paris
4th October 1910

(To Dr. Uhlemayr)

Yesterday was festivity—to-day comes depression—I profit by it to write you a letter, for that will ease my heart.

The day of the Mi-Carême I carried on like a character out of Zola. I went on the razzle, and now to-day I repent and wish to be pure. After those violent joys—after such monstrosities I find myself in the most pessimistic state of mind, just ripe to deny that life holds any interest or happiness. My circumstances, which only yesterday seemed not at all unjust, appear to-day as bitter as one of those good wines turned rancid. I suppose that will make you laugh, but I assure you it's horribly true. This is what I have always noticed for the last few years since I learnt to look at life in a fairly abstract way, and became able to analyse my own feelings: with me every big pleasure, or rather, every big deviation from my usual life, is followed by a deviation in the opposite direction, and this is the reason for the pessimism and optimism which I hold in spite of myself. My natural state, my every-day feeling, is between the two. It is a succession of little variations, tiny contrasts, perhaps, but which all the same exist. I am never without a little joy and a little sadness. These small moments stretch out for several days, some cause or other favouring the intensive development of one of these two states, and this is what happened this morning after I had come home.

As a rule, when I go to sleep I am glad to wake and see the day and look at a lovely engraving by Steinlen or a poster by Toulouse-Lautrec which I have, then I quickly get to work before I have to start for the office and the translations which prolong my material existence.[1]

To-day, nothing of this.

I got in at six, tired, weak, annoyed with myself for having shouted all the afternoon in a 'rag', and for having wallowed all the night. I felt phenomenally lazy and depressed in spirit. To-morrow, however, that will be all right. Already I feel the change coming over me.

I have been reading Taine's *Philosophy of Art*. His theory does not seem to me to be very sound. It is true that environment does have an influence, but what has a much greater effect on the artist is love or hatred. He uses his setting to express these things—that is how I see it. Take, for example, Forain—the best of draughtsmen, in my opinion. This man has been made spiteful by the misery of his early years; he began his work in a spirit of implacable raillery against the customs and manners of his contemporaries; to-day the influence of his surroundings is modified enormously—he is rich. The setting has changed, but the artist has become even more in-transigent and malicious than before. His drawings breathe the strength of a perfect anarchy. This powerful personality dominat-ing its surroundings is a thing which Taine never explains. I do not believe that it is possible or useful to describe art in so rigorously

[1] Gaudier had gone back to work in an office.

scientific a way. To begin with, you lose the whole of the pleasure when you only look at a work to discover all the causes which went to its making—then art is so subtle and capricious a thing, so different in the hands of people who have developed together, that, considering the rarity of good work, one should find the pleasure it gives a sufficient justification for it.

I have started to read Bergson's *Evolution Créatrice*—it is an entirely abstract work, and so profound that I must study it carefully, and, above all, meditate about it before I can discuss it with you.

You will remember that last summer I deplored the lack in France of an illustrated anarchist review which should equal *Simplicissimus* in artistic value. This review now exists—it is *Les Hommes du Jour*, which for Art and Literature does what the *Guerre Sociale* does for Politics.

We are forming an anti-parliamentary insurrectional committee, who have in view a revolution only possible by force. Young people will come to us, and it is all that we need. . . .

You will think me very revolutionary. I am. Each day I grow more convinced of the necessity of a radical sweeping away—especially of machines, which must be utterly destroyed. It is mechanism which is now our master. To make matter obey him, man must abandon the wish to do colossal things. The other day I visited an exhibition of Japanese prints and sword-hilts. Since then I have not stopped proclaiming, in the teeth of opposition, that the yellow civilization is better than our own. Had it not been so they would not have so adeptly appropriated our infernal machinery for our own destruction. . . .

HEAD OF A MAN

Miss Brzeska now persuaded Henri to leave Paris, and a month in the country brought back most of his natural vigour. Sophie was better, too, and decided to stay on in Royon all the winter. Henri, whose doctor would not allow him to paint, and advised him to stay in the country for another two months, implored her to come to him. He found her a charming little cottage not far from his parents' house, and after much deliberation and with many forebodings Sophie decided to go. There Henri came to see her every afternoon. He would arrive early while Miss Brzeska lay on her bed, a practice which helped her to digest her dinner. One day he told her that his mother was beginning to be annoyed by his daily visits; that she had accused Sophie of debauching Henri and so making him ill, and had added that soon there would be evil gossip amongst the neighbouring farmers. Sophie felt that there might be some reason in Madame Gaudier's vexation, and persuaded Henri not to come the next day, particularly as his visits occupied much of her time, and she was anxious to get on with a book which she was writing.

Next day Henri came as usual and said that he could not stay away, that it was so dull at home, that no one understood him, and anyhow, why should they be separated? Sophie was lying on her bed, and Henri, who sat in a chair by her side, got up every now and then tenderly to caress her mouth or her forehead with his lips. Although Sophie had never allowed him the passionate kisses of a lover, she did not feel that she need refuse him the indulgence of this small caress which he seemed so much to need.

While they were thus together there was a knock at the door;

Sophie expected no one, but without getting up called out, 'Come in.' It was her landlord, out of breath and red in the face. 'Come downstairs quickly,' he said, 'the police have come with an anony-mous letter'; and before she understood what he meant, the police were in the room. With furtive glances at the bed, they asked her to read the letter, which accused her of using her house for the improper reception of men.

It seems that some farmer, who had unsuccessfully tried to rent the house in which Miss Brzeska was living, had started this scan-dal in order to revenge himself on the landlord. Henri and Sophie were very much upset by this incident, and spent a great deal of time and energy, though without any satisfactory results, in trying to have the originator of this slander punished.

Henri's reaction expresses itself in a letter to Dr. Uhlemayr:

St. Jean de Braye
11th November 1910

You will be surprised to see that I am in the country. I have been ill—anæmia—the result of all the energy I've put into this hate-ful battle for existence. All the same, I have won, for from the muddy channels of commerce I have risen to the less seamy realm of 'Kunstgewerbe'. It is as a designer of fabrics that I now earn my living, and it is in this way that I shall continue through a long and tempestuous future.

But enough of myself—I want to speak of 'la belle France'. It is indeed a lovely country, but the people who live in it are utterly degraded. Men more malicious, more treacherous, more miserly and grasping, you will find nowhere. I begin to establish certain maxims for my personal use: 'Beautiful countries are given over to savages.' 'Religion is a necessity to frighten ferocious beasts.' If our peasants feared an imaginary God, they would not act so wickedly. I have got mixed up in the most abominable affairs,[1] of which I will tell you later, and I have been able to judge for myself the value of a pure republican justice. I believe that my country has never before been in so advanced a state of decadence. The Latin race is rotten to the core. Its flag has become violet, yellow, and green, the colours of the putrescence which fills the romantic paintings of Delacroix, presaging storms, wind, destruction, and carnage. The French disgust me more and more by their idleness, their heedlessness, and their excess of bad taste—I have irrevocably decided to leave them to the Furies and to get quickly to the frontier.

I have tried to place caricatures in the Parisian papers; they took a few for *Le Rire* and *Charivari*—I don't know if they published them, but they paid well. I shall try again, particularly since my ideas become more crisp and precise, but there's the rub—at nineteen one is scarcely more than a child, and the battle is hard. One's line lacks snap and vigour, and one's outlook is narrow, there is a want of coherence. There are parts which seem free and original, and others which are full of outside influences and childishness. The editors see this clearly enough, and it is better for their papers, but it sometimes drives me to despair. Still, one has to sacrifice oneself a bit. One only has to take three vows: poverty, chastity, abstinence, and everything goes well. One leads the life of an ascetic, and art becomes the sole inspiration—and that is the only way to development—by cultivating one's own innate powers. . . .

[1] The slander against Miss Brzeska.

Worn out and disgusted by persecution and injustice, they decided to leave France, particularly as it was almost time for Henri to start his military service; a duty he was determined not to do, his convictions as well as his character not easily submitting themselves to these years of slavery.

England seemed to be the most suitable country; for Henri, because he had already spent two years there, thought that with the help of friends he would be able to find work. Sophie, who believed in his glowing accounts of the English, agreed to accompany him. First of all, however, they went back to Paris, where they stayed for two months.

Henri looked for work without success, and Sophie had to provide rooms, clothes, and food, since he would accept nothing from his parents after the way in which they had behaved about Miss Brzeska.

They were not peaceful, these two months; Henri was nervous and irritated, and Sophie was frightened to find her small savings rapidly decreasing. There were many angry quarrels, with as many reconciliations, until at the end of 1910 they crossed over to London, where for the next four years, until Gaudier's death, these two were to live together under the name of Gaudier-Brzeska,[1] as brother and sister; each in his or her way passionately fond of the other, but seldom rising sufficiently above the daily grind of poverty to be able fully to appreciate each other's friendship.

[1] So far as I know, the linking of their two names into one was never more than a personal arrangement.

CHAPTER IV
THE FIRST MONTHS IN LONDON

PART I

IN LONDON, Gaudier did not find work so quickly as he had hoped; his poverty-stricken boots and frayed collars frightened the few acquaintances on whose help he had counted. Sophie had drawn heavily on her savings for the expenses of the journey, and had to continue doing so to pay for the necessities of their daily life; this naturally alarmed her, because the precarious state of her health always made her desperately anxious to keep by her a small fund in case of need.

At one moment they were reduced to such poverty that while Henri was out, Miss Brzeska made a doll, took a shawl, which she wrapped round herself and 'her baby', and went to the street corner to beg. She collected sixpence in pennies, and with it she bought some bread, margarine, and tea; because Henri was fond of cakes, she also bought one small cake. When Henri got home he found an excellent tea all ready for him, and he asked Sophie how she had done it; she told him, and to her surprise he was very angry, saying that she must never do such things again. Instead, they visited the various public-houses of the neighbourhood, and Henri did drawings of the customers at a penny each.

At last, after two months of searching, during which they came very near starvation, Henri found work as a typist and foreign correspondent with a Norwegian in the City at a salary of six pounds a month. A month later Sophie got a temporary post as a governess at Felixstowe, in exchange for board and lodging.

The two months in London without work for either of them, and the consequent poverty and worry, had exhausted her, so it was a relief to be in the country, though at the same time she was very

47

anxious about Henri's health. He had no idea of the value of money, and quickly got through the six pounds he was earning, which left nothing for food; he had little rest, since his business occupied him all day, and his evenings were spent in drawing and study, so that he became enervated, underfed, hollow-eyed, thin in the face, and subject to dreadful fits of crying and anger. The doctor he had seen in France had told him that he would find it good for his health if he went occasionally to prostitutes; and Sophie encouraged this idea, even although it cost five shillings every time; but her economical sense was outraged, though her heart was touched when Henri returned, having given the woman five shillings, and then been too disgusted and horrified to have anything to do with her.

He was very lonely when Sophie went away, and wrote her long letters full of love and affection. These letters give a very true picture of his life during the next month.

C/o W. and Co.
22nd April 1911

Mamusin dearest,

I expect you are feeling better by now—I know Pik is; he was very miserable yesterday, but he slept for ages the night you left, and last night, too. Wulfs [1] only came back yesterday evening at five o'clock, so you see I have had a quiet time.

I have disobeyed Mamus! I didn't go to the Park, but went to the Museum instead, where I found some marvellous casts of Michelangelo's study of a slave. I only worked from five till nine, and half an hour afterwards I was in bed. Yesterday evening I bought the

[1] Wulfsberg was his employer.

frames (eightpence three-farthings each), and also a little brooch for sixpence—it is silver with blue enamel. I didn't choose one with brilliants, because they were very small and badly made—no use at all.

I have something very amusing—comic, rather—to tell you; the love affairs of the Jewess Rachel, the celebrated actress. It relates to the first time she lost her virtue. The Prince of Joinville, son of Louis Philippe, Admiral of France, had just brought home Napoleon's ashes. At a gala night at the Comédie française, given in his honour, he saw our Rachel. He at once sent a message to her box with the words: 'Où? Quand? Combien?' to which the actress replied, 'Ce soir, chez toi, pour rien', and our two had a gay time.

And now for our own affairs. This morning I received replies [from J. A. Dickinson & Co.] to my advertisement of last week. They ask me to send them specimens of my work, and if it is suitable, they will give me a commission. So I am again going to disobey my Mamus. I shall work all this afternoon, this evening, and all day to-morrow, without taking much of a walk, just as far as the river, perhaps. You must forgive me, Mamus, because it would be stupid to miss a good opportunity. If I am successful it will be a help to you—so you see, you stupid little Madka! I won't write any more now, it excites me too much, and I must keep very quiet. I wish you the best of luck and health, and send you my blessing. Every day I say our prayer to the great sun, and he shines splendidly. I ask him always for endless benefits for Zosienka—that she may be happy, contented, sweet, and beloved. I send you a copy of the letter which I'll send to-morrow with the drawings in reply to the advertisement, and also a Polish study.

Pipik.

P.S.—Dickinsons addressed me as 'H. A. GANDER'—'Mr. Jars, mâle de l'oie en français'.

Horsden Hill, Berks
Sunday, 23rd April 1911

Zosienka Darling,

I am always the 'p'tit blagueur français'. Having proposed to work all yesterday afternoon and all to-day, I only managed to draw from five a.m. till one to-day. I was dreadfully upset with Mamus's departure, and the move to new rooms, and then here I wasted ages hunting after subjects none of which pleased me. I have come miles out, far into the fields, and the lovely sun blazes. I have been very lonely since Mamus went away so quickly, but I am keeping myself well in hand. When I am in my new rooms, everything will change, and as I have heaps of work to do, I am sure to forget a little. What a curious thing life is: in order to have any peace at all, one must always forget. Don't you think, little Mother, that life would be marvellous if one were always allowed to remember? But for the moment we must work, and knowing this, I am sticking at it.

I went on with the study of form and the arrangement of Michel-angelo's noted planes, but without discovering anything new; I only convinced myself that what I felt yesterday was true. There are always a dozen little 'kids' around me when I draw the Slaves. They are, no doubt, astonished by my methods, because I write as much as I draw; for a long time I look at the thing I want to under-

stand, and then draw by system. What intrigues them beyond anything is that instead of drawing the fellow straight off, as they are
used to seeing everyone else do, I draw square boxes, adjusting the
sizes, one for each plane, and then suddenly by joining the boxes
with a few little lines, they see the statue emerge. They look at me
with terror—with respect, perhaps—I don't know if it is because
they find me so severe, or because of the drawings. Whatever it is,
they amuse me highly. I believe, in the end, it is the drawing, because men respect and reverence, or rather fear, what they don't
understand, and consequently what astonishes them.

When I tired of drawing Michelangelo—about eight o'clock—
I went to see the Goyas. He is a Spanish painter—the first since
Rembrandt who knew how to use aquatint with mastery. He did
three series of engravings: 'Los Capricos', 'Los Desastres de la
Guerra', and 'La Tauromáquia'. Last night I only looked at the
first two series. Mamus would delight in them, because although
they are, for the most part, very scrupulous studies of life and movement; they are, at the same time, real drawings, and are all impregnated with a very strong philosophy and sarcasm. In the 'Capricos',
for instance, he has drawn the most outrageous things: an old woman, fat, abominable, naked, held by devils, who carry her in the
air, and underneath he has written: '¿Adonde va Mama?'[1] ...
The words he uses are so short, so strong, and so intimately connected with the drawings that it is impossible not to be bowled
over with admiration. I tell you this, dear little Mamus, thinking
that it will interest you, for it has thrilled me—I am quite captivated

[1] The letter here contains many detailed descriptions of Goya's engravings.

by it. The drawing is magnificent, and I believe that the best draughtsmen in this manner—Goya, Daumier, Gavarni, Toulouse-Lautrec, Phil May, Keene, Forain, Belcher—have been, or are still,
the profoundest thinkers. So you see, we have heaps of lovely things
to look at when we are together again in the winter: Japanese prints,
French paintings, Belgian and German engravings, Goya, and
many other things which I shall no doubt find. You will be quite
confused by hearing of so much all at the same time, funny little
Mamus; what with the orchids, the palm-trees, the drawings, you
won't need Pipik any more, and to think you didn't want to come
to London!

It is very annoying that I should have to reply to the advertisement just now, when I never felt so good for nothing, so empty-
headed, jumpy, over-excited and 'zweifelhaft'. All the same, I have
done a drawing, but as I have already told you, it took me from
five this morning until one o'clock this afternoon. The little larks
are singing all around me, and that makes me live in company with
my precious Zosienka. You will see, little Mamus, we shall be happier soon, so have courage—for me particularly, as I am so easily
depressed. I soon pick up again, but these sudden changes make
me suffer physically very much.   Pik.

Still at 'Fifille'
25th April 1911

Pickna Zosienka,
You will scarcely be able to imagine the tremendous joy I had
last night, when I found your dear letter in my room; just like my
beloved little Maman, I have been terribly over-excited and ill—

although I feel a bit better now. It is strange that we should influence each other to such a degree.[1] Knowing this, I do everything in my power to be very quiet at these moments, I study the old masters, and so straighten out all the stupid ideas which upset my mind. The 'zweifelhaft' worried me dreadfully yesterday. After taking all the morning over a drawing, I decided that I would go out somewhere in the afternoon. But where? To the Tate Gallery? No. Museums make me sick. I should see nothing. To Kew? No, there would be such crowds there. Then where on earth? Perhaps to the Tate after all—no, I'll decide on Kew. All this took an hour at least, until, furious with myself, I took my head in my hands and shook it to bring back my wandering wits. I left for the train, and only at the station decided to go to Sudbury Hill, far away in Berkshire, in the west.

I saw the most magnificent country from the top of the hill—all central England, even the good old Blagdon Hills that I loved so much in Somersetshire; the South Downs as far as Portsmouth and, close up in the valley, Windsor Castle. Beyond all this, I imagined France lying far behind the Downs which fell away in front of me, and I was comforted, alone with the memory of Zosia, and with the phantasmagoria of Goya y Lucientes. The great, beautiful sun sank to rest behind all the expanse of meadows and trees, and I prayed to him, the great artist, to make us prosperous. I should never be happy all day if I did not, each morning when I get up, kneel down before him and communicate with you, good little Mamuska. I am always very enthusiastic, but very weak, and this is

[1] See letter of 19th May 1911, p. 63.

why I need a beloved Maman, and a beautiful great God. We only follow the fine and natural religion of the ancients, and no one can laugh at us, for our prayers are addressed to a Being, true and real.

Do you know what I saw yesterday in the City? An old book by Emerson, in German, and the title was *Die Sonne regiert die Welt*. If Matuska will allow me, I will buy it later, but only if I can't find it in one of the Libraries, for I already possess too much. I notice this particularly during a removal, though I am getting on all right with this one. Already I have half my things at Sterndale.[1] The rest are tied up here, and after three more journeys there will be nothing left. To-night I will sleep in your bed, and this will pleasantly crown the memories of this happy week. I shan't need a man to help me move the box, which we are destroying, and I shall have enough pennies to last me until April 30th, which is Sunday. I shall be bucked if W. pays me on the 29th. He probably will. I put myself out for Wulfs much more than I have done in other places, because I am fond of him, and so I work conscientiously for him. He is trying to get a certain job in order to do in a filthy pig of a 'business man', a hideous liar, woman-hunter, and rotter; so, sweet Mamus, you will pray for Wulf's success, won't you?

Don't be too disappointed that I haven't been learning Polish, and that we haven't spoken much. We will discuss all these things in our letters. We have been together for so short a time that we are quite justified in letting ourselves go a bit. We have so many things to talk about. At Kew, for instance, we could only talk of the flowers and the trees, and when we stayed at home there was so much to

[1] 39 Sterndale Road.

say—Mamus had to tell all that happened to her at Felixstowe,[1] and since that Tuesday Pik has seen little of her; so you see, sweet dear, you must not get anxious.

I promise you, Mamus, to look after myself better next month. In addition to the two pints of 'Lolo', I will eat raw eggs every day, and, if I can get it, some raw meat too. Although I may control myself ever so much, I can't possibly promise not to be an enthusiast—it would be impossible. For that, I would need to see nothing, to read nothing, and never to think. I must get stronger, I agree, but it must be a relative strength, don't you see, my little Mamus? For certain things I shall do, as I have already told you dozens of times, I shall follow my instinct, and think as little as possible about them; and, little Mother, don't worry about the drawings, nor about your writings. You see that advertisement may easily lead to something, and now that I am feeling better and have not got to think again about changing my lodgings, I shall, through the help of the 'Architect', get to know other people, so that, without having an Abbey—you greedy kid—we will at least have a little house, or even a little flat for the two of us. The little Mother is, of course, an excellent housewife, and she must have her little nest. Is it in order to powder her nose? Pik isn't so ambitious on that head, although it is true he is just as keen—for his greatest joy would be to have a studio, also for powdering—people—in plaster!

Let's keep up our spirits with the big sun as our guide. You know Pik is very, very young, and Mamus is young too—we will have time to do such a lot.

[1] During her visit for an interview.

Heaps of love, kisses, and sweet things to you, poor love. I will get better all the time now, little Zosienka.

Pik.

Tes énormes fautes
horrible petite gribouilleuse.

'lui laissant la charge *de* gosses'—des gosses.

un nombre vague, indéfini (il peut en avoir 10 comme 20, 30).

Par contre, *de* 3 gosses—*de* quelques gosses, *de* plusieurs gosses.

'je suis forcée d'avoir des mioches':

c'est très bien là—pourquoi pas dans le 1er cas? *étourdie*.

la nature n'est pas *magnanime*, mais *magnifique:* magnanime—seulement pour les individus.

'loin *de* méchants h. . . .', *des*—comme pour gosses.

abaye—abbaye.

pourvue—'pourvu que' est toujours invariable, car c'est une conjonction.

ammonceler—avec un seul 'm'.

'S' à la seconde personne sing. pour les verbes s.v.p.—'tu te soign*e*' —'te surmèn*e*'.

que veut dire 'compete'—sans doute l'anglais 'compete', 'fait concurrence'.

39 Sterndale Road
13th May 1911

Beloved Maman,

First of all, I must give you a good spanking for having wished to go away from Pik so soon. She doesn't want him to work for her, she would like to earn her own living—stop there! Madama,

THE WRESTLER

it is high time that you settled down; you have collected quite enough material by now to construct something, and it is impossible that you should go on any longer dragging from place to place. I am very young, and I ought to study, but while doing so, I will earn a little. If Mamus would only consider her Pik as part of herself, she would not talk of being 'kept'—as if it were a question of two different people, of a fellow who had a woman for his kitchen and his bed. No, it is a question of art, and I'm your Pikus, as you know. I shall be desperate if you really wish to do what you say in your letter.[1] It is this splendid sunshine that has puffed you up with enthusiasm and recklessness. At heart you are still poor little Madka, who needs a good Pik to do all in his power to aid her to realize her wishes; he will do it, so give him your promise. Pipik takes your advice, you know, whenever it is possible, and to-day he took his first sunbath. We are a couple of miserable little insects—for I also thought he would shine just because we worshipped him—who is going to whip us for our presumption? Between you and me, I think it is the only way, all the same. It is lovely weather—magnificent—a most delicious springtime. The lilac is in flower in the gardens, and each evening I inhale deep marvellous scents which put me in a frenzy. You are quite right about my eyes; they used to say to me in France—mother in particular—'Why don't you look like everyone else? You have the eyes of a wicked madman. People will think that you want to steal something', etc. And, certainly, it is true—and it is the Soul that I wish to capture.

[1] Miss Brzeska was looking for a permanent position as a teacher in a school.

Now let's talk about art. You say that it is monotonous to see [single] statues standing or seated.

We have:

Victory:	standing
The Slave:	"
St. John:	"

and these are the best.

You are bungling the whole thing when you say that design and colour do not require much thought. It is only as a result of knowledge and ability that simple things are discovered. Philosophy is inherent in man. It comes long before these exact expressions. We always come back to the same thing, belovedest, that beauty can only be arrived at through truth of form and colour. It is not a scrap of use theorizing in front of a mass of modelling clay. Life must come out of the clay by means of its external surface, and this is the *design*. If you discover fine design, it will bring with it life, and herein lies Art. No one will shake my belief in this. Conceptions, subjects, are but the frames of pictures—secondary things on which one should not count.

It is true that before beginning even a portrait I should know what the work will be, but if I am unable to render what I conceived, people will say that I am not an artist—thus art does not lie in the dream, but in the marriage of the dream with the material. Work, always work. And in order to work well you need a big intelligence, and that is all I can tell you, little Mamusienka.

I have been reading about the Neo-Impressionists. They are, like all artists, very idealistic: too idealistic, I think—mystical and not at all independent. They are like Christian savages of the Middle Ages. Their principle is that drawing (painting, sculpture, architecture) should not represent such and such an object, but by means of some indications should convey to the mind the memory of a form, heighten the imagination and make you think of the thing represented. Example: a laughing man: they would not draw the features, but only make you think that the man laughs. This is a decadence, because they are mixing painting with music—an art altogether idealistic, since it exists to evoke, nothing else—while the rôle of drawing is to be pleasing to the senses in giving them

réalisme　　*néoimpressionisme*

something palpable, solid; in other words, in giving a representation. If the representation is of a living thing and if it is true, it will be alive, but under no consideration should one imagine that it belongs firstly to the soul—that is a false trail. One's fingers should feel delight in touching the undulations of a statue, the eyes in beholding a painting. Philosophize after, to satisfy your humanity, but not before. In Art one must absolutely respect its limits and its logic—otherwise one arrives at nothing worth doing. The great masters are there to instruct us, and I wish to remain faithful to their tradition.

I heard Keir Hardie, the great English socialist—a magnificent old man—very enthusiastic. He was holding an open-air meeting in Trafalgar Square, and spoke of the exploitation of the miners by the owners of the mines. I'll send you the sketches I did of him and a little revolutionary prospectus, copies of which were distributed.

I write in haste this evening so that you will get it to-morrow morning.

I beseech you, little Mamus, to forget what you said about plans for next winter. I do absolutely wish to help Mamus, and she ought to accept, otherwise it will be I who can do nothing because of the torment I shall be in on your account. Be a good little Madka, and since we so affectionately promised to live one for the other, you *must* accept. Poor little Mamusienka, you have made me very sad

and I shall worry myself all to-morrow, poor devil that I am, and shall be able to do nothing.

Pik.

14th May 1911

I write again, little Maman, because my heart is very full. I feel very discouraged by your queer tone of independence. Up till now I have gone happily to business with the delightful vision in my mind of making it possible for little Madka to work quietly during the next year, of making her happy and of finally giving her this miserable little home that she covets. This evening she herself upsets everything.

Why, oh why, do you say such things to me?

I can't prevent myself from crying and upsetting myself dreadfully. I won't feel light-hearted in the City any longer, for I shall regret the sculptor's chisel so much more. Anyhow, everything looks black at this moment, when outside all is so beautiful, and I ought to be feeling stronger; it is another gift of the moon, I half expected it—the thirteenth of the month—a pinch still of superstition! I don't care much for myself—for my poor, broken carcase, so that it requires something more than my own personal comfort to enable me to sacrifice myself to office work. For this I had my darling Zosienka, and now she won't allow it any longer, becomes disagreeable, and, for low-down, shabby questions of money, capable only of interesting hideous middle-class people, she gives me pain. I implore you on both knees, dear Maman, as the only creature who loves me, for the good of us both, to promise to think of yourself as a part of your Pik; otherwise, in spite of himself, he will go to the dogs through depression and disgust, and through all the devilish horde of troubles which upset his health. So for your own sake, you must absolutely stay, Zosienka. You can't go away from Pipik. I implore you, darling. I am an ass to upset myself like this, I know it; but these things make such an impression on me at the moment. I forgive poor Mamus, because she hasn't done it on purpose. Perhaps it was only by a kind of modesty or politeness—I understand my little Zosik—but she ought to be my own madka, for I am nothing but her pik, belong only to her, and am ready to sacrifice everything in order that she may feel better and be able to work—if she fails me I shall fail too, for I shall be incapable of doing anything. She will call me capricious—but I am not, Maminska, it is because I love you and I don't want to suffer for nothing. If I make myself stupid at a typewriter, I desire at least that Mamus shall profit; unless she does, I shouldn't have the strength to keep it up.

I got too upset last night, for I was very tired. My English colleague has gone away on his holidays and I have to do all his work —that is why I have written this sentimental tirade to-day. As it is wet, I have stayed in my room, reading and resting, and I understand better now what little Madka means—but Mamus, you must not compare yourself with Sarah Bernhardt, for she is stronger, she does not suffer as you do, and is not tormented by illness every month. Already this week you have had to stay in bed three days: Friday, Saturday, and Sunday. Think it over. I will be very quiet for your sake, poor little soul, and don't refuse Pik's aid, because he is your own boy and not a vulgar outsider. Darling, do write to me as soon as you can, for I shall be frantic, what with this and the awful heat that we are now having in London.

Pik.

Friday, 19th May 1911

Adorable Maman,

Surely poor Zosienka is in pain, for since mid-day to-day Pik has suffered from every ill. What with a headache and a hideous stomach ache I listened so badly to what Wulfs was saying that I have had to do over again a third of my correspondence, which isn't exactly a help, since I am all alone to do everything. I've been upset since about two o'clock yesterday, when things started going wrong, and this morning I broke the big white jug from my room. It happened when I was in the bath: the old fools have turned out the bathroom, and taken out all the planks, leaving only the bath. It's been like that for a week, and Pik has refrained all this time from having a sponge down. But this morning, because he felt more rotten than usual, he went into the bathroom—the beastly affair gave a great shake while he was pouring water down his back, and it made him jump out of his skin.

I dropped the jug, which broke into atoms, but happily did not cut me. What would have continued this litany of accidents would

 have been the second print in the Goya book—'The Pig has broken the Pitcher' —but there was no Mamus to beat Pik's bottom with a slipper. I shall keep very quiet for the rest of to-day, to-morrow and Sunday, for since there is such telepathy between us, we must be sensible, mustn't we, Mumsie dear ? We so often gain by it, that when we don't, we mustn't complain; it shows that we love each other in a perfect way, that our souls and bodies make one—Mamuspikus—so let's be happy, very happy; Pipik never expected to be so loved, and neither did little Mamuska.

For several nights I've dreamt about my beloved Maman—such lovely things, like the dreams of quite little children: little Mamus, magnificent, radiant with great suns all around her, bending low over Pik to bless him—and the sentimental Pikus who always takes the mask to bed with him, wakes in the morning kissing it, in the belief that it is his real Maman. He gets up at once, washes and then says his prayer for Mamus and himself—with the sun so pure, he can only pray after having purified himself of dust and dirt, and then, naked, he adores; clothes are not creatures of the sun—only our bodies. I love to pray thus before so great a god, for I become one with my beloved and that fills me with voluptuousness.

Before that I had several nights of ugly dreams—that is, ugly afterwards, for I had 'enjoyment' during these nights. Pik had horrid temptations with stupid women, and once with men: he even committed the act with them, but he doesn't remember if that gave him pleasure. He was always very annoyed with himself when he woke, and washed three times as hard as usual, for all these things are repugnant horrors sent only by the moon.

All the time and quite regularly I am learning Polish, and by next winter I shall be able to read, for already I can manage without difficulty little things on the history of Poland and those stupid conversations at the end of the exercises. . . .

Evening

Dearest, if I said that you must come to me while you are writing the 'Trilogy', that was only so as not to shock you, because you would never let me say 'for always' on account of my sculpture; but I desire, and absolutely must see, that this Trilogy is written and well written. Even if for that I have to sacrifice art, study, every‑ thing, in order that Matka may work, I will do so—that's all I wanted to say to my precious Mamusin.

Now it's understood that when little Mamus grows old Pik will look after her as if she were his daughter, and will always adore her. While he has a drop of blood he will fight for his Mamus, just as his Zosienko will do for him—so don't let's torment ourselves any more—anyhow, I wrote that 'tartine' because I was enormously tired and these obscenities all came to upset me, but last Sunday's letter has put all right. I am much too sensitive a chap, have too much the characteristics and manners of a schoolgirl, and Mamus must often scold me—but you see, Matka, it is being obsessed by art which leads to these stupidities, for art leaves no room to culti‑ vate secondary ideas—so give me many 'thrashings'.

I am very sad also about Delannoy's death.[1] I am very fond of his way of drawing: it is strong, and now I understand why his latest things weren't so good as the first ones, it's because the poor devil was ill. I have most reverently put by the portrait; it's rather weak, but all the same one can see that he had character. You see Mamus I'm right again: that a fine and noble artist must also be a simple, good, and beautiful man. I will never give this up, and you can cry out that it is presumption to judge by a face, quoting the proverb 'il ne faut pas juger les gens sur la mine'. It isn't presumption, but knowledge and judgement—humility is no good, you know that quite well, and preach it yourself, poor old Mamusin. Let's pray to the beautiful sun for Delannoy.

[1] Aristide Delannoy, born 1874, died 5th May 1911.

Dearest, the mistake you make is to confuse 'expression' with the successive appearances of the face. Expression, as I tried to say, is the sum total of the vices and virtues of the whole [inner] life which shows in the aspect of each individual. I might no doubt say that one person has more expression than another if his enthusiasm, his anger, his passions are more lively in his face, if there is more sarcasm or gaiety in his laughter and more sadness in his tears; but the laughter and those tears are mere accidents caused by nervous excitements, in the course of which the whole expression is not changed, but coloured, or, if you like, veers towards a note of gaiety or sorrow. When I say that Mamus changes her *expression*, I only mean that her gayest laugh follows her blackest woe without transition, that her nervous excitements are so great and so varied that her real, innate, unchangeable expression, that of a good and energetic little mamiska, is constantly taking a different *colour*. When you laugh or cry you do not cease to be the little mamus.

A loathsome personality—like that pupil of yours for instance—can laugh, make pretty faces, or work herself up as much as she likes, her *expression* doesn't change, you still see her filthiness show through her coarse lips, her vileness through her low forehead or her ill-shaped nose, her stupidity and malice through her eyes. That is what expression is, and it can certainly no more be distinguished from features than the soul from the body. Now little Mumsie speaks without really thinking of all these enormous possibilities. It is true that a man can and does change the appearance of his face, as also his body—unconsciously in most people—and that this change directly follows his ethics. When Nero was young he was attractive to look at, but through debauch, slaughter and cruelty, he developed a bull's neck, hideous eyes, and a wicked mouth, thereby stigmatizing on the outside all that was within. How is it that depraved men and women develop these eyes, lips, and noses? They weren't like that when they were young, and if they had kept themselves from vice they would not have grown like that. One sees this side chiefly, as more people go from virtue to vice than from vice to virtue.

Now for statuary, I like best the 'Jean': I admire Michelangelo's 'Slave' for its magnitude, because heroism, creative energy, astonishes me; the Samothrace 'Victory' because its poetry pleases my senses; but I don't really understand one or the other, although I often make out that I do. I can't look at them for long without getting tired; but Rodin's 'John the Baptist', on the other hand, would hold me for days on end.

My aim has always been to convince you that a chosen subject may be very well executed, but for all that, doesn't make a work of art. I agree, Mamus, absolutely agree so long as this subject has been lived—like your Trilogy, for instance—which is a very good subject into which you can weave many sensations; but never introduce purely legendary incidents. Beware of your imagination—make it serve you to a good end by mating it with your observation, your knowledge of real life, true things that are beautiful because they exist. As I have told you, its conception is natural, it stands by itself as a portrait, so that's that. A St. John by Rodin is a subject, an old woman is a subject, a man with a broken nose is a subject, everything is a subject; but it has no need to be an old woman dressed up in the garb of mythology; indeed, it ought not to be; *finita la comedia.*

You are certainly right in saying that the beautiful and good are innate in the Primitives—yes, but they are very weak, and civilization must develop them so that ethics and æsthetics become their product. We find the truth of this not in savagery but in civilization. The savage acts by rage, vengeance, hatred; in a word, he is natural and spontaneous, he has no laws, it does not matter to him that his daughter should do as she likes, she is probably his wife and many other people's too. The rich Greek makes a law—he thinks of his fortune, his power, which he does not wish to lessen, and so he forbids his children to ally themselves with others, on pain of death, since this is the only thing which will stop them. This is criminal, not savage—it is criminal, not because the death penalty is brought in, but because a man takes it upon himself to dispose of the liberty of many others. There you have civilization, and just as I hold no brief for a civilization which admits slavery, human sacrifice, etc., I do not wish a system of æsthetics, equally false, based on so absurd and illusory a thing as line. Line is a bar, a limit, an infraction of liberty, a slavery—while mass is free, and can be multiplied infinitely, treated in a thousand ways. It leaves me free, and on top of all that, it is true, it exists.

Æsthetics are certainly a product of civilization, because one judges an epoch as much by its Art as by its customs; one wishes to see the level certain people have reached in their rendering and their comprehension of the beautiful. Our taste in all this has been falsified by a badly understood tradition which has always taught blind adoration of the Greeks and the Romans. Certainly they reached a high level, but we can and do arrive at an equally high degree without imitating them, 'sklavisch nachahmen'. In my opinion the St. John is more beautiful than the Venus of Milo, for I understand beauty differently from Phidias and his followers. He is a beggar who walks along, who speaks and gesticulates—he belongs to my own time, is in my epoch, he has a twentieth-century workman's body just as I see it and know it; in a word, it's a lovely statue. I like it better than the others, because I believe that Art should be seen in the present, looked for in the present, and not in the past. I keep my head high before anyone who reproaches me for not having 'seen' the Greeks. 'Sir,' I would say, 'had you made me then I would have been able to see them'; but it would be my greatest shame if anyone could accuse me of not being able to see what was around me. I should have no excuse.

Mamus feels all that instinctively, and she has never asked herself why she does not place her novel amongst the knights of the Crusades. It would, of course, be ridiculous, and it would be equally stupid for me to draw according to ideas which came from the minds of antiquity, and which were brought into life by circumstances which are not in force to-day. That's what I want to arrive at and to hold until the end—that in art the sentimental subject has no place, and any imitation of a past time is an enormous fault. Flaxman added nothing to the human collection, for he imitated Phidias. Stevens nothing, for he imitated Michelangelo. If to-day we have only beggars, let us only sculpt beggars; if subjects suitable for gigantic paintings no longer appear, don't let us do gigantic paintings, for our successors should not be able to accuse us of having falsified our age. My belief in the eternity of life (but on this earth, in the breaking-up of life's forces to renew itself) makes me count it a crime to lie in this way, because I am surely also made of the past which I must respect, and of the future which I should venerate, since it is more important.

Artistic vision, sensation if you like, is not called forth because some picture is labelled 'The Battle of Hermann', in which Romans and Germans kill each other, but by some beautiful form which it contains. Now what I object to in such representational subjects is that the artist, not having been in it, cannot convey all the artistic feeling; his work lacks interest, and to gain ground he indulges in theatricalities and sentimentalities: in fellows who bleed, in children with torn throats, in women who cry, etc., not to mention the sweeter sides. Imagination exists to help us understand the present, not to create things of herself. I talk now like Mamus for the pleasure of talking, not to convince her, because at heart she is already convinced. If she had not this sense of the contemporary, this appreciation of art in immediate things, this working from the present in which alone I believe, she would not write a novel which is beautiful and vibrating with life though tragically true, but one full of soft beauties (of a knight Jehan who kills another knight at a tournament for the hand of a 'damoiseau beau et gente que sera son noble épouse'). She can speak thus of mythological things, stories which are in other people's worlds, but in her own world she would not dream of doing so, and in Pik's it is utterly forbidden to express anything other than that which is real. That, little

Mamus, is what makes the greatness of Phidias and of Michelangelo, they did not represent Egyptians nor Gauls but their contemporaries. Rodin will be as big a man for the twentieth century as Michelangelo is for the sixteenth—but you must not compare one with the other—do you see, Mamuska? Yesterday I drew 'St. Jean' for you, and here it is. I would certainly prevent Mamus from writing rot; that is to say, things without sense because unreal and out of date; and on her side she should save me from presumption (since she finds it in me) and from unreality.

I enclose you a drawing [1] which is worth ten thousand times all the Prometheuses because it is alive, its forms are right, as I have seen with my own eyes and felt in my own soul.

I need to discuss; but little Mamus is always saying to me: 'Modesty, modesty'. I am modest, but not humble; that is a Christian stupidity; I know what to do, and when I do something really good, or even only fairly good, I say so without hesitation; but I see my faults, and the proof of this is that when I do something bad I burn it. Mamus jumps with rage during these *autos-da-fé*, but they must be, for none of this piggish trash must remain. You say, 'Pipik, perhaps you may make a mistake and believe a bad thing to be good'. Impossible in a drawing, though not in science. I may make a mistake in a calculation, but I see at a glance if the completed thing is good or not; there is an instinct inside me. To be modest is not to be puffed up—tell me, Mamus, have I ever boasted of myself as an artist? Never any more than you—this thing is so sacred that we would not dream of sullying it. I draw firstly out of love, then from

---

[1] Drawing of little old seated woman, since lost.

ENID BAGNOLD

egoism, and I wish that it should be good out of dignity, so as not to offend myself first and afterwards others, but so long as I do not offend myself I'm blest if I really care.

. . . .

Beloved,

I don't want to accuse Uhlemayr before being quite sure that he hasn't replied.[1] I haven't yet been to see at South Kensington. Usually Uhl. does not write more than once every two or three months. I don't think he would be so rotten, and I hope for the best. ——, ——, and —— are idiots and I shall give them a miss, and if others act in this way I shall ignore them also—but always and in spite of everything I shall be pik to matus, just as she will be matus to pipik, although he is capricious, unstable in his thoughts, changeable in his ideas, but only superficially—at heart he is solid, about art in particular.

It is already eleven o'clock, and I have been writing and drawing for you during four hours, dear Zosienka, and I am happy, content, and quiet, although ill; but since you, poor dear, are ill too, I will not make things worse by grumbling—if the 'old boy' wishes to 'couler qu'il coule, "et l'on s'en fout la tire re lire re lon"', etc. Just as at the Panthéon—you remember those 'rags'!

I will bring anything you like, and I will have enough cash at the end of the month to come to you! Pik must be economical; since

---

[1] Dr. Uhlemayr had not written to Gaudier for a long while because at this time he was extremely busy. Gaudier feared that he might have been offended by the Gaudier-Brzeska arrangement.

the most stupid fools can manage on tiny means, why shouldn't we, who are more intelligent than all of them?

There is a market in Leadenhall Street where they sell dogs, cats and birds. I go there, and I love to see the tiny dogs amusing themselves; it is much pleasanter than the heart-rending slaughter-houses of Whitechapel, with hideous Jews. When you write on Monday tell me what you think of Keir Hardie and of the pamphlet I sent. I hate those swine who upset you, and I pray the lovely sun to send them to sleep by its heat, so that you shall be left for a little in peace, poor darling.

your own Pik.

PART II

Beloved little Mamus,

It's you who are a stupid old boaster—what paradoxes you do fling at me!

'The true artist neither desires to be nor is aware of being one.' That is equivalent to saying that Michelangelo, a great artist, never knew that he was a better sculptor than Desiderio da Settignano or Giovanni da Bologna, who were his contemporaries, and that he could only do his Slaves well 'without being aware of it', and this after he had spent years in making studies to get into them the greatest possible amount of life, of rich modelling—or that Shakespeare never knew that he wrote far better than Marlowe or Milton,[1] and that his arrangement was always unconscious—or again that Rodin doesn't know in his heart that he is bigger than the others. Blast it all, if he hadn't known this he would never have struggled for so long. The truth is that a great artist is conscious of the talent and the power he possesses, otherwise he would not see his faults, and so would not be able to improve.

You ascribe strange laws to beauty—that's because, like the early Christians, you believe that the soul is separate from the body, and that pushes you to say that expression is a different thing from features. You give the paradoxical example of two people who have similar features but different expressions. What are features—what is expression? The features are a certain composition made by the nose, the mouth, the eyes of an individual, the expression is the

---

[1] *Sic.* Shakespeare died before Milton had published anything.

sensation which is thrown off by these features; now if two people have practically similar features, their expressions cannot certainly vary as much as if one was beautiful and the other ugly. It would only be possible if the features, although apparently similar (that is to say, the form of the nose, of the mouth and of the eyes), were *really* absolutely different (composition). The profane would say: 'See two people curiously alike', and the 'wise man' would deny it to the last. As I have told you and will always maintain, the expression is inherent in the form and colour, and made by them; to arrive at it one must model and colour *truthfully*.

You say that Rodin's 'Old Woman' is ugly because shrivelled. It is age, and it seems to me vicious to generalize over life and beauty. A strong, vigorous man whose arms have been cut off is ugly; a tree fallen in the full plenitude of its life is ugly; a slaughtered lamb is ugly—because all that disturbs the design of life is ugly. An old man, decrepit (not disabled, for that is unnatural, a man with a wooden leg or crutches being ugly) is beautiful; a body, which has died naturally in old age, is beautiful, a wellsetup child, a sound man is beautiful, and Rodin's 'Old Woman' is beautiful—for beauty is life and life has three phases: Birth, Maturity, Death, all of which are equally beautiful. The forms of this Old Woman are lovely because they have character, like your hands, which are lovely; and just as you cannot see your hands as other than having character, it is impossible for you to speculate on what the statue might have been had it been void of character.

You talk of an artist's 'aim' and 'pleasure', *life*, you say. But it is so in the essence of man, in his being, that in truth he has neither aim nor pleasure, but a *passion* to accomplish in order to accomplish, and where look for subjects if not in '*Life*' (since as I understand it there is no opposition between life and death), since only life surrounds us?

Now to get back to the Greeks and the beauty of the Greeks. I see that you won't give up your blessed lines. The Victory is beautiful, not because its silhouette is abominably weak and monotonous, but because the masses of which it is composed have sufficient truth in their disposition to give the sensation of many rhythms: life, movement, wind, water, which are pleasing to the eyes. Phidias' statues are beautiful because the planes are well disposed, but the manner in which the work is done, the insipid draperies on the 'Three Fates' with their mawkish lines, are absolutely beneath consideration. Phidias' most beautiful statue is the Ilissos, and he at least has not got sweet lines, concession to an animal voluptuousness of the basest and most barbaric kind. True voluptuousness springs at the same time from the soul and from the body, and two people who love, and perform the act, will naturally have more pleasure if they have bones, muscles, nerves, furrows of skin to caress, than those who have soft contours to press against, for in this latter case the human body would become mixed with the cushions on which it reposes.

Line is nothing but a decoy—it does not exist, and although the Greeks are praised for having put it to so good a use, I—and you can call me presumptuous—am sure that it has nothing essentially to do with beauty. There are few things so detestable as the Venus of Milo—and exactly because she is no more than a line enjoyed by pigs—an enormous stomach if you like, without lumps, without holes, without hardness, without angles, without mystery, and without force—a flabby thing made of wool, which goes in if you lean against it, and what's worse, makes a fellow hot. Then in God's name tell me what hands could be more abominable than those of the Venus of Cnidos: tapering hands, butter fingers which flow without joints, without phalanges, without tendons, and with which she hides her 'cucu', that marvellous thing, that wonderfully divine delight? I loathe Praxiteles, for he, better than any other, has rounded the angles and levelled the depressions: stumps of marble very polished, very sweet, Mr. Praxiteles, Sir Scopas idem. But these are not men, only well-oiled corpses which one has set up; and they give pleasure because they are corpses, they are not forms which can give a local rhythm, do not evoke the base or the sublime, have no vibrating life-force; and that is why all the Greeks, with the exception of Phidias, of Polycletus and of Lysippus, are nothing but vulgar hewers of marble.

Your code for an honest life is conventional and was acquired by legions of individuals in the past, a perpetual adaptation to the needs of the moment. For Plato it is perfectly right for a father to kill his daughter if she does not wish to marry a particular person, or his son if he does not obey him: to me this is odious, and in the same way why should I, in æsthetics, necessarily be obliged to accept certain parts of their laws which to my senses are equally horrible and seem to me to be nothing but relics of barbarism?

That the Greeks were entirely right in balancing the masses, in studying planes and rhythm, yes, it was in this their grandeur lay; but that they were equally right for form in general, sweet lines, suave mouths, little feet, big breasts, no; there was their mistake, and I see no reason why I should adopt such ramblings. I understand beauty in a way which I feel to be better than theirs, and history and observation convince me that I am right; that is why I am so enraged against their damnable lines which have falsified people's taste, even that of my own little Mamusienka. Michelangelo has not manifested life in all its aspects, far from it. He has taken one aspect, and that without *desiring* it, but because it admirably served his technique—that is to say, the latent life of a man who thinks before acting: David, Night, Dawn, Evening, and Day, the Slaves, all without a definite and positive movement, all undecided. Rodin has put into the St. John what he saw in his beggar, with less certainty it is true, because he is not perfect, and life is.

The single statue is the only true way, standing or seated, whatever you may say about its monotony. The greatest masters have only made single statues, groups are always inferior; that is why Carpeaux, big though he was, is less so than Rodin, for he never knew how to make single statues. He did not know how to find his rhythm in the arrangement of the shapes of one body, but obtained it by the disposition of several. The great sculptors are there to prove this. Think of the masterpieces which we like most, all standing or seated, and one at a time, and they are not in the least monotonous. The connoisseur loves one spicy cake, but the glutton requires at least six to stimulate his pleasure.

The great thing is:

That sculpture consists in placing planes according to a rhythm.

That painting   ”   ”   colours   ”   ”   ”

That literature   ”   ”   stories   ”   ”   ”

That music   ”   ”   sounds   ”   ”   ”

and that movement outside any one of these is not permitted, that they are severely confined and limited, and that any incursion of one into the domain of another is a fault in taste and comprehension.

.   .   .   .   .   .

Now Matka is far more presumptuous than Pik, for she will never admit herself to be in the wrong. Although the stories would never have been published in February, she still repeats to Pik that if he had subscribed, as she advised him to, she would have seen in the January number the advertisement which she has just read, ask-ing for contributions by the end of May; yet if, having subscribed, she had seen it, she would have sworn the most foul oaths; for she would no longer be receiving the paper when the stories were pub-lished in July. Oh, you wretched little Matulenka, I did very well not to subscribe from January. I have always believed and thought that it would take at least three or four months to correct the answers and to distribute the rewards. Mamus has always mocked at me about this, we even had a row over it at Edith Road; I remember only too well, and in the end who is right? Mamus, naturally! Eh, you beloved old stupid! Prepare yourself to receive a spanking at Pentecost—learn from to-day how to lift your petticoats properly. Apart from that, I pray the sun, most fervently, to help us and to bring us a prize, even if it is not the first, in July when the results are published.

To criticize your work Mamus is too bitter against men—males in general. The really intelligent have always taken women into their confidence, it is only the vulgar who have despised them—see Julius Cæsar, Napoleon, Ulysses (if one is to believe Homer), Michelangelo and Colonna, and nearer to us, Curie.

Tell me that you will be pleased that Pipik should earn some money so that you can write your Trilogy, and tell me what you think about the question of Line—think it out logically and you will see that beauty doesn't depend on it in the least.

Devotedly, Pik.

Saturday, 3rd June 1911

I am at the Museum, Mamus dear, and here is a sentence by Rodin himself which exonerates the presumptuous Pikus, and plunges the poor 'vieille' into outer darkness: 'only one thing is important in sculpture—to express life', etc. . . . .

I have just got your letter, beloved. I must speak of Rodin first. You—you do nothing but blaspheme—that's the worst of you literary fellows: you judge everything by your own little standards.

I shall always maintain tenaciously that Michelangelo was wrong in his mannered proportions, which make 'supermen'. That's an unfortunate word which I don't like. If a man is imperfect you qualify him according to his merits, base, brutal, false, otherwise he is perfect—but if he is a 'superman' it must be that he is inhuman.

Paradox—you reproach me with it, but little Mamus, it's a way of amusing oneself which is no worse than wit and lying, and is more cultivated, and with Pik quite natural, he curbs himself tremendously, but all the same it often darts out. It is funny, Mauclair is worried by just the same thing in Rodin, he says that all aspirations of the sculptor to be simply realistic are paradoxical—but my only feeling is that you idealists, with possibilities stretching before you as wide as the universe, take immediate fright at the idea of limitation and combat it. Our sculpture is limited—it is a mathematical art—if we take off a millimetre from ten there only remain nine; if you take a line out of a chapter it wouldn't be missed. To make reliefs *tell* you must exaggerate the forms—that is the logical upshot of our discussions and it shocks you—you say that it's a paradox. Poor little Mamus will again say presumptuous little ass, lunatic who is always reverting to old ideas, etc., but, Mamus, I cannot possibly get away from them, they are instinctive and necessary. I must deduce things mathematically, for in my head everything unconsciously takes the form of a cube so many centimetres wide, while in that of my little Mamus everything is a long vaporous trail. That sets up a balance; beloved Matka must always strain after ideas and be cooled down by the concrete outlook of her pikus, Pik should sedulously force himself into form and be warmed by the ideas of his good little Zosienka.

So I'm very pleased with this 'Wortstreit', it does us both good. Matka is on the side of Mirabeau (sometimes), of Mauclair always, and of Anatole France, Marx, etc.—they are great in literature. Pik is on the side of Rodin, and asserts that sculpture is far simpler than

what these vain theorists ? ? ? ? ?!!! keep repeating over and over
again.

I was in bed, and got up to shout you down. Will you please
understand, dearest, once for all, that beauty does not lie in oily
lines nor in the sugared accents of the voice. It's a mannerism in
Mamus to find everything in herself ugly 'because people have always said so'. You must judge for yourself and let others be damned,
but I know that deep down you don't really think yourself ugly. I
don't know enough about music to be able to say whether or not
your voice is true—but I love the dear voice of Maman, it is rugged
and tempestuous, but alive and full of feeling, it expresses all the
loveliness held in her dear heart and all the ideas in her little head—
it is infinitely varied, as are all beautiful things, it changes completely
with her changing moods, with her pleasure in Pipik or her rage
against him, but above all it is sincere, and sincerity and truth are
beauty—that is why in statuary the true copy of nature (not the ser-
vile one) is beautiful. Leave me in peace, you, with your oils and
your flabby flesh of reverend academicians—remember that on their
side is the woman with big breasts, and that on mine you will see
her bones and her muscles. Beauty is character, truth, nothing else.
This 'bura' is now finished!

I have thought a great deal about the *Studio* and you will rant
against my want of courage, but it is childish to waste one or two
hours of one's precious time, and a penny, which is the important
thing (we are poor and already my little toothbrush hasn't any hairs
left), and to fuss oneself to death for fools that I have never seen.
I'll have the most fulminating rows with fellows who know me,

with people who may be moved, but with the *Studio* . . . who will read what I say? Some kid who opens the letters, and it will only make him laugh—it isn't worth it. The world is corrupt, and the way for me to make it better is not writing letters, but joining my efforts with those of others to produce a work of beauty. If Mamus wishes to write herself, let her, for she is better at cursing than I am; also it will give her practice, it's part of her job. To me it is most profoundly repugnant.

I shan't be sending any more German exercises, we will do them next winter; at present Polish is as much as my head will stand, and as I've been pretty poorly I've not even done this since Thursday. It's most regrettable that this disgusting moon drives me to all sorts of things.

Yesterday I bought two little copperplates for engraving, 3 frs. 50, but if I had had your letter I should have spent the 3 frs. 50 in quite another way—I should have sent them for Delannoy's portrait. But all is not lost. Instead of going to Richmond on Sunday, I will only go to Battersea Park, and so save about 2 frs. 50. On Tuesday I will post the order and tell them to send the portrait direct to Mamus—it will be a souvenir of the anniversary of our love, and of the birthday of the charming Zosienka. I want this letter to bring you every tenderness, specially distilled in my heart for the 6th of June, day which gave you birth.

The beastly moon is up, as I have already told you, and it has scarcely brought me luck: on the contrary everything is rotten. Not only the 'old boy' comes into the game, but also my nose has been bleeding . . . Anyhow I do practically no work, eat very well, have a bit of a headache, am as irritable as the devil; but all the same happy, since the sunshine is lovely and Matuska beloved and good. She must not get at all worried because of these accidents—it will probably get better bit by bit.

You write in your story, 'Qui sait si à un moment donné elle n'aurait pas pris un gros bonhomme . . . et qui sait si à un moment donné elle ne s'est pas fait immensément de mauvais sang à cause de cela'. Poor dear Matka, you must indeed have suffered to have let yourself go so completely—but you must not think of it any more now—you see you have a rotten little pikus, and the warm sunshine caresses us.

I must impress on you once again the mathematical side of sculpture. Take a cube—it is beautiful because it has light and shade—now here is a collection of cubes which delights me—I can inscribe the body of a woman. It is not beautiful because it's a woman of such and such a type, but because it catches the light in certain ways. If you want to dream in front of it so much the better, but you must on no account tax the sculptor with having primarily wished to express vice or virtue. His first wish has been to make a beautiful statue, from a material point of view. What puts you people wrong is that the most characteristic types are represented by the most beautiful statues, and for this reason. Christians and Pantheists may insist that the soul is separate from the body, but this is not true. There is a live body, that is all. Now if the forms are fine in the sense of refined it is because they are allied to a fine and refined moral life, and these exquisite forms reflect an exquisite light; and the result is a beautiful statue. You are the compiler, not I.

I long to make a statue of a single body, an absolute truthful
copy—something so true that it will live when it is made, even as

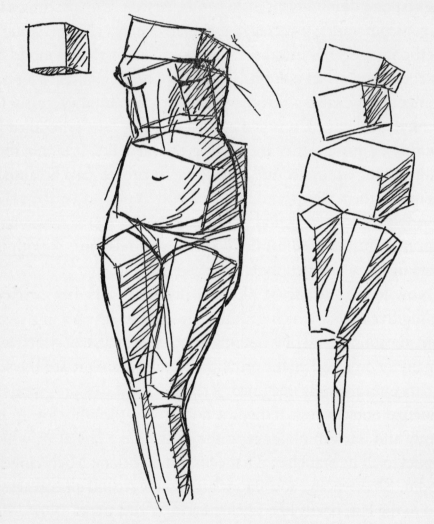

the model himself lives. The statue has nothing to say—it should
only have planes in the right place—no more.

You make a dreadful mistake in trying to compare Shakespeare with Rodin, it plunges you into an inextricable confusion, for one is a writer and the other a sculptor. You are wrong too, because Shakespeare didn't invent his subjects, he took them as settings for his contemporaries, 'überzeugt' that man does not change throughout the ages. Queen Elizabeth might well have served as model for Macbeth, and when you read *Hamlet* or *Othello* you don't for one moment ask when or where they take place, because they are true for eternity; and why? Because they are pure, they aren't muddled by painting or music—they are nothing but literature. It is only these adulterations which are dull. One quickly tires of Zola because he has mixed them all up, and his work only applies to a certain class of people, to a given period, and is not eternal. In the same way a man is disgusted with his body after sexual relations, or with his entire being when he is morally diseased.

Now for Baudelaire—I like him just because he has sacrificed the fugitive to that which endures. He encloses his idea in a severe form, the sonnet, and puts nothing but the essential, that which will remain for ever. When the principal features are expressed the secondary ones are easily imagined; if only the secondary are given, the principal ones are lost. If they are both given, then they lose in intensity and one can no longer distinguish. It is a law of art which applies to all its branches. To the first group belong Michelangelo, Rodin, Shakespeare, and Baudelaire, to the second all bad artists, and to the last, devils like Dickens and Walter Scott. Now I like Baudelaire and Chopin, for as I have told you music should only express those mysteries which sleep in the deep recesses of our hearts; and if I am a complete being I am satisfied, for I have different pleasures. I am sensual, voluptuous, materialistic in front of a statue, drunk with the play of light and with the harmonious or discordant colouring before a painting, I think profoundly when reading a book, and when listening to music I dream and am exalted. You, you don't know how to enjoy, for you don't recognize differences, and judge always on a basis of your literary idea—which is fundamentally impossible, for whatever you may say, your sensations are different when you read or when you listen to music or when you look at statues—different at their root, of a different species if you like; and these differences form our taste, which will be proportionately heightened in accordance with the profundity of our differing sensations.

It is no use for Mamus to waste herself in theories, for she lies to herself all the time. All that she says consciously is at war with her talent, which comes from her unconscious self. It's of little use for you to bewail the periods which have gone by without art; and here let me tell you, if there are periods without great artists it is that they were not sufficiently interesting to come into the history of art, and we ought not to worry our heads about them. You write what you know about, what you have lived—you blame yourself for only writing your Trilogy because you have suffered, and because that so burns within you that you cannot choose but tell it. So much the better, for had you not this living idea you could do nothing, you would write historical stupidities without any life. Notice a point though—in your Trilogy you could call the characters by Greek names, place them in Aulis if you liked, that wouldn't alter it at all; that is only setting, as in the case of Shakespeare; it is the fugitive,

GAUDIER *working on the Ezra Pound statue*

the famous 'local colour' which should be sacrificed to the universal colour, inspired genius ? ? ? ? ?!!!....

In Art one must exaggerate; as the sculptor deepens a depression,
or accentuates a relief, so the writer accentuates a vice, diminishes
some quality, according to his needs; and it is only here that the
imagination comes into play. Grandiosity, sublimity and luxury
with which you overwhelmingly reproach me goes with that necessary exaggeration of the facts which helps to secure greater truth,
and that is what I mean by a well-thought-out copying of nature.

Mamus really must think more deeply, she is too superficial in
all that she says, it's because the poor little one has never grown
accustomed to look at different things in different ways—she mud-
dles them all together, and that's why I ask her to be more careful
about her style....

Monday, 5th June 1911

I went to Kew yesterday afternoon and had an absolute orgy of
beauty, and was happy that Mamus was seeing things even more
beautiful. It is very hot, and I have but little courage. I'll do some
drawings in the morning, and in the afternoon I'll go out again—
probably to Kew, for I can make sketches of lovers who roll in the
grass—you know how. I've been very lucky lately, for I've seen
some lovely creatures—two superb women dressed so lightly that
one could see their big bodies without corsets and their breasts small
and well-placed on either side of their chests. One was a Hindoo
and the other, I don't know, probably a Russian, but certainly not
English; and for a man, again a beautiful Hindoo. He had a mouth

so delicate and voluptuous that it looked like a ripe fig burst open in the sunshine: he had scarcely any clothes on either, and only the thinnest of vests covered a most marvellous chest. He walked like a tiger, proud and haughty, with eyes that flashed like steel. I think he was the most lovely man I have ever seen, the sight of him made me wild with pleasure; and, would you believe it, the English, with their hideous mugs, laughed like idiots as he went by. In this country it's a kind of crime to be beautiful. Pik would have loved to kiss that lovely mouth.

I have found some more coincidences with Rodin—he sees statues in the clouds, in the old trunks of trees, in flowers; vases, insects and birds, in the bodies of women—just like the Mamus! Now, don't be too proud, you rotten little Matusienka.

Pik.

Wednesday evening, 14th June 1911

Dear adored Mamuska,

I will arrive on Thursday morning, 22nd June, 11.1 a.m., at Felixstowe Town (I'm getting a five days' ticket costing 7/6) and will leave on the following Sunday evening at 7.33, so that I shall have three nights and four days with you my own beloved. It was thanks to you that I got four days. I was going to ask my boss for them bang out when a good wind filled with 'kruczki polskie Zosienkie Brzeskie' blew in my ears; and without showing it, but looking a picture of innocence, I asked Wulfsberg if we were going to have Friday 23rd, the day after the Coronation. I knew quite well that we should, but I wanted to make him speak, and I fully succeeded—'Oh yes, Gaudier, it's only a question of Saturday, we will shut on the 22nd and 23rd—are you going to the country?' 'No, Mr. Wulfsberg, I ought to go to Paris, and you see if we have Saturday it will give me four days, otherwise only two.' 'Well you know I'm very pleased with you and you've worked well, so I'll give you from Wednesday evening until Monday morning.' I said thank you, and off I am to Paris—Felixstowe—to see the Mamusi —it's all the same so long as it contains the Mamus. I'm so pleased, for the air will do me good—I'm about in the same state as I was last year when you came to Combleux. I couldn't get out this evening, for yesterday I caught a cold coming back from the country, or perhaps it was only because I am so run down, and to-day I've been very unhappy—always 'la bas'—I smelt bad and was afraid the others would notice it. I often went down to the wash-room and upset myself thoroughly. I'll go to bed at 9 and will get up and go for a walk from 5–8 to-morrow morning like Mamus' good little Pikusik. I've got lots of things to tell you about Mrs. Harriet Beecher Stowe, whose centenary is to-day—also about modern Tokio. I'll write all that to-morrow. Good-night, Mamusin—I'll have a long sleep, and rest in your arms for the night.

Thursday morning

I haven't gone for a walk, for I have only just woken up, and it's 7.30. It was little Mamus who put me to sleep, dear gentle Zosia, and I feel much better than yesterday, fresh and rested, and I'm in a delirium of joy that in a week from to-day I shall press to my heart the real little Mamus of flesh and bone. I'll pamper her no end and make her very happy—we will wander along by the edge of the sea, we will bathe in the swift waves—at least Pik will, very early in the morning when there is no one about—what orgies of nature we will have together! It is so beautiful that it is almost unbelievable after the sordidness of this dirty old town. . . .

'People still recall Mrs. Stowe during her visits to England as a pleasant little lady with corkscrew curls and a quiet dignified manner. She had an earnest religious manner, *and took her mission as a writer very seriously and had little taste for the lighter social graces. Her highly-strung nervous temperament and habit of absent-mindedness made her averse to crowded receptions, and she was content to leave most of the talking to her amusing and jovial husband, who had a fund of racy New England anecdote.*' There is a strong analogy with Matka in her face and in her constitution too; see how she writes of herself: 'a little bit of a woman somewhat more than forty, about as thin and dry as a pinch of snuff—never very much to look at in my best days, and looking like a used-up article now.' This was at the moment when she wrote *Uncle Tom's Cabin*, one of the most decisive books of all times, for it played an eminent part in bringing about the War of Secession and the emancipation of the American negroes. You see Mamus is just the right age, '40', and the right appearance, 'thin and dry', to write a book just as decisive, but better literature, more beautiful than hers. Have courage, little Mamus, it will come, work hard and I pray the good sun every day to bless you.

I will talk about Modern Tokio another time, for it's already late this morning and it would take too long. With regard to my making up to the old women, arrange just what you think best. I'll do exactly as you like, for Matka shouldn't be made to suffer because of these idiots. So you will decide whether or no you need introduce me to them, etc.—feel quite free and Pik will behave superbly, even to praising to the skies their pasty colour!

Remember I leave London at 8.10 on the morning of the 22nd and should be at Fel. at 11.1. The train will probably be half an hour late, so don't get worried.

Pikus.

P.S.—I think that as I am coming next week I will bring the Grammar book instead of sending it this morning for 3d.

For the last week I've looked every day in the *Morning Post*,[1] but there is nothing—At Whitsun there are many demands for London, but as I've told you already you must apply in person.

I kiss you passionately, my sweet Mamusienka, on your lovely mouth and on your impish eyes—I fold you to me in gentle affection and hope that you will be quiet and calm during your illness.

Saturday, 17th. Evening

Poor beloved pet,

I was sure last Thursday that you were ill. You see I caught cold on Wednesday evening through lying out on a bank in the country. I was ill all through the night, and the next day was a kind of martyrdom, as I bled again and got enervated, so that it's probably all my fault that Mamus is ill. I'm better to-day, but in the night was much worse. God, what a horror all this is, but let us hope that

[1] For a situation for Miss Brzeska.

some day it will all go away, my dear one; we will be strong and healthy and able to work. I also am happy and pleased to come back to be nursed in those dear maternal arms and to be able to cheer up my dear companion a little. I have lots of news—I will tell you 'of how' one day I ran into —— and his Jewess in the middle of the street, 'of how' he came to see me the next day, and I reproached him for all his rottenness to us and said that I would never go near his Jewesses. 'They have never liked you,' he said with *naïveté*. His editor is a fellow who knows 'Simpson', the artist who did those two fine advertisements for 'Oxo', as well as the man with a black hat and red feather. Simpson has seen the —— Magazine and admired Pik's drawing, and wants to know Pik and see more drawings. So I gave —— some posters and some drawings to hand to the editor fellow. Let's profit all we can—he is rotten and I'll be generous with my rottenness to him—I want to give Mamus a nice companion for the winter. The old beast suggested starting again the 'leçons françaises' but I absolutely refused him. He has no dignity, for if he loves his Jewesses he ought not to speak to me again after all I said to him about them. He doesn't seem to notice it. He hopes to have drawings for his magazine—the blood sucker—you wait, old fool—I shall know Simpson and that's all.

Pik.

Richmond Park
18th June 1911

I am very anxious about Mamus although she says she is better and not worrying. The same worries I had on Thursday came again a little while ago (about 11 o'clock), I very much fear that the same

CHAPTER V
LIVING TOGETHER

A QUICK series of postcards altered all these arrangements. Pik suddenly thought it would be better to go to a place nearer London than Felixstowe, and told Zosik that he would make inquiries. On Wednesday 21st June, she heard from him that Southend was a good place, that she was to find rooms, and expect him the next morning. She took her ticket, but heard in the train that Southend was a much-frequented and noisy town. Nothing in the world would induce her to go to such a place, and at the next station she darted out of the train and implored the station-master to tell her of a spot which was both small and quiet. He suggested Burnham-on-Crouch, saying that it was a quiet little yachting centre, very beautiful without being expensive.

In her carriage was a young girl who came from Burnham, and she told Miss Brzeska that it was several miles from the sea, but all the same there was a salt water river, where she would be able to bathe. It was unbearably hot, and when Miss Brzeska got out at Burnham, she was so overcome by the heat and so flustered by her journey, that she forgot her luggage in the train, and went away with only her handbag and food-basket. Stunned and stupefied, her face so red that she looked as though she were drunk, she wandered about the streets searching for a room. In some houses the people did not like the look of her, elsewhere there were numberless children and dirt, and again in others the prices did not suit her. At the end of one little street she saw some green bushes, and instinctively went towards them. There, in the shade, she took off her shoes and stockings, which burnt her feet, and refreshed herself with fruit out of her basket. About six in the evening, when it was slightly

99

cooler, she again took up her search. This time she found rooms in the house of two old maids, and next day Pik joined her. They bought their own provisions, which their landladies were to cook for them, and which these women stole most flagrantly. When Sophie tried to convey to them, by little exclamations of surprise, that she saw what was happening, they put on the table a large silver mug whose inscription proclaimed that it had been won by their brother for his honesty!

While they were at Burnham, Pik did his best to persuade Sophie not to try for another post, but to come and live with him in London. He told her he wanted her all the time, and that he had no one to speak to after he left his 'damnable box of an office'. It was surely sufficient, he said, that one of them should groan under the yoke; and if he had to submit to this 'business', which he loathed, he would at least like to have the satisfaction of feeling that he was enabling her to be free. Sophie had only about eighty pounds left, and she felt that this must on no account be touched except in the case of some real emergency; but Pik explained that to furnish a room they would need so little, scarcely more than a bed.

'What do you mean, a bed? Are we not two?' cried Zosik.

'Yes, but I will sleep in a hammock.'

Zosik protested that this was insanity, that no one could sleep in a hammock.

'What, no one? Aristocrats, perhaps, or middle-class folk wouldn't, but I'm an artist, and artists must lead a Bohemian life and not make themselves weak by comforts. I tell you, I shall sleep

in a hammock, or if need be on the floor, so you need not count a
bed for me.'

Zosik said that she would need a bed, anyhow, and also tables,
chairs, and a cupboard.

It was now Pik's turn to protest:

'What, tables and cupboards! Why not heavy armchairs and
carpets right away? If that's your idea of an artist's life, I pity you;
a table and two chairs, perhaps, but even that is not necessary'.

'Oh, of course not. We can eat off the floor.'

'Well, why not? We can buy a few sugar-boxes, which will do
splendidly.'

'But with winter coming on we shall need blankets, we cannot
sleep in newspapers.'

'Pshaw,' said Pik, 'there are four months still before the winter
comes; by that time I shall be earning more money as a draughtsman, and we shall be able to indulge in these luxuries.'

In the end, Sophie was persuaded, but first she made him promise not to put her in a rage—she was weak and nervy, and did not
want to ruin her health after having more or less established it at
Felixstowe.

'I promise you, on the faith of an artist, to be a good Pikus to his
Mamus,' said Pik, and the matter was settled.

The sunshine and the enjoyment of their first freedom together in
England were too exciting to allow of arguments, and they had four
lovely days together, bathing, and running in the fields. They over-
did it, of course, and their health was no better in the end. Zosik
threw herself about and jumped in the water as if she were mad, and

Pik ran round far too much in the heat. The river water was dirty and unhealthy, and once Pik fell into a ditch of green, stagnant mud, which gave him rheumatism.

Before Pik left, it was decided that Zosik should stay on at Burnham until the end of August, and that he should find suitable rooms for them in London. A week or so later, he wrote to say that he had found two splendid rooms, far cheaper than they had anticipated: they were seven shillings a week, and what was more, his boss had raised his pay from six pounds to seven pounds a month, so that in future they would be rich, and able to live together in comfort. He asked her to come at once, and said he would meet her at the station.

Sophie started, full of misgivings. How would it be? Would they get on any better than in their first Kensington rooms? As usual on important occasions, she became nervous and superstitious. She told herself that if he met her at the station it would augur their happiness; if he didn't she would know that she had taken a wrong step. At the station there was no Pik to be seen. She waited and waited, and then decided to look for him; and so, with all her luggage, trundled round the noisy station. After half an hour she was in despair and went to the waiting-room, where she stayed patiently for some time. In the end she got annoyed: she began talking aloud to herself, and the other women in the waiting-room looked at her as though they thought she was possessed. Pik finally found her, having himself searched for her during the last hour.

Pik's enthusiasm and gay excitement were, however, in no way daunted, and Zosik had to go round then and there to see the new palace. There was no gas, a smoking lamp lit the stairs. The rooms smelt and were dreadfully damp. Sad at heart, Zosik returned to sleep in Pik's room, while he went out to buy himself a deck-chair and slept at the new premises. Next day he went along to see Sophie, enchanted with his night's rest; the chair was lovely, he had bought it in the King's Road for five shillings, and you could see by the marks on it that it had already made long voyages; it had even been to India.

In the afternoon they went out to buy a few necessaries. Henri always knew best about everything, or so it seemed, for he was of a very decided nature. Sophie was trying to get a clean second-hand bed or a cheap new one.

'Why on earth do you want to spend a pound on a bed?' cried Pik. 'It's crass folly, middle-class luxury. In one of these streets I saw a notice advertising a bed and everything complete for five shillings.'

Sophie suggested that at that price it would be 'walking'.

'Anyhow, we can go and see,' said Pik.

The man in the shop said it was hardly a bed for a lady to sleep on—it had no springs, and the mattress was worn.

'You can, at any rate, show it us,' said Pik.

In an old, dilapidated room where the boards squeaked and sagged they found a huge *bahut de famille*. An enormous bed, *délabré*, *égratigné*, which a hundred years ago had been new. The brown sack which called itself a mattress contained a few handfuls of rags which flaunted themselves at their ease in this tattered cover, giving the most distressing qualms as to its cleanliness. The idea of sleeping on such a *grabat* gave Sophie a shudder throughout her body, but Pik had energy for two and said:

'We can take it, it isn't very dirty, and, anyhow, one wouldn't sleep on it without spreading a cloth.'

'How can we tell who has slept on this bed?' said Zosik, and the shopman hastily replied that he could guarantee that nobody nasty had been in it—his wife had taken gentlemen *en pension*, and now they wished to let unfurnished rooms, so the bed was for sale.

'There, you see, Zosik,' broke in Henri, 'take it. We're so poor. We need other things as well—we shall never find elsewhere anything so cheap as this.' And as he saw Sophie hesitate, he said with an air of assurance: 'Well, I think we'll take it.'

Seeing the business settled, Sophie wished to get the thing a little cheaper, but Pik, with a lordly air and a cutting look, told her to be quiet with her saving of pennies, for it was cheap enough already; so that it was with some difficulty that she managed to have this ruined structure delivered without further charge.

They installed themselves that day—a small table for Miss Brzeska's work, two chairs, the deck-chair, a tub, and the famous bed made their complete outfit.

They soon found that their hoped-for little Paradise was a regular hell; there was a garage immediately outside Pik's room, and a chicken-run outside Sophie's. Sophie was particularly upset by all kinds of noise, and this situation soon drove her to a frenzy, greatly aggravated by the discovery of bugs in their rooms. On top of this, after three days Pik could stand his deck-chair no longer, and confessed that he could not do with another night of such torture. He

WOMAN AND CHILD

was ill and tired, and as it looked as if they would soon be leaving, Zosik was against buying another bed, which would have to be moved, so Pik had to share hers. It was a strange loading—these two in this ancient sarcophagus of a bed, bug-ridden and held together by bits of string. Across the threadbare mattress by the wall Miss Brzeska had put her old travelling-rugs, sewn together and padded with what she could find, while Pik lay on the bare mattress at the foot on a lower level. Nights of torture; for with every movement each disturbed the other. The days were no relief, for there was a continuous noise, and horror of the dirt made the place seem worse than a thousand hells.

In a couple of weeks they moved to a house in Paulton Square, but conditions were not much better. They were dreadfully underfed, Zosik cooking all the food on Monday—meat and potatoes and herrings—to be eaten cold for the rest of the week, augmented by milk and bread in small supplies. It is little wonder that she found life a constant irritation, and one quarrel culminated in Pik's throwing a herring at her. He was horrified by his action, and there was a most tender reconciliation. Throughout all this time Pik never complained, but was full of exuberance and excitement over the future. He was often touchingly attentive to Sophie, and with the money which she gave him for his fare he would bring her flowers and other small surprises.

Each month Pik would hand over to Zosik his seven pounds earned in the City, and as they endeavoured to spend each month a pound on things for daily life, cooking utensils, etc., they were often at the end of the month left with absolutely nothing,

save the untouchable savings which Miss Brzeska held in reserve.

Their enchantment knew no bounds when they made their first
friend. It was now October 1911, and they had been in London
for over nine months, but had found no one to speak to. One day,
outside the Victoria and Albert Museum, they saw a man who
looked like an Indian, and Henri felt attracted by him. A few days
later they found themselves together in the vestibule of the National
Gallery, and all looked at each other, but were too shy to speak. A
week later they were walking to the British Museum, and there
was their friend ahead of them. Pik again hung back, but Zosik
went to him and said that her brother was so anxious to know him.
He was delighted, and they arranged for him to come to tea on the
day after next. He was an Italian from Verona, called Arrigo Le-
vasti, and he came very often to see them, for he seemed as lonely as
they were. Then Pik, feeling it was wrong to hold anything from a
friend, told him that he and Zosik were not brother and sister, and
Zosik added that so far there had been nothing but a platonic love
between them. Pik immediately said, 'That's not true', which throws
an interesting light on Henri's character; for later on, when they
were to relate their history to Katherine Mansfield and Middleton
Murry, he again made the same statement, adding that he and
Zosik had often slept together. It shows that although he and Zosik
lived together as brother and sister, he was ashamed for anyone to
think it who knew they were not. After this their Italian friend's
visits became rare, and by Christmas had ceased altogether, so that
they were again left without anyone to talk to.

At Christmas Wulfsberg gave Pik five pounds as a Christmas-box, and Pik's first action was to buy Zosik a small porcelain oil-stove on which for several months she had set her heart. At the same time Pik's pay was raised by two pounds a month. In consequence of these sudden riches he and Zosik arranged to spend the following Saturday in buying Pik a trousseau, as he had had nothing since he came to London. They got a suit for twenty-six shillings, and Pik, ever so pleased to be so smart, thanked Zosik for getting him the suit. She found it very charming in him to thank her for buying him something with his own money.

He was always full of enthusiasm for the future, but Zosik's mind was of a matter-of-fact order and could not easily take in Pik's quick flights. For instance, he had a habit of lying: he said that lies were interesting and quite indispensable to an artist; she believed in what might be called a boring truth. This led to many disputes. Also Henri was very definite; everything with him was positive or negative, and the less he knew about a thing the more emphatic he became. Naturally his ideas would often change, and Zosik, with her added twenty years, did not always make allowances for this. Whatever you asked him he was always ready with an answer, and made it with such assurance that it was impossible to contradict it. Next day he might be just as emphatic in an entirely opposite direction.

Out of his 'Christmas-box' Pik sent ten shillings to his youngest sister Renée, and his letter to her shows the simple quality of his nature and his enthusiasm for art.

.   .   .   .

45 Paulton's Square, Chelsea
28th December 1911

My dear little Renée,

You will be tired of waiting for news of me, but I was hoping to receive Henriette's letter which Papa said was coming, before I replied. I send you a little present for your birthday, and this is how you will get the money. Go to the post-office the day after you get this letter—tell them your name: Renée Gaudier, and when they ask you who is sending the money you will say: 'Henri Gaudier, 45 Paulton's Square, Chelsea, Londres, S.W.' Don't make a mistake and they will give you 12 frs. 25 to 12 frs. 50, for it is ten shillings and not 10 frs. I am sending. Perhaps you had better ask Papa or Henriette to go with you. When you have got it you should give a little to Henriette so that she can bring you from Orleans a block of white paper (folio), there is some very good at the corner of the Rue Jeanne Darc and the Place de la Cathédrale at 40 or 50 centimes the block—a bottle of Chinese ink (marked J. M. Paillard) at 60 centimes—a pennyworth of good nibs (Gillott) and a nice new penholder. On top of that give her 1 fr. 50 so that she can buy you one of the series 'chefs d'œuvre illustrés' or 'Maîtres de la peinture'. She will get you *Puvis de Chavannes*, and if they haven't that, *Giotto*, and if they have no *Giotto*, then *Botticelli*, or *Fra Filippo Lippi* or *Uccello*, *Ghirlandajo* or *Cimabue*, and if they have none of these, any Italian she can find with the exception of *Raphael*, *Veronese*, *Carracci*, *Romano*, *Titian* or *Tiepolo*, and of all the French, English, German, and Spanish. But surely she will be able to get *Puvis de Chavannes* or *Giotto* or *Cimabue* at Loddé's in the Jeanne Darc. Also she must bring you a box of 5 elementary Bourgeois water-colours for 40 centimes from the Galeries Orléannais and a good brush, not too fine, for 30 centimes, also at the Galeries where they sell double ones, and a big mug.

So

A Book	1.50	
Paper	50	
Pens	30	
Colours	40	anyhow about 3 frs. 50
Brush	30	
Mug	40	
	3.40	

With the rest you can buy 2 francs' worth of good chocolate to celebrate New Year's Day, or jujubes—just as you like, and save the rest carefully in your money-box, and if you haven't got one, in any little box.

As I've already advised you, don't draw anything except from nature. Draw branches now that there are no leaves, birds, the cat, particularly since he's so fat and beautiful according to Henriette. But for every drawing take an entire new sheet of folio paper. The little page which you sent me was very pretty, but too minutely drawn.

Thus—with big strokes, boldly. Don't be frightened, make mistakes, as many as you like, but all the time draw very very strongly.

Do things like these, anything you like in Chinese ink without using a pencil, and get used to colouring them afterwards just as you think, but if you put a lot of *yellow* remember that you should have *violet* near by, if *red*, then have *green*, if *blue*, then *orange*.

Yellow with red and blue
Blue   " red and yellow
Red   " blue and yellow

so that one colour always looks well with a mixture of the two others. In the box which Henriette will bring you, you should keep only the carmine, the Prussian blue and the gamboge—throw away the black and the sky blue. . . .[1]

Pik had an absolute passion for creating and, not content himself with doing new things each day, he spurred Zosik on to finish books

[1] The remainder of this letter is lost.

and articles. He hoped to see them published and known by the world from one day to the next, but Sophie found their rooms far too noisy to be able to concentrate on her work. Pik for some months

had been doing nothing but posters, and he was certain that he would sell these for large sums of money.

In the meantime they knew no one, and suffered greatly from the cold and from hunger. Although he was now earning nine pounds a month, they found it very little for the two of them to live on. They had clothes to buy, a bed for Pik, and extra bedding, and in addition to this, Pik was trying to pay Sophie back all the money she had spent during their first months together. They thought they ought to make every effort to re-establish her small reserve fund.

Their landlady used constantly to poke her head into their room: she was obviously insulted by their having no furniture, but as they paid their rent regularly and kept their rooms clean, she could say nothing. She was nearly eighty years old, this landlady, and constantly the worse for drink. Often Pik and Zosik, after hearing a terrific crash in the basement, would go down, to find her lying unconscious on the floor, and with great difficulty they would undress her and put her to bed. She never thanked them for these attentions, but seemed rather to bear them an increased grudge, keeping out of their way afterwards.

CHAPTER VI
FRIENDS

IT WAS not until January of 1912 that Gaudier first met an English man publicly interested in Art. He had seen an article by Haldane Macfall in the *English Review*, and was very much struck by certain statements, although he thought it weakly written and long winded. Mr. Macfall had said, amongst other things, that he would fight anyone whose ideas were contrary to his, whether he were a bishop, a butcher or a burglar. Gaudier wrote to Mr. Macfall, telling him that he was a French artist, all alone in London, and earning his living in the City, and that he would be immensely pleased to make Mr. Macfall's acquaintance.

One day he came back from work full of excitement, and little by little, with much playfulness, he told the whole incident to Zosik. 'He certainly won't reply; such fortune could not possibly come to us,' said Sophie.

'That's just where you make a mistake,' said Pik, pulling a card from his pocket. 'The old fellow has already replied, and I'm to go and see him next Saturday; what's more, he will help me to sell my posters; we will take a nice house with a studio, and then I shall start to do some sculpture. Not a bad prospect, eh?'

They waited for Saturday in the utmost excitement. Pik put on his new twenty-six shilling suit, and Zosik bought him a special tie for one and sixpence. They felt that the doors of Paradise were to be opened to them at last, and they built fantastic castles in the air of how they would get a footing in many interesting houses, and both be universally recognized as great artists.

At 2 a.m. Henri returned from his first visit in the 'World'. Zosik was waiting anxiously for his news, but he said that he would tell her in the morning: he was too tired, and also it would only excite her and keep her from sleep. In the morning Zosik was early awake, and eager for his story as soon as he had opened his eyes.

'Well, disappointment is the lot of little sparrows like us. The author whom we thought so big, genial, and famous has none of these qualities, and lacks refinement and culture. To begin with, I was frightened of him—he has an atrocious mouth, a cow-like head . . . and a moustache brushed up *à la Guillaume d'Allemagne.* He seemed extremely alive, talked a great deal, gesticulated, and was very much taken up with himself. All the same, he's not a bad chap, and I'm very glad to have met him. His wife, too, who smoked like a factory chimney, seemed a pleasant, intelligent woman.'

Gaudier's accounts of people were nearly always brutal, and his anarchistic temperament made him speak particularly harshly of Mr. Macfall, who was a retired Army officer.

One result of this visit to the Macfalls was that Gaudier was to go there with Miss Brzeska on the following Wednesday, and take with him some of his drawings; and more immediately, two men whom he had met there, Hardinge and Alfree, were to call on them that very evening at nine.

Zosik leapt from her bed. 'What! You tell me this right at the end instead of at once, so that I could jump for joy! Oh, what a devilish little tease you are; you wait till I pull your stork-like nose!' and Pik huddled under his blanket to escape her impetuosity.

They were very happy all that day, and Sophie used all her in-genuity in making their rooms look as nice as possible. The idea that people might pity them for their poverty, or think them dirty because poor, humiliated and tormented her. But Pik said that these were only stupid, sentimental ideas, that artists did not pay attention to such things, and that her being unable to work when things were in a mess was the one thing which made him feel that she was not a real artist; for himself, he could work under any conditions, and soon he would be famous. Henri felt that he owed nothing whatever to Providence, that it was sheer will-power and perseverance which had won him his scholarship, and that only submissive people were imposed upon. 'I have always been in revolt,' he said; 'even when I was a child, I would fight my parents until they had to give in.'

Hardinge and Alfree were to come about nine, but at ten forty-five no one had arrived, and Zosik decided to go to bed. At eleven, when all the room was disarranged, there was a ring at the door. Hurriedly they covered up the bed, slipped various objects out of sight, and scrambled into their clothes. Pik ran downstairs to open the door for their visitors, while Zosik tried to collect her wits. She was very anxious not to appear a fool before Hardinge, who was a writer.

They were both full of enthusiasm over Pik's drawings and posters; he had never shown them to anyone in England before, and though at the worst of times he was certain of fortune, he now felt that he had indeed arrived. After a quarter of an hour they left, and Zosik and Pik were no longer alone in the world.

Next day a postcard came from Macfall telling Henri to take his posters to ——, adding that he would pay well. They would make at least fifty pounds—how rich they would be! They would go to Canterbury and see the Cathedral.

That day Pik went to work singing. He came back very dejected: they did not want any of his things. His Negress, being naked, was therefore indecent, the Bagpiper was too crude, and the Mermaid had not got a pretty enough face. This was their first disappointment, but it was soon forgotten, since each day there was a regular rain of postcards from Macfall, suggesting an orgy of prospective fortune.

His encouragement, sincere as it was, did not seem to lead to anything material, though it tided Henri and Sophie over a very difficult time by keeping their hope at white heat, and so numbing the pain of their daily life. Mr. Macfall tried very hard to get help for Gaudier. He introduced him to many people, and it was entirely due to him that Gaudier began to be known. He was not in a position to do anything big, and certainly he never realized that quite small help would have made all the difference in their lives. This was, I think, the case with most of the people who met them.

Henri would never ask for anything, or suggest that he was in any way poor. If he showed his drawings and they were liked, he would offer them as a gift. He was so generous and enthusiastic that the idea of there being any immediate necessity for help simply did not occur to anyone. Miss Brzeska had saved several remnants of furs and silks from the past, and always tried to make an impression of financial ease. She pretended she had a bank account, talked of cheques which had got mislaid, and of money orders which were on the way from France or Austria; while Pik's untidiness, on the other hand, would pass for a manifestation of the artistic tempera‐ment.

Miss Brzeska, who during the last year and a half had been of so much use to Henri, now began to stand in his way. Her disposition was too difficult to allow of her being generally accepted, and many people who would have liked to befriend Henri refrained for fear of Sophie. Henri, on his side, was always so loyal to her that he preferred to keep people at a distance rather than have her feelings hurt.

Sophie's visit to the Macfalls was not a success. The fatigue of getting there, the heat of the rooms, and the unwonted meeting with a number of people, went to her head, and she became over‐hilari‐ous. In the course of the evening she dirtied her hands on some charcoal, and Mrs. Macfall took her upstairs to wash. She was there persuaded to have a glass of whiskey to steady her, but instead of doing so it made her ten times more excitable. When they returned, Mr. Macfall was telling one of the guests, Miss Bagnold, that a drawing she had made was full of genius (he had set his guests to do caricatures of each other), and Sophie, unable to control her irrita‐tion any longer, said in a loud voice: 'Not at all, her drawings are stiff and photographic, their only merit is that they strike a likeness. Miss Bagnold is a writer, not an artist.' Her manner was strident in this drawing‐room, and soon everyone was on his feet to leave; and Mrs. Macfall was telling her that she would miss her last bus, and Mr. Macfall was holding her coat for her.

Miss Bagnold describes one of these dispersals:

'One night we came from Macfalls', Dolly and Lovat and I, and some others whose names and faces are gone, and we were again on a Tube railway station. Though we still expected it, the last train had gone. It was winter, and a wind like a wolf galloped down the Tube tunnel. We stood in its passage, Gaudier talking. He did not drop a subject when he had added a little to it. He did not throw a word in here and there, and make a crisp sentence sum up a bale of thought. What had been talked of a quarter of an hour before at Macfalls' was still being followed up. Gaudier, his long front hair hanging in a string down the side of his white brow, was throwing his future and his past and his passion into the discussion. We lazier English stood and shivered, and tried to back out of the wind. Gaudier felt our bodies moving, grouped, away from him, and I remember as he talked, and his eyes and pale face shone, he put out his thin arms and surrounded us and held us fast in the wind so that our edging movements should not distract him.

'Lovat was the first to have the wit to be excited about him. But they soon quarrelled. His young vanity could not stomach Gaudier's blows.

'I did not really like him. But that is no judgement on either of us. Gaudier never seemed to like anyone. He rushed at people. He held them in his mind. He poured his thought over them, he burnt his black eyes into them, but when in response they had said ten words, they were jabbed and wounded, and blood flowed.'

To us who know in what poverty they had to live—having to count each penny and make full use of every scrap they had— Sophie's account of Mrs. Macfall's visit to them a few weeks later is full of humour. She came with her husband and Mr. Hare one

BRODZKY

evening about half-past ten. While Pik showed his drawings to the men, Zosik answered her questions.

'Don't you suffer from the cold like this, without a carpet?'

'Well, you see, we are just leaving' (there was no question of a move at this time), 'and as my brother is occupied all day at his office, we have taken the chance of the week-end to roll up the mats and covers.'

'Oh, so you have mats and covers as well?'

'Yes, we have mats for the floor and covers for the beds,' said Zosik with absolute assurance, although she knew that Hardinge must have reported quite otherwise.

Then looking at their awful bed, terribly bent and untidy, Mrs. Macfall asked:

'Is this your brother's bed or yours?'

'It is his. This is his room. Mine is across the passage.'

'Oh, really! Have you got a good landlady? Does she do your meals for you?'

'Yes, sometimes, but when we are tired of home cooking we go to a restaurant, or we buy cooked foods, ham or cold chicken.' (Cold meats and potatoes cooked once a week!)

'Have you got a good charwoman to come in and do the rooms?'

'She is not over-good. I always have to supervise her, and even do the work after her; but what can you expect, they're all alike.'

This was too much for Pik, who had been listening to all this with one ear while talking to the two men, and with an impertinent laugh he said:

'Why are you telling all these fibs? You haven't got any char-woman.'

Poor Zosik was quite confused, but almost at once replied with force: 'Don't you meddle with my affairs: you are out all day, you know nothing of who does the work.'

Pik subsided and the conversation continued:

'Why don't you take one of these self-contained flats, like ours, for instance? They don't cost much, only about seventy pounds a year.'

'Yes, certainly that's very little, but then, you see, your husband doesn't need a studio, whereas my brother must have one, and that would make our rent a hundred pounds or more!'

'I suppose that *would* be too much?'

'Yes, just at the moment, for Pik isn't earning much, and I daren't plunge more deeply into my own capital; I've already had to go pretty far, since for a long time after we arrived Pik could get no work at all', etc.

Mr. Macfall and Mr. Hare were very encouraging to Henri, and the party broke up with warm hopes that they would all meet on the following Wednesday. Mr. Hare tells me that Mr. Macfall, in writ-ing to him about Gaudier, spoke of him as a young genius, but said that Miss Brzeska was a far bigger person, and wrote amazingly good stories; a remark which, when she heard it, gave Sophie a great deal of pleasure.

Mr. MacFall interested Lovat Fraser in Henri Gaudier, and Fraser called to see Henri, and ordered a large mask from him, for which he paid five pounds. Henri went back with him to his studio, and was enchanted with his work, but Sophie did not like Fraser at all. She thought him affected and moon-faced. He told Pik that he should give up everything and be a sculptor, and Pik explained that he really was a sculptor, but had been doing posters as a pastime.

One evening, just as they had packed up their few belongings and were going to leave for other lodgings, there was a ring at the bell. It was Mrs. Hare, who brought with her particulars of a real live commission. There was a proposal to make a small statue of Madame Maria Carmi, who was then taking the part of the Madonna in *The Miracle* at Olympia. Mr. Hare had spoken to Lord Northcliffe and a few others, and Lord Northcliffe had already said he would give fifty pounds. It was hoped that they would raise a subscription of two hundred pounds, and they would like Gaudier-Brzeska to do the statue.

With some difficulty they managed to accomplish their removal, and to get to Mr. Hare's house in Kensington in time to be taken to the show. At first Henri could not get into the right mood, and spent his time drawing horses, but towards the middle of the performance he took fire and did many excellent drawings of Madame Carmi. Mrs. Hare has a very beautiful one, which reveals in an amazing way his sculptor's instinct. He did a statuette, and two plaster casts were made, one of which Gaudier coloured.

Lord Northcliffe did not like them, gave Mr. Hare five pounds for the artist, and the idea was dropped. Mr. Hare bought one, and the other was sold at the Leicester Galleries in Gaudier's posthumous Exhibition.

Gaudier now began on busts of Mr. Macfall and Major Smythies, a friend of the Macfalls. He had said that he didn't require his sitters to sit, and indeed liked them to walk about; but Zosik noticed that it was a great relief to him when Macfall said he would prefer to sit down. The beginning of this bust did not go well, and Henri was about to destroy it when, much to his disgust, Macfall leapt up to save it, and carried it away.

The work on Major Smythies was more successful. The Major watched the building up of his head with great interest, but objected to everything, as is, perhaps, not surprising: his nose was too flat, his forehead too high, and so on. At first Gaudier took no notice, but after a bit changed his tactics. 'I believe you're right. See, I will alter it.' And taking up some clay, he proceeded to make the alteration. After Major Smythies had gone, Zosik protested against his being so weak-minded as to be deflected in his own vision by an outsider.

'Poor Zosik,' said Pik, 'to be so blind. I only took up a little clay and put it on the bust so as to satisfy him, and then, when he wasn't looking, took it off again, and he never noticed.'

Gaudier was to do these busts for ten shillings each, and he hoped that Major Smythies would have his cast in bronze, which he did at a cost of twelve pounds.[1]

When Sophie told Pik that he should not dispose of his work so cheaply, he said: 'I'm a sculptor. I need clay to work with. For ten shillings I can get two hundred pounds of clay. I'm too poor to buy

[1] This bronze was presented by Major Smythies in 1922, through the National Art Collections Fund, to the Manchester City Art Gallery.

this otherwise, so it's better to take the money and create a work of art, than to be puffed up with dignity and achieve nothing.'

These two busts caused some little talk in London, and Pik hoped, through the help of Macfall, to do several of Oxford under-graduates; but this seems to have come to nothing, though it kept him in a ferment of excitement.

Sophie made several attempts to interest someone in her writings: she lent a specimen to Mrs. Hare. A few days later Mrs. Hare sug-gested to her that she should take a house, and have a few paying guests, so as to live more comfortably. Zosik took this suggestion that she should become a landlady as a direct reflection on the qual-ity of her work, and was bitterly hurt. She was convinced that she was a great writer, and her whole energy went in trying to crystallize her ideas; but her surroundings and the lack of food were too much for her, and she achieved nothing; nor was she fortunate enough to meet anyone, save Pik, and for a brief moment Mr. Macfall, who would encourage her in her work, for her insistent nature drove people away from her.

In spite of this lack of sympathy from outside, her life with Henri was founded on the idea that they were both artists—she a writer and he a sculptor—and much of their time was spent in helping each other. Henri once said to her: 'Without my Mamus, I should have had nothing to show anyone; for as soon as I have done any-thing it disgusts me, and if you had not saved my works, I should have destroyed them all.'

One of these works was a 'Woman and Child', which Mrs. Hare bought for three pounds. She had asked Henri how much he wanted, and he, in his usual way, had said: 'Oh, do take it as a present if it pleases you.' Its casting had cost him twenty-five shillings, but nothing would have induced him to mention this; and when Mrs. Hare offered him three pounds, he felt rich indeed.

Henri found the Hares' friendship a great comfort, and had it not been for Sophie there is no doubt that they would have better understood the difficulties of his life, and contrived some way to alleviate them. But Sophie had to be reckoned with, and Henri's friends found this too difficult a task.

It was at the Macfalls', as we have seen, that Pik met Miss Enid Bagnold, and he thought her extremely beautiful. She came to sit to him, and he expected that she would come every day; but her own activities diverted her attention, and week after week went by, filled with excuses and postponements. She herself tells the story of her finally sitting to him.

'It's a horrid story. I went to his room in Chelsea—a little, bare room at the top of a house—it was winter, and the daylight would not last long. While I sat still, idle and uncomfortable on a wooden chair, Gaudier's thin body faced me, standing in his overall behind the lump of clay, at which he worked with feverish haste. We talked a little, and then fell silent; from time to time, but not very often, his black eyes shot over my face and neck, while his hands flew round the clay. After a time his nose began to bleed, but he made no attempt to stop it; he appeared insensible to it, and the blood fell on to his overall. At last, unable to stand it any longer, I said: "Your nose is bleeding". He replied: "I know, you'll find something to stop it in that bag on the wall"; and all the time he went on working, while the light got less and less. The bag was full of clothes belonging to Gaudier and Miss Brzeska, most of them dirty, most of them torn. I chose something, long-legged drawers, I think, and tied them round his nose and mouth and behind his neck. "Lower!" he said impatiently, wrenching at it, unable to see properly. I went to my seat, but after a time the cloth became soaked through with blood. The light had gone, and in the street outside there was a terrific noise. It was a dog-fight, one large dog pinning another by the throat, and Gaudier left his work to come and watch it. He watched it to the finish with dark, interested eyes, his head against the window, and the street-lamp shining on his bloody bandages.'

Gaudier had found the previous uncertainty of Miss Bagnold's sittings a great trial to him, since he could not start a new work while he was expecting her from day to day; he therefore decided to give it up, and asked Zosik to sit for him instead. The history of this sitting throws an interesting light on their personal lives.

Gaudier's attempts to do Zosik had always resulted in such solemn effigies that this time she decided she would do her utmost to encourage a gay one. Although she was very tired with her work, and her nerves were on edge with the perpetual noise outside their rooms, she spent the sitting singing old songs from Roumania, Poland, France, and Russia. They were both for the moment in a frenzy of delight, and forgot that any cloud had ever dimmed the edge of their horizon. All their first happiness came back, care-free. The sitting lasted a long time, and in the end Zosik was terribly tired; but the portrait was a miracle, and they kissed each other for joy. Then, next day, came a little dispute. Zosik had given Gaudier two shillings for his fare, and he had promised to return one and ninepence. In the evening he came back with nothing—he had spent the money on sending photographs to people in Germany. Sophie was annoyed at his having broken his promise, and bitter words followed. Sophie went out for a walk. It was late when she returned, and Pik called to her from his bed with a gentle voice, but she would not go to him. He got up and came to her: 'Don't be angry with me, Sisik—I was very annoyed when you went out, but I'm sorry now, and I broke ——.' Sophie's mind flew to a vase they had bought, of which she was very fond, and she would listen no more. She flung invective upon invective at him, and in the end they separated for the night. After a sleepless night, she went into Pik's room, and he welcomed her with his usual happy 'good morning'. She repulsed him, but he pursued her until her rage burst forth once more, and entirely destroyed her self-control. After many bitter remarks from Zosik, Pik said:

'Well, since you hate me, I'll finish my work,' and taking the wet cloth from the bust of Zosik, he gave the forehead a half-hearted hit.

It was only then that she realized it was not the vase he had broken, but that he had taken his vengeance on the bust. It had, as a matter of fact, only a few dents in it, which were no doubt reparable, but Zosik was overwhelmed by the idea that, unable to beat her in his rage, he should have vented his anger on the clay head; she remembered the hours she had sat, the trouble she had taken, and with one wild leap she fell upon it with her fists, beating it as if she were threshing corn.

'See,' she shrieked, 'I'll help you in your work!' and blow after blow fell upon the bust, until it was again nothing but a lump of clay.

Pik watched her with a little smile—timid and naïve: then he ran after her, but she fled exhausted to her room, and locked the door. Later on, when she was quiet again, she came out, and Pik said in his calm way:

'I'm not angry that you spoilt the bust—it didn't really satisfy me. I'll do another, a better one. Sisik will sit again.'

The next excitement and disappointment for Henri arose through a simple misunderstanding. Mr. Macfall introduced him to Mr. Benington, a photographer in the West End. Mr. Benington had seen Gaudier's head of Macfall, and had expressed his enthusiasm. Mr. Macfall had passed this on to Henri, and hinted that Mr. Benington would have his head modelled for thirty pounds, and most likely have his wife done too. Gaudier was almost beyond excitement, but as Mr. Benington had never had any thought of sitting for his portrait, and did not know that Henri had any such expectation, many weeks passed without any conclusion being reached. In the end, he took several photographs of Gaudier and of his work,[1] but still did not know that more had been looked for.

Henri also met two Canadians, who suggested that he should go with them to Canada, where a sculptor was badly needed, and where they would all make their fortunes. With so many distractions, Henri began to be casual about his office—he arrived late and

[1] Mr. Benington made a much larger series of photographs in 1918, at the time of Gaudier's posthumous Exhibition.

left early, and talked of nothing but escaping from so paralysing a position.

He was still interested in his small sister's art training, and sent her some of Mr. Benington's photographs, as the following letter shows:

15 Redburn Street, Chelsea
19th June 1912

Dear little Renée,

I am so glad that you have passed your exam—you see now how easy it is, and you probably had great fun that day at Chécy's with your little friends.

Your drawings were good, and you should do them all the time, concentrating each time more. I send you a small money-order with this so that you can buy yourself colours, etc.

I thought you would like to have photographs of the statues which I have done lately. I give them to you because you are so good and so pretty. I am up to my eyes in work, but I shall try to come one of these Sundays. Keep well, water your little garden if it doesn't rain, and my love to you.

Henri Gaudier.

Do you eat lots of raspberries, you greedy one, and do you pick the roses? Give Maman a good kiss for me, and Papa and Henriette.

CHAPTER VII
MORE FRIENDS

IT WAS at this time that Henri became intimate with Middleton Murry and Katherine Mansfield, the editors of *Rhythm*, who had asked Mr. Macfall to introduce Gaudier to them, as they wanted his drawings for their paper. Pik went to see them, and came back enchanted. He had never met anyone so charming or so sympathetic. They were both young, he said, very young: Middleton Murry was strong in body, with refined features and a magnificent head like a Greek god, an Apollo or Mars; while Katherine Mansfield was not at all silly or vindictive; she hated women, particularly English women, finding them heartrendingly conventional. She was a curiously beautiful person, Slav in appearance, and very strong-minded.

Pik had never seen anyone like her before, and he did a drawing for Zosik, who was all impatience to know what she was like; and from the drawing Zosik thought that she must be like Catherine of Russia. 'I am sure that we shall become enormous friends,' said Pik, 'they are very fond of me and told me so, and Katherine Mansfield gave me an Indian knife as a token of her friendship.'

It is not surprising that they should have been drawn to Henri Gaudier. He was at this time full of a youthful attraction, like a young eagle flying in space. He was delicate of build, soft and feline but of a sinuous strength, with large, piercing eyes like a leopard's.

They had promised to call next day. Zosik was all excitement to see these demi-gods, and awaited their arrival in a ferment of nerves. It was raining in torrents, and Pik went out to buy a few plates and glasses; for so important an occasion they did not think their two tin plates and broken mugs sufficient. The visit was a great success;

133

they praised Gaudier's drawings and talked nicely with Sophie. They went away in high spirits, arranging for the Brzeskas to come to them the next day.

When they had gone, Pik and Zosik were full of their praises, Pik saying that he was ready to have his head cut off for them. He wanted to sit down at once and write them a letter.

'What, now, almost before they are out of the house?' cried Zosik.

'Yes, they are such darlings, Sisik dear, that we must tell them about us—but I won't write, I'll tell them to-morrow when I see them.'

Zosik asked him to wait for a week or so, but Pik felt that that would be dishonest, since they loved them; and then—flip—before she knew it, it was done.

In exchange, Katherine Mansfield told her own experience, which ended with these words:

'And then we got into this bed and we laughed and we laughed and we laughed without stopping, and since that time we have always slept together. But perhaps I am scandalizing you by talking of such things.'

'Not at all,' said Pik. 'We have also already slept together.'

They spent several hours in happy conversation, and Pik in an access of affection pressed Middleton Murry in his arms and fondled his head with his hands. Katherine Mansfield joined them in this demonstration of love, while Sophie sat at some distance in her chair. During this first visit Sophie talked far too much, and also Pik persuaded her to sing, which made her over-excited. After that it was

Katherine Mansfield's turn; she had a sore throat, and went to sing in an adjoining room. When Middleton Murry said how good her voice was, Zosik replied with disconcerting frankness: 'Do leave the poor child alone. You can hear she has a bad throat and can do nothing.' Pik refused to leave until long after midnight, and they had to walk home in drenching rain.

Pik wanted to model their heads, but Katherine Mansfield said that they were going away in a couple of days to Sussex. They asked him if he would come to stay with them, but he said that he could not promise, as the week-ends were the only free times he had, and he could not spare them for pleasure alone, if it were to the detriment of his work. Few things could have been pleasanter for him than a visit to people he loved, living in a nice country house, and his refusal shows in a marked degree how seriously he took his work. He suggested, however, that they should take 'this poor girl Zosik' for a few weeks, which produced, after prolonged blankness, an 'Oh yes, yes, do come'. Pik thought them perfect, and told Sophie that to be suspicious of them was as futile as objecting to spots in the sun.

Middleton Murry and Katherine Mansfield were often in town, and Gaudier began a head of Murry. They talked of going to live together on a Pacific island, and Pik laughingly told Zosik that she must, of course, come in order to teach them to cook. Pik got it hot from Zosik for putting her at so venal a valuation. While they were bickering Katherine looked puzzled, and Sophie said: 'You are surprised to see us so quarrelsome.'

'No, you fascinate me, I can't make you out, you interest me tremendously.'

Encouraged by this remark, Sophie felt that while Pik was work-ing on Middleton Murry she could confide in Katherine Mansfield; she felt that at last in her she had found a friend to whom she could open the pent-up torrent of her heart. She launched into a most intimate recital of their ascetic life, the daily routine, the poverty, the nervous irritations, their platonic love and her fears for Henri's health, his headaches, and his useless expeditions to King's Cross. Katherine listened to her with a strained expression, and then Sophie, in order to get closer touch and give herself assurance, took her hand and pressed it warmly in hers. Katherine Mansfield gave a slight shudder but remained silent, and Sophie, in order to break down this wall of ice, opened the deepest abysses of her mortified soul; she made her own heart bleed in living over a second time all these past torments, and, as she lived them again, they seemed to become part of herself, and to be conquered. Suddenly Katherine Mansfield, with a more marked shudder than the first, withdrew her hand; Miss Brzeska received a moral shock, slowed down in her out-pouring, and then stopped altogether.

Katherine Mansfield was looking at Middleton Murry with queer eyes, questioning, enigmatic; then he got up with: 'Tiger, darling, we must go.' Before they left, she said to Sophie: 'A Polish writer is coming next Wednesday, you must come then and finish your Polish tale.'

Pik was as enthusiastic as ever. 'They *are* darlings—I've not made his head half magnificent enough.'

But Zosik protested that they disliked her, to which Pik replied that it was impossible that such dear people should not like his Sisik

SLEEPING FAUN

—he would, however, speak to them about it when they met on Wednesday.

Zosik was very excited by the idea of meeting a Pole, who might, incidentally, help her with her work; but she dreamt that when they got to Murry's house they found the door barred by a huge cat. When she told this dream to Pik he laughed at her fears. Just as they were leaving, a telegram arrived, saying that Katherine was feeling unwell and would they please not come, and that a letter would follow. Day after day passed and no letter arrived. Pik was in the utmost distress; he wandered about their rooms and in the passage like a lost soul, and finally wrote to ask for a reason. Then came an express letter to Pik from Middleton Murry to say that he had been forced to telegraph at the last minute, for Katherine had come in late and very tired, and had not been able to bear the idea of sitting for an evening with Miss Brzeska; would Pik forgive them and come alone that very evening. The letter ended by saying: 'You are a most exceptional boy, and I am sure that one day you will be great; every moment I spend with you is for me an immense pleasure. Wire if you can come.'

Gaudier felt very much annoyed and quite disillusioned, but he decided to go and settle the matter by a personal explanation. 'I still love Middleton Murry,' he said, 'since all this fuss is only an intrigue worked up by Katherine Mansfield, whom I have never really liked; and although nothing would have induced me to write such a letter to him, it only means that he is weak-minded and not that he is a fool.'

Zosik told him that it was his own fault, since, had he supported her in public instead of abusing her, they would never have dared to write in such a way.

Next morning he told Zosik that although they had been very nice to him he had been bored to death, and had been very distant all the time. He thought that they must, after all, be stupid people; for, incredible though it sounded, they had never noticed the statue of Charles I in Trafalgar Square, and they were people who considered themselves to be artists.

He said that Katherine Mansfield had suspected him of being homosexual, and had begun by asking him if he had not a passionate nature; in order to lead her on he had said 'No'; on which she had plunged deeper, suggesting that he sometimes had peculiar longings like the great French sculptor, or like the English writer who was driven out of England. 'Perhaps,' said Pik, while laughing in his sleeve. He thought that she was too cunning to drive him away from Middleton, since she saw how useful he could be to them. He felt sorry for Murry, who seemed to be entirely in the hands of Katherine Mansfield, who made love to him all the time, until he was squeezed dry.

They were both coming the next day, Middleton Murry to sit for his portrait and Katherine Mansfield to make it up with Zosik. Sophie said that she would go and rest, and would only come in for a few minutes at the end of the sitting.

At about four Pik called to her, but she took no notice; he then put his head in at the door with: 'Come on, it's all right, she isn't here.' Poor Murry looked like a ghost, and Zosik at once felt tenderly towards him and made him some mint tea. He told her that he was terribly upset by Katherine's nervous behaviour. Miss Brzeska described the rest of the episode thus:

' "You won't be angry with me, will you, because I love you—I love you really," and taking my hand, he kissed it.

'Pik was much touched by this, and came over and enfolded us both in his arms, and there we stayed a little while with my head on Middleton's shoulder. I longed to give him a maternal kiss, but feared to disgust him. Then with a little hug we all separated, and with rich handshakes, we swore eternal friendship.'

On the first of September *Rhythm* was published. Gaudier expected to get a few copies, as it was the first time his drawings had been reproduced in this paper, and he wished to send them to a few friends in France. He was very much upset because his name was wrongly spelt 'Gaudier-Bizeska'; he thought that Katherine Mansfield had done this on purpose, so that Zosik's name should not appear. By the tenth two copies arrived. Murry had been out of town some little while, and the friendship had suffered so severe a shock that Henri, who was going away for a week's holiday to a place near Murry's country house, swore he would not see them.

A week later he returned, full of life and energy, and there was no end to all that he and Sisik had to say to each other. He had been to stay a night at Murry's place—they had met each other on the cliffs. Before dinner he had overheard the following conversation relating to Sophie:

M. M.: 'I think she should come here now, there is plenty of room. Just let us speak to Gaudier about it.'

K. M. : 'Oh, no. I don't want to see her here—she's too violent—I won't have her.'

M. M.: 'But, Tiger, look here, she's not like that—I don't see why——'

K. M. (violently): 'Leave me alone, I don't like her and I don't want to see her—she'll make me ill again.'

This was a relief to both Henri and Sophie, for they now knew where they were, and Sophie found much solace in the fact that Middleton Murry had spoken nicely of her at a moment when there was no reason to do so except that of genuine good feeling.

The worries of the last few months had been, all the same, too much for Sophie, and she decided that she must go away to the country, recuperate her strength and get seriously settled to her work. After a good deal of letter-writing to and fro she decided, on the enthusiastic advice of Pik, to go to an old house in Frowlesworth. Her experiences there, and her meeting with a woman she called Niemczura, are most interestingly described in some of her writings, and were the topic of an amusing set of drawings in one of Gaudier's letters.[1]

Gaudier's last letter to Middleton Murry is a characteristic one, and it is quoted almost at length, since it throws rather a special light on his nature. It is a pity that a letter which Henri wrote earlier cannot also be quoted, and which Middleton Murry said was so charming and so interesting that he would keep it until Henri was famous. When he was asked for it he replied: 'I am sorry that I have

[1] Page 161.

not the letter which Gaudier wrote me in 1912. Probably I destroyed it at the time of our quarrel, as young fools do.'

November 1912

My dear Murry,[1]

I was last night with M. . . . and was most surprised to hear you
were in town. You apparently did not think fit to let me know,
just as in the same filthy way you never informed me of the *Rhythm*
show, against your promise, nor sent it to me either last month or
this. Your acquaintance has been for me one long suffering—not
only for me but also for the object of my love, which is twice worse.
I met you at a dangerous turning, the brains burned by the recent
summer, thirsty for good friendship, only with one drawback: poverty. Being then freshly strong, promising all kinds of things and
favours, you behaved stupidly, thinking I was lashed to you, and
that I would not mind any dirt. I was confirmed into my thought
of the wickedness of Katherine Mansfield by a conversation I overheard when at Runcton. It was about my poor Zosik. You pleaded,
and this to your honour, that you could receive her in your house,
but K. M., with a fiendish jealousy, upheld to the end that Zosik
was too *violent*. You will remember the whole story, which I need
not trace more. I was wounded, and if I came once more it was only
to take my Zosik's MSS., which with the same prejudice have
been absolutely misjudged. I kept my mouth shut all this time

[1] This letter is the rough draft of a letter which was probably never sent, since
Gaudier thought it best to obtain the return of some books before sending it.
It was written in English. Middleton Murry does not remember if he received it,
but has still one of the books.

because I knew you were in devilish difficulties all the while. Now you have got over it and there is no reason why I should not say what I think and feel.

I loved you innerly and still sympathize with you as a poor boy, chased by the Furies, but I must reproach you your lack of courage, discrimination and honour. Katherine Mansfield I never wish to see any more. I must ask you to kindly send back to me three books that my Sisik lent you, *Bubu de Montparnasse, Poil de Carotte, Cantilènes du Malheur*, against receipt of which I shall let you have *The Cherry Orchard*. I cannot send you your book and wait for you to send mine on—you have no word whatever and I cannot trust you in the least.

You must not think for one minute that I want *Rhythm*—it is vice-versa. My drawings have been amongst the best that have appeared in your paper, and more in the ideal of it than the putrid trash you exhibit this month of Yeats and Peploe. I will not barter the purity of my love, nor my conscience, for a halfpenny worth of *réclame*. You had promised me money for what had appeared, and you might have thought me anxious only for this money's sake— you are not in a position now to give me this money, and you might think I retire for this simple reason. It would be bad for you, but I suspect it greatly, so you will please me to retain Heal's £2—for the advertisement in this month's towards the paper expenses. I shall never more contribute, and wish to cease all relations whatsoever, until being free from the thraldom of your present love you reflect upon your actions and find yourself a much better and more reliable man.

Before putting the seal upon our short but unhappy acquaintance

I wish to point out to you, as a friendly counsel, that the less K. M. writes for you the better it will be, either under Petrosky's name or her own—for it is not sincere but pure affectation: no Art. Also that you discriminate more in matters poetical and pictorial and never insert any such rabble as Simpson's drawings or any such that do not represent concentrically Fergusson's idea—the only man with a real will in your agglomeration.

I wish you to read this letter twice over as I cannot express myself well in writing. My Zosik has been a month already in a most lovely Worcestershire cottage, on a hill, where she works, is free, and has not the sorrow to see herself insulted as she was in the gross-est way, by whom you know.

H. G. B.

CHAPTER VIII
A GROUP OF LETTERS

PART I

DURING THE last three months of 1912, while Henri was for the second time alone in London, his letters to Sophie again vividly convey his thoughts and his actions. During this period he received letters from France, summoning him to return for military duty, but against this he had steadfastly set his mind, and would listen neither to argument nor to exhortation.

For the week-end of November 10th, he managed to go to see Sophie at Dodford, where she had gone after leaving Frowlesworth. She was in nice rooms at a farm-house, and Henri had heaps of gossip to tell her, amongst other things that Macfall had spoken of her as beautiful. This delighted her, and Pik was charmed that she could still be pleased with anything so frivolous. Miss Brzeska said that 'he was affectionate, animated, and vigorous, and his eyes blazed like torches'. They forgot how quickly the time had passed, and it was one a.m. before Pik went on tiptoe to his own room. The next day they went for a long walk in the country. In the garden of their house there were some old jars and a fifteenth-century Christ, which they decided to buy if they could get them very cheaply. Zosik had already bought four Indian curtains costing thirty shillings, and these were going to adorn a charming flat in London.

This week-end visit had rather a special value for them: their love for each other found peace in which to flower, and had Henri not feared to lose her continued companionship, he might have awakened in her a return of that physical love which he himself had always felt for her, but to which he had, so far, never confessed. As it was, he went away full of fondness for her, which became a little dulled through being perpetually unsatisfied.

15 *Redburn Street, Chelsea*
Friday, 11th October 1912

Dear Old Thing,

I miss you terribly—this place seems so big without my Zosik, and I'm very far from working well. I have every good intention, but I sleep much too much and can't break myself of this. Yesterday evening I made a fairly good composition for Tomsy[1] and I will paint it on Sunday. I don't feel fit for much—to begin with I'm put out by this damned military service, my running away from which seems to irritate them most terribly. Secondly, your portrait doesn't progress very well, poor darling, anyhow I'm about dished with it, and then that ass ——, the fellow I met at the British Museum, is supposed to come here to-morrow, and that takes away the last grain of hope that I had. But on Sunday I feel that I am going to work well, and I hope that next week will not be so sterile as this one. May it be the same for you too, my great big girl, and may the good sun protect you. It is a shame that all I do turns out so badly, particularly when it is for you, dear Zosik. I went to the Luggage-in-Advance office and they assured me that you should have your luggage to-day. If not, send a line to the station-masters at Ullesthorpe and Lutterworth to ask them what the Hell they are up to.

Zosiulo, don't be angry with me . . . in shaking the kettle to make the water come out I've broken the handle, and yesterday the lamp-glass burst in my face without any apparent cause, and I spent half an hour looking for the little bits of glass—my cauliflower was

[1] Mr. Hare.

full of them—for I was having dinner. I take baths, like Sisik, only
with less hot water, for it's more refreshing. I'm sorry that everything
is so dirty in your Boarding House, and I'm afraid you will blame
me for having got you into it, but you will remember, Sisik, that
I told you not to go unless you wanted to. If you can't find anything
else it would perhaps be better for you to go to Worcestershire, or
even somewhere in Belgium, if you prefer that. I feel that it would
be nice in the Ardennes—it's like the Black Forest, but we will go
into all that later, and in the meantime I wish it was Christmas so
that I might be with my Sisik, and that I was ten years older in order
to be richer, and that my Sik had a lovely country house of her own.
Don't you worry about 'Poorhouses', my Zosisik, your pipik won't
let you go to one. If I am still poor when I am old I would kill us
both rather than go into such charnel houses.

They are dirty devils who wish to frighten my Sisik. Stay where
you are as long as you can—rest yourself—take a bit of breathing-
space, or clear out quickly if it seems to you a better idea and you can
get something advantageous. Good-night, old darling, I send you
thousands and thousands of kisses and now I'm going to bed, as
to-morrow they wash the place.

Good-night dear Zosikmaly—the fog is so thick that you can't
see the lights of Radnor Street, and it comes in through the cracks
of the windows, and if you stop them up it comes down the chimney.

I have been a soldier since three o'clock this afternoon and consequently beyond benefit of civil law—may the good sun burst all
the officers of this filthy regiment! Good-night.

Saturday morning

P.S.—Your card must have come while I was in bed—I got it this morning at 6.30, and I'm anxious about the luggage. Poor dear, you absolutely must get away if everything is so disgusting that you can't sleep. Your rascal of a piknis sleeps far too well in your bed— I'm tired out, and this is perhaps the reason. Next week will slip away more easily—there won't be so many distractions, and perhaps I shall manage to get in some work. Zosiulenko, who is this Niemczura? A cook or some kind of servant, 'albo? dama?'

P.P.S.—I add this little page so that there shall be three. I dreamt about Wulfs last night and about my Zosik. He wanted to have novels and stories by Zosik for his daughter . . . and then stupidities, for we found ourselves, he and I, in a great room full of enormous machines, etc. Dear Mamus, I do not feel alone because I have a good Zosik, and I kiss her tenderly and warmly. Be good, dear love, and don't stay any longer in that foul hole where you were stuck by the moon. Good-bye, Zosiulik.

Pikusurinia.

15 Redburn Street, Chelsea
Sunday, 13th October 1912

Zosisikoiv Smarkoisowi,

I've been reading your letter over again, and you do seem to have got into a beastly hole, my poor dear, to be so embittered. Poor, poor darling—the old woman with cancer, the workhouse, the Vicar, the Niemczura, etc., and bad food and a rotten bed—it's really disgusting. My dear, I understand so well how you get annoyed with me, and I'm sorry I took all you said so seriously, and particularly that I scolded you about it. I am also furious that I haven't enough money to send you a box of food—but I'll do that as soon as possible. That ass Fraser is doing such rotten things, affected and stupid and crude in colour. It is true that the colours are brilliant, but they have no relation to each other.

It only costs 10s. to 12s. 6d. to go to Belgium by boat from London. If we have a few days at Christmas or the New Year we could perhaps go there together.

Your Pipik who loves you intensely, who loves you more each day,

Pikuś obesrany
if you wish him for a friend.

Monday, 14th October 1912

Zosik,

The Lousadas don't come back for a fortnight—I telephoned. I got 10s. for overtime last Saturday and I send it to you, for I expect you need it, poor dear, since you left with only £2. Send me a p.c. to say how much you will need before the end of the month, and I will borrow it off the rent. . . .

Mother now writes to say that she thinks I have acted wisely [in refusing to do his military service], and that her first letter was wrong, which cheers me up very considerably.

I've done an illustration for Tommy and finished your 'glowa szkaradna', which I'm pleased with. I saw the bronze group at Parlanti's on Saturday, and I agree it's a scandal that such a beautiful little group should be flung away for a profit of £7—still it is better than nothing. I hope that you are getting more sleep and that you are feeling quieter. Poor darling, may the good sun bless you.

Your Pipik.
H. Gaudier-Brzeska.

P.S.—Naturally, no *Rhythm* yet. Oh, the rotters!! I am writing from the studio. The boss is at Cardiff from this afternoon until Wednesday. I'm going to work hard. I will write a long letter at the end of the week, for this is only a line to go with the ten little shillings. Don't worry, Zosik, we are very near each other. I get your letters the day you write them. I work hard in order not to get depressed. I had potatoes and rice, which gave me wind in the belly, but I have had some peppermint and feel better.

16th October 1912

Sweet Heart,

There is a hurdy-gurdy playing blithely outside, the Scot and the Scotswoman are dancing, and Pik has made a crackling fire to cook an 'ogonek'.

For the last two years Pik has never vacillated nor oscillated about militarism. Naturally when I receive such a letter as the one I sent you, I can't help inveighing against all the prejudices with which the rich stuff the poor in order to keep them in slavery. I've written a strong but very dignified reply. I have said that I do not recognize any patriotic duty; that if they did not wish to wrangle with me they should not have meddled with my affairs, and that if my sisters, particularly the elder, because the young one seems to have said

THE FALLEN WORKMAN

nothing, make such a fuss, let them go to the Devil. The final touch to the whole thing was getting this letter from G——, which I enclose:

St. Jean de Braye
'le 13 Octobre 1912

Conseil Général du Loiret.
'Mon cher Gaudier,

'Je viens de voir votre père qui m'a mis au courant de ce qui vous concerne. Je n'ai pas besoin de vous dire quel coup votre décision lui a porté. Vous l'avez rendu profondément malheureux, si malheureux que je dois vous l'écrire. Je vous ai, d'ailleurs, témoigné toujours assez d'intérêt pour avoir le droit encore de vous donner un conseil.

'Je sais les raisons que vous avez données à votre père. Laissezmoi vous dire qu'elles ne sont pas sérieuses. Dans tous les cas, ce n'est pas à vous de vous en faire juge. Mon plus jeune frère vient de finir son service militaire. Les deux années qu'il a passées au régiment ne lui paraissaient pas moins dures qu'à vous; il avait aux jambes des varices qui l'ont fait beaucoup souffrir pendant et après les marches. Il n'en a pas moins fait allégrement ses deux années, sans se plaindre, heureux d'accomplir son devoir. Il faut vous dire que le service militaire est un devoir, et qu'on est toujours heureux de faire son devoir.

'Puis, dans quelle situation vous mettez-vous? Vous vous fermez les portes de la France; vous ne pourrez plus revenir à St. Jean de Braye; s'il survenait dans votre famille qui a été si bonne pour vous et où tout le monde vous adore, vous le savez bien,—s'il survenait, dis-je, quelque malheur dans votre famille, vous ne pourriez même pas accourir au chevet d'un malade qui pourrait mourir sans que vous auriez la consolation de l'avoir vu. Mon pauvre enfant, avez-vous bien réfléchi que, par là, vous vous mettez hors de la patrie et hors de la famille ?

'Vous travaillez, vous avez du talent; je crois que vous réussirez. Vous êtes-vous dit que votre situation nuira à votre succès d'avenir ? Je ne sais si vous avez suivi, il y a à peu près deux ans, les histoires d'un auteur dramatique de grand talent, Henry Bernstein, qui avait fait précisément ce que vous avez fait, et qui a eu l'humiliation, dans son succès, d'être contraint de faire amende honorable publique. J'aurais voulu avoir conservé la lettre qu'il écrivit alors; vous l'au-riez lue, et vous auriez compris quel poids vous vous attachez pour la vie!

'Vous savez tout ce que votre père a fait pour vous; vous savez combien il vous aime. Votre décision l'a peiné à un point que je ne saurais dire; elle l'a beaucoup vieilli; je vous assure que je n'exa-gère pas. Je vous en prie, revenez sur votre décision tandis qu'il est temps encore.

'Il est tard, il n'est pas trop tard. Vous serez évidemment puni, mais j'interviendrai de mon mieux pour que les choses n'aillent pas trop loin. Ce sera quelques mauvais jours à passer, mais vous vous éviterez tous de regrets pour l'avenir, et vous enlèverez à ceux qui vous aiment un souci si douloureux.

'Croyez bien que c'est un ami qui vous parle, et qui vous parle parcequ'il a de l'affection pour vous. Je crois vous en donner en ce moment la preuve la meilleure.

'Venez vite, mon cher enfant, réparer la faute que vous avez commise; je souhaite vous avoir persuadé. C'est le meilleur vœu que puissent former mon amitié pour votre père et ma sympathie pour vous,   'G.

'Personne ne sait rien encore dans le pays, que moi, qui ne dirai rien.'

I have answered in a cold, strong, dignified manner:

'le 16 Octobre 1912

'Monsieur (pas cher et autre),

'Votre lettre fait preuve de très grde. sentimentalité. Vous êtes un barbare si vous vous glorifiez de votre frère qui souffrait tant de ses varices. Votre sympathie pour moi s'est montrée à mon retour d'Allemagne. Vous m'avez proposé une place de 50 frs. en disant c'est un peu de vache enragée à manger. Je ne vous reconnais aucun droit de me donner des conseils—je n'ai commis aucune faute envers qui que ce soit. J'ai reçu du gouvt. français 3000 frs. avec lesquels je me suis formé, vous et autres politiciens ont. . . . Je considère ces 3000 frs. comme venant du peuple, et je les rends au peuple par l'art.

'Je serai naturalisé anglais dans 2 ans et si je ne puis pas un jour travailler à Paris, n'ayez crainte que je fasse comme Bernstein— j'irai droite en Allemagne, et vous aurez alors le piteux spectacle d'un artiste français érigeant un monument commémorant une dé- faite française pour se venger de la bassesse et étroitesse d'esprit de ses contemporains.' Etc.

About eight large pages of abuse of this sort in short pointed sentences. Christ! What a brute! None of this is for one's father or for friendship or anything of that kind, but purely for himself, because he is the Maire of S. Jean de Braye, and he must see to it that there are no 'bad examples' in his district. Oh, I let him have it at the end, where I said, 'C'est malheureux, déplorable, que la jeunesse française ne se révolte pas en masse contre cette infâme conscription.'

Will that make the Zosik pet happy? Naturally I have not written to Middleton. I will buy a copy of *Rhythm* in order to have a record of my drawings, but I won't ask for anything nor lower myself. If he pays me, as he said he would, so much the better—if not, fft! Anyhow, I'm not going to humble myself any further, and if he pays me and writes to me I shall tell him quite clearly what I think,[1] as I have just done to G——.

I'll have £7 or £8 from the group. You know that the casting of Tommy's two plasters is not yet paid for, and that will be £2 or £2 10s., and the bronze brings £10. Wretched Zosieki! believing that I wanted to hide £2 from her in order to buy chocolate. You look out for yourself if I ever catch you!

And now, my dear, it is really impossible that we should continue to live apart—stay for a month where you are to set yourself up, and then come back. I'm doing everything now—it is all quite clean, I don't waste time and I'm working hard. I shall be able to do just the same when you come back, and we shall get along beautifully. Zosik only needs a rest and change of air. I really can't live for three months without my Sisik. I miss her so that I cry most of the night (without knowing it at the time, since I sleep well—but

[1] Letter printed at the end of Chapter VII.

in the morning my pillow is wet and my eyes all swollen). We must come to some arrangement, once and for all.

I've done a little jungle cat that I like, and I'm going to do another at once.

À bientôt, my unhappy and beloved darling. Najukochanek, you will come back to your pisukonik at least after Christmas for two or three months, won't you? That is if you can work well, for I don't want to allow myself to be led away by sentimentality to sacrifice your work. You are the more intelligent, and it is you who must decide. I don't want to have any responsibility in the matter.

Pikus Gaudier-Brzeska.

Chelsea
24th October 1912

Najukochanisku Zosisik,

Your letter made me very unhappy. From one end to the other you do all you can to find fault with me, and you don't enter at all deeply into what you say; and what is more you cite instances that are historically false; the case of Rodin for one. I am more bothered by the thought of your ridiculous 'moral aim' than by your attacks against me. I have certainly got many faults—indeed, like everyone else, I have got every fault in a greater or lesser degree. Yes, I know I'm a spendthrift, but conceited, to the degree of having a wicked letter piled up against me in order to prove it? Never. Since you are so good a partisan of the old mystic philosophies which search into cause and effect, why don't you weigh a little what you are saying? You accuse me of being conceited, and then in the next

line you say that I am perpetually changing my ideas and my opinions, even about art.

Surely this very fact proves that I am not at all conceited. Life,
according to Bergson and the later philosophers, is simply intuition
of the passing moment, and time, which flows continually, eternally, makes itself known by change. The conceited man is one
who stops at a certain phase of his work or of his thought, and cries
out loud, like you, 'When I say something, I believe it—I'm sure
of myself', etc. I'm not a bit like that. I look at things a great deal and
I draw a great deal. I notice how everything differs, mingles with
and knocks up against everything else. I am never sure that what I
think is true, still less that which I have thought or said is true; and
I can't bring myself to sacrifice new ideas, quite different from those
I had yesterday, just because the old ones happened to have the
honour of passing through my head and I advocated them ferociously.

You can talk till you are blue in the face,[1] Art has no moral aim,
and when it has been great has never had one, in any of its phases.
It is simply an interpretation of life; and life has no moral aim either
—though one can draw a certain amount of morality from it to help
the intellect in its battle with the elements. Ethics are a very secondary thing, but the consciousness of change is of the utmost importance, for without this, work cannot renew itself, art is gloomy and
sad, and is no longer art.

When you have fully realized once for all that I am a poor Pikus
for whom the only country in which he can work for the next few

[1] 'chante autant que tu voudras.'

years is ENGLAND, perhaps you will at last understand. You don't, I think, realize that I have to be in a filthy office all day long, and that every minute I am devoured by the most torturing desire to be cutting stone, painting walls, and casting statues? You always seem to forget this, and that isn't at all nice of you. I only know stupid people, but through these I may be able to get out of the hell of shipbroking, etc., and naturally I won't risk my chances of this for the sake of the 'senseless honours' of pride. I hold Machiavelli's opinion that when you wish to attain an end you must use every possible means, and when you consider everything with a clear understanding, the misery I endure in business is far greater than the little troubles of the soul and mind which I experience in my dealings with these fellows whom I have to see.

You have a very good example of this—I too—this example being yourself. You have ruined the best part of your life because of this pride which you place above the work which you could and should accomplish. This leads you inevitably to that narrowest kind of egoism which puts the self on a pedestal, labelled *Don't touch*, and makes hay with the primordial conception of the individual as part of a society, having relations with the other individuals who compose it.

All you say against me makes me mad, because none of it is my fault—but yours—caused by the falseness of your principles about life itself. My love for you is entirely intuitive, whereas yours for me is a reasoned thing, and therein lies the first obstacle, causing all our differences of opinion. As you are so set on being alone, please stay alone and I, on my side, will manage as best I can. You insist that

I am not sufficiently interested in your work—that I don't ask you questions—that I haven't read anything of yours since people here said it wasn't worth anything. That is a hideous lie. What can I ask you? During the two years that we have been together your work has only been in a state of preparation, and but for slight alterations, is always practically the same—except that it gets more drawn out and amplified. You never set yourself a limit, and of its final form you seldom speak. Since I know the story from A to Z, what is the use of asking you questions about it? I have, as a matter of fact, read all the little notes you have put in the margin, and that is more than you can say for yourself about my drawings, which you never dream of looking at unless you want me to give you one, and then you go and hide it. The whole fuss is, of course, only a trifle, but you seem entirely unconscious of the fact that I work very hard to earn our living, and don't want to stop my artistic activity. You exaggerate every little fault; you never try to understand why I do this or that, but you expect me to fall in with all your quite arbitrary actions, which are the result of conceit and egoism, and utterly lacking in importance. It is this particularly that upsets me, and if it goes on too long it will wear down my love for you. I can't see why you don't adapt yourself a little more to circumstances. You reproach me again with not having written to you—this is utter madness, for I wrote you three letters at the end of last week. Then you say I never tell you about what I read. What time have I to read? You know quite well I have scarcely the time to work. All the same I am sending you some newspapers this morning, not because of your scolding, please note, but because I had already thought of sending them to you. You ask too late for provisions—I haven't enough money, and you will have to wait a bit. It is just as well, perhaps, not to send anything to Frowlesworth—but rather to Bromsgrove —however, please yourself.

I have seen a lot of fellows who know Murry, and they all say that he was quite a different person a year ago—gay, strong, alert. . . . In spite of all Sisik may say, I'm sorry for Murry, and I don't at all hate him. As for *Rhythm*, no one knows exactly what has happened. . . .

Macfall has produced a hideous article—'The Splendid Wayfaring', which you will find in the *Art Chronicle*. He asked me for drawings to adorn it, and I gave him about sixty. The stupid editors made a fuss because my monkey had only three legs. Macfall had to go to them three or four times in order to convince them, but I believe all the same he himself wished I would put in a fourth.

The Lousadas come back next Sunday evening, and I shall probably have some ready money the week after. . . .

25th October 1912

My dear, why do you say so many horrid things about your Pipik, who doesn't deserve them—it is not really nice of you—still, poor little one, you are hungry and alone, tortured by this Niemczura and this clergyman, so that it is silly of me to take it so much to heart.

I'm always very sincere with you, Zosik mia, only, as I always point out to you, I don't attach any importance whatever to what I have said or done, but only to the present. You know very well, beloved, that I love you with all my heart, so don't be sad, and clear your mind of all these horrid black ideas which keep coming to you incessantly. When you are a bit rested you will be quite happy again, and come back to your Pipik—you wait and see. I shall be so happy when Christmas comes and I can talk with my Zosisik. I am working a great deal and hope that you are doing the same in Ambrosia.[1]

Your Pipik, who loves you dearly and who is always near you.

Pikusik.

Chelsea
Monday, 28th October 1912

Mon bon Dziecko Ukochany,

I will go to Euston to-morrow evening and try to find out what I can about the hours of the country trains. I enclose a letter from the old woman at Bromsgrove which came at the same time as yours. Naturally my Sisik likes feather beds—get a big bedstead, 'będsiemy spać mitsammen' at Christmas ! ! ! ! !

It is absolutely true, without any doubt whatever, that you talk through your hat—you place Bergson with Nietzsche, Schopenhauer, etc. Bergson expressly demonstrates that the world is positive, real; and that it is pernicious and useless to rack your brains to find out if the world was created by a God or not. He emphasizes intuition as more valuable than reason—for reason is scientific and leads to the absurd. . . . To make this clearer for you, I send you a little book which you really ought to read.

[1] A reference to Ambrosia Cottage, where Miss Brzeska was staying.

I regret much that I have said and done. You see, Zosik, I have only just opened my eyes on the world, and I'm dazzled. My feelings do not agree with my reason—my words fail to convey just what I am longing to say. My touch with all things is very slight, and the primitiveness of my nature always gets the upper hand. As a punishment, I have sworn to translate the whole of the *Divine Comedy* for Sisik, for I see that Dante suffered just as I do from this curiously ambiguous situation.[1]

As to my ideas about art, I'm perpetually modifying them, and I am very glad I do. If I stuck to some fixed idea, I should grow mannered, and so spoil the whole of my development. As far as I can see at this moment, I believe that art is the interpretation of emotions, and consequently of the idea. For this emotion I recognize as necessary only the discipline of technique, and at this moment I think the idea comes better the more the technique is simple and limited; on the other hand, I fully recognize that the more you limit your technique, the greater danger you run of falling into mannerism, which is the negation of all the emotion which we experience in front of nature.

Again, in this emotion I see three divisions, linear emotion, produced by the rhythm of outlines and of strokes, sculptural emotion, rendered by the balance of masses, such as they are revealed by light and shade, and lastly, pictorial emotion, produced by various

[1] Gaudier translated only the first five Cantos of the *Inferno*, a work which Miss Brzeska spoke of as 'œuvre très mièvre—ennuyeuse jusqu' à l'indigestion d'Esprit et du tête'. He had a Tuscan edition with a 'hideous English translation', which helped him where the passages were obscure.

coloured pigments. These three technical emotions seem to be very closely united in a vast intellectual emotion, which I do not know, but which, in the corresponding realm of spirit, I feel, in the form of pleasure, suffering, sorrow, joy, etc., and that's where the mystery lies. I used to think that to reproduce each form exactly was enough; then I thought it was only the light that mattered, and that if each variety of light was rendered perfectly, that which it lit would be thus rendered also. You will see for yourself that it is best for me to free myself gradually from all these prejudices—that I should deny, so to say, all that I have thought instead of becoming ridiculously engulfed—an example of pigheadedness. To tell the truth, I am sure of nothing, since it is only now that I am beginning truly to feel life.

According to the little book which I am reading about Dante, 'the devil lived on very good terms with very few people, because of his terrible tendency to invective and reproach, and his extraordinary gift for irony and irresistible sarcasm'—just like my own funny little Sisik.

To be quite honest, Sisik, I love you passionately, from the depth of all my being, and I feel instinctively bound to you; what may often make me seem nasty to you is a kind of disagreeable horror that you don't love me nearly so much as I love you, and that you are always on the point of leaving me—however, the more I know you, the more I realize that you do love me very deeply.

Cheer up, Sik, dear. I'm feeling well and looking after myself— for example, last Sunday, the landlady cooked me a good joint and potatoes. I have provided myself with lots of vegetables and fruit.

Yesterday morning I got up at six o'clock—had a bath, went to the Park for an hour, and got back to the house at eight o'clock. I worked hard until seven in the evening, went out for an hour, and to bed at eight. Next morning I was up at six again. I did a fairly big canvas in oils yesterday without any hesitation—I did it in one go, and am pleased with its colour and composition. It is a White-chapel Jew, selling his wares.[1] In the afternoon I half-finished the plaster group: two women running. Now that it is finished it seems to me like an allegory—the Spirit of Liberty drawing women to-wards a nobler life. Since you left I have done innumerable draw-ings—about 600 to 1000, your portrait, which I have begun three times, and which has taken me ages (it is finished now, and I am delighted with the beauty which comes out of it, and the absolutely refined charm of the face), a little statue of a monkey, one of a lynx, one of a puma, the group, the picture mentioned above, and several illustrations of the Tomego Zajaia.[2]

I know a bookseller, Rider, a pleasant fellow. It is he who has put me in touch with [Frank] Harris. He has suggested that I should show in his shop little statues and pictures for sale—I'll take him my Jew and the plaster groups of Russian dancers. Zosik was right: Parlanti has given me back the plaster group—*mea maxima culpa!* Lousada has come back. I spoke to him on the telephone this eve-ning; he is going to send me a card telling me what evening he can see me, and I will take him the bronze that Parlanti is bringing

[1] This canvas was reversed later, and the bas-relief of Wrestlers worked on the new surface, so that the painting of the Jew is now at the back of the Wrestlers.

[2] Drawings for Mr. Hare.

to-morrow. The Hares always ask for news of you directly they see me, and I think it would be nice if you wrote a little letter to Tommy. I don't think very much will come of Tommy's mythological stunt, and that's all to the good, since I about burst myself over each blasted design. I'm much better working at my own personal ideas. . . .

Wulfsberg has promised to make a contract with me before the 1st of November. There is a rumour in the office that he is going to take me with him to Christiania (he said something about it to the Norwegian, but it is very doubtful). If he does propose it, how-ever, I really ought to refuse, for in Christiania we would have to work from 8 a.m. to 9 p.m., and on Sundays until 2 or 3 o'clock in the afternoon. The town is a frightful nest of 'cancans', where everyone knows his neighbour, and where it would be impossible for me to do any kind of work. I ran off to see Tommy to ask him to keep an eye open for a job for me. I'll also have a look round myself, and I'll ask Lousada and also Rider, who, with Frank Harris, is running the new review, *Hearth and Home*. It pays well, and there might be an opening there. All these are safety measures, for I don't think for a moment that Wulfs means to take me to Norway—it would cost him far too much.

You are quite right in thinking that the Past continues in the Present, and forms the Future. This is one of Bergson's big prem-ises, and his theory of change is based on that. On the other hand, you have no right to judge me so severely. I am very young, and you are grown up, 'nel mezzo del camin di nostra vita', as Dante said of the man between thirty-five and forty years; quite formed, while I am only in the making. What is more, when you first knew me, I was ill—then when I found work, I fell into another abnormality, the one in which I now am—driven nearly mad by too much work, and wishing all the time—no matter how—to get out of business. . . .[1]

My little darling, a thousand kisses on your sweet body. Keep cool! I only added feather-bed, large bedstead, on your card, because I understood that you would have two rooms—see? I enfold you in a profound embrace, and send much love from your insufferable but loving

Pikus.

Chelsea
31st October 1912

Ukochano Brzesko Brzescych,

By all that's marvellous I send you four fat sovereigns, all in gold in this sweet letter from your beloved? ? ? pipik.[2] I will send you your little package to Dodford—it will probably be there on Monday—I will do it up this evening, and send it off to-morrow morning. I will put in it:

deux pains à 2 lbs. Allinson
beaucoup *des* citrons (il n'y a pas encore des oranges)
beaucoup *des* bananes
2 douzaines *des* punaises bien vivantes!
une boîte des allumettes vestas en cire

[1] The letter here contains three pages and a map about the Balkan War.
[2] See Note at the end of this letter.

but I can't send you any acid to clean your washbowl—it's too dangerous. To begin with, it might get broken on the journey and burn everything in the box, and besides, some always remains in the basin, particularly if it is not very good, 'et çà te ferait tomber les kouaki de la pisia et te donnerait la colique'. I send you some soda instead—it is the best. And what will my old donkey say if it finds chocolate from an A.B.C.[1] and good apples?? Eh?? You old miser!!

Don't miss your train on Saturday and don't tire yourself out by worrying. If you take the ten o'clock train, which I suggest, you will do very well, because you will have a little rest at Leicester and again at Birmingham—enough, but not too much.

You will find with this the third Canto of Hell. I am tremendously interested in this *Divine Comedy* and also in Dante's personality. He had something akin to Shakespeare in that he didn't rack his brains to find new things, but borrowed all the old Troubadour songs, and particularly those of Pons de Capdiul and Guiraut de Borneil, adding to them his own ideas. It was the same thing for the Hell. Much is taken from Virgil's *Aeneid*, but whatever is used brings out Dante's idea.

I send in the box of fruits a little Life of him similar to the one about Bergson. . . .

Pik.

Note to the previous Letter

The four sovereigns which Henri gave to her played a very prominent part in one of the many trials of Miss Brzeska's life.

[1] Aërated Bread Company Restaurant.

MATERNITY GROUP

In 1918, she had come up to town to make some arrangement about Henri's posthumous Exhibition at the Leicester Galleries. She went to stay with the Pissarros in Hammersmith, and was to go on to dinner with Mrs. Bevan in Hampstead.

A little before luncheon some discussion arose, and Mrs. Pissarro laughed. Miss Brzeska, quite mistakenly, thought that she was laughing at her, and left the room without a word. It seems that she went upstairs, fetched her handbag, and, not waiting to put on a hat, rushed into the street with the intention of going at once to Mrs. Bevan. Her poor mind was in so sudden and complete a state of confusion that she could not think of her direction, and some time in the afternoon found herself in Hyde Park. She walked all over the Park, and on into Kensington Gardens, talking aloud to herself all the while. She walked about all through the night, searching for the way to Mrs. Bevan's, and by morning, tired and exhausted, but talking and swearing more loudly than ever, she dropped into an A.B.C.[1] near Paddington Station to have some coffee before catching the early train to her home at Wootton-under-Edge. While she was in the A.B.C.[1] the police came, and took her to the Paddington Infirmary.

Mrs. Bevan was informed, and went to see her, and the Doctor in charge thought her well enough to go home—Mrs. Bevan arranged to take her to the station and see her into the train. Before leaving, Miss Brzeska asked for her things, which had been taken away from her the day before, and these were returned, with the exception of her money, amongst which were these four golden

[1] Aërated Bread Company Restaurant.

sovereigns given to her by Henri in 1912, and since then most jealously guarded by her. Although several people wrote to the police, pointing out that these sovereigns were more in the nature of a keepsake than money, offering notes in their stead, they were not able to obtain their return. From ten in the morning until nearly one Miss Brzeska endeavoured by argument and invective to get her sovereigns back, but in the end had to take the train to Gloucestershire, feeling again at the edge of her sanity.

City

My dear child,   *31st October 1912*

I hope that you are no longer feeling so poorly, and that you aren't tired. I have sent you this morning four sovereigns well done up in an envelope, and registered; you will probably get them at the same time as this.

Savoff, the Bulgarian, has fought the Turks 50 kilometres from Constantinople. The battle has gone on for the last four days, and is not yet finished. The principal armies are engaged. Apart from that, Turkey is in the hands of the Slavs, who say quite openly that they will divide it among themselves, and Austria accepts. This is all very good news, because after this war, there can be no further excuse for another.

Pipik.

15 Red. Street

Beloved,   *Sunday, 3rd November 1912*

For many months I have been a martyr to my need for music, and I have just satisfied this desire. I have heard with the utmost ecstasy

Beethoven's 5th Symphony. There were very few people in the Albert Hall, which is immense, and I sat alone in a corner with my eyes shut, and didn't open them until the last note. I can't describe the Symphony to you, but the whole has a suave amplitude, and gives the impression of a very beautiful young woman's torso, firm but soft, seen at first by rarefied lights, and then with strong light and shade something like this, but with sounds instead of tones.

Beethoven has my complete admiration. I like his music more than any other.

To tell the truth, I haven't worked very well this week—my eyes have hurt me—I have drawn intermittently, and have done a little sculpture. I stuck at the little group which I told you about, and finished it this morning once for all, after having changed it for the better by broadening the planes.

On Friday evening I washed out the big room, and as I had made a fire, I profited by it to have a good bath, which set me up. Yesterday I wasted a good hour in 'zweifelscheissem' in the French quarter, looking for gingerbread for my Sisik, and didn't in the end find any. I didn't want to waste money on the 'bus, so another hour and a half was lost in getting home. I did up the parcel for Sisik, sent it off, and by then it was dark. I went out to buy paper, and in the shop heard of a studio where for 5s. I can go and draw from the nude from 8 till 10, Tuesdays and Fridays, for five weeks. That works out at 3d. per hour, which is ripping. When I began to wonder what I was going to do, there was only time left to go to the Museum. I rushed off filled with shame at the thought of half a day lost, and plunged with vigour into *Art*, a book on Rodin. I read it all through. I read it all between 5 and 10 o'clock, passionately and with understanding, and found heaps of things in it that interested me.[1]

All our sympathies are with Rodin, are they not, my Zosik? Things used to be much worse in the Middle Ages. The other day I read of Van Eyck, who was sent to Portugal to paint the portrait of a Princess, betrothed to the son of his patron, the Duke of Burgundy. Van Eyck had already painted the Retables at Bruges, and was in the maturity of his talent. The story tells of the journey, the festivities, the lords, the tournaments, and at the end, 'et certain maistre Jean Van Eyck, petit valet de Monseigneur de Bourgoygne, qui, dit-on, sait peindre sur bois à la couleur à olle qu'il a inventée, et auquel dame l'Enfante fit insigne honneur et trop grande grâce de lui laisser peindre son portrait'. On the journey he slept with the servants, and attended to the horses.

Speaking of horses, I went this morning to Hyde Park to the famous Rotten Row. My God! A rottener lot of broken-winded old hacks you never saw anywhere! To get over my disgust with these horses, I made a pilgrimage to Kensington Gardens to Watts'

---

[1] Gaudier here gives Miss Brzeska a five-page précis of *Art*.

statue, which looks splendid under the airy lights between the big walks.

Yesterday evening I delighted my heart with the 'St. Jean Baptiste', this afternoon with Beethoven. I also had a superb pomegranate, pink, large and beautiful like a lovely 'pisia' of dear Sisik, which I kiss distractedly, so much does she delight me. I have my doubts all the same! I am now going to the Library, will eat when I come back, then go for a walk, and so to bye-byes.

Pipik.

P.S.—I kiss my dear Zosik, all over her dear body, and I recommend her to the care of the beneficent sun. I couldn't put the bananas in, it would have made it too heavy: 5–15 lbs., 2s., 15–20 lbs., 4s., and it was almost exactly 14 lbs. Next time I will put in other good things: the old man promised me that you would get them on Monday.

Ten thousand kisses full of love, close caresses, kisses, kisses— Zosienkoju. The Bulgarians are at Constantinople—good-night, darling.

Pik.

15 Redburn Street, Chelsea

Dear Old Thing,   *5th November 1912*

Our little differences are most excusable—not only are we of different sexes, but also of different nationalities. We are not the same age, nor have we had the same experience, nor do our talents follow the same course. In spite of all this, one thing remains. My Zosik loves me so much, and she is right in saying that if I have perfect

confidence in her, and love her, it is because of her intelligence. I
know I'm a queer devil. I try to excuse myself, and Sisik only tries
to make me see where I am wrong in order that I may correct it
once for all. When I am in a good mood, and have thought things
over properly, I see that on the whole she is right. So let's finish all
these harangues, and we will always love each other, just we two,
because this is the only happiness on which we can count.

You mustn't get worried about bad dreams. In these last three
years, while we have been in a weak and nervy condition, we have
had dreadful nightmares each night, but they have never come to
anything, for, say what you will, our situation is getting better. Last
night, for instance, I dreamt that, with my Sisik, I saw lions on a
plain. We had a hut, and it was raining; all that we noticed was
that we were able to go inside the hut, and we were delighted to
think that we should have fur coats made of lion skins—we started
off with our guns well loaded and—not a lion to be seen! It's only
the reaction of the imagination and of nerves too highly strung.
Don't worry about the boss, that will be all right. He has dismissed
the little English fellow, saying that —— and I are quite able to do
the work without him. He goes to Norway on the 25th, and won't
be back until April 15th, so that he will probably arrange everything before he goes away. To-day he is in Paris running after a
wood contract for next year.

If you are happy where you are, don't put yourself out, but work
well, care-free; whatever happens, I will be prudent, and won't
indulge in any stupidity, such as: taking a studio, giving up commerce, etc., in fact, anything which might worry you, and prevent

you from writing well; for if there is one thing which I consider a labour of love for my Sisik, it is to enable the poor darling to work. I am so pleased that this time you have struck a good place,[1] and I commend you to the great beautiful SUN, that he may help you.

My dear, it is much too much '*du* luxe' to take your baths in front of a glowing fire, it is not at all good for you, brings on all sorts of dreadful illnesses—you should have cold water—really cold. I take a cold bath every morning, at first I used to add a little hot, but that was sheer cowardice, and it didn't go on long.

I have taken the Nijinsky to Bob Rider,[2] and have promised him 4s. in the £, so long as he sells it as best he can—also the head of Smythies, in order to try to get some commissions for portraits—when my 'Jew' is ready, I will take it too. This evening I am going to the life class, and I shall enjoy it. I shall see 'panis toutes nues', blast it all, and good ones too.

Leave the sweet little flowers to grow where they are—when the poor things arrive they are all mutilated, squashed, lifeless—they cry and make me sad. Send me only your good kisses; kiss the little flowers for me, but do not destroy them, 'ou gare à ton sale cucu quand je viendrai'.

I am going to start to do coloured drawings for tiles, and paint friezes for wall-paper; it amuses me much more than doing illustrations, and perhaps I can make something of it, for with the people I am in with at present, there is nothing to be got except by being exploited, and for the little statues I have to have ready money. All

---

[1] Miss Brzeska had gone to Dodford.
[2] Gaudier wrote of Mr. Dan Rider as Bob Rider.

good things to you, beloved. I embrace you most passionately, and will write more to-morrow.

Thursday

Madroźka Milośé, I didn't go to draw at that class the other evening, because I got a letter from Lousada asking me to take him the bronze. I send you only £5, for I must keep a little for plaster for a portrait which Bob Rider has got me, a commission not yet definitely decided. The fellow is a friend of Rider's, and likes the portrait of Smythies, but he can't pay £10 for the plaster, because he is poor, so Bob is going to arrange with him for £5. Marsh[1] has written to me again, asking me to dinner at the 'Moulin d'Or' next Wednesday. Shall I square that by giving him 2 or 3 drawings, or not? What do you think?

I think I shall be able to sell some of the drawings for decorative tiles. Keep well, my Mamusienka, dear love. Be happy. Are you working well? Have you received the little parcel?

Pik.

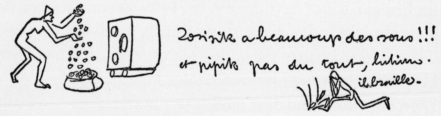

Mordo jedna napisaj mnie że "tu as bien reçu cette lettre avec les pieniądze."

Zorżik a beaucoup des sous !!! et pipik pas du tout, lilium. il braille.

---

[1] Mr. Edward Marsh. In replying to one of W. Marsh's letters Gaudier says: 'Your envelope bearing the Admiralty seal gave me a sort of fright—I had a vague idea I was going to be arrested for some reason or other—the look of governmental authority is always more or less frightening to people not accustomed to it.'

PART II

12th November 1912

My dear love,

Now that I have got over all the fatigues of the journey,[1] two real impressions remain with me. In the first place, that sweet sensation of perfect and profound love which unites us one to the other, and next, the pleasantness of Sisik's curtains, and the grace of all the sculptures which decorate the garden. Dear, you are in a charming place, and the air is making you much stronger. All the lovely country, not grand but very intimate, very human, and rather Celt-ic, with a gaiety of its own, has made a great impression on me, and even more on the Zosik, because she has had longer with it. . . .

The terra-cotta mask which I took away has no charm in a room, and I'm sorry I brought it—it's a good work, but to come into all its beauty, it needs the open air—the side of a hill. The four walls of a dirty room spoil the poor thing. I have hidden it so that I shan't be annoyed.

Yesterday I finished the two tiles which I had in hand—they are the best in colour I have done so far. I have seven. I'll go on doing them until the end of the year, and then try to sell them in January. This evening I started the nude—but there, again, I don't feel too happy, for now that I have communed with the body of my dear Dziecko, I don't find these models very beautiful, or even desirable to see. Anyhow, one must work, and put little Eros under the lash, when he tries too hard to tyrannize. I now feel just the same towards

[1] Gaudier had been to see Miss Brzeska for the week-end.

my good Zosik as I did during those first days at Combleux, when even to speak to someone seemed to me a sin against our love. . . .

I read that the place left empty by the Gioconda has been filled by the portrait of Baldassare Castiglione, the perfect gentleman of the Renaissance, the author of a book very celebrated at that time, *The Courtier*. . . .[1]

I feel compelled to tell all this to my good child because it pleases me so much. I adore all those rich stories of the Italian Renaissance. They savour in a peculiar manner of the lovely Latin civilization, which reveals the ancient customs of Rome, and are deeply impregnated with one's own pagan Christianity—of which Christ and the Virgin are the supreme gods, and in which each saint has his own special and well-defined province.

My old dear wished to see her Pikus until the last moment, so she stretched her poor head and only looked at the front of the train. Although I cried out 'Zosik!' and made the most vigorous signals of distress, she would never look round to my end, and so, my poor darling, I saw you longer than you saw me.

I had £5 4s. 2d. from the Boss for my expenses, so with the money I gave you, I have gained 30s. on the trip[2]—not counting the celestial joy of spending two such good days with my sweet lover. It was therefore one of the most splendid windfalls of our life. My dear heart of Zosienka, I kiss you with such passion, I lavish upon your lovely body all the deepest expressions of my love, and my soul is inseparably held in yours. . . .

[1] Gaudier here gives a short Life of Castiglione.
[2] Gaudier included this week-end in some business he had to do for his firm.

14th *November 1912*

My precious love,

I called on Marsh last night, and there saw the most magnificent examples of Girtin's work—it impressed me immensely, and Constable and Turner and Cotman—in fact, all the best 18th to 19th century English landscape. I am still enchanted with it all. . . .

I went with Marsh to see Gibson—he isn't at all the sort of chap I thought he was, but much more sympathetic. All the poets have joined together to hire a big house near the British Museum, where they live and work, and have underneath it a shop where they sell poetry by the pound—and talk to the intellectuals. Some of them have huge, vast rooms, while those like Gibson have only a tiny hole. He is boxed in a room, over the door of which is written, 'In case of fire, access to the roof through this room'. I have asked him to come and see me some day, so that I can see what sort of a fellow he is. Marsh thinks he is very talented.

This morning I had a letter from Frank Harris. He says that he will come on Sunday, and I have laid in two cwts. of clay. He continues, 'I would be very glad indeed for you to model my bust, if it is worth doing, but I go to New York to lecture at the end of the week, and I don't know whether you could do it this Saturday or Sunday. I would put a room at your disposal here, or I would come to you, whichever you prefer, please let me know. I have known Rodin for 25 years; I bought a dozen bronzes from him quite 25 years ago, and have admired him this side idolatry ever since. It is twenty years since he asked me if he could model me, and I did not think I had done anything that deserved such an honour, so I refused.' It seems to me that to seek out a sentence like that last one, a man must be pretty conceited and pleased with himself. By special arrangement, there is a portrait of him by Fergusson in the last *Rhythm*. I admire this enormously—Marsh says that he would never have recognized Harris—Murry swears that it is the spit of him. In any case, for Fergusson to have knocked off so good a picture, the old chap must be a jolly good model, and we will put him through the mill with pleasure,[1] particularly as I am now dying to do a portrait.

I have been reading the doings of the Prince de Condé in the *Revue des Deux Mondes*, and I was very much interested. What corruption under Louis XV! [etc.] . . .

The Lousadas want to change the colour of the group to light green. It has now a marvellous patine of old bronze. I have written to Parlanti to make it green like the leaves of a cabbage. We will laugh, for they are so close that they will never buy anything big from me,[2] so I may permit myself the pleasure of letting them go to the devil.

It is Maud Lousada who writes in the name of the Holy Duality, of which she is the Divine Spirit.

I went to the life class. It is kept by four stupid old women. The model—a lovely young boy—wore a tiny little cloth, and the quick sketch wasn't a quick sketch at all. The model takes his own pose—which is, of course, a good thing—and keeps it for ten or fifteen

---

[1] Et nous le stigmatiserons avec plaisir.

[2] The £20 which the Lousadas paid for this group (*L'Oiseau de Feu*) was, all the same, the highest price paid for any of Gaudier's works during his lifetime.

minutes. I should have liked to have a model who didn't pose at all, but did everything he wanted to, walked, ran, danced, sat, etc. To-morrow we shall probably have a woman.

My dear love, you are surely not working so assiduously that you couldn't find time to send me even a postcard, and me away from you and all, and so very anxious to have a word. You know very well the agony of being lonely, and you want me to write to you in the middle of the week. I have far less leisure than you have, and it makes me sad to see that you forget me. So make honourable amends next week by sending me a little postcard. I have not had time yet to translate 'Hell' for you. Monday, 2 tiles; Tuesday, class; Wednesday, Marsh; Thursday, cleaning the rooms; to-morrow, class; Saturday, Zoo and the Museum; Sunday, Frank Harris; and the rest of the time sleep and the office, from which I am now writing to you, in a moment of leisure. I love you so much, little Zosik dear, and I kiss you passionately from the head to the foot of your lovely body, and pray the warm sun for your happiness and the success of your work. I love you tenderly, and wait feverishly for the first chance of seeing you again, of possessing you fully and fondly.

Friday

I cleaned all yesterday, and then had a hot bath in front of a good fire, and slept without my clothes, in order to make believe that I was with my Sisik.

Don't talk to Tommy about the vases; he might want to have a share in the transaction, and we want it for ourselves—don't speak to anyone. As for the agate, I forgot to tell you that it is only volcano lava. I examined it very carefully and it is entirely without value. The stone Christ is certainly 15th century or earlier; I believe that without going wrong you could put it at the 12th or 13th century. English sculpture has always been behind the French of the Middle Ages by a couple of centuries. In French Art, this style of Christ would be of the 9th century, considering the crown and the form of the cross and the work around the eyes and cheeks, but the moustache and beard are of a 12th or 13th century French style, so you might say that the whole piece, which is English, existed at the end of the 15th century and the beginning of it might go back as early as the 12th century. You must not dream of paying more than 15s. or 20s. for it—that is why I telegraphed.

Of the pottery vases, only consider the one with the smiling figures—the one standing alone in the garden, not either of those at the foot of the little stairs, and don't pay more than 10s. to 15s. After these purchases let's buy nothing more—for this reason—if we carry on like a couple of profane collectors we won't be able to enjoy the little money we have—there is nothing more horrid than lots of repulsive fragments which have no relation to each other all huddled in one dwelling. One ends by hiding them, and then they are no use. My Zosik is too much infected with the desire for property. The curtains and pots are quite enough, and it is not really worth your while to go charging all over the country for the remains of antiquity. We want neither to tie up our capital in antiquities nor to set up as antiquaries. We have need of all our activities to carry on our own affairs, and to publish your book. Remember, dear

Zosik, that for that you will need a very great deal—so better buy
nothing at all if you are not already committed, and leave the pots
where they are. The memory of them and the desire they provoked

ZOSIK

are better than the possession. I don't believe that it is at all desirable to have them, and as for considering it an investment, they are not worth the trouble we should have—we should never sell them unless we had to, and then no one would buy them. I hope so very much that you have not yet committed yourself to anything.

I implore my Zosik to work hard and regularly, at least five hours a day. You must remember that each month you lose a week by your illness, and we are such poor devils that we must keep ourselves very much in hand and not waste our time but produce.

My Zosik disappointed me—I had looked for a long letter, but there was nothing. You don't seem to have cared to hear about Castiglione—it makes me feel that it is no use bothering to tell you about things. You complained at the beginning that I never talked to you about things—but how can I if you pass it all over in silence?

It distresses me to see how you waste the good sunlight. You don't get through all your affairs until 11 a.m. and then you go for a walk until 12—lunch 1 o'clock, and you don't get up from your rest until half-past two—and there's the day spoilt, you haven't time to write to me, and you ought to—whereas I, with many more preoccupations, visits and work, am expected to talk to you about all that is going on, keep you up to date, etc., and you give me no encouragement, for you don't seem to notice it at all.

Zosik love, please be a little sweeter and a little more noticing. I'm not at all annoyed—I know you are a dawdler, and I wish you weren't. If you want to make me happy at Christmas you ought to be through a good quarter of *Madka*.[1]

[1] One part of Miss Brzeska's *Trilogy*.

THE DANCER

I kiss you a thousand times, dear beloved, and wait with great impatience for your news—send me a postcard on Wednesday—I shall get it on Thursday. Dear love and affection.

Pik.

P.S.—The wills I made are wrong. I will do them again, and they need 6d. stamps.

16th November 1912

Dearest and Best,

I went to the Zoo. The beasts had a curious effect on me, which I haven't hitherto experienced; I have always admired them, but now I hate them—the dreadful savagery of these wild animals who hurl themselves on their food is too horribly like the ways of humans. What moved me most was a group of four chimpanzees. They were like primitive men, they walked helping themselves with their hands, and looked like old men, their backs all bent. They discussed things in little groups, shared their food without dispute but with much wisdom—the strongest giving bread and carrots for the oranges and bananas belonging to the others. It's most depressing thus to see our own origin—depressing, not because we sprang from this, but that we may so easily slip back to it. Our knowledge is great, but how empty! How ephemeral! So small a thing, and we lose all. We no longer know chemistry as did the men of the Italian Renaissance, and it will be a long while before we re-discover their secrets. Art comes instinctively to us, but it is so uncertain. I have in front of me photographs of all Rodin's best works; the more I admire them the further I feel myself removed from all art, it seems so easy, so limited! We are part of the world creation, and we ourselves create nothing. Our knowledge allows us to make use of all the forces already in existence—our art to interpret emotions already felt; a big war, an epidemic, and we collapse into ignorance and darkness, fit sons of chimpanzees. Our one consolation is Love, confidence, the embracing of spirit and of body. When we are united we think neither of outer darkness nor of animal brutality. Our human superiority vibrates through our passions, and we love the world—but how insignificant we really are, and how subject to universal law! Mere midgets in the wide universe, but masters of our particular planet. Oh, Zosik, Zosik, how strange it all is; in my memory, I compare the slender springing grace of a lovely man with this hairy mass of monkey flesh, the mastery of an energetic head, full of individual character, with the stupid masks of chimpanzees who can scarcely raise the beginnings of a smile. These comparisons are so terrible, so formidable in the mind; for if the blind masses of humanity, which always persecute their pioneer spirits, had the desire, or rather the power, then would our tall and erect stature be bent, and we should be covered with hideous fur; the grass would grow over our finest works, and we should return to bestiality.

These wicked people who are so ignorant, we hate them—don't we, dear love? These brutes who have eyes for nothing save their animal passions, who think only of eating, who fight each other, and wallow in dirt—foul, disgusting fellows who only crush people of our kind, whose instinct is for beauty, for ideas and for reflection. Sweet dear, I am so blessed in being able to love you, and blessed be the day when the great sun guided me to you; without your love I should have been flung into an outer darkness, where bones rot, and where man is subject to the same law as beasts— final destruction, the humiliation of extinction. Dear, dear love, I press you to me with all my force, and only your help enables me to work. I thank you, dear Sun, lovely Star, for having created women and men that we may be united, mingle our personalities, melt together our hearts and, by the union of our passionate bodies, better liberate our souls, making of us a single creature—the absolute human which you have endowed with so many gifts.

Goodnight, dear heart, sweet Sister, Mother. Think that we are together in the same bed, and by our perfect union, making prayer to God.

Sunday, 17th November

I woke up full of life, and was quickly at work. I painted. Yesterday afternoon I went to the Zoo and drew a little, not so much as I would have liked, because of the dark day and the distraction of my thoughts—all the same, I have a few drawings, and I painted two buffaloes, one white and one black, each against the other, and I am happy.

I am sorry that I did not take Smythies sooner to Bob's. I should have been ready to sculpt Harris. He promised to come today, but a telegram has called him to America; he says he will come in January. On Friday evening I met at Bob's a young actor called Wheeler. The same sort of type as Murry. He works like Pik by day, and acts in the evenings and on Sundays. . . .

I went to the class again on Friday, they had a man again, but old, brutal, with a great belly. I worked well, and I asked the old woman when we were going to have a woman to draw. She promises one for this week. I am anxious to see if the old bitch will make her wear a rag as she did the boy—just as if she were in her 'suiski czerwone'—for all I know, they'll hang another over her breasts. The people in the class are so stupid, they only do two or three drawings in two or three hours, and think me mad because I work without stopping—especially while the model is resting, because that is much more interesting than the poses. I do from 150 to 200 drawings each time, and that intrigues them no end.

Zosik love, I really must stop writing to you for to-day, for my little fire is already almost out and I must cook my supper on it, as they haven't yet put in the gas.

I have hung my beloved's mask above my bed, and the shadow it makes on the wall is so utterly like my Sisik's that I am constantly startled, thinking it is she. Kisses, sweet dear, I hold you to me in love and tenderness.

Tuesday

Sweetheart, the lousadsiny invited me to supper last night, and they are coming here one of these days. I have only got £1 10s. left for the month, and, poor love, I cannot send you the stove, etc., but if I sell something, as I hope to do, then I will. Pet, I want so much to write to you this morning, but I have heaps to do and really must stop. I kiss you incessantly, I'm filled with longing and am always thinking of my Sisik and want so much to make love with her. 'Je suis lourd à cause de cela et je vais essayer encore une 'tite putain quand j'aurai des siousions ("Five shillings, lay your

money down, sir! Lay your money down!"), à la santé de ma mamus, car ça m'empêche de bien travailler——

'Zosisik, ne sera pas zalouse, n'est-ce pas bon petit amour, c'est
seulement pour vider ces vilains workis——'

Friday 22nd

Dear love, you can't imagine what a state of mental depression I
have been in lately. I am a bit better this morning. I have no real
reason for detesting Tommy and Chuckie. They've always been
very kind to me; it is just my own stupid ideas. I went to see them
last night, and I like them better than ever. Fraser asked very anxiously after my Zosik, if she were well, etc.

Dearest, I can't make any headway, these cheap lodgings depress
me, and I'm going to clear out in the first week of December. I will
take a nice little studio, not on the ground floor, because ground
floors will always have the same disturbing effect, and will be so
much money lost.

Boss won't make a contract, either with Watkins or with me,
and that's all to the good; but what isn't good is that he is only
going to give us a £1 rise—we are going to try our best to leave him
while he is in Norway. Zosik mustn't worry herself about anything.
I shall always find work of some sort or other, and she has only to
breathe the good air, and not force herself to work until the New
Year. It is better to have an end in view, don't you think? Poor
darling, don't write such long letters, it only makes you over-tired.
I am a graceless creature who always will clamour for more honey,
though the poor bee gives her very guts to provide it. Sometimes I

am too hasty with my Mamus, and sometimes I accuse her of wickedness just to stimulate her to reply. How strange these sensations of
love are—I almost become jealous of myself! . . .

Poor darling, I haven't even a little sovereign to send you. I should
have to borrow, and you wouldn't like that. Next Saturday is
November 30th, and I shall then be able to send a little. I went to
see Rider at his house in Hammersmith, and he spoke of Harris,
but this for next week. Ten thousand kisses.

Pik.

My dear Love,   *Sunday, 24th November*

I am going to have a rest to-day, and I profit by it to write a long
letter to you. Darling, when I say I am jealous of myself, it does
not at all mean that I doubt your affection, it only means that I love
you so much that I don't wish to see or speak to anyone. Zosiumo,
you are such an intelligent Zosik that you should have understood
that when I wrote to you as I did last week, I wasn't in a normal
condition. The truth is that since my return I have been utterly upset—one day I was full of the most exuberant joy, and the next in
the worst of depressions.

I came back overstrung by sex feelings which have lasted almost
until now, and it is because of that that I am taking to-day quietly.
I won't work at all. I shall buy slippers and an umbrella and stock
my larder from the 'Home and Colonial'[1] and soon be all right
again, so don't worry about me. . . .

[1] Henri had a horror of umbrellas, and all this is only a figure of speech for
coddling himself.

Wheeler came yesterday to help me take the Bagnold head to Fraser's studio. We hired a little hand-cart, and we laughed enough to piddle our pants. Wheeler has an engineer brother, who is going to try to get me some regular and paying work in Birmingham, little ornaments, heads of lions, etc. He's buying a tiny statue for himself for £2. Fraser's studio is a magnificent place, a huge room with two walls entirely taken up by windows, a gallery at one end, and two rooms above—all lit by electricity.

He has got a lot of pictures, but all scenes of carnival, a life superficial and automatic, with no kind of depth or idea. In order to flatter me, he has had a beautiful book bound, and stuck in the drawings which I gave him in the hopes of further passes to the Zoo. On the cover he has put in huge letters of gold, 'Studies by Henri Gaudier-Brzeska, 1912'. The tiles and the masks which I did at his house last March are framed in white passepartout, and look very well. Now don't you go accusing me of inconsistency, and of flattering Fraser. There is nothing of that. For the last six weeks I've made no attempt to see him, and then last Thursday I met him at Bob's, and he asked me to come with the Hares on Saturday and bring the head of Bagnold—she wants to have it cast, and is ashamed to ask me, because she has left it so long. I was full of curiosity to see Fraser's place, and also glad to get rid of these big heads of Bagnold and Murry.[1]

You remember my speaking of ——, he is a queer devil. I told him I should like to see a couple in the act of love, and so he is going to arrange a meeting, but the difficulty is to find a woman. He

[1] Gaudier afterwards destroyed the head of Murry by throwing stones at it.

suggested that I might draw his children—the little two-year-old girl is very beautiful, he says, lovely limbs—I must profit by this. I have worked well these last two evenings at the class. Tuesday a girl, without a rag, and Friday a beautiful youth with a wrestler's loin-cloth of black silk bordered with a lovely Indian stuff. If they all wore that sort of thing it would be all right, but a tiny covering is ridiculous.

On Friday I found waiting for me a reply-paid telegram from Marsh, inviting me to dinner. As I had the class and was terribly keen to work, I sent a letter yesterday morning returning the reply for 6d., inventing the little lie that I only returned at 10 p.m., and his telegram asked me for 8. One must follow the advice of Sisik and make oneself 'hoped for'.

This afternoon I am going to see some Americans, Gaylord Wilshire at Hampstead, a syndicalist—very keen on the bust of Haldane Macfall. A well-known collector, Judge Evans, is also very taken with the bust, he is going to come to see me in a fort-night's time, when I am settled in my studio. On Wednesday, I went to look up Dan Rider, and he took me to the Café Royal, and there I drew while he slept, because he had a ghastly headache; after that he took me to his house in Hammersmith, where we had a magnificent evening. He is very natural and open, and we soon became good friends, when we found that we were both passion-ate naturalists. Like Pik, he has studied and adored ferns, the re-production of plants, sea-stars, the collection and life of shell-fish, flowers, insects. He talked a great deal about Harris, whom he ad-mires tremendously. According to him, he is a most honest man of the Castiglione type. He knows all the big bugs, is an intimate friend of the Princess of Monaco, of Lord Howard de Walden, of whom you will have received Rodin's portrait before you got this letter, and Bob really thinks that he will try to push me, because he liked enormously my Nijinsky and Smythies. It was Bob who introduced Fraser to Harris, and though Harris hates Fraser's affected ways, he has introduced him in many places, and has done a great deal for his reputation. Bob thinks me much better than Fraser, 'un dieu sur une pelle à pain', which naturally pleases the old Pikus, who loves to be admired, but who, at the same time, sees its exaggerated stupidity, and is amused by it.

Zosiuno, you need have nothing to fear—whatever happens we shall be much better off than we were two years ago, when we knew no one but Slocombe. Poor darling, I am sorry to have bothered you by speaking to you of your work. Don't harass yourself, dear. Stay quietly in the little spot where you are, and I will fight in London, as far as in me lies, for our common good. We ought to be successful, because we are one with the dear sun, and that great god of ours has not ceased to shine since I began writing to you. I kiss you so lovingly.

Pik.

More to follow.

Monday

After I wrote to you yesterday I went to see Epstein. While I was ringing at the front door his missus stuck her head out of the window to see who I was. Epstein came to the door and asked me to come upstairs. There is an enormous difference between old Epstein's place and that of Fraser & Co.—Little Epstein, dirty and dusty and covered with plaster, sitting on the sill of his window cutting at marble. In the room, two bunks mean and miserable (like Pikus' chair), one bigger than the other—a little table, very small, and nothing else. No picture nor image, nothing on the large white walls, only the torso of a woman, half-broken, in a corner. He spoke to me about his Oscar Wilde in Paris. When he arrived he found that the sexual organs had been covered over with plaster —later the Prefect of the Seine covered the whole monument over with straw, as being altogether indecent. Epstein took off the straw, then the plaster, and restored to his Wilde his couilles de taureau, which hung down at least half a yard, and through the petition of some artists he was able to get the better of the Civil authorities. Later on he showed me a little bronze, very beautiful, quite the nicest work of his I have seen—alive and sincere—a seated woman with her arms above her head. . . . We smoked together, talked of castings and marbles as usual, and I left.

I had no sooner got back to my room than I hared off to Hampstead—it is a beautiful suburb, built like Rome on seven or eight hills. I walked for two hours on the Heath in the fresh air, and discovered magnificent views of hills, like those of Malvern, but much more numerous, closer together and covered with trees. I went to the Americans' and was pleasantly surprised. I expected to see only business men from Wall Street, clean-shaven, hideously square shoulders, puffy skin and nasal accents. He is a little fellow about fifty years old, with a beard, a shy appearance, delicate, and not annoying to look at. She, a large woman and more interesting. American skin, but hard, red, with few lines—you know, 'peau de buffle', hair dressed 'à l'Allemande' in bandeaux, with a turned-up nose. In their room were assembled about thirty people, French and English. An elderly author, very interesting and sympathetic, with white hair and beard, Whiting his name is and *No. 5 John Street* his work. I must try to read it: his ideas on Art are sound and he spoke very clearly, I had a long talk with him and I like him. The party was freer than any I've been to before, it was possible to get into little groups and speak for a long time independently.

A Russian actress, ——, a woman with a monocle and pretty stupid, asked me in French to explain to her futurism and cubism. When for a joke I made her believe that it had something to do with homosexuality, she asked me to go and see her on Thursday evening after dinner. She is at home on Wednesday afternoons, and as the Boss is going to Cardiff this Wednesday, I rang up to say I was coming in the afternoon, which suits me better. She had asked me to come alone with Mrs. Wilshire, and it would have been no fun for me to have a *tete-a-tete* with the two of them; by going in the afternoon I have always a chance of meeting other people.

There was at the Wilshires' an old French woman characteristic of all that dirty middle-class race, dropsical, double-chinned, skin speckled with these little coalish black spots that you only see in the Latins—toads' paws on dirty tripe, and she lording it about —I wished her to the moon and the devil. I will write to you after Wednesday about the Russian, she speaks very good French, German and English, and is an actress. . . .

I have been telling the tallest stories. The Americans call me Brzeska, and several of the French when they heard that I was 'polonais' said to me that I spoke French and English like a Russian, and several others who had thought I was Italian saw very clearly from my type and my walk that I was Slav. What fools! What asses! It amuses me once in a while, and I shall go once more before I have my studio.

Pik.

Thursday, 28th November 1912

My dear good love,

Yesterday I went to the Russian; she is rather stupid, and I won't go again. In the afternoon I went to see Wheeler's brother, who is a director of —— and a pleasant fellow; he has travelled a great deal and is particularly fond of the Poles. Making use of Sisik's description, I talked to him of Cracow and Zakopane, which he knew, and he was very keen on the Tatra: so all this affair served to adorn the conversation and prepare the ground. He gets big contracts of copper, wire, carriages, motors, etc., for firms in Birmingham, and he has a great deal of influence with these people. He is going to give me an introduction to one for motor mascots: they have already complained that they have to get them from France, because there was no one here who could make them. He has recommended me to another for electric radiator ornaments. On top of this he is very much interested in sport, and has commissioned me to make two little statues in plaster—one of a wrestler and the other of a bather—which he will have cast in bronze by one of his firms. In his office he has the very wrestler that I liked so much—a wonderful boy, strong, taut and finely square. I am going to see wrestling in the evenings two or three times, which will give me good sketches; I am also going to see some boxing matches and diving, and I'm terribly excited about it.

I will do him two little statues, the height of your little dancer, for £4 and 30s. extra for the plaster; I shall make £4 nett. Not much, I know, but the devil of it is that I must hit it off with him in order to get more work. He has promised also to give me some introductions for advertisements. He seems very honest, and I don't think he is promising all this in order to get a couple of works cheap. Anyhow, I'm prepared to expect the worst and count no chickens, save those of seeing beautiful athletes in action. The old hag at my evening class promised a magnificent model for to-morrow—a beautiful Frenchwoman. The fellow who was there on Tuesday was a poor little Italian workman, and it is from him that I have made my best studies. The old woman and the other idiots in the class think I am mad. As I have already told you, I work all through the evening without a stop in order to get my full six-pennyworth. They try to talk to me during the rests, but I don't reply. Only when I have finished, if they speak to me I reply, and if they don't, I just clear off, saying 'good-evening'. For fun I speak to the Italian models in Spanish, this gives me prestige and makes me seem queerer to the class—but I do it really from a desire to speak nicely to these poor devils, who seem frightened in the midst of such unimaginable brutes. It is impossible for you to picture these asses.

This drawing[1] is very far from the mark and will give you only the dimmest idea of this band of coconuts. There is amongst them

[1] Page 198.

a young blood who has always something to show or say in order to draw attention to his stupid person. One day it was a Russian ikon, which he neither understood nor admired, and another day

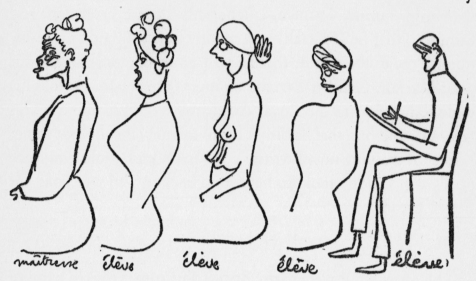

maîtresse   *élève*   *élève*   *élève*   *élève*

it was a German amber and meerschaum pipe; but what took the cake was on Tuesday. It was raining cats and dogs, and the fool came in a hideous pair of suède boots, quite new. He fidgeted about so with these boots that the old hag complimented him on his footwear—he took them off and showed them to everyone—not to me though, for I have sent him packing a couple of times already, and he doesn't dare come near me. He kept saying, 'It was when I was going to Russia some years ago, I bought them in Sweden for shooting, you know they are very comfortable for shooting'. Pah! I can see the fool from here! *Un très sale coco.* Anyhow, it didn't interrupt me, because I forgot it all as soon as I began working.

Yesterday, after I had been to the Russian's, I went to Macfall's,

he lives quite close. He spoke again of his hideous painting, accusing Fergusson of having copied it; that Fergusson only did his still
life under the influence of Macfall; that he (Macfall) introduced to
the world Turner, Steinlen, Nicholson, Orpen, Fergusson, and
Simpson; that he (Macfall) is very busy, but will find time to introduce me to the world; that he will write an article on me, the
great Macfall, Gaudier-Brzeska no more than a toad. He told me
to do something for the Royal Academy. At this I laughed in his
face, and told him that he didn't begin to know the slightest thing,
neither of drawing nor of writing. . . . In the end, I told him quite
gently that I didn't look for help from anyone, and we parted the
best of friends.[1]

Pik.

This afternoon I went to the British Museum. I looked particularly at all the primitive statues—negro, yellow, red, and the white
races, Gothic and Greek, and I am glad to say I was at last convinced of a thing which had for a long time bothered me. I had
never felt sure whether the very conventional form of the primitives,
which gives only an enormous sensation of serene joy or exaggerated
sorrow—always with a large movement, synthetized and directed
towards one end—had not a comprehension more true, more one
with nature: in other words, ampler and bigger, than modern sculpture from the Pisani through Donatello up to Rodin and the French
of to-day. Having very carefully studied the two aspects, at the moment I think not. Up to what point I am absolutely justified I can't

[1] 'Amis comme cochons'.

at all say. My first reason, and the one I consider most sound, is that primitive sculpture seen in large quantities bores me, whereas modern European sculpture seen in the same quantity interests me infinitely, without boring me, and if I go away from it, it is because the strain of looking at it and understanding it upsets me, tires me. I have to go away, but with regret and with the firm intention to come back soon. All that seems to mean that I am an individual— a pik gaudierBrzeska—and it is my individual feeling which counts the most. Why? I do not know nor do I wish to know. I accept it as a fact which does not need explanation.

Now, when I think it out I see that in modern sculpture the movement, without being so big, is nearer to the truth. Men do not move in one movement as with the primitives: the movement is composed, is an uninterrupted sequence of other movements themselves divisible, and different parts of the body may move in opposed directions and with diverse speeds. Movement is the translation of life, and if art depicts life, movement should come into art, since we are only aware of life because it moves. Our expressions belong to this same big movement, and they show the most interesting aspects of the individual; his character, his personality. What kept me in doubt was, I think, the very simplicity of the early primitives in rendering movement, their conception of things in general being very simple, that of the modern being more complex. To-day it all seems to me the other way round—the movement of the primitive is a misconception of true movement, is a fabrication of his mind, an automatic creation which corresponds in no way with the natural movement of the living being. In one word, it is complicated

STUDY

because he does not take the trouble to probe deeply, but invents, creates for himself. The movement of the modern seems to me to be simple because, putting aside all his natural capacity as a human automaton, he uses his energy to see well, in order to render well what he has felt well in seeing well. . . . To conclude, in order not to afflict my Zosik's ears too much, I am in entire sympathy with the modern European movement—to the exclusion always of those moderns who belong to the other class, those who invent things in-stead of translating them.

Pipik.

London
Saturday, 30th November 1912

Dear Sisik,

At last I send you the gingerbreads, poor dear. It seems a long time to have to wait for four wretched buns. Yesterday evening I met Enid Bagnold in the King's Road;[1] she asked me to do a plaster cast of her head, and I told her it would cost £3, so I shall make 35s. on her, which will do for casting a statue, which I will begin to-morrow—I have sent Parlanti to get the model from Fraser. She asked after you and wishes you etc. etc., anything you like. She asked me if I wasn't lonely. I replied rather evasively that I was working. That made her laugh in a rather cynical way and say, 'O well, I don't think you mind much'. . . . 'Sale garce abomi-nable!' I'm not quick at repartee, and while I was chewing over what to say, she started talking of something else. The girl at the

---

[1] Miss Bagnold was studying painting with Mr. Walter Sickert.

Library also asked after you. I told her you were in the country and she said, 'Oh, that's nice', and that you wouldn't come back for several months, 'Oh, that's nice'—everlastingly 'Oh, that's nice'. . . .

Tommy is still trying to do business with the 'Madonna' since Carmi is in London in a ghastly piece called *Venetian Night* . . . .

Many kisses and my love in your heart, dear Zosik.

H. Pik Gaudier-Brzeska.

15 Redburn Street, Chelsea, S. W.
Tuesday, 3rd December 1912

Sisik dear,

I went back to Hampstead on Sunday, worked in the morning, and needed some fresh air by 5 o'clock. I talked all the evening to an American woman: she has a pleasant face, but there is always this twist of the lips in speaking—this nasal tone that drives you mad. She is receptive, admires artists, because they can probe to the depths of existence; admires good music and interested me very much with stories of the customs of Red Indians and with their music. They weren't snobs, these American devils I saw—but there is plenty of that to make up for it in the English who go there. There is something queer about them all. There is no need to be sincere with any of them. The Wilshire woman is intelligent; he is very reserved, smiling, and rather shy—they both have a bit of a lost look. I can't make them out. Anyhow, one can always study people, as there are always new ones there, so I'm told, and you always can talk to one or two people without being disturbed during the whole evening.

You are a wretch. You write me two very abusive postcards, and you carry on like a fiend instead of keeping quiet. My poor darling is very upset I know, but I cannot help feeling that the excursion to Bromsgrove was terribly rash, and to be so afraid of getting the old illness again is unworthy of a courageous Sisik like mine. Anyhow, another time Sisik won't go on like this, but will behave like a sane person. As for the buns, etc., I couldn't get them on Saturday for two reasons: (1) I had to look for a studio and had a rendezvous at 2.30, and I knew you weren't dying of hunger; (2) I couldn't get the books, as all the shops shut at twelve and I only got out at one, and also I knew that you didn't need books any more than bread.

Friday

Beloved, I am very tired; I have done nothing but rush from one place to another, and on top of that have done a lot of work. Last night I went to see the wrestlers—God! I have seldom seen anything so lovely—two athletic types, large shoulders, taut, big necks like bulls, small in the build with firm thighs and slender ankles, feet sensitive as hands, and not tall. They fought with amazing vivacity and spirit, turning in the air, falling back on their heads, and in a flash were up again on the other side, utterly incomprehensible. They have reached such a state of perfection that one can take the other by a foot and, without exaggeration, can whirl him five times round and round himself, and then let go so that the other flies off like a ball and falls on his head—but he is up in a moment and back again more ferocious than ever to the fight—and Pik, who thought he would be smashed to bits!

I stayed and drew for two hours and am going to begin the statuettes on Sunday. The negotiations for the £50 studio have fallen through. I must look for another. On Wednesday evening I went to see the Bagnold because of the plaster cast. She is staying with Dollie and another girl whom I don't know. There was a boy there called Lunn; we spoke of Murry but I don't want to see him again: I don't dislike a person easily, but when at last I do, it's for good. We arranged with the Bagnold that she should take the plaster for £3—with what is left over I will bake one or two little statues and buy a decent book for Christmas. The Bagnold still has the same peculiarity. In the middle of a conversation she rushed away to the Embankment without saying a word. Affected, of course —but in spite of that she is the most interesting of girls—she at least tries to understand and to get into touch with things.

I learn through the *Guerre Sociale* that Kropotkin, the great Anarchist, lives in London. I have heard the Wilshires speak of him and must ask them for his address—I should be the happiest devil if I could do his portrait. I enclose an article about him, although you haven't been interested in politics for the last two weeks.

I'm half asleep, dear love, and I don't remember what I meant to say. It will come into next Sunday's letter, and you shall have a long one next week. I am in a state of creative effervescence. I'm looking after myself well, I sleep well (for the last 7 or 8 days I haven't got up until 8 o'clock). The Boss doesn't come to work until 11 a.m. and to-morrow he leaves for Norway.

I kiss you with all my heart, press you and hug you, dear love. I pray the Sun for you, your health and your work. I'm very happy about the hysteria and all that you tell me. I kiss you a thousand times.

Your Pik.

P.S.—Tommy, when referring to you, speaks in a general way of nerve maladies, which shows clearly that you must seem very nervy, for I have never said that you were ill in any kind of way. Tommy and Chuquie have put quite a pace on to find me a studio. They still want me to take the £50 one, and they say that the other ones further out are no good at all—that one needs a big one in a good position. As they insist so and as they are morally responsible I have left them to it. Tommy, with his knowing air, has given me to understand that if I take the studio he wants me to take he will get me some orders for illustrations—if not he will do nothing. That is the 'hoped-for change' he speaks of in his letter to you. 'La Chuquie' is already bucked at the idea of helping me to move and of putting things in order, while Tommy will arrange terms, etc.

Oh, Sisik, do for goodness sake calm yourself—I suppose not before our bread is assured from some other source.

Good-bye, 10,000 . . . kisses.

Zosik dear, I kiss you, I kiss you.

Pik Brzeska.

Sappho, I understand that the important thing for you is intellectual intransigence, but for me the important thing is sculptural
intransigence. Till you can understand this there will be no possibility of our discussing things with any accuracy and consequent
possibility of agreeing. As usual, your pride detaches itself in its
omnipotence, and you don't take the trouble to think of what you
are writing. Your wailings on what I wrote to you are ill-placed—
those on the Bagnold erroneous, those on the studio, etc., unreason-
able. I will write all about it in a letter—Sisik sees the dark side of
everything too much—herself included, and I repeat that if I were
to carry on as she does, I should never do a statue in my life. Get into
your head once for all that I'm a workman, and it is nothing to me
to be 'hoflieferant' so long as I produce. Tender kisses.

Pik.

[*Postcard*] *4 p.m. 7th December 1912*

Sappho—Wulfs has left and I have just made a contract with
him for a year at £10 per month. I can't leave him before the end of
next year, nor can he send me away before then. It is better than two
years—one is a little freer, although I am such a queer, bad Pik,
who makes Zosik unhappy. But, Zosik, it is never intentional, and
you are a little too pessimistic, for you often scold unreasonably when
you get on your high horse. As to the studio, there were some concessions I didn't want to make, so I am looking for another, more
modest, at £25 to £30, in Chiswick. I don't want to upset the
Hares and so alienate them. Lousada telephoned to ask if I had

any statues, and I said No. I had better wait a little. I will get him to come in January. Much love.

Pikusik.

[Postcard] 9th December 1912

I have refused the studio because it is damp and I should have to pay £50 plus rates and taxes. I have another to look at, as big as Epstein's—gas and water all included at £36 a year, but no bedroom. I suppose I could make one inside. Next door there is a smaller studio which is, even so, at least twice as big as Fraser's used to be, at £26 a year, and probably I ought to take that and hire a room at 3s. a week, but I am awfully attracted by the big one, which has a furnace to do plaster moulds. I went to the Wilshires' again yesterday and met two charming people there, an actor and his wife—very sound ideas about Art. They have been in England for 9 years and now that they have the chance they are clearing out, they detest it so much. They are Scotch, and they are going to America, where they say the people are just as stupid, but there is more freedom. I am writing you a long letter, kisses,

Pik.

CHAPTER IX
STUDIO LIFE

AT CHRISTMAS Henri went to Dodford again, but he and Sophie did not recapture the joy which they had found the time before. Sophie was feeling ill during these few days, and Pik caught a dreadful cold. It rained all the time, and they sat together in a room without talking. The landlady, it seems, hurried all the farm-hands to bed so that Pik and Zosik might be left undisturbed, and Zosik said she believed the landlady suspected they were not brother and sister, and if not, it was a typical example of English purity—ready even to encourage incest so long as it did not become obvious.

Pik stayed with her for four days, irritable and contrary all the time, and then, just before he left, told her that he was fonder of her than he had ever been before; he implored her to come and live with him in London. He said platonic love could not last for ever—that she had made excuses from month to month, from year to year, and with all this waiting his passion had died down—and then he hurried away to catch his train. Zosik was left very much disturbed, and Pik's letters only added to her worries. He complained much of feeling ill, he bled a great deal at the nose, didn't take regular meals, and suffered from the cold.

With the help of the Hares, he at last found a studio, and he wrote to Sophie:

The studio is a marvellous place, and I feel as if I had been lifted from Hell into Heaven, I am filled with inspiration, and burn with the holy and sacred fire of creation. What infinite peace after the hellish din of Redburn Street!

Ideas keep rushing to my head in torrents—my mind is filled with a thousand plans for different statues, I'm in the midst of three, and have just finished one of them, a wrestler, which I think is very good. I'm also doing sketches for a dozen others. God, it's good to have a studio! It's disgusting that so fine a hole should remain empty while I am at this filthy 'business'. Zosik could be quiet here, and would write better than while stowed away in the country. . . .

A little later he wrote to Dr. Uhlemayr:

454a Fulham Road, Studio 5
6th January 1913

On the advice of some friends and patrons, English *mécènes* without generosity, I have taken this studio in the hope that it will bring me more work. Anyhow, I can work better here than in ordinary rooms—though what I really want to do is to sculpt a large statue in hard stone, and for that I must first get a commission. All this year I have been reduced to doing little statues in plaster and bronze, and portraits, which haven't in the least satisfied my desires or my ability.

The struggle for life is hard here, worse than elsewhere, because all these wretched people are without sensibility, without heart, attracted only by what is eccentric and odiously pretty. To get anywhere one must either wait for ages or prostitute one's art. The only advantage is that art fetches a higher price here than elsewhere, but against that food and lodgings are very dear. I would willingly go elsewhere, but where? I can't go back to France, for last October I deserted their Army, slaughterers of the Arabs, and if I return it is

I whom they will slaughter. In Belgium there is nothing doing. Germany swarms with artists, and I'm not sure that the stupid law would leave me alone. It's better to persevere here, for in another three years I shall be a British subject and definitely free; after that we will see, perhaps I could go to Munich, Berlin or Vienna, it's my greatest desire, and when I have reached my full vigour, at 40 or so, I shall set up in France. Philosophically, if I forget my surroundings, I enjoy life and I feel that I am gaining an enormous experience, and in matters of art a very delicate sensibility. Life normally is so lovely, although filled with grave doubts; an artist always suffers, mostly because of the enslaved people who surround him, bleating like a lot of sheep. I still work uncongenially during the daytime at tapestries and calicoes, silks and carpets, but there it is—we must have bread, and in good times to come these will only be happy memories. . . .

One day at a friend's he met a girl with a demon-like expression, who, when he was alone with her in the studio, looked at him with wicked eyes, and complained that the old days of Bacchanalian debauch were over. Pik was again suffering from pains in his head, and in telling Sophie of this incident, he said that he had asked the girl to bring some of her friends to his studio, where they would indulge in some of the 'exercise' she seemed to want—it would do him good, 'and the old Sisik, who has so often recommended this to her Pik, will surely not mind'.

To Sophie's surprise, although she had formerly persuaded herself to the contrary, she found that now she did mind—she was terrified of Pik's getting into the hands of some girl who would tarnish his innocent nature. She gave greater consideration to all that Pik had said to her, and for the first time she began to feel, mingled with her fondness for him, the magnetism of a physical affection. Pik said that his studio would make a charming home, that it had a small kitchen, and everything of the utmost convenience. Sophie decided to join him, and in February 1913 arrived in London.

The first blow which met Miss Brzeska on her arrival was Pik's telling her they could only sleep in the studio for a day or two, since the solicitors had said it was only to be used as a studio and not as a domicile. They would have to find a room somewhere for Zosik, and Pik could sleep in the studio on a camp bed which he would turn into a chair by day. Pik had promised before she came to clean the place, so as to receive her regally; but there had been other things to do, and when she arrived the studio was in the utmost dilapidation. There was a pool of water on the floor.

'Oh,' said Pik, 'that's nothing, the roof fell in two days ago and the rain came in, but they have repaired it now—don't let us worry about such things, let's have supper. I'll run and get a bottle of wine—eh! Sisik, darling, and then we will have a little love and then to bed.'

Sophie describes the situation: 'I had to wash all the plates and forks before we could start supper, everything was covered with indescribable filth—the Underground trains which passed just outside the window made a row enough to split my head in two, the draughts on all sides were as if we were on a lighthouse in the open sea, soot from the stove suffocated my nose and throat, and the general untidiness threw me into a nervous exhaustion.'

All night long in this strange room the light from a street lamp shone through its high window, and an old torn blind flapped and gesticulated in the gusts of wind which entered through a broken pane.

For the next fortnight Sophie lay ill with influenza. When she was better, she looked for a room and found what, at night, seemed to be a dream of quietness. She took it, only to find next day that she was surrounded with noises and, what was more, the landlord proved to be a milkman who, at 4 a.m. each day, was up and rattling his pails just outside her room.

She tried again to get a post as a governess, but she was always turned down, which is no wonder, since the demands were for a 'strong, young, cheerful, domesticated woman'.

Miss Brzeska had gold fillings in her teeth, and when she went to see friends or people she wished to impress with her importance, she would smile in order to show the gold; but when speaking to prospective landladies, she took great care to keep her mouth closed as much as possible, so that they should not suspect a millionairess, and raise their prices.

Henri Gaudier was very happy during these months, never daunted in his enthusiasm, always expecting a regular flood of orders which would be sure to burst upon them from one day to another. He calculated only in hundreds. They would take a magnificent flat and have a house in the country, spend the summer in Switzerland and the winter in Florence, London, etc.

These air-blown castles were perhaps due to the influence of Frank Harris, who had returned from America and was seeing a good deal of Gaudier. He must have found Gaudier's aliveness a great help, as also his sure judgement on quality. Gaudier, on his side, gained impetus from the financially larger life of Frank Harris. Harris came several times to sit, and at one of the sittings Zosik met him. They seem to have got on rather well at this first meeting, and she and Pik were invited to dinner on the following Tuesday. Zosik had many misgivings—she hadn't unpacked her clothes, she had nothing suitable to wear, and for three nights she had hardly slept. Then Pik came home to get ready, and somehow before they could stop it they found themselves angrily bickering. In the end, Pik said:

'Zosik, don't be angry—see, we've again said dreadful things to each other, things we don't at all mean.'

She protested that she was now too tired to go out, but he persuaded her. She dressed in some strange, high-necked, tight-waisted red blouse with silver trimmings, and Pik was shocked, asking why she had got herself up like a landlady. There were then more words, which concluded by Pik's not minding what she wore, but Sophie said she wasn't going to sit opposite him and feel his critical eye upon her all the evening, to avoid which she dragged out of the bottom of her box a collar of old lace which had belonged to some Polish ancestress.

They arrived at the Harrises punctual to the minute, but Frank Harris was busy, and they waited an hour. They occupied themselves by studying the things in the drawing-room. There was a

MR. FRANK HARRIS

statue of two lovers by Rodin which Mrs. Harris, according to Pik, was always hiding behind vases. Pik pulled it out into the middle of the mantelpiece, and Zosik said that if Mrs. Harris moved it back she would tell her what she thought about it. At last came what Zosik calls the 'Triumphal Entry', Mrs. Harris on her husband's arm. The opening of dinner is amusing as Miss Brzeska described it.

' "What do you drink at dinner?" asked Mrs. Harris, who spoke to me with the utmost sweetness, never separating herself from her smile all the evening.

' "Well, really, I shouldn't drink at all, because of the state of my nerves."

' "Just make an exception for this evening," threw in Pik, who was also smiling. The smile of a lovely and gracious lady is contagious, so we were all smiling as if some beatitude had fallen upon us from on high.'

They had champagne, it seems, and a very nice dinner, and everyone was in excellent form. Afterwards, they had great discussions about books, and Zosik said that she couldn't abide Balzac; that five times she had tried to read him but could never get to the end; that he was overdone and long-winded. Harris rose in his defence, and so the hours passed, until finally he suggested to his wife that it was time she went to bed. Pik on these occasions would never go, and it always ended by their being shown the door and, what is more, having to walk home, since the last bus had gone.

At the end of a long, revolutionary political letter to Dr. Uhlemayr, Gaudier refers to the people he is meeting:

12th March 1913

I've lately met people who have a little more influence than those I've known before, and I'm to be introduced into the best circles of English *mécènes* (you can imagine their mugs), the Lord —— (who protects Ibsen because he is dead and Rodin because he no longer needs it), Lord ——, Lord ——, etc., who wish to buy things cheaply, keep them for a few years and probably sell at a large price —anyhow, I have no illusions—Illusion is a winged girl, but the English fog is so heavy that she can scarcely shake her feathers. I am in the midst of a portrait of a writer called Frank Harris, and he promises that in a few months everything will be going well with me. It's about time, for I am a little discouraged, I have suffered frightfully from all manner of miseries since I left Germany, doing all kinds of jobs, but if in the end I can give myself up entirely to my art I shall be the happiest man in London. . . .

Then Frank Harris went away, and things seemed to stand still —Pik dropped out of London life, and no one came near the studio. About August he was much disappointed at hearing that Harris would only have his bust done in plaster, but revived with the idea that he was an Artist, and Harris just a middle-class nonentity who would be too greatly honoured if Gaudier-Brzeska were to worry over his stupidities.

At this period the Brzeskas' friendship with Brodzky made an amusing interlude in their lives. Brodzky was a great relief to them, for he did not mind their joking at his expense, yet he irritated as well as amused them. He gave them a sense of solidity, for he seemed a person so much less rooted than they were that they could offer him their protection; and they were able entirely to follow their own bent, since he was too indolent to interfere.

Gaudier started a portrait of Brodzky for the Albert Hall Exhibition, and he suggested to Sisik that she should come to the studio to meet him. 'He is a Pole, born in Australia and brought up in America, not very clever, but a pleasant enough, amusing fellow', Pik explained.

'I suppose, since he's a Jew, he's very materialistic,' said Zosik.

'Yes, frightfully. I tell you that the first time he came to see me, I was in the midst of arranging my drawings, and there were quantities spread all over the floor; he had hardly crossed the doorstep before he cried out, without even stopping to wish me good day: "Aou! What are you doing? Walking on your drawings? There are mines of gold in them. How wasteful you are!"'

Sophie found Brodzky lying at full length in the basket chair; he seemed half asleep, and could not bring himself to get up to welcome her. She was reminded of a big serpent warming itself in the sun. Pik, in his presence, seemed to be thrown into a vivid energy. He kept darting about, and every now and then would rush at Brodzky, leap on him, wrestle with him, or thump him about. Brodzky would defend himself as best he could, calling him 'Savage' and 'Redskin'. It pleased Pik to be thought an elemental, and Brodzky and Zosik would call him 'Savage Messiah', a name deliciously apropos.

Once when Pik came back to the studio, Brodzky leapt up, seized his hat and hung it on a peg to save it from the spirit of destruction which consumed the master of the house. He might easily treat it as he had treated his own, new a month before and now a crumpled piece of felt. Pik always looked like a scavenger who had spent the night on the floor of a pub—he thought that a man could not be clean and at the same time an artist.

Mr. Pound says that Gaudier once burst out about Epstein: 'Work! Work? I know he does not work. His hands are clean!'

It was arranged that Brodzky should paint a portrait of Sophie, for which Pik bought a canvas. It went on for weeks, and got worse at every sitting, until Pik was horrified, and called it a regular 'academy' piece. Pik's friendship for Brodzky was often strained, and Brodzky's attitude towards this portrait was more than usually trying to him. Although they were very friendly, when they met there was always a slight antagonism on Gaudier's side. On one occasion, before a dinner party to which they had invited Cournos, Pik said:

'I hope that this time you haven't asked Brodzky.'

Zosik had, and Pik swore that he would go to the Museum and stay there until eleven o'clock in the evening. Zosik had thought that Pik was fond of Brodzky, but Pik said:

'Because I fool about with him, it does not mean that I love him. He is stupid and materialistic, and has no talent at all.'

Pik stayed all the same, for his outbursts did not mean much, and Sophie prepared a nice meal of hors-d'œuvres, meat, vegetables, fruit, and biscuits, with a good French wine to go with it. But all was spoilt, for Pik was insufferable: gobbled his food and behaved like a bear, chipped in whenever Zosik wanted to speak, and contradicted her from beginning to end; to have any say at all, she had to raise her voice to a scream, which frightened Cournos. Brodzky, according to Miss Brzeska, spoke little at dinner, since he was too much occupied with eating, though, from time to time, he encour⁄aged Pik in his savage explosions. At eleven he left, and Cournos soon after, evidently with the fear that Pik and Zosik might come to blows in front of him.

Gaudier admired Brodzky's drawings, but used to tell him that he would never know anything about painting, and that he had really better give it up.

There was great excitement over Brodzky's expected millions from America,[1] and Zosik and Pik were delighted that he took the prospect of riches so calmly. They had a big 'beano' in Pik's studio to celebrate Brodzky's good fortune, and they became very merry: Sophie had not laughed so much for many a year.

Frank Harris now returned from America, and though Pik had not heard from him while he was away, he at once expected great things from his return. They did not see much of each other, but when they met, Frank Harris was full of promises, and said he would buy the marble dog for five pounds, or the high relief in red and yellow. One of Harris's projects was that Henri should go with him to China. He was extremely friendly and full of ideas, on the strength of which Gaudier gave up his work in the City. This was, of course, a daring move, and for the first two months no one bought anything from him. Mrs. Hare tells me that in order to earn a little ready money, Henri obtained work as a porter at Covent Garden, getting up in the small hours and carrying baskets of fruit and flowers; he

[1] A newspaper report that Brodzky had inherited millions.

was not very strong, and found this work a great strain, but it brought in a little money, and gave him his day in which to work at his sculpture.

Zosik's nerves were giving her much trouble, and she told Pik never to accept any invitations for her, but always say that she had a cold.

'Shut up,' said Pik, 'I am a sculptor, not a bloody diplomatist,' and when Zosik called him an egotist, he said: 'I love myself better than anyone else—everyone loves himself best.'

One evening he called on the Harrises after dinner, and Mrs. Harris took him to the dining-room to give him a meal, but although he was hungry, he said he had already eaten. They all thought he was looking very ill, thin, like a ghost, and the Simpsons, who were there, tried to persuade him to go to the seaside. Harris said that as soon as he had his paper he would give him the job of caricaturist, and that he expected this would be in a fortnight; but so many fortnights had gone by, with the same project in view, that Pik had begun to lose heart.

In September Gaudier had had his studio for nine months, but hadn't managed to earn the forty pounds which would pay the rent.

One day they had arranged to go to Richmond with Brodzky for a picnic, when Henri received a telegram from Mr. Harris: 'Good news for you will be with you soon after three'. Zosik and Brodzky had to go alone to Richmond, leaving Pik to join them later, for so exciting a telegram must mean at least a fortune which it would never do to miss. When Pik came he whispered into Zosik's ear that it was the French Ambassador, which threw Zosik into a tremendous flutter of excitement. She thought that France had at last realized what a splendid artist they had in Gaudier; the Ambassador himself had come to congratulate Henri, and tell him that he would be able to go back to Paris without fear of military service.

After half an hour Pik said: 'It wasn't exactly the Ambassador, but his secretary. He says that he will get the Ambassador to sit for me.'

The secretary was Paul Morand; he had been very enthusiastic over Pik's work, and thought that he might help Gaudier to place some of his drawings in France. He suggested that through his father, who was then Director of the Arts Décoratifs in Paris, he would show some of Henri's drawings to Rodin, or perhaps to Maillol. After this first visit he did not come back for so long that Pik and Zosik had given him up, until one day, on going into the studio, Zosik found a young man of about twenty-four, who looked a little like a Japanese, but whom, to her surprise, Pik introduced as Monsieur Morand. He was intending to bring the Ranee of Sarawak to see Pik, and told Miss Brzeska that she was an English lady brought up in India, to which Zosik replied that she was then probably far more intelligent than people brought up in this country. M. Morand passed over this undiplomatic remark in silence, and Zosik, understanding her *faux pas*, bit her tongue for shame.

When M. Morand took the Ranee of Sarawak to Pik's studio, she admired his sculpture, thinking it simple and alive, though she did not buy any. She chose a dozen of his most recent drawings, and when she asked the price, Pik, according to formula, said that he would be delighted if she would accept them as a present. She took them away, and later on sent ten pounds to Gaudier through M. Morand. He tried also to sell for Gaudier 'La Chanteuse Triste', now in the National Gallery, Millbank, but wrote to say that the lady to whom he had hoped to sell it had jumped out of her skin with horror at the sight of such a manifestation of modern art.

Wolmark also encouraged Gaudier a good deal at this time, and they did each other's portraits. Wolmark did two portraits of Henri, one a small one, now in America, representing him naked to the waist, with a statue and a big sculptor's knife; the other large, and conspicuous at the International Exhibition of 1913, where it was first shown as 'The Man with the Green Face'.

Henri at this time was wearing a scarlet Russian tunic and a heavy black cloak and sombrero, and Wolmark shows him thus in the portrait.

One day he arrived at Wolmark's with his face terribly swollen, unable to speak or to eat. After some hours he began painfully to jerk out his story. As he had passed through Soho, a carter had flung some insult at him, and Gaudier had naturally answered back. The carter got down from his cart and went for Gaudier, thinking him only a puny youngster, but Henri, throwing back his cloak, gave him such a blow that he fell unconscious in the street. At this moment some man came out of a public-house behind, and hit Henri on the jaw, dislocating it. Henri had the presence of mind to force his jaw back into its place, and then ran away before he was surrounded by a crowd. 'But before I left, I dug my foot into the carter's chest as a parting gift, and I heard his bones scrunch.' Wolmark says that he will never forget Gaudier, scarcely able to speak, describing in a whisper this last ferocious thrust.

Wolmark introduced Gaudier to several people, and amongst others to Mr. Kohnstamm, who very much liked the Maternity statue, now in the collection of Mr. Eumorfopoulos. His interest seemed to flag when Pik said he wanted forty pounds for the group. Gaudier's erratic pride often prevented his making a little money at a time when he badly needed it. At times he would give a statue away for a song, and at others he would ask what was then a quite exorbitant price.

Mr. Edward Marsh says that when he went to Henri's studio, he never saw any drawings, that at that time he did not even know that Gaudier did drawings, save for two or three slight ones which Gaudier had once sent him in a letter. All that was on view was a series of rather large pieces of sculpture, each costing about fifty pounds, quite a formidable sum in pre-war money.

CHAPTER X
A HOLIDAY

TOWARDS THE end of September 1913, ill-health and the Ranee of Sarawak's unexpected ten pounds decided Pik and Zosik to take a holiday at Littlehampton, and Pik was in a heaven of joy at the prospect, since he hadn't seen the sea for over a year. They made each other endless promises: Zosik not to get excited, and Pik not to force Zosik to run about, since it was better for her to keep quiet. They decided to take only one room, and to use the money saved for some excursion. Pik said he would sleep quietly on one side all night, and never jump about.

Their holiday started badly, for Zosik had indigestion and could eat nothing; she was tired out with packing and anticipation, while Pik, on the other hand, had got it into his head that they would be late for the train; so they rushed like madmen through the streets, to find themselves at the station with two hours to spare. Pik was like that. When he got an idea into his head, were it catching a train or cutting a piece of marble, he could think of nothing else, even though he might feel dead with fatigue. On their arrival at Littlehampton, Pik was so excited that he forgot all his promises and was for rushing Zosik down to the sea without either rest or refreshment.

It was a curious life that these two spent, strangely wrapped up in each other, and yet, because of the hardness of their lives, constantly angry with each other. Their arrival at Littlehampton was typical. They had been up since early morning, and it was mid-afternoon, they had had nothing to eat, and were naturally tired.

Zosik: 'Don't be so rough—you're just a hooligan, without any sense of decency.'

Pik: 'And as for you, you're nothing but a stupid old woman,

229

full of imaginary illnesses—you think of nothing but your nerves and your stomach and the devil knows what.'

Zosik: 'Oh! You disgusting egoist—you know quite well that it is now three o'clock and that I've not been able to eat anything since yesterday, and you won't even take me somewhere to have a little hot milk.'

Pik: 'Hot milk! What crass stupidity! Let's get down on the beach and see the sea.'

Zosik: 'That's all very fine for you, since you're hungry, and have a basketful of provisions that I can't touch.'

Then they went and had some milk, and ten minutes later were sitting side by side in the sunshine as happy with each other as two children who are the best of friends.

They left looking for a room until the sun had set, and they then had to drag from place to place, finding everything so expensive that in the end they were forced to accept a dingy room with a bed which was a regular implement of torture and fit to kill a saint. Pik had insisted on paying a week's rent in advance in case they lost their money; which meant that they could not leave, but had to endure the torture of their bed. According to Miss Brzeska, Pik bounded about as if he had St. Vitus's Dance, and each morning they both ached from head to foot with the pain of sleeping on the iron bars of the bed. Each evening as they went to bed it was: 'Three more nights of torture.' 'Only two more nights', etc.

It was hard work to keep Henri interested on this holiday, for almost at once he wished to rush back to town and start cutting stone again. At first he bought a fishing-rod, but after a fishless day and a half he found it a boring occupation. Then Zosik set him to doing embroidery in coloured cottons for a blouse she was making. This was an excellent idea, and Pik was enchanted; he sat at it from early morning until late at night and could scarcely be dragged away. Next day, he was up with the lark and already at his sewing. He kept comparing it with Zosik's: his was the more brilliant; had the better design; he would do lots and lots; it would be a delightful occupation for the evenings when he got back to London. For several days they sat together on the beach working at this blouse, then Pik became restless and life was again a turmoil.

One day they decided to go for the day to Arundel Park. As usual, the excitement of the project upset Sophie, and she could not concentrate on getting ready; she dawdled about and fussed with one thing and another, while Pik waited, impatient to be gone. At last he could stand it no longer and started off alone. Zosik followed him, feeling hurt and angry that he had not waited for her. When she caught him up, Pik told her that she would never make an artist, since she was so much concerned with all her little affairs —so much on her high horse over absurd futilities; and for the hundredth time they found themselves saying the most dreadful things to each other. Pik, in a moment of fury, flung down the provisions he was carrying, and apples and sandwiches were spread in the dust, while he strode on ahead. He looked back, to see Zosik on her knees, picking everything up, but he didn't stop, and she toiled after him with the bags of food. One of the bags broke, the apples fell into a ditch and Zosik had great difficulty in getting at them. Henri saw her in this predicament and rushed to help her.

'Zosik, darling, don't let us quarrel; we're only tired and hungry; let's be happy! We're a couple of queer fish—but it's quite natural—artists can't have the same nature as common bourgeois folk. We are capricious and proud and it makes things harder—don't you think so, Sisik?'

Very soon they were sitting in the park, transported by the beauty of it all; the lake and the hills with woods spread over their slopes. They took off their shoes and stockings so that the sun might warm them better, and they ate their lunch amongst a flock of peacocks, which took food out of their hands. Later they found a crystal stream and refreshed themselves with its bright cold water. It was one of the happiest days they had ever had, and in the evening, as they left the park, they watched the deer on the hillside.

One big stag was calling deeply and beating the branches of trees and the long grass with his antlers. Zosik was frightened, but Pik told her that it was the setting sun that gave him this longing. They followed him at a distance, and he looked magnificent with his great antlers sweeping the air and his rich colour outlined against the green of the hillside. He went over to a group of does who were feeding with some young stags nearby, and the young stags fled

RED STONE DANCER

before so regal an approach, while the does allowed themselves to be driven, like sheep before a sheep-dog, into a small, wooded enclosure, where the royal stag would make love to them through the night.

Many of Gaudier's best drawings and the two pieces of sculpture by which he is usually known are the result of this vision of deer, and it was with joy in his heart at so pleasant an experience that he returned to London next day, leaving Zosik to stay on for a week or two more.

His first letter came to her a few days later:

454a Fulham Road, No. 5
Sweet little Sosisiko, *8th October 1913*
I don't know where to begin, there are so many things to tell you. First of all, the Jew from Cracow is at Wolmark's—he is really intelligent; he knows all the artists from Cracow, and has very good taste. He is fed up with the English. He thought he was going to find people full of energy, etc., etc. He has never done saying how stupid they are. I went to the Wagner concert with them—the Cracovic and Wolmark. They played all the best parts of *Lohengrin*, *Tannhäuser*, *Tristan* and *Parsifal* and *Götterdämmerung*, and it's an insult to God, the stupidity of this rotten composition is unsurpassed —there is no kind of unity—no agreement, no depth. The melodies are dull, slow and sentimental, with inevitable claps of thunder. I convinced Wolmark that Wagner is neither great, nor even an artist. The other argues that Wagner is good, and as he speaks well, he may be forgiven. Afterwards they took me to a '*café à putains*'.

We cleared out at once and ran into Epstein. He praised Strind-
berg's *Cabaret*. Yesterday I had been with one Jew to see the other
Jew, Epstein; he's doing most extraordinary statues, absolute copies
of Polynesian work with Brancusi-like noses. We stayed there all
the afternoon and then 'Crac' came round here and wanted to buy
my little alabaster Venus for £3. I let him have it because it will go
to Cracow—otherwise he certainly wouldn't have got it so cheap.
He then took me to Wolmark's, where we had dinner, and from
there we went to the Café Royal because we had invited Epstein.
On the way we met Brodzky. We sat with Epstein, his wife, a
French engraver called Norbel, and Augustus John, who looked
as if he would burst. While we were drinking someone called me
and I looked round, to find Marsh, with Mark Gertler—I talked
to him and he invited me to dinner next week. Although Sisik
won't like it, I accepted. On Monday morning I arranged my garret in Bishop's Road, and yesterday I went with Fabrucci to Putney, so it is only to-day that I have been able to see Harris and ——
about the money due to me. Tippets has written for the rent, which
I can't pay him, so that I *must* pick up something from somewhere.
To-morrow is the International, and the day after I have an interview with a big dealer—Duveen—to make some garden ornaments.
Wolmark has got me this and has also one or two other ideas on
foot, so these two days have been very much occupied and I've
been able to do very little work.

Epstein told me that Brancusi is a Rumanian and not an Italian
—to-morrow I'll send you more gossip.

Your devoted Pik.

454a *Fulham Road, Studio* 5
13th October 1913

Thanks awfully for your sweetness—as usual your love becomes clouded over once there's a question of money. Well, if there's any reason for blowing me up for going to that Café it's because I lost hours of sleep, but never did I spend a penny. Wolmark saddled me with the Jew, asked me to look after him, and as he is intelligent I said I would, and he's sufficiently sensitive to see that I found it awkward, so he insisted on paying. As for ———, I've asked him several times before yesterday—but what can I do, he is almost bankrupt. His place no longer exists, for the bailiffs have sold his books —not all, but some of them. I went in last night, as he was going to give me a statement, but as he only wished to part with £1 I said 'No', for I needed at least £3, for which I would come again on Saturday. But what can I do? He hasn't got a farthing. Harris says he has owed him . . .

As for Brodzky, he's been ill and has spent the little money he had; it's hardly my fault if he can't pay me what he owes.

You are angry with me about the little statue, but in this I thought I should be giving you pleasure, since it would go to Poland. It's at this moment that I need money if I've ever needed it, and what will really put you in a fury is that I shan't even be paid for the statue until the end of the month. Rant and scream as much as you like—it makes no impression on me so long as your worry is to do with material things. If you want to stay at Littlehampton I don't want to beg you to come to me—no fear! Your little ways are far too gentle—particularly at this moment! Naturally I haven't paid

Tippets, because I need first to 'get myself good food', according to your instructions. I'm just fed up and don't care what happens—if I break my neck so much the better. Since you tell me to go to the devil, I return so charming a compliment with interest.

Henri Gaudier-Brzeska.

Does it interest you to know that Wolmarca had a boy yesterday morning?

CHAPTER XI
PEOPLE AND EXHIBITIONS

WHILE SOPHIE was left alone at Littlehampton she became very much worried about Pik's inability to look after money, and the way he allowed several people to be his debtors, and did not call upon them for payment. She realized that her own savings were nearly at an end, and Pik had earned practically nothing for so long that it was small wonder she got into a panic over their finances. She had decided not to go back to London, but when she wrote to tell Pik of this, his calm way of taking it made her feel that she was, perhaps, losing her power over him, besides, it seemed to her stupid to be spending twelve shillings for a room in Littlehampton while Pik was paying for rooms and a studio in London. This, taken with the fact that Pik would spend less if she were there than if he were alone, made her decide at a moment's notice to come up to town. She had not time to warn Pik, and he had gone out. His rooms and his studio were locked, and she had no money left in her purse. She ran from one place to the other, hoping to meet him, and finally had to wait up in the landlady's kitchen until Henri's return at 2 a.m., a none too good beginning for their renewed life together.

When Zosik was pessimistic and complained of the hardness of life, Pik would say: 'I cannot complain, if I am earning nothing at the moment, that doesn't matter at all; it is sure to come. I despise people who complain. I have always had good luck because I know how to defend myself. I never have any debts, and am never despondent. Everyone is his own master, and the weak naturally perish because they haven't the strength to fight.'

Just before Miss Brzeska's return from Littlehampton, Gaudier

239

had noticed a girl standing in front of his 'Wrestler'. He spoke to
her, and found her intelligent, not prudish nor hypocritical, and
she agreed to sit for him. The story of this first sitting is striking.
After she had sat for some time, and Henri had done a dozen drawings or so, he said suddenly: 'Now it is your turn', and quick as a
flash, he had taken off all his clothes, seized a large piece of marble,
struck an attitude, and told her to start drawing. Pik was delighted
to have a model, and they were soon great friends. One of the first
things she told Pik was that she had no pretensions to being a pure
woman, and that she had felt very much annoyed with some man
who had lectured her on the beauty of virginity.

Sophie said that she was trying to seduce Pik, but this was not
the case, for their friendship was a Platonic one. Pik answered Sophie's comments with: 'Well, of course, I intend to make love to
her, since my Zosik is no use, and keeps me waiting so long.' Zosik
gave him her blessing, and said that she must be allowed to be behind a screen, and when Pik asked her if this wouldn't make her
jealous, she replied that since she was unable to satisfy his wishes,
she would not be so mean as to hinder his pleasures with others.
'Good Sisik,' said Pik, 'you will always be the favourite, and she
will be the concubine.'

Pik was always very anxious to please his new friend when she
came to his studio, and kept asking Zosik for shillings to buy cakes
for 'ma —— qui est pauvre'. Miss Brzeska acidly suggested that
Miss —— would not be so poor if she did not smoke so much.
After several weeks Pik brought her to see Sophie. Miss Brzeska was
feeling particularly irritated by the noise around her, had stopped

up her ears with cotton-wool, and was sitting right up against the wall, with her back to the room, so as not to see its bare misery, and was singing at the top of her voice. Pik had to call her two or three times before she turned round.

A little after this, ——went to Paris for a few weeks, and came back with sensational tales of how she had danced naked, greatly to the delight of the artists there; how Isadora Duncan had wanted to meet her, and how several theatres had offered to engage her. Also Modigliani had wanted to sleep with her, but she had refused because he drank and had no money. She was going back to Paris in a few days. Pik was charmed, he thought her dashing and brilliant, and admired her unconventionality.

Gaudier and Sophie had many discussions over Rodin, who had at one time been such a God in Pik's life. He considered that his head of Smythies was as good as any Rodin, and that those of Brodzky and Wolmark were probably better, and quite original.

'I am an artist,' he said, 'and nothing but art has any interest for me. So long as I do good sculpture, I don't care how I arrive at it.'

This last remark annoyed Sophie, who said that it did not accord with what he used to think, to which he replied that what he had said yesterday was no precedent for what he might say to-day—that he was only twenty-two, and that she must realize that he was developing. He brought her some of his drawings, men with Brancusi-like heads, but he denied that they were derived from Brancusi, and said that they were a direct evolution from his old work, and that his sculpture had by now become quite abstract. This made Zosik fear that he would sell nothing; but Pik's reply was that he wasn't a dealer, but an artist. To Major Smythies, who protested against Gaudier's abstract work, he wrote:

'We are of different opinion about naturalism, I treat it as a hollow accomplishment: the artificial is full of metaphysical meaning, which is all-important.'

Nina Hamnett, who was one of Gaudier's friends at this time, obtained for him some sculpture lessons in Hampstead at two and sixpence an hour, and she also introduced him to Roger Fry. Fry had said that he would like to meet him, and that he could, perhaps, give him some work at the Omega Shop.

'What is this Fry?' asked Miss Brzeska.

'A very advanced painter, who has started the Omega workshop for modern art in decoration, furniture, and other things: a fine man, who has put his capital into giving work to artists, into making their existence easier. He is entirely disinterested, and when I see him to-morrow, I shall show him my most advanced works, which, to tell the truth, are only old-fashioned, neo-impressionist work.'

Fry, it seems, was much pleased with the poster for *Macbeth* and with the alabaster 'Boy', and said that he could sell this latter for twenty pounds. He ordered a special poster, and also a tray, for which Pik might expect a few pounds, though he did not know how much, for, as he put it to Sophie, 'one can't bargain with a splendid fellow like Fry'.

At the Alpine Club Exhibition, organized by Fry, Gaudier exhibited five works; his red stone 'Dancer'[1] he likened to Ezra Pound's poems, and when Zosik asked for an explanation of this, he said:

[1] National Gallery, Millbank, London.

'Well, if you can't understand it, I can't explain it to you. I just feel it, and there's an end of it.'

He felt that his work was not simple enough, and his search for greater simplicity often resulted in an added complexity of form. He exhibited also the Torso, now in the Victoria and Albert Museum: 'a marble statue,' he wrote to Major Smythies, 'of a girl in the natural way, in order to show my accomplishment as a sculptor'.

He thought that Duncan Grant, with his big picture of Adam and Eve, shown at the Alpine Exhibition, was the Phœnix of English painting, and Miss Brzeska suggested that Fry's pictures were thoroughly academic and chocolate-coloured, 'a family trait, since he is a nephew or son of Chocolate Fry'.

Pik sold his 'Fawn', which gave him tremendous pleasure, and later Cournos told him that someone wished to buy two statues of his for fifteen pounds. Pik agreed, but when he heard that this 'someone' was Ezra Pound, 'the abstract poet', his joy knew no bounds.

There was some talk of Mr. Kohnstamm buying 'La Chanteuse Triste', but this must have fallen through, for he purchased an alabaster relief instead. Mr. Sydney Schiff went to visit Gaudier at his studio in Putney, and bought the 'Dancer', which he presented later through Miss Brzeska to the Victoria and Albert Museum.

Mr. Schiff had two bronzes made of this statue, and Gaudier wrote to him:

'I am naturally glad that Mme. Schiff likes the statuette. It is a sincere expression of a certain disposition of my mind, but you must know that it is by no means the simplest nor the last. The consistency in me lies in the design, and the quality of surface—whereas the treatment of the planes tends to overshadow it.'

Mr. Stanley Casson, in his book, *Some Modern Sculptors*, writes:

'In his [Gaudier's] interpretation of movement, he really achieves a new style in modern sculpture. The Dancer is a figure in which movement is detected rather than seen, and detected at a moment when it is neither static nor in motion: when it is potential, and yet not stopped. No sculptor, to my knowledge, has ever depicted a figure thus *descending* out of one movement into another. Rodin's definition of movement as "transition" is here carried out more clearly than he could ever have wished, and more effectively than he could ever have achieved. There is no representation of motion here, only its full and direct expression.'

Gaudier had a profound belief in himself; he would often say: 'It was an honour for So-and-so to be in my company.' He said also: 'You will never make me believe that a man who is strong and healthy minded cannot accomplish his ends. I have always done everything that I wanted to do. So long as I have tools and stone to cut, nothing can worry me, nothing can make me miserable. I have never felt happier than at this moment; you must take happiness where you can find it, it's no good waiting until it comes and offers itself to you.'

This was near the beginning of 1914, and apart from his studio expenses, Pik was only supplying twenty-six shillings a week for their rooms, their food, their clothes; and Zosik had to use her own savings, which by now had dwindled again to about sixty pounds.

Their rooms were very cold: they had only a tiny oil-stove, and Pik suffered from this discomfort. Zosik was able to do less and less of her literary work: she was entirely occupied with mending and cooking and cleaning and being ill, until she came to wonder if she was only destined to be mentioned in the annals of great twentieth-century men as someone who had had an influence on one of their lives.

Gaudier was now great friends with Ezra Pound, and this friendship lasted until Gaudier's death. It was the strongest attachment that he made in England. Mr. Pound describes their first meeting in his book on Gaudier. Henri was enchanted that Pound should have bought two of his works, and in addition to these he was to make him a marble box for five pounds. He was also at work on a large bust of Ezra Pound which he hoped would one day find a place in the Metropolitan Museum, New York.

Miss Brzeska described an evening she and Henri spent with Ezra Pound. As usual, she was very nervous and excited before starting, while Pik added to her worries by pressing her to hurry, and by objecting to all she put on. He did not want her to wear goloshes, and hated her to take an umbrella. 'Quoi! Tu penses à emporter ce sale meuble? Affreuse vieille bonne femme—pourquoi ne pas emporter tes fourchettes ou ta commode?'

He refused to carry her umbrella, saying that he was not a lackey. When the wind blew hard, he took the umbrella from her and closed it angrily, so that she arrived at Pound's tired, wet, and bedraggled.

Pik had these swift ferocities: it was due to their difference of age, their poverty, and their sexual estrangement. Afterwards he would be so sorry, and she too would make resolutions to be much more patient; and then, as she said, 'my nerves got the better of me, and all resolutions went to the winds'.

At the Café Royal, Zosik's excitement led her into talking very loudly, and it is small wonder that Mr. Pound wished to escape from her company. He had been extremely attentive to her all the evening, and on the way home Pik actually offered to carry her umbrella, having seen Pound do so, but this time Sophie kept it to herself.

Gaudier hoped now that Pound would buy the 'Stags', which were to be exhibited at the London Group, and a friend of Pound's ordered two marble charms at ten pounds each. Again Pik felt that life would be full of ease, and he arranged for Zosik to go away for a splendid holiday in France. She badly needed this holiday, for she was very run down and, amongst other things, had a sudden feeling that she was mad, which was a great shock to her. But she had to wait until they received the money and, as usual, the idea proved but a castle in the air.

At the London Group Exhibition, held at the Goupil Gallery, Gaudier was exhibiting, amongst other things, the 'Stags', the 'Dancer', and the 'Maternity Group', which last Konody at the time called 'affectation in stone'. Pik was very much excited about going to this Exhibition, and Miss Brzeska says that when they asked him at the door who he was, his voice trembled as he replied: 'I am Gaudier-Brzeska, who is exhibiting here'.

The London Group closed in March 1914, and Gaudier had

sold nothing. There is a detailed account of his financial position at this moment. From October until the end of March, he had earned forty-seven pounds nineteen shillings, and out of that he had spent twenty-four pounds twelve shillings for materials, tools, studio, and exhibitions, leaving less than four pounds a month for their life together, washing, clothes, food, and rooms. Again Henri found Sophie useful to him, for her slender savings made life possible. The months of May and June were very peaceful, and they often went together to Richmond Park, where they enjoyed the flowers. One day Pik was so much entranced with the beauty of nature, that he said that he would probably return to a naturalistic style in his work.

Henri went home much more often in the evenings, talked and read to Zosik, and did not get angry because the washing was hung out to dry in the room. He praised Zosik's careful economy, which enabled them to continue as independent beings.

CHAPTER XII
THE WAR

WHEN SUMMER came, their hard-won domestic peace was over, for with the heat their rooms became infested by bugs. It was too much, and Zosik broke down entirely, for though each morning they exterminated every bug, by the evening new ones had come. They took other rooms, and Miss Brzeska went again to Little-hampton, where she found a charming landlady, a Spaniard, who was a great comfort to her.

Pik, who now found himself entirely without money, went round to his various friends to ask them to pay their debts, but for one reason or another he could get none of them to pay. He wrote to Sophie: 'Send me ten shillings, —— promised to pay me to-day, but has disappointed me. I have asked him so often. He seems always to have enough for his girls, and for the Café Royal, but as far as I am concerned, I can die of hunger. Since you left, I have only had three pounds, and most of that I have had to spend on things for my work, so for the last four days my cat and I have lived on milk and eggs given me on credit, and it isn't enough; my stomach is already dreadfully upset, and I haven't a halfpenny.'

Zosik sent him some money, and at the same time his friends seem to have paid their debts. Paul Morand came again to see him and suggested that Gaudier should call on the Ranee, whom he had brought before. But Gaudier, however hard up, could never ask people to buy things from him, nor would he visit people in the hope that they would buy.

Then Zosik came back to London with a plan. They had a friend, a French girl, whose sister was coming to London. She suggested that they should take larger rooms in a quieter place, buying the necessary furniture with her last pounds, and taking these two girls as boarders. The three of them would do the house-work in turn, thereby giving each of them a fortnight's freedom for her work. Pik was enthusiastic, rooms were found, the money was spent and all nicely arranged, when, a week later, war was declared, and the girls rushed back to France, leaving Miss Brzeska with her rooms and her surplus furniture. This is a typical example of the ill luck which had beset her all through her life, and it is small wonder that she believed that the Furies were against her.

The outbreak of war was a great shock to them both, and Pik at once wanted to go to the Consul for his passport. For a little while Zosik dissuaded him, saying that the war would soon be over, that it was a full moon,[1] which would surely bring bad luck, that he owed nothing to France, and so on. They had both, at different periods, long before, dreamt that Pik would be killed in a war, and this added greatly to their fears; but after a couple of weeks Pik could stand it no longer, and said: 'One has to die some time; if it is in bed or in the war, what does it matter?' So he got his passport and left for France.

Zosik was in despair—she felt for the first time that she had always been very hard on Pik, that her recriminations had been small-minded, and that every time it had been Pik who had taken the first steps to make up any quarrel. She longed beyond endurance to have him back that she might be really charming to him.

Next day, when she was going to sit in the Park, whom should

---

[1] Miss Brzeska had a half-moon in her family crest, and felt that it was this which had brought her ill luck throughout her life.

she meet but Pik. She thought it was a spirit and ran away, but he called after her: 'Zosik, Zosik, I have come back'. He then told her what had happened.

'When I arrived in France I was told that I was a deserter and that I should get twelve years' imprisonment. They didn't want my kind at the Front. So they whisked me off to a prison, and told me that I should be shot by the sentry outside if I attempted to escape. There was a tiny window in my cell, with a bar across the middle, and as I had one of my chisels with me, I managed after many hours to get the bar loose. I looked out, and saw no sentry; so being small, I succeeded in squeezing out, scaled a wall and ran across many fields. I ran for several hours until I got back to Calais, where I lay concealed until it was dark. I then slipped into the harbour, having persuaded the man at the gate that I had come with baggage that morning. I even made him believe that he remembered my lighting his cigarette for him. I told him that I had been in the town for a bit and that I must get back to England by the night boat —and here I am.'

It all seemed fantastic and miraculous, and they were so happy to be together again that for some time there were no disagreements. Pik thought that he would not try again to go to the Front, and Zosik remembered how desolate she had felt without him. Pik tried to persuade her to be his lover in a fuller sense, but she said that she was ill and tired, that she would give him her intellectual and spiritual love, and that he must be satisfied with that.

After a while, some dispute arose—Pik found her clothes old-fashioned, her shoes worn out; she was particularly ill at the moment, and forgot her resolutions to be patient. Pik went to live in his studio,[1] while she stayed in her room.

Early one morning in September, he came and knocked at her door; he had come to say good-bye, for he was off to the Front again, having obtained a new and more satisfactory passport. Sophie thought it a trick to get into her room, and would not open to him; after half an hour he went away. She then rushed to her window and called him back as he was half-way down the street. They had a very happy last two days; she did not try again to shake his determination to go, and though all his friends said that it was stupid to go a second time, he said: 'I'm going, I absolutely must; there's no more to be said about it, and nothing else to do'.

Unfortunately, none of his letters to Miss Brzeska from the Front have been preserved; but Mr. Pound, in his book, quotes several written to friends, which throw a very interesting light on his reactions to the war. Four letters, hitherto unpublished, one to Mr. Edward Marsh and three to his home, take him to the end of 1914.

[Copy of letter to Mr. E. Marsh.]

1st October 1914

My dear Eddie,[2]

Here I am face to the foe. I have been at the Front for the last fortnight and have seen both latent and active fighting. By latent I mean staying days in trenches under heavy artillery fire, keeping

---

[1] During this period Gaudier was great friends with T. E. Hulme, who also was killed in the war.

[2] The original of this letter is in English.

ready for any eventuality [such] as a raid or an unforeseen forward movement from the enemy—by active, a nice little night attack that we made last Saturday night upon an entrenched position. We crept through a wood as dark as pitch, fixed bayonets and pushed some 500 yards amid fields until we came to a wood—There we opened fire and in a bound we were along the bank of the road where the Prussians stood. We shot at each other some quarter of an hour at a distance of 12–15 yards and the work was deadly. I brought down two great giants who stood against a burning heap of straw—my corporal accounted for four more, and so on all along the line. They had as much luck, unhappily, for out of 12 of my squad that went we found ourselves five after the engagement, and on the whole company the toll was heavy. . . .

Confident in ultimate success, I remain,

Yours ever,

Henri Gaudier.

Au front: par Le Hâvre (French army at the front)

4th October 1914

Dear Parents,

I've been in the trenches for 15 days, and in spite of a most bloody night attack and four days' exposure to a regular hail of shells I've managed to reach the age of 23 to-day.

I am now resting with my battalion in a little fortress of which the only rottenness is having to sleep in the cellars. This sleeping out all over the place and in any weather has given us all diarrhœa, and the drugs which they give us aren't much use. Apart from this

everything is all right—naturally life is very monotonous and animal, one hasn't the energy nor the desire to think, and one is too
disturbed to concentrate anyhow. I kiss you all tenderly and hope
to see you soon.

                                                        Henri.

Dear Father,   *9th November 1914*
    Thank you for your card—I have already told you that I am in
front of the town sacred to the Kings, that should explain and I
cannot say more. The Cathedral burnt in front of my eyes, now
you will understand. I had a good laugh last night. My Lieutenant
sent me to repair some barbed wire between our trenches and the
enemy's. I went through the mist with two chaps. I was lying on
my back under the obstacle when pop, out came the moon, then
the Boches saw me and well! pan pan pan! Then they broke the
entanglement over my head, which fell on me and trapped me.
I took my butcher's knife and hacked at it a dozen times. My
companions had got back to the trench and said I was dead, so the
Lieutenant, in order to avenge me, ordered a volley of fire, the Boches
did the same and the artillery joined in, with me bang in the middle.
I got back to my trench, crawling on my stomach, with my roll of
barbed wire and my rifle. The Lieutenant was dumbfounded and
I shall never forget his face. When things had quieted down I went
out again, did my job and got back at 5 a.m.
                    Henri Gaudier   Soldat
                        Iᵉ Section 7ᵉ Cie 129ᵉ de Ligne
                            3ᵉ corps au front par Le Hâvre.

Dear Father, *12th November 1914*

Thank you for your letter of the 6th. The day before yesterday I wrote you a card telling you of my adventure in a barbed wire entanglement. At the time I hadn't noticed it, but I find that I have two wounds, one tear on the right leg made by the wire, and a bullet wound in the right heel. I put some iodine on it when I was in the trench, and yesterday I had it bathed, but it doesn't prevent me from walking as well as before.

Everything was all right in your parcel, nothing was pillaged. You must not send me any more clothes—every week I get some from London and I'm expecting another parcel at this moment. The only thing I want is tobacco at 50 centimes.

I'm not at all bored in the trenches. I am doing some little pieces of sculpture. A few days ago I did a small Maternity statue out of the butt-end of a German rifle, it's magnificent walnut wood and I managed to cut it quite successfully with an ordinary knife. The Captain had asked me to do it to give as a present to someone.[1] I can't tell you the names of the officers, etc.—anyhow, there's no need, you will know later on, and they are most sporting fellows.

Love to you all and thank you for your good wishes.

Henri.

By the New Year Gaudier had been made a corporal, and a few weeks later, a sergeant. A letter which he wrote to Mr. Schiff shows that his energy was as much alive as ever.

[1] Monsieur Ménager (Gaudier's Captain) tells me that Gaudier did three or four small bits of sculpture in the trenches, either from the butts of rifles or in soft stone, using only his penknife. These works were preserved for a little while, and then thrown away to make room for clothing.

26th February 1915

I learnt of Currie's death while in the trenches near Rheims some time in November, I believe, and of course I was not surprised; he had tried once when I was at his place. He was a great painter, and a magnificent fellow; in ordinary times, I should naturally have been more afflicted, but as you may imagine, death is here a daily happening, and one is expecting it every minute. . . .

These last twelve days I have succeeded in making the enemy angry—we were only 50 yards off, and I got a bugle to blow false alarms, then I insulted them, and went out of the trench with a French newspaper. A German came out to meet me, and gave me the *Hanover Zeitung* and *Kieler Nachrichten* in exchange; it was very amusing, but I profited by the excursion to discover an outpost, on which I directed our artillery. At 3 p.m. four big shells fell on it, and the twenty chaps in it went up to heaven. I also brought one down with my rifle the next day. . . .

In April Mr. Schiff sent him some money, and he replied: 'I can only thank you for the note, and consider it as an advance on account of work you want me to do for you.'

This is, I believe, the only instance of his having accepted any money by way of a gift, and even here, in the emotional climax of war, there is no question of not repaying its full value. He sent ten shillings to Zosik, and told her that life at the Front was curing him of many faults. His last letter to Mrs. Bevan arranges for news of his death, should it occur, to be given to Sophie: 'As I may fall, I should be grateful if you would ask for news of me from Capitaine

Ménager, Commandant, 7ᵉ Compagnie, 129ᵉ Infant., 3ᵉ Corps, to convey it to my sister, but only if I have been at least six weeks without sending any news.'

Monsieur Ménager writes of Gaudier in a letter dated 9th March 1929:

Nous admirions tous Gaudier, non seulement pour sa bravoure, qui était légendaire, mais aussi et surtout pour sa vive intelligence et la haute idée qu'il avait de ses devoirs. . . . A ma compagnie il était aimé de tous, et je le tenais en particulière estime car à cette époque de guerre de tranchées j'étais certain que—grâce à l'exemple qu'il donnerait à ses camarades—là où était Gaudier les Boches ne passeraient pas.

In the meantime, Miss Brzeska went away to teach at a girls' school. The food was miserable, and the noise, to her, appalling, so that after a few months she had to leave. She found a small attic in the neighbourhood for very little money, and six times a week she went to teach French to the children of Lady G., at a house five miles away. For this she received six shillings a week; it was a two hours' walk each way, and she had to leave at eight o'clock in the morning and walk all through the mud of the country lanes. Lady G., she said, was very kind to her, and spoke to her sympathetically on her arrival.

Miss Brzeska was back in London when she heard of Henri's death in June 1915.[1] He had written to her saying that he longed to

[1] Henri Gaudier was killed at about one o'clock in the afternoon of June 5th, 1915, during the attack on Neuville St. Vaast.

come back, and that when he did, he wanted her to be his wife. In the meantime, she had been feeling terribly desolate, and had sent him a letter, which crossed his, blaming him for her life in England, and demanding that he should come back and take her away. After hearing from him she spent some time thinking of his proposition, and finally replied most sympathetically, but did not post it at once, adding here and there new thoughts and new hopes for their future happiness together.

Before she was ready to post this letter, she received the information that Henri had been killed. She felt that her first complaining letter had perhaps driven him into danger, and the torture resulting from this thought is a constantly recurring theme in the closely-written diary which she kept for the next seven years.

Many people will remember Miss Brzeska in the streets of London, a strange, gaunt woman with short hair, no hat, and shoes cut into the form of sandals. She felt that the world was against her, and never for an instant did she forget the tragic loss of her 'little son'. He became for her the whole of her life, but a life consumed by remorse, in that she had not been to him a companion more complete, more lively, and more sympathetic.

Henri Gaudier, on the other hand, had regretted nothing, always using his energy to the full and feeling sure of ultimate success.

Date Due

THE COMPLETE ILLUSTRATED HISTORY OF
KNIGHTS&
CRUSADES

A vivid account of the life and times of the medieval knight, an
examination of the code of chivalry, and a detailed history of the crusades

CHARLES PHILLIPS
CONSULTANT: DR. CRAIG TAYLOR

HERMES
HOUSE

© 2013 by Anness Publishing Ltd

Illustrations © 2013 by Anness Publishing Ltd

This 2013 edition is published for Barnes & Noble, Inc.
by Anness Publishing Ltd

Publisher: Joanna Lorenz

Editorial Director: Helen Sudell

Executive Editor: Joanne Rippin

Designer: Nigel Partridge

Artworks: Simon Smith

Production Controller: Wendy Lawson

ISBN 978-1-4351-4861-1

Manufactured in China.

2 4 6 8 10 9 7 5 3 1

NOTE

Although the information in this book is believed to be accurate
and true at the time of going to press, neither the authors nor the
copyright holder can accept any legal responsibility or liability for
any errors or omissions that may have been made.

CONTENTS

(continued overleaf)

INTRODUCTION

They bear weapons suitable for war, they have the cross of Christ on their right shoulder or between their shoulders, and with a unified voice they give issue to the cry, "God wills it! God wills it! God wills it!" This was the description – according to an anonymous chronicle of the First Crusade, the *Gesta Francorum* ('Deeds of the Franks') of *c*.1100 – given to the Norman lord Bohemond of Taranto when he asked for information about the army marching across Europe in 1096, bound for the Holy Land. The army had arisen in response to a call from Pope Urban II, in November 1095, for the fighting men of Europe to hurry to the aid of Christians in the East, who were being persecuted by Muslim Seljuk Turks, and to liberate the sacred places of Jerusalem. Bohemond was inspired to follow them. Pope Urban's sermon at Clermont was one of the most powerful and influential in history. Its depiction of the humiliation of Christians by Turks and the

▼ *Fighting in the name and under the cross of Christ. Godfrey of Bouillon was the first ruler of the Latin Kingdom of Jerusalem.*

▲ *The Third Crusade (1189–92) achieved the Muslim surrender of Acre to King Philip II of France and Richard the Lionheart.*

Muslim possession of Jerusalem – represented as the taking 'into slavery of the Holy City of Christ' – inspired an outpouring of religious anger and energy sufficient to mobilize Christians in their thousands to leave their homes and march across continents risking all for Christ and the Church. Particularly persuasive was Urban's promise that participation made personal salvation almost certain – he said, according to an account of his speech by Robert the Monk: 'Take on this journey for the remission of sins, in confidence of the undying glory of God's kingdom.'

The speech launched the popular movement of pilgrims and soldiers described above – known as the People's Crusade by historians – and a second wave of armies led by leading nobles and minor royalty, called the Princes' Crusade, in which Bohemond of Taranto took part. These two waves of people converged on Constantinople, capital of the Christian Byzantine Empire, where they arrived between August 1096 and May 1097. A little over two years later, in July 1099,

after many gruelling marches, desperate sieges and brutal battles, and reportedly having been helped at Antioch by heavenly armies led by St George, the survivors of these crusader forces succeeded in capturing Jerusalem from Fatimid Muslims amid scenes of deplorable ferocity yet nevertheless in the belief that they were doing God's will. The crusade leaders reported to the pope: 'The Lord … made a gift to us of the city, along with his foes … in the portico of Solomon and in his Temple, our men rode in the blood of the Saracens even up to the knees of their horses.'

TWO CENTURIES, NINE CRUSADES

These events were celebrated as a glorious triumph in Europe and led to the establishment of a Christian Kingdom of Jerusalem in Palestine and Syria that survived in various forms until 1291. They inspired a whole series of crusading expeditions not only to the Holy Land but also to north Africa and within Europe itself.

Traditionally historians identified nine crusades. According to this reckoning, the First Crusade of 1095–99, which ended with the taking of Jerusalem and the establishment of the Kingdom of Jerusalem, was followed by a second (1147–49), called by Pope Eugenius III (ruled 1145–53) in response to the capture by Muslim forces of Christian-held Edessa. Led by King Louis VII of France and Conrad III of Germany, it ended dismally in a humiliating failure to take Damascus.

The Third Crusade (1189–92) was called in 1187 by Pope Gregory VIII (ruled October–December 1187) following the devastating defeat of the army of the Kingdom of Jerusalem by Muslim general Saladin at the Battle of the Horns of Hattin in July 1187 and Saladin's subsequent capture of Jerusalem. The crusade was led by Holy Roman Emperor Frederick I, King Philip II of France and

▲ *In the encounters between Christian crusaders and their Muslim enemies, both sides called on God to support their cause.*

King Richard I Coeur de Lion ('the Lion Hearted') of England. Frederick died en route, Philip and Richard were delayed in Sicily and Cyprus and then quarrelled, and although King Richard performed a number of heroic acts and won a great victory over Saladin in the Battle of Arsuf, the crusade ended in a negotiated settlement without the hoped-for recapture of the city of Jerusalem.

The Fourth Crusade (1202–04) was called by Pope Innocent III (ruled 1198–1216), with the aim of attacking the Holy Land by way of Egypt, but it fell under the control of the city of Venice, which provided the fleet for the crusader army, and diverted to attack the Christian city of Zara and then the Byzantine capital, Constantinople. The Fifth Crusade (1217–21) attacked Egypt and succeeded in capturing the port of Damietta, but then made an unwise attempt to attack Cairo that ended in defeat by the Egyptian sultan al-Kamil, bringing a humiliating end to what had been a promising campaign. In the course of this crusade, the papal legate Pelagius was offered possession of Jerusalem – indeed, the return to the borders of the Latin Kingdom of Jerusalem as

they had stood before the disastrous defeat at the Battle of the Horns of Hattin – but declined on the grounds that the Holy City must be won by the sword and not by negotiation with the infidel.

The Sixth Crusade (1228–29) was led by Holy Roman Emperor Frederick II while he was excommunicated following a quarrel with the pope and it was remarkably successful: through diplomacy rather than military might, he regained posses-

▼ *In November 1095, in the market place of Clermont, Pope Urban II makes the call to arms that results in the First Crusade.*

sion of Jerusalem, Nazareth and Bethlehem. The Seventh Crusade (1248–54) was led by King Louis IX of France in response to the fall of Jerusalem to the Khwarezmian Turks in 1244. Once again attacking Egypt and capturing Damietta, it again ended in failure for the Christians. Louis was captured and ransomed at enormous expense, after which he travelled to Acre in Palestine and remained there for some years.

The Eighth Crusade (1270) was again led by Louis IX. It set out for Syria but diverted to attack Tunis, where Louis died either of bubonic plague or dysentery and where the crusade came to nothing. The Ninth Crusade (1271–72) consisted of a campaign to the Holy Land led by the future King Edward I of England, in the course of which he made a few minor territorial gains – and famously survived an assassination attempt.

OTHER CRUSADES

The labelling of the nine crusades is arbitrary. There were not only a large number of other smaller crusades between those summarized above, but also many other campaigns that were promoted as crusades with the grant of indulgences after 1271 – at least until the Battle of Lepanto in 1571, between the Christian 'Holy League' (of the papal states, Spain, Venice, Genoa, the Duchy of Savoy and the Knights of Malta) and the fleet of the Ottoman empire, if not even later.

Moreover, the nine crusades in the traditional list include: one (the Fourth) that got no farther than Constantinople, two (the Fifth and the Seventh) directed not at the Holy Land but at Egypt, and one (the Eighth) that diverted to Tunisia and ran out of steam there. There were also many other crusades in Europe that do not make it into the traditional list. These were fought in Spain and Portugal against Muslims, in the Baltic region against pagans, in southern France and Bohemia against Christians declared heretics by the Catholic Church, and in Italy against enemies of the papacy.

As a result of these complications, modern historians question the traditional numbering. Some identify the Sixth Crusade (1228–29), the campaign by Holy Roman Emperor Frederick II, on

▼ *The reputation of Richard Coeur de Lion, one of the leaders of the Third Crusade, made much of his ferocity. Stories were told of the crusader king's fondness not only for killing but also for eating Saracens.*

▲ *Louis IX's ships on the Nile battle against the Saracens during the Seventh Crusade.*

which he regained possession of Jerusalem and Bethlehem through diplomacy, as part of the Fifth Crusade (1217–21), the campaign to Egypt under the command of papal legate Pelagius – for Frederick was pledged to join the Fifth Crusade but did not arrive despite the fact that a German army was in Egypt awaiting his command. Some see the Ninth Crusade (1271–72), on which the future King Edward I of England campaigned briefly in the Holy Land, as part of the Eighth Crusade (1270), the all-too-brief campaign during which King Louis IX of France died during the siege of Tunis.

Historians therefore also disagree as to the total number of crusades. In the 18th century some counted eight crusades while some insisted there were just five (the First, Second, Third, Fifth and Seventh). Many modern historians also limit the numbered crusades to just five, but usually number only the first five from the traditional list and then describe the rest by name.

In this book, for reasons of clarity and ease of comparison with other reference sources, we will follow the traditional numbering from the First to Ninth Crusades and refer to other campaigns by

name (usually that of the destination or leader) and date. Minor (unnumbered) crusades to the Holy Land or those aimed at restoring Christian power in the Holy Land are treated in the progression of the main narrative, but the crusades directed against Muslims in the Iberian Peninsula, against pagans and heretic Christians in central and northern Europe and Bohemia and against enemies of the Church in Italy are treated in a separate chapter.

BROTHERS IN ARMS

In the aftermath of the success of the First Crusade, the monastic order of the Knights Hospitaller of St John of Jerusalem was established in Jerusalem. It had responsibility for the defence of the Holy Land and had grown from a hospice (guesthouse) or hospital for pilgrims to Jerusalem. The brotherhood was recognized in 1113 by Pope Paschal II (ruled 1099–1118) as the Hospitallers of St John of Jerusalem. This was followed shortly afterwards by the establishment of the order of the Poor Knights of Christ and the Temple of Solomon – later known as

▲ *The Knights of St John defend the island of Rhodes against Ottoman attack in 1480.*

the Knights Templar, recognized in 1129 at the Council of Troyes and confirmed by Pope Innocent III in 1139. More brotherhoods followed, including the Teutonic Knights and the Knights of St Lazarus.

These monastic military brotherhoods won a reputation for great bravery and ferocity in defence of the Christian settlements in the Kingdom of Jerusalem, where they built and garrisoned many great castles. Later, the Knights Templar were charged with heresy and suppressed by the Catholic Church in the early 14th century, and most of their very considerable assets were passed to the Knights Hospitaller, who went on to win wide acclaim and admiration for their heroics in defending first Rhodes and then Malta against the Ottoman Turks. The warrior brotherhoods were an institution intimately connected with the crusading spirit and unique to the culture of chivalry.

ROMANCE OF CHIVALRY

By the 14th century the events of the First Crusade were a distant, romanticized memory. In this later era kings, princes and gentlemen soldiers looked back on the knights of the 11th century – and the knights' imagined precursors in earlier years – as embodiments of military and even of religious perfection.

In August 1346 Edward Prince of Wales, the recently knighted 15-year-old son of King Edward III of England, covered himself in glory at the Battle of Crécy as he helped the English army to a famous victory over a French force that outnumbered them by three times.

One among as many as 30,000 casualties in the French army was King John of Bohemia, a major figure of 14th-century European chivalry who had insisted on proceeding into the thick of the battle with his men at arms despite the fact that he was almost completely blind. His corpse was found on the battlefield the next day surrounded by the bodies of his men, who

▼ *The Battle of Crécy. According to one account, Prince Edward was forced to his knees in the mêlée and was only saved from capture by Sir Richard Fitzsimon.*

had died defending him and had tied the reins of their bridles to each other so that they would not be driven apart in the mêlée of the conflict.

After the battle, Prince Edward (later known as the 'Black Prince', probably because he fought in black armour) paid tribute to King John, who had been killed fighting the Prince and his men, by adopting John's personal crest of an ostrich feather and his motto *Ich dien* (a short version of German *Ich diene*, 'I serve'). In adapted form this crest and motto remains that of the Prince of Wales to this day. Returning to England in October 1347, after besieging and capturing Calais and negotiating a truce, King Edward and the Black Prince celebrated Christmas at Guildford then held a great series of chivalric tournaments in 1348.

At one tournament, in Windsor, the king founded the Most Noble Order of the Garter, dedicated to the Virgin Mary and St George and conceived as a 'Round Table' of knights in tribute to the mythical chivalric warriors of King Arthur.

The founder members of the Order of the Garter were mostly veterans of Crécy and cherished companions and opponents of King Edward and the Black Prince at chivalric tournaments. One later but celebrated story explaining the origin of the Order's badge (a garter) and motto *Honi soit qui mal y pense* ('Shame come to him who thinks evil of it') was that it arose from an act of gallantry performed by the king when he swept up the garter that had fallen from the leg of his mistress the Countess of Salisbury and put it on his own leg with those words.

This sequence of events, from the Battle of Crécy to the foundation of the Order of the Garter, captures a great deal of the romance of medieval knighthood and encompasses many of the most glamorous aspects of its code of chivalry: triumph in battle for a newly made knight – often called 'winning his spurs'; King John's determination to seek glory as a warrior; the devoted service – even unto death – of his men at arms; the Black Prince's generosity in victory; the siege and capture of a foreign city; jousting in tournaments before admiring ladies of the court; the foundation of an order of knights in celebration of the legends of King Arthur and the knights of the Round Table, but also

▲ *By the reign of Edward III of England (left), the cult of St George (right) as patron of knights was well established. George was originally an Eastern Orthodox saint.*

as a mark of religious devotion to the Virgin Mary and St George; and the gallantry of a knight, in this case King Edward, towards his lady. Yet it presents only one face of medieval chivalry, which

in the course of about 500 years across many countries had many varied aspects.

At one time historians tended to treat the medieval institution of knighthood as if it were unchanging from the time of its development under the Normans in England during the second half of the 11th century, throughout the medieval period. However, it is important to emphasize that knighthood and knights' understanding of chivalry changed over the 250 or so years from the late 11th century to the mid-14th century and again over the next 200 to 250 years from the time of King Edward III of England to the last flowerings of chivalry in the later 16th and early 17th century. One key change was that knighthood became more exclusive: at one time a brotherhood of warriors to which the greatest martial figures could be raised, it became associated with inherited rank, and increasingly limited only to the descendants of knights.

A MOUNTED WARRIOR

In origin the knight was a mounted warrior. The word for knight in French (*chevalier*), Spanish (*caballero*) and

▼ *Edward III made St George the patron of the Order of the Garter.*

German (*ritter*) means in every case 'horse-man'. The knight had a relationship of near-religious intensity with his weapons (principally his lance and sword) and with his horse. In chivalric chansons ('songs') and romances, from which we learn so much of knights' received wisdom about chivalric warfare, King Arthur had his revered sword Excalibur, and Roland (leading knight of the Frankish king Charlemagne) fought with a magnificent weapon named Durandel. The chanson hero Renaud of Montauban had his famous magical horse Bayard, which could grow bigger or smaller to accommodate riders of different sizes, and the Spanish war captain Don Rodrigo Diaz de Vivar ('El Cid') had his extraordinary steed Bavieca, which refused ever to take another rider after Don Rodrigo's death.

However, the knights who rode as 'soldiers of Christ' to the Holy Land on crusade and those who jousted in the lists to win the favour of their lady were more than just mounted warriors. They certainly honoured bravery and courage, and praised prowess in battle (or in the lists at

▲ *The Arthurian knight Sir Galahad was more spiritual aspirant than bloodthirsty warrior. In the Grail cycle of legends, Galahad was praised as innocent and pure.*

▼ *Loyalty and honour often led to death. Knights drew inspiration from Roland, who fought to the end to prevent his sword Durandel falling into the hands of Saracens.*

chivalric tournaments). But they also aspired to a range of qualities such as Christian faith, courtesy, generosity, loyalty and moderation that were connected to a world of social and religious obligations rather than to life in the saddle.

AT YOUR SERVICE

The English word 'knight' is derived from the Anglo-Saxon *cniht*, meaning servant or young man, and service was a key element in the medieval institution of knighthood and the accompanying code of chivalry. Knight service was the name for the land-holding arrangement within the feudal system, under which knights were given the right to hold land in return for serving as a mounted soldier, usually for 40 days a year. The knight provided this obligation of military service to his suzerain (superior within the feudal system) or the king, to whom, initially at least, the land ultimately belonged.

◄ *Sir Lancelot, first knight of Arthur's round table, seen here capturing the castle Dolorous Garde, had all the qualities of the perfect knight, but his adultery with Guinevere was a grave failing.*

kings Charles Martel and Charlemagne. But these Macedonian, Roman or Frankish warriors were not knights in the way of the medieval knights, such as the mid-14th-century English knight Sir John Chandos, renowned for his diplomacy as well as his martial spirit and hailed in the chronicles of Froissart as 'the most courteous knight alive'. Or of 15th–16th century French knight Pierre de Terrail, Seigneur de Bayard, who was known for his spotless honour and carefree manner and was declared *Le chevalier sans peur et sans reproche* ('The fearless and blameless knight'), Or indeed of great knights in the chivalric literature, such as Roland, or the figures of the Arthurian tradition such as Lancelot or Percival.

INSPIRATION TO CHIVALRY

Literary representations of knightly virtue were essential to the development of the institution of knighthood. Great deeds of knights were presented by poets and chroniclers as an inspiration to further great deeds of chivalry. The Spanish law codes *Las Siete Partidas*, promulgated in the mid-13th century by Alfonso 'the Wise' of Castile, declared that 'accounts of brave feats of arms should be declaimed before knights while they ate', to promote deeds of chivalry by generating a desire to outdo great deeds of the past.

Figures such as the 12th-century French poet and writer of romances Chrétien de Troyes, the author of five Arthurian romances and the writer who introduced Sir Lancelot into the cycle, played a key role in formulating prevailing images of knighthood. The most important patrons for Chrétien de Troyes and other poets of the time were lords such as Henry I, Count of Champagne (husband of Marie de Champagne, and thus son-in-law of Henry II of England's

▼ *French knight Bertrand du Guesclin was famous for rising from relatively humble origins to achieve high office.*

As the social and religious institution of knighthood developed, however, knightly service acquired other important aspects: service to Christ by fighting for the Christian faith; service to the weak and vulnerable by enforcing the peace; service to the knight's lady by winning honour either in combat at a tournament or by embarking on a journey of challenges as a 'knight errant'.

CHIVALRIC CODE

The medieval knight's devotion to service, and to the ethical and spiritual aspects of the chivalric code, made him different from a mounted soldier of earlier ages. We shall see that the medieval knights had precursors in the aristocratic elite of the hetairoi (companions) who rode into battle with spear and sword alongside the 4th-century BC Macedonian king and general Alexander the Great; they had forerunners also in the cavalry of the Parthian and Roman empires, and in the mounted warriors of the great Frankish

crusader armies has an undeniable heroic element. A good number of those who participated may have merely professed to be taking the cross for religious reasons while secretly hoping to find land, wealth or simply adventure. But another large contingent of crusaders genuinely committed themselves to crusading for religious reasons, and for these people, taking the cross was an act of self-denial, of committing to a larger cause.

This book celebrates the world of the medieval knight, his golden age but also his decline, and examines the knight as a symbol, a literary figure and a heroic ideal. The archetype of the knight lives on through the continuing popularity of chivalric romances – particularly of the Arthurian tradition – and beyond into the age of adventure movies and computer games. He has survived as an inspirational figure; an embodiment of the noble virtues of bravery, strength of character and simplicity of spirit.

wife Eleanor of Aquitaine), and Philip, Count of Flanders. These powerful figures were not only supporters of the arts, but financers and patrons of the chivalric sport of tourneying.

Chivalric literature and tournaments developed side by side with martial prowess. Inside noble courts, castles and, later, manor houses, knights and their retainers, exhausted after a physically demanding day of jousting in the lists, would settle down in the evening to listen to tales of chivalry. The audience had a taste for tales of arms in various settings, whether the Arthurian court, the Holy Land towns familiar to Crusaders, the classical world of Alexander the Great or Hector of Troy, or the battles against hordes of Saracens (Muslim warriors) fought by Charlemagne and his knights.

▲ *In tournaments knights proved their martial skills before appreciative courtiers. They fought first with lances, then swords.*

▼ *Early artillery cannon were difficult to load and inaccurate but still had a devastating effect against armoured knights.*

CONTINUING RESONANCE

The accounts of the crusades and of the exploits of knights that inspired generations in the Middle Ages retain an appeal today. The extraordinary enterprise of the

PART ONE

THE WORLD OF THE MEDIEVAL KNIGHT

The knight who won glory charging with couched lance on the battlefield or jousting in the lists at tournament had usually undergone a rigorous training, learning courtesy and the ways of war over many years as a page in a noble household and a squire in the service of a knight. As a result his skills as warrior and horseman were beyond question, and he understood his duties. In times of both war and peace, his principal task was to serve: to fight in the company of his feudal lord, to protect the Church by guarding the vulnerable and keeping the peace, and if by good fortune he were tied to the service of a noble lady, to honour her by feats of arms and knight errantry. Knightly service was a matter of great pride: a squire might have to wait many years to be knighted, but from the moment he was made a knight he would be driven by the desire to prove himself worthy of the honour.

▲ *In 1450, during the course of the Hundred Years War, the English surrendered Cherbourg to the French.*

▶ *The siege of the castle of Jean de Derval during the Hundred Years' War (1337–1453) between France and England. On the right of the picture, French knight and national hero Bertrand du Guesclin sits on a white horse; on the left, in front of his tent, Louis d'Anjou receives a royal order.*

TIMELINE OF MEDIEVAL CHIVALRY

732AD In the Battle of Poitiers (Tours), western France, a Frankish army commanded by Charles Martel defeats a Muslim force of the Umayyad Caliphate in Spain, ending a series of Muslim raids northwards into France.

768–814 Charlemagne reigns as King of the Franks. He is later celebrated as a great Christian king and exemplar of medieval chivalric values.

778 A Frankish army commanded by Charlemagne is defeated by Muslim or Basque raiders in a skirmish in the Pass of Roncesvalles in the Pyrenees mountains. Charlemagne's knight Roland is killed.

842 'War games' at Strasbourg to celebrate the alliance of Charlemagne's grandsons, Louis the German and Charles the Bald, are a forerunner of the tournament.

911 Viking chief Rollo or Robert is granted land in western France by King Charles II. His descendants, the Normans, establish an early form of knighthood and a feudal society in Normandy.

955 King Otto I of the Germans uses heavy cavalry to defeat the Magyars in the Battle of Augsburg, a victory celebrated by contemporaries as a great triumph for Christian knights.

1066 The Normans invade England and defeat King Harold at the Battle of Hastings. William, Duke of Normandy, becomes King William I of England and imports a feudal society and the Norman form of knighthood.

1095 Pope Urban II calls the knights of Christendom to liberate Jerusalem from Muslims, launching the First Crusade.

1099 The First Crusade ends in triumph as Christian knights capture Jerusalem. In its aftermath the religious brotherhoods of the Knights Templar and the Knights Hospitaller are founded.

1100–35 From the time of Henry I of England (r.1100–35) onwards, kings use paid soldiers as well as knights performing feudal service. They accept 'scutage'

▲ *A battle scene at the walls of Jerusalem.*

(payment) in lieu of feudal military service, and use the money to pay soldiers.

1128 The Council of Troyes approves the rule of the military brotherhood of the Knights Templar.

1130 Pope Innocent II bans tournaments.

*c.*1130 The earliest of the *chansons de geste*, *The Song of Roland* was written by this date, but may have been in circulation as early as 1050.

1135–39 Geoffrey of Monmouth's *History of the Kings of Britain* establishes Arthurian legend. Arthur was celebrated in Welsh poems as early as the 6th century AD.

1139 Pope Innocent II condemns 'the deadly art, which God hates, of cross-bowmen and archers'.

1140 Roger II, Norman King of Sicily, forbids the knighting of men who are liable to disturb the peace.

1142 The Spanish *Song of My Cid* is written down, but has been current in oral form for decades.

1147 Troops setting out on the Second Crusade stop in Portugal and capture Lisbon from its Muslim rulers.

1147–49 The Second Crusade is a failure.

1152 A German decree excludes peasants from being knights.

*c.*1160 Benoit de Sainte-Maure writes *The Romance of Troy*, establishing a genre, the *romans d'antiquités*, of poems of the feudal age featuring classical warriors.

*c.*1160 The French romance *Floire and Blancheflor* tells of the love between a Saracen knight and a Christian lady.

1170–91 French poet Chrétien de Troyes writes five Arthurian romances. They introduce the character of Sir Perceval and the theme of the quest for the Holy Grail.

1186 Holy Roman Emperor Frederick I bans the sons of peasants and the sons of priests from being knighted.

1189–92 The Third Crusade. Also known as the Kings' Crusade: Kings Richard I of England and Philip II of France and Holy Roman Emperor Frederick I all take part.

1194 King Richard I of England defies the papal ban and introduces a licensing system under which tournaments can be legally held in England.

*c.*1200 Norman poet Alexander of Bernay writes *The Alexander Romance*, about the Macedonian king Alexander the Great.

*c.*1200 The great German epic poem *The Song of the Nibelungs* is written.

*c.*1200–1220 German poet Wolfram von Eschenbach writes his masterpiece *Parzival*, a version of the Sir Perceval story.

1202–04 The Fourth Crusade attacks Zara (Hungary) and Constantinople.

1209–1229 The Catholic Church fights the Albigensian Crusade against the heretical Cathars of Occitania (southern France).

1212 The Children's Crusade. A tiny minority reach the Holy Land.

*c.*1215 German poet Gottfried von Strassburg writes *Tristan und Isolt*, a version of the story of Arthurian knight Tristan and Irish princess Iseult.

1217–21 The Fifth Crusade attacks Muslim Egypt but ends in failure.

1223 A 'Round Table' tournament at which knights act out the parts of King Arthur and his knights is held by John of Ibelin, Lord of Beirut, in Cyprus.

c.1225 French poem *The Order of Chivalry* describes an idealized knighting ceremony.
c.1225 Anglo-Norman poem *The History of William Marshal* celebrates the life of the great English knight (1146–1219).
1228–29 Largely through diplomacy rather than fighting, Holy Roman Emperor Frederick II gains Jerusalem, Nazareth and Bethlehem on the Sixth Crusade.
1235 The Cortes of Catalonia declares that only the sons of knights can be knighted.
1248–54 The Seventh Crusade, led by Louis IX of France, attacks Egypt.
c.1250 The Anglo-Norman *Romance of Richard Coeur de Lion* is written. Just 50 years after his death in 1199 , Richard I of England is a figure of legend.
c.1260 *The Golden Legend* by Jacobus de Voragine popularizes the story of St George and the dragon.
1265 Majorcan poet and philosopher Ramon Llull writes the *Book of the Order of Chivalry*, a handbook for knights.
1270 Louis IX leads the Eighth Crusade against Muslim North Africa. He dies in Tunis and the crusade fails.
1271–72 Prince Edward of England leads the Ninth Crusade but achieves little.
1278 A lavish Arthurian tournament is held at Le Hem, Picardy. It is described in the poem *The Book of Le Hem* by Anglo-Norman trouvère Sarrasin.
1285–1314 King Philip IV of France (r.1285–1314) has a considerable part of his army in paid rather than feudal service.
1303 The Catalan Company founded by Italian adventurer Roger de Flor is among the first groups of mercenary knights.
1312 The *chanson de geste*, *A Peacock's Vows* introduces the 'Nine Worthies' of chivalry. These are: three biblical figures – Joshua, David and Judas Maccabeus; three classical warriors – Hector of Troy, Alexander the Great and Julius Caesar; and three of the Christian era – Arthur, Charlemagne and Godfrey of Bouillon.
1316 The papal ban on tournaments is lifted by Pope John XXII.
1325 King Charles of Hungary establishes the Order of St George.
1326 The city of Florence acquires two cannon for its defences. This is the first known record of artillery guns in Europe.
c.1330 The first plate armour suits appear.
1332 King Alfonso XI of Castile and Leon (r.1312–50) establishes the Order of the Sash brotherhood of knights.
c.1335 The chivalric Order of St Catherine is formed in the Dauphiné, France.
1337–1453 The armies in the Hundred Years War contain many paid soldiers. They are mainly infantry and bowmen rather than knights, although Charles VII of France has 1500 cavalry on fixed pay.
23 Apr 1348 King Edward III of England and his son form the chivalric order of the Most Noble Order of the Garter.
c.1350 French knight Geoffroi de Charny writes the *Book of Chivalry*.
c.1350 Another company of mercenary knights, the Grand Company, is formed.
1351 In the celebrated 'Combat of the Thirty', two teams of thirty knights joust in Brittany.
1352 The French chivalric order, The Order of the Star is formed.
1356 The English defeat the French at Poitiers; in this victory, and at Crécy, knights are deployed to fight on foot.
1364 At the Battle of Auray English knight Sir John Chandos captures the great French knight Bertrand du Guesclin.

▼ *The battle of Crécy, 1346, with Edward the Black Prince in the centre.*

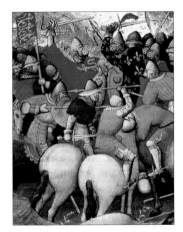

1367 Chandos, and Edward the Black Prince, take du Guesclin captive a second time. He is ransomed for 100,000 francs.
1369–1400 French poet and historian Jean Froissart writes his *Chronicles*, one of the most important sources on chivalry.
1382–87 Provençal writer Honoré Bonet composes *The Tree of Battles*.
1390 In the Jousts of St Inglevert in northern France four French knights occupy the lists for 30 days and fight all-comers.
1399 French knight Marshal de Boucicaut founds the order of the Enterprise of the Green Shield of the White Lady, with 12 members, sworn to protect women.
c.1400 The tilt or central barrier on the tournament lists is in common use from about this date.
1430 Philip the Good, Duke of Burgundy, establishes the chivalric Order of the Golden Fleece.
1434 Duarte, King of Portugal, writes *The Art of Good Horsemanship*, a manual on jousting and managing horses.
c.1450 René I of Naples, known as René d'Anjou, writes *The Book of Tournaments*.
c.1450 The first state infantry regiments are formed in France, part of a general movement at the time towards the establishment of professional standing armies.
1485 Sir Thomas Malory's *Le Morte d'Arthur*, one of the great English sources for the Arthurian tradition, is published.
1495 Matteo Maria Boiardo's *Orlando Innamorato* ('Roland in Love') is published.
1513–18 Italian courtier and diplomat Baldassare Castiglione writes *The Courtier*, a guide to being a gentleman, part of a movement away from chivalry to courtesy.
1515 French knight Pierre de Terrail, also known as the Chevalier de Bayard, knights his king, Francis I, after the Battle of Marignano.
1516 Lodovico Ariosto's *Orlando Furioso* ('Roland Maddened') is published.
1520 Kings Francis I of France and Henry VIII of England host the Field of the Cloth of Gold. Entertainments included jousting and wrestling and feasting.
1559 King Henry II of France sustains a fatal injury while jousting in Paris.

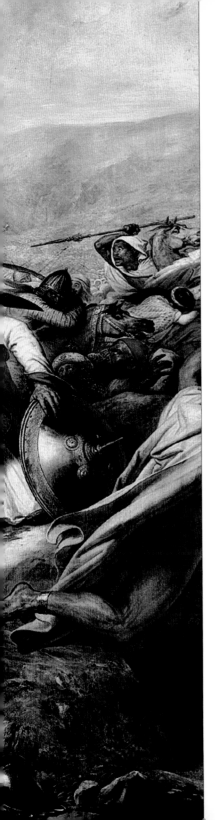

CHAPTER ONE

THE ORIGINS OF KNIGHTHOOD

In 732AD near Tours in what is now western France, the army of the Franks, commanded by the redoubtable Charles Martel, won a famous victory over a great Muslim force commanded by Abdul Rahman Al Ghafiqi. The Muslim army, with its powerful cavalry, was carrying out the largest in a series of northward invasions from the Umayyad Caliphate, an Islamic territory established in what is now Spain after an invasion from north Africa in 711. After this defeat, the Muslims abandoned all hope of invading northern Europe and settled in the Iberian peninsula, where their descendants lived until 1492.

The Battle of Tours has also been celebrated as a key stage in the history of chivalry, because it helped to establish the power of the Franks, whose heavy cavalry would be such an effective military tool in the hands of Charlemagne, King of the Franks 768–814, and because its demonstration of the steadfast bravery of Christian warriors fighting a great Islamic army struck a strong chord with audiences of the crusading era in the 11th century and afterwards.

Yet the Battle of Tours was not won by the Frankish cavalry. Charles Martel ordered his cavalry to dismount and fight alongside his infantry in a square. There, as footsoldiers, they stood firm in the face of repeated charges by the Islamic cavalry – in the words of the Muslim Mozarabic Chronicle 'unmoving as a solid wall, holding fast like a great ice block'.

▲ *Emperor Charlemagne leads his knights into battle in Agolant, Spain.*

◀ *The Battle of Tours in AD732 was a defining moment in European history, and can perhaps be seen as the conception of knighthood.*

THE WORLD BEFORE KNIGHTS

EARLY MOUNTED WARRIORS

Knights of the Middle Ages were not the first warriors to ride into battle on horseback, nor were their predecessors the mounted cavalry of the Franks. The use of horses in war extends back thousands of years, almost into prehistory.

PRECURSORS OF THE CAVALRY

People may have tamed and begun to ride the horse as long ago as 4000BC. We know that as far back as the 2nd millennium BC warriors fought in horse-drawn chariots: the Indo-Iranian nomads who overran the ancient civilization of northern India and Pakistan in c.1500BC fought with war chariots and iron weapons. The use of the war chariot was invented in the homeland of the Indo-Iranian peoples, probably the steppes of Central Asia, and they spread its use as they fanned out in at least two waves of migration from their original

▼ *Between the 9th and 7th centuries BC, the Assyrian cavalry were famed for their speed and strength in combat. They were armed with bows and arrows and spears.*

homeland in c.1500BC and c.800BC. The chariots were adopted in the Assyrian, Babylonian and ancient Egyptian empires.

In the 9th century BC the Assyrian army had a powerful cavalry. The Assyrian mounted warriors fought principally with bows, and arrows, although they also carried shields and swords. They rode without the benefit of saddles, stirrups or spurs. The warriors needed to be highly skilled riders because handling weapons while moving at speed on horseback was an extremely demanding task. They rode in pairs, taking it in turns to hold the reins of both horses, while the other prepared his bow and fired an arrow.

From the 5th to 3rd century BC the Scythians – originally another group of Indo-Iranian steppe nomads – were famed for their prowess as mounted warriors. Like the Assyrians, they rode bareback, fighting with bows and arrows. The Scythians were truly bloodthirsty fighters who beheaded and scalped any warriors they caught, scraped out the skulls and used the hollowed bone as a drinking cup.

▲ *With the help of his cavalry squadrons, the Macedonian king Alexander – known to history as 'the Great' – built a vast empire.*

ALEXANDER'S COMPANIONS

The armies of ancient Greece relied principally on infantry, but cavalry was a key part of the army of Alexander the Great, the 4th-century BC Macedonian king. He achieved extraordinary conquests and would later become a celebrated figure in medieval chivalric romances.

Alexander's cavalry was strikingly similar to the cadre of noble knights who fought alongside their lord in the Middle Ages. The main component of cavalry in Alexander's army was an aristocratic elite called the *hetairoi* (companions), equipped with a long spear for mounted combat and a slashing sword and a straight sword to use if they were forced to dismount. They also wore a helmet and a linen or bronze cuirass (protective jacket).

Alexander rode into battle at the head of his companions when they charged. He would use his infantry to immobilize the enemy and then attack with the companions on the enemy's right flank or from behind, while another lesser group of cavalry attacked on the left.

THE CATAPHRACT

The mounted soldiers of the Parthian empire, at its height in the 1st century BC, struck fear into the hearts of their enemies, including the armies of Ancient Rome. The mounted Parthian warriors rode armoured steeds and were famous for firing arrows over their shoulders as they rode away – a tactic known ever afterwards as the 'Parthian shot'. The Parthians – and their successors, the Seleucid and Sassanid empires of Iran – also used small units of armed cavalry fighting with lances, a formation called *kataphraktos* ('protected by a barrier') in Greek, and which came to be more commonly known as the 'cataphract'.

The Roman army also had cavalry. In the early years of the Roman republic, the cavalry was filled by wealthy landowners, the *equites*, who could afford a horse as well as the necessary weapons, but increasingly the *equites* became an elite social group and the cavalry was filled with foreign fighters from the tribes of the Iberians, Gauls and Numidians (Berber tribesmen from northern Africa). For a long period the Roman cavalry was used mainly for scouting and skirmishing rather than as an arm of the military in battle. However, during the Battle of Carrhae

▲ *The ancient Roman army combined the speed of lance-bearing horsemen with the tenacity of legionary footsoldiers.*

▼ *Mounted warriors in the Persian army sat on large, coloured blankets. They did not wear armour or carry shields.*

(modern Harran, Turkey) in 53BC, where Roman general Crassus was humiliatingly defeated by the Parthian general Spahbod Surena, the Romans saw how effectively large groups of cavalry – especially lance-bearing cataphracts – could be used in war. Thereafter they used more cavalry with better-trained men and began to deploy cataphracts of their own.

GOTHIC HORSEMEN

As the Roman Empire collapsed in the west in the 5th century AD, a number of Germanic tribes prospered in Europe. The Goths and Vandals who sacked Rome used powerful cavalry. A little earlier, at the Battle of Adrianople (modern Edirne, Turkey) in AD378, the Gothic cavalry had imposed a devastating defeat on the Roman army. This battle is traditionally seen as one of the first great triumphs for heavy cavalry and also as the conflict that initiated the final collapse of the Roman Empire in the west.

In the eastern Roman Empire, based on Constantinople (modern Istanbul), heavy cavalry became an important part of the imperial army. Under the command of Flavius Belisarius, 6th-century general to

Byzantine Emperor Justinian I, bands of heavy cavalry were a powerful weapon, fighting with javelins, bows and arrows.

In Europe, too, the use of armed cavalry spread. The Franks, a Germanic tribe who took control of most of the former Roman colony of Gaul and who would serve as highly effective mounted warriors under Charlemagne, initially fought on foot. They learned the use of cavalry from the Goths and many years later would pass it on to the Vikings – whose descendants, the Normans, were such accomplished practitioners of cavalry warfare.

By the time of the Battle of Tours in 732 the Franks were beginning to ride horses to war. The horses they used were little better than carthorses and their principal effectiveness was as beasts of burden rather than fighting animals. Wealthier Franks would ride horses to battle, then dismount to fight. They would be fresher for battle than their enemies, who might have marched for many days to reach the battlefield.

FEUDAL WARRIORS
THE RISE OF THE FRANKS AND THE EARLY FEUDAL SYSTEM

The nobles who fought in the heavy cavalry of Charlemagne, King of the Franks (r. 768–814), served their monarch in times of war in a way that prefigured the bonds of medieval knights to their lord. The Frankish nobles were tied to their lord by an early form of the feudal system, in which they were granted land in return for military service.

THE EMERGENCE OF THE FRANKS

The Franks were a federation of Germanic tribes, first known in history as settlers on the east bank of the Lower Rhine river in the 3rd century AD. They gained former Roman territories in what is now Belgium in the mid-4th century, and some of their leaders became allies of Rome, acting as guards of the empire's frontiers. They were already known as redoubtable warriors, and many of them served as auxiliaries in the Roman army.

▼ *The baptism of King Clovis by Bishop Remigius of Reims in 496 began the Franks' long association with the Catholic Church. The 6th-century historian Gregory of Tours likened Clovis to the biblical King David as father of his people and faith.*

▲ *Pepin III, son of Charles Martel and father of Charlemagne, was crowned by Pope Boniface I in 751. He was the first Frankish king to receive papal blessing.*

During the 5th century, as Rome's hold on its empire in Europe grew weaker, the Franks took control of north-eastern parts of the former Roman colony of Gaul (modern France). Clovis I (r. 481–511), king of the Salian Franks, one branch of the Frankish federation, conquered the rival groups, uniting all the Franks as he built an empire encompassing all of Gaul, save Burgundy and what is now Provence. He founded the Merovingian line of kings (named after his grandfather Merovech) that ruled until the rise of the Carolingian kings of the Franks in 751.

A CATHOLIC PRINCE

Clovis I also began the Franks' long association with the Catholic Church, converting to Catholic Christianity on his marriage to a Catholic Burgundian princess, Clotilde. At this time many other Germanic tribes had converted to the Arian form of Christianity (named after 4th-century theologian, Arius), which held that Christ was a created being rather than an equal presence with God the Father from the beginning of all things. Arianism was generally viewed as a heresy. However, the Franks, following the example of their leader, converted in large numbers from their pagan beliefs to Catholicism. Because

he united the Frankish tribes and the territories of Gaul, Clovis is often celebrated as the founder of France.

Following his death in 511, however, inheritance disputes broke up the Frankish empire into a number of competing kingdoms. The authority of the Merovingian kings withered and then power resided increasingly in the hand of the *Major Palatii* ('Mayor of the Palace') in each kingdom. This position had arisen from one current in the Roman Empire, that of *Major Domus* ('Household Supervisor') appointed by landowners to manage a number of estates.

RENEWED EXPANSION OF THE FRANKS

In the late 7th century, Pépin, Mayor of the Palace in the Frankish kingdom of Austrasia (the north-east part of the former empire), embarked on a campaign

---

COMMENDATION

A vassal swore loyalty in a special ceremony called the 'commendation'. The vassal knelt and put both his hands in those of the lord as he swore the oath of fealty, promising to be loyal to the lord and to provide military or other service, such as farming land. The lord kissed his vassal and pulled him to his feet. He handed him a symbol of the agreement – sometimes a piece of earth. The vassal was granted the lord's protection – an important consideration at a time when central authority was often weak and raiders such as the Vikings were at large. In early times the vassal might become part of the lord's retinue, but by the 9th century the oath required the vassal to provide mounted military service with lance, shield and sword.

▲ *The Frankish empire, initially won on the battlefield, was subsequently fractured by war. Charlemagne's grandson Lothair I was crowned emperor by Pope Paschal I in 823, and expected to inherit, but military defeats forced him to share power with his brothers.*

of territorial expansion. He took control of the neighbouring kingdom of Neustria (the north-west part of the former empire) and defeated the Frisians to the north of Austrasia. On Pépin's death in 714, his illegitimate son, Charles, succeeded as mayor and continued Frankish expansion. His military exploits won him a resounding reputation as Charles Martel ('the Hammer'). It was he who in 732 stopped the northward expansion of Islamic warriors at the bruising Battle of Tours.

VASSALAGE AND EARLY FORMS OF FEUDALISM

The principle in Frankish territories was that every free Frank was required to fight for the king. In addition Frankish kings kept groups of sworn warriors, called *antrustiones*, or vassals. These men swore loyalty to the ruler and promised him military service; in return they could expect to be equipped and fed, and would receive a share of war plunder. This arrangement had grown out of the *comitatus*, a group of sworn warriors serving and fighting for a leader in Germanic tribes. The antrustiones were given leading administrative positions as a *comes* (count) and military positions as a *dux* (duke).

In the 8th century, trade and an economy based on money had broken down in the Frankish territories, and wealth was measured in land. The principal landholders were the king, the Church and Frankish lords, to whom the king delegated control of sections of territory. The kings parcelled out land in the form of a benefice, a grant of full ownership for the lifetime of the recipient.

Under the Frankish kings the granting of benefices came to be associated with vassalage in the form of the fiefdom: the land given to the vassal remained the king's but rights over it were granted to the vassals in return for an oath of lifelong loyalty to the lord and the promise of military service.

The fiefdom tied to sworn military service became the basis of the feudal system that structured early medieval society. The lord–vassal relationship could be found at all social levels: between the king and his leading counts and dukes; between these men and the tenants on their land; and equally further down between the holder of a small fief and the vassals who held sections of his smallholding.

It became customary for the holders of fiefdoms to be able to bequeath them to their sons, and the holding of land in the form of the inheritable fiefdom allowed noble families to gradually build up considerable territories and pass them on after death. Some families became so powerful that they could begin to challenge the authority of the king. The right of holders of fiefdoms to pass the land on to their sons was accepted, but not legal until Charlemagne's grandson, King Charles the Bald, decreed that if a count died when the king was away on campaign, the count's son could inherit.

▼ *Charles Martel was impressed by Muslim horsemen at the Battle of Tours. He set about strengthening the Frankish cavalry, taking Church land and distributing it among his sworn followers to increase the number of landowners wealthy enough to equip themselves as mounted warriors.*

A CHRISTIAN EMPIRE IN EUROPE

THE HOLY ROMAN EMPIRE OF CHARLEMAGNE

Charles Martel's descendants – notably his grandson, Charles I, King of the Franks from AD768 – created a great empire that encompassed much of western and central Europe. They allied themselves with the Christian Church, and accepted the blessing of the pope in Rome on their rule, and through their conquests spread the faith, imposing Christianity on pagan tribes such as the Saxons in what is now northern Germany.

The Frankish armies built their success on the exploits of a highly mobile, well-equipped cavalry. Charles I was known as Charles the Great, in Latin *Carolus Magnus* and therefore as Charlemagne.

THE CAROLINGIAN DYNASTY

Charles Martel had ruled as king in all but name: he was Mayor of the Palace, and nominally subject to the Merovingian kings, descendants of Clovis I. In 751, however, Martel's son Pépin the Short ousted the last of the Merovingians, Childeric III, and became king in his own right. He founded the Carolingian dynasty (named from the Latin form of Charles, *Carolus*, in honour of his father Charles Martel and his son, Charlemagne).

Pépin was anointed twice, first by the Christian missionary St Boniface and then in 754, together with his two sons Carloman and Charlemagne, by Pope Stephen II in a magnificent ceremony at the Saint Denis Basilica in Paris. Pépin defeated the Lombards of northern Italy, and gave territories he had won to the papacy. He also brought Aquitaine (southwestern France) into the Frankish realm. He was succeeded by his sons in 768, but when Carloman died in 771, Charlemagne ruled alone.

CHRISTIAN WARRIORS

One of Charlemagne's first campaigns was to invade once more the kingdom of the Lombards in northern Italy, where

▲ *The papacy supported the rise of Frankish power. Charlemagne seized control in northern Italy in 774 and had his rule blessed by Pope Adrian I in Milan.*

Carloman's widow had fled seeking help. Charlemagne defeated and deposed the Lombard king, Desiderius, and seized the crown for himself in 774. He took possession of his nephews, who had a claim to power via their father, and they subsequently disappeared – presumably disposed of. He appointed Frankish lords to key positions in the Lombards' territory. In the course of this campaign he celebrated Easter in Rome with the pope and reaffirmed the alliance between the Franks and the papacy.

The association of Frankish rule with the Catholic Church was a crucial element in the development of knighthood. The mounted warriors of Charlemagne's army fought in the name of Christ. The Church developed theories under which violence could be seen as holy if committed in a sacred cause.

FIGHTING FOR CHRIST

Charlemagne saw it as a king's duty to spread the Christian faith. He rode into battle with an elite cadre of mounted warriors to fight for the Cross. In 772 he launched an attack on the pagan Saxons, a fiercely independent Germanic group, rivals to the Franks, in an attempt to bring them within his Christian realm. The Saxons proved to be of stern stuff: Charlemagne's onslaught against them lasted on and off for 32 years, until 804. He led no fewer than 18 campaigns himself at the head of his elite unit of soldiers.

He must have thought he was close to his goal when he oversaw a series of mass baptisms of Saxons in 775–77, but despite signing a treaty of allegiance in 777 the Saxons rebelled again, and Charlemagne unleashed a terrible punishment in the mass execution in 782 of no fewer than 4,500 Saxons. In the course of his reign he succeeded in bending all the other Germanic tribes to his will – defeating the Bavarians, the Frisians, the Alemanni and the Thuringians.

DEFEAT AND CHRISTIANIZATION OF THE AVARS

In the late 790s Charlemagne launched an onslaught on the Avars, a nomadic tribe from Asia who had settled in what is now Hungary and had launched raids into the eastern part of the Frankish realm. (The Avars were called 'Huns' by Charlemagne's biographer Einhard.) Charlemagne personally led a devastating rout of the Avars in 790–91. Further campaigns led by Charlemagne's second son Pépin (known as Pépin of Italy) and Duke Eric of Friull defeated the Avars decisively, and their leaders submitted, swearing fealty to Charlemagne as his vassals and accepting his Christian faith.

THE WESTERN ROMAN EMPIRE REVIVED

Charlemagne set out at first to maintain good relations with both the pope in Rome and the rulers of the Byzantine or eastern Roman empire in Constantinople. He was in Rome once more in 781, for the anointing of his sons Pépin and Louis as kings of the Lombards and of the

▼ *Christian warriors led by Charlemagne were overcome by Muslims in the Battle of Roncesvalles in Spain (778). The defeat was treated elegiacally in the* Song of Roland.

Aquitanians respectively. He recognized the Byzantine empress Irene – and the two rulers even entered into negotiations for the arranged marriage of Charlemagne's daughter Rotrude to Irene's son (the future Byzantine emperor Constantine VI) but the negotiations failed and the arrangement was broken off.

In 799 he gave refuge to Pope Leo III who had fled a revolt by Italian nobles; Charlemagne had him escorted safely back

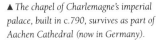

▲ *The chapel of Charlemagne's imperial palace, built in c.790, survives as part of Aachen Cathedral (now in Germany).*

to Rome. The following year, Charlemagne visited Rome and Leo crowned him 'August Emperor'. This was an attempt to revive the Roman Empire in the west as a Christian realm.

It was a challenge to the Byzantine Empire, for nominally the popes and the Franks were subjects of the eastern empire, and the Byzantine emperor was seen as the ruler of all Christians. Briefly it seemed possible that the two halves of the empire might be reunited: Charlemagne proposed marriage to Empress Irene, but the negotiations failed and she died in 802. Subsequently there was a stand-off, and then the two sides fought an intermittent war over Byzantine-held territories in Italy. Finally in 812 Byzantine emperor Michael I recognized Charlemagne as emperor under the title of *Imperator Romanorum gubernans imperium* ('Emperor governing the lands of the Romans'). The following year Charlemagne declared his son Louis to be co-emperor and his chosen successor. Charlemagne himself died in 814.

PARAGON OF CHIVALRY

CHARLEMAGNE THE GREAT

In medieval Europe Charlemagne was seen as the model Christian king or emperor. A superb military tactician, he marshalled large armies and made effective use of the power of mounted warriors with his cavalry. He rode into battle with his elite cadre of mounted warriors, in whom medieval knights saw their forerunners. He was a Christian warrior, who fought to spread the faith of Christ: all the peoples he defeated accepted Christianity as part of their submission. Centuries later, he was celebrated as a chivalric hero in *chansons de geste* (chivalric poems) and a perfect knight, perhaps history's first great exemplar of the chivalric code.

CHARLEMAGNE'S FAITH

In his early campaign of AD774 against the Lombards, when he deposed the Lombard king Desiderius, took the crown for himself, eliminated his brother's sons as

▼ *Charlemagne attends Mass while on campaign. The wars he waged against pagan Germanic tribes were fought in Christ's name to spread the Gospel.*

potential rivals and renewed the Franks' alliance with the pope, Charlemagne demonstrated several of his key qualities: strategic intelligence, decisiveness, military force, and an element of ruthlessness in negating the claim to power of his nephews. The events of 774 also demonstrated his combination of political manoeuvring and religious faith – for while his alliance with the papacy was politically expedient, his commitment to the Christian faith was genuine.

Charlemagne was driven by a desire for power, but he believed himself to be doing God's will. He did not accept that the pope had any sovereignty over him: in his laws he described himself as *Imperator a Deo Coronatus* ('Emperor Crowned by God'), indicating that he was subject only to God.

AT COURT AND AS A PATRON

Not least among the qualities that contributed to Charlemagne's enduring reputation in the Middle Ages was his commitment to the Church and to learning. He was a great patron of the Church and of education and oversaw a revival of

art and learning known to history as the 'Carolingian Renaissance'.

He gathered many of the great minds of contemporary Europe at his court in Aachen, among them the Anglo-Saxon monk Alcuin who reorganized education within Charlemagne's vast realms. Alcuin reintroduced the study of the seven liberal arts of music, astronomy, geometry, logic, arithmetic, grammar and rhetoric, which had been studied in ancient Rome.

Another key figure among the courtiers at Aachen was the monk Einhard, originally a pupil of Alcuin, who wrote a biography of the emperor. From Einhard's account, we know that Charlemagne was well-built and unusually tall – his height was noted to be seven times the length of his feet. He had large eyes and nose, a full head of grey hair and a cheerful face. He walked purposefully and spoke with a higher voice than an observer might expect. From other sources we know that although he had rough manners, he enjoyed debating with the learned men he had gathered around him and was always keen to learn.

A FAMOUS DEFEAT IN SPAIN

Under Charlemagne, the Frankish army was a military machine of awesome effectiveness. Yet one of the great *chansons de geste* that celebrated medieval chivalric heroes focused on a rare defeat for this warrior king.

This setback took place in the Pyrenees mountains in 778. Charlemagne had invaded northern Spain at the urging of some Muslim emissaries whose request for help against the Umayyad emir of Córdoba had appealed to him as an opportunity to add lustre to his military reputation while also expanding the reach of Christianity into largely Muslim Spain. The campaign, during which he besieged and failed to capture Zaragoza, was not a success, but worse was to follow – for, as

▲ *Charlemagne refused to accept that his power was dependent upon papal approval. To emphasize this, he used the words 'Emperor Crowned by God' in his laws.*

he led his army back through the Pyrenees, they were ambushed by Basque fighters (perhaps in alliance with Muslim warriors) and many in Charlemagne's army were killed. One of these was Hroudland or Roland, Warden of the border territories with Brittany, and the warrior who gave his name to the 11th-century epic poem the *Chanson de Roland* (the *Song of Roland*), a masterpiece of medieval literature that makes a great celebration of this defeat.

CHARLEMAGNE THE WARRIOR

We know plenty about Charlemagne's campaigns, his political manoeuvring and his commitment to education, but we have little certain information about him as a warrior. Yet this aspect of his life was important in the Middle Ages, when he was revered as a knight, and in works such as the *Song of Roland* his relationship with his elite companions in his cavalry was presented as the epitome of chivalry, the perfection of chivalric relationship between a lord and his knights.

We do, however, have a description of Charlemagne dressed for battle. Notker of St Gall, a 9th-century Benedictine monk at the Abbey of St Gall (at modern St Gallen, Switzerland), left in his work *Gesta Caroli Magni* (*Life of Charlemagne*) a description of the king equipped for the battlefield. It refers to him as 'the Iron King': saying that his armour consisted of an iron helm, with sleeves of iron armour and a chain mail tunic; his upper legs also were covered with chain mail, with iron greaves on the lower leg.

KING WITH KNIGHTLY VIRTUES

Totila, King of the Ostrogoths in the mid-6th century, was celebrated as a great early precursor of chivalry in much the same way as Charlemagne was seen as an early example of the ideal knight. In the 540s Totila recaptured for the Goths most of central and southern Italy, which had been taken by the Byzantine or eastern Roman Empire. In near contemporary accounts, Totila was celebrated for his humanity and fairness in dealing with defeated enemies – later important chivalric virtues. He was also a great mounted warrior and a figure of heroic appearance. The 6th-century Byzantine historian Procopius described

Totila's magnificent attire: gold armour, with adornments hanging from the cheek pieces, and a purple helmet and lance. He also praised the king's horsemanship and weapon-handling: in front of the armies arrayed on the field of battle, he danced on his horse and was able to throw and catch his spear while parading on horseback. Totila's name was Baduila, but chronicles suggest he fought under the name Totila.

▼ *On 21 March 543 Totila paid a visit at Monte Cassino to Benedict of Nursia, founder of the Benedictine monastic rule. Three years later, Totila took Rome.*

THE EMPEROR'S CAVALRY
MOUNTED WARRIORS IN THE CAROLINGIAN ARMY

Charlemagne's triumphant military success depended on his use of very large, well-equipped and superbly disciplined armies. They contained a large contingent of light cavalry and a smaller elite section of heavy cavalry. Some estimates of the number of mounted warriors in the Frankish army go as high as 35,000 men. Charlemagne issued detailed edicts laying out requirements for how the armies should be raised, equipped and supplied with food and weapons.

A MILITARY MACHINE

Charlemagne was a great tactician, but a major part of his armies' effectiveness depended on organization. Many of his army manoeuvres were only possible because his military machine was so big and so well organized that he was able to keep two or more large armies in the field at once.

As well as fighting on more than one front at once, his armies could undertake long-range campaigns of conquest – beyond the river Rhine, across the Alps in

▼ *A bearded, regal Charlemagne elevates a warrior to the cavalry. The illustration is from the 14th century and is coloured by notions of chivalry from this later age.*

Italy, in the far west of Brittany and once even across the Pyrenees in northern Spain (although this campaign was the scene of the celebrated failure in the Pass of Roncesvalles). In battle Charlemagne's armies were large enough to split into separate units. It was a favourite tactic of his – used in 778 in Spain, in 787 in Bavaria and in 791 in Pannonia – to outflank the enemy with columns of troops.

Charlemagne did not usually wage war during the winter. His custom was to gather his army at Easter, prior to embarking on campaigns in the summer months. Sometimes, however, he remained in the territory he was intent on subjugating for

▲ *Wearing the typical conical helmets of the day, mounted warriors in Charlemagne's army follow the baggage train on campaign.*

the winter break. In 776, for example, he defeated the Saxons at Lippespringe and forcibly baptized them, but they rose up in revolt, throwing off the Christian faith which they had accepted, almost at once. That winter he kept his court in Saxony – and, unusually, he kept up regular raids against Saxon targets during the winter months.

RAISING AN ARMY

Each count was held responsible for bringing with him all the warriors who were his vassals – save four, whom he could leave behind to guard his property and protect his wife. Bishops and abbots also had to give military service, with all their vassals – although they, too, could leave a pair of warriors to protect their possessions. A royal vassal at court did not have to perform military service, but he was responsible for ensuring that all his vassals joined up.

During the course of Charlemagne's reign, selective service became accepted: three vassals might join together to equip a fourth, who would go on campaign. One of the emperor's edicts, issued in Saxony

in 806, required five Saxons to equip a sixth to fight for the king in a projected Spanish campaign, and for two more men to equip another warrior to serve in Bohemia.

Charlemagne's armies were always well supplied, and his campaigns were usually well planned. He ordered his mounted warriors to bring three months' worth of food and six months' worth of military clothing and weapons. The decree even specified that these three months would begin when the army assembled on campaign rather than when the warriors embarked from their homes. Herds of livestock for food were part of an army's baggage train.

During the Saxon campaigns the troops were well enough equipped to build bridges and forts; the army had collapsible boats for crossing the river Ebro on the Spanish campaign of 778 and carried a moveable bridge for its 792 campaign against the Avars. When he had forces fighting simultaneously in Hungary and Saxony he tried – though without success – to dig a canal between the Danube and the Rhine.

▼ *Charlemagne's forces fight at Pamplona, Spain, during the ill-fated campaign that ended in defeat in the Pass of Roncesvalles.*

▲ *Fighting beneath a heavenly apparition of the Cross, Charlemagne's cavalry and the sheer might of his army defeat the pagan Avars, who were superbly skilled horsemen themselves, near the river Danube in 791.*

FORTS AND PLUNDER

In conquered territories he ordered the building of permanent garrisoned fortifications – forerunners of the castles built by medieval knights. Plundering enemy riches was an accepted part of campaigning. The campaign against the Avars in 790–91 produced so much booty that 15 wagons were needed to carry it back to the court at Aachen.

Discipline was strict. Drunkenness was officially forbidden. There was a stiff fine for those who failed to attend when required. Desertion was punished with seizing all of a warrior's property followed by execution.

EQUIPMENT AND WEAPONS

Charlemagne laid down strict requirements for the military equipment his troops should have. In 792 his edict required mounted warriors to have a lance, a shield and both long and short swords, in addition to a horse. In 802 the warriors were ordered to bring body armour as well. In 805 he decreed that each mounted soldier in possession of at least 300 acres (121 hectares) had to bring a *byrnie* (tunic of chain mail). The decree also stated that warriors who had chain mail armour but did not bring it to battle risked punishment by losing their fiefdom.

A typical mounted warrior in one of Charlemagne's armies had a chain mail tunic that extended down to his knees and was slit at the side to allow greater ease of movement. Some had a scale overshirt instead – a jacket of leather or fabric with metal or horn pieces attached to it. The warrior wore a conical helmet and carried a round shield with a spike in the centre, so that it could be used as a thrusting weapon as well as for defence. He had a long lance, used for thrusting – in this era, groups of mounted warriors did not yet charge with couched lance. His sword had a rounded end, and was effective for cutting but not for stabbing.

A TIME OF UNREST
THE PROTECTIVE ROLE OF MOUNTED WARRIORS IN AN UNRULY WORLD

In the years after Charlemagne's death in 814 his empire swiftly disintegrated in power struggles among his sons and their descendants. At the same time his former territories were assailed by violent raiders: from the north, Vikings came by sea and river in their longships; from the east, the reckless Magyars came on horseback; from the south and west (from North Africa and the Iberian Peninsula) came fierce Islamic raiders. It was a lawless time, seemingly lacking effective central authority.

Monasteries and churches were as much the raiders' targets as palaces and farms, and churchmen as well as lords looked to mounted warriors for protection. This led to the first idealizations of the warrior-horsemen as defenders of the Church and of right against lawless pagans. It was a key stage in the progression from the mounted warrior of Charlemagne's army to the knight of the 11th and 12th centuries, who was seen as a *miles Christi* ('soldier of Christ').

▼ *Viking attacks by sea were hard to defend against because their swift, powerful ships swept in, looted and departed before local defences could be organized.*

THE FIRST TRUE CAVALRY ENGAGEMENTS

Charlemagne's son Louis the Pious reigned for 26 years, 814–40. Early in his reign he attempted to settle the question of the succession among his descendants, but not to their satisfaction: he was twice deposed in major revolts by his sons, then subsequently reinstalled. After his death his three surviving sons fought amongst themselves, then divided the empire into three under the Treaty of Verdun (843). The former East Frankish kingdom became Francia Orientalis and was taken by Louis the German; the West Frankish kingdom became Francia Occidentalis, and was given to Charles the Bald. A central strip called Francia Media and the title of emperor was given to Lothair. (Francia Occidentalis and Francia Orientalis were later the basis of the countries of France and Germany respectively.)

These wars saw the first true mounted warrior engagements as cavalries from opposing armies met in full charge. By this stage the stirrup had been widely adopted, but the mounted warriors had not yet developed the technique of charging with couched lance.

A NEW WARRIOR CLASS

Power struggles continued for decades. All the time the authority and influence of the royal house grew weaker; meanwhile, Magyars and Vikings struck repeatedly. The most effective resistance came from local lords, whose power grew steadily as they built a large territorial holding, often through the grant by weak kings of hereditary fiefdoms. These lords in turn granted fiefdoms to their warrior supporters. An elite class of landholding warrior-knights began to develop.

These warriors' principal loyalty was to their lord rather than the king. In 792–93 Charlemagne had been able to impose an oath of loyalty to the king on all royal vassals and required the vassals to make their vassals swear it also. But as royal authority collapsed, and counts became more powerful as they accumulated land, it began to be accepted that vassals would fight for their lord against the king.

VIKING RAIDS AND CONSOLIDATING LOCAL POWER

From the 830s through to 910 Viking raids were a persistent threat to the western Frankish lands. They hit coastal targets

THE BATTLE OF AUGSBURG

King Otto I of the Germans unleashed heavy cavalry against the Magyar horsemen at the Battle of Augsburg on the river Lech in 955. Chronicle accounts claim that Otto's army numbered around 10,000 while the Magyars fielded 50,000 warriors, but modern historians believe that the true figures were perhaps 1,000 against 5,000. Initially the Magyars gained the upper hand, and appeared to have outflanked Otto's army, but many Magyars dismounted to begin looting the Frankish baggage train and Otto sent his knights to ride them down. The main part of the battle was marked by the disciplined charge of Otto's knights, who drove back and overwhelmed the Magyar horsemen, and then ruthlessly pursued them from the field – according to some accounts – for two days. The Magyars were routed, and never again raided Frankish territories; Otto's victory was hailed by contemporaries as a great triumph for Christian knights.

▲ *The Magyar mounted warriors were expert at ambushing troops, and often pretended to retreat before turning suddenly on their pursuers.*

as well as any settlements that could be reached by river. In *c.*840 they raided Nourmoutier, Utrecht and Antwerp; in 841 they razed Rouen; in 843 they attacked Nantes and sailed up the river Loire. By the 850s they had set up camps on the Seine, Loire and Garonne. In 847, 861 and 865 they attacked Paris.

Frankish kings relied on local counts and dukes to repel the threat. Charles the Bald of the western Frankish kingdom (r. 844–70) made fiefdoms hereditary as a means of maintaining the loyalty of local lords who had proved their worth in countering the Vikings. Local lords who benefited in this way included Baldwin 'Iron-Arm' who made his name combating the Vikings in Flanders and was made *margrave* (ruler) of Flanders by Charles the Bald in 864. Similarly Richard the Justiciar, who defeated the Vikings in

Burgundy in 888 and relieved the Viking siege of Chartres in 911, was established as the first margrave of Burgundy.

Raids on the western Frankish kingdom largely came to an end after the early 10th century, when a settlement of Vikings was established by Charles III the Simple in what became Normandy, as a buffer zone to protect against future raiding.

MAGYAR HORSEMEN

The Magyars were warlike descendants of nomadic people originally from the region of the Ural Mountains, who had settled in what is now Ukraine in *c.*830. They began launching mounted raids on the eastern Frankish territories in 862.

They were superb horsemen and archers, who fought mainly with bows and arrows but also with lassos and javelins. They would pour into an area,

looting widely, then disappear just as quickly. Otto I (r. 936–73) of the eastern Frankish kingdom (around this time generally described as Germany) ended the Magyar threat once and for all at the Battle of Ausgburg in 955 (see box).

WAR BY SEA

For much of the 9th century, Islamic raiders dominated the Mediterranean. They captured Bari in Italy, the island of Crete and part of Sicily (where they developed Palermo as a great cosmopolitan city). They established bases in what is now southern France, including Farakshanit (Fraxinet) near modern St Tropez, and raided up the river Rhone as far as Upper and Lower Burgundy.

The Europeans called them infidels (people of no faith) or Saracens from the Arabic word *sharqiyin* ('Easterners'). In southern France feudal lords defended local populations against the raiders, and achieved increasing independence from Frankish or Byzantine authority in building fortifications to hold the raiders at bay.

ALFRED THE GREAT AND ENGLISH MILITIAS
KNIGHTHOOD IN ENGLAND BEFORE THE NORMAN CONQUEST

Alfred of Wessex (r. 871–99) is the only king in English history to be honoured with the epithet 'the Great'. As with Charlemagne in Europe, Alfred has been revered by later generations in England as a great warrior monarch, military reformer, administrator, lawgiver and educator. Like Charlemagne, Alfred was a close ally of the Church, and celebrated as a defender and promoter of the Christian faith against pagan enemies. Throughout the age of chivalry he was celebrated as a pioneer of knightly virtues such as bravery, charity and magnanimity, as a giver of laws, and as an inspirational example of a king and general who achieved victory when all seemed lost.

MILITARY REFORMS
In 871 Anglo-Saxon England appeared to be at the mercy of Danish Vikings: a great Viking army had landed in 865 and won control of York, Northumbria and East

Anglia. Alfred, still a prince, led the armies of his brother King Aethelred of Wessex in a stirring victory over the Danes on the Ridgeway at Ashdown in Berkshire on 8 January 871. However, the Danes quickly regrouped afterwards and won important victories. Alfred meanwhile acceded to the throne on the death of Aethelred.

Alfred bought peace by bribing the invaders, but the Vikings, after conquering the Anglo-Saxon kingdom of Mercia, attacked again in 877, penetrating far into Wessex. Alfred fought back, initially conducting a guerrilla war from a base deep in the impenetrable wetlands of Somerset, then the following year leading a West Saxon army to another great victory over the Danes, in the Battle of Edington on Salisbury Plain. Alfred's men harried the Danes for more than 15 miles (24km) back to the invaders' base at Chippenham, which surrendered after a siege of 14 days. Alfred later freed London from the Danes.

The Viking leader Guthrum and his army pledged not to attack Wessex, but the invaders remained in England, established in the eastern region of the country, between the rivers Thames and Tees, in the area known as the Danelaw. Alfred set about improving his kingdom's defences and the effectiveness of its army. He split the *fyrd* (militia) into two, and thereafter ensured that one half was always ready for action while the other half rested at home. He adopted the tactics of the invaders, introducing mobile groups of mounted warriors as part of the army.

▲ *Alfred is a great figure in the traditions of English law as well as in the country's military history. His* Book of Laws *was based on three Saxon law codes.*

Alfred also revamped the navy and introduced a heavier, 60-oar boat that he had designed. Most importantly, he ordered the building of a string of defensive forts, or burghs, around his kingdom. He decreed that there should be a fort within 20 miles of every settlement. Some of the burghs were newly built, others were based on old Roman or Iron Age forts; some were small, others appear to have been planned from the start as fortified towns.

◀ *King Alfred discusses his new ship design with associates. The heavy boats, when made, ran aground on their first use.*

▶ *This iron ceremonial helmet was buried with an Anglo-Saxon chief at Sutton Hoo, Suffolk, in the 7th century. The Anglo-Saxon warriors were footsoldiers, but their army did use Celtic-British cavalry units.*

▲ *The two sides of a silver penny issued by King Alfred in c.880.*

NECESSARY KNOWLEDGE

Alfred believed that the violent visitations of the Vikings were God's judgement on an ignorant people, and saw it as his Christian duty to revive learning in the kingdom. Probably inspired by the example of Charlemagne, he invited scholars to his court, and established schools. He had those books that he considered 'most necessary for all men to know' translated from Latin into the native tongue. He himself learned Latin and translated the *Cura Pastoralis* (*Pastoral Rule*) of Pope Gregory the Great. He sponsored the creation of the *Anglo-Saxon Chronicle*, a history running back to Roman times, so that his people could know their history. He tried to establish justice, introducing a code of law, attempting to limit the prosecution of blood quarrels and introducing strict penalties for breaking an oath.

ALFRED AND KNIGHTHOOD

In Alfred's time during the late 9th century early forms of knighthood were beginning to take shape in mainland Europe with the emergence of a military elite of mounted warriors rewarded for fighting with the possession of land. In Anglo-Saxon England, the army consisted largely of thegns – warriors bound to their aristocratic lords who took responsibility for maintaining them. Alfred's reign saw the beginning of the theory that warriors were a self-contained group whose existence was essential for good government and a stable society. From the time of the Church Fathers in the 1st–5th centuries AD, it was normal for scholars to debate the right ordering of society and to propose a threefold division – such as clergy,

monks and laity; or nobility, freemen and slaves. As part of his campaign to improve education in his kingdom, King Alfred learned Latin and translated *On Consolation* by the 6th-century Roman philosopher Boethius. To the translation Alfred added the statement that good government required a land that has a good number of people containing (in Anglo-Saxon) '*geberdmen, fyrdmen and weorcmen*' (men who pray, men who fight and men who work). This theory would play an important part in the Church's later view of knights and in the code of chivalry.

ALFRED AS A CHIVALRIC WARRIOR

After the Battle of Edington in 878 Alfred showed considerable forbearance to the defeated Danish force. The Saxon victory came after a period of desperate guerrilla warfare and a great victorious charge across country – it might have been understandable for Alfred and his army to slaughter their enemies. Instead they behaved with restraint.

However, like Charlemagne's defeated Germanic enemies, the Vikings discovered that the price of their defeat was conversion to Christianity. Danish leader Guthrum was baptized with Alfred standing as his godfather and personally raising him from the baptismal waters. Afterwards Alfred recognized Guthrum as an adoptive son. This ability to exhibit generosity in victory, and to recognize the noble qualities of his defeated opponent,

▶ *This heroic statue of King Alfred stands in Winchester, southern England, the place of the king's burial after his death on 26 October 899. The facts of his life were quickly embroidered with legend.*

was subsequently made the hallmark of a chivalric warrior fighting according to the code of chivalry.

In his lifetime, as well as after his death, Alfred's contemporaries celebrated him as a Christian warrior. His leading soldiers fought with swords that were decorated with the cross and his troops said prayers on the field of battle; as a contrast, monks recording his exploits always made a point of describing the Danes as pagans. The Welsh monk Asser, who wrote Alfred's biography in 893, called him 'ruler of all Christians in the island of Britain'.

THE RISE OF THE NORMANS

THE EXPORTERS OF KNIGHTHOOD

The Normans who invaded England in 1066 were descendants of the Viking warrior chieftain Rollo, or Robert, who was granted land in western France in 911 by King Charles III the Simple of West Francia. Between 911 and 1066, Rollo's descendants established a feudal society in Normandy. In warfare they used heavy cavalry and built castles. Following the conquest they imposed feudalism in England, and their descendants later exported it to the Holy Land on the First Crusade from 1095 to 1099.

ARRIVAL OF THE NORTHMEN

Scholars disagree as to whether Duke Rollo was originally Norwegian or Danish. He took part in an unsuccessful Viking siege of Paris in 886 and afterwards established a settlement at the mouth of the river Seine. Charles the Simple established this area as a buffer state against further Viking attacks by granting the lands to Rollo. As well as agreeing to fend off further Viking incursions, Rollo paid feudal homage to King Charles III and accepted baptism as a Christian under the name Robert. The deal was sealed in the Treaty of St Claire-sur-Epte in 911 and Robert married Charles's daughter.

Robert and the settlers were originally known as Northmen or Norsemen, and subsequently as Normans. They quickly

▼ *Viking raiders arrive off the coast of France in the late 9th century. Their war band mentality fed into Norman and later chivalric culture.*

expanded their territory, moving west, and Robert gained middle Normandy (Bassin, Bayeux, L'Huernin and Le Mans) from the king in 924 and Robert's son and successor, William Longsword (Duke William I of Normandy), was granted the seaboard of the Avranchin (the area near Mont St Michel) and the Contentin (the north part of the peninsula) in 933.

DUKE RICHARD I OF NORMANDY

William Longsword was murdered in 942 and a power struggle ensued, but William's illegitimate son finally regained control of Normandy as Duke Richard I. Richard I was known as Richard Sans Peur ('the Fearless'), and in his long reign (942–96) the feudal system was begun in his lands. Normandy was a wealthy realm, with the city of Rouen established as a successful trading centre. Coins bearing the name of Duke Richard I have been found as far afield as Russia and Scotland.

EXPANDING MILITARY POWER

Richard I was succeeded by his illegitimate son Duke Richard II, known as 'the Good'. In his reign Normandy became a great military power: many of his feudal vassals were powerful counts, with large bodies of mounted warriors in their service. Normandy also became a player on the international stage. Duke Richard II established political links with English royalty through the marriage of his sister, Emma of Normandy, to King Aethelred in 1002. However, in the same period he also allowed Danish Vikings to use ports in Normandy as their bases for repeated raids on England.

In 1013 the Danes invaded England, and Emma's sons by King Aethelred, Edward (later Edward the Confessor) and Alfred Atheling, went to Normandy as exiles. Emma remained in England and after Aethelred's death in 1016 went on to marry England's Danish king, Canute.

KING WILLIAM'S FATHER

Richard II was succeeded by his son as Duke Richard III, but Richard III died after just a year in power, and his brother Robert became Duke Robert II of Normandy. Some sources suggest he murdered Richard and he is sometimes known as Robert le Diable ('the Devil') for this reason; he may be connected to the legendary Norman knight of that name, who in the 12th–14th-century tales was the devil's own son and lived a life of the greatest depravity before seeking forgiveness from the pope and saving Rome three times from Islamic attack.

After providing military support for King Henry I of France, Duke Robert II was rewarded with the territory of the Vexin, near Rouen. (Around this time historians generally begin to identify the lands of Francia Occidentalis or West Francia as France and those of Francia Orientalis or East Francia as Germany.) However, despite his nickname of 'the devil', Robert II was clearly also a religious man. He was a sponsor of reform for monasteries in Normandy along the lines

▲ *The ability of Duke William's mounted warriors to launch a swift counter-attack made the difference between defeat and victory at the Battle of Hastings in 1066. This image of Norman cavalry preparing to charge is from the Bayeux Tapestry.*

of the new practices promoted by the Abbey of Cluny, and made a pilgrimage to Jerusalem. It was on his return from this voyage that he died in Nicaea (modern Iznik, Turkey) in 1035.

DUKE WILLIAM OF NORMANDY

Robert II fathered an illegitimate son, William, by Herleva, daughter of a tanner or embalmer from Falaise. On his father's death William le Bâtard ('the Bastard') succeeded to the dukedom of Normandy at the age of just eight. He was raised in the household of his late father's steward, Osbern Herfasston, and appears to have had an education alongside several other martial youths in the Norman ways of war, including sword-fighting, the skills of mounted horsemanship and even castle-building – like that of later generations of knights-to-be, as first page and then as squire.

Duke William's biographer, William of Poitiers, described William in his youth as being masterful in the saddle, cutting the air with his sword, grasping his shining shield, and striking fear into his opponent with his fearsome use of the lance. He was knighted by King Henry I of France at the age of 15, in c.1042–43. Before he invaded

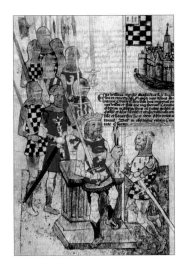

▼ *Duke William of Normandy, enthroned as King William I of England, makes a grant of lands to Alain de Brittany in return for the promise of feudal military service.*

England in 1066, William had proved himself a forceful warrior and leader of men, with victories in Brittany, Maine and Ponthieu.

FEUDAL INVASION

The Norman invasion of England in 1066 could be termed a 'feudal war'. William's noble vassals were fighting for the promise of titles and land if the invasion was a success. At the crucial Battle of Hastings King Harold's army fought entirely on foot behind a wall of shields, while William's cavalry played an important part in the victory – hitting the Anglo-Saxons with a mounted charge after some had lost their discipline and broken out to pursue a feigned Norman retreat. From the very start of the occupation of England, the Normans raised castles to hold conquered territory and frighten the populace, and imposed their own feudal society in place of England's existing nobility.

THE FIRST KNIGHTS

AN EXCLUSIVE FRATERNITY

In the decades after the Norman conquest, in the feudal societies of France, Germany and Norman England, we see the emergence of the first true knights – men who were made knights in a formal ceremony that admitted them to an elite group of warriors. Modern historians argue that soldiers fighting on horseback in the 9th and 10th centuries should be viewed as mounted warriors, rather than true knights. These mounted warriors were, as we have seen, bound to their lords in the developing feudal system, in which they provided military service in return for the right to land. However, an essential element of knighthood was absent: the idea of the making of a knight through the formal admission to a chivalric brotherhood.

Within this view, figures such as Charlemagne and Alfred the Great can be seen as remarkable warrior-kings, as precursors of chivalry, but not as knights; and likewise while mounted soldiers

▼ *Feudal service was rewarded with grants of land, so more prominent knights were able to establish themselves on large estates.*

riding in the heavy cavalry of Duke Richard II of Normandy, for example, had many qualities of knights, their comradeship as bonded vassals of their lord lacked this quality of a brotherhood following a chivalric code.

SOCIAL STATUS OF KNIGHTS

As both feudalism and knighthood developed, knights became established as one level in an enormously stratified social grouping that also included the barons on their great estates, and poorer mounted warriors who were not admitted to knighthood and provided military service as squires. The relative social status of those formally called 'knights' was constantly shifting as it was challenged from above and below.

EQUALITY AND EXCLUSIVENESS

In theory, according to the code of chivalry, the brotherhood of knights was an elite, but all within it were equal. This equality probably derived from that of the knights' predecessors among the freemen who fought side by side for the Frankish kings. In this tradition knighthood was a reward

▲ *The Christian Church sanctioned violence when it was performed in Christ's service. This 12th-century illustration is entitled 'The faithful knight leaving to battle Satan'.*

for the brave, and all brave knights were equal. Only a knight could make a knight – but knighthood could be conferred upon anyone who had proved himself worthy of the accolade.

Yet knights were also often a social elite. This was in large part because their feudal rewards for military service set them up as wealthy landowners, who were able to use their position to acquire more land and pass great territories down the generations. On a practical level, it was also because the cost of a knight's equipment excluded poorer warriors.

It became a matter of official policy to maintain the exclusiveness of the knightly fraternity and to exert control over who might confer knighthood. From the early 12th century, royal pronouncements excluded various groups from being knighted. Some of the earlier exclusions were designed to keep the peace by preventing any rowdy elements from becoming knights, and in particular to prevent nobles quickly raising a rebel force through a mass knighting ceremony. For example, a German decree of 1152 excluded peasants from being knights, and in 1140 Roger II, Norman king of Sicily,

▶ *In this manuscript illustration, also from the 12th century, the devils represent vices and heresies. Drawing his sword, the knight prepares to impose Christian law.*

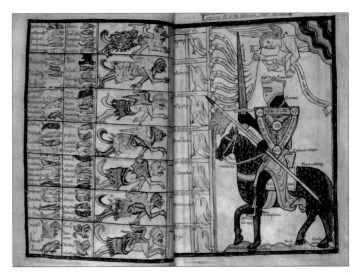

forbade the knighting of men who were liable to disturb the peace. In 1186 Holy Roman Emperor Frederick I banned both the sons of peasants and the sons of priests from being knighted – the latter on the grounds that since priests officially could not marry, their sons were illegitimate.

INHERITED QUALITIES

Gradually the idea developed that the qualities needed to be a knight could only be transmitted through inheritance: only the descendants of knights could be knights. In 1235 the Cortes of Catalonia declared: 'We establish that no man can be knighted unless he is the son of a knight.' Sometimes the ability or right to raise to knighthood those not descended from knights was restricted to kings. For example, Holy Roman Emperor Frederick II declared in 1231: 'No man who is not of knightly descent shall be made a knight except by our licence or permission.' The royal prerogative could be valuable (see box). These kinds of exclusions were not in force in England. Moreover, even in Germany and France knights were still sometimes 'made' by other knights on the field of battle as a reward for valour.

A LEISURED CLASS

The feudal system delivered knights a leisured life. When not on campaign, they lived in grand style in their castles and fortified manor houses, subsidised by the hard labour of the peasants who worked the land on the grand estates. Knights were free to hunt and hawk, to practise their military skills in tournaments and to develop their taste for literature and music – songs of knightly bravery. In these circumstances the literature and ethos of chivalry developed.

A COMPLEX BOND

In its mature form, from the late 11th century – when European knights rode out against the warriors of Islam in the First Crusade (1095–99) – knighthood was a complex bond, a combination of a badge of warrior honour, a social distinction, an ethical challenge and a religious calling. To be a knight was often a sign of valorous achievement, while it could also be a title inherited by birth, giving right to certain lands. A knight also voluntarily adopted a code of honour, a duty of service, and was blessed by the Church as a defender of the Christian faith, or *miles Christi* ('soldier of Christ').

▼ *According to chivalric theory, the knight offered his military service to God. Knights and their swords were blessed in church.*

KNIGHTHOODS FOR SALE

Once it was accepted that generally men could not rise to knighthood from lower social ranks, except by royal licence, kings faced the temptation of raising money by putting knighthoods up for sale. This very unchivalric practice was particularly common in France, where for example the king, Philip IV (r. 1285–1314), announced his willingness to grant knighthoods for sums of money. In France in this era, a wealthy merchant might purchase a knighthood as a financial investment since being a knight brought exemptions from tax. Knighthoods were also sold by the Imperial crown in 14th-century Germany, by Charles IV, Holy Roman Emperor in 1355–78, and his subsequent successors.

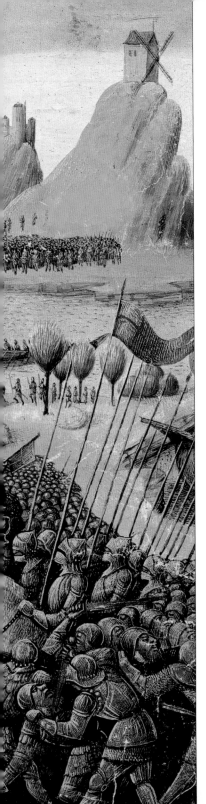

CHAPTER TWO

HOLY WAR

Knights such as Godfrey of Bouillon and Robert of Flanders won
enduring fame on the First Crusade of 1096–99, their exploits
quickly embroidered in legends. Yet for every knight such as
Godfrey or Robert there were many other crusaders who died
uncelebrated and in wretched circumstances – of starvation, of
disease, in battle or ambush – many having brought financial ruin
on themselves after borrowing very heavily to make the trip. It can
be difficult at a distance of several centuries to see why so many
men (and women) were moved to risk so much on such a venture.
A key explanation is that they were inspired to view the enterprise
as a holy war – they saw themselves as the latterday counterparts of
the Israelites, whose struggles against enemies of their faith were an
inspirational prototype of the crusades. The biblical warrior Judas
Maccabeus is said, according to the Second Book of Maccabees, to
have gone into battle with a golden sword given to him in a vision
by the prophet Jeremiah with words that could happily have given
service as a blessing for medieval knights: 'Take this holy sword, a
gift from God, wherewith thou shalt overthrow the adversaries of
my people Israel'. Judas's soldiers followed him into battle in a
manner that was equally suited as inspiration for the crusaders'
assault on Jerusalem: 'Thus being exhorted with the words of
Judas, which were very good, and proper to stir up the courage,
and strengthen the hearts of the young men, they resolved to fight,
and set upon them manfully; that valour might decide the matter,
because the Holy City and the temple were in danger.'

▲ *The pope had the spiritual authority to judge even royal sinners.*

◄ *The army of Bohemond of Taranto comes under attack while trying to cross the River
Vardar en route to fight in the First Crusade. The journey was long and arduous.*

FIGHTING A HOLY WAR

THEORIES OF JUST AND SACRED WARS

The Benedictine historian Guibert, Abbot of Nogent-sous-Coucy, author in the early 12th century of a chronicle of the First Crusade, declared that 'God has instituted in these days sacred wars, so that the body of knights … can find a means of winning their salvation'. Guibert may have suggested that holy wars were created in his era by a watchful God, but in truth the idea of fighting a just and divinely sanctioned war had its origins centuries earlier, and had roots as far back as the biblical era.

THE EXAMPLE OF THE OLD TESTAMENT

There are many examples in the Old Testament of the Bible of warfare waged on God's instructions or in his name. The God celebrated in the Old Testament appeared to use warfare to achieve his ends; he himself dealt in death. According to the Book of Exodus (Chapter 15), after

▼ *The anger of Israel's warlike God brought ruin on the Egyptians when the Red Sea closed over them, allowing the Israelites to travel on towards the Promised Land.*

escaping from captivity in Egypt the Israelites sang a hymn of praise in which they joyously celebrated their miraculous escape, the parting of the Red Sea and the death of their enemies in its waters: 'The Lord is a man of war: the Lord is his name … Pharaoh's chariots and his host hath he cast into the sea … the depths have covered them: they sank into the bottom as a stone. Thy right hand, O Lord, is become glorious in power: thy right hand, O Lord, hath dashed in pieces the enemy.'

The Old Testament God did call on his people to kill on his behalf – for example, when he instructed King Saul (David's predecessor as the king of Israel): 'Thus saith the Lord of hosts, I remember that which Amalek did to Israel, how he laid wait for him in the way, when he came up from Egypt. Now go and smite Amalek, utterly destroy all that they have, and spare them not; but slay both man and woman, infant and suckling, ox, sheep, camel and ass' (1 Samuel 15: verses 2–3).

A gallery of Israelite warriors, including David, Gideon and Joshua, were venerated as proponents of righteous warfare, even as exemplars of the knightly

▲ *'And I beheld when He had opened the sixth seal, and, lo, there was a great earthquake …' Martial language, such as this quote from the Book of Revelation, encouraged Christians to believe that God sanctioned the use of violence.*

code of chivalry; chief among them and celebrated alongside David and Joshua among the 'Nine Worthies' of the biblical, classical and chivalric worlds was Judas Maccabeus, guerrilla fighter against Seleucid overlords of Jerusalem in the 2nd century BC.

Judas Maccabeus was said to have led his warriors into battle 'fighting with their hands, but praying to the Lord with their hearts' and in battle 'they slew no less than five and thirty thousand'; in the midst of this carnage they were 'greatly cheered with the presence of God'. This quotation is from Chapter 15 of the Second Book of Maccabees, part of the Old Testament for Roman Catholics and Eastern Orthodox Christians but in modern times usually considered by Protestant Christians to be in the Apocrypha, a selection of texts that is associated with the Bible but not seen as part of it.

the 1st-century BC Roman statesman Cicero, who argued that a just war had to be fought using just means or in the right way – for example, with bravery. As developed by St Augustine, the Christian theory of a just or holy war required that it be fought in self-defence or to recover a seized territory or possession, on proper authority, and with the right intentions and means by all involved. Augustine added that wars fought on God's authority did not breach the commandment forbidding killing.

These ideas of sanctioned violence, of just and sacred war, applied to public bodies, such as State or Church. Individuals were required to be obedient to these public bodies, and to fight if commanded to do so. But in their individual lives violence was not sanctioned, and here Christ's troubling commands to love thy neighbour and to show forgiveness applied. Here was the distinction between sanctioned violence carried out in defence of the Church under vows to maintain the peace of God, and private wars, the secular clashes between knights that were condemned by the Church.

▲ St Augustine, kneeling, was inspired by the preaching of St Ambrose, right, the Bishop of Milan. Both men were great intellectuals and rhetoricians who developed theories of a just use of violence.

▼ Augustine urged Christians to focus on a mystical heavenly Jerusalem in his work The City of God, *written shortly after 410.*

VIOLENCE OF THE LAST DAYS

In the New Testament, Christian knights and their clerical supporters drew on the warlike imagery of descriptions of the Day of Judgement in the Book of Revelation, in which celestial armies gave expression to the righteous anger of God, which was likened to a winepress. Many of the knights, clerics and ordinary people who travelled to the Holy Land on the First Crusade had a strong sense that they were living in the last days before the Second Coming of Christ, which gave a great sense of urgency to the need to achieve remission of sins. Moreover, a key incentive for travelling to Jerusalem was that the events of the Last Judgement were expected to be played out in the city where Christ died and was buried.

JUSTIFICATION OF HOLY WAR

Theoretical justifications of holy war drew on 4th- and 5th-century AD Christian writers, such as St Ambrose, Bishop of Milan, and his pupil St Augustine, Bishop of Hippo. These theologians drew on classical philosophy: in particular those of the 4th-century BC ancient Greek philosopher Aristotle, who developed the notion of a 'just war' waged for the purpose of maintaining peace; ancient Roman ideas that wars could justly be fought to defend oneself, to recover seized territory or property, or to inflict punishment on a wrongdoer as long as the war was fought with proper authority (of the state); and the theory of

DEFENDERS OF THE FAITH

CHRISTIAN WARRIORS IN A HOLY WAR

The great Norman crusader lord Tancred of Hauteville was filled with energy, according to his biographer Radulph of Caen, by Pope Urban II's call to the First Crusade. Before departing on crusade, Radulph writes, Tancred was disturbed by the disjunction between on the one hand the demands of life as a feudal knight, which required him to wage war, and on the other the teaching of Christ to turn the other cheek and act with generosity to the needy. The new idea of crusading, in which waging war against pagans was presented as a form of devotional penance for Christian knights, was tailor-made to address such a difficulty, and Tancred responded with enthusiasm: in Radulph's words, 'as if he had previously been asleep, he came awake, his energy was aroused, his strength increased, his seeing grew sharper and his bravery was born'.

In the context of energizing knights to fight for the Church in distant lands, Pope Urban's conflation of waging war and doing penance was a stroke of genius, and a new departure. But the idea of fighting a holy war – and of being a holy warrior – was not a new one: Radulph may well have been overstating Tancred's sense of discomfort at the disjunction between his life as a knight and his life as a devout Christian. For the knights who travelled on the First Crusade were descendants of Germanic tribes whose warrior-band philosophy, incorporating celebration of the military lord and of feats of martial vigour, had had a profound effect on thinking and writing about the Christian faith in the centuries since they had been converted in the 5th and 6th centuries AD.

▲ *In the 5th century, King Clovis of the Salian Franks began his people's long association with the Catholic Church when he converted to Christianity in order to marry Princess Clotilde. The faith became increasingly militarized.*

Figures such as Clovis I, the first Frankish king to convert to Christianity, and his successor, Charlemagne, were viewed as warrior heroes as much as they were Christian kings. Christian language and thought became infused with Germanic warrior imagery. For example, in the masterful 8th-century Anglo-Saxon poem *The Dream of the Rood*, the poet uses very military language in describing his dream of seeing Christ on the cross, calling Christ the 'young hero', 'the warrior', 'the Prince' and 'the Lord of Victories', and envisages Christ's actions on the cross as those of a fearless warrior.

HOLY WAR AND DIPLOMACY

One key divide between the westerners, or 'Latins', who travelled on crusade and the easterners, or 'Greeks', they went to help, derived from a distinctly different outlook on life, particularly when it came to diplomacy and war.

The Latins had a developed theory of the just, or holy, war and of the righteousness of combat, but the Greeks viewed conflict only as a last resort and preferred to settle disagreements through diplomacy and compromise. Many of the Latins were only a few generations separated from forebears among the Viking raiders, and the Greeks saw them as uncultured barbarians; for their part, the Latins viewed the Greeks as untrustworthy – particularly in their willingness to negotiate and sign treaties with Muslim powers.

FIGHTING TO PROMOTE CHRISTIANITY

Battle imagery invaded Christian thought, and Christian practices found a place on the battlefield. King Alfred of Wessex prayed with his commanders before battle and his warriors had Christian images on their weapons; in chronicles his wars were always presented as being for Christianity against pagans. Likewise, Charlemagne's battles against pagan enemies such as the Saxons were presented as holy wars. For the 'pagans', the price of defeat by Alfred or by Charlemagne was forcible conversion to Christianity. Such a war was self-evidently a holy one, fought in order to spread the faith. The empire that Charlemagne built was an explicitly Christian one.

FIGHTING TO DEFEND CHRISTIANITY AND THE CHURCH

From c.850 onwards when Charlemagne's empire began to fall apart, the chief foes were marauding pagans – Vikings, 'Saracens' (Muslim Arabs and Berbers) and Magyars. Fighting against these raiders

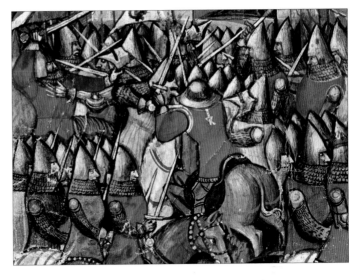

▲ *Christian Emperor Charlemagne leads his army at the walls of Pamplona, Spain, 778, from a 14th-century manuscript.*

was a defence of Christianity and the idea of 'Christendom' began to inform debate. The community of European peoples who had once been united under the Frankish empire were now bound by their common Christian faith and their opposition to non-Christian, pagan enemies.

In the 9th and 10th centuries, moreover, in increasingly lawless times, church authorities began to promote the theory that armed warriors had a responsibility to protect the weak, and particularly the Church. The churchmen promoted the Peace of God, under which warriors would swear to protect those who were not equipped to protect themselves – principally clergy and monks. In this context, fighting was a form of piety.

This initiative did more than condemn attacks on church property, going as far as to encourage violence in the interests of preventing lawless attacks. As with Urban's call to arms at Clermont, in the Peace of God initiative the Church was not simply giving its blessing to violence, it was rather bringing violence into being.

Throughout the period there were also those churchmen who resisted the glorification of violence, who continued to promote the monastic or clerical life as the ideal Christian one. Killing remained officially a sin. The Norman soldiers who fought at Hastings under William the Conqueror were required to do penance for the blood they had spilled, despite the fact that they were fighting under a papal banner (with the pope's backing) and the explicit approval of their clergy.

▼ *At Hastings in 1066 Christian Normans fought Christian Anglo-Saxons. Duke William's men were supported by the pope.*

MUSLIM EMPIRES
THE SPREAD OF ISLAM

In the late 11th century, prior to the First Crusade, control of the eastern Mediterranean was divided between the Christian Byzantine Empire based in Constantinople, the Sunni Muslim Seljuk Turks nominally ruled from Baghdad, rival Seljuk groups in Anatolia with a capital at Nicaea, and Shi'ite Muslim Fatimids from northern Africa. In eastern Anatolia the Muslim Turkish Danishmends were also a force to be reckoned with.

THE ISLAMIC EXPANSION

The great expansion of Islam began from the Arabian Peninsula in the 7th century AD. In the hundred years following the death of the Prophet Muhammad – founder of the faith – in 632, Muslim warriors created a vast empire stretching from Spain in the west to parts of China and India in the east, and encompassing Palestine, Syria and Mesopotamia.

▼ *Islamic warriors spread north, taking on the Persian and Byzantine empires, then eastwards across Africa to Spain by 711.*

THE PROPHET AND HIS TEACHING

The Prophet Muhammad was born in c.570 in the caravan city of Mecca, Arabia, a member of the Quaraish tribe. He began to preach in around 613 and established the new faith of Islam in exile from Mecca at Yathrib (later known as Medina, the City of the Prophet) in 620–30, before returning to Mecca from 630 until his death two years later.

Muhammad taught that there was one God, named Allah, Creator of all that existed, who demanded honour and submission from humans – the word *Islam* means 'surrender' (that is, to the will of Allah), while *Muslims* are so called from the Arabic for 'those who submit'. *Allah* was another name for the 'God of the Christians and the Jews'. Muhammad's teachings were gathered in the Koran, which his followers said completed and superseded the Christian and Jewish books; Muhammad was the final prophet in a sequence that also included Noah, Abraham and Jesus.

▲ *Angels Gabriel, Michael, Israfil and Azrail attend on the Prophet as he travels to Mecca. One of a set of 16th-century Ottoman illustrations on Muhammad's life.*

THE FIRST ISLAMIC LEADERS

Following the death of Muhammad in Mecca in 632, one of his followers, named Abu Bakr, a merchant and member of a minor clan in the Prophet's Quaraish tribe,

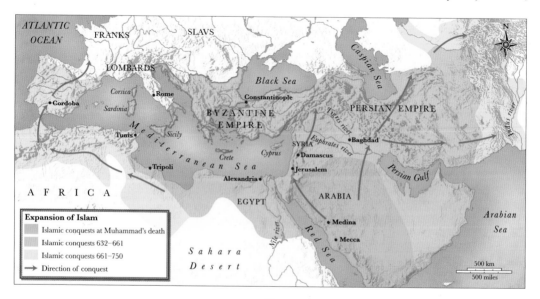

Expansion of Islam
- Islamic conquests at Muhammad's death
- Islamic conquests 632–661
- Islamic conquests 661–750
- → Direction of conquest

was elected as *khalifat rasul Allah* (Successor to God's Prophet) or 'caliph': the spiritual and political leader of the faithful. He died in 634, but before his death appointed a successor, another merchant and a member of the Quaraish, named Omar bin Khattab.

Under Caliph Omar's rule (634–44), Muslim Bedouin tribesmen won astonishing victories against the Byzantine and Persian empires, defeating the Byzantines in Syria and the Persians in Mesopotamia. They took Damascus in 635. In 637 they captured the Persian capital Ctesiphon. In 638 they took Jerusalem. In the 640s they established themselves in Egypt, capturing Alexandria in 646. By this time Omar was dead. Disputes over the succession gave rise to schism and centuries-long enmity between Sunni and Shi'ite Islam.

SUNNI AND SHI'ITE SPLIT

Omar was succeeded by Othman ibn Affan, another merchant and also one of Muhammad's original converts and once again a member of Quaraish tribe of Mecca. There was opposition to his appointment, gathered around the Prophet's cousin and son-in-law Ali, husband of Muhammad's daughter Fatima. When Othman was murdered in 656, two rival caliphs vied to replace him: on the

▼ *This image of a Moorish army is from a manuscript made for King Alfonso X of Castile and Leon (r.1252–84).*

one hand Ali, and on the other, Mu'awiyah, a member of Umayyad clan, who had earlier been appointed Governor of Syria by Othman. In 661 both Ali and Mu'awiyah were stabbed as they prayed in mosques in separate cities – Ali later died, but Mu'awiyah survived. Ali's supporters appointed his son Hassan caliph, but in a confrontation with Mu'awiyah he backed down; then when Mu'awiyah died in 680, Ali's second son Hussein claimed the caliphate. In an encounter with Mu'awiyah's son Yazid on 10 October 680, Hussein and all his followers were killed.

The split between Shi'ite and Sunni Muslims derived from this power struggle. Sunnis backed the descendants of Mu'awiyah – the Umayyad caliphs – as the rightful leaders of Islam, but Shi'ites declared them usurpers and argued that Ali had inherited the spirit of Muhammad and that leadership of Islam should be from his descendants. The Shi'ites' name came from that of the followers of Ali in the 7th century – the *shi'at Ali* (the party of Ali), whereas the Sunni were so called because they said they were following the *sunna* (example) of Muhammad.

AN ISLAMIC EMPIRE IN SPAIN

Muslim Arabs spread westwards from Egypt through northern Africa. Their advance was temporarily held up by the Berbers of the Atlas Mountains but after constructing the fortified city of Kairouan (in modern Tunisia) they subdued the Maghreb region of north and north-western Africa, then under the great Arab general Tariw ibn-Ziyad, crossed the Straits of Gibraltar and in just five years took virtually the whole Iberian Peninsula from its previous rulers, the Visigoths.

Arabs began to raid beyond the Pyrenees Mountains into southern and western France. In 732 at the Battle of Tours the marauding Arabs finally met their match in a redoubtable army commanded by Charles Martel ('the Hammer'), King of the Franks. Thereafter the Arabs withdrew into Spain and consolidated their possessions there.

▲ *St James makes a miraculous appearance in the legendary Battle of Clavijo in 844.*

UMAYYADS, ABBASIDS AND FATIMIDS

In the east the Umayyad descendants of Caliph Mu'awiyah ruled the Islamic empire from Damascus until they were ousted in 750 by their cousins and rivals the Abbasids, who established the capital of the empire at Baghdad in Iraq. The Abbasids came to power with Shi'ite support but ruled as Sunni Muslims. In 909 militant Shi'ite Muslims established a rival Fatimid dynasty (claiming direct descent from the Prophet's daughter Fatima) in Tunis and built their capital at Cairo.

By the second half of the 10th century the balance of power in the western Mediterranean was between a resurgent Byzantine empire, which had re-established itself in Syria; the increasingly weak Abbasid caliphate in Baghdad, which had nominal control over Iran, Iraq and the remainder of Syria; and the Fatimids of Cairo, who had extended their territory up through Palestine.

THE RISE OF THE SELJUKS

Then the Seljuk Turks erupted onto the scene. Originally from central Asia, these Turkmen tribes converted to Sunni Islam, conquered Afghanistan and eastern Iran, and in 1055 took control of Baghdad. In the 1070s the Seljuks delivered a crushing blow to the Byzantine army at the Battle of Manzikert, capturing Syria and most of Palestine from the Fatimids.

CHRISTIANS IN THE EAST

THE 'EMPIRE OF THE GREEKS'

The Latin Christians led by the pope in Rome, the faithful who were summoned by Urban II to the First Crusade, did not have a close or easy relationship with their counterparts in the Eastern Church and the Byzantine Empire.

CHRISTIAN ORIGINS IN THE EAST

Christian presence in the eastern Mediterranean dates back to the 1st century AD, when saints Peter, Paul and Barnabus established the first Christian community in Antioch – its members were the first people in history to be called 'Christians'. The origins of the Christian Byzantine Empire lie in the 4th century, when Constantine, the first Roman emperor to support Christianity, established the city of Constantinople as a new capital for the Roman Empire.

Constantine built the city as Nova Roma (New Rome) on the site of the trading city of Byzantium, according to legend created in 667BC by Greek colonists led by

▼ According to tradition, St Peter was the first Bishop of Antioch, then Bishop of Rome – and, as such, was the first pope.

King Byzantas (or Byzas); New Rome was renamed Constantinople (the city of Constantine) after Constantine's death in AD337. In contrast to previous Roman emperors, who had persecuted Christians, Constantine announced that Christianity would be tolerated in the empire in 313 – traditionally he had won power after a vision had inspired him to fight under the sign of the Christian cross. He then laid the groundwork for the establishment of a Christian culture in the empire, although he was not himself baptized until shortly before his death. He called the Church's first ecumenical meeting, the Council of Nicaea, in 325. This council drew up the first statement of uniform Christian doctrine, the Nicene Creed.

Situated on the Bosphorus between the Black Sea and the Sea of Marmara, at the intersection of the mercantile routes of Asia and eastern Europe, Constantinople grew fabulously wealthy on the profits of trade. After the death of Emperor Theodosius I in 395, the Roman Empire was permanently split into eastern and western halves, ruled from Rome and Constantinople, respectively. Following the sacking of Rome by the Visigoths in 410 and the collapse of the eastern empire in Europe culminating in the deposition

▲ *Constantine the Great (left) founded Constantinople, while his mother St Helena (right) played an important part in Jerusalem's rise as a centre of pilgrimage.*

of the last emperor in Rome, Romulus Augustus, in 476 by the Germanic king Odoacer, the city of Constantine was the capital of the Byzantine Empire.

EXPANSION AND DECLINE

In the 7th and 8th centuries the Byzantine Empire came under repeated attack by the swiftly expanding Muslim empire. Several times, from 674, the Arabs attempted to take Constantinople itself, but without success; they were finally driven back from the city when the siege of 717 was decisively defeated by the Byzantine emperor Leo III. In the period 863–1025 the Byzantine Empire expanded greatly and at one point in 976 the Arabs were driven back as far as the very gates of Jerusalem. But after the death of Emperor Basil II in 1025, the empire's fortunes declined once more, and in the mid-11th century the Seljuk Turks erupted into the region, culminating in the severe defeat of the Byzantine army by the Seljuks at Manzikert in Armenia in 1071. This defeat lost the empire all its lands in Anatolia.

▲ *St Mark, author of the Gospel of Mark, is revered by Christians in north Africa, and was Bishop of Alexandria.*

CONFLICT WITHIN

The name 'Byzantine Empire', it should be noted, dates from the 16th century, when it was first used by a German historian. The rulers and citizens of the empire called it 'Roman', whereas those in western Europe called it the 'Empire of the Greeks'. From the 9th century onwards the great powers of Europe were increasingly in competition with the Byzantine Empire to determine who was the successor of ancient Rome – as well as being in dispute over territories in Italy. In 800 Charlemagne was crowned *Imperator Augustus* (August Emperor) by Pope Leo III in Rome, in an attempt to revive the Roman Empire in the west; he also bore the title *Patricius Romanorum* (Protector of the Romans). In the 10th century Otto II of the Germans married a Byzantine

princess – Theopanu, niece of the Byzantine emperor John I Tzimisces – but was in conflict with the eastern empire and declared himself 'Roman emperor'.

TENSION BETWEEN WESTERN AND EASTERN CHURCHES

There was also conflict between the Church hierarchies of west and east. In 1054, the leaders of the Churches – Pope Leo IX in Rome and Patriarch Michael Cerularius in Constantinople – excommunicated one another. The tension went right back to the 5th century, when, following the fall of Rome, the pope assumed the mantle of protector of Christians in the west. Rome was the burial place of the Apostle Peter and the popes claimed direct succession from him and ultimate authority over the entire Church; but the patriarchs of Constantinople claimed they were the highest authority, since Constantinople was the seat of the eastern Roman Empire.

Matters of doctrine also caused controversy: the Eastern Church allowed married priests but the Latin Church insisted officially on celibacy of the priesthood; the Latin Church allowed the use of unleavened bread in the Mass but the Eastern Church was against this. Another major disagreement arose over whether in the Christian Trinity of Father, Son and Holy Spirit, the Spirit derived from the Father or from both the Father and the Son. The Nicene Creed had declared 'I believe in the Holy Spirit, the Lord the giver of Life, who proceedeth from the Father', but western churches had added the words 'and the Son'. This *filioque* clause (so called from the Latin word meaning 'from the Son') had first been used in Spain in the 7th century, then had been backed by Charlemagne, and had finally been accepted by the papacy in 1014; but it was vehemently rejected by the Eastern Church as heresy. In 1089 Urban II sent an embassy to Constantinople asking for full relations to recommence between Western and Eastern Churches but the division – later known to historians as the 'Great Schism' – endured.

▼ *The Byzantine Empire held territory in Italy. At Ravenna, the basilica of San Vitale contains this beautiful mosaic of Christ.*

THE POWER OF THE PAPACY

POPES STRUGGLE FOR INDEPENDENCE

The second half of the 11th century saw concerted attempts by the papacy to establish the Church in a strong position independent of secular power. The idea of fighting as a form of Christian devotion was taken a stage further when popes presented struggles in support of the papacy as holy wars.

Pope Leo IX (ruled 1049–54) personally led troops to war against Norman adventurers in southern Italy in 1053. He set the precedent of promising his soldiers absolution of their sins and remission of penance as their reward. In this campaign the papal army was defeated at the Battle of Civitate by a Norman force led by Humphrey of Hauteville and containing Robert Guiscard. Ten years later the Normans were papal allies: after Pope Nicholas II (ruled 1059–61) invested

▼ *Pope Gregory VII grants absolution to German emperor Henry IV in 1077. This was an important but temporary victory for the papacy in the long struggle to establish its independence from secular rulers.*

▲ *Cluny Abbey in France was at the forefront of Church reform in the 10th to 12th centuries and its abbot was second in power only to the pope. Otho of Lagery, later known as Pope Urban II, was a prior there. As pope, he visited the abbey in 1095.*

Robert Guiscard as duke of Apulia, Calabria and Sicily, the Norman army fought under a papal banner in invading Muslim Sicily. Another branch of the Norman family also had a papal banner for William of Normandy's invasion of England in 1066.

GREGORY VII AND ST PETER'S SOLDIERS

Pope Gregory VII (ruled 1073–85) became embroiled in a long-running dispute with the German emperor Henry IV (reigned 1056–1105). The main issue of contention in what is known to historians as 'the Investiture Controversy' was whether Henry or Gregory should control

▶ *Pope Leo X and Patriarch Michael Cerularius of Constantinople excommunicated one another in 1054. The quarrel had begun centuries before in a dispute over which church had primacy.*

the church: it was focused on who should have control over bishops' investiture (appointment and presentation of symbols of office) in the German church; it followed a period in which the papacy had been very weak, and Henry IV's predecessor, Henry III, had appointed three German popes. Gregory set out to mobilize his own papal force, the *Militia Sancti*

Petri (the 'army of St Peter'). He told the knights in his service that they were 'vassals of Saint Peter' and as reward would receive Peter's blessing 'in this life and the life to come'.

Gregory and Henry IV clashed dramatically. In 1076 Gregory excommunicated Henry and declared him *anathema*, which meant he was excluded from the community of Christian believers and that none of his subjects had to keep oaths made to him. German nobles forced Henry to back down and in January 1077 he travelled to the pope's castle at Canossa in northern Italy, where Gregory made him wait outside, barefoot and clad in a hair shirt in the snow, before finally allowing him in to receive forgiveness. This decisively changed the balance of power between pope and emperor, but only in the short term: Henry and Gregory clashed again and Gregory excommunicated Henry again in 1080; Henry attacked Rome three times between 1081 and 1084 and on the third occasion Gregory had to be rescued from his castle of Castel Sant'Angelo in the city by his ally and vassal, the Norman adventurer Robert Guiscard.

REFORM AND PAPAL POWER

Gregory is remembered as a 'reforming pope', because he attacked such abuses in the church as simony (the sale of Church offices) and tried to impose celibacy on the priesthood. Both these campaigns were tied up with his efforts to establish the absolute supremacy of the papacy – simony was beneficial to secular leaders who used it to bring about the appointment of their own supporters in key positions, and he made use of the campaign for celibacy to counter the power of rebel bishops who allowed married priests. He was passionately committed to the spiritual renewal of the Church.

GREGORY VII'S 'CRUSADE'

Gregory is also notable for his attempt to launch a forerunner of the crusades – a military expedition to help Constantinople and the Christians in the East in 1074.

THE ISSUING OF INDULGENCES

Popes used the promise of forgiveness, the remission of penances and the granting of indulgences as a lure to mobilize armies in their support. The issuing of indulgences derived from the idea that a punishment remained due for a sinner even when he or she had won forgiveness for a sin through repentance and confession; a sinner might win God's eternal forgiveness through genuine repentance but still be liable for a temporal punishment.

In the early Christian Church 'canonical penances' were calculated to wipe a sinner's slate clean, to do away with the temporal punishment; then in the early medieval Church, parts of the canonical penance were commuted – a repentant sinner was told he or she would achieve the same benefit by donating a specified amount of money to the Church, by giving alms to the poor or by spending an allotted period of time in fasting or prayer. Indulgences were usually partial – they commuted part of the punishment. The first recorded instance of an absolute or plenary indulgence that promised the complete avoidance of temporal punishment was the speech by Urban II at Clermont in 1095, when he issued his call to arms in the First Crusade. He declared: 'Whoever, acting out of devotion and not for the sake of winning honour or riches, travels to Jerusalem to free the Church of God may substitute this sacred journey for all penance.'

▼ *Pope Urban II at Clermont, where he issued his call to take up arms.*

Gregory made the attempt in response to a call in 1073 from Byzantine emperor Michael VII for help against the Seljuk Turks. In a manner that would have many echoes in Urban II's declaration at Clermont in 1095, Gregory promoted the enterprise in 1074 as an act of charity on behalf of those he hoped to involve, and claimed that they would be following the example of Christ, acting under the mandate of God himself; he also offered the promise of 'eternal reward'. Gregory did manage to raise an army but the enterprise foundered and the expedition did not set out.

The First Crusade was a direct descendant of the holy wars that were fought in the name of the papacy, since it was launched by the pope and fought with the aim of establishing his supremacy over the Eastern Church and his rule over a united Christendom. From the outset it was conceived by those involved in it as an expression of papal power.

THE HOLY CITY OF JERUSALEM
PLACE OF CHRIST'S PASSION, SACRED TO THREE FAITHS

Several medieval maps survive to the present day in which Jerusalem is represented as the centre of the Earth, which was at that time believed to be flat. To Christians of this era, the city was the holiest spot in the world, the place where God, through his son Jesus Christ, had redeemed the fallen creation.

Jerusalem was and is sacred to Jews and Muslims, as well as to the followers of Christ. Jews revere Jerusalem as the city of David, founder of the united kingdom of Israel and Judah, and the place where his successor, Solomon, built a great temple. To Muslims Jerusalem is traditionally the third most sacred city in the world after Mecca, the Prophet's birthplace, and Yathrib, or Medina, the city in which he established the Islamic faith in AD620–30. Jerusalem is said to be the place from which the Prophet made an ascent into heaven – according to Muslim tradition,

▼ The Church of the Holy Sepulchre, believed to be built on the spot where Christ was crucified, was the crusaders' goal.

Muhammad was taken up from Mecca by the Angel Gabriel one night in 620 and transported to Jerusalem, from where he ascended a golden ladder to heaven.

REPEATED VIOLENCE
By the time of the First Crusade in the 11th century, the city already had a long and bloody history. Following the era of David and Solomon the city was sacked by the Egyptian pharaoh Sheshonk I in 922BC, and then both city and Temple were destroyed by Nebuchadnezzar of Babylon in 587BC. This cataclysmic event, which resulted in the exile of the Jews in Babylon, was followed eventually by their return under Cyrus the Great of Persia and the building of a second Temple in 515BC.

Under the rule of the Seleucids (the rulers of a kingdom that grew out of the empire of Alexander the Great) in the 2nd century BC, Judas Maccabeus led his celebrated revolt to reclaim the city and cleanse the Temple. In the era of chivalry he became an unlikely role model for the crusader knights as a religious warrior.

ROMAN CITY
At the time of Christ, Jerusalem was part of the province of Judea in the Roman Empire. A Jewish revolt in AD66 resulted in a devastating attack led by the future emperor Titus, in which the city was almost completely destroyed and the Temple once again reduced to ruins. A new city named Aelia Capitolina was built by Emperor Hadrian, provoking another revolt in 132–35, put down again by Roman might; at this time Hadrian renamed the Roman province of Judea 'Syria Palaestina' after the Philistines named in the Bible. Jerusalem remained under Roman rule until the 7th century, although from the 4th century onwards this was under Christian emperors. The city became a well-established site of pilgrimage for Christians.

▲ Jerusalem was depicted as being at the centre of the world in this map from an English psalter c.1262. Christ and two angels preside. The east is at the top, Europe and Africa at the bottom.

CHURCH OF THE HOLY SEPULCHRE
Built by Emperor Constantine in c.325, the Church of the Holy Sepulchre was said to mark the site of Golgotha, or the Hill of Calvary, where Christ was crucified and then buried.

The church consisted of three parts: a basilica named the *Martyrium* built over the place of crucifixion, a colonnade called the *Triportico* built around the Hill of Calvary, and a rotunda called the *Anastasis* (Resurrection) containing the actual cave in which Christ was said to have been buried. The tomb itself was enclosed in a special structure beneath the rotunda called the 'edicule' (from Latin *aediculum*, meaning 'small structure'), and visiting the edicule understandably became a major focus for Christian pilgrims and subsequently crusaders.

AN ARAB CITY

Jerusalem was captured by Bedouin Arabs under Omar bin Khattab, the second caliph, or leader, of Islam, in 638. His successors, the Umayyad caliphs of Damascus and their successors, the Abbasid caliphs of Baghdad, ruled over Jerusalem for more than 600 years, until 969. These regimes were both supporters of mainstream Sunni Islam, but in 969 the rival Fatimid caliphs of Cairo in Egypt, who were Shi'ite Muslims, took control of the city.

THE DOME OF THE ROCK

The city's principal Muslim holy site, the Dome of the Rock, was constructed in 685–91 by the Umayyad caliph Abd al-Malik. It was a mosque built as a *masshad* (pilgrimage shrine) for Muslims, on the reputed site from which Muhammad ascended to heaven on his Night Journey. The site was also sacred on three counts for Jews: as the place where the patriarch

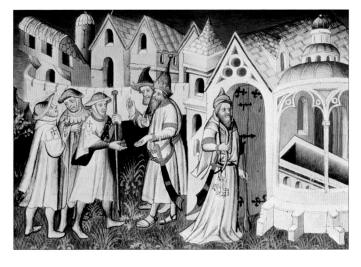

▼ The army of Nebuchadnezzar, king of Babylon c.605–562BC, brings death and destruction to the city of Jerusalem. The illustration is from the Commentary on the Apocalypse *(c.776) by Spanish monk Beatus of Liébana.*

Abraham had readied himself to sacrifice his son Isaac to please God; as the rock on which Jacob had dreamt of a ladder ascending to heaven; and as the site of King Solomon's Temple. The al-Aqsa Mosque was built nearby at around the same time. In the crusader era, contemporary reports suggest that many Christian pilgrims, ignorant of their history, believed the Dome of the Rock to be the biblical Temple of Solomon.

▲ Christ's empty tomb is visible within the Church of the Holy Sepulchre in this 14th-century view of pilgrims visiting Jerusalem.

The Umayyad, Abbasid and Fatimid caliphs were mostly liberal towards Christian pilgrims. There was a major outbreak of persecution in the early 11th century, when the Fatimid caliph al-Hakim ordered the destruction of Christian shrines, including the Church of the Holy Sepulchre in 1010. This aggression proved to be short-lived, however, and in the 1040s the church was reconstructed by Byzantine builders with the permission of Fatimid caliph Ma'ad al-Mustansir Billah.

In 1071, however, the Fatimids were ousted from Jerusalem by the Seljuk Turks, who were far less tolerant of Christianity, and were unwilling to allow pilgrims to come and go unmolested. The reported attacks by Seljuk Turks on Christian pilgrims to Jerusalem was one of the provocations and justifications of the First Crusade.

Immediately prior to the First Crusade, Jerusalem was in the hands of the Seljuk Turks, but during the crusade (in 1098) it was recaptured by the Fatimid Muslims, so it was from the Fatimids that the crusaders took it in July 1099.

THE PENITENTIAL JOURNEY
A LONG HISTORY OF PILGRIMAGE

The religious tradition of the pilgrimage, or penitential journey, has roots that travel down deep into history. Christians in the 10th and 11th centuries enthusiastically embraced the crusade as a form of pilgrimage, as a means of expiating their sins.

The tradition of making religious journeys to visit shrines dates back to at least the world of ancient Greece, when people would travel to visit the Temple of Diana at Ephesus in Asia Minor (now western Turkey) and other sacred sites. Christ's birthplace, Bethlehem, and the scene of his Passion, Jerusalem, were places of pilgrimage for Christians from as early as the 2nd century AD.

FIRST CHRISTIAN PILGRIMS TO JERUSALEM

Eusebius, an early 4th-century Bishop of Caesarea, made references in his *Historia Ecclesiastica* (History of the Christian Church) to travelling Christians making

▼ *Devout pilgrims patiently wait to receive a papal blessing before embarking on their voyage to the holy places in the East.*

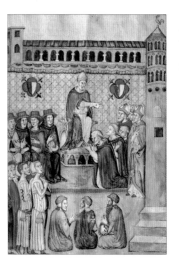

religious visits to Jerusalem. In truth, there was little for Christians to see in the city before Constantine the Great began a programme of identifying sacred sites and building churches.

Before Constantine's time the Jerusalem of Christ's era was almost entirely covered with the new city of Aelia Capitolina built by Hadrian following the near-total destruction of the earlier city by the future emperor Titus in AD70. The only known site associated with Christ's Passion was the cenacle, or supper room, reputedly the place in which Christ shared his last earthly meal with his disciples and gave them the basis of the Christian Mass, or Communion service. The cenacle was in the house said to have belonged to Mary,

▲ *The 'True Cross' is identified when it miraculously heals a sick woman during St Helena's pilgrimage to Jerusalem.*

mother of Saint Mark, author of the biblical Gospel of Mark; she was a prominent early Christian and the house was a meeting place for the disciples and followers after Christ's resurrection.

Constantine identified the site of Christ's burial in an area that, according to Bishop Eusebius, had been built up with earth and used as the site for a temple of the Roman goddess Venus, probably during Hadrian's rebuilding of the city. Constantine excavated the mound and found a cave that was then identified as the place where Joseph of Arimathaea placed Christ's body after it was taken down from the cross. There, Constantine constructed the Church of the Holy Sepulchre in c.AD325.

THE 'TRUE CROSS'

According to a tradition first recorded by the late 4th-century Christian writer Socrates Scholasticus, Constantine's mother Helena – who also converted to Christianity – made a pilgrimage to Jerusalem in c.312–30 and, under the guidance of a local Jew, found Christ's cross together with those of the two robbers who were crucified alongside him. A miracle revealed which one of the three was the cross used to crucify Christ: each of the crosses was laid on a very sick woman and one of them, imbued with divine power because Christ's blood had been spilt on it, brought about a cure. Helena also supposedly found the inscription hung above Christ's head on the cross, which identified him as 'King of the Jews', and the nails used to fix Jesus to the cross: the relics were sent to Constantinople, where the nails were beaten to form the emperor's bridle and helmet.

According to some accounts Helena also took the cross itself back with her to Constantinople, but other versions indicate that parts of the cross were kept in the Church of the Holy Sepulchre: pilgrims were venerating relics of the cross there by about c.380. Shortly afterwards, accounts of pilgrimages indicate that religious travellers were also being told that they could see the Holy Lance that pierced Christ's side, the crown of thorns He wore and the pillar at which He was whipped.

A fragment of the cross was taken from Jerusalem by Persian Sassanid emperor Khosrau II when he took the city in 614, then recaptured by Byzantine emperor Heraclius when he defeated Khosrau in battle. After keeping the relic briefly in Constantinople, Heraclius returned it to Jerusalem, where it remained. It was hidden by Christians early in the 11th century, and reputedly found in August 1099 by Arnulf of Choques, the city's first

Latin Patriarch. The fragment became the principal sacred relic of the Kingdom of Jerusalem, kept in the Church of the Holy Sepulchre, and carried into battle by the crusader armies. This was the relic whose loss to Saladin's army during the Battle of Hattin in 1187 caused such lasting concern and consternation.

PILGRIMAGE AS PENANCE

The pilgrimage was a form of penitential discipline. Making a pilgrimage was a form of penance, that is an act performed to win forgiveness of sins. A priest, or in more serious cases a bishop, would specify the particular pilgrimage that a penitent must undertake in order to earn forgiveness. While travelling, the pilgrim might be required to wear a heavy chain or a hair shirt to add to the penance.

THE POWER OF RELICS

The institution of the pilgrimage was supported by the belief – already powerful as we have seen by the 5th century, and strong right through the Middle Ages – in the spiritual force of physical relics of Christ and his saints. In addition to fragments of objects such as the Cross or the Crown of Thorns, pilgrims travelled to venerate miraculously preserved body parts of sacred figures, such as fingers or hair clippings. These relics were believed to be imbued with divine power and regularly, like Helena's piece of the cross, effected extraordinary cures. Pilgrimages did not have to be to Jerusalem or the Holy Land: penitents could make journeys to a wide range of sites closer to home that were associated with the lives of saints or sanctified by the possession of a holy relic.

THE GOLDEN LEGEND OF THE TRUE CROSS

The pilgrims who venerated pieces of the True Cross in various locations were eager to tell and hear stories of its origin. A story developed linking the wood from which the cross was made to the Tree of Life that grew in the Garden of Eden; the form in which this tale has survived is the *Golden Legend* written by Jacopo of Voragine, Bishop of Genoa, in

1260. According to this story, the cross was made of wood grown from a seed of the Tree of Life: as he lay dying, Adam persuaded his son Seth to get the seed from the archangel Michael; when he returned with it, Seth placed it in Adam's mouth. Adam was buried after he died and a great tree grew from the seed and lived for many hundreds of years. Finally it was cut down: the wood was used to build a bridge. It happened that the biblical Queen of Sheba crossed the bridge on her way to visit King Solomon: she saw the wood's true nature and worshipped it, then told Solomon that a piece of the wood would be instrumental in the establishment of a new covenant between God and the Jews. Solomon was afraid and had the wood buried, but 14 generations later it was unearthed and made into the Holy Cross on which Christ died.

◄ *The Queen of Sheba kisses the wood of the Cross in a fresco of the story by Piero della Francesca in the Church of San Francesco, Arezzo, Italy.*

CRUSADER PILGRIMS

A SACRED ENTERPRISE

Access to Jerusalem was the ultimate prize for the crusader armies, for their journey was a pilgrimage as well as a military campaign. Each crusader who took the cross vowed to enter the Church of the Holy Sepulchre and pray there.

PILGRIMS BEARING ARMS

At low points during the First Crusade, such as the long siege of Antioch and the delay following its capture, the rank and file of the army were inspired to endure by their desire to fulfil their pilgrimage vows. Following the taking of Jerusalem, and their visit to the Church of the Holy Sepulchre, many felt that their enterprise was complete and took off for home, despite the fact that the crusaders' hold on Jerusalem was tenuous and that a formi-

▼ *Amid brutal violence, the soldiers who recaptured Jerusalem at the climax of the First Crusade celebrated ecstatically. Their pilgrimage had reached its goal.*

dable Egyptian relief army under the command of Fatimid vizier al-Afdal Shahanshah was marching on the city.

Before the crusades, there was already, as we have seen, a well-established Christian tradition of the pilgrimage as a form of penitential discipline. There was also a precedent for armed pilgrimage: in 1064, 7,000 armed German pilgrims under the command of two archbishops and two bishops marched to Jerusalem – some apparently wearing crosses. In 1095 Pope Urban II conflated the idea of a holy war fought in the name of God and the papacy with the benefits of a penitential journey. Part of the explanation for the response to his call to take the cross and travel on armed expedition to Jerusalem was that it met a keenly felt need – it allowed people to make their piety public and to seek expiation for their sins.

For many, the highest expression of Christian faith in action remained the monastic or clerical life. For example,

▲ *Preaching the Second Crusade in 1146, Bernard of Clairvaux urges Christians to take up the cross of Christ, and demonstrate their willingness to share in His suffering.*

Aelfric Grammaticus (the Grammarian), 10th-century abbot of Eynsham in southern England, declared that monks were the proper soldiers of Christ, those who fought with the words of prayers rather than with the metal of swords. But not all

THE GERMAN PILGRIMAGE OF 1064–65

Various chronicle accounts survive of the German pilgrimage of 1064. It was led by Siegfried, Archbishop of Mainz, and William, Archbishop of Trier, supported by Otto, Bishop of Regensburg and Gunther, Bishop of Bamberg. According to one report, Bishop Gunther cut such a splendid figure on this voyage that when the pilgrims came to Constantinople the people suspected that he must be the Holy Roman Emperor himself, travelling in disguise.

As they moved on towards Jerusalem, the pilgrims met returning travellers who told horror stories about the treatment of Christians by Arabs. On Good Friday 1065 the German pilgrims themselves were attacked by Arab bandits and then besieged at an isolated farmhouse over the entire Easter weekend. But, inspired by their archbishops and

bishops, the pilgrims trusted in God and in their weapons and drove back the besiegers on Easter Sunday, despite having gone three days without food or water. They captured some leading Arabs who had broken into the enclosure and used these men as hostages.

Another much-reported and horrific episode on the pilgrimage involved the rape of an abbess in full view of the travelling pilgrims by a gang of Arabs. The abbess was so badly injured that she died. One account of the pilgrimage, contained in the *Life of Bishop Altmann of Passau*, commented: 'Brought down by events like this and other humiliations in Christ's name, the travelling faithful won high praise in all quarters, from men and from angels above, because they elected to enter God's kingdom, suffering many tribulations.'

were willing to share in the suffering of Christ; what pain and difficulty they had to endure en route to victory would only improve the effectiveness of the enterprise in winning salvation for them.

In a sermonizing letter, which he despatched to the people of France and Bavaria in 1146, Bernard called the crusade 'Christ's business, in which is found our salvation' and called for urgency – 'now is the right time, now is the day of total salvation'. He summoned the vision of pagans defiling the Holy City, the place where so many Christian pilgrims had 'confessed their wrongdoings with tears and won forgiveness'; he said that the all-powerful God could of course cleanse the city with a battalion of angels, but that he preferred to test the mettle of his faithful Christian soldiers.

Bernard concluded with the following exhortation 'since your land is bursting with courageous men and is celebrated for the strength of its young warriors, gird yourselves like men and take up arms joyfully in the name of Christ.'

could follow this path. As Guibert, the Benedictine abbot of Nogent-sous-Coucy in France, wrote after praising the holy wars of the crusades as giving knights a chance to win their salvation: 'In this way they are not forced to give up secular affairs entirely by entering the monastic life of the clerical professions, as was once the normal practice, but can reach in some degree God's grace while following their own careers, with the freedom and in the dress to which they are used.'

THE CROSS OF SUFFERING

The men (and women) who took the cross did not call themselves crusaders. They were known by contemporaries as *cruces-ignati* – people marked with the cross. Nor did they call the enterprise a crusade. It was variously called a business, a journey or way and a pilgrimage. Urban principally promoted it as a military expedition.

When Bernard of Clairvaux came to preach the Second Crusade in 1146 – with such dramatic effectiveness that his sermons were viewed as a 'divine augury' and

a 'miracle' – he emphasized the expedition to Jerusalem he was urging as an opportunity for Christians to win salvation and, on an individual level, to demonstrate their repentance. In his vision, the cross worn by the crusaders was a sign that they

▼ *Bernard of Clairvaux and other crusade preachers painted a picture of terrible outrages perpetrated by Muslim 'Saracens' against the Christians in the East.*

CHAPTER THREE

BECOMING A KNIGHT

The knight was a specialist in mounted fighting. He was well equipped, and often superbly well trained. Many knights underwent a long and difficult apprenticeship in the arts of war, and the thoroughness of this training set them apart from their contemporaries. Although some great martial figures were able to break into knighthood through acts of great chivalry, knights were generally a social elite of princes, magnates or the sons of knights.

In the 13th century the chivalric handbooks that provided instructions on proper knightly behaviour set guidelines on the kind of people who might properly aspire to knighthood. The most celebrated, the *Libre del Orde de Cavalleria* (*Book of the Order of Chivalry*), was written in *c*.1265 by the remarkable Majorcan troubadour, philosopher, novelist, mystic and missionary Ramon Llull. The book also teaches that it is essential for knights to come from a noble family because such families have an established tradition of chivalric virtue going back generations.

Another handbook, the *Livre de Chevalerie*, or *Book of Chivalry*, was written in *c*.1350 by French knight Geoffroi de Charny. He stresses the role of chivalric warriors in keeping the peace, and presents them as an arm of the Church alongside the priesthood. Chivalry (the class of knights and men at arms) supports the divinely sanctioned social structure, by making it possible for God's representatives on earth, the king and the Church authorities, to exercise authority and ensure that justice is done.

▲ *The late medieval Bodiam Castle, in East Sussex, England.*

◄ *By tradition, a squire was expected to keep vigil on the last night before he was elevated to the brotherhood of knights.*

ACQUIRING COURTESY

LIFE AS A PAGE

In theory the son of a knight was educated for knighthood from birth. Until the age of seven he was in the care of his mother and her women of the household, then he began the first stage of his knightly training as a page, either at home or in another noble house. Life as a page lasted for seven years before, at around the age of 14, a page moved on to complete his apprenticeship by serving a true knight day by day as his squire. In the later period of his life as a page he was sometimes known as a *damoiseau*, or valet.

▼ *The education of children was divided strictly by gender. While girls learned to spin, sew and manage the household, boys were instructed in martial arts, as shown in this 15th-century illustration.*

FIGHTING AND HUNTING

Squires of the household instructed the pages in horse-riding, tilting at the quintain (riding at and striking a target with a couched lance), tilting at the ring (striking a smaller round target), wrestling, boxing and running. The quintain was a human-shaped dummy holding a shield, and suspended on a stick: the page had to hit the shield right in the centre. The dummy would swing round and round and the page had to be careful to get swiftly out of the way.

The pages also learned how to handle a sword, practising their strokes against a 'pell', or wooden stake. They were trained in hunting techniques, such as caring for the hawks and falcons, and how to use a bow and arrow in competition

GEOFFREY CHAUCER

English poet Geoffrey Chaucer, whose portraits of a knight and a squire in *The Canterbury Tales* are celebrated for their authenticity, was a page at the court of Elizabeth de Burgh, countess of Ulster. The countess was married to Prince Lionel, duke of Clarence and second son of King Edward III of England, and Chaucer served as a squire in Lionel's company during the Hundred Years War in France. Captured while fighting at the siege of Rheims in 1360, Chaucer was ransomed for a handsome sum – the king himself contributed £16 to the fee. After these early military adventures, Chaucer spent most of his life as a courtier – like many young men who passed through the chivalric education system, he did not progress beyond being a squire and was never knighted. Chaucer was clearly an extraordinarily gifted and talented man, and it is apparent from his later work, which shows that he could read Latin and French, that the quality of education available to all pages and squires in the royal and noble households of this period was of a very high standard – in book learning as well as in chivalric accomplishments.

les 2 enfans de octouers

with their peers. They learned how to handle animal carcasses and prepare them for the kitchen – for example how to cut up a deer.

By watching and helping the squire, the pages also learned to perform the duties that would be required of them when they were older, whether serving knights in hall, working in the kennels and hawkpens, tending horses in the stable or cleaning and storing helmets, armour and weapons in the armoury. They learned

▶ *Pages were trained to serve alongside squires and kitchen staff during banquets. The guest of honour at this feast is Edward the Confessor.*

how to wait at table and carve meat and how to clean armour, weapons and chain mail by rubbing it in a barrel of sand.

In addition the squires were responsible for the pages' training in the courtly arts of singing, dancing, playing the pipes and the harp, and learning Latin and French. These skills were important accomplishments for a mature knight, so it was vital that this area of a page's education was not neglected. The actual teaching of writing and singing was entrusted to minor clergy and to travelling troubadours. The visiting priest would also give the pages religious education.

CORRECTION

If pages were unwilling to learn any part of their studies, squires were permitted to 'correct' them with physical force. No doubt squires were able to get away with a good deal under cover of 'corrections' and probably made themselves feel better

▼ *As well as teaching the pages to read and write, priests made sure that the young men had a proper grounding in Christianity.*

about their own mistreatment when they were pages by handing out orders and harsh punishments.

The pages had a gentler time with the ladies of the household, who also took an interest in the young men's education in chivalric arts, helping with writing and teaching dancing, courtly manners and gallant behaviour. They taught the pages necessary skills of hygiene and personal grooming. The ladies also played chess and other games with them.

BOARDING SCHOOL FOR PAGES

It was normal practice for a son to be sent to the house of his father's *suzerain* (his superior within the feudal system) to undergo his chivalric education in the company of the children of other knights. A lord's son was generally sent to the castle of another great lord or bishop – for example, Stephen of Blois (the future King Stephen of England, and the son of Stephen of Blois who was one of the leaders of the First Crusade) was sent to the court of his uncle, King Henry I of England, at about the age of ten, in 1106. Prominent churchmen took princes and the sons of noble houses into their establishments, to instruct them in the ways of chivalry. Thomas Becket received Henry II's son Henry (later 'the Young King')

alongside princes and nobles of neighbouring kingdoms. He oversaw their education until they attained knighthood.

Above all, pages learned 'courtesy', meaning the kind of behaviour that could only be picked up at a lordly or princely court. The Latin word *curialitas* can be translated as 'courtesy' or 'courtliness', the behaviour practised at the *curia*, or court.

▼ *Pages were expected to learn how to feed, groom and soothe horses belonging to the squires and the knight they served.*

AT A KNIGHT'S RIGHT HAND

LIFE AS A SQUIRE

The second stage of a chivalric education, after seven years living as a page, was often seven or more years' senior service to a knight as a squire. Typically, this began at around the age of 14. In these cases, squires cared for their lords, the knights whom they served, in all things. They attended to the knights' needs in the castle or manor house, at chivalric tournaments and on the field of battle.

It is important to note, however, that not all squires were trainee knights. There were many mounted warriors who, having progressed from being a page to becoming a squire, remained squires into mature adulthood, and even for their whole lives, because they were never formally dubbed into knighthood. Many had all the skill, bravery and chivalric

accomplishments of their knightly counterparts. At the same time, many more junior squires served in the knightly household and oversaw the education of pages as described on the previous section and below.

▼ As well as serving wine and food at mealtimes, one of a squire's duties in the banqueting hall was to bring water for guests to wash their hands.

▲ Life as a knight or a squire required a fit, strong body. Practice was needed to develop the skills with sword and lance.

AT HOME

When a squire was young, and still learning the arts of chivalry in the service of his lord, he generally lived in the castle alongside his fellows, usually sharing sleeping quarters. The young men took turns to serve the lord and other knights. In the hall the squires carved meat, and served food and wine at banquets. They also worked in the knight's bedchamber, making the bed, helping the knight dress and bringing a *vin de coucher* (draught of wine before sleep). It was also one of the squire's duties to sleep in the knight's chamber or at his door if requested. Squires worked with the animals in the kennels and stables and looked after the armoury. They also taught the pages in the house.

Squires also served the ladies of the castle. They were permitted to mingle with them quite freely, playing chess, walking in the garden, going hunting and hawking in their company. It was quite common for scandals to arise when these interactions became too intimate.

▲ *Three knights are dressed and armed by their squires, prior to a knighting ceremony.*

AT TOURNAMENTS AND ON CAMPAIGN

If the knight travelled to a tournament, the squire accompanied him. The squire fought in the mêlée, the mock battle that was held at the start of some tournaments. For jousting he had to prepare the knight's horses and be on hand to provide fresh lances and equipment. The squires gathered behind the barriers at the edge of the lists or tournament competition area, ready to rush to the knight's assistance if needed.

When the knight went on military campaign, two squires served him together. They fought alongside him, and were responsible for ensuring he had a good supply of weapons and fresh horses.

Another key part of the squire's training was learning and practising the arts of fighting, jousting and horse-riding. Squires began by fighting without chain mail or other armour in order to accustom themselves to handling the great lances and heavy swords that were used at tournaments and in battle. For example, they would practise hitting targets with their lances while running. Then they would move on to practising with the weapons while wearing armour. The young men needed to be fit and strong to cope with chain mail, for example, because it could weigh as much as 22.5kg (50lb) and the suit's entire weight was felt on the shoulders. Finally they would be ready to practise fighting and jousting while on horseback.

The squires were also educated in other aspects of courtly life and chivalry such as hunting, hawking, dancing and the appreciation of poetry and music. Some learned to read. They were introduced to historical chronicles, books on hunting and battlefield chivalry and treatises on how to be a knight such as Ramon Llull's *Book of the Order of Chivalry*, as well as chivalric romances and songs of courtly love. Squires also learned the basics of blazonry – the language of heraldry, the science of recognizing and interpreting coats of arms. Squires were also responsible for overseeing the education of pages in all these aspects of chivalric life.

LIFELONG SERVICE AS A SQUIRE

As mentioned earlier, not all squires progressed to become knights. Some seem to have fought in campaign after campaign alongside knights and remained squires. Some came from families that could not afford the expense of the ceremony and the equipment needed to be a knight. There were certainly plenty of opportunities for men of this class, well educated in the ways of chivalry, to serve at royal and noble courts throughout Europe whether as warrior squires, heralds or – if they had literary talent – as poets or chroniclers. Examples of notable men of letters who did not progress beyond being squires are Geoffrey Chaucer, author of *The Canterbury Tales*, and Ramon Llull, author of the *Book of the Order of Chivalry*.

KNIGHTING

The ceremony of knighting marked the end of the chivalric apprenticeship as page and then squire. Squires who were princes or the sons of great lords could look forward to being knighted in a great courtly ceremony. A prince would often be knighted with a host of his fellow squires to make the ceremony more magnificent. In 1306, for example, Edward of Caernarfon (the future King Edward II of England) was knighted in a ceremony involving 276 squires. He followed the prescribed rituals for preparing to be knighted, including keeping vigil overnight, then was knighted by his father before he himself knighted all the other participants. The main ceremony was held in the grounds of the London Temple, and tents were raised there to accommodate the great crowd of squires. Even so, the space was so full that two knights died in the crush, several others collapsed in a faint, and there was even a fight. There were many other similar examples – such as that of Ulrich von Lichtenstein, knight and poet, who was one of 250 squires raised to knighthood when Duke Leopold of Austria celebrated the wedding of his daughter in 1222.

Some squires of a modest background but with great martial ability were able to win knighthood on the basis of their deeds – for it was possible to be knighted on the field of battle after achieving a great feat or prior to the beginning of fighting.

▼ *Squires attended to a knight's needs in the heat of battle and on campaign, helping him with his weapons and armour.*

'ARISE, SIR KNIGHT'

THE ORIGINS AND DEVELOPMENT OF THE KNIGHTING CEREMONY

The central event in a knight's life was the occasion on which he was knighted. In this proud moment, he was admitted to an elite international group, a brotherhood of equals bound by the demanding code of chivalry. He dedicated himself to serving God, the Church, his king and his lord.

The ceremonies of knighting developed from ceremonial rites of passage practised in ancient Rome and among Germanic tribes in the Roman Empire. In Rome, when a boy was of age to become a man he was given the *toga virilis*, a white toga worn by citizens of the empire. Among Germanic tribes of the 1st and 2nd centuries AD, according to the Roman historian Tacitus, when a young man was ready to assume adult status he was given a sword and shield in a public ceremony by his father, a relative or the tribal chief. Afterwards he was counted among the tribe's warriors.

▼ *According to some accounts, it was in the Norman tradition that only knights could make others knights, and the Anglo-Saxon tradition was to be knighted by a priest.*

INVESTED WITH A SWORD

In the 8th and 9th centuries, a similar coming-of-age ceremony was used among the Germanic tribes for their princes and young lords: the young man was presented with a sword or a sword-belt. Charlemagne's son Louis the Pious, for example, was ceremonially invested with his sword in 791 at Regensburg, in preparation for going on a military campaign with his great father against the Avars. By the late 10th and early 11th centuries, in France and Norman England, the ceremony was being used to describe the elevation of a footsoldier into a mounted warrior; in the ceremony the footsoldier was given the equipment he would need to serve as a knight.

This was originally a secular event, but it became imbued with religious significance as the Christian Church developed doctrines that sanctified violence if performed in the defence of the Church and of God, and knights began to be seen as 'soldiers of Christ'. In Mainz, as early as the mid-10th century, the blessing of a sword and creation of a knight was incorporated into the Christian Mass: the sword was laid on the altar before the reading of the Holy Gospel and this prayer was read: 'Hearken, we pray, O Lord, to our intercessions, and bless with the right hand of thy greatness this sword, with which thy Servant wishes to be girded, that it may be used to defend churches, widows and orphaned children, and all thy people against the attacks of pagans, and that it may strike terror into doers of evil and may be used in justice both to attack and to defend.' Attendants then girded the sword on the aspirant knight.

DUBBING A KNIGHT

Elaborate protocol grew up around the knighting ceremony. The experience of being knighted could be very different depending on the circumstances or the

▲ *After a squire was knighted it was a matter of honour for him to seek an opportunity to prove himself worthy of his knighthood.*

custom prevailing at various times in the chivalric period. For some princely or lordly warriors, knighting took place in the courtly and religious ceremony of investiture, in the presence of a bishop and often at the hand of a king, among many noble peers. For others it was a simpler, though still religiously charged event involving confession and attendance at Mass, while for some squires, knighting was performed on the battlefield – in the simple act of dubbing – either before fighting began or else during or after the battle as a reward for an act of valour.

Dubbing consisted of striking the aspirant knight a blow either with the hand or a sword. In French the blow was known as the *collée* or *paumée* – later it was known in English as an 'accolade'. The striking of the blow may have derived from the ancient Roman practice of slapping a slave to set him or her free, or else from a Germanic tradition of hitting the

witnesses to a legal agreement (presumably this was to ensure that they did not forget what they had seen).

THE MEANING OF DUBBING

From at least the 11th century in England and France, dubbing was an important part of knighting ceremonies, both at court and on campaign – the earliest known use of the verb 'to dub' comes in the *Anglo-Saxon Chronicle* for 1086, which records that at Whitsuntide that year King William I 'dubbed his son Henry in making him a knight'. Until the mid-14th century dubbing was found only in England and France, but subsequently it became accepted as one of the essential parts of any knighting ceremony, whether simple or grand.

There is considerable debate among historians about the meaning of the dubbing ceremony. In addition to admitting warriors to the chivalric elite and providing them with the status and equipment that would enable them to function as a knight, the ceremony often also marked the delegation from a lord to the new knight of legal authority to perform

▶ *One of the parallels of the chivalric knighting ceremony was the practice in the 10th century of 'making a knight' by presenting him with military equipment needed to fight in battles and tournaments.*

▲ *Armed soldiers look on as Charlemagne invests a young man as a member of his warrior band. Earlier rituals like this lay behind the development of the formal knighting ceremonies of the Middle Ages.*

feudal duties in his name. In the 11th century the class of knights was increasingly presented as a body created by God to keep order, as a secular arm of His Church. From around this time, bishops were present at formal knighting ceremonies. However, the involvement of

▲ *By the late 15th century, the investiture of knights had developed from the days of Charlemagne into a much more complex ritual, with specific stages that all had distinct religious overtones.*

ordained clergy, and the development of a religious rationale for knightly warfare, did not alter one key element of knighting: only a knight could make a knight. Entrance to the chivalric brotherhood could only be conferred by one who was already a member.

'BE THOU A KNIGHT!'
ACHIEVING KNIGHTHOOD

Accounts in chronicles and romances make it clear that the simplest form of knighting, performed on the battlefield in the immediate aftermath of some great military feat, with the blood still wet on the weapons, was the most highly prized of all. It was probably a very simple ceremony – perhaps no more than a *collée* or blow accompanied by the words 'Be thou a knight'.

If it were possible to achieve this, undergoing such a battlefield ceremony before the fighting began was a very good option for a squire of modest means. Not only did it avoid the need for a costly courtly ceremony, but it also greatly improved the squire's prospects in battle:

a knight could earn more per day than a squire, and was also far less likely to be killed if he were captured in the fighting – for his status as a knight would ensure that he was treated with great respect and ransomed.

KNIGHTED AFTER AN ACT OF GREAT BRAVERY

The great Breton warrior Bertrand du Guesclin, who was a French commander during the Hundred Years War between France and England, was a member of the select band of warriors to be knighted on the battlefield.

Serving Marshal Arnoul d'Audrehem, the French king's lieutenant in Normandy,

du Guesclin was honoured at Easter in 1354 after he defeated a raid led by the English knight Sir Hugh Calverley. Du Guesclin and the Marshal were on reconnaissance in Brittany and staying in the castle of Montmauron, 6 miles (10km) from the key English stronghold of Bécherel, which was commanded by Sir Hugh. Guessing that Sir Hugh might launch an assault on the castle in a bid to capture Marshal d'Audrehem, du Guesclin

▼ *According to chronicler Jean Froissart, at the Battle of Aljubarrota in 1385 between Portugal and Castile, 140 Castilians and 60 Portuguese were knighted. The Portuguese knights, fighting in the front rank, prevailed.*

hid a group of archers beside the route from Bécherel to Montmauron. When the attack came, du Guesclin heard his archers fighting the English and rode out with Marshal d'Audrehem to take part in the battle. In the course of the conflict, Sir Hugh Calverley was flung to the ground and taken prisoner, and afterwards du Guesclin was knighted on the field of battle by Eslatre des Mares, Captain of Caen Castle.

KNIGHTED BEFORE BATTLE

Many squires were knighted at the start of a campaign or before battle commenced. This was partly done for practical reasons – tradition demanded that a squire be knighted before he could command troops in battle.

Sometimes squires were knighted in a great hurry as a battle was about to start. According to historian Jean Froissart (c.1337–1410) in his *Chronicles*, several knights were made in this way in the English army at Vironfosse in 1338. The French and English forces were arrayed in the field, and the morning passed without battle being joined, but at around noon a hare broke from cover in the front part of the French army and ran hither and thither, causing the soldiers there to shout and laugh; this noise was interpreted in the rear part of the English army as the sound of the first fighting of the day, and

▼ *Breton knight Bertrand du Guesclin kneels before King Charles V. He was raised from humble origins by his bravery and skill.*

▲ *This 15th-century illustration of the Battle of Crécy from an edition of Froissart's Chronicles gives the foreground to English longbowmen. The battle was a famous victory for the English and for Edward, the Black Prince.*

several squires were knighted there and then in order to take part in the battle as knights. The Earl of Hainault made 14 knights in this way; afterwards when it was revealed what had happened these men became known as the 'Knights of the Hare'.

Sir James Douglas, the Scottish knight named the 'Black Douglas' by the English for his fierce border raiding, was another great warrior dubbed on the battlefield – in his case, prior to battle, on 24 June 1314 at Bannockburn.

THE BLACK PRINCE AT CRÉCY

Another knight who swiftly proved his worth as a chivalric warrior was Edward Prince of Wales (later known as 'the Black Prince'), the 16-year-old son of King Edward III of England. The king knighted the prince along with several of the young man's peers at the start of the French campaign of 1346; then on 26 August, at the Battle of Crécy, he placed his young son in charge of the right wing of his army, with Sir Godfrey Harcourt to assist him, and he himself stood back watching the engagement from a windmill nearby.

According to the account in Froissart's *Chronicles*, the fighting was very hard on the Black Prince's wing of the army, and Sir Godfrey Harcourt called for reinforcements, but Edward III refused, saying 'let the boy win his spurs'. By this Edward (or more likely Froissart, who put the words in his mouth) meant that the prince should prove himself worthy of the gilded spurs that were a mark of knighthood.

He did so. The prince fought on and the English prevailed in the battle. When fighting at Crécy finished, after dark, the French had lost no fewer than 1,542 knights. The battle was remembered as significant in two ways – a humiliating disaster for France and a great triumph for the English army – and proof beyond doubt that Prince Edward had a great future ahead of him as a knight.

THE MEANING OF KNIGHTING

THE RELIGIOUS SYMBOLISM OF THE KNIGHTING CEREMONY

In his *Book of Chivalry* (c.1350) Geoffroi de Charny gives an idealized account of the knighting ceremony. His version is based on that given a little over a century earlier in an anonymous French poem called *L'Ordre de Chevalerie* (c.1225), and presents an account of what should, or ideally might, happen rather than what did routinely occur. The kind of ceremony he describes is rich in religious symbolism. De Charny also provides detailed explanations of the significance of the various parts of the ritual.

RETREAT AND PREPARATION

According to de Charny, a squire was expected to prepare himself to join the blessed company of knights by confessing his sins and receiving communion. On the day before the ceremony, the squire was to take a bath, then rest in a bed newly made with perfectly white sheets. At the given hour, knights were to come to the squire's bedroom to dress him in new white linen, scarlet robes and black stockings, with a white girdle and a scarlet cloak. They would lead him in the evening to church, where he would spend the night in lonely vigil.

In the morning the knights would accompany him to Mass, at which he should pray for divine grace to make him fit to serve as a knight. After Mass, the knights would lead the squire into the presence of the knight who was to confer the order of knighthood upon him. This knight would attach a gilded spur to the squire's foot, gird the squire with a sword and kiss him to confirm the conferral of knighthood. Finally the knight would dub the squire, delivering the accolade or *collée* on his shoulder.

The *Book of Chivalry* explains the knighting ceremony as follows. When the squire takes a bath on the day before he is to be knighted, he washes away the accumulated sins of a lifetime and emerges

with a clean conscience. Then when he rests in a bed newly made with white sheets, this symbolizes the deep sense of peace that arises when his conscience is clean, and he has won God's forgiveness for past wrongdoing. When he is dressed in new white clothes these symbolize his new virtue, while the scarlet robes signify the blood he must be willing to spill in defending Christianity and the Church. The black stockings stand for the earth from which the squire came and to which he will return, and the fact that since he cannot know the hour of his own death he should turn away resolutely from pride and vainglory. His white girdle signifies chastity, and his scarlet cloak is a traditional sign of humility.

Then he keeps a vigil through the night, and this symbolizes that he must be

▼ *King Edward III of England, enthroned, looks on as Edward the Black Prince is invested as a knight of the Most Noble Order of the Garter in 1348. Members wore the garter on their armour in battle or in tournaments as a badge of honour.*

always watchful and renounce evil. When he is given a golden spur in the moment of knighting, this signifies that he must never be covetous, for gold is the most precious and widely coveted of metals but the knight wears it on his foot rather than on his head or close to his heart. When he is girded with a sword, this signifies that he must support justice and reason, defending both the Christian faith and the Church, and when the knight kisses him it is a sign of peace, loyalty and love. The accolade or blow on the shoulder signifies that he should not forget that he is now a knight and must behave henceforth in accordance with the laws of chivalry.

CHIVALRIC SYMBOLISM IN *THE ORDER OF CHIVALRY*

The anonymous French poem, *L'Ordre de Chevalerie*, that provided de Charny with the basis of his inspirational account, describes a fictional encounter between a Christian knight and the great Kurdish Muslim warrior and general Saladin, who captured Jerusalem in 1187 and fought against King Richard I of England during the Third Crusade (1189–1192). The Christian knight, Hue de Tabarie, is captured by Saladin, who was renowned for his chivalric behaviour but, as a non-Christian, could not be expected to know the ceremonies of knighthood. Saladin offers to set Hue free if he will instruct him in the meanings of knighthood and then make him a knight. Hue is not keen to agree this bargain, for he knows that Saladin cannot truly become a knight because he does not accept the Christian faith, but as a prisoner he has little choice.

Hue de Tabarie cuts Saladin's hair and beard, then leads the way to a bath that signifies – as it did for the knight in the *Book of Chivalry* – the washing away of sins, here specifically identified with the Christian rite of baptism. Afterwards Hue takes Saladin to a magnificent bed, which

▶ *Saladin, the crusaders' greatest Muslim foe, exhibited such magnanimity and chivalry in victory that he was hailed as a 'Saracen knight'. He is said to have been knighted in 1167 by Humphrey III of Toron, Constable of the Kingdom of Jerusalem.*

is said to symbolize the place in Paradise that each true knight will attain, then dresses him in white and a scarlet robe, again signifying the willingness to shed blood in chivalric encounters. He then girds on the sword but stops short of giving Saladin the accolade on the grounds that he cannot administer this because he is Saladin's prisoner.

THE SYMBOLISM OF KNIGHTLY FIGHTING EQUIPMENT

Knighting rituals developed from simpler ceremonies in which young men were given the equipment they needed to be warriors or mounted knights. In the literature of chivalry, symbolism was attached not only to the elements of

the knighting ceremony but also to the fighting equipment a knight used. In the French prose romance *Lancelot* (c.1225), also known as the *Prose Lancelot*, the Arthurian knight Sir Lancelot is instructed in the symbolism of his armour by the Lady of the Lake. She tells him that his armour signifies various aspects of the

duty that he and every Christian knight owes to the Church. His hauberk, or mail tunic, protects his body just as he should defend the Church; his helmet covers his head and symbolizes the way in which he should guard the Church; as his great lance, expertly wielded, strikes fear into wicked men, so it stands for his power to keep the enemies of the Church at bay. His mighty sword has two edges, which stand for the fact that he serves both God and the people, and a sharp point, which signifies that the people must be obedient and follow his leadership. The horse on which he rides stands for the people of the Christian world who support him and follow his guidance, just as a horse follows the directions of its rider.

▼ *King Francis I of France considered it a great honour when he was dubbed a knight by French chivalric hero Pierre du Terrail, the Chevalier de Bayard. This romanticized depiction suggests that the event was blessed by a shaft of light falling from heaven.*

'HOTSPUR'

SIR HENRY PERCY

Sir Henry Percy was probably the greatest knight of the late 14th century, whose effectiveness in patrolling England's border with Scotland – and especially his speed of movement and willingness to attack – won him the nickname 'Hotspur' from his Scottish foes. He was a valued servant and trusted military leader for the English kings Richard II and Henry IV, although he eventually rebelled against both. He was renowned for his knightly prowess, both in the lists and on the field of battle. The chronicler Jean Froissart declared that Hotspur 'desired feats of arms above all other things, and was always first into action at the barriers'.

A PRODIGIOUS YOUTH

Hotspur was raised to arms. He was born at Alnwick Castle, Northumberland, in 1364, the son of another Henry Percy, 1st Earl of Northumberland, and the earl's

▼ *Hotspur was England's hero at the Battle of Otterburn in 1388. This two-panelled illustration is to a line from the poet Robert Burns's celebration of the battle, 'But Persie wi his gude braid sword'.*

SIR HENRY PERCY
Born: 20 May 1364
Died: 21 July 1403
Knighted: 1377
Famous for: raiding victories against Scots on England's northern border
Greatest achievement: victory in Battle of Homildon Hill, 1402

wife Margaret, who was of the proud Neville family of Raby. Contrary to normal practice, Hotspur was knighted at the age of just 13 in 1377 by King Edward III. The following year, aged 14, he fought alongside his father in retaking Berwick Castle from Scottish raiders.

In 1379 Hotspur married Elizabeth Mortimer, daughter of Edmund Mortimer, 3rd Earl of March, and in 1380 he campaigned with his father-in-law in Ireland. In 1383 Hotspur went on crusade in Prussia against pagan Lithuanians – at this time, the military order of the Teutonic Knights organized crusading trips in Prussia and the Baltic region for the nobility of Europe.

SCOURGE OF THE SCOTS

In 1385 King Richard II of England appointed Hotspur the Warden of the East March (border region) of Scotland, charged with controlling Scottish raiders in the region. In the same year Hotspur accompanied the king's army into Scotland. In 1386 Richard sent him to the aid of the English garrison in Calais, France, because an attack was expected from the French; while there, Hotspur led a number of raids in Picardy.

In 1388 Hotspur was nominated as a Knight of the Garter and returned to the Scottish border. That year he rode into Scotland and fought James Douglas, 2nd Earl of Douglas, at the Battle of Otterburn, which was partly fought in moonlight, and was celebrated by Froissart for being 'as hard a meeting, as well-fought a struggle as ever was'. In this heroic clash, Douglas was killed but Hotspur was captured and ransomed by the Scots. The greater part of his substantial ransom – 7,000 marks – was paid from royal funds and by a subscription from Parliament.

Hotspur's reputation as a knight continued to grow. He took on his fellows in chivalric tournaments, and won admiration for his performance in the lists, notably in the Jousts of St Inglevert that were held near Calais in 1390, and at Smithfield, London, during the celebration of Richard II's 1396 marriage to Isabella of France. He was entrusted by the king with diplomatic missions to Cyprus, to the duchy of Aquitaine and to Calais in 1394–96, and in 1396 was once again appointed Warden of the East March, this time for a period of ten years.

REBEL KNIGHT

Yet despite so much evidence of royal favour, Hotspur turned against Richard II and sided with his opponent Henry Bolingbroke. Hotspur and his father may

▶ *Alnwick Castle, Hotspur's birthplace, was built in the late 11th century to guard England's northern border against the Scots. The Percy family bought it in 1309 and it remains in the family's hands to this day.*

have felt that Richard was undermining their authority in the border region, for he took the town of Berwick out of their control; they may have believed that the king was acting in tyrannical fashion in his campaign against the Duke of Gloucester, his nephew Henry Bolingbroke and the earls of Arundel and Warwick. When in 1399 Bolingbroke returned from the exile into which Richard had cast him in an attempt to seize the throne, Hotspur threw his lot in with Henry, meeting him at Doncaster and riding south in his support.

Once established as King Henry IV, Bolingbroke rewarded Hotspur handsomely. He made him Sheriff of Northumberland, Lord of Bamburgh and Justiciar of North Wales and Chester, as well as giving him a further appointment

▼ *Hotspur had undoubted greatness as a military commander and as a knight in the saddle. But he displayed little loyalty, twice rebelling against his king – Richard II in 1399 and Henry IV in 1403. This is his effigy, at Wells Cathedral, Somerset.*

as Warden of the East March. The appointment in Wales brought him control of the great castles of Beaumaris, Caernarfon, Chester, Conway and Flint. In 1401 Hotspur again proved his prowess by capturing Conway Castle, which had fallen to Welsh rebels, and in the next year trounced the Scots at the Battle of Homildon Hill, capturing several lords including Archibald, Earl of Douglas.

KILLED AT SHREWSBURY

In the wake of this success he rebelled against Henry IV, accusing him of tyrannical government and the breaking of oaths. Hotspur was angry at various royal decisions that he perceived as slights, including Henry's establishment of a military command in Wales under Henry, Prince of Wales. Open conflict ensued. Hotspur led an army south to fight forces under the command of the Prince of Wales at Shrewsbury, but on arriving was surprised to discover a larger royal army led by King Henry IV himself. In the battle that followed, Hotspur was killed – reputedly when he raised the visor of his helmet to gulp some air and was shot in the mouth by an arrow. On seeing the death of their proud leader, the Percy forces abandoned the fight.

Despite the rebellion, King Henry wept when he saw the corpse of his former friend. He ordered Hotspur's burial at Whitchurch in Shropshire, but then had him disinterred. Henry wanted to display the body to counter rumours that Hotspur was still alive and also to make an example of him as a rebel against royal authority. He put Hotspur's corpse on display in Shrewsbury marketplace supported by a pair of millstones, and afterwards had his body cut into four and sent to the four corners of the kingdom. The former knight's head was displayed on a pole at the gates of York.

SHAKESPEARE'S HOTSPUR

Hotspur's fame among later generations rests in part on his appearance as a character in William Shakespeare's historical play *King Henry IV Part I*. Shakespeare rewrites history by making the knight the same age as Prince Henry ('Hal') whereas in reality Hotspur was a good deal older than the future king. The play contrasts Prince Hal's seeming indolence as a young man with Hotspur's great energy, force and bravery.

HOW TO BE A KNIGHT

MANUALS OF CHIVALRY

In the 14th and 15th centuries chivalric manuals such as Ramon Llull's *Book of the Order of Chivalry* were read at courts across Europe. Written in Majorca in the Catalan language in *c.*1265, Llull's book was widely translated and editions have survived that were published in France, Scotland and London – the last a translation by English printer William Caxton, printed in 1484, the year after he published the second edition of Geoffrey Chaucer's *The Canterbury Tales* and the year before he published Sir Thomas Malory's *Le Morte d'Arthur*.

The *Book of the Order of Chivalry* describes an encounter between a hermit and a squire at the former's forest hermitage. The hermit was once a great and wise knight, who had enjoyed a long and glorious chivalric career, in the course of which he had won many renowned victories in battle and excelled at tournaments held for the pleasure of kings and

RAMON LLULL

Ramon Llull, author of the *Book of the Order of Chivalry*, was a remarkable man with many very powerful talents. He is celebrated as a philosopher and religious mystic, as a poet and the author in 1284 of the allegorical novel *Blanquerna*, the first major work of literature in the Catalan language. But perhaps above all he is remembered as the developer of a means of marshalling information by combining attributes from lists: he developed the method, which he published in the *Ars inveniendi veritatis* ('Art of Finding Truth') and the *Ars Magna* ('Great Art'), as a way to reduce doctrine to first principles for use in attempts to convert Muslims to Christianity. His method – claimed by some as an antecedent of modern information science – is commonly

known by the name *ars combinatoria,* applied to it by the 17th-century German philosopher Gottfried Liebniz.

Born in Ciutat de Majorca (probably Palma) in Majorca in *c.*1232, Llull had a chivalric education as page and squire at the royal court of Majorca. He married, then at the age of about 30 (just before he wrote his chivalric manual) had five visions of Christ crucified, that inspired him to become a lay Franciscan and later a missionary to Muslims in northern Africa and Asia Minor. He visited North Africa three times on mission, on one occasion carrying out reconnaissance for a possible crusade, and according to legend was stoned by angry Muslims at Bejaïa (Bougie) – or perhaps at Tunis – and died in 1315 a Christian martyr on the voyage home.

▲ *Like the hermit knight in the* Book of the Order of Chivalry, *Arthurian knight Sir Lancelot spent a large part of his life in rural retreat. Lancelot was cared for and educated by the Lady of the Lake.*

princes and their ladies. He had often risked his life for the glory of knighthood and in all his dealings had shown wisdom and nobility of character as well as courage and physical strength. Nearing the end of his career, he was aware that his physical strength was failing and rather than attempt to perform acts of chivalry at a level below his customary excellence, he had chosen to retire to a hermitage. A young squire, meanwhile, was riding through the forest on his way to the king's winter court nearby, but he failed to keep his wits about him and fell asleep in the saddle; his horse wandered off the path into the depths of the forest and came to the hermitage.

DEFENDERS OF HONOUR

When the two met, and explained their positions, the hermit offered to teach the young squire all he could need to know about chivalry. He gave the squire a copy of a book on the subject, which contained all his wisdom.

The book explains that long ago, knights were picked from the general population, one from every thousand men, as defenders of justice; and the horse was placed at the service of the knight because of its beauty, speed and strength. It says that knights were an order set apart, coming in the natural social hierarchy above the people, and below the prince, whom the knights must serve alongside God. The knight's principal duties were to defend the honour of the prince and of the Church, and to uphold justice. It is right, the book says, for knights to strike fear into the hearts of the ordinary people, because this prevents the populace doing wrong. In the same way, as knights are placed in an elevated position of trust, it is therefore far worse when a knight does evil than when an ordinary peasant or farmer is wicked.

▼ *Chivalric manuals described how a knight should behave towards the poor, who might need charity as well as protection.*

▲ *Knights were expected to be skilled in the arts of hawking and hunting. Here a hunting party sets out from a castle.*

KNIGHTLY SKILLS

Knights must be taught and must practise essential chivalric skills such as horse-riding, jousting, sword fighting, and the hunting of lions, bears, stags and rabbits. These activities are important for a knight because they keep him fit for fulfilling his duties of chivalric service. A knight who despises the practice of knightly skills is one who despises the very institution of knighthood.

LARGESSE AND COURTESY

Other notable guides to chivalric behaviour include Geoffroi de Charny's *Book of Chivalry*, and an anonymous early 13th-century poem *Roman des Eles*. The *Roman des Eles* argues that chivalric courtesy derives from God and is possessed by knights. The poem has two key aspects: largesse and courtesy. All knights should be able to demonstrate largesse, it states; they should give freely, with boldness and even carelessness. Knights should demonstrate their courtesy by never displaying boastful behaviour, envy, slanderous talk and greed. Rather, they should take pleasure in music and songs, and always honour the Church.

De Charny addresses much of his teaching to men-at-arms, a group of chivalric warriors distinct from knights, from which he himself had emerged. He went on to become one of France's most prominent knights in the service of King John II. He was a member of the Order of the Star and was granted the honour of bearing the Oriflamme, the French standard, into battle. In his *Book of Chivalry* he argues that chivalric warriors should spend their lives striving; even the greatest of them should be seeking to achieve remarkable deeds that would bring them more honour still. He also argues that they can be driven to greater deeds by the fire of courtly love: they should love their lady for love's sake and achieve greatness in the quest for her love.

THE KNIGHT AT HOME

When a knight was not at war, he lived in his castle. If he were a substantial lord he kept his own castle, and if he were less well established he served with honour in the castle of his feudal superior. During peacetime he enjoyed strenuous pastimes such as hunting and tourneying (fighting in tournaments), which helped keep him ready for battle. The knightly class to which he belonged was supported by the labour of the peasants who farmed the lands of the fief, or feudal landholding, and whose agricultural produce supplemented the meat the knights caught in hunting. The knight therefore had plenty of leisure time in which to feast and enjoy the chivalric songs of travelling poets. He also had peacetime responsibilities and duties to carry out.

The knight's role in peacetime changed as feudalism developed. In the early years, he was a mounted soldier and little more, and in periods of peace his main job was to ride out in service of his feudal lord if the need arose, to protect the lord's interests or impose his authority. The knight had a duty to administer and govern his feudal domain or manor, but this work was usually done by his steward or bailiff. In later years, the senior knights, keepers of castles, had more developed duties in the administration of the law and the keeping of the peace, sitting as local judges and, particularly in England and Germany, often having a duty to keep the peace beyond the confines of their feudal domain.

▲ *Courtly banquets were designed to impress, with lavish displays of food and drink.*

◀ *Home and feudal stronghold – the castle of a great lord dominated the country for miles around. Pontefract Castle in west Yorkshire, shown here, was founded in c.1070. It was greatly developed by John of Gaunt and was the scene of King Richard II's murder.*

A LORD IN HIS MANOR
A KNIGHT'S RIGHTS AND DUTIES AT HOME

Knighthood did not necessarily bring a large estate with it. Some knights were in possession of fiefs too small to support them adequately and exploited their military training and skill to make a living through tournaments and on the field of battle by ransoming defeated enemies. But ideally a great knight was master of a substantial landholding.

THE NOBILITY OF LORDSHIP

A great knight was lord to a large number of retainers and lived in great style. This was seen as proper in the chivalric world. Ramon Llull wrote in his *Book of the Order of Chivalry* that knights rightly should be 'made lord of many men, for in seignory is much nobleness'. A lord would take pride in seeing his retainers wearing his arms on their clothing. The larger the household, the greater the glory.

Medieval philosophers held that feudal society was divided into three estates or conditions: the Church was the first estate; the nobility, the knights and lords who held feudal properties were members of

▼ *The main hall of a medieval castle was its central public space, where a lord would eat, dispense justice and entertain.*

▲ *Peasants build a fence on their lord's land while in the background one of their fellows ploughs a field on the farm.*

the second; and the peasantry was the third. It was proper, ordained by God, that the members of the third estate should labour to support the members of the other two. Another image, developed by lawyers in the late medieval period, was that society rightly ordered was like a great pyramid, with the peasants at the bottom, the clergy above them and the knights beneath the king at the top. Above the king was only God himself, and this social structure – in which each man knew his place – was believed to have been blessed and to be sustained by God.

GOVERNOR OF THE MANOR

Under the system introduced in England by the Normans, and current in much of western and central Europe, the knight's landholding as a feudal lord was called a manor, or in France a *seigneurie*. The feudal lord (*seigneur*) had legal and economic power within his manor.

Typically, a manor contained a village and arable and pasture land farmed in strips by the lord's tenants. Some of the land was the lord's and some was farmed on their own behalf by the peasants. The peasants had to farm the lord's lands and in addition had to pay 'taxes', usually 'in kind' in the form of a proportion of the agricultural produce grown on their own strips of land. The lord had duties and

responsibilities to govern his tenants. He presided at a manor court. His manor was a self-sufficient community.

The fief-holder supported by his land tenants could be a secular knight or a prominent clergyman such as a bishop or abbot. Many bishops and abbots were knights, and fought in feudal armies. The feudal households described in this chapter could be secular or ecclesiastical.

A NOBLE HOUSEHOLD

From the 12th century, a leading knight's household would contain a range of administrative positions. The *seneschal*, or steward, was in overall charge of food and drink for his lord, while the butler managed its storage. The chamberlain was guardian and manager of the lord's private chambers and their contents, with the help of subordinate valets and janitors. The priest was likely to be one of the few literate people in the castle: he ran the chapel, said religious services and kept the lord's written records in order. The constable and marshal oversaw the security of the castle, and managed the garrison and other troops as well as overseeing the running of the mews and stables.

Among those who provided service to a king or great lord were powerful knights. Chivalry honoured service; there was nothing demeaning about it. In Arthurian literature, King Arthur's seneschal was Sir Kay, who was one of the knights of the Round Table. This arrangement was typical of the period. Knights might provide service in the hall, the stables, the tilt-yard, the armoury and the hunting park. Such was the size of these feudal households that lords with grand positions such as Marshal or Master of the Horse had many more menial staff beneath them. Some of the lower positions were filled by squires.

Those knights and noblemen who occupied elite positions in the inner household were free to offer advice to the lord they served, both as individuals, and gathered together in council. The lord might disregard their opinions, just as the king could go against the will of his

barons, as happened frequently – notably in 13th-century England, under King John and King Henry III.

SPECIALIZATION OF ROLES

During the 13th–15th centuries, the roles of officials in the larger noble households became more specialized and titles were changed. In the 13th century the treasurer took charge of finances, while the role of steward was divided in two, with one managing the lord's estates and tenants and a second in charge of food and provisions. In the 14th century this position was often called the chamberlain, while a clerk managed the butler's store of food.

In a large household of the 15th century, the seneschal was often the lord's deputy, in charge of key roles such as the dispensing of justice when the lord was absent – as he frequently was, either at another of his manors or on campaign.

▲ *A feudal estate was a self-sufficient unit, in which each person had a role and a strictly defined social position.*

The seneschal was assisted by a chancellor, responsible for keeping administrative documents, writing letters, charters and legal papers. By this time the chamberlain often focused mainly on financial affairs, while the steward managed the estate. The highest authority in the lord's absence was the constable, who was the 'keeper' of the castle and responsible for its defence.

KEEPING A GRAND HOUSE

It was honourable for a feudal lord to entertain men of rank. Even a prince could enhance his status by offering hospitality to a knight. Llull declared that: 'Any baron or lord who honours a knight in his court, in his meetings of council and at his meals does honour to himself'.

KEEPER OF THE PEACE

A KNIGHT'S ROLE IN GOVERNMENT

As feudalism developed, many knights across Europe accepted it as their duty to maintain order in peacetime and to administer the king's law. The knights and their castle strongholds became symbols of a stern authority that demanded respect and kept lawlessness at bay.

JURY SERVICE

By the mid-13th century many leading English knights were no longer simply a warrior caste in the king's service, but were part of the royal administration. They had a major role in delivering justice, both local and national. As we have seen, they presided over manorial courts; they also had to provide jury members for grand assize – the travelling royal court held periodically in English counties. This jury work involved, in addition to attending the hearings, demanding administrative work and in criminal cases law enforcement duties. Such duties were not taken

on by all knights, and those members of the chivalric class who did shoulder these responsibilities shared them with other nobles who were not knights.

▲ The king's law had to be administered as well as enforced around the country and knights contributed to the work of travelling courts that brought justice to the shires.

Some knights had a similar role in France and Germany. In France some made a good living as administrators for the king, for these tasks were well paid there. In Germany *ministeriales* were 'serf-knights' who worked mainly as stewards, judges and administrators. Originally the *ministeriales* were not free men, since they were tied to the land on which they served and were without legal rights beyond that domain. But they gradually acquired the right to own property and generate wealth, and in time became members of the knightly class, with the right to hold fiefdoms in the gift of other lords in addition to their original suzerain.

KNIGHTS OF THE SHIRE

In the 13th century English knights attended the royal council that was the precursor to Parliament. Two knights from each shire were summoned to the governmental council called by English

---

SYMBOL OF ORDER

In chivalric literature the castle is frequently a symbol of order. Within its walls, and on the feudal estate, all is well – the lord and his retainers live in comfort, each knowing his place and providing service. Outside the island of order are all the terrors of an unruly world – symbolized in chivalric literature by the forest, with its monsters and

rogue knights. The medieval world had a fear of disorder – raids by Vikings, Magyars and Saracens were still fresh in folk memory. The castle's structures and discipline would keep the darkness of the forest at bay, while the structures of feudal society guaranteed social order.

▼ Leeds Castle, Kent, begun in 1119.

▶ *A convocation of lords enforces the power of the French monarchy, hearing the trial of John II, duke of Alençon, for treason against Charles VII. Alençon was sentenced to death in 1458 but the sentence was not carried out; he died in prison in 1476.*

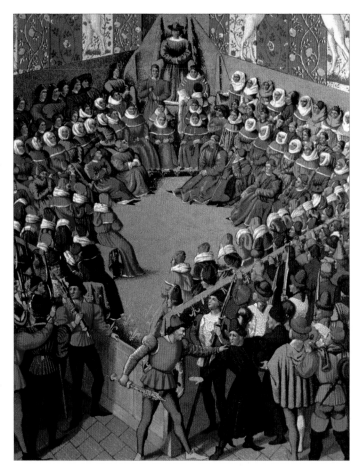

nobleman Simon de Montfort when he was briefly in power in 1263–65, having deposed King Henry III. De Montfort was then defeated and killed by Henry III's son, the future Edward I, at the Battle of Evesham and his experiment ended, but it had set a precedent. In 1295 Edward I called a representative council later termed the 'Model Parliament' by historians, because it was the first representative English parliament.

The Model Parliament included, in addition to magnates and churchmen, representatives of lesser clergy, two knights from each county, two burgesses from each borough and two citizens from every city. The council began to be called Parliament (from the old French *parlement*, 'a talk') at around this time, and in the reign of King Edward III (1327–77) split into its current format: the House of Commons and the House of Lords. At that point, the knights of the shire, the lesser clergy and the burgesses formed the House of Commons, while the nobles and high clergy formed the House of Lords.

PROTECTORS OF THE WEAK

All knights also had a general duty to provide protection for the Church, widows, children and others unable to protect themselves. In the writings of philosophers and churchmen, knights' elevated position within the feudal system was justified by this role as protectors.

Knights had a particular duty to protect pilgrims. Pilgrimage played a central role in religious life in the Middle Ages. As an act of penance or an expression of Christian devotion, men and women uprooted themselves and travelled along the well-worn routes to shrines such as Canterbury, Santiago de Compostela in Spain, Rome and Jerusalem. They

travelled in large numbers: as early as 1064 a party of 7,000 travelled to Jerusalem, which at this stage was in Muslim hands. After the First Crusade in 1096–99 resulted in the recapture of Jerusalem, the number of pilgrims to the Holy Land increased further. All pilgrimages could be dangerous, but the voyage to Jerusalem was particularly long and difficult. The knightly brotherhood of the Knights Templar was established in *c.*1119 to protect pilgrims to the Holy Land.

THE EXPRESSION OF LORDSHIP

The castle was an expression in stone of the knight's mastery and authority. Many castles were built around a great central

tower or keep, known as the *donjon*, a French word derived from the Latin *dominium*, meaning lordship. (The English equivalent is 'dungeon'; this word did not come to have its modern meaning, of a dank underground jail room, until later.)

Even when the knight was not in residence – as was often the case, when he was away on campaign, or perhaps visiting another of his residences – the forbidding walls of his castle proclaimed both the greatness of the knight and the solidity of the rule of law that he enforced. The castle was a standing warning to law breakers of the military might that could be brought against them if they rebelled against the lord's authority.

CASTLES AND MANOR HOUSES

LIFE ON A FEUDAL ESTATE

Castles were military instruments, used as bases for expansion and afterwards for dominating conquered territory, but they were also domestic environments. They were a show of power, and a statement of authority, but were also knightly residences, set at the heart of great feudal estates or manors.

EVERYTHING A LORD NEEDED

The great estates were virtually self-sufficient. The castle or fortified house was surrounded by pasture and crop fields, with hundreds of peasants working the land to produce corn and hay, raising animals for the lord's table and chopping the wood needed for fires. On some estates even the cloth worn by the lord and his household was woven on site, but if not, wool produced by sheep on the estate was taken to a nearby centre to be exchanged or woven.

Anything that could not be produced on the estate – salt, say, or iron goods – could be purchased from itinerant merchants or at fairs held in the larger market towns. Larger fairs attracted merchants from as far away as Italy, France and Germany, some selling goods all the way from the far eastern countries of the Muslim world. At the larger markets, a lord's household staff could buy spices, gold, silks, dyes, French or Spanish wine, furs, Flemish cloth and so on.

AN EMPTY HOME

Kings in this period had to keep mobile in order to keep themselves abreast of developments and to maintain their authority. They carried their court with them as they travelled from household to household. Likewise, princes and the greater lords had more than one castle and moved from one to another. Much of their wealth consisted

of land, and its produce, paid to them as rents-in-kind. As the court, and lesser lords, moved from one property to another, their rents – in the form of harvested food and hunted animals – kept them and their courtiers well fed.

When they were away at another house, or indeed on campaign or crusade, the castle was guarded and administered by a castellan, or governor, with a defensive garrison of knights and crossbowmen alongside a team of artisans such as carpenters, smiths and masons to maintain the buildings. The peasants working the estate would of course stay where they were, but the majority of the lord's household would travel with him – necessarily, for they would be needed to provide service in the next location.

DEFENSIVE DESIGNS

Castles took many forms, designed primarily for defence. The Normans who pioneered castle-building often built to a 'motte and bailey' design: the motte was an artificial or natural mound within or adjacent to a wider area called the bailey, set inside a defensive wall and ditch or moat. On the motte stood a tower – made of wood in early castles, later of stone – which usually housed the lord's living quarters and that was a stronghold to which the lord and his garrison could retreat if the castle came under attack and the outer defences were breached.

Later castle-builders – in England and Wales, most notably King Edward I and his builder Master James of St Georges – improved upon this basic pattern. The

◄ *The hall at Penshurst Place, a fortified manor house in Kent, southern England, was completed in 1341. A medieval hall was a space that the lord shared with his retainers, guests and animals. It would be noisy, crowded and full of smoke from the central fire.*

▲ The kitchens were generally just off the main hall. Often a carved wooden screen disguised the passageway that led from the hall to the larders, kitchens and offices.

the Knights Hospitaller during the Crusades, and Beaumaris Castle in North Wales built by Edward I and Master James of St Georges.

▲ Banquets were seen by noble households as an opportunity to display wealth and influence, and they would be as lavish and impressive as possible.

perfection of medieval fortress design was the concentric castle that had two sets of walls: a taller inner set, surrounding the 'inner bailey', and a lower outer set, surrounding the 'outer bailey'. To capture a concentric castle, attackers would have first to defeat the defenders of the outer walls, then cross the outer bailey under fire and begin their assault on the inner, more heavily fortified walls. Fine examples of the concentric castle include the Krak des Chevaliers (near Homs in Syria) which was built and garrisoned by

▼ This view of Salzburg in 1493 shows how the medieval castle and the fortified cathedral – symbols of the dual powers of State and Church – dominate the city.

DOMESTIC BUILDINGS

The large empty baileys or yards that we see in many castles today were once filled with domestic buildings. These were usually constructed of wattle and daub or timber and were either destroyed in conflict or have decayed naturally. They would have included stables, an armoury, a smithy, a servants' hall, the kitchens and the buttery (a storeroom for wines, so called because casks of wine were called butts). In some castles, certain of these halls and rooms were built into the walls surrounding the bailey and so their remains can still be viewed.

The lord of a great castle would have lavish accommodation. His rooms were always in the safest part of the fortress –

initially in the keep or donjon, then, as castle design developed, in the strongly fortified inner bailey. Also in the inner bailey, close to the lord's rooms, would be the chapel and the great hall, the centre of castle life. Even the greatest lord would eat with his retainers in the hall. Robert Grosseteste, scholar and Bishop of Lincoln under King Henry III of England, wrote that it was not proper for a lord to eat alone.

The lord, his family, companions and notable visitors would eat at the high table on finer foods than were served to the mass of soldiers and other vassals in the main part of the room. At the far end of the hall, opposite the high table, was often a raised minstrels' gallery from where musicians entertained diners. In between meals the hall was also a place of business used for judicial hearings and estate management, and by night many of the castle's large population slept there.

Some castles contained more than one chapel. In the lord's private chapel, he and his family would attend a service each morning. A larger chapel in the outer bailey would serve the needs of the members of the garrison. Many castles had a heavily fortified gatehouse guarding the entrance. This usually contained rooms for the castellan, and perhaps a smaller version of the great hall used for receiving visitors and emissaries.

KNIGHTS AT LEISURE
FAVOURED PASTIMES OF THE CHIVALRIC CLASS

Knights had duties both in peace and in war, but they also had plenty of time for leisure. They spent much of this time in pursuits that improved their military skill or their understanding of their knightly calling, although they were also fond of lavish feasts.

THE HUNT

Hunting provided a key opportunity for developing fitness and strength and practising horsemanship as well as the skilled use of weapons such as the bow and arrow, the spear and the sword. The *Anglo-Saxon Chronicle* reports that King William I of England enclosed vast tracts of forest and 'loved the tall stags as if he were father unto them'. The 13th-century English chronicler William Rishanger, a Benedictine monk from St Albans also known as Chronigraphus, described how as a young man Prince Edward (the future warrior-king Edward I) loved to hunt stags on horseback, and when he had chased one down he would kill it at close quarters with his sword rather than from a safe distance with a spear. This was presented as a sign of his bravery and martial spirit.

Manuals on hunting were circulated to complement the handbooks on chivalry. The French nobleman Count Gaston III of Foix-Béarn wrote a treatise on hunting, *Le Livre de Chasse* ('The Book of the Hunt') c.1387. Gaston was a great chivalric figure, who wrote that the three main delights of his life were 'arms, love, and hunting', and whose court in southern France was described in all its knightly splendour by French chronicler Jean Froissart. *Le Livre de Chasse* covered all aspects of hunting in the 14th century, listing the open and close seasons for animals, the best kinds of bait and traps to use, the different kinds of pursuit, including a discussion of which hounds to use for which animal, and even ideal arrangements for dining in the forest.

▲ *A hunting party gathers outside the castle walls. Ladies often rode on the hunt alongside men. Hunting dogs were used to track, chase and kill prey; greyhounds were particularly prized for their speed.*

HUNTING RESERVES

Kings, noblemen and leading knights kept hunting reserves that were strictly guarded. The *Anglo-Saxon Chronicle* reports that William I imposed blinding as the punishment for anyone who killed deer from his forests. They employed specialists to care for the lands, maintain the wild animals and look after the hounds. Hunting was considered a noble pastime and positions involving the management of horse, hounds or the hunt were quite appropriate ones for a knight to take in the household of his feudal superior. The nobles developed a hierarchy among the animals: the noblest target was the stag, then, in descending order, the boar, the female deer, the wolf and the bear, the fox and the hare.

HAWKING

Another favoured pastime of the royal and knightly class was hawking, the use of trained birds of prey such as eagles, falcons and hawks to pursue game. Some contemporary sources suggest that the crusader knights learned of the sport in the Holy Land and brought it back to

Tancarville, Chamberlain of Normandy, Marshal was nicknamed *gaste-viande* ('glutton') for, unless otherwise occupied, he filled every waking hour with eating. But the biography makes clear that this was no indication of slothfulness and laziness, noting that de Tancarville predicted a great future for the young man. Likewise in one romance, English knight Guy de Bourgogne made quite an impact on the Saracens merely with his appetite, which was said to be equivalent to that of four normal men – and he demonstrated the general truth that 'a man who eats heartily will never prove to be a coward'.

As many as ten courses would be served on a great occasion. These included such dishes as boar, swan, peacock, fowl, fish, cheese, fruit and pastries, with plenty of wine, cider, spiced mead and sometimes beer to keep spirits high. A medieval document that lists the 'Fifteen Joys of a Knight' identifies the first and foremost of these joys as 'eating well and going swiftly through the supplies of wine'.

Music was usually played by minstrels during the meal and afterwards knights might play at dice or chess. But their favourite after-dinner event was a recitation by a travelling minstrel of *chansons de geste* or *chansons d'amour*, accounts of great

▲ *Minstrels were generally employed at the castle, but the troubadours who sang songs of courtly love were wandering musicians.*

Europe, but there is evidence to suggest that in fact it was practised by both Anglo-Saxon and Norman lords before that time. In the 1240s Holy Roman Emperor Frederick II was the patron for a translation of an Arabic treatise on hunting with birds, and he then wrote a book himself on the subject – incorporating some of the translated Arab text and supplementing it with information gleaned from his own lifelong devotion to the sport.

FEASTING AND POETRY

Days could be long in the castle. A favourite way to pass the time was in feasting and drinking. A vast appetite was not considered inappropriate for a great knight – indeed, it was almost a virtue, a sign of a warrior virility and forcefulness. The verse biography of 12th-century English knight William Marshal reveals that in his youth when he was serving as a squire in the household of his uncle, William de

▶ *Chivalric tournaments provided much excitement and colour. A Dutch illumination of c.1475 represents knights and ladies riding through the streets of London to a tournament.*

▲ *Chess was invented in India and spread via the Arab world to Europe by c.1000. It was so popular among the nobility that it became known as the 'royal game'.*

knightly doings in battle or romances of courtly love. The 'Fifteen Joys of a Knight' indicates that a knight would always show hospitality to a wandering poet. In this way the knight was sustained in his daily life by the poems and romances of chivalry, which functioned as a mythology of knighthood.

MARRIAGES AND ALLIANCES

THE INCREASING IMPORTANCE OF SOCIAL STANDING

Knights dreamed of doing the great chivalric deeds described in the many chansons, and some had the excitement of riding out on heroic campaigns and fighting great battles, but they also lived in the day-to-day world of social and financial obligations. In this world a knight's standing and that of his family could be a pressing concern.

In the higher levels of feudal society occupied by knights, marriages were normally based on considerations of social standing and wealth, and marital engagements were arranged in order to acquire property or to make a political alliance

with a powerful lord. A good marriage for a knight or his daughters could bring with it great landholdings.

THE ROLL OF ARMS

Knights of this era rode into battle and into tournaments bearing their coat of arms on their shield, surcoat or other tunic and horsecloths. These coats of arms developed from simple symbols worn by early knights to identify themselves in battle, and gradually became more complex. When a knight acquired new lands through marriage a new title and coat of arms would come with them; he would

then add the new 'arms' to his own coat of arms. In battles and particularly at tournaments heralds were the experts on these arms. A herald might work for a great lord and have jurisdiction throughout the area of his power: he would keep a 'roll of arms' listing the different coats of arms for all the knights in the area.

WILLIAM MARSHAL'S RISE

The great 12th-century English knight William Marshal was the model for those needing to better themselves. He rose from relatively humble origins to be the equal of the leading knights and nobles by dint of his prowess in tournaments and on the field of battle. From a position where, as a junior knight in the house of William de Tancarville, he had to sell his clothes to buy a new horse, he achieved such status within the world of chivalry that in 1189 he married one of the richest women in England, the 17-year-old Isabel de Clare, heiress to Richard de Clare, 2nd Earl of Pembroke. Marshal was made earl and he went on to become Marshal of England and Protector of the Kingdom in the minority of King Henry III.

DAUGHTERS OF A POOR KNIGHT

A rise such as Marshal's was an inspiring dream, of course, but also an exception to the rule. Many knights lived in relatively straitened circumstances, and found it difficult to maintain a good position for themselves and their families in the world of the noble elite. Impoverished or struggling knights were common figures in the literature of chivalry.

In the 12th-century Spanish epic poem *Cantar del Mio Cid* ('Song of the Cid'), the poem's hero, great Spanish warrior Don

◀ *A roll of arms of Yorkshire lords, recorded in c.1483 by William Ballard, March King of Arms under the English kings Edward IV and Richard III.*

▲ *Philip the Bold, Duke of Burgundy, made a highly advantageous alliance when he married Marguerite, Countess of Flanders, in 1369, after which he became Count of Flanders and of Artois.*

Rodrigo Diaz de Vivar ('El Cid') goes to war in part to provide for his family. He needs to furnish his daughters with suitable dowries, and to find fitting husbands for them. He achieves his aim by raising tribute from Muslim leaders, capturing Valencia and giving his daughters in marriage to the kings of Navarre and Aragon.

In the Arthurian romance *Érec et Énide* ('Eric and Enid') by the 12th-century French poet Chrétien de Troyes, the Lady Enid's father is a knight fallen on hard times, who is too poor to provide a dowry for her or to dress her in finery. Enid is ashamed of her worn clothes, but her father is not a figure of ridicule in the poem: he is presented as pleasing, generous, forthright, attractive – he possesses the virtues of a good knight, despite being poor. The plight of his family is presented with sympathy.

Chivalric literature describes the interaction of the ideal code of chivalry with the real world. According to the code, knightly virtues matter far more than worldly wealth, but the poems make clear that there may be unpleasant consequences of failing to acquire wealth alongside virtue.

CHIVALRIC WEDDINGS

Within noble society, marriages were celebrated with all the trappings of chivalry. Some of the greatest of medieval tournaments were held as celebrations of the weddings of noble lords or their daughters. In 1359 the wedding of John of Gaunt to Blanche of Lancaster at Reading was marked by a tournament in which King Edward III, his sons and 19 other nobles entered the lists clad as the mayor and aldermen of London, and fought against all comers.

▶ *Extravagant gestures and declarations of love were an integral part of the social interaction of a court. Attachments were made to single and married women alike.*

LOVE AT COURT

In a world in which marriages were made principally in the light of considerations of political expedience or property holdings, love may have seemed like a luxury. Some matrimonial matches began as diplomatic arrangements but became deeply loving. For example, the marriage of the future Edward I of England and Eleanor of Castile started as a diplomatic alliance when he was 15 years old and she was only nine, but ended as a powerful relationship, honoured by Edward after the queen's death in 1290 with the erection of 12 memorial crosses marking the spots at which her funeral cortége stopped on its route from her place of death at Harby, in Nottinghamshire, and her place of burial, Westminster Abbey in London. (Charing Cross in central London is a replica of one of these memorials.) In mourning, Edward wrote: 'In life I dearly loved her and I will not stop loving her in death'.

These deeply loving matches were, however, exceptions to the general rule. The cult of courtly love gave an outlet to romantic passion within the chivalric world. The lady to whom knights would dedicate their service in the courtly love tradition was usually already married to a great lord. The knight may have felt a deep passion for her on account of the connection, and may have expressed his longing for physical union with his beloved, yet very few of the relationships celebrated in these poems would have come to physical consummation.

LIFE IN A KNIGHTLY BROTHERHOOD

DAY-TO-DAY LIFE FOR A KNIGHT TEMPLAR OR A HOSPITALLER

Like other knights, the members of the great chivalric brotherhoods such as the Knights Hospitaller and the Knights Templar also spent periods 'at home', away from the excitement and difficulties of life on the battlefield. For much of the time, they lived a life not unlike that of the monks in Cistercian or Benedictine houses.

Those joining up to military orders took the monastic vows of poverty, chastity and obedience. (One brotherhood, the Spanish Order of Santiago, allowed married men to join.) Mostly the brothers lived a communal existence, in quarters designed like those in a conventional monastery, eating in a refectory and sleeping in a dormitory. They followed the monastic hours and were required to attend services.

The monks were largely lay brethren, many of them illiterate. In addition, there were literate clerical brothers who would serve as chaplains and recite the services or daily offices while the others listened. A typical rule required the lay brothers to repeat the *pater noster* (the Lord's Prayer), a number of times at each of the set offices.

▲ *The Templars wore Christ's cross into battle on clothing, shields and horse coverings. Their full name was 'Poor Fellow-Soldiers of Christ and of the Temple of Solomon'.*

▼ *Krak des Chevaliers, a fortress originally built in 1031 for the Emir of Aleppo, was given to the Knights Hospitaller in 1144, who rebuilt it as the largest crusader castle in the Levant.*

A NOBLE CALLING

It was not an easy life for the knights of these brotherhoods. The address or statement read out before an applicant to the Hospitaller order made it clear that he would have to be willing to sacrifice his own desires and needs and devote himself to the service of the order. It said that to enter the order was a great and noble calling, but that he should not expect to have a magnificent steed or to be kept in comfort. It said that he would find that when he wanted to sleep, the order might require him to be on watch, and when he wanted to eat he might have to fast. The knight would have to be able and willing to travel far away, 'to places that will not be pleasing', and that he would often find it necessary 'to abandon [his] desires in order to fulfil those of another'.

MILITARY RANKS

In the principal knightly orders, the lay brothers were divided into two ranks: sergeants and knights. There were two kinds of sergeant: non-fighting sergeants and sergeants-at-arms. In the monastery the sergeants performed necessary farming and household work, but the knights were of higher rank and were spared this labour. The brothers undertook military exercises to keep themselves prepared for war. Knights had better armour and three or four horses, while sergeants-at-arms made do with basic protection and only a single horse. The sergeants would sometimes fight as infantry alongside their brother-knights. The brothers in the different orders built or repaired and garrisoned many castles.

RULES OF LIVING

The warrior-monks followed a less strict diet than that of their contemporaries in the non-military orders. They were allowed to eat meat, normally on three days a week, in order to keep up their strength for military activities.

Other rules were very strict. Most orders required silence at mealtimes. The favourite leisure activities of secular knights, such as hunting, hawking and fighting in tournaments, were all outlawed – although, as we shall see in Chapter Five, brothers in the Knights Templar were

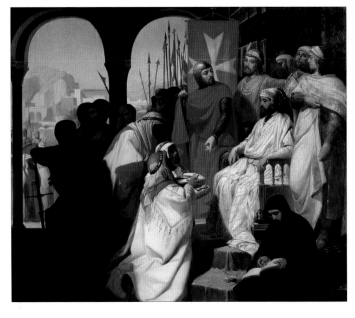

allowed to take part in *bohorts*, the form of tournament in which there was no physical conflict, presumably as a way of maintaining their fitness and good horsemanship. Another exception to the general rule was made in the case of the brothers of the Spanish military order of Calatrava, who lived in a barren landscape, and were allowed to hunt in order to secure food.

There were strict rules on clothing, which should normally be plain and of

▲ *In 1347–48, the Knights Hospitallers, by then based on Rhodes and known as the Knights of Rhodes, came to the aid of King Constantine III of Armenian Cilicia in his conflict with the Mamluk Sultan of Egypt.*

wool. It appears that these kinds of rules may have been honoured more in the breach than in the observance – in the 13th century the statutes of the Knights Hospitallers often found it necessary to denounce the use of embroidery on any clothing and even of silver and gold adornment on military equipment. The Templars allowed the brothers in Syria to wear linen, rather than wool, in the hot summer months.

In many of the orders, there was no probationary period or novitiate of the kind followed in the non-military orders. This must have made it difficult to establish whether applicants were really suited to the communal life of the brotherhood. The strict rules were enforced with fierce penalties, which ranged from being expelled to receiving a beating or merely being asked to perform a few days of penitential activities.

YOUNGER SONS

In feudal society property was inherited by the oldest son, which generally made it difficult for younger sons to make their way in the world. At one time, historians argued that many of these relatively poor younger sons went on crusade seeking their fortune, but modern scholars have stressed the enormous expense and financial risk of travelling on crusade and argued that normally only the wealthy could have made the decision to take the cross and become a crusader. The brotherhoods of the warrior-monks, however, offered a way in which younger sons and even those from non-noble families could make a career as a knight; up to the mid-13th century applicants from outside the nobility were able to enter the brotherhoods. There they received very good military training. Their financial position probably meant that they would not have been able to marry outside the order, so that they were not giving up the chance of a wedded life when they took the order's vow of chastity.

CHAPTER FIVE

A KNIGHT AT ARMS

Mounted knights riding with couched lances in cavalry charges, and wielding mace and sword in close combat, dominate popular visions of battles in the age of chivalry. In reality the exploits of individual knights were usually far less important than we may think in determining the outcome of battles. Accounts in poems, romances and even chronicles were written to praise and memorialize feats of arms by knights, and they exaggerated the number who fought and their importance in battle.

These accounts also overplayed the importance of battles themselves. Pitched battles were rare in the Middle Ages and wars were often conducted through a series of sieges with attacking armies trying to draw out their opponents. However, knights were occasionally the difference between victory and defeat on the battlefield. A celebrated example of such a conflict is the Battle of Bouvines, northern France, on 27 July 1214, in which Philip IV of France was victorious over a German–Flemish army led by Holy Roman Emperor Otto IV. The battle was fought on a front over a mile long, with three areas of fighting: on the two wings and in the centre, where initially the Flemish infantry got the upper hand, but the French recovered and Philip led the cavalry charge. The battle was decided in this central area between the two groups of mounted knights, with daggers and swords. Otto was unhorsed and his imperial standard was captured, but he was saved from capture by the bravery of a group of Saxon knights.

▲ *The reality of medieval warfare involved plunder and looting.*

◀ *After the brutal clash of armies in battle, courtesy was restored in ransom and peace talks. This chivalric encounter is the aftermath of Philip IV's victory at Bouvines in 1214.*

THE MOUNTED WARRIOR

A KNIGHT IN BATTLE

The mounted warriors who fought alongside Duke William of Normandy at the Battle of Hastings in 1066 wore chain mail coats that extended to the knees and the elbows, and were split at the sides and front to make it easier to move. On their heads the warriors wore a conical metal helmet with a single downward protrusion to protect the nose. They carried a long shield shaped like a kite, which when used on horseback offered them protection from head to toe.

▼ *The Norman knights of the 10th and 11th centuries would be dressed in chain mail, which made mounting and dismounting possible in the thick of battle.*

CHAIN MAIL

The basic chain mail tunic (hauberk) or long robe (byrnie), made of circular interlocking links of iron, had changed little since the time of Charlemagne, and continued as the basic defensive armour until the end of the 13th century. Additions were made to it to increase protection. These included a chain mail hood (camail or coif); a chain mail mouth flap (ventail) to protect the lower face; chain mail mittens; and quilted cuisses with metal sewn in to protect the upper legs.

CHARGING WITH A LANCE

Anna Comnena, daughter of Byzantine emperor Alexius Comnenus, was powerfully impressed by the impact of charging crusader knights, which she witnessed at Byzantium in 1096–97. She wrote that the 'first shock' was 'irresistible' and conjectured that they could 'make a hole in the walls of Babylon'. Chronicle accounts may exaggerate the importance of knights in determining the outcome of battles, but there is no denying the force of mounted, armoured knights at full charge.

The knights described by Anna Comnena were charging in a coordinated unit with couched lance. This manoeuvre was developed in the second half of the 11th century in northern France – probably by the Normans. It is a key technique of the age of chivalry, seen both in the lists at tournaments and on the field of battle.

▲ *Norman knights charge at the Battle of Hastings. They use their lances as spears rather than 'couched' under the right arm.*

Mounted soldiers, dressed in chain mail in earlier armies, had used the lance as a spear for overarm throwing when mounted, and for jabbing when fighting on the ground. Knights, however, learned to hold the lance firmly beneath their arm and use it as a weapon of impact. The full force of the knight's charge was delivered at the point of impact, and the knight retained his lance, so that after a charge he could wheel away with the weapon and charge again. Another advantage of the new technique was that the knights could use a heavier lance, because they did not have to lift the weapon up to throw it or jab with it. Lances kept the enemy at a distance, making a knight less vulnerable.

A MIGHTY CHALLENGE

Handling both horse and weapons on the battlefield was extremely difficult. A knight needed to have the ability to control the horse when riding at speed, and when changing direction, through a crowded field if necessary. The knight would be quickly despatched if he were not physically fit and highly skilled in the use of his mount and equipment. For this reason, chivalric literature stressed repeatedly the need for knights to train in the arts of war: tournaments provided an

SADDLE AND STIRRUP

Warriors rode horses in battle for centuries before the solid saddle and the stirrups made them secure on their mounts. The Assyrian cavalry developed the first saddle in about 800–700BC. It was no more than a simple cloth tied around the horse, giving the rider a better grip. The Scythians used an improved, padded saddle. The Nubian mercenaries in the Roman army used a solid saddle built high at the front (pommel) and back (cantle). Of partic-

ular relevance for the massed charge was the use of a high pommel, invaluable for helping the knight to stay mounted at the shuddering moment of impact.

Stirrups made the rider much more secure and allowed him to fight energetically. It is not known for sure when and where the stirrup was invented. Around 500BC, soldiers in India were using a simple leather loop, and the Sarmatians – nomadic contemporaries of the Scythians – used one stirrup-like loop as a help in mounting. The oldest evidence for the use of twin stirrups, one on each side, was in an ancient Chinese tomb of AD322.

From their use by the nomadic groups from Asia, notably the Avars who rode into what is now Hungary, stirrups were gradually adopted in Europe, and more generally by the 8th century.

◄ *An early pair of Avarian stirrups from the 8th century.*

by knocking his knee or ankle. At the end of the hilt was the pommel, a heavy rounded extension, which could also be used as a weapon.

In the late 13th century knights fought with a lance around 2.4m (8ft) in length, and 14th-century lances became longer still – typically 3m (10ft). The spearhead was strong enough to pierce armour.

DAGGER AND MACE

In close combat knights also used daggers and one-handed battle-axes. One type of dagger had a straight blade with a single cutting edge, and was called a misericorde from the Latin *misericordia* ('mercy') because it was used to finish off a badly wounded knight – perhaps by stabbing through the helmet visor or under the gorget. Another dagger was the anelace, a broad double-edged tapering dagger with a blade of up to 45cm (18in).

A knight could also attack a nearby opponent by hitting him with a mace – a wooden club with a metal or stone head. A blow from a mace was often enough to stun an opponent and was the favoured weapon of clerics in battle, for while they were expected to fight, they were not supposed to shed blood. Some spiked maces, such as the flanged mace and morning star mace, could penetrate armour.

The battle-axe was an effective weapon when used with force: at the Battle of Bannockburn, Robert the Bruce reputedly killed the knight Sir Henry de Bohun with a single blow to his head.

▼ *From top: battle-axe, 'morning star' mace, anelace dagger and broadsword.*

essential opportunity to practise, in addition to being an opportunity for self-display and courtly manoeuvring.

A knight could not have fought like this without specialized weapons and equipment. Probably most important of all to the effectiveness of mounted warfare were the saddle and stirrups. Also relevant is that horseshoes were developed in the late 11th century. Horses with horseshoes could travel farther and cross rougher country than those without them.

SWORD AND LANCE

A mounted warrior in the early Middle Ages carried a light sword, weighing less than 1.5kg (3lb), which he used mainly for cutting and slashing. From the 11th and 12th centuries, the sword was usually a little longer with a sharper point so he could thrust with it as well. In the late 13th century a typical knight's sword had a blade of 80cm (2ft 6in) with a handle of

around 20cm (8in). In the following century they used a two-handed broadsword that was almost twice as long, measuring 1.8m (6ft) in total.

All sword handles (hilts) featured a cross-guard, a pair of extensions (quillions) at the blade end of the handle that prevented the hand sliding off the handle. Sometimes knights would reverse the sword when fighting – holding the sword by the covered blade they used the quillions to undermine an opponent's balance

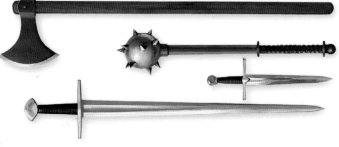

THE ARMOURED KNIGHT
PROTECTION IN BATTLE

The main advantages of chain mail were that it was not too heavy and allowed considerable freedom of movement. However, it could not stop the point of a lance or the edge of a sword. In the 12th century, knights began to wear a padded jerkin beneath the mail, which

▼ In the 13th century knights began to wear pieces of metal plate armour in conjunction with chain mail. The leg piece is jointed just below the knee for ease of movement.

helped to absorb the shock of blows, but was still easily penetrated. In addition, a heavy blow, even if it did not break the mail, could force pieces of chain into the wound, making injury and bleeding worse. Chain mail was also difficult to clean and keep rust-free.

THE 'COAT OF ARMS'
The custom of wearing a surcoat, a cloth garment worn over the chain mail, was probably brought back by the crusaders from the Holy Land, where they learned its use from Muslim armies. Soldiers and knights – both in battle and at tournaments – wore coats of arms on their surcoats as a means of identification.

SUITS OF ARMOUR
The first steps towards suits of solid plate armour were taken in the 13th century. Initially chest and back plates of hardened leather were tried, and small pieces of solid metal were attached to the chain mail suit at the elbows, armpits and knees. The next stage was to attach jointed plates of metal to a leather base, making a jacket for the entire upper body.

The first suits of armour in c.1330 consisted of many pieces, often connected by complex lacing, which together provided layered protection for the body. It took a long time to put a suit like this on, and there are several accounts of knights being unprepared if an army was surprised.

These suits were gradually improved to counter the devastating effects of the longbow and the crossbow. The breastplate was introduced in the late 1300s, and the gorget to protect the throat, neck and shoulders came in at the start of the 15th century. It was not until the mid-15th century that princes and great lords – the elite among knights – were riding to battle wearing complete suits of plate armour of the kind we may associate with medieval knights

▲ From top left: the coif, made of chain mail covering the shoulders as well as the head, the chain mail tunic, and the Aketon, a quilted jacket worn beneath armour.

through depictions in Victorian paintings. The best plate armour was made in Italy and Germany, especially at the Missaglia workshop in Milan. It was made from heat-treated steel, and at vulnerable spots between the main plates were protective roundels – or sometimes pieces of mail were worn beneath the suit.

Armour suits were highly prized, and it was accepted practice for a captured knight to give up his armour as part of his ransom. Froissart reports in his *Chronicles* that at Tournai in 1339, Pope Clement's nephew Raymond was killed after he had surrendered, slain for no better reason than that his captors coveted his beautiful armour – and this unchivalrous act 'drove many good men to anger'. The very best plate armour was superbly well made. Its chief purpose was as protection, but almost as important was its function as a status symbol – a badge of knightly pre-eminence. Plate armour was also remarkably light – hardly any heavier than chain mail. Some of the finest suits weighed as little as 25kg (55lb).

HELMETS AND SHIELDS

The simple conical helmet worn by the Normans at Hastings was gradually developed to protect the head more and more.

▼ By the 14th century the many pieces of plate provided good protection, although the lack of a breastplate and gorget (neck piece) left knights vulnerable to the bowmen.

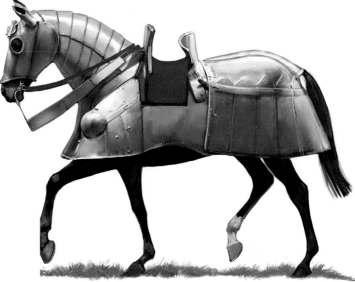

▲ Horse protection in the 1200s was made of cloth, but horse armour, first of boiled leather and then of plate metal, was developed in the course of the 15th century.

At first soldiers wore a chain mail coif, or hood, with a padded cap beneath, then in the early 13th century they added a cylindrical helmet with a flat upper surface, a slit at eye level and tiny holes in front of nose and mouth to allow for breathing. Curved helmets were in use by c.1270 as experience had shown that a curved upper surface deflected blows better than a flat one. The first helmets with moveable visors were introduced at around the same time. In the 14th century pointed Italian helmets called bascinets became popular – they had a projecting 'snout' covering the mouth and were popularly known as 'hounskulls' (hounds' skulls) or 'pig-faces'.

The long kite-shaped shields carried by Normans were also used by the crusader knights. These shields generally had a

▶ Open-face helmets were superseded first by flat-topped helmets with eye-slits, then by curved-topped ones, then by helmets with hinged visors.

rounded top, and were made of wood covered in leather boiled until it was very hard. During the 12th century shields were made with a flatter top. As armour improved the shield was made smaller, and by the 14th century knights carried a compact arm-shield in the shape of a flat-iron known as a 'heater-shield'. By the 15th century, knights in full plate armour no longer needed to carry a shield at all, but shields were still used in tournaments.

A KNIGHT'S ROLE IN BATTLE

HOW KNIGHTS WERE DEPLOYED

The basic pattern of all battles during the age of chivalry was the same: the cavalry attacked in waves, while the infantry was primarily arrayed as a defensive block. If an attack went well, infantry poured forward to support the cavalry.

Knights were usually organized in groups of 30 to 40 fighting beneath a banner. These groups were called *conrois* and several together formed a 'battle', and two or three 'battles' might enter the conflict at once. If a feigned retreat was planned, a further battle would be held in reserve to attack unexpectedly once the enemy had broken out of his defensive position in pursuit of the retreating force.

THE NEED FOR DISCIPLINE

If the cavalry charged too soon, this could spell disaster. Leading knights were sometimes deluded by over-confidence or driven by an intense desire to achieve individual feats of glory: they led attacks

▼ *Christian forces crushed the Almohad army at the Battle of Las Navas de Tolosa in 1212. The battle was fought as part of a crusade called by Pope Innocent III.*

against impossible odds, disregarding the better judgement of more cautious fellow knights. In 1187 at the Battle of Cresson near Nazareth – shortly before the Christians' devastating defeat by Saladin at the Horns of Hattin – Templar knight Gerard of Ridefort led a mere 100 knights in a charge against a large Muslim force. Only three of the knights survived, one of whom was the architect of the disaster, Gerard himself.

Even if a cavalry charge were not against impossible odds it could still spell disaster if it were badly timed. In battlefield conditions it could be very difficult for a group of knights to reform and charge a second time. In the confused mêlée of fighting, an individual knight would have to look for the banner under which he was fighting, and might have to fight his way back to it. Effectively, the charge needed to succeed the first time.

VICTORY – OR DISASTER

Battles could be won quickly with a well-timed charge, but a position of strength could also be thrown away by impulsive knights. If the defending army weathered

the charge, it could launch its own counter-attack, often to devastating effect. It could be difficult for military commanders to maintain discipline within an army containing many proud lords and separate groups in order to prevent this kind of thing happening. For example, on crusades the knightly brotherhoods often competed for the greatest glory.

BATTLEFIELD STANDOFF

Where discipline was maintained, armies sometimes showed great reluctance to make the first move. In Spain in 1212 at the Battle of Las Navas de Tolosa the combined armies of the Christian kings of Castile, Aragon, Navarre and Portugal were arrayed for two full days in opposition to the vast force of the Muslim Almohads before fighting began. These battles often started with preliminary skirmishes between individuals or small groups who rode forward between the two armies, taunting the enemy and trying to tempt a charge. In this case Almohad warriors did just that, trying to goad the Christians into an angry response. But the Christians held firm. The attack when it came was crushingly effective, resulting in a Christian victory that killed or took prisoner 100,000 opponents.

THE EFFECT OF ARMOUR

The development of armour – from mail hauberks and byrnies to full plate armour in the 14th–15th centuries – necessarily had an effect on how knights fought. Different kinds of armour allowed for greater or lesser freedom of movement. It is a common misconception that after the development of plate armour, knights were virtually immobilized by heavy suits of armour and had to be lifted into their saddles using a small crane. In fact the armour was light and they could run and jump on to their horse wearing this equipment. Yet it is true that plate armour in both this final and its various earlier developments did tend to limit the effectiveness of a dismounted knight on the field of battle – he could not move about as easily as his predecessors had in a byrnie, simply because the plate armour was designed to be worn by a mounted warrior and not one fighting on the ground.

KNIGHTS ON FOOT

If a knight in armour were knocked from his horse, he often struggled to regain his mount, and was forced to fight on foot, when he was at a disadvantage. In the Battle of Bouvines, both Philip IV and Otto IV were unhorsed in the close fighting: Otto was saved by the bravery of his Saxon guard, but Philip – who was young and fit – managed to regain his mount and fight on. At the Battle of Poitiers in 1356, many French knights had their horses killed beneath them by English archers and were forced to try to cope on foot – with little success.

A footsoldier could quite easily bring a knight down by stabbing with his dagger through any gaps in the armour or

▼ *At the Battle of Bouvines in 1214, French cavalry power won the day in direct and bruising confrontations with the German-Flemish knights of Otto IV's army.*

at the joints between armour pieces. In the mid-14th century, at the time of the Battle of Poitiers, plate armour was gradually being developed and many knights wore both chain mail and plate armour in this period. This double armour weighed heavily upon them, and thus they were very severely handicapped once they had been unhorsed.

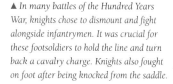

▲ *In many battles of the Hundred Years War, knights chose to dismount and fight alongside infantrymen. It was crucial for these footsoldiers to hold the line and turn back a cavalry charge. Knights also fought on foot after being knocked from the saddle.*

THE INFANTRY'S EFFECTIVENESS

In most battles the infantry held the key. The knights in a cavalry charge hoped to scatter the footsoldiers they rode towards, or at least to kill enough of them to break the infantry's unity as a defensive formation. If the infantry were broken up into twos and threes, then the knights could pick them off, but if the footsoldiers were able to maintain their discipline, there was little the attacking cavalry could do to best them – once knight and horse were fighting at close quarters with a solid formation of footsoldiers they were quite vulnerable. At the Battle of Hastings in 1066, the initial Norman cavalry charges had little effect and the Anglo-Saxon footsoldiers, fighting behind a wall of shields, might have carried the day had they held firm rather than breaking out to follow the feigned Norman retreat.

COEUR DE LION

KING RICHARD I OF ENGLAND

King Richard I of England is one of the most celebrated figures in the history of knighthood, hailed as Richard Coeur de Lion ('the Lionheart') for his exploits on the Third Crusade of 1190–92 when he defeated and then wisely negotiated with the great Muslim military leader Saladin. Richard was a superb general who repeatedly took the correct strategic decisions rather than clouding his judgement by a thirst for glory. Yet, like many leading figures of the era, he often did not live according to the code of chivalric honour or the doctrines of Christianity. His actions were often self-seeking and disreputable – he took part in looting, was accused of rape and suspected of murder, and rebelled twice against his own father.

▼ *This statue of Richard I outside England's Houses of Parliament perfectly depicts his heroic status in the English psyche.*

RICHARD I
Born: 8 September 1157
Died: 6 April 1199
Knighted: 1173
Famous for: his charisma, bravery in battle and his ability as a general
Greatest achievement: Defeat of Saladin, Arsuf, 7 September 1191

A TASTE FOR CHIVALRY

Born in Beaumont Palace, Oxford, in 1157, the son of King Henry II and his queen, Eleanor of Aquitaine, Richard evidently had a good education. His mother's influence was strong. She had travelled on the Second Crusade (1147–49) with her first husband, King Louis VII of France, and was a keen patroness of chivalric literature. Richard followed his mother on this path: as well as taking the Cross as a crusader, he was a major patron of poets; he himself wrote poetry in French and Occitan (a French dialect used in romances); and, according to Muslim sources, he had an interest in Arabic culture. By repute, he was a handsome man: tall, with reddish-blond hair and pale skin. He was universally praised for his bravery.

FIRST TASTE OF WAR

Richard's loyalty and sense of responsibility were certainly poorly developed. In 1173, encouraged by his mother, he joined his brothers Henry the Young King and Geoffrey, Count of Brittany, in a revolt against his father, King Henry II. The three sons gathered at the court of Eleanor's first husband, Louis VII of France. At this time, Richard was knighted by Louis, at the age of 15, and then in July 1173 rode out on his first military campaign, an invasion of eastern Normandy. The revolt failed: Henry II succeeded in imposing his authority and in 1174 Richard begged pardon and swore an oath of subservience.

▲ *Richard was a very effective leader. When he landed at Acre on the Third Crusade in April 1191, the town had been besieged for 20 months. He captured it in five weeks.*

A BRILLIANT STRATEGIST

In this period of his life Richard was duke of Aquitaine and count of Poitou, both in France. He quickly proved himself to be an outstanding warrior and general in putting down revolts by the barons in Aquitaine. The troubadour Bertran de Born wrote of the young count, 'he lays sieges and pursues his enemies, seizing their castles, smashing and burning in all directions'.

A particular example of Richard's ruthless and effective military strategy came when he took the castle of Taillebourg, near the river Charente, which was considered impregnable because it had cliff-faces around it on three sides and a town laid out on the other. He ravaged the town, farms and landscape all about, terrifying the garrison into risking all by coming out to confront him. In open battle he defeated them, and entered the castle, which he destroyed. He was merciless in wiping out the challenge of

▶ *In the Holy Land, Richard came face to face with the other great chivalric figure of his age – the Muslim general Saladin. In 1191 Richard won a great victory at Arsuf. They agreed peace terms at Jaffa in 1192.*

the barons, according to some accounts even taking their wives and forcing them to serve as prostitutes for his leading knights and then afterwards for the army.

CRUSADER KING

In 1187 Richard allied himself with Philip II of France, and then the following year again revolted against Henry II. Richard and Philip defeated Henry's forces, and Henry named his son his heir before dying. Richard was crowned King of England in Westminster Abbey on 3 September 1189 and at once set about raising money for a crusade. In 1190 he departed on crusade with Philip II.

Richard's first act on crusade was to help capture the port of Acre in June 1191. He was very ill with scurvy and laid out on a stretcher, but is said to have been strong enough to shoot down the guards on the city walls one by one using a crossbow, while his retainers carried the stretcher here and there. The garrison surrendered. Meanwhile, Philip II abandoned the crusade he started with Richard.

After Acre Richard marched his army south towards Jaffa. Saladin launched a major attack at Arsuf, but Richard inflicted a famous defeat on the great Muslim general. Later he might have marched on Jerusalem, but seeing that he would not be able to hold the city even if he were to succeed in taking it, instead opened peace negotiations. This decision is typical of Richard's practical realism as a military commander. He agreed a treaty with

Saladin under which Jerusalem remained in Muslim hands but pilgrims could have access to it, and embarked for Europe in September 1192.

His homecoming was humiliating. He was shipwrecked, captured, imprisoned by Holy Roman Emperor Henry VI and ransomed for 150,000 marks.

DEATH AT CHALUS

After a brief visit to England in April 1194, when he was crowned king for a second time, he spent the final five years of his life fighting over his French possessions. He died after he was shot in the neck with a crossbow bolt at the castle of Chalus and the wound became gangrenous.

REPUTATION AND CHARACTER

Contemporary accounts suggest that as well as being an intelligent strategist, Richard was a charismatic commander, beloved of his men. He repeatedly showed his bravery in combat and once rode into great danger to rescue a foraging party, with the words: 'I despatched those men there. If they die without me, then I should never again be called king.' According to the 12th-century chronicler Richard of Devizes, King Richard's men were willing to 'wade in blood to the Pillars of Hercules' at his command.

In the 20th century the idea developed that Richard was homosexual: he spent very little time with his wife, and had no children by her – although he had an illegitimate son. Some historians suggest he had a love affair with Philip II, and that this explains the ferocity of their quarrels, and it has been proposed that his wife's brother (later Sancho VII of Navarre) was another of Richard's lovers. Modern historians cast doubt on these arguments – which they say were based on a misreading of texts – and suggest that there is insufficient evidence to make conclusions about his sexuality one way or another.

◀ *Richard was buried beside his father Henry II and mother Eleanor of Aquitaine at Fontrevault Abbey near Chinon. His brain was interred separately, at Rouen.*

THE SPECTACLE OF WAR
PAGEANTRY ON THE BATTLEFIELD

Armies arrayed on a battlefield in the age of chivalry made a stirring sight. Infantry probably impressed mostly by their solid mass, and sometimes their large numbers gathered beneath fluttering banners, but the knights were an imposing sight, in helmet and armour and surcoat, mounted on powerful horses, with a colourful shield bearing a coat of arms or other armorial badge, and sword and lance and other weapons glinting in the light. In chivalric literature and in chronicles – from which we glean so much of our knowledge about how knights saw them-selves and understood their calling – a knight's physical appearance was an integral part of the impact he made.

CHIVALRIC DISPLAY
Display was all-important for a knight. His armour's chief purpose was of course protection, but almost as important was its function as a status symbol – the uniform of an elite. In battle, knights were also parading their wealth and seeking to win a glorious reputation – just as they did in the mêlée conflict or individual jousts at a tournament.

▼ *Royal or noble members of the chivalric class used fine equipment as a symbol of status. Some even wore golden armour.*

In the pages of medieval epics, romances and chronicles, battles were pre-sented as being scarcely distinguishable from tournaments – as opportunities for display and knightly encounters. The accounts are full of the glorious spectacle of knighthood in action.

ARMOUR BURNING LIKE FIRE
In the 87th *laisse* or verse-paragraph of the epic *Song of Roland*, for instance, the poet describes the army of Charlemagne as it rides through the Pass of Roncesvalles in the Pyrenees mountains. He reports that the evening sun was reflecting from their armour, so that their helmets and hauberks seemed to be made of fire, while their bright shields, painted with flowers, and their bannerets and pennons, fluttering in the breeze, made a gorgeous vision. Likewise, the Muslim army of King Marsiliun, which sweeps down to engulf Charlemagne's rearguard and kill Roland, is said to present a wondrous sight – the warriors wore golden helmets set with jewels and mail coats varnished with gilt, and carried gleaming shields. Similarly, Froissart in his *Chronicles*, describing

▲ *Italian adventurer Roger de Flor parades into Constantinople with a splendidly attired army of Almogavar Spanish mercenaries – the 'Catalan Company' – to fight for Byzantine Emperor Andronicus II Palaeologus against the Ottoman Turks.*

knights and their squires progressing forward, spear in hand, at Noya in Spain in 1387, declares: 'To tell the truth, this was a beautiful sight'.

In battle, chivalric display – wearing the finest armour, using magnificent weapons, and demonstrating great skill in using them – was a way to intimidate the enemy. According to some chronicle accounts of the Battle of Hastings, before the fighting began one of Duke William's knights rode out between the two armies to display his prowess – as a taunting expression of Norman superiority. The knight, a minstrel named Ivo Taillefer, sang a version of the *Song of Roland* while throwing his lance and sword in the air and catching them. An Anglo-Saxon warrior came forth to fight, but Taillefer killed and decapitated him – and paraded the head as proof that God was on the side of the Normans.

THE KNIGHT'S SWORD

The finest weapons were also a sign of chivalric grandeur. The sword, indeed, was the symbol of the knight's calling. In romance literature great knights had magnificent swords, that possessed within them an element of the hero's bravery and nobility: Charlemagne had Joyeuse, his knight Roland had Durendal, King Arthur had Excalibur.

The sword was a precious item, often inlaid with silver in the blade and jewels in the hilt. It was also sacred. The most common design had a sizeable crossbar between blade and hilt so that it took the shape of the Christian cross when held point downwards; squires would pray over the sword before they were knighted and then, when they were knights, before conflict. The sword itself was often blessed during the knighting ceremony.

▶ *The sword a knight carried into battle and stained with blood was a reminder of his calling as Christ's warrior, especially when used as a crucifix during prayer.*

MASSED RANKS

Aside from the wealth on display among the fighting noblemen, another aspect stressed repeatedly in chivalric literature and chronicles is the sheer size of the spectacle. King Marsiliun's army in the *Song of Roland* is a 'vast host' divided into no fewer than 20 battle formations – this is a force that attacks in a narrow mountain pass. Similarly, various chronicle accounts of the Battle of Bouvines claim that Philip IV's army included around 60,000 French – with no fewer than 9,000 knights – while Otto IV's imperial force totalled 250,000. In reality, even though the battle was fought on a much larger scale than most clashes of the 12th and 13th centuries, Philip's army probably contained no more than 1,200 knights and about 5,000 infantry, while Otto's forces had around 1,500 knights and 6,000 footsoldiers.

USE OF BANNERS

Among the colourful elements on the battlefield were the banners raised above the fighting men. They served a very necessary purpose as a rallying point for knights dispersed after a cavalry charge or by close fighting. These knights often had to fight their way back to their own banner, and it must have been very difficult for a group to reform once they were dispersed. Although military brotherhoods were in competition for glory on the field of battle, the rule of the Knights Templar laid down that if a Templar were cut off from his own banner he should seek out that of the Knights Hospitaller, or failing that any other Christian banner.

▼ *Banners flutter above the mêlée of knights and infantrymen as the English and French armies clash at the Battle of Poitiers on 9 September 1356. Edward the Black Prince led the English to a great victory.*

THE AGE OF SIEGE WARFARE

THE TECHNIQUES USED TO CAPTURE A CASTLE

In early medieval warfare the possession of castles usually provided the key to victory. Military campaigns often entailed a series of sieges. These could last for months at a time, and the fighting when it broke out was often dirty and desperate.

LOCAL STRONGHOLDS

The Normans built castles when invading, initially as a base from which to operate in subduing the territory. Once the land was conquered they used the castle as a consolidating position: its presence dominated the surrounding countryside, intimidating local people. Moreover, if an enemy approached, the castle garrison would not only stoutly defend the fortification but could venture forth from safety to harass the enemy with raids.

For this reason an army could not safely bypass a castle and move on to a more distant target because that would leave its rear and its supply lines wide open to raids from the castle garrison. An invading army had to capture castles, either eliminating or forcing the surrender of the garrison before moving on.

ATTACK OR SIEGE

Castles were designed to withstand attack. An attacking army had two main options: to launch an assault quickly or to mount a siege, cut off supplies and reduce the garrison to desperation.

There were several difficulties with mounting a siege. In a prolonged siege, it could be difficult to hold the besieging army together – feudal levies might come to an end of their period of service and depart for home. It is noticeable that King Henry II of England, who mounted many successful sieges, used mercenary troops who were happy to remain and be paid, however long the siege went on. There was also the risk of sickness setting in amongst the besiegers, as happened to the crusaders at Acre in 1189–91.

Moreover, a well-sited castle could be well-nigh impossible to isolate totally – for example, King Edward I of England established his formidable Welsh castles so that they could be supplied by sea. It was due to this that in the Welsh rebellion led by Madoc ap Llywelyn in 1294 none of the rebels' sieges of the castles was successful.

In 1401, by contrast, Owain Glyndwr, self-styled 'Prince of Wales', succeeded in taking Harlech Castle after a siege because he was able to mount a total blockade – by his own troops on land and by a fleet supplied by his French allies at sea.

SIEGE EQUIPMENT

Attackers often used specialist siege equipment to try to make a hole in the castle defences – machines such as the mangonel and trebuchet, which hurled stones at the walls of the castle. They sometimes used battering rams to try to knock the walls down; at others they tried to scale the walls using ladders – a technique known as escalade. This was highly dangerous since as they mounted, the attackers were liable to be wounded or killed by arrows, missiles or liquids sent their way by members of the garrison on the castle walls.

▼ *The concentric fortifications of Harlech Castle in Wales stand atop a 60m (200ft) rock. The English garrison survived a major siege by the forces of Madoc ap Llywelyn during the Welsh revolt of 1294–95.*

A better technique was to use a belfry, a tall tower that was set up against the besieged castle's walls. The belfry was usually built taller than the defensive walls so that the attackers could climb to the top, then fire down on the garrison before clambering over the walls along a bridge lowered from the belfry top. The belfry was usually made of wood, but covered in water-drenched animal skins to make it harder for the defenders to set fire to it as a way of repelling the assault.

The tactics used to break the spirit of a defending garrison were often highly unchivalrous. For example, King Henry V of England captured Rouen, France, in 1418–19 because he had cut off its water supplies and thrown dead animals into the accessible wells. Eventually a plague broke out in the city and the garrison was forced to surrender.

THE ROLE OF KNIGHTS

Knights did not frequently play much of a role in the initial stages of a siege. Specialist soldiers usually operated the siege equipment such as the mangonel, trebuchet or battering ram. Knights would then lead an assault, clambering up the belfry or pouring through a breach in the

▲ *English troops fire from a siege tower and pour over a ladder into a French town in the Hundred Years War. On the walls the defenders put up a desperate resistance.*

▼ *Three crusader armies – those of the kingdom of Jerusalem (upper left), of France (lower left) and of Germany (right) combine at the Siege of Damascus during the Second Crusade. The abject failure of their attack brought the crusade to an end.*

walls once one was made. On the other side knights were often members of the besieged castle garrison, so once battle was joined over or through the walls chivalric encounters did occur between the two groups of knights.

FIGHTING IN A MINE

Another means of attack was to try to make the walls collapse by digging beneath them. The attackers would dig a mine; within, the defenders would dig a counter-mine in order to repel them. The defenders would place a bowl of water on the ground at various points within the outer walls and if they saw ripples on the water this indicated that digging was going on underground and that a mine was nearby. Where two mines met, it was – rather strangely – the custom for knights on opposing sides to meet in individual combat in the mines. In the autumn of 1420, during his siege of the town of Melun in France, King Henry V of England took part in mounted combat in a mine dug beneath the town walls that was lit by torches along the walls of the mine. These encounters were a good opportunity for acts of high chivalry, and it was the custom for the knights who fought in them to become lifelong chivalric associates – 'brothers in arms'.

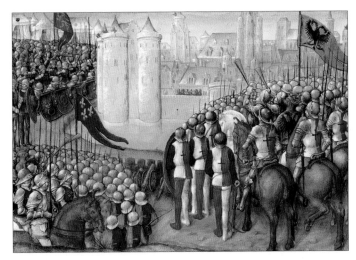

PILLAGING AND BURNING
THE REALITY OF MEDIEVAL WARFARE

Many medieval campaigns featured the ravaging of countryside and cities, particularly in the mid-14th century during the Hundred Years War between England and France. These pillaging raids were known as *chevauchée* (from the French term for a 'charge of horses', presumably because the small raiding army moved at great speed across the countryside). The raids were planned as a form of economic warfare to undermine the enemy's capacity to continue the fight by attacking their supplies and resources. Moreover, in an age when the leading generals were often reluctant to risk their infantry and knights in a pitched fight on the field of battle, chevauchée raiding was designed to force a defending army to leave the relative safety of a beseiged castle or a fortified town, and to come out to fight in the field.

▼ *When an invading army swept across the countryside, setting homes and farms ablaze, frightened locals were powerless to stand in its way.*

THE PILLAGING OF NORMANDY
In July 1346 King Edward III of England and his son Edward Prince of Wales (later known as 'the Black Prince') landed in Normandy and marched their army along the Contentin Peninsula and westwards to Caen, raiding and pillaging as they went.

▲ *The sack of Aalst and Grammont by the inhabitants of Ghent in 1380, in an illustration from a manuscript of 'Chroniques', by Jean de Froissart.*

With support from an English fleet out at sea, Edward mounted a swift and brutal attack on Caen. His soldiers poured through the streets, taking their pleasure and plundering the city's wealth. If the chronicle reports that Edward had banned maltreatment of women, children and religious houses are to be believed, then the ban was disregarded during the brutal sacking of the city.

Caen was a scene of devastation and rapine. Chronicler Jean Froissart, as always emphasizing chivalric deeds by great knights, reported in his *Chronicles* that Sir Thomas Holland rode through the town, and managed to save the lives of many women, children, nuns and monks from the maddened English mob. The booty was loaded on to the ships of the fleet to be taken back across the Channel – Froissart notes that the ships were 'weighed down with fine clothes, precious jewels, and silver or gold objects'.

SCORCHED EARTH

Chevauchée warfare resulted not only in looting but in wanton destruction and the burning of great swathes of countryside. In 1339 during an early campaign using the chevauchée tactic led by Edward III, a chronicler climbed at night to the top of a church tower in the vicinity of Cambrai, northern France, and saw the countryside ablaze in all directions for many miles around – a vision of hell risen to the earth's surface.

The raids deliberately undermined the capacity of the enemy to fight back by depriving him of resources and support. In 1355–57 Edward the Black Prince led a chevauchée campaign in France specifically designed to hit towns that were strong financial supporters of the French monarchy. Sir John Wingfield, the Black Prince's steward and councillor, wrote that the lands and towns destroyed in the raids 'found for the king of France each year more to maintain his war than did half his kingdom'.

POLITICAL CHALLENGE

If an English army raided with apparent impunity in France it was a demonstration of the power of the English crown, and a calculated insult to the king of France. In the summer of 1370 Sir Robert Knowles (or Knollys) marched unchallenged from Calais to the Île de France (Paris), laying waste the countryside en route, and then taunting the French king in his capital city.

The raids were designed to undermine the French monarch's support among his citizens in the ravaged area. When the local people saw that royal protection counted for nothing, they would lose faith in their king. Often, indeed, the raids forced the enemy to launch reprisals.

Both of the chevauchée campaigns that were conducted by Edward, the Black Prince, in 1346 and 1355–57, drew a military response from the French in the field – they resulted in the celebrated English victories at the Battle of Crécy (1346) and Poitiers (1356). Indeed, this was a principal part of their purpose, for the

English – with their widely feared archers – were confident of victory in the pitched battles that occurred during the Hundred Years War.

ECONOMICAL WARFARE

Chevauchée was extremely profitable because it resulted in the capture of mounds of booty and hundreds of ransomed prisoners. Moreover, it was an economical way to wage war because the raids could be carried out by small armies of a few thousand men and did not call for the expense of long campaigns involving major battles or prolonged sieges. The raids delivered effective blows to the enemy's finances and morale but did not result in conquests that had to be defended with permanent and expensive garrisons.

THE BRUTALITY OF WILLIAM I

Chevauchée is particularly associated by historians with the mid-14th century campaigns in the Hundred Years' War, but

▲ *Women and children, as well as defenders, faced a dreadful fate when a fortified town fell to its besiegers. Army commanders would often turn a blind eye to the activities of their looting soldiers.*

punitive raiding was certainly used elsewhere as an aspect of military policy. For example, William I used similar tactics in his infamous 'Harrying of the North' in 1069–70, when his army burned villages, destroyed the crops and livestock, and devastated the populations across much of northern England. He is reckoned to have killed 150,000 people, with more succumbing to starvation and plague in the course of the long winter that followed in a ravaged landscape. The crusaders also made use of the tactic in the Holy Land. It was also adopted during the raiding in the mid-14th century across the English–Scottish border, when both English and Scots used merciless violence in ravaging the countryside.

'THE BLACK DOUGLAS'

SIR JAMES DOUGLAS, LORD OF DOUGLAS

Sir James Douglas, a great knight in the Scottish wars of independence in the early 14th century, was a brilliant exponent of guerrilla warfare, a man whose violent raids on English castles and towns in the Scottish borders won him the affection of his countrymen and the hatred of his English enemies – the Scots knew him as 'Good Sir James', while the English called him 'the Black Douglas'. He was a close battle companion of Robert the Bruce (King Robert I of Scots). He died fighting against the Saracens in Spain en route to the Holy Land, where he had promised to bury Robert the Bruce's embalmed heart.

SQUIRE IN PARIS

Sir James's father was Sir William Douglas the Hardy (also 'the Bold'), who was Governor of Berwick Castle when it was brutally sacked by the army of King Edward I of England on Good Friday 1296. Sir William was subsequently freed, and supported the Scots freedom fighter Sir William Wallace, but was recaptured and died in captivity in 1298 in the Tower of London. In this period the youthful James Douglas was in Paris, where he had been sent by his family to be safe, and where he entered the service of William Lamberton, Bishop of St Andrews, as a squire. When he returned to Scotland in 1306 with Bishop William, Douglas found that his family estates had been taken and given to one of Edward I's loyal soldiers, Robert de Clifford.

Bishop William introduced Douglas at the English court, but when Edward refused to contemplate restoring the family estates to the young man, Douglas allied himself with Robert the Bruce, who had claimed the Scottish crown after killing his principal rival John Comyn. It was during these years that Douglas learned the guerrilla warfare that he would put to such devastating use.

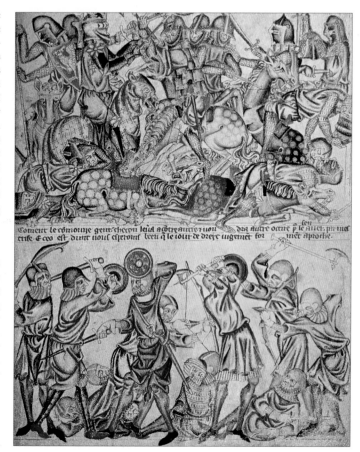

▲ *At Bannockburn in 1314, Sir James – on the very day of his knighting – commanded one of the four divisions of the 6,500-strong Scottish army of Robert the Bruce.*

THE 'DOUGLAS LARDER'

On Palm Sunday, 19 March 1307, Douglas led a brutal assault on the English garrison in Douglas Castle, the stronghold that should rightfully have been his own possession. He and his troops surprised the garrison celebrating the holy day, breaking into the church with the battle-cry 'Douglas! Douglas!' and slaying many

there and then. Afterwards he beheaded the surviving garrison members, and cast their corpses atop a great fire that he had built from wine casks taken from the castle cellar. He poisoned the wells by throwing dead horses and salt into them. The attack was known as 'the Douglas larder'.

He struck again to capture the English-held Roxburgh Castle in 1314. He ordered his men to approach the castle in the dark on the night of Shrove Tuesday, crawling beneath their cloaks – when the guards looked out from the battlements in the darkness they thought the dark shapes were nothing more threatening than wandering cattle. Suddenly the Scots soldiers threw hooked scaling ladders up the walls, and poured into the castle, surprising the garrison – who were distracted by their pre-Lenten celebrations. He then slighted the castle (damaged its defences so that it was indefensible by the garrison).

A KNIGHT AT BANNOCKBURN

Later that year Douglas fought alongside the Bruce in the Scots' famous victory at Bannockburn over a much larger English army. On the morning of the battle, 24 June, Douglas was knighted – surprisingly late in life, given his many great military exploits, but an interesting example of how many men fought on as squires for several years.

It was in the years after Bannockburn that Douglas won his reputation as 'the Black Douglas' through his relentless raiding of northern England. On these raids he and his men rode on ponies called 'hobbins' and dismounted to fight on foot – soldier and horse together were called 'hobelars'. Douglas defeated many notable

▼ *An English archer leads an assault on Berwick Castle, whose position in the English and Scottish borders meant it changed hands many times. Sir James endured a siege there by the army of King Edward II in 1318–19.*

> **JAMES DOUGLAS**
> **Born**: 1286
> **Died**: 25 August 1330
> **Knighted**: 24 June 1314
> **Famous for**: his lightning raids on northern England
> **Greatest achievement**: defeat of Sir Robert Neville of Middleham, 1318

opponents in these conflicts including Sir Robert Neville of Middleham, known as 'the Peacock of the North'.

'DOUGLAS! DOUGLAS!'

In April 1318 Douglas took part in the capture of Berwick Castle, then England's last notable possession in Scotland. Edward II of England rode north with an army to take it back, bringing his queen, Isabella, with him as far as York. In 1319, with the English army encamped outside Berwick, Douglas led a raid into Yorkshire, forcing Isabella to flee southwards, and defeated an English army raised by the Archbishop of York that mainly consisted of clergy, in the Battle of Myton.

Douglas continued to be a thorn in the side of the English. In 1327 when the teenage King Edward III led an army northwards, Douglas launched a night raid on their camp at Stanhope in northern England, his men roaring through the camp with the terrifying shout of 'Douglas! Douglas!', killing 300 Englishmen and almost taking the king himself prisoner.

DEATH IN SPAIN

King Robert the Bruce died in 1329, but before he died he asked Sir James, by now his oldest companion in arms, to take his heart to the Holy Sepulchre in Jerusalem. Sir James set out in 1330, with the dead king's embalmed heart enclosed in a silver casket hung around his neck.

On the way he and his companions heard that King Alfonso XI of Castile and León had declared a crusade against the Saracens in Spain and – as good knights, being ever hungry for glory in the service

---

of Christ – diverted there. In a battle at Teba, Douglas went to the aid of a fellow knight surrounded by Saracens. They were badly outnumbered, but Douglas plunged into the thick of the conflict, throwing the silver casket with Bruce's heart ahead of him, and shouted 'You go ahead, as was our custom, and I will follow you – even into death!' Douglas was indeed killed and afterwards his body, and the Bruce's heart, were taken back to Scotland. Douglas was buried in St Bride's Kirk, Douglas, and the Bruce's heart was buried at Melrose Abbey.

CHIVALRY IN PRACTICE

Sir James was a celebrated knight of his day, but it cannot be said that he fought according to the laws of chivalry. His favoured method of guerrilla warfare was both necessary, given limited Scottish resources, and very effective, but it relied on subterfuge, deception and ruthlessness. His stirring life story is by no means unique in the medieval period in providing many examples of how the code of chivalry was an ideal that many knights had often to abandon in order to thrive.

▼ *This tower is all that remains today of Douglas Castle, scene of Sir James's Easter attack on the English garrison in 1307. At that time the castle was just 19 years old, having been built in 1288.*

THE BUSINESS OF WAR

HOW KNIGHTS MADE MONEY ON CAMPAIGN AND IN TOURNAMENTS

In raiding and through the raising of ransoms, knights could acquire great wealth. While chivalry emphasized purer motives for fighting, such as seeking glory or exhibiting loyalty to a noble lord, in practice knights accepted the rewards that came their way.

RANSOMS

A knight captured in battle was ransomed, often for very large sums of money. There was a generally accepted understanding that the ransom should not be set at so high a level that the knight would be ruined, and thereafter be unable to keep maintaining himself as a knight.

A king's ransom could be vast. King Richard I of England, captured in 1192 on his way home from the Third Crusade, and imprisoned by Duke Leopold of Austria and Holy Roman Emperor Henry VI, was ransomed for 150,000 marks –

▼ Many knights, including Bertrand du Guesclin, seen here being made High Constable of France by King Charles IV , made great fortunes through accumulating the legitimate spoils of war.

RANSOMS AND THE KNIGHTLY CODE

Honoré Bonet, the late-14th-century Provençal prior and writer on chivalry, considered in his *Arbre des Batailles* ('Tree of Battles', 1382–87) whether the setting of ransoms was consistent with chivalric conduct and concluded that it was, declaring: 'All that a soldier can win from his opponent in lawful war he has the right to retain', adding that the act of taking ransom from a prisoner had been 'approved' by 'custom and usage'. He went on, however, to complain that many knights acted without pity or mercy in demanding excessive ransoms, and suggested that they should limit themselves to a 'reasonable and knightly' amount.

---

equivalent to 35 tonnes of gold, and about three times the English crown's annual income. This vast sum was raised from his English subjects by Chief Justiciar Hubert Walter through the seizing of valuable church plate and the imposition of swingeing taxes (a quarter of the value of property) on both clergy and lay people.

After King John II 'the Good' of France was captured at the Battle of Poitiers in 1356, a ransom of 3,000,000 marks was demanded. This was never paid as John was released, with his son Louis held in Calais as a hostage, in order to raise the sum, and then when Louis escaped, John voluntarily gave himself up into captivity once more.

RANSOMS AND HONOUR

A high ransom was in one sense a sign of honour. When the 'Eagle of Brittany', the great Breton knight Bertrand du Guesclin, was captured by Edward the Black Prince at the Battle of Najera (Navarette) in Spain

---

▲ Son of a Florentine merchant, Pippo Spano was a knight in the service of Sigismund, King of Hungary and Holy Roman Emperor from 1433 to 1437. Sigismund rewarded Pippo with the control of all the gold mines in Hungary.

in April 1367, he taunted his captor saying he would not dare grant him his freedom. The Black Prince responded by telling du Guesclin to name his own ransom and he set it at the vastly inflated level of 100,000 francs – boasting that in France he was so highly regarded that even the peasant women would contribute to his ransom. In the event even this enormous payment was given by the French king.

At the other end of the scale, a poor knight might be required to raise a few crowns for his ransom. Sometimes a knight merely forfeited his armour and his horse and weapons and was allowed to go free – even this penalty was considerable, for the cost of horse and equipment was high.

NECESSARY FINANCES

Seeking land and wealth has been a motive in going to war from time immemorial. The mounted warriors of Duke William of Normandy's army at Hastings were not required to be there by feudal loyalty, for their vows of service did not extend beyond the lord's territory: they were drawn, as countless warriors before them, by the promise of the riches they could acquire through conquest. Similarly, one among the many motives for knights going on crusade was seeking riches in the Holy Land.

Throughout the age of chivalry, many lesser knights – those whose fiefs were too small to support them adequately – knew that the wealth acquired with sword and lance was necessary for their very survival. There were knights who rose from a humble beginning to positions of extraordinary power, such as the impoverished Italian knight, Pippo Spano, who became the confidant, trusted strategist and general of the King of Hungary, and as such was granted large portions of land, noble titles, and national assets such as control of Hungary's gold mines, that guaranteed him a substantial income.

In chivalric tournaments, as well as on the field of battle, and in feudal politics, knights could make a living from their martial skills – for defeated opponents in the mêlée and joust could be required to pay ransom and to surrender their horse and equipment. Battles between Christian knights in the European theatre of war,

battles in which there was limited risk of dying because the conflict was not pursued to the death, were thus in many ways highly comparable to tournaments – good opportunities for establishing a public reputation for chivalry and a private fortune.

SHARING OUT THE BOOTY

In the 14th century, when a town was formally besieged and its occupants did not take the opportunity to surrender, according to the laws of chivalry its riches were forfeit to the invaders, save that

▲ *King John II is taken captive at the Battle of Poitiers. Lords had little to fear as their ransoms ensured they were treated well.*

clergy and churches were spared. The normal custom was for spoils to be divided three ways, with the first part being divided among the soldiery and knights, the second part being reserved for the commander, and the remainder sent home to the king. Not all these sieges ended in a frenzied sacking as at Caen – often there was an ordered entry and taking of booty. A more formal system was introduced in England in the second half of the 14th century under the indentures of war. In accordance with these, the commander was required to give up to the king the most important castles, towns and prisoners and he would be rewarded for this. The remaining spoil was split, two-thirds to the commander and one-third to the crown.

◄ *A commander would reward his leading knights and soldiers out of his two-third share of a conquered town's spoils.*

CHIVALRY IN WARFARE
THE CODE OF CHIVALRY ON THE BATTLEFIELD

The code of chivalric behaviour laid down the boundaries of good conduct both on the battlefield and during sieges. However, in practice, fighting was often dirtier than chivalry would readily countenance. In addition, success in war depended on qualities such as discipline that were at odds with chivalry's emphasis on the pursuit of individual glory.

DEMANDS OF CHIVALRY
In battles of the age of chivalry, fighting to the death was only normal in wars against 'the infidel' – meaning those who were not Christians, principally the Islamic soldiers in the Holy Land and in Spain, or pagan fighters in the Baltic region. In conflicts such as the Hundred Years War, particularly in clashes between noble knights, it was normal to take prisoners and to ransom them at great profit.

▼ A Breton warrior surrenders to a French knight at the Battle of Saint-Aubin-du-Cormier in 1488. In such moments of chivalry the brute energy of the medieval battlefield was suddenly stilled.

When a town or castle was besieged, chivalry demanded that the siege be declared by a herald. Once this was done, the garrison or the townspeople could surrender at any point up to the scaling of the walls. There are numerous examples of garrisons and populations being treated with great clemency, in accordance with these rules – such as cases of fighting

▲ When a town fell, its inhabitants were at the mercy of the victorious troops. Even within the code of chivalry, at the end of a siege soldiers could lawfully run riot.

being suspended to allow populations who had taken refuge in a castle to exit while the garrison remained behind to carry on the fight. King Edward III of England allowed non-soldiers free exit from Calais in northern France, when he was besieging the town in 1346; he even gave them food and money. If defenders remained defiant, then when the assault finally came the soldiers of the invading army were entitled to help themselves to the riches within the walls – except that church buildings, priests, monks and nuns could not be touched.

THE SACKING OF LIMOGES
Often when a long siege came to an end the victorious besiegers ran out of control, inflicting dreadful suffering on the garrison or townsfolk. The knights of the First Crusade when entering Jerusalem in 1099 set a terrible example, slaughtering men, women and children until the streets reputedly ran with blood. As we have

seen, Edward III and the Black Prince oversaw the horrific sacking of Caen in 1346, while – according to Froissart – at Limoges in 1370 the Black Prince himself took part in a savage raid on the city following the conclusion of the siege. Froissart's account of the attack on Limoges suggests that the prince was maddened with anger that his old ally, the Bishop of Limoges, had gone over to the French side – and ordered the sacking of the city in which more than 3,000 men, women and children were slaughtered.

FAILURE OF DISCIPLINE

On many occasions, it appears that knights were unable to control their men. Armies often contained a good proportion of unruly elements – not least because the English armies in France during the Hundred Years War contained criminals who had been offered a free pardon in return for volunteering for service.

Moreover, it may be that knights felt that the misbehaviour of the lower orders in the army did not reflect badly on them – that the code of chivalry principally bound the noblemen who were knights, and that it was understandable that the lower classes would be unable to live up to chivalry's high standards. This is the view put forward by Froissart when describing the devastation at Caen – that the rampaging mob was full of 'wicked fellows and doers of evil, the sort you inevitably find in a royal army'.

Yet there were also occasions on which knights could not control themselves – when they also took part in the sacking of towns and profited greatly from them; and when they did not adhere to the code of chivalry in battle, abandoning its ties in moments of rage or in the physical excitement and turmoil of the battlefield.

QUEST FOR GLORY

In one important sense self-discipline and the chivalric code were at odds. Knights were expected to seek glory; the code of chivalry demanded that they should be eager to prove again and again their

knightly status through acts of martial endeavour. In battle they were ready to seize any opportunity to do this. Yet then as now, armies required discipline, and to be most effective usually needed to function as a unit. There are countless examples of knights acting rashly and against the interests of their commanders in order to seek glory for themselves or for their knightly brotherhood.

The Templar knights were often a law unto themselves in this regard. In the siege of Ascalon (Ashkelon in Israel) mounted by Baldwin III of Jerusalem in 1153, the Templars even fought against their own side in the search for glory: when a breach was made in the walls opposite the Templar quarters in the camp, a group of 40 knights led by Bernard of Tremblay went in to take the city, while others prevented non-Templars from joining. In the event, the 40 Templar knights had taken

on too much, and they were defeated, captured and killed, and their heads were hung from the city walls.

During the Seventh Crusade at Al Mansourah in Egypt in 1250, the Templar Robert I, Count of Artois, led a charge of fellow members of the brotherhood despite specific orders to hold back. He surprised part of the Egyptian army but then his troops swept on into the streets of the town, where they were ambushed and he was killed; the Egyptians were able to launch a counter-offensive against the main army, which robbed the crusaders of the land they had just won.

▼ *Templar knights pour forward, despite a hail of arrows, towards their Saracen foes. The Templars and Hospitallers were an often unpredictable part of the crusade armies, liable to launch independent attacks in search of their own glory.*

PART TWO

THE FIRST AND SECOND CRUSADES

When Pope Urban II finished the great speech at Clermont in 1095 in which he called knights to the First Crusade, those who rushed to obey his summons at once began to adorn their clothing with the sign of the cross – and the cross was soon established as the sign beneath which the crusader knights rode into battle. In its original biblical context the cross was a symbol of Christ's intense physical suffering, and of his refusal to foment violence and take up arms; through centuries it became emblematic of the power of God and of Christianity, and was worn by pilgrims. But in the hands of the crusade preachers and the knights they inspired, the cross turned into a symbol of dedication and military vigour – an icon that inspired faith, a badge of honour to be worn by those who signed up for the perilous journey to the Holy Land and a sign of the salvation they were seeking. It symbolized the faith and obedience embodied in the cry 'God wills it!' that arose following Urban II's speech, the shout that became the battle cry of the crusader knights on campaign.

▲ *Muslim horsemen often pretended to flee. Crusaders lost many a battle by charging recklessly in pursuit of a feigned retreat.*

▶ *The knights who responded to Urban's call to arms were inspired by tales of the religious campaigns of Charlemagne and his knights, seen here besieging the walls of Pamplona in AD778.*

TIMELINE OF THE FIRST CRUSADES

March 1095 Byzantine Emperor Alexius Comnenus I sends envoys asking Pope Urban II for help against the Seljuk Turks.

27 November 1095 At Clermont, Pope Urban II calls Christian knights to arms, launching the First Crusade.

1095 Pope Urban declares that Christians fighting Moors in Spain would win full crusading privileges.

April 1096 The first two waves of the People's Crusade, one led by Walter Sans Avoir and one by Peter the Hermit, depart for the Holy Land.

May 1096 Crusaders under Count Emicho of Leisingen carry out attacks on Jewish communities in the Rhineland.

1 August 1096 The armies of the People's Crusade arrive in Constantinople.

21 October 1096 The People's Crusade is routed by Seljuk Turks in Anatolia.

November 1096–May 1097 Crusade armies led by Hugh of Vermandois, Godfrey of Bouillon, Bohemond of Taranto, Raymond of Toulouse and Robert of Normandy arrive in Constantinople.

6 May 1097 Crusaders begin siege of Nicaea, capital of the sultanate of Rum.

19 June 1097 Following secret negotiations, Nicaea surrenders – to Byzantine emperor Alexius Comnenus I.

1 July 1097 Crusaders defeat Seljuk Turks at the Battle of Dorylaeum.

21 October 1097 Crusaders begin the siege of Antioch.

December 1097 Bohemond of Taranto and Robert of Flanders defeat a Turkish army under Sultan Duqaq of Damascus.

January 1098 Morale is low among the crusaders, who suffer severe famine; many, including Peter the Hermit, desert.

9 February 1098 Bohemond of Taranto defeats a relief army under Radwan, Seljuk ruler of Aleppo at Harenc, 25 miles (40km) from Antioch.

10 March 1098 Baldwin of Boulogne creates crusader state: the County of Edessa.

April 1098 Embassy from Fatimid Egypt

▲ *Moors besiege a Christian castle in Spain.*

arrives at Antioch, offering crusaders possession of Syria if they agree not to attack Jerusalem. The crusaders decline the offer.

2 June 1098 Stephen of Blois begins march north to Constantinople.

3 June 1098 Crusaders capture Antioch. The citadel remains in Turkish hands.

6 June 1098 Relief army led by Sultan Kerbogha of Mosul arrives at Antioch and begins siege of crusaders within city.

14 June 1098 Peter Bartholomew claims to have discovered the Holy Lance in the city of Antioch.

28 June 1098 Crusaders defeat Sultan Kerbogha in battle outside Antioch. The citadel surrenders.

December 1098 Crusaders from Antioch capture nearby Maarrat an-Numan.

January 1099 Raymond of Toulouse leads the crusade army south from Antioch, bound for Jerusalem.

January 1099 Bohemond of Taranto establishes the second crusader state, the Principality of Antioch.

8 April 1099 Peter Bartholomew undergoes 'Ordeal By Fire' in an attempt to prove that his claimed discovery of the Holy Lance in Antioch was genuine. He is severely injured and dies on 20 April.

May 1099 Crusaders capture Tortosa and march down the coast as far as Arsuf.

5-6 June 1099 Tancred of Hauteville and Baldwin of Le Bourg capture Bethlehem, birthplace of Christ.

7 June 1099 Crusaders begin the siege of the city of Jerusalem.

13 June 1099 Crusade army fails in assault on Jerusalem.

7–9 July 1099 Crusaders hold a three-day penitential fast prior to renewing their assault on the city.

15 July 1099 The crusaders capture Jerusalem. For two days, 15–16 July, they run amok, killing and looting.

22 July 1099 Godfrey of Bouillon is elected Defender of the Holy Sepulchre.

1 August 1099 Arnulf of Choques is elected Patriarch of Jerusalem.

5 August 1099 Patriarch Arnulf announces he has found a piece of the True Cross (the cross on which Christ was crucified) in Jerusalem.

12 August 1099 Godfrey of Bouillon consolidates the victory in Jerusalem by defeating a 50,000-strong Fatimid relief army in the Battle of Ascalon.

1100 Pope Paschal II calls a new crusade in response to calls from crusader lords for reinforcements.

18 July 1100 Godfrey of Bouillon dies; his brother Baldwin of Edessa is elected his replacement.

September 1100 Crusader troops are mobilized in response to Pope Paschal's call to arms depart from Italy.

25 December 1100 Baldwin of Edessa is crowned King of Jerusalem.

1100 Patriarch Arnulf is replaced by Dagobert of Pisa, the new papal legate. Arnulf becomes Archdeacon of Jerusalem.

June 1101 The Italian crusaders, fighting alongside Byzantine troops commanded by Raymond of Toulouse and a French–Burgundian–German force under Stephen of Blois, are routed by Seljuks.

1101 The Kingdom of Jerusalem captures Caesarea and Arsuf.

May 1104 The Kingdom is further expanded with the capture of Acre.

1107 King Sigurd I of Norway embarks on crusade.

12 July 1109 After a long siege Tripoli surrenders to crusaders and Bertrand, illegitimate son of crusader lord Raymond of Toulouse, becomes ruler of the fourth crusader state, the County of Tripoli.

May 1110 The Kingdom of Jerusalem captures Beirut.

4 December 1110 King Baldwin I and King Sigurd I of Norway capture Sidon.

1110 Tancred of Hauteville, veteran of the First Crusade and regent of Antioch, captures the castle of Krak des Chevaliers.

15 February 1113 Pope Paschal II recognizes the monastic order of the Hospitallers of St John of Jerusalem.

1113 Paschal II recognizes the Equestrian order of the Holy Sepulchre of Jerusalem.

1114 In Spain Count Berenguer of Barcelona leads a crusade against the Muslim-held Balearic islands.

1118 Pope Gelasius II declares a crusade against the Moors in Spain.

2 April 1118 King Baldwin I of Jerusalem dies and is succeeded by his cousin Baldwin of Le Bourg as Baldwin II.

19 December 1118 Crusaders in Spain capture the city of Saragossa.

28 June 1119 Artuqid Turkish ruler Ilghazi inflicts crushing defeat on Christian army in the Battle of the Field of Blood.

1122 Pope Calixtus II calls crusades to the Holy Land and Spain. A large fleet sails for Jerusalem from Venice.

c.1123 The brotherhood of the Order of St Lazarus of Jerusalem is established.

1124 With the help of Venetian crusaders, the Kingdom of Jerusalem captures Tyre.

January 1128 Knights Templar recognized at the Council of Troyes.

21 August 1131 King Baldwin II of Jerusalem dies and is succeeded by his daughter Melisende and her husband Fulk of Anjou. They rule as Queen Melisende and King Fulk.

1135 Pope Innocent III offers crusade indulgences for those fighting antipope Anacletus II.

13 Nov 1143 King Fulk of Jerusalem dies and is succeeded by his wife Melisende, co-ruling with their son Baldwin III.

24 December 1144 Turkish general Imad

ed-Din Zengi captures the capital of the crusader state of Edessa.

1 December 1145 Pope Eugenius III calls the Second Crusade.

1 March 1146 Eugenius III reissues his call to arms, authorizing Bernard of Clairvaux to preach the crusade.

Easter Day 1146 Bernard preaches the crusade at Vezelay in central France. King Louis VII takes the cross.

25 December 1146 Another crusade sermon by Bernard of Clairvaux inspires Conrad II of Germany to take the cross.

1146 While the Second Crusade is being preached, violence breaks out against Jews in the Rhineland.

13 April 1147 Pope Eugenius III guarantees full crusading privileges to those fighting pagan Wends in the Baltic.

May–June 1147 Armies of the Second Crusade set out for the Holy Land.

July–September 1147 German crusaders campaign against pagan Wends.

mid-September 1147 German crusade army arrives at Constantinople.

24 October 1147 Crusaders aid in the capture of Lisbon from the Moors.

25 October 1147 In Anatolia German

▼ *Kurdish general Saladin the Great.*

crusaders are defeated by Seljuk Turks.

8 January 1148 French crusaders are defeated by Seljuk Turks in Turkey.

19 March 1148 King Louis VII of France arrives in Antioch.

24 June 1148 The Council of Acre determines the future direction of the Second Crusade and decides to attack Damascus.

23 July 1148 Crusader armies arrive at Damascus and lay siege to the city.

28 July 1148 After the arrival of a relief army under Nur ed-Din, crusaders abandon the siege of Damascus. This marks the end of the Second Crusade.

29 June 1149 Nur ed-Din defeats and kills Raymond, Prince of Antioch.

1153 Baldwin III takes power in his own right as King of Jerusalem.

1154 Nur ed-Din captures Damascus.

10 February 1162 King Baldwin III of Jerusalem is succeeded by King Amalric I.

26 September 1164 Pope Alexander III recognizes the Spanish military brotherhood of the Order of Calatrava.

1164–69 A power struggle in Egypt ends in March 1169 with Salah ed-Din Yusuf (later called Saladin) as vizier of Egypt.

c.1170 Spanish military brotherhood of Order of Santiago is established.

11 July 1174 King Amalric I of Jerusalem is succeeded by his son Baldwin IV.

October 1174 Saladin takes Damascus.

25 November 1177 Baldwin IV defeats Saladin at the Battle of Montgisard.

1180 Pope Alexander III approves the establishment of the Knights of Our Lady of Mountjoie in Jerusalem.

1185 Baldwin IV dies and is succeeded by his nephew Baldwin V with Raymond of Tripoli as regent.

1186 Baldwin V dies and is succeeded by his mother Sibylla. She rules as Queen with Guy of Lusignan as her consort.

4 July 1187 Saladin wins a decisive victory in the Battle of the Horns of Hattin.

8 July 1187 Acre surrenders to Saladin.

4 September 1187 Saladin takes Ascalon.

20 September 1187 Saladin besieges the city of Jerusalem.

2 October 1187 Saladin succeeds in recapturing Jerusalem.

CHAPTER SIX

A CALL TO ARMS

On 27 November 1095, in a stirring speech to a great crowd at Clermont in France, Pope Urban II set in motion preparations for the First Crusade, which was to prove the start of centuries of violence between European Christians and Eastern Muslims in the Holy Land. Of course, he did not know that his speech was the beginning of hundreds of years of religious conflict, and the pious knights and other European warriors who responded to his call to arms were not aware that they were embarking on the first of a series of wars of the cross – indeed, they were encouraged to believe that the war would be final, victory total and glorious. Urban made the claim that Christ offered the ultimate reward to the knights and infantrymen he was seeking to mobilize. According to the version of the speech recorded by eyewitness Fulcher of Chartres, Urban urged those who waged war to take their courage and martial vigour abroad and put it to good use in combating 'barbarians' and cleansing the Holy Land: 'Let those who have been used to fighting without justice in private wars against faithful men and women, now embark against the faithless infidel and bring to an end with a great victory this war which should have been launched long ago ... Let those who have been earning mercenary pay instead earn eternal reward.' This reward, promised by the pope on behalf of God, was the complete remission of sins, the glory of heaven.

▲ *The People's Crusade sets out for the Holy Land, led by Peter the Hermit.*

◀ *The wealthy and deeply devout Count Raymond IV of Toulouse was the first European nobleman to obey Christ's command – as relayed by Pope Urban – to take the cross. Many pilgrims travelled in his party.*

CONSTANTINOPLE UNDER THREAT

EMPEROR ALEXIUS'S CRY FOR HELP

In March 1095 Alexius I Comnenus, ruler of the Byzantine Empire, despatched envoys to the Council of Piacenza in Italy to ask Pope Urban II for help in fighting the Seljuk Turks. This appeal either convinced Urban to promote a holy war to come to the aid of Christians in the East and reclaim the Holy Land, or else gave him ammunition to justify a decision he had already made to ask the chivalry of Europe to fight for the cross in the East.

Alexius's appeal was one of a number he made in the 1090s. He wanted military help in launching a counter-attack against the formidable Seljuk Turks, who had defeated the Byzantine Empire at the Battle of Manzikert in 1071 and had established the Sultanate of Rum in central Anatolia in 1077. Since becoming Byzantine emperor in 1081, Alexius had succeeded

in halting the invasion of Byzantine lands in Greece by the southern Italian Norman lord Robert Guiscard in 1081–82, then in beating back the incursions of the Turkish Pecheneg nomads in the Balkans. He saw an opportunity in the death in 1092 of the Turkish sultan of Baghdad, Malik Shah, and the collapse of his empire in Iraq, Syria and Palestine. The time appeared to

▲ Alexius made much of the barbarity of the Seljuk Turks. They were fierce warriors, but maintained a highly civilized court.

be ripe to strike back against the Seljuks and to reassert Byzantine authority across many of its former lands.

To win the support of Western nobles, Alexius and his envoys emphasized the

▼ Pilgrims arrive at Jaffa (top) and pay a toll before entering Tyre (bottom). Both cities attracted pilgrims because of their role in biblical and early Christian history, and became crusader strongholds.

ALEXIUS I COMNENUS

Alexius I Comnenus, who ruled as Byzantine emperor from 1081 to 1118, proved himself one of the leading statesmen of his era. He came to power, by seizing the throne from Nicephorus III, just ten years after the empire's catastrophic defeat at the Battle of Manzikert by the Seljuk Turks, and ruled through the period of the First Crusade and the establishment of the crusader states of Jerusalem, Antioch, Edessa and Tripoli.

He made the crusader lords swear an oath to return to him the lands they gained on campaign and, although this was not honoured, by the crusaders' efforts he regained control of many cities including Nicaea, Sardis and Ephesus, as well as much of Anatolia. In his 37-year reign he restored the Byzantine Empire to a position of relative strength following its series of defeats at the hands of Normans and Turks. He founded the Comnenian dynasty of Byzantine emperors, who ruled until the late 12th century. In the words of an anonymous Greek biographer, he was a man 'great both in the power of his will and in deeds'.

◄ The likeness of Alexius I Comnenus, Byzantine emperor between 1081 and 1118, adorns one side of this gold Byzantine soldo (penny coin).

threat to Christians and their holy places posed by the pagan Turks. But he did not envisage a holy war – he wanted a mercenary army, whose soldiers he could control with financial incentives. He did not foresee the struggle for the Holy Land launched by the pope; fighting to recapture Jerusalem was never part of his plan – the city had, after all, been in Muslim hands since 638.

LETTER TO COUNT ROBERT OF FLANDERS

One of Alexius's appeals survives in the form of a letter dated 1093 written to Count Robert II of Flanders. Count Robert's father – Count Robert I of Flanders – had stayed with Alexius in Constantinople on his return from a pilgrimage and Alexius had reportedly been impressed by the strength of his escort. His letter tried to appeal on several different fronts, seeking to generate not only righteous anger but also a lust for riches.

The letter described how the Patzinaks (or Pechenegs) and Turks carried out forced circumcision of Christian babies and boys above the baptismal font, and forced them to urinate into its waters; it suggested that they not only abducted and raped Christian women (both virgins and

▲ *The crusaders were awestruck by the beauty and ancient treasures of the walled city of Constantinople. This map was made in c.1485 by the Italian cartographer Cristoforo Buondelmonti.*

venerable matrons), but also performed acts of sodomy on Byzantine men – including Christian clergy, monks and even bishops. He compared their acts to those of the 'impious Babylonians', who, according to biblical accounts, had mistreated the Jews in exile – suggesting

thereby that under the threat of the Turks, the Christian Byzantines were effectively in exile in their own lands.

Alexis lamented that the great expanses of the Byzantine Empire had been snatched away and suggested that the invaders were on the verge of capturing Constantinople itself, 'unless the help of God and faithful Latin Christians should come quickly to us'. He pointed out that the cities of the East – and notably Constantinople – were rich in holy relics and that God would punish any brave lord who refused to come to their protection; those who did come, he said, would win reward in heaven.

Later in the letter, however, Alexius also emphasized that these cities were additionally full of treasures and gold, and of beautiful women – 'Greek women possess a beauty beyond compare that would be a good enough reason to lure the brave armies of the Franks to Thrace'. The Latin Christian lords should not allow these beauties – neither treasures nor flesh and blood – to fall into pagan hands.

▼ *Byzantine forces besiege Messina in Sicily. In Italy, the Byzantines had for centuries been at odds with the Normans and other Europeans, whose help they now requested.*

RIGHTEOUS WARFARE

POPE URBAN II PREACHES THE FIRST CRUSADE

On Tuesday 27 November 1095 at the close of the Council of Clermont in central France, Pope Urban II issued a rousing call to arms, urging the Christian knights of Europe to travel to the aid of their brothers in the East and liberate the holy places of Jerusalem from unbelievers. The speech was the high point of a months-long tour of France promoting the crusade between August 1095 and September 1096.

The Council of Clermont, an assembly for church reform, had been running since 18 November and had been attended by around 300 prominent clerics. They had deliberated on clerical marriage, the elimination of simony (the practice of selling Church positions) and the excommunication of King Philip of France for committing adultery.

Word must have been circulated that the pope was planning to make a great announcement, for the crowd that gathered to hear him was too large to fit into the Cathedral at Clermont and the papal

▼ *Urban is escorted to Clermont, where he asked bishops and abbots to bring the leading lords in their areas to the council.*

▲ *In Fulcher of Chartres's account of the speech, Urban declared 'Let men who have grown used to waging private war against fellow Christians go now against the infidel and win a great victory in this war that should have been started long ago.'*

throne was therefore moved to a field just outside the city. There, Urban delivered the passionate address that launched the First Crusade.

URBAN'S SPEECH

We know that Urban was a highly intelligent man and a great orator and can tell from the response that the speech had an electrifying effect. But it is impossible to know for sure what he said. Five separate substantial accounts of Urban's speech survive, but all were written in the early 12th century in the light of later assumptions about the enterprise and after the First Crusade had ended in triumph at Jerusalem in 1099.

The earliest account was in the anonymous chronicle *Gesta Francorum* (Deeds of the Franks), probably written by a follower of Bohemond of Taranto in *c.*1100. This was used as a source by the other reports. Shortly afterwards, perhaps in 1101, Fulcher of Chartres, an ecclesiastic who travelled on crusade in the party of

Stephen of Blois and Robert of Normandy, wrote a history of the First Crusade that also included a major report of the speech; it is probable that Fulcher was actually present at the Council of Clermont. Another very important description of the speech was given by Robert the Monk, who reworked the *Gesta Francorum* in *c.*1106; he was almost certainly not present at Clermont.

A fourth account was written by the Benedictine historian Guibert, Abbot of Nogent-sous-Coucy, in his *Dei gesta per Francos* (Deeds of God carried out by the Franks) of *c.*1108. He used the *Gesta Francorum* as a principal source but also used material gleaned from discussions with crusaders he knew; he, too, was present at the Council of Clermont, so must have included his memories as an eyewitness in the report. A fifth version of Urban's speech was given by Balderic, Archbishop of Dol-en-Bretagne from 1107–30, who based his account – written 10–20 years after the speech – on the *Gesta Francorum*.

According to the account in the *Gesta Francorum*, Urban primarily focused on the instruction of Christ to his followers that they should take up the cross and follow him, and described how men should seek to save their soul and find reward in heaven by finding the way to the Holy Sepulchre in Jerusalem.

In Fulcher of Chartres's report, Urban presented the expedition as an opportunity for secular warriors to become soldiers in Christ's service. He condemned lawlessness and the actions of robbers and urged that the Truce of God, the general peace agreed on Church authority, should be honoured. Then he called on all present to hurry to the aid of Christians in the East against 'Turks and Arabs', and to 'drive that vile race from the territories of our friends'. He said: 'All who die on the journey, overland or across seas, or in fighting against pagans, shall be rewarded with immediate remission of sins.'

In Robert the Monk's account, meanwhile, Urban emphasized the need to fight for the conquest of the Holy Land more than hurry to the aid of the Christians in the East. He repeated many of the descriptions of pagan infamy listed in the supposed letter of Alexis I to Count Robert II of Flanders – such as forced circumcision of Christian boys, spilling of human blood in the font and brutal rape of Christian women.

▼ *According to Balderic, Urban called on knights to defend the Church of the Holy Sepulchre and other Eastern churches as they would defend their mother.*

▲ *Robert the Monk described Urban calling on Christians to go to the aid of their brethren because, in the words that became the battle cry of the crusaders, 'God wills it!'*

In Robert's account, the pope also emphasized the great history of the Franks and their pedigree as a fighting race – they were above all other nations in arms, and should be inspired by the deeds of their ancestors, great warriors such as Charlemagne: 'O bravest of soldiers, the sons of invincible forebears, do not forget the valour of your ancestors.' He added that France was crowded with men, nd that inevitable competition bred conflict, but that the Holy Land to which he called them was – as noted in the Bible – one that 'floweth with milk and honey'; it was 'a paradise of many delights' and, moreover, a place consecrated by the suffering of Christ. He personified the city of Jerusalem, which he said lay at the centre of the world: 'from you,' he said, 'she asks for help!' He added: 'Take on this journey for the remission of sins, in confidence of the undying glory of God's kingdom.'

Balderic of Dol's version emphasized particularly the desecration of holy places in Jerusalem by pagans and called powerfully on Christian knights to stop fighting one another and, instead, to combat Turks and others in the Holy Land. In this account, Urban declared 'may you find it is a beautiful thing to give your life for Christ in the city in which he gave his life for us all'; fighting Saracens, he said, was 'righteous warfare', and would deliver 'everlasting glory'. He also pointed out, however, that worldly wealth would be an auxiliary prize – for the enemy was in possession of great riches.

The account of Guibert of Nogent emphasized the notion, current in the 10th and 11th centuries, that the 'Last Days' were at hand prior to the Second Coming of Christ as described in the biblical Book of Revelation and suggested that Christian knights should go to Jerusalem to oppose pagans as part of this final conflict. In this version, Urban described the many sufferings of Christian pilgrims to the Holy Land at the hands of pagans. He promised that knights fighting in the holy war would have Christ as 'standard bearer and inseparable leader'.

GOD WILLS IT! GOD WILLS IT!

THE RUSH TO TAKE THE CROSS

At the end of Urban's speech, a great shout went up among those in the crowd: 'God wills it! God wills it! God wills it!' Adhemar, Bishop of Le Puy, stepped forward and fell to his knees before Urban, and asked to be allowed to take part in an expedition to the East. Urban appointed him to serve on the pope's behalf as leader of the crusade. Some men trembled and wept in the crowd, and others discussed Urban's words earnestly: almost at once, many came forward in imitation of Adhemar to pledge themselves to undertake the task to which Urban called them.

TAKING THE CROSS

According to some accounts volunteers at once began to mark themselves out by attaching a cross to their clothes, in homage to the cross of Christ; clerics and monks surrendered their cloaks to provide

▼ *A monk bestows the cross on a crusader. The symbol of Christ gave weight and meaning to each knight's journey eastwards.*

material from which people cut the crosses. Fulcher of Chartres reported that as soon as people took the oath to go on the expedition, they made 'shining crosses' from cloth of gold or silk and attached them to their shoulders.

It seems obvious from contemporary accounts that the events at Clermont were carefully stage-managed: doubtless Urban had instructed a cleric to set up the chant of 'God wills it! God wills it!' and arranged in advance that Adhemar would step forward and be the first to take a vow. According to Robert the Monk, Urban whipped up the crowd further by claiming that the fact that they all chanted the one phrase was evidence that God was at work among them, in line with Christ's promise that 'Where two or three are gathered together in my name there am I in the midst of them': though the words were issuing from many mouths, they had their origin in one place, in God. And he proceeded to specify that these words should become the battle cry of the crusading armies when they went to war in the East.

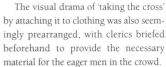

▲ *Crusader knights of the Minutolo family kneel in prayer, in a fresco from San Gennaro Cathedral, Naples. Over centuries families became associated with crusading as fathers and sons, uncles and nephews took the cross on different campaigns.*

The visual drama of 'taking the cross' by attaching it to clothing was also seemingly prearranged, with clerics briefed beforehand to provide the necessary material for the eager men in the crowd.

The taking of the cross was a symbolic visual act that gave added physical weight to the verbal vow taken by the participants. The *Gesta Francorum* reported that the Franks who undertook to make the expedition sewed the cross of Christ on their right shoulders. According to Robert the Monk, Urban instructed all those taking the vow to mark themselves with the sign of Christ's cross either on their forehead or on their chest, and said that when they had accomplished what he asked them to do, they should wear the cross on their back between their shoulders. Guibert of Nogent also reported that it was

JERUSALEM ENSLAVED
In December 1095 Urban wrote an open letter to crusaders waiting in Flanders, describing his sermons and in particular his call at Clermont to holy war. In it, he described again how the churches of the East and Jerusalem, the 'Holy City of Christ, made glorious by his Passion and Resurrection', were in 'intolerable slavery' and needed to be freed. He reiterated that the crusade would be in remission of sins, and that Adhemar, Bishop of Le Puy, would be leader of the undertaking in the Pope's place.

▼ *Urban was archdeacon of Rheims and prior at Cluny Abbey before he became pope.*

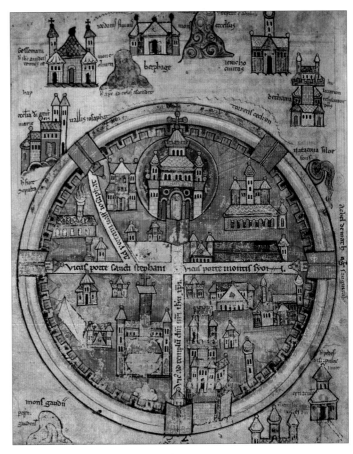

Pope Urban's order that people sew the cross, made of any material, on their shirt, cloak or chain mail tunic. In this version, Urban added that any person who took the vow and then did not travel would be an outlaw for all time.

THE REMISSION OF SINS
Although the accounts of the speech at Clermont vary, we can be certain that Urban's appeal did promise the remission of sins for those who took part – the journey itself would bring the same benefits as a pilgrimage to Jerusalem.

The issues of sin and forgiveness were very important for people of all classes at this time, not least because it was commonly held that the expected Second Coming of Christ was imminent, and that the 'Last Days' of the world as described in the Bible were at hand. This meant that the feared Day of Judgement was also imminent, and that it was a matter of even greater than normal urgency to find officially sanctioned ways of seeking forgiveness for wrongdoing.

FIGHTING WITH GOD'S BLESSING
Urban II, who came from the minor nobility of the Champagne region of France, knew how to address the knightly class, and his appeal at Clermont and throughout the preaching tour of which it was a part struck a note that rang true with the warriors in his audience. The Church's initial response to the emergence of knights

▲ *Jerusalem, the Holy City, and navel of God's creation, was said to be calling out in her distress to the knights of Europe, begging to be freed.*

had been to try to stifle their enthusiasm for fighting – in the Peace of God and Truce of God movements, to limit knightly conflict to prescribed periods. But on the expedition Urban proposed should take place to the East, knights would be encouraged to fight, and would do so with the full blessing of the Church and of God. Moreover, in doing so they would gain spiritual blessings as well as impunity – as Christ's soldiers they would win forgiveness of their sins and ultimately their salvation after death.

THE QUEST FOR GLORY

MOTIVES OF THE KNIGHTS WHO UNDERTOOK THE FIRST CRUSADE

The primary motivation of the knights who departed on the First Crusade was religious. Taking the cross was an act of piety, a statement of faith.

Taking the cross as a knight was likened to becoming a monk, which in this period was put forward as the spiritual ideal for a Christian life. Those who took the cross were treated like the clergy, and acquired certain associated privileges – while on crusade they did not, for example, have to pay taxes or settle debts or carry out feudal military service. It was understandably a matter of concern for those considering going on crusade that they were leaving their family and property behind, but the Church promised protection on their behalf. In the account of Urban's speech at Clermont given by Guibert of Nogent, the pope announced that anyone who molested the property or family of a soldier of Christ while he was on pilgrimage to the Holy Land would be subject to 'a fearful anathema' – that is, excommunication.

▼ Before embarking upon crusade a knight receives Holy Communion. Crusading was comparable to the quests in search of honour taken by knights in chivalric poems.

GLAMOUR AND HONOUR

But there were also secular attractions for the crusaders in addition to these primary religious motives. The knights were seeking honour and glory as well. Glamour was attached to the crusade proposed by Urban: it was an adventure and, as we have seen, it allowed the knights of Europe to indulge their taste for conflict.

The code of chivalry, which in the late 11th century was in the early stages of its development, taught that knights must seek opportunities to practise their martial skills and to prove themselves worthy of the honour of being a knight. In Europe they could be frustrated in doing this by the Peace of God and by secular or ecclesiastical authority, but on crusade they were encouraged to do so. The knights were – and saw themselves as – an international elite: the landowners of northern France and of England and of southern Italy had more in common with each other than they had with their countrymen; the crusade gave them an enemy and a target, and the opportunity to ride out among their peers seeking glory.

THE LURE OF WEALTH?

For many decades historians argued that the crusaders also rode eastward in search of a fortune. The accounts we have of the appeal that was made to the knights of Europe certainly included the promise of wealth. Alexius Comnenus's letter to Count Robert II of Flanders pretended that in Constantinople there was more gold than anywhere else in the world – and that the city's churches were overflowing with silver and precious stones and fine silks as well as gold; moreover, he claimed that the riches of all the emperors of the ancient Roman Empire were hidden in the palaces of the city. In Balderic of Dol's account of Pope Urban's speech at Clermont, the pope promised the crusaders the spoils of the enemy: 'the

▲ A knight offers his service to God. This celebrated crusading image is from the English Westminster Psalter of c.1250.

possessions of the enemy will be yours, too,' he said, 'since you will make their treasures your spoils'.

The knights, of course, were happy to take what spoils of war came their way in line with conventional practice in the medieval period. But they did not set out principally to seek their fortune.

At one time, historians argued that crusade armies contained many younger sons, men who seized on Urban's call to reclaim the Holy Land as a chance to make a place for themselves in the world and win a fortune. This traditional account pointed out that within the feudal system in northern France and England, younger sons in noble families could not inherit their father's wealth and had limited opportunities for self-advancement. And even in southern Europe, where inheritances were shared out among all sons, many found their prospects were poor because the property was split so many times among

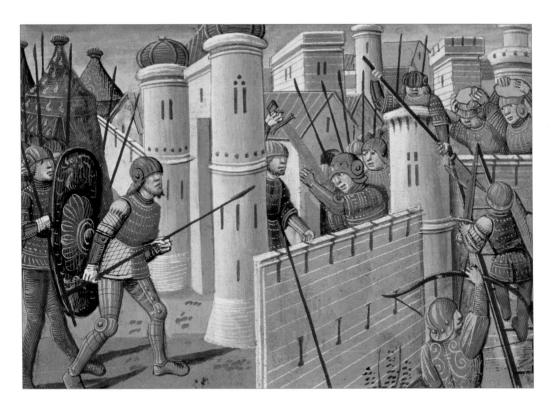

▲ *Committing to crusade required bravery, a willingness to risk all fighting far from home. Most knights were sustained by their faith that they were carrying out God's will.*

descendants that it became insignificant. However, modern historians dismiss this argument, pointing out the great expense of equipping oneself to go on crusade. To travel on crusade cost a knight many times his annual income.

From surviving charters and other documents we can see that the great majority of crusaders intended to return, if they did not die on the adventure overseas, and were not deliberately setting out to make a new life in a strange land. Moreover, it is simply not true that younger sons rather

▶ *Knights had to equip themselves at great expense with a horse, weapons and finery. Crusading was a chance to demonstrate social standing and chivalric qualities.*

than their older siblings went on crusade – great lords and eldest sons travelled as well as their younger brothers. It is true that following the success of the First Crusade and the establishment of the crusader kingdoms of Jerusalem, Edessa, Antioch and Tripoli, a number of Europeans settled in the Middle East. But

historians now question whether these settlers were primarily crusaders, as was once assumed, or whether they were emigrants after the crusade taking advantage of the new opportunities.

There were certainly individual cases of young men who made their name and fortune on crusade, but they were not a general type among the crusaders. Many knights, in fact, made significant financial sacrifices to go on crusade – some had to mortgage their property to pay for the expedition – and pay high rates of interest on the loan; others sold their land – and often accepted a poor price because in France, for example, the 1090s were a time of agricultural depression. The fact that so many knights made substantial sacrifices to take the cross is testament to the power of Pope Urban's stirring appeal and runs quite counter to the proposal that knights travelled to the Holy Land out of financial self-interest.

WALKING TO THE HOLY LAND

THE PEOPLE'S CRUSADE

The sermon at Clermont may have been meticulously planned and the accompanying pageantry carefully staged, but the response to Urban's plea took him by surprise. In addition to a well-equipped military force of great princes, lords and knights of the kind Urban had hoped to mobilize, a vast army of peasants and poor townspeople also left their homes, determined to put their trust in God and make their way to the Holy Land.

PETER THE HERMIT

A monk and popular preacher from Amiens named Peter the Hermit toured northern France and Flanders on a donkey, calling for crusade volunteers. He was a small man, known as 'Little Peter' by his contemporaries, with a long thin face, like

▼ *Peter shows knights their duty. Byzantine princess Anna Comnena wrote that Peter had tried before to make a pilgrimage to Jerusalem, but had been tortured by Turks.*

that of his donkey, and eccentric habits – he dressed only in a cloak, was often unwashed and lived on nothing but wine and fish. Yet Peter had the orator's gift, the ability to transfix a large crowd; according to Guibert of Nogent, who met him, Peter's charisma was such that his acts and deeds seemed 'half divine'. Peter claimed that Christ himself had appointed him to preach the crusade – and even pretended that he had a letter from God to prove it. The crowds flocked after him.

This first wave of crusaders contained many hangers-on with little or no military equipment or experience of fighting, although the core of the group was adequately fitted out with horses and weapons. But remarkably there were only eight knights. The most notable of these was the experienced Walter of Sans Avoir in the Seine Valley. (He was not, as is commonly written, a penniless knight. This traditional reputation derives from a misunderstanding of his name – for

generations historians interpreted Walter Sans Avoir to mean he had nothing, that he was penniless; in fact, it refers to his feudal base, a place of that name in the Seine Valley.)

DEPARTURE FOR THE HOLY LAND

Pope Urban had declared the Feast of the Assumption of the Blessed Virgin Mary (15 August 1096) to be the starting point for the expedition, but the people who gathered to travel on what historians call the People's Crusade were impatient to depart. Peter the Hermit assembled his followers at Cologne, Germany on 12 April. His plan was to gather more followers by preaching among the Germans.

A French contingent of a few thousand under the leadership of Walter Sans Avoir could not brook even this minor delay and departed at once. They followed an overland route, and were in Hungary by 8 May. They then proceeded without incident as far as Belgrade, on the border of Byzantine lands. However, the governor of Belgrade refused them entry and the French crusaders looted the countryside – in the market town of Semlin, 16 of them were captured and stripped of their armour, which was hung from the walls of the castle there. Eventually the main group reached Nish (now in Serbia) and waited for a troop escort from the Byzantine emperor in Constantinople.

A second wave of around 20,000 left Cologne under Peter the Hermit's leadership on 20 April and followed the same route as the French pilgrims who had gone before. The first part of their journey was uneventful, but when they reached Semlin and saw the armour of the earlier crusaders hanging from the castle walls, they rioted and attacked the city, killing 4,000 locals. Afterwards, they crossed the River Save before attacking and looting Belgrade. At Nish, where they arrived on 3 July, the garrison commander was

initially peaceable and promised an escort to Constantinople if the crusaders would move quickly on, but then a skirmish broke out between locals and some German crusaders and the commander unleashed the full force of his garrison, routing the motley crusader force and killing about 5,000 crusaders. Peter the Hermit and the chastened survivors carried on, and on 12 July arrived at Sofia (now in Bulgaria), where they awaited a military escort from Constantinople.

CRUSADES AGAINST THE JEWS

Some sections of the great population mobilized for a crusade did not travel to the Holy Land, but carried out attacks against Jewish communities in France and Germany. The most serious slaughter was carried out by a 10,000-strong army commanded by Count Emicho of Leisingen, who claimed that Christ had appeared to him and promised to make him emperor if he would convert the Jews of Europe. The Church authorities largely tried to protect the Jews, but Jews were forcibly converted or killed in their thousands by

▲ *Faith drove them on. The unlikely looking forces of the People's Crusade march across Europe in an image from the 15th-century* Les Passages faits Outremer.

the crusaders – especially in the Rhineland, where there were dreadful massacres in Worms, Mainz, Cologne and Trier. Count Emicho's troops massacred 800 Jews at Worms on 18 May and at least 1,100 at Mainz on 27 May.

Anti-Semitism had been current for centuries, but these were the first organized attacks against the Jews in European history. Some of the crusaders, including Count Emicho himself, felt that the Jews – culpable for the crucifixion of Christ – were just as much enemies of the cross as the Muslims, and believed that the crusading spirit could be given expression close to home. Feeling was also running high against the Jews among crusaders who had to borrow money to finance the crusade since, because money-lending was forbidden among Christians, they usually had entered into debts with Jewish lenders. Many of these crusaders now grew rich by stealing the Jews' money. Some historians refer to these attacks as the 'First Holocaust', linking them to the official attempt to exterminate the Jews by the Nazi government of Germany during the 1930s and World War II.

WHY DID SO MANY PEOPLE JOIN THE PEOPLE'S CRUSADE?

In the late 11th century there was a resurgence of belief that the Second Coming of Christ was imminent. This fired a popular desire to make a mass pilgrimage to Jerusalem and to return the Holy City to Christian control. At the same time, a series of celestial events – including a comet, a lunar eclipse and a meteor shower – seemed to reinforce the sense that the enterprise preached by Pope Urban and Peter the Hermit had God's blessing. In addition, there had been an outbreak of ergotism, or 'St Anthony's fire', food poisoning (caused by long-term consumption of cereals

containing fungi). This poisoning results in convulsions and gangrene, and it was interpreted as evidence of God's displeasure and made people desire to expiate their sins by making a pilgrimage. Some historians argue that in the years prior to 1096, the peasants of northern Europe had been suffering very severely as a result of the plague, drought and famine and were seeking escape from these terrible conditions.

▶ *For most people in Europe, life was harsh. Some may have seen the crusade as a chance for a new beginning.*

CHAPTER SEVEN

THE JOURNEY TO PALESTINE

The vast contingent of pilgrims and soldiers led by the monk Peter the Hermit and the knight Walter of Sans Avoir was followed to Constantinople by no fewer than five armies commanded by minor royals and some of the leading noblemen of Europe – including Duke Robert of Normandy, eldest son of King William I of England, and Hugh of Vermandois, younger brother of King Philip I of France, as well as counts and noblemen such as Raymond of Toulouse, Godfrey of Bouillon and Bohemond of Taranto. The second wave of armies, some of whom travelled overland and some by sea, is known to historians as the Princes' Crusade to distinguish it from the earlier People's Crusade, which was so called because it contained many unarmed pilgrims and peasants. As had the People's Crusaders before them, the Princes' armies endured their share of mishaps and disasters before they ever arrived at the glittering capital of the Byzantine Empire; and, arriving there confident in the knowledge that they were riding to the help of beleaguered Christians, their leaders faced an uncertain welcome from an emperor suspicious of their motives, who in particular feared that they aimed to establish themselves as rulers in his territory. In the event, the two crusades merged – after a catastrophic defeat at the hands of the Seljuk Turks in Anatolia, the chastened remnant of the People's Crusade returned to Constantinople, joined up with the still fresh and confident armies of the Princes' Crusade and set off for Jerusalem.

▲ *A messenger is sent for help at the siege of Antioch.*

◄ *The main strength of a crusader army was in its mounted cavalry bearing lances, but the soldiers were also a very effective force when battle broke down into hand-to-hand combat.*

MORE THAN THE STARS OF HEAVEN
THE PEOPLE'S CRUSADE ARRIVES IN CONSTANTINOPLE

The two main branches of the People's Crusade, one under the leadership of impoverished knight Walter Sans Avoir and the other following charismatic monk Peter the Hermit, had both arrived at Constantinople by 1 August 1096.

Anna Comnena, daughter of the Byzantine emperor Alexius I, described how the armed contingent was accompanied by a vast crowd of crusader-pilgrims 'outnumbering the grains of sand on the sea shore or the stars sparkling in the sky, carrying palms and crosses on their shoulders'. This group included many women, children and old people. She wrote that 'to look upon them was like watching powerful rivers flooding from all sides to a confluence'.

▼ *Peter the Hermit's charismatic preaching convinced many to abandon home and loved ones to honour the cross. Arriving in the East, they began to realize the immense difficulty of the task they had taken on.*

ACROSS THE BOSPHORUS

Alexius had expected a disciplined and cohesive army to be sent from Europe; instead he was confronted with a motley band of largely ill-equipped travellers who expected to be fed and given assistance. He refused them entry into the city, and made them camp outside the city walls. Within five days he had ferried them all across the Bosphorus into Anatolia.

It may be that the emperor simply wanted to be rid of them, and sent them on without much help to face almost certain death; on the other hand, it is possible that the crusaders insisted on marching on towards Jerusalem despite his best efforts to dissuade them. Anna Comnena – whose account in the *Alexiad* (c.1148), a biography of her father, understandably cast Alexius in a sympathetic light – claimed that the emperor tried to persuade Peter to await the arrival of reinforcements before moving on, but that Peter insisted on crossing into Anatolia and pressing on

towards Jerusalem. Alexius also warned the hermit not to be drawn into battle, because he saw that the crusaders were evidently no match for the Turkish army.

The crusaders were joined by several contingents of Italians, newly arrived from home. The group marched on, pillaging the towns they came to until they reached Nicomedia (now Izmit in Turkey), where they quarrelled. The Italians and Germans, under the command of an Italian by the name of Rainald, separated themselves from the French under Geoffrey Burel. Peter the Hermit and Walter Sans Avoir were no longer in control of events.

RAIDS IN ANATOLIA

The crusaders established a camp at Civetot, on the Sea of Marmara (the inland body of water that connects the Black and Aegean seas). Groups set out from the main crusader camp, competing with one another in attempts to progress the crusade. A French contingent marched as far as Nicaea, wealthy capital of the Turkish sultanate of Rum, and looted the edge of the city – according to Anna Comnena's colourful version of events, they committed atrocities there, torturing venerable old men, killing children and even cooking babies over spits and eating them.

Meanwhile, a 6,000-strong German troupe took the city of Xerigordon. In response the Turks sent an army to lay seige to Xerigordon, which captured the only source of water, located outside the city walls. The Germans lasted eight days, and surrendered only after they were reduced to drinking their own urine and the blood of their donkeys to survive. In defeat, they were slaughtered, or forced to convert to Islam and sold into slavery.

CRUSADERS MASSACRED

The Turks then set a trap for the remainder of the crusaders. In the main camp at Civetot, Turkish spies spread a rumour

▲ *The dreams of glory summoned by Peter the Hermit fell apart in the unfamiliar territory of Anatolia, where the crusaders were ravaged by the Seljuk Turks.*

that the Germans had not only triumphed at Xerigordon, but had also taken Nicaea. The rumour spread like wildfire, and generated a clamour to travel swiftly on to Nicaea and share in the looting. Peter the Hermit was absent, having travelled back to Constantinople to negotiate for supplies; Geoffrey Burel convinced the entire remainder of the force, some 20,000 strong, that they should move out at once.

On 21 October at dawn they marched out of the camp towards Nicaea. Anna Comnena commented at this juncture that the 'Latins' (Italians and Europeans) were known for their love of money, and that when they went on a military campaign their lust for wealth grew even stronger, becoming so overpowering that it robbed them of their judgement and made them rush headlong, as here, into trouble. In her account, they simply ran out of the camp towards Nicaea, without arming themselves, clamouring for money, with no semblance of discipline: they were entirely unprepared for what followed.

The Turks had laid an ambush in a narrow valley just 3 miles (5km) from the crusader camp. There they set on the army led by Geoffrey Burel, provoking a wave of blind panic among them. The slaughter was most terrible. Anna Comnena reported that when after the battle men went to clear the battlefield they gathered together the corpses of the fallen crusaders and made not merely a mound or a hill but a grisly flyblown mountain. Only 3,000 crusaders survived, and they took refuge in an abandoned castle. The Turks pursued them there and laid siege, but in time a Byzantine force sailed across from Constantinople, chased the Turks off and freed the crusaders.

A RABBLE OR AN ARMY?

The conventional view of the People's Crusade has been that the people who made this long and fruitless pilgrimage were little more than a rabble roused by an unscrupulous charismatic preacher, and that their 'armies' contained no more than a handful of properly equipped and trained soldiers. However, it is worth considering that this first wave of crusaders maintained their discipline sufficiently to march all the way across Europe as far as

▲ *Peter distributes crosses to eager volunteers. He convinced many of his poorer followers that a host of angels would defend them if they came under attack.*

Constantinople and that in Anatolia they did win military victories before their ultimate defeat. Even granted this, however, the ill-conceived People's Crusade cannot ultimately be adjudged anything more than a disaster. Scores of thousands of people lost their lives – the 3,000 crusaders who survived defeat in Anatolia were the only survivors of the crusade.

After they were freed by the Byzantine relief force from the castle in which they had taken refuge, the survivors made their way slowly back to Constantinople, where they eventually joined up with the better equipped armies that had followed them from Europe.

▼ *The crusaders arrive in Constantinople. A significant proportion of the peasants on the People's Crusade died of starvation or were sold into slavery.*

PRINCES ON CRUSADE
THE LEADERS OF THE FIRST CRUSADE

The European princes and nobles who responded to Pope Urban's call to crusade travelled in five main armies to Constantinople by different routes. They began to leave in mid-summer 1096 and arrived at Constantinople at various times between November 1096 and May 1097.

The first army to arrive was that of Hugh of Vermandois, who as younger brother of King Philip I of France was a prince of a royal house and one of the highest-ranking of the crusaders. He was reputedly convinced to embark on the crusade by an eclipse of the moon in February 1096, which he interpreted as divine guidance. The chronicler William of Tyre called him 'Hugh Magnus' (Hugh the Great), but despite high birth Hugh did very little of note, being an ineffective soldier and leader. He certainly had a high opinion of himself, however: according to Anna Comnena, he sent a breathtakingly arrogant letter to Alexius, in which he declared: 'Be advised, O Emperor, that I am the King of kings, highest-ranking of

all beneath the sky. My will is that you should attend me upon my arrival and give me the magnificent welcome that is fitting for a visitor of the noblest birth.'

Hugh's army travelled by way of Italy, where they were joined by a number of soldiers previously under the command of Count Emicho, leader of the German Crusade against the Jews – soldiers who had been dispersed by a Hungarian army. The army set sail from Bari across the Adriatic Sea, but were shipwrecked off the Byzantine port of Dyrrhachium (now Durres in Albania) and had to be rescued by the Byzantine governor of that locality before being escorted to Constantinople, arriving in November 1096.

GODFREY OF BOUILLON
The second army was from northern France and Belgium, led by Godfrey, Lord of Bouillon and duke of Lower Lorraine, with his younger brother Baldwin and his older brother Eustace III, Count of Boulogne. The army, perhaps 40,000 strong, set out from Lorraine in August

▼ *Godfrey of Bouillon. The crusade made him into a figure of legend, celebrated in literature as one of the 'Nine Worthies'.*

▲ *Bohemond of Taranto's crusading feats won him the hand of Constance, daughter of King Philip I of France, in 1104.*

1096 bound for Constantinople: they followed largely the same route as the People's Crusade, through Hungary and the Balkans (part of the Byzantine Empire), where they crossed the River Danube at Belgrade and proceeded via Sofia and Adrianople (modern Edirne in Turkey) and arrived at the Sea of Marmara in mid-December. On 23 December they pitched their camp beneath the walls of Constantinople. In some accounts, this army was referred to as 'the Lorrainers'.

BOHEMOND OF TARANTO
The third army was made up of Normans from southern Italy and led by Bohemond of Taranto. Bohemond was the son of Norman adventurer Robert Guiscard and was an old enemy of Emperor Alexius, having fought against him during his father's failed invasion of the Byzantine Empire in the early 1080s. In his company

was his nephew Tancred, the son of Bohemond's sister, Emma of Apulia.

Bohemond did not hear Pope Urban's call to arms. He joined the crusade only in October 1097 after he encountered knights making their way towards the Holy Land by way of southern Italy, where he and his army – including Tancred – were besieging the town of Amalfi, which had rebelled against his authority. Among these knights was Tancred's brother William: learning of the purpose of their journey, the Normans under Bohemond elected to join the crusade. The army set sail in October 1096, crossing the Adriatic from Brindisi to Avlona (a seaport now in Albania) and marched overland to Constantinople, where it arrived on 9 April 1097.

RAYMOND OF TOULOUSE

The fourth army belonged to Raymond, Count of Toulouse, Duke of Narbonne and Margrave of Provence. He was the first noble knight to take the cross after Pope Urban's speech at Clermont, and was profoundly religious: according to one account in an Armenian chronicle, he had made a pilgrimage to Jerusalem before the First Crusade, and during the course of this journey lost an eye; he had also fought in Spain against Muslim armies. He was 55, the oldest and also the wealthiest of the crusading lords, and he might have expected to be named leader of the expedition, but Pope Urban gave no special position to any of the secular lords, vesting his authority in the papal legate Adhemar, Bishop of Le Puy, who travelled in Raymond's party.

Raymond, in the company of his third wife Elvira (the illegitimate daughter of King Alfonso VI of Castile) and Bishop Adhemar, departed from Toulouse with a large army and a significant contingent of unarmed pilgrims in October 1096. They took an overland route by way of Genoa and Venice and along the coast as far as Dyrrhachium, before heading inland. They arrived at the gates of Constantinople on 27 April 1097.

DUKE ROBERT OF NORMANDY

The fifth main army was jointly led by Duke Robert of Normandy, his brother-in-law Stephen, Count of Blois, and Count Robert II of Flanders.

Duke Robert of Normandy was the eldest son of King William I of England, who, on his deathbed, had bequeathed the duchy of Normandy to Robert and the English throne to his second son, William Rufus. The two brothers had been at war on and off since William Rufus had become King of England on the Conqueror's death in 1087: in September 1096, Robert pawned the duchy of Normandy to William Rufus in return for 10,000 silver marks, which he used to fund his part in the crusade.

Stephen, Count of Blois, was married to Robert's sister, the formidable Adela of Normandy, and according to contemporary accounts went on the crusade only because he was ordered to do so by his wife. (He was to be father of a king of England, for his son Stephen – born at

▲ Robert II, Count of Flanders, was one of the co-leaders of Robert of Normandy's section of the crusading army.

Blois in 1096 before the crusade – was King Stephen of England from 1135–54.) Count Robert of Flanders was an experienced campaigner and skilled knight, who had proved his worth by governing Flanders while his father had been away on a pilgrimage to Jerusalem from 1085–91. Also in this army was Bishop Odo of Bayeux.

This fifth army left northern France in October 1096, but was waylaid in southern Italy where Duke Robert and Count Stephen settled for the winter, enjoying the hospitality of local lords. But Count Robert of Flanders pressed on with his force, sailing from Brindisi and marching overland to Constantinople. The remainder of the army followed in the spring, leaving Brindisi in April and arriving in Constantinople in May 1097, just a month behind Raymond's army.

THE CRUSADERS IN CONSTANTINOPLE
NEGOTIATIONS WITH EMPEROR ALEXIUS

Alexius quite naturally viewed the princely crusaders with suspicion. The princes and lords had mobilized great armies and brought them on to imperial Byzantine territory officially to supply help to Christians in the East, but it was difficult to be sure of their true motives.

The emperor could not be certain that the Latin lords were not plotting to capture pieces of his empire for themselves. In any case, the crusaders were also talking of capturing Jerusalem, which Alexius still viewed as a possession of the Byzantine Empire, even if one that was temporarily in Muslim hands. Moreover, among the leaders was a major former adversary, Bohemond of Taranto.

Alexius determined to make each of the crusader lords swear an oath of allegiance to him, under which they would pledge to be his vassals and would promise to return any Byzantine lands that they won in the course of the crusade. In return, he would supply the crusade with provisions, money, horses, guides and a supporting

▲ *Constantinople had formidable defences. Its magnificent double walls, with 142 fortified towers and 11 gates, were built in 412–22 during the reign of Theodosius II.*

military force. In demanding personal oaths of loyalty, Alexius adopted the established practices of Europe: in his own domain he could expect the total obedience of his subjects, but in the feudal lands from which these lords had come, he knew, great men generally held they were bound only by oaths they swore in person to an emperor, a king or a suzerain (feudal superior).

HUGH OF VERMANDOIS

The first of the princely crusaders to arrive, Hugh of Vermandois, expected a grand welcome; Alexius was happy to provide gifts and to spout honeyed words, but he kept Hugh under close supervision – virtually as a prisoner – in a monastery. For all his self-aggrandizement, Hugh did not object when asked to swear an oath of loyalty as vassal to the emperor.

GODFREY OF BOUILLON

When the second main army arrived under Godfrey of Bouillon and his brothers, Alexius made them camp outside the

---

THE IMPACT OF CONSTANTINOPLE

The city of Constantinople amazed the crusaders. Emperor Alexius had decided to make the armies camp outside Constantinople's great city walls, but he

allowed small groups of five or six at a time to enter the city in order to pray in the churches and see the sights. They were astonished by what they found – by the

city's size and wealth, by its baths and sanitation and by the beauty of the churches and the rich collections of treasures and of sacred relics. Fulcher of Chartres wrote: 'Oh what a splendid and noble city! What fine monasteries, what elegant palaces we saw, what superb workmanship! How many superb works … It would take too long to describe the richness of all kinds of goods, of silver and gold, fine clothes and sacred relics.' The Frankish lords were also suspicious of, and perhaps a little intimidated by, the courtly ritual of the Byzantine Empire.

◄ *Constantinople retained its great beauty through centuries of conflict.*

▲ *Godfrey of Bouillon and his army praise God as they make the passage across the Bosphorus into Anatolia, moving closer to their ultimate destination, Jerusalem.*

city walls. Godfrey was unwilling to swear the proposed oath of loyalty, maintaining that he could not became a vassal of Alexius since his feudal lord was the German emperor Henry IV. He attempted to play for time, since he wanted to wait for the other European lords to arrive. Alexius, on the other hand, was concerned about what might happen if Godfrey, Bohemond of Taranto and other lords marshalled their armies at Constantinople at the same time: he was absolutely determined to move on Godfrey's troops before Bohemond arrived, but he could not do so until Godfrey agreed to swear the oath. Alexius cut off the food supplies to the crusader camp, but when this provoked an outburst of looting and then scavenging he began to provide food once more.

The waiting game continued until, growing desperate, Alexius cut off the food to the camp again. This time Godfrey and his army launched a military attack on Constantinople, which provoked panic

among the citizens. Alexius decided to move the army on without requiring Godfrey to swear the oath but the men he sent with this message were attacked by the crusaders before they could deliver the information. Finally, Alexius lost his patience and unleashed the imperial military on the crusader camp. This was enough to bring Godfrey and his brothers to heel and on Easter Sunday, 5 April 1097 they swore the required oaths, recognizing Alexius as their overlord and promising to return to him any conquests they made in former Byzantine territories. The next day, Godfrey and his troops were transported across the Bosphorus.

THE NORMAN CONTINGENT

Three days later, on 9 April, Bohemond of Taranto arrived. According to contemporary sources, Bohemond declared 'I come by my own free will to be a friend to your Majesty'; Alexius housed him in magnificent quarters and gave him splendid gifts. Contemporary accounts report that Bohemond asked to be named as deputy or chief commander to Alexius in Asia, but Alexius was noncommittal. Bohemond was happy to swear the oath that Alexius

suggested, although he set little store by it and had no intention of keeping it. They moved on: on 26 April the Norman army was transported across the Bosphorus and joined the troops of Godfrey of Bouillon in Anatolia. Bohemond's nephew Tancred, however, had refused to swear the oath and slipped out of Constantinople by night to escape having to do so.

RAYMOND OF TOULOUSE AND ROBERT OF NORMANDY

That very same day saw the arrival at Constantinople of the army of Raymond of Toulouse. It had not had an easy march, and had even come under attack from imperial forces. Raymond refused to swear an oath to Alexius as his overlord, but promised to return conquered lands.

The final groups of arrivals, Duke Robert of Normandy, his brother-in-law Stephen, Count of Blois, and Count Robert II of Flanders agreed to swear the oath. According to chronicler Fulcher of Chartres, who travelled in their company, swearing the oath was 'essential to make good our friendship with the emperor, for without his advice and help we would not be able to make the journey we planned'.

THE SIEGE OF NICAEA
THE CRUSADERS MAKE THEIR MARK

The princely and noble leaders of the First Crusade were now gathered in Anatolia at the head of an army of perhaps 60,000 men. They agreed that they should move first against Nicaea, the capital of the Turkish sultanate of Rum, for it was clear that the crusade could not safely advance beyond Nicaea towards Jerusalem if the city remained in Turkish hands.

The crusaders were not a united force, for there were many rivalries between lords, and regional, cultural and linguistic differences among the knights and

▼ Under heavy attack by the forces of the Seljuk sultan, Kilij Arslan, the crusaders' rally was later attributed to heavenly aid.

soldiers. In addition to the main army there were many non-combatants – women and children, some of them families of crusaders, as well as aged pilgrims and clergy – and the battered remnants of the People's Crusade. There was also a Byzantine force, around 2,000 strong, supplied by Alexius and under the command of an experienced general named Taticius; Alexius's order was that the crusaders would give the command of cities and territories they captured to Taticius.

CRUSADERS ENCAMP AT NICAEA

The crusader army arrived at Nicaea in instalments – the first groups, under Godfrey of Bouillon, Robert of Flanders,

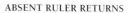

▲ During the siege of Nicaea, the crusaders lobbed the heads of corpses into the city.

Tancred and Taticius arrived on 6 May and were reinforced a few days later by Bohemond of Taranto. On 14 May a large force under Raymond of Toulouse swelled their numbers, and the final contingent, under Robert of Normandy and Stephen of Blois, joined the camp on 3 June.

The city of Nicaea, on the eastern side of Lake Iznik, was an ancient Christian town, where, in AD325, the Church's first General Council had agreed the statement of Catholic Christian beliefs still known as the Nicene Creed. Situated just 50 miles (80km) from Constantinople, it was for centuries part of the Byzantine Empire, but had been captured by the Seljuk Turks in 1077. The crusaders surrounded it on three sides and settled in for a siege; they were unable, however, to blockade the lake approaches so the city could still bring in supplies. Emperor Alexius provided the crusader army with supplies and siege equipment.

ABSENT RULER RETURNS

Kilij Arslan, the Sultan of Rum, was not present to defend his capital. Not expecting any greater threat from the new wave of crusaders than he had experienced from the ineffective armies of the People's Crusade, he had departed to fight rival ruler Ghazi ibn Danishmend in Sivas (also

known as Sebastea), several hundred miles away at the eastern edge of his territory. (The Danishmends were named after dynastic founder Ghazi ibn Danishmend; he had captured the Roman city of Sebastea and renamed it Sivas, making it his capital in c.1080.) When Kilij Arslan received messages to the effect that a large and apparently well-equipped army was besieging Nicaea, he made a hurried peace with Danishmend and rushed back.

By mid-May Kilij Arslan was in the vicinity of Nicaea, viewing the crusader forces with dismay. On 16 May he launched a surprise attack on the recently arrived army of Raymond of Toulouse, which was still setting up camp to the south of the town. It was a fierce clash, in which Raymond showed great skill to hold his force together until reinforcements sent by Godfrey of Bouillon arrived and decided the conflict in the crusaders' favour. A notable casualty, according to the account in a letter written by Stephen of Blois, was Baldwin, Count of Ghent. Kilij Arslan withdrew and gathered his forces in the hills to fight another day.

The siege of Nicaea lasted six weeks. The crusaders had only lightweight siege equipment and were unable to do significant damage to the town walls; they were

▼ *Nicaea's walls, about 32ft (10m) tall, ran for a total of 3 miles (5km). The west wall gave directly on to the lake.*

limited to hurling small rocks, flaming missiles, beehives, the heads of corpses and other foul objects at the defenders. They could not smash their way into the town and since the town garrison could bring in supplies across the water of the lake, there was no hope of starving them out. There seemed to be no end in sight.

OUTMANOEUVRED BY ALEXIUS

Emperor Alexius was keeping a close watch on events from a camp at Pelecanum nearby. He wanted to regain control of Nicaea in good condition for the Byzantine Empire, and so wanted to prevent the crusaders destroying its defences, overrunning the city and looting its wealth. With typical cunning, he went behind the backs of the crusaders, opening secret negotiations with the Turks in Nicaea. He promised them good treatment if they would surrender to him; if they did, he would protect them with his own troops against the crusaders.

On the morning of 19 June the crusaders prepared to launch a major attack on the town and saw to their initial puzzlement and then dismay that the Byzantine standard was flying above the walls. The Byzantine troops were in control of the city. They acted as guards, only

▲ *Nicaea was an important city for Christians, where a groundbreaking council had taken place in AD325 to formulate what became known as the Nicene Creed.*

allowing the crusaders inside the walls in small groups. Alexius laid on food and wine for the crusading army and made gifts of jewels and gold to the leaders, but the crusaders remained deeply unhappy at having been outmanoeuvred and denied the riches they had expected to gain from looting.

In the aftermath, Alexius had a stand-off with Tancred: he refused to give Tancred his share of the gold unless the prince swore an oath of fealty. Tancred insisted that his loyalty was to Bohemond, not to Alexius; and he demanded as much gold as all the other lords put together, plus the amount it would take to fill Alexius's campaign tent. The tense situation was only resolved when Bohemond persuaded Tancred to give way.

Despite the crusaders' disappointment at the outcome in Nicaea, the future looked bright. Stephen of Blois wrote to his wife Countess Adela declaring they would be in Jerusalem in just five weeks. In fact, the crusaders' journey to the Holy City was to take more than two years.

MEN OF IRON
THE BATTLE OF DORYLAEUM

Near Dorylaeum (modern Eskiehir) on the Anatolian plateau, the crusaders were attacked by a Seljuk Turkish army led by Kilij Arslan, Sultan of Rum. The battle, on 1 July 1097, was fierce and long – from the third hour to the ninth, according to the Frankish chronicle the *Gesta Francorum*. After weathering a Turkish assault, the crusaders were reinforced when the rear of their army caught up and turned the tables to win a great victory.

BUILD-UP TO THE BATTLE
Following the capture of Nicaea, the crusaders set out eastwards across the Anatolian plateau towards their ultimate goal, Jerusalem. In the vanguard of the army were around 20,000 Normans under Bohemond of Taranto, his nephew Tancred and other noblemen; in the rear, around a day behind, were some 30,000 Franks led by Raymond of Toulouse, Godfrey of Bouillon and other lords. Kilij Arslan, who was smarting at the loss of his

capital city Nicaea, had retreated to the mountains and, in alliance with Ghazi ibn Danishmend, prepared an ambush for the Christian invaders. The Turkish army was probably about 20,000–30,000 strong – although the contemporary crusader accounts claim it was much bigger, with Raymond of Aguilers suggesting 150,000 and Fulcher of Chartres reporting 360,000 men under Kilij Arslan's command.

Bohemond noticed that Turkish scouts were watching the crusaders' vanguard, and on the evening of 30 June, three days' march out of Nicaea, set up a defensive camp near the town of Dorylaeum. At once, he sent a messenger riding at breakneck speed back to the army's rearguard, with an urgent summons for the Franks to come to the rescue of their comrades.

DAWN ONSLAUGHT
The Turks attacked at dawn the next day, 1 July. Bohemond ordered his knights to form a defensive line, while the foot

soldiers and women took refuge in the camp. He ordered that no one was to try to charge the attackers – they were to put all their efforts into holding them at bay. The plan was to defend the camp until the rest of the army caught up.

Rather than engaging the crusaders in a pitched battle of foot soldiers and cavalry of the kind fought in Europe, the Turks surrounded the camp and attacked from all sides. The Turkish army was all cavalry: its horsemen swept in from every direction, then swerved away at the last moment, sending a storm of spears and arrows into the camp. The attack was strange and terrifying for the crusaders – as Fulcher of Chartres wrote, 'this form of warfare was not known to us'. The *Gesta*

▼ *Heavily armoured crusaders clash head on with the Turks. At Dorylaeum the Franks were amazed at the size of the Turkish army, while the Turks marvelled at the ferocity of the crusaders' charge.*

▲ *When properly deployed, a fully armoured cavalry backed up by foot soldiers and archers was a formidable force.*

Francorum reported, 'the Turks were attacking us from all sides … we were not able to resist or weather the force of so many'. The defence was brave, but seemed ultimately hopeless.

Many of the pilgrims who accompanied the soldiers were killed, and those huddled in the camp feared that they would be slain. According to contemporary accounts, while some women ran tirelessly back and forward bringing water to the cavalry, others seem to have been quickly convinced that defeat was inevitable and set about making themselves as attractive as possible as a way of averting death by winning admirers among the Turks.

REINFORCEMENTS TO THE RESCUE

For six hours the army of Kilij Arslan and his allies kept up the assault. They were breaking through the crusaders' defences and an end to the battle was in sight. But at this moment, the rear of the crusaders' army rode in to the rescue.

On their arrival, a group of knights under Raymond of Toulouse attacked the Turks from the flank. Then the crusader cavalry drew up swiftly in battle formation, with Godfrey of Bouillon and Hugh

of Vermandois aligning themselves to the right of Bohemond, and Stephen of Blois and Robert of Normandy to the left. They attacked, a great wall of cavalry, bristling with lances, thundering across the field.

THE LURE OF RICHES

The battle continued. The crusaders were no longer in desperate straits, but they were unable to drive the Turks off. According to the *Gesta Francorum*, the crusaders marvelled at the size of the Turkish army and knowing that these essentially nomadic men carried their riches with them, they looked forward to seizing some of the wealth they had missed out on when they had been denied the chance to sack Nicaea. They declared: 'Let us all be one in faith in Christ and in the victory of the Holy Cross because this day, God willing it, we shall become rich!'

Then knights under the papal legate Bishop Adhemar of

Le Puy launched a surprise attack on the Turks from the rear, having ridden round under cover of some low hills. The army of Kilij Arslan, now tiring, and fearing being surrounded, broke and fled. The crusaders rode in triumph through the enemy camp, setting it afire and looting the riches in its tents.

VICTORY FOR THE 'MEN OF IRON'

The Turks' casualties were very heavy. Probably around 4,000 crusaders died; among them was Tancred's brother, William. Disaster had been very close at Dorylaeum: defeat would have brought the crusade to a premature end, but victory reinforced the crusaders' belief in their holy mission.

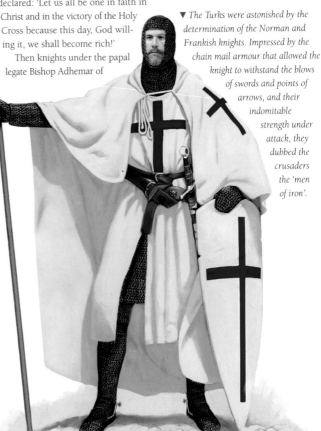

▼ *The Turks were astonished by the determination of the Norman and Frankish knights. Impressed by the chain mail armour that allowed the knight to withstand the blows of swords and points of arrows, and their indomitable strength under attack, they dubbed the crusaders the 'men of iron'.*

DEFENDER OF JERUSALEM
GODFREY OF BOUILLON

French knight Godfrey of Bouillon did not play a leading role in the First Crusade until its final stages, when he was one of the first Christians into Jerusalem on 15 July 1099 and after its capture became the first ruler of the Latin Kingdom of Jerusalem. He died only a year later, but he succeeded in consolidating the kingdom, and within a century of his death had become a hero of medieval legend, celebrated in chansons about the crusade that were told by *trouvères* (troubadours) at the noble courts of Europe as early as the 12th century.

Born in 1060 in northern France or Belgium, perhaps in Boulogne-sur-Mer, Godfrey was lord of Bouillon, a castle and village in the Ardennes forest of France, and from 1087 duke of Lower Lorraine. Most of Godfrey's life before he left in his

▼ When Jerusalem was taken by the Christians on 15 July 1099, Godfrey is said to have been one of the first knights to scale the battlements of the city.

mid-30s on crusade was spent asserting his right to the lordship of Lower Lorraine against attempts by Henry IV, King of Germany and ultimately Holy Roman Emperor, to take these territories away.

FINANCING THE CRUSADE
In 1095, inspired by Pope Urban's call to crusade, Godfrey either sold or agreed loans against his substantial landholdings and thereby raised a large force of knights. He also accepted money from Jewish communities in the Rhineland who were desperately attempting to buy safety in the face of repeated atrocities by crusaders. With his brothers Baldwin and Eustace, Godfrey embarked with an army of perhaps 40,000 from Lorraine in August 1096. They reached Constantinople in November, the second of the princely armies to arrive, following that of Hugh of Vermandois, brother of Philip I of France.

When the following year the crusaders set out for Jerusalem, Godfrey and his knights played only a supporting role in

the conflicts en route, such as the capture of Nicaea and Antioch, while in between those two events, he and his contingent were part of the force that rode to the rescue of the beleaguered vanguard of the crusader army at the Battle of Dorylaeum. After Antioch, he took part in the march on Jerusalem and the siege of the city and was one of the first knights to climb the walls when it was taken on 15 July 1099.

DEFENDER OF THE HOLY SEPULCHRE
A week later, in a meeting of the crusade leaders in the Church of the Holy Sepulchre in Jerusalem on 22 July, Godfrey was elected ruler of the newly established Latin Kingdom of Jerusalem. He did not accept the title of king in a city where the crusaders believed that Christ himself was the only true ruler, and was known either as *Princeps* (Prince) or as *Advocatus Sancti Sepulchri* (Defender of the Holy Sepulchre).

According to the *Gesta Francorum*, Godfrey's task as ruler was to 'subdue the pagans and defend the Christians'. He set about ensuring the survival of the new kingdom, which was by no means certain, for the great majority of the crusaders departed, leaving him with a force of only 300 knights and 2,000 infantry and without a fleet with which to mount naval blockades of Muslim cities along the coast. He agreed truces with the cities of Acre, Ascalon and Caesarea and, most important of all in the short term, succeeded in defeating the Egyptian army in the Battle of Ascalon.

DEATH AND LEGACY
On 18 July, less than a year after his election, Godfrey died in Jerusalem. He was around 40 years old. Accounts of how he died differ: the Muslim chronicler Ibn al-Qalansi reported that Godfrey was shot by an arrow while besieging Acre, but

Christian chroniclers wrote that he fell ill in Caesarea in June and succumbed to the illness on 18 July in Jerusalem – some versions allege he was poisoned by the emir of Caesarea.

Godfrey was succeeded by his younger brother Baldwin – according to the chronicler Radulph of Caen, before he died he called the Patriarch of Jerusalem and leading secular lords and warned them, saying they needed to consider formally who should succeed him, but they asked him to nominate his successor and when he named Baldwin they were pleased and pledged to be loyal subjects to him.

THE LEGEND OF GODFREY OF BOUILLON

It was Godfrey's position as the first ruler of Jerusalem and his achievement in securing the future of the Latin kingdom there that established his towering reputation in medieval legend. In the stories that

▼ The enduring fame and memory of Godfrey of Bouillon is honoured by a fine equestrian statue in Place Royale, Brussels.

▲ The clergy, knights and citizens of the young Kingdom of Jerusalem mourn Godfrey at his funeral on 23 July 1100.

quickly began to circulate, he was presented as an exemplar of fearless chivalry and a man of immense strength – in one story he wrestled a bear into submission, in another he beheaded a camel with one skilful stroke of his sword. William of Tyre, whose chronicle of the Kingdom of Jerusalem was written in the late 12th century when the myth of Godfrey was already established, described him as taller than average, with solid limbs, a brawny chest and 'strong beyond any comparison'; William reported that the hero was good-looking, with blond hair and beard. Godfrey was certainly an intelligent man and a forceful character, but there is little evidence that he was truly devout, and he was certainly not the paragon of Christian virtue that he became in his legend.

THE MARCH ACROSS ANATOLIA

AND THE ESTABLISHMENT OF THE COUNTY OF EDESSA

Following their victory in the Battle of Dorylaeum, the crusaders rested for two days and then marched onwards to the south. They headed across the Anatolian plateau bound for Antioch in Pisidia and thence on to Iconium.

A HELLISH SUMMER

It was summer and the gruelling heat took a heavy toll on the army. According to chronicler Albert of Aix, the suffering was terrible: children, women, animals and soldiers died at the roadside from thirst and heat exhaustion; some women gave birth in the dust and were too weak to do anything but stagger on, abandoning their babies in the roadway; when a river was reached, many more people and their ani-

mals died from drinking too much. Albert claims that 500 people died in a single day from the effects of the heat. It seemed to the crusaders that far from arriving in the paradise of a land flowing in milk and honey, as promised by Urban II, they had arrived in hell.

Near Heraclea, the crusaders had to muster the strength to fight a Turkish army under two emirs from Cappadocia; the battle was soon over, for the Turkish army – perhaps made nervous by reports of the crusaders' exploits at Dorylaeum – dispersed and fled when Bohemond gathered his finest knights and charged at speed with couched lance.

In September the crusaders arrived at the Cilician Gates, the daunting pass

▲ *The people of Edessa pay homage to Baldwin I, King of Jerusalem.*

through the snow-covered Taurus Mountains that lay between the Anatolian plateau and the Mediterranean coast. By this stage almost all the travellers' pack animals had died and many knights were without horses, having to ride on oxen and force dogs to pull carts.

The weather was still hot and dry and the crusaders decided that if they took the pass, they would be vulnerable to guerrilla attacks from the Turks. The main body of the army now marched north-east, away from the Cilician Gates, into easier wooded country towards Armenian lands. In these territories, the crusaders could expect a welcome: the Armenians were Christians who had been evicted from their lands in the southern Caucasus by Byzantine forces and so had little affection for the emperor of Constantinople. They were also enemies of the Turks.

FIGHTING OVER TARSUS

A smaller force of around 100 knights and 200 foot soldiers under Tancred elected to split off from the main army, risk the passage through the Cilician Gates and attempt an assault on the Turkish-garrisoned town of Tarsus on the plain beyond. At Tarsus, Tancred succeeded in driving out the Turks and raising his own banner, with the help of reinforcements of 500 knights and 2,000 foot soldiers led by

---

FIRST-HAND ACCOUNTS OF THE FIRST CRUSADE

Such was the impact made by the crusaders' success in librating Jerusalem that several histories were written soon afterwards. *Gesta Francorum* (Deeds of the Franks) was written almost immediately after the capture of Jerusalem in *c.*1100 by an anonymous follower of Bohemond of Taranto. Fulcher of Chartres, a churchman who travelled in the party of Stephen of Blois, also wrote a history of the crusade perhaps as early as 1101–06. The history of Raymond of Aguilers, chaplain to Raymond, Count of Toulouse, is rich in accounts of visions and miracles – including the discovery of the Holy Lance at Antioch. Radulph of Caen was chaplain to Bohemond of Taranto and he wrote a biography of Bohemond's nephew, Tancred, in *c.*1112. Albert of Aix (also known as Albert of Aachen) wrote a 12-volume history of the First Crusade and the early history of the Latin Kingdom of Jerusalem in *c.*1125–50; Albert's is the most detailed chronicle of the First

Crusade. Among other first-hand accounts of events of the time are Anna Comnena's biography of her father, Emperor Alexius, and the writings of Armenian Christian Matthew of Edessa. There are also later accounts of events of the First Crusade written by Muslim chroniclers, including Ibn al-Athir and Sibt Ibn al-Jawsi.

▼ *In the aftermath of the crusade, churchmen recorded God's triumphs.*

Baldwin of Boulogne, brother of Godfrey of Bouillon. The two knights then disputed the spoils: Baldwin had led his men through the Cilician Gates not to help Tancred but in order to prevent him (and thereby his uncle Bohemond) from taking control of the coast.

Rival lords were coming into open and bitter conflict as they disputed control of captured territories. In this instance, Baldwin had many more knights and soldiers than Tancred, so Tancred gave way. When more of Bohemond's knights arrived at Tarsus, Baldwin refused to open the city gates and they were put to the sword in an attack by Turkish troops. Tancred moved on and took control first of Adana and then of Mamistra. Baldwin followed. The two armies fought, but finally agreed to withdraw from the coast.

ON TO ANTIOCH

The main army had a terrible time crossing the Anti-Taurus Mountains that stood inland, behind the Taurus range. By this time it was October and heavy rains had begun – in wet conditions, the steep tracks were almost impassable. The army limped across the mountains and moved on

▼ *During the lengthy siege of Antioch, various plots to take the city by stealth were attempted, and rumours of secret truces and intercepted messengers were rife.*

towards the city of Antioch. Tancred, meanwhile, had captured Alexandretta, crossed into Syria and was reunited with the main army as they prepared to besiege Antioch in October 1097.

BALDWIN ESTABLISHES THE COUNTY OF EDESSA

For his part, Baldwin headed north-east to the town of Edessa, an important and wealthy Armenian town to the east of the River Euphrates, while the main army settled in for the siege of Antioch. Edessa was governed by an Armenian Christian

▲ *Baldwin of Boulogne, seen here in a particularly viciously fought battle against the Seljuk Turks, became the King of Jerusalem in 1100.*

named Thoros, who had only two years earlier captured it from the Turks. Thoros's position was far from secure: he was surrounded on all sides by Seljuk emirs who were all too keen to depose him. He was happy to welcome a fellow Christian in Baldwin, and to accept the support of his fighting men. Baldwin, clearly sensing possibility, demanded that Thoros adopt him as his son and heir, which he did in a public ceremony.

Shortly afterwards, Thoros was killed during a revolt by the townspeople, who were said to hate him because he was a Greek Orthodox rather than an Armenian Orthodox Christian. Baldwin became ruler, calling himself Count of Edessa. Thoros's death was highly convenient for Baldwin, but we do not know for sure that he masterminded it – indeed, his contemporary supporters vehemently denied that he had any involvement.

Baldwin thereby established the County of Edessa, the first of the crusader territories that would be created in the course of the First Crusade.

CHAPTER EIGHT

BOUND FOR JERUSALEM

The extraordinary events of June 1098 at Antioch were the turning point of the First Crusade. In that month the crusaders twice went from despair to wild elation. At the start of June they were bogged down in a siege of the city that they had been enforcing since October 1097 with little progress, and were expecting the arrival within days of a vast Seljuk Turkish army led by Sultan Kerbogha of Mosul, who had every intention of lifting the siege. One of their leaders, Stephen of Blois, abandoned the enterprise and departed for home. They were starving, and frightened, and desperate. Then they took the city through cunning and subterfuge on the night of 2 June, and rejoiced wildly and raucously. But within three days they were plunged into despair again, when Kerbogha arrived and besieged them. Within the city they wondered if the entire crusade would come to nothing, but after visions of St Andrew and the discovery of what was purportedly the Holy Lance – the spear with which Christ's side was pierced on the cross – morale soared. On 28 June the crusaders threw open the gates of Antioch and rode out behind Bishop Adhemar bearing the Holy Lance to take on the huge army of Sultan Kerbogha. Despite being vastly outnumbered, they won, and claimed it as a miracle. Antioch was safe, and as soldiers of Christ riding in a divinely ordained mission to liberate Jerusalem; the crusaders must triumph.

▲ *The town of Latakia was one of the key ports in Syria. The crusader armies were dependent on it for the delivery of supplies.*

◄ *The crusaders at last reach Jerusalem, and give thanks and praise to God for a hard-won achievement that has taken so much longer than expected.*

THE SIEGE OF ANTIOCH

A LONG STRUGGLE TO WEAR DOWN THE CITY'S DEFENCES

The crusader army drew up before Antioch in October 1097. The city lay in a vital position on the route from Anatolia into Syria, and the crusader lords knew that they had to capture it before moving southwards through Syria and on down the Mediterranean coast towards the city of Jerusalem.

FORBIDDING DEFENCES

At once the crusader lords saw that capturing Antioch was a daunting task, for it had 400 towers set in 25 miles (40km) of defensive walls running across very hostile terrain. A siege would be difficult – the city stood on the bank of the River Orontes, so was very well supplied with water, and there were even areas of pasture set safely within the forbidding walls. Military attack was impossible from the north, because of the river, and from the south because of the forbidding bulk of Mount Silphius, site of Antioch's citadel. Writing home, Stephen of Blois called the city 'unassailable' and by general consensus the city was deemed to be impossible to take by force: the Arabs had captured it in AD637, and since that time it had only been taken twice – by the Byzantine Empire from Arabs in 969 and by Seljuk Turks from the Byzantines in the 1080s – both times by treachery.

In October 1097 when the crusaders set up camp before the city, Antioch was in the hands of a Turkish governor, Yaghi-Siyan, ruling on behalf of the Seljuk sultan in Baghdad, Barkiyaroq. The citizens were mostly Christians, a combination of Orthodox Greeks, Armenians and Syrians, most of whom disliked their governor heartily. Taking a precaution against possible treachery, Yaghi-Siyan made himself more unpopular by expelling the leading Christian citizens and jailing the Patriarch of Antioch, a very senior ecclesiastic on a par with the patriarchs of Constantinople and of Jerusalem.

TO ATTACK OR TO BESIEGE?

The crusader lords discussed how to proceed: Raymond of Toulouse argued for a military assault, but Bohemond urged a siege and an attempt to foster treachery within the city. Caution prevailed, and the army settled in for a siege. As autumn passed into winter, they had to deal with dwindling food supplies, regular sallies by the garrison and the taunting behaviour of Yaghi-Siyan, who put the Patriarch of Antioch in a cage, and hung it from the walls to enrage the Christians without. Stephen of Blois wrote to his wife, reporting that: 'We have lived through great

▲ *Like the cities of Nicaea and Jerusalem, Antioch was surrounded by massive walls that demanded the construction of siege towers for any attack to be successful.*

suffering and evils beyond counting. Many people have exhausted their finances, and others were saved from starvation only by the kindness of God. The cold is excessive and there are terrible deluges of rain.' In these months, having come so far, thousands of the poorer crusaders died of starvation; some people ate their horses, while there were even reports of cannibalism among the most desperate.

TWO RELIEF ARMIES ROUTED

The need for food grew so severe that in late December Bohemond and Robert of Flanders risked riding out on a foraging expedition up the fertile valley of the River Orontes. There they encountered a large Turkish army under Sultan Duqaq that was marching from Damascus to raise the siege of Antioch. In a tense battle, the crusaders recovered from a disastrous start, in which Robert of Flanders and his men were almost defeated, to launch a powerful counter-attack that drove the Turks off. Bohemond and Robert returned safely to Antioch, but without the supplies they had been seeking.

The New Year brought little comfort. Godfrey of Bouillon and Raymond of Toulouse fell ill. Robert of Normandy left the siege, withdrawing to Laodicea in Anatolia (near modern Eskihisar in Turkey). In February the Byzantine general Taticius took his troops north, either in search of supplies or else because he judged it more important to consolidate Byzantine gains in Anatolia than continue

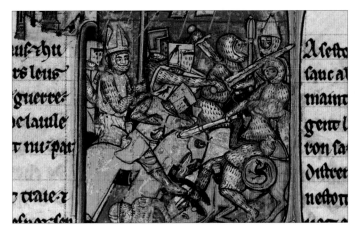

▲ Wearing his mitre in battle, papal legate Adhemar of Le Puy takes the battle to the Seljuks at Antioch. He carries the Holy Lance discovered within the city.

▼ During the long months of the siege at Antioch, the crusaders spent a great deal of time building siege equipment to drive home their assault, but they made little progress.

a hopeless siege. Many began to despair, losing their faith in what they were doing; some deserted, including Peter the Hermit who was caught and forcibly brought back to Antioch by Tancred.

Then a fresh threat emerged: news arrived that a large relief army under Radwan, Seljuk ruler of Aleppo, had approached and had set up camp at Harenc, only 25 miles (40km) from Antioch, in preparation for launching an attack on the besieging army. The crusaders struck first: Bohemond led a company of knights out by night and surprised Radwan's army, winning a stunning victory despite being vastly outnumbered.

SIEGE EQUIPMENT

In March an English fleet under Edgar the Atheling, a claimant to the throne of England, arrived at St Symeon, the port of Antioch, with supplies, siege equipment and building materials. The crusaders tightened their grip on the city by building tall siege towers and a fort called the 'Castle of Raymond' opposite the city's Bridge Gate; Tancred established a position in a monastery opposite St George's Gate. Spring turned to summer and although the city was almost entirely encircled, the crusaders were no closer to taking it by force. It was clear that they would need to find someone in the city who was willing to betray his masters.

THE FALL OF ANTIOCH
THE CRUSADERS CAPTURE THE CITY

Sultan Kerbogha's imminent arrival had forced the invading Christians to take fright and abandon the enterprise, or else to lift the siege in order to fight Kerbogha's army in open countryside.

But in the middle of the night, the treacherous watchman Firuz let down a rope beside the Gate of St George and allowed Bohemond to climb into the city. At the top, in the darkness, Bohemond felt his hand seized by another and heard a voice whisper: 'Long life to this hand.' He was followed in by a group of 60 knights. They succeeded in surprising the watchmen and guards and at dawn opened the Gates of St George and of the Bridge.

LOOTING AND DESTRUCTION

Meanwhile the main army had returned under cover of darkness and now they swept into the city. Terrible scenes followed, as the starving crusaders gave vent to their fear and greed, raping and killing, looting and burning. Many of the Christian citizens burst out from their houses into the streets to seek revenge against the Turkish overlords, but were killed in the confusion and lawlessness by the blood-crazed crusaders.

In May 1098 the crusading army encamped around Antioch received news that a mighty relief army was approaching under the command of the powerful Sultan Kerbogha of Mosul. It was clear that they needed to take the city before Kerbogha arrived, otherwise his force would either destroy the crusader army or drive it away – and all their efforts and suffering during the eight-month siege would have been wasted.

THE CRUSADERS ABANDONED

At this crucial moment Stephen of Blois, who had been elected commander-in-chief of the besieging army, abandoned the crusade. Deciding that the enterprise was doomed to failure and taking a sizeable contingent of French soldiers with him, he marched back towards Constantinople to take a ship for Europe.

▲ Betrayed to its besiegers, Antioch is overrun. The city has a European look in this 15th-century French illustration.

His timing could not have been worse, for Bohemond had found the ally he had been seeking within Antioch. This man was an Armenian, a Christian convert to Islam named Firuz, who commanded key defence towers overlooking the Gate of St George. Firuz had been fined for hoarding foods and according to some versions had discovered that his wife had been seduced by his superior officer. He was happy to have his revenge and profit by it.

BOHEMOND TAKES THE CITY

On the night of 2 June 1098 the crusading army feigned a retreat from the city walls. To Antioch's Turkish governor, Yaghi-Siyan, it looked as if the news of

A few Turks survived by taking refuge in the citadel under the command of a son of Yaghi-Siyan. As for Yaghi-Siyan himself, he escaped on horseback, but fell and was knocked unconscious during his flight to the mountains; his companions left him for dead, but some Armenians found him and, recognizing his face, cut off his head. They brought the corpse and its head to Bohemond in Antioch and were given a substantial reward.

The crusaders, when their heads cleared, praised God. Another victory had been achieved that had seemed impossible. They had taken the impregnable city of Antioch. It was beginning to seem as if their success in the crusade truly was to be guaranteed by God.

THE TAFURS

The most intense members of the crusader army were the Tafurs, poor soldiers originally part of the People's Crusade who were fired with wild religious fanaticism. According to Guibert of Nogent they marched barefoot and without weapons, living on the roots of plants, as a kind of holy army, and led by their own king of the Tafurs. They were notorious among the enemy – their name comes from the Arabic *tafuria*, meaning 'poverty-stricken'. They were always associated with the most extreme behaviour of the army, for instance performing acts of cannibalism during the siege of Antioch or later at Maarrat an-Numan, and were said to have urged on soldiers to acts of cruelty against the enemy at Antioch and in Jerusalem. The Tafurs were later celebrated as the deserving poor in the crusade chanson, the *Chanson d'Antioch*, which suggested that God had led the crusaders to victory because of the Tafurs' religious devotion.

▶ *The 'king' of the Tafurs was reputedly a wealthy Norman knight, who took pity on their plight and gave up his position and comforts to become their leader.*

TRAPPED INSIDE THE CITY

But in the days following their victory, the Christians' delight turned to fear once more. Sultan Kerbogha arrived on 6 June and set his army before the city. The besiegers became the besieged.

There was little food within Antioch. Kerbogha's troops took possession of the citadel and the crusaders had to fight determinedly to prevent them flooding over its walls into the city.

The crusaders pinned their hopes increasingly desperately on relief from Emperor Alexius, who had set out with an army from Constantinople in the spring. But these hopes were empty: Alexius had met the fleeing Stephen of Blois, who had described the critical situation at Antioch. Alexius, convinced that the crusaders' cause was lost, had turned back.

The crusaders' numbers were cut further by desertions – those who fled were derided as 'rope-danglers', presumably because they used ropes to climb from the city walls. By this stage, the Christian army probably numbered no more than 30,000. The crusaders' position was desperate.

▶ *Flooding into the city after months of frustration, the crusaders ran amok. Terrified citizens jumped to their deaths to avoid being torn limb from limb.*

MIRACLES AT ANTIOCH

FIRED WITH BELIEF, THE CRUSADERS DEFEAT SULTAN KERBOGHA

In early June, as we have seen, the crusaders were at the lowest of ebbs. Once the euphoria of breaking into Antioch had died down, they found themselves besieged and starving in the city.

Then, on 11 June, a priest named Stephen of Valence reported to the papal legate Bishop Adhemar that he had had a vision of the Blessed Virgin Mary and of Christ himself and that Christ had promised to come to the army's aid. Around the same time, a Provençal peasant named Peter Bartholomew reported that he had had a whole series of visions of St Andrew, who had revealed that the Holy Lance – the spear with which Christ's side was pierced on the cross – was within Antioch, buried beneath the Church of St Peter. There were other portents, including a meteor that seemed to fall directly on to Sultan Kerbogha's besieging army.

▼ Soldiers fall to their knees in awe as Peter Bartholomew presents the Holy Lance (the spear that pierced Christ's side on the cross). The illustration is from an edition of William of Tyre's crusade history made for King Edward IV of England.

THE DISCOVERY OF THE HOLY LANCE

On 14 June an excavation was carried out in the Church of St Peter: at first the digging soldiers found nothing, but then Peter leapt into the hole, dressed only in a shirt, and triumphantly brandished a length of metal that he declared to be the lance. A few sceptics doubted, but most were swept up in a wave of delirious rejoicing. Here was proof that God was on their side. They need fear no more.

THE DEFEAT OF KERBOGHA

The leaders prepared for battle and on 20 June elected Bohemond commander-in-chief. Bishop Adhemar ordered a three-day fast (not much of a challenge, since most were already without food) in repentance of their sins and preparation for battle. At first light on 28 June the soldiers attended Mass then flung open the city gates and marched out to take on the army of Sultan Kerbogha.

They marched behind Bishop Adhemar holding the Holy Lance and priests dressed in white and carrying crosses

▲ Reported visions of the Blessed Virgin Mary and of Christ himself in Antioch, together with the discovery of the Holy Lance, raised feelings among the crusaders to such a fever pitch that they came to believe themselves invincible.

while they prayed aloud. Their chances of success seemed to be nil. The encircling army was vast. The crusaders were weak from hunger. In previous encounters on crusade, their strength had been the mounted charge of knights with couched lances, but now they had only around 200 horses left alive. Many of the knights had to fight on foot.

According to the *Gesta Francorum,* as the crusaders emerged from the city they saw a great host on white horses and bearing pure white banners charging to their aid. This was – they afterwards reported in awe – nothing less than a heavenly army commanded by saints George, Demetrius and Mercury riding in to ensure that God's will was done. This was in line with the prophecies of the Last Days in the biblical Book of Revelation,

▶ *At Antioch the crusaders built this façade in front of a cave believed to have been used as the very first Christian place of worship by St Peter and followers in c.AD40–50.*

which declared that the heavenly armies following the Word of God 'were upon white horses, clothed in fine linen, white and clean'.

The crusaders, calling on God's name, charged the Turkish army. Amazingly, the Turks broke up and fled. A letter written by the leaders of the crusade to Pope Urban II, describing the victory, declared 'from the very first clash on the battlefield we drove the enemy back'.

Kerbogha had split his force between an advance group near Antioch's Bridge Gate and a main camp no less than 3 miles (5km) away. Charged by the crusaders, the advance group fled just as Kerbogha arrived with the main army from the camp. The main force then also abandoned the battle – perhaps partly because they were surprised by the discipline and ferocity of the crusaders' assault but principally, according to Islamic sources, because the sultan's rivals in the army wanted to prevent Kerbogha capturing Antioch and so called off their men at the very last moment.

Finally Kerbogha set fire to the sun-dried battlefield in a last desperate attempt to change the course of the conflict, but to no avail. The crusaders were afire with belief, and fought like men possessed; they had no desire to flee since behind them was only the empty city where they had been starving to death. In the citadel above the city, the Turkish garrison watched Sultan Kerbogha's army flee and knew that their chance had gone. They sent a message of surrender to Raymond of Toulouse. The crusaders had complete control of the city. The letter to Pope Urban II continued: 'the right hand of God fought on our side ... our Lord Jesus Christ brought the entire city of Antioch to the Roman religion and faith.'

THE HOLY LANCE AND ITS EFFECT ON THE CRUSADERS

In the medieval era Christians had a deep and powerful belief in the miraculous powers of relics of the life of Christ and other biblical figures. The astonishing effect of the Holy Lance on the crusaders can partly be explained as an effect of this belief. In addition, the majority of the crusaders were under extreme mental and physical stress – starving and desperate for hope – which would increase the likelihood of mass hysteria. The relic supposedly discovered by Peter Bartholomew was presented as the lance used by a Roman soldier to pierce the side of Christ while he was hanging on the cross, an event described only in the Gospel of St John and said to be the fulfilment of a prophecy in the Book of Psalms concerning the Messiah. Many crusaders in Antioch must have known and chosen to forget that a spear said to be the Holy Lance had been found in Jerusalem, where it was seen by many Christian pilgrims in and around the 5th–6th centuries AD; by the time of the First Crusade, this other spear was being kept in Constantinople.

▶ *In John's Gospel, the soldier was said to have pierced Christ's side with the lance rather than break his legs, which was normal practice with the crucified.*

THE PRINCE OF ANTIOCH

BOHEMOND OF TARANTO

Bohemond of Taranto, the Calabrian-born Norman knight who established himself as Prince of Antioch, was an inspirational leader of men and by far the most effective general among the knights of the First Crusade. He was also powerfully ambitious and primarily self-interested; the realization of his dream of establishing a personal principality meant far more to him than the official aims of the First Crusade. He did not even take part in the triumphant conclusion of the crusade, the capture of Jerusalem, having remained in Antioch to consolidate his position there.

BOHEMOND'S APPEARANCE AND CHARACTER

Anna Comnena, daughter of the Emperor Alexius, met Bohemond in Constantinople at the start of the First Crusade and left a vivid portrait of the man. She reported that Bohemond was astonishingly tall – she claimed he was 18 inches (45cm) taller than the tallest men; he had a narrow waist but broad chest and shoulders and very strong arms; he had a sturdy frame, she said, but a slightly stooping stance. His skin, she reported, was noticeably white, but his cheeks were red; his hair was light brown and worn shorter than was normal among the crusaders, cut just above the ears. He had grey eyes, which suggested (according to Anna) that he was a man of indomitable courage and great dignity. People were astonished at the sight of him.

Anna noted that Bohemond's size and strength made him frightening – even his laugh, she remembered, caused people to be nervous; in fact the mere mention of his name made people jittery. But he certainly also had charm. It was clear that courage and love ran deep in him, and he found expression for both these qualities in warfare. His intelligence was sharp – he always made ambiguous, non-committal replies to questions, and his mind 'ran

▲ *Bohemond climbs into Antioch on the night of 2 June 1098 after the watchman let down a rope ladder. He then threw the gates open to admit his fellow crusaders.*

over all possible outcomes' and 'dared all things'; his actions were often unpredictable, for he rushed into undertakings. Overall, he was 'like no other man ever found in the Byzantine Empire, whether a foreigner or a Greek'. It is a measure of the impression that Bohemond made that Anna's account, with its vivid details, was written around 40 years after she met him and that he was the only one of the crusader lords she described so closely.

THE YOUTHFUL GENERAL

Bohemond's father was the powerful Norman adventurer Robert Guiscard. As a baby, the future prince of Antioch was christened 'Mark' but as he grew was given the name 'Bohemond' by Guiscard in tribute to a legendary giant of that name. In 1080–85, in his early 20s, Bohemond proved himself a great general during Guiscard's daring invasion of the Byzantine Empire, and in 1082–84 while commanding the Norman army when

Guiscard was recalled to Italy, he won two major victories over Emperor Alexius. Bohemond was forced to abandon the campaign in 1084 through illness, and returned to Italy. Guiscard's death in 1085 was followed by a succession conflict in which Bohemond fought his half-brother Roger; this was ended by a settlement, favourable to Bohemond, imposed by Pope Urban II.

In 1096 Bohemond joined the First Crusade: in some accounts, he was besieging the rebel town of Amalfi (near Naples) when he encountered knights riding to the crusade and, impressed by their zeal, opted to join them. In other versions, such as that of the 11th-century Benedictine chronicler Geoffrey Malaterra, Bohemond saw the crusade from the start as a chance to continue his father's attack upon the Byzantine Empire and to carve out a principality there for himself.

A LEADER OF MEN

Throughout the early part of the First Crusade, Bohemond was the effective commander of the enterprise, an inspirational general and leader for the crusaders. At Dorylaeum through his quick thinking and tactical nous he averted disaster and held off the Turkish attacks until the main force of the crusader army could arrive. During the difficult months of the siege of Antioch Bohemond again proved his excellence as a general – not only defeating a large force under Sultan Duqaq that he encountered during a foraging mission, but also routing and driving back a substantial relief army under Radwan, Seljuk ruler of Aleppo.

Bohemond then almost single-handedly brought about the capture of Antioch through clandestine negotiations with the rebel Firuz within the city and a daring night-time raid. Afterwards, when the crusaders were besieged within the city by Sultan Kerbogha, when despair was

▲ *The crusader army had feigned a retreat but turned around and flooded into Antioch after Bohemond had opened the gates.*

mounting and desertions were common-place, he remained inspirationally upbeat, touring the defensive positions, making sure that they were manned and lifting the spirits of the defenders with the example of his courage and self-belief.

After the discovery of the Holy Lance, Bohemond was privately sceptical that a miracle had occurred, but he knew well enough how to marshal the outpouring of emotion among the rank and file: he was elected commander-in-chief of the army by the lords, and in this capacity planned the army's tactics and oversaw the aston-ishing victory over the besiegers on 28 June 1098.

SEEKING CONTROL IN ANTIOCH

Throughout this period, however, Bohemond was also plotting to outma-noeuvre the other crusader lords and establish a private holding in his name at

Antioch. He was even apparently willing to put this objective above the success of the crusade itself: during the siege his men spread discontent within the crusader camp, suggesting that a military assault would never succeed and that their cause was hopeless, so that when he established contact with an ally within the city and with the news that Sultan Kerbogha was approaching fast, he could negotiate hard, knowing that he held all the cards. From the other leaders he wrung the concession that he could keep Antioch if they won it. He proceeded with the capture of the city only when he knew that it would be his.

Bohemond remained in Antioch when the main crusading force marched on towards Jerusalem in January 1099. He watched the conquest from afar, and then visited Jerusalem at Christmas 1099 to ful-fil his vows. On this occasion, wily as ever, he engineered the election of Dagobert of Pisa as Patriarch of Jerusalem to counter-act the strength of the Lorrainer faction under Godfrey of Bouillon, who was by that time the effective king of Jerusalem.

AFTER THE CRUSADE

In 1100 Bohemond launched an attack on Danishmend, the warlike emir of Sivas (Sebastea), but was captured and thrown in jail. He stayed there for three whole years until being ransomed in 1103 by Baldwin of Le Bourg, at that time Count of Edessa and later King Baldwin II of Jerusalem. In the following year, Bohemond was heavily defeated by a Seljuk army after he attacked and besieged the city of Harran. After this setback Bohemond returned to Europe, where in 1105–06 he was hailed as a conquering hero for his part in the crusade.

Now Bohemond felt that he was poised for enduring greatness and after raising a large army he launched an attack on the Byzantine Empire. The enterprise failed, and Bohemond was forced to accept a peace treaty in 1108 by which he became the emperor's vassal. He died, humiliated and with his dream of creating a powerful independent principality broken.

However, he was able to pass Antioch on to his heirs, and was assured of everlasting fame for his reputation as a charismatic diplomat and general. Without his leadership, the crusade would have foundered at Dorylaeum or Antioch before it ever reached Jerusalem.

▼ *On his death in 1111, Bohemond was buried in this mausoleum at the Cathedral of San Sabino in Canosa di Puglia, Italy.*

THE WAY TO THE HOLY CITY
DELAY IN ANTIOCH PRECEDES THE MARCH SOUTH

The capture of Antioch appeared to open the way to Jerusalem. The army's morale was sky high, bolstered by the conviction that with the Holy Lance in their possession they were invincible because they fought with God's blessing. But this impetus and energy was wasted, allowed to drain away, while the princely and noble leaders of the crusade were locked in dispute over what should be done with Antioch.

Raymond of Toulouse insisted that Antioch be returned to Alexius in order to honour the vow that he and other lords, including Bohemond, had made while in Constantinople, to return captured lands to the Byzantine Empire. Bohemond claimed the city for himself and, as we have seen, before beginning the assault he had negotiated an agreement with the other lords that he should keep it; he argued that because Alexius had not come to the crusaders' aid when they were besieged in Antioch, and left them to God's mercy, that the vow no longer held. Nevertheless, Raymond sent a message to Alexius with Hugh of Vermandois to the effect that they would return Antioch to the empire if the emperor now agreed to bring an army to help them in the conquest of Jerusalem.

THE UNTIMELY DEATH OF BISHOP ADHEMAR

Just over a month after the capture of Antioch, the crusaders lost their spiritual leader when Bishop Adhemar, the papal legate, died of a plague that swept through the city. Adhemar's death was a great setback, for he had been a guiding presence, presiding over councils of leading lords, reminding all involved of the original purpose of the undertaking and attempting to restrain the leading lords from personal conflicts that might derail the crusade.

He had also been a visible leader of the army and played a major part in determining battle tactics. For example, prior to the siege of Antioch a crusader force under Robert of Normandy captured the Iron Bridge across the River Orontes 15 miles (24km) from Antioch, defeating a garrison sent from the city to do so; in this battle, on Bishop Adhemar's advice, they used a tortoise formation – the crusaders held their shields above their heads to form a protective barrier to hold off arrows fired by the defenders, and were able to advance largely unscathed and overpower the garrison. The formation was inspired by the *testudo* formation of the ancient Roman army, which the bishop probably read about in a Roman military treatise.

▲ *The crusader army finally began its march southwards from Antioch towards Jerusalem. Rank and file soldiers were convinced Heaven was lighting their way.*

THE ATTACK ON MAARRAT AN-NUMAN

The months dragged on, with little happening. Groups of crusaders raided the countryside around Antioch; some went north to join Count Baldwin in Edessa. In December an expedition was mounted to take the strategically significant town of Maarrat an-Numan to the south of Antioch. The army captured the town and slaughtered its 20,000 population and then, finding little or no food, they were allegedly reduced to cooking and eating some of the freshly slain inhabitants.

JERUSALEM BECKONS

The Holy City to which the crusaders were ultimately headed was no longer in the hands of the Seljuks. In 1098, while the crusaders were occupied at Antioch, an army of the Fatimid Vizier of Egypt, Al-Afdal Shahanshah, had retaken Jerusalem and Palestine as far north as Beirut – lands which they had only lost to the Seljuks in the early 1070s. The Fatimids had

---

CANNIBALISM AMONG THE CRUSADERS

According to accounts by Tancred's biogapher Radulph of Caen, and in a letter to Pope Urban II, the troops at Maarrat an-Numan were driven by desperation and maddening hunger to commit acts of cannibalism. Guibert of Nogent, who discussed incidents of cannibalism in his *Historia Hierosolymitana*, reported that perhaps because of incidents such as this or perhaps because of wild rumour and speculation, the Turks and other 'Saracens' became convinced that it was common practice among the crusaders, whom they regarded as savages, to eat the flesh of their dead enemies. He then described an act of provocation by the Tafurs, who openly spit-roasted a slain Turkish prisoner in view of the Turks in order to madden and anger them – they had no intention of eating the man's flesh. It is probable that accounts of crusaders eating flesh were propaganda on behalf of Christian writers seeking to make the crusaders seem fierce.

declared that the city was open to Christian pilgrims, who could come and go safely – the city's holy places did not need rescuing.

Although the crusaders did not know this, the Byzantine emperor Alexius had effectively disowned them, declaring to the Vizier that he could not control and did not support them, and renewing an alliance with Fatimid Egypt. Yet the bulk of the crusaders were desperate to march on Jerusalem, determined to fulfil their vows to reach the city and worship in the Church of the Holy Sepulchre, and driven by the conviction that they were engaged in a divinely inspired war fighting for Christ and his saints.

While the leading crusaders continued to hesitate, the lesser lords and knights – together with members of the army's rank and file – urged the continuation of the crusade. They offered to recognize Raymond of Toulouse as leader of the crusade if he would command them on the way to Jerusalem. Raymond accepted, giving way in the stand-off and allowing Bohemond to keep Antioch.

Finally, in mid-January 1099, walking barefoot as a pilgrim, Raymond finally left Antioch and began the journey southwards towards Jerusalem, leading a force of 5,000 crusaders. Tancred and Robert of Normandy followed with their troops almost immediately, while Robert of Normandy and Godfrey of Bouillon caught up around a month later.

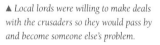

PROGRESS SOUTHWARDS

The crusaders encountered little opposition as they marched south, partly because local lords – following the defeat of Kerbogha and the advance of the Fatimids – thought that dealing with the Christians was a way of exploiting the changing balance of power to their own advantage, and partly because the rulers simply wanted

▼ *As the crusader army advanced through the Holy Land, its reputation for ferocity and acts of barbarity preceded it.*

▲ *Local lords were willing to make deals with the crusaders so they would pass by and become someone else's problem.*

to keep the crusaders moving on, avoiding the devastation that would follow from conflict, and making the bedraggled army another ruler's problem.

The crusaders captured the port of Tortosa, strategically important for maintaining their supply line, and then passed Tripoli on the coast of Lebanon on 16 May without attacking, after its emir agreed to pay them protection money and supplied them with horses and provisions. They proceeded down the coast past Beirut and into Fatimid-held territory, past Acre and Caesarea to Arsuf, about 50 miles (80km) north-west of Jerusalem, from where they headed inland towards the Holy City.

They stopped for four days at the town of Ramla, which they found deserted of its Muslim garrison but well supplied with food. Here, according to Fulcher of Chartres, they installed a bishop in the Church of St George and left a Christian garrison holding the fortress before setting out once more for Jerusalem on 6 June.

ROBERT OF JERUSALEM

CRUSADER KNIGHT COUNT ROBERT II OF FLANDERS

French knight Robert of Flanders fought bravely in the major sieges and battles of the First Crusade, including the capture of Jerusalem in 1099, and when he returned to Europe after fulfilling his vows he won acclaim and adulation for his part in events that were quickly becoming the stuff of legend. Hailed as Robertus Hierosolimitanus (Robert of Jerusalem) and as 'Robert the Crusader', in the ensuing decades his fame was almost equal to that of Godfrey of Bouillon.

THE 'ARDENT WARRIOR'

The eldest son of Robert I, Count of Flanders (the nobleman known also as Robert the Frisian), Robert the younger had ruled the county as regent while his father had undertaken a pilgrimage to Jerusalem in 1085–91. After his father's

death in 1093 he took power as Count Robert II, but within two years had committed to the First Crusade. He was already an experienced knight, and on the crusade he proved himself a great general and soldier, often in close association with Bohemond of Taranto. *Gesta Francorum* described Robert as an 'ardent warrior'.

EXPLOITS ON CRUSADE

Robert travelled on crusade in the company of Godfrey of Bouillon, leaving northern France in October 1096. In Constantinople he was easily persuaded to swear the oath of loyalty to Emperor Alexius in the company of Bohemond and Godfrey. After taking part in the siege of Nicaea, Robert marched on in the vanguard of the crusader army with Bohemond of Taranto – the part of the

---

THE CULT OF ST GEORGE

Robert played a significant part in the establishment of the cult of St George in Europe, for on his return he brought with him a precious relic, supposedly the arm of St George, which had been given to him as a gift by Emperor Alexius. Robert gave the relic to the Church of Anchin in Flanders, which established the church as a pilgrimage centre. He also founded the Monastery of St Andrew at Betferkerke near Bruges.

▼ *An artist's impression of Count Robert and Godfrey of Bouillon depositing trophies, supposedly won in the Battle of Ascalon, in the city of Jerusalem.*

army that came under attack in the Battle of Dorylaeum. He and his men fought bravely to keep the Seljuk Turks under Kilij Arslan at bay until the arrival of the main part of the crusader force, then fought on in the centre section of the crusader army alongside Raymond of Toulouse, when it launched the counter-attack that managed to decisively break the Turkish advance.

In the long siege of Antioch, Robert took part in key manoeuvres at the side of Bohemond of Taranto. In December they rode out to forage for food in the fertile valley of the River Orontes and, on 30 December, they together encountered and defeated a relief army sent by Duqaq, the Seljuk ruler of Damascus. As at Dorylaeum earlier, the charge of the Frankish and Norman knights riding with lances couched was too much for the Turkish horsemen to endure. When Antioch was subsequently taken, Robert was among the first of the crusaders to enter the city with Bohemond.

Then on 28 June 1098, when the Christian army broke out of the city to attack Sultan Kerbogha's besieging force – behind the Holy Lance, to the sound of prayers chanted by priests and in the face of a blinding vision of heavenly warriors under St George riding to their rescue – Robert together with Hugh of Vermandois commanded the first regiment to emerge, which deployed along the riverbank in a line. Contemporary accounts of the battle suggest that leadership was exemplary, for the crusader deployment and tactics were highly disciplined. After this battle, Robert took part with Bohemond in the capture of the citadel of Antioch, which had held out against the crusaders when the rest of the city had fallen.

LOYAL TO BOHEMOND OF TARANTO

Subsequently, Robert backed Bohemond in the dispute with Raymond of Toulouse over whether the crusaders could keep the city or must return it to Alexius. In December that year he rode out with

Raymond of Toulouse to attack the strategically important town of Maarrat an-Numan to the south of Antioch: Robert took part in the siege and capture of the town and presumably also in the massacre of its 20,000 inhabitants. He probably did not become involved in the alleged instances of cannibalism in which, according to Radulph of Caen, the starving crusaders cooked and ate the freshly slaughtered locals, both adults and children – this was most likely limited to the rank and file, while the nobles and commanders would have had the resources to buy scarce and overpriced food.

The crusaders recommenced their movement towards Jerusalem in January 1099, led by Raymond of Toulouse. Robert of Normandy and Tancred swore oaths to become Raymond's vassals and marched in his army, but Robert of Flanders and Godfrey of Bouillon refused to swear and initially remained in Antioch with Bohemond, subsequently joining the army at the siege of Arqa in March.

Robert largely remained with the army all the way down the coast to Jerusalem, except that at one point he and Tancred made a diversion into Samaria to find wood for building siege engines to use in the expected siege of Jerusalem. Robert then took part in the siege and capture of Jerusalem and in the subsequent Battle

▲ *The ancient port of Latakia in Syria, taken by Count Robert and Raymond of Toulouse in 1099, became an important holding of the Principality of Antioch.*

of Ascalon, in which the crusaders drove off a Fatimid army commanded by al-Afdal Shahanshah, Vizier of Egypt. Having been warned of the approach of the Fatimid army, the crusaders rode out to meet them and caught them by surprise in their camp near Ascalon. In this battle, he fought in the centre of the crusader force with Tancred, Robert of Normandy, Eustace of Boulogne and Gaston of Bearn, while Godfrey of Bouillon commanded the left wing and Raymond of Toulouse led the right flank. The crusaders triumphed despite being outnumbered by as many as five to one.

HOMEWARD BOUND

Robert of Flanders left Jerusalem in the company of Robert of Normandy and Raymond of Toulouse at the close of August 1099. On route to Constantinople, they conquered the Syrian port of Latakia, which became part of the crusader Principality of Antioch. In Constantinople, both Roberts declined an offer from Emperor Alexius to remain there in his service and took ship for Europe and a wildly enthusiastic homecoming.

JERUSALEM! JERUSALEM!

ARRIVAL AT AND BESIEGING OF THE HOLY CITY

As spring turned to summer in 1099 the crusaders neared their goal day by day. They were encountering little opposition, and even receiving a welcome of sorts, but they got an inkling of the locals' true attitude when a carrier pigeon was killed by a hawk above their camp and was found to have been carrying a message from the governor of Acre calling on faithful Muslims to take up arms and repel the Christian invasion.

A WELCOME IN BETHLEHEM

Christian inhabitants of Bethlehem sent out envoys begging the crusaders to liberate them from Egyptian occupation. Tancred and Baldwin of Le Bourg accepted the call and were welcomed as a liberating army by citizens and priests. The sight of their banner flying above Christ's birthplace was an enormous boost to the

crusaders. They were further cheered by an eclipse of the Moon that occurred at that very time – they interpreted it as portending the imminent eclipse of the crescent, the symbol of Islam.

'MOUNT JOY'

On 7 June 1099, the very day after the taking of Bethlehem, the crusader force crossed the hill known as Mountjoie ('Mount Joy') to generations of pilgrims and saw the walls of Jerusalem before them. 'Jerusalem!' went up the cry, and echoed down the lines. According to William of Tyre, the crusader-pilgrims fell to their knees and sobbed tears of joy, offering prayers of gratitude that God had led them to their destination; they cast off their shoes and bowed low to the ground in order to kiss the earth of the Holy Land. It had taken them three years to get there,

▲ At last the crusaders see the cherished city of Jerusalem. They offer prayers to God for having delivered them to their goal.

a long period of suffering and desperate exertions in which the pull of the Holy City and of their pilgrims' vows had inspired them to carry on. Now Jerusalem's walls were spread out before them. But their task remained a daunting one, for this city was one of the world's most strongly fortified, in a commanding position with deep valleys on two sides, to the east and west.

Assault was really only feasible from the north, for in the south on Mount Zion conditions could not support anything other than a small encampment. Expecting a siege, its governor, Iftikhar al-Daula, had prepared well, bringing in provisions and poisoning wells around the city, and sending urgent communication to Cairo calling for a Muslim relief army. He also expelled the city's Christian inhabitants to prevent any of them betraying Jerusalem to the crusaders.

AN ATTACK IN FAITH

The crusader army was not large enough to surround the city fully. On the northern wall, Godfrey of Bouillon arrayed his troops, alongside those of Robert of Flanders and Robert of Normandy, while to the south was the army of Raymond of Toulouse. In the gruelling heat of the summer and with very little water available, the crusaders decided to act quickly. They launched an attack on 13 June, although they had insufficient siege equipment. They had been spurred on by a hermit who reported that he had been told in a vision that if they proved their faith by attacking at once even without the necessary equipment God would grant them instant success. The attack failed, and brought home to the besiegers their urgent need for wood and other equipment with which to build proper siege towers.

Then, as if in answer to their prayers, Tancred found a hidden collection of

timber in a cave, and six English and Genoese ships put in at Jaffa bearing wood, nails, bolts, ropes and other supplies. Hidden from sight of the Jerusalem garrison, the crusaders set to work building two siege towers. They even took apart two ships to get more wood.

THE EXAMPLE OF JOSHUA

As at Antioch, they were working against time, for they received a warning that Governor Iftikhar al-Daula's cry for help had been answered, and a large relief army

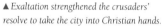

▲ Exaltation strengthened the crusaders' resolve to take the city into Christian hands.

was on its way from Egypt. But they found time to mount a penitential procession around the city. A crusader priest named Peter Desiderius had been visited by the late Bishop Adhemar in a vision, and been instructed that if the army marched barefoot around the city walls Jerusalem would fall within nine days. This was inspired by the example of Joshua, Israelite leader in c.1200BC, who, according to biblical accounts, led his army seven times around the city of Jericho – and, as promised by God, the walls of the city fell down and the Israelites captured it. The entire crusader army held a three-day fast and on the second day, Friday 8 July, marched barefoot around the city, singing hymns. Members of the garrison gathered on the walls to jeer at the soldiers, who proceeded to the Mount of Olives to hear sermons by Peter the Hermit and others.

Five days later, the siege towers were ready. The plan was to mount the main assault on the north wall, using the two towers, one commanded by Godfrey of Bouillon and the other by Robert of Normandy, while a second assault was led by Raymond's force from the south side.

▼ Godfrey rallies foot soldiers and knights at Jerusalem. Victory now seemed as certain as that of Joshua at Jericho.

THE HOLY CITY CAPTURED

THE CRUSADERS' TRIUMPH – AND SHAME

After dark on the night of 13 July, the crusaders began to move their siege towers up to the walls of Jerusalem. They worked beneath a murderous storm of arrows, missiles, pitch and Greek fire. All night and all the next day, while behind them the mangonel hurled great rocks at the walls of Jerusalem, sweating and toiling beneath a searingly hot sun and through great clouds of dust, they laboured at hauling the machines forward.

At last, on the morning of 15 July, Godfrey of Bouillon's tower was close enough to the wall to make a bridge across on to the city ramparts near Herod's Gate. Godfrey and his brother Baldwin fought bravely on the tower. At around noon, despite the defenders' desperate attempts to repel them using fire and boiling water, the first crusaders made it on to the ramparts from Godfrey's tower. Among the first across were two brothers from Flanders, Lethold and Gilbert of Tournai. Just afterwards, the second tower under Robert of Normandy established a bridgehead to the wall.

THE CITY TAKEN

The defenders on the north wall retreated in order to take refuge in the al Aqsa mosque. Crusaders clambered over the walls and opened gates from within, and their comrades flooded into Jerusalem, unleashing a frenzy of bloodletting.

During the long struggle to get the towers up to the walls, according to the author of the *Gesta Francorum*, the crusaders had been surprised by how difficult it was, 'numbed with astonishment and extremely frightened'. Now, in the moment of triumph they had dreamt of for years, they unleashed their pent-up emotions in a bloodbath. According to the same author, 'the defenders of the city fled … and our men, following Lethold, ran after them, slaughtering them and dismembering them all the way to the Temple of Solomon. And in that place there was so much killing that the blood

▼ *The besiegers endured a heavy assault from the battlements as they moved their siege towers, little by little, up to the walls.*

came up to our ankles.' According to the Provençal chronicler Raymond of Aguilers, 'in the streets and squares of the city, piles of heads, hands and feet could be seen. People were making their way over the corpses of men and horses. But this is only to describe the minor horrors …'

The defenders of the north wall were pursued by Tancred and his men, and surrendered to him, promising to pay a large ransom. They took refuge in the al Aqsa mosque praying for their lives. Tancred claimed the Temple quarter in his name, and set his banner flying above the building. The Jews of the city also fled for their lives, taking refuge in their main synagogue, by the Western Wall.

The *Gesta Francorum* account goes on to describe how the pilgrims followed the soldiers into the city and also slew 'Saracens' indiscriminately to left and right. At the Temple of Solomon, it reports, attackers and defenders 'fought a furious battle all day so that their blood flooded all over the Temple. At last the pagans were defeated and our men took a good number of men and women prisoner in the Temple. They killed whichever prisoners they wished and chose to allow others to live.'

THE HONOUR OF RAYMOND OF TOULOUSE

On the south wall, meanwhile, the defenders kept Raymond of Toulouse's attack at bay until they saw that behind them the city had been lost. Then they made a swift retreat to the citadel, the Tower of David, and finally surrendered there to Raymond. He gave his word that they would have safe passage out of the city – and, remarkably, amid such chaos was able to honour it, escorting them from Jerusalem as far as the Muslim garrison in the port of Ascalon. This honourable enactment of the safe escort was a brief interlude of restraint.

THE CITY IS STRIPPED

The account given by Fulcher of Chartres describes how crusaders ran into deserted houses and seized whatever they found. Whoever was first into a building was able to claim it – 'in this way, many poor folk became rich'. For it was a frenzy of greed, as well as of bloodletting. According to the *Gesta Francorum*, 'the crusaders seized silver and gold, mules and horses, and buildings full of all manner of riches'.

A VIOLENT CLEANSING

It was normal practice in 11th-century warfare for an army to loot a city it had conquered after a long siege. The attack on the inhabitants of Jerusalem had an extra intensity, fuelled as it was by papal and priestly rhetoric about the need to sweep the city clean of 'Saracens'. After the killing, the soldiers and pilgrims piously gave thanks to God in the Church of the Holy Sepulchre. Fulcher of Chartres presented this dreadful slaughter as a purgative cleansing: 'O day so fiercely longed for! ... O deed above all other deeds! ... [the crusaders] desired that this place, for so long made unclean by the pagan practices of its inhabitants, should be cleaned of its filth.' Raymond of Aguilers declared that: 'after the city had

been taken, it was a rich reward to see the devotion of the pilgrims at the Holy Sepulchre; the manner in which they clapped in their exulting, singing a new song to the Lord.'

The slaughter continued for almost two days. Tancred was not able to protect the Muslims in the al Aqsa mosque. On 16 July the crusaders forced their way into the building and killed every man, woman and child. The synagogue, filled with refugees, was burned to the ground. A letter from the crusade leaders to the pope declared proudly that in the portico of Solomon and in his Temple, 'our men rode in the blood of the Saracens even up to the knees of their horses'. A reference, perhaps, to the Book of Revelation, whose apocalyptic accounts of the Last Judgement were familiar to the crusaders: 'And the winepress was trodden without the city, and blood came out of the winepress, even unto the horses' bridles.'

▼ *In the 15th century, when this illustration was drawn, the battle for Jerusalem was reimagined as a civilized encounter.*

▲ *The crusaders dedicated their attack to Christ and proclaimed a desire to win Jerusalem for God.*

▼ *In the heat of the moment, bloodlust took over from pious righteousness, and one act of barbarity was followed by another.*

AFTER THE VICTORY

THE CITY SECURED WITH TRIUMPH AT ASCALON

In the immediate aftermath of the slaughter of 15–16 July, the crusaders had had to deal with cleaning the city, since the piles of corpses made such a terrible stench. The *Gesta Francorum* reports that the bodies of the Saracens were dragged out of the city and burned in huge pyramids. The smoke hung over the city in a dreadful pall.

DEFENDER OF THE HOLY SEPULCHRE

On 22 July, the eighth day after the taking of Jerusalem, the crusaders elected Godfrey of Bouillon to rule the city as Defender of the Holy Sepulchre. The first choice had been Count Raymond of Toulouse as king, but he declined the offer saying no mortal man should wear a crown in the city that belonged to Christ. Godfrey agreed with this statement, but came up with a compromise title that allowed him to take power.

▼ *With the city of Jerusalem secured, normal rules of pillage did not apply, and the victors became rich overnight.*

In many ways, Godfrey was an understandable choice. He had proved himself pious, steadfast and brave. Among the other lords, Bohemond had established himself in Antioch and Baldwin in Edessa, while Robert of Normandy had truly joined the crusade in order to liberate Jerusalem and was now set on returning to France. Raymond's refusal of power in Jerusalem is less easy to understand, given that he had shown himself elsewhere to be ambitious and not averse to putting political ambition above Christian piety. It is possible that his refusal was a ploy to prevent any of the lords claiming the kingship or that he considered Jerusalem too difficult a prize to defend and was planning to establish a principality in Tripoli.

JERUSALEM'S FIRST LATIN PATRIARCH

Then on 1 August Arnulf of Choques, the chaplain in Robert of Normandy's army, was elected Patriarch of Jerusalem. Arnulf had been one of the most prominent sceptics voicing doubts about the validity of Peter Bartholomew's claims that he had

▲ *When the Church of the Holy Sepulchre gave up a piece of the True Cross it was seen as a further validation of the attack.*

discovered a piece of the Holy Lance in Antioch, and his opposition had played a major part in forcing Peter to undergo a trial by fire in April during the march south, after which the visionary had died. During the siege of Jerusalem, Arnulf had made a statue of Christ to stand on one of the siege engines. Then, on 5 August, he announced that he had discovered a piece of the True Cross (the cross on which Christ had been crucified) in the Church of the Holy Sepulchre. This became one of the most treasured possessions of the Kingdom of Jerusalem.

Arnulf's election was supported by Godfrey, and in return Arnulf backed Godfrey's decision to make the Kingdom of Jerusalem a secular state rather than one under Church – and ultimately papal – rule. He imposed the Latin form of Christianity, barring the priests of other denominations, such as the Orthodox Greeks and the Coptic, Armenian or Georgian Christians, from the Church of

the Holy Sepulchre. He also reportedly authorized the torture of other Christians to force them to reveal where they had hidden other parts of the True Cross. The events of these first weeks of the Kingdom of Jerusalem created a fierce hatred in the Eastern churches for the Latin Christians that would endure for centuries.

BATTLE OF ASCALON

Godfrey's first job as ruler was to repel the Fatimid relief army summoned from Egypt by Jerusalem's governor, Iftikhar al-Daula, before the fall of the city. The Fatimids had raised a force of perhaps 50,000 men under the command of Vizier al-Afdal Shahanshah, who intended to mount a siege of Jerusalem. On 10 August, Godfrey received reports from scouts that the Muslim army was massing in the vicinity of Ascalon, a port about 35 miles (55km) east of Jerusalem. Godfrey led his army out of Jerusalem to confront the Fatimid force, with Robert of Flanders and Arnulf; they were followed the next day by Raymond of Toulouse and Robert of Normandy. On the way, at Ramla, they met up with Tancred and Eustace of Boulogne, Godfey's brother.

In total, the crusader force numbers totalled around 10,000, with probably as few as 1,200 knights and the rest infantry. They were severely outnumbered by the Fatimids, although not as badly as is suggested in the *Gesta Francorum*, which claims the Egyptian army was 200,000-strong. The crusaders had their relics to comfort them: they marched behind Arnulf carrying the piece of the True Cross he had found and Raymond of Aguilers carrying the relic of the Holy Lance.

On 11 August the crusaders discovered a large number of goats, cattle, sheep and even camels grazing near Ascalon: they presumed the creatures were intended as a source for food for the large Fatimid army, although a few captives taken in a small encounter by Tancred indicated that the animals were intended as a decoy in the hope that the crusader army would lose its discipline and begin pillaging.

▲ *The crusaders rejoice as the symbol of Christ's Passion is raised at the end of their long and desperate campaign.*

When the crusader scouts discovered the precise location of the Fatimid force, the Christian army marched on with the animals in tow, making their army seem larger than it otherwise would have done.

The two forces met in open conflict outside Ascalon. Most contemporary accounts suggest that the crusaders caught the Fatimids unprepared and that the battle was quickly over. It began with an exchange of arrows, and then the two main contingents fought at close quarters with lances, the kind of battle in which the crusaders were at their best. The Fatimids broke and fled, some into the city, some into the sea. They abandoned their camp, and all its treasures, which were claimed by Tancred and Robert of Normandy.

QUARREL OVER ASCALON

The crusaders rejoiced, but prepared for a second battle. However, after spending the night in the abandoned Fatimid camp, they discovered the next day that the Fatimid survivors had begun a retreat to Egypt. The city lay at their mercy, but its garrison declared that it would only surrender to Raymond of Toulouse – doubtless because he had behaved honourably in providing safe escort for Iftikhar al-Daula and his troops during

the capture of Jerusalem. Raymond and Godfrey quarrelled over the spoils: Godfrey refused to accept the surrender on these terms, declaring that the city should come to him as ruler of Jerusalem, Raymond, furious at being thwarted again by Godfrey; marched back to Jerusalem, with Robert of Normandy. Godfrey alone was not strong enough to capture Ascalon, and so it remained in Muslim hands. Allowing this to happen was a grave mistake, for taking Ascalon would have been an important step towards consolidating the fledgling Kingdom of Jerusalem.

CRUSADE COMPLETED

For the great majority of the crusaders, the enterprise was now at an end and most went home. At the end of 1099 Godfrey remained in Jerusalem with only around 2,000 foot soldiers plus perhaps just 300 knights – in the estimation of William of Tyre. Robert of Normandy and Robert of Flanders were among those who departed for Europe and with them Godfrey sent word that the Kingdom of Jerusalem needed reinforcements.

CHAPTER NINE

THE LAND OVERSEAS

The many settlers who stayed after the First Crusade in 1099 created an outpost of Latin Christendom in the East. The land in which they made their homes became known as *Outremer* – from the French word meaning 'overseas'. Outremer encompassed the four crusader states established during or as a result of the First Crusade: the County of Edessa; the Principality of Antioch; the Kingdom of Jerusalem; and the County of Tripoli.

The settlers organized life along familiar lines, introducing the feudal system and imposing the rites of the Latin Church on other Christians. But in many respects, also, they went native. Fulcher of Chartres, who became chaplain to King Baldwin I of Jerusalem, wrote: 'We were once Westerners, but now we are men of the East. You may once have identified yourself as a Roman or a Frenchman, but here, in the present, you are a man of Galilee or of Palestine.... For we do not remember the lands of our birth; to the majority of us they are unfamiliar, foreign lands.' He went on to describe how the lords of the new estates came to appreciate local customs and food and married local women, whether Armenians, Syrians or even 'Saracens' – of course, he added, 'only to those who have been baptized'. It is clear that for the settlers life in Outremer represented the start of something permanent. When the soldiers of the Second Crusade arrived in 1148, they were shocked to find that the leading men of Outremer in their eyes were more like 'Saracens' than Christian princes.

▲ *The coastal crusader citadel of Sidon, in Lebanon.*

◄ *The impressive remains of Krak des Chevaliers at Qal'at al-Hisn in Syria are an enduring symbol of the might of the military orders and the kingdoms of Outremer.*

THE KINGDOMS OF PALESTINE

To understand the movements of the great crusading armies, and appreciate the drama of their adventures, it is helpful to know the routes they took and the boundaries they crossed.

Tracing the long and dangerous journey made on the First Crusade underlines the enterprise's vast ambition and daring (shown on the map below). From central and northern Europe, some from as far north as England, or from southern France, by a variety of routes – across the Holy Roman Empire and Hungary, or through Italy and by sea across the southern Adriatic – the great armies marched under the banner of the cross to Constantinople, capital of the Byzantine empire, then on across Anatolia and down the Mediterranean coast towards their glittering goal, the Holy City of Jerusalem.

Across these thousands of miles trailed many, many thousand men (and some women), first the somewhat ragged forces of the People's Crusade – according to Byzantine princess Anna Comnena, to see them was 'like looking at rivers flooding together from all directions' – then no fewer than five princely armies. The routes of the four main princely armies are detailed on the map. Faith and the inspirational words of Urban II and the crusade preachers drove them on and helped them keep their nerve: this was a great adventure but also a daunting and frequently terrifying challenge. In taking the cross many had cried 'God wills it!' and the belief that they were destined to achieve their goal bore the core of the crusaders onward in the face of hardship, defeats and the deaths of comrades. More than

three years elapsed between the departure of the first elements of the People's Crusade in April 1096 and the bloody capture of Jerusalem in July 1099.

JERUSALEM

With the Holy City in Christian hands for the first time since AD638, the crusaders began building. They erected a palace beside the al-Aqsa Mosque, in the place

▼ *The first of the main princely armies to depart was that of Godfrey of Bouillon, who left Lorraine in August 1096. Bohemond of Taranto set sail from Bari in October 1096. At the same time Raymond of Toulouse left southern France and Robert of Flanders set out from the north. Their combined forces took Nicaea in June 1097 and marched across the Sultanate of Rum.*

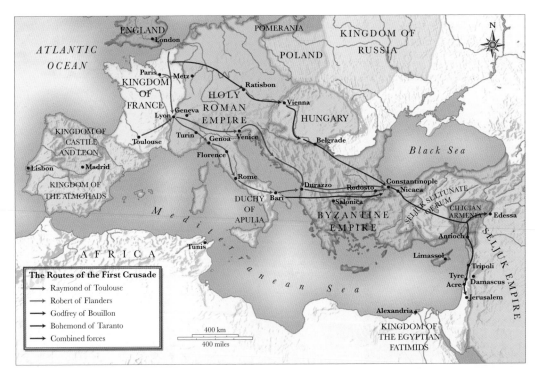

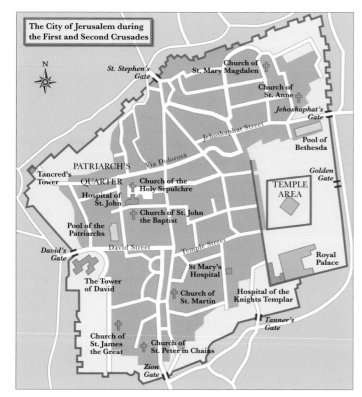

The City of Jerusalem during the First and Second Crusades

Saladin and his troops captured Acre and other strongholds along the Mediterranean coast: from Acre he headed north and took Sidon and Beirut, then marched south and took Jaffa and Ascalon before moving inland to capture Jerusalem on 2 October 1187. He campaigned again in 1188, in the north, and won several further victories, including the capture of the fortress of Saone. But he did not take Tyre, and this would be an invaluable foothold for a Christian revival in the Holy Land.

▼ *Saladin campaigned at great speed, determined not to allow the Christians to regroup. He took Acre just four days after the victory at the Horns of Hattin, then captured Ascalon, during a solar eclipse, exactly two months after Hattin. By 20 September he had marched inland to begin the siege of Jerusalem.*

▲ *Pilgrims entered the city by David's Gate in the west and went directly to the Church of the Holy Sepulchre. Christ reputedly entered the city on Palm Sunday through the Golden Gate, beside the Temple Area.*

crucified, and the site of his tomb. Pilgrims visiting Jerusalem could follow the 'Way of the Cross' from the site of Pontius Pilate's palace on Jehoshaphat Street to the site of Christ's crucifixion and burial.

THE CONQUESTS OF SALADIN
Less then a century later, beginning in July 1187, Muslim leader Saladin won a series of victories that brought the Christian Kingdom of Jerusalem close to extinction (shown in the map right). Crossing the River Jordan from the east with an army of around 30,000 on 30 June 1187, Saladin defeated Guy of Lusignan, King of Jerusalem, and a 20,000-strong army in the Battle of the Horns of Hattin on 4 July. Jerusalem was an easy target after this victory, in which the crusaders famously lost their treasured relic of the 'True Cross' on which Christ died, for the Kingdom's military force was all but wiped out.

believed to be the site of the ancient Temple. Later this became the headquarters of the Knights Templar, and a new palace was built in the west of the city at the Tower of David, by David's Gate. In this place King David had reputedly written the Book of Psalms in the 11th-10th century BC. Under the Muslims, bells had been banned from churches, but now they were restored and rang out over the capital of a Christian kingdom in the Holy Land, a city perceived as the centre of the world.

In the course of 50 years to c.1150 the crusaders built the great Romanesque Church of the Holy Sepulchre, containing the rock of Calvary on which Christ was

THE FOUNDATION OF OUTREMER

EDESSA, ANTIOCH, JERUSALEM AND TRIPOLI

The first crusader states had been established in 1098 en route to Jerusalem, when Baldwin of Boulogne created the County of Edessa based on the ancient city of that name (now Urfa, Turkey), and Bohemond of Taranto established the Principality of Antioch in Syria.

THE KINGDOM OF JERUSALEM

The third state, the Kingdom of Jerusalem, did not technically come into existence until 17 months after the Christian conquest of Jerusalem on 15 July 1099. As we have seen, Godfrey of Bouillon, refused to be called king in the city where Christ wore a crown of thorns and took the title 'Defender of the Holy Sepulchre'. But following Godfrey's death in July 1100 his brother Baldwin, no longer 'of Boulogne' but 'of Edessa', had no such qualms, and was crowned king on 25 December 1100 by Daimbert, Patriarch of Jerusalem.

Daimbert had arrived in Jerusalem from Rome in 1099. The Archbishop of Pisa, he had been sent from Italy as the new papal legate, the replacement for Bishop

▲ *The crusaders called this fortress on Mount Hermon 'L'Asibebe'. In English it is called Nimrod Fortress after the biblical hunter – and 'Citadel of the Mosquitoes'.*

▼ *Baldwin of Boulogne became Baldwin of Edessa and then, on the death of his brother Godfrey, King Baldwin I of Jerusalem.*

Adhemar of Le Puy, who had died of the plague in Antioch. Daimbert engineered the removal from office of the recently elected Patriarch of Jerusalem, Arnulf of Choques, on the grounds that Arnulf's election had been illegal, and took his place. He allowed Arnulf to occupy the lesser position of Archdeacon.

Then Daimbert set to work to bring about the creation of the papal state in the Holy Land that had been Pope Urban II's dream. He recognized the rule of Bohemond as Prince of Antioch and Tancred as Prince of Galilee, thus guaranteeing their independence from Jerusalem. From Godfrey he won the assurance that on his death the church would inherit control of Jerusalem – according to William of Tyre, Godfrey's plan was to cede rule to the Church in the Kingdom of Jerusalem and to carry on crusader conquest as far as Egypt, where he would establish his own secular kingdom.

But when Godfrey died unexpectedly, fate and conspiracy among the secular lords combined to prevent Daimbert achieving his and the papacy's wish of establishing a theocracy (a state ruled by God through churchmen). At the time of Godfrey's death, Daimbert was away on a campaign with Tancred against Haifa, and Baldwin was secretly summoned to come to Jerusalem and take power. When

Daimbert heard that Godfrey had died and that Baldwin was marching on Jerusalem, he wrote to Bohemond offering him rule of Palestine under Daimbert's authority – and asking him to prevent Baldwin reaching Jerusalem. The letter was intercepted, however, and Bohemond was captured while attempting an attack on Danishmend, emir of Sivas (Sebastea).

Baldwin marched into Jerusalem and secured his power base. Daimbert was forced to crown him king. Baldwin gave his previous holding, the County of Edessa, to his cousin Baldwin of Le Bourg. Early in 1101 Tancred abandoned his rule as Prince of Galilee, moving to take up power in Antioch – he reigned as regent for Bohemond, who was in Danishmend's jail (where he remained until 1103).

THE FOURTH CRUSADER STATE

The crusader state of the County of Tripoli was created in the course of the war waged by Raymond of Toulouse, from 1102 onwards, against Fakhr al-Mulk, emir of the coastal city of Tripoli (now in Lebanon), in power there as a vassal of the Fatimid caliphs in Cairo. Raymond died in 1105, before the city fell, naming his cousin William-Jordan as regent and his infant son Alfonso-Jordan as heir; but subsequently, one of his illegitimate sons, Bertrand, who had been serving as regent of Toulouse in his father's absence, arrived in the Holy Land. Bertrand and William-Jordan agreed, as a result of King Baldwin I's intervention, that they would each keep the conquests they individually made. Bertrand was the main beneficiary, for he captured Tripoli and became sole ruler when William-Jordan died a little while afterwards; Alfonso-Jordan meanwhile returned to France with his mother.

Bertrand ruled the County of Tripoli as a vassal of the king of Jerusalem. Within his realm, the castle of Krak des Chevaliers was given to the military order of the Knights Hospitaller in 1142.

THE GEOGRAPHY OF OUTREMER

The County of Edessa was the farthest north of the crusader states and set in a remote, landlocked position, with half of its territory lying far away from the Mediterranean, on the east bank of the River Euphrates; the other three states were all coastal domains. The Edessa territory west of the Euphrates was governed from the castle of Turbessel, strongly fortified against attacks from the Seljuk Turks of the Sultanate of Rum, which lay to the north. To the west lay Armenian Cilicia, parts of the Byzantine Empire where the crusaders had made conquests, including the city of Tarsus.

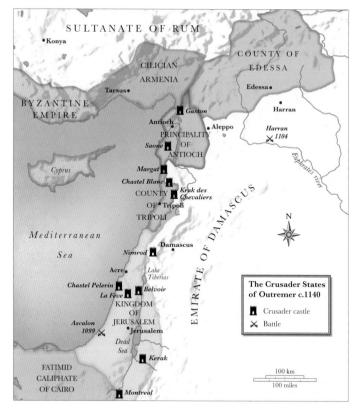

▲ *The majority of Outremer territories were coastal, and the Christian lords grew rich on trade passing through their ports.*

▼ *Krak des Chevaliers, the 'Castle of the Knights', in the County of Tripoli, was the foremost crusader fortress of Outremer.*

The Principality of Antioch bordered the County of Edessa to the south-west, and ran down to the Mediterranean coast. When Tancred was regent in 1100–03 he expanded the Principality north-west to take the cities of Tarsus and Latakia from the Byzantines. To the south was the County of Tripoli, leading south again to the Kingdom of Jerusalem. By the mid-1100s, when the Kingdom was at its largest, it extended north to south from Beirut (now capital of Lebanon) to Rafia (modern Rafah in the Gaza Strip). In the north it was separated by the district of Lebanon from the Emirate of Damascus; in the south-east it ran all the way to the Arabian desert and even encompassed the Red Sea port of Aila (modern Elat). After the First Crusade, some parts of Cilicia remained in European hands, but they never formed into a state or principality.

GOVERNMENT OF THE CRUSADER STATES

THE FEUDAL HIERARCHY IS EXPORTED TO OUTREMER

The crusader states were governed on the lines of the feudal system. The crusaders imported this social system from Europe because in their eyes it had God's blessing as the perfect way to create stability within a hierarchy of duties and responsibilities. Each man had his place, by divine plan, beneath the king. Detailed accounts of the government of the Kingdom of Jerusalem survive, and we know that the other crusader states had a parallel system.

THE KING OF JERUSALEM

Within the Kingdom of Jerusalem, the king was paramount. Great lords held land as his tenants in chief – men such as Tancred, Prince of Galilee, or Eustace Grenier, Lord of Caesarea. These lords in turn packaged land out to their tenants or rear-vassals. Only Catholic Christians were permitted to hold fiefs – Jews, Muslims and all other Christians were excluded from the system.

As in Europe, the lords and their vassals were required to provide military service – for example, Caesarea was required to provide 100 knights, as was Galilee; even the inhospitable lordship of

▼ *The port of Caesarea, a major crusader possession on the Mediterranean coast, dates back to around the time of Christ. It was built by Herod the Great in c.25BC.*

Oultrejourdain (the land east of the Jordan river containing the Negev Desert) had to raise 60 knights.

In 1166 the second tier of tenants, the rear vassals, took vows of liege homage to the king – at that time, Amalric. The chief city of Jerusalem was naturally reserved for the king himself, part of a royal domain that he governed directly.

THE KING'S POWER STRUCTURE

The king's most senior officers were: a seneschal, with control of royal castles and the treasury; a butler, in control of the royal household; and a constable, in charge of the military establishment. The collection of revenue from the countryside largely used pre-crusade methods, and then the moneys were passed via scribes and bailiffs, through local treasuries to the Grant Secrete, or principal treasury.

The king's power was limited by the great lords as tenants-in-chief and the rear-vassals, in their capacity as members of the High Court. The king took an oath in its presence, and was forbidden to seize any lord's fief-holding unless the decision was approved by the Court. The High Court, and not the king, made the kingdom's laws or assizes – the Assizes of Jerusalem. (These are sometimes wrongly said to have been drawn up by Godfrey of Bouillon.) Under these assizes, if the king broke his oaths, his feudal dependants had the legal

right to resist. In addition, if two members of the royal family came into dispute over succession to the throne, the Court had the power to determine the new king. However, the Court met only when summoned by the king so, if necessary, he was able to sideline its powers.

The High Court also functioned as the kingdom's highest legal tribunal, and there was no appeal against its judgements. Beneath it was a network of burgess courts to judge cases involving Western settlers; these courts had the power to impose the death penalty or to send offenders into exile. In addition, within the larger fiefs there were courts of knights and burgesses. These courts were limited to Latin Christians. Other Christians used a separate group of port and market courts. For Muslims and Jews, cases were divided into spiritual or secular: spiritual cases were judged by the existing religious authorities of qadis or rabbis, while secular ones went to newly established native courts called the Courts of the Syrians.

Assemblies of leading citizens – including senior churchmen, top members of the military orders and prominent townsmen as well as the king and nobles – were occasionally held to debate matters of consequence such as the necessity of levying taxes to pay for wars or policy problems such as where help could most profitably be requested among western lords. These meetings were called *parlements*.

THE INDEPENDENCE OF MAJOR LANDOWNERS

As in feudal Europe, the king often struggled to impose his will on the most powerful lords, who possessed strongly fortified castles and their own military forces – for example, Reynald of Châtillon, lord of the important fief of Montreal from 1174, was largely a law unto himself and waged a private war against Muslims, ignoring the royal policy of his king,

Baldwin VI. The lordship of Montreal was a wealthy one, for its main castle, Al-Shaubak (also known as Montreal) controlled lucrative caravan routes from Damascus to the Red Sea and Egypt.

THE RICHES OF THE KING

This difficulty was balanced by the fact that the king's domain made him richer than any of his lords: it contained the ports of Tyre and Acre as well as the city of Jerusalem. The king imposed customs duties at ports along the Mediterranean coast, and taxed overland trade caravans; he also had a monopoly on some local industries and was the only lord permitted to coin money in the realm; he had the right to claim shipwrecks; he could also, with the approval of his *parlement* or the High Court, levy one-off taxes – as when, in 1182, Baldwin IV imposed a tax of 2 per cent on all incomes, including those of the Latin Church, in order to raise money to fight Saladin. These large and varied incomes made the kingship of Jerusalem very profitable indeed: the king of this small eastern kingdom was probably richer than most European princes in the 12th century. And he was able to use his wealth to hire mercenaries.

THE POWER OF THE CHURCH

After the king, the Patriarch of Jerusalem was the most important person in the kingdom. The Latin Church in Palestine quickly became powerful, establishing a number of monasteries on land donated by wealthy crusaders and ruthlessly

▲ *The prosperity of Outremer depended on trade. The king of Jerusalem amassed great wealth from taxes on desert caravans.*

sidelining other Christians, such as the Coptic, Syrian, Greek Orthodox and others. The Patriarch was elected by the clergy, then acclaimed by the people: his position was subject to the approval of the pope, who would confirm the Patriarch's powers after the election.

▼ *The city of Tyre, an important port on the Mediterranean coast, had a Christian community from the 2nd century onwards. Its Muslim rulers surrendered in 1124.*

THE MILITARY ORDERS

One of the principal difficulties for the crusader authorities was the low number of settlers. They made repeated attempts to attract immigration from Europe, but they remained vastly outnumbered – a ruling minority with a very large subject population of Syrians, Greeks and Muslim Arabs who could not be relied on if the kingdom came under attack. By the 1180s, only an estimated 35 per cent of the population was European in origin.

The establishment of the military orders such as the Knights Hospitaller, the Knights Templar and the Teutonic Knights helped to boost the Kingdom's strength. The increasingly wealthy orders, funded by lavish donations in Europe, were able to buy castles and land from impoverished noblemen among the settlers and were an important means of maintaining order.

However, the ultimate loyalty of the military orders was to the papacy; they were not bound by feudal ties to the king, and technically did not owe military service in the defence of the kingdom, although in practice they fought in all the major campaigns. They also had the right to negotiate directly with Muslims.

LIFE IN THE CRUSADER STATES
THE RICH ENJOY LOCAL LUXURIES

In Jerusalem and other cities of the crusader states, the great lords and many of their retainers lived in fine style. They had their pick of the cargoes of Chinese silk, rare stones and spices that were brought to the Mediterranean coast overland from central Asia by camel caravan; in addition, they chose from the finest locally produced cotton and glassware.

In their city dwellings and their castles, they surrounded themselves with the finest luxuries, including silk wall hangings, woven carpets and beautifully carved Arabian furniture; the richest even used gold and silver plates. They adapted to the local diet, learning to enjoy dates, olives, watermelons, lemons, oranges and sugar cane, and to spice up their foods with pepper, ginger and cinnamon; they dressed in flowing robes, and began to wear open-toed sandals; some even adopted the turban. They married beauties among the local womenfolk – often in addition to European wives. Many lords kept elaborate Arabian-style gardens as havens from the dust and heat.

▲ *In this image of Bertrand of Saint-Gilles receiving submission from Seljuk qadi Fakhr al-Mulk it can be seen how the Westerners adapted their lifestyle to the climate and landscape of Outremer.*

LIFE IN THE COUNTRYSIDE

The majority of the Europeans lived in cities and castles but there was some settlement in the countryside. Some occupied existing villages and towns. In the Mediterranean port of Caesarea, for example, the crusaders who captured the town in 1101 simply drove out the Muslim population and made their homes in the existing city. Initially they just adapted mosques to use them as churches. In the longer term, they dismantled the Great Mosque and built in its place the Catholic Cathedral of St Peter.

There were also new settlements, in which land was given to European peasants in return for a 10 per cent tithe paid to the local secular or religious landowner. For example, the village of Magna Mahumeria (modern day al-Bira) north of

Jerusalem was established on these lines in 1120 by canons of the Church of the Holy Sepulchre on land bequeathed to them by Godfrey of Bouillon.

For poor Eastern Christians and Jews in the parched countryside, however, life probably seemed to have changed very little as a result of the crusade: their Muslim landlords had been replaced by Christian lords, but little else was different. The Muslims, of course, had to come to terms with being cast among the poor.

One way in which the feudal system in the East was different to that in Europe was that the Christian lords were largely absentees, for they chose to live in Jerusalem or other cities rather than on their estates. Although technically they were the property of the Latin Christian master who owned their land, the Muslims, Jews and Eastern Christians had a significant amount of freedom. There was freedom of religion in that in the countryside, Jews, Muslims and Eastern

---

THE KING'S ARMY

The king's feudal subjects were required to perform military service, but unlike in Europe there was no time limit set on this; as a result, knights and soldiers were rewarded with pay. But the feudal army, given the small Western population of the kingdom, was always likely to be too small to mount an effective defence of Jerusalem and its environs. In addition to perhaps a few hundred knights, the king of Jerusalem used his immense wealth to hire a large force of mercenaries, including Seljuk or Greek mounted archers called *Turkopoles* (from the Greek for 'offspring of Turks'), Lebanese archers and Armenian and Syrian infantry. This force numbered around 20,000.

▲ *The crusaders drove the local inhabitants out of Caesarea in 1101 and simply took what they found for their own use.*

Christians could follow their own faith and in religious matters at least were subject to their own authorities.

The farmers grew cereals and summer crops such as maize and millet. They kept vineyards, orchards and olive groves, and a few grew sugar and cotton. They paid a tax of up to one-third of their arable crops and one-half of the produce from olive groves and vineyards.

RELIGIOUS FREEDOM

In the cities, Muslims, Jews and Eastern Christians had their freedom – except that Jews and Muslims were allowed only to visit Jerusalem and were officially not permitted to live there. The Armenians, Jacobites and Maronite Christians were allowed to worship according to their own rites, but as we have seen were excluded from the Church of the Holy Sepulchre.

The degree of tolerance that developed between the Catholic Christians and other groups was a matter of necessity. For example, trade connections had to be made with Muslims and Jews. The Catholics' treatment of Jews was considerably better in the crusader states than in 11th–12th-century Europe, and there were no pogroms against the Jews in the crusader states.

MERCHANT ENCLAVES

Within the cities – particularly the coastal ports, such as Tyre and Acre – were colonies of merchants from the cities of Genoa, Venice, Pisa, Marseille, Narbonne and so on, who lived in independent, self-contained districts under the control of their own consul; they were not subject to the feudal system and did not have to perform military service. These merchant colonies had landholdings on the edges of cities, where they grew sugar cane and cotton. They were allowed a monopoly on trade between the Kingdom and Europe and sent home ships heavily laden with highly profitable cargoes. Ships from European ports brought goods necessary to the settlers' way of life, although most adapted quickly to local conditions.

The ports grew very rich. Traders from the Byzantine Empire, Syria, Iraq and north Africa worked alongside those from the European mercantile cities of Europe. Taxes imposed by the authorities could be as high as 25 per cent. The most valuable trade of all was in spices leaving the Mediterranean ports bound first for Constantinople and then on to the towns and cities of western Europe. Among the richest and most profitable of the ports was Acre. The Muslim geographer Ibn Jubayr, born in Valencia, described Acre in 1185 as 'a trading stop for all ships. It is a major attraction for vessels and caravans, the meeting place for Christian and Muslim traders from all around the area. Its streets are hard to walk, so crowded are they by men from all countries.'

▼ *Acre was a key crusader city, which was taken, lost and recaptured many times.*

PRINCE OF GALILEE
TANCRED OF HAUTEVILLE

A Norman lord from southern Italy, Tancred of Hauteville rode on the First Crusade with his uncle Bohemond of Taranto and afterwards established himself first as Prince of Galilee and then as regent of the Principality of Antioch and the County of Edessa. Through his feats of bravery leading up to, during and after the capture of Jerusalem in 1099, and his staunch defence of the independence of the crusader state of Antioch against the Byzantine Empire, Tancred won enduring fame as a knight that made his name resonate down the centuries.

Grandson of the great Norman–Italian adventurer Robert Guiscard, Tancred shared his name with the founding father of the Hauteville clan, the relatively minor 11th-century nobleman from near Coutances in Normandy, whose sons – including William Iron-Arm, Guiscard himself and Roger, Count of Sicily – travelled south to achieve greatness. Tancred

▼ *Tancred (right) meets King Philip I of France prior to marrying the king's daughter, Cecile.*

the Crusader certainly lived up to the expectations that such ancestry aroused. His life was recorded in the *Gesta Tancredi in Expeditione Hierosolymitana* (The Deeds of Tancred on Crusade to Jerusalem), written in Latin by Norman churchman Radulph of Caen in the years after 1112, based on eyewitness accounts.

IN CONSTANTINOPLE AND CILICIA
Tancred took part in the early episodes of the crusade. Notably in Constantinople, when other crusader princes swore oaths to Alexius in which they promised to return any conquered lands to the Byzantine Empire, doubtless with the full intention of breaking them, Tancred avoided taking the oath at all by slipping out of the city at night.

He took part in the siege of Nicaea and the Battle of Dorylaeum, but Tancred first made his name on the crusade when taking Tarsus during an excursion in Cilicia in 1097; in this part of the crusade he came into open conflict with Baldwin of Boulogne (later King Baldwin I of

Jerusalem). Tancred went on to capture Adana, Mamistra and Alexandretta, before taking part in the siege of Antioch.

In the course of the siege at Antioch, when spirits in the camp were very low and members of the crusader armies were sorely tempted to abandon the adventure, Tancred encountered no less a figure than Peter the Hermit attempting to flee and make his way back to Constantinople. Peter was the itinerant French monk who had preached the crusade so enthusiastically in Europe and become one of the leaders of the 'People's Crusade'. Tancred forced him to return to the crusaders' camp before Antioch.

A BROKEN PROMISE TO PROTECT MUSLIM PRISONERS
During the capture of Jerusalem in 1099 Tancred took hundreds of Muslim prisoners and famously pledged to protect them from the rampaging soldiers who had taken over the city, in return for the offer of a large ransom. He flew his banner over the al Aqsa mosque where the prisoners were gathered, but on the second day of looting he allowed the Muslims to be slain – man, woman and child.

AFTER THE FIRST CRUSADE
In the aftermath of victory, Godfrey of Bouillon, newly elected as Defender of the Holy Sepulchre, gave Tancred the title Prince of Galilee. Then, in the following year, when his uncle Bohemond was taken prisoner during an ill-fated military expedition against Danishmend, the emir of Sivas (Sebastea) in eastern Anatolia, Tancred became regent of the Principality of Antioch. He extended its territories by seizing land from the Byzantine Empire, and resisted attempts by Emperor Alexius to bring him to heel.

In 1104 Tancred also became regent of the County of Edessa, when its ruler Baldwin of Le Bourg was taken prisoner

▲ *Tancred raises his banner above Bethlehem. He and Baldwin of Le Bourg established a crusader presence in Christ's birthplace before the attack on Jerusalem.*

by the Seljuk Turks at the Battle of Harran. In 1105–06 when Bohemond, having been released, returned to Europe to raise reinforcements, Tancred remained as regent in Antioch. He attempted to hold on to the regency of Edessa when Baldwin was released in 1107, but later agreed to relinquish his claim.

HUSBAND OF A PRINCESS

Around this time, Tancred married Cecile, daughter of King Philip I of France; she had travelled to the Holy Land to become the wife of Bohemond of Taranto, but that marriage had not taken place. He remained very powerful in Antioch and staunchly defended the Principality's independence from the Byzantine Empire – despite the fact that Bohemond, having been defeated in battle by Emperor Alexius, had signed the humiliating Treaty of Devol in 1108, in which he agreed that Antioch should be a vassal state of the empire. In 1100, moreover, Tancred gained a foothold in the crusader state of Tripoli when he gained possession of the powerful castle of Krak des Chevaliers.

DEATH AND REPUTATION

Just two years later, however, Tancred died of typhoid while still in power in Antioch. He had no children, but his memory was kept alive in Radulph of Caen's *Gesta Tancredi*. In addition to his status as a warrior in the key engagements of the crusade, Tancred demonstrated considerable strength of purpose and political nous, as he carved out a position for himself as the pre-eminent Catholic Christian magnate in northern Syria.

AFTERLIFE OF A CRUSADER

In the 16th century, Tancred was a hero of the epic poem *La Gerusalemme Liberata* (Jerusalem Delivered) by Italian poet Torquato Tasso. The poem used historical events from the First Crusade as a frame on which to hang a chivalric romance, and borrowed many narrative elements from the *Orlando Furioso* of Tasso's fellow-Italian, Ludovico Ariosto. In Tasso's work, the character of Tancredi falls in love with a Muslim warrior maiden, Clorinda, a character based on Bradamante in the Orlando; Tancredi himself is loved by Princess Erminia of Antioch, who betrays her city to the crusaders because of her love for him.

Italian composer Claudio Monteverdi used parts of Tasso's poem in his operatic dialogue *Il Combattimento die Tancredi e Clorinda* (The Fight Between Tancred and Clorinda), composed in 1624. In 1759 French writer Voltaire wrote a tragedy about the hero called simply *Tancrède*, and this, together with Tasso's poem, formed the basis of the opera *Tancredi in Siracusa* by Gioacchino Rossini in 1813.

▼ *In* La Gerusalemme Liberata *the distraught Erminia finds Tancredi heartbroken by the death of Clorinda.*

KRAK DES CHEVALIERS
AND OTHER GREAT CRUSADER CASTLES

The crusaders built a string of formidable castles in Outremer. Like castles in Europe, these functioned both as garrison points from which to dominate the surrounding countryside and as strongholds to which troops could retreat when under attack; they were either maintained as lordly residences or were garrisoned by the military brotherhoods. The foremost of all the crusader castles was Krak des Chevaliers (Castle of the Knights), built at Qal'at al-Hisn in Syria, and today celebrated as one of the finest surviving medieval castles in the world.

The first fortress on the site, which occupied a commanding position 2,300ft (700m) above sea level and dominating the valley between Tripoli and Homs, was built in 1031 for the Muslim emir of Aleppo. It had a Kurdish garrison and in Muslim chronicles was known as the 'Castle of the Kurds'. During the First Crusade, Raymond of Toulouse captured it in 1099 then abandoned it when he headed southwards with the rest of the

▼ The inner enclosure at Krak des Chevaliers, enlarged by the Knights Hospitaller, incorporated some of the stonework of the original structure.

crusader force to Jerusalem; Tancred, Prince of Galilee, then took the fortress in 1110 when he was regent of Antioch. Raymond II, Count of Tripoli, gave the castle to the Knights Hospitaller in 1144.

It was during its time under the care of the Hospitallers, who held it until it was taken by the Mamluk Sultan Baibars in 1271, that Krak was developed into the largest crusader castle in Outremer. The Hospitallers built an outer wall with a thickness of 10ft (3m) and with seven guard towers to make the fortress a con-

▲ According to legend the crusaders found the Holy Grail at Caesarea. They built a castle there, but in 1265 the Mamluks razed it after taking the city.

centric castle. (A concentric castle has two sets of defensive fortifications, a lower outer wall enclosing an outer bailey overlooked by a higher inner wall protecting the inner bailey. Its garrison would initially man the outer walls, but under heavy attack could retreat to the inner bailey and then any attacking force would have to

WELSH CRUSADER CASTLES
The future King Edward I of England visited Krak des Chevaliers when he travelled on crusade in 1271–72. He was impressed with its formidable concentric defences and, with the help of architect Master James of St Georges, reproduced them where possible in the castles he raised in Wales. Master James was so called after the castle of St Georges d'Espéranches that he built, but his masterpiece is considered to be Beaumaris, the concentric castle on the isle of Anglesey.

OTHER CRUSADER CASTLES

Belvoir, another concentric Hospitaller stronghold, was situated around 12 miles (20km) south of the Sea of Galilee and controlling the Jordan Valley. Following the Battle of the Horns of Hattin in July 1187, Belvoir withstood a siege by Saladin's forces for 18 months, before finally surrendering on 5 January 1189.

Margat, on the route between Tripoli and the port of Latakia and overlooking the Mediterranean, was the Hospitallers' headquarters in Syria. Originally an Arab fortress, it was captured by the Byzantines in 1104, then taken by Tancred and made part of the Principality of Antioch before being passed to the Hospitallers in 1186.

Montreal in the Transjordan (on the eastern side of the River Jordan) was built by King Baldwin I of Jerusalem on a hill dominating the plain of Edom and overlooking Muslim pilgrimage and caravan routes from Syria to Arabia. Reynald of Châtillon gained possession of the castle on his marriage to Stephanie, daughter of Philip of Milly, in 1183. From this stronghold Reynald emerged to raid Muslim caravans, and even planned an attack over

▲ At Krak des Chevaliers the Knights Hospitaller built a vast central keep with a superb vaulted stone roof. The castle is one of the best-preserved crusader fortresses.

cross the outer walls and outer bailey under heavy attack from the garrison before even beginning their assault on the formidable walls of the inner bailey.)

The Hospitallers refashioned the buildings of the inner ward in the Gothic style. They included a storage chamber almost 400ft (120m) in length and stables with the capacity to hold 1,000 horses, in addition to a well, bakery and a sizeable meeting hall and chapel.

Historians have estimated that there was room in the fortress for a garrison of up to 60 Hospitaller knights and around 2,000 infantrymen and that the storage chamber, supplemented by further storerooms that had been excavated in the cliff beneath the fortress, could hold enough supplies to enable the garrison to survive a siege of five years.

After Krak was rebuilt by the Hospitallers it never fell to military assault: the one time it was captured was through trickery, when Sultan Baibars forged a letter purporting to be from the garrison's commander in Tripoli, which commanded the defending knights to resign.

▲ Steps lead to an inner retreat at the Castle of Saint-Gilles in Tripoli, named in honour of crusader lord Raymond of St Gilles, Count of Toulouse and of Tripoli.

the Red Sea on Mecca; his repeated provocations reputedly enraged Saladin. After defeating the crusaders at the Horns of Hattin, Saladin personally executed Reynald; then, after taking Jerusalem in October 1187, he made it his business to capture Montreal. It took him almost two years, but the castle fell at last in May 1189 – after a devastating siege in which the defenders reputedly went blind from a severe lack of salt in their diet, and also were said to have sold their children and their wives to obtain food.

Saone, around 15 miles (24km) northeast and inland of Latakia in north Syria, was one of the biggest of the crusader fortresses, covering 12 acres (5ha) in a triangular fortification atop a rocky outcrop surrounded by precipices. On the eastern side, the crusaders dug an extraordinary defensive ditch 90ft (27m) deep, 60ft (18m) wide and 450ft (140m) long. In its construction, they shifted an estimated 2.4 million cubic feet (70,000 cubic metres) of rock, which they used in raising the castle's great towers and walls. Saone was besieged and captured by Saladin.

▼ The 90ft (27m)-deep ditch at Saone Castle near Latakia in Syria is a powerful deterrent to attackers. But Saladin succeeded in taking the fortress in 1188, and it is also called 'the Castle of Saladin'.

BY SEA FROM ITALY

CRUSADING PILGRIMAGES OF THE EARLY 12TH CENTURY

Several expeditions were mounted from Europe to Jerusalem in the aftermath of the First Crusade. Some were armed pilgrimages, others were called by the pope and preached as military crusades.

THE CRUSADE OF 1101

The first of these, generally known as 'the Crusade of 1101', set out almost immediately after the end of the First Crusade in response to calls for reinforcements from the original crusader lords. After the capture of Jerusalem and the defeat of the Egyptian army at Ascalon in 1099, the crusaders sent word back to Europe that they needed strengthening if they were to hold on to what they had won.

According to Genoese soldier and historian Caffaro di Caschifellone, two Genoese traders named William and Primus Embriaco had in the summer of 1099 sailed to Jaffa with two galleys, which were broken up to provide wood for making the siege machines used to take Jerusalem. Afterwards, they acquired vast riches at the Battle of Ascalon from the abandoned camp of al-Afdal Shahanshah, vizier of Cairo, and with this treasure and messages calling for reinforcements had sailed for Europe, arriving in Genoa on Christmas Day 1099.

▼ *The exploits of the crusaders were depicted proudly all over Europe, but the disastrous failure of the Crusade of 1101 in Anatolia brought a change in attitude.*

As a result of the call for help, a new crusade was called by Pope Paschal II, the successor to Pope Urban II. In particular, he urged the crusade on those who had taken part in the First Crusade but turned back, and those who had taken the vow in 1096, but not departed. The crusade had three main parts, all of which were crushed by Turkish armies in Anatolia.

The first phase began when an army consisting largely of Lombard peasants under Archbishop Anselm IV of Milan departed Milan in September 1100. On arriving in the East, the army pillaged Byzantine territory and even parts of Constantinople itself, so Emperor Alexius swiftly moved them on across the Bosphorus, where they waited for reinforcements. In May 1101 this first army was joined by a French–Burgundian–German force under Stephen of Blois (the same count who had travelled on the First Crusade) and a Byzantine army under Raymond of Toulouse, who was now in the service of Emperor Alexius. The combined crusader force suffered a devastating defeat at the hands of a Seljuk army at the Battle of Mersivan in June 1101; Raymond and Stephen of Blois both escaped and fled back to Constantinople.

▲ *The establishment of the Kingdom of Jerusalem, and in particular its capture of Mediterranean ports, opened a sea route from Europe to the Holy Land. It was taken by pilgrims and later crusaders.*

Meanwhile, a second crusader army from Nevers in France had arrived, but failed to meet up with the first; the second army was trounced by Seljuk leader Kilij Arslan at Heraclea Cybistra. A third army under Hugh of Vermandois and William IX of Aquitaine then arrived: around half of the force was again slaughtered by the Seljuks, although the other half travelled by ship directly to Palestine; Hugh of Vermandois was mortally injured in the battle with the Seljuks and died at Tarsus in October 1101.

Survivors of all three waves united and pressed on, but the expedition was by this stage more pilgrimage than crusade. They arrived in Jerusalem at Easter 1102. Many then went home, but some remained to fight with King Baldwin I of Jerusalem against an Egyptian army at Ramla, a battle in which Stephen of Blois was killed.

The First Crusade had given the crusader armies an aura of invincibility, but the Seljuk Turks' devastating victories in

1101 proved to the Muslim world that the armies of Europe were in fact far from unbeatable. The major consequence of the defeats was that the land route to Jerusalem from Constantinople could no longer be made safe, and so passage to the crusader states had to be by sea. With Jerusalem under Christian rule, ever larger numbers of Europeans wanted to make a pilgrimage there, and merchants from the Italian cities such as Venice and Genoa grew rich transporting them there.

THE EXPLOITS OF 'SIGURD THE CRUSADER'

In 1107–11 King Sigurd I Magnusson of Norway led an armed expedition to support the Kingdom of Jerusalem. Sailing with 60 ships, en route to the Holy Land he visited Lisbon and fought Moorish pirates off the Balearic islands; after arriving in Jerusalem, he fought alongside Baldwin I in 1110, helping the crusaders capture the coastal city of Sidon (modern Sayda, Lebanon). He returned home the following year, taking as a gift from Baldwin a piece of the True Cross that he housed in a castle at Konghelle (modern Kungälv, Sweden). Sigurd's adventure

▼ *Sidon, an ancient city on the coast of Lebanon, became a major lordship within the Kingdom of Jerusalem following its capture by crusaders including King Sigurd I Magnusson of Norway in 1110.*

earned him the title of Sigurd Jerusalemfarer (the Crusader), although his expedition was really more pilgrimage than crusade.

BOHEMOND'S 'CRUSADE' OF 1107–08

Around the same time, Bohemond of Taranto led a military expedition from Europe that is sometimes identified as a crusade. Bohemond was one of the leaders of the First Crusade who had established himself as Prince of Antioch, but after defeats at the hands of Muslim powers he had returned to Europe to raise an army in 1105–06. He led a military expedition to the East in 1107–08, but rather than using it to consolidate the position of Antioch he launched an attack on Emperor Alexius and was again defeated. The episode was ended in 1108 by the Treaty of Devol, in which Bohemond became a vassal of Alexius and agreed to allow a Greek Orthodox Patriarch to have authority in Antioch.

Two further crusades took place in the 1120s. The first was proclaimed by Pope Calixtus II in 1122 and is also known as the 'Venetian Crusade' because the main response came from the city of Venice. The city sent a large fleet, which was waylaid at Corfu before finally reaching the Holy Land, where it took part in the siege of Tyre. Tyre was captured in 1124 and became one of the key trading posts for

▲ *In a highly charged atmosphere, Doge Dandolo of Venice forced the crusade leaders to swear an oath to support an attack on Zara. From this point, Venice rose to wealth and prominence through trade with the Byzantine Empire.*

the Kingdom of Jerusalem. Calixtus also offered Christian soldiers fighting Muslims in Spain 'the same remission of sins we have offered to the defenders of the Church in the East' and the crusade he called had also found expression in campaigns against Spanish Islam waged by Alfonso I of Aragon in 1125.

Another crusade was launched in 1128, partly recruited by Hugues of Payens, the French knight who was a co-founder of the Knights Templar. This expedition attacked Damascus in November 1129 but failed to take the city.

CONTROL OF THE COAST

Partly with the help of these expeditions and partly by their own strength, the armies of the crusader states won control of the key ports along the Mediterranean coast of what are now Syria, Lebanon, Israel and Palestine in the quarter century after 1099. In 1101 they took Arsuf and Caesarea, Haifa and Acre in 1104, Beiry and Sidon in 1110 and Tyre in 1124. The only significant port left was Ascalon.

CHAPTER TEN

MUSLIM RESURGENCE AND THE SECOND CRUSADE

The Europeans who fought in the First Crusade and subsequently established the crusader states of Jerusalem, Antioch, Edessa and Tripoli benefited from division among their opponents. Fierce rivalries between Muslim lords meant that in many cases, they preferred to ally themselves with the crusaders than with their countrymen. But in the 12th century great Muslim generals such as Ilghazi, Zengi, Nur ed-Din and Saladin began to develop unity and inflict great defeats on the Christians. These men mobilized their armies and people with the call to jihad, or holy war. The capture of Edessa at Christmas 1144 provoked European Christians to mount the Second Crusade of 1147–49; the abject failure of that enterprise only boosted Muslim morale and inspired Nur ed-Din to further great exploits of jihad. Then, in 1187, Saladin annihilated the strength of the crusader states at the Battle of the Horns of Hattin, and later that year recaptured Jerusalem. According to his biographer Imad ed-din al-Isfahani, Saladin envisaged an even more sweeping holy war. After Hattin he declared: 'When Allah grants me possession of the rest of Palestine I shall divide my lands, make a will laying down my wishes, and then embark by sea to the Franks' faraway lands, and pursue them there, so as to clean the earth of all those who do not believe in Allah.'

▲ *Qalaat ar-Rahba in Syria was built by the great Muslim general Shirkuh.*

◄ *The culmination of the Islamic fight back in the Holy Land was the recapture of Jerusalem by Saladin's army on 2 October 1187, seen here through the eyes of a 19th-century artist.*

THE FIELD OF BLOOD

A GREAT TURKISH VICTORY NEAR ALEPPO

The first major victory in the Muslims' fightback against the crusaders came in 1119, when a vast Turkish army assembled by the emir of Damascus and the Artuqid Turkish ruler and general Ilghazi entirely devastated a Christian army commanded by Roger of Antioch. The defeat was so heavy that it became known to Western chroniclers as *Ager Sanguinis* (Field of Blood).

BACKGROUND TO THE CONFLICT

Things looked very grim for the Muslims of northern Syria at the close of the 12th century's first decade. In 1109 the crusaders captured and sacked Tripoli after a siege of five years. In May 1110 they took Beirut. On 4 December Sidon also fell and was sacked. In Baghdad the Seljuk Turkish sultan, Muhammad, faced calls to mount a jihad, or holy war, against the invaders.

Muhammad sent his general Mawdud, who was also governor of Mosul, to attack the crusader state of Edessa. The attack failed but there were many Christian

▼ *Imposing city walls embody the power of the Artuqid dynasty at Diyarbakir, Turkey.*

casualties. In 1113 Mawdud raised another army to mount a new wave of jihad, but the enterprise came to a premature end when he was murdered in Damascus by a militant Shi'ite assassin. Fulcher of Chartres recorded Christian relief – 'the Lord had allowed this man to be a scourge unto us for some time, but afterwards His will was that the general should die a lowly death by the actions of an unimportant man.'

Mawdud's place as leader of jihad was taken by Ilghazi, a highly gifted general who had fought in Mawdud's army. The Artuqid dynasty to which Ilghazi belonged had been established in the late 11th century by Artuq ibn Ekseb. Starting out in the service of the Seljuk Turkish sultanate, Artuq's descendants built an independent powerbase in the province of Diyarbakir (now south-eastern Turkey).

Ilghazi took power at Mardin in that province in 1108. In 1118 the citizens of Aleppo asked Ilghazi to become ruler of their city, which was in turmoil: Aleppo's ruler Alp Arslan had been assassinated by his eunuch, who had seized power and then been killed himself.

THE BUILD-UP TO THE BATTLE

The following year Ilghazi marched on Antioch. The Principality of Antioch was in the hands of Roger of Salerno, nephew of Tancred; Roger had succeeded his uncle as regent when Tancred died in 1112.

Roger brought trouble upon himself: when Ilghazi marched into the Principality, Roger and his army were safely ensconced in the fortress of Artah, near to the city of Antioch, and he overconfidently ventured forth to meet Ilghazi, ignoring orders from King Baldwin II to wait for reinforcements from Jerusalem, and advice from the Latin Patriarch of Antioch, Bernard of Valence, that they should remain in Artah. As a result, the Christian army was vastly outnumbered by the Turks. Roger established himself in the mountain pass of Sarmada, while Ilghazi was engaged in besieging the fortress of al-Artharib. Roger sent a contingent under Robert of Vieux Pont to try to lift the siege but they were outmanoeuvred when Ilghazi feigned a retreat and were easily defeated.

On the morning of Saturday 28 June 1119 Roger's army awoke in their camp at the Pass of Sarmada to find themselves

Western historians suggest the more sober figure of around 3,700, but accept that only a handful of Christians survived.

THE AFTERMATH OF AGER SANGUINIS

Although the city of Antioch had been left wide open to attack, Ilghazi failed to press home his advantage by advancing, and instead, he returned to Aleppo to celebrate his victory. Yet the total victory at the Field of Blood was of major significance: it delivered a great shock to the crusaders, and it proved to the Muslim world that their armies did not have to rely on the might of the Seljuk forces to defeat the European soldiers.

entirely surrounded by Ilgahzi's men. They may have suspected that this day might be their last and went to their deaths after the archbishop of Apamea had heard the confessions of the whole army.

THE BATTLE

Descriptions of the battle survive from both sides. The Christian perspective was given in an account by Walter the Chancellor, the Norman crusader who served as chancellor of the Principality of Antioch, in his *Bella Antiochena* (Antioch Wars); the Muslim view was recorded by Kamal ad-Din, a Muslim historian of Aleppo. When battle was joined, the crusaders began well but then fell into disarray when their Turcopole mounted archers were driven back into the main line under Roger's command. Roger, who was fighting under a great jewelled cross as his standard, was slain, slashed in the face with a sword and his head sliced open down to the nose. His army fled – according to ad-Din 'the arrows flew thick as a locust swarm, falling on cavalry and infantry alike' and forced the Christians into disorganized retreat. They were pursued without mercy, and cut down in the hillside vineyards nearby.

Ad-Din claims that Roger's army numbered 15,000 and that all but 20 were killed in the battle and the ensuing chase.

▲ *The power of mounted soldiers – especially the devastatingly effective Turcopole archers – was decisive at the Battle of the Field of Blood.*

▼ *Armies on the march in crusader-era Syria relied on roads and bridges built by the Romans. This bridge, across the River Afrin in northern Syria, dates to c.3AD.*

THE CAPTURE OF EDESSA

THE RISE OF IMAD ED-DIN ZENGI

Turkish general Imad ed-Din Zengi stunned the Christian world on Christmas Eve 1144 when he succeeded in capturing the capital of the crusader state of Edessa. In the 25 years since the defeat of Roger of Antioch by Ilghazi at the devastating *Ager Sanguinis*, there had been defeats for the crusader lords, notably at the hands of Ilghazi's fearless nephew Balak, but always the status quo was more or less maintained in the crusader states. Now Zengi's triumph at Edessa cast doubt on the very survival of Outremer, the Christian kingdom overseas. Among Muslims, Zengi was hailed as *al-Malik al-Mansur*, the 'victorious king'.

BALAK

Ilghazi did not long survive his triumph at the Ager Sanguinis – he died three years later, in 1122, having never risen to those heights of military success again – but his nephew Balak took up the torch and swiftly became a scourge of the crusader kingdoms. In 1122 he captured Joscelin of Courtenay, Count of Edessa, and the following year took captive no less a person than Baldwin II, King of Jerusalem.

In 1124 Balak became ruler of Aleppo and began to retake territory from the crusaders in northern Syria. But he died the same year, having been shot in the chest with an arrow while besieging the castle of Manbij. In a few years he had made a great impression on the crusaders – after recording the news of his death, Fulcher of Chartres wrote in his chronicle: 'Then we all gave thanks to God because Balak, the furious dragon who had stamped on Christianity, was brought low at last.'

THE ORIGINS AND EMERGENCE OF ZENGI

In Balak's wake, Imad ed-Din Zengi leapt to prominence. Zengi was the son of a governor of Aleppo who, after his father's execution for treason against the Seljuk sultan Malik Shah in the late 11th century, had been raised in Mosul. According to legend, Zengi was the son of Ida of Austria, mother of Leopold III, who had travelled with the Crusade of 1101 and disappeared, presumed dead, during the crusaders' defeat at Heraclea Cybistra by Kilij Arslan. The legend recounted that rather than being killed she was carried

▲ *The formidable citadel of Aleppo. The city was Imad ed-Din Zengi's base when he established his power after 1128.*

off to life in a harem, where she later gave birth to Zengi. However, this tall story is impossible on grounds of chronology, and cannot be true.

Zengi established himself as ruler in Mosul in 1127, then in Aleppo the following year. Over the next 15 years or so he worked tirelessly to extend his power in the region, fighting whoever came his way – his Turkish rivals, the Byzantine emperor or the crusader lords. Zengi repeatedly attempted to gain control in Damascus and in 1137, when the Damascenes allied with the crusaders, he ambushed the army of King Fulk of Jerusalem and then besieged them in the fortress of Barin, north-east of Tripoli, before allowing Fulk to buy his freedom and return home to Jerusalem.

ATTACK ON EDESSA

King Fulk's death in 1143 led to a joint succession by his wife Melisende (daughter of King Baldwin II) and his son

Baldwin III, but Melisende effectively ruled alone, with the help of the Constable of Jerusalem, Manasses of Hierges, and initially largely excluded Baldwin III from power. Zengi sought to take advantage of this situation and in 1144 turned against the County of Edessa.

Joscelin II, Count of Edessa, had made an alliance with Kara Aslan, the Artuqid Turkish ruler of Diyarbakir and had marched the bulk of his army out of Edessa to support Kara Aslan in a campaign against Aleppo. Zengi moved swiftly, mounting a siege of the city of Edessa in November 1144. Within its walls Hugh II, the Catholic archbishop, and Basil, the Armenian bishop, combined to lead the defence; Count Joscelin II, hearing of the developments, went to the town of Turbessel, (now Tilbesar in Turkey) and sent out a plea for help from the other crusader states. Queen Melisende sent an army led by Manasses, but Raymond of Antioch was unable to help.

At Edessa, Zengi built siege engines and set to work undermining the walls of the city. The defences were poor, for the population of the city, according to chronicler William of Tyre, were traders who 'knew

▼ *Fulk of Anjou became King of Jerusalem when he married Melisende, daughter of King Baldwin II, on 2 June 1129. Fulk was closely associated with the Knights Templar.*

THE FIRST FIVE KINGS OF JERUSALEM

Godfrey of Bouillon is regarded as the first king of Jerusalem although he was known as Defender of the Holy Sepulchre. Godfrey was succeeded in 1100 by his brother, Baldwin of Boulogne, who ruled as Baldwin I until he died in 1118. Baldwin's cousin, Baldwin of Le Bourg, then Count of Edessa, became Baldwin II of Jerusalem. He died in 1131 and was succeeded by his son-in-law, Fulk of Anjou, who ruled as King Fulk of Jerusalem. He died in 1143 following a hunting accident while on holiday in Acre, and was succeeded by his

▲ *Baldwin III, King of Jerusalem at the time of the disastrous Second Crusade.*

wife Melisende (Baldwin II's daughter) and his eldest son, who ruled as Baldwin III of Jerusalem until 1162.

nothing of using weapons and understood only the business of buying and selling'. They had to rely on mercenaries to man the walls, and their numbers were dwindling because Archbishop Hugh was a miser who hoarded the city's great wealth rather than put it to sensible use in paying for the defence of the walls.

On Christmas Eve 1144, Zengi's mining operations were complete and he gave the command to set fire to the wooden posts that supported the tunnels beneath the walls near the Gate of the Hours. The tunnels collapsed, the walls fell down, and Zengi's troops poured into the city.

THE ENEMY OF LATIN CHRISTIANS

Thousands were killed in the taking of Edessa before Zengi intervened, ordering his men to stop the slaughter. He made it very clear that his war was only against the Latin Christians or Franks: and he went on to execute all the Latin Christians who had been taken prisoner, but spared all the other Christians, whom he allowed to live on in the city as before. He appointed one of his commanders, Zayn ad-Din Ali Kutchuk, as the city's governor and allowed the Armenian bishop, Basil, to continue in his position. He destroyed the Latin Christian church buildings, but allowed the remainder to stand.

Subsequently Zengi captured Saruj (now Suruç in Turkey) but then retreated to Mosul when the army of Jerusalem at last arrived. He did not attempt to consolidate his power in the County of Edessa nor to attack Antioch, as many had feared. But his capture of Edessa sent shockwaves through Christendom and led to the calling of the Second Crusade. Zengi himself died in 1146, when he was stabbed to death by his eunuch slave during a siege at Qalat Jabar. He was remembered by Muslims as 'the great, the just, the helper of God … the pillar of religion, destroyer of infidels, rebels and atheists'.

SOLDIERS OF ISLAM
WEAPONS AND TACTICS

Many of the Muslim armies faced by the crusaders in the late 11th and 12th centuries were enormously large and contained a wide range of troops, including untrained, poorly armed peasants alongside professional soldiers with the finest equipment. The core of the armies was made up of crack Turkish troops.

The Turks were famous for their cavalry. They were quick and lightly armed. They wore lighter chain mail than the crusaders and conical helmets that were often inscribed with inspirational words from the Koran. They carried small, round shields that were much less burdensome than the elongated kite-shaped shields used by the crusaders.

They fought with clubs, swords and lances, but their principal weapon was the bow and arrow. They were highly skilled and trained horsemen who had entirely mastered the art of shooting from the saddle – they could fire off arrows while

▼ *Two Turkish cavalrymen practise the use of sword and lance while on horseback. Both also carry a bow and a sheath of arrows. Wearing light armour, they were generally no match for the crusaders in close fighting.*

riding at full speed, and could even fire over their shoulders as they rode away, a version of the famous Parthian shot. The arrows they loosed were not highly penetrative, but they were fired in such numbers that they caused panic and disarray among the Christian armies – various accounts of battle liken the arrows to a plague of locusts, a storm of rain or a thick cloud that blocked out the sun.

SPEED AND MOBILITY

The use of long-range weapons, such as the bow and arrow, and the mobility of the cavalry were the key to the Turkish tactics. Typically they attacked in the rear and the flank of the crusader army. According to contemporary accounts, the Turkish horses were quicker and lighter than the crusader's animals; their speed and movement were a constant threat.

They tried to avoid encountering the European knights' mounted charge, since they were not heavily enough armed to fight on these terms; however, they saw that once the crusader knights had charged the line they tended to dissolve in disarray, leaving them vulnerable to counter-attack and leaving the European

infantry open to assault. A favourite stratagem, used effectively again and again, was to pretend to retreat, leading the European knights on and encouraging them to charge. The Muslim cavalry would then either draw the crusaders on into an ambush or turn quickly to launch a devastating counter-attack.

The heavily armoured and armed crusaders were stronger than the Muslims in close combat, so the Muslim tactics tended to avoid hand-to-hand fighting if they could by holding off and using the lightning cavalry attacks and bombardment with arrows to punish the Europeans; they would only commit to close-quarters combat when they could be confident of success. Eyewitness accounts of the Battle of Dorylaeum in 1097, during the First Crusade, reveal that the crusaders' long chain mail body armour provided a very

▲ *The crusaders were feared for their cavalry assault, but the Muslim warriors, on light and fast horses, were often able to outmanoeuvre them and drive them back.*

effective defence against the light swords carried by the Seljuks – and also against their arrows, unless these were fired from straight ahead when they were able to pierce the armour. If the crusaders were able to draw any of the attackers into close combat, they found they could usually get the upper hand.

FIGHTING IN GOD'S NAME

The Muslim armies were fighting to spread Islam through jihad, or holy war, just as the Christians had gone to war in the name of Christ. Eyewitness accounts of the Battle of the Field of Blood in 1119 reveal that prior to the battle the ra'is, or mayor, of Aleppo, Abu al-Fadi ibn al-Khashshab, rode out before Ilghazi's army and delivered a stirring speech, urging the soldiers to fight jihad without fear. His words reduced hardened soldiers to tears. Meanwhile, Prince Roger addressed his men as 'soldiers of Christ' and urged them to fight to the death if that were God's will.

Likewise, Norman eyewitness accounts of the earlier Battle of Dorylaeum in 1097 report that Seljuk Turks shouted as they came forward, 'calling in great voices in their own language a devilish word that I could not understand'. We know from Radulph of Caen, biographer of Tancred, that this word was 'Allachibar!' – far from devilish, it was a form of the Muslim holy words *Allah Akhbar* (God is Great). For their part, again according to eyewitness accounts, the crusaders were calling out 'God wills it!' 'God wills it!' as they fought.

◄ *The Turkish cavalrymen were renowned for their ability to fire arrows as they rode at full speed in battle. Feigning retreat, they often lured crusaders into rash charges.*

CALL TO A SECOND CRUSADE

BERNARD OF CLAIRVAUX APPEALS TO THE RULERS OF THE WEST

On 1 December 1145 Pope Eugenius III responded to the news that Turkish general Imad ed-Din Zengi had captured Edessa by calling a new crusade.

THE LOSS OF EDESSA

The first news of Edessa's fall had been brought back by pilgrims and then had been confirmed by Bishop Hugh of the Syrian town of Jabala, who was sent as part of an official embassy to Rome by Raymond of Antioch. In Italy, Bishop Hugh had an audience with the pope; he also informed the historian Otto of Friesling that a Christian king of India was ready to come to the aid of the crusader states – this was the first documented appearance of the enduring medieval myth of Prester John (*see* box).

▼ *'I opened my mouth; I preached; and the crusaders have multiplied beyond counting!' Peerless orator Bernard of Clairvaux casts his spell over a vast crowd at Vézelay.*

A CALL TO ARMS

Eugenius issued his rallying call in a bull, or papal letter, known as *Quantum praedecessores* and addressed to King Louis VII of France and his people. (Papal bulls were untitled and are named from their first words. In this case, *Quantum praedecessores nostri Romani pontifices* is the beginning of a phrase that translates 'The extent to which our predecessors the pontiffs of Rome did work to free the Eastern Church, we have learned from the accounts of older writers and by studying their deeds.') The bull recalled the heroic achievements of the crusaders of 1096–99 and offered remission (forgiveness) of sins for those who took the cross together with church protection of their possessions and relatives while they were away on crusade.

In France, King Louis was already planning a crusade, or perhaps a pilgrimage, and announced his plans at his court at Bourges at Christmas 1145, probably before hearing of Eugenius's bull. He encountered opposition at home, but after liaising with French preacher Abbot Bernard of Clairvaux, who referred him to the pope, Louis received Eugenius's enthusiastic blessing on the enterprise. The papal bull was reissued on 1 March 1146 and Bernard was authorized by the papacy to preach the crusade through Europe.

BERNARD PREACHES THE CRUSADE

On Easter Day 1146 Bernard preached before a vast crowd at Vézelay in central France. He was a great orator and he succeeded in whipping the crowd up into an absolute frenzy of enthusiasm. At the conclusion of his sermon, they leapt up almost to a man, shouting 'Crosses! Give us crosses!' Bernard had these prepared in advance, but even so he ran out – and reputedly then tore off his own clothing to make more crosses for the eager knights and infantrymen.

▲ *Frederick, Duke of Swabia, seen here being crowned emperor in 1155, took the cross at Spires in south-west Germany.*

Louis VII and his nobles were among those who took the cross: Louis received a cloth cross blessed by the pope, and people also flocked to the cause. Bernard wrote to the pope: 'I opened my mouth; I preached; and the crusaders have multiplied beyond counting. The countryside is deserted. You will hardly find one man for every seven womenfolk. In every place you will find widows whose husbands are far from dead.'

He continued the tour, preaching in Switzerland and Germany. Conrad III of Germany was initially unmoved by Bernard's pleas, but on Christmas Day at the Diet of Spires the abbot preached a second sermon to the German king, in which he took the part of Christ himself and asked Conrad directly: 'O Man, what should I have done for you that I have not

▼ *Louis VII, depicted here on his royal seal, was another head of state persuaded by Bernard of Clairvaux to take the cross.*

PRESTER JOHN

Legends of Prester John, a priest-king ruling over a Christian realm somewhere in the Orient, were popular from the 1100s until the 17th century.

The first mention of the king is found in the *Chronicon* of 1145 by Bishop Otto of Friesling, who reported that he had heard of the king from Bishop Hugh of Jaballa at the papal court in Viterbo, Italy, in that year. According to this version, the priest-king was a descendant of the Three Wise Men, or Magi, and after defeating the Muslim rulers of Persia had intended to free Jerusalem but had been waylaid by trouble crossing the River Tigris. The origin of the legend may have been in reports of successes against Muslim Persia by Central Asian Mongol rulers, one of whose queens and many of whose subjects were Christians.

The king soon became the subject of colourful legends that placed him in 'the three Indies' as ruler of a peaceful realm, sometimes said to contain the Fountain of Youth and to be adjacent to the Garden of Eden. One 12th-century document identified him as guardian of a

▲ *Prester John was still a legend around 1550 when he appeared as one of the wonders of the Orient on this mariners' chart of the Indian Ocean.*

shrine to the biblical apostle St Thomas at Mylapore, India. Later versions of the legend located Prester John's realm in Ethiopia. The goal of finding Prester John's kingdom inspired generations of eastbound adventurers, including the 13th-century Venetian, Marco Polo.

done?' Conrad was so deeply moved that he burst into tears: he and several of his noblemen, including Frederick, Duke of Swabia (later Emperor Frederick I Barbarossa), took the cross on the spot. Many ordinary Germans also joined up for the expedition.

As at the time of the First Crusade, the crusade sermons provoked anti-Jewish rioting in Germany. They were particularly inspired by an anti-Semitic monk named Rudolf who whipped up popular feeling by declaring that the Jews were not making any contribution to the rescue of the Holy Land. Abbot Bernard was eventually able to bring this outburst of violence to an end, persuading many of the rioters to join the official crusade, and ordering Rudolf to return to his monastery.

THE KINGS' CRUSADE

The departure date for the crusade was set for the summer of 1147. Bernard had recruited an impressive cast of Europe's royalty and nobility. In addition to two kings, Louis VII of France and Conrad III of Germany, Louis's wife, the celebrated Eleanor of Aquitaine and his brother Robert I of Dreux travelled on the crusade; other leading figures were William II, Count of Nevers; William of Warennes, 3rd Earl of Surrey; and Hugh VII 'the Brown' of Lusignan.

Another notable participant on the Second Crusade was Alfonso Jordan, a son of Raymond of Toulouse; Alfonso was born in Tripoli in 1103 but returned to Europe with his mother at the age of five and became Count of Toulouse.

CRUSADERS SET OUT

FROM EUROPE TO CONSTANTINOPLE

The armies of the Second Crusade set out in three waves in May and June 1147. The first departure in mid-May was from England and consisted of Norman, English, Scottish, Flemish and a few German crusaders. They were followed later the same month by a larger, mainly German army under Conrad III and then in June by a French force led by King Louis, containing armies from Aquitaine, Brittany, Burgundy and Lorraine.

EUROPEAN CRUSADES

In addition to its main theatre in the Holy Land, the Second Crusade had two European fronts, for Pope Eugenius also authorized holy wars in Germanic territories against the pagan Wends and in Spain against Muslims. He promised the knights

▼ *The first part of this itinerary to Jerusalem guides a prospective crusader from London to Dover. On the Second Crusade, many English knights travelled no farther than Lisbon in Portugal.*

and infantrymen who fought in these wars the same crusading indulgences he had offered for the war in the Holy Land.

The first wave of crusaders left England by sea, sailing around Brittany and the Iberian Peninsula, and were driven by bad weather to make landfall in June in Porto, where the local bishop persuaded them to make a diversion to Lisbon. There they backed King Alfonso I of Portugal in a four-month siege of the city, and looted it raucously after it fell on 24 October. Thereafter, some elected to remain in Portugal, and an English priest named Gilbert of Hastings was named the first Bishop of Lisbon, but most of the crusaders travelled on by sea to the Holy Land, departing in February 1148.

VIEW FROM THE EAST

In the Byzantine Empire memories of the First Crusade 50 years earlier were naturally still strong. When the new crusade was being planned, Emperor Manuel I Comnenus had given permission for its armies to pass through the empire, but he did not trust them – fearing that they had designs on his territories. He broke off a war against the Seljuk sultanate of Rum in spring 1147, signing a peace treaty with Sultan Mesud I, so that he could give his full attention to defending his lands against the crusaders.

The Muslim scholar and writer Ibn al-Qalanisi, mayor and chronicler of Damascus, described the sense of mounting fear in Syria as news filtered through that another wave of crusaders was about to break in the Holy Land. He wrote: 'The news was coming in from Constantinople, from the lands of the Franks and from neighbouring countries, too, that the kings of the Franks were travelling from their homeland to attack the land of Islam. They had left their own lands empty, without defenders, and brought with them great wealth.'

▲ *Manuel I Comnenus managed the Second Crusade's passage through his lands very successfully. He was reputedly a great jouster and fearsome warrior.*

THE PROGRESS OF THE GERMANS

The German army travelled by land through Hungary without much incident. Alongside Conrad in the royal party were his nephew, the haughty Frederick, Duke of Swabia, and the kings of Poland and Bohemia. Some contemporary accounts reported excitedly that this force numbered as many as one million, but in truth it was probably only about 20,000 strong. Before passing into Bulgaria, then part of the Byzantine Empire, Conrad swore an oath of loyalty to Byzantine emperor Manuel I Comnenus, pledging that he would do nothing likely to harm the emperor or his territory.

The army was given a Byzantine military escort, but this did not prevent it pillaging and looting as it went. At Philippopolis (modern Plovdiv, Bulgaria) a riot erupted after crusaders accused a local of witchcraft, and the outer part of

▲ *Kneeling humbly, King Louis VII receives a pilgrim's staff from Pope Eugenius III in the abbey church of St Denis in June 1147.*

the town was burned to the ground; then at Adrianople (modern Edirne, western Turkey), local robbers killed a German noble outside a monastery and Frederick of Swabia launched murderous reprisals, burning down the monastery and killing all the monks. Conrad then ignored the emperor's request to pass into Anatolia by the Dardanelles, and instead marched the ill-disciplined troop to Constantinople, where they arrived in mid-September.

KING LOUIS THE PILGRIM

On 8 June 1147 King Louis VII formally handed control of France to Abbot Suger of St Denis in a candle-lit service at the abbey church attended by the pope. Dressed as a pilgrim in a black tunic with red cross, Louis received the pope's blessing and, before a cheering congregation, was handed a pilgrim's staff and wallet. Leaving from Metz, the French army marched in the wake of Conrad's German

force across Hungary, with the contingent from Lorraine marching ahead of the main force. The Provençal army under Alfonso of Toulouse waited behind, having decided to depart in August and go by sea.

In early October the French army arrived at Constantinople. There was some trouble at first, when the contingent from Lorraine clashed with the rear of Conrad's army outside the walls of Constantinople. But the Germans were already in the process of moving on, at the emperor's insistence, into Anatolia. In addition, some of the French wanted to attack the city on the grounds that the emperor had made a truce with the Seljuks, but the papal legates restored peace. King Louis was royally welcomed and entertained within the city. Manuel prevailed on him to swear an oath under which the crusaders would return to the Byzantine Empire any lands they captured on the crusade.

Troops from Savoy, Montferrat and Auvergne joined up with Louis at Constantinople. They had come overland through Italy, then by sea from Brindisi to Byzantine territory. Thus bolstered, the

French army travelled across the Bosphorus into Anatolia. Unlike his grandfather Alexius at the time of the First Crusade, Manuel did not provide the crusaders with an army. The French marched on, accompanied only by a few Byzantine scouts, to meet their fate.

▼ *Abbot Suger acted as co-regent during the reign of Louis VII, when the king was absent on the Second Crusade.*

DISASTER AT DORYLAEUM
AND THE CRUSADERS' DIFFICULT PROGRESS TO ATTALIA

At Dorylaeum, the scene of the European armies' first victory in 1097 during the First Crusade, the bulk of the German army suffered a devastating defeat at the hands of the Seljuks, led by Kilij Arslan II, the son of the Seljuk ruler defeated there in 1097.

▼ *Warrior of the cross. Conrad survived defeat at Dorylaeum and a serious illness to take part in the final stages of the crusade.*

DIVIDED AND DEFEATED

When the German army reached Nicaea, Conrad decided to split it in two. He sent the largely non-combatant contingent of pilgrims led by Bishop Otto of Friesing, along a safer, but longer, route through Byzantine territory, while he and his army headed straight across Anatolia towards the Seljuk realm. Meanwhile, Seljuk scouts were keeping close tabs on the German progress. The main German army stopped to rest at Dorylaeum after a gruelling march and were ill-prepared for the Seljuk attack when it came out of the blue.

In the battle, the Europeans were out-thought and outmanoeuvred. The Seljuks once again tricked the European warriors by feigning retreat, luring the German knights into what they thought was a triumphant charge – only to be surrounded and utterly defeated by the Seljuks. The German army was virtually wiped out at a stroke. Conrad, Frederick and a few survivors, at most a tenth of the original army, began the retreat to Constantinople.

FRENCH PROGRESS

At Nicaea the German survivors joined up with the French army under Louis. They then marched along the western, largely coastal route already followed by Bishop Otto of Friesing as far as Ephesus. Conrad fell badly ill and was forced to return to Constantinople to convalesce; he was cared for there under the personal supervision of Manuel.

The French force marched on and succeeded in defeating a Turkish army in a minor skirmish outside Ephesus. As they pressed on through difficult winter conditions, under constant harassment by the Turks, discipline became ragged and morale very low.

In the region of Laodicea (near modern Denizli, in south-western Turkey) on 8 January 1148 the French army suffered a heavy defeat at the hands of the Turks. This setback came just a few days after a similarly damaging defeat nearby for the pilgrim contingent under Bishop Otto von Friesing.

RAYMOND OF ANTIOCH

Raymond of Poitiers took power as Prince of Antioch in 1136 on his marriage to the 10-year-old Constance, daughter of and heir to Bohemond II of Antioch, and was co-ruler with Constance. Raymond was the second son of William IX, Duke of Aquitaine and Count of Poitou, the French nobleman celebrated as the first troubadour poet, and was uncle to Duke William's granddaughter, Eleanor of Aquitaine. His rule in Antioch was not successful, for he was twice forced to pay homage to the Byzantine emperor and was unable to contain the threat of Nur ed-Din. Moreover he failed to divert the Second Crusade towards an attack on Nur ed-Din's powerbase at Aleppo.

Raymond was, however, one of the greatest courtly noblemen of his time. William of Tyre described him as being 'of noble descent, tall and stylish in figure, the finest-looking of earthly princes, a man of great charm and wit, generous and magnificent beyond measure.' Raymond was also a patron of literature – he was responsible for funding the composition of the crusade poem the *Chanson des chétifs*. He was a most generous host when Louis VII and Eleanor of Aquitaine made their visit during the Second Crusade – to the extent that rumours ran rife that he was Eleanor's lover. William of Tyre rehearsed this story, but modern historians tend to discount it as being unfounded.

BY SEA FROM ATTALIA

Louis and the survivors pressed doggedly on until they reached the port of Attalia (modern Antalya), close to where Byzantine territory gave way to Seljuk lands. Food was short, the army starving and desperate. The plan had been for the whole army to embark by sea from Attalia for Syria, but the fleet supplied by Emperor Manuel was far too small.

Louis took the available ships for himself, his household and the leading knights and essentially abandoned the remainder of the army to its fate. Although he left money with the Governor of Attalia to feed them, the soldiers and pilgrims had little alternative but to press on by land largely unprotected by knights through dangerous Seljuk territory to Tarsus. Most of the army's remnant was killed before reaching Tarsus.

Meanwhile Louis and his elite corps reached St Simeon, and were received with lavish hospitality by Raymond of Antioch. Escorted by Raymond, they arrived – exhausted and weary of both battles and voyaging – at the capital of the principality on 19 March.

▼ *King Louis, Conrad and the leading lords of Outremer arrive in Antioch. Here they took time to recover from the hardships of campaign, and debate the crusade's future.*

▲ *The main part of the French army had to make its own way, without king or knights, to Tarsus, travelling through country that had been the ruin of many before them.*

IN ANTIOCH

Louis considered what to do next. Raymond was keen to divert what force remained in the crusade against the rising power of Nur ed-Din, the Zengid ruler of Aleppo in Syria. Joscelin of Edessa, meanwhile, urged Louis to make the reconquest of Edessa his primary goal, arguing that the fall of Edessa had precipitated the crusade and therefore its recovery should be the expedition's primary goal. Louis himself was preoccupied by his pilgrim's vows and wanted to press on to Jerusalem.

For a while the French lords and their ladies enjoyed the comforts of court life. Louis's wife, the intelligent and fiercely independent Eleanor of Aquitaine, was a keen advocate of her uncle Raymond's policy; in later years it was alleged that she was having an incestuous love affair in Antioch at this time with Raymond. But Louis was not minded to listen to her and when Fulk, the Patriarch of Jerusalem, arrived with an invitation from Queen Melisende and King Baldwin III, urging Louis's presence in Jerusalem, the French king began to make preparations for his departure. The royal couple argued – Eleanor stating that she would remain behind in Antioch and ask for a divorce. Louis reportedly dragged Eleanor forcibly out of the palace and made her come with him to Acre. Eleanor was not the only one who was angry – Raymond refused to take any part in the remainder of the crusade.

THE COUNCIL OF ACRE

AND THE HUMILIATING SIEGE OF DAMASCUS

When King Louis VII and Eleanor arrived in Acre, a great council was convened there on St John's Day (24 June) 1148 to discuss the future direction of the crusade. At this council the assembled lords agreed to attack Damascus, and the abject failure of this expedition was to bring the Second Crusade to an end.

CRUSADERS IN JERUSALEM

By the time Louis reached Acre, the remnants of the German pilgrim contingent under Bishop Otto had reached Jerusalem. Also in the Holy City was their king, Conrad III, who had recovered in Constantinople from his sickness and sailed directly as far as Tyre before travelling on to Jerusalem.

Other crusader groups had also made it to the Holy Land. Those who remained of the first wave of crusaders who had fought in the siege of Lisbon had arrived by sea, and the Provençal army that had

▼ On three thrones, Louis VII of France, Conrad III of Germany and Baldwin III of Jerusalem hold court at the Council of Acre.

▲ This illustration from William of Tyre's History of Outremer (c.1280) shows the three kings at Acre and, below, the siege of Damascus that they decided to attempt.

departed under Alfonso Jordan, Count of Toulouse, had landed. Alfonso almost immediately met his end, reputedly poisoned while at Caesarea by Raymond II, Count of Tripoli, who was fearful that Alfonso had come to claim the lands in Tripoli he had held in his infancy as the legitimate son of Raymond of Toulouse. (Count Raymond II was, in fact, Raymond

of Toulouse's great-grandson, descended through an illegitimate brother of Alfonso Jordan named Bertrand of Toulouse. This made him Alfonso Jordan's great-nephew.)

The council in Acre was officially a meeting of the High Court of the Kingdom of Jerusalem. In attendance were: Queen Melisende and her son King Baldwin of Jerusalem; Manasses of Hierges, the constable of Jerusalem; Patriarch Fulk of Jerusalem; Louis VII; Conrad III; Bishop Otto of Freising; Duke Frederick of Swabia; and Henry II, Margrave of Austria. In addition, the masters of the military orders were there – Robert of Craon, master of the Knights Templar, and Raymond du Puy of Provence, master of the Knights Hospitaller. Other leading nobles of Outremer at the council included Walter Grenier, lord of Caesarea, Philip of Milly, lord of Nablus and Humphrey II, lord of Toron; but none of the lords of Antioch, Tripoli or Edessa were in attendance.

King Baldwin and the Knights Templar urged an attack on Damascus. Several local lords argued against this line of action, particularly on the grounds that

Mu'in ad-Din Unur, emir of Damascus, was an ally of the Christians against the Zengid lords of Syria – including the increasingly formidable Nur ed-Din of Aleppo. King Louis and King Conrad, however, were persuaded to back the attack on Damascus; the European lords, unversed in local politics and diplomacy, could not readily accept arguments in favour of making alliances with Muslim rulers and wanted principally to pursue a holy war against 'the infidel'. Moreover, while Aleppo meant nothing to them, Damascus was a city they knew from the Bible. An army was raised and in July assembled at Tiberias.

THE ORCHARDS OF DAMASCUS

The crusader lords decided to attack Damascus from the west, where a thick band of orchards would provide them with a steady food supply. They arrived there on 23 July, with the troops of the Kingdom of Jerusalem leading the way, followed by Louis and the French and then Conrad and the remainder of the German contingent in the rear. Emir Unur was warned of their approach, and had poisoned water sources, taken steps to strengthen his fortifications and sent out appeals for help to rival Muslim lords.

Taking the orchards was the crusaders' first task, but it was not an easy one: according to William of Tyre, they stretched for more than five miles 'like a dense, gloomy forest', the trees growing close together and accessible only by way of narrow footpaths between mud walls; in addition, there were defensive towers set at regular intervals. The crusaders poured into this difficult terrain, losing many men to arrow shots from the towers or to sudden attacks with spears from the darkness between the trees. They also had to face the city defenders who poured out of Damascus across the Barada river.

Both sides fought fiercely – according to a contemporary account, Conrad III made himself the talk of the entire army by dealing an overwhelming blow to a Turkish warrior that sliced through his

entire body, cutting off his head, neck and left shoulder. By the end of July 24 the crusaders had prevailed, taking control of the orchards and driving the Damascene defenders back behind their city walls.

Within the city, the people began to build barricades in the streets, fearing that they would be overrun. But at this point the crusaders paid the price for not encircling the city, for a relief army began to arrive from Aleppo in response to Emir Unur's cry for help – and this force, approaching from the north, was able to march right up to the city and enter through its North Gate. They began to launch counter-attacks on the Christian position in the orchards.

EASTERN APPROACHES

On 27 July the crusader lords took the fateful decision to move the army around the city to its open east side. Here they thought they might better be able to defend their camp. But – as they discovered the moment they arrived – there was

▲ *The crusader armies fought bravely at Damascus, but were undone by their leaders' bad tactical and strategic decisions.*

little or no food or water available there, and the eastern section of the city wall was very heavily fortified.

The crusaders and their leaders must have looked about in dismay. They could not return to the orchards, for by this stage Nur ed-Din himself had arrived and encamped his army there. In the burning heat of July, with insufficient water and the city strongly reinforced, their chances of taking Damascus had melted away; their position became untenable.

At dawn on 28 July, the Christian army began to abandon the siege, retreating in despair and disarray, harried all the way by the Turks. They lost many more men and horses during this humiliating retreat, and according to local chroniclers the human and animal corpses that lined the road sent up a stench powerful enough to make birds fall from the sky.

DESPAIR AND RECRIMINATIONS
THE AFTERMATH OF THE SECOND CRUSADE'S FAILURE

The crusaders' shambolic retreat from Damascus spelled the end of the Second Crusade, which fell apart in bitter recriminations. The failure of this enterprise had important and enduring consequences for the crusader states of Outremer and for their relations with the kingdoms of Europe.

In the immediate aftermath of Damascus, unity among the Christian forces was destroyed. Conrad took his troops to Ascalon, with the plan of taking that important port, but when none of the other parts of the army came to his aid he had to make another retreat. He headed home in September, but broke his journey to spend Christmas 1148 as a guest of Emperor Manuel in Constantinople. Louis, meanwhile, returned to Jerusalem. He did not embark for Europe until June 1149, then stopped on the way with King Roger of Sicily in Calabria, and with Pope Eugenius in Rome, before arriving back in Paris on 11 November.

THE FAULT OF OUTREMER LORDS
The crusaders felt bitterness towards both the native lords of Outremer and the Greeks of the Byzantine Empire. They asked how it was that the army had abandoned its hard-won position of strength in the orchards of Damascus, with the city almost at their mercy, to occupy an exposed and badly supplied position on the city's east side. They blamed the decision on bad advice from local lords, and began to circulate allegations that these lords had deliberately thrown away the military advantage.

One theory was that the lords had been outraged on discovering that the crusaders planned to grant the city to Count Thierry of Flanders and had secretly plotted to scupper the attack for this reason; another was that the lords were in league with Emir Unur of Damascus and had received payment for their part in making the siege

▲ *St Bernard of Clairvaux was a great teacher and inspiring preacher, but his reputation was ultimately damaged by the failure of the enterprise that he had done so much to instigate.*

fail. A third theory was that the lords had been plotting with Raymond of Antioch, who was still fuming at Louis's decision not to help him against Aleppo.

One of the central complaints of the crusaders was that both the lords of Outremer and the Byzantines had entered into alliances with Muslim rulers – in the case of Jerusalem with Emir Unur of Damascus, in the case of the Byzantine Empire with the Seljuk sultan Mesud I. This was inexplicable to the crusaders, fired as they were by the rhetoric of Bernard of Clairvaux.

BYZANTINE TREACHERY

The crusaders also had a string of complaints against Emperor Manuel and the Greeks of the Byzantine Empire. Some claimed that Byzantine scouts had deliberately led the German army into a Seljuk ambush at Dorylaeum – they asked whether perhaps Emperor Manuel had agreed this deal as part of the treaty he signed with Seljuks in 1147. In addition, they bemoaned the lack of support from Constantinople during the march of the French army across Anatolia and the fact that the fleet sent to King Louis in the port of Attalia was too small even for the much reduced army that had made it that far. Odo of Deuil, Louis VII's chaplain on the crusade, claimed that Manuel had betrayed the crusaders because Louis was an ally of Manuel's enemy Roger of Sicily.

CRITICISM IN EUROPE

In Europe Bernard of Clairvaux was at a loss fully to explain how the enterprise he had promoted as being devised and blessed in heaven could end in such abject failure. He attempted to blame the treachery of the Byzantines, but also said that the failure must have occurred because the sins of the crusaders had caused God to withdraw his support. Bernard participated in an attempt, driven by Abbot Suger of St Denis, to start a new crusade; at a meeting in Chartres in 1150, Bernard himself was elected leader of the enterprise. However, it came to nothing. Bernard was by now around 60 years old and having undergone many severe austerities as part of his spiritual life was far too frail to become a warrior monk.

Wider attempts to understand the crusade's failure led to criticism of almost all its aspects in Europe. There was denunciation of those, including Bernard, who had preached the enterprise. The anonymous Annalist of Wurzburg in Germany declared that the crusade preachers were 'witnesses of anti-Christ' who had misled good Christian folk. Other critics blamed the crusade leaders or the greed of Frankish lords in Outremer.

One idea with important consequences was that the considerable number of non-combatant pilgrims who had accompanied the crusade had been a major hindrance. The preaching of later crusades was focused more narrowly on mobilizing knights and infantry and avoided stirring up the passions of the people; indeed, after this crusade attempts were made to prevent pilgrims who could not fight or support themselves from travelling with armies to the East.

A WEAKENED OUTREMER

In the wake of the crusade's failure, the Kingdom of Jerusalem was in a far weaker position. The attack on Damascus had destroyed a valuable alliance, boosted Muslim morale and greatly strengthened the position of Nur ed-Din.

Moreover, the souring of relations between the crusader kingdoms and Europe meant that the leading knights among the European nobility were far less willing than previously to come to the aid of Outremer. Crusading and making a pilgrimage to the Holy Land suffered a severe decline in popularity. The success of the First Crusade had give the idea glamour and force, but these were dissipated by the failure of the Second. William of Tyre commented that after the Second Crusade Europeans 'looked askance at our leaders' ways' and 'showed complete indifference about the business of the kingdom'; this attitude spread – 'their influence caused others who had not been there to loosen their love for the kingdom' and so 'fewer folk, and those less committed in spirit, made the pilgrimage after this time'.

A QUARREL WITH CONSEQUENCES

The violent quarrel between Louis VII and his wife, Eleanor of Aquitaine, in Antioch during the Second Crusade had consequences that were still being felt in Europe in the 15th century. Eleanor tried but failed to get Pope Eugenius to grant a divorce on the couple's way home, but in March 1152 an annulment was granted on the basis of consanguinity (they were third cousins, once removed, as common descendants of Robert II of France). Just six weeks later, Eleanor married Henry, Count of Anjou and Duke of Normandy, who would become King Henry II of England in 1154. Because under Aquitaine law women would inherit property and her father's will had specified that the duchy should remain in the hands of her heirs, Eleanor brought vast and wealthy possessions in south-western France into the hands of the English crown.

▶ *Louis VII was both learned and devout. His wife, Eleanor, is said to have declared that she had thought she was marrying a king but found she had married a monk.*

Disputes over this land between England and France led to centuries of conflict, running right down to the Hundred Years War of 1337–1453. The royal couple had certainly begun to be estranged before travelling on the Second Crusade, but the quarrel in Antioch appears to have been a decisive moment, marking a split from which they did not recover.

NUR ED-DIN AND A UNIFIED SYRIA

MUSLIMS UNITE IN JIHAD

Buoyed by the abject failure of the Second Crusade, Nur ed-Din, whose personal reputation was enhanced by his part in driving back the crusaders at Damascus, prepared a new attack on the Principality of Antioch. His ultimate goal, however, was to capture Damascus and so unite Syria.

THE RISE OF NUR ED-DIN

Nur ed-Din was born in 1118, the second son of the great Turkish Muslim general Imad ed-Din Zengi, ruler of Aleppo and Mosul in Syria. On his father's death in 1146, Nur ed-Din took power in Aleppo while his brother Saif ed-Din became the ruler of Mosul. Nur ed-Din was already establishing himself as a scourge of the crusader lords, capturing a number of castles in the Principality of Antioch and also in November 1146 defeating an attempt by Joscelin of Courtenay, the ousted count of Edessa, to recapture his capital. In 1147 he formed an alliance with Emir Unur of

▼ *Knights ride out to battle in Syria. Nur ed-Din plotted his rise to power carefully, using diplomacy as much as warfare.*

Damascus as part of an attempt to create a united Muslim front against the advancing crusaders, but the two leaders were suspicious of each other's motives. Nevertheless, in 1148, as we have seen, Nur ed-Din came to Emir Unur's rescue when he brought his army to relieve the ill-conceived siege of Damascus that had been mounted by the crusader lords.

In the wake of the events at Damascus, Nur ed-Din's name was trumpeted far and wide. It was proclaimed that the crusaders had fled at the approach of his army. The victory of the city's defenders was recorded and celebrated as a triumph of jihad.

VICTORY IN ANTIOCH

In 1149, with help from Emir Unur of Damascus, he moved against Antioch, attacking the crusader castle of Inab in the Principality. Raymond, Prince of Antioch, rode out with an army to defend the citadel and was heavily defeated on 29 June 1149. Raymond was killed during the battle; afterward his head was cut off by Nur ed-Din's general Shirkuh and despatched by Nur ed-Din in a silver casket to the Abbasid caliph of Baghdad.

▲ *A wall painting depicts Templar Hugh IX the Brown of Lusignan, who died at Damietta on the Fifth Crusade. Nur ed-Din's campaigns had strengthened the Muslim defence for 40 years after his death.*

This victory put much of the territory of the principality in Nur ed-Din's hands and he marked his triumph by marching as far as the sea and having a celebratory swim in the Mediterranean. He did not move against the city of Antioch itself, however. He possessed the Principality east of the Orontes River and seemingly was happy for the capital of the state to remain in crusader hands: perhaps he did not want to get drawn into conflict over its possession with the Byzantine Empire, for Emperor Manuel Comnenus claimed it as his possession.

In 1149 Nur ed-Din's brother Saif ed-Din died and was succeeded as ruler of Mosul by another brother, Qutb ed-Din. The new ruler recognized Nur ed-Din as overlord of Mosul. Nur ed-Din's main concern was now to take control of Damascus and so create a united Muslim Syria.

TRIUMPH IN DAMASCUS

He besieged Damascus four times in 1150–54 without launching an assault on the city. By this time, Mu'in ad-Din Unur had died and been succeeded by a weaker ruler, Mujir ad-Din, who agreed to pay tribute to the king of Jerusalem. Finally, in 1154, the people and the garrison turned against their ruler, who they felt had betrayed Islam by making a demeaning treaty with the Christians, and opened the city gates to Nur ed-Din.

For once, the end of a siege was not marked by rioting and bloodshed. Nur ed-Din promised the leading citizens that he would protect their livelihoods; he provided food for the poor. He even cut taxes, and began a public building programme.

Nur ed-Din proceeded with caution. He did not march on Jerusalem, in fact he reaffirmed the treaty that had caused controversy and continued to pay tribute. He went on chipping away at the crusaders, in 1157 besieging the Knights Hospitaller at the Castle of Banias and trouncing a

▲ *Nur ed-Din besieged the formidable walls of Damascus four times. A map from 1620 shows what a challenge this was.*

▼ *The leaning minaret, 170ft (52m) high, is all that remains of the mosque of Nur ed-Din at Mosul in Syria.*

relief army despatched from Jerusalem. In 1160 he captured Reynald of Châtillon, Prince of Antioch, who he kept in prison for 16 years. He also became involved in conflicts to the north, in 1159 agreeing an alliance with the Byzantine emperor Manuel Comnenus against the Seljuk Turks and the same year mounting an attack on the Seljuk sultan Kilij Arslan II.

THE RULE OF NUR ED-DIN

Nur ed-Din was celebrated for his piety and his just rule. A staunch follower of Sunni Islam, he did not make personal use of the wealth he generated through conquest, but poured it into the building of mosques, madrasas (religious schools), hospitals, public baths and caravansaries (lodges for Islamic travellers). He established fairer taxation and an effective civil service and justice system. He also built a network of khanqas, centres for Sufis, followers of a mystical branch of Islam. And he improved communication by introducing the use of carrier pigeons.

SUFISM

This branch of Islam outlines a path to God through self-purification, inner exploration and mystical experience. It probably developed at some time under the Umayyad caliphate in AD660-750, although all Sufi traditions trace their history right back to the time of the Prophet Muhammad (c.AD570-632); teachings were reputedly passed down the generations from master to pupil. Early Sufis were careful to stress their path as a complementary way to God alongside the Shariah (religious law), but from the late 12th century onwards Sufism and Shariah began to separate. Sufism is known for its magnificent collections of religious love poetry.

THE BATTLE FOR EGYPT

SYRIA LOOKS TO EXTEND MUSLIM POWER

In 1162, with Syria secure against intervention from the crusader lords, Nur ed-Din went on pilgrimage to Mecca. He had achieved his ambition of uniting Syria. His eyes – and those of his nominal masters, the Abbasid caliphs of Baghdad – began to turn to Egypt, and to view the possibility of overthrowing the Shi'ite Fatimid caliphate there and establishing a united Sunni Muslim state of Syria and Egypt. The same year, a new king mounted the throne in Jerusalem – Amalric I, brother of Baldwin III.

POWER STRUGGLE IN CAIRO

In Egypt, although rule was nominally by the religious leader or caliph, real power lay in the hands of the chief administrator, or vizier. In 1163, at a time when the caliph was the inexperienced 14-year-old al-Adid, the vizier Shawar was ousted and replaced by Dirgham. King Amalric of Jerusalem, seeing an opportunity,

mounted an expedition into Egypt claiming that the Fatimids were not paying tribute that had been pledged during the reign of Baldwin III. This campaign failed and he was forced to withdraw to Jerusalem. Meanwhile, Shawar visited the court of Nur ed-Din begging for military help to restore himself to power, and offering lavish rewards.

In 1164 Nur ed-Din sent an army under his leading general Asad ed-Din Shirkuh bin Shadhi to Egypt. Shirkuh had risen from relatively humble origins by dint of his energy, leadership qualities and military excellence. His name, of Kurdish-Iranian origin, meant 'Mountain Lion'. William of Tyre described him as a short and 'very stout' man, and already in the early 1160s 'advanced in years', with a cataract in one eye; he presented him as a formidable leader, experienced in military affairs, possessed of 'great endurance in the face of hardships' and beloved of his

men because of his profound generosity. With him to Egypt rode his nephew, Salah ed-Din Yusuf (later known as Saladin).

Shirkuh did his job: Dirgham was killed and Shawar reinstated. But at once Shawar reneged on his promises and entered an alliance with Amalric against the Syrians. Amalric invaded Egypt once more and with Shawar's troops besieged Shirkuh in the fortress of Bilbeis.

CRUSADERS HUMILIATED IN ANTIOCH

In response, Nur ed-Din launched an attack on the Principality of Antioch, where he besieged the castle of Harim and won a crushing victory against the crusader armies of Tripoli and Antioch. He

▼ *Qalaat ar-Rahba in Syria was one of the strongholds of the 'Mountain Lion' Asad ed-Din Shirkuh, general in the service of Nur ed-Din and uncle of the great Saladin.*

captured a roll-call of crusader lords: Bohemond III, Prince of Antioch; Raymond III, Count of Tripoli; Joscelin III, Count of Edessa; and French nobleman Hugh VIII of Lusignan, who had recently arrived on pilgrimage. Nur ed-Din had them all led in chains into Aleppo and cast into jail there. As many as 10,000 were killed in the crusader army, according to the Arab historian Ibn al-Athir.

But Nur ed-Din did not capture Antioch itself; it remained officially a Byzantine possession and he did not want to provoke Emperor Manuel Comnenus, with whom he had lately agreed a treaty. He did, however, capture Banias, and then kept up a constant harrying of the crusader states for the following two years. Meanwhile in Egypt, Amalric and Shirkuh made terms, agreeing to lift the siege and return home.

EGYPTIAN BATTLES

But in 1167 Shirkuh and Saladin invaded Egypt again. They were followed by Amalric's army in 1167. Initially there was a stand-off between the Christians and Shirkuh's army at Cairo. Shirkuh offered Shawar the chance to make a deal and unite against the crusaders, but he turned it down and instead renewed his alliance with Amalric. Shirkuh then led his men south, followed by the crusader army. The

▲ *View of Cairo and the valley of the River Nile from the citadel constructed in the city by Saladin after he became vizier of Egypt.*

two sides fought without clear result: Shirkuh occupied Alexandria, where he was welcomed by the largely Sunni Muslim population, but was then besieged by the crusader army.

Shirkuh broke out of the city in the hope that the crusader troops would follow him and engage in battle. But they sat tight, and Saladin was left in control of a starving population within the besieged city. Finally the standoff was broken not by a battle, but a truce; Saladin played no small part in brokering a deal under which both leaders took their armies home.

THE TAKING OF CAIRO

In 1168 Amalric entered an alliance with the Byzantine Empire and invaded Egypt once more. He captured Bilbeis, massacred the inhabitants and then besieged Cairo. Shawar changed sides once more, turning to Nur ed-Din and the great Shirkuh for help. Shirkuh and Saladin responded with all speed to the summons, marching south with an army containing 8,000 cavalry. The crusader army, badly outnumbered, withdrew once more and Shirkuh entered Cairo in triumph on 9 January 1169.

THE KURDS

Originally a pastoral people living in the mountains to the north and north east of what is now Iraq, the Kurds were subjects of the Abbasid Empire who established independent warrior principalities when the power of Baghdad waned in the 11th century. These states were overwhelmed by the invasion of the Seljuk Turks, but in the 12th century the Kurds rose to prominence again as soldiers of fortune in the pay of the Syrian rulers Imad ed-Din Zengi and Nur ed-Din. The brothers Najm ed-Din Ayub and Asad ed-Din Shirkuh made their names under Nur ed-Din: Ayub was governor of Damascus while Shirkuh was Nur ed-Din's leading general. Saladin was Ayub's son.

▼ *Kurdish mounted warriors battle against Arab counterparts.*

At first Shirkuh dealt amicably with Shawar, but then, ten days later, Shawar was killed after Saladin and his associates dragged him from his horse and had him beheaded – notionally on the orders of the caliph. Shirkuh then became vizier of Egypt. But within thee months Shirkuh had died, reportedly from overeating, and Saladin was in power in his place.

THE CHIVALROUS INFIDEL

SALADIN

Saladin was undoubtedly the leading Muslim figure of the entire crusading era. He inspired fear and awestruck admiration among the Westerners he repeatedly defeated in battle, while his magnanimous behaviour in victory won him a reputation as a chivalrous infidel, a seeming contradiction in contemporary Christian terms. He rose from relatively humble origins to become ruler of Egypt and Syria, and won undying fame in the Muslim world as the man who recaptured the Holy City of Jerusalem from the crusaders.

SALADIN'S YOUTH AND RISE TO PROMINENCE

The son of Najm ed-Din Ayub, governor of Damascus, Saladin lived as a young man at the splendid court of Nur ed-Din in that city, studying Islamic law, rhetoric and Arabic grammar, and developing a reputation as a brilliant all-rounder. Hee was a refined courtier who was skilled in debate, elegant in conversation, well versed in the traditions and military achievements of the Arab tribes, knowledgeable about the genealogies of the finest Arabian horses and a superb player of polo. This game was the equivalent at

▼ *Saladin was reputed to be equally at home pursuing learned discussion at court as he was directing armies in battle and making strategic decisions on campaign.*

Muslim courts of the chivalric tournament in Europe, a proving ground for young lords and a way of making a reputation among the political–military elite: Saladin achieved the distinction of being invited to join Nur ed-Din's own polo team.

He served his military apprenticeship in the service of his uncle Shirkuh, already established as Nur ed-Din's foremost general. Alongside Shirkuh he invaded Egypt three times, in 1164, 1167 and 1168–69. On the second of these occasions, Saladin was in command of the city of Alexandria while it was besieged by the crusader army – he later recalled: 'I endured many hardships at Alexandria that I can never forget.' Subsequently he took a leading role in the negotiations that brought the siege to an end and allowed both the Syrian and the crusader armies to go home with heads held high.

During these negotiations, Saladin's skill and nobility of character greatly impressed the crusader lords; he spent some time in the crusader camp after the siege was lifted, and according to some accounts was knighted by Humphrey II of Toron, Constable of the Kingdom of Jerusalem. The enduring myth of Saladin the infidel knight was born at this time.

VIZIER OF EGYPT

During the invasion of 1168–69, Saladin killed the vizier of Egypt, Shawar, and General Shirkuh became vizier in his place. When Shirkuh died on 22 March 1169 Saladin triumphed in politics within the Syrian army and took power for himself.

Saladin had triumphed in Egypt as a soldier of Syrian ruler Nur ed-Din, but his relationship with his nominal overlord became increasingly strained as it grew clear that Saladin was determined to rule in Cairo on his own terms, independently of influence from Damascus. In particular, he refrained from immediately removing the Shi'ite Fatimid caliph, while Nur ed-

▲ *Saladin gives thanks to Allah after his conquest of Jerusalem returned the city to Muslim control.*

Din was impatient for Sunni Islam to be imposed on Egypt. Finally, in September 1171, when the Fatimid caliph al-Adid died, Saladin abolished the Fatimid caliphate and proclaimed the name of the Abbasid caliph of Baghdad, Al-Mustadi.

Saladin's barely concealed ambition was to unite Egypt and Syria in an Islamic empire. He had been joined in Egypt by his father, a trusted intimate of Nur ed-Din, and on his father's advice did not make open moves against Syria and publicly behaved as if he were no more than Nur ed-Din's servant. But Nur ed-Din was not fooled and his anger with Saladin grew, especially when Saladin twice retreated from invasions of the crusader Kingdom of Jerusalem that he had been ordered to undertake. A clash between the two was averted in 1174, when Nur ed-Din, preparing to invade Egypt, died of a fever resulting from a throat infection.

The heir to Damascus was Nur ed-Din's ten-year-old son, al-Salih, and Syrian emirs began a scramble for power. Saladin marched on Damascus, according to some accounts following an invitation from local lords. His reputation went before him: when he arrived in October 1174, he was welcomed into the city by the people. He bolstered his position by marrying Nur ed-Din's widow and reinforced his popularity among his devoutly Muslim populace by vigorously promoting himself as a committed leader of jihad against the crusaders. Initially he did not have authority over Syria's other leading centres of power, but he imposed his authority on Aleppo in 1176 and on Mosul in 1186. By this stage he was close to his ultimate victory over the Kingdom of Jerusalem.

CONFLICT WITH JERUSALEM

Saladin had been reluctant to attack the Kingdom of Jerusalem while Nur ed-Din was alive: he was well aware that if he attacked from Egypt in the south while Nur ed-Din invaded from Syria, their combined force could wipe the crusader state off the map – but the outcome would then have been that Nur ed-Din, officially still Saladin's overlord, would have become immeasurably more powerful. But after Nur ed-Din's death, any victory over Jerusalem was only going to boost Saladin's own power base; moreover, he had committed himself to attack the crusaders by public proclamations of his enthusiasm for jihad.

In November 1177 he marched north from Egypt against the Kingdom of Jerusalem. The new king of Jerusalem, Baldwin IV, who had succeeded his father Amalric I in 1174, had installed himself with 375 knights at Ascalon expecting a siege; but Saladin bypassed the city, sending a force to surround it, and moved on towards Jerusalem itself. Baldwin bravely broke out through the surrounding army and rode with a force of about 80 Knights Templar and a few thousand infantry to intersect Saladin's progress.

DEFEAT AT MONTGISARD

The Christian knights took Saladin's much larger army entirely by surprise near the fortress of Montgisard on 25 November and inflicted a devastating defeat on them that was celebrated for years; the Old French translation of William of Tyre's chronicle said that the Christians found St George riding into battle at their side. Saladin lost his entire bodyguard and only just escaped with his life – according to contemporary accounts, because he was mounted on a racing camel and was able to outrun his pursuers. Only around 3,000 Muslim troops from an army of 30,000 or more limped back to Egypt.

Two years later Saladin had revenge of sorts. In a show of defiance, Baldwin had begun constructing a great castle at Jacob's Ford at the only crossing of the Jordan on the route from Damascus towards the Kingdom of Jerusalem. The king's men managed to complete the castle's outer walls, which stood 32ft (10m) in height, before Saladin marshalled his resources to attack. When the onslaught began Baldwin was in Tiberias: Saladin managed to breach the walls and killed 800 members of the castle's vast garrison, captured another 700 crusader soldiers and poisoned the water sources.

▼ *With an inferior force Baldwin surprised and defeated Saladin at Montgisard. The king fought left-handed since his leprosy had affected his right arm.*

CRUSADERS DESTROYED
SALADIN'S VICTORY AT THE HORNS OF HATTIN

In July 1187 Saladin moved again against the Kingdom of Jerusalem. On 4 July he annihilated the crusader army at the Battle of the Horns of Hattin, on one day destroying the Kingdom's united military capability and making inevitable his triumphant capture of Jerusalem later in the same year.

THE PROVOCATION OF REYNALD OF CHÂTILLON
Following Saladin's defeat at the Battle of Montgisard in 1177 and his revenge at Jacob's Ford in 1179, conflict between Saladin and the crusaders continued throughout the 1180s. A constant provocation was Reynald of Châtillon, a highly controversial figure in his own lifetime and beyond, the former Prince of Antioch (1153–60) who had spent 16 years in jail in Aleppo after being captured by Nur

▼ Guy of Lusignan was crowned King of Jerusalem in 1180. He came to the throne as consort of Sibylla, daughter of Amalric I and sister of the leper-king Baldwin IV.

ed-Din in 1160. Following the death of his wife, Reynald had made a powerful second marriage in 1183 when he wed Stephanie of Milly, heiress of the lordship of Oultrejordain, which included the powerful fortress of Montreal. From here, Reynald repeatedly attacked Muslim trade and pilgrim caravans, provoking Saladin to besiege the castle without success in 1183 and 1184. Reynald briefly practised restraint, but he was soon back to his old ways, attacking a caravan of pilgrims making the *hajj* (pilgrimage) to Mecca in 1185. (According to the 13th-century Old French *Continuation of the Chronicle of William of Tyre*, in this attack Reynald captured no less a figure than the sister of Saladin, but this is probably an invention since it is not confirmed in any of the contemporary accounts.) In May 1187 he attacked again, sweeping down from Montreal to attack a Muslim trade caravan from Cairo headed for Damascus. Saladin decided to act. He reputedly swore then that if he were ever to capture Reynald, he would kill him with his own hand.

THE SUCCESSION DISPUTE IN JERUSALEM
Saladin was also encouraged to attack by the weakness of the regime in Jerusalem, which had been undermined by a succession dispute. The dispute had begun in the reign of Amalric I's son, Baldwin IV, who, although a great military commander, was also a leper and was often too ill to govern and was unable to leave an heir. Two factions fought over the succession: on one side was Baldwin's eldest sister Sibylla and her ambitious husband Guy of Lusignan, supported by (among others) Reynald of Châtillon; on the other side was Raymond of Tripoli and the powerful Ibelin family, who backed the cause of Baldwin and Sibylla's half-sister Isabella, whose mother, Maria Comnena (widow of Amalric I), had married Balian of Ibelin.

▲ Guy of Lusignan was banished from France by the future King Richard I of England. Guy arrived in the Holy Land some time after 1174, and can be seen here at his coronation as King of Jerusalem.

Baldwin IV had Sibylla's young son Baldwin V crowned as co-ruler and heir in 1183 and when Baldwin IV died in spring 1185 the boy became king at the age of 8, with Raymond of Tripoli as regent. Baldwin V lasted less than 18 months: he died in summer 1186, and in the aftermath, Sibylla and Guy won the power struggle and Sibylla was crowned Queen with Guy as her consort.

A RECKLESS ADVANCE
Saladin gathered his army in May–June 1187 and on July 2 attacked Tiberias. The Christians gathered their forces at Sephoria under the leadership of Guy of Jerusalem (as Guy of Lusignan was known following the coronation of his wife Sibylla as Queen of Jerusalem). The army numbered around 1,200 knights and perhaps 20,000 infantry, representing the entire military strength of the Kingdom of Jerusalem. In attendance was the Bishop of Acre carrying a piece of the True Cross, the Kingdom's most sacred relic.

The position at Sephoria was a strong one, but Saladin was hoping that by his attack on Tiberias he could lure the crusaders out into open country. He got his way. Guy ignored advice from Raymond of Tripoli who counselled him not to risk a pitched battle against Saladin, and – urged on by the hot-headed Reynald of Châtillon – advanced towards Tiberias on 3 July. This was desert country, and the crusaders marched for hours without food or water, being harassed by Saladin's advance troops, until in the evening they encamped just to the south of the twin-peaked hill known as the Horns of Hattin.

SURROUNDED IN THE DESERT

In the morning they found that they were surrounded. Ahead of them, within sight, was a green valley and a lake, but Saladin's army barred the way. Saladin's men set fire to the dry grass around the crusaders, increasing the searing heat. Thirst maddened the crusaders, smoke billowed around them and arrows rained down on them from the sky. Saladin's secretary and chronicler Imad ed-din al-Isfahani later

▼ *Knights of the Kingdom of Jerusalem lie dead on the battlefield following the defeat at Hattin. By tradition, a heavenly light shone over them for three nights.*

recalled that: 'the people of the Trinity were eaten up by a worldly fire of three kinds, each irresistible and overwhelming: the fire of racing flames, the fire of raging thirst and the fire of whistling arrows.'

The crusaders tried to drive back the advancing army of Saladin, but without success. Only one sortie succeeded: Raymond of Tripoli, Reynald of Sidon and Balian of Ibelin broke out but were then unable to rejoin the battle; they rode away, knowing that Guy's rashness had brought the Kingdom to the brink of extinction.

Back in the heat of battle, the crusader army was driven up the hill towards the tent of King Guy, visible on the summit. To the despair of all, while fighting, the Bishop of Acre was robbed of the relic of the True Cross. Templars and Hospitallers fought bravely but they could not prevent the inevitable and eventually King Guy's tent fell and the battle was over.

HONOUR AND REVENGE

Guy and Reynald of Châtillon were still alive and were brought to Saladin's tent. Saladin gave the thirst-maddened Guy a drink of iced rosewater and the king

▲ *The crusaders were overrun and all but wiped out by Saladin's army at the Battle of the Horns of Hattin. Fires set by Saladin's men swept smoke across the battlefield.*

handed it to Reynald. Saladin grew angry, and made it clear that he had not offered the drink to his enemy Reynald – for by the Muslim warriors' code of war if a prisoner were offered food or drink by his captor his life had to be spared. Saladin did spare Guy, but slew Reynald by his own hand. 'Kings do not kill kings,' he said to Guy, but looking at Reynald added, 'that man's insolence went beyond what can be tolerated.'

On the following day Saladin ordered the execution of the surviving warriors among the Knights Templar and the Knights Hospitaller. Muslim holy men and Sufi mystics, who had joined the army in answer to the call to take part in jihad, begged to be allowed to perform the deed. Saladin seated himself on a mounted platform and watched, with his assembled soldiers, as the Christian warriors were put to death agonizingly slowly by these inexperienced swordsmen.

JERUSALEM RECAPTURED

SALADIN TAKES THE HOLY CITY

On 2 October 1187 Saladin and his army recaptured Jerusalem, ending almost 90 years of Christian rule.

CONTROL OF THE KINGDOM

Defeat at the Horns of Hattin had wiped out the crusader states' military strength and Saladin proceeded through the Kingdom virtually unopposed. Acre surrendered within days of the battle, and shortly afterwards Saladin's brother Al-Adil captured Jaffa. Nazareth, Caesarea and Haifa were taken and on 4 September Saladin captured Ascalon. Darkness fell by day because there was an eclipse of the sun; Christians who had heard of the eclipse of the moon witnessed before the capture of Jerusalem in 1099 may have seen this as an omen – and shuddered.

On 20 September 1187 Saladin began a siege of Jerusalem. The city's defence was

In triumph the Muslim army was highly disciplined. Saladin had his enemies at his mercy but treated them respectfully. There was no repeat of the lawlessness of 1099.

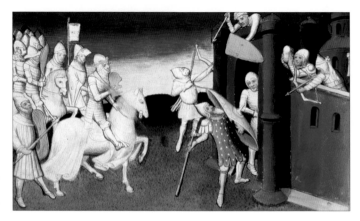

the responsibility of Balian of Ibelin, one of the knights who had broken out of the Muslim encirclement at the Horns of Hattin; he had returned to the city in order to rescue his wife Maria Comnena (the city's former queen and widow of Amalric I). He did not have sufficient manpower to mount an effective defence of the city walls – according to one contemporary account, there were only two other knights and a limited number of men-at-arms. Nevertheless, he inspired the defenders to hold out for nine days.

TERMS OF SURRENDER

On 30 September, after the Muslim siege equipment had made a breach in the wall near the Gate of the Column, Balian rode out to Saladin's camp to discuss terms under which the city might be given up. At first Saladin did not want to negotiate. He reminded Balian of the terrible behaviour of the Christian knights in taking Jerusalem in 1099. He wanted nothing less then unconditional surrender.

Balian responded by threatening that if they could not agree a truce and ransom, he would order the Christians within the city to slaughter the 5,000-odd Muslim slaves and prisoners, then to kill their own wives and children, destroy their valuable

Within Jerusalem, Balian of Ibelin led a few knights in desperate resistance to the siege, but they were vastly outnumbered. The Holy City passed into Saladin's hands.

possessions, attack the Muslim holy places and then fight to the death on the city walls. The city would be a bloodbath, loot would be destroyed, sacred places desecrated, and many of Saladin's soldiers would be killed unnecessarily in taking the city by force.

Saladin wanted to capture the city intact and did not want to cause the deaths of his fellow Muslims, so he agreed a ransom deal with Balian: ten dinars for each man, five for each woman and one for each child, with a lump sum of 30,000 dinars payable for 7,000 of the population who were too poor to pay their own ransom, the remainder of the unransomable poor were to be sold into slavery.

THE REOCCUPATION OF JERUSALEM

On 2 October 1187 Saladin and his disciplined army took the city peacefully. He was true to his word and the Franks were allowed to leave unmolested. Saladin sent groups of armed soldiers into the city to ensure that there was no looting or

Saladin was celebrated for his lively mind and sense of honour. Crusaders praised him for his generosity in victory and his wit in negotiation. His Muslim biographer Baha ed-Din ibn Shaddad wrote of him that he was a mine of fascinating information in conversation, a caring leader who would always ask after friends, and attempt to raise people's spirits. He would not allow fellow Muslims to be criticized in his presence, wanting to hear of people's good qualities instead. When he encountered orphans he always made sure that they were helped. Baha ed-Din ibn Shaddad recounted the story of how a distraught crusader woman demanded to see Saladin after her daughter had been stolen by Muslim soldiers: Saladin not only saw her and listened to her, but also sent men to scour the markets to see if they could find the girl; they did and he reunited her with her mother.

▼ *A monument to Saladin in Damascus.*

▲ *An illustration of c.1400 looks back to the fight for Jerusalem in 1187. The besieging Islamic army has been reimagined as a conventional European force.*

to pilgrims. The manner in which they reoccupied Jerusalem was a great and lasting credit to Saladin and his men, and should have shamed the Christian knights of 1099 had they been alive to see it.

Saladin's reputation for magnanimity and piety were enhanced by his treatment of the ransomed prisoners. Forty days were allowed for the Christians to raise the necessary ransoms. Throughout, Saladin behaved with the utmost generosity: when his brother, growing distressed at the vast numbers of captives, asked for some to be spared, Saladin freed 1,000; he gave another 700 their freedom in response to a request by the Patriarch of Jerusalem; and set another 500 free as a tribute to Balian. He then went even further, freeing the elderly and the infirm and all the husbands of women already freed.

MUSLIM JOY

According to Imad ed-din al-Isfahani, Saladin held a joyful court in the days after his retaking of Jerusalem, and was visited by many leading Muslims who 'covered

his carpet with kisses'. He maintained a sober and dignified bearing, but his face was 'bright with joy' and 'his expression shone'; the great triumph he had achieved, Imad ed-din wrote, appeared to give him a halo of moonlight.

CHRISTIAN DESPAIR

The Kingdom of Jerusalem appeared to be close to extinction. In the two years following the Battle of the Horns of Hattin, Saladin captured more than 50 crusader strongholds. He did not move against Tripoli or Antioch and Tyre remained in Christian hands, but the taking of Jerusalem was a great propaganda victory that suggested there was no future for the Christians in Palestine.

News of the defeat at the Horns of Hattin and the loss of Jerusalem reached Europe in the autumn of 1187 and Pope Urban III is reported to have died of grief. Writers and preachers lamented the terrible turn of events. One declared: '... on that day, October 2, 1187, the queen among all the cities in the world was cast into slavery.' It was an end, but also a beginning – within weeks, Urban's successor Pope Gregory VIII issued a call for a fresh military expedition to the Holy Land and a new crusade began.

rampage. He then set about cleaning up the city, restoring the al Aqsa mosque and the Dome of the Rock to sacred use for Muslims. Although he was urged by his compatriots to destroy the Church of the Holy Sepulchre, he merely ordered it to be closed for three days, then reopened

PART THREE

THE LATER AND EUROPEAN CRUSADES

The kings, princes and knights who conducted the Third Crusade of 1189–92 – and those of the ensuing centuries – were inspired by tales of the heroic deeds of Christian warriors on the First and Second Crusades (1096–99 and 1147–49). In particular, they were driven by a desire to repeat the extraordinary achievement of the knights of the First Crusade, who succeeded against all odds in capturing Jerusalem for Christ and for the Western Church. They had little political or economic motive in fighting in the East – they were inspired principally by religious motives. The later crusades in the Holy Land were paralleled by wars of the cross fought against pagans of middle and northern Europe, against the Muslim 'Moors' of the Iberian Peninsula, against enemies of the Catholic Church in Italy, and against the French dualist Cathars and other Christians denounced as 'heretics' – a collection of campaigns characterized by historians as Baltic or European Crusades to distinguish them from those in the East. These crusades were different in character: while the Eastern Crusades remained essentially wars of religion, the European Crusades were mostly political or economic struggles, in which the powerful religious rhetoric was merged with political agendas and causes.

▲ *Holding key ports was essential in the crusading era so that vital supplies could be shipped in to maintain the long sieges.*

▶ *In 1249, on the Seventh Crusade, an army led by Louis IX of France landed in Egypt, aiming to destroy Muslim power in north Africa before attacking Syria.*

TIMELINE OF THE LATER CRUSADES

29 October 1187 Pope Gregory VIII calls the Third Crusade.

January 1188 Kings Philip II of France and Henry II of England take the cross.

March 1188 Frederick I of Germany takes the cross.

11 May 1189 German crusaders under Frederick I depart.

6 July 1189 Henry II of England dies; his successor Richard I sets about raising money to go on crusade.

27 August 1189 King Guy of Jerusalem begins siege of Acre.

17 May 1190 German crusaders defeat Seljuks and capture Iconium.

10 June 1190 Frederick I drowns in River Saleph (modern Göksu).

25 July 1190 Queen Sibylla of Jerusalem dies, sparking succession dispute.

20 April 1191 Philip II arrives at Acre.

8 June 1191 Richard I arrives at Acre.

12 July 1191 Acre surrenders.

7 September 1191 Richard I defeats Saladin in the Battle of Arsuf.

April 1192 Sibylla's sister Isabella and her husband Count Henry II of Champagne take power in Jerusalem.

5 August 1192 King Richard I defeats Saladin at Jaffa.

2 September 1192 Richard I and Saladin agree a peace treaty that brings an end to the Third Crusade.

4 March 1193 Saladin dies.

25 July 1195 Pope Celestine III calls a new crusade; German emperor Henry VI takes the cross and a crusade sails in 1197 but melts away following Henry's death in Sicily in September 1197.

August 1198 Pope Innocent III calls the Fourth Crusade.

October 1202 The armies of the Fourth Crusade set off.

24 November 1202 Crusaders sack the Christian city of Zara in Hungary (modern Zadar in Croatia).

1202 The military order of the Livonian Brothers of the Sword is established.

12–15 April 1204 Forces of the Fourth Crusade sack Constantinople.

16 May 1204 Count Baldwin of Flanders is crowned emperor of the new Latin Empire of Constantinople in the Church of Haghia Sophia, Constantinople.

1208 Pope Innocent III declares a crusade against the Cathars, a heretical Christian sect of southern France.

July 1209 A crusade army takes Béziers from the Cathars, killing 20,000.

15 August 1209 The crusaders capture Carcassonne and evict the Cathars from the city.

1212 Pope Innocent III proclaims a crusade in Spain against the Almohad caliphs.

16 July 1212 A Christian army led by Alfonso VIII of Castile and Sancho VII of Navarre defeats the Almohads under their caliph Muhammad al-Nasir in the Battle of Las Navas de Tolosa.

April 1213 Pope Innocent III proclaims the Fifth Crusade.

November 1219 The Fifth Crusade army captures and sacks Damietta, Egypt.

July 1221 The Fifth Crusade army is defeated by Ayyubid sultan al-Kamil after

▼ *Soldiers at the gates of Jerusalem, from 13th-century manuscript* Velislavovy.

its attempt to march on Cairo is stopped by the flooding of the River Nile.

*c.*1228 The Prussian Cavaliers of Christ Jesus are established to maintain a permanent military presence in Prussia.

1228 Despite having been excommunicated, Holy Roman Emperor Frederick II embarks on the Sixth Crusade.

17 March 1229 At the climax of the Sixth Crusade Frederick II takes possession of Jerusalem for Christendom. He triumphs through diplomacy rather than military force.

1233 Pope Gregory IX establishes an Inquisition to counter the continuing activity of the Cathars in southern France.

1233–34 Pope Gregory IX calls a crusade against pagan Prussians, led by the Teutonic Knights. The knights build fortresses at Marienwerder and Rehden.

1236 King Ferdinand III of Castile and León captures the city of Córdoba from the Moors as the Christian Reconquista in Spain continues.

March 1244 The Cathar stronghold of Montségur castle is taken by French royalist forces.

August 1244 Khwarismian Turks take Jerusalem. Only 300 Christians escape.

17–18 October 1244 In the two-day Battle of La Forbie, a Turkish–Egyptian army commanded by Baybars (the future Mamluk sultan of Egypt) crushes a Christian–Syrian army.

1245 Pope Innocent IV grants the Teutonic Knights the right to issue crusading indulgences to those fighting on their behalf.

1248 King Ferdinand III of Castile and León captures Seville.

25 August 1248 King Louis IX of France embarks on the Seventh Crusade.

6 June 1249 The armies of the Seventh Crusade capture Damietta, Egypt.

6 April 1250 After a failed advance, the crusade army surrenders and Louis IX is captured by Ayyubid sultan Turan Shah.

May 1251 Louis IX is released from captivity in Egypt after payment of a large ransom. He sails to Acre.

April 1254 After three years in the Holy Land, Louis returns to France.

1255 The Cathars abandon their last stronghold at Quéribus in southern France, and flee.

3 September 1260 Mamluk general Baybars defeats a Mongol army in the Battle of Ain Jalut in Galilee. Later the same year, he seizes power as sultan.

1265 Baybars invades Outremer, taking Caesarea and Arsuf.

24 March 1267 Responding to Baybars' attacks, Louis IX of France takes the cross once more.

May 1268 Baybars captures Antioch.

July 1270 Louis IX and the army of the Eighth Crusade besiege the city of Tunis, in north Africa.

25 August 1270 Louis IX dies during the siege of Tunis.

30 October 1270 The army of the Eighth Crusade lifts the siege of Tunis.

May 1271 Prince Edward (the future King Edward I of England) lands in Acre leading the Ninth Crusade, causing Baybars to abandon the siege of Tripoli.

May 1272 King Hugh of Jerusalem agrees a truce with Baybars.

16 June 1272 An assassin sent by Sultan Baybars fails in an attempt to kill Prince Edward in Acre.

24 September 1272 Edward quits Palestine and departs for England.

1289 Tripoli is captured by Mamluk sultan Qalawun.

11 April 1291 Mamluk sultan Khalil begins the siege of Acre.

18 May 1291 The Christians are driven out of the Holy Land as Acre is captured by Khalil.

22 November 1307 King Philip IV of France orders the arrest of Jacques of Molay, Grand Master of the Knights Templar, and other French Templars.

1309 Having left the Holy Land following the fall of Acre in 1291, the Teutonic Knights build a new headquarters at Marienberg, Prussia.

▲ *Copies of Albigensian books are burned by monks of the Dominican order, under orders from the Inquisition.*

1312 With support from King Philip IV of France, Pope Clement V dissolves the Order of the Knights Templar.

1330 King Alfonso IX of Castile defeats Sultan Muhammad IV of Granada in the battle of Teba in Andalusia; Sir James Douglas, boon companion of the late Robert the Bruce, dies in this battle.

1332 King Alfonso founds the chivalric Order of the Sash.

30 October 1340 King Alfonso defeats a Marinid army in the Battle of Rio Salado.

1344 King Alfonso captures Algeciras from the Moors.

27 June 1365 King Peter I of Cyprus leads a crusade against Mamluk Egypt.

9 October 1365 King Peter's army captures and sacks Alexandria. Shortly afterwards, the army melts away as many of its leading members return home, and Peter has to abandon the city.

1390 Count Louis of Bourbon leads a crusade against Mahdia, Tunisia, a base for Muslim pirates attacking Genoan ships. It ends in a profitable settlement.

25 September 1396 Ottoman Sultan Bayezid I trounces a European crusading army at the Battle of Nicopolis.

1420 The First anti-Hussite Crusade is mounted against the followers of executed preacher Jan Hus, in Bohemia.

6 January 1422 Jan Zizka leads a Hussite army to defeat the Second anti-Hussite Crusade at the Battle of Nemecky Brod.

1422–31 The Third, Fourth and Fifth anti-Hussite Crusades are mounted but come to nothing.

10 November 1444 At the Battle of Varna Sultan Murad II's Ottoman army defeats a European Christian army.

29 May 1453 Ottoman sultan Mehmed II captures Constantinople. This marks the end of the Byzantine Empire.

21–22 July 1456 In the 'miracle of Belgrade', a vast army commanded by Sultan Mehmed II fails to capture the city. Belgrade's Christian defenders are led by Janos Hunyadi of Hungary and Italian monk Giovanni da Capistrano.

26 September 1459 Pope Pius II calls a new crusade, but it comes to nothing.

28 July 1480 Mehmed II abandons his attempt to capture Rhodes having been repulsed by the Knights Hospitaller.

1485 As part of a final push to drive the Moors from Spain, the army of King Ferdinand II of Aragon and Queen Isabella I of Castile takes Ronda.

1487 Ferdinand and Isabella capture the island of Malaga.

1491 Ferdinand and Isabella besiege the Muslim stronghold of Granada.

2 January 1492 King Ferdinand II of Aragon and Queen Isabella I of Castile take possession of Granada, marking the end of the centuries-long Reconquista.

22 December 1522 The Knights Hospitaller surrender Rhodes to Ottoman sultan Suleyman I 'the Magnificent' after a six-month siege.

Sept 1565 The Ottomans fail to take Malta from the Knights Hospitaller.

7 October 1571 The Christian Holy League defeats the Ottoman fleet in the naval Battle of Lepanto in the Ionian Sea.

1588 Spanish forces fight for English Roman Catholic insurgents against the ruling Protestant establishment, with the support of crusading privileges.

CHAPTER ELEVEN

RICHARD THE LIONHEART AND THE THIRD CRUSADE

On 7 September 1191, during the Third Crusade, King Richard I of England won a stunning victory over the great Saracen general Saladin at the Battle of Arsuf. Richard's battle tactics, which demanded total discipline from his knights in holding back from attacking under enormous provocation, were almost spoiled by a hasty charge led by the Knights Hospitaller, but ultimately were triumphantly vindicated as the Christians swept the Saracens off the battlefield in three unstoppable mounted advances.

The Third Crusade is forever associated with Richard I and his encounters with Saladin. The Battle of Arsuf was one of three victories Richard won over Saladin – and they had other memorable diplomatic encounters. In the chivalric literature of chansons and of chronicles, the clash of these great generals shines as an example of chivalry at its finest. The origins of the Third Crusade were notably different from those of the first two crusades, since it was called by the will of secular rulers as much as by that of the pope. Richard's participation – along with King Philip II of France and Emperor Frederick I of Germany – made the 'Kings' Crusade' one of the greatest and most glamorous of the wars of the cross – but, equally, the involvement of these monarchs was its undoing, for they were unable to put aside their fierce rivalries.

▲ *Frederick Barbarossa, King of Germany, invades Italy by sea in 1157.*

◄ *According to* jongleur *Ambroise, an eyewitness of the Battle of Arsuf, Richard was like a crossbow bolt fired against the enemy, who cut down his foes like a farmer harvesting wheat.*

THE CATHOLIC EXPANSION

The sense of glorious achievement felt by the Christian world after the success of the First Crusade was never to be repeated. Later crusades in the Holy Land and Europe were more complex and often severely compromised by mixed or deliberately duplicitous motives. The Fourth Crusade spiralled out of control amid political machinations and ended in the sacking and looting of Constantinople. In Europe, the crusading model was applied both to the fight against Muslim power in the Iberian peninsula and to campaigns waged against enemies both religious and political. The religious exaltation felt in 1100 did not accompany these events.

THE FOURTH CRUSADE

The Fourth Crusade was called by Pope Innocent III in August 1198. Its forces, which took some time to gather, departed from Venice in October 1202, bound initially for the former Venetian colony of Zara, which had become part of Hungary in 1186. (Today the city, on the Adriatic coast of Croatia, is called Zadar.) The crusade was vastly in debt to the city of

Venice after negotiating an extravagant deal to supply a crusade fleet, and paid off part of the money owed by attacking and capturing Zara; from this point on they lost papal backing, for Zara was under the protection of a Roman Catholic monarch, King Emeric of Hungary, and Pope Innocent III had outlawed attacks on Christian cities. Some crusaders wanted no more to do with the enterprise and sailed directly from Zara to the Holy Land, but the bulk of this now badly flawed expedition became embroiled in the attempt by exiled Byzantine prince Alexius Angelus to oust Emperor Alexius III and claim the throne for himself.

Promised great wealth – nominally to help fund the recapture of Jerusalem – the crusaders left Zara on Easter Monday 1203 and arrived at Constantinople on 24 June that year. They landed on the far side of the Bosphorus but on 5 July crossed in transports and began a siege of the city. They took the Byzantine capital on 17 July, but then were forced to wait in their encampment for several months while the former Prince Alexius (now Emperor

Alexius IV) raised the money he had promised them. Before he could do so, Alexius was deposed and a courtier named Alexius Doukas took power as Alexius V. A new siege began. The crusaders captured the city on 13 April 1204 and looted it wildly over three days. They established the Latin Empire of Constantinople; Count Baldwin of Flanders was elected Emperor Baldwin I. The crusade did not move on to the Holy Land.

RECONQUISTA

The *Reconquista* (Reconquest) of the Iberian Peninsula from its Muslim rulers was regularly promoted as a crusade from the 1090s onwards. The war against Islam in what became Spain and Portugal had

▼ *The papacy lost control of the Fourth Crusade, an enterprise in which religious crusading rhetoric was used to mask nakedly political motives. After the capture of the Byzantine imperial city, and the establishment of the Latin Empire of Constantinople, a large part of southern Greece was captured in winter 1204–05.*

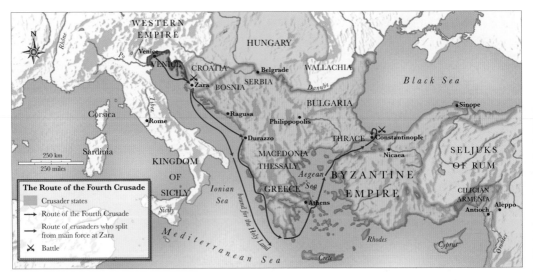

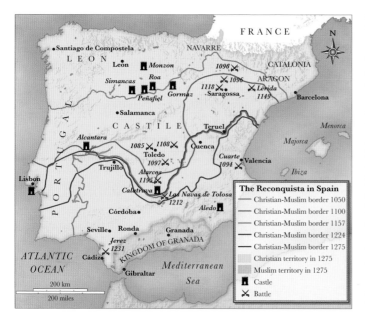

The Reconquista in Spain
— Christian-Muslim border 1050
— Christian-Muslim border 1100
— Christian-Muslim border 1157
— Christian-Muslim border 1224
— Christian-Muslim border 1275
  Christian territory in 1275
  Muslim territory in 1275
  Castle
  Battle

conquered by King Ferdinand and Queen Isabella of a united Castile and Aragon in 1482–92. With the capture of the city of Granada on 2 January 1492 the monarchs of the fledgling Spain ended 750 years of reconquest.

CATHAR CRUSADES

The first major battle of the decades-long Albigensian Crusade against the Cathar heretics of southern France was at Béziers on 21 July 1209: around 20,000 were killed. Carcassonne surrendered the next month. A Cathar fightback, supported by Peter II of Aragon, was defeated at Muret near Toulouse in September 1213. After 1216 the Cathars under Raymond VI of Toulouse and his son, Raymond VII, did win back a good deal of territory.

The war ended in 1229 but the fight against heresy continued through the often brutal activities of the Dominican Inquisition. The final Cathar strongholds in the hills and mountains east of Perpignan were captured in 1240–55.

▲ *The final war waged by Ferdinand and Isabella was explicitly a Christian crusade, and their army – as well as being equipped with the latest artillery – was reinforced by Christian troops from around Europe.*

actually begun almost 400 years earlier, not long after Arabs and north African Berbers seized most of the Christian kingdom of the Visigoths in AD711–716. Catalonia was recaptured in the late 8th century and became known as the 'Spanish March'. By the late 9th century Christian territory extended right across the north of the Iberian Peninsula; the remainder of what is now Spain and Portugal was ruled by a Muslim caliph from Córdoba.

After the Caliphate of Córdoba collapsed in 1002, the 30 or so independent Muslim kingdoms that succeeded it proved vulnerable to Christian advance: King Alfonso VI of Léon took Toledo in 1085 and looked set to recapture the entire peninsula but was defeated by the Almoravids of north-west Africa in the Battle of Sagrajas in 1086. They made southern Spain and Portugal part of the

Almoravid Empire, but this too collapsed after 1140 and was succeeded by the Almohad Caliphate, which held roughly the southern third of the country. The Muslims were pushed farther and farther south by the expansion of Christian Castile, Aragon and Portugal – until by the last quarter of the 13th century the Muslims held only the small Kingdom of Granada in the far south. This territory survived for 200 years until it was finally

▼ *The Cathars were especially numerous in what is now western Mediterranean France, then part of the Kingdom of Aragon. Although Cathar ideas did not originate in Languedoc, one of the most urbanized and populated areas of Europe at the time, it was there that their theology found its most spectacular success.*

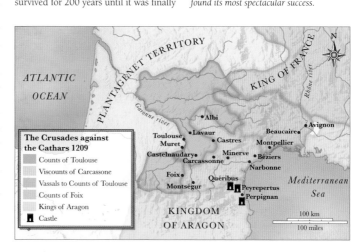

The Crusades against the Cathars 1209
  Counts of Toulouse
  Viscounts of Carcassone
  Vassals to Counts of Toulouse
  Counts of Foix
  Kings of Aragon
  Castle

ONCE MORE TO JERUSALEM

A THIRD CRUSADE IS CALLED

On 29 October 1187, in Ferrara, Pope Gregory VIII issued a crusading bull known to historians from its first words in Latin, *Audita tremendi* (the first part of a Latin phrase that translates as 'On hearing of the dreadful and profound judgement inflicted on the land of Jerusalem by the divine hand'). The papal bull was issued in response to the defeat at the Battle of the Horns of Hattin in July, before news of the fall of Jerusalem had reached Europe.

The bull called the defeat at Hattin and the loss of the relic of the True Cross in the battle 'a terrible judgement inflicted by the Lord on the land of Jerusalem' and declared that the news – which had reputedly ended Pope Urban III's life, by bringing on a heart attack – had thrown his successor as pope and other church leaders into confusion and left them battered by 'such a deep horror and resounding grief that it was not apparent what we should do'. But it called for all to maintain their faith and to believe that God 'once softened by our repentance' would bring 'gladness after grief'; Christian warriors should see this as 'a chance to repent and do a good deed', offering themselves and their wealth for recovery of 'the land where Truth itself was born from the earth in order to bring about our salvation'.

Those who made the journey with 'humble and contrite heart' or who died 'in repentance of their wrongdoing and in the right faith' would earn a plenary indulgence and eternal life 'by the mercy of God Himself, on the authority of the apostles Peter and Paul' and that of the papacy. As in previous crusades, the property of those who took the cross would be protected by the Church and those who incurred debts making the journey should be free of the requirement to pay interest. The bull also urged those travelling to avoid ostentation and aim for simplicity – not to take dogs,

▲ *When elected to the papacy Alberto di Morra took the name Gregory in honour of Pope Gregory VII (r.1073-85), pictured here, a key establisher of papal primacy.*

hawks and expensive clothes but to have plain robes and equipment, to make clear that they are travelling in penitence rather than indulging idle vanity.

CRUSADE SERMONS

A Church campaign to preach the new crusade was put in train. In the British Isles, the Archbishop of Canterbury, Baldwin of Exeter, made a tour of Wales in 1188 to preach the cross. Baldwin's journey was described by the colourful Norman–Welsh churchman and chronicler Giraldus Cambrensis, or 'Gerald of Wales', in his *Itinerarium Cambriae*, written in 1191.

According to Giraldus Cambrensis Baldwin convinced 3,000 men-at-arms to take the cross. The sermons were delivered in Latin and French, sometimes with a Welsh interpreter, but even when the crowd could not have understood the words, knights and men-at-arms still rushed forward to take the cross. According to Gerald, a miracle occurred that showed God's blessing on the enterprise and the holiness of Archbishop Baldwin – in the area near Haverfordwest,

an old lady who had been blind for many years was cured when she rubbed her face with earth upon which the archbishop had stood when giving the sermon.

SALADIN TRIUMPHANT

In Outremer in July 1187, in the immediate aftermath of Saladin's victory at the Battle of the Horns of Hattin, the Muslim general's armies marched virtually unchallenged and imposed his will where they went. City after city passed out of crusader control. But the important port of Tyre was saved at the last moment following quick thinking by the charismatic European lord Conrad of Montferrat.

Conrad had sailed from Italy for Jerusalem in 1185 in order to join his father, William V of Montferrat, but he had been waylaid in Constantinople, where he had married Princess Theodora, sister of Byzantine emperor Isaac II Angelus. In July 1187 Conrad set out for the Kingdom of Jerusalem, probably fearing reprisals after he killed a rebel general named Alexios Branas when putting down a rebellion on behalf of Isaac. He set sail on board a Genoese merchant ship.

When Conrad arrived by sea at Acre on 14 July he found the place eerily quiet and cautiously dropped anchor offshore; then he and his companions saw Saladin's standards above the walls – the town had just fallen to the Muslim general. When messengers from the port approached by ship, Conrad pretended to be a merchant ally of Saladin; he promised to bring his goods ashore the next morning. But in the night he lifted anchor and inched away, setting sail for Tyre.

TYRE SAVED FROM SALADIN

There are differing versions of precisely what happened next. According to the 13th-century Old French *Continuation of the Chronicle of William of Tyre*, Conrad arrived in Tyre just as the port, which was

▲ *At Tyre, Saladin and his apparently invincible army were defeated for the first time since the Battle of the Horns of Hattin.*

in the hands of crusader lord Reginald of Sidon, was preparing to mark its surrender to Saladin by raising his banners. But Conrad – resolute, determined and charismatic – threw the banners into the city ditch and convinced the people to transfer their allegiance to him; when they did so he led them to a last-gasp defence.

The truth may have been more prosaic. Other accounts suggest that Conrad arrived in advance of Saladin's army while Reginald was absent seeking to fortify his castle of Belfort; Conrad strengthened the town's defences and inspired its merchant community and other residents to put up a stout defence. Whatever truly happened, Saladin's attempt to take the city of Tyre was repulsed and he moved on to take Caesarea, Arsuf and Jaffa.

In November Conrad repulsed another, larger-scale attack on Tyre by Saladin, who

▼ *The victory at Tyre, snatched as it was from seemingly inevitable defeat, was the kind of triumph against all odds that had occurred on the First Crusade and inspired later generations to try to emulate it.*

had blockaded the city by land with his troops and by sea using an Egyptian fleet. Saladin paraded Conrad's aged father, William, who had been captured at the Battle of the Horns of Hattin, before the walls of Tyre and threatened to kill him if Conrad did not surrender; but Conrad was unmoved, declaring that his father had already lived a long life, and even – it is said – aimed a crossbow at the old man. His bluff worked, Saladin backed down and later released William. Again Conrad drove him off, leading an assault on the Egyptian fleet, and then a brave charge out of the city gates that surprised the besiegers and forced them to retreat.

The saving of Tyre was a turning point for the crusaders. This strategically placed port was to be a vital point of access for Western ships bringing supplies and troops in order to make the Third Crusade possible. Saladin's decision not to press home his advantage by taking Tyre was one of the very few strategic mistakes he made in a long and glorious career.

KINGS OF EUROPE TAKE THE CROSS

HENRY II, PHILIP II AND FREDERICK I JOIN THE CRUSADE

At Gisors, north-west of Paris, in January 1188 a crusading sermon by Archbishop Joscius of Tyre convinced two kings, Philip II of France and Henry II of England, to take the cross. According to the account given by the English chronicler Roger of Howden in his *Chronica* (*c.*1191), the sermon was accompanied by a miracle, when the Cross of Christ appeared in the sky above the kings.

Joscius had been sent to the west by Conrad of Montferrat after Conrad had repulsed Saladin's initial assault on Tyre. Joscius sailed in a ship with black sails to spread the news of Saladin's victories and call for urgent help and, according to Arabic accounts, carried with him pictures designed to outrage the Christians in Europe – for example, one of Saladin's army horses urinating in stables he had supposedly set up within the Church of the Holy Sepulchre, and another of a 'Saracen' hitting Christ in the face.

Roger added that the kings, who had been at war, were inspired by Joscius to put aside their enmity and agreed to

▼ *Frederick Barbarossa and his crusaders are called on to liberate the Holy Land, and begin their journey in 1157.*

pursue a common goal in the Holy Land – as Roger commented: 'those who were once enemies were persuaded to become friends on that day, through his preaching and the help of God'. At their meeting the kings also agreed on distinctive crosses to be worn by their armies to help tell them apart on campaign: the English army would wear a white cross, while the French would wear a red one. The troops of Philip, Count of Flanders, who also took the cross on this day, would wear a green cross.

DECISIONS AT LE MANS

In a meeting at Le Mans in February, Henry and Philip discussed ways to finance the crusade and decided on a tax of 10 per cent on income and property for an entire year to be applied to both Church and laity. This tax became known as the 'Saladin tithe' because it was imposed to raise money for a campaign against the Muslim general. It was administered by the Church rather than by lay authorities; clerics and knights who took the cross were exempt from the tax, but those who refused either to go on crusade or to pay the tax were excommunicated. The tax was extremely unpopular, and sparked fears that it was not a one-off but the beginning of a permanent taxation of the people; Philip II was faced with such opposition that he had to issue a proclamation in summer 1189 to the effect that the tax was an extraordinary measure and would not be perpetuated.

The kings also agreed on a sober code of conduct for the crusading armies. In order to generate a penitent and suitably sombre mood, furs and other fine clothes, games of dice and swearing were all outlawed; in addition, no knight or yeoman was permitted to bring a woman with him – 'save possibly a washerwoman on foot, to be beyond suspicion'. Anyone who died on crusade would be required to give up

▲ *Clockwise from top left: King Henry II, 1133–89, Richard I, 1157–99, John, 1167–1216, Henry III, 1207–72, from Matthew Paris',* Historia Anglorum, *1250.*

the money he carried with him: it would be divided to meet immediate needs, such as maintaining his bondmen, helping the land of Jerusalem or feeding the poor.

FREDERICK TAKES THE CROSS

At Pentecost – the church festival celebrating the descent of the Holy Spirit on early Christians – in 1188, Emperor Frederick I of Germany took the cross at a special 'Court of Jesus Christ' convened in Mainz. By now in his mid-sixties, Frederick was a veteran of the Second Crusade on which he had travelled, as Duke of Swabia, in the company of his uncle, Emperor Conrad III. He had called the court the previous December, when, according to contemporary reports, he was visibly moved by a sermon at Strasburg (modern Strasbourg, now in France) that

▲ *A stained-glass window in St Stephen's Cathedral, Vienna, represents Holy Roman Emperor Frederick I taking the cross.*

cast Christ in the role of a feudal lord wronged by his enemies and left unsupported by his liegemen.

On that day of Pentecost, around 13,000 princes, bishops, dukes, margraves, counts, nobles as well as many lesser knights took the cross alongside Frederick and his son Frederick, Duke of Swabia. According to the author of the anonymous *Historia de Expeditione Frederici* (Narrative of Frederick's Expedition), many men were in tears as they listened to a reading of Pope Gregory's encyclical, and a sermon from Bishop Godfrey of Würzburg. Frederick put himself forward as leader and standard-bearer for the crusade. No warlike man in Germany ignored the call, said the chronicler, and those who took the cross: 'burned with a great passion for fighting. For them, life was in Christ and death was a prize to be gained.' They set the departure for St George's Day (23 April) 1189.

WAR OF WORDS

Frederick traced his descent from Charlemagne himself and in 1165 had brought about the elevation to sainthood of that great leader, the creator of a Christian empire. Frederick had also, since 1157, used the term *Sacrum Imperium* (Holy Empire) to describe his own territories; and he believed it was the necessary and rightful task of a leader of a Christian empire to come to the aid of the faithful in the East against their 'infidel' opponents. He had even in 1165 considered launching a crusade on his own initiative.

Now, according to the crusade history called the *Itinerarium Regis Ricardi* (The Voyage of King Richard), he sent a proud missive to Saladin, demanding his retreat from the Holy Land and threatening a 'trial by battle' on 1 November 1189, 'by the merit of the life-giving Cross of Christ'. He claimed that Saladin would be shocked by the ferocity and strength of the warriors of the German empire: the untamed warriors of the Rhine, young soldiers from the Danube who would never flee, the towering Bavarians and canny Swabians, Saxons expert with the sword, circumspect Franconians, Bohemians unafraid of death, men from Bologna wilder even than their own beasts. And he said that he himself could still enforce his imperial will with a sword, for his arm was not wearied by age.

The *Itinerarium* also gave details of Saladin's equally proud response, in which he boasted that only three cities – those of Tyre, Tripoli and Antioch – remained in Christian hands in all the lands of Outremer and that 'these will inevitably be captured'. He also said that he was quite happy to undergo a trial by battle but that peace was a possible outcome if the three cities were handed over; in which case, he would allow Christian pilgrims to come and go freely.

▼ *Passions run high at Mainz on Pentecost 1188 when Frederick I accepted the call to take up the cross once more, together with many great men of the empire.*

BARBAROSSA'S CRUSADE

THE CAMPAIGN LED BY FREDERICK I OF GERMANY

The German army under Frederick I was the first crusading force to depart, leaving on 11 May 1189. Contemporary reports claim that his army was 100,000 or even 150,000 in number – easily the largest ever to set off on crusade – and took three days to march past an observer.

DISCIPLINE AND BELIEF

Frederick, now 67, must have had a good amount of grey in the red beard that gave him his nickname 'Barbarossa', but he still cut an imposing figure at the head of his vast force. He attempted to maintain strict discipline, reportedly turning away a group of 500 small-time criminals at Vienna and accepting into the army only those who could prove their capacity to support themselves. He had absolute confidence in his ability to regain Jerusalem and the Holy Land for Christianity: in common with the soldiers of the First Crusade, he believed that the Last Days

▼ *An idealized portrait from the 19th century of Frederick I Barbarossa, Holy Roman Emperor.*

▲ *Frederick and his vast army survived a long overland journey, with many difficulties, and then boarded ships in Constantinople to sail across the Hellespont to Anatolia.*

as described in the Bible were upon humankind, and that when the emperor laid his sceptre down in Jerusalem the final act would begin with a reign by the Anti-Christ prior to the triumphant Second Coming of Jesus.

BY LAND ACROSS EUROPE

The German army departed from Ratisbon (modern Regensburg, in Bavaria, Germany) and followed the overland route to Constantinople taken by the soldiers of the First Crusade almost a hundred years earlier. Frederick led the way through Hungary and Serbia into Byzantine territory. Frederick had planned ahead, and conducted prolonged negotiations with Byzantine emperor Isaac II Angelus to ensure the crusader army's safe passage across Byzantine territory, but they did not receive the warm welcome they expected. Isaac was in negotiations with Saladin, who wanted Constantinople's troops to

impede the progress of the crusader army in return for support against the Seljuk Turks in Anatolia and his help in ensuring that the church in Palestine would be under Orthodox Christian control. The Byzantine emperor was also suspicious of Frederick's motives – and reports reached him that parts of the army wanted to conquer his empire for Latin Christianity.

CONFLICT WITH BYZANTIUM

In October there were several open clashes between German and Byzantine troops in the Balkans. Frederick reported in a letter to his son Henry (the future Emperor Henry VI) that the crusader army had endured 'plundering' and 'massacre', and

▲ *After setting out from Germany in a spirit of religious devotion, Frederick had a rude awakening when he encountered what seemed to be attempts by the Byzantine emperor to undermine the crusade.*

that attacks had been 'obviously instigated by none other than the emperor'. They were, he wrote, attacked by bandits, had their way blocked with great rocks and felled trees and even found castles fortified against them. Nevertheless, they progressed and spent the winter of 1189–90 in Philippopolis (modern Plovdiv, Bulgaria).

In the letter Frederick indicated that Isaac 'with little concern for his reputation' had also imprisoned German ambassadors in Constantinople and seized 'upwards of two thousand marks' of their money – and that relations had deteriorated to the extent that Frederick was planning to attack Constantinople. He asked Henry

to gather a fresh force of knights to embark by sea to help in the battle. He instructed him to send more money to Tyre, where he would collect it – and he also asked to be remembered in Henry's prayers and those of the people at home.

In the event, full-scale war between Germans and Byzantines was averted, the German army bypassed Constantinople, and crossed the Hellespont into Anatolia – on board transport ships provided by Isaac – on 28 March 1190. They marched across Anatolia and won a great victory over the Seljuks, capturing the capital of the Sultanate of Rum at Iconium (modern Konya in Turkey) on 17 May. They stayed in the city for almost a week, restocking the army with horses and supplies, before moving on towards Armenian-held Cilicia. They also captured the town of Laranda (modern Karaman) around 60 miles (100km) farther south and just to the north of the Taurus Mountains.

At this point the crusade seemed well-starred. The army had survived a difficult passage from Europe, had won a great victory and appeared to be on the threshold of great deeds in the Holy Land. But in a twist of fate on 10 June, Frederick died when he fell from his horse while crossing the River Saleph (now called the Göksu) and drowned in its icy though shallow waters. In that moment, all the energy and conviction went out of the German wave of the crusade.

Saladin and the other Muslim leaders declared that Frederick's death was the work of Allah, who had acted to deliver them from a great impending threat; to the Christians it appeared that God was not supporting their march on Jerusalem. Many Germans gave up and returned to Europe; some were reportedly so shocked that they renounced Christianity entirely.

Barbarossa's son Frederick of Swabia took control of the army and marched on to join the crusader siege of Acre, where they arrived in October 1190.

▼ *Frederick drowns in the icy River Saleph – like many crusaders before and after, he died in humiliating circumstances far from home, without having achieved the crusading mission he saw as his destiny.*

IN SICILY AND CYPRUS
RICHARD I AND PHILIP II STOP EN ROUTE TO THE HOLY LAND

The kings of France and England did not follow the German army to the Holy Land until July 1190. Although in their meeting at Gisors in January 1188 Henry II and Philip II had agreed to put disagreements to one side in the interests of Jerusalem, feuding had resurfaced.

In particular Henry II's eldest surviving son, Richard of Poitou, had allied with Philip II and invaded Henry's territory in Anjou. Henry was defeated, and was broken by this, the latest of a series of rebellions involving his sons, and he died at Chinon on 6 July 1189. He was succeeded by the Count of Poitou, who became King Richard I of England. Richard set about raising money for the crusade: he cancelled the Treaty of Falaise

▼ *On 24 June 1190, Philip II receives the royal standard in the abbey church of St Denis prior to embarking on the crusade.*

of 1174, thus freeing the Scots from their acknowledgment of English overlordship, and in return received a payment of 10,000 marks from King William of Scots.

FROM FRANCE TO SICILY

Richard and Philip II embarked together from southern France, bound initially for Sicily, where, following the death of William II of Sicily, his successor Tancred, Count of Lecce, had imprisoned William's widow, Joan of England (Richard's sister), seized her dowry and stolen a legacy intended for Richard himself.

Arriving in Sicily in September 1190, the crusader armies came into conflict with the locals; but they were given an outlet for their energies when on 4 October Richard captured and sacked the capital city of Messina. The *Itinerarium Regis Ricardi* reported that the attack was so swift and easy that it took less time than

▲ *Leaving on crusade, Richard appointed William of Mandeville, Earl of Essex, and Bishop Hugh of Durham as his regents. But William died and his position was taken by the chancellor, William Longchamp.*

a priest needs to sing the Mass; Richard spared the citizens, but his army seized vast quantities of loot. Tancred backed down, freed Joan and returned the moneys he had taken.

But Philip and Richard quarrelled fiercely about who should take most credit for the victory, with Philip enraged that Richard flew his standard above the walls rather then Philip's banner. In the end, on 8 October they made up and swore an oath to defend one another and each other's armies on the campaign ahead. Nevertheless, the differences between the two kings would dog the entire crusade.

The armies of France and England then spent the winter on the island, while their leaders continued to squabble – principally now over a marriage, for Richard had pledged to wed Philip's sister Alys, but then proposed to renege on that promise in order to marry Princess Berengaria, the daughter of the king of Navarre. According to the *Chronica* of Roger of Howden, Richard took time in Sicily to listen to the prophecies of Joachim, Abbot of the Cistercian monastery at Corazzo,

who had visions of St John the Evangelist, and declared to Richard: 'the Lord is to grant you a great victory over his enemies, and will raise your name above that of any other prince on the Earth'.

THE KINGS PART COMPANY

Finally the two kings went their separate ways. Philip left Sicily on 30 March 1191, and landed at Tyre in the middle of May. He moved on towards Acre, and joined the crusader siege of that city on 20 April. Richard made another diversion, for several of his ships – including the one carrying his intended wife Berengaria and his sister – had been caught in a storm and put in to Cyprus. There, the Cypriot ruler, Isaac Dukas Comnenus, had seized a large load of treasure that Richard was carrying and had imprisoned many of Richard's men.

Isaac Comnenus had come to power by treachery and trickery and ruled as a tyrant, so when Richard landed and

▼ *Philip and Richard swore a vow like that of chivalric brothers in arms after their quarrel in Sicily. They promised to protect one another throughout the crusade. But they would soon be at loggerheads again.*

ANTI-SEMITIC RIOTS IN ENGLAND

The Third Crusade was no different to its two predecessors in that the preaching of the cross sparked widespread anti-Jewish rioting. The violence afflicted England particularly, where Richard's coronation was marred by a major anti-Semitic riot in London, sparked when onlookers saw wealthy Jews apparently gaining access to the celebration. The following year violence against the Jews swept the country. The

▲ *Members of the London mob run riot in a Jew's house during Richard I's reign. Crusading rhetoric drove violence at home as well as in the disputed territories of Outremer.*

worst outbreak was in York, where on 16 March around 150 Jews committed suicide by setting fire to the tower in which they had taken refuge rather than face the mob in the streets below.

attacked Limassol the people welcomed him as a bringer of freedom. Isaac agreed to return the treasure and pledged to add 500 troops to the crusading army.

Once he had ensconced himself within his castle of Famagusta, however, Isaac attempted to take a hard line, ordering Richard's departure from the island. At this point, a ship arrived from the crusader camp at Acre, seeking news of Richard; on board were leading members of the Knights Templar, to whom Isaac owed a large amount of money. With their backing and encouragement, Richard led the conquest of the island, which was thereafter to be an important ally of the

crusader states in Palestine. The campaign took 15 days and, according to the *Itinerarium Regis Ricardi*, Richard found extraordinary stores of wealth that had been hoarded by the miserly Isaac – treasure was piled high in the castles of the island: the king and his knights found golden cups, silver jars, gilded saddles, precious spurs, silken cloth and fine scarlet robes, and they took them all, thinking it a gift of God to help finance the crusade.

Also during his stay on Cyprus, on 12 May, Richard married Berengaria at the port of Limassol and made her his queen. Richard finally left Cyprus and arrived at Acre on 8 June 1191.

A SICK WINTER

CRUSADERS SUFFER DURING THE LONG SIEGE OF ACRE

While King Richard and King Philip were occupied on Sicily in the winter of 1190–91, the crusader forces in the Holy Land were enduring terrible suffering as they doggedly besieged the port of Acre, while they were themselves besieged by the army of Saladin.

THE START OF THE SIEGE

The siege had begun in the summer of 1189. Saladin had imprisoned Guy of Lusignan, former king of Jerusalem, in Damascus, but in 1188 released him on condition that Guy promise to take himself overseas and never again make war against Islam. However, having sworn this oath, Guy disregarded it at once, and set about trying to rebuild his power base. He marched to Tyre, where he attempted to take control of the city but was refused by Conrad of Montferrat, who had saved the city from Saladin and saw the opportunity to establish his own territory. Then Guy, with the help of fleets from Pisa and Sicily, moved on to Acre and began a siege. A fleet of 50 ships arrived, bearing powerful Danish and Frisian warriors to bolster his army. Louis of Thuringia managed to prevail on Conrad of Montferrat to take part in the siege, and bring men from Tyre to further boost the Christian army.

▲ *Crusaders mixed with Saracens outside the walls of Acre and, by holding jousting bouts, tested in sport the fighting skills they would soon use in earnest.*

SALADIN'S ASSAULT

Saladin had considered attacking while Guy was marching south from Tyre, but he held off until the Christian army was encamped before Acre. He arrived at Acre just a few days after the crusaders at the end of August and settled in behind them. There was only desultory fighting between the two armies in September, and an atmosphere akin to that of a European tournament developed. There was even a staged contest between two boys from the Christian army and two from the city garrison; one of the Christian youths was defeated and had to be ransomed by a crusader lord for two dinars.

Battle was joined by Christians and Saracens on 4 October. After an initial success in which the Christians drove back the centre and right wing of Saladin's army, the crusaders threw away their advantage and began looting the Muslim camp; they

▼ *Men and supplies arrived at Acre to strengthen the hand of the besieging army.*

▲ *Hunger was a recurring problem for the crusaders. According to tradition, parts of the German army on the Third Crusade lost hope and flung themselves down in the shape of the cross to await starvation.*

were then themselves forced back by a combined assault from Saladin's besiegers and the garrison of the city, who had broken out to attack. The battle was ultimately indecisive, but was certainly costly. The crusaders lost as many as 7,000 men with many Knights Templar, including their Grand Master, Gerard of Ridefort, killed. Conrad of Montferrat was isolated and had to be saved by Guy of Lusignan.

THE CRUSADERS STARVE

The siege dragged on and on. Trapped between the city walls and Saladin's army, unable to break out and forage in the countryside, the Christian army became desperately short of food. According to the *Itinerarium Regis Ricardi*, the soldiers fought over bread, and those who could afford it would pay 12 shillings for a fowl or a 100 gold pieces for a measure of wheat. They grew so desperate that they killed the finest horses for food.

A SUCCESSION DISPUTE

There were repeated outbreaks of fever and dysentery. During a stalemate in fighting in the summer of 1190, probably on 25 July, Queen Sibylla of Jerusalem died in the camp, and this sparked a succession dispute over the throne of Jerusalem.

Sibylla was the eldest daughter of King Amalric I (by Agnes of Courtenay) and was the wife of Guy of Lusignan, who had held power in the kingdom as her consort; on her death, the crown rightly passed to her half-sister, Isabella, Amalric's daughter with his second wife, Maria Comnena. But Guy refused to concede the crown and demanded to be recognized as king. Conrad of Montferrat launched an attempt to take control by marrying Isabella. At Acre, rumours circulated that Conrad was supplying food only to those in the camp who were his allies and accomplices, and that those who backed Guy of Lusignan's claim were left to starve.

In October 1190 spirits in the crusader camp were raised when the remnant of the German crusade arrived under the command of Duke Frederick of Swabia. These men were bedraggled and severely reduced in numbers, but their arrival was taken as a sign that the European armies were on their way. A little while afterwards, an English contingent arrived under the command of Baldwin, Archbishop of Canterbury. The crusaders launched a fresh assault on the city, and knocked down part of the walls with a pair of battering rams, but the garrison held firm and the attackers made no further progress.

HARD WINTER MONTHS

The winter was very hard on the Christian army. Wells and other water sources became contaminated and disease was rife in the camp. Frederick, Duke of Swabia, Theobald, Count of Blois, Stephen, Count of Sancerre, Archbishop Baldwin of Canterbury and Patriarch Heraclius of Jerusalem all died of sickness. Count Henry II of Jerusalem (the future Henry I of Jerusalem, 1192–97) was very seriously ill for several weeks, but finally recovered.

New hope came with the spring. Duke Leopold V of Austria arrived by sea in March and took control of the army. He brought the news that King Philip II of France and King Richard I of England were on their way.

▼ *A fresh assault following the arrival of Archbishop Baldwin of Canterbury came close to success but Acre's garrison did just enough to drive back the attackers.*

THE CAPTURE OF ACRE
RICHARD I'S ARRIVAL BRINGS LONG SIEGE TO AN END

◀ *The turning point in the seemingly endless siege at Acre came with the arrival of the charismatic Richard Coeur de Lion. Sure of success, the crusaders celebrated.*

Philip II arrived at Acre on 20 April 1191 with a Genoese fleet. He was followed on June 8, by Richard I with an English fleet carrying a force of 8,000 men. Within five weeks of Richard's arrival, the city of Acre, which had steadfastly withstood a siege since August 1189, fell to the crusader army.

Richard's reputation had preceded him to Palestine. Saladin knew from his military intelligence that although Philip II was the highest-ranking of the European kings on the crusade, Richard was the leader in terms of battle prowess and charisma, a far more powerful warrior than his rival, driven by a burning desire for warfare. For several weeks before Richard arrived, Saladin and his officers heard boasts from crusader lords in the besieging camp to the effect that when this king of England arrived, the siege of Acre would be swiftly brought to its conclusion. The day of his arrival turned into a

festival. According to the *Itinerarium Regis Ricardi*, trumpets, pipes and drums sounded out 'until the earth shook with the happiness of the Christians'; as darkness fell, people celebrated with carousing and dancing and lit bonfires that burned so brightly that the garrison of Acre thought the land around them was on fire.

SIEGE TIGHTENED

After his arrival in April, Philip II had put in train the construction of several powerful new siege engines, and Richard now personally supervised the erection and use of many more as the crusader army stepped up its attacks on the city. One of his military catapults had sufficient range to hurl great stones far over the walls and into the heart of the city; it reputedly killed 12 men with one shot. Richard fought in the front line: he had his men build a moveable protective shed beneath which the army's foremost crossbowmen

could shelter as they fired; he himself worked a crossbow and killed many of the defenders manning the walls.

The garrison fought back forcefully, using Greek fire to consume the laboriously constructed siege towers and engines, manning the battlements and clearing the ditches, but they were outnumbered and increasingly desperate. On 3 July the crusaders made a substantial breach in the walls. There was intense fighting at close quarters as the crusader army, containing many hastily armed lords, including the Earl of Leicester and the Bishop of Salisbury, tried to enter the city – but the Turks rallied strongly and held them at bay. On 4 July the city's defenders offered their surrender, but Richard was unhappy with the terms: the crusaders were asking for the Kingdom of Jerusalem to be restored to its boundaries prior to the Battle of the Horns of Hattin.

ACRE SURRENDERS

On 7 July the garrison sent a message to Saladin indicating that if he did not come to their aid they would be forced to surrender. Saladin attacked the crusaders once more on 11 July but without driving them off and on 12 July the garrison formally surrendered.

They did so without the agreement of Saladin, who reportedly wept tears of frustration and grief when he heard the news, for he had just received yet more reinforcements and was confident that a final assault might drive the crusaders off and save Acre. The garrison, moreover, had agreed punitive terms on Saladin's behalf, as negotiated by Conrad of Montferrat (or of Tyre, as he was often now known): a vast ransom of 200,000 gold dinars for the lives of the garrison, 3,000 of whom would be held as prisoners; the cherished relic of the True Cross, in Saladin's possession since it had been captured at the Battle of the Horns of Hattin, would be returned, and around 2,000 Christians held prisoner by the Muslim army would be released; the city, all its possessions and the ships in its harbour would be handed over to the crusaders. Despite his anger, Saladin felt honour-bound to accept the terms agreed in his name.

The English army took possession of the city. King Philip II installed himself in the Acre mansion of the Templars, while Richard made himself at home in what had been the royal palace. Almost at once Richard quarrelled openly and fiercely with Duke Leopold of Austria – in a disagreement almost identical to the one that

▼ *Their long months of suffering at an end, the crusaders establish themselves in Acre after the garrison's formal surrender.*

had followed his capture of Messina. Duke Leopold saw himself as the commander of the German contingent on the crusade, for Frederick Barbarossa had died in Cilicia and his son Frederick, Duke of Swabia, had died during the siege; Leopold, therefore, demanded equal ranking with Philip II and Richard I. He issued an order that his standard should fly alongside that of

▲ *Saladin was impressed by the valour of Hubert Walter, Bishop of Salisbury, at Acre and later asked to meet him. On returning from crusade to England, Walter was named Archbishop of Canterbury.*

Richard on the city walls; but shortly afterwards the standard was found in the ditch, having been torn down and thrown over the wall. The result was that Leopold and the force at his command abandoned the crusade and set off for home.

KING PHILIP'S DEPARTURE

Philip II also left shortly afterwards. He had been severely ill with dysentery and also needed to settle the succession in Vermandois and Flanders, for the lord of that region, Philip of Alsace, had died in the camp at Acre and left no heirs. Philip left behind in Acre a French army of 10,000 under the command of Duke Hugh III of Burgundy and set sail for Genoa, bound for France. His departure greatly displeased Richard, who declared: 'It is a pity and a shame on my lord to leave this place without having brought to an end the enterprise that brought him here. But if he finds himself in bad health, and in fear perhaps lest he should die here, his will must be done.' His displeasure was no doubt principally caused by the knowledge that his territorial possessions in northern France would be open to interference from Philip while he himself was engaged in pursuing the crusade.

ATROCITY AT ACRE?

RICHARD I AND THE MASSACRE OF MUSLIM PRISONERS

On 20 August Richard had 2,700 Muslim prisoners from Acre beheaded on the plain in front of the city, in full view of Saladin's camp. He said that he did it because Saladin was refusing to honour the agreed terms of the surrender.

The prisoners killed included soldiers from the garrison, but also women and children. Many historians have expressed horror at the deed, contrasting it with Saladin's frequent magnanimity in victory. The Muslim army launched an attack in an attempt to stop the killing, but were driven back.

▼ *Kings Philip II and Richard I oversee the surrender of Acre and the taking of the city's garrison and people into captivity.*

It may be that Richard's decision was a justified act of war. It is certainly true that Saladin was dragging out the settlement of the ransom payment. Saladin had made an initial payment of the ransom fee on 11 August but according to the 12–13th-century Muslim historian Baha ad-Din ibn Shaddad, the general had then refused to hand over the next instalment until all the garrison prisoners had been released, and had wanted to provide a new batch of prisoners from his own camp to stand in place of the members of the Acre garrison. His motive was probably to make the settlement of the agreement drag out so long that the campaigning season would end before Richard could succeed in launching an attack on Jerusalem.

A LION IN A HURRY

Richard, on the other hand, was in a hurry. He had seen Philip II set sail for home, and had had time to consider the possible ramifications of the king of France being at large in Europe unchecked by the presence there of the king of England – Richard himself. He wanted to hasten the crusade towards its conclusion, so that he could return to manage his European affairs. He wrote to his justiciar in England from Acre on 6 August describing his victories on campaign, but indicating that he would soon be returning home – 'as soon as we have brought Syria back to its previous position'. He promised to be back in English waters by the following Lent.

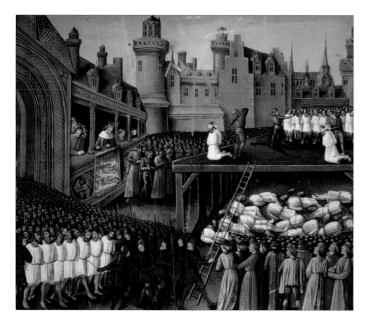

▲ *Barbarous act or necessary military decision? On Richard's orders, one by one, 2,700 Muslim prisoners are put to death.*

He was in any case a decisive man who liked to act swiftly: already on the crusade he had conducted two whirlwind campaigns, one in southern Italy, where he had captured several Byzantine possessions, and one in Cyprus, where he had captured the island in just a fortnight.

He wanted to move on from Acre, and he did not have sufficient manpower to leave an army behind to guard the prisoners. Among the garrison were many crack Turkish soldiers who had fought bravely and with great skill to prolong the siege – he could not allow these men to escape or be released and then rejoin Saladin's army. Some writers have argued that the killing of the prisoners was an act of barbarity, but it can be viewed as a sensible and necessary strategic decision.

ALL THINGS FAIR IN WAR?

Moreover, it would appear from Saladin's later friendly relations with Richard that the Muslim general did not view the killing at Acre as an act of brutality – he did not conceive a contemptuous hatred for Richard as he had done for Reynald of Châtillon. While Saladin was certainly often notable for his clemency in victory, he, too, was capable of acts of great ferocity, such as when he ordered the beheading of the captured Knights Templar and Hospitaller after their defeat at the Battle of the Horns of Hattin. On that occasion, the killing of the knights was made into an amusing spectacle, as the Muslim army jeered and laughed while untrained and unskilled army followers hacked at the knights.

Richard's actions did, however, have consequences that cannot have been good for army morale. The killing of the prisoners naturally brought an end to negotiations. As a result, the 2,000-odd Christian prisoners in the Muslim camp were not released and the sacred relic of the True Cross, captured at the Horns of Hattin and held in Saladin's camp, was not returned to the crusaders. However, the failed attack by the Muslim army left the crusaders in even stronger control of Acre than previously.

FIERCE AND RUTHLESS

Throughout his career, Richard demonstrated ruthlessness and decisiveness and a knack for making correct strategic decisions. In most ways the man known as *Coeur de Lion* was the very type of the chivalric knight – a great leader of men, charismatic, brave, strong, skilful, good-looking, hearty, and not lacking courtly accomplishments as a well-educated lover of poetry and song. But he was not the kind of knight who placed a greater importance on chivalry than on victory.

The massacre at Acre should probably be viewed in this light, seen alongside his treachery towards his father, Henry II of England, or his ruthlessness on European campaigns as another example among many of a clear-eyed desire for victory – a willingness to do whatever is necessary to win. The killing of the prisoners freed the crusader army to move on swiftly from Acre and impressed his ferocity and strength of purpose on his opponents. (Later, Saladin was unable to garrison Ascalon against Richard, for his men were too frightened by reports of Richard's behaviour at Acre to volunteer.) *Coeur de Lion's* heart was not only brave and strong, but also ferocious – and dangerous.

▼ *Ruthless in victory, Richard does away with the prisoners. He saw them as a threat that had to be eliminated.*

RICHARD'S MARCH TO JAFFA
AND A GREAT VICTORY AT THE BATTLE OF ARSUF

Richard set out from Acre on 22 August with the intention of moving swiftly on to Jerusalem. He led his army southwards along the coast to Jaffa (modern Tel Aviv-Jafo), accompanied at sea by a fleet carrying supplies and water. But Saladin's troops shadowed them all the way and launched wave after wave of skirmishing attacks. In a pitched battle at Arsuf on September 7, the crusaders drove off their persecutors, winning a resounding victory over the Muslim force.

THE MARCH

Richard imposed absolute discipline on his army. He knew that over-enthusiasm and a lack of respect for the harshness of climate and terrain had led to disaster at the Horns of Hattin: for this reason, he decreed that the army would march no more than 4–5 miles (6–8km) per day, moving only in the cooler hours of the morning and making camp each afternoon by a source of water.

On the march Richard insisted that his men kept in a tight formation, with the infantry on the landward side to fend off attacks by the Muslim army and protect the mounted knights riding in the centre of the column. The infantrymen carried large crusader shields and wore heavy armour over thick felt jerkins. According to Muslim historian Baha ed-Din, the arrows of the Turkish archers could make little impression on them: 'I saw,' he wrote, 'warriors with no fewer than ten arrows stuck in their back armour, marching on unperturbed without breaking rank.' Periodically, the infantrymen on the landward side were replaced by fresher men who had been marching on the seaward side, where there were no attacks.

In the centre of the main column was the royal standard, mounted in a wagon and guarded by an elite reserve. In front of this rode the Knights Templar and behind it the Knights Hospitaller. The rear of the army had to cope with repeated attacks, and take care not to fall behind. The Muslim force harried the column, hoping to force the crusaders to break rank, but they failed. King Richard was constantly vigilant, barking our orders, tirelessly riding out to meet attacks with his great sword shining in the harsh sun.

▼ *Richard's troops make their way in searing heat and through bare desert from Acre to Jaffa, his men under strict orders not to respond to attacks by Saladin's army.*

▲ *The crusaders fought fiercely, but it was Richard's ability to make instant tactical decisions that triumphed at Arsuf. When the Hospitallers broke rank it was a potential disaster, but with a swift general charge Richard won the day.*

There was no great crowd of camp-followers as there had been on previous crusades – only this strictly disciplined column. Baha ed-Din described the Muslims' frustration at being unable to break the self-control of the Christians: 'You could not help but admire the patience of these soldiers, who put up with the most extreme difficulties.' Richard would not allow women to accompany the army, save for a corps of washer-women who were responsible for cleaning the soldiers' linen, washing their hair and delousing them.

THE ATTACK AT CAESAREA

The crusader army reached Caesarea on 30 August. A major Muslim attack succeeded briefly in isolating the rear of the crusader column under Hugh III, Duke of Burgundy, but with the help of Richard himself they managed to drive off the attack and reunite the column. As they fought the crusaders called out 'Help us, Holy Sepulchre!'

THE BATTLE OF ARSUF

On 7 September Saladin unleashed a full-scale onslaught on the crusader army at Arsuf. His plan was to draw the Christian knights out into a series of charges, and then attack and overpower them once they were split up into small groups.

The first attack came at nine in the morning, accompanied by a fearful noise of gongs, cymbals and trumpets and by the Muslim soldiers screaming. A second attack concentrated on the Hospitallers in the rear of the army column. Each attack came in waves: first Nubian and Bedouin soldiers unleashed a storm of arrows and javelins, and then moved aside to allow a follow-up onslaught from the Turkish mounted archers who rode swiftly forward before wheeling away in the hope of drawing out a charge. Here and there along the columns were pockets of fierce hand-to-hand fighting.

All this time the crusaders continued to march forwards towards Arsuf. Richard's plan was to hold the line and keep his

▼ *Richard was everywhere at Arsuf, leading his men by personal example and trying to ensure that they kept their discipline.*

knights back for one overwhelming charge. This demanded extraordinary discipline, for the Christians were under extreme pressure and the natural response of many of the knights in the army was to break out and charge.

In mid-afternoon, the vanguard of the Christian army marched into Arsuf just as the Hospitallers in the rear came under very severe attack. The Hospitaller general, Garnier of Nablus, begged Richard for the order to charge but the king commanded men to hold the line. But at this point discipline snapped: the Hospitallers charged, with a great shout of 'St George!' They were followed by the French knights who were just ahead of them in the line.

Richard acted decisively, making the best of what had happened by ordering a Templar-led charge right along the line. Saladin's army was driven back, but regrouped; Richard managed to gather his knights for a second charge and the Muslim force scattered. According to the *Itinerarium Regis Ricardi*, Richard led by example: the author likened Richard's sword to a sickle, harvesting a crop of warriors: he claimed that Richard covered the battlefield with Muslim corpses.

▲ *Saladin's attack was carefully planned at Arsuf. He thought he had Richard trapped, but the crusaders turned the tables on him.*

The crusaders still had to weather one more storm, for Saladin's nephew Taqi al-Din led an attack on the left flank, but Richard managed to regroup his knights for a third charge. This time Saladin's army fled in disarray into the hills. Richard's knights mounted his standard on the hill where Saladin's had flown and looted the abandoned Muslim camp. Since darkness was now falling Richard ordered his men to abandon the chase.

A GREAT BUT NOT DECISIVE VICTORY

The Battle of Arsuf was a major victory. It blew a hole in Saladin's reputation for invincibility and demonstrated Richard's superb generalship and personal bravery. But it was not a victory on the scale of the Horns of Hattin, for it wasn't a decisive blow against Saladin's military strength. The Muslim general prepared to block the route to Jerusalem: Richard's triumph at Arsuf did not leave the way open to the Holy City as Saladin's victory at the Horns of Hattin had done. In the short term, instead of marching on Jerusalem Richard occupied and refortified Jaffa.

AN UNCERTAIN FUTURE

RICHARD'S NEGOTIATIONS WITH SALADIN, AND THE JERUSALEM SUCCESSION

After the immense demands of the siege of Acre, the difficult march down the coast and heroic victory in the bruising Battle of Arsuf, Richard and his army recuperated in Jaffa. Saladin went to Ascalon and broke down the fortification to prevent Richard taking it and using it as a stronghold. In October Richard opened negotiations with Saladin in search of a diplomatic solution to bring the war to an end.

With the year drawing to a close, Richard saw the difficulty of mounting a swift campaign to capture Jerusalem, given Saladin's surviving military strength and the fact that elements of Richard's own army had drifted back to Acre. He also saw that lack of manpower would make it virtually impossible to defend the Holy City even if he succeeded in capturing it, especially because many in his army were crusader-pilgrims and could be expected to return to Europe having entered Jerusalem and worshipped in the Church of the Holy Sepulchre. On 1 October 1191 Richard wrote to the abbot of Clairvaux, describing his successes at Arsuf and reoccupation of Jaffa, and look-

▼ *Richard and Saladin were exemplars of chivalry throughout the medieval period. These tiles representing the adversaries date from the 13th century.*

ing hopefully forward to future conquests. Richard indicated that he and his men were exhausted and that the land of Palestine needed reinforcement, for if they captured more territory they would need men to hold it: he asked the abbot to inspire more European lords and yeomen to travel to the Holy Land.

NEGOTIATIONS AT JAFFA

Meanwhile, Saladin sent his brother al-Adil to Jaffa to carry out the negotiations. Richard was negotiating from a position of relative strength, and initially made a remarkably bold demand: the handover of Jerusalem together with all the territory between the coast and the River Jordan, and the return of the sacred relic of the True Cross, which was still in Saladin's possession following the breakdown of negotiations after the slaughter of prisoners at Acre. Saladin returned a cautious response, noting that Jerusalem was as much a Muslim as a Christian city, that the wider territory in Palestine had been in the possession of the crusaders for only a century or so and that he was willing to hand over the True Cross if he received something of equal value in return.

Then Richard made a shockingly original suggestion to al-Adil. He proposed that al-Adil marry Richard's sister, Joan of England, who, since the death of William

II of Sicily, had been the Dowager Queen of Sicily. Richard would give them possession of Acre and Jaffa and Saladin, should he agree, would give them the remainder of Palestine: then together they would rule the entire country from Jerusalem. Richard would return to England; the war would be over. The only problem he could see, Richard said, was that the pope would not agree: in which case, Richard suggested, one of his nieces could take the place of Joan.

Saladin, remarkably enough, agreed to this proposal – although according to Baha ed-Din, only because he knew it was a practical joke. But Joan of England refused to marry a Muslim; and Richard's suggestion to al-Adil that he convert to Christianity was also rejected. The negotiations ended amicably but without lasting results.

MARCH ON JERUSALEM

Richard then marched to Ascalon and began to rebuild the fortifications that Saladin had dismantled. In the winter, when Saladin had largely disbanded his army, Richard marched the crusader force towards Jerusalem. He got within 12 miles (20km) of the Holy City in January 1192, but in terrible weather that made rivers of the roads he decided not to risk an assault; the waterlogged, mountainous terrain did not play to the strengths of the crusader cavalry and instead favoured the mobile Turkish horsemen and archers. He returned to Ascalon.

Negotiations continued. Richard felt an increasingly urgent need to return to Europe to safeguard his possessions, for he was receiving reports that his brother John was seeking to seize power in England while Philip II was eyeing Normandy. At the end of March a workable compromise seemed to have been reached: the crusaders would retain Acre, Jaffa and Ascalon and would have the relic

◄ *Richard's decision to pull back from an assault on Jerusalem in 1191–92 may be a sign of his willingness to compromise.*

Isabella's consort from 1192 to 1197, although for unknown reasons he was never crowned.

Rumours soon began to circulate as to who had been behind Conrad's murder, with some claiming that Richard had hired the Assassins to do the deed. But it seems unlikely, given that he did not try to force Guy of Lusignan on the kingdom but accepted the elevation of the kingship to Henry of Champagne. More likely the cause lay in conflict between Genoese merchants who had Conrad's backing and their rivals from Pisa who would have been excluded by a Genoese monopoly had Conrad succeeded, but under Henry won important concessions in Acre.

of the True Cross returned; in addition, they would have the right to visit Jerusalem as pilgrims and maintain priests there. On Palm Sunday, 29 March, Richard knighted al-Adil in a splendid ceremony.

THE JERUSALEM SUCCESSION

In April the long-running succession dispute between Guy of Lusignan (also known as Guy of Jerusalem), the husband of the deceased Queen Sibylla, and Conrad of Tyre (also known as Conrad of Montferrat), husband of Sibylla's younger sister Isabella, was decided in Conrad's favour at a meeting of a council of Jerusalem's leading knights and barons. Richard had backed Guy but Guy received no votes at all in council. Richard subsequently arranged for him to buy the Kingdom of Cyprus. But then, on April 28, before he could be crowned, Conrad was killed in the streets of Tyre by two Assassins (*see* box).

Within a week of Conrad's death Henry II, Count of Champagne, nephew to both Richard I of England and Philip II of France, had married Conrad's wife Isabella and been acclaimed King of Jerusalem. He ruled as king on account of being Queen

THE ASSASSINS

The Assassins who killed Conrad were members of a militant Shi'ite Muslim sect, founded in 1094 in opposition to the new Shi'ite Fatimid caliph in Cairo and in support of his deposed brother Nisar. They believed in terrorist murder as a sacred duty, and were known as *hashshashin* in Arabic, from their reported practice of smoking hashish before embarking on suicide murder missions. The English word 'assassin' comes from *hashshashin*.

The Assassins carried out deadly missions against Sunni and certain Shi'ite Muslims whom they considered religious enemies as well as against crusaders. Their first leader, Hasan-e Sabbah, oversaw the establishment of a string of castle strongholds in Iran and Iraq from which terrorist killers emerged on missions. In the 12th century they captured several fortresses in Syria,

▶ *The fortress that became the Assassins' castle at Masyaf in Syria was originally built by the Byzantines.*

including the celebrated castle of Masyaf, from which their Syrian chief Rashid ad-Din as-Sinan and his successors sent men out on a series of murder missions. Sinan and his successors were called *shaykh al-jabal* (mountain chieftain in Arabic), which the crusaders rendered into English as the 'Old Man of the Mountain'.

THE TREATY OF JAFFA

LAST BATTLES AND FINAL TREATY OF THE THIRD CRUSADE

In May–June 1192, when Richard and his troops came within striking distance of Jerusalem for the second time in just six months, Richard elected not to launch an assault. Subsequently, back on the coast, he won two astonishing victories over Saladin before agreeing the terms of the Treaty of Jaffa, which brought the crusade to an end.

SECOND APPROACH TO JERUSALEM

In May 1192 Richard marched southwards down the coast from Ascalon and captured the fortress of Darum. Then he marched inland towards Jerusalem and encamped in the hills about 12 miles

▼ *In war and diplomacy Richard and Saladin treated each other with respect, each aware of the other's prowess. Chivalric authors and storytellers ever since have imagined encounters between the two men.*

(20km) from the city. Two events occurred in the hills before Richard ordered a surprising retreat to the coast.

The first was that he attacked a trade caravan heading from Egypt to Jerusalem and seized rich booty, including several hundred camels and horses – according to Saladin's secretary, Imad ed-din al-Isfahani, Richard disguised himself as an Arab in order to reconnoitre the landscape as the caravan approached. On another occasion, while pursuing some Turks in the hills he looked up and saw the Holy City in the distance. This was to be the only time he saw Jerusalem – and because he had made a vow that he would look on the city only as its conqueror, he raised his shield in front of his eyes to block off the view and rode away.

After the attack on the caravan, Saladin expected an assault on Jerusalem and prepared for a siege by poisoning water sources around the city and calling his

military advisers to a council of war. But on 5 July he received reports from his scouts that the crusaders had broken their camp in the hills nearby and were marching away from Jerusalem, back to the coast. Saladin rode out to watch the retreat. Many in the crusader army were puzzled and angered by Richard's decision. It would appear that he again decided that it would be pointless to launch a major assault against a target that he could not hope to hold even if he won it.

THE BATTLES OF JAFFA

Richard retired to Acre, expecting the stand-off to continue, but Saladin launched a heavy attack on Jaffa. Here, for once, the great Muslim general lost control of his men, who ran amok looting and plundering in defiance of Saladin's orders to allow the Christians to leave the city peacefully with their possessions. Some contemporary reports suggest that Saladin urgently communicated with the Christian garrison, encouraging them to take refuge in the citadel while he struggled to impose order on his troops.

Richard meanwhile gathered a small force and sailed along the coast from Acre to Jaffa. Arriving on 31 July he anchored off the city: a priest from the garrison, seeing the royal standard, swam bravely out to the ships to let Richard know that, although the city was in Saracen hands, the garrison was holding out in the citadel and negotiating terms of surrender.

What followed was truly the stuff of chivalric legend. Richard leapt immediately from the boat and swam ashore, loyally followed by his knights. This force of just the king and 54 others succeeded against all odds in driving the Saracen forces back. Richard and his knights camped outside the city, for inside it was in ruins following its earlier sacking and the stench of corpses in the streets made it uninhabitable. At dawn on 5 August

Saladin launched an attack with 7,000 cavalry; Richard and his knights had just 15 horses between them but – supported by around 2,000 Italian crossbowmen – they went resolutely forward to defend the edge of their camp, which was marked by a line of sharpened tent pegs. That day the crusaders won another extraordinary victory, holding the camp and the city against the Saracen attack. Saladin abandoned the campaign and retreated to Jerusalem.

Richard and Saladin were both exhausted, and both fell ill in the days after the extraordinary battles of Jaffa.

▼ *Richard's heroic assault on Jaffa with just 54 knights really was an occasion when history matched the brave feats of legend.*

▲ *These stones, in the gateway to the Old City at Jaffa, witnessed the clash of armies and the great deeds of kings and knights.*

With typical chivalry, Saladin sent fruit and mountain snow to Richard to speed his recovery.

PEACE AT LAST

Negotiations for a peace settlement were reopened and the two leaders reached agreement and signed the Treaty of Jaffa on 2 September. Under its terms, there would be a three-year truce between the two sides. The Christians agreed to demolish Ascalon and not rebuild it in those three years; they were to keep the coastal lands from Acre down to Jaffa, as well as the Principality of Antioch and the County of Tripoli; they would be allowed access as pilgrims to the churches and shrines of Jerusalem; and Roman priests would be able to celebrate services in the city.

In the weeks following the agreement, hundreds of crusaders made their way to Jerusalem to fulfil their vows. But Richard refused, declaring that he could not enter the city since God had denied him the chance to do so as conqueror. He was in any case very keen to return to Europe to look after his possessions there. He set sail on 9 October.

AFTER THE THIRD CRUSADE

THE AFTERMATH AND LEGACY OF THE 1189–92 CAMPAIGN

The Third Crusade ended in 1192 without the capture of Jerusalem. The crusade did not have a dramatic conclusion, and although it succeeded in preventing the complete destruction of the Latin Kingdom of Jerusalem, there remained in many quarters a sense of unfinished business. Just three years later, in 1195, another crusade was being organized by Pope Celestine III (ruled 1191–98) and German emperor Henry VI.

▼ *Coeur de Lion's martial prowess counts for nothing as he is fatally injured by a crossbow bolt from Chalus-Chabrol castle.*

RICHARD LEAVES PALESTINE

Richard I's homeward journey from the Holy Land was a disaster. Shipwrecked in the Adriatic, he attempted to cross the lands of the Holy Roman Empire in disguise, well aware that he could not expect a hospitable welcome from either Duke Leopold of Austria (with whom he had quarrelled violently at Acre) or German emperor Henry VI (angry that Richard had recognized Tancred as King of Sicily). By rights, these lords should have offered Richard immunity from attack because he was returning from the crusades, but both were keen to punish and to profit by him.

Richard was betrayed to Leopold who passed him on to Henry. Richard languished in prison for months before being ransomed for 150,000 silver marks.

His great opponent, Saladin, died after morning prayers on 4 March 1193 in Damascus, just five months after Richard's departure from Acre. Baha ed-Din ibn Shaddad declared that the Islamic world was filled with a grief so profound that only Allah himself could plumb its depths. Famed for his generosity, Saladin died bankrupt – at his death his treasury contained a gold coin and 47 pieces of silver – not enough to pay for his funeral.

Saladin's death presented an opportunity for the crusaders at an extremely inopportune moment. The great general's army was dispersed, and his power evaporated in family squabbles as one of his sons, al-Afdal Nureddin, marched on Damascus, while a second son, al-Aziz Uthman, was besieged in Cairo by Saladin's brother, al-Adil. Had Richard I waited in the Holy Land just six months longer, he would almost certainly have been able to capitalize on Saladin's death by capturing Jerusalem and re-establishing it as a Christian city. In the event, it took al-Adil ten years to reunite Saladin's territorial possessions.

Richard was never to return to the Holy Land. He spent most of the remainder of his life fighting over his French possessions with Philip II and died in April 1199 aged 41 after being shot in the neck by an archer during a siege of the unimportant castle of Chalus-Chabrol in the Limousin.

THE 'CRUSADE' OF 1195

On 25 July 1195 Pope Celestine III issued a call to arms for a fresh crusade. His letter, as reported by English chronicler Ralph of Diceto, declared that although the most recent crusade had not entirely succeeded in its aims, Christian folk should be strong in faith that God would

'exalt in his miracles' and 'instruct their hands in battle and their fingers in fighting'. As his predecessors had done before him, Celestine promised a plenary indulgence for the crusaders' sins 'and afterwards eternal life'.

German Emperor Henry VI, the son of Frederick I Barbarossa, responded to the call. Between October 1195 and March 1196 a great throng of Germans took the cross; they departed from southern Italy for the Holy Land in spring 1197. The army, sent by Henry, Duke of Brabant, landed at Acre in September 1197 and occupied Beirut and Sidon. But Henry died of malaria in September 1197 in Messina while campaigning in Sicily; and the German crusaders, as their predecessors had in 1189, simply melted away when they heard the news of the emperor's untimely death. The crusade of 1195 ended in a hurried truce.

LEGACY OF THE THIRD CRUSADE

The Third Crusade did not succeed in achieving one of its principal targets, capturing Jerusalem, but in many ways it was a success. At the outset in 1187 Saladin appeared to be invincible and it seemed

only a matter of time before the greatest of Muslim generals drove the Latin settlers out of Palestine altogether. Yet Richard I managed to inflict stunning defeats on this towering figure at Acre, Arsuf and Jaffa and in the process re-established the Kingdom of Jerusalem on a relatively secure footing. Moreover, the island of Cyprus, which Richard captured in 1191, proved to be a very valuable conquest,

▼ *Saladin died in Damascus, where he was buried close to the Umayyad Mosque.*

▲ *German crusaders capture Beirut in 1197, but the victory was to be short lived.*

since it provided a vital long-term partner for the Latin states in the Holy Land.

The Third Crusade set the pattern for future crusades to the Holy Land. After the campaign of 1189–92, crusaders no longer made their way to Palestine by way of Constantinople and Anatolia, but by sea directly to the ports of Acre or Tyre. In the first two crusades the European soldiers had chosen violence over diplomacy in every impasse, but after the use by Richard of truces and negotiated settlements with Saladin, relations between the crusaders and the Muslims were transformed. Moreover, just as the crusade had failed to capture Jerusalem, but still achieved certain valuable goals in consolidating the Latin presence in Palestine, so in future crusades the focus shifted away from the earlier narrow focus on liberating Jerusalem to a more general focus on aiding the Christian settlers in the Holy Land.

In 1198 a young, power-hungry pope, Innocent III, began to organize another crusade. The fruit of his labours would be the Fourth Crusade of 1202–04.

CHAPTER TWELVE

CRUSADES OF THE EARLY 13TH CENTURY

In the first three decades of the 13th century, popes Innocent III (ruled 1198–1216), Honorius III (ruled 1216–27) and Gregory IX (ruled 1227–41) oversaw three major crusades to the East – the Fourth of 1202–04, the Fifth of 1217–21 and the Sixth of 1228. In his 18-year reign Innocent III also proclaimed a whole series of European crusades, including two against fellow Christians (the German lord Markward of Anweiler and the Albigensian heretics of southern France), one against Baltic pagans in northern Europe and one against the Muslim Almohad caliphs in Spain. In all of these encounters, Innocent and his successors worked with their utmost force to maintain papal control, for they saw crusading as a means to extend the power of Rome.

But the popes often failed to keep control of the powerful lords and complex alliances engaged in the crusades to the East. Of the three major Eastern crusades in these years, only the Fifth can be said to have remained under papal control through the office of papal legate Pelagius. It ended in abject failure, with the agreement of a humiliating peace treaty. Of the others, the Fourth slipped entirely from the papal control and ended up as little more than a pillaging expedition, while the Sixth ended as a seeming success, with Jerusalem in Christian hands and the position of Outremer bolstered. However, these successes had been achieved by the fiercely independent Frederick II of Germany working quite unilaterally to the papacy.

▲ *Venetian and French lords take stock after the sacking of Constantinople in 1204.*

◄ *The armies of the Fourth Crusade ignored an excommunication threat from Innocent III when they sacked the city of Zara in 1202.*

FIGHTING FOR VENICE

CRUSADERS DIVERT TO ATTACK ZARA

The newly elected Pope Innocent III called for another crusade to reclaim the Holy Land in August 1198. French barons responded to the call in 1201 and, choosing to travel by sea, negotiated with the doge of Venice, Enrico Dandolo, to transport them to the Holy Land. Failures of organization and recruitment resulted in them being in such severe debt to Venice that they had to agree to divert the crusaders to fight on the doge's behalf against the city of Zara, in Dalmatia (Croatia).

INNOCENT'S CALL TO ARMS

Pope Innocent's call to arms was largely directed at knights and noblemen rather than royalty. Like many others, Innocent believed that the Third Crusade had failed to liberate Jerusalem because it had been led by kings, and principally because of the inability of Richard I and Philip II to overcome their rivalries. This time the pope set out to establish the crusade as one strictly under papal control and nominated two legates, Soffredo of Pisa and Peter of Capuano, to be leaders 'humbly and religiously' of the crusade. Innocent

▼ *Venice rose to prominence as a centre for trade between western Europe and the rest of the known world – both the Byzantine Empire and Islamic territories beyond.*

later authorized the preaching of the crusade by a French priest named Fulk of Neuilly, a gifted orator.

The response to Innocent's call to arms was initially underwhelming, but then in November 1199 at a grand chivalric tournament at Ecry-sur-Aisne in Champagne, the 22-year-old host, Count Theobald of Champagne, and one of the leading competitors, the 27-year-old Count Louis of Blois, both took the cross after hearing a crusade sermon by Fulk of Neuilly. (Theobald was the younger brother of Henry of Champagne, then reigning as king of Jerusalem since he was the husband of Queen Isabella of Jerusalem, having married Isabella right after the assassination of her previous husband, Conrad of Montferrat.)

Theobald and Louis were followed by other noblemen, including Count Baldwin of Flanders and Simon of Montfort, 5th Earl of Leicester. (Simon was later captain general of French forces in the Albigensian Crusade and father of the Simon of Montfort who led baronial opposition to King Henry III of England and briefly ruled the country in the 1260s.) Also among the French noblemen who took the cross was Geoffrey of Villehardouin, who wrote an account of the crusade. Count Theobald was elected leader.

▲ *Earlier in his career, wily Venetian leader Enrico Dandolo had served his city as an ambassador to the Byzantine Empire. He knew the wealth of Constantinople.*

NEGOTIATIONS WITH VENICE

Theobald, Louis and Baldwin appointed six envoys to negotiate the necessary practical arrangements. The envoys approached Venice, the world's leading maritime power at the close of the 12th century, and commissioned a fleet to transport the crusader army to the Holy Land. They asked for sufficient ships to transport an army of 33,500 men – a wildly ambitious number, no less than seven times larger than the force taken by Philip II in 1190. The proposed army was to consist of 4,500 knights (with their horses), 9,000 squires and 20,000 infantry.

To supply a fleet to carry this army, plus nine months' supply of food and fodder, the Venetians demanded 85,000 marks; in addition they offered to provide 50 additional armed galleys 'for the love of God', on the condition that the city be granted one-half of any plunder that was seized by, either by land or sea. The deal was agreed, and consecrated in a lavish service in St Mark's, Venice.

The envoys' overambitious planning was to have severe consequences. The envoys also secretly agreed among themselves that the initial target for the crusade should be Egypt rather than Palestine. It had been proposed before, not least by Richard I during the Third Crusade, that the key to undermining Muslim strength in the Holy Land would be found in attacking Egypt. However, the revised target was kept secret because the majority of the knights and others who had taken the cross had done so with Jerusalem as their inspiration and goal.

A NEW LEADER

In May 1201, crusade leader Count Theobald died of a mysterious malady. He was replaced by the Italian count Boniface of Montferrat. In June 1202 crusaders began gathering in Venice. Only around 11,000 men had arrived by October, partly because some had sailed directly from ports in southern France; the original target of 33,500 had been far too ambitious. The fleet of ships was ready – but the crusaders could not pay for it in full. After a prolonged stalemate, the Venetian doge offered to postpone full

▼ *Pope Innocent III felt the Christian church had to strengthen its position against heretics within it.*

▲ *Baldwin of Flanders played a leading role in the Fourth Crusade from start to shameful finish. He was made emperor of the Latin Empire of Constantinople.*

payment of the shortfall until the crusaders were able to raise the money through looting, but only if the crusaders came to the aid of Venice by reconquering its former colony of Zara in Hungary (modern Zadar in Croatia). This was a Christian city, under the protection of the Roman Catholic king, Emeric of Hungary, who had himself taken the cross.

The crusaders effectively had no choice. The doge, Enrico Dandolo, elected to take the cross and sail with them – despite being in his 80s and virtually blind. He was an extremely capable and intelligent man, and remarkable healthy for his age.

THE ATTACK ON ZARA

The crusade fleet sailed in November 1202, bound for Zara. The papal legate Peter Capuano approved the deal as the only way to prevent the crusade foundering altogether, but Pope Innocent III wrote a letter threatening the crusade leaders with excommunication if they attacked fellow Christians. The citizens of Zara hung banners emblazoned with the cross from their windows and on the city walls in the hope of forestalling the assault. But the attack went ahead.

After a siege of five days, Zara surrendered to the crusade leaders, and accepted Venice's claim of suzerainty. The victorious army entered the city and systematically looted it. They then decided to spend the winter there before proceeding with the crusade.

ON TO CONSTANTINOPLE

CRUSADERS AGREE TO RESTORE DEPOSED EMPEROR TO THRONE

After the sacking of Zara, the crusaders took another unexpected diversion. Exiled Byzantine prince Alexius Angelus offered their leaders astonishing levels of funding and military support for the remainder of the expedition if they agreed first to sail to Constantinople and depose the emperor, Alexius III.

BYZANTINE NEGOTIATIONS

Emperor Isaac II Angelus had in 1195 been blinded, deposed and imprisoned by his own brother, who took the throne as Emperor Alexius III. The deposed emperor's son, Prince Alexius Angelus, had escaped into exile and was seeking support to restore his father to the throne. In the winter of 1202 he was a guest of Philip of Swabia, who was his brother-in-law, having married Alexius's sister Irene in May 1197.

At Philip's court, Alexius met Boniface of Montferrat, the elected leader of the Fourth Crusade, who had left his fellow crusaders in Venice before they embarked to make the attack on Zara. (Philip was the youngest son of Emperor Frederick I Barbarossa and was king of Germany; he had been elected Holy Roman emperor in 1198 following the death of Henry VI, but Pope Innocent opposed his succession, preferring the rival claim of Otto, son of Henry the Lion, Duke of Saxony. Boniface was one of Philip's leading feudal vassals.)

Prince Alexius made a remarkable offer to Boniface: if the crusaders diverted the expedition to Constantinople in order forcibly to right the wrongs brought about by the usurper emperor Alexius III, he would provide 200,000 silver marks to meet the army's current expenses, supply food for the entire force, send 10,000 men and 20 galleys to support the planned crusading expedition against Egypt for an entire year, establish a permanent force of 500 Byzantine knights in the Holy Land – and put the Greek Orthodox Church under the authority of the pope in Rome.

Boniface of Montferrat returned to the crusaders, with Prince Alexius in his party, and news of his very generous offer. The main leaders agreed to the plan, arguing that this diversion was the only way to bring about the crusade's ultimate aims, but it was far from universally popular. Several noblemen, including the French knight Simon of Montfort, withdrew in disgust; when news of the decision reached Rome, Pope Innocent sent letters forbidding an attack on Constantinople.

However, these letters arrived after the main body of the crusade set sail for Constantinople on Easter Monday 1203, too late; in any case, the crusaders had so many reasons to move against the Byzantines that it is doubtful whether or not the letters would have had any effect.

REASONS TO ATTACK THE BYZANTINE EMPIRE

Venice had a longstanding quarrel with the Byzantine emperor, dating back to the 1170s, when Emperor Manuel I Comnenus had arrested Venetian merchants and confiscated their valuable goods. Moreover, the current usurper emperor, Alexius III, was granting preferable trading terms to Venice's rivals, Genoa and Pisa.

Boniface of Montferrat also had a quarrel with the Byzantine Empire. His younger brother Rainier had in 1179 married Maria Comnena, daughter of Emperor Manuel I Comnenus, and had been given the title 'Caesar'. Both Rainier and Maria had then been killed by poison in Constantinople in 1182 and Boniface claimed that Byzantine territory that he believed had been given to Rainier was now rightfully his.

Another important factor, although not one that can have been discussed openly, was that launching the planned attack on Egypt was not in the interests of the Venetians, who had a trading colony in Alexandria; according to some interpretations of contemporary documents, the Venetians may have secretly made a treaty in 1202 with Saladin's brother al-Adil, in power in Egypt, to divert a crusading attack away from Egypt in return for improved trading privileges there.

◄ *Zara surrenders to Venetian control. Venice had twice invaded Zara in the 12th century before the opportunity arose to impose its will on the city.*

▲ *After spurning orders from Pope Alexius III to move on to Jerusalem, the huge Venetian fleet of over 200 ships, attacked the great walls of Constantinople.*

On top of these considerations, relations had been extremely strained between the 'Latins' in the European crusader army and the 'Greeks' of the Byzantine Empire, from the time of the First Crusade.

But probably most pressing of all reasons was that the crusaders in Zara did not manage to raise enough money in looting the city to pay off their debt to the city of Venice. They needed to generate wealth, and the diversion to Constantinople, although officially being launched to restore the deposed emperor, also raised the tantalizing prospect of looting the imperial capital.

ARRIVAL AT CONSTANTINOPLE

The vast crusade fleet, consisting of 60 war galleys as well as 50 large transports and 100 horse transports, arrived at Constantinople on St John the Baptist's Day, 24 June 1203. The ships did not land before the city, but sailed on to capture and install themselves in Chalcedon and Chrysopolis on the other side of the Bosphorus.

There they were visited by an envoy from Emperor Alexius III declaring that he would provide money and supplies if they moved swiftly on towards Jerusalem, but they sent back the reply that they did not recognize his authority and that the lands he ruled belonged to his nephew who was in the crusader camp. Then the crusaders sent young Alexius to the city with ten galleys of soldiers, to ask the

inhabitants of the city, who were arrayed on its walls, whether they would recognize the rule of the deposed Isaac II Angelus and his son. They replied that they did not know these names, and jeered at the soldiers.

On 5 July – to the sound of trumpets, tabors and kettledrums – the full might of the crusader army embarked on to transports to cross the Bosphorus and begin the siege of the city. According to the eyewitness account of a crusader knight from Picardy, named Robert of Clari, the people of Constantinople armed themselves and climbed on the roofs of their houses and up the many towers of the city. They saw the vast fleet. 'It seemed to them,' Robert wrote, 'that the ocean and the land were shaking, and that the wide waves were covered over entirely with ships.'

THE SACK OF CONSTANTINOPLE

RAPE, MURDER AND LOOTING AS CRUSADERS SHAME THE CROSS

The Fourth Crusade's diversion to Constantinople, officially performed to restore the deposed Emperor Isaac II Angelus to the imperial throne, degenerated into a full-scale attack on the city, followed by three lawless days of rampant looting. The greed-driven ransacking of this historic Christian city must rival the savage slaughter of the inhabitants of Jerusalem in 1099 as the nadir of the entire crusading era.

THE FIRST SIEGE OF CONSTANTINOPLE

When the crusaders crossed the Bosphorus to attack Constantinople on 5 July 1203, the usurper emperor Alexius III led his army to the Bosphorus shore to fight, but such was the intimidating might of the crusader and Venetian fleets that the Byzantine troops fled before the crusaders landed. The knights had embarked on their transports already mounted on

horseback and now were able to gallop right off the ships, along platforms lowered on to the beach. They chased the terrified Greeks as far as the city walls.

The crusaders settled in for a siege that lasted until 17 July. On that day, they launched a two-pronged attack by land and sea. The Venetians captured the Tower of Galata on the northern side of the Golden Horn, which allowed them to break the protective chain that stretched across the harbour preventing ships sailing in. The fleet then passed easily into the harbour. The aged doge of Venice rode in the foremost Venetian ship, with the city banner of St Mark before him, urging his men on, and then clambered on to land and planted the banner in the soil.

▼ *Piety was nowhere to be found as the crusaders ran amok in the historic city of Constantinople, looting, drinking, raping and wrecking treasures they could not carry.*

RESTORATION OF ISAAC II

The usurper Alexius III fled, with as many jewels and as much imperial treasure as he could take from the treasury. The Greeks of Constantinople then took former emperor Isaac II, blind and bewildered after so many years in prison, and restored him to the throne, hoping to pre-empt any actions by the Venetians. But the invaders needed Alexius to be in power, so he could make good his lavish promises to them. They engineered his election as co-emperor alongside his father. Isaac II and Alexius IV were so crowned on 1 August 1203 in the Church of Hagia Sophia.

With the treasury severely depleted, however, Alexius IV was unable to honour the promises made in Zara. He asked the crusaders to extend their stay for six more months to help him consolidate his position on the throne and to raise money from his subjects.

REVOLT OF ALEXIUS DOUKAS

The crusaders and Venetians agreed reluctantly for they could not afford to leave without Alexius's finance. They camped outside the city, but often ventured into it to seek entertainment, on one occasion starting a fire that raged for an entire week. The people of Constantinople grew restless, and rebelled against their joint emperors in January 1204: Isaac and Alexius barricaded themselves in the palace, sending a courtier named Alexius Doukas or Murtzuphlus to seek help from the crusaders. But Murtzuphlus – who was a popular figure, having taken part in number of skirmishes against the crusaders – seized his opportunity: he deposed the emperors and took the crown for himself, to great popular acclaim. He took power as Alexius V, strangling Alexius IV; the weak and aged Isaac II died in prison a few days later, probably of natural causes.

▲ *Baldwin of Flanders is elected emperor in*
Constantinople on 16 May, 1204.

THE SECOND SIEGE OF
CONSTANTINOPLE

Now the crusaders and Venetians had no
chance of receiving the wealth and military help they had been promised. They
determined to take the city by force. The
pope declared that Christians could be
attacked if they were actively preventing
the furtherance of the crusade – and it was
possible to argue that the people of
Constantinople had done this by depos-
ing the emperor who had promised to
help in the holy war.

The besieging army agreed that six
Venetians and six crusaders would form
an electoral college to elect a new emperor,
who would have a quarter of the empire.
The other three-quarters would be split
between Venice and the crusaders. The
crusade's clergymen came up with justifications for the attack, suggesting that the
people of Constantinople deserved to be
punished for committing the mortal sin of
murdering their anointed emperor, and

that in any case they should be forcibly
brought into the Roman Catholic Church.
They declared, moreover, that knights and
soldiers who died in the attack would benefit from the indulgence granted by the
pope as if they had carried the crusade to
its conclusion.

THE CITY IS SACKED

The Venetians and crusaders embarked on
a second siege of Constantinople on 6
April and took the city just seven days
later, on 13 April. Emperor Alexius V fled;
the crusader leaders and the doge of
Venice installed themselves in his abandoned palace. The army was allowed three
days of looting.

They went on the rampage, committing
murder and rape, stealing indiscriminately,
ransacking churches, destroying ancient
objects of art, and taking sacred relics.
Drunken soldiers were joined in the looting by knights, noblemen, priests and
bishops. According to Geoffrey of
Villehardouin, more booty was seized in
the sacking of Constantinople than ever
before in the entire history of the world.

THE LATIN EMPIRE OF
CONSTANTINOPLE

In the aftermath, the papal legate absolved
the crusaders of their vow to carry the
expedition on to the Holy Land. The crusaders and Venetians set about creating a
new government in Constantinople.
Count Baldwin of Flanders was elected
emperor and crowned in the Church of
Hagia Sophia on 16 May 1204 by the
papal legate. Baldwin declared himself a
vassal of the Pope, and received the recognition of Rome. Thomas Morosini, a priest
from Venice, was appointed the first Latin
Patriarch of Constantinople. European-
style feudalism was introduced, with 600
knights being granted fiefdoms.

Boniface of Montferrat had probably
expected to be elected emperor himself,
but he had to make do with a kingdom
formed from Byzantine territory and based
on Salonica (modern Thessaloniki). The
doge stayed on in Constantinople overseeing Venetian interests. He died there in
1205, aged 97, and was buried in the
Church of Hagia Sophia.

▼ *The bronze horses seized from the*
Hippodrome were sent back to Venice and
erected in St Mark's Square. They are
visible within the cupola of this plan.

A NEW VIEW OF CRUSADING

CRUSADING REFORMS AND INNOVATIONS OF POPE INNOCENT III

Pope Innocent III, who reigned for 18 years from 1198 to 1216, established crusading on a new footing. He preached two holy wars in the East and proclaimed crusades against pagan Europeans, heretic Christians and political enemies as well against Muslims. In every single year of his rule, a crusade was being fought somewhere in the world, officially in his name.

PAPAL POWER

Educated in Rome, Paris and Bologna, Lothar dei Conti di Segni was elected Pope Innocent III at the age of just 37 on 8 January 1198. He had a brilliant mind, a rare gift for canon law, and a powerful desire to build on the Church reforms of Pope Gregory VII and establish the papacy as the pre-eminent religious and political force. Almost at once he set about promoting a crusade to the Holy Land. He also began negotiations with the Byzantine emperor to unite the Eastern and Western churches under papal control in Rome.

This plan was ruined when in 1202–04 the Fourth Crusade spiralled out of his control, with the army effectively serving the aged doge of Venice and diverting to Zara in Hungary and then to an attack on

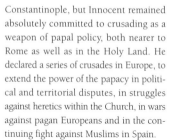

▲ *Pope Innocent III, like his predecessors, proclaimed various crusades, but uniquely he sanctioned military campaigns against non-Muslim powers and heretic Christians.*

▼ *In 1209 Innocent III gave St Francis of Assisi permission to found a religious order. Francis was loyal to church and clergy and Innocent may have wanted to utilize his itinerant monks to counter heresy.*

Constantinople, but Innocent remained absolutely committed to crusading as a weapon of papal policy, both nearer to Rome as well as in the Holy Land. He declared a series of crusades in Europe, to extend the power of the papacy in political and territorial disputes, in struggles against heretics within the Church, in wars against pagan Europeans and in the continuing fight against Muslims in Spain.

Already in 1199 he had declared a crusade against Markward of Anweiler, a follower of the recently deceased Holy Roman Emperor Henry VI, who had come into direct conflict with papal policy in southern Italy and Sicily: Innocent declared Markward 'another Saladin', an enemy of Christianity who was attempting to undermine the Fourth Crusade; he promised those who fought Markward the same indulgences available to those who travelled to the Holy Land.

In 1204 Innocent launched a crusade against pagans in the Baltic region of northern Europe: in a letter to the archbishop of Bremen he offered the same indulgence available for a Holy Land crusade to those who attempted to convert Baltic pagans by force. Then, in 1208, he called a crusade against the Albigensians, a group of heretical Christians in southern France, and again promised those who fought in his service the same indulgences available for a Holy Land crusade. In this case, the indulgence would be granted in return for just 40 days of military service.

In 1212 he proclaimed a crusade in Spain against the Muslim Almohad caliphs, and that year crusader knights and infantrymen from southern France and Spain, fighting alongside the armies of Sancho VII of Navarre, Peter II of Aragon and Alfonso VIII of Castile, won a resounding victory over a Muslim army at the Battle of Las Navas de Tolosa. This was a crucial Christian victory in the centuries-long struggle against Muslims in Spain.

The following year, in 1213, Innocent began to organize the Fifth Crusade to the Holy Land and he died in 1216, while preaching the crusade in Perugia. In addition to promoting crusading in so many guises, Innocent also made a number of changes and clarifications in the financing and organization of these holy wars.

CRUSADING TAXES

Seeing that the cost of crusading put off many potential holy warriors/soldiers of Christ, Innocent set out to establish a secure financial basis for the crusading movement. In promoting the Fourth Crusade in 1199 he imposed a tax on clerical incomes – one-fortieth of their annual revenue for one year – to raise money for the expedition. He said that this would not set a precedent, but in fact it did – and clerical taxes were subsequently imposed in 1215 for the Fifth Crusade (one-twentieth of revenue for three years), in 1245, after Jerusalem had fallen to the Khwarismian Turks (another tax of one-twentieth for three years), and again in 1263 and 1274.

Innocent made a major innovation in 1213, while promoting the Fifth Crusade, when he ruled that crusade vows could be redeemed by payment of money. This meant that those Christians who could not take the cross because of age, infirmity, physical weakness or lack of equipment could pay for others to go on their behalf – and have a part in the spiritual benefit of the crusade without leaving home.

Innocent also sought to improve the arrangements for the promotion of crusades, introducing new procedures and appointments for preaching the cross. For the Fourth Crusade, he despatched Cistercian monks to give crusade sermons, while for the Fifth Crusade he sent out a group of trained reformers to promote the expedition. Innocent even set out to boost attendance at crusade sermons by offering a 'partial indulgence' (the cancellation of part of a penance due) simply for listening to a preacher's attempts to convince people to take the cross.

CRUSADER PRIVILEGES

Pope Innocent also codified and clarified the privileges available to crusaders, notably in the appendix *Ad liberandum* to the decrees of the Fourth Lateran Council of 1215. The most important was the indulgence. Previous indulgences had been given on the understanding that – by the pope's authority – God would view the crusader's sufferings on crusade as 'satisfactory', meaning that they cancelled debts due for previous sins. This sparked debate among canon lawyers as to whether any penance could be satisfactory in this way. Under Innocent III, the indulgence guaranteed a crusader that all punishment for previous sins would be remitted (both in this world and the next) whether or not as a penance it proved to be satisfactory in God's eyes; the guarantee was given on God's behalf by the pope. Other notable privileges included: a crusader's property

and dependents would be protected by the Church; a crusader would be freed of the obligation to settle debts or pay interest on them while away on crusade; he would also be exempted from feudal service, taxes and tolls for the duration of the crusade; a crusader would have the right to hospitality from the Church while on crusade; anyone who had been excommunicated would be freed from his punishment by taking the cross, and while on crusade could interact with excommunicated Christians without fear of punishment; and a crusader could take a crusade vow in place of another vow or instead of returning stolen goods.

▼ *Innocent sent a monk named Dominic to dispute with the Albigensians. In a trial by fire, Dominic's books were miraculously saved from the flames while others burned. But Dominic could not persuade them.*

THE CHILDREN'S CRUSADES

SPONTANEOUS OUTBURSTS OF ENTHUSIASM FOR HOLY WAR

According to chronicle accounts, in 1212 thousands of poor children were inspired by charismatic preachers to leave their homes in France and Germany to travel to Jerusalem on crusade and save the holy places there. This was not a holy war: none of these crusaders envisaged using force, for they believed that through faith the power of God would be enough to achieve their purpose.

FROM FRANCE AND GERMANY

There were two waves to the Children's Crusade, one issuing from northern France and one beginning in Germany. The story goes that in May 1212 a shepherd boy named Stephen from Cloyes-sur-le-Loir (near Châteaudun in the Vermandois) walked to see King Philip at Saint-Denis and reported that he had had a vision of Christ instructing him to lead a crusade to Jerusalem. Philip attempted to send the boy home, but Stephen embarked on a preaching tour of the countryside and gathered many followers among the youth and children of the area.

▼ *Christ Pantocrator (Ruler of all). Both German and French Children's Crusades were called in His name.*

He promised them that because Christ had called the crusade, He would supply food and water on the march and bring them safely to the Holy Land, and that if they followed Stephen to the south of France they would find that Christ would part the waters of the Mediterranean to enable them to walk all the way.

Around the same time, a German youth named Nicholas of Cologne mobilized a similar pilgrim army in the Rhineland. He called for the liberation of the Holy Sepulchre and, like Stephen, promised that the seas would be parted by God as they made their way to the Holy Land, demonstrating their faith by trusting in His deliverance. Stephen's followers were mainly children and youths, although there were also adults and priests in the company. People of both sexes joined up – according to the contemporary Annals of Marbach, as the crusaders marched through the countryside young people simply downed tools in the fields or abandoned the flocks they were minding and joined the march.

THE FRENCH MARCH SOUTH

The French group headed southwards towards the Mediterranean coast under Stephen's leadership. The group contained principally children and young people, mostly under the age of 15, both from very poor and more prosperous backgrounds; there were also a few priests and other adults in Stephen's following. Many died of exhaustion, illness or starvation on the way, and others simply drifted away, but when they reached Marseilles they were still as many as 30,000 in number.

The waters did not part as promised. Some pilgrims became disillusioned and wandered off, but many waited on, believing that God would still deliver them. Finally two merchants from the city, named Hugh Ferreus (Iron Hugh) and William Porcus (Pig William), offered to

▲ *Following in the footsteps of the Tafurs (the pious peasants who accompanied the First Crusade) the participants in the Children's Crusades are said to have believed that their faith would be enough to bring success.*

carry them by ship to the Holy Land and Stephen embarked with the still sizeable remnant of his following in seven ships. They were never seen again in France, but later reports (supposedly based on an eyewitness account by a survivor of the expedition) revealed that after two ships were lost in a storm near Sardinia the other merchants sailed to Bougie and Alexandria in northern Africa, where they sold the surviving children into slavery among the Saracens.

THE GERMAN CHILDREN'S CRUSADE

Meanwhile, the German contingent made its way across the Alps into northern Italy and proceeded to Genoa. Some participants settled in Genoa, others went on to Pisa and some made it all the way to Rome, where they had an audience with Innocent III. Innocent told them to return home, but to that they should preserve

▲ Philip II travelled on the Third Crusade but afterwards was not interested in crusading. He did not help Innocent III in his holy war against Albigensians in southern France.

their enthusiasm for crusading and put it to use in adulthood. From Pisa, two shiploads of German children embarked but were never heard of again.

A POPULAR LEGEND?

Some modern historians suggest that these accounts may be largely popular legends based on memories of the mass movement of country poor in the early 13th century. According to this theory, the poor forced into wandering by poverty were called *pueri* (Latin for 'boys') in some accounts, and this was misinterpreted by later chroniclers as a movement of children when in fact it was a migration of adults. Moreover, the largely secular movements of the poor seeking food and work were cast as pilgrimages, and even crusades, under the influence of the thriving popular cult of the Innocents. These were the children who were slaughtered, according to the Gospel of St Matthew, on the orders of King Herod, in response to a prophecy that a newborn 'King of the Jews' was destined to seize his throne. The Innocents were celebrated as the first Christian martyrs as part of a celebration of poverty and simple piety, which was also fed by memories of the poor but ferociously pious Tafurs of the First Crusade, and it may be that in the light of this cult the mass migrations of country poor were reimagined as a crusade of the Innocents.

THE PIED PIPER OF HAMELIN

According to some historians, the German folktale of the Pied Piper of Hamelin has its origins in the events of the Children's Crusade. In the folktale, the people of the German town of Hamelin were plagued by rats, and accepted the offer of a vagrant in colourful clothes that he would clear the town of vermin for a fixed sum; he played a marvellous tune on his pipe and the rats followed him out of the town to the river, where they drowned. The people of Hamelin then refused to pay up the agreed fee, and so the piper returned when the folk were all in church and, playing his pipe once more, led all the town's children away. They were never seen again. The first known appearance of the piper of Hamelin is in a church window in Hamelin dated to *c.*1300, but this window – now destroyed – simply showed the piper leading away several children dressed in white; the rats were not added to the story until the late 1500s. Another theory is that the folktale is based on memories of the 13th-century migration of people to settle in eastern Europe.

▼ The Pied Piper leads the children of the village of Hamelin on their merry dance of no return. Was he based on a folk memory of the preachers who led off the young on the Children's Crusades?

THE FIFTH CRUSADE
CRUSADERS HUMILIATED IN EGYPT

In April 1213 Innocent III proclaimed another crusade to the Holy Land in the papal bull *Quia major*. The pope was determined to bring about the recovery of the Holy Sepulchre in Jerusalem as a symbol of papal supremacy throughout Christendom. In the event, the crusade fleet sailed to Egypt, where after taking the port of Damietta they marched to a humiliating defeat at the hands of Saladin's nephew, Sultan al-Kamil.

The crusade was promoted enthusiastically by travelling preachers, and regular processions. Innocent made the call again at the fourth Lateran Council of 1215; the departure date for the new crusade was set for 1217. Innocent died in May 1216, and his successor Pope Honorius III took over the organization of the expedition.

THE FIRST WAVE OF CRUSADERS

The first armies to depart were led by Duke Leopold VI of Austria and King Andrew II of Hungary, in 1217. They sailed to Acre, and mobilized with John of Brienne, King of Jerusalem, Prince Bohemond IV of Antioch and King Hugh I of Cyprus to fight Ayyubid descendants of Saladin in Syria – principally the great general's brother al-Adil, who had succeeded him as sultan. Very little was achieved on this expedition, although a number of sacred relics were captured. In January 1218 King Andrew headed home by way of Constantinople.

THE SIEGE OF DAMIETTA

In 1218 a contingent of German crusaders arrived in Acre. Now the target was switched to Ayyubid possessions in Egypt. In May 1218 German troops under the command of John of Brienne sailed to Egypt and besieged the port of Damietta. Their plan was to take this city as a supply base before moving on to attack Cairo.

On 25 August they captured the tower just outside Damietta, but did not push

▲ *Francis of Assisi attempts to convince al-Kamil of the merits of Christianity during the meeting he was granted with the sultan.*

on and take the city itself, preferring to wait for reinforcements – for news had reached them that a French and English army was sailing from Genoa while the Spanish cardinal Pelagius of Albano had embarked from Brindisi.

Pelagius arrived in mid-September, but struggled to impose his authority, for he was not a military man and the assembled army looked to John of Brienne as its leader. German soldiers also had another claim on their loyalty: they were expecting the arrival of Frederick II, who had taken the cross as early as 1215, but had since focused his energies on consolidating his position in Germany and Italy.

In October the English and French arrived: still the crusaders, hampered by lack of leadership and a badly organized siege, did not take the city. Their camp was flooded following storms in November and December and hit by an epidemic in which as many as 10 per cent of their number died – including English cardinal Robert of Courçon, one of the principal crusade preachers.

OFFER OF PEACE

By this time, al-Adil had died and his son al-Kamil had taken his position as sultan. In spring 1219, judging it inevitable that the crusaders would take Damietta, Sultan al-Kamil made overtures of peace – if the crusaders agreed to lift the siege of Damietta and leave Egypt, he promised to give them possession of Jerusalem, and the entire Kingdom as it had been before the Battle of the Horns of Hattin, and also to return the relic of the True Cross – which had been in Muslim hands ever since that battle. All he wanted to retain was the fortresses of Oultrejordain and the territory they controlled, so that the two main parts of his empire, Egypt and Syria, could maintain contact – for this territory he would pay tribute of 30,000 bezants. In the Holy Land, al-Kamil's brother al-Mu'azzam, the ruler of Syria, dismantled the fortifications of Jerusalem so that the Christians would not be able to defend it.

King John of Jerusalem and the barons of his kingdom urged acceptance. So did the crusader knights of Germany, France and England, for it seemed to them that the offer delivered the prize for which the crusade had been mobilized. But Pelagius made the judgement that the Holy City could not be bartered for and that the Christian army should not negotiate with the infidel. He had the support of the knights of the military orders, who were unhappy at the proposed loss of their treasured castles of Krak and Montreal in Oultrejordain, and of the Italians, who were determined to capture Damietta in order to establish a trading position there.

A SAINTLY VISITOR

The siege continued. In August or September, the saintly monk Francis of Assisi arrived in order to argue for non-violence. He had an audience with al-Kamil and so impressed the sultan that he was allowed to preach to his subjects.

and waiting, Pelagius and the crusade leaders suddenly became decisive – and ordered a march up the river Nile towards Cairo, with the idea of making the manoeuvre before the beginning of the river's annual floods.

DEFEAT IN THE MUD

The sultan brought his troops out to meet the crusade army and the advance was stalled. Then the river began to rise and the crusaders became cut off from their supply ships by Egyptian vessels.

Pelagius saw that the campaign had gone badly wrong and ordered a retreat, but Sultan al-Kamil destroyed flood control barriers and the waters swept in, stranding the crusader troops in the thick Nile mud. When Al-Kamil launched a night attack, the crusade army suffered very heavy losses and Pelagius had to negotiate a humiliating peace treaty under which the crusaders evacuated Damietta, agreed an eight-year truce and left Egypt. All they had in return was a promise that the piece of the True Cross would be handed over – but when it came to it, the Muslims could not find this most sacred of Christian relics.

A STRONG POSITION LOST

Finally in November 1219 the crusaders captured Damietta and, true to form, sacked and looted the city. Had they marched swiftly south against Cairo they would probably have ended the rule of Sultan al-Kamil and made Egypt a Christian country. Instead they became embroiled in a quarrel over who had the right to claim Damietta, with John of Brienne declaring the town to be his possession and legate Pelagius claiming it on behalf of Rome.

The army was still expecting the imminent arrival of Emperor Frederick II, and for no less than 20 months the crusaders sat in Damietta. From Rome came official confirmation of Pelagius as commander-in-chief of the crusading army. John of Brienne returned to Acre.

In June 1221 Sultan al-Kamil made a fresh peace offer, on largely the same terms as before. Again Pelagius refused. Finally in July, Emperor Frederick's advance party arrived under the command of Duke

▲ *Crusader troops land prior to launching an assault on the port of Damietta.*

Louis I of Bavaria – the emperor himself sent orders to await his arrival. John of Brienne returned from Acre. But then, after more than 18 months of indecision

▼ *The crusaders suffered a heavy defeat as they tried to retreat following their ill-judged advance up the river Nile.*

JERUSALEM REGAINED

THE SIXTH CRUSADE OF 1228–29

The Sixth Crusade was led by Holy Roman Emperor Frederick II. Without even engaging the army of Ayyubid sultan al-Kamil in battle, he negotiated the return of Jerusalem (as well as Nazareth, Jaffa, Sidon and Bethlehem) to Christian control, although under the terms of the agreement the Temple Mount area of Jerusalem, which includes the Dome of the Rock and the al-Aqsa mosque, was to remain in Muslim hands.

KING OF GERMANY TAKES THE CROSS

Frederick II was crowned King of Germany in 1215, and in that year first took the cross as a young man of just 19 in response to the April 1213 call to arms made by Pope Innocent III. As we have seen, he was repeatedly said to be preparing to embark to take part in the disastrous Fifth Crusade to Egypt, and even sent an advance party of his force in 1221. It is probable that had he gone in

▼ *Frederick II Stupor Mundi – 'the wonder of the world' – was his own master and kept the Sixth Crusade free of papal control.*

person to Egypt he would have been able to oust the papal prelate Pelagius from control of the army and under more effective leadership the crusaders might have taken Cairo and defeated Sultan al-Kamil – and the crusade would have ended in triumph rather than disaster. However, he was embroiled in consolidating his position in Germany and Italy and did not go.

HOLY ROMAN EMPEROR – AND KING OF JERUSALEM

In 1220, before the end of the Fifth Crusade, Frederick was crowned Holy Roman Emperor by Pope Honorius III on 22 November 1220. At this point he renewed his promise to go on crusade, but it was to be 1228 before he finally arrived in the Holy Land.

By the time he did so he was notionally king of Jerusalem, for in 1225 he had married Isabella (or Yolande), Queen of Jerusalem. Isabella was the daughter of Maria of Montferrat, the previous Queen of Jerusalem, and of King John of Brienne, who had ruled as King of Jerusalem on account of his marriage to Maria. Isabella had become Queen of Jerusalem as an infant on the death of her mother in 1212. In 1225 Frederick married her in a magnificent ceremony at Brindisi Cathedral, then despatched a message to John of Brienne, who was already in his late 70s, that as a result of the marriage the Holy Roman Emperor was now also King of Jerusalem.

STUPOR MUNDI

The grandson of Frederick I Barbarossa, Frederick II was an extraordinary figure, known to his contemporaries as *Stupor Mundi*, 'Wonder of the World'. He was fluent in six languages – German, Italian, French, Greek, Latin and Arabic; he was a mathematician and philosopher and a great patron of the arts. He was worldly, ferociously intelligent and scathing of

▲ *Frederick was twice crowned king, in 1212 and 1215, before he was crowned Holy Roman Emperor in Rome in 1220.*

religion – he reportedly declared that 'Moses, Christ and Muhammad were all imposters' and intimated that the pope had been found on a dunghill. At Palermo he kept a harem in the style of Oriental rulers – and to this he despatched his young bride immediately after the wedding. This was not a man who could easily be forced to become a papal agent.

CONFLICT WITH THE PAPACY

A key reason for Frederick's repeated delaying of his crusade was that he was embroiled in a long-running struggle with Rome, both over lands in Italy and over the centuries-old issue of whether pope or Holy Roman emperor was the rightful leader of Christendom. When he first took the cross in 1215, the then pope, Innocent III, wanted to stop him going – he was determined to maintain control of the crusade and wanted to avoid the involvement of so powerful and independent a man as Frederick. Subsequent popes, however, were willing to countenance his involvement in the holy war as they believed he would bring success. Moreover, when he finally departed for the Holy Land the territories in Italy would be left unprotected.

Frederick embarked for the Holy Land in 1227, but an epidemic struck his fleet and he himself was laid low with fever, so

▲ *Gregory IX was nephew to Pope Innocent III and also attempted to maintain a strong papal authority. Frederick defied him.*

the crusaders returned to Italy. The new pope, Gregory IX, excommunicated him for breaking his crusader vows.

AN ALLIANCE WITH EGYPT

In Italy, Frederick received a diplomatic mission at Palermo from Sultan al-Kamil seeking military help against his own brother, al-Mu'azzam, and offering Jerusalem as a reward. This played right into Frederick's hands – all along he had wanted to lead a crusade on his own terms, not as an instrument of papal power but as emperor, secular ruler of Christendom. Despite the excommunication, which technically meant that he could not lead a crusade, he finally embarked. Pope Gregory issued a ringing condemnation of the emperor's actions.

He sailed via Cyprus, where he quarrelled with the regent John of Ibelin, lord of Beirut and Arsuf. Frederick imposed rule in his name by a group of five local knights (*baillis*) and then sailed for Acre, the capital of the Kingdom of Jerusalem.

SUCCESS IN THE HOLY LAND

On arrival, Frederick did not receive undivided support: he had alienated the important Ibelin group, and the Church hierarchy led by Patriarch Gerald of Lausanne followed the leadership of the pope by being hostile. His only supporters were the barons of the Kingdom, the Teutonic knights and the German army.

Sultan al-Kamil in fact no longer needed Frederick's support, for al-Mu'azzam had died. But after Frederick made a show of force by marching down the Mediterranean coast from Acre to Jaffa with a crusader army of around 3,000, al-Kamil agreed to honour the proposed deal and Jerusalem was returned to Latin control in a treaty signed on 18 February 1229. The treaty also established a ten-year truce and guaranteed Muslims free access to Jerusalem to visit their shrines on the Temple Mount; as well as Nazareth and Bethlehem, the Christians received a corridor of land linking Jerusalem to Acre.

TRIUMPH IN JERUSALEM

Frederick marched into Jerusalem on 17 March 1229. He took part in a crowning of sorts the following day, and proclaimed himself Lord of Jerusalem. It was not a formal coronation because the Patriarch was still opposed to these events, and had remained in Acre – in fact, Frederick lifted the crown on to his own head and, according to some, used the imperial crown, not that of Jerusalem.

The treaty was generally highly unpopular on both sides. The Muslims felt cheated by their sultan – the imams in Egypt and Damascus proclaimed a period of public mourning because Islam had been betrayed. The Christian knights felt that the treaty was far less favourable than the terms offered and turned down at Damietta. Moreover, as Pelagius and their predecessors had argued, they felt that the Kingdom of Jerusalem should have been won back by the sword and not through negotiation. The Latin settlers argued that the narrow corridor of land between Acre and Jerusalem was impracticable since it could not be adequately defended. In spite of this dissent, the fact remains that Frederick had achieved the crusade's ultimate aim by putting the Holy City back in Christian hands.

Frederick left Jerusalem in May and returned to Italy. He had to drive out papal troops commanded by John of Brienne, which had invaded his Italian territories. Later in the year the pope, humbled by defeat in battle, lifted the excommunication. But the struggle between pope and emperor was far from over – and a decade later, Frederick not only found himself excommunicated a second time, but also had a crusade declared against his territorial holdings in Italy.

▼ *At Frederick's coronation (1229) as King of Jerusalem, he is said to have placed the crown on his own head.*

KINGDOM OF JERUSALEM REBUILT
BUT RACKED BY BITTER DISPUTES

The success of the Sixth Crusade was part of a short-lived re-establishment of the crusader states of Outremer during the first half of the 13th century. Although the Christians who lived in the restored kingdom were bitterly at odds, for a short while the Kingdom appeared to have a brighter future. But in 1244 control of Jerusalem was lost once more and after this it would not be in European hands again until 1917.

CHRISTIAN DISPUTES
Almost as soon as Frederick had returned to Europe after regaining Jerusalem, in 1229, John of Ibelin overthrew imperial rule in Cyprus and assumed control himself. Frederick for his part was embroiled in fighting papal forces in Italy, and John of Ibelin established himself as the effective king of both Cyprus and Jerusalem.

In 1230 Frederick attempted to deal with this challenge to his authority, sending an army east under the command of Riccardo Filanghieri, Marshal of the Empire, but John defeated the imperial army at the Battle of Agridi in Cyprus on 15 June 1232. In Acre, moreover, the local barons sided with John against Frederick: they formed a commune and elected John their mayor. Nevertheless, Filanghieri established himself in Tyre and in Jerusalem itself.

The conflict continued after Henry of Lusignan came of age as Henry I of Cyprus; in 1234 Pope Gregory IX excommunicated John of Ibelin. John was then killed when his horse fell on him during a campaign against Muslim forces in 1236.

CRUSADE OF 1239–41
A further European crusade, not usually given a number, was called by Theobald I of Navarre (also known as Count Theobald IV of Champagne) and Richard, Earl of Cornwall. In 1239 possession of a large region of Palestine, including

▲ *During the fight for Jerusalem the sanction of the Church was at first seen as a vital component of the struggle.*

Jerusalem, came under dispute once more on the expiry of Frederick II's treaty with Sultan al-Kamil; embarking in that year, Theobald recaptured Ascalon, Beaufort and Safed, but suffered a major defeat by an Egyptian army at Gaza in November 1239 and returned to Europe in 1240 before the arrival from England of Prince Richard, Earl of Cornwall, the younger brother of Henry III of England.

The crusade of 1239–40 was a relatively minor event in the life of Theobald, who is remembered as one of the greatest of aristocratic troubadours and wrote no fewer than 60 surviving lyrics. He was rumoured to have fallen passionately in love with the formidable Blanche of Castile (mother of 'Saint Louis', King Louis IX), and to have poisoned her husband, King Louis VIII; many of his poems are believed to be addressed to Blanche.

When Richard, Earl of Cornwall, arrived in Acre with a fine company of English knights he was welcomed by the Knights Hospitaller and stayed in their accommodation in the city. He then moved on to Jaffa and proposed to its population that they accompany him to Ascalon and help him refortify that place. This they did, and after Richard had rebuilt the defences and arranged for a garrison, he handed over control to the emperor's representative and returned to England. Also during his stay in the Holy Land, Richard negotiated the release of 33 noblemen, 50 knights and many lower-ranking Christian prisoners captured during Theobald's defeat at Gaza; he collected the unburied remains of many killed in the battle and had them buried in the cemetery at Ascalon. He finalized a treaty initially negotiated by Theobald

▼ *At Sidon the crusaders built a sea castle in the 13th century on a small island connected to the mainland by a bridge.*

▲ *This 15th-century illustration shows Christians fighting to retake Jerusalem with bowmen and siege towers to the fore.*

with Sultan as-Salih Ayyub of Egypt that settled wider borders for the Kingdom of Jerusalem than any since 1187.

The Kingdom of Jerusalem appeared to be thriving and have a sustainable future. The ports of Tyre and Acre were very rich, and the Kingdom was also less isolated than previously: Cyprus and the Kingdom of Armenia in Cilicia were Christian neighbours, offering a degree of security – Armenia had even accepted Latin Christianity and religious rule from Rome. But the Latin Christians were too badly split to take advantage of this opportunity: Tyre and Acre, for all their prosperity, existed in a state of open competition that was akin to warfare, while the Templars and Hospitallers even came to blows. In 1244 this future was swept away by the

invasion of Khwarismian Turks, who seized Jerusalem in August that year, and by a cataclysmic defeat of the Kingdom's army by the troops of Egypt at the Battle of La Forbie near Gaza.

THE BATTLE OF LA FORBIE

The sacking of Jerusalem was savage and brutal. Only 300 Christians escaped to tell the story of how the Turks swept into the city, looting and burning the churches. Christians of the crusader states reacted to the loss of Jerusalem in August by making an alliance with al-Mansur of Damascus against Sultan as-Salih Ayyub of Egypt.

An allied Christian–Syrian army drew up at La Forbie commanded by al-Mansur and Walter of Brienne, Count of Jaffa and Ascalon, against a joint force of Khwarismian Turks and Egyptians commanded by a young Turkish soldier named Rukn al-Zahir Baybars (who shortly afterwards would overthrow Sultan

as-Salih Ayyub and found the Mamluk sultanate of Egypt). The battle was launched by Templar charges on 17 October and fought all through that day and the next.

The Christian–Syrian defeat was absolutely crushing: al-Mansur had just 280 survivors out of more than 2,000 cavalry and many more infantry; the Christian knights were virtually wiped out, with only 33 Templars, 27 Hospitallers and three Teutonic knights surviving the slaughter. Among the dead was Armand of Perigord, Grand Master of the Knights Templar. His Hospitaller counterpart, William of Chatelneuf, was captured.

La Forbie was the most severe and significant defeat for the Latin Christians in the Holy Land since the Battle of the Horns of Hattin. Baybars rose to power as the first of the Mamluk sultans of Egypt in 1260 and swiftly drove the Kingdom of Jerusalem almost to extinction, reducing it to a tiny strip of coastal territory.

CHAPTER THIRTEEN

CRUSADES OF THE MID-13TH TO 15TH CENTURIES

For the most part, the news of the fall of Jerusalem to the Khwarismian Turks and the devastating defeat of the armies of Outremer and Damascus at the Battle of La Forbie had little effect in Europe, but it did provoke one very powerful man to plan a military response. In December 1244. Louis IX of France was revered by contemporaries as the embodiment of Christian chivalry, the perfect Christian ruler. He was fiercely devout, a great leader, respected by knights and men-at-arms – but even he could not bring success to the crusading cause. In fact, he led two crusades, the Seventh of 1248–54, and the Eighth of 1270. The Seventh Crusade, to Egypt, ended with a humiliating surrender. The Eighth Crusade, in Tunisia, ended in his death and the abandonment of the enterprise with only a trade treaty with the city of Tunis to show for it. The year after Louis's death saw the expedition traditionally regarded as the Ninth and last Crusade, led by Prince Edward (the future King Edward I of England). This enterprise brought about a ten-year peace treaty between Christians and Muslims in the Holy Land, but it was followed through the 14th and even 15th centuries by further crusading expeditions despatched from Europe to counter the power of the Mamluk sultanate of Egypt and then later of the Ottoman Turks.

▲ *Rukn al-Zahir Baybars destroys a Christian-Syrian army at the devastating Battle of La Forbie near Gaza in 1244.*

◄ *After four years' preparation, Louis IX of France embarked on the Seventh Crusade in 1248, heading to Cyprus and then to Egypt.*

CRUSADE IN EGYPT

KING LOUIS IX CALLS THE SEVENTH CRUSADE

King Louis IX declared his intention to lead a crusade to the East in 1245. But he certainly did not rush to war, for he spent no less than four years recruiting and preparing, raising money and even building a special port at the sleepy village of Aigues-Mortes in southern France, before he finally embarked in 1248.

Louis imposed a swingeing tax on the French Church, demanding one-tenth of ecclesiastical revenues for five years, raising 950,000 livres tournois. (The livre tournois, or 'pound of Tours', was one of a number of currencies used in France in Louis's time.) He demanded municipal grants from the towns of his royal domain, raising another 275,000 livres tournois. In all, he raised around 1.5 million livres tournois – a sum so vast that he campaigned in the East for four years before he needed to borrow more money.

FRENCH LORDS

Louis's recruitment campaign resulted in many of France's great lords taking the cross, including: Peter of Vendôme; Hugh X of Lusignan (Count of La Marche); John of Montfort; and Louis's brothers Alphonse of Poitou, Robert of Artois and Charles of Anjou. Many of these great lords' feudal dependants and blood relatives also joined the crusade. Another notable participant who joined the crusade in France was John, lord of Joinville in Champagne, who later wrote a life of King Louis that is a major source for our knowledge of the Seventh Crusade.

The army that finally embarked from southern France in 1248 numbered around 15,000 and included some 2,500 knights as well as 5,000-odd crossbowmen. As many as half of those who travelled received loans or agreed contracts

▲ *The holy warrior-king, as seen by his enemies. This image of Louis IX on horseback is from a 13th-century Egyptian or Syrian brass medallion inlaid with silver.*

from Louis, meaning that they were effectively subsidized by the king. Practical arrangements included the advance purchase of supplies and equipment, and the contracting of 36 ships from Marseilles and Genoa to carry the army.

DEPARTURE

The French crusade army left from Marseilles and from the specially built port and arsenal at the Aigues-Mortes on 25 August 1248 and sailed initially to Cyprus. They landed at Limassol on 17 September, and there united by prior arrangement with various other crusade participants, including Scottish and Italian forces, around 200 English knights led by William, Earl of Salisbury, and barons from Outremer led by Guillaume of Sonnac, Grand Master of the Knights Templar. The crusade leaders agreed that their first target should be Muslim Egypt: the plan was to defeat the sultan's army there before moving against Syria.

◀ *Louis IX of France embarks at Aigues-Mortes on the 7th Crusade. This depiction is from a mid-16th century stained-glass window in Champigny-sur-Veude, France.*

▲ *Encamped before Damietta in June 1249, Louis and his barons pray for the triumphant ending they envisaged for their painstakingly planned enterprise.*

DAMIETTA

Having overwintered on Cyprus, they embarked for Egypt on 14 May 1249. The fleet, which by now numbered as many as a hundred ships, was scattered by a storm, but the royal ships held together and arrived off the beaches near the target of Damietta (modern Damyut) in early June. They saw an Egyptian Muslim army drawn up on land. Disregarding the advice of senior campaigners to wait for reinforcements, Louis led an immediate assault that drove back the Muslim force in the course of a fierce battle on 5 June.

The Muslims retreated along a pontoon bridge of boats to Damietta and that night, in a panic, the Damietta garrison of Bedouin troops and the town's Muslim population fled. The following day, having been alerted to this development by Christians in Damietta, the French army marched in triumph, unopposed across the bridge of boats, into the port.

▶ *This 17th-century Ottoman map shows Muslim power bases around the Mediterranean as well as the movements and origins of crusaders, marking Jerusalem with an image of Christ.*

JOHN, LORD OF JOINVILLE, AND FRIEND OF LOUIS IX

John came from a family of lesser nobles from the Champagne region of France who, nevertheless, had a proud history of crusading – and is a good example of the way taking the cross became a tradition in certain families. John's grandfather, Geoffrey of Joinville, had travelled on the Third Crusade and was killed during the siege of Acre in 1189; John's father, Simon, had crusaded against the Cathars in southern France and fought on the Fifth Crusade, taking part in the capture of Damietta; he also had two uncles who had gone on crusade. John himself took the cross in 1244. In the catastrophic defeat that ended the Seventh Crusade he was later captured with King Louis and travelled with him to Acre, where he became friends with the king before returning in the royal party to France in 1254. He served as seneschal of Champagne, and lived both at the royal court and in Joinville. In 1270 he refused to take part in the ill-fated Eighth Crusade (on which Louis died): before Louis departed, John told him the enterprise was folly. He began writing his life of

▲ *This statue of Louis IX is believed to be true to life. The king was canonized in 1297, just 27 years after his death. He is revered as the perfect Christian king.*

King Louis in the 1270s, but did not complete it until 1309, when it was presented to Louis X. By this time, Louis IX had been canonized and the work was called the *Histoire de Saint-Louis* (The Story of St Louis).

A KING'S RANSOM

THE CRUSADE FAILS AND KING LOUIS IS CAPTURED

After the capture of Damietta on 6 June 1249 the sultan of Egypt, al-Salih Ayyub, offered to swap possession of the town for the Holy City of Jerusalem, as his predecessor al-Kamil had in 1219 and 1221. But Louis rejected the offer, as Pelagius had done before, on the grounds that possession of Jerusalem could not be bartered for. Louis knew, also, that al-Salih Ayyub was seriously ill with tuberculosis and that Egyptian morale was very low. He no doubt believed that with God's help the French army was poised to take complete control of Egypt as a precursor to defeating Muslim Syria and winning Jerusalem.

Initially Louis sat tight in Damietta. It was the start of the season for the flooding of the River Nile, and the king had learned the lessons of the Fifth Crusade when papal legate Pelagius and John of Brienne had been trapped in the Nile mud and forced to surrender. He waited for the waters to subside. In the interim he oversaw the reconsecration of the town's Great Mosque as a cathedral, and the establishment of an archbishopric there. In October, reinforcements from France arrived and the following month, on 20 November, Louis marched towards Cairo.

BATTLE OF AL-MANSOURAH

As the French army proceeded southwards, Sultan al-Salih Ayyub died. In mid-December the crusaders drew up on the bank of the al-Bahr al-Saghir river, opposite the fortress of al-Mansourah, where a 70,000-strong Ayyubid army was encamped. But the crusaders could not find a way across, and remained there for six weeks engaged in the construction

▲ *Louis received Robert of Nantes, the Latin Patriarch of Jerusalem, in Damietta in 1249. The king established an archbishopric in Damietta under the Patriarch's authority.*

of a causeway. Then in early February 1249, a local Coptic Christian alerted them to the existence of an undefended ford a little way downstream, and on 8 February the army's vanguard led the advance on al-Mansourah.

Under the command of Louis's brother, Count Robert of Artois, the French vanguard (with a contingent of Templars and of English knights under Earl William of Salisbury) launched a surprise attack on the Ayyubid camp. The Ayyubid troops fled and Count Robert and his fellow commanders, ignoring orders to wait, and driven by the chivalric urge to glory, rode after them into Damietta. But in the town the Egyptians were rallied by the brilliant commander Rukn al-Zahir Baybars (victor at the Battle of La Forbie) and turned on their pursuers. They cut down the small band of crusaders – who were

◄ *This celebrated portrait of St Louis was painted by Spanish-Greek artist El Greco in c.1592. In Louis's lifetime the French king was the most powerful of the monarchs of Europe.*

▲ *Scenes from a 13th-century book show Pope Innocent IV at the Ecumenical Council of Lyon in 1246 (top left), Louis (top right) receiving the blessing of the church, and the Battle of Gaza, on 12 October 1244.*

disoriented and unable to manoeuvre easily in the narrow streets – in a devastating slaughter. Most of the English knights, including Earl William and all but five Templars, were killed. Count Robert was also slain, with the members of his bodyguard. Through lack of discipline they had thrown away the advantage.

Meanwhile, the main part of the French army was still crossing the ford. Around half the army had crossed when the Egyptians, commanded by Baybars, poured out of Damietta once more to attack. A fierce battle ensued. The crusaders just about managed to hold their ground and finally the Egyptians retreated into al-Mansourah.

SIEGE OF MANY MONTHS
Louis settled in for a siege, hopeful that in the aftermath of the death of Sultan al-Salih Ayyub infighting over the succession would distract the Egyptians from the matter in hand and open the path to a victory for the Christians.

However, a new sultan, Turan Shah, arrived from Damascus to take command, and he quickly imposed his authority on the Egyptian force.

Over the following months the Egyptians effectively undermined the crusader position – principally by venturing out to destroy, one after another, the barges bringing supplies downriver from Damietta. Dysentery and typhoid spread through the crusader camp, and starvation loomed. Louis tried to reopen negotiations, but found that possession of Jerusalem was no longer on offer. His

advisers urged him to make a swift retreat, with just his bodyguard in attendance, but he refused to abandon his army of crusaders to its fate.

RETREAT – AND SURRENDER
On 5 April 1250 Louis accepted the inevitable and ordered a general retreat to Damietta, with the sick going in the front and the remnant of the army marching behind. As they limped northwards, the army was repeatedly attacked by Egyptian horsemen. On only the second day of the march, 6 April, Louis fell seriously ill and became delirious. The army was surrounded, and surrendered.

Under the terms of the surrender, Damietta was returned to the sultan. Those among the crusaders who had been reduced to weakness by disease were killed. Sultan Turan Shah decided there were too many prisoners to control and feed: and ordered that every day for a week 300 of the able-bodied Christians be marched out of the camp and executed. Louis himself was seized and marched in chains to al-Mansourah. The sultan demanded a ransom of 800,000 gold bezants, sending Louis's cloak to Damascus as proof of his triumph.

▼ *The crusade reaches a humiliating end as Louis is captured (left of picture) and then cast into a common jail (right) by his captor.*

THE EIGHTH CRUSADE
KING LOUIS'S FINAL ENDEAVOUR

In the mid-1260s devastating attacks by Egyptian sultan Baybars on Christian holdings in Syria and Palestine reduced Outremer to little more than the port of Acre in Syria. Louis IX of France was inspired by these events to launch another crusade, but it got no further than its very first engagement, the siege of the north African city of Tunis, which had been planned as a preliminary to an attack on Egypt prior to an assault on Muslim strongholds in the Holy Land.

AFTER THE SEVENTH CRUSADE

The failure of the Seventh Crusade in Egypt and the capture of Louis IX by Sultan Turan Shah in April 1250 provoked an outpouring of grief in France. The peasants of northern France rose up in a protest movement that presented itself as a crusade to free their pious king from humiliating captivity among the infidel, but which was really a social uprising and a protest against the failure of the French nobility and the Church to go to Louis's aid (see box).

Meanwhile in May 1251, on the payment of his vast ransom, Louis was released and departed from Egypt, bound for Acre. He stayed in the Holy Land for three years, effectively ruling the Kingdom of Jerusalem and holding his court in Acre. In his time there he refortified Acre, Caesarea, Jaffa and Sidon. He made several diplomatic attempts to improve the standing of the states of Outremer. In April 1254 he had to return to France on the death of his mother, Blanche of Castile, who had been serving as his regent.

OUTREMER UNDER PRESSURE

In the early 13th century Genghis Khan had led a devastating expansion from Mongolia and founded a vast empire. His grandson Hulagu inherited the Mongol territories in Persia and Armenia and in 1260 he captured Damascus.

Meanwhile, the general Baybars had risen up against Sultan Turan Shah in Egypt and founded a new sultanate of Mamluks (a military caste of former slaves converted to Islam). Baybars was originally himself a victim of the Mongols: he was a Kipchak Turk from the northern coasts of the Black Sea, who was sold into slavery in Egypt after his lands were overrun by Mongols in *c.*1240. In the service of the Ayyubid Egyptian sultan al-Salih, he rose to prominence, and defeated crusader armies at La Forbie and al-Mansourah.

In 1260, after taking Damascus, Hulagu sent his principal general, Kitboga, southwards to defeat Egypt. The Mongols met their match in Baybars, who led the

▲ Angels lead the way across the waves as the saintly Louis IX embarks on crusade from the port of Aigues-Mortes in France.

Egyptian army to victory in the Battle of Ain Jalut in Galilee on 3 September 1260. That same year Baybars plotted the death of the Mamluk sultan, Qutuz, and seized power for himself. He marched into Syria and took Damascus. He now had control both of Egypt and of Syria and united them in a single state.

In 1265 Baybars repaired and refortified the Syrian fortresses earlier destroyed by the Mongols, then launched an invasion of Outremer. That year he took the town of Caesarea and seized Arsuf from its garrison of Knights Hospitaller. The garrison surrendered on the promise that survivors would be freed, and then were slaughtered to a man. In 1266 Baybars captured Safed from the Knights Templar – again Baybars promised safe passage to members of the garrison, only to behead them. He took Toron, also in 1266. In 1268 he invaded Outremer once more, and captured Jaffa and Antioch. Both were utterly destroyed, their populations either slaughtered or sold into slavery.

LOUIS'S SECOND ATTEMPT

Baybars' devastation of Outremer inspired Louis IX to take the cross a second time, on 24 March 1267. Recruitment this time proved much more difficult than in 1245–48. Nevertheless, three years later Louis embarked from Aigues-Mortes with an army of around 10,000 men bound initially for Sardinia. He was persuaded by his brother, Charles of Anjou, to direct the attack first against Tunis, then to move against Baybars' power base in Egypt.

The crusaders landed in northern Africa in July, and besieged Tunis. Almost at once, a large part of the army became sick after drinking dirty water; Louis himself was struck down so badly that he

▲ *While in Outremer in 1251–54, Louis oversaw the building of fortifications at Caesarea, surrounded by a deep moat.*

died, on 25 August, just one day after Charles of Anjou had arrived to lend his support. By tradition, Louis's dying word was 'Jerusalem!' Louis's 25-year-old son Philip, Count of Orleans, was proclaimed King Philip III of France; Charles of Anjou took on leadership of the crusade.

The crusaders failed to take Tunis. On 30 October they lifted the siege after negotiating a favourable settlement under which Christian merchants could enjoy free trade with the city and priests and monks were given rights of residence there. About this time Prince Edward of England arrived. He moved swiftly on Acre, the only surviving crusader territory in Syria. His actions there are considered to form the Ninth Crusade.

▼ *Louis is struck down by dysentery near Tunis. He died without fulfilling his desire to reclaim the Holy City, and the legend arose that his last word was 'Jerusalem!'*

THE SHEPHERDS' CRUSADE OF 1251

French popular unrest over the capture of Louis IX in Egypt was focused into a protest by a Hungarian monk known as le Maître de Hongrie (The Hungarian Master). He declared that the Blessed Virgin Mary, Mother of Christ, had visited him in a dream with instructions to mobilize the shepherds of France and lead them in a crusade to free the saintly king from captivity.

Chronicle accounts suggest that the 'shepherd' army, which contained all kinds of rural poor, including women and children, numbered 60,000. The monk led them to Paris but Louis's mother, Blanche of Castile, who was acting as regent, sent them on their way.

(English chronicler Matthew Paris met the monk and afterwards declared him an imposter; Matthew believed that the man was a rabble-rouser, and a survivor of the so-called Children's Crusade of 1212.) The crusaders went to Rouen, where they attacked priests, and Tours, where they used violence against monasteries. Later in Amiens and Bourges they attacked Jews. At this point the regent, Blanche of Castile, gave orders that the wandering crusaders be dispersed; in a fight outside Bourges, the Master was killed and his followers then broke up of their own accord. Some of them are believed to have taken the cross and gone to the Holy Land.

SAINT LOUIS
KING LOUIS IX OF FRANCE

Louis IX led two crusades, both utter disasters. But his ascetism, the obvious strength of his religious faith, and the way he conducted himself on campaign and in negotiations meant that, remarkably, his reputation was not destroyed by his failures. He was, indeed, esteemed by both sides: by the Christians for his great leadership and his refusal to abandon his men, and by the Muslims for his noble bearing and generosity of spirit. He was canonized in 1297 by Pope Boniface VIII and is the only French king to be a saint.

A POWERFUL MOTHER
The son of Louis VIII of France and Blanche of Castille, Louis became king aged 12 on his father's death in 1226. His mother, Blanche, the powerful granddaughter of King Henry II of England and Eleanor of Aquitaine, was regent and she single-handedly secured the kingdom against baronial unrest in 1226 and an attempted invasion by the youthful King Henry III of England in 1230. Four years later, Louis came of age, began to rule in his own right and married Marguerite of Provence, but he remained under

▲ *Louis arrives at Notre Dame, Paris, with his mother, Blanche of Castile. He owed his kingdom to her bravery and resolution during his minority.*

▼ *The formidable Blanche of Castile was a powerful influence throughout Louis's life. But he defied her wishes when he went on the Seventh Crusade in 1248.*

Blanche's influence right up to her death in 1252. She served as regent a second time, just as effectively, from 1248–52, while Louis was on the Seventh Crusade; indeed, Louis returned to France from his rule in Acre in 1254 because of her death.

NEGOTIATING WITH THE ENEMY
Louis also attempted to advance the cause of Christianity in the East by attempting to make alliances against Muslim rulers. He twice sent ambassadors to the Mongols, in the belief that he could form a powerful alliance against the Abbasid caliphate in Baghdad. The first time was in 1248–49: Louis received an approach from Eljigidel, Mongol ruler of Armenia and Persia, suggesting that if Louis attacked

Egypt, Eljigidel would attack Baghdad, splitting Muslim power; he responded by sending a Dominican priest named Andre of Longjumeau as his ambassador to the court of the Great Khan Guyuk (the grandson of Genghis Khan) in Mongolia. Unfortunately Guyuk died before the envoy arrived, and his widow sent an insulting message back to Louis, demanding that he send financial tribute.

The second time was in 1253 when Louis sent a Franciscan friar named William of Rubruck to visit the Great

▶ *One of Louis's many distinctions is that he founded the* Parlement *(council of the king) in Paris. It met within the royal palace on the Ile de la Cité. On this altarpiece Louis is shown in Paris with St John the Baptist.*

Khan Mongke in Mongolia. Mongke also demanded tribute and suggested that Louis should accept Mongol authority. These were only two of several attempts by Christian powers to engage the Mongols as allies against Muslim Egypt and Syria: for while the Mongols mostly followed a folk religion based on shamanism, they had Christians among their followers and forces and were clearly enemies of Islam. Earlier, Pope Innocent IV had sent two embassies, in 1245 and 1247, and later Prince Edward negotiated with them in 1271 and Pope Gregory X did so later in the 1270s.

RELIGIOUS PASSION

Louis was celebrated for his kindness, his piety and the strength of his religious devotion. His faith did have positive consequences as well as the failed crusades and inconsequential diplomatic contact with the Mongols. One glorious product was the Sainte Chappelle (Holy Chapel) on the Ile de la Cité in Paris. He built the chapel to house two sacred relics, bought

▼ *Sultan Turan Shah returns home to a hero's welcome and fanfares of trumpets. He becomes known as the Conqueror of Louis; France's humiliation is complete.*

at inordinate cost from Byzantine emperor Baldwin II in 1239–41: these purported to be the Crown of Thorns that Christ was forced to wear after his arrest, and a fragment of the True Cross (on which Christ was crucified). These supreme relics greatly enhanced Louis's standing and that of the French crown, and made Paris the most famous city of Europe.

ON CAMPAIGN

There was no doubt as to Louis's standing as a knight and general. Prior to going on crusade, Louis proved himself in battle against French vassals. On the Eighth Crusade he fought with inspirational bravery, as reported by contemporary chroniclers. On landing at Damietta he personally led the disembarkation and planted the sacred standard of St Denis, the oriflamme, into the sand, rousing his troops to perform fearless acts of bravery by his example. Outside al-Mansourah, according to John of Joinville, Louis once again demonstrated the greatest bravery – at one point he was almost captured when six Egyptians seized his horse's bridle but he set about them with his sword and freed himself to fight on. Joinville reports that the Christians took heart at seeing their king fighting with such ferocity and

bravery. At the end of the battle, when he heard the news of his brother Robert's death and on being reminded of the victory he had won, Louis wept in the saddle.

PERFECT CHRISTIAN RULER

In his life and his death while on crusade Louis was seen by contemporaries as the perfect Christian monarch – indeed, as an embodiment of Christendom. After his death from sickness at Tunis on the Eighth Crusade, his entrails were reputedly buried at his place of death near Tunis, where a shrine raised to him still stands today. The rest of his corpse was returned to France and buried at Saint-Denis. A gilt brass tomb was raised over his remains in the late 14th century but this was destroyed and his body lost in the French Wars of Religion (1562–98). Louis was canonized in 1297. His friend and biographer John of Joinville gave evidence at the papal inquest into his life.

A mischievous Tunisian tradition however, holds that the king did not die at Tunis, but instead was inspired to convert to Islam after falling in love with a Berber princess. According to this story, he then took the name 'Sidi Bou Said'. The episode is commemorated in the name of a town in Tunisia.

THE NINTH CRUSADE

PRINCE EDWARD IN ACRE

Prince Edward of England (the future King Edward I) led an English army to the Holy Land to support the beleaguered remnants of Christian Outremer, principally Acre and Tripoli, in 1271–72. The crusade led to the signing of two ten-year truces with the warlike Egyptian sultan Baybars, and the settlement of disputes between Christians in the Holy Land – but it did nothing to secure the long-term future of Outremer. While in Acre, Edward also famously survived an assassination attempt sponsored by Baybars.

FIRST TO TUNIS

Edward had responded to King Louis IX's calling of a new crusade in response to attacks by Sultan Baybars of Egypt on the few remaining Christian strongholds in the East. He arrived in north Africa too late to take part in that crusade, which came to nothing, and after Louis IX's death of dysentery and the subsequent lifting of the

▼ *At Acre the Knights Hospitaller built a formidable citadel, which was part of the north wall of the city. Beneath the citadel they excavated a series of large halls.*

▲ *Edward was a proven warrior before he went on crusade. At the age of 24, he had commanded the cavalry in the army of his father, Henry III, at the Battle of Lewes.*

siege of Tunis in October 1270, Edward and his English knights, together with the remnant of the crusader army commanded by the late king's brother Charles of Anjou, sailed on to overwinter in Sicily before the English contingent alone pressed on to Acre. Edward travelled on crusade with his beloved wife Eleanor of Castile, whom he had married when he was 15 and she was 9 in 1254.

TRIPOLI SAVED

Sultan Baybars's capture of Antioch in May 1268 was as ruthless as any before it: the garrison and population were slaughtered or sold into slavery, the city razed to the ground. It was news of this calamity, which left the crusader County of Tripoli in a very vulnerable position, that inspired Prince Edward to take the cross. When Edward landed in May 1271, Baybars had just taken the formidable fortress of Krak des Chevaliers and was already besieging

Tripoli. But the landing of Edward's army, coupled with crusader expeditions against the Egyptian army's supply lines, caused Baybars to lift the siege and agree a ten-year truce with Tripoli.

EMBASSY TO THE MONGOLS

In June Baybars captured Montfort Castle, near Acre, from the Teutonic Knights; for once he honoured his promise to let the garrison escape alive – he marched them up to the walls of Acre before releasing them. Within the city, the knights and men-at-arms clamoured for Edward to lead a sortie against Baybars and his army – but, seeing the enormous size and strength of the Egyptian sultan's force, Edward elected to stay put. Later in the month Edward led a brief raid on St Georges-de-Lebeyne, a mere 15 miles (24km) from Acre: his army captured and looted the settlement, but the troops were badly affected by food poisoning and extreme heat.

In the same month, June 1271, Edward sent an embassy to the Mongol ruler of Iran, Iraq and parts of Anatolia, Il Khan Abagha, seeking an alliance against Sultan Baybars. While in Acre, Edward also attempted to defuse quarrels among the Christians of Outremer and Cyprus, saying that unless they could present a united front against the military threat of Baybars, they were certainly doomed. For instance, he acted as arbitrator in a dispute between King Hugh III of Jerusalem and Cyprus, and Hugh's knights, members of the powerful Ibelin family, who challenged Hugh's claim that they should fight for him in Outremer as well as in Cyprus.

THE SECOND EXPEDITION FROM ACRE

In the autumn, the Christian position in Outremer was strengthened when Edward's embassy to the Mongols bore fruit in a Mongol attack on Mamluk Syria, and reinforcements from England arrived under the command of Prince Edmund. In November, Edward led a second military expedition from Acre, marching with

▲ *Stabbed by a would-be assassin, Edward overpowered the man and so saved his own life. Acre might have been Edward's place of death, and England would have been deprived of one of its great kings.*

the support of local barons and members of the military orders around 45 miles (70km) to attack the Muslim-held castle of Qaqun. He and his troops won a victory over a Turkoman army but were unable to defeat the garrison and take the castle and retreated again to the safety of Acre. There he oversaw the building of a new tower and the foundation of a new military order, that of St Edward of Acre.

A TRUCE – AND AN ASSASSIN

The following year, in May 1272, King Hugh agreed a truce with Sultan Baybars, establishing that the Kingdom of Jerusalem would maintain its borders for ten years, ten months, ten days and ten hours. According to some accounts, Edward was unhappy at this peace treaty, and did not plan to honour it.

The following month, in any case, Sultan Baybars sent an assassin into Acre

in the guise of a Muslim seeking conversion to Christianity; on 16 June this man managed to get into Prince Edward's quarters and stabbed the prince with a poisoned dagger as he slept; Edward woke, kicked out and won possession of the dagger before killing the assassin.

In the traditional account, Edward's wife Eleanor of Castile then saved his life by sucking the poison from his wound before spitting it out. However, this part of the tale was made up; in truth what happened was that Edward's wound became so badly infected that it threatened his life, and an English doctor performed an operation to cut the diseased flesh away.

Afterwards, Edward prepared to attack Jerusalem, but the news that his father, Henry III, had died, making the prince King Edward I of England, forced him to abandon these plans and head home. On 24 September 1272 Edward and Eleanor embarked for Europe, sailing initially to southern Italy, and travelling home by way of Savoy, Paris and Gascony. They landed in England on 2 August 1274 and Edward was crowned King Edward I of England on 19 August in Westminster Abbey.

THE FALL OF TRIPOLI AND ACRE
THE END OF OUTREMER

The ten-year truces signed by Tripoli and Acre with Muslim Egypt were essentially worthless, for neither Sultan Baybars nor his successors in Cairo were the type of men to be bound by such a nicety as a peace treaty. Following the death of Baybars in 1277, sultans Qalawun and Khalil led the Mamluk Egyptian army to the conquest of Tripoli in 1289 and of Acre in 1291.

CRUSADING INITIATIVES
In the immediate aftermath of the Ninth Crusade there were further attempts in Europe to mount expeditions to come to the aid of Outremer. Pope Gregory X entered negotiations with the Mongols to mount a combined campaign in the Holy Land and preached a crusade in 1274, but the plans came to nothing following

▼ In Tripoli the forbidding Castle of Raymond of St Gilles, named for the leader of the First Crusade, was expanded by the Mamluks after they captured it in 1289.

Gregory's death in January 1276. In 1282 Louis IX's brother, Charles of Anjou, King of Sicily and in name King of Jerusalem (after he had bought the succession rights from Mary of Antioch) attempted to mount a campaign to retake Constantinople for Latin Christianity. (Constantinople had been recaptured by the Byzantine Greeks under Emperor Michael VIII Palaeologus in 1261 – *see* box.) But Charles had to abandon the campaign to deal with an uprising against his rule in the War of the Sicilian Vespers.

THE MAMLUK SUCCESSION
In the year of his death, in 1277, Sultan Baybars achieved two final triumphs: the defeat of a combined Mongol–Seljuk Turk army and the capture of Caesarea. When he died in June of that year, Baybars was initially succeeded by his son Baraka, who was forced to abdicate by a revolt in Egypt. He was replaced by Salamish, his seven-year-old brother – then Qalawun, established himself as regent from 1279.

▲ Acre was held by the crusaders from 1104 until 1187, when it was taken by Saladin, and from 1191 to 1291. For its last century in Christian hands, Acre was the capital of the Kingdom of Jerusalem.

EVENTS IN OUTREMER
Charles of Anjou died in 1285, and King Henry III of Cyprus was crowned King of Jerusalem at Acre on 15 August 1286. After two weeks of celebrations including an 'Arthurian Round Table' chivalric tournament, Henry returned to Cyprus leaving his uncle, Philip of Ibelin, to rule in Acre as his bailiff. Then, in 1287, Bohemond VIII, Count of Tripoli, died. The citizens of Tripoli chose to become a republic rather than accept the accession of Bohemond's sister Lucia and asked the republic of Genoa to send its fleet.

This was the impetus for Sultan Qalawun to march on Tripoli with a vast army and settle in for a siege. He had earlier moved against the remaining crusader possessions, capturing the Hospitaller fortress of Margat in 1285 and taking the main Syrian port, Latakia, in 1287. The siege of Tripoli lasted less than a month. Qalawun's troops slaughtered the population and destroyed the city and its port so that a new wave of crusaders would have nothing to inherit.

THE RECOVERY OF THE BYZANTINE EMPIRE

Following the sacking of Constantinople in 1204 during the Fourth Crusade, and the establishment there of the Latin empire of Constantinople, the Byzantine Empire moved its capital to Nicaea. There, Constantine Laskaris established a new dynasty of emperors – the Laskarid. This dynasty ruled until 1261, when the child-emperor John IV Laskaris, was deposed by an aristocrat who declared himself Emperor Michael VIII Palaeologus. Emperor Michael captured Constantinople from the final Latin ruler, Baldwin III, on 25 July 1261. Threatened in the 1270s by Charles of Anjou's scheme to reclaim Constantinople under the authority of Rome, Michael offered to engineer the reunification of the Christian Church and to place Orthodox Christianity under papal rule. However, he was unable to force this on his outraged subjects, and had to back down, leading to his excommunication by Pope Martin IV. Michael – and Constantinople – were then saved from attack at the hands of Pope Martin's ally, Charles of Anjou, by the War of the Sicilian Vespers, which Michael himself had secretly incited. Subsequently, Michael continued to reign until his death in 1282: he established the Palaeologian Dynasty of Byzantine emperors, who ruled the empire until the Ottoman Turks captured Constantinople under Mehmed 'the Conqueror' in 1453.

THE FALL OF ACRE

Determined to achieve the destruction of the crusader states, Qalawun next moved against Acre. But he died in November 1290 before he could effect its capture. His son and successor, Khalil, began the siege, bringing an army perhaps 75,000 strong and a huge siege train containing more than 90 mangonels and trebuchets. The siege began on 11 April 1291.

The garrison numbered 800 knights and 14,000 infantry. From Europe came a contingent of English knights sent by Edward I of England under the command of Odo of Savoy, and a contingent of French knights under Jean of Grailly. The defenders manned Acre's double line of walls, with the Templars on the northern section, the Hospitallers alongside them, the French on the southern walls and Venetians, Genoans and Pisans defending the port area. Further reinforcements under King Henry II of Cyprus and Jerusalem arrived on 4 May.

The besiegers set up their great engines: one directed at the quarter defended by the Templars, another aimed at the Hospitallers' area of walls and a third wheeled machine trained on the Accursed Tower, on the eastern wall and defended by knights of Cyprus and Syria.

Early in the siege Frankish envoys rode into the Egyptian camp and spoke to the Sultan, asking him to have mercy on the poor and vulnerable of the city. He made them an offer: abandon the city and he would let them leave freely. They refused to negotiate, perhaps remembering the many promises broken by Sultan Baybars.

The knights of the military orders made two night-time sorties – the first (by the Templars) was essentially successful, although it did not result in the hoped-for destruction of siege equipment, but the second (by the Hospitallers) was met with fierce resistance.

The continual assault by the siege engines and the digging of sappers beneath the walls inevitably had its effect. On 15 May, following the collapse of the towers of Blois, of St Nicholas and of Henry II, the defenders were forced to abandon the outer walls and retreat to the inner defences. On 18 May Sultan Khalil ordered a general assault, which was launched before dawn to the beating of a kettledrum and accompanied by a hail of Greek fire and a storm of arrows. The Accursed Tower was the first to be taken by the attackers, and in the bitter struggle the Grand Master of the Knights Templar, William of Beaujeu, was killed in the fighting. The attackers poured through and overran the city. Acre fell to Sultan Khalil on 18 May 1291. Only a small group of Knights Templar, in the Templars' palace, carried on the resistance – but they were forced to surrender after a week. The population of the city was put to the sword, and its buildings, including the warehouse and port, were utterly destroyed.

END OF OUTREMER

In the days following the fall of Acre, the crusader towns of Beirut, Tyre, Haifa and Tortosa were all abandoned by their defenders. A few thousand refugees managed to escape in ships bound for Cyprus, which remained in crusader hands; other survivors were sold into slavery. A little less than two centuries after the First Crusade, the Latin Christians had been expelled from the Holy Land. Outremer was a thing of the past.

▼ *William of Clermont at the forefront of the last stand in defence of the Kingdom of Jerusalem on the walls of Acre.*

THE ATTACK ON ALEXANDRIA

CRUSADES OF THE 14TH CENTURY

The fall of Acre in 1291 is traditionally taken as the end of the crusades, but people continued to take the cross for centuries afterward. Christian rulers and adventurers made a number of attempts to revive the attack on Islam in the course of the 14th century.

CRUSADING LEAGUES

In the Aegean region, Western powers such as the Knights Hospitaller, Cypriots and Venetian trading colonies attempted to form maritime crusading leagues to combat the power of Turkish emirates that had emerged along the western coast of Anatolia following Mongol devastation of the Seljuk Sultanate. These leagues had papal blessing and assembled small fleets to take the fight to the Turks by sea; they went to war under crusading indulgences and tax exemptions. The first league was formed in 1334 and defeated a Turkish fleet at Adramyttium.

A second league was established ten years later and made a significant capture

▲ *The background to the early 14th-century crusades was the dissolution of the Knights Templar by Pope Clement V (left) in 1312. He transferred the Templars' vast wealth to the Knights Hospitaller, now on Rhodes.*

by taking the port of Smyrna. In the wake of this, French lord Humbert II, Dauphin of Viennois (the region near Vienne in west-central France), attempted to gather a crusading army in northern Italy to consolidate Smyrna and then take further territory. But his efforts came to nothing, principally because of enduring hostility between the rival trading cities of Venice and Genoa.

A third league was gathered in 1359 and under the papal legate to the East, the French-born Carmelite Peter Thomas, won a victory at Lampsacus, an ancient Greek city on the eastern Hellespont (near Lapseki in Turkey). The league supported the efforts by Peter I of Cyprus to repel the Turkish coastal emirates, which were launching attacks on his territories. Gaining the fortified harbour of Corycus (modern Kizkalesi, Turkey) in 1360, he

captured the port of Adalia (now Antalya in south-western Turkey) in 1361, and in 1362 led raids on Myra, Anamour, Siki and other ports along the Mediterranean coast of what is now southern Turkey.

KING PETER'S CRUSADE

Bolstered by these successes, but frustrated that the paucity of Cypriot resources prevented him doing more, he embarked on a tour of Europe in 1362, attempting with papal support to win the backing of European knights and rulers for a crusade. He visited Poland, Bohemia, Germany, France, England and the Low Countries.

▼ *Alexandria's library was established by Ptolemy II in the 3rd century BC. By the time of King Peter's Crusade it was far from the institution it had been. The crusaders claimed that all the books were burned after Muslims conquered the city in AD642.*

The result was the embarkation of a crusading army at Venice on 27 June 1365. The enterprise was called 'King Peter's Crusade' by contemporaries.

The army sailed to Rhodes, where they joined forces with Knights Hospitaller. Peter had heard of plans for an attack from Mamluk Egypt on Cyprus and drew up a plan to pre-empt this campaign by seizing the Egyptian port of Alexandria and then negotiating to swap possession of the Egyptian port for the Holy City of Jerusalem. The combined army, embarked in a fleet of 165 mainly Cypriot and Italian ships, set sail under his command in October 1365 bound for northern Africa.

On 9 October they made a difficult landing under heavy attack from the shore: Muslim bowmen kept up a thick rain of arrows on to the crusader galleys as they neared land and warriors, undeterred by crossbow bolts fired from the ships, came into the sea up to their chests fighting desperately to drive the crusaders off. Finally a brave contingent of Peter's army established a beachhead and began to drive the Muslims back.

The retreating Mamluks closed the city gates and manned the battlements against Peter's invaders. Peter set a great fire before the gates and caused sufficient damage to enable his army to break into the city. An orgy of violence and looting followed. The crusaders rampaged through Alexandria stealing indiscriminately and even sacking the city's celebrated library.

According to the account of French musician-poet William of Machaut, more than 20,000 Saracens were killed in the attack and many others fled. The victory, he claimed, was a triumph for the Christian faith, one ordained by God and given as a reward to King Peter for his dedication to the cause of Christianity.

PETER ABANDONED

But in the aftermath of victory, Peter found that his army of adventurers did not have the stomach to stay and defend what they had won, and virtually to a man they took their booty and departed for home.

William of Machaut reports that the Viscount of Turenne made a speech warning against staying and the crusaders followed his advice. The viscount declared that King Peter did not have sufficient men to defend the city, that his army did not have food, supplies or adequate artillery and that they would soon be faced with an army raised by the sultan of Egypt, al-Ashraf Nasir, who would bring 'five hundred times five hundred thousand men' to win back the city. William notes that Peter was extremely upset, not least because before embarking on the crusade the viscount had promised to serve Peter for a year in defence of any lands conquered on the expedition. Another contemporary comment on the endeavour was made by the great poet Francesco Petrarcha (Petrarch), who wrote to his fellow writer Giovanni Boccaccio that the city of Alexandria, once taken, could have been a great base for Christianity in driving back the Saracens in Africa, but that the enterprise failed because too many of the crusaders were from northern climes – people, according to Petrarch, who begin enterprises full of energy, but cannot carry them through. The crusaders, now immeasurably richer, abandoned Alexandria and headed for home, followed by the exasperated King Peter.

PLANS TO REGAIN THE HOLY LAND

European men of letters of the 14th century drew up a range of plans for re-establishing the Kingdom of Jerusalem. The Venetian Marino Sanuto Torsello, for example, argued that the best means of achieving this end was to outlaw trade with Muslim Egypt: traders would be barred from delivering their cargoes of children, timber and iron to Egypt and from collecting cargoes of sugar, cotton and spices. He pointed out that a similar embargo on sea trade had been imposed in 1187 on trading with the empire of Saladin. He argued that this time the embargo should be maintained on land and sea.

▲ Sanuto envisaged that after a trade embargo brought Egypt low, Christian knights could win back the Holy Land.

▼ This illustration from Sanuto's treatise shows traders carrying supplies to and from the Holy Land.

PETER I OF CYPRUS

THE CRUSADER KING

Peter of Cyprus is known to history as the crusading king, who briefly in the mid-14th century made Cyprus a major participant in international affairs. He reigned for just 11 years, 1358–69, but established himself as a well-known figure of chivalry, the founder of a chivalric order and leader of holy war against Egypt of 1365. This enterprise was known by contemporaries as 'King Peter's Crusade'.

THE ORDER OF THE SWORD

Peter, sometimes also called Pierre I of Lusignan, was the second son of King Hugh IV of Cyprus and had the title of King of Jerusalem from 1358–69. Born in 1328 in Nicosia, Peter was just 19 when, in 1347, he had a religious vision that inspired him to found the chivalric Order of the Sword. According to the account given by French poet and musician William of Machaut (*see* box), Peter had a vision of a cross floating in mid-air, venerated by many as the cross on which the Good Thief hung. (The Gospels report that Christ was crucified between two thieves, one of whom railed against Christ, but the second of whom rebuked his fellow thief and addressed Christ as Lord; in later Christian tradition he was known as

the 'Good Thief' or St Dismas.) Peter heard a voice addressing him as 'Son' and urging him to wage holy war to regain the lands promised by God to the holy patriarchs; as a result, he founded the Order of the Sword for knights professing a determination to regain the promised land and for men-at-arms with the desire to save their souls. The emblem of the order was a silver sword, set with the point downward to resemble a crucifix, against a blue background and the words 'With this maintain loyalty' inscribed in gold.

Two years later Peter left secretly for Europe with one of his brothers, perhaps with the intention of trying to raise or join a crusade. But his father, King Hugh, tracked the pair down and had them brought back to Cyprus, where he jailed them for having left without permission.

SEA RAIDS

Following his father's abdication in 1358, Peter assumed power and was crowned King of Cyprus and titular King of Jerusalem in Famagusta in 1360. He achieved a number of successes against Muslim Turkish emirs along the eastern seaboard of the Mediterranean. In 1360 he was invited by the citizens of Corycos,

▲ *King Peter's Crusade in 1365 ended in disarray but Peter himself, seen here issuing orders to his men, had a great reputation a military strategist and leader.*

in Armenian Cilicia, to take control of their harbour settlement and protect them against Turkish attacks. Peter accepted and sent a Cypriot force commanded by Robert of Lusignan to defend the port. The city was then besieged by Turkish forces, but the garrison held firm and Corycos was made part of the Kingdom of Cyprus.

Peter was now seen as a threat by the Turkish emirs on the mainland, and these men united to plan a maritime attack on Cyprus. Peter, however, received news of the plan and launched a pre-emptive strike with the help of the Knights Hospitaller on Rhodes, and some European and papal forces. With a fleet of 120 ships, he attacked and besieged Adalia (now Antalya in south-western Turkey) and forced the Turks to sue for peace. He made them pay a yearly tribute to Cyprus.

TOUR OF EUROPE

The following year Peter embarked on a trip to Europe, intending to generate enthusiasm for a general crusade for the

▲ *Pope Urban V told Peter to bring the 1365 crusade to an end after it broke down, and in the wake of violent reprisals against Christian merchants in Egypt and in Syria.*

recapture of the Holy Land. He took part in a succession of chivalric tournaments and was hospitably received by monarchs and princes, but was unable to win the widespread support he had hoped for.

Nevertheless, by 1365 Peter had managed to raise an army of sorts, and he embarked on his crusade against Egypt in October of that year. As we have seen, the enterprise began well, with the taking of the city of Alexandria, but this quickly degenerated into ill-disciplined looting before the crusaders departed for home, refusing to obey Peter's command to march on Cairo. In contemporary accounts of the events, Peter's own participation was highly praised – he was represented not only as an inspirational leader, but also as a brave warrior and a

▶ *Peter was represented (back row, second from right) with Emperor Charles IV and Pope Urban V (third and fourth from right) in Andrea Bonaiuti's fresco of 'The Church Militant' at St Maria Novella in Florence.*

skilled and capable general who achieved what could have been a significant gain for Christendom if he had not been let down by greedy and self-interested troops.

Peter returned to Cyprus, where he continued to mount raids on Turkish holdings along the coasts of what is now Turkey and Syria. He raided Tripoli and was preparing an attack inland, on Damascus, but abandoned that venture after Venetian merchants – afraid of damage to trade – bribed him handsomely not to carry it through. In 1367 he made another trip to Europe, again to try to raise a crusade force, but without success. Increasingly he ruled with an iron hand: when he discovered that his wife Eleanor had conducted an adulterous affair with John of Morphou, Count of Edessa, he embarked on a bitter campaign against her favourite members of the nobility. Some began to question his sanity.

ASSASSINATION AND LEGACY

On 17 January 1369 Peter was assassinated. Two of his knights allowed conspirators – including Philip of Ibelin, lord of Arsuf, and Henry of Jubail – access to the king's bedchamber early in the morning. There, half-dressed, he was repeatedly stabbed, then beheaded and even had his genitals mutilated by an angry knight, James of Nores.

> ### WILLIAM OF MACHAUT
>
> Born in *c.*1300 in Champagne, the poet William of Machaut was in his mid-70s when he wrote his account of the crusade to Alexandria. He was a celebrated figure, who had served one of the great chivalric monarchs of the age, King John of Bohemia. John insisted on fighting on the French side at the Battle of Poitiers in 1356 despite being almost blind and was killed and then honoured by Edward the Black Prince, who took his emblem of an ostrich feather and motto *Ich Dien* (I serve) as his own. William wrote several poems in praise of royal knighthood and also composed many lays and ballads.

Peter's reign was brief and he died a humiliating death. His crusading endeavours achieved little – the only real effect of the attack on Alexandria was to provoke the Sultan of Egypt and damage trade. Nevertheless, because of his devotion to crusading ideals, the fact that he founded a chivalric brotherhood and cut a impressive figure in the courts of Europe (as well as when fighting during the crusade to Alexandria), he was remembered as a paragon of 14th-century chivalry.

CRUSADE TO MAHDIA
ATTACK ON TUNISIA UNITES WARRING CHRISTIANS, 1390

In 1378 the Catholic Church split, in an event known as the Great Schism: there was one pope in Rome and one in Avignon, and the schism continued until 1417 when rule by a single pope was reintroduced. The rival popes combined in 1390, however, to call a crusade against the town of Mahdia, in Tunisia, home to a corsair fleet.

CHRISTIANS DIVIDED
In 1305, at a time when Italy was riven by the papacy's conflict with the Holy Roman Empire, Pope Clement V moved the Roman curia (papal court) from Rome to Poitiers in France, and then in 1309 moved on to Avignon. In 1378 Pope Gregory XI moved back to Rome, but died the same year; there was a dispute over the succession and while Bartolomeo Prignano took power as Pope Urban VI in Rome, in France cardinals elected Robert of Geneva

▲ *John of Gaunt is received by the citizens of Bayonne. John campaigned in Europe in the 1360s–70s, fought with Edward, the Black Prince, in the Battle of Najera (1367) and led a 'crusade' to Portugal in 1386, which ended in a financial settlement.*

▼ *John of Gaunt was the fourth son of King Edward III of England and was father of King Henry IV. Lady Margaret Beaufort, mother of the first Tudor king (Henry VII) was Gaunt's great-granddaughter.*

as a rival pope to rule from Avignon. Robert took the papal name of, Clement VII, and swiftly excommunicated Urban, declaring him to be the Antichrist.

CRUSADES OF THE GREAT SCHISM
In the years following the Great Schism, supporters of the rival popes fought crusades against one another. In general terms, the Avignon pope enjoyed the support of France and her allies Scotland and Castile, while the pope in Rome had the backing of most of the rest of Europe. In 1383 Sir Henry Despenser, Bishop of Norwich in England, a supporter of Rome and a veteran of papal wars in Italy, led a crusade against Louis of Mâle, Count of Flanders and a supporter of Avignon. In a bloody campaign, beginning in May 1383, Sir Henry took Gravelines, Bourbourg, Dunkirk, Diksmuide and other coastal towns, as well as many castles and a fortified church at Veume. He then drove off

an army raised by the Count of Flanders at Dunkirk and laid siege to Ypres. However, the crusade army became bogged down in the siege and after eight weeks, hearing that the French army under Charles VI was approaching, retreated to Dunkirk. In the end, Sir Henry left for England after a negotiated settlement and the crusade came to nothing – although the settlement with Charles VI reportedly made the bishop and his leading knights considerably richer.

A second crusade took place in 1386 when John of Gaunt, 1st Duke of Lancaster, led a campaign in alliance with Portugal on behalf of Rome against Castile. The enterprise doubled as an attempt to enforce Gaunt's claim to the Castilian throne (through his marriage to Constanza, daughter of the late King Pedro I of Castile), and before he left he was formally recognized as King of Castile by King Richard II of England. However, like its forerunner of 1383, this crusade was settled by a financial agreement under which Gaunt abandoned his claim to the Castile in return for a substantial payment.

CRUSADE OF 1390

The warring halves of Christendom were united by proposals for a crusade against Tunisia in 1390. The idea of the crusade came from Genoese traders whose Mediterranean ships had been raided repeatedly by corsairs from the town of Mahdia, Tunisia. The Genoese, supporters of Pope Boniface IX (Urban VI's successor in Rome), won the backing for the project of King Charles VI of France, who supported Clement VII in Avignon. The proposal was then enthusiastically taken up in France and won the backing of both Boniface IX and Clement VII. Contingents joined from the Low Countries, England and Spain to bolster the mainly French and Genoese army. The leader was named as Count Louis of Bourbon.

▼ *Boniface IX, second Roman pope of the Great Schism of 1378–1417, is crowned. The 1390 crusade, which had his backing, showed the benefits of Christian unity.*

The crusaders set sail from Marseilles and went by way of Genoa to northern Africa. They expected to have a fierce fight on their hands when they landed before Mahdia, but they disembarked unopposed and began a siege, with Count Louis's army surrounding three sides of the city by land and the Genoan fleet blockading the seaward wide. The inhabitants of the town waited three days before launching any attack: when it came, it was easily beaten back by Count Louis's troops, who drove the Mahdians back and reached as far as the gates of the city, fighting fiercely, but unable to force their way into the city.

After that the crusade went on for nine weeks, until finally the Genoans negotiated a peace treaty with Ahmad, emir of Tunis, under which the Tunisians would pay handsome taxes to Genoa for 15 years as well as furnishing them with 12,000 gold sovereigns to cover the cost of this campaign. The crusade turned out well for Genoa, but achieved none of its wider goals – although it certainly had benefits for Christian morale at a time of schism. Its success probably lay in the fact that it gave considerable weight to the argument that the disputes of the Great Schism would be best solved not by wars between rival camps but by creating a united front against the Turks. A further crusade would be proclaimed by Avignon and Rome in 1394 – this time against the rising power of the Ottoman Turks.

▲ *In 1417 the Great Schism was over and the Church was reunified with the deposition of two popes, the abdication of a third and the election of Pope Martin V, seen here at the Council of Constance, 1418.*

THE ENDURING SCHISM

The division within Christianity continued, however. Indeed, the two-way split became a three-way one in 1409, when patriarchs, cardinals and bishops at the Council of Pisa declared the Holy See to be vacant and elected Peter Phillarges as Pope Alexander V. Finally in 1417, at the Council of Constance, Pope John XXIII (successor to Alexander V) was deposed, the Avignon Pope Benedict XIII was deposed, Pope Gregory XII abdicated and Pope Martin V was elected as sole pope.

DEFEAT AT NICOPOLIS
THE RISE OF THE OTTOMANS

As the 14th century progressed the Christian powers of Europe were increasingly aware of the rising threat posed by the Muslim Ottoman state as it expanded from its original base in Anatolia into the Balkans and towards the lands of the mighty Holy Roman Empire. In the 1390s the Ottomans, under their great general Bayezid I, took Salonika (modern Thessaloniki) in Greece, blockaded Constantinople and invaded Hungary. The Christian response was a major Venetian–Hungarian crusade, with the backing of both the Avignon and Roman popes, in 1396. It ended in yet another crusading humiliation, a crushing victory for Bayezid and his Ottoman army at the Battle of Nicopolis.

OTTOMAN ORIGINS AND EXPANSION
The Ottomans were descended from Turkmen tribes driven from their homes in Turkestan in the early years of the 13th century by the raids of the Mongols. They took their name from Osman I, who reigned from 1299–1326, and was known

The Ottomans became a major naval power, mostly acquiring their ships by theft. They stole an entire fleet from the Byzantines in the course of a daring night raid in 1356 led by Sultan Murad's brother Süleyman.

as Uthman or 'Ottoman' in Arabic. He was the son of Ertogrul, chief of a principality in Anatolia based at Sögüt (now in Turkey); Osman greatly expanded the principality, taking a series of towns including Eskisehir, Yenisehir and Bursa from the Byzantine Empire. Osman's son Orhan (r.1324–60) continued the expansion, capturing Nicaea (modern Iznik) in 1331 and Nicomedia (Izmit) in 1334.

In 1341–47 Orhan intervened in a Byzantine succession crisis, providing the military support that enabled John VI Cantacuzenus to overcome his rival John V Palaeologus. As a reward for this, John Cantacuzenus gave Orhan the hand of his daughter, princess Theodora, and allowed him to raid Byzantine lands in Thrace and Macedonia. Under Orhan, and as a result of the policy of John Cantacuzenus, the Ottomans won their first permanent holding in Europe, taking Gallipoli in 1354.

In 1361 Orhan's son, Murad I, captured Adrianople and Philippopolis in Thrace

▲ *King Sigismund of Hungary was forced to retreat at Nicopolis and took refuge in Venetian shipping. He was frustrated that the crusaders, refusing to listen to the advice of those familiar with Ottoman battle tactics, brought defeat upon themselves.*

and forced the Byzantine emperor (by now John V Palaeologus once more) to become a vassal. Making Adrianople his capital, renaming it Edirne, Murad then expanded deep into Serbia and Bulgaria, making local princes accept him as their overlord.

CRUSADE OF 1366
In 1366 Murad faced a crusade from Venice under the command of Italian nobleman Amadeus of Savoy. This small enterprise, which set sail with just 15 ships and 1,700 troops, was intended to restore Byzantine power in the face of Ottoman expansion and to help John Palaeologus, who was Amadeus's second cousin. Amadeus allied with Francesco I of the Aegean island of Lesbos and together they drove the Turks from Gallipoli; afterwards Amadeus, discovering that John Palaeologus had been taken captive by the Bulgarians, captured the ports of Mesembria and Sozopolis on the

Black Sea and besieged Varna, demanding his release. Finally the emperor was freed and the crusade saw no further action.

THE THUNDERBOLT STRIKES

Murad's son was Bayezid I, nicknamed *Yildirim* (the Thunderbolt) for the speed of his military campaigns. He came to power following the death of Murad in battle against Bosnian, Serbian and Bulgarian princes at Kosovo in 1389, and just two years later began a siege of Constantinople, the principal buffer between the Ottoman power base in Anatolia and Europe. He also began to extend Ottoman power towards and into Europe, capturing most of the Balkans and expelling Bulgarian tsar Ivan Shishman from his capital, Nicopolis.

A crusade was proclaimed by both Pope Boniface IX in Rome and his rival, the Avignon pope Clement VII. Kings Richard II of England, Charles VI of France and Sigismund of Hungary (who was later to be Holy Roman Emperor, 1433–37) backed the enterprise: initially the plan was for Charles and Richard to fight on the crusade, but in the event an army of 10,000 French, 1,000 English and around 6,000 from the German states gathered under Sigismund in Buda (now part of the Hungarian capital Budapest) in

▼ *The Battle of Nicopolis became a rout. Admiral of France, Jean de Vienne, fought off attackers trying to capture the French standard six times. In the end he was killed.*

TAMERLAINE AND BAYEZID

The seemingly invincible Bayezid met his match in the Turkish–Mongolian warlord Timur, or Tamerlaine. In 1402 Bayezid again abandoned his siege of Constantinople to deal with a troublesome enemy, but this time was heavily defeated by Tamerlaine at the Battle of Ankara. Bayezid was taken prisoner and kept in captivity by Tamerlaine.

Colourful contemporary reports suggested that the Ottoman sultan was kept chained in a cage but this is thought to be false. Bayezid certainly died in captivity, however, one year later; his sons, who had escaped to Serbia after the Battle of Ankara, were later able to re-establish Ottoman rule. In the 16th century English playwright Christopher

▲ *Bayezid died after a year in captivity.*

Marlowe wrote a celebrated play, *Tamburlaine the Great*, about the warlord's exploits. He was also the hero of an opera of 1724, *Tamerlano*, by Handel.

July 1396. The plan was to force the Turks from the Balkans, relieve the siege of Constantinople, and then march across Anatolia and Syria to take Jerusalem for Christ. Mircea, Prince of Wallachia, joined the crusade with a substantial army despite being an Orthodox Christian rather than a Roman Catholic; a contingent from Transylvania also joined up. Venetian and Genoese fleets and a contingent of Hospitaller knights from Rhodes also arrived to lend their support.

The army marched southwards, pillaging towns and massacring locals, before settling in to a siege of Nicopolis, the

Bulgarian capital recently taken by the Turks. Bayezid then showed why he was called 'the Thunderbolt', acting with astonishing decisiveness and speed in lifting his siege of Constantinople and marching against the crusade army. He met them in battle near Nicopolis on 25 September.

Wallachian prince Mircea, who was familiar with Ottoman tactics and had won previous victories against Bayezid, proposed that he should lead an initial assault with his skilled Wallachian light cavalry prior to a main charge by the Western army. But the crusade leaders were suspicious of his motives and instead chose to make a full-scale frontal assault. The battle was a disaster for the crusaders: although the French knights won initial successes against the Ottoman vanguard, they were overwhelmed by the main bulk of Bayezid's men; the Wallachians and Transylvanians deserted and Sigismund escaped. It was a triumph for Bayezid serving to consolidate the Ottomans in the Balkans, and leaving Constantinople even more vulnerable. Bayezid built the magnificent Ulu Mosque in Bursa to commemorate his victory in what became known as the Crusade of Nicopolis.

THE END OF BYZANTIUM

CRUSADERS FAIL TO SAVE CONSTANTINOPLE

The Ottomans repeatedly threatened Constantinople, and Western powers sent intermittent expeditions to the aid of the city. The most significant, in 1444, ended in another heavy defeat for the crusaders at Varna. Then, on 29 May 1453, the Ottomans under Sultan Mehmed II 'the Conqueror' captured Constantinople, marking the end of the Byzantine Empire.

CRUSADES OF BOUCICAUT

French knight Jean Le Meingre, Marshal of France and known as 'Boucicaut', had taken part in the Christians' defeat by Ottoman sultan Bayezid at the Battle of Nicopolis in 1396. Boucicaut was captured in the battle and later ransomed. Then, in 1399, the same year in which he established his chivalric order, the *Emprise de l'Escu Vert à la Dame Blanche* (Enterprise of the Green Shield of the White Lady), he sailed once more to the East. With 21 galleys, three transports and six ships and around 1,200 men, he succeeded in lifting the Ottoman blockade of Constantinople and rescuing the embattled Byzantine emperor, Manuel II

Palaeologus. Manuel then returned with Boucicaut to Europe to try to drum up interest for a further crusade.

In 1401 Boucicaut was made French Governor of Genoa and in 1403 he sailed to Rhodes with a fleet of 16 Genoese ships and from there led a series of raids against ports in Anatolia and Syria held by the Ottomans and the Mamluk Sultanate of Egypt. He attacked Ottoman Alanya in Anatolia, then (with the help of the Knights Hospitaller from Rhodes) raided Mamluk-held Batroun, Tripoli and Beirut.

A NEW CRUSADE

In 1443 Pope Eugenius IV (ruled 1431–47) issued a rallying call to Christians in the West to go to the aid of their brethren in the East against the Ottomans. Murad II, grandson of Bayezid 'the Thunderbolt', had re-established Ottoman supremacy after a period of decline and in-fighting following Bayezid's defeat by the Turkish-Mongolian general Tamerlaine in 1402 and his subsequent death in captivity. Murad II defeated two rivals, forced the Byzantine Empire to pay

▲ *Pope Eugenius IV did much to restore the power of the papacy after the Great Schism. The crusade he called in 1443 almost ended in success at Varna in 1444.*

tribute, and in 1430 recaptured Salonika (Thessaloniki) from the Venetians. Then he annexed Serbia in 1439.

However, the Hungarian army, commanded by King Ladislas of Hungary and his illegitimate son Janos Hunyadi, known as the 'White Knight', won victories against the Ottomans at Nis, Sofia and Snaim in 1443, on the celebrated 'long campaign', and again at Jalowaz in 1444, encouraging Christendom to dream once more of a lasting victory over Islam. A motley collection of crusaders gathered in the Balkans in 1444: the force included Hungarians, Poles, Germans, Ukrainians, Lithuanians, Croatians, Bulgarians and Bosnians. The plan was for a fleet of Genoese, Venetian and papal ships to blockade the Dardanelles to prevent Murad crossing from Anatolia into Europe to fight the crusaders; the fleet and the crusader army would rendezvous at Varna in Bulgaria, then march and sail down the coast of the Black Sea to Constantinople and relieve the siege there, pushing the Ottomans out of Europe in the process. However, the blockade of the Dardanelles failed, and Murad marched to meet the crusaders at Varna.

BATTLE OF VARNA

In the Battle of Varna on 10 November 1444 Murad's Ottoman army of around 60,000 men faced a much smaller crusade army of no more than 20,000 troops commanded by Ladislas and Janos Hunyadi. Not only were the Christians outnumbered, but they also had an unbalanced army, with very few foot soldiers and a great preponderance of heavy cavalry.

The Christians pinned their hopes on the arrival of reinforcements by sea from Constantinople. The papal legate on the crusade, Cardinal Julian Cesarini, called on the army to retreat, but they were in a difficult position, trapped by the enemy between the Black Sea, Lake Varna and the hills. The cardinal then proposed that they attempt to defend their position until they were relieved by Christian reinforcements, but Ladislas and Janos Hunyadi argued for attack – famously declaring: 'Escape is not possible, surrender inconceivable, so let us fight bravely and do honour to the arms we bear!'

The plan almost worked. The crusaders came close to victory: a group of around 500 Polish knights smashed the centre of the Ottoman deployment, breaking through the elite Janissary infantry; Sultan Murad began to flee on horseback but a soldier seized his reins to prevent him, and Murad regained his composure; Janos Hunyadi and his cavalry devastated a company of Sipahis (Ottoman cavalry) and drove them from the battlefield; King Ladislas went in pursuit of Murad, but was cut down by the Ottoman imperial

bodyguard, also of Janissaries. Ladislas was beheaded on the battlefield and, seeing the king cut down, the Polish cavalry lost heart and retreated. Janos Hunyadi escaped. King Ladislas's head was subsequently carried off to the Ottoman court.

SECOND BATTLE OF KOSOVO

In 1448 Janos Hunyadi raised another mainly Hungarian Christian army and fought Murad II again, in the Second Battle of Kosovo, which ran over two days in October. (The clash is known as the Second Battle of Kosovo to distinguish it from the earlier battle at the site between a Serbian army led by Prince Lazar and an Ottoman force under Murad I in 1389 – the battle in which Murad I died.)

Once again, as at Varna, Hunyadi was badly outnumbered by Murad II's Ottoman army, and once again he almost won the battle despite this numerical disadvantage; and, as at Varna, it was the

resilience and bravery of the sultan's elite Janissary corps that won the day. The battle began with an attack by Hunyadi's flanks that was driven back, but this was followed by a strong assault by the main part of his army. This defeated the Janissaries and reached as far as the Ottoman camp before falling back; during this latter part of the battle, with Hunyadi's forces retreating, the Janissaries recovered from their earlier setback and delivered a powerful attack that killed many of the finest Hungarian knights and forced Hunyadi himself to flee. Fighting went on with missiles and artillery fire through the night; on the next day the Ottomans launched a final and decisive attack.

The Christians' defeat in this battle left the Ottomans in the ascendant in the Balkans, with the Byzantine Empire at their mercy. Within five years, Murad II's son and successor, Mehmed II 'the Conqueror', had captured Constantinople.

▶ 'The White Knight' Janos Hunyadi was a formidable opponent of the Ottomans for 20 years from the 1430s to his death in 1456. He was regent of Hungary in 1446–53.

THE CONQUEROR
OTTOMAN SULTAN MEHMED II

Mehmed II, son of Murad II, was celebrated as 'the Conqueror' because he achieved the long-standing Ottoman ambition of taking Constantinople. He was just 21 when he led Ottoman troops into the city on 29 May 1453. On that day the city of Constantine, founded as New Rome in AD330 to be a new capital for the Roman Empire, and for centuries the centre of the Christian Byzantine Empire, became the Islamic city of Istanbul, capital of the Ottoman Empire. The venerable 6th-century Hagia Sophia (Church of Holy Wisdom) was made into a mosque. The leaders of the West were appalled.

BOY EMPEROR

Mehmed II first came to the throne at the age of 12 in 1444. His father Murad II, having suffered defeats at the hands of the Hungarian-led Christian alliance in the Balkans, notably at Jalowaz in 1444,

▼ *Constantinople, former capital of the eastern Roman Empire, falls to Mehmed's troops. By tradition the conquest was foretold by the Prophet Muhammad.*

signed a ten-year peace treaty at Edirne in June 1444. The Western powers then broke the treaty and gathered a crusading army. Murad – who had retired to rural contemplation – returned to power and led the Ottomans to decisive victories over the Christians at Varna in 1444 and in the Second Battle of Kosovo in 1448.

EYES SET ON CONSTANTINOPLE

In 1451 Murad died, and Mehmed became sultan for a second time. Almost at once, in spring 1452, he set about preparing to capture Constantinople. He had a vast cannon cast, raised an army of no fewer than 250,000 Janissaries and built a fleet of 280 ships.

Constantine had barely men enough to defend the walls of the city when Mehmed began his siege on 6 April 1453, and the siege seemed destined to succeed. According to Niccolo Barbaro, a ship's doctor from Venice who was an eyewitness to these events, those in the city became convinced that the Ottomans would succeed after a portent was seen on the night of 22 May 1453: it was a time of

▲ *Rumeli Hisari, the great fortress Mehmed built in 1452 on the European side of the Bosphorus, was also known as 'strait blocker' because it dominated the sea.*

full moon, but the moon rose as a crescent before becoming full later in the night. Outside the walls the besiegers rejoiced, for the Ottomans held the crescent moon to be their symbol.

Mehmed delivered a stirring speech in which he reminded his troops of the greatness of their forebear Bayezid the Thunderbolt. He spoke of their suffering after Bayezid's defeat by Tamerlaine, and of how the Byzantine Empire had played, and continued to play, a major part in all their woes, constantly seeking to create dissension and set Turks against one another. And all the warriors acclaimed him and cheered his plan to attack.

THE CITY TAKEN

At Mehmed's command the Ottoman army began its assault at sunset on 28 May, with the setting sun at their backs shining directly into the faces of the defenders. The assault began with a

terrifying cacophony of pipes, cymbals and trumpets, followed by a barrage of arrows and missiles. Then the walls were attacked and close hand-to-hand fighting followed around the city perimeter. Fighting continued through the night. A Genoese soldier named Giustinianni was leading the defence of the city and when he was shot and fell down dead the defenders around him fled.

At dawn on Tuesday, 29 May 1453, Mehmed himself led a fresh wave of attacks, clasping an iron club, with the Janissaries behind him and at their back a corps of executioners ready to put to death by beheading anyone who attempted to flee. Constantine XI, last in the long line of Byzantine emperors, was killed attempting to prevent this last part of the assault.

The city secured, Mehmed later made a formal entry on horseback at around noon. He entered the Hagia Sophia; it is said by tradition that when he made his way into the Palace of the Caesars, established more than a millennium earlier by Constantine the Great, he quoted from Persian poetry: 'The spider makes his frail curtains in the grand palace of the Caesars, the owl calls softly the watches of the night in the towers of Afrasiab.'

CONQUESTS AND REFORMS

The capture of Constantinople was only the first of Mehmed's many military victories. He went on to conquer Serbia, Bosnia, Albania and Greece, and the great part of the territory around the Black Sea.

▲ *Byzantium, forerunner of Constantinople, was founded by Greek traders. Mehmed visited Troy and announced that he had avenged the Trojans when he beat the Byzantine descendants of the Greeks.*

In 1480, poised to invade Italy, he sent a vast Turkish fleet to besiege the island of Rhodes, stronghold of the Knights Hospitaller. Here he met his match, and after a three-month siege was forced to abandon the attempt to capture the island, having lost no fewer than 9,000 men in the assault. That same year he died.

As well as being a great general, Mehmed was a notable administrator. He rebuilt the city of Constantinople and brought in a new tax system, promulgated a new law code, and set up a group of advisers known as the *ulama* (meaning 'wise' in Arabic), all of whom were fluent in Arabic and Persian as well as Turkish and were learned in Islamic holy law.

Mehmed died in 1481 and was succeeded by his son Bayezid II, who led the Ottomans to a series of further triumphs against Poland, Hungary, Venice, Egypt and Persia (Iran).

◄ *After taking Constantinople, Mehmed II claimed the title of 'Caesar' for himself, implying that the Ottomans were by virtue of conquest rightful heirs of ancient Rome.*

DRACULA

In 1462 Mehmed had an encounter with Prince Vlad III the Impaler. That year Mehmed invaded Wallachia in an attempt to remove its ruler Vlad, who had raided Ottoman territory and killed 20,000 people. Mehmed brought a great army with him, and occupied the Wallachian capital, but Vlad kept up a fierce guerrilla war against the invaders. In one incident on the night of 16–17 June Vlad entered the Ottoman camp with his men and came close to assassinating Mehmed. Subsequently, Mehmed installed Vlad's brother Radu in power. Vlad (below) was the inspiration for Dracula, the vampire created by Bram Stoker in his 1897 novel.

THE MIRACLE OF BELGRADE

CRUSADERS SAVE HUNGARY, 1456

After capturing Constantinople on 1453, the Ottomans under their war-like sultan Mehmed II continued to seek new conquests, both for the glory of Islam and the enrichment of their empire. But the Christian West was encouraged once more to believe in the power of holy war when a makeshift crusading army raised by the sermons of a Franciscan friar named Giovanni da Capistrano succeeded in turning back the Ottomans at the siege of Belgrade in 1456. This event was celebrated as the 'miracle of Belgrade'.

BELGRADE FORTIFIED

The 'White Knight' Janos Hunyadi, great foe of the Ottomans in the early 1440s, was an illegitimate son of the late King Ladislas and had been regent of the Kingdom of Hungary since 1446. He foresaw that Mehmed would move to conquer Hungary, and that to do so the Ottoman

▼ *Mehmed II brought a vast army, heavy artillery and a sizeable fleet to take Belgrade. The unlikely Christian victory seemed a triumph of faith that began to restore belief in the crusading enterprise.*

army would have to take the border fortress of Belgrade (today the capital of the Republic of Serbia). He set about strengthening its defences and laying in provisions, and raised a sizeable garrison force that he placed under the command of his brother Mihaly Szilagyi and his own son Laszlo. He also raised a relief force and a fleet of 200 light warships. His army consisted mainly of battle-hardened mercenaries and a selection of mounted knights from the European nobility.

He was helped in these preparations by the Italian-born Franciscan friar Giovanni da Capistrano. This venerable figure had been used widely by earlier popes as a legate and had preached vehemently against heresies, notably those of the followers of Jan Hus in Bohemia; in 1454, at the age of 70, he was sent by Pope Nicholas V to preach a crusade against the Ottomans at the Diet of Frankfurt. The following year Giovanni was sent by the pope to Hungary and Transylvania to preach the crusade.

There he managed to raise an army and it marched, with Capistrano himself at the head of one division, to support Janos Hunyadi. Capistrano's army consisted of a motley crew, many of them yeomen, armed with scythes and slings, but they were driven and inspired by the preacher's words to believe that God would deliver victory in return or their faith.

SIEGE SET

Mehmed II brought an army of around 70,000 and began his siege of Belgrade on 4 July 1456. He also had 300 cannon and he used his 200 ships to prevent the arrival of reinforcements and supplies by way of the river Danube. The garrison was well armed and motivated but numbered only around 7,000.

The relief army under Janos Hunyadi and Giovanni da Capistrano arrived at Belgrade on 14 July. That same day they

▲ *Franciscan friar and crusade preacher Giovanni da Capistrano raised an army of ill-armed peasants to defend Belgrade. One in a long line of militant churchmen, he led the troops himself into the battle.*

managed to break through Mehmed's naval blockade of the city, sinking a total of seven large and 20 smaller Ottoman ships. They were able to bring troops and supplies into the city. Mehmed then launched a week-long bombardment by his artillery and on the evening of 21 July ordered an all-out attack.

NIGHT FIGHT

The Ottoman attack continued through the night, with desperate fighting on both sides. The Christians managed to hold the attackers at bay and a large contingent of Mehmed's elite Janissaries were put to the sword. In one celebrated incident, a Turkish soldier tried to raise the sultan's banner on a bastion of the fortress when a Hungarian soldier named Titus Dugovic attacked him and the two men fell together from the wall – Dugovic was later celebrated as a hero and his son was raised to the nobility.

On the following day the large body of peasant crusaders that Giovanni da Capistrano had raised took matters into their own hands, launching an impromptu attack on the besieging army. Giovanni da Capistrano tried to call them back, but finding it impossible to impose discipline rode into the conflict himself, reputedly declaring 'The Lord God, who brought about this beginning, will see to the end!' Janos Hunyadi also led a lightning attack, aiming to seize Turkish artillery positions. The main part of the Ottoman army fled.

OTTOMANS SHAMED

The sultan's bodyguard fought heroically, but were overwhelmed by Hunyadi's cavalry. Mehmed delivered a fatal blow to a Christian knight, but then was shot in the leg by a bowman and fell unconscious on the battlefield. Shortly afterwards darkness fell, and by night the Turks lifted the siege and retreated. They needed 140 wagons

▼ *Christians triumph at Belgrade. Pope Calixtus III ordered the church bells to be rung as a call to arms, but it became a celebration. The battle is commemorated to this day by the ringing of a noon bell.*

to bear their wounded away from the city they had expected to take with ease. One of them was Mehmed, still unconscious.

The sultan recovered in the city of Sarona. Contemporary reports tell that he was plunged into despair when he learned that the Ottoman army had been so completely humiliated and so many of his greatest warriors had lost their lives, and had to be prevented by his aides from taking his own life with poison. He then retreated to Constantinople.

▲ *In the 1480s Western powers tried to destabilize the Ottomans by supporting Cem, brother of Bayezid II, seen here meeting with the Knights Hospitaller.*

AFTERMATH OF BELGRADE

The Christian West rejoiced. The relief of the city against all odds evoked the spirit of the First Crusade, when unexpected victories convinced knights and churchmen that their battle was blessed by God. Janos Hunyadi and Giovanni da Capistrano believed that the time was a ripe for a crusading push to drive the Ottomans back, to take Constantinople and perhaps even go on to regain Jerusalem. However, neither man lived to further these ambitious plans. Both fell victim to bubonic plague: Janos Hunyadi died on 11 August, three weeks after the victory; Giovanni da Capistrano followed on 23 October.

Pope Pius II (ruled 1458–64) was inspired by the victory to call a new crusade on 26 September 1459 in Mantua. The following January he proclaimed the crusade for a period of three years. But despite the 'miracle of Belgrade' there was little enthusiasm among the powers of Western Europe and the expedition came to nothing after Pius died in August 1464.

CHAPTER FOURTEEN

THE WARRIOR MONKS

On 1 May 1187 a small Christian force of foot soldiers and 140 knights under Gerard of Ridefort, Master of the Knights Templar, encountered a Muslim Ayyubid army of 7,000 in the Battle of Cresson near Nazareth. When the Ayyubid horsemen feigned a retreat Gerard rashly ordered a charge, his knights were isolated from the foot soldiers and the two parts of the army cut down. The account in the crusade chronicle *Itinerarium Regis Ricardi* (The Voyage of King Richard) describes the extraordinary heroism and death of Templar knight Jakelin of Mailly, who reportedly fought to the last, surrounded by Muslim soldiers and entirely alone, until he sank to the ground and his soul rose at once to heaven, wearing a martyr's crown and covered in glory.

The Knights Templar and other monastic military brotherhoods – such as the Knights Hospitaller, the Teutonic Knights, the Knights of St Lazarus or the Knights of St Thomas Acon – were famed for their ferocity in battle and the powerful commitment to the crusading cause celebrated in the account of Jakelin of Mailly's death. In battle, they provided a highly disciplined, well-trained fighting force, although their leaders often were drawn by overconfidence or the desire for glory into rash and even disastrous acts. The monastic military brotherhood – consisting of men who like Jakelin of Mailly sought salvation through their exploits in religious warfare – was an institution unique to European chivalry of the Middle Ages, without counterpart in other cultures or eras.

▲ *At Cresson in 1187, Templar Jakelin of Mailly fought to the end.*

◀ *The defence of Rhodes by Fulkes of Villaret and the Knights Hospitaller, against Sultan Osman I in 1307. The Knights held the island until 1522.*

KNIGHTS OF ST JOHN

FOUNDATION AND EARLY YEARS OF 'THE HOSPITALLERS'

The monastic order of the Knights Hospitaller of St John of Jerusalem was established in the wake of the First Crusade with responsibility for the defence of the Holy Land. It had its origins in a hospital or hospice (guesthouse) founded in Jerusalem to care for Christian pilgrims, and was formally recognized in a papal bull of 15 February 1113 issued by Pope Paschal II (ruled 1099–1118).

Paschal's bull gave the order the name of the 'Hospitallers of St John of Jerusalem', but its members were often referred to as 'Knights of St John' or 'Knights Hospitaller', and over the centuries the order has also had many other names – including the 'Knights of Rhodes' and the 'Knights of Malta', reflecting the Hospitallers' residence on those islands. (The order's modern name, in use since the introduction of a new constitution in 1961, combines all these in the title of the 'Sovereign Military Hospitaller Order of St John of Jerusalem'.)

▼ *The order of the Knights of St John was founded after the First Crusade and the triumphant gain of Jerusalem.*

▲ *The brothers built the imposing Church of St John of the Hospitallers in Sidon in the 13th century. Today it is a mosque.*

ORIGINS OF THE HOSPITAL

The hospital in Jerusalem was established by merchants from Amalfi and Salerno in Italy in 1023, with permission from Caliph Ali az-Zahir of Egypt, who ruled Jerusalem at the time. Benedictine monks served the establishment, housing and caring for the pilgrims who came to see the holy sites in Jerusalem. The hospital became associated with St John because it stood close to the site of the monastery of St John the Baptist.

The Jerusalem hospital, in fact, had a long history prior to the 11th century. Its forerunner was established as early as AD600 by a certain Abbot Probus, on the authority of Pope Gregory the Great (ruled 590–604), and was intended from the start to house and care for Christian pilgrims to the Holy Land. Then, in c.800, Charlemagne, the King of the Franks, promoter of learning and 'August Emperor', who wanted to establish himself as ruler of all Christendom, expanded the hospital and installed a library there. But in 1010 the hospital was destroyed as part of the demolition of many Christian shrines – including the Church of the Holy Sepulchre – ordered by the sixth Fatimid caliph of Egypt, Al-Hakim bi-Amr Allah. The building raised by the Italian merchants in 1023 was the replacement for the earlier hospital.

▲ Raymond du Puy was the order's second Grand Master but the first to use the title. He was the man who established the Hospitallers on a firm footing. He fought in the siege of Ascalon in 1153.

FOUNDER OF THE ORDER

In the immediate aftermath of the capture of Jerusalem by the soldiers of the First Crusade in 1099, a Christian knight or merchant named Gerard Thom became guardian, or superior, of the hospital. Later known as 'Blessed Gerard', he founded the religious order of St John of Jerusalem, under the Benedictine rule, and then travelled to Europe to raise money and gather support – crucially winning the backing of Pope Paschal II. Paschal decreed that the order would not be subject to the authority of the King of Jerusalem, but was to be subservient only to the papacy; he granted it exemption from paying tithes to the Church and the right to own its religious buildings.

Gerard also established associated hostels for pilgrims at cities in Provence and Italy that were on the pilgrim route to the Holy Land. In the Holy Land, the warrior

▶ The Knights Hospitaller wore the eight-pointed Maltese cross. This example is on a coin issued by John of Brienne, King of Jerusalem in the years 1210–1225.

monks of the order branched out from housing and caring for pilgrims into providing them with an armed escort on dangerous parts of their journey, when they were liable to attack by bandits or enemy soldiers.

SECOND GRAND MASTER

Gerard was succeeded as Grand Master of the order in 1120 by French knight Raymond du Puy of Provence. Raymond was related to Adhemar of Le Puy, papal legate on the First Crusade, and was the son of the leading crusade knight Hughes du Puy, who fought as a general of Godfrey of Bouillon and was named Governor of Acre. Over 40 years as Grand Master (1120–60), Gerard established the order as a significant military force: he divided the brothers into military, medical and clerical divisions; he established the

order's first infirmary in Jerusalem, close to the Church of the Holy Sepulchre; and he moved the order from the Benedictine to the Augustinian rule.

Gerard also made the eight-pointed cross of Amalfi in Salerno the order's symbol, in honour of the hospital's founders from that town. This symbol later became known as the Maltese cross because of the residence of the Hospitallers on the island of Malta after 1530. The knights went into battle wearing black surcoats marked in white with the eight-pointed cross.

EQUESTRIAN ORDER OF THE HOLY SEPULCHRE OF JERUSALEM

The Equestrian Order of the Holy Sepulchre of Jerusalem is a chivalric order that, like the Order of the Knights of St John, traces its history back to the time of the First Crusade. At that time, Godfrey of Bouillon, the first ruler of the Kingdom of Jerusalem, gathered a body of knights to protect the canons in the Church of the Holy Sepulchre. They fought under the banner of a red cross on a white background. In 1113 Pope Paschal II gave the order official recognition, and in 1122 Pope Callixtus II granted it status as a lay religious order with the duty to defend the Church of the Holy Sepulchre and the city of Jerusalem against attack by Muslims.

▶ Godfrey, lord of Bouillon, first leader of the Kingdom of Jerusalem, is recognized as the founder of the Equestrian Order.

HOSPITALLERS SAVE RHODES

KNIGHTS OF ST JOHN DEFEAT MEHMET THE CONQUEROR

After the loss of Jerusalem in 1187 the Knights of St John removed to Acre and, following the fall of Acre in 1291, took up residence on the island of Cyprus, so maintaining a presence in the East. The Hospitallers did not stay long in Cyprus. Within 20 years they had transferred to the island of Rhodes, where they would remain for more than 200 years, in that time twice defeating seaborne armies – one in 1444 from Muslim Egypt and a second in 1480 from the Ottoman sultan Mehmet II 'the Conqueror'.

ESTABLISHMENT ON RHODES

On being driven from the Holy Land following the fall of Acre in 1291, the leading figures in the hierarchy of the Hospitallers saw that the sea would inevitably play an important part in the order's future. The admiral of the Hospitaller fleet, Fulkes of Villaret, joined the inner council of the order in 1299. In 1307 the knights captured Rhodes, in part to curb the operations of Muslim corsairs who used the island as a base of operations for raiding Christian shipping in the East, but also perhaps with an eye to establishing their own landholding.

The knights found it difficult to maintain their independence from court politics on Cyprus and elected to move permanently to Rhodes in 1310. By now Fulkes of Villaret was Grand Master. The order also took control of a number of small neighbouring islands, including Bodrum and Kastellorizo. Using these bases, the Hospitaller knights waged a determined sea war against Muslim corsairs from northern Africa who preyed on Christian shipping in the western Mediterranean. (These ruthless Muslim operators were also known as 'Barbary pirates' because the north African coast from which they emanated was called the Barbary coast.)

The Hospitallers also took part in the various minor crusades of the 14th cen-

▲ *The Ottoman fleet, commanded by Palaeologos Pasha, approaches Rhodes, at the top right of this picture. The island appears secure behind stout walls.*

tury, notably those of 1345 in which Smyrna was captured; 'King Peter's Crusade' of 1365, which degenerated into the sacking of Alexandria; and the Nicopolis Crusade of 1396.

A NEW ORGANIZATION

In this period, the order also became immeasurably richer: after the Knights Templar were disbanded in 1312, all their property was assigned to the Hospitallers by Pope Clement V (ruled 1305–14). The Hospitallers organized their new territory

well, dividing their landholdings into eight *langues*, or 'tongues' (Provence, Italy, Germany, France, England, Castile, Auvergne and Aragon), each with its own prior and with key positions of authority in the order distributed among the langues. In this way, the Knights Hospitaller avoided difficulties caused by national feelings at a time when such feelings were increasingly powerful in Europe.

On Rhodes the brothers of different langues lived in their own *auberges*, or hostels, within an enclosed area of the city known as the *collachium*. They fortified both the city and the island's main harbour and established a commercial area, as well as inviting Latin and Greek farmers from the mainland to settle.

ATTACK ON RHODES

In 1426 Cyprus was conquered by Muslim Egypt and Rhodes was more than ever isolated and vulnerable. In 1435 the warlike Egyptian sultan Baybars planned an invasion of Rhodes, and the Knights brought reinforcements in from Europe at full speed, but the threat came to nothing. In 1444 the Egyptians tried again, mounting an invasion of the island and a month-long siege of the town of Rhodes.

In 1480 Ottoman sultan Mehmet II 'the Conqueror' launched a major attack on Rhodes – ostensibly because Muslims on the islands had reported being persecuted, but really as part of military expansion towards southern Italy. A vast Ottoman fleet, reputedly carrying 70,000–100,000 men, appeared off Rhodes in May. It was commanded by Palaeologos Pasha.

On the island, the garrison, under the command of Grand Master Pierre d'Aubusson, had just received reinforcements of around 2,000 foot soldiers and 500 knights from France. D'Aubusson had been vigilant and had prepared well against possible attack, laying in substantial supplies and military equipment.

The Ottomans settled in to a siege. Coming under attack from the citadel, where the garrison was ensconced, the Ottomans launched an assault: they succeeded in building a bridge from the boats in the harbour to the citadel walls but as their men began to pour across it to attack, this makeshift structure collapsed and thousands were drowned in the ensuing panic. A second attack was more successful and some of the Ottoman troops succeeded in raising the sultan's standard on the walls.

HEAVENLY ARMY

Accounts differ as to what happened next. According to the version given by Flemish writer Guillaume Caoursin, the Ottomans were terrified by a vision of the Virgin Mary and a saintly army in the sky above the citadel. Caoursin reports that the Knights had raised banners showing Christ, the Virgin Mary and St John the Baptist on the walls of the citadel, but that when the Ottoman attack was at its height a golden cross appeared in the clear sky above these banners, together with a miraculous image of the Virgin Mary carrying a spear and a shield and next to her a man in simple clothing standing before a great host of warriors of light. The Ottomans were paralyzed with fear and the Hospitallers were able to cut them down and drive them back.

The Ottoman account, however, suggests that their soldiers were poised for victory when their commander issued the order that there was to be no looting since the wealth of the citadel, and the merchants in the town, belonged to the sultan. This apparently caused the Ottoman warriors to stop fighting and many were slain in their moment of wavering.

OTRANTO PUNISHED

In the wake of this defeat, the Ottoman fleet lifted the siege of Rhodes and sailed away on 28 July 1480. On the island, the merchants, farmers and knights of the Hospitaller garrison rejoiced at their delivery by a seeming miracle from a force of such size. The Ottomans, for their part, sailed on and wreaked a terrible vengeance for the frustration at Rhodes on the people of Otranto in Italy. Having overrun the port, they killed Archbishop Stefano Agricoli in the cathedral and slaughtered 800 citizens of the town who refused to convert to Islam.

▼ *The Ottoman forces preparing for battle outside the walls of Rhodes in 1480. Their attack failed, reputedly after an appearance by the Virgin Mary.*

SULEYMAN TAKES RHODES

BUT THE HOSPITALLERS HOLD MALTA

In 1522, the Hospitaller garrison on Rhodes was forced to surrender after a six-month siege by Ottoman sultan Suleyman I 'the Magnificent' and his army. The Hospitallers departed Rhodes to take up residence on Malta.

PREPARATIONS FOR THE SIEGE

Philippe of L'Isle-Adam was elected Grand Master of the order in 1521 and began at once to prepare for the defence of Rhodes. He sent out an appeal throughout Europe for reinforcements to defend this outpost of Christendom, but received no response save a small contingent from Venice and Crete. He laid in a year of provisions and organized the defence of the town's reconstructed walls and bastions with most particular care, assigning the protection of different areas to groups of knights.

▼ *The Hospitallers had a powerful fleet and were a force to be reckoned with at sea.*

The Ottoman fleet arrived on 26 June under the command of Mustafa Pasha; Sultan Suleyman sailed in around a month afterwards to take command. The Turks launched a concerted assault on a section of the town walls defended by knights of Aragon and England, using both artillery and the digging of mines. This went on for as much as a month, with little progress, but on 4 September the Ottoman attack opened a breach almost 40ft (12m) across beside the bastion of England. The Ottomans gained control of this area, but then a fearless Hospitaller assault led by English knight Nicholas Hussey managed to force the Turks back.

GENERAL ATTACK

On 24 September the Turks mounted a general assault on the town, with particular concentration of fire against the bastions of England, Italy, Provence and Spain. Twice in one day the bastion of Spain was captured by the Ottomans and then retaken by the Hospitallers. After hours of fierce fighting, with the garrison's powerful cannon killing vast numbers of Ottoman warriors, the attack was at last called off. Suleyman was enraged and ordered the execution of Mustafa Pasha because he had failed to take the city despite his vast numerical advantage; the sultan was persuaded to spare Mustafa, but he replaced him with Ahmed Pasha.

The Ottomans launched another powerful attack in late November, but it was driven back once more. However, the Knights and the townspeople of Rhodes were close to exhaustion and by mid-December were ready to negotiate terms of peace. A truce was called on 11–13 December, but when the townspeople asked for further reassurances regarding their safety, Suleyman ordered the artillery attacks to begin again. His troops took the bastion of Spain on 17 December – and from this point on there seemed no doubt the city would eventually be taken.

PEACE AT LAST

On 20 December Grand Master of L'Isle-Adam requested another truce and on 22 December a peace treaty was agreed under which the Knights who wished to depart would be allowed 12 days to leave the island in peace, with their weapons and religious relics, while the islanders would be permitted to leave for up to three years. Suleyman was very impressed with the fight put up by the Knights and the bearing of Grand Master of L'Isle-Adam. After the peace negotiations, the sultan is reported to have said of of L'Isle-Adam 'it gives me no pleasure to force this fearless old man from his home' and when he entered Rhodes he dismissed his imperial bodyguard, declaring that he had his safety guaranteed on the honour of the Grand Master of the Hospitallers, and that this was 'worth more than all the world's

armies'. A further tribute to the heroism and faith of the Hospitallers came from Holy Roman Emperor Charles V, who declared: 'Nothing in the world was ever so well lost as Rhodes.'

IN MALTA

After leaving Rhodes, the Knights Hospitaller took up residence in Sicily, but in 1530 moved on to Malta, which was given them as a fief, along with the nearby island of Gozo and the port of Tripoli in north Africa, by Holy Roman Emperor Charles V (r.1519–56). In return, they were required to send one falcon a year to the Viceroy of Sicily and to celebrate Mass for Charles on All Saints Day.

From their new base they launched regular attacks on Muslim shipping, and fought a running war against the Muslim corsairs who operated from north Africa across the Mediterranean. In 1551 the corsair Turgut Reis and the Ottoman admiral Sinan combined in an attack on Malta: they did not take the main island, but captured Gozo and, also during the same campaign, drove the Hospitaller garrison from Tripoli. In response the Knights greatly expanded and strengthened fortifications on Malta. In 1559, the Knights took part in an expedition organized by

▼ *Jean Parisot of Valette masterminded the defence of Malta. He was a veteran of the Hospitallers' campaigns in Rhodes.*

Philip II of Spain to drive Turgut Reis from Tripoli. It was a significant enterprise – involving more than 50 galleys and 14,000 men – but ended in a heavy defeat in the Battle of Djerba in May 1560.

THE ASSAULT ON MALTA

Nevertheless, the Hospitallers kept up their attacks on Muslim shipping, and in 1565 Suleyman determined to stop them once and for all. A vast Ottoman war-fleet landed a force of around 40,000–50,000 men on Malta in mid-May. Grand Master Jean Parisot of Valette had sent out a summons to members of the order around the world, but even so its defending garrison numbered no more than around 6,000. He further strengthened the fortifications on the three main forts of Malta – St Elmo, Fort St Michael and Fort St Angelo.

The Ottomans could not use the mining that had worked so well on Rhodes because the fortresses on Malta were built on solid rock. Instead they relied on their mighty artillery, training their guns on the fortress of St Elmo at the entrance to the Grand Harbour. The Ottomans launched three major attacks on St Elmo, on 3, 10 and 16 June, and each time were driven back by the determined defenders; the attackers suffered very heavy losses, and many of the elite Janissary troops were killed. But finally on 23 June, in another major attack, the entire defending garrison of that fort was killed – even the

▲ *In the defence of Malta the Hospitallers fought with heroic courage.*

wounded men who had fought heroically to the last, sitting on chairs on the ramparts. The fort was taken.

Next the Turks attacked the Senglea Peninsula to the south of Fort St Angelo. There was fierce fighting over several days in early August, but the Ottomans were driven back. Another attack on Fort St Michael and the town of Birgu on 7 August seemed to have brought the Turks close to victory when they made a breach in the walls, but they had to retreat to defend their camp against a daring attack by Hospitaller cavalry from Mdina.

THE OTTOMANS DEPART

Further attacks on Fort St Michael and on Mdina also failed and in early September the Ottomans abandoned the attack when a relief force arrived from Sicily. The holding of Malta against seemingly impossible odds was an extraordinary and famous victory that ranked alongside any of the Hospitallers' other feats.

The Knights Hospitaller continued to fight for Christendom at sea and in land wars in eastern Europe and on Crete. They were to remain on Malta until 1798, when they were finally driven out by French general Napoleon en route to Egypt, on the expedition that was to discover the Rosetta Stone.

KNIGHTS OF THE TEMPLE OF SOLOMON
FOUNDATION OF THE KNIGHTS TEMPLAR

The military brotherhood of the Knights Templar was founded in the aftermath of the First Crusade, initially for the care of Christian pilgrims travelling to Jerusalem. The order received the official blessing of the Church at the Council of Troyes in 1129 and this was confirmed and many privileges granted to the order by Pope Innocent II in 1139.

French knights Hugues of Payens and Godfrey of Saint-Omer, both veterans of the First Crusade, took on the responsibility of protecting pilgrims on the road between the port of Jaffa and the Holy City, and in c.1120 proposed the formation of a religious brotherhood to perform this task. King Baldwin II of Jerusalem gave them his backing and provided space for a headquarters in the former al-Aqsa mosque on Temple Mount. At the time, this building was believed to stand on the ruins of the biblical Temple of Solomon and the brotherhood took the name of the 'Poor Knights of Christ and the Temple of Solomon'. Initially there were nine knights in the brotherhood and they had very few resources; their emblem, which shows two

▼ *With the backing of Bernard of Clairvaux, the Templars received the ceremonial blessing of the Roman Catholic Church at the Council of Troyes in 1129.*

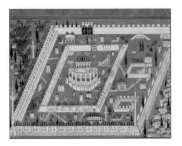

▲ *In crusader Jerusalem the al-Aqsa mosque was used as a palace. The Knights Templar were given space in one wing.*

knights mounted on a single horse, reflects their poverty-stricken beginnings. They took vows of poverty, chastity and obedience and agreed to share all their property.

BERNARD OF CLAIRVAUX

In 1126 Hugues of Payens, by now known as *Magister militum Templi* (Master of the Temple Soldiery) travelled to Europe to raise finances and seek Church support. He had a powerful ally in the Cistercian monk Bernard of Clairvaux, founder and first abbot of the Cistercian Abbey of Clairvaux in north-eastern France, who was also nephew to Andre of Montbard, one of the initial members of the brotherhood. Bernard wrote a pamphlet called *De Laude Novae Militiae* (In Praise of the New Soldiery), in which he set up the Templar knights as ideal exemplars of chivalry and contrasted their Christian poverty and religious devotion with the lack of these qualities in the secular knights of the day, men who expended their God-given energy in private quarrels driven by greed.

The pamphlet took up the imagery used by St Paul in his *Epistle to the Ephesians*, which urged readers to put on 'the whole armour of God' and 'the breastplate of righteousness', to use 'the shield of faith' and 'the helmet of salvation' and fight with 'the sword of the spirit'. Bernard

FOUNDER MEMBERS
Hugues of Payens was initially a vassal of (and cousin to) Count Hugues of Champagne in France and fought alongside his suzerain on the First Crusade, probably in the army of Godfrey of Bouillon. In addition to Godfrey of Saint-Omer, there were seven other founding members of the order: Payen of Montdidier; Archambaud of St Agnan; Andre of Montbard (Bernard of Clairvaux's uncle); Geoffrey Bisot; two knights known as Gondamer and Rossal; and an unknown knight – who may perhaps have been Count Hugues of Champagne himself. Legend tells that the image on the Templar seal of two knights on a single horse (seen below) in fact represents the actual practice of Hugues of Payens and Godfrey of Saint-Omer, who shared a horse because in the early days of the order they could not afford one each.

wrote of the new 'fearless knight, secure in every direction, who dons the breastplate of faith to protect his soul just as he dons an iron breastplate on his body'; he added that with this 'double armour' knights need fear nothing, and urged them to go forward in safety, with undaunted spirits, to fight back those who oppose the Cross of Christ.

Hugues of Payens, almost certainly with Bernard's help, drew up a rule for the new order, which was to be committed to protecting pilgrims and the holy places in Jerusalem, and this was approved at the Council of Troyes in January 1129. Five Templars, led by Hugues of Payens, attended the council and received the rule from Bernard. The rule was based on that of the Cistercians.

On his trip of 1128–29, Hugues of Payens also visited England and Scotland, where he established the first Templar house in London and also one close to Edinburgh on land granted to the order by King David I at Balantrodoch (now known as Temple, in Midlothian).

ROBERT OF CRAON

Hugues of Payens died in 1136 and was succeeded as Grand Master by Robert of Craon. Robert won papal approval for the order in 1139. In his bull *Omne Datum Optimum*, Pope Innocent II confirmed the order's rule and granted the Templars exemption from local laws and taxation and also from all secular and religious authority save that of the papacy. He wrote: 'since your religious order and your

▼ *The Templars meet, with great ceremony, in Paris in April 1147, shortly after they were granted privileges by the Church.*

ancient institution is praised throughout the whole world ... you should be regarded especially as part of God's knighthood.' By this date, the order was well established, having already received several substantial gifts of land and finance from the nobility of Europe, many as a result of Bernard of Clairvaux's tract in praise of the order.

The Templars gained further significant privileges in the papal bulls *Milites Templi* of 1144 (issued by Pope Celestine II, who ruled 1143–44) and *Militia Dei* of 1145 (issued by Pope Eugenius III, who ruled 1145–53), which permitted them to build

▲ *Burgundian nobleman Jacques of Molay is inaugrated into the Knights Templar. He became Grand Master in 1292, and was also the last Grand Master, for the order was accused of heresy and dissolved in 1312 under his leadership.*

their own places of worship, to bury their dead in the grounds of these establishments and to gather taxes on Templar property once each year. In 1147 Eugenius III granted the knights to right to wear a red splayed cross (one with spreading ends) on their white surplice. The sacred design was sewn above the heart.

ORGANIZATION

The head of the order was the Grand Master. Major decisions were taken by the Grand Chapter, a council of leading officers. Only the Grand Chapter could agree treaties or declare war. Its officers included the Marshal, in charge of military affairs, and the Seneschal, in control of administration, plus eight provincial masters in Aragon, Apulia, England, France, Poitiers, Hungary, Portugal and Scotland.

KNIGHTS TEMPLAR IN THE FIELD

BRAVE BUT OFTEN RECKLESS

The Knights Templar were famed for their bravery and martial prowess – as exemplified by the extraordinary heroism of Jakelin de Mailly, who fought until he was the last knight standing at the Battle of Cresson (1187). However, as a self-contained unit within crusader armies they often fought for the glory of the order above all other considerations. Within the order discipline was extremely strict – and this made the Templars a formidable fighting unit; but in a campaigning army they often undermined overall discipline by acting on their own initiative, seeking their own glory at the expense of strategy.

AT ASCALON

One celebrated example occurred during King Baldwin III of Jerusalem's siege of Ascalon (modern Ashkelon in Israel) in 1153. Baldwin brought a vast army, including the Templars and Hospitallers

▼ *Jakelin of Mailly, who reputedly fought on single-handedly when overwhelmed by Ayyubid troops at Cresson (1187), was the paragon of Templar bravery in battle.*

and all the great barons of the Kingdom of Jerusalem, as well as a contingent of pilgrims and Patriarch Fulcher of Jerusalem carrying a piece of the True Cross; but the city was well garrisoned and supplied with food to endure a long siege. Thus, it was particularly galling that when chance (or some might say the hand of God) gave the crusaders an opportunity, the self-interest of the Templars worked directly against the crusader army's long-term interests.

The Egyptian garrison attempted to burn down one of the crusaders' siege towers but the wind blew the flames back on the city defences and started a conflagration that made a section of the wall collapse. This part happened to be the one assigned to the Templars to attack. The Templars' Grand Master, Bernard of Tremblay, led an assault with 40 of his elite knights but did not tell King Baldwin. He even mounted a guard to prevent other crusaders joining the assault. Some accounts suggest that this was because the Templars wanted to have the glory all for themselves; according to chronicler William of Tyre, Bernard wanted to have

the spoils of the city to enrich the order's coffers. In the event, the 40 knights were overwhelmed by the garrison, the breach was repaired and the crusader army lost its advantage. The heads of Bernard and the Templar knights were displayed on the city walls.

AT AL-MANSOURAH

Another often cited example of Templar rashness in conflict was at the Battle of al-Mansourah during the Seventh Crusade when, following success in a surprise attack on the enemy camp, the Templars and members of other brotherhoods swept into the town of al-Mansourah against the orders of crusade leader King Louis IX of France. Their attack was a failure and jeopardized the entire campaign. All but five Templar knights were killed.

AT HATTIN

The Templar leadership also played a significant – and disastrous – role in the events leading up to the cataclysmic crusader defeat at the Battle of the Horns of Hattin in July 1187. Following Saladin's attack on 2 July on the Castle of Tiberias, King Guy of Jerusalem encamped with a vast army at Sephoria, around 18 miles (29km) away from the castle; initially Guy and his military council were minded to attack Saladin, but Sephoria was a strong defensive position and Count Raymond of Tripoli, who was master of Tiberias and knew the land, urged caution. Raymond insisted that even if he were to lose his castle, and his wife who was within it, he would prefer this outcome to putting the entire Kingdom of Jerusalem at risk by launching an ill-timed and ill-advised assault in difficult terrain.

The council accepted his advice, but that night Templar Grand Master Gerard of Ridefort managed to persuade King Guy to launch an assault on Saladin's army – by convincing him that Raymond was a traitor who had agreed a secret deal with Saladin. The army made a reckless advance, was surrounded by Saladin's troops, and suffered a devastating defeat. The relic of the True Cross was captured and the military strength of the Kingdom of Jerusalem was annihilated.

THE MIGHT OF THE CROSS

At the Horns of Hattin – as at the Battle of Cresson shortly beforehand – Gerard placed his confidence in the might of the cross and showed himself willing to risk all in order to win glory. The Templars and other warrior brotherhoods took pride in waging war by the sword against the armies of Islam and had no time for the methods of negotiation and diplomacy that were increasingly favoured by the lords of the Kingdom of Jerusalem.

In 1148 at the Council of Acre, Templar Grand Master Robert of Craon was one of the voices urging an attack on Damascus while local lords argued rather for building an alliance with Mu'in ad-Din Unur, emir of Damascus, against the Zengid lords of Syria, notably the formidable Nur ed-Din of Aleppo: the resulting siege of

▼ *In 1299 Templar Grand Master, Jacques of Molay, fought the Mamluks in Armenia.*

▲ *The Templar chapel at Cressac, south of Angouleme, France, is decorated with scenes of the Templars fighting in Syria.*

Damascus was a disaster and brought the Second Crusade to a miserable end. In 1172, similarly, the Templars refused to back an alliance between King Amalric of Jerusalem and the Muslim Assassin sect against Nur ed-Din: they were annoyed that the proposed alliance would damage their income, for Templar taxes on Assassin villages were to be waived, and a body of Templar knights murdered a group of Assassins shouting 'No diplomacy with the infidel!' Their action effectively scuppered the deal. According to one chronicler, King Amalric was so angry that he declared his intention to ask the pope to dissolve the Templar order.

In the later crusades in Egypt, the Templars were likewise among those who refused to enter negotiations for the return of Jerusalem on the grounds that the Holy City must be won by the sword and the Christian knights must not negotiate with those of Islam. On the Fifth Crusade the Templars backed the papal legate Pelagius against King John of Jerusalem and the barons of his kingdom when Pelagius turned down the offer of Sultan al-Kamil in Egypt to give possession of Jerusalem and the entire Kingdom of Jerusalem as it

had been before the Battle of the Horns of Hattin if they would return Damietta and leave Egypt.

BROTHERS AT WAR

Such was the rivalry between Templars and Hospitallers over glory and resources that they became effectively enemies on sight. In the 13th century a Templar would draw his sword when he encountered a Hospitaller in the streets; in 1242, the two orders were actually drawn into a sword battle in the streets of Acre. In this period the Templars and Hospitallers secretly worked against one another in their dealings with the enemy.

BRAVERY AT ACRE

In 1291 in the siege of Acre, the last great military engagement of the Kingdom of Jerusalem, the Templars were defending the northern part of the city walls and showed all the bravery and indomitable fighting spirit of old. The Grand Master, William of Beaujeu, gave his life in the struggle at the walls and even after the city fell on 18 May the Templars carried on the fight for a full ten days from their headquarters within the city. By the time they were finally overrun by the invading army, attacks had reduced the Templar palace in Acre to a ruin, and it collapsed, killing defenders and attackers alike.

TEMPLAR BUILDERS

CASTLES AND CHURCHES

The Templars were involved in building from the first years of the brotherhood. When King Baldwin II of Jerusalem gave the founding Templars the Temple Mount as their headquarters in c.1120 he allowed them to develop the area as they pleased. In 1139 a key privilege granted to the order was the freedom to build their own churches and graveyards. In the early-to-mid 12th century they began to build castles to help in the protection of pilgrims and Christian sacred sites in Outremer.

TEMPLAR CASTLES

On the road to Jerusalem from Jaffa, the Templars manned the Castle of Castrum Arnaldi, first erected by the Patriarch and citizens of Jerusalem in c.1130 but subsequently given to the knights. Protecting the southern route to Jerusalem they had the Castle of Le Toron des Chevaliers, or Latrûn: built by Count Rodrigo Gonzalez of Toledo in Spain in 1137–41, during an armed pilgrimage to the Holy Land, and then given to the Templars. Midway between Jerusalem and Jericho, the Templars built a castle at Cisterna Rubea, complemented by a tower close to Jericho.

▼ *The Keep of the imposing Templar castle of Chastel Blanc at Safita (north-western Syria) has walls 9 feet (3 metres) thick.*

The Templars were responsible for protecting the mountains to the north of Antioch, the area known as the Amanus March, and they built or garrisoned a number of impressive castles in the region. These included the Castle of Gaston (now known as Baghras), which the Templars manned from c.1154. They lost it to Saladin on 26 September 1188 and he dismantled the fortress, but the Templars regained the repaired castle in 1216. Shortly afterwards, however, they burned it when they had to retreat from the army of Egyptian sultan Baybars.

In Galilee the Templars themselves built the Castle of La Fève before 1172 and perhaps a good deal earlier. When this fortress was captured by Saladin in 1187, it was praised by an Islamic chronicler as 'the finest castle and most strongly fortified, the best supplied with men and munitions … for the Templars this was a powerful castle, a place of refuge and a pillar of strength'. He added that it had a fine pasture and a fountain, and was regularly used by the Templars as a meeting place and a pasture for their horses. We know that the Castle of La Fève was used as a base for armies on campaign. From La Fève, Templar knights under the command of Gerard of Ridefort rode to defeat at the Battle of Cresson.

▲ *The impressive five-towered Monzon Castle, on a hilltop in Aragon (in northern Spain), was given to the Templars in 1143.*

The Templars also manned the fortress of Gaza, originally built by King Baldwin III of Jerusalem, who gave it to the knights in 1149 as a base for raids against the Muslim garrison in Ascalon and to protect the Kingdom of Jerusalem's southern frontier against attacks from Muslim Egypt. At a crossing of the upper River Jordan, the Templars began building the formidable

▼ *The Templars built fortifications in Europe as well as in the Holy Land. Their vast castle at Ponferrada in the kingdom of Léon was constructed in c.1290.*

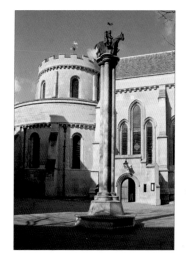

▲ *Building began on the Temple Church in London in 1166, and finished in February 1185. A statue outside shows the Templar symbol, two knights riding on one horse.*

▲ *The imposing Convent of Christ in Tomar, Portugal, was built by Gualdim Pais, provincial master of the order, in 1160. The Templars were fighting against the Moors.*

Castle of Le Chastellet or Jacob's Ford. The position of the castle was a potential threat to Saladin because it guarded the only crossing of the Jordan and the way necessarily taken from Saladin's territory to the Kingdom of Jerusalem; the sultan offered King Baldwin IV a bribe of 100,000 dinars to tear the castle down and when he was refused he prepared to attack. The castle was still unfinished when the attack came in August 1169 and Saladin's sappers were able to bring the incomplete outer wall down. His men poured through the tun-

nel they had excavated and killed 800 of the garrison. Another 700 Templars were executed by Saladin. He dismantled the remains of the castle before he left.

TEMPLAR CHURCHES

The Templars understood that the former al-Aqsa mosque, which they had made their Jerusalem headquarters, was built on the remains of the Temple of Solomon, and they called it the *Templum Solomonis* (Temple of Solomon) or *Templum Domini* (Temple of the Lord). The temple itself, or

perhaps the Church of the Holy Sepulchre in Jerusalem, was the inspiration for a number of Templar churches with round naves in Europe.

These included the Church of the Holy Sepulchre, or 'Round Church', in Cambridge, England, built in 1130, and the Templars' own London headquarters, Temple Church in central London, both of which are still standing. Originally Temple Church was lavishly decorated within; it was the order's second London base, built when the brotherhood moved from a smaller headquarters in High Holborn, also in central London, and it had a very grand consecration service performed by no less a figure than Patriarch Heraclius of Jerusalem on 10 February 1185, probably in the presence of King Henry II.

The Templars did not build only round churches – the chapel at their castle of Chastel Pelerin (built *c.*1218), now in Israel, had 12 sides and that at Safad Castle (built 1240–60) also had many sides; nor were the Templars the only creators of round churches – the Knights Hospitaller also built chapels and churches in this form. The majority of Templar churches, moreover, are rectangular and undecorated, in line with Bernard of Clairvaux's call for simple architecture.

TEMPLAR BANKERS

The Templars pioneered many methods of banking still in use today. Because the Templars received lavish gifts and had privileges exempting them from taxation, they grew immensely rich and became established as money lenders, providing funds for many monarchs and the Church to finance cathedral building. They used their network of monastic houses, or preceptories, to

facilitate the safe transfer of funds for merchants: funds could be paid in at one Templar preceptory, and the credit note issued could be cashed at another preceptory halfway around the world. Money lending or usury was forbidden for Christians, so Templars did not call the fees they charged 'interest' – instead they compared the activity to being a landlord and called the charge 'rent'.

DOWNFALL OF THE TEMPLARS

ACCUSED OF HERESY AND DISBANDED

In the early 14th century the Templars came under a fierce and sustained attack on charges of heresy, pressed particularly by King Philip IV of France (r.1285–1314). The order was dissolved by papal bull *Vox in excelso* of 1312, issued by Pope Clement V (ruled 1305–14).

After the fall of Acre in 1291 the military monastic orders faced an uncertain and difficult future: with no possessions to defend in the Holy Land, their purpose was unclear; the Teutonic Knights and the Hospitallers established monastic states, in Prussia and Rhodes respectively, but the Templars did not. The Templars also faced criticism for the lavish lifestyle of some members, funded by wealth generated from banking and property; they were also subject to attack because many people were in debt to them.

▲ *Arrested at dawn. Grand Master Jacques of Molay and thousands of French Templars are taken into royal custody.*

MERGER PROPOSAL

One popular solution was the merger of the Templars and the Hospitallers. This proposal was made by, among others, Norman lawyer and pamphleteer Pierre Dubois and by Majorcan novelist, poet and author on chivalry Ramon Llull. King Philip IV of France was strongly in favour, seeing an opportunity to escape his very substantial debts to the Templars, and he proposed that the kings of France should become hereditary masters of a combined order; under this plan, Philip was to lead the knights of the combined order on a new crusade to recover the Holy Land.

In 1305 Bertrand of Goth, Archbishop of Bordeaux, was elected Pope Clement V. He was strongly under the influence of King Philip IV of France, and he established the papal curia not in Rome but in France, first at Poitiers and then, from 1309, at Avignon. In 1306 Clement summoned the two Grand Masters, Jacques of Molay of the Templars and Fulk of Villaret of the Hospitallers, to Poitiers to consider the merger; Jacques arrived in 1307 but Fulk was delayed. Clement raised the

matter with the Templar Master and also discussed accusations of heresy against the Templars that had been made by former Templar knights Esquin of Floyan, Bernard Pelet and Gérard of Byzol. It would appear that Clement was convinced that the charges were false, but he asked Philip IV to investigate.

ON TRIAL

Philip IV saw an opportunity to bring about the downfall of the Templars, cancel his vast debts, and engineer the merger of the monastic orders that he favoured. Philip issued secret orders and in dawn raids on Friday 13 October 1307, 5,000 Templars in France, including Jacques of

▼ *After executing Jacques of Molay in early 1314, Philip ruled for only a few months. He met an untimely death, mauled by a boar while out hunting in November 1314.*

TEMPLARS IN AMERICA

Some rather fanciful accounts suggest that Knights Templar were in fact the first Europeans to sail to the New World of North America (after the Vikings in c.1000). The theory goes that the Templars sailed from Scotland (or perhaps from their port of La Rochelle in western France) after the downfall of the order and settled in Nova Scotia (Latin for 'New Scotland') in 1398, and then moved on to New England in 1399 – almost a century before the voyages of Christopher Columbus, the Genoan explorer usually credited with discovering America. There are gravestones in Nova Scotia that bear crusader crosses, and a hand-cut gravestone in Westford, Massachusetts, is marked with Templar imagery. The Templar Rossyln Chapel in Scotland is reportedly decorated with carvings in stone of American plants such as the *aloe vera*; the chapel was completed in 1486, six years before Columbus's first voyage in 1492.

Molay, were arrested on charges of heresy, blasphemy and sodomy. The accusations centred on the Templars' secret initiation ceremony: it was alleged that an initiate was required to spit on the cross, to deny Christ three times and to kiss the officer who admitted him. There were also claims that initiates worshipped a pagan idol and that knights were not permitted to refuse to have sexual relations with one another. Most Templars admitted to these or similar charges under severe torture.

On 22 November Clement called on all Christian rulers to arrest Templars and to take possession of their assets. He also commanded the French Templars to be released from imprisonment and be given into the care of papal commissioners. In hearings before a papal committee beginning on 24 December 1307 Jacques of Molay and other senior Templars retracted their confessions on the grounds that they had been extracted under torture.

Trials began in 1309 and ran on and off for five years. Before the commission in November 1309 Jacques of Molay declared that he wanted to mount a defence of the order, but had doubts that he could – since he was illiterate and the order did not contain a single lawyer; he

▼ *Philip IV used his influence over Pope Clement V to bring about the downfall of the Templars, to whom he was in debt.*

▲ *The condemned Templars are executed in Paris on 18 March 1314. In 2001 a document uncovered at the Vatican revealed that Pope Clement had secretly absolved Jacques and other Templars in 1308.*

put his faith in the pope and seems to have believed, perhaps with the confidence of the innocent, that he and his men would be cleared in the end. Under questioning he declared that the Templars had always been generous in charitable donations, that Templar liturgy was more beautiful than that in any other churches, and that in no other order had the knights shed their blood more readily in defence of the cross of Christ.

One accusation against the Templars that was most widely confessed was that they spat on the cross and denied Christ during their initiation ceremonies. Some historians suggest that this claim may have been true, and was perhaps required as a demonstration of the initiate's total loyalty to the order – overriding all other claims, even that of religious faith.

At the Council of Vienne in 1312 Pope Clement issued the bull *Vox in excelso*, dissolving the Templars, and a second bull, *Ad Providam*, transferring most of the Templars' assets to the Knights Hospitaller. However, a paper found in Vatican archives in 2001 suggests that privately Clement absolved Jacques of Molay, the Templar order and all its knights of guilt.

JACQUES OF MOLAY EXECUTED

On 18 March 1314 at a trial hearing in Paris, Jacques of Molay and leading templar Geoffrey of Charney, Preceptor of Normandy, publicly withdrew their confessions once more and were sentenced to death as relapsed heretics by burning at the stake in central Paris. On his own insistence, Molay was tied facing the cathedral of Notre Dame, and with his hands raised in prayer; legend recounts that at his death he declared that Pope Clement and King Philip would soon meet him before the throne of God. Both men were indeed dead by the end of the year.

Of the remaining Templars some joined the Knights Hospitaller; others probably quietly returned to the secular world. Still others fled beyond the reach of papal power – to Switzerland or to Scotland, which had been excommunicated; some, perhaps, sailed to America (*see* box). In Portugal, the Templars carried on as the Knights of Christ, and in Spain as knights of the Order of Montesa.

▼ *Rosslyn Chapel in Midlothian, Scotland, reputedly has Templar connections and secret coded decorations, but many scholars dispute the link to the Templars.*

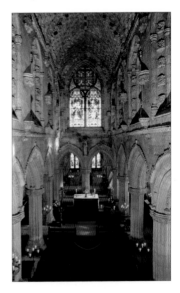

TEUTONIC KNIGHTS
GERMANIC BROTHERHOOD

The German order of the Teutonic Knights was established in Acre in the late 12th century and granted approval by Pope Celestine III (ruled 1191–98) in 1192. In the 13th century the order established itself in Prussia, initially as part of a crusade against pagans in the region and subsequently against the non-Christian people of central and northern Europe. The order suffered a crushing defeat at the hands of a Polish–Lithuanian force at the Battle of Tannenberg in 1410 and became gradually secularized.

ORIGINS AND FOUNDATION

The earliest origins of the order of the Teutonic Knights lie in a hospital for German pilgrims run in Jerusalem from c.1140 by German knights under the overall control of the Knights Hospitaller. It was known as the *Domus Teutonicorum* (House of the Germans). In 1189–90 during the siege of Acre on the Third Crusade, German merchants from Lübeck and Bremen set up a sister German hospital in the crusader camp. After the

▼ *The Teutonic Knights' Montfort Castle was originally so called from the French for 'strong mountain'. The Knights' name for it, Starkenberg, means the same in German.*

▲ *Holy Roman Emperor and sometime King of Jerusalem, Frederick II, seen here receiving a delegation of Arabs in 1230, was a major patron of the Teutonic Knights. His chancellor, Petrus of Vinea, pictured on the left, was a Master of the Order.*

capture of Acre in 1191 the hospital was established as a permanent institution in Acre, known as the Hospital of St Mary of the German House in Jerusalem. Initially a simple monastic brotherhood, as recognized by Pope Celestine III in 1192, it became a military order with the approval of King Amalric II of Jerusalem in 1198.

The Teutonic Order received substantial grants of land from popes Celestine III and Innocent III in the Latin Kingdom of Jerusalem and in Germany, Italy and elsewhere. It was Innocent III who, in 1205, granted the knights the use of their white habits, or surplices, decorated with a black cross. The order based its organization on that of the Knights Templar and its head was known as the Grand Master.

MONTFORT

The order's original base was in Acre, but in 1220 the brotherhood bought the Castle of Montfort, or Starkenberg, to the north-east of the city and on the route between the Mediterranean coast and Jerusalem. From 1229 this was the principal seat of the Teutonic Grand Masters, as well as the home of the order's treasury and archive. In 1266 the Knights repelled an attack by Mamluk sultan Baybars, but when he returned in 1271 the garrison surrendered at the end of a seven-day siege. Baybars for once honoured his promise made during negotiations to allow the knights to leave Montfort with their belongings. They returned to Acre.

IN TRANSYLVANIA

Hermann von Salza, Grand Master of the Teutonic Order in 1210–39, was a close friend of Holy Roman Emperor Frederick II. Under von Salza's leadership, the brotherhood began to transfer its operations from the Holy Land to central Europe.

▲ *The Teutonic Knights' days of glory ended when, under Grand Master Ulrich von Jungingen, they were roundly defeated at the First Battle of Tannenberg in July 1410.*

In 1211 the Teutonic Knights entered the service of King Andrew II of Hungary (r.1205–35) and settled on land he gave them in Burzenland, Transylvania; his aim was to establish a buffer against the border incursions of the nomadic Turkish Cuman people. However, when the Teutonic Knights attempted to establish an independent principality on the territory by appealing to Pope Honorius III (ruled 1216–27) to be placed under his authority rather than that of the Hungarian crown, King Andrew expelled them from the country.

IN PRUSSIA

In 1226 the Teutonic Knights answered a call from Duke Konrad I of Masovia in Poland to fight on his borders against the pagan Prussians who had been provoked to violent uprising by the first Prussian Crusade of 1221. Over 50 years between 1233 and 1283 the knights fought with great ferocity for the conversion of the Prussians. From 1245 the order even had the power to grant crusade indulgences in this struggle without prior papal approval.

The Teutonic Knights governed Prussia as a sovereign 'monastic state' under charters from the Holy Roman Emperor and the papacy. They founded several fortress settlements including Konigsberg (now in the Russian enclave of Kaliningrad Oblast, situated between Poland and Lithuania), Elbing (modern Elblag in northern Poland), Allenstein (modern Olsztyn in north-east Poland) and Memel (modern Klaipeda in Lithuania). But they faced sustained and brutal opposition from pagan Prussians, who (according to the order's chronicles) would 'roast' captured knights in their armour over fires 'like chestnuts'. The order also tried to expand eastwards to convert Russia to Roman Catholicism, but suffered a devastating defeat at the hands of Alexander Nevsky in the Battle of Lake Peipus, 1242.

MARIENBURG

The knights maintained their presence in the Holy Land at Acre but following the fall of that port in 1291 and the final collapse of Outremer, they briefly made their main base in Venice, Italy, from where they planned ways to retake the Holy Land. In 1309, however, they built a vast castle in Prussia named Marienburg (Mary's Castle)

▼ *Teutonic Knights encounter pagan east German farmers during their attempts to impose Christianity in the region.*

in honour of the Virgin Mary. This place (now Malbork in Poland) was thereafter their main base. In the 14th century they waged a long war against pagans in the Baltic, in the area known as Livonia (now Lithuania, Latvia and Estonia).

The knights were also engaged in wars against Poland, because their expansion cut the country off from its access to the Baltic Sea, and with Lithuania even after that country's conversion to Christianity in 1387. In 1410 Poland and Lithuania joined forces and defeated the Teutonic Knights at the Battle of Tannenberg. The brotherhood ceded territory to Poland, and further landholdings in 1466 following defeat by the Poles and the knights' own Prussian vassals in the Thirteen Years War (1454–66). The order survived in East Prussia, but the Grand Master held the land as a vassal of the Polish king.

DECLINE AND REBIRTH

In 1525 Grand Master Albert of Brandenberg dissolved the order and founded a secular duchy in Prussia under his own rule. Gradually over the ensuing 400 years, the order's territories were ceded to secular authorities. In 1809 the French emperor Napoleon dissolved the order entirely and seized its remaining holdings. However, the Teutonic Knights enjoyed a rebirth in Vienna in 1834 as an ecclesiastical body engaged in charitable work.

WARRIORS OF THE RECONQUISTA

SPANISH AND PORTUGUESE ORDERS OF KNIGHTHOOD

A number of military brotherhoods were formed in Spain and Portugal as part of the *Reconquista* (Reconquest), the 770-year war waged between 722 and 1492 to win back those countries from Muslim control.

The first Spanish military brotherhoods were formed shortly after the establishment of the Knights Hospitaller and the Knights Templar in 1110–20. In the 1130s a number of Templar foundations were made in Spain, and on his death in 1134 King Alfonso I *El Batallador* (the Warrior) of Aragon and Navarre left the entire kingdom of Aragon to be shared between the Templars and Hospitallers.

The bequest was annulled, and in the event the Templars and Hospitallers took on the care and defence of a number of castles both in Aragon and elsewhere in Spain; however, they were generally not keen to be drawn into the war against Muslims in Spain because their main interest was to use European landholdings to raise money and men to fight for the cross in the Holy Land.

THE ORDER OF CALATRAVA

In 1157 the Templars told King Alfonso VII of León and Castile that for this reason they were abandoning the Castle of Calatrava in southern Castile. At this point

Raymond, Abbot of the Cistercian monastery of Fitero, offered to man and defend the castle with Cistercian lay brothers; he had been persuaded to do so by a former knight turned monk named Diego Valasquez. The monks held Calatrava until Raymond's death in 1163, after which some withdrew to the monastery of Cirvelos. The remainder stayed on, elected Don Garcia as their first Grand Master and established the Order of Calatrava.

The order was recognized as a militia by Pope Alexander III (ruled 1159–81) on 26 September 1164. The brothers' rule,

▼ *The Knights of Calatrava had monastic beginnings, but repeatedly proved their worth in battle against the Moors.*

▲ *King Alfonso IX of the Spanish kingdom of León conquered Alcantara on the River Tagus from the Moors and gave it into the protection of the Knights of Calatrava. The town's imposing Convent of St Benedict was built later, in the 16th century.*

based on that of Cistercian lay brothers, was approved in 1187 by Pope Gregory VIII (pope for less than two months in 1187). It included the requirement that the brothers keep silent when eating and sleeping and sleep in their armour. Unlike the Templars and Hospitallers, the order was subject to secular authority and its Grand Master took an oath of loyalty to the King of Castile.

The Knights of Calatrava had mixed fortunes on the field of battle. Alongside the Castilian army they suffered a heavy defeat at the hands of the Moors at the Battle of Alarcos in 1195 and as a result lost the Castle of Calatrava; the survivors settled in the Cistercian monastery of Cirvelos, and then built a new stronghold at Salvatierra in 1198. They also lost this castle to the Moors in 1209, but in 1212 recaptured Calatrava and then fought in the great Christian victory of that year at the Battle of Las Navas de Tolosa. After which they built a new headquarters, Calatrava La Nueva just 8 miles (12km) from their original home.

▲ *A Spanish nobleman wears the cross of Alcantara on his court clothes. By the 16th century, when this portrait was painted, the knights no longer lived as monks.*

THE ORDER OF ALCANTARA

The knights of the Order of Alcantara, which grew from a brotherhood established in the 12th century in the Kingdom of Leon, came under the protection of the Order of Calatrava in c.1218. Its knights were originally called the Knights of St Julian of Pereiro: according to tradition, St Julian was a hermit who inspired a group of knights to build and garrison a castle on the River Tagus. They were known to have existed in 1176 and were recognized by Pope Celestine III in 1197; in 1218 they took over the defence of the Castle of Alcantara from the Order of Calatrava. Like the Calatrava brothers, the Alcantara knights followed the Cistercian rule.

THE ORDER OF AVIZ

The Portuguese knights of the Order of Aviz were also under the protection of the knights of Calatrava. Originally known as the Brothers of Santa Maria of Evora, the Order of Aviz had possession of the town of Evora, taken from the Moors in 1211; they subsequently took possession of the Castle of Aviz and named themselves after it, the Knights of St Benedict of Aviz. They

followed the Benedictine, then the Cistercian rule. The knights of Calatrava passed control of a number of their castles in Portugal to the Order of Aviz.

THE ORDER OF SANTIAGO

Established in c.1170, the Order of Santiago had its origins in a brotherhood of knights founded to protect pilgrims travelling to the shrine of Saint James (Santiago) at Compostela. Also known as the Order of Saint James of Compostela, it had its headquarters at Uclés in Castile. It followed the rule of the canons of Saint Augustine. The order was unusual in that, unlike other military orders, from the start the knights of Santiago had the right to marry. In the mid-13th century the knights of Santiago won a great reputation fighting in the campaigns of King Ferdinand III of Castile (reigned 1217–52) against the Moors in southern Spain and they played a notable part in the siege and capture of Seville in 1247–48.

▼ *Knights of the Order of St James of Compostela were granted their first monastic rule in 1171 by Cardinal Jacinto, who later became Pope Celestine III.*

OTHER SPANISH ORDERS

The Order of the Knights of Our Lady of Mountjoie was established by Spanish knight Count Rodrigo and received official approval from Pope Alexander III (ruled 1159–81) in 1180. It was named after the hill of Mountjoie, the 'hill of joy' from which the men of the First Crusade first saw Jerusalem. The brothers – all Spaniards – had their headquarters on Mountjoie and also had landholdings in Castile and Aragon and had responsibility for protecting pilgrims there. Their emblem was a red-and-white cross.

The brotherhood had difficulty with recruitment and was renamed the Order of Trufac in 1187. Several of its knights were killed at the disastrous Battle of Hattin in 1187 and the remainder left the Holy Land and settled in Aragon. In 1221 King Ferdinand of Aragon merged it with the Order of Calatrava.

Other Spanish brotherhoods included the Order of Montegaudio, founded in Aragon in c.1173; that of Saint George of Alfama, established in c.1200; and that of Saint Mary of Spain, created in c.1270. The Order of Montegaudio merged with the Knights Templar in 1196. The Order of Saint Mary of Spain combined with the Order of Santiago in 1280. The Order of the Blessed Virgin Mary of Mercy was established in 1218 in Barcelona.

KNIGHTS OF ST THOMAS

THE HOSPITALLERS OF ST THOMAS OF CANTERBURY AT ACRE

The English military brotherhood of the Knights of St Thomas of Canterbury at Acre was established after the capture of the city by crusader armies led by King Richard I of England (r.1189–99) and King Philip II of France (r.1180–1223) in 1191. Some sources suggest its founder was a certain William, chaplain to the Dean of St Paul's Cathedral, London, although there is also evidence that the knights celebrated no less a figure than Richard Coeur de Lion himself as their founder. Their brotherhood was named in honour of Saint Thomas Becket, the Archbishop of Canterbury who had been slain in his own cathedral by English knights in 1170 and canonized in 1173 (see box). The order survived for around 340 years, until it was wound up by King Henry VIII of England (r.1509–47) as part of the Dissolution of the Monasteries in 1538.

▼ *The Fifth Crusade was mainly against Ayyubid Egypt, but its initial stages took place in the Holy Land, and at this time Peter Roches established the Knights of St Thomas as a military order.*

CARING FOR THE SICK

In its first years the brotherhood was a religious rather than a military order, dedicated to caring for the wounded and sick, burying the knights who had died in the wars of the cross and seeking to raise funds in order to ransom Christian warriors who had been taken prisoner by Saladin and his Muslim generals. The

◀ *Peter Roches, Bishop of Winchester and the man who transformed the St Thomas brotherhood from monks to knights, founded Titchfield Abbey in Hampshire in c.1222.*

brothers took vows of poverty, chastity and obedience like their counterparts in other monastic orders. In Acre they built a church and a hospital, both dedicated to St Thomas of Canterbury.

The brotherhood was made into a military order by Peter Roches, Bishop of Winchester, when he was in the Holy Land for the Fifth Crusade of 1217–21. He established the brotherhood under the rule of the Teutonic Knights with the backing of the Latin Patriarch of Jerusalem and leading magnates of Outremer. The brotherhood was recognized by Pope Gregory IX (ruled 1227–41) in 1236. The order became more generally known as the Knights of St Thomas Acon (the last word being an anglicized form of Acre). In the first 80 years or so of its existence, the brotherhood had a prior as its senior figure, but from *c*.1279 – reflecting increasing militarization – the pre-eminent individual was the master.

Historians are not certain why members of religious brotherhoods initially dedicated to providing medical and other care for pilgrims and soldiers became themselves soldiers. It is likely that the constant shortage of warriors in Outremer was an important incentive for the brothers to take up arms and further the Christian cause themselves. Bishop Peter Roches would surely have been encouraged in his militarization of the Order of St Thomas of Acre when he sought the counsel of Outremer's leading barons, for these men faced a constant struggle to find enough soldiers to fight their wars and maintain hard-won territories.

The brothers fought in defence of Christian holdings in the Holy Land and, in particular, to protect Acre. They did not become wealthy. In 1279 they were forced to appeal to King Edward I of England (r.1272–1307) for funds. But they did succeed in establishing a house in London and various provincial quarters in both England and Ireland.

▼ Mercers Hall in Ironmonger Lane, London, stood on the site of the former Hospital of St Thomas Acon, which was destroyed in the Great Fire of London (1666). The hall as shown here was itself destroyed by German bombs in May 1941.

THE CULT OF ST THOMAS BECKET

King Henry II of England (r.1154–89) elevated Thomas Becket to greatness, making him Chancellor in 1155 and Archbishop of Canterbury in 1162 but the pair quarrelled over Henry's attempts to impose his authority on the Church and, despite an apparent reconciliation, four knights claiming to be acting on Henry's wishes killed Becket in Canterbury Cathedral on 29 December 1170. The whole of Christendom was outraged and in 1173 Pope Alexander III (ruled 1159–81) canonized the archbishop. Becket's cult was immediately very strong and his tomb at Canterbury became a major draw for pilgrims. For his part, Henry II strongly denied having ordered the murder of his archbishop, but was forced to make a public demonstration of penance at the saint's tomb in July 1174.

▲ *Two murderous knights violate the sanctuary at Canterbury Cathedral and slay Thomas Becket at his prayers.*

IN CYPRUS

After the fall of Acre in 1291 the brothers removed, with the Knights Templar, to Cyprus. There they built the fine Church of St Nicholas in Nicosia. But very difficult times followed. In the early 14th century the London house of the Knights of St Thomas was reported to be in ruins and the brothers had to fight off two proposed takeovers, firstly by the Knights Templar and secondly by the convent of Bonhommes at Ashridge, Hertfordshire.

In *c.*1320 the master of the order in Cyprus, Henry of Bedford, removed to London and established himself in power there. He sent a deputy to rule in Cyprus, but the brothers rejected this man and there was a spilt in the order. Overall power briefly returned to Cyprus after Henry's death, but in *c.*1360 it was finally confirmed in London; there are no records of a master in Nicosia after this date.

From this period onwards, the brothers appear to have abandoned their military role and exchanged the rule of the Teutonic Knights for that of the monastic

rule of the Augustinians. They concentrated on charitable and educational work in London, where they established St Thomas of Acres grammar school in the city in *c.*1450. The order was dissolved by Henry VIII in 1538 in the Dissolution.

MERCERS

Henry put the brothers' London hospital and chapel up for sale and the buildings were bought by the Worshipful Company of Mercers. Incorporated under royal charter in 1394, the Worshipful Company of Mercers was established as a trade association for merchants in the cloth trade, especially importers of velvet and silk and exporters of wool. The Mercers had already established links with the Knights of St Thomas and had been worshipping in the brotherhood's London chapel for some years. This was destroyed in the Great Fire of London in 1666, but a statue of Christ was salvaged and reused both in the second Mercer's Hall and Chapel (destroyed in World War I) and in its modern replacement.

THE ORDER OF ST LAZARUS

AND OTHER MINOR CHIVALRIC ORDERS

A number of smaller chivalric orders complemented the major brotherhoods of the Knights Templar, the Knights Hospitaller and the Teutonic Knights. Among these, as we have seen, was the brotherhood of the Knights of St Thomas at Acre. Others included the Order of St Lazarus of Jerusalem, established *c.*1123, and the Order of the Sword, founded by King Peter of Cyprus in 1347.

THE ORDER OF ST LAZARUS

Another group of knights in the Holy Land who were dedicated to relieving the suffering of pilgrims and soldiers in the wars of the cross belonged to the Order of St Lazarus of Jerusalem, which specialized in the care of lepers. Like the Order of St John (Hospitallers), St Lazarus grew into a military order from a brotherhood offering hospitality and medical care. Under the Templar rule, any Templar knights who contracted leprosy were required to transfer to the Order of St Lazarus, and

▲ Henry II of England was an important patron of the Order of St Lazarus. His effigy is at Fontevrault Abbey, France.

these Templars trained the St Lazarus brothers in military ways. The Order of St Lazarus of Jerusalem was established as a military brotherhood in *c.*1123.

The order became very wealthy, and was left endowments by European kings including Louis VII of France (r.1137–80), Henry II of England (r.1154–89) and Holy Roman Emperor Frederick II (r.1220–50). The order followed the Augustinian rule. Knights of the Order fought at the Battle of La Forbie in 1244 against the alliance of Khwarismian Turks and Sultan as-Salih Ayyub of Egypt (r.1240–49), in the army of the Seventh Crusade led by King Louis IX of France (r.1226–70) and at the fall of Acre in 1291.

The order received papal recognition under Augustinian rule in 1255 in the reign of Pope Alexander IV (ruled 1254–61), and was granted the same privileges and exemptions as the principal monastic orders in 1262 under Pope Urban IV (ruled 1261–64). Its numbers were swelled after 1265 when Pope Clement IV (ruled 1265–68) issued an order that Catholic clergy send all lepers to the houses of St Lazarus.

After the loss of Jerusalem in 1187, the Knights of St Lazarus (like the Hospitaller counterparts) removed to Acre. Then, following the fall of Acre in 1291, the Order

of St Lazarus disappeared from the East altogether while the Hospitallers as we have seen took up residence on Cyprus. The Knights of St Lazarus continued to maintain leper hospitals in Europe.

THE ORDER OF THE SWORD

The future Peter I of Cyprus, the titular King of Jerusalem in 1358–69 and the monarch known as the 'Crusading king', led a military expedition in 1365 against Muslim Egypt. He founded the chivalric brotherhood of the Order of the Sword

▼ The Knights of St Lazarus are named after the man raised from the dead by Christ, as told in the Gospel of St John.

▼ Those afflicted with leprosy, who entered the Order of St Lazarus, were required to pass their worldly goods to the brothers.

▲ *Mary the mother of Christ, was honoured in the brotherhood of Our Lady Of Bethlehem, established to counter the power of the Ottomans in the mid-15th century.*

in 1347. In a powerful mystical experience, Peter had a vision of a floating cross and heard a voice urging him to liberate the Holy Land: the order he formed was for knights and men-at-arms prepared to dedicate themselves to freeing Jerusalem and other parts of Outremer from Muslim control. Its emblem was a silver sword, point down, against a blue backing inscribed with the words 'With this maintain loyalty'.

THE ORDER OF OUR LADY OF BETHLEHEM

After the Ottoman Turks under Sultan Mehmed II 'the Conqueror' (r.1444–46, 1451–81) captured Constantinople in 1453, Pope Pius II (ruled 1458–64) established the Order of Our Lady of Bethlehem on the island of Lemnos in the Aegean Sea. Its knights were charged with defending the island against the Ottomans and countering the Turks' activity in the Aegean and Hellespont. The knights of the order wore a white surplice with a red cross and followed a rule similar to that of the Knights Hospitaller.

Pope Pius suppressed a number of orders, including that of St Lazarus, in order to provide the knights of Our Lady of Bethlehem with property and revenues.

But the enterprise came to nothing when the Ottomans succeed in capturing Lemnos. The orders Pius had suppressed were re-established.

OTHER GERMANIC ORDERS

A number of minor Germanic military-monastic orders of knighthood were established in the 13th century. The Order of Dobrzyn, also known as the *Fratres Milites Christi de Prussia*, (the Prussian Cavaliers of Christ Jesus), was created in the 1220s by Christian of Oliva, the first Bishop of Prussia, in order to fight against raids on Masovia by pagan Prussians who had risen in defiance of Duke Konrad I of Masovia's efforts to force them to convert

to Christianity. The establishment of the order was approved by Pope Gregory IX (ruled 1227–41) in 1228. The order was granted possession of the town of Dobrzyn and surrounding regions (Dobrzyn Land). The order initially had 15 German knights in membership under the command of Master Brunon. In 1235 the majority of the knights joined the Teutonic Order.

The monastic order of the Livonian Brothers of the Sword was established by Albert of Buxhoeveden, third Bishop of Riga in Livonia, in 1202 and was granted official sanction by Pope Innocent III in 1204. Bishop Albert wanted the German warrior monks to help in the forcible conversion to Christianity of pagan Curonians, Livonians and others in the region. The knights, who were also known as 'Christ Knights', 'Sword Brethren' and 'The Militia of Christ of Livonia', made their headquarters at Fellin (modern Viljandi in Estonia) and the remains of their Grand Master's castle can still be seen there. They suffered a heavy defeat by Lithuanians at the Battle of Schaulen in 1236 and in 1237 most of the members joined the Teutonic Order.

▼ *Two minor Germanic orders – those of Dobrzyn and of the Livonian Brothers of the Sword – were established by bishops.*

CHAPTER FIFTEEN

THE EUROPEAN CRUSADES

Christian wars were waged against Muslims in Spain from as early as the 8th century, and against the pagan peoples of northern Europe from the time of the Second Crusade (1147–49) up until the 14th century. In southern France the Albigensian Crusade of the 13th century brutally attacked the Cathars, who were denounced as heretics by the papacy; in Bohemia the Hussites (followers of Czech nationalist preacher Jan Hus) were likewise declared heretics and attacked by crusaders in 1420–32; and in Italy during the 12th–14th centuries, several holy wars were called against enemies of the Catholic Church.

Many of these wars were thinly disguised secular struggles – those in Italy, for example, were fought to promote the territorial interests of the papacy. They were different in kind to the crusades in the Holy Land, and would probably have been fought even if the ideology of crusading was not deployed. One of them, the war to reconquer Spain, predated the crusading era, for it began in the immediate aftermath of the Muslim conquest of the Iberian Peninsula in the early 8th century. Yet, once available, crusading rhetoric and the apparatus of crusade indulgences and taxes were enthusiastically applied to this Spanish struggle from the time of the First Crusade in the 1090s. The call to fight for the cross also gave an added force and charge to all the struggles termed as the Northern Crusades against Muslims, heretics or pagans.

▲ *King Alfonso XI of Castile waged war against Muslims in Spain with such determination he was called 'the Implacable'.*

◄ *After the conquest in 1492 of Granada, the last remaining Muslim territory in Spain, Ferdinand and Isabella receive Arab tributes.*

THE RECONQUISTA
THE STRUGGLE IN SPAIN

◄ At the Battle of Guadalete (711) in the far south of the Iberian Peninsula, invading Muslim cavalry routed the Visigoths.

The *Reconquista* – from the word in Spanish and Portuguese for 'reconquest' – was the struggle by the Christians of Europe to retake the Iberian Peninsula from its Moorish rulers. The Reconquista lasted a full 750 years, from the early 8th century, when Muslim Arabs and Berbers captured the peninsula from the Visigoths, to 1492, when the combined armies of Aragon and Castile conquered the city of Granada, the last Muslim territory in the peninsula. These Iberian wars were promoted as holy wars by popes who offered crusading privileges to those taking part in the struggle.

VISIGOTHS AND MUSLIMS
In the 5th century AD the Visigoths, an East Germanic tribe, took power in the Roman province of Hispania (incorporating the whole of the Iberian Peninsula and part of southern France) under the auspices of Rome. After the fall of the Roman Empire in the west, the Visigoth territory became an independent territory.

A Muslim army of Arabs and north African Berber tribesmen invaded the southern part of the peninsula in 711 and in five years captured most of the large Visigoth kingdom. The Muslims then attempted to push on northwards but were defeated by Odo, Duke of Aquitaine, at the Battle of Toulouse in 721 and by Frankish leader Charles Martel in the Battle of Tours in 732. Thereafter they largely abandoned attempts at northward expansion and settled in what is now Spain and Portugal.

Only in the north of the Iberian Peninsula did the Visigoths maintain a foothold. The Visigoth nobleman Pelayo established the Kingdom of Asturias, which was subsequently to be an important base for the reconquest of Spain. His defeat of a Muslim army in the Battle of Covadonga (722) is often identified as the first conflict of the Reconquista.

AL-ANDALUS AND THE MOORS
The Muslim state in the Iberian Peninsula was known by the Arabic name al-Andalus – and its people were known by the Christians as 'Moors'.

Al-Andalus was at first nominally subject to the Umayyad caliph in Damascus, Syria. 'Caliph' was the title for the leader of Islam as a successor to the founder of the faith, the Prophet Mohammad; the

Umayyads were the successors of the fourth caliph, Mu'awiyah, a member of the Umayyad clan of caravan merchants.

In 750 the Umayyad caliph Marwan II was defeated by a rival leader, Abu al-Abbas, who established the Abbasid caliphate. Abu al-Abbas was known as *as-Saffah* ('the Bloodshedder') on account of the ruthlessness with which he eliminated his rivals, but one prominent Umayyad, Abd ar-Rahman, escaped to Spain and established himself in Córdoba. His successors were in theory subordinate to the Abbasid caliphs, who were now based in Baghdad, in Iraq, but were in practice independent and ruled as emirs of Córdoba. When Abbasid power declined sharply and their realm fell into anarchy in the early 10th century, the then emir, Abd ar-Rahman III, declared himself the

▼ The Arabs capture Córdoba. Under their rule it became one of the world's largest cities, home to as many as 500,000 people.

independent caliph of Córdoba in 929. Historians call al-Andalus the Umayyad caliphate province from 711 to 750, the Emirate of Córdoba fom 750 to 929, and the Caliphate of Córdoba from 929 to 1031. After 1031, the caliphate broke up into small Muslim kingdoms.

ST JAMES THE GREAT

Descendants of King Pelayo of Asturias seized territory in Galicia (the north-west part of the peninsula). In the reign of King Alfonso II of Asturias (r.791–842), the bones of St James were reputedly discovered at Compostela, which became established as one of Europe's foremost pilgrimage sites. St James the Great was one of Christ's 12 Apostles and traditionally brought the Christian Gospel to the Iberian Peninsula. According to legend, his bodily remains were brought to what is now Spain by sea after his death. In 844 the saint then supposedly made a miraculous appearance to lead the Christian army of King Ramiro I of Asturias (r.842–50) against the Moors of Córdoba in the Battle of Clavijo.

PROGRESS IN THE RECONQUISTA

Gerona and Barcelona were taken from the Muslims in 785 and 801 by Carolingian armies from France, and the region of Catalonia became part of the Carolingian realm known as 'the Spanish March'. After 850 the Christian buffer between southern France and the Iberian Peninsula established by the Kings of Asturias was expanded to the valley of the River Duero. In 913 the rulers of Asturias moved their seat of power from Oviedo to León and the kingdom became known as León. Christian kingdoms were also established in Pamplona and Aragon.

In 1002 the caliphate of Córdoba collapsed and divided into around 30 small *taifa* (successor) kingdoms that were to prove vulnerable to the continuing Christian recovery. In 1029 the independent kingdom of Castile was founded in what had been a county within the kingdom of León.

ALFONSO VI AND EL CID

King Alfonso VI of León temporarily reunited his kingdom with Castile, reigning as king of Castile and León from 1072, until his death in 1109. When he captured Toledo in May 1085, he appeared to be on the brink of a major onslaught against the taifa kingdoms: in 1077 he had declared himself Emperor of Spain. But the beleaguered rulers of the taifas appealed to the Muslim Almoravids of north-west Africa, and Almoravid armies defeated Alfonso at Sagrajas in 1086 and Ucles in 1108.

In this period, Don Rodrigo Diaz of Vivar, the Spanish knight celebrated as 'El Cid', performed his great feats of chivalry. He was cast into exile by King Alfonso in 1081, entered the service of al-Mu'tamin, Moorish king of Saragossa, and then fought for al-Mu'tamin and his successor al-Musta'in II for almost ten years, before returning to Alfonso's service and capturing the Muslim kingdom of Valencia in 1090–94; he ruled Valencia until his death in 1099, when it was captured by the Almoravids. (León and Castile remained reunited until 1157.)

▼ *In the legendary Battle of Clavijo, a Christian army was vastly outnumbered by the Moors but triumphed nonetheless after a miraculous appearance by St James.*

CRUSADING PRIVILEGES

War against Muslims in Spain was promoted as crusading, with privileges identical to those offered for military service in the Holy Land, from the 1090s onwards. In 1095 Pope Urban II (ruled 1088–99) urged the Spanish to respond to his call to crusade by fighting the Muslims in their own land rather than by travelling to Palestine. In 1123 Pope Callixtus II (ruled 1119–24) declared a crusade in Spain at the same time as he called a fresh military expedition to the Holy Land.

At the time of the Second Crusade during 1145, Pope Eugenius III (ruled 1145–53) also called a crusade in Spain, guaranteeing King Alfonso VII of León and Castile (r. 1126–57) the same indulgence he had given to the French crusader knights. In 1147 crusader armies from England, Scotland, Normandy and Germany stopped in Spain and Portugal en route to the Holy Land and helped to recapture the city of Lisbon; around the same time, as part of the crusading campaign, Alfonso VII of Castile and Count Ramon Berenguer IV of Barcelona conquered Almeria in south-eastern Spain from the Moors. The next major crusading activity in the Iberian Peninsula was to come in 1212.

THE SPANISH CRUSADE OF 1212
AND OTHER 13TH-CENTURY CRUSADES IN SPAIN AND PORTUGAL

In 1212 Pope Innocent III (ruled 1198–1216) proclaimed a crusade in Spain against the Almohad caliphs. The Almohads had ousted their Almoravid predecessors and defeated the kingdom of Castile in the Battle of Alarcos on 19 July 1195. With the support of troops from the Spanish kingdoms of Aragon and Navarre and with crusaders from France, King Alfonso VIII of Castile (r.1158–1214) won a resounding victory over the Almohads at the Battle of Las Navas de Tolosa, one of the greatest and most important Christian victories in the entire period of the Reconquista.

RISE OF THE ALMOHADS

The Almohads were originally followers of a Berber religious teacher named Ibn Tumart from the Atlas Mountains of

▼ *King Alfonso VIII led the army of Castile and a vast force of crusaders and Knights Templar to victory over the Almohads at the Battle of Las Navas de Tolosa in July 1212.*

Morocco. Ibn Tumart established the Almohads as a religious order dedicated to bringing purity back into the faith of Islam, and after declaring himself the *mahdi* (a promised Islamic redeemer) in 1121, he led armed resistance against the Almoravid caliphs ruling in northern Africa. His successor, Abd al-Mu'min, defeated the Almoravids by 1147 and made himself Emir of Marrakech in 1149; another Almohad leader, Abu Ya'qub Yusuf (r.1163–84), conquered the Almoravid empire in Spain and established a capital in Seville.

Meanwhile King Alfonso VIII of Castile led resistance to the Almohads in Spain. In 1190, following a defeat, Alfonso was forced to agree an armistice, but when this expired in 1194 he attacked the Almohad province of Seville. Almohad caliph Abu Yusuf gathered an army and inflicted a heavy defeat on Alfonso near the fortress of Alarcos, making the Castilian king retreat to Toledo.

In the aftermath of this defeat, the Almohads took a great deal of territory – capturing Trujillo, Talavera, Cuenca, Ucles and the fortress of Calatrava, stronghold of the Spanish monastic military brotherhood the Order of Calatrava. These Muslim successes forced the border between Muslim and Christian Spain many miles northwards, until it lay in the hills just south of Toledo.

Alfonso's ally Rodrigo Jiménez of Rada, Archbishop of Toledo, sought Church backing for a crusading response. Pope Innocent III issued a call to arms, and in 1212 crusaders – including Frankish knights under Archbishop Arnold of Narbonne and members of the military-monastic brotherhood of the Knights Templar – arrived at Toledo. They marched southwards, accompanied by the armies of Aragon, León and Castile. They captured Calatrava, Alarcos and Benevente before they met the Almohad army.

GLORY OF NAVARRE

According to legend, King Sancho VII of Navarre broke into the Almohad caliph's camp at the climax of the Battle of Las Navas de Tolosa. The story goes that the caliph had surrounded his tent with a defensive barrier made of slaves chained together, but that Sancho cut through the barrier and burst into the tent. To celebrate his feat of arms, Navarre changed its coats of arms to one showing a golden chain, below.

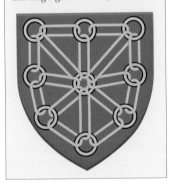

LAS NAVAS DE TOLOSA

The Almohad caliph, Muhammad al-Nasir, gathered his army on the plains of Las Navas de Tolosa. The Christians, trying to reach them though the mountain pass of La Llosa, found it heavily guarded, but then with the help of a local shepherd found a different route through the Despenaperros Pass.

After a prolonged stand-off, the two armies clashed. King Alfonso led the Christian forces into battle, and they won a famous victory – killing, wounding or capturing no fewer than 100,000 of the Almohads at the cost of 2,000 of their own men dead or wounded. Tradition has it that King Sancho VII of Navarre (r.1194–1234) humiliated the Almohad emir in his tent following an act of great

▲ *King Ferdinand III of Castile and León receives homage from a Moor after taking Seville in 1248. The city had been in Moorish hands since its conquest in 712.*

bravery (*see* box). The Almohad caliph, al-Nasir, fled to Marrakech in Morocco, where he died shortly afterwards. Alfonso went on to capture the southern towns of Baeza and Ubeda.

CHRISTIAN TRIUMPHS

In the following years, the victory at Las Navas de Tolosa proved to have been a truly significant one, for the Almohad empire fell apart in dynastic struggles after 1224 and without strong leadership was unable to hold back the armies of the Christian reconquest. King Alfonso IX of León (r.1188–1230) captured Caceres (1227) and Merida and Badajoz (1230), opening the way to the recapturing of Seville. Ferdinand III, who reigned as King of Castile 1217–52 and of León 1230–52, captured Córdoba in 1236), Jaen in 1246 and Seville in 1248. (Ferdinand is celebrated as San Fernando after he was canonized on 4 February 1671.)

King Alfonso X of Castile and León (r.1252–84) defeated the Muslim emirates in Niebla and Murcia. (Alfonso was the father of Eleanor of Castile, beloved wife of King Edward I of England, and it was at his court that the law code known as the *Siete Partidas*, or Seven-Part Code, was composed; he was a great patron of learning and is remembered as Alfonso 'the Wise' or 'the Learned'.)

King James I of Aragon (r.1213–76) captured the Balearic Islands (1229–35) and the kingdom of Valencia (1233–38). Both these campaigns were crusades. James was renowned as *El Conquistador* (the Conqueror). In Portugal, King Sancho II (r.1223–47) reconquered from the Moors a number of cities in Alentejo (south-central Portugal) and the Algarve (the southernmost part of the country). By the close of the 13th century, the kingdom of Granada was the only part of the entire peninsula to remain under Muslim rule.

▼ *Knights embark by sea for the Holy Land on crusade. The illustration is from a book made for Alfonso X of Castile and León, a great patron of court learning who also played his part in the Reconquista.*

THE CONQUEST OF GRANADA
FINAL STAGE OF THE RECONQUISTA

In the 14th and 15th centuries the Muslim kingdom of Granada in southern Spain was the only surviving part of al-Andalus. In theory subordinate to the kingdom of Castile, its ruler a feudal vassal of the King of Castile from the time of King Ferdinand III onwards in the mid-13th century, its days seemed numbered. But remarkably, Granada survived until 1492 when the might of a united Spain, formed by the union of Castile and Aragon, finally brought to an end almost 800 years of Muslim rule in Spain.

MUSLIM HOLY WAR

In Morocco, the Marinids ousted the Almohads, with the aid of Christian mercenaries, in the mid-13th century, taking Fes in 1248 and Marrakech in 1269. The Marinids were fundamentalist Muslims who declared a jihad on the Kingdom of Castile in 1275 and formed an alliance with the Nasrid sultans of Granada; Marinid soldiers helped Granada to protect its borders and even won back some fortified settlements that had fallen to the Christians. The Nasrid sultans ceded the Spanish city of Algeciras to the Marinids.

▼ *Crusading monarchs. This stained glass window celebrates the capture of Malaga by Ferdinand and Isabella's army in 1487.*

SIR JAMES DOUGLAS AND THE BATTLE OF TEBA

King Alfonso XI 'the Implacable' of Castile (r.1312–50) took up the battle against Granada. In 1330 he defeated Sultan Muhammad IV of Granada at the Battle of Teba in Andalusia. In this battle Sir James Douglas, friend of Robert the Bruce, King of Scots, was killed. Douglas had departed from Scotland bearing the Bruce's embalmed heart in order to fulfil his promise to the late king to carry it to the Holy Land; en route he had diverted to Spain to help Alfonso in his struggle against Granada. After the battle, Douglas's body and the Bruce's heart were returned to Scotland, where they were buried.

In the immediate aftermath of his victory at Teba, Alfonso captured the nearby Castle of the Star and installed knights of the military monastic brotherhood of the Order of Santiago as its garrison. Two years later in 1332, in Vittoria, the king founded the chivalric Order of the Sash.

BATTLE OF RIO SALADO

In 1340 Alfonso – together with King Afonso IV 'the Brave' of Portugal (r.1325–57) – defeated a large Marinid army at Rio Salado. The Marinids had amassed a vast army and they crossed the Straits of Gibraltar to mount an invasion with the

▲ *King Ferdinand I of Aragon, the ruler celebrated as 'He of Antequera' after he captured that town from the Muslims as part of the Reconquista, issued this ducat during his brief reign in Aragon, 1412–16.*

aim of establishing their own permanent kingdom in Spain. They captured Gibraltar, defeating a Christian fleet, then moved inland to meet the two Christian kings near Tarifa on the Salado river.

Following a resounding victory over the invaders, Alfonso proceeded to attack Algeciras, which he retook after a two-year siege in 1344. This siege drew Christian volunteers from all over Europe. The defeat of the Marinids at Rio Salado marked the end of the last attempted Muslim invasion of Spain and seemed to clear the way for a final push against Granada. After 1350, however, Alfonso's successors were distracted from the Reconquista by civil war in Castile, and Granada made a number of inroads into Christian territory, taking the city of Jaen, among other strongholds.

In the first part of the 15th century, the Spanish Christian kingdoms moved once more against the Muslim presence. In 1410 the future King Ferdinand I of Aragon (r.1412–16) captured the fortified town of Antequera from Granada while he was regent for his nephew, the infant King John II of Castile. For this feat, he was

▲ After the end of the Reconquista in 1492, the Jews were expelled from Spain by decree of Ferdinand and Isabella.

elected to the throne of Aragon and was known as *El de Antequera* (He of Antequera). In 1430 Ferdinand's nephew King John II of Castile (r.1406–54) launched a campaign against Granada that culminated in a victory over the Nasrid sultan Muhammad IX at the Battle of Higuerela, in July 1431.

For almost 50 years thereafter there was no major offensive against Granada. Spanish military brotherhoods, such as the orders of Calatrava and of Santiago, and leading Castilian noblemen conducted a raiding and skirmishing war along the frontier between Castile and Granada, intermittently joined by crusaders seeking glory, riches and crusading privileges.

BIRTH OF SPAIN

In 1469 Ferdinand, heir to the throne of Aragon, married Princess Isabella, heir to the throne of Castile. He became king consort in Castile in 1474 when Isabella became queen following the death of her brother King Henry IV of Castile, and when Ferdinand succeeded his father,

King John II of Aragon (r.1458–79), in 1479, the couple ruled a united kingdom of Aragon and Castile. This marked the birth of the nation of Spain. Within three years they moved against Granada and in a ten-year war, 1482–92, won the final victory of the Reconquista. Ferdinand and Isabella made sure that their army was

equipped with the latest artillery guns and cannon. They promoted the campaign as a religious war – on several occasions Isabella led prayers on or near the field of battle, declaring her burning desire that God's will be performed; soldiers came from several European countries to join the crusade. In Spain, money was raised to cover expenses through the imposition of crusade taxes and the sale of crusade indulgences. The crusaders besieged and captured Ronda in 1485 and took Loja the next year. In 1487 they captured Malaga and in 1489 Baza.

They laid siege to the city of Granada in 1491. After their camp was destroyed by fire, they rebuilt it in stone in the shape of a giant cross, had it painted white and named it Santa Fe (Sacred Faith). At the end of 1491 Sultan Boabdil surrendered the city. Ferdinand and Isabella made a formal entry into Granada on 2 January 1492 and oversaw the reconsecration of the city's main mosque as a church.

▼ At the gorgeous Alhambra palace in the city of Granada, Sultan Boabdil consults with advisers in 1492, prior to surrendering to the army of Ferdinand and Isabella.

THE ALBIGENSIAN CRUSADE

WAR ON HERESY

In 1208 a papal legate named Pierre of Castelnau was murdered in the Languedoc region of southern France and Pope Innocent III (ruled 1198–1216) declared a crusade against the Cathars of that region, who were viewed as heretics by the Catholic Church. The Cathars were subsequently called the Albigensians (from the town of Albi that was inaccurately identified as their headquarters).

The Albigensian crusade lasted 20 years, from 1209 to 1229, and although it began as a religious war aimed at curbing what the Church hierarchy saw as a popular and dangerous heresy, it became little more than an exercise in territorial expansion by northern French barons. The

▲ *The seal of Raymond VI of Toulouse. It was his vassal who murdered Pierre of Castelnau and provoked Pope Innocent to declare his crusade against the Cathars.*

▼ *St Dominic worked for years to convince the Cathars that their beliefs were heretical. After the celebrated trial by fire, in which Cathar books burned while orthodox Catholic volumes were spared, he gave one of the orthodox books to the Cathars.*

religious victory over the Cathars when it came was achieved not in battle but through the efforts of the Dominican Inquisition (a tribunal to investigate heresy), established in 1233. Military action against the Cathars continued inter-

mittently until 1255. The Cathars were driven from France into Italy, where they died out and were heard of no more after the end of the 14th century.

CATHAR BELIEFS AND BACKGROUND

The Cathars took their name from the Greek word *katharos*, meaning 'pure'. They were dualists, believing in two gods – an ultimate embodiment of goodness, and a lesser and evil creator god who had made the material world. They believed the material world therefore to be evil: the human soul was naturally good and trapped in this evil creation; people should seek salvation through extreme asceticism. Cathars avoided meat and animal products, were sexually chaste, lived in poverty and were pacifists.

Cathars divided themselves into two groups: 'the perfect' and 'the believers'. The perfect passed through an initiation ceremony called the *consolamentum* and

lived lives of extreme asceticism, devoting their energy to contemplation. The believers were not required to attain the very high standards of asceticism and religious devotion attained by the perfect.

ROOTS IN GNOSTICISM

Cathar beliefs may have derived from ancient Gnosticism, a dualist faith system popular in the Mediterranean and Middle East from the last centuries BC onward, but suppressed in the Christian Roman Empire from the 4th century AD. Like Cathars, Gnostics believed in dual divinities. The highest god was good and the lesser one evil; the evil one had created the material world. Humans were divine souls trapped in the material world, from which they could only escape through *gnosis* or knowledge held by the elite. The Cathars did not place strong emphasis on spiritual knowledge, but they did have an initiation ceremony, and an initiated elite.

BOGOMILS AND PAULICIANS

The Cathars certainly had links with the Gnostic-influenced Christian groups of the Bogomils and the Paulicians. The Bogomils had emerged in the 10th century in Bulgaria and spread from there into the Byzantine Empire, as well as into Italy and France: they were dualists, who rejected the doctrine of Christ's divine birth and the veneration of the Virgin Mary and declared that reverence for the cross and for saintly relics was no more than idolatry.

The Paulicians had their origins earlier, in the 7th–9th centuries, in Armenia: they rejected the Old Testament, veneration of the Virgin Mary, worship of the Cross and the sacraments of Baptism and Communion. The Cathars for their part denied the divinity of Christ and declared him to have been an angel come to earth; they said that his apparent sufferings and death as a human being were an illusion. Cathar teaching also rejected the doctrines of purgatory and hell and that of the resurrection of the body, arguing in favour of reincarnation.

▲ *Pope Innocent III sent out wandering preachers to bring heretics back to the true faith. He gave St Dominic and St Francis (shown here) his blessing to do this work.*

The Cathars were first established in Flanders, northern Italy and western Germany in 1000–50. They expanded in 1140–70, particularly under the influence of a resurgent Bogomil Church that sent missionaries throughout Europe; historians also believe that soldiers and pilgrims on the First Crusade picked up dualist ideas and brought them back to Europe in the early 12th century. In the 1140s the Cathars established themselves as a church: their first bishop in *c*.1149 was in northern France, but soon afterward he was joined by counterparts in Lombardy and in Albi. By 1200 they had five bishops in France and six in Italy.

SERIOUS THREAT

Remarkably, in the Languedoc Catharism became a popular religion – unlike many sects, attracting a wide following among the nobility, educated townspeople and the peasantry. Cathars attacked the wealth and corruption of the Church, while rejecting the authority of Catholic priests and of the pope; they posed a threat to the very structure of society, for they rejected the taking of oaths that was one of the central features of the feudal system. Moreover, the fact that they had many followers among both nobility and peasantry served to undo the natural, God-given social hierarchy that orthodox believers saw in the feudal system.

Pope Innocent III initially tried to bring the Cathars back to orthodoxy by peaceful means, sending preachers – including Dominic Guzman (later St Dominic), founder of the Dominican Order – to attempt to convert the heretics. The preachers had little success. Innocent then found that local nobles and even bishops were protecting the Cathars. In 1204 he suspended the bishops and replaced them with papal legates, and he demanded that Philip II of France (r.1180–1223) force the nobles to return to Catholicism. Philip refused to take action. Innocent demanded that the powerful local count, Raymond VI of Toulouse, take action but he, too, refused and was excommunicated.

In January 1208 Raymond held a meeting with the papal legate, Pierre of Castelnau, which ended angrily. The following day Pierre of Castelnau was murdered by one of Raymond's vassals. Pope Innocent III declared war, issuing a call to a crusade against the Cathars.

Innocent offered a full crusade indulgence to all who responded to his call to take up arms against the Cathars. He also declared that they would have the right to seize the land of the heretics, which attracted a number of northern French barons to the cause. It should be noted that the indulgence offered to the anti-Cathar crusaders was remarkably generous – the annulment of sins was being offered for a mere 40 days campaigning (the normal period of feudal military service) and for a war fought in nearby southern France rather than for a potentially very hazardous journey over land and sea to the Holy Land.

MASSACRE OF THE CATHARS

TWENTY YEARS OF BRUTAL WAR, 1209–1229

The crusade armies raised against the Cathars by Pope Innocent III won a series of brutal victories in 1209–15, in which local people – both Cathars and Catholics – were slaughtered in their thousands. During the next ten years, many of these bloody victories were overturned by rebels, but in 1226 King Louis VIII of France (r.1223–26) entered the fray on the side of the Church and following his death in November that year, his son Louis IX (r.1226–70) took up the fight. The Languedoc region was conquered by 1229 and peace finally agreed in the Treaty of Paris that year.

COUNT RAYMOND RECANTS

In 1209 a crusade army of around 10,000 massed in Lyon and marched south under the leadership of papal legate Arnaul Amalric, Abbot of Cîteaux. Suddenly persuaded of the error of his ways, Raymond VI of Toulouse agreed at last to move against the Cathars and was reconciled to the Church in a ceremony before carvings of the Passion of Christ on the west front

▼ At the Battle of Muret on 12 September 1213, Simon of Montfort's small crusader force roundly defeated the much larger army of Peter II of Aragon and Raymond of Toulouse. Peter was killed in action.

of the Benedictine abbey church of Saint-Gilles. The crusaders then marched towards Montpellier; Raymond-Roger Trencavel, viscount of Béziers and Albi and a vassal of Raymond VI of Toulouse, attempted to make peace with them but was refused an audience. He fled back to Carcassonne to arrange its defence.

THE SLAUGHTER AT BÉZIERS

The crusade army marched to Béziers, where it arrived on 21 July 1209. The soldiers demanded the surrender of the Cathars and the submission of any local Catholics; both groups refused. But the crusaders gained access to the town when an attempted sortie by the defenders went wrong and they burned Béziers to the ground and savagely killed every man, woman and child.

According to one account, soldiers asked the Abbot of Cîteaux how they would tell Cathars from Catholics and the abbot replied: 'Kill them all. God will recognize his own.' Afterwards the Abbot wrote gleefully to the Pope: 'Our soldiers spared neither rank, nor sex, nor elderly. About 20,000 people lost their lives … the entire city was put to the sword. Thus did God's vengeance vent its wondrous rage.'

CATHARS EVICTED FROM CARCASSONNE

Many settlements were terrified into submission and surrendered to the army. The crusaders marched on Carcassonne and took it after a two-week siege on 15 August 1209. The Cathars were forcibly evicted, having been stripped naked to humiliate them. At this point, French nobleman Simon of Montfort took charge of the crusade army and was granted territory that included the Cathar strongholds of Carcassonne, Albi and Béziers. (Simon of Montfort, a veteran of the Fourth Crusade, was the father of Simon of Montfort, 6th Earl of Leicester and main

▲ Fighting during the siege of Carcassonne. In the rear the Cathars emerge from the city to take on the besieging crusaders.

leader of baronial opposition to King Henry III of England; the 6th Earl was the effective ruler of England in 1263–64 and is remembered as a pioneer of parliamentary democracy.)

Town after town surrendered or was conquered by the crusader army over the following months. In June–July 1210 the city of Minerve put up a brave resistance but finally surrendered on 22 July; many Cathars accepted Catholicism, but fully 140 remained defiant and were burned at the stake. In 1211 Raymond of Toulouse was again excommunicated after he fell out with Simon of Montfort. In May hundreds of Cathars were burned at the stake and Aimery of Montréal was hanged after his castle fell to Montfort.

The crusaders besieged Raymond in Toulouse, but the siege failed and the army withdrew. Raymond then led a successful rebellion, capturing Castelnaudary from Simon of Montfort and 'freeing' more than 30 towns for the Cathar cause.

THE BATTLE OF MURET

In 1212, however, much of Toulouse was captured. In 1213 King Peter II of Aragon (r.1196–1213), famous victor over the Moors at the battle of Las Navas de Tolosa, led an army in support of Raymond, who was his brother-in-law. With Raymond, he besieged Montfort in Muret, but was defeated and killed in the ensuing battle. The Aragonese army broke and fled on seeing their king slain.

In 1214, Raymond was forced to flee to England and his lands were given by the pope to Philip II, who became involved in the war. In 1214–16 Montfort captured the remaining Cathar strongholds and also ceded his lands to Philip II.

CATHAR RESURGENCE

In 1216 the tide began to turn. In that year, Pope Innocent III died and was replaced by Honorius III (r.1216–27), who was not so strongly committed to waging war on the Cathars. Raymond returned from exile and captured first Beaucaire and then, in 1217, Toulouse. Montfort besieged him there and was killed in fighting outside the city on 25 June 1218, his head crushed by a stone hurled from a mangonel. The Cathar side made a number of gains, including

▼ The Cathar stronghold of Carcassonne had grown from a Roman fortification, and parts of its northern walls date from when France was under Roman rule.

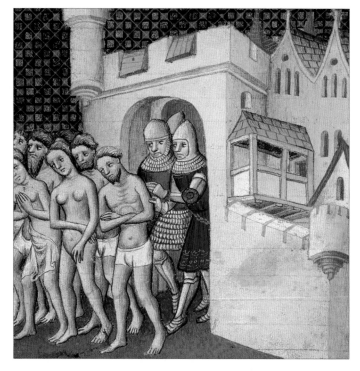

Castelnaudary, Montreal and Fanjeaux and, in 1224, Carcassonne. Raymond VI of Toulouse had died in 1222 , and been succeeded by his son, another Raymond; and Philip II had died, in 1223, and been succeeded by King Louis VIII. Amaury of Montfort, son of Simon, offered his claim to territory in the Languedoc to the new French king, who took up the challenge.

▲ Naked and frightened, the Cathars were expelled from Carcassonne after the city fell to the crusader army in August 1209.

Louis led a new crusade army into the region in June 1226. Many castles and towns surrendered without a fight but it took a three-month siege to capture Avignon. That same autumn, Louis VIII died and was succeeded by his son, Louis IX, at the age of just 12. Louis VIII's widow, Blanche of Castile, acted as regent and ordered the continuation of the crusade under the command of Humbert of Beaujeu. The crusaders crushed Cathar resistance, taking Labécède in 1227 and Toulouse in 1228.

A peace treaty was finally agreed in 1229 under which Count Raymond was recognized as ruler of Toulouse, but was forced to agree to hand his castles over into royal control, to dismantle the defences of Toulouse and to attempt to suppress the Cathars.

THE CATHAR INQUISITION

THE FAITHFUL BESIEGED – WITH SECRET TREASURE?

In 1233 Pope Gregory IX (ruled 1227–41) established a papal Inquisition (or investigative tribunal) staffed by Dominican friars charged with stamping out the Cathars. Many of the heretics were burned at the stake, while others fled the Inquisition to northern Italy. A few Cathar communities survived in isolated fortresses in the Pyrenees but these were gradually captured by the royalist forces. The Castle of Montségur was taken in March 1244 after a nine-month siege, while the small fort of Quéribus, probably the last surviving Cathar stronghold, was taken in August 1255.

The Dominican Inquisition was given substantial powers to stamp out heresy by burning Cathars where they were found and even in some cases digging up the bodies of former heretics to burn them. In a letter of 1233, the pope denounced the preachers of the Cathar faith as 'evil min-

▲ *The mountaintop Castle of Quéribus may have been the Cathars' last refuge. It was rebuilt by the French as one of five castles that guarded the French border with Spain.*

▼ *An enthroned Pope Gregory IX hears the report of a Dominican inquisitor.*

isters of Satan ... they appear to be pious but they entirely deny all virtue. Their sermons are smoother than the oil of crushed olives; but they are as dangerous as javelins and their words have a sting in the tail like that of a scorpion.' He urged the Dominican priors to 'root out ... the wickedness of heresy', 'to work assiduously against all who receive, help or defend any who are excommunicated'; he encouraged them to 'lay sentences of interdict' on the lands of those behaved in this way. But he also encouraged them to give absolution to those that 'wish to come back to the unity of the church'. He made a promise that all who came to listen to the sermons of the friars would be granted freedom from 20 days' penance.

CATHAR REVOLTS

The Cathars continued to resist. They drove the friars of the Inquisition out of Narbonne, Toulouse and Albi in 1235. Another Raymond, son of Roger Trencavel, led a revolt in 1240 and

attempted to capture Carcassonne. But he was driven off and then besieged by the forces of King Louis IX in the Castle of Montréal. Raymond escaped and fled into exile in Aragon. (Later he surrendered to Louis, and accompanied the king on the Seventh Crusade.)

In 1242 Count Raymond VIII of Toulouse tried to mount a revolt in alliance with the English, but the campaign faltered, the English were defeated by Louis IX at Taillebourg and the rebellion came to nothing. Count Raymond surrendered to Louis and asked for his excommunication to be lifted. Many Cathars took refuge in mountain strongholds such as Montségur. The Council of Béziers determined in the spring of 1243 to attack the castle there as an attempt to wipe out Catharism once and for all.

SIEGE OF MONTSÉGUR

The Castle of Montségur was perched atop a rock at an altitude of 3,900ft (1,200m) in the Languedoc near the Pyrenees Mountains. It was built on the ruins of an earlier fortress by Raymond of Pereille in c.1210. According to some accounts, it was the headquarters of the Cathars in the Languedoc region.

▲ *Roman Catholic monks rejoice at the burning of the Cathars at Montségur.*

From May 1243 to March 1244 it was besieged by a royalist army of around 10,000 commanded by Hugh of Arcis, Louis IX's Seneschal of Carcassonne. On 1 March 1244 the defenders, offered terms of surrender, asked for a two-week truce to consider them; in return they provided hostages whose lives would be forfeit if the defenders tried to flee. On March 14, the defenders reportedly celebrated a festival coinciding with the spring equinox. On the next day the truce expired, and around 220 Cathars, all members of their initiated elite group 'the perfect', were taken down the mountainside and burned as heretics in a large stockade at the foot of the hill. In the two-week period, an additional 25 of the Cathars had joined the ranks of 'the perfect' and were therefore put to death.

ESCAPE WITH TREASURE?

In the final days of the siege, it is said that four of the castle defenders slipped unnoticed though the siege lines carrying some unidentified treasure. This treasure may have been esoteric writings, Cathar riches or, as some claim, the Holy Grail.

One tradition claims that the Knights Templar when building on Temple Mount in Jerusalem discovered extraordinary treasure that they then passed to the Cathars, and that these treasures were among those smuggled out of Montségur. Some writers claim that the castle may have been the actual Holy Grail castle celebrated in chivalric romances and poems such as *Parzival* by Wolfram von Eschenbach (written only decades earlier, in 1200–10) – where the Grail castle is called Monsalvat, strikingly similar to Montségur. (The Castle of Montségur that survives today is not the one that was occupied by the Cathars, for that fortress was entirely destroyed by the royalist army in 1244. The building seen today was built over the ensuing centuries and has many characteristics typical of the 1600s.)

The few surviving Cathars gathered in another hilltop stronghold at Quéribus. When a French army was despatched to deal with them in 1255 they fled the castle without a fight and left the country, dispersing to take refuge either in Aragon or in northern Italy.

LINKS TO TEMPLARS?

One reason that the Knights Templar came under such fierce attack in the early 14th century was that they were accused of fraternizing with and protecting heretics. The sixth Templar Grand Master, Bertrand of Blanchefort (Grand Master 1156–69) was reputedly from a Cathar family and from his time the Templars accepted Cathars into the order. The Templars accepted many heretics into their ranks because recruitment was always difficult, but they had a significant number of Cathar members from France. During the Albigensian Crusade the Templars gave refuge to Cathars fleeing the crusaders – and allowed them to bury their dead in their Templar graveyards.

▼ *Was the Cathar fortress at Montségur in south-western France the original Grail castle? The current castle was erected on the ruins of the Cathar one in the 1600s.*

THE BALTIC CRUSADES

HOLY WAR AGAINST NORTHERN PAGANS

The Baltic Crusades were military campaigns against the pagan peoples on the southern and eastern shores of the Baltic Sea. They were cast as wars of religion but were often fought to gain territory for local bishops and feudal lords. The Baltic Crusades are often said to have started in the 1190s when popes Celestine III and Innocent III called what became a standing crusade. Its purpose was to support the Catholic Church in the region of Livonia (now Estonia, Lithuania and Latvia), but as early as 1147 crusading privileges had been officially granted to Saxon, Danish and Polish Christians fighting against the pagan Wends of the Baltic.

THE WENDISH CRUSADE

In 1147 when Bernard of Clairvaux was preaching the Second Crusade to the Holy Land on behalf of Pope Eugenius III, he was told by the north German Saxons that they were not willing to travel to the Holy Land but wanted to conduct a holy war against the pagan Wends in the Baltic. Eugenius sent out the *Divina dispensatione*

bull, on 13 April 1147, guaranteeing those fighting on this Baltic crusade the same benefits as those who took the cross to fight in the Holy Land. Bernard himself wrote of the crusaders' attack on the Wends: 'We expressly forbid that for any cause they should agree peace with these people until either their false religion or their nation has been destroyed.'

Papal legate Anselm of Havelberg was put in command of an army that included Danes and Poles as well as Saxons. Some of these crusaders were genuinely fighting in order to convert the pagans, but many bishops and lords were primarily seeking to increase their landholding in the region.

◄ *The Wends of the Baltic region were descendants of Slavic tribes who settled in eastern Germany in the 5th century AD. King Wandalus was a mythical ancestor, and was supposedly originally a Trojan.*

▲ *The Baltic Crusades had begun as much as 50 years before Pope Celestine III called a crusade in Livonia following the failure of a Church mission to the region.*

The campaign followed the annexation by Count Adolph of Holstein of Wendish lands, which he had parcelled out among Christian immigrants from western Germany. Wendish leader Niklot led an invasion of Wagria (now eastern Holstein in northern Germany) and Adolph fought back with part of the crusader army. This part of the campaign was swiftly over, and ended in a peace treaty, but other crusaders attacked Dobin and Demmin. At Dobin, the members of the Wendish garrison were baptized following a siege. The crusade army marching on Demmin sacked a castle and pagan temple at Malchow, but their siege of Demmin was unsuccessful and so they marched on into

Pomerania on the Baltic coast where, reaching the Christian city of Stettin (now in Poland), they were greeted by Bishop Albert of Pomerania and Prince Ratorbor I of Pomerania and then disbanded.

The crusade achieved a few conversions, but many of these Christianized Wends reverted to their own religion after the crusaders left. It had the effect of strengthening Christian landholdings in the region and of weakening the resistance of the local people to future campaigns.

THE CRUSADE IN LIVONIA

Before Celestine and Innocent unleashed the power of the crusading machine on Livonia in the 1190s, the Church had made peaceful efforts to convert the local populace. In the 11th century Adalbert, Archbishop of Bremen in 1045–72, had sent missionaries into the region, but with little effect. In 1180 an Augustinian monk called Meinhard led missionary work at Uxhull (modern Ikskile) on the River Dvina (now called the Daugava) and established himself as bishop.

▼ Prince Niklot, who fought against the crusade army in 1147, had renounced Christianity and reverted to paganism. He is an ancestor of the dukes of Mecklenburg, and is honoured with this statue in their castle at Schwerin, north-eastern Germany.

▲ The Livonian Brothers of the Sword fought in Finland in 1232 on the orders of Pope Gregory IX. After they merged with the Teutonic Knights in 1236, they still had their own Master. He was subject to the Grand Master of the Teutonic Knights.

After Meinhard's successor, Berthold, reported that the mission to Livonia was close to failure, Pope Celestine III called a crusade in the area. A Saxon crusading army led by Berthold won a battle against the Livonians in 1198, but Berthold was killed. Subsequently the crusaders went home and the missionary monks had to abandon their work after the Livonians issued death threats against them.

In 1199 the Archbishop Hartwig of Bremen appointed his nephew Albert of Buxhoeveden as Bishop of Livonia, with instructions to conquer the region and impose Christianity on its people. Albert embarked on a tour to preach a crusade in Livonia, and Pope Innocent III issued a papal bull guaranteeing those who fought in Livonia the same crusading privileges as knights and men-at-arms fighting in the Holy Land. At the bishop's request, Innocent also dedicated the Baltic region to the Virgin Mary, in order to encourage recruits to the cause, and the area is still sometimes known as 'Mary's Land'.

In 1200 Albert landed at the mouth of the River Dvina with a crusade army of around 1,500 men aboard a fleet of 23 vessels. In the next year he abandoned his mission station at Uxhull and founded the trading settlement of Riga at the mouth of the river. Previous efforts at conquest had foundered when temporary crusading armies disbanded, so in 1202 he founded the military order of the Livonian Brothers of the Sword to ensure a continuous military presence. (Albert founded the Cathedral of Riga in 1215; he was later named a Prince of the Holy Roman Empire, with Livonia as his fief, and was known as a 'Prince-Bishop'.) The Livonian Brothers of the Sword suffered a heavy defeat at the hands of a Livonian army in 1236 and the order's few survivors joined the Teutonic Knights.

For more than 25 years, until his death in 1229, Albert was engaged in the conquest of Livonia. He converted some of the locals – for example the Livs accepted Christianity when Bishop Albert guaranteed them military protection against incursion by rival Lithuanians and Estonian tribes; he also achieved the conversion of some Latvians. Otherwise he achieved his goals by military means. By c.1230 the conquest and conversion of Livonia was complete.

▼ The seal of the Livonian Brothers of the Sword. They were called Fratres militiae Christi Livoniae in Latin.

IN PRUSSIA AND LITHUANIA

EUROPEAN CRUSADES OF THE TEUTONIC KNIGHTS

Over a period of 50 years of brutal campaigning from *c*.1230 onwards, the military brotherhood of the Teutonic Knights imposed Christianity on the pagan peoples of Prussia. The Teutonic Knights, who had been founded in the Holy Land but were seeking to establish themselves in central Europe, entered Prussia under an agreement that allowed them to keep their initial landholding and all that they conquered. As a result they built up a substantial territory, which they ruled as a sovereign monastic state, answerable only to the Holy Roman Emperor and the papacy. In the 14th century, having conquered Prussia, they led a series of campaigns against Lithuania. These campaigns attracted knights from France and England to test their chivalric attributes in battle.

In 1209 Christian, a Cistercian monk from the monastery of Oliva (modern Oliwa, part of Gdasnk in northern Poland)

▼ *Grand Master of the Teutonic Knights. The brotherhood needed shrewd leadership as it attempted to find a new role and a new base in Europe in the 1200s.*

HENRY BOLINGBROKE'S CRUSADE

In 1390, after taking part in the celebrated Jousts of St Ingelvert near Calais, Henry intended to lead a small army of around 120 men on a crusade against Muslims in Tunisia, but because he was not granted safe conduct through France he joined the Teutonic Knights on a *reysen* against the Lithuanians. With 32 knights and squires he sailed to Danzig (now northern Poland), arriving on 10 August and joining the knights' march up the River Niemen. He took part in the siege of Vilnius from 4 September and after its failure returned to the Teutonic Knights' headquarters at Marienburg (now Malbork in Poland), where he remained for the winter, enjoying the feasting, hunting and other

▲ *Henry Bolingbroke (right) accompanies King Richard II as he enters London.*

chivalric entertainments. He departed at the end of March 1391. We know from royal records that the expedition cost him no less than £4,360.

---

was appointed by Pope Innocent III to lead missions in Prussia. He was named the first Bishop of Prussia in 1212. The mission came under repeated attacks from pagan Prussians and in 1217 Pope Honorius III (r.1216–27) called a crusade in the region.

The Prussians launched another major attack in 1218, in the course of which they sacked no fewer than 300 churches and cathedrals. A crusade army gathered in Masovia (now eastern Poland) from 1219 onwards and engaged the enemy without fighting a major campaign; the bishopric of Prussia was given a number of territories by Christian lords, meanwhile, in the area of Chelmno Land (now central Poland). The Prussians launched another devastating attack on Chelmno Land and Masovia in 1223.

Bishop Christian and Duke Konrad I of Masovia decided to establish an intimidating and permanent military presence to deter further Prussian raids. In 1225–28, on the border between Masovia

and Prussia (modern Dobrzyn Land in Poland), Christian established the Order of Dobrzyn, also known as the *Fratres Milites Christi de Prussia* or 'the Prussian Cavaliers of Christ Jesus'. At around the same time, Konrad invited the Teutonic Knights to help defend his borders against the Prussian raiders.

TEUTONIC KNIGHTS

The Teutonic Knights had been founded in 1192 as a monastic brotherhood in charge of a German hospital in Acre and then become a military brotherhood in Outremer in 1198. At the start of the 13th century they had established a presence in eastern Europe, entering the service of King Andrew II of Hungary in 1211, but after a disagreement Andrew had expelled the brothers from the territory he had granted them in Burzenland, Transylvania.

When Duke Konrad invited the Teutonic Knights to Masovia, the brotherhood was still heavily committed in Outremer: the first contingent of Teutonic

Knights despatched to Masovia numbered just seven knights and around 100 squires and sergeants. From an initial base at Vogelsang, south of the River Vistula, they concentrated on establishing timber fortresses along the line of the river. Reinforcements, numbering around 20 knights and 200 sergeants, arrived at Vogelsang in *c*.1230. They campaigned only when German and Polish crusaders arrived to swell their numbers. By 1232 the Knights and crusaders had defeated the Prussians in Chelmno Land.

Pope Gregory IX (ruled 1227–41) called for crusaders to back the Teutonic Knights in their struggle and a crusade army of 10,000 men gathered in the summer of 1233. In 1233–34 they won significant territorial gains, consolidated with fortresses at Marienwerder (now Kwidzyn in northern Poland) and Rehden (modern Radzyn Chelminski).

On these foundations the Teutonic Knights built a great edifice. In the course of many long and bloody campaigns over no less than 50 years they gradually defeated the Prussians. There were several Prussian uprisings: in 1242, most seriously in 1260–74, and again in 1286 and in 1295, but by the end of the 13th century the Knights had imposed their authority completely on Prussia.

ASSIMILATING OTHER ORDERS

The Order of Dobrzyn did not have a long or glorious existence. The initial membership was just 15 knights, and at its largest the order had only 35 knights. In *c*.1235 most of the knights joined the Teutonic Order. In the following year, 1236, the Livonian Brothers of the Sword, the brotherhood established by Albert of Buxhoeveden in 1202, was comprehensively defeated by an army of pagan Samogitians at the Battle of Saule and was also assimilated by the Teutonic Knights.

MONASTIC STATE

The Teutonic Knights had moved to Prussia on the understanding that they would be given a base in Chelmno Land

as a permanent territory of their own and would be allowed to keep any land they conquered. This agreement was not recognized by Duke Konrad or Bishop Christian, but was guaranteed by Holy Roman Emperor Frederick II in the 'Golden Bull of Rimini' of 1226 and by Pope Gregory IX in the 'Golden Bull of Rieti' of 1234. The Knights governed the territory they carved out for themselves in Prussia as a 'monastic state'. They were subject only to the Holy Roman Emperor and the papacy.

14TH-CENTURY CRUSADES

Throughout the 14th century the Teutonic Knights led a series of crusading campaigns against the pagan Lithuanians. Following the fall of Acre in 1291 to the Mamluks, the great knights of Europe had no outlet in the Holy Land for their crusading ambitions and they saw the Teutonic Knights' annual manoeuvres in Lithuania as an opportunity to prove their martial prowess, have a taste of crusading glory – and perhaps relive some of the storied exploits of past knights of the cross.

The Teutonic Knights ran their campaigns like adventure holidays, laying on feasts, courtly hunting expeditions and prizes. Knights came from all over Europe – especially from England and France – to take part; in Chaucer's *The Canterbury Tales* his Knight takes part in one of the Teutonic adventures. The campaigns were called *reysen* (voyages): those who took

▲ *The Teutonic Knights built a vast castle as their new headquarters at Marienburg (Mary's Castle) in Prussia in 1309.*

part had to cross a 100 mile (160km) wide area of swampland and forest, which they called 'the wilderness' before engaging the enemy.

It was in the interests of all involved in the *reysen* to maintain the pretence that these annual chivalric adventures were genuine crusades, fought to bring the Christian faith to an obdurately pagan people. The campaigns became so popular that they continued even after the Lithuanians were converted to Christianity in 1386. For all that fantasy played its part, the military element, it must be stressed, was real enough – the fighting when it came was as brutal as in any war, and prisoners taken were treated with contempt since they were pagan.

Among the many great names connected to the *reysen* were French knight Jean Le Meingre, Marshal of France and known as 'Boucicaut', who fought on three campaigns in Lithuania as a young man, and King Henry IV of England, who in his youth (while Henry Bolingbroke, Earl of Derby) took part in a campaign of 1390 that culminated in the siege of the Lithuanian capital, Vilnius. He subsequently looked back with great pleasure on the experience; he was still talking of the Teutonic Knights with warmth and affection some 17 years later, in 1407.

CRUSADES AGAINST THE HUSSITES
BOHEMIA UNDER ATTACK

◄ Hus defends his beliefs at the Council of Constance. His execution fanned discontent in Bohemia and led to the Hussite Revolt.

Five crusades were launched against the Hussites in Bohemia in 1420–32. Followers of a university lecturer and preacher, Jan Hus, who had been burned at the stake for heresy in 1415, the Hussites were inspired by the beginnings of Czech nationalist feeling and challenged the rule of King Sigismund of Hungary in their homeland. None of the crusades achieved its goal and Sigismund was forced to agree a compromise in 1436.

HUS

Jan Hus was Dean of the philosophical faculty at Prague University from 1401 and a supporter of reform of the Roman Catholic Church in Bohemia. He established himself as a popular preacher through his sermons in Czech (rather than Latin) at the Bethlehem Chapel in Prague and was a leader of a national reform movement. He was excommunicated by Pope Alexander V (ruled 1409–10) in 1409 after refusing to accept a papal ban on preaching in private chapels. He was called to the Council of Constance in 1415

and promised safe conduct, but while he was there he was condemned as a heretic and burned at the stake.

His execution sparked protests in Bohemia, where Bohemian knights and nobility made a formal protest, the *protestatio Bohemorum*, and offered support and protection to people persecuted for their religious faith. When King Wenceslaus IV of Bohemia died in 1419, his half-brother King Sigismund of Hungary (later Holy Roman Emperor, 1433–37) claimed the throne. The Bohemian nobles rejected his claim, however, and installed their own government, starting the 'Hussite Revolt', which had the support of reforming clergy and townspeople as well as the nobility.

THE FIRST CRUSADE (1420)

In a bull of 17 March 1420 Pope Martin V (ruled 1417–31) called a crusade against the Hussites, to be led by Sigismund with the support of German princes. Sigismund marched an army swelled by crusaders from all over Europe towards Prague, and besieged the Hussites there at the end of

June, but without success. He had himself crowned king of Bohemia in the fortress of Hradcany Castle, but was defeated by the Hussites on 1 November near Pankrac. The Hussites gained control of most of Bohemia after Sigismund withdrew.

HUSSITE DEMANDS AND DIVISIONS

Following the siege of Prague in 1420, Hus's successor at the Bethlehem Chapel, Jakoubek of Stribo, drew up the Four Articles of Prague, which helped establish common ground for the Hussite movement. They called for: freedom in preaching; support for the doctrine of Ultraquism, which required that the faithful should be given both bread and wine in the communion service; the clergy to adopt a lifestyle of poverty; and mortal sins to be prohibited and punished.

▼ Jan Zizka, inspirational Hussite leader and a great general, commands the rebels in an attack on a small town in Bohemia.

► *Sigismund I of Hungary leads an army against the rebels during the Second Anti-Hussite Crusade, early in 1421. The venture ended in a heavy defeat for the crusaders at the Battle of Nemecky Brod.*

Almost from the beginning, however, the Hussites were split into two camps. Moderate Hussites were called 'Utraquists' from their support for the doctrine of Ultraquism; but there was a more radical wing, often known as 'Taborites' after the city of Tabor. Led by Jan Zizka, the Taborites believed the Millennium or New Age of Christ was at hand and called for a return to innocence and the establishment of a communist-style society in which servants and masters would be no more.

THE SECOND ANTI-HUSSITE CRUSADE (1421)

A German army arrived in Bohemia in August 1421 and besieged Zatec, but after a failed attempt to take the town retreated to avoid an approaching Hussite army. After Sigismund joined the crusaders at the end of the year, he seized the town of Kutna Hora, but on 6 January 1422 was utterly defeated by a Hussite army led by Jan Zizka at the Battle of Nemecky Brod.

THE THIRD CRUSADE FAILS

In 1422–23 there was civil war between the rival Hussite groups in Bohemia: on 27 April 1423 a Taborite army led by Jan Zizka defeated the Utraquist forces at the Battle of Horic. A third crusade had been called, meanwhile, and an army gathered, but it came to nothing amid dissension, and the force dispersed without even attempting to invade Bohemia.

Zizka won further victories over the Utraquists in 1423–24, but died of the plague on 11 October 1424 as he was preparing an invasion of Moravia. Chronicle accounts report that his last wish was for his skin to be made into drums, so that he could continue to lead his men into battle. His soldiers were so distraught at his passing that from that time they called themselves 'the Orphans'.

THE FOURTH AND FIFTH CRUSADES (1427 AND 1431)

Under the leadership of Zizka's successor, Prokop the Great, the Hussite army conducted a series of military raids – which they called 'beautiful rides' – into neighbouring territories. Two further crusades in 1427 and 1431 came to nothing. On the first occasion a crusader army under Frederick, Margrave of Brandenburg, and Cardinal Henry Beaufort, Archbishop-elect of Trier, was defeated at Tachov. In this battle, the crusaders attempted to use the Hussite tactics of the Wagenburg, but were defeated. On the second crusade, a large crusader force entered Bohemia but fled before a Hussite army under Prokop.

PEACE AT LAST

Internal Hussite conflicts were brought to an end at the Battle of Lipany (or Cesky Brod) on 30 May 1434 when the Taborite army under Prokop the Great was roundly defeated by an alliance of Utraquist nobles and Catholics (the 'Bohemian League'). Finally, with more moderate Hussites having won the day, a peace was agreed with Sigismund on 5 July 1436.

HUSSITE BATTLE TACTICS

A key to the Hussite success in battle was the use of *wagenburg* (war wagon) tactics. Horse-drawn war wagons were set in a defensive circle, and a ditch dug around the formation. Each wagon had a crew of 22 foot soldiers and bowmen: eight crossbowmen, two gunners, eight men armed with pikes and flails, two drivers and two shield carriers. In the first phase they used the wagons as a defensive barrier, from behind which they fired their small cannon and handguns; usually the enemy knights were drawn into an attack and the wagenburgers were able to cause carnage among them. The second stage was to burst out from behind the wagons and attack the enemy on the flanks with pikes while the gunners kept up the barrage of fire from behind the wagons.

► *Military historians see the wagenburg as the forerunner of the tank.*

CRUSADES IN ITALY

WARS IN THE PAPAL INTEREST

In the 12th–14th centuries a series of crusades were called against Christian princes and noblemen who had been declared enemies of the Catholic Church in Italy. Many of these enterprises were in fact thinly disguised attempts to enforce the interests of the papacy.

TERRITORIAL CONFLICTS

In the 12th century the popes established themselves as secular rulers of a strip of territory across the middle of what is now Italy – bound to the north by a collection of independent city-states in Tuscany and Lombardy, and to the south by the Kingdom of Sicily, which at this time included the southern part of the mainland as well as the island of Sicily. As early as the 1120s, crusading indulgences were offered to those fighting the opponents of the papacy, King Roger II of Sicily, for example, who had a crusade declared against him by Pope Honorius II.

▼ *Farinata degli Uberti, a 13th-century Ghibelline leader from Florence, fights the pro-papal Guelphs at the Battle of Serchio.*

In the 12th and 13th centuries, Italy was divided between the Guelphs (those who supported the papacy) and the Ghibellines (who supported the rule in Italy of the Holy Roman Emperors). The conflict between Holy Roman Empire and papacy in Italy went back to the investiture conflict between Holy Roman Emperor Henry IV (r.1084–1106) and Pope Gregory VII (ruled 1073–85) over control of church appointments. The names of the Guelphs and Ghibellines probably derived from rallying cries used at the Battle of Weinsberg (1140) between the house of Hohenstaufen, who called the name of a castle, 'Waiblingen!' (later Ghibelline) and the rival house of Welf, who shouted 'Welf!' (later Guelph), which had the support of the papacy.

MARKWARD OF ANWEILER

At the close of the 12th century Pope Innocent III (ruled 1198–1216) called a crusade against Markward of Anweiler, a former follower of Hohenstaufen emperors Frederick I 'Barbarossa' and Henry VI. Markward was appointed Margrave of

▲ *This coin was issued by the Ghibelline government of Genoa, northern Italy.*

Ancona and Count of Abruzzo by Henry; his service to the emperor in Italy brought him into territorial conflict with the papacy and he was excommunicated by both Celestine III and Innocent III.

Following Henry's death he entered the service of the emperor's brother, Philip of Swabia, by whom he was granted the lordship of Palermo in Sicily. In 1198 Henry VI's widow, Constance of Sicily, died, placing her son, the future Emperor Frederick II (r.1212–50), in the care of Pope Innocent III. Markward challenged the pope, however, and established himself as guardian of the heir and Regent of Sicily.

In 1199 Innocent declared a crusade against Markward, likening him to the greatest of defenders of Islam by calling him 'another Saladin' and claiming that Markward was working in alliance with Muslims resident in Sicily and attempting to undermine preparations for the Fourth Crusade, which had just been proclaimed. Knights who joined up to fight Markward were to receive the same indulgences as those who travelled to the Holy Land on crusade; Innocent declared that because Markward was attempting to hinder the crusade, fighting him was as crucial as actually going to Jerusalem.

▲ *Prominent Ghibelline Ezzelino III da Romano was* podestà *(magistrate and representative of the Holy Roman Emperor) in first Verona, then Vicenza, then Padua.*

When he had earlier excommunicated Markward, Innocent had placed him under anathema, cursed him and damned him to hell. For all that, however, and although he suggested that Markward was in league with Muslims, in calling the crusade Innocent did not accuse Markward of being a heretic, and so the cause of the war remained transparently political rather than religious; many historians identify it as the first purely political crusade. The crusade itself did not really come to anything, although an army under Walter of Palear, Chancellor of Sicily, fought against Markward in 1202 as a result of Innocent's call to arms.

CRUSADE OF CHARLES OF ANJOU

For the next 70-odd years, the papacy preached a series of crusades in Italy, most aimed at countering the power of Emperor Fredrick II and his Hohenstaufen descendants in Sicily. Most notable was the holy war waged in Sicily in 1265 by Charles of Anjou, brother of King Louis IX of France.

Following Frederick II's death in 1250 and the death of his heir Conrad in 1254, Frederick's illegitimate son Manfred

(Conrad's brother) had seized power in Sicily and declared himself regent, then entered an alliance with the Saracens to defeat a papal army at Foggia. Pope Alexander IV (ruled 1254–61) excommunicated Manfred, and his successor, Urban IV (ruled 1261–64), offered the crown of Sicily to Charles of Anjou.

Urban's successor, Clement IV (ruled 1265–68), had Charles declared King of Sicily in Rome in May 1265. Charles led his army on campaign and defeated and killed Manfred at the Battle of Benevento on 26 February 1266 to become King of Sicily in fact as well as in name.

WARS OF THE SICILIAN VESPERS

Charles was driven out of Sicily in 1282 and the people allied themselves with the royal house of Aragon. Almost 20 years of fighting followed, known as the Wars of the Sicilian Vespers (1283–1302), and in this period the papacy called a series of crusades in an attempt to restore the rule of Charles and his Angevin descendants. (Charles's descendants were known as the Second Angevin Dynasty, since the first was that otherwise known as the House of Plantagenet, established in England by King Henry II in 1154.) None of these crusades succeeded and, in 1302, the

Treaty of Caltabellotta divided the old Kingdom of Sicily into a mainland portion, to be ruled by the Angevins (and subsequently known to historians as the Kingdom of Naples), and the island of Sicily itself, to be ruled by Aragon.

CRUSADES OF AN EXILED PAPACY

In 1305, the papacy established itself in France, first at Poitiers and then from 1309 at Avignon. Through the period of the papacy's French exile (until 1378), various popes in exile declared crusades against the Ghibellines in Italy. Crusades were launched against the Ghibelline Visconti lords of Florence, for example, in the 1320s and 1360s. But none of these crusading initiatives succeeded in defeating the Ghibellines.

During the ensuing Great Papal Schism of 1378–1417, when there were rival popes in Rome and Avignon, the two sides used crusades against one another with no success. After this date, the holy war as an instrument of papal policy was little seen, found only occasionally in the 16th century under popes such as Julius II.

▼ *War of the Sicilian Vespers. The people of Sicily rise up against Charles I and his French followers on the island in 1282.*

PART FOUR

THE GLORY OF CHIVALRY

The Christian Church and the brotherhood of knights were the two main institutions of the Middle Ages. Christianity and the code of chivalry together moulded the motives and inspired the actions of the dominant figures of the era. Knights drew inspiration from portrayals of knighthood in the literature of chivalry – in heroic *chansons de geste*, poems of courtly love and prose and verse romances that told of knights' great deeds in war and love. The knights judged themselves and their own behaviour in terms of the ideals portrayed in poems and romances. At the same time, romance leaked into reality – chronicles of the age, biographies of knights and practical handbooks on chivalric behaviour were strongly influenced by fictional portrayals. Together the books of chivalric literature embodied a vision of how knights should and could behave. They amounted to nothing less than a mythology of knighthood.

▲ *The death of Roland, legendary knight of Charlemagne.*

▶ *King Arthur and the Knights of the Round Table, ideals of romantic notions of chivalry, depicted in the 15th-century French manuscript of* Le roman du roi Arthur et les Compagnons de la Table Ronde *(Book of King Arthur and the Knights of the Round Table) by Chrétien de Troyes.*

TIMELINE OF CHIVALRY

938 King Henry I of Germany reputedly holds glamorous tournaments in Magdeburg. However, this is according to a possibly unreliable account in the 16th-century *Book of Tournaments* (c.1530).

c.975 Mock battles fought by Frankish cavalrymen across open countryside in northern France are a forerunner of the chivalric tournament.

1062 Norman knights are said to take part in a tournament fight during a siege in Sicily, according to chronicler Geoffrey of Malaterra.

1066 Another later chronicle claims that Frankish nobleman Geoffrey de Preilly invented the tournament in this year.

1095 According to a 12th-century church history, Count Henry III of Brabant is killed in a tournament between his warriors and those of Tournai in 1095.

1095–99 On the First Crusade, Frankish knights train between battles by 'tilting at the quintain' (riding towards a target with a couched lance).

1095–1291 In the period of the Crusades, the crusading knight embodies the ideal of religious chivalry. He is seen as a warrior in Christ's service.

1114 A law issued by Count Baldwin III of Hainaut contains the first known use of the word 'tournament' to mean martial competition.

c.1125 In early tournaments jousting was less common than the mêlée, a pitched battle fought between two teams of knights in an enclosure.

1127 Jousts are held during a siege of Würzburg in Germany.

1130 In banning tournaments, Pope Innocent III issues a declaration that says 'We firmly prohibit those detestable markets or fairs at which knights … show off their strength and boldness.'

January–February 1141 Knights engage in jousting during the siege of Lincoln Castle by King Stephen's forces.

1167–68 William Marshall and another

▲ *Sir Perceval, one of the legendary knights of King Arthur's round table, came to represent the embodiment of chivalry.*

unnamed knight show that tourneying can be profitable: in a ten-month partnership they capture 103 knights, together with their costly horses and equipment.

1170–91 In his Arthurian romances (entitled *Narratives of the Knights of the Round Table of Legendary British King Arthur*) French poet Chrétien de Troyes promotes holy innocence – as embodied by one of the knights, Sir Perceval – as a key chivalric quality.

1180–1207 In *The Epic Letter* Raimbaut de Vaqueiras, court poet at the court of Montferrat, praises Boniface of Montferrat (leader of the Fourth Crusade in 1202–04) for embodying key chivalric virtues including compassion and generosity as well as military prowess.

1186 Geoffrey Duke of Brittany, King Henry II of England's fourth son, is trampled to death at a tournament near Paris.

1194 King Richard I of England licenses tournaments in England in defiance of Pope Innocent's ban of 1130. Richard sees

tournaments as a training ground for knights, and wants to improve the martial skills of English knights.

1197 During a truce to halt fighting at Tours, the army of King Richard I holds a tournament.

c.1200 Another form of tournament is a pitched battle or contest of horsemanship known as a bohort.

1207 Peter II of Aragon hosts a tournament at Montpellier to honour his mistress. This is the first recorded instance of a tournament in honour of a lady, which later becomes common.

1219 Prior to his death in 1219 and in fulfilment of a vow he made while on crusade in 1183–86, English knight William Marshall – described as 'the greatest knight who ever lived' – is invested in the Knights Templar.

1240 German knight Ulrich von Lichtenstein takes part in a tournament at Neustadt: six knights from his Round Table fight against 17 attackers.

1241 Eighty knights die from suffocation fighting in heavy suits of armour at a tournament in very hot and dusty conditions at Neuss, Germany.

c.1250 The Bishop of Acre denounces tournaments, declaring that knights who take part in them commit all seven deadly sins – pride, envy, anger, greed, lust, sloth and avarice.

c.1250–1284 King Alfonso X of Castile and Leon compiles *Cantigas de Santa Maria* ('Songs to the Virgin Mary'), a collection of 427 songs celebrating courtly and sacred love. Alfonso writes many of the songs himself. Other poets include Airas Nunez.

1258 Edward I fights in his first tournament, at Blyth. He wears padded armour.

1285 A lavish tournament at Chauvency, France, is described by the trouvère Jacques Bretel.

September 1293 King Edward I holds a tournament at Bristol to celebrate the wedding of his daughter, Eleanor, to Count Henri III of Bar.

c.1300 Jousting is commonly the main event in tournaments by this period. Some tournaments feature only jousting.

c.1300–c.1500 The knightly class share a more secular conception of chivalry, contrasting with the religious chivalry celebrated in the era of the crusades. Knights fight more in the service of kings and worldly leaders than in the cause of Christ and the Church.

February 1308 King Edward II of England holds a tournament as part of his coronation at Westminster.

1316 One hundred and eighty–six years after it was imposed by Pope Innocent III in 1130, the papal ban on tournaments is raised by Pope John XXII.

1332 The statutes of the Order of the Sash brotherhood of knights, created by King Alfonso XI of Castile and Leon in this year, declare truthfulness and loyalty to be the qualities essential to knightly behaviour.

1334 King Alfonso XI of Castile and Leon fights incognito in a tournament at Valladolid among the knights of his brotherhood of knights, the Order of the Sash, against a team of challengers.

1336 King Edward III of England successfully rescues Katherine, Countess of Atholl, from a besieged Highlands castle during a Scottish campaign; the very stuff of chivalry.

January 1344 King Edward III announces his intention to form the Most Noble Order of the Garter during a tournament and feast at Windsor. The order is established in 1348.

1344 Henry 3rd Earl of Lancaster founds a 'tournament society', whose knights commit to gather for jousting at Lincoln each Whit Monday.

1346 According to chronicler Jean Froissart, Edward III sees his teenage son Edward the Black Prince come under great pressure at the Battle of Crécy, and declares 'let the boy win his spurs'.

1347 Chronicle accounts describe how King Edward III chivalrously spares the lives of six leading citizens of the besieged town of Calais at the request of his lady, Queen Philippa.

1350 French royal official, poet and legal expert Philippe de Beaumanoir affirms a knight's right to use violence in a good cause, saying: 'A knight can wage war in line with tradition.'

c.1350 Under the rule of Holy Roman Emperor Charles IV a knight is entitled to wage war in pursuit of his own ends, provided he gives his enemy three days' notice of attack.

1353 According to chronicle accounts, half the knights of the French Order of the Star are killed in a single battle in Brittany; they had sworn never to retreat in battle.

1357 At Rennes the Breton knight Bertrand Du Guesclin fights a series of jousts against an English opponent during the siege of the town by an English army commanded by Henry of Grosmont, Duke of Lancaster.

1370 English knight Sir John Chandos, a great figure in English chivalry and a

▼ *Edward III established the Order of the Garter in 1344, here he confers the Black Prince at Windsor on 23 April 1349.*

lifelong follower of Edward the 'Black Prince', dies. According to Jean Froissart, Chandos was 'the most courteous and gentle knight alive'. Chandos was celebrated also for his moderation and self-control.

1370 John of Gaunt, duke of Lancaster, jousts against French knight Jean de Villemur in tunnels dug beneath the city walls during the siege of Limoges.

c.1375 Lavish themed tournaments known as *pas d'armes* ('passages of arms') are held in this period by leading royals and nobles.

1390 Scottish knight Sir David Lindsay of Glenesk defeats Lord de Welles, England's ambassador to Scotland, in a trial of strength on London Bridge. He spares his defeated opponent and visits him daily through a long convalescence. Sir David's conduct is praised as exemplary.

1391 Sir William Neville and Sir John Clanvowe, both Knights of the Garter, die and are buried alongside each another in 1391 near Constantinople. They epitomize the 'brotherhood of arms' between a pair of knights.

1398 Seven French knights issue an open 'challenge to arms' to any seven English knights, open for three years, for a fight with lance, sword, axe then dagger.

1421 Two squires in King Henry V's army, Nicolas Molyneux and John Winter, swear to become brothers in arms in the Church of St Martin at Harfleur: each is liable to find the first £1,000 if the other needs to be ransomed.

1430 Duke Philip the Good of Burgundy holds a banquet and six-day tournament in Bruges to mark his marriage to Isabella, daughter of King John I of Portugal.

1466 Sir John Tiptoft's *Ordinances* provides details of rules for scoring at a tournament. The highest score is given for knocking your opponent's horse down with him.

1468 Duke Charles the Bold of Burgundy hosts a lavish 14-day tournament at Bruges to mark his third marriage, to Princess Margaret of York. Its theme is 'Florimont: the Knight of the Golden Tree'.

CHAPTER SIXTEEN

THE GOLDEN AGE OF THE CHIVALRIC KNIGHT

In the 14th century, Jean Froissart wrote in the preamble to his *Chronicles* that he intended to record 'the honourable adventures, noble enterprises and feats of arms' achieved in the long wars of his era between England and France. He wanted to do this, he wrote, in order that the deeds should be 'held in perpetual remembrance' and act as an example and encouragement to fearless men. These wars were hard-fought, often in a quite unchivalric manner, with brutal raiding campaigns that used 'scorched earth' tactics, and frequent incidences of murder, theft and rape during the sacking of towns. Yet Froissart saw 'noble enterprises' because he viewed them through the lens of chivalry.

By the time Froissart was writing, the code of chivalry had been established for 300 years as a guide to the behaviour of knights, inspiring them to exhibit qualities of loyalty, bravery, courtesy, generosity and humility in both war and peace. The code emerged in the late 11th century and endured as a powerful ideal and ethic for many centuries. That this code was often at odds with the way knights behaved does not diminish its importance: it coloured and influenced all aspects of knights' lives, determining their self-image and aspirations, rather as religious faith affects a person's life even if he or she does not always live up to its codes of behaviour.

▲ *The return of King John II of France to London in 1362.*

◀ *Jean Froissart presents a copy of his* Chronicles *to the duchess of Burgundy. He saw noble knights performing acts of chivalry where a viewer with a different perspective might have seen battle-hardened warriors often driven by necessity to act cruelly.*

A KNIGHT LOYAL AND BRAVE

LOYALTY, COURAGE, PROWESS AND HONOUR

On the field of battle, in tournaments and on the quests described in chivalric literature, a knight welcomed the difficulties that he often encountered as opportunities to prove his courage. He knew that he should always act out of loyalty and be true to his lord, his faith and his lady. Bravery and loyalty were key virtues of the chivalric code.

COURAGE AND LOYALTY

In *The Book of the Order of Chivalry* (*c.*1265) Ramon Llull described courage as the knight's primary virtue, and promoted loyalty as one of the ways in which he could prove his bravery. The 13th-century German knight Wolfram von Eschenbach, author of the poem *Parzifal*, a masterpiece among medieval romances, put the main emphasis on loyalty among chivalric virtues. In *Parzifal* Sir Perceval, one of the knights of King Arthur's Round Table, learned through many adventures

and on the quest for the Holy Grail the key importance of loyal faithfulness – in love, to God and Christianity and to his fellow knights. In the vision of *Parzifal*, the essential chivalric virtue of loyalty guided the knight in love, in religion and in the secular world of service as a knight.

The statutes of the Castilian chivalric brotherhood, the Order of the Sash – which was established in 1332 in Vittoria, Castile, by King Alfonso XI of Castile and León (r. 1312–50) – had a similar interpretation of chivalry. The order declared that 'of all in the world the qualities most appertaining to a knight are truthfulness and loyalty'.

PROWESS

A knight needed prowess to exhibit his bravery to its fullest extent: prowess meant skill in arms, and to an extent this depended upon natural ability of the kind possessed in abundance by great knights

such as William Marshal, Jacques de Lalaing or the Black Prince. To a lesser extent, however, prowess could be developed through practice, and knights were expected to work at their horsemanship and weapon-handling.

THE EXPRESSION OF CHIVALRY

In the medieval period, there were three principal arenas in which knights could exhibit the qualities of this ideal. In the different arenas the knight might express key chivalric qualities in different ways.

The first was the knight's life as a feudal warrior – his loyalty was to his lord, and he would exhibit courage in his lord's service in battle. The second arena was the knight's life as a religious warrior – his

▼ *It was natural that kings such as King Alfonso XI of Castile and León (1311–50), founder of the Order of the Sash, should emphasize loyalty among chivalric virtues.*

loyalty was to Christ, and he would be expected to show bravery in fighting against Saracens and other infidels, and in protecting the Church, pilgrims, women and children. The third arena was the knight's life as a noble lover, within the context of the conventions of courtly love – his loyalty was to his lady, and he would demonstrate his bravery in showing obedience to her and striving to win her favour on quests and in tournaments.

THE MEANINGS OF CHIVALRY

The word chivalry appeared in a wide variety of documents from the 11th to the 15th centuries, with various meanings. At times the word was used as a collective noun to refer to a group of medieval knights armed for battle, and as an alternative term for 'knighthood' – a label for the position of being a knight. In a romance, or chanson, chivalry might mean knightly action performed in battle. Beginning in the late 11th century, the idea of a code of chivalry developed as a guide to knightly behaviour. Chivalry began occasionally to be used to refer to the actions and life of an ideal knight. Finally, it came to have its modern meaning, as an aspect of this type of behaviour – a kind of gallantry and honourable conduct.

▲ *Before Wolfram von Eschenbach's Parzival, an earlier poem about Sir Perceval (written by Chrétien de Troyes in c.1181–91) emphasized his holy innocence. The story has similarities with a Welsh tale in which an innocent, raised like Perceval in the forest, rides out to learn about chivalry.*

▼ *One of the knights most revered as the epitome of chivalric virtues was Sir Galahad of King Arthur's court.*

There were distinct periods within the history of chivalry. The ideal of religious chivalry was at its height from the late 11th to the 13th century – the period of the Crusades. The crusader was in theory the perfect incarnation of chivalry, who used his weapons not in political struggles between princes or barons, nor in search of glory at tournaments, but in the service of Christ and his Church. This period of religious chivalry was followed by one of secular chivalry, the time of the struggles of the Hundred Years War in the 14th and 15th centuries, when the ideal of the crusading knight was in decline and knights fought principally for king and country. Before the end of the first period, courtly love began to rival religious ardour as the

inspiring ideal for many knights. A further development was that of courtly chivalry: secular chivalric brotherhoods such as the Order of the Garter and the Order of the Star were founded in the 14th and 15th centuries, when knights were courtiers who took vows of service not to God or the brotherhood of knights but to their monarch, and distinctions of rank began to appear among them.

CRUSADER KING

KING EDWARD I OF ENGLAND

A great knight from his youth, Edward took part in the Ninth Crusade (1271–72) while still a prince and was hailed by contemporary chroniclers as the new Richard Coeur de Lion. After he became King Edward I of England, he directed his military attentions particularly against his country's neighbours in Wales and Scotland, and following his death in 1307 his marble tomb in Westminster Abbey was marked with the tribute *Edwardus Primus, Scottorum Malleus* ('Edward I, Hammer of the Scots'). This inscription was probably added in the 16th century, by which time the king's status as a great exemplar of English chivalry was well established – he was the subject of a play *The Famous Chronicle of King Edward the First* by 16th-century dramatist George Peele.

KNIGHTING AND FIRST EXPLOITS

Edward was knighted at the age of 15 by King Alfonso X of Castile, prior to his marriage to Alfonso's 13-year-old daughter Eleanor on 1 November 1254. He first proved himself in battle aged 20 fighting in his father's campaigns against Welsh

---

KING EDWARD I OF ENGLAND
Born: 17 June 1239
Died: 7 July 1307
Knighted: 1254
Famous for: conqueror of Wales and persistent enemy to the Scots
Greatest achievement: the subjugation of Wales

---

prince Llywelyn ap Gruffydd in 1259, and in 1265 exhibited sound strategic sense in isolating the small army of the rebel knight Simon de Montfort in order to defeat him at the Battle of Evesham in Worcestershire.

CRUSADER KNIGHT

In 1268 he travelled with around 130 knights to take part in the Eighth Crusade alongside King Louis IX of France. The crusade was called to relieve the Christian-held port of Acre, the capital of what remained of the Kingdom of Jerusalem, but was diverted to Tunis in Africa; Louis died of disease before Edward even arrived and the crusade came to nothing.

However, Edward pressed on to Acre in a campaign that became known as the Ninth Crusade. He succeeded in lifting the siege of Tripoli and survived an assassination attempt during negotiations for a truce. He was preparing to abandon negotiations and launch an attack on Jerusalem when the news arrived that his father Henry III had died; the treaty was swiftly signed so that he could depart for England to be crowned King Edward I.

WARS IN WALES AND SCOTLAND

Edward proved himself a great general and strategist in wars against the Welsh. In 1276–77 he crushed Welsh resistance raised by Llywelyn ap Gruffydd and again in 1282–83 defeated Llywelyn's brother Dafydd. He raised ten castles to enforce English control of Wales, including those

at Beaumaris, Caernarfon and Harlech. In 1284 Wales became part of England under the Statute of Rhuddlan.

In relations with Scotland he was equally forceful, storming Berwick in 1296 in an attack that killed almost the entire population, and then defeating a Scottish army at Dunbar before taking the Scottish coronation stone, the Stone of Scone, to London. He forced the abdication of King John Balliol, and stripped him of his finery and crown in a humiliating ceremony.

He was determined to conquer Scotland and bring it into England but Scottish resistance could not be broken as the Welsh had been, and Edward had to fight several other campaigns on and beyond his northern borders, including in 1298 when he defeated Scottish freedom fighter Sir William Wallace at the Battle of Falkirk; indeed, when Edward died from the effects of dysentery in 1307 he was near Carlisle on his way north to combat the Scots once more. It would appear that he was sorely troubled by the unfinished business of the conquest of Scotland, for according to the chroniclers, he wanted to have his bones carried on campaign in

▼ *Edward was crowned on 19 August 1274 in Westminster Abbey.*

▼ *King Edward's crusading partner, King Louis IX of France, died in 1270.*

▲ *Kings of Edward's era were expected to demonstrate piety. Edward complied.*

Scotland, and was buried in a lead casket, asking to be moved to the gold casket of the kind reserved for kings only when Scotland was finally conquered.

EDWARD AND CHIVALRY

Physically Edward was extremely imposing: he stood 6ft 2in (1.9m) tall, which was a remarkable height in the 13th century, and had thick curly hair, which was blond in youth. He was nicknamed 'Longshanks'. He may have been lacking in some aspects of military chivalry. He was merciless in his treatment of defeated enemies: Simon de Montfort in 1265, Prince Dafydd of Gwynedd in 1283 and Sir William Wallace in 1305 were horribly mutilated in death. But in other ways his life was a model of chivalry.

He was certainly possessed of knightly prowess and was fond of chivalric pastimes, notably hunting and hawking. According to tradition, he had three favourite horses: a war horse named Lyard; a hunting horse named Ferrault; and his favourite, named Bayard after the great horse of Renaud de Montauban.

He was a very keen tourneyer from his teenage years on, and was deeply interested in Arthurian tradition. He was responsible for the reburying of what were believed to be the bodies of Arthur and Guinevere, found at Glastonbury and reinterred in the abbey there in 1278; he held an Arthurian 'Round Table' at Nefyn in Wales in 1284, to celebrate the conquest of Wales, and resided over several others at Kenilworth in 1279, Warwick in 1281 and Falkirk in 1302.

He also exhibited religious devotion, most notably in founding Vale Royal Abbey in 1277 in Cheshire, allegedly in honour of a vow he made to build an abbey for the Cistercian monks after he was saved from shipwreck during a Channel crossing in 1263–64. He supposedly brought back from the Ninth Crusade a piece of the cross on which Christ was crucified, and gave it to the monks. He was as devoted to his lady as

▲ *Edward was married in a Castilian convent to Eleanor of Castile in 1254.*

any knight could be, particularly to his first wife Eleanor of Castile, who travelled with him whenever she could, even on crusade. On her death in 1290 he built a magnificent series of 12 memorial crosses to mark the places at which her funeral cortège stopped on its route from her place of death in Nottinghamshire to her burial place in Westminster Abbey.

▼ *The construction of Beaumaris Castle was begun in 1295. It is the greatest of the castles built by Edward to consolidate his conquest of Wales.*

THE GENTLE QUALITIES OF A KNIGHT
COURTESY, GENEROSITY AND HUMILITY

In addition to courage, loyalty and prowess, other qualities were deemed to be proper in a knight. These included *largesse* or 'generosity', *mesure* or 'moderation', and *franchise* or 'noble bearing'.

There was never a definitive statement of the qualities of behaviour associated with the code of chivalry. Various authorities – some active knights, others religious commentators or philosophers, others, poets whose works praised acts of chivalry – put emphasis on different qualities according to the focus they brought to bear. Philosopher of chivalry Ramon Llull took care in *The Book of the Order of Chivalry* to stress the variety of ways in which a knight could give expression to his bravery. Llull warned against the showiness of display that was often an aspect of knightly behaviour. He wrote that a knight should not devote himself to fine speech, for this could be misleading;

▼ *Sir Lancelot – otherwise the embodiment of perfection in chivalry – stained his name when he embarked upon adulterous relations with Queen Guinevere. In this 15th-century illustration other knights see Lancelot creep out of the queen's bedroom.*

▲ *On his adventures Lancelot encountered many hermits and treated them with courtesy. From one he learned that the perfect knight Sir Galahad was his son.*

he should not believe that fine armour and splendid horse trappings were necessarily signs of true courage, for they could conceal cowardice. Courage, he wrote, was not guaranteed by fine equipment, but must be genuine and find expression in qualities such as 'faithfulness, hope, charitable love, a commitment to justice, physical strength, moderation and loyalty'.

THE QUALITIES OF LANCELOT
In Sir Thomas Malory's 15th-century masterpiece of chivalric literature, *Le Morte d'Arthur*, Sir Ector gave a moving lament for Sir Lancelot that provides an insight into the range of gentle virtues to which a medieval knight was expected to aspire. Sir Ector called Sir Lancelot the 'head of all Christian knights' and declared that he was 'the most courteous knight who ever carried a shield', 'the truest friend who ever rode a horse', the 'most honest lover that ever honoured a woman', the 'kindest warrior who ever fought with a sword', 'the goodliest person among the whole body of knights', the 'meekest man and the most gentle among knights gathered to dine in the company of ladies'.

In addition to all these gentle qualities, Sir Ector said, Sir Lancelot was also fierce in battle – 'the sternest knight who ever took up lance' when faced with his enemy. In Malory, Sir Lancelot was presented as the knight without equal, the epitome of chivalry, despite other parts of Arthurian literature undermining his greatness by his adulterous love for Guinevere.

LARGESSE
It was an important element of the code of chivalry that knights should give freely. Generosity, or *largesse*, was interpreted as demanding lavish, even sometimes reckless spending. This principally took the form of large payments to reward military followers and retainers for loyal service and deeds of arms – as we have seen, the Black Prince rewarded Sir John Chandos and Sir James Audley very generously after the Poitiers campaign of 1356. But a great lord could also demonstrate his nobility

of character and social standing by spending extravagantly on hospitality and entertainment. King John's son Richard, 1st Earl of Cornwall, reputedly had 30,000 separate dishes of meat at his wedding ceremony when he married Princess Sanchia, daughter of Ramon Berenguer IV, Count of Provence, in 1240. The great French knight, the Chevalier de Bayard (1473–1524) maintained his generosity, according to his biography, even when he did not have ten crowns himself.

MESURE AND FRANCHISE

The code also emphasized the counterbalancing virtue of *mesure* ('moderation'). English knight Sir John Chandos, negotiator of several truces in the Hundred Years War between England and France, was as well known for his diplomacy as he was for his abilities as a war captain. A key aspect of his sense of chivalry was *mesure*: he had the other key chivalric virtues such as bravery, loyalty and courtesy, but, according to Jean Froissart, moderation, self-control and a disciplined spirit were qualities that marked him out from other knights. Froissart noted approvingly that his strong sense of duty prevented him from indulging in 'acts of high romance'.

Knights were also expected to exhibit *franchise*, meaning 'noble bearing'. The word's roots were associated with freedom from servitude but the concept became associated with nobility. It began to be seen as part of the noble character of a knight and one of the reasons why young men had to be descended from chivalric families to be considered fit for the honour of being knighted.

VIRTUES OF A COURTLY KNIGHT

Boniface of Montferrat, leader of the Fourth Crusade and a great chivalric patron, was praised for his embodiment of the courtly virtues of generosity, elegance, honesty and compassion, as well as the martial ones of force, bravery and prowess. The *Epic Letter*, a poem by Boniface's friend and court poet, the Provençal troubadour Rambaut de Vaqueiras (1180–1207), gave a stirring account of the virtues, courtly as well as martial, that were thought to embody the highest expression of chivalry at Montferrat, which was one of the most celebrated knightly courts of the late 12th and early 13th centuries.

The *Epic Letter* praised Boniface's understanding of all aspects of courtly life, the elegance of the clothing, the beauty of the armour, the sophistication of games, the quality of the music and poetry and the richness of the table at the court of Montferrat. It also underlined Boniface's good judgement as a lord: it said that he never listened to slander from a dishonest man's lips, but always knew how to distinguish between good and evil, raising up the deserving and exiling the wicked.

▼ *Troubadours praised deeds of knights in love and war but often knew little of military life. This illustration of poet-singers is from the fine 13th-century Portuguese collection* Songs to the Virgin Mary, *which combines poems of sacred and courtly love.*

THE GENEROSITY OF A PATRON

Of great importance among Boniface's many chivalric virtues, the *Epic Letter* said, was generosity. Rambaut said his lord had always been generous at his table, and beyond that had shown compassion to those who were in need, helping widows and orphans. On a personal level, Boniface had raised the troubadour up from a 'nobody' to a 'highly valued knight, always welcome at court and worthy of the praises of ladies'.

For the poets who played a key part in formulating the code of chivalric conduct, generosity was of course an essential virtue in a patron. At Montferrat both Boniface and his sister Azalais, the Marchioness of Saluzzo, were noted patrons of courtly poetry and literature. In addition to the court poet Rambaut de Vaqueiras, they supported the poets Peire Vidal (a favourite of Raimon V of Toulouse), Gaucelm Faidit (author of a celebrated lament on the death of King Richard I of England), and Arnaut de Mareuil (who was another troubadour particularly associated with the court at Toulouse).

'THE MOST COURTEOUS KNIGHT ALIVE'

SIR JOHN CHANDOS

In the mid-14th century, English knight Sir John Chandos was revered for his sense of chivalry. Jean Froissart reported that at the height of Sir John's fame, in *c.*1350–70, he was the most courteous and gentle knight alive.

NORMAN DESCENT

Like many of his peers among the great knights of medieval Europe, Chandos had a long chivalric heritage: he was descended from the Norman knight Robert de Chandos, one of the close companions of King William I. Born in Derbyshire, John made his name at the very start of the Hundred Years War when he fought in single combat against a French squire at the siege of Cambrai in 1339, and attracted great renown. In the same year he was knighted, and given an annual annuity of 20 marks to support himself 'in the estate of knight'.

JOUSTER AND DIPLOMAT

In the 1340s Sir John established himself as a lively leading chivalric figure at the court of King Edward III. He won a great reputation fighting in the king's tournaments from 1344 onwards, and was a close associate of Edward Prince of Wales (later 'the Black Prince'). He was kept lavishly, receiving royal gifts of horses and jewellery and wearing the prince's livery. In August 1346 he fought alongside the prince in the English vanguard at the

▲ *In the Battle of Poitiers in 1356, Chandos was one of Edward the Black Prince's key advisors and fought alongside the prince.*

Battle of Crécy. In 1350 at the naval battle off Winchelsea he sang a ballad, on the king's orders, before fighting began – and the minstrels played a new German dance that Sir John had introduced at court. In 1348 he was a founder member of the Order of the Garter, although curiously he was one of the 12 companions on King Edward's side rather than the 12 on the Black Prince's side.

In 1356 during the campaign that culminated in English victory at the Battle of Poitiers, he and Sir John Audley had charge of scouting in the Black Prince's army. On this campaign Chandos first demonstrated the great diplomatic skills for which he was later renowned, negotiating a truce before the battle proper during which peace talks took place. He then fought bravely at Poitiers and was richly rewarded by his royal master with the grant of two English manors, together with an annual sum of £40, in addition to a one-off payment of 600 crowns.

Sir John again led negotiations with the French in 1357 and 1359. In 1360 he won the admiration of the great French

knight Bertrand du Guesclin when he negotiated the release of du Guesclin's brother Olivier, who had been captured by the English during a period of truce.

DEFEAT OF DU GUESCLIN

Sir John oversaw the establishment of English rule in the duchy of Aquitaine in 1361–63. In 1364 he supported John de Montfort, Duke of Brittany and a supporter of English rule, in the Breton War of Succession against Charles, Duke of Blois. At the Battle of Auray in September that year, Chandos helped defeat the French and captured Bertrand du Guesclin. The bulk of the very large ransom of 40,000 gold francs set for the French knight came to Sir John, establishing him as a wealthy man once and for all. He served King Edward III as lieutenant in France and constable of Aquitaine, and was made viscount of Saint-Sauveur-le-Vicomte in Normandy.

SIR JOHN CHANDOS

Born: unknown

Died: 1 January 1370

Knighted: 1339

Famous for: his diplomacy and chivalric *mesure* (moderation)

Greatest achievement: capture of French knight Bertrand du Guesclin at the Battle of Auray, 1364

CHANDOS'S HERALD

Sir John Chandos's herald wrote a life of Edward, the Black Prince, which is greatly valued by historians as a source for the events of the period. It describes the Hundred Years War and the civil war in Castile, during which Chandos and the prince helped to reinstate King Pedro. After Sir John's death his herald became king-of-arms in the service of King Richard II.

▶ *King Richard II, seen here with his father, Edward, the Black Prince, both dressed in heraldic robes.*

THE PASS OF RONCESVALLES

In 1366 Sir John served alongside the Black Prince in his campaign in Spain to reinstate King Pedro on the throne of Castile, after the king had been driven out by his illegitimate brother Henry of Trastamera. En route Sir John (as constable of the army) followed in the footsteps of Charlemagne in leading the vanguard of the force through the Pass of Roncesvalles in the Pyrenees, the scene of the events so beautifully described in the *Song of Roland*. At the Battle of Najera in April 1367, Chandos and the Black Prince defeated Henry and once again took Bertrand du Guesclin captive. This was the occasion, described in Chapter Four, when the Black Prince allowed du Guesclin to name his own vastly inflated ransom – and received no less than 100,000 francs as a result.

DEATH IN THE WINTER ICE

Back in France, Sir John apparently quarrelled with the Black Prince and retired to his estate at Saint-Sauveur-le-Vicomte. He was fatally injured in a skirmish on New Year's Eve 1369 at Lussac-les-Châteaux near Poitiers. Froissart's account gives colourful details: Sir John gallantly led an attack against the French, but slipped on his surcoat and fell on the frozen ground; before he could recover he was stabbed in the face by a French squire – he could not see the blow coming because he was blind in one eye from an old wound. He died the next day, 1 January 1370.

According to Froissart, French knights mourned Sir John's passing because they believed he might have been capable of establishing peace between France and England; Sir Thomas Walsingham reported that King Charles V of France commented that Chandos's death meant there was 'no knight left capable of bringing peace between France and England'.

▼ *In 1369 Sir John Chandos and Sir Robert Knowles successfully besieged Domme, a bastide (fortified town) founded by King Philip III 'the Bold' of France in the Dordogne in 1283.*

A CHRISTIAN WARRIOR

FAITH, HUMILITY AND HONOUR

True knights were inspired by a strong Christian faith, exhibited through great deeds in fighting for the Church. They were expected also to cultivate Christian virtues such as humility and truthfulness.

FAITH

The ideal knight channelled his martial skills into the service of Christ, and the crusader fighting for the cross was regarded as the embodiment of this ideal. In this context religious faith could be manifested in bloodthirsty violence, if it were directed against the Saracen enemy, as in the case of Charlemagne's knights in the *Song of Roland*, or Richard Coeur de Lion, who was celebrated in the romance of his life for the relish with which he killed Saracens, even eating their flesh as a sign of his enthusiasm.

PURITY AND PRACTICALITY

The chivalric code also celebrated purity of life and mind, most notably in the figures of Sir Perceval and Sir Galahad in the Arthurian tales, who were presented in some versions as sexual innocents and

travellers on a mystical path of self-denial. But these qualities had to be balanced by martial energy and strength in conflict.

The practicalities of life as a knight, even in a religious brotherhood, were emphasized in a sermon by 13th-century French theologian Jacques de Vitry to the Knights Templars. He spoke of a brother knight who paid a great deal of attention to self-denial and private devotions, but whose performance in battle suffered as a result: characterized as 'Lord Bread and Water', this knight was so weak after his self-denial in the refectory that he was defeated by the first blow of the lance he received from his Saracen enemy, and had to be rescued by a fellow Templar; put back in the saddle, he rode back into battle and was knocked down again at

◀ *The cross, once a symbol of Christ's love, became the sign under which Christian wars were waged. 'Taking the cross' came to mean swearing an oath to go on crusade.*

▲ *According to the Arthurian romances, the pure Sir Galahad was the first knight to carry the white shield with a red cross, later used by the Knights Templar.*

the first Saracen blow. The same knight rescued him a second time, and told him to eat more heartily in future, for he was not about to rescue him a third time. The sermon commented: 'You ought not to put God to the test, but do what you are capable of, following behind as Heaven leads the way, and then you can safely go to your death for Christ's sake.'

HONOUR

The ideal quality of honour was central to chivalry as a focus for a knight's actions. Maintaining honour was a knight's main goal: to do so he had to win renown and behave always in line with the rules of good conduct. If a knight swore on his word of honour to do a deed there was no going back – it was his most solemn and

▲ *The Battle of Pavia in 1525 was a crushing defeat for French King Francis I, when his knights were shot down by Spanish gunmen and his 28,000-strong army was annihilated. Yet he felt that because he had not disgraced himself, his honour survived.*

kept his honour safe, all other things could be lost. King Francis I of France famously declared after his humiliating defeat in the Battle of Pavia, northern Italy, in 1525, 'All is lost save honour'.

HOW REAL WAS CHIVALRY?

There were so many occasions on which knights did not live up to the code of chivalry that we are justified in asking to what extent they believed in it. Many institutions presented as noble expressions of chivalry had a very mundane side: for example, in one light, the 'brotherhood of arms' was little more than a very practical risk-sharing and profit-sharing arrangement, in which knights agreed to pay one another's ransoms and also to split any money they made. While the chronicles wrote up deeds of high chivalry, knights were indulging in pillage and looting, and often making great fortunes as a result. It could be argued that knights used chivalry as a smokescreen behind which they were happy to fight dirty wars.

Yet knights did often act in accordance with chivalry when dealing with one another – for example they went to great lengths and into personal danger to keep their honour. They saw knighthood as an international elite body, and it appears that they believed in the code of chivalry only as it applied to other members of the elite.

pressing vow. It depended upon honesty. In theory, honour reigned in both history and literature, as countless deeds were done because a knight had given his word of honour. For example, Sir Walter Manny led a contingent of just 50 knights in a highly dangerous attack on the French in 1339 because he had made a vow to be the first into combat in the war that had recently been declared (which became the epic Hundred Years War).

In reality, many a blind eye must have been turned to knights' actual behaviour. For instance, Sir John Talbot – one of the great English commanders in the Hundred Years War – was mourned at his death in 1453 as one of a dying breed of great knights, exemplars of chivalry, yet in his lifetime he was also known as a disturber of the peace and a ruthless operator.

Honour was all, the supreme concept of the chivalric code. Thus, if a knight

AFTER THE FALL

Medieval philosophers traced the origin of warfare and violence to the biblical Fall. According to the account in the Book of Genesis, our first ancestors Adam and Eve were expelled from the paradise of the Garden of Eden after they had defied God's commandment not to eat from the Tree of Knowledge in the garden. The Fall referred to this lapse from the original state of grace, living alongside God in the Garden, to the familiar conditions of life in the world. The medieval writers argued that war was the result of the Fall, and that God oversaw the rise of knights and the development of chivalry in order to regulate violence and defend those who

▶ *Warfare followed the Fall and knights had to keep order and protect virtue.*

were defenceless in the fallen world. Some authorities saw the origin of the knight in the Roman era, when they believed armed forces of 1,000 expert warriors were created.

TALES OF WAR AND LOVE

HOW EPIC CHANSONS, ROMANCES AND COURTLY POEMS SHAPED CHIVALRY

By the *chansons de geste* and prose or poetry romances of chivalric literature, knights were educated in chivalry. As they listened to tales of great deeds, of battles won, tournaments fought, quests pursued or dread marvels encountered and overcome, they participated in the growing development of a vision of knighthood that would have a major influence on their own behaviour as knights.

THE MYTHS SURROUNDING KNIGHTHOOD

This vision embodied how knights should behave and how they should conduct themselves in an ideal world. These ideals often filtered through stories about how knights used to behave in a legendary or quasi-historical golden age of the past. Tales of Charlemagne and his paladins, of King Arthur and his knights, of biblical or classical warriors such as the Jewish freedom fighter Judas Maccabeus or the Macedonian conqueror Alexander the Great, were expositions of knightly virtue.

HEROIC DEEDS FROM A GOLDEN PAST

The first flowering of chivalric literature came in the 12th century, with the appearance of *chansons de geste* ('songs of heroic deeds'). These were epic poems in Old French that celebrated the exploits of Christian knights fighting for Charlemagne and other Frankish kings against warriors of Islam from Spain, usually called 'Saracens' (a word traditionally said to be derived from the Arabic *sharqiyin*, which meant 'easterners').

Some of the great deeds celebrated were based on historical fact – like those recounted in the first and greatest *chanson de geste*: the *Chanson de Roland* (*Song of Roland*) of *c*.1130–70, which as we have

▲ Minnesänger, *the German musician poets, were counterparts of the Provençal troubadours. Their songs included some written by kings and other leading nobles.*

seen was inspired by an ill-fated expedition to Spain led by Charlemagne in 778. The poems usually looked back to a lost golden age when knights behaved better, and so had an elegiac quality that is a strong part of their appeal.

The chansons were recited and sung by *jongleurs*, or minstrels, who would usually accompany themselves on a *vielle* – the medieval version of the violin. Chansons were probably composed and performed for around 200 years before the mid-12th century, the date of the oldest surviving manuscript. Around 100 chansons survive in manuscripts dating from the 12th to the 15th century.

◀ *The warlike feats and noble deeds of Charlemagne, seen here on the right, and his retainers, were the subject of many* chansons de geste, *most famously in the* Song of Roland, *illustrated here.*

RISE OF ROMANCE

Alongside the *chansons de geste*, and ultimately superseding them, arose chivalric romances – narratives of heroic deeds written in prose or poetry. The romances flourished from the mid-12th century onwards throughout the age of chivalry – right up to the 16th and 17th centuries – but were at their most popular in *c.*1150–1300. According to the 12th-century Old-French poet Jean Bodel, there were three principal subjects for romances: 'the Matter of Rome', narratives about heroes of the classical world such as Julius Caesar; 'the Matter of France', principally stories about Charlemagne, his great knight Roland and other paladins; and 'the Matter of Britain', recounting the doings of King Arthur and the Knights of the Round Table. There was some common ground between chansons and the early romances. Both were written not in Latin, the language then used for scholarly and ecclesiastical writing, but in vernacular languages; the Old French word *romanz* means 'the language of the people'. A great

▲ *In the tradition of courtly love, knights were inspired to deeds of chivalry by their burning desire to prove themselves worthy of their lady's love.*

literary figure such as Chrétien de Troyes was the author of both romances and chansons, and they could have very similar subject matter. But one key difference was that chansons were performance poems that were sung to an audience by a professional troubadour, while romances were written down in a book and then read aloud.

COURTLY LOVE

In the late 11th century, in what is now southern France, poets developed a new emphasis in songs about knights. Working at the largely peaceful and prosperous courts of princes and dukes in Aquitaine, Burgundy, Champagne and Provence, the poets sang about knights' intense devotion to noble ladies. The knights conceived a fierce love for the ladies at court, who were often already married; the poets said

that the knights were bound to the ladies by the bonds of feudal service, as a knight conventionally was to his feudal lord.

This culture or literary convention has been known as one of 'courtly love' since the Frenchman Gaston Paris first used the term in the 19th century. It referred to the fact that the conventions flourished at royal and noble courts, and also to the supposed 'courts of love' at which, according to some of the poems, ladies sat in judgement on the exploits of their devoted admirers. Modern historians point out that the term 'courtly love' appeared only once in chivalric literature – in the form *cortez amor* in the 12th-century poem written by Pierre d'Alvernhe – and some writers prefer the name *fin'amors* ('fine love'), which was used frequently in poems of the period. It was an elevated form of love, characterized by the knight's feelings of devotion, almost to the point of religious worship, for the lady, and by humility and courtesy; it did have a sexual element, but actual physical consummation was not its principal goal.

NOBLE WARFARE

FIGHTING TO KEEP GOD'S PEACE

Knights believed that armed conflict was a quite proper way to settle disputes. It was honest and noble to confront an enemy in a trial of strength and martial skill. The chivalric attitude was that war is man's natural condition.

The 14th-century Provençal writer on chivalry, Honoré Bonet, declared in his *Arbre des Batailles* ('Tree of Battles') from 1382–87: 'Fighting is not a bad thing, but excellent and full of virtue, for it cannot be denied that war only seeks to put wrongs right, and turn disagreement to concord, in line with the teachings of Scripture'. Bonet's book, which is based on the *Tractatus de Bello* ('Theories of War') by the 14th-century Italian canon lawyer Giovanni da Legnano, argued not that all fighting was good, but that in the right context and for the right purpose, warfare was a noble and just cause. Churchmen and those who wrote on chivalric issues

▲ *A French manuscript illumination from c.1310–25 depicts the belief in those times that the crusaders were the knights of Christ in their campaign against Islam.*

generally agreed with this position, and argued that knights were ordained by God to keep order and peace while protecting and fighting in the Church's interests.

ATTEMPTS TO CONTROL PRIVATE WAR

There were often incidental victims when knights worked out their disagreements in 'private wars'. Peasants or churchmen might have livestock killed or lands ravaged in the fighting; they were not equipped to defend themselves against a lord and his well-armed warriors. From the 10th century onwards, the Church aimed to control rather than prevent the knights' outbursts of martial energy. Through the 'Peace of God' and the 'Truce of God' movements, churchmen tried to guarantee exemption from violence for certain groups such as peasants and clergy and attempted to outlaw fighting between knights on certain days – initially, Sundays and holy days and later the period of Lent.

Repeatedly kings, too, attempted to end the fighting of private wars, but with very limited success. The waging of private war remained a jealously guarded chivalric right – less in England, where knights did

▼ *In his youth Holy Roman Emperor Charles IV was wounded at Crécy; later he was known chiefly for his diplomatic skills and dedication to learning.*

not fight in this way after the 1200s, than in France and Germany. In France c.1350 the knight's right to wage war was reaffirmed by the French royal official, poet and legal expert Philippe de Beaumanoir, who wrote: 'A knight can wage war in line with tradition.' This entitlement was governed by certain rules: before attacking, a knight had to make a formal complaint against another, giving due cause, and the combatants were not permitted to burn or ravage property. In Germany private war also had a legal basis in the mid-14th century: Holy Roman Emperor Charles IV accepted the knight's entitlement to wage private war provided he gave his enemy three days' notice of attack.

PURSUING A QUARREL

Even when knights did not openly pursue private wars, there were many opportunities for them to settle grievances or seek out old opponents. When knights fought at tournaments, they had a good chance

▲ *Medieval writers generally agreed that knights could justly wage war to keep the peace or protect the Church, but these battles could involve the knights in political manoeuvrings – such as the campaigns to promote the interests of the papacy in Italy.*

to come up once more against former adversaries. Private war could also be fought under cover of national war – many old quarrels were pursued during the Hundred Years War or the Scottish border raids on northern England.

Knights who fought private wars or who sought out former foes in this way were not merely pursuing a grudge, for often there was a strong chivalric element to the conflict: the knight who tracked down an old foe might not so much be seeking to get even as to pit himself once more against an honoured adversary in a 'joust of war' or a 'feat of arms'.

CHIVALRY IN COMBAT

In one of the most celebrated feats of arms, Scottish knight Sir David Lindsay of Glenesk fought Lord de Welles, England's ambassador to Scotland, on St George's Day 1390 on London Bridge in the presence of a great crowd and of King Richard II of England. Lord de Welles had boasted of English chivalry and so Sir David had challenged him to a test of strength, the rules of which called for a joust.

When the two knights met in the charge their lances both splintered, and onlookers taunted Sir David by calling out that he was tied to the saddle in contravention of the rules of conflict. To prove them wrong, the Scottish knight leapt from his horse then vaulted back into the saddle unaided before riding on.

At the second charge both lances again shattered; at the third joust, Sir David unseated Lord de Welles, who fell heavily

but recovered in time to fight on foot, when he was again defeated and this time quite badly injured. The Scots knight had Lord de Welles at his mercy but rather than press home his advantage, he revived his opponent – and after the contest visited him daily for three months during the lord's recuperation.

Sir David was widely praised for his gallantry – and chroniclers noted that he had fought in the true chivalric manner, not from anger but seeking glory. Later Sir David served as Scotland's ambassador to England, and he also commemorated his victory on St George's Day by founding a chantry at Dundee.

Three years afterwards, a second match between the leading lights of Scottish and English chivalry was held at London Bridge. On this occasion the English knights were the victors, in a conflict once again fought in the spirit of chivalry.

▼ *How a knight fought was as important as why he did so – he was called upon to conduct himself bravely and to demonstrate that glory was more important to him than mere victory.*

A KNIGHT FEARLESS AND BLAMELESS

PIERRE DE TERRAIL, CHEVALIER DE BAYARD

French knight Pierre de Terrail achieved remarkable feats of chivalry while in the service of Kings Charles VIII, Louis XII and Francis I of France in the late 15th and early 16th centuries. In an age when chivalry appeared to be in severe decline, and when many knights were fighting as mercenaries for whoever paid the most, he was revered as a great example of the knightly creed and an unconditionally loyal servant of the French crown.

Pierre de Terrail was hailed as *le chevalier sans peur et sans reproche* ('the fearless and blameless knight'), and was the subject of a romanticizing biography by Jacques de Mailles.

▼ *The Chevalier de Bayard acted with typical gallantry in the siege of Brescia in 1512, when he was wounded, but his fellows in the victorious French army embarked upon a five-day sacking of the city, killing thousands.*

PIERRE DE TERRAIL

Born: 1473
Died: 30 April 1524
Knighted: 1495
Famous for: chivalrous bearing at all times
Greatest achievement: the defence of Mézières with a force of just 1,000 men against an army of 35,000

PAGE, SQUIRE AND KNIGHT

Born at Château Bayard in the Dauphiné, Pierre came from a great chivalric family, and in his youth served as page to Charles the Warrior, Duke of Savoy, before, at the age of 14, becoming a squire in the service of King Charles VIII of France. Even at a young age he was renowned for his handsome looks and his courteous and charming manners, as well as for his bravery and skill at jousting. He was a squire

in Charles's army at the start of the Italian Wars, launched by the French king against the kingdom of Naples, and fought in the Battle of Fornovo in 1495. The French lost the battle against a combined army from Venice, Milan and Mantua, but Terrail won glory when he captured an enemy standard, and afterwards he was knighted on the field of battle for his prowess. Subsequently Terrail was captured when pursuing an enemy, alone, into Milan, but he impressed and charmed his captor Ludovico Sforza, Duke of Milan, so much that the duke released the knight without demanding ransom.

HERO OF THE ITALIAN WARS

Terrail won repeated acclaim for his feats of bravery and chivalric deeds during the Italian Wars, on one occasion being the hero of a contest that took place between 12 French and 12 German knights, on another reputedly holding a bridge over

the river Garigliano in central Italy alone against a force of 200 Spanish knights. As in the chronicle accounts of Jean Froissart, the romantic nature of chivalry must have coloured the telling of his life story.

He was praised for his part in the sieges of Genoa in 1508 and of Padua in 1509 and was injured attempting to be the first on to the ramparts at the siege of Brescia in 1512. He was left unable to defend himself, but his soldiers took him to safety in the house of a nobleman; even severely wounded, he managed to do enough to prevent the nobleman's family from being insulted later in the siege. Then, before he was even properly recovered, he rode from Brescia to fight in the Battle of Ravenna under Gaston de Foix, Duke of Nemours.

In addition to bravery in combat, the Chevalier was known for his careful planning and sound knowledge of enemy movements gathered through painstaking reconnaissance and the use of spies.

▼ *A king kneels before a knight at Marignano, in 1515, when the Chevalier de Bayard knights young King Francis I.*

CAPTIVE OF KING HENRY VIII

The following year, in the wake of the French army's heavy defeat by King Henry VIII of England at the Battle of the Spurs, he attempted to rally the French but was isolated on the battlefield and, unwilling to surrender, he rode up to an English captain and demanded that he instead surrender; when the Englishman did so, the Chevalier de Bayard gave himself up. Henry VIII was delighted by the French knight's courtesy and chivalry and once again Terrail was released without ransom. He gave the English king his *parole*, or word of honour, that he would not fight in the war for a period of six weeks.

SAVIOUR OF FRANCE

In 1515 after playing a great part in the French victory in the battle of Marignano against a Swiss army in Italy, Terrail had the honour of knighting his own king, the 21-year-old Francis I. His biographer noted that despite the Chevalier's relative lack of social status, his bravery in battle meant that there was no one knight more worthy to raise the king to knighthood.

The Chevalier de Bayard was appointed Lieutenant-General of the Dauphiné and in 1521 defended the town of Mézières in northern France against the invading army of Holy Roman Emperor Charles V. For six weeks Terrail and his small garrison defied the imperial army, until eventually they lifted the siege. His actions prevented the invasion of central France and won time for Francis I to collect the army that would go on to defeat the imperial forces in 1521. He was hailed as France's saviour and made a knight of the Order of St Michael. He was given his own command of a unit of 100 mounted cavalry – an honour only previously given to scions of the royal family.

A CHIVALRIC DEATH IN ITALY

In Italy once more, in 1524, he took command of the French army after Admiral Guillaume de Bonnivet was wounded at Robecco. Terrail was himself fatally injured on 30 April when he was hit by a ball fired

▲ *Perhaps the Chevalier's finest achievement was inspiring a garrison of just 1,000 men to hold Mézières for six weeks against a 35,000-strong army of the Holy Roman Empire in 1521.*

from an arquebus (an early gun) during a skirmish at the crossing of the River Sesia. Like the English knight Sir John Talbot, he was killed by a gun, a fact that only reinforced the sense that here was one of the last of a dying breed of chivalric knights, representatives of an old and increasingly outmoded way of fighting. In Terrail's case, another important part of his appeal for contemporaries was that in addition to great prowess and spotless honour, he also showed kindness and had a light, carefree and charming manner. His second nickname was *le bon chevalier* ('the good knight').

The Chevalier died in the middle of battle, amidst his enemies, and attended by his old comrade in arms, Charles, Duke of Bourbon. Tradition has it that his dying words were as purely chivalric as his life: 'Do not pity me, for I died an honourable death while doing my duty. Pity rather those who fight against their king, their country or the sworn oath.'

BROTHERHOOD OF ARMS

A PARTNERSHIP BETWEEN KNIGHTS

The chivalric virtue of faithfulness was given powerful expression in the custom of the brotherhood of arms. Two knights pledged loyalty to one another, even to death.

BLOOD BROTHERS

Knights who swore to be brothers in arms took an oath to support one another in war and in peace: they would fight together, in some cases sharing the same coat of arms. Their vows meant that an enemy of one would be an enemy of the other, and likewise they would share friends and allies. The oath was stronger than any other tie that bound them except for the feudal duty to lord or king. It even took precedence over a knight's promises to his lady.

The custom probably had ancient roots that run back to the bonds of blood brotherhood made between Germanic and ancient Greek warriors who mixed their blood and swore to brave injury and death in defending one another. The medieval brotherhood of arms was usually formalized in a written document and to mark this contract the two men would take the Sacrament of Holy Communion as well as mixing their blood. They also exchanged a 'kiss of peace'.

KNIGHTS BOUND IN DEATH

The bond of Sir William Neville and Sir John Clanvowe epitomized the brotherhood of arms – although the written document giving evidence of their union unfortunately did not survive. The two men, both Knights of the Garter, died and were buried alongside one another in 1391 near Constantinople – and their tombstones are now exhibited in Istanbul's archaeological museum.

The stones depict the men's coats of arms combined, so that both bear the same shield showing the Neville and Clanvowe arms side by side – in heraldry

▲ *Chivalric encounters took place in the intervals between bouts of fighting during sieges and on campaign. Remarkably, even the tunnels excavated beneath castle walls to weaken the fortifications were large enough to be used for jousting.*

this is called 'impalement' and was customarily done to the arms of married couples. Sir William and Sir John were

prominent knights who were constantly in each other's company from 1378 onwards, and their deaths were recorded in the chronicle of Westminster Abbey; we know from this source that when Sir John died, Sir William pined away – refusing to eat, weakening swiftly and dying himself just two days later. The chronicle refers to Sir William as Sir John's 'companion on the march'.

SHARING THE KISS OF PEACE

Many leading knights and princes were brothers in arms through the age of chivalry. As early as the 10th century, according to the chronicler Henry of Huntingdon, the kiss of peace was shared by Edmund Ironside and King Canute. In the 11th century Godfrey of Bouillon and the Prince of Edessa became brothers in arms. In the 14th century the great French warriors Bertrand du Guesclin and Olivier de Clisson made an agreement of this kind. They swore to guard one another as brothers, and to keep the other apprised of any impending threat. In the 15th century King Louis XI of France became brother in arms to Charles the Bold, Duke of Burgundy.

BROTHERS NO MORE

Although the agreement, like that made by a married couple, was 'till death', there is a notable example of a brotherhood in arms being cancelled. As Earl of Hereford, Henry Bolingbroke swore to be brother in arms with Louis, Duke of Orleans, but when Henry deposed King Richard II of England to become King Henry IV in 1399, Louis cancelled the treaty of brotherhood. The brothers became enemies as Louis challenged King Henry to meet him at any place in France for combat with 100 knights and squires in each company. Although he deposed his king, Henry was a great chivalric figure and was renowned as one of the foremost jousters and fighters at tournaments in his day.

PROFIT-SHARING AGREEMENT

Chivalry cast a glow over the real world. Its ideal forms often had a very practical side. The brotherhood in arms was an expression of faith and martial brotherhood, but among kings, princes and leading nobles it could be a very useful diplomatic tool, used to promote or cement alliances.

The brotherhood sometimes had strong elements of a business arrangement. As part of their brotherhood agreement, described above, the French knights

Olivier de Clisson and Bertrand du Guesclin swore to share equally all the lands and ransoms gained in conflict. Similarly, two squires in the army of King Henry V, Nicolas Molyneux and John Winter, agreed detailed financial arrangements when they swore to become brothers in arms in the church of St Martin at Harfleur in 1421: for example, they were each pledged to find the first £1,000 if the other needed to be ransomed, and they agreed that any money they made while on campaigning should be despatched quickly to England to the safety of London banks.

In this context, the brotherhood is comparable to a profit-sharing agreement made by knights in tournaments. As we have seen, William Marshal and Roger de Gaugi, a knight in the household of his royal master Henry the Young King, made a substantial fortune competing in tournaments of 1177–79.

BROTHERS IN THE MINES

During the sieges of castles, when the attackers dug mines in an attempt to undermine the walls, the defenders would excavate countermines, thereby creating tunnels in which fighting took place. The conflict, strangely, usually took the form of formal jousting between knights on the opposing sides – and it was the custom for the knights who fought in this way to afterwards become brothers in arms. At Limoges in 1370 John of Gaunt, Duke of Lancaster, reputedly fought French knight Jean de Villemur in this way, and subsequently it appears that de Villemur was spared when the city was captured.

GODFATHER IN ARMS

The *Siete Partidas* (Seven-Part Code), a law code composed in the reign of King Alfonso X 'the Wise' of Castile (1252–84), described a relationship between knights that was comparable to the brotherhood of arms. The man who ungirded the sword of a new knight would thereafter stand as the knight's 'godfather in arms': the knight was forbidden to fight against his godfather in arms or in any way work to his detriment; he was expected to support his godfather in arms in any conflict unless it were against his feudal lord or one of the members of his own family. As well as formulating statutory codes, the Seven-Part Code also contained writings on philosophy and theology.

▼ *Alfonso, King of Spain – known also as 'the Learned' – set up a school of translators in Toledo, whose work accelerated the transmission of Arabic and ancient Greek learning into Europe.*

KING OF CHIVALRY

KING EDWARD III OF ENGLAND

King Edward III of England was an internationally renowned chivalric figure, celebrated as the foremost Christian warrior of the mid-14th century. He did a great deal to foster chivalry in England. As an inspirational general, he led his army to major military victories in France; he was father to the warrior-prince Edward the Black Prince; he presided over many tournaments and he founded the Order of the Garter, which was openly based upon the Round Table of King Arthur.

PROTECTOR OF THE REALM

In his youth Edward had a solid education in the practical skills of knighthood, and he learned to read and write Latin and to speak French and English. However, as a teenager he became a pawn in the power struggle between his father Edward II and his mother Queen Isabella, supported by

---

EDWARD III

Born: 12 November 1312
Died: 21 June 1377
Knighted: 1 February 1327
Famous for: embodiment of chivalry, a great general, co-founder of the Order of the Garter
Greatest achievement: victory at Crécy (1346)

---

her lover Roger Mortimer. Isabella and Mortimer used him to depose Edward II and he became 'Protector of the Realm' at the age of 14. He was knighted by the Earl of Lancaster prior to his coronation on 1 February 1327.

EARLY HUMILIATION

Edward's first military campaign, against the Scots in 1327, was not a success and almost resulted in his capture by a raiding party led by Sir James Douglas; when the English prepared to retaliate, the Scots fled, reputedly making Edward weep tears

of frustration. England agreed a peace with the Scots that recognized Robert the Bruce as King Robert I, but the humiliation of the campaign and the treaty rankled with Edward for many years.

In 1330 Edward seized power in England, aged 18, when he launched a night raid on Nottingham Castle and surprised his mother and Mortimer in their bedchamber. He sent Mortimer to the Tower of London and exiled his mother at Castle Rising, Norfolk.

TOURNAMENTS

From the start Edward was an enthusiastic tourneyer, and used the tournaments he organized and attended as opportunities to consolidate relations with the leading knights. In 1330 he attended tournaments at Dartford, Stepney and Cheapside.

In 1331 he attended three days of jousts at Stepney: 26 defending knights and 26 challengers, all dressed in costumes bearing a motif of a golden arrow, rode through London to St Paul's and said prayers before jousting in the marketplace. For another three-day joust in the same year, at Cheapside in London, all the defenders were dressed as Tartar knights and were led through the streets by a lady in costume as a 'damsel'. The king's enthusiasm for tournaments and the store he set by them as opportunities to foster unity can be seen in the fact that for both these events, he ordered all able-bodied knights in the country to attend.

IN SCOTLAND

Edward soon built a military reputation for himself. In the war against the Scots in 1333, he won a resounding victory over Sir Archibald Douglas and a Scottish army at the Battle of Halidon Hill by using the new defensive tactics that combined dismounted knights with archers. Edward fought again in Scotland in 1334–35 and 1336, during which he achieved an act

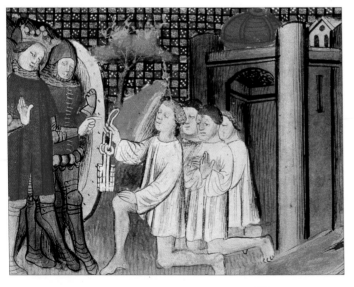

▼ *The surrender of the Burghers at Calais, 1347, to the English army. Six townsmen offered their lives to King Edward III if the besieged populace could be spared.*

of high chivalry by rescuing Katherine, Countess of Atholl, from the besieged castle of Lochindorb in the Highlands, but thereafter his attention was largely taken up with wars against France.

CLAIM TO THE FRENCH THRONE

From the start of his reign Edward had been pressing his claim to the French throne. This followed the death without issue in 1328 of his uncle Charles IV of France. In 1340 Edward declared himself King of France, defeated a French fleet in the naval Battle of Sluys, and invaded France – with little success on land. His first major victory came in 1346 with the campaign in Normandy that saw him win the famous Battle of Crécy, achieved by using the same defensive tactics that he had used at Halidon Hill 13 years earlier.

The triumph of Crécy was followed by the surrender of besieged Calais in 1347, and the defeat of the Scots (in Edward's absence) near Durham, where the Scottish king, David II, was captured. At Calais, according to chroniclers, Edward held six

▼ King Edward III released David II (right) from captivity in 1357. The Scots paid a ransom of 100,000 marks for their king.

▲ Edward laid claim to the French throne prior to the campaign that led to his famous victory in the naval battle of Sluys in 1340.

leading citizens of Calais as hostages, and was preparing to put the men to death when Queen Philippa begged him to spare them. Ever the chivalrous knight, he acceded to the wishes of the lady and the citizens were spared. (Chroniclers made much of Queen Philippa's involvement, but she was not in fact at Calais.)

CHIVALRIC CELEBRATIONS

These military successes in France and Scotland were celebrated with a great series of chivalric events that were used as an opportunity to parade prisoners of war and to make a statement of the king's international power. In 1348 Edward hosted tournaments in various cities, and it was during a Windsor event that he began the brotherhood of the Order of the Garter. The founding knights were all veterans of Crécy and tourneying companions of the king and the Black Prince, and the two 'sides' of knights (one led by the king and one led by the Black Prince) may have

been based on tournament teams. The year 1356 brought further military triumphs, including victory at Poitiers in which the Black Prince led an 8,000-strong army to victory over 50,000 French, and captured King Jean II. This year may have been the high point of Edward's international standing. He was unable to translate his successes into lasting gains in France: in 1360 Jean was released for a ransom of 3 million gold crowns and Edward renounced the claim to the French throne. Over the next two decades the land in France that Edward held was gradually lost to a resurgent French military.

A CHIVALROUS KING

Edward's standing in Europe was built on his success as a warrior and his status as a chivalric figure. The chronicler Jean le Bel of Liège called him 'noble', and most contemporary accounts stressed his honourable behaviour – especially in his dealings with women. Stories of the Countess of Atholl's rescue and Edward's giving way to Queen Philippa's plea for the lives of the Calais hostages presented him as a model of chivalry.

ORDERS OF CHIVALRY

KNIGHTLY IDEALS AND THE LAY CHIVALRIC BROTHERHOODS

From a distance, the 14th century's lay chivalric brotherhoods, such as the English Order of the Garter and the Castilian Order of the Banda, appear to be a stirring embodiment of knightly romance. However, their creation as national organizations with oaths of loyalty to the king ran counter to the international ideals of religious chivalry that found expression both in the stateless class of knights mobilized to fight the crusades, and in the deeply religious brotherhoods like the Orders of the Templars and the Knights Hospitallers.

▼ *The establishment of the Order of the Garter was a celebration of Edward III's famous victory at the Battle of Crécy, as well as a statement of the power and nobility of English knighthood.*

KNIGHTS OF THE GARTER

The model for the secular brotherhoods was the Round Table of knights described in the romances of King Arthur. King Edward III initially emphasized the romance of his proposed brotherhood. He announced his intention to form it at a feast and tournament held at Windsor Castle in January 1344. He invited knights and their ladies from throughout the realm; and the king, his minstrels and no fewer than 200 squires and knights were decked out in fine tunics for the occasion. After a day of feasting and jousting, on the second morning of the festival Edward and Queen Philippa attended Mass, then the king solemnly swore upon the Bible that he would found a brotherhood of knights of similar type and standing to the one established by King Arthur. He said

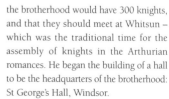

▲ *Edward III confers the Order of the Garter on the Black Prince. The order's first meeting was at Windsor on 23 April 1349.*

the brotherhood would have 300 knights, and that they should meet at Whitsun – which was the traditional time for the assembly of knights in the Arthurian romances. He began the building of a hall to be the headquarters of the brotherhood: St George's Hall, Windsor.

However, when the Order of the Garter was finally established in 1348, it was at least as much a ploy in support of Edward's claim to the French throne as it was a tribute to the legendary chivalric feats of King Arthur and the knights of Camelot. The knights were each given a blue and yellow garter – in the colours of France – and their motto *Honi soit qui mal y pense* ('Shame come to him who thinks evil of it') was almost certainly a reference to the king's claim in France, a suggestion that only those who backed Edward in his designs on France could be his brothers in chivalry. The colourful account of the

motto being the king's response to an embarrassment for his mistress (see box) was a later embellishment.

The Order had only 26 members instead of the proposed 300. They were King Edward and the Black Prince, with 12 knights each in their company. The knights selected by King Edward and the Black Prince were their brothers in arms, who had fought beside one another at the Battle of Crécy two years earlier and won honour in the lists at the king's many tournaments. The creation of the order was a celebration of the great victory at Crécy and a statement of the power of English knighthood. The statutes of the order established that Edward would call on the Knights of the Garter first when he was planning a war campaign or any other act of chivalry – France should beware.

ENDURING FAME OF THE ORDER OF THE GARTER

Other secular chivalric brotherhoods of the 14th century included, as we have seen in Chapter Five, the Order of St George (created in Hungary in 1325), the Order of the Sash (created in Castile in

▼ French knights of the Order of the Star take their oath before its founder, John II of France, then celebrate at a banquet.

▲ Philip III the Good, Duke of Burgundy, wears the jewel-encrusted collar of his chivalric Order of the Golden Fleece.

1332), the Order of St Catherine (created in the Dauphiné in the 1330s) and the Order of the Star (created in France in 1352). None of these achieved the reputation or enduring glory of the Order of the Garter. The Order of the Star failed principally because it required its knights to swear that they would never retreat in battle, and according to one chronicler half of its member-knights were killed in one battle in Brittany in 1353. Another reason was that its founder, King John II, was very unpopular among the nobility of his country, after clashes with leading nobles earlier in his reign.

CHIVALRY AND DIPLOMACY

The Order of the Golden Fleece, created by Philip the Good, Duke of Burgundy, in 1430, was modelled on the Order of the Garter. Duke Philip's brotherhood initially had 24 members plus the king, but this number was raised to 30 in 1433 and 50 in 1516. Its badge was a piece of sheepskin hanging from a jewel-encrusted collar and its motto was *Pretium laborum non vile*

('The reward of labour is not cheap'). The order's statutes provided that all disputes among members would be settled by the order and that the king was required to take the advice of the knights before embarking on a war.

The original membership of the Order of the Garter included three French knights who had served the English cause in France. It became common practice for other secular brotherhoods, especially the Order of the Golden Fleece, to use offers of membership as a tool in diplomatic negotiations.

THE ORDER OF THE GARTER

The most widely told story about the origin of the emblem and motto of the Order of the Garter (shown below) dates from the 16th century, in the work of historian Polydore Vergil. Edward was dancing with his mistress, the Countess of Salisbury, when her garter fell to the floor. Edward pre-empted any laughter among the company by picking it up and putting it on his own leg with the phrase *'Honi soit qui mal y pense'*. Another tale told that Richard I tied garters around the legs of his knights before a battle, which they then won, and that Edward was commemorating this event. An important aspect of the garter from the point of view of chivalric life was that it could be tied on to armour as a badge of honour.

THE BLACK PRINCE

EDWARD OF WOODSTOCK, PRINCE OF WALES

Edward the Black Prince was a central figure of English knighthood in the mid-14th century. Eldest son of King Edward III of England, he was famed for his martial prowess: he 'won his spurs' aged 16 in the great victory at Crécy in 1346, was a founder member of the Order of the Garter and was celebrated as a conquering hero for his part in the Battle of Poitiers ten years later, when he captured the French king Jean II.

THE YOUNG KNIGHT

Son of a great devotee of chivalry, Edward was truly born to knighthood. He had his own suit of armour by the age of seven, and was already a friend of knights by the age of ten, in 1340, when he lost money at gambling to Sir John Chandos. At the age of 13 he went with his father on military campaigns abroad, and in 1346 he fought at Crécy, where he acquitted himself superbly in the vanguard of the army and became a hero of the English while little more than a boy.

At one point in the battle, he was knocked to his knees and was captured by the count of Hainault, but almost at once was freed by English knight Sir Richard Fitzsimon. One report suggests that King Edward, seeing his son under pressure, sent knights to his aid, but that when they arrived at the spot they found the prince and his companions leaning nonchalantly on their swords. (The account of the battle

▲ *The Black Prince is celebrated for his crushing victories over the French at Crécy and Poitiers. The French lost more nobles in these two battles than to the Black Death.*

in Froissart's *Chronicles*, which suggests that King Edward watched while the prince's section of the army came under powerful attack and refused to send help with the words 'Let the boy win his spurs', is believed to be a legend.)

After the battle, Edward paid a tribute to King John of Bohemia, a great chivalric figure who had been killed fighting on the French side. Prince Edward adopted King John's emblem, an ostrich feather, and motto *Ich Dien* ('I serve') as his own; at first the prince's badge showed a single feather but later versions had three feathers, and this has remained the emblem of the Prince of Wales to this day.

RETURN FROM POITIERS

At the Battle of Poitiers in 1356, Prince Edward captured the French king Jean II and afterwards, according to the account by Jean Froissart, behaved with great

chivalry – serving the king at table, and praising the sovereign's performance in battle, as having outdone that of all the great French knights. Afterwards Edward took Jean to Bordeaux, where they were delayed by three months of peace negotiations, and then by sea to Plymouth, where the party arrived in May 1357.

▼ *Victory at Poitiers was helped by great leadership from Edward and superb discipline among his troops.*

THE BLACK PRINCE

Born: 15 June 1330
Died: 8 June 1376
Knighted: 12 July 1346
Famous for: bravery in battle, co-founder of the Order of the Garter
Greatest achievement: victory at the Battle of Poitiers, 1356, and capture of the French king, Jean II

Edward made a magnificent triumphal entry into London later that month amid great pageantry: on the road, he was 'attacked' by 500 knights disguised as bandits in a mock ambush, and in London he was welcomed by the city guilds in streets decorated with armour and beside fountains running with wine. His reputation and chivalric prestige could get no higher.

PRINCE EDWARD AND CHIVALRY

In many ways, Edward was an exemplar of chivalry. In addition to his treatment of Jean II, he was a great jouster and was noted for his generosity, his willingness to exhibit the knightly virtue of *largesse*. After Poitiers he rewarded his leading knights Sir James Audley and Sir John Chandos with gifts of 600 crowns, in addition to large annuities. He was also known for his piety – he made pilgrimages before campaigns (to Walsingham and Canterbury in 1345 and again to Walsingham in 1354), and made a number of generous donations to Canterbury Cathedral. He is believed to have been devoted to the Holy Trinity and is represented in a lead badge doing religious homage.

Prince Edward was surely destined to be one of England's greatest kings, but the length of his father's 50-year reign (1327–77) and the prince's own death in

▲ After being captured at Poitiers by Prince Edward, John II of France was escorted in style to captivity in England. He was valued at no less than 3 million crowns by his English ransomers.

his mid-40s from dysentery denied him that honour. In his time he was England's most famous knight. His use of some unchivalric methods, such as chevauchée raiding, was common in his time.

NAMED FOR HIS ARMOUR

In his lifetime the prince was called 'Edward of Woodstock' after his place of birth. The name of 'the Black Prince' was first used in an English chronicle that was

published by the Tudor printer Richard Grafton. Modern historians suggest that the name may have been made up by French chroniclers, and referred to his string of victories over the French or the cruelty of the chevauchée raiding he planned. The traditional view, however, is that the name was used because of an ornate black cuirass, or breastplate, given to the young prince by his father at the Battle of Crécy.

▼ A gilt-copper effigy of the Black Prince surmounts the knight's tomb in Canterbury Cathedral. Above the tomb is a panel of the Holy Trinity, to which Edward dedicated his chivalric achievements.

CHAPTER SEVENTEEN

KNIGHT OF THE TOURNEY

In January 1430 Philip the Good, Duke of Burgundy, hosted a magnificent banquet followed by a six-day tournament to celebrate his marriage to Isabella, daughter of King John I of Portugal. To welcome the new duchess to Bruges he hung vermilion cloth in the streets, laid on fountains of wine and built a magnificent temporary banqueting hall containing a gilded tree hung with his heraldic arms. During the tournament two teams of knights jousted in three sets of lists built in the city's marketplace. Each day a golden chain or sparkling jewel was presented to the best knight and squire of each team. At the end of the tournament Philip announced the creation of a new chivalric order, the Order of the Golden Fleece. The duke's tournament was one of the most lavish of the entire Middle Ages, and the culmination of a long tradition of chivalric competitions. Tournaments were absolutely central to the world of medieval knights. They developed from martial manoeuvres, and throughout their history were always valued by knights as a form of military training. Crucially, also, they provided a setting for knights to display their chivalric virtues such as bravery, courtesy, humility and generosity. They were inspired by, and themselves inspired, the developing culture of chivalry and courtly love, an arena where knights competed for the approval of watching ladies. The tournament was also a place of opportunity, for knights could grow rich on the winnings.

▲ *Medieval jousts were the extravagant entertainment spectacles of the day.*

◄ *Sir Tristan and Sir Palomides fight in the lists as other knights of the Round Table look on. According to Arthurian legend, Palomides was inspired by a glimpse of the lady he adored, Iseult, to become unbeatable in the tournament – despite the fact that she loved Tristan.*

MARTIAL GAMES
THE ORIGIN OF TOURNAMENTS

A spectacle incorporating military training, tournaments have precursors going back to the classical world. In the medieval era the lavish and formal courtly entertainments of the kind held by Philip the Good developed from the rough and tumble of cross-country cavalry manoeuvres.

THE EXAMPLE OF ROME
From the time of ancient Greece and Rome, if not earlier, soldiers and their generals understood the need for martial games and manoeuvres as part of military training. The young men of Sparta and of Rome developed their strength and their soldierly prowess in mock combats. In the medieval period, knights and writers on chivalry saw tournaments as emulating the fighting contests of the classical world. Tournaments, particularly when they took the form of a pair of knights jousting in the lists, also had forerunners in classical and pre-medieval combats, such as the gladiatorial contests so popular in ancient Rome and in the trials by combat used by Germanic tribes to resolve their disputes.

▼ *Most gladiators in ancient Rome were slaves. Like a joust, gladiatorial combat was both a trial of strength and entertainment.*

▲ *The city-state of Sparta rose to power in the 8th–5th centuries BC with an army of super-fit soldiers who fought mock battles to develop their skills – similarly, tournaments honed the prowess a knight needed for war.*

FRANKISH CAVALRY MANOEUVRES
The Frankish cavalry practised riding at speed, changing direction sharply and controlling a horse among a crowd of many others. One celebrated account of these manoeuvres describes 'war games' held at Strasbourg in 842 to celebrate the alliance of Charlemagne's grandsons, Louis the German and Charles the Bald.

In the games, groups of cavalry rode fast towards each other, then one group wheeled away, protecting themselves with shields, and pretending to flee, drawing their opponents into a charge before suddenly turning and driving back the charge. Finally the kings, Louis and Charles, rode into the battle with their lances aloft, urging on the two sides. Frankish historian Nithard described the event, noting that the encounter was a great sight, partly due to the many nobles taking part and also because they were so well ordered. Some modern historians have claimed this was the first medieval tournament, although it was not a true tourney because it was not a combat – the two sides charged and fled but did not fight.

BATTLES IN OPEN COUNTRY
The first proper tournaments were probably mock battles that took place between groups of Frankish cavalry in France in the late 11th century. Two sets of knights, often from different areas, fought across open countryside. They rode across farmland and forests and took full advantage of the opportunities for ambush provided by buildings and natural features. There were often as many as 200 knights on each side, led by the same lords they followed in war. The purpose of the game was to capture and then ransom as many knights as possible from the other team.

The knights fought with real weapons including lances, bows and arrows – and injuries were common. There were no rules, save that fighting must not be to the death, and that knights could take refuge and rest in fenced-off neutral areas.

▲ When tournaments were held in the streets, onlookers ran the risk of being hurt by the galloping horses and flailing knights.

TOURNEYING ON CRUSADE

Formal tournaments developed out of these cross-country battles. The Franks probably carried the sport with them when they went on the First Crusade – the chronicler Robert the Monk noted that when not fighting they practised tilting at the quintain (riding towards a target with a couched lance). Tournaments, indeed, emerged at the time that the Franks or Normans began using the couched lance in battle, a very demanding technique that required a lot of practice – and it may well be that tournaments developed initially out of the need to practise it.

FIRST REFERENCES

The first use of the word 'tournament' is in legislation of 1114, issued by Count Baldwin III of Hainaut, which describes keepers of the peace neglecting their jobs and leaving the town of Valenciennes to partake in 'javelin games, tournaments and similar sports'. Around the same time, in *c*.1115–20, the Benedictine monk and chronicler Geoffrey of Malaterra observed that in campaigns in Sicily by his fellow Normans, the young knights tourneyed during the course of a siege in the year 1062 – this indicates that tournaments were being held in *c*.1120, when he was

writing, even if his account of 1062 is fictitious. Then in the 1140s, a history of the Church of St Martin of Tournai referred to the death of Count Henry III of Brabant in a tournament between his warriors and those of Tournai in 1095.

CREATIVE ACCOUNTS

Caution is advised when reading accounts of early tournaments since in later years a way of proving knightly heritage was to demonstrate that one's ancestors had fought in tournaments for generations; medieval chroniclers often rewrote the

past, inventing great encounters at tournaments to add lustre to the reputation of their lords. The 16th-century herald Georg Ruexner claimed in his *Book of Tournaments* (*c*.1530) that King Henry I of Germany held glamorous tournaments in 938 in Magdeburg; but certain details in his description cast doubt on his account. The chronicle of St Martin of Tours refers to the supposed origin of tournaments: it says that a nobleman named Geoffrey de Preilly, who it says was ambushed and killed at Angers in 1066, should be remembered as the inventor of the sport.

WHAT WAS A TOURNAMENT?

Strictly speaking a tournament was a mock battle between two sets of knights – the combat also known as a mêlée. The knights fought as units, just as in battle, with the aim of defeating the other side and so winning their opponents' equipment and horses. In France and England this was often also called a *hastilude* ('spear contest'), and it was the principal form of the tournament in England in the 13th century when Sir William Marshal rose to prominence due to his martial skills. It was a distinct

contest from jousting. However, the word 'tournament' began to be used, especially in Germany, for the courtly events that encompassed both mêlées and jousting, and it certainly has the more general meaning in modern usage.

▶ Two teams of knights from Arthur's Round Table compete as groups in the form of the tournament known as a hastilude.

PROWESS ON DISPLAY

TYPES OF TOURNAMENT

The 12th-century English chronicler Roger of Hoveden defined tournaments as 'military exercises performed not in a hostile spirit but only to practise and put prowess on display'. Across the centuries of the chivalric period, the tournament took a number of forms – most, in line with Roger's definition, devoted to the sport of mounted contests, but some much closer to actual warfare.

THE MÊLÉE

The earliest formal tournaments seem to have taken the form of mock battles of the kind fought by the Franks in the fields of northern France, but in an enclosed area rather than in open country. In this type

▼ *Knights take an oath before participating in the tournament. The competitors are split into two 'teams' to fight in the mêlée.*

of encounter, called a mêlée, two teams of knights fought with couched lances.

The two groups represented home and away teams – the 'defenders' (those associated with the town or region in which the tournament was being held) and the 'attackers' (visitors from elsewhere). The two sides first paraded into position and called out their cries of war, then rested briefly while in the land between the two sides young knights charged at one another in individual jousts.

At a signal the main charge began: the two groups headed for one another with couched lances, then turned swiftly to fight individually or in small groups. The word 'tournament' is believed to derive from the French *tournement* ('turning'), a reference to the quick reversal of direction. Squires stood by to offer up to three replacement lances to their lords.

From an account in Wolfram von Eschenbach's great 13th-century poem *Parzifal* we learn that a knight in one of these charges aimed for his opponent to the left and carried his couched lance across the neck of his mount, aiming at his rival's shield. After the charge, the mêlée often spread out beyond the original lists into a designated area of countryside or even into the streets of the town as knights carried on the fight, trying to take as many of their opponents captive as possible.

THE JOUST

The mêlée was quite dangerous and often resulted in serious injury or death. Over time it became less common and tournaments primarily featured jousting between two knights. In a joust the knights rode towards one another with couched lance, each aiming to unhorse his opponent.

From about 1400, in an attempt to limit injuries, the knights rode either side of a central barrier called the tilt. Probably developed in Spain or Portugal, the tilt spread throughout Europe during the 15th century; it was already common in France by 1430. At first it seems to have been no more than a cloth hanging from a rope, but quickly this became a stout wooden barrier with padding.

In the 11th–12th centuries individual jousting was often a sideshow to the main event, which was the mêlée. Jousting might take place on the eve of the tournament or on the morning of the contest, prior to the main combat. The 13th and 14th centuries saw jousting becoming more popular, and some tournaments featured only individual combat with lances.

Although the conditions of the mêlée provided better practice for battle than did a joust, knights tended to prefer jousting because their individual prowess was more obvious in individual combat. Jousting certainly had its dangers but it was generally safer than the mêlée, with less danger of the horses trampling unseated riders.

THE BOHORT

Less formal contests between mounted knights continued to be held alongside tournaments. One of these was the *béhouard*, also known as the *buhurt* (in 12th-century German) or, in English, the bohort. This was more sport than conflict, an encounter between knights relying principally on their horsemanship, and using weapons less than in a tournament. For this reason, while the tournament was often condemned by state and Church authorities, the bohort was viewed more kindly. The rules of the Knights Templar stated that brothers must not compete in tournaments but were allowed to take part in bohorts. Sometimes bohorts were enacted by squires rather than knights.

Bohorts were described often in chivalric literature, where they were the natural conclusion to a wedding or knighting ceremony. In Geoffrey of Monmouth's *History of the Kings of Britain*, King Arthur's knights

are described as riding out to hold an impromptu bohort after feasting at one of the king's courts: and while the ladies cheered from the town walls, the knights sported in the meadows, riding and throwing lances and competing with bows and arrows. Geoffrey emphasizes that the competition was only for sport, and never in earnest, and that it did not provoke the smallest display of bad feeling.

PRACTICE MEETINGS

New knights needed practice before they entered the very demanding mêlée arena and the jousting lists. Practice sessions called vespers were often laid on for the inexperienced on the eve of major tournaments, but sometimes entire contests were held specifically to give the young knights practice. In Germany this type of tournament was called the *tirocinium*.

PAS D'ARMES AND CHALLENGES TO ARMS

In the late 14th and 15th centuries very lavish tournaments called *pas d'armes* ('passage of arms') were held. These were so magnificent in conception and presentation that only kings, princes and leading nobles could afford to mount them. Examples include the tournament held by Philip the Good in 1430.

▲ *Jousts were often fought until a specified number of lances had been broken. In this tournament, fought in the reign of King Charles V of France (1338–80), broken lances litter the ground in the lists.*

Poorer knights, who could not afford to organize a *pas d'armes*, arranged their own chivalric contests by issuing 'challenges to arms'. A good example is the open challenge issued by seven knights of France in 1398 to any seven knights from England. The French knights agreed to wear a diamond on their armour for three years and to be ready to fight on challenge by an English knight, with lance, then sword, then axe, then dagger. Should the English knight win, he could keep the diamond, but should he lose he would be required to supply seven golden rods, one for each of the French victors, for them to pass on to their devoted ladies. We have no record of the result of this challenge.

Four French knights travelled to Parliament in London to issue a challenge for jousts at Calais, and the king granted licences to English knights to respond. Another example is the celebrated Joust of St Inglevert in northern France in 1390, when four knights proclaimed that they would occupy the lists for a period of 30 days and fight all comers.

HERALDS AND CHALLENGES
WHEN AND HOW TOURNAMENTS WERE HELD

Tournaments were often held to add pageantry and colour to great royal or noble state occasions. These entertainments needed careful organization.

COURTLY CELEBRATIONS

At royal and noble courts tournaments were associated, first and foremost, with weddings. The chivalric Edward I held a tournament at Bristol in September 1293 to celebrate the wedding of his daughter, Eleanor, to Count Henri III of Bar. Nobles also laid on tournaments to entertain their wedding guests, as we have seen in the example of Duke Philip the Good of Burgundy in 1430.

The tournament was also considered fitting for a royal coronation. King Edward II of England had a tournament at his

▼ *The tournament survived into the 17th century. This one was held in Turin in 1619 to mark the marriage of Victor, Duke of Savoy and Prince of Piedmont, to Christine, third daughter of King Henry IV of France.*

coronation in Westminster in February 1308. Farther afield, at Acre in 1286, the crusaders fought an Arthurian 'Round Table' tournament in honour of the coronation of King Hugh III of Cyprus as King of Jerusalem. Events were also a frequent addition to diplomatic meetings as late as 1520 – King Francis I of France and King Henry VIII of England met with ceremony, feasting and jousting at the Field of the Cloth of Gold near Calais in France.

Tournaments were also associated with festivals of the Church year – particularly at Shrovetide, the celebrations prior to the self-denial of Lent, as well as at Easter and Christmas. Sometimes tournaments were also held in late autumn, prior to the onset of winter, notably on St Martin's Day, 11 November, the festival of the 4th-century churchman Martin of Tours.

Tournaments could last for a week or more, often beginning on Monday or Tuesday. They were not held on Sundays or Fridays, which were kept sacred, or on holy days of the Church calendar.

SEEKING GLORY

Between the 11th and 13th centuries knights would often travel in search of tournaments. Young noblemen and royals such as King Henry II of England's sons Henry the Young King and Geoffrey, Duke of Brittany, kept a permanent group of knights and squires for competing. In the summer of 1260, the 21-year-old Prince Edward (the future Edward I) travelled to France with a company of 80 companions to seek glory by fighting in tournaments – surprisingly, given his later status as a warrior, with little success. At this time it is probable that events were publicized by word of mouth among the participants, who before leaving at the end of a tourney would arrange to meet again in the future at a particular time and place.

More formal arrangements for planning and publicizing the events came into use in the 14th and 15th centuries. King René I of Naples, known as René d'Anjou and an artist and poet as well as a patron, gave details of tournament organization in his book *Le Livre des Tournois* (*The Book of Tournaments*), written in *c.*1450.

ISSUING A CHALLENGE

Often letters were sent out to particular knights to advise them of a coming tournament. Heralds rode out to proclaim the date, place and duration of the tournament; the rules under which it would be fought; the type of arms and armour to be used; and the arrangement of the tournament area – known as the lists. This would be announced at least a fortnight before the tournament was due to start.

Sometimes an invitation to a particular knight was issued by a challenge: the herald would ride to the court of the king, prince or noble knight to be invited, and present to him a blunt sword (the kind used in some tournaments), and taking the sword would signify acceptance of the challenge by the recipient. It was expected

▶ *In the close and highly dangerous combat of the mêlée, brute strength counted for as much as skill. This manuscript depicts a German tournament of the early 1300s.*

that he swear to fight not out of anger or a desire for violence, but in order to please his challengers and the ladies of the tournament court. The recipient then chose four judges of the tournament from a list of eight carried by the herald.

Invitations were often sent far and wide. For King Edward III of England's 1344 tournament at Windsor, the invitation was proclaimed by heralds as far afield as Brabant (in the Netherlands), Burgundy, Flanders, France, Hainault (in the Low Countries) and Scotland. Knights were promised safe conduct to and from the event. For a 1358 tournament, Edward spent £32 on sending heralds to Scotland, Flanders, Brabant, Germany and France.

GATHERING FOR THE EVENT

The knights who wanted to take part in a tournament gathered at least four days before the event was due to start. The

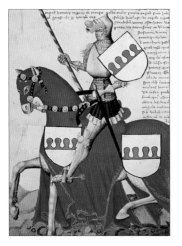

▼ *Knights usually made sure they could be identified in the lists by their coat of arms on shields and horse coverings. Occasionally knights deliberately avoided being identified – and competed as 'an unknown knight'.*

more important would make a formal processional entry into the city or town where the event was taking place. The appointed judges were required to take up residence in a local monastery or other religious establishment. All the knights planning to fight had to display their escutcheon, or shield, bearing their coat of arms, in the window of the inn and in the courtyard of the judges' residence. They also had to display it on the place they were staying, whether that was a room or a tent.

This gave knights or others the chance to make a complaint against particular contestants: a 'blot on the escutcheon' was a stain on a knight's reputation. On the eve of the contest the shields were inspected by the judges and if a complaint were upheld, then the knight in question would be excluded. There were a number of complaints liable to cause exclusion – for example being a proven murderer or a fugitive, having slandered a woman or broken a knight's duty to be honest, or having been excommunicated.

Tournaments also attracted merchants, who would gather in the days before jousting started. These included horse traders, sellers of fine clothes and moneylenders offering knights help in covering a possible ransom. Entertainers such as jugglers and fortune tellers also attended, giving the events the atmosphere of a fair.

THE LISTS

Lists, usually rectangular or oval, were set out within barriers either in a town – perhaps the marketplace – or in open countryside. Stands were set up for noble spectators. A strong wooden barrier was built around the lists to keep the spectators safe. This soon became a double fence, and in the area between the fences the squires stood, ready to rush to the assistance of the knights whom they served. The ground in lists was covered with dung, straw and sometimes sand.

A SEA OF COLOURS

THE PAGEANTRY OF THE TOURNAMENT

Tournaments were a magnificent sight, drenched in gorgeous colours, full of dramatic movement. They also had the extra spice of the passions of courtly love between knight and lady, and the promise of martial combat, even serious violence.

From specially constructed stands or balconies decorated with pennants and tapestries, lavishly dressed ladies and eager courtiers looked down on the knights and the poorer spectators gathered below, sometimes throwing coins into the crowd as an expression of their benevolence. Pavilions, also decked with flags, often lined the edge of the lists – the area laid out for competition. The knights wore elaborate armour sometimes decked only with the 'tokens' – the scarves, gloves or veils – of the ladies they represented, sometimes partly covered with colourful surcoats bearing the armorial bearings that adorned their shield as well as the horse-cloths and trappings. Heralds, who were familiar with the coats of arms of the contestants, proclaimed the names of knights as they entered the lists. We draw much of our knowledge of tournaments from accounts in chansons and romances, which presented an idealized version of tourneying. In practice, of course, there was great variety in the type of tournaments held, and many must have been far less splendid than the very grand ones glorified in chivalric literature.

FIGHTING IN COSTUME

Display was central to the event. Knights often fought in disguise, dressed as monks, cardinals, ancient Romans and women – but most often as knights from chivalric literature. When assuming a character, knights must have had a 'costume' simple enough to slip over their armour without affecting their ability to fight – perhaps a simple coat bearing a crest or arms, plus a symbol on horsecloths and trappings.

▼ *The colour and excitement of tournaments are evident in this scene from a 14th-century event. A herald (right) is master of ceremonies; in the grandstands, ladies and courtiers debate the outcome.*

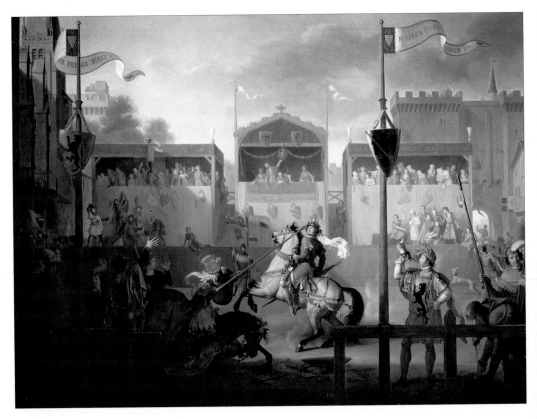

Frequently, in the 13th–15th centuries, tournaments were devised as theatrical celebrations of chivalry, and those taking part either represented great knights of history or played out typical scenes from romance literature. In 1468 Charles the Bold, Duke of Burgundy, celebrated his third marriage, to Princess Margaret of York, with a lavish 14-day tournament at Bruges. It was set within a romance narrative, based on the story of Florimont, the Knight of the Golden Tree, whose service was to the Lady of the Secret Isle. A tree was erected in the market place in Bruges and a champion knight defended it against four challengers every day for eight days. The tree was guarded by a dwarf dressed in white and red satin and by a giant; each challenger had to knock four times on a barrier and identify himself to a herald before taking a lance from those proffered. He would then fight in the lists with the Knight of the Golden Tree, for a defined period of 30 minutes: the knight who broke the largest number of lances was to be the winner. The dwarf sounded a horn to begin the 30-minute challenge. After the eight days of jousting the tournament culminated in a mêlée for two competing teams of 25 knights on the final day.

Ladies and courtiers watching the main action of the tournament also dressed in costume and finery. To preside over her wedding jousts Princess Margaret, for instance, wore a glorious golden coronet set with pearls and precious stones and the white roses of York made from enamel – with her initials and those of Duke Charles picked out alongside lovers' knots.

ARTHURIAN 'ROUND TABLES'

There was a whole series of 'Round Table' tournaments in which knights played the parts of Arthur's leading warriors. In 1223 the crusader knight John of Ibelin, Lord of Beirut, held the first, a 'Round Table' in Cyprus to celebrate the knighting of his son. The German Ulrich von Lichtenstein took part in one at Neustadt in 1240, when six knights from his 'Round Table' fought against 17 attackers; it was planned

▲ In the evenings, after vigorous exercise in the lists, the knights joined their ladies for courtly entertainments, dancing and feasting. The lower part of this fresco of c.1390 depicts this other part of tourneying.

as jousting, one to one, but was fought rather more loosely, with knights competing two against one, in an event halfway between a joust and a mêlée. The fighting was fierce – Ulrich records that more than 100 spears ended up broken.

King Edward I of England held two 'Round Table' tournaments – once while a prince (in 1254) and once as king (in 1284). Perhaps the most celebrated of all is the one held at Windsor by Edward III of England in 1244, where he announced the formation of a secular chivalric brotherhood. The Most Noble Order of the Garter was formed four years later, in June 1348: it consisted of 26 knights, Edward and his son, the Black Prince, with 12 companions each.

SCENERY, PROPS AND DANCING

These events used props and scenery as well as costumes. It is probable, for instance, that the celebrated 5.5m (18ft)-diameter Round Table at Winchester was made for Edward III to use at one of his Arthurian tournaments; the design on the table, which features the names of Arthur's knights, was painted in the mid-16th century, probably for another royal devotee of chivalry, King Henry VIII. In 1328 Roger Mortimer, Earl of March, erected a castle

made from canvas as scenery for one of the tournaments he arranged to celebrate his engineering of the accession of the teenage Edward III to replace Edward II (the deposed king was later horribly murdered in Berkeley Castle, Gloucestershire). At the tournament held in 1430 by Philip the Good, described in the introduction to this chapter, there were many 'stage props' and large amounts of scenery, including a vast wooden lion and sculptures of a stag and a unicorn that dispensed drinks.

Such tournaments were important social events in the medieval calendar. They were accompanied by feasting and dancing from as early as the 12th century – we know that there was dancing at the tournaments in which William Marshal (1146–1219) competed. It became a tradition for there to be dancing on the night before the tournament began, and at many events – such as during a celebrated tournament held at Chauvency, France, in 1285 – there was dancing every night.

QUEEN OF THE TOURNAMENT
THE IMPORTANCE OF LADIES TO THE EVENT

Ladies played a central role in the tournament. As well as providing an audience, they were often patronesses of tournaments, which were proclaimed as being held in their honour, and served as inspiration for the competing knights. They were also, nominally at least, judges of the jousting and often awarded prizes to the best-performing knights.

A GLAMOROUS AUDIENCE
The first tournaments were more military manoeuvres than courtly entertainments and did not cater for audiences, but ladies were increasingly present as spectators and as patronesses of tournaments from the 13th century. The first record of an event held to honour a lady is from 1207, when Peter II of Aragon hosted a tournament at Montpellier to bring glory to his mistress.

In England the presence of ladies at tournaments was certainly the norm by

▼ The king and queen look on from the royal box as two knights break their lances in combat. Note the sturdy wooden barrier (the 'tilt') built down the centre of the lists.

c.1330. King Edward III's queen, Philippa of Hainault, was a regular attendee at her husband's tournaments after their marriage in 1328 and she probably helped popularize the attendance of noble ladies at the events. Earlier than this, however, English ladies were involved in themed events; for

▲ Within the code of courtly love, a knight was driven to acts of bravery in tournament and in battle by the fact that his passion for his lady was pure and impossible.

example, King Edward I of England's Round Table at Kenilworth Castle in 1279 was for 100 knights and their ladies.

As we have seen, tournaments were very often associated with grand courtly celebrations with dancing and feasting. King Edward III's great tournament at Windsor in 1344 began with a feast in the castle for the queen and her ladies, while the knights ate equally lavishly in specially erected pavilions. After the banquet came an evening of dancing; the jousting took place over the following three days.

ARTHUR'S QUEEN
In the elaborate tournaments planned on Arthurian and other themes, ladies took a part as queen, princess or damsel within the chivalric make-believe. At Le Hem, Picardy, in 1278 a two-day Arthurian tournament was held in honour of a lady portraying Queen Guinevere; it was

described in some detail in the poem 'Le Roman du Hem' written by an Anglo-Norman *trouvère* named Sarrasin. All the knights had to bring a lady with them, as a knight-errant in a romance would bring a damsel, and the tournament was opened by Dame Courtoisie ('Lady Courtesy').

The tournament, held by the lords of Bazentin and Longueval, provided a narrative setting for the jousting. At the start, seven knights of Guinevere humbled themselves before their queen, reporting that they had all been bested by a noble warrior named the Knight with the Lion. Immediately, this knight arrived, bringing a number of damsels in Guinevere's service, whom he had saved from a dreadful fate, and also a live lion. He was intended to represent Yvain, and was played by Robert II, Count of Artois, a devoted tourneyer who took part in the event despite having been excommunicated for attending tournaments while they were officially banned. He would later lead the French army to a heavy defeat by the Flemish at the Battle of Courtrai in 1302.

Subsequently, a noble lady claimed that these knights of Guinevere were the best in the world, but her lord angrily challenged her and ordered her to be beaten in public. Guinevere's knights were then able to prove themselves by defeating this lady's champion one at a time. The event was less a performance before an audience than a shared theatrical experience, for all those present were required to act in the pretence that these events were taking place at the court of King Arthur.

THE LADY AS INSPIRATION

As the courtly love tradition developed, knights often fought to honour a lady. The knight would enter the lists wearing a 'favour' – a token such as a scarf that she had given him. The knight's desire to win the lady's favour inspired him to fight more bravely. She became his protector. In Thomas Malory's *Morte d'Arthur*, Sir Palomides – who, like Sir Tristan, loves Iseult – becomes unbeatable in the lists after a glimpse of Iseult laughing in a window overlooking the contest – 'he struck down with his sword or his spear every knight he encountered'. In this case, Palomides is inspired, despite the fact that Iseult's love is for Tristan – the laugh he saw was prompted by the sight of Sir Tristan riding past in his knightly finery.

▲ *A knight pays homage to the lady who is presiding over the tournament. These brief, formal encounters, bound by convention, were the very stuff of chivalric romance.*

PRIZEGIVERS

The lady or ladies presiding over an event were often asked to give prizes for the best performances in the mêlée and the jousts. Some accounts suggest that they chose the winners, but it is more likely that they just presented the prizes to winners who were chosen by heralds and other nominated judges familiar with the complex rules and scoring for a tournament.

▼ *This illustration of a 15th-century Italian tournament depicts the knights competing fiercely in a mêlée.*

WAR AND PEACE

TOURNEYS ON CAMPAIGN AND PEACETIME REGULATION OF EVENTS

Jousts and mêlées were often fought by knights during wartime as a diversion while they were far from their home on a campaign. In peacetime, because of the not infrequent deaths and attendant violence, tournaments provoked opposition from state and Church authorities.

JOUSTS OF WAR

From the very earliest days of tournaments, knights fought mêlées and jousts during military campaigns – particularly at a time of truce or during the longueurs of a siege. We have seen that, according to chronicler Geoffrey of Malaterra, Norman knights fought a tournament during a siege in Sicily as early as 1062; in the 12th century, jousts were held during sieges at Würzburg (Germany) in 1127, and at Lincoln during the siege of the castle by King Stephen's forces in January–February 1141; and in 1197, the army of Richard I held a tournament at Tours during a truce. Other examples include that of the great Breton knight Bertrand du Guesclin, who

▼ *Although the Church disapproved of them, tournaments were often a recruiting ground for holy war, when knights agreed to undertake a crusade to the Holy Land.*

in 1357 at Rennes fought a series of jousts against an English opponent, while he was also masterminding the defence of the town against a besieging English army commanded by Henry of Grosmont, Duke of Lancaster.

In England's 14th-century border conflicts with Scotland there were often prolonged periods of inactivity between engagements because the Scots used guerrilla tactics and could be difficult to engage. Knights from opposite sides arranged to hold jousts of war during these periods, which were neither really truces nor periods of full war. In 1341 at Berwick, jousts between 20 knights on each side left three dead and many injured, but nevertheless were ended with the giving of prizes to the best knights, as if it were a peacetime tournament.

CHIVALRIC ARENA OR DEN OF SINNERS?

For a knight the tournament was the chivalric arena par excellence in peacetime, a place in which he could display the key chivalric virtues of *prouesse* (prowess) and courage in fighting, and *courtoisie* (courtesy) in his dealings with the ladies; he could show *franchise* and *debonnaireté*

▲ *Pope Innocent II, who banned tourneying in 1130, had to use violence in his struggle to win the papacy from rival claimant Anacletus II. Innocent sent German king Lothair II to Italy to fight on his behalf.*

(good breeding and noble manners), and exhibit *largesse* (generosity) in dealing generously with crowds at the tournament.

For the Church, on the other hand, the tournament was a sinful indulgence in violence and pride. In the mid-13th century the bishop of Acre wrote that knights at a tournament committed all of the seven deadly sins, for they felt pride when they were praised, and envy when others were lauded more highly; they allowed themselves to feel and act on anger in the combat of the lists; they were avaricious because they greedily eyed the horses and shining equipment of other knights; they indulged in lust when they set out to please ungodly women by wearing their favours; they were slothful when they were defeated and slunk back to their

quarters; and they were gluttonous at the feasting that followed the fighting.

In the light of this sermonizing, it would appear that at a 1362 tournament in Cheapside, London, seven knights meant mischief when they entered the lists in the guise of the seven deadly sins and fought against challengers.

TOURNAMENTS BANNED

Pope Innocent II banned tournaments in 1130. At the Council of Clermont in that year he declared: 'we firmly prohibit those detestable markets or fairs at which knights … show off their strength and boldness,' adding that aside from the real danger of death or serious injury there were many 'dangers to the soul' in attending a tournament. Those who ignored the prohibition risked excommunication. Knights killed at tournaments were denied a church burial.

Kings added their authority to that of the Church in outlawing tourneying. The bans were of variable effectiveness: in England, strong kings such as Henry I and Henry II were able to enforce their will but a weak ruler such as King Stephen could not, and as a result in the reigns of the two Henrys (1100–35 and 1154–89), English knights routinely travelled to France to tourney, while under King Stephen (1135–54), knights took on themselves the right to fight at tournaments and Stephen could do nothing about it.

REGULATION OF TOURNAMENTS

In 1194 King Richard I of England defied the papal ban and introduced a licensing arrangement under which tournaments could be legally held in England. Richard, though a great knight and a devoted chivalric patron, was not himself a keen tourneyer. While in France, before he was king, he devoted his martial energies to fighting wars in the duchy of Aquitaine rather than competing in tournaments. But he reputedly saw the benefit of tournaments as training for knights, and wanted to establish them in England to improve military skills.

Under Richard's scheme there were to be five licensed tournament areas in England: Wiltshire, Warwickshire, Suffolk, Northamptonshire and Nottinghamshire. A knight who wished to hold a tournament in one of these areas had to buy a charter and a personal licence. Knights from outside England were not permitted. Historians note that Richard I was continually short of funds as king, due partly to his expensive crusading campaigns, and no doubt designed the scheme partly because of the income it would generate through licences and charters – and also through the hefty fines imposed on those who ignored the regulations.

▲ *Depictions of dancing (bottom) and feasting (top) join riding out to war and competing in tournaments among the works of the devil in this illustration from an early 14th-century manuscript.*

In France, where the kings had a closer relationship with the papacy, kings continued to ban tourneying – with little effect. The papal ban on the sport stayed in place until it was eventually lifted in 1316 by Pope John XXII, the second pope of the Avignon Papacy (the period in the 14th century when seven successive popes, all French, made their residence at Avignon in France).

DEATH AND DANGER
THE RISK OF DEFEAT IN A TOURNAMENT

Especially in the early years, tournaments were dangerous and knights were sometimes killed in the full-blooded encounters of the mêlée. Even in later, more stylized events, a knight's defeat in a tournament could bring ruin and humiliation, severe injury or occasionally death.

KILLED IN THE LISTS

Several knights died as a result of the conditions in which early tournaments were fought. Some were killed by frightened or stampeding horses – King Henry II of England's fourth son, Geoffrey, Duke of Brittany, was trampled to death in 1186 at a tournament near Paris. Sometimes, in hot and dry conditions, the heat and dust during a tournament could be overpowering – in 1241 at Neuss, in Germany, as many as 80 knights died from suffocation.

Many knights also lost their lives because of the force of the conflict. In 1344 Sir William Montagu, 1st Earl of

▲ *The main danger in the lists was being injured in the head by the other knight's lance. Jousters might also be badly hurt if knocked at high speed from the saddle.*

▼ *The shuddering impact between two knights hurls one to the ground. This graphic woodcut of c.1516 is thought to be by the great German artist Albrecht Dürer.*

Salisbury, died from severe bruising he had received after fighting in a tournament at Windsor. The Montagu family suffered badly in this regard – in 1383 Sir William's grandson, another Sir William Montagu, also died from wounds received in a Windsor tournament – the injuries were delivered by his own father Sir William Montagu, the 2nd Earl, a veteran of the Battle of Poitiers and one of the first Knights of the Garter. Earlier, in 1252, Sir Roger of Leybourne killed Sir Arnulf de

Munteny, a knight in King Henry III of England's household, in a tournament at Walden. Sir Roger, seeking revenge for a slight by Sir Arnulf at an earlier tournament, used a sharpened lance, which struck Sir Arnulf under the helmet. Sir Roger recovered from this early disgrace by taking the cross and going on crusade. He succeeded in winning the king's forgiveness, and had a long and chequered chivalric career, fighting both with Simon de Montfort and for the royalist cause in the 1260s.

TRAGIC ACCIDENT

Late in the history of chivalry, King Henry II of France sustained a fatal injury while jousting in July 1559. The tournament, in the Place des Vosges in Paris, was held to celebrate his daughter's marriage to King Philip II of Spain, as well as the Peace Treaty of Cateau-Cambrésis that ended the Italian War of 1551–59. During a joust the lance carried by Henry's opponent, Gabriel, Count of Montgomery, shattered – and a piece of it went through the king's

▲ *With pride, a great deal of status and personal safety at stake, jousts and subsequent sword fights could become very heated. Judges were on hand to intervene if a contest got out of hand.*

visor and through his brain. The king lived for nine days in agony, and although he was able to absolve Gabriel of blame, the royal physicians were unable to save him and he succumbed to the injury.

JOUSTS OF WAR

Several died in the jousts of war that were fought between knights during breaks in military campaigns. In 1341 Scottish knight Sir William Douglas was killed in a joust between four Scottish and four English knights at Roxburgh. In 1351 in the celebrated Combat of the Thirty, two teams of 30 knights competed near Ploërmel, Brittany: a French force of 30 Bretons against an English group of English, Germans and Bretons. (The two groups were garrisons attached to rival lords disputing possession of the duchy of Brittany.) In this event, at least three of the French knights were killed, while no fewer than nine of the English knights died including the English commander, Sir Robert Bramborough.

RUIN IN DEFEAT

When a knight was unhorsed, his opponent had to dismount to continue the fight: the pair abandoned their lances and fought on with maces and swords. They would fight until one was unable to carry on through injury or exhaustion and cried 'quits' to end the contest. A judge or patron(ess) of a fight could also intervene to stop it. A defeated knight was liable to pay a ransom for his freedom and would also be expected to give up his horse, his armour and his weapons. To be released he had to pledge to raise the ransom fee – he would give his *parole* (word of honour) to do this, and be released 'on parole'.

A knight who was repeatedly defeated would soon build up a sizeable debt in promised ransoms. The 15th-century French nobleman Robert de Baudricourt reported of a relative who often lost at tournaments and was able to survive only because his wife, remaining behind on the family estate, was so careful with the money that she was able to meet these commitments on his behalf. On the other hand, a knight who regularly won could quickly build a fortune – not through the acquisition of prizes, which were small, but through ransoms and seizing his opponent's arms, armour and horses.

JOUSTS À OUTRANCE, JOUSTS À PLAISANCE

The jousts of war were the most dangerous form of the sport, fought with sharpened weapons, and clearly in some encounters to the death. They were termed jousts *à outrance* ('to the uttermost'). Alongside them in the 14th and 15th centuries courtly tournaments were often fought *à plaisance* ('for the pleasure of the encounter'), with blunted ('rebated') lances, maces and swords.

▼ *At tournaments, even with blunted weapons, deaths were common.*

'THE GREATEST KNIGHT THAT EVER LIVED'

SIR WILLIAM MARSHAL

Sir William Marshal rose from humble origins to become a great knight and statesman, initially establishing his reputation through his astonishing prowess at tournaments. Some claim that in the many tournaments he fought he remained undefeated. Stephen Langton, Archbishop of Canterbury (1207–28), declared him 'the greatest knight that ever lived'.

After Sir William's death in 1219, his son William Marshal II and his squire and executor John d'Earley commissioned a biography of the great man. The result, *L'Histoire du Guillaume le Maréchal*, was a 19,214-line poem, written in rhyming couplets, giving a full account of the exploits of this remarkable figure.

AN EARLY ESCAPE

In 1152, aged just six, William was given up as hostage by his father John Marshal when John's castle at Newbury was besieged by the army of King Stephen. The king lifted the blockade, expecting surrender negotiations to begin, but John – apparently untroubled about the safety of his son – instead used the opportunity to bring provisions into the castle. Stephen

▲ *William Marshal was largely responsible for raising the first stone fortifications at Pembroke Castle in Wales. He built on the site of a wooden structure erected in 1093.*

tried several times to convince John that he would kill young William if he did not co-operate but John reputedly replied: 'I have a hammer and anvil on which I can forge better sons than he!' In the end, Stephen spared William and kept him at court as a royal ward until 1153.

In c.1159–66 William underwent his chivalric education as a squire at the court of William de Tancarville, Chamberlain of Normandy, who was his mother's cousin. In 1166, aged about 20, he was knighted. His first engagement was in war, that same year, when with de Tancarville and as part of the garrison of the castle at Neufchâtel-en-Bray, he fought in a frontier war between King Henry II and the counts of Boulogne, Flanders and Ponthieu. His bravery almost got the better of him – his master called him back at one stage of the conflict and told him not to be a 'hothead', and he lost his horse to an opponent.

HIS FIRST TOURNAMENT

He was at a low ebb. De Tancarville, clearly displeased, refused to supply him with a new horse and he was of such

◀ *King Stephen, who threatened to kill the 6-year-old William in order to force the cooperation of his father, John Marshal.*

limited means himself that he had to sell his clothes to procure one. But shortly afterwards, his life changed when he fought in his first tournament, at Le Mans. He was an immediate success: in the mêlée he captured a number of prisoners including a notable Scottish courtier, and at the end was richer to the tune of four horses, with a half-share in another.

William spent two years, 1167–68, winning repeatedly (and growing rich) on the tournament circuit of France. He went into partnership with another talented knight in the party of King Henry II's second son, Henry the Young King. In ten months, William and his partner captured no fewer than 103 knights along with their horses and equipment.

In 1168 William entered the service of his uncle, Patrick, Earl of Salisbury, and while fighting on his side in Poitou was injured and captured by soldiers serving Guy de Lusignan (the French knight who later became king of Jerusalem). William was imprisoned, but was ransomed by Henry II's queen, Eleanor of Aquitaine.

ROYAL SERVICE AND CRUSADES

In 1170 William was appointed tutor in arms to the 15-year-old Henry the Young King. Over the next decade they fought together often at tournaments and William became rich enough to maintain his own household knights. However, he was banished from the Young King's court in 1182, accused of having become too intimate with the Young King's wife, Margaret. This was probably a false accusation put about by jealous courtiers, but we cannot be sure.

The following year Henry and Marshal were reconciled and Marshal returned but only in time to see the Young King die of dysentery in June 1183. The Young King had taken the cross, and on his deathbed he gave William Marshal his cloak and made him promise to take it to Jerusalem. William thereafter went on crusade, and in the Holy Land made a solemn vow that his burial would be as a Knight Templar.

FIGHTING THE COEUR DE LION

On his return to Europe he served King Henry II from 1186 until the king's death in July 1189. Marshal fought in the king's household guard on campaigns against Philip II of France and Henry's rebellious

sons. He reputedly had the chance to kill Prince Richard (the future King Richard I of England) when the latter was suddenly isolated – an encounter between perhaps the two most celebrated chivalric men of the 12th century. Richard is said to have begged for his life and Marshal chose to kill the rebel prince's horse instead.

As king, Richard chose to honour Marshal. In 1189 he arranged Marshal's marriage to the 17-year-old Isabel de Clare, heiress to Richard de Clare, 2nd Earl of Pembroke. Marshal, now a great magnate, undertook substantial building at the de Clares' Pembroke and Chepstow castles.

PROMINENT NOBLE

For the rest of his long life, Marshal was one of the leading men in England. He was on the council of regency while King Richard I was away on the Third Crusade (1189–92), then was named Marshal of the Kingdom. After Richard's death he served King John, supported Magna Carta (he was a signatory) and on John's death was named as Protector of the Kingdom during the minority of King Henry III.

He was by now an old man of 70, but still fought with astonishing vigour in Henry's army against the rebel barons at the Battle of Lincoln of 1217. He died in 1219 and, in fulfilment of his vow while he was on crusade, was invested as a Knight Templar on his deathbed. He is buried in the Temple Church in London, where a fine effigy of this great knight lies with those of his sons.

▲ *The signing of Magna Carta by King John in June 1215. Sir William Marshal was also a signatory.*

WILLIAM MARSHAL
Born: *c.*1146
Died: 14 May 1219
Knighted: 1166
Famous for: sparing Richard Coeur de Lion's life and rising from obscurity to be Marshal of the Kingdom
Greatest achievement: remained undefeated in European tournaments

▼ *Temple Church, London, where William Marshal was buried in 1219.*

▼ *The effigy of William Marshal in Temple Church, London.*

RULES OF THE GAME

TOURNAMENT LAWS AND TECHNIQUES

The rules governing the fighting in a tournament were created as the sport developed. If the first tournaments were effectively war without the killing, the more refined events that took place from the mid-15th century onwards were governed by complex rules. These covered how to score points, and detailed the manoeuvres that were illegal and would lead to disqualification.

WAR GAMES

In tournaments of the 12th century, as in the Franks' very first countryside battles of the mid-11th century, knights could use any techniques to unhorse and then defeat an opponent, but should not fight to the death nor deliberately aim even to injure one another. There were fenced-off areas where engagement was suspended and knights could take a rest for their horses or themselves. In these early tournaments ordinary weapons were used – knights

▼ *By the 15th century tournaments were much better regulated, with rules of entry, engagement and scoring.*

could use lances, swords, battle-axes, maces, and bows and arrows.

Some of the techniques and tactics reported seem scarcely chivalrous. For example, the 12th-century noble Philip of Alsace, Count of Flanders, was renowned for refusing to take part in the mêlée until the other knights involved were near to exhaustion – he would then sweep into the lists to attack a group of opponents from the flank and claim a large number of easy ransoms. (Philip later went twice on crusade, once in 1177, and once in 1190 on the Third Crusade, when he died during the Siege of Acre from sickness.)

RULES OF ENGAGEMENT

There exists only limited evidence of the rules of engagement for tournaments in the 13th and 14th centuries. It would seem that there was a developing set of general rules and also that rules were agreed for individual tournaments. At the 'Round Table' events, so popular in the 13th century and afterwards, knights agreed to rules laid down when they entered the tournament.

Typical rules in these 'Round Table' tournaments specified the use of blunted weapons, and said that knights should not have concealed weapons. They also set the limit on the number of squires who were allowed to enter the lists to assist a knight in the tournament, and usually required that the squires and all other supporting retainers must be unarmed. The rules often declared that once a knight had surrendered he could not be attacked further, or launch another attack himself. The early 13th century saw the first use of blunted weapons, which greatly helped in making the combat in tournaments safer, and the rounded coronal head was used on the lance in place of a point from the mid-13th century.

The rules usually also laid down details about the kind of armour worn and the length of the lance. It was the normal practice for knights to use lances supplied by the defending knight to ensure that they were both fighting with identical equipment and challengers could gain no secret advantage by using their own weapon. It is known from the account in the romance of Fulk Fitzwarin (c.1230) that judges were in charge of settling any disputes in the tournament by the early to mid-13th century.

SCORES AND DISQUALIFICATION

Complex scoring rules were in use at some tournaments by the mid-15th century. They are detailed in Sir John Tiptoft's *Ordinances* of 1466. According to this list, the best score was achieved by the knight who knocked his opponent from his horse and brought the horse down with him. The next best point-scoring move was to make two spears break by the collision of their coronals or rounded tips. The third best score was achieved by hitting an opponent's visor three times, and the fourth best score was gained by breaking the largest number of spears.

▲ *Charles the Bold, Duke of Burgundy (1433–77), dressed in the splendid robes of the Order of the Golden Fleece.*

We have seen that in the 1468 tournament in Bruges held by Charles the Bold, Duke of Burgundy, the knights jousted for a set period of 30 minutes, measured on an hourglass, and the winner was the one who broke the most lances. However, this arrangement was unusual, and completely unknown in tournaments before the mid-15th century, when knights generally competed for a set number of jousts, agreed in advance.

Sir John Tiptoft's *Ordinances* also indicated that a knight could be disqualified if he struck a horse, struck an unarmed knight or one who had turned his back, hit the tilt (the central barrier in the competition area) three times, or took off his helmet twice, unless this was caused by trouble with his mount. When fighting in a general mêlée, knights were required to give up their sword for inspection by the judges before entering the fight, and they could be disqualified if they dropped a sword, tied the sword to their hand, hit an opponent beneath the waist with a pike, or rested on the barrier.

TECHNIQUES IN THE LISTS

Duarte, King of Portugal, wrote a manual on jousting and the management of horses, *The Art of Good Horsemanship*, in 1434. The book contains detailed advice on how to hold and support the lance, the best type of equipment to use, the training methods needed for effective jousting and even, perhaps most interestingly, on the mental strength needed to supplement physical bravery if a knight were to succeed in jousting.

Duarte stresses the importance of balancing the lance and, among a number of options for carrying it, suggests that the best way in a tournament is on the leg, supported by a bag placed on the saddle bow or on the leg itself. He adds that a knight should never use a lance that is too heavy for him to handle comfortably. He writes that it is a useful technique to aim slightly below the point of impact – this method enables a knight to see the exact place he intends to strike as clearly as possible, and prevents the frequent error of pulling the lance too far down at the last moment.

In addition, King Duarte stresses that it is important to banish fear and to maintain steadfast commitment in the lists: many jousters fail, he writes, because they look away or close their eyes or pull the lance imperceptibly off target just prior to impact. But it is important, he adds, not to be too tense because this may also cause the jouster to pull the lance off target. A knight should be confident in his abilities and able to ride into the impact with his eyes open and trained right to the last on the place on his opponent he intends to hit. Furthermore, he adds, a knight should never seek unfair advantage – and if he perceives that he is far better equipped than his opponent, he should lower his shield to even things up a little. He writes: 'I believe that you cannot prove yourself a skilled jouster if you are unwilling to take a risk.'

▼ *The squire's role in a tournament was an important one, and tourney rules reflected this by including various regulations on how many squires could attend, and how they should be armed.*

PROTECTION IN THE LISTS

TOURNAMENT ARMOUR AND EQUIPMENT

In the tournaments of the 11th and 12th centuries and for much of the 13th century, knights used the same armour and equipment in tournaments as they did in battle. Conditions of combat in a mêlée were similar to those on a battlefield, so there was no need to develop specialist tournament equipment. But from the late 13th century, the elite armour makers who

▼ In early tournaments knights wore chain mail, often with a surcoat for identification over the top. The great helm gave better protection but restricted the wearer's view.

served kings, princes and leading knights began to make specialist armour and other equipment designed for use in jousting.

EARLY ARMOUR

Knights at the first tournaments wore a chain mail hauberk and camail, or mail hood, with a simple conical helmet with nose piece of the kind shown on Norman knights in the Bayeux Tapestry. Gradually they began to use chain mail sleeves that also protected the wrist and hand – although the palms were necessarily left exposed to make it easier to hold and manipulate the lance and other weapons.

A full helmet design was introduced in the late 12th or early 13th century, and is commonly known as the 'great helmet'. These helmets were generally flat-topped and cylindrical in shape and provided much better protection, but had definite drawbacks – it was very hard to see out through the two small eye-slits, and also difficult to breathe through the holes situated near the mouth.

CRESTS AND COATS OF ARMS

When knights began wearing a full helmet, it became impossible to tell them apart. They started to sport armorial bearings to proclaim their identity. It was important to do so because the display of individual *prouesse* (prowess) was a key motive for fighting in the tournament. One of these identifiers was the crest, worn on top of the helmet. This could be a few feathers or else a heraldic beast or symbolic feature, made probably from cloth and wood. Another was the surcoat, a cloth garment worn over the armour and decorated with coats of arms.

LINEN AND LEATHER ARMOUR

A knight or soldier who received a heavy blow when wearing chain mail could be very badly bruised. In the 13th century, knights at tournament began to

▲ A knight takes leave of his lady. He does not wear a surcoat but has his coat of arms emblazoned on his horsecloth.

wear padded linen armour instead: as the use of blunted or rebated weapons spread, knights at tournament needed protection not against cutting and penetration, as they did in battle, but against bruising following heavy impact. Bruising was a very serious problem: Sir William Longespee was very badly bruised while jousting in 1256 and reportedly never fully recovered. Prince Edward (the future King Edward I of England) wore padded linen armour in his first tournament, at Blyth in 1258.

In the late 13th century, armour makers experimented with other materials including plates of metal, horn, whalebone and leather. The last of these became a popular choice – the leather was boiled and soaked in hot wax so it was soft enough to be fashioned into pieces that fitted tightly, but it was also sufficiently hard to repel a blow by a lance or sword, and it was light. Armour made from *cuir bouilli* (boiled leather) was popular until the 15th century; King Edward I of England held a bohort tournament at Windsor in 1258 in which participants were only permitted leather armour. A particularly popular piece of leather armour was the cuirass, a moulded piece that protected the chest, stomach and back, and was worn beneath the surcoat.

PLATE ARMOUR

As we have seen in Chapter Four, the first suits of plate armour, which appeared in c.1330, consisted of several plates of tempered steel, either laced in place or sewn on to a coat of leather or cloth and worn

▼ *Tournaments were flamboyant public displays of a knight's wealth, as well as their military prowess and skill, and helmet plumes became an expression of both.*

beneath the surcoat. They also included gauntlets, sabatons or shoes, and pieces to protect the throat and the upper and lower arms. The first solid breastplates were developed very quickly, probably as early as c.1340.

SPECIALIST TOURNAMENT ARMOUR

At around the same time, amid this rapid development of new types of armour, there appeared the first pieces designed for use in tournaments. These included the *maindefer* and *poitrine pur justes* – we do not know for sure what they were, but they were probably a gauntlet made to hold a lance, and a breastplate with a support on which to rest the lance. In the years of the late 14th to

the mid-15th century, knights could wear full suits of jointed plate armour. At this time, the original great helmet was widely replaced by a smaller design called the 'frog-mouthed helmet' (so called because of its profile), with a rounded top and curved front. As pageantry played an increasingly important role in tournaments, knights needed armour not only for protection but also to give them a splendid and glamorous appearance. Heraldic devices were emblazoned on surcoats and horse trappings, and elaborate, attention-seeking plumes adorned helms.

WEAPONS AND SHIELDS

In early mêlées and later jousts of war, knights fought with the ordinary weapons of contemporary warfare: lances, axes, maces and swords. In jousts of peace they used weapons with blunted blades; in par-

ticular, the sharp end of the lance was replaced with a coronal, shaped like a tiny crown with three short protrusions, from the mid-13th century. In battle, knights of this era carried a triangular shield, but in jousts of peace they used the oval ecranché shield, which had a part missing on the right-hand side to allow aiming of the lance. In the 16th and 17th centuries, as tournaments became displays more than contests, knights began to use mechanical devices that produced memorable effects for spectators. Chief among these was the spring-mounted shield that shattered dramatically into pieces when it was struck by the opponent's lance. During this period elite competitors such as King Henry VIII of England and the Holy Roman Emperor Maximilian I wore magnificent, highly ornamented jousting armour, with delicate chasing and fluting. This type of armour is so closely associated with the emperor that it is called 'Maximilian armour'.

▶ *The two most common kinds of horse used for jousting were chargers and destriers. Chargers were medium-weight horses bred and trained for agility and stamina, while destriers were heavy war horses.*

BROTHERS IN ARMS
CHIVALRIC ORDERS AND TOURNAMENTS

Beginning in the mid-14th century, a number of lay chivalric brotherhoods were formed. They were modelled on the religious brotherhoods such as those of the Knights Templar and Knights Hospitallers, which had come into existence in the era of the First Crusade (1196–99). However, these lay orders required members to swear an oath of loyalty to their secular lord and to fight on his behalf in war. Most of these orders were closely connected to tournaments.

▼ *The cult of St George, a soldier in the Roman army who was martyred in AD303, was popularized by knights returning from the First Crusade. The story of George and the dragon was recast within the conventions of medieval chivalry, with the saint riding a white horse and using a lance.*

THE ORDER OF ST GEORGE
The first of these was probably the Order of St George, founded in Hungary by King Charles in 1325. It was a brotherly union of knights who swore to defend the realm and protect the king, and to follow him in 'pastimes and knightly sports' – doubtless a reference to tournaments they contested. Unlike the later orders, described below, the Order of St George did not have the monarch at its head.

THE ORDER OF THE BANDA
In 1332 in Vittoria, Castile, King Alfonso XI of Castile and León (r. 1312–50) established the first lay brotherhood of knights, the Order of the Banda – or Sash. The members wore a white surcoat with a broad vermilion sash running diagonally from the left shoulder down to the waist.

▲ *Knights at a session of the Order of the Golden Fleece, formed in 1430 by Philip the Good, Duke of Burgundy. Philip based the brotherhood on the Order of the Garter.*

They swore an oath of loyalty to the king, and were to be grouped together in an elite unit within the royal army when at war. They also promised to love their fellow knights as brothers, and to avoid conflict among themselves.

The order was specifically linked to fighting in tournaments: it was a duty for each member knight to attend any tournament within a day's ride of where he was if he were summoned by the king. Moreover, it was laid down as an expectation that every meeting of the order would include a tournament. Chronicle reports reveal that Alfonso was a dedicated tourneyer and believed tournaments to be a valuable means of keeping his knights trained up and ready for war. He made new members by giving a surcoat and sash to any knight who performed great deeds in war against his enemies.

At a tournament held in Valladolid at Easter 1334, Alfonso fought incognito among the Banda knights against a team of challengers. Great deeds of chivalry were performed, and the fighting became so heated that the four appointed judges had to break the contest up for fear that the king would be badly hurt – according to the chronicles, he was receiving bruising blows in the midst of the press. The combat then moved to a second location, at a bridge just outside the town, and again the judges had to break the fighting up because it was so fierce.

The knights of the Banda are also reported to have fought at the pilgrim destination of Santiago de Compostela in 1332 and many years later at a Christmas tournament in Seville held by King Henry II of Castile and León (r. 1369–79) in 1375. But the prime of the order lasted no more than 20 years, and after Alfonso's death in 1350 it was in decline although it continued to exist for around 100 years.

THE ORDER OF ST CATHERINE

Formed in the Dauphiné, south-eastern France, in the 1330s, the Order of St Catherine was another lay brotherhood. Its knights swore to serve the lord of the Dauphiné and were committed to help one another and to be ready to lend one another horses and jousting equipment at tournaments. They carried a shield bearing an image of St Catherine, and were required to attend celebrations on her feast day at Côte-St-André each year – only those who were not able-bodied or who were more than three days' journey distant were excused.

THE ORDER OF THE GARTER

The most celebrated of these lay orders is certainly the Most Noble Order of the Garter, established at Windsor Castle on St George's Day, 23 April, 1348 by King Edward III of England. It consisted of 26 knights – Edward and his son, the Black Prince, with 12 companions each.

Four years earlier, during a tournament held at Windsor, Edward had vowed to form an order of Arthurian knights called the Order of the Round Table. Initially, the plan was for 300 knights to be in the

▲ *These illustrations of the badges of King Edward III, Richard II and Henry IV are from Writhe's Garter Book, a late-15th-century heraldic and genealogical volume.*

order, but Edward had scaled down the plans (perhaps influenced by the Order of the Banda) by the time he created the Order of the Garter. The 1348 foundation established a college of 12 canons and an almshouse for impoverished knights at Windsor. The vows of the order required knights never to fight on opposing sides, never to leave England without the king's permission, and not to be seen in public without the insignia of the order – a dark blue garter. Edward inaugurated the order with a feast and tournament at Windsor. The founding knights were regular contestants at Edward's tournaments in this period – and most had fought alongside Edward and the Black Prince at the Battle of Crécy in 1346.

THE ORDER OF THE STAR

This French order was formed in 1352, with 500 knights. It was dedicated to the Virgin Mary, and its motto was *Monstrat regibus astra viam* ('Kings see their way by the stars'). Its stated aims were to promote chivalry and increase honour.

TOURNAMENT SOCIETIES

In Germany in the mid-14th century groups of knights would gather in tournament societies. Tournaments were organized among these groups, with one society issuing a challenge to another. A similar body was formed in England in 1344 by Henry, 3rd Earl of Lancaster. The knights in Henry's society made a commitment to meet for jousting at Lincoln once a year on Whit Monday, and under a royal licence they were permitted to hold tournaments even during times of war or during a general ban.

▼ *Early shields bore very simple designs.*

KNIGHTS OF GOOD STANDING
THE USES OF HERALDRY

From open beginnings in the 11th–12th centuries, tournaments became socially more exclusive. Heraldry, or the practice of making and displaying family coats of arms, developed alongside this evolution of the tournament.

KNIGHTLY HERITAGE
The earliest tournaments seem to have been open to all-comers, as long as they possessed a suit of chain mail armour. In practical terms, this often limited entry to knights and squires, and the rule that only knights could take part in tournaments was gradually formalized. This became the general rule in England, France and Spain, but did not hold everywhere – ordinary citizens would joust in the Baltic towns, in the Low Countries and in the cities of south Germany.

By the 14th century in England, France and Spain, tournaments were often only open to knights who could trace knightly ancestry back to their grandparents. In Germany, perhaps as a reaction to the involvement of citizens in some urban

▼ *The Heralds' Roll of shields and coats of arms was drawn up in England c.1270–80.*

jousts, even more highly exclusive tournaments began to be held, until by *c.*1480 only those whose forebears had actually been fighting in tournaments for three generations back (as far back as the great-grandfather) were permitted to take part in the tournaments. This was a reflection of a social change in the 14th and 15th centuries in which status resided ever increasingly in one's descent.

SOCIAL SHAMING
As we have seen, procedures were also introduced to exclude knights who were guilty of wrongdoing – such as adulterers, perjurers or robber knights. Exclusions also included those considered unworthy for social reasons – for example those who had married outside the nobility, illegitimate sons, traders and moneylenders.

In some tournaments the punishment for a knight found guilty of these offences was to beat him, confiscate his horse, then put him on his saddle on the barrier around the lists and make him stay there for the entire tournament. The same punishment lay in store for a knight who made accusations against another that proved to be false. In some of the most

▲ *These shields are from the Carlisle Roll, a heraldic document listing the 277 knights who took part in King Edward III's military campaign against Scotland in 1335.*

exclusive German tournaments, a knight could be beaten and excluded simply for not having the proof that his forebears had tourneyed within the past 50 years.

HERALDRY AND PROOF OF DESCENT
Heraldry developed from the need to identify oneself in battle or in the lists. The 'coat of arms' was so called because it was originally a surcoat or tunic emblazoned with a device and worn over the armour. The first coats of arms in the 13th century were simple stripes or crosses. Later ones usually included images of animals – typically lions, birds, boars, deer and dragons; flowers such as the fleur-de-lis and the rose were also popular. In time, knights also included representations of weapons or chivalric equipment such as swords, spurs and horseshoes. In tournaments knights generally bore their coats of arms on their shield, as well as on their surcoat and their horsecloths.

The first coats of arms were personal, but with the emphasis on descent they came to be treated as hereditary. As this process continued over generations, and families intermarried, coats of arms were combined. The combination of elements from two coats of arms was called compounding. This might be necessary if a knight married, acquired new property or received a particular honour. Quartering involved splitting a shield into four parts to combine the insignia of different coats of arms in one design.

THE ROLE OF HERALDS

Heralds began as public speakers, sent out to announce dates and times of tournaments, and were then required to act as commentators for the events themselves – to announce the arrival of particular knights in the lists and to interpret events for those watching. To do this job they had to be familiar with contestants' armorial bearings. As coats of arms became more complicated and more significant as a badge of knightly descent to allow entry into a tournament, heralds became acknowledged experts on family history and the technicalities of coats of arms. The heralds had to be well educated, knowledgeable about the arms of historical knights that had been established by convention, and the symbolism of colours, plants and animals used in the designs.

Initially heralds were probably itinerants who sought work at tournaments

▲ In this scene of a tournament in the 14th century this herald is shown dressed in all his heraldic finery.

when they were held, but they were soon attached to particular lords and would wear their master's livery as they travelled to proclaim his tournament. They became experts in armoury as well as coats of arms.

They travelled on campaign as well, where they were granted safe passage by the armies of both sides. Part of their job was to keep a record of squires knighted before and after battle, of acts of chivalry and of deaths during battles. They also served as diplomats, carrying messages

ROYAL ARMS

King Richard I of England was the first English monarch to have a heraldic device: it was originally two lions 'rampant' (standing on their hind legs in profile); in 1195 he put a third lion in place, and three golden lions 'passant' (arranged horizontally, a if striding) set on a red background became the royal arms of England.

from one army to the other. Another role was in the dramas of courtly love, when heralds were often used to carry messages between lovers.

HERALDIC DISPUTES

The 14th century saw the frequent appearance of heraldic treatises, usually written by heralds themselves. The heralds became involved in regulating coats of arms and their use. One knight could not simply use another's armorial bearings, or elements from its design, in his own coat of arms. By the 14th century, there were regulations in place in England to prevent a knight adopting a particular coat of arms unless it had royal approval or that of a high-ranking herald. In England, disputes were settled in the Court of Chivalry, founded in the 14th century.

▼ A 15th-century manuscript illustrates some of the heraldic devices of the time.

PART FIVE

LEGENDARY KNIGHTS

In medieval chronicles, chivalric biographies, poems or romances, writers amplified the feats of arms performed by historical figures such as Godfrey of Bouillon, Sir William Marshal or King Richard I of England. Godfrey was an 11th-century French knight, a leader of the First Crusade of 1095–99 and the first 'Defender of the Holy Sepulchre'. William Marshal, 12th–13th-century Englishman, was a peerless fighter at tournaments who was dubbed the 'greatest knight who ever lived'. King Richard, celebrated as we have seen under the name Coeur de Lion for his endeavours on the Third Crusade of 1189–92, was a mighty warrior on the battlefield. Ancient figures from the biblical and classical worlds also featured in the works of these medieval poets, warriors such as the Jewish freedom fighter Judas Maccabeus, Hector of Troy, or Julius Caesar were reimagined as knights of chivalry and so presented as exemplars for medieval warriors. Other more legendary figures such as Roland, the Germanic warrior Siegfried, the British heroes King Arthur or Guy of Warwick were likewise presented as protagonists in affairs of the heart at court, as heroes in tournaments or on the field of battle, even as 'soldiers of Christ' on crusade. Medieval knights listened – and were inspired.

▲ *The legendary figure of Roland, knight of Charlemagne, blew his horn to request aid but help came too late to save him.*

▶ *The fate of a noble knight was often entangled with a beautiful damsel, and there were many tales of unwary and impressionable young knights being lured into fairy kingdoms, robbed of all energy and purpose or used in some wicked scheme against the maiden's enemies.*

TIMELINE OF LEGENDARY KNIGHTS

c.500 A British war leader who achieves a significant victory over the Saxons at 'Mount Badon' may be the historical basis of the legendary King Arthur.

c.550 Arthur is a hero in Welsh works by poets Aneirin and Taliesin.

778 In the Pass of Roncesvalles in the Pyrenees, Basques or Muslims attack the army of Frankish king Charlemagne.

793 William of Gellone (Charlemagne's cousin and Count of Toulouse 790–811) defeats the Muslim 'Saracens' of Spain at Orange in southern France. This is the basis of the 12th-century chanson *La Prise d'Orange* ('The Taking of Orange'). He is known as 'William of Orange'.

c.817–30 The *Vita Karoli Magni*, a biography of Charlemagne by Einhard, identifies 'Hroudland' or 'Roland' as one of those killed in a skirmish at Roncesvalles in 778.

c.830 Welsh monk Nennius mentions Arthur in his *History of the Britons*. He lists 12 battles in which Arthur fought the Saxons, including a famous victory at Mons Badonicus (Mount Badon).

c.950 The anonymous *Annals of Wales* report that Arthur won victory at Mount Badon in 516 and was killed fighting at Mount Camlann in 539.

973 William I, Count of Provence (another model for William of Orange in later chansons), defeats Saracens at the Battle of Tourtour.

c.1050–1130 The *Chanson de Roland* ('Song of Roland') mourns the loss and celebrates the heroism of a knight in the service of Frankish king Charlemagne, and is one of the first of the *chansons de geste* ('songs of heroic deeds').

c.1050–1150 The legend of Arthur develops in Welsh legend *Culhwch and Olwen*, which describes Arthur as foremost among a band of warriors with a court at Kelliwic ('wooded grove') in Cornwall; this may be Callington (near Launceston).

1096–99 The feats of Norman knight Robert Guiscard are celebrated by Norman

▲ *King Arthur, a knightly legend who features repeatedly, and for centuries, throughout historical and literary works.*

chronicler William of Apulia in *The Deeds of Robert Guiscard*.

1099 Spanish knight Don Dodrigo Diaz de Vivar dies in Valencia. His exploits in the service of the Spanish crown and in that of the Moors (Muslim Saracens) are the subject of the 12th-century poem *Song of My Cid*.

1100–50 Alberic of Besançon writes the oldest surviving romance about Alexander the Great. His work is a key source for the *Alexander Romance*, written before 1200 by Norman poet Alexander of Bernay.

1126–71 Henry de Blois, abbot of Glastonbury, orders a search of Glastonbury Tor for King Arthur's remains. A coffin is reputedly found inscribed with the legend 'Here is found the grave of King Arthur, buried in the Isle of Avalon'.

1130–90 French troubadour Bernart de Ventadorn is active.

c.1150–1300 Chivalric romances – accounts of knightly deeds in prose or poetry – are at the height of their popularity. They will remain a notable art form throughout the age of chivalry, right up to the 16th and 17th centuries.

1155 The *Roman de Brut* by Anglo-Norman chronicler Wace of Jersey is a translation of the *History of the Kings of Britain* (c.1135–39) by Geoffrey of Monmouth and transmits Welsh/British traditions about King Arthur to continental Europe.

c.1155–60 *Tristan* by Anglo-Norman poet known as 'Thomas of Britain', and another roughly contemporary poem of the same name by Norman poet Béroul, are the oldest surviving versions of the story of Tristan and Iseult.

c.1160 The Romance of Aeneas, the Romance of Thebes and the Romance of Troy, all attributed to trouvère Benoit de Sainte-Maure, are early examples of the roman d'antiquité, romances about figures from the classical world.

c.1160–1215 Marie de France writes several songs including the *Lay of Lanval*.

1170 *Erec and Enide*, a 7,000-line poem by French poet Chrétien de Troyes, is the first Arthurian romance. Sir Erec is also known as Sir Geraint in other contexts.

1176–81 Chrétien de Troyes's poem *Lancelot, the Knight of the Cart* develops the story of Sir Lancelot and is the first work in the Arthurian tradition to mention Arthur's court at Camelot.

c.1180 In his chanson *Girart de Vienne*, troubadour Bertrand de Bar-sur-Aube identifies three cycles for chansons: the *Geste du roi*, (mainly about Charlemagne), the *Geste de Garin de Monglane* (mainly about William of Orange) and the *Geste de Doon de Mayence* (about rebellions against royal authority).

1180 *The Four Sons of Aymon*, also known

as *Renaud of Montauban*, is one of the most popular *chansons de geste* in the Geste de Doon de Mayence.

c.1180 The Chanson d'Antioche ('Song of Antioch') by trouvère Bertrand de Bar-sur-Aube features Godfrey of Bouillon and other knights of the First Crusade and is based on a poem reputedly written by Richard the Pilgrim during the crusade.

1181–91 Chrétien de Troyes's poem Perceval, the Story of the Grail introduces the story of Sir Perceval and the search for the Holy Grail. It is dedicated to Count Philip of Flanders.

1190 French churchman and courtier Andreas Capellanus ('Andrew the Chaplain') writes *The Art of Courtly Love*.

1191-1202 French poet Robert de Boron's *Joseph of Arimathea* develops the story of the Holy Grail. Around the same time, his Merlin is the first Arthurian tale to describe the sword that could be drawn from the stone only by the rightful king.

c.1194 The romance *Lanzelet* by Swiss cleric Ulrich von Zatzikhoven is the first work in the Arthurian tradition to describe Sir Lancelot's upbringing by the Lady of the Lake. His work is based on an Anglo-Norman original.

c.1200–20 In his poem *Parzival* (another version of the story of Arthurian knight Sir Perceval) German poet Wolfram von Eschenbach promotes loyalty as the foremost chivalric virtue.

1210 Old French poet Jean Bodel (1167–1210) identifies three proper subjects for chivalric romances: 'the Matter of Rome' (on heroes of the classical world), 'the Matter of France' (about Charlemagne and his knights) and 'the Matter of Britain' (about King Arthur and his knights).

c.1220 The attitudes and engagements of courtly love are described in French poet Jean Renart's narrative poem *The Lay of the Shadow*.

c.1225 *The Search for the Holy Grail* presents Galahad as the unique perfection of chivalry, who gradually comes to understand the meaning of the Holy Grail.

1225–26 The Anglo-Norman poem *History of William Marshall* describes the exploits of the man described as 'the greatest knight who ever lived'.

c.1250 In the Welsh collection *Triads of the Island of Britain*, Arthurian knight Sir Kay is celebrated as a great enchanter – able to grow as tall as an oak tree.

1254 The future King Edward I of England, later a great chivalric figure, is knighted at age 15 by King Alfonso X of Castile prior to marrying Princess Eleanor of Castile. He later fights on the Ninth Crusade (1271–72) and takes great interest in the Arthurian tradition. He holds several Arthurian 'Round Tables' (jousting tournaments) in 1279–1302.

1255 Ulrich von Lichtenstein, a noble from the Duchy of Styria (now southern Austria), writes the courtly love poem *In Service of the Lady*.

1278 The supposed remains of King Arthur and Queen Guinevere are reburied in the presence of King Edward I in front of the High Altar in Glastonbury Abbey.

1279 King Edward I holds a 'Round Table' tournament at Kenilworth Castle for 100 knights and their ladies.

1286 Crusaders compete in an Arthurian

'Round Table' tournament in Acre to mark the coronation of King Hugh III of Cyprus as King of Jerusalem.

c.1300 Middle English poem *Sir Orfeo* transports the ancient Greek myth of Orpheus to the medieval world. It is probably based on a now lost Old French Breton lay or song.

c.1310–14 In *The Divine Comedy* the poet Dante Alighieri celebrates Norman knight Robert Guiscard as one of the greatest of all knights.

1312 Jacques de Longuyon, from Lorraine, is the first to list the 'Nine Worthies', figures from the biblical and classical world celebrated as exemplars of chivalry: three biblical figures (Joshua, David and Judas Maccabeus), three classical warriors (Hector of Troy, Alexander the Great and Julius Caesar) and three Christian leaders (King Arthur, Charlemagne and Godfrey of Bouillon, leading knight of the First Crusade).

c.1320 *The Deeds of the Romans*, probably written by monks, features classical figures including Alexander the Great.

1330–44 Roman general Julius Caesar is portrayed as a medieval knight in the courtly love tradition in the 14th-century French romance *Perceforest*.

1348 King Edward III of England makes St George the patron of his knightly brotherhood the Order of the Garter.

c.1375 In the English poem *Sir Gawain and the Green Knight*, Gawain is the first figure to be called 'knight errant'.

1380 *The Chronicle of Bertrand du Guesclin*, a poem by Cuvelier, celebrates the life of the Breton knight.

1485 In Sir Thomas Malory's Arthurian masterpiece *Le Morte d'Arthur*, Sir Lancelot is celebrated as the foremost Christian knight, embodying key chivalric virtues of courtesy, loyalty, honesty, kindness and humility – as well as ferocity in conflict.

1493 Louis de Hédouville hosts an Arthurian *pas d'armes* at Sandricourt set in locations from romance narratives.

◀ *Sir Lancelot became known as the knight who embodies all aspects of chivalry.*

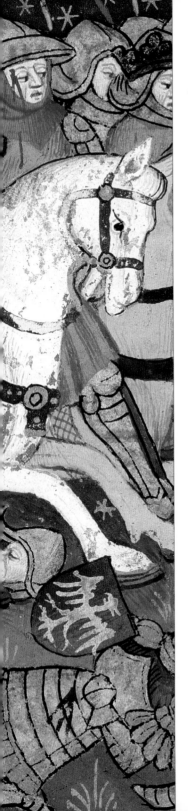

CHAPTER EIGHTEEN

KNIGHTLY HEROES OF THE BIBLICAL AND CLASSICAL WORLDS

In his *Historia Regum Britanniae* (*History of the Kings of Britain*), written in *c*.1135–39, the chronicler Geoffrey of Monmouth claimed that the people of Britain were descended from Brutus, great-grandson of Aeneas of Troy. Geoffrey wrote that Brutus and his fellow Trojan Corineus were the first settlers of the British Isles: Brutus founded the city of Troia Nova ('New Troy'), which became London, while Corineus gave his name to Cornwall. Britain was thereby linked to the heroic past of legend, and perhaps also to the Roman Empire, which according to some was founded by Aeneas.

In the same way the strand of knightly poems and romances centred on classical heroes and biblical warriors added glory to contemporary knights by creating an ancient pedigree. Romance authors described the classical and biblical warriors as if they were medieval knights. Characters in the stories were intended to inspire knights to perform similar acts of chivalry.

For the purposes of this book, great figures such as the Jewish King David or the Greek warrior Achilles are of interest not in their own right as warriors, although their reputation makes them major figures in military history, but because the way they were presented in chivalric literature gives us important insights into how medieval authors and knights understood chivalry and their own world.

▲ *Medieval-style Trojans setting off for battle in a 15th-century manuscript.*

◄ *In the 15th century Alexander the Great was depicted riding into battle against the Persians in the manner of a late medieval king, with 12th-century armour and weapons.*

GOD'S SOLDIERS

AN INSPIRATION TO CRUSADERS

Knights of the Middle Ages saw the Jewish warriors of the Old Testament as exemplars of chivalry. Chief among these biblical prototypes of the medieval knight were King David, Judas Maccabeus, Joshua and Gideon.

THE CITY OF DAVID

In the 10th century BC David became the second king of Israel (after Saul) and created a united kingdom with a capital at Jerusalem (later called 'the city of David'). David was a great warrior as well as a king. The most famous of the many celebrated biblical stories featuring him was doubtless his slaying of the Philistine giant Goliath in single combat, using a stone from his sling. In the medieval Christian tradition he was likened to Christ himself, and his victory over Goliath was said to be the precursor of Christ's victory over evil in the form of Satan.

David was also a poet and musician – and is traditionally believed to be the author of much of the Book of Psalms in the Bible. He was one of the prototypes for those ideal chivalric figures and historical knights – such as King Richard I – who wrote poetry and songs as well as being great warriors.

THE HAMMER

Judas Maccabeus was a Jewish guerrilla fighter of the 2nd century BC, who led a revolt against the Seleucid empire, the Hellenistic state stretching from Thrace to India that followed Alexander the Great's empire. The Seleucid King Antiochus IV Epiphanes had attempted to prevent the Jews from practising their religion, had defaced the Temple in Jerusalem and rededicated it to the Greek god Zeus. Judas's rebellion against the Seleucids was celebrated for having saved Judaism.

Using mainly guerrilla tactics, Judas defeated four Seleucid armies and restored the Temple in Jerusalem. The name Maccabeus was given to him in his lifetime, and is thought to derive from the Aramaic word *maqqaba* ('hammer') – a reference to his fierceness in battle. In later years both Frankish king Charles Martel (Charles 'the Hammer') and English monarch Edward I (known as *Scottorum Malleus* – 'the Hammer of the Scots' – because of his victories in Scotland) were similarly honoured.

Judas's achievements were described in Books 1 and 2 Maccabees, which were part of the Bible in the medieval period. (The books are still part of the Old Testament in the Roman Catholic and Eastern Orthodox Christian traditions, but not in the Hebrew Bible. Protestant Christians usually consider them to be part of the Apochrypha, a group of texts associated with the Bible but not included in it.) Judas featured also in the history written by the 1st-century AD Jewish priest and historian Josephus.

AN EXAMPLE FOR CRUSADERS

Judas Maccabeus was celebrated for his strength, bravery and piety, and the combination of these qualities made him the ideal model for knights. In defending his faith of Judaism (seen as the forerunner of Christianity) and driving imposters

◀ *An illustration in a 16th-century French manuscript shows the Jewish warrior Judas Maccabeus giving money to pay for services for those killed in battle.*

◄ The Israelites commanded by Joshua sack the city of Ai (top), and (below) the people of Gibeon, afraid of the receiving the same treatment, make peace with Joshua. Both images are from a 13th-century manuscript of the Old Testament.

Sadly, in victory the crusaders also followed the example of Joshua's army, when his men slaughtered every living person in Jericho except for a woman, Rahab, and her family who had helped spies sent ahead by Joshua before the attack. Once in Jerusalem, the crusaders likewise went on a violent rampage, until the streets ran with blood. (Joshua's exploits were described in the Bible, chiefly in the books of Exodus, Numbers and Joshua.)

Another great biblical warrior, Gideon, was hailed by medieval writers for his combination of martial power and deep religious faith. As described in the Bible's Book of Judges, he restored the true faith in God after his fellow Jews had turned to the worship of the Canaanite god Baal. Gideon won a great victory over a tribe of desert raiders called the Midianites. His name meant 'Great Warrior'.

out of the holy city of Jerusalem, he was a prototype for the knights of the crusades.

The example of the biblical warrior Joshua was also a model for the crusader knights, particularly those on the First Crusade. After the Israelites had escaped from captivity in Egypt in *c.*1200BC, Joshua succeeded Moses as their leader and led them into the 'Promised Land' of Canaan (the eastern Mediterranean shore, from southern Turkey to Egypt).

On arrival in Canaan, Joshua famously inspired the Israelites to attempt to capture the fortified city of Jericho. This was done by ordering the army to march around the city for seven days – after which the walls miraculously collapsed. In 1099 the priest Peter Desiderius convinced the crusaders to employ the same tactics at Jerusalem – and reputedly they were again successful.

THE NINE WORTHIES

Joshua, David, and Judas Maccabeus were celebrated as the three great exemplars of chivalry of the biblical age in the list of the Nine Worthies accepted by medieval writers. The idea of the Nine Worthies was introduced in a *chanson de geste* called *Les Voeux du Paon* ('A Peacock's Vows'), written in 1312 for the Bishop of Liège; the poem was traditionally said to have been written by Jacques de Longuyon from Lorraine, but this claim has been shown to be false. The list of the Nine Worthies also includes figures from the classical world – Hector of Troy, Alexander the Great and Julius Caesar; and the Christian era – King Arthur, Charlemagne, and crusader knight Godfrey of Bouillon.

▲ The warrior Judas Maccabeus, portrayed as one of the Nine Worthies.

HEROES OF ANCIENT GREECE
ANCIENT WARRIORS PRESENTED AS FEUDAL KNIGHTS

The 12th-century trouvère Benoit de Sainte-Maure gave the classical story of the Trojan War a feudal setting in his poem *Le Roman de Troie* (*The Romance of Troy*). In Benoit's 40,000-line poem, written in *c*.1160, all the Greek and Roman heroes of the narrative behaved as feudal warriors. They had abbeys and castles, and they fought according to 12th-century techniques of war.

The story of the Trojan War, which describes historical events that occurred in Anatolia in the 13th century BC, is principally familiar to modern audiences through the *Iliad*, by the ancient Greek poet Homer. However, Benoit de Sainte-Maure did not have access to the works of Homer, since these were not rediscovered until the 15th century in Italy. He had two main sources: a Latin history believed in the Middle Ages to have been written by Dares the Phrygian, a participant in the events described, which in fact probably dated from the 5th century AD; and another Latin account, supposedly written by a second contemporary, Dictys of Crete, but in fact dating from the 4th century AD.

Benoit's version was strikingly different from the accounts familiar to modern readers because it did not include the frequent interventions in the story by Greek gods and goddesses. It made the Trojan warrior Hector, rather than the Greek warrior Achilles, the main hero of

▲ *Hector leads the mounted warriors of Troy into the kind of battle fought by knights in the 15th century, when this edition of Benoit's Trojan poem was published.*

the narrative. This was in line with the prevailing enthusiasm for Troy and its heroes – Hector was celebrated, as we have seen, as one of three principal warriors and chivalric figures of the classical age in the list of Nine Worthies.

THE *ROMANS D'ANTIQUITÉ*
Benoit's poem inspired an entire literary genre, the *romans d'antiquité*, which consisted of poems of the feudal age featuring classical warriors – the 'Matter of Rome' described by Jean Bodel. Of these ancient warriors, the Greek Achilles and the Trojan

Hector were viewed as the finest exemplars of chivalry. The poems were intended to inspire contemporary warriors in the audience by their examples of great chivalric behaviour. The poets who wrote them invented love affairs for their protagonists so they could treat themes of courtly love, and added episodes of knight-errantry and fighting of tournaments so they could describe acts of gallantry and chivalry. Classical narratives of this kind were, alongside Arthurian stories, the favourite subjects for enactment in tournaments and the courtly pageants that surrounded them.

Benoit was attached to the court of King Henry II of England and dedicated *Le Roman de Troie* to Henry's queen, the

◄ *An illustration from an edition of Benoit de Sainte-Maure's* Romance of Troy *shows the Trojans building their city.*

▲ *This portrait of Hector of Troy is from a fresco of the Nine Worthies made in c.1430.*

great royal patroness of chivalric literature, Eleanor of Aquitaine. He may also have been the author of a slightly earlier romance called *Le Roman de Thèbes* (*The Romance of Thebes*), a 10,000-line account of the assaults by the city of Argos on the city of Thebes. It was based on an abridgement of the Latin poem the *Thebaid*, written in the 1st century AD by Publius Papinius Statius, and again represented the Greeks using 12th-century methods of warfare and behaving according to the dictates of courtly love.

Another near-contemporary poem is the 2,000-verse *Le Roman d'Eneas* (*The Romance of Aeneas*), again sometimes attributed to Benoit. Written in c.1160, it was presented as a translation of the Latin poem the *Aeneid* (written in the 1st century BC by Roman poet Virgil). However, rather than reproducing Virgil's account of the travels of Trojan warrior Aeneas from Troy to Italy and his defeat of the Latin people there, it instead concentrated on a medieval courtly love affair between Aeneas and Lavinia, daughter of Latinus, King of the Latins.

TROILUS AND CRESSIDA

Benoit's *Le Roman de Troie* imported the concerns of 12th-century courtly love into the world of the Greek war against Troy. He invented a love affair between a Trojan prince and Briseida, the daughter of a Trojan priest, and this was the first telling of the story of Troilus and Cressida, which was later retold by three major writers.

In Homer's narrative (which, as we have seen, was not available to Benoit) Troilus was the son of King Priam and Queen Hecuba of Troy, and was killed before the Trojan War began. In other ancient versions Troilus was killed by the Greek hero Achilles. In Benoit's poem, Troilus was presented as a young and innocent warrior, who fell deeply in love with the beautiful Briseida, but was betrayed by her when she took up with the Greek warrior Diomedes. The heroine was renamed Cressida in the three later accounts of the tale: the 14th-century version *Il Filostrato* (c.1335) by the Italian poet Giovanni Boccaccio; Englishman Geoffrey Chaucer took Boccaccio's work as the outline for his poem *Troilus and Criseyde*, written c.1385–90; and then, in the 17th century, William Shakespeare used Chaucer's poem as the source for his play *Troilus and Cressida* (c.1602).

In Boccaccio's poem, Cressida mourned for her father, Calcas, who had powers of prophecy and had seen the future defeat of Troy and so taken up residence in the Greek camp. Troilus noticed her at a festival and fell passionately in love with her. With the help of his friend Pandarus, a cousin of Cressida, he was able to meet her. As part of a truce agreement Cressida was then allowed to join her father in the camp, leaving Troilus in the city. He begged her to elope with him, but she said he should remain to defend Troy. She promised to guard her honour closely and meet him again after ten days.

Subsequently, however, Cressida was seduced by the Greek warrior Diomedes and she did not keep her promise to return to Troilus. He suspected the worst, and although Cressida sent him letters promising continuing love his fears were confirmed when his brother Deiphobus returned from battle with a piece of Diomedes' clothing – it had a favour from Cressida attached to it. Troilus sought revenge in battle, and fought for many hours against Diomedes, and in the style of a hero of chivalric romance killed no fewer than a thousand warriors in his righteous anger, but did not kill his rival. He was finally despatched by Achilles.

▼ *The go-between Pandarus talks to Cressida on behalf of her courtly lover Troilus. This image is from an edition of Giovanni Boccaccio's poem* Il Filostrato, *printed c.1475.*

THE ADVENTURES OF ALEXANDER
MEDIEVAL ROMANCES ABOUT ALEXANDER THE GREAT

A series of medieval romances recounted the larger-than-life exploits of Alexander the Great, the 4th-century BC Macedonian warrior who conquered the Persian Empire and northern India. The Alexander romances – like the *romans d'antiquités* that featured narratives of the heroes of Greece and Troy – used an anachronistic approach, presenting the great general and other ancient heroes as feudal warriors. They were also full of marvels and enchantments, monsters and magic, and tales of the Orient that appealed strongly to a noble audience that had developed a taste for the exoticism of the East, by listening to eye-witness accounts of grizzled crusaders.

Alexander's extraordinary career combined stirring military achievements with explorations far into the east, beyond the limits of the known world. Even in his lifetime, colourful legends collected around his name and following his death in 323BC, a folklore rich in exotic oriental marvels grew up. A number of these stories, written in Greek, were gathered in

c.AD300 by an author masquerading as one of Alexander's own generals named Callisthenes, and the scholars call the text the pseudo-Callisthenes; many translations of this source in Latin were available to the authors of the romances in the 12th and 13th centuries.

ALBERIC OF BESANÇON
The oldest surviving medieval version of the life of Alexander was written in c.1100–1150 by Alberic of Besançon. Alberic told how Alexander's birth was

▲ According to legend, the great warrior had a remarkable education. A French edition of The Alexander Romance, *c.1400, shows him with his tutor Aristotle.*

marked by marvels: the sky grew dark as the sea raged and the rain fell red as blood, but with the birth of the baby who was destined to be a conqueror all fell quiet. According to the legend recounted by Alberic, Alexander's father King Philip II of Macedon appointed great men of the age of antiquity including Homer, Aristotle and Ptolemy to be tutors to Alexander in his youth; and they saw to it that he had a good chivalric education, of the kind enjoyed by the nobles in the audience for the poem, combining knowledge of letters with training in the arts of knighthood such as swordplay, jousting and hunting – as well as singing and playing music.

THE ALEXANDER ROMANCE
Alberic's work survives only in a fragment of 105 lines, but it was one of the major sources for other medieval stories about the legendary general, notably *Le Roman d'Alexandre* (*The Alexander Romance*), a

◄ The people of Babylon give the keys of their city to Alexander. The world-conquering general died in Babylon, perhaps of food or alcohol poisoning, aged 33 in June 323BC.

poem in lines of 12 syllables written by the Norman poet Alexander of Bernay, also known as Alexander of Paris, before 1200. (The 12-syllable lines he used to such good effect were named 'alexandrines' in his honour.)

EXTRAORDINARY FEATS

One section of *The Alexander Romance* told how as a youth the future general prefigured his wide conquests on land by claiming the heavens as his own. It happened that one day as he rode to hunt he saw two gryphons, creatures of Greek myth that combined a lion's body with an eagle's head and wings. He was seized by a desire to fly the creatures as high as the sun, and called a squire to him, commanding the young man to capture and starve the gryphons for two days, so that on the third day they would be willing to obey his commands if he brought them food. Meanwhile he constructed a chair and added a canopy to guard against the light when he was near the sun.

When the day came, he easily mastered the gryphons, tied the chair to them, and by luring them with juicy meat suspended just out of their reach he drove them into the sky as easily as he was able to make his horse gallop and turn in the hunt. He flew so high that the gryphons' wings were burned and the creatures swooped down away from the great heat; Alexander mastered them once more and brought them safely to land in his father Philip's fields.

Another episode recalls how he went on campaign to the land of the Amazons, the race of terrifying female warriors in Greek mythology, and forced them to pay tribute. Their queen, Thalestris, was so impressed with the general that she came to him with 300 women hoping to breed children in his image – she herself waited on him for 13 days and nights, in hopes that she might conceive a daughter by him.

THE WISDOM OF INDIA

Two other tales recounted incidents that occurred during Alexander's campaigns in India. In the first, Alexander encountered

a group of Indian sages, who informed him that they were not afraid of him because in their village there was nothing to steal except wisdom – and for all his strength, he could not take that from them against their will. In the story, Alexander reacted with grace and intelligence, allowing his army to rest in a camp and sitting with the sages in order to learn from them. They told him that all his campaigning would in the end be for nothing since he, like all men and women, would die, and another man would come and take what he had worked so hard to conquer; but they also taught him that death was not the end, for although darkness covered the soul when a person died, soon the soul would rise to new life just as the sun rose at the end of night.

▲ *After being impressed by war elephants in the Persian army during his victory at the Battle of Gaugamela in 331BC, Alexander incorporated the animals into his own forces and used them in battle charges.*

In the second story, which was framed as a letter from Alexander to his tutor Aristotle, the great general encountered in India a holy grove containing talking trees that were sacred to the moon and sun gods. The trees delivered the chilling news that Alexander would be killed by his own men and that his death would come in Babylon – a prophecy that proved only half-right, for although Alexander did die in Babylon in 323BC at just 33 years of age, it was from fever rather than as a result of treachery.

KNIGHT OF ROME

JULIUS CAESAR

Another great general of the classical world revered as an embodiment of chivalry was Julius Caesar, the Roman general and statesman, conqueror of France (then known as Gaul) in 58–50BC and invader of Britain in 55BC and 54BC.

ALL FOR LOVE

As we have seen, Caesar was one of the Nine Worthies who were presented as exemplars of chivalry. In the 14th-century French romance *Perceforest* (c.1330–44), he was portrayed as a young knight in the courtly love tradition, who decided to invade Britain because one of his own knights named Luces had fallen passionately in love with the wife of Perceforest, King of England.

The seeds of Caesar's death were sown in the invasion: after Caesar killed a British knight with a lance, the knight's nephew Orsus Bouchesuave vowed revenge, and taking the lance, made 12 iron weapons from its head. These were the weapons used by Brutus and his allies (with Orsus in their number) to kill Caesar on the Ides of March in 44BC.

The romance also found room for Alexander the Great: it claimed that he conquered Britain, but then set out for Babylon and left Perceforest in charge;

Perceforest then converted Britain to Christianity and ruled over a golden age, with bands of great knights in his service.

GEOFFREY OF MONMOUTH'S 'HISTORY' OF CAESAR

Geoffrey of Monmouth included an account of the Roman general's invasions of Britain in his *History of the Kings of*

▲ *A 15th-century French manuscript of the* Deeds of the Romans *depicts Caesar's army in full medieval armour preparing to disembark after defeating a Breton army.*

Britain (c.1135–39). To the various existing accounts by early medieval writers such as Bede and Nennius, Geoffrey added a number of legendary elements that reflected the preoccupations of the medieval knights in his audience.

According to Geoffrey's account, Julius Caesar decided to invade Britain after he had conquered Gaul (whereas in reality he undertook the invasions while still engaged in the conquest of Gaul) and dispatched a letter demanding tribute to Cassibelaunus, the King of Britain. (Cassibelaunus was Geoffrey's literary version of the historical British chieftain

◀ *The Roman army uses medieval siege engines and ladders to break into a fortress in this illustration from a 14th-century French edition of the* Deeds of the Romans.

Cassivellaunus of the Catuvellauni tribe, who led British resistance to the second Caesarian invasion that occurred in 54BC.) Cassibelaunus refused to pay tribute and claimed equality with Caesar, on account of the Romans' and Britons' common descent from the heroes of Troy.

CAESAR'S MAGICAL SWORD

Caesar then invaded via the Thames estuary and during the ensuing battle engaged in a hand-to-hand duel with Nennius, Cassibelaunus's brother. In the course of the struggle, Caesar struck Nennius a brutal blow to the head and then his sword *Crocea Mors* ('Yellow Death') became stuck in Nennius's shield. Nennius kept the weapon and – like the swords carried by great chivalric figures such as Charlemagne or King Arthur – it proved to be a sword of magical power that laid low any person that Nennius encountered during the remainder of the battle. The Britons fought with such heroism that Caesar was forced to take flight and sailed back to France. Nennius, however, survived for only 15 days after the battle and died from the effects of the head wound. He was buried in Trinovantum (London) with the magical sword beside him.

BRITONS BETRAYED

Subsequently, according to Geoffrey, Caesar invaded a second time and was driven back once more. The British used the cunning tactic of driving stakes into the Thames mud so they were hidden beneath the water at high tide and holed the Roman ships. During the victory celebrations after this triumph, however, the seeds of future disaster were sown when Cassibelaunus's nephew Hirelglas was killed by Cuelinus, the nephew of another royal, Androgeus, during a bout of wrestling. In Caesar's third invasion, Androgeus betrayed Cassibelaunus by

▲ Caesar's assassination on the Ides of March 44BC is reimagined as a moment of 15th-century Italian court life in this panel of c.1450 by Giovanni di Tommaso Angelo.

launching an attack on the rear of the British, and driving Cassibelaunus into retreat. Finally Cassibelaunus agreed to pay tribute to Caesar and became his friend.

AN ISLAND FOR A HORSE

Caesar and the invasion were also covered in the *Welsh Triads of the Islands of Britain*, a 13th-century collection of history, mythology and folklore. In this version, Cassibelaunus (here called Caswallawn) travelled to Rome to find his lover Fflur and initially allowed Caesar to land in Britain, in return for a horse of great strength and beauty named Meinlas.

ANCIENT VERSUS MEDIEVAL

Also in the 13th century a French work, *Le Faits des Romains (Deeds of the Romans)* detailed Caesar's invasion of Britain. In this the invaders overcame the underwater stakes by burning them with Greek fire. The mysterious Greek fire was a sulphur-based weapon developed in c.AD670 and used by the Byzantine Greeks. The use of the stakes was a partial invention of the medieval writers: in the historic invasion, the Britons did use sharpened stakes and did conceal some beneath the waterline, but they intended them as a defence against Roman infantry, not the ships.

ONE OF THE NINE WORTHIES

As with all the Nine Worthies, Julius Caesar (depicted below second left in an early 15th-century fresco) represents all facets of the perfect warrior. All, with the exception of Hector of Troy and arguably King Arthur, are conquering heroes. Most came from royal families.

All brought glory and honour to their nations and were noted for their prowess in arms. As individuals, each displayed some outstanding chivalric quality which, in combination with their historical context, made them exemplars of knighthood.

SIR ORFEO

CHIVALRIC LORD, LOYAL HUSBAND AND COURTLY MUSICIAN

An English poem from the 13th and 14th centuries transposed the Greek myth of Orpheus and Eurydice to the world of medieval England. The hero and heroine, in the Greek myth a minstrel and his beloved wife, a tree-spirit, became Sir Orfeo, ruler of a medieval kingdom, and his queen, Heurodis. The poem *Sir Orfeo* appeared to be derived from an earlier Old French Breton lay or song and it showed the strong influence of Celtic folktales about faery kingdoms existing alongside the day-to-day world.

WHAT MEDIEVAL POETS KNEW OF THE GREEK MYTH

The earliest surviving manuscript of *Sir Orfeo* dates from *c.*1330. There are references to a Breton lay about Orpheus in earlier French narratives, such as the 12th-century romance *Floire et Blanchefleur* (*Floris and Blanchefleur*) and the 13th-century *Prose Lancelot*, but this version of the story has not survived. The ancient Greek myth of Orpheus and Eurydice

▼ *According to the ancient Greek myth, Orpheus was killed by Maenads, female worshippers of the mystery god Dionysius. They were angry that after Eurydice's death he had abandoned the love of women.*

dates back to at least the 6th century BC, and would have been available to the medieval period poets through the Roman poets Virgil and Ovid.

In the Greek myth Orpheus was a musician from Thrace so gifted that animals, and even trees and stones, would come to listen to his playing of the lyre. When his wife Eurydice was killed by a snakebite he followed her into the underworld, and there played so beautifully that the god of the dead, Hades, allowed him to have Eurydice back – on the condition that as he led her out of the land of the dead, back to the world of the living, he did not look back. In older versions of the myth he succeeded, and Eurydice was restored to life, but in the better known, and less happy versions (found in Ovid and Virgil) he looked back – and Eurydice dissolved into mist.

FROM WINCHESTER TO THE OTHERWORLD

The poet of *Sir Orfeo* began by situating the narrative in England, declaring that Thrace (Orfeo's kingdom) was in fact an old title for Winchester, King Alfred the Great's capital. The king lost his beloved wife, Heurodis, when she was stolen by the king of the fairies from under an apple tree haunted by spirits. In this version, she did not die, but was taken at the moment before death to a faery Otherworld.

Sir Orfeo was undone by grief, and renounced his kingdom in order to search for Heurodis. Like a good feudal lord he thought of the well-being of his vassals, and left his steward in charge of the kingdom; he announced that the people should hold an assembly to elect a new ruler if they heard reports of his death. Then he cast off his fine clothes and put on the simple robes of a pilgrim, and retreated into the forest. He took only one thing with him: his harp. In his solitude and grief, deep in the woods, he played

▲ *Orpheus and Eurydice in elaborate medieval courtly dress, from an illustration to a c.1412 edition of the works of Venetian female writer Christine de Pizan.*

songs of unearthly beauty on this instrument, and even the wild animals were charmed to stillness.

Ten years passed, then one day Sir Orfeo saw Heurodis riding by in the fairy king's hunting expedition, and followed her into the Otherworld. There he played songs of exquisite beauty on his harp and the king offered him one 'boon', or favour. Seizing his chance, Sir Orfeo chose Heurodis and led her back to the earth.

With Heurodis safely restored to him, Sir Orfeo returned, rejoicing, to Winchester. He remained disguised as a poor beggar in order to test the loyalty of his steward, and finding the man to be honest and true, he then revealed his identity and resumed his rule as king.

▶ *The myth of Orpheus, with the journey to the underworld realm of the dead and the celebration of the power of music from above, has remained a symbolic tale of loss and redemption through the centuries.*

CHRISTIAN INTERPRETATIONS

The abduction of mortals by fairies, the appearance of the fairy hunt and the idea of an Otherworld that mortal men and women could travel to and return from, were all traditional motifs that appeared in Celtic folklore. At the time of the poem's composition, there were many Christian commentaries written on the original myth. One 14th-century interpretation identified Eurydice as the soul of a Christian, the king of the underworld as Satan, and Orpheus as Christ (who travelled to hell to save lost souls after his death on the Cross).

Another interpretation of the story from the same period saw Orpheus as a Christian and Eurydice as his soul; in the version in which Orpheus lost Eurydice by looking back, this interpretation said that after regaining his soul through leading a religious life and turning away from the things of the world, the Christian was tempted once more by temporal concerns and in looking back lost his soul to Satan.

CHIVALRIC MEANINGS

For the medieval audience of *Sir Orfeo,* the harp that the king played was both a courtly and a sacred instrument, and would recall the lyre played by the biblical psalmist, and paragon of chivalry, King David. Sir Orfeo's withdrawal into the forest was suggestive for the audience of a religious retreat or pilgrimage – indeed, after his temporary abdication, the king wore pilgrim robes; moreover, the fact that Sir Orfeo was granted a glimpse of Heurodis (on the fairy ride) while he was on retreat rather than on a quest would suggest the grace of God in granting spiritual benefit to pilgrims.

In addition to supporting such a religious interpretation, *Sir Orfeo* could be understood in the light of the code of

chivalry and of courtly love. The knight's loyalty to his lady, tested to the utmost limit when he gave up his worldly preeminence and lived in the wilderness of the forest for ten years, proved that he was worthy of her love. He demonstrated great bravery in his journey to the unknown

faery Otherworld, and his prowess (in this case with the harp rather than lance or the mace) won him his reward. In addition, he proved himself a worthy ruler, putting his people in the care of a trusty steward, and arranging for them to elect a new king if necessary.

CHAPTER NINETEEN

KING ARTHUR AND THE KNIGHTS OF THE ROUND TABLE

King Arthur and the knights of the Round Table at Camelot were honoured in the Middle Ages as the epitome of chivalry. The knights who took inspiration from the medieval cycles of Arthurian romances sought to emulate the deeds of Sir Lancelot or Sir Galahad, while many kings, princes and lords used the Round Table as the model for the organization of tournament knights or chivalric brotherhoods. As early as 1223 the Crusader knight John of Ibelin, Lord of Beirut, used the deeds of the knights of the Round Table as an inspiration for a 'Round Table' of jousting in Cyprus. Knights looked on Camelot with pride, admiration – and sadness, for the golden age of King Arthur contained within it the seeds of its own decline and failure. The medieval romances told of the great adventures of Arthur's knights, but also of the adulterous love between his queen, Guinevere, and his most trusted knight, Sir Lancelot. Their treachery, combined with the chivalric quest for the Holy Grail – the cup used by Christ at the Last Supper – led to the dissolving of the Round Table fellowship, Arthur's death and the passing of his glorious kingdom. Taken as a whole, the romances – and the wider body of Arthurian legend – were coloured with a deeply affecting elegiac tone, the sense that all great things, such as the age of Camelot, must pass away.

▲ *The Lady of the Lake meeting Guinevere, from 'The Story of Lancelot'.*

◄ *The Round Table – at which no knight could claim precedence – was presented as the ideal organization for a body of brave warriors, but when the knights departed on the Grail quest the brotherhood of fellow knights was fractured.*

LORD OF CAMELOT

KING ARTHUR'S HISTORICAL ROOTS AND THE GROWTH OF HIS LEGEND

In the great body of medieval literature celebrating Arthur and his knights, the king was cast in a number of roles – as squire called to greatness, noble ruler, peerless warrior, perfection of knighthood and the emblem of a perfect past who might one day return to lead his fallen people into a glorious future. The origins of this figure, whose appeal endures to this day, are found in an uncertain blend of Celtic history and legend.

ARTHUR'S GRAVE

Medieval knights in England were in no doubt that King Arthur was part of their history. In the 12th century a search was mounted for his place of burial.

The familiar tales of his life told that he was carried away for burial on the Isle of Avalon. This has been associated with St Michael's Mount, a sea island just off the coast in Cornwall, and L'Ile d'Aval off the coast of Brittany, but a parallel tradition, current from the early 11th century, held that Avalon was Glastonbury Tor, a hill that looked like an island among the water meadows of Somerset before the meadows were drained.

In the time of Henry II of England, Henry de Blois, abbot of Glastonbury in 1126–71, ordered a search of the Tor for Arthur's remains. Reputedly a coffin was found buried in the hillside inscribed with the legend *Hic jacet sepultus inclitus rex*

Arthurus in insula Avalonia ('Here is found the grave of King Arthur, buried in the Isle of Avalon'). In the 13th century the remains were reburied in front of the high altar in Glastonbury Abbey, in the presence of King Edward I. They were visited by pilgrims until well into the Tudor era.

HISTORICAL ROOTS

Most modern historians believe that the legend of King Arthur grew up around the military achievements of a minor British or Welsh prince of the 5th or 6th century, who led a united resistance to the invasions of the Saxons. He may have been the leader of a British army that won a celebrated victory over the Saxons at 'Mount Badon' in *c*.500.

The earliest references to Arthur are Welsh. He was named in poems of the late 6th century by Welsh poets Aneirin and Taliesin, which praised his bravery and referred to him as the 'great holder of feasts'. In the *Historia Brittonum* (*History of the Britons*) of *c*.830, the Welsh monk Nennius catalogued no fewer than 12 battles in which Arthur fought the Saxons, and mentioned the great victory at Mons Badonicus (Mount Badon); in the following century the anonymous chronicler of

▼ *Glastonbury Tor, proposed as the site of the Isle of Avalon, takes its name from the Celtic word (tor) for a cone-shaped hill.*

▲ *In his youth Arthur thought himself a mere squire, but without knowing it he was, in fact, a prince, destined to wear the crown.*

the *Annales Cambriae* ('Annals of Wales') stated that Arthur won a battle at Mount Badon in 516 but was slain in fighting at Mount Camlann in 539. The Annals also mentioned that a warrior named Medraut (a Latin form of Mordred) met his end in this fateful battle. Arthur's name appeared in 11th- and 12th-century Welsh accounts of the lives of the saints, in which he was portrayed as a great warrior.

Mount Badon is identified by many historians as the hill fort of Little Solsbury Hill near the city of Bath in southern England. Archaeologists have uncovered evidence that the fort was in use by the British at the close of the 4th century. Other theories hold that Camlann, the proposed place of Arthur's death, might

be in northern England at Bidoswald in Cumbria, which was called Camboglanna in the Roman era.

ARTHUR THE BEAR GOD

Other historians, however, disagree that there was a single historical figure at the heart of the Arthurian legend. Arthur's name may mean 'bear man' from the Welsh *art* ('bear'), and some experts argue that Arthur was originally a Celtic bear god who was given a historical setting in legends. Others suggest that the name may have been a *nom de guerre* adopted by a succession of war leaders who fought against invaders.

THE LEGEND IS BORN

The legend of Arthur developed in Welsh folklore and early romances. Perhaps the earliest of these was *Culhwch and Olwen* (11th–12th century), which described Arthur as the leader of a band of heroes (forerunners of the knights of the Round Table) and placed his court at Kelliwic ('forest grove') in Cornwall; this has been identified as Callington (near Launceston) or as Castle Killibury, a hill fort near Wadebridge in North Cornwall.

The Arthurian legend was established by Geoffrey of Monmouth in his *Historia Regum Britanniae (History of the Kings of Britain)* in *c.*1135–39. In his fictionalized account, which was highly influential across Europe, many now familiar elements of the Arthurian cycle were present: the magician Merlin gave the British King Uther Pendragon the appearance of Gorloise, Duke of Cornwall, so that Uther could satisfy his desire to sleep with Ygerna, Gorloise's beautiful wife; as a result of this union, Arthur was born; he became king when his country was at the mercy of Saxon invaders, but drove them back decisively; he married the beautiful Guinevere and his rule was a golden age of peace and chivalry. But Camelot could not last forever: when the Roman Emperor Lucius Tiberius demanded that Britain pay tribute, Arthur travelled to France to defeat a Roman army, leaving the country

▲ *A stained glass window depicts King Arthur beside his foremost knight, Lancelot.*

in the care of his nephew Mordred; ungrateful and unchivalrous, Mordred seduced Guinevere and seized the throne. Arthur returned and killed Mordred but was fatally wounded in the last battle, at Camlann, and his body was borne off to the Isle of Avalon (which Geoffrey said meant 'island of apples').

THE ROUND TABLE AND THE GRAIL QUEST

The Anglo-Norman author Wace of Jersey translated Geoffrey of Monmouth's *History* into French as the *Roman de Brut* (1155). This work was the first to describe the round table at King Arthur's court. The French author Chrétien de Troyes, author of five Arthurian romances (*c.*1165–80), introduced the theme of the quest for the Holy Grail, the cup used in the Last Supper, which Christ had supposedly given to Joseph of Arimathaea who had brought it to Europe.

The legend was further developed in French romances of the 13th century, which added the narratives of Arthur's childhood and how his destiny as king was revealed when he drew the sword Excalibur from the stone; of the liaison between Guinevere and Arthur's most trusted knight, Lancelot; and of Lancelot's son, Sir Galahad, whose purity allowed him to succeed as far as possible in the Grail quest. These legends were made available to English audiences by the 15th-century knight Sir Thomas Malory in his *Le Morte d'Arthur* (*c.*1470).

In the development of the Arthurian legend, very little changed in the main story between Geoffrey of Monmouth and Sir Thomas Malory. One key change came with the development of the code of chivalry and theories of knighthood: Arthur himself, a warrior in the early legends and in Geoffrey of Monmouth's account, became a more courtly figure, a chivalric patron and lord of the Round Table, rather than a knight finding sport in tournaments and on the battlefield.

A KING BETRAYED

SIR TRISTAN AND LADY ISEULT

Sir Tristan was the hero of a Celtic legend about a warrior's love affair with his lord's wife. This was recast in the 12th century by Anglo-Norman poets within the conventions of courtly love, then assimilated in the first quarter of the 13th century into the cycle of Arthurian romance, so that Sir Tristan became a knight of the Round Table, where he was a rival of Sir Lancelot and participated in the quest for the Holy Grail. The story of Tristan's joyful but doomed adulterous love affair with Iseult, wife of King Mark of Cornwall, came before and probably influenced the narrative of Sir Lancelot's affair with Guinevere, wife of King Arthur.

TRISTAN'S CELTIC LEGEND

The earliest surviving versions of the story of Tristan and Iseult are in the Old French poem *Tristan* (c.1155–60), by Anglo-Norman poet Thomas of Britain, and the 12th-century Norman poem *Tristan* by Norman poet Béroul. An earlier story in Celtic folklore, from which all later versions were derived, is now lost but can be reconstructed with confidence.

▲ *Returning from Ireland with Lady Iseult, Sir Tristan mistakenly drinks the potion that makes him risk all for his lady's love.*

According to this version, Sir Tristan was a knight in the service of his uncle, King Mark of Cornwall, and was himself prince of the kingdom of Lyonesse. He was Mark's champion, and after defeating an Irish knight named Marhaus in a duel, was sent to Ireland to seek the hand of Princess Iseult on Mark's behalf.

In Ireland Sir Tristan killed a dragon that had been terrifying the local population, then set sail for Cornwall with the princess. On their journey they mistakenly drank a love potion that Iseult's mother had prepared for her daughter to share with Mark, and were swept away by a deep love that could not be denied.

Iseult married King Mark, whom both she and Sir Tristan liked and honoured, but secretly she carried on her love affair with Tristan. Mark was suspicious and many times tried to catch the lovers out, but they used trickery to maintain an appearance of innocence.

Finally Mark had proof of his suspicions, and sent Tristan to death at the stake and Iseult to a leper colony. But Tristan made a miraculous escape by leaping from a clifftop chapel and rescued Iseult, and the lovers took refuge in the forest of Morrois, where they lived a life of simple fulfilment.

There Mark discovered them again, sleeping naked together with a drawn sword laid between them. Shortly afterwards, remarkably, the three made peace: Iseult returned to Mark's court as his wife and Tristan departed for Brittany, where he married a second Iseult, 'for her name as well as her beauty' – Lady Iseult of the White Hands, the daughter of Duke Hoel of Brittany.

The story ended in tragedy, however: Tristan fought Morholt, uncle of the original Iseult (of Ireland) and although he performed heroically and killed Morholt, he was stabbed with a poisoned spear in the struggle; only Iseult of Ireland knew the magic to draw this poison and save his life, so he sent for her from his sickbed with the message that if she could come she should sail in a ship with white sails, whereas if she could not come the ship should sail with black sails.

Tristan called out to his wife, Iseult of the White Hands, from his bed to tell him whether the ship was coming, and she, jealous of his undying love for her rival, lied to him, telling him that the ship had

---

PAS DE LA JOYEUSE GARDE

▲ *René d'Anjou, Duke of Anjou was a chivalric legend in his own lifetime. The epitome of a knight, he excelled in all the necessary skills and accomplishments.*

Typical of the elaborate 15th-century *pas d'armes* devised to dramatize scenes from the Arthurian cycle was the *Pas de la Joyeuse Garde* held in Anjou in 1446. A castle was built from wood near Saumur in imitation of the 'castle of love' in which, according to various versions, both King Arthur and Queen Guinevere and Tristan and Iseult took refuge. The pageant included two 'Turks', two real lions, a company of musicians mounted on horseback, a dwarf and Duke René d'Anjou on a horse led by a maiden. The best jouster won a gold clasp adorned with rubies and diamonds.

hoisted black sails. So Tristan, believing himself abandoned by his one true love, turned to the wall and died.

When Iseult of Ireland arrived, and discovered Tristan was dead, she was inconsolable – and herself died in a final embrace with her lover. Two trees, one honeysuckle and one hazel, were planted on the lovers' grave, and their branches intertwined as a symbol of their undying love: although King Mark tried three times to cut and separate the branches, they grew back and linked once more so he allowed them to grow.

PRINCE OF LOTHIAN?

Tristan's name (which also appears as Drystan or Drustanus) was a common Pictish name, while his kingdom of Lyonesse may be a transcription into French of Lothian (a region in south-east Scotland, once part of Pictish territory). King Mark of Cornwall was a historical figure who ruled in the early 6th century, and it is possible that the legend of Tristan grew up around a historical Pictish prince

▲ The legend of Tristan and Iseult's doomed love has inspired many reworkings. German composer Richard Wagner's opera Tristan und Isolde *was first performed in 1865.*

who was sent to the Cornish court. Another theory is that Lyonesse refers to the Isles of Scilly off south-west Cornwall.

The earliest versions of the Tristan legend probably had no connection to the Arthurian legend cycle. However, the names of Tristan and Iseult are found in early Welsh poems in connection with King Arthur's court: Iseult was listed as one of the key figures at the court in the 11th-century *Culhwch and Olwen*, while Tristan was identified as one of Arthur's advisers in the 12th- or 13th-century *Dream of Rhonabwy*.

In the early versions of the story, King Mark was a sympathetic character, wronged by circumstance; Mark, Tristan and Iseult all honoured one another – as in the later narrative of Arthur, Lancelot and Guinevere. Tristan loved and honoured Mark as his king and lord; Mark

loved both Iseult and Tristan as nephew and wife; and Iseult loved Mark as her husband. Typically in the earlier versions, with the strongest influence of the magical elements in Celtic folklore, Tristan and Iseult were viewed as being under the power of the love potion and so not morally responsible for their adultery.

In the prose romance versions of the story, however, Mark became a villain who raped and murdered his niece and killed his brother Baldwin. He also slew Tristan – in this version, Tristan did not die in Brittany, but at King Mark's court: the king crept upon him and stabbed him while the knight played his harp beneath a tree.

RETURN FROM EXILE

In some versions Tristan returned from exile to visit Iseult. Two 12th-century poems, now known as the *Folie Tristan*, told of how the knight came back to King Mark's court disguised as a fool or madman, while another called the *Luite Tristan* recounts how he made his return in the guise of a minstrel. The 12th-century poet Marie de France told in her lay *Chèvrefoil* (*Honeysuckle*) of how Tristan signalled to Iseult by leaving out a hazelnut branch inscribed with the legend *Ni moi sans vous, ni vous sans moi* ('I cannot live without you, nor can you live without me').

▼ King Mark was present at the funeral of Tristan and Iseult, according to this 15th-century manuscript version of the story.

KING ARTHUR'S SQUIRE AND SENESCHAL

SIR KAY

ir Kay was the son of Arthur's foster father Sir Ector, and so was the future king's foster brother. Kay's character differed markedly in different versions of the Arthurian legends, ranging from being one of the first and bravest of the knights of the Round Table to being a boastful fool and even a treacherous coward. He appeared often with Sir Bedivere, the knight who returned Arthur's magical sword Excalibur to the mysterious Lady of the Lake.

Sir Kay was best known in the guise presented by the French Arthurian prose romances and in Sir Thomas Malory's *Le Morte d'Arthur*. As an infant, Arthur was removed by Merlin the magician from his true parents, King Uther Pendragon and Ygrayne, and placed in the care of Sir Ector. Arthur grew up in the company of Sir Ector's son, Sir Kay, and came to serve as his squire. At a tournament in London, Arthur lost Kay's sword and thought he could replace it by drawing the magical weapon Excalibur from the stone. In so doing he revealed that he was destined to be King of the Britons. Initially Sir Kay tried to claim that he had drawn the sword himself, but in the end had to admit that it was his foster brother, Arthur, who was the chosen one. The tables were turned: Sir Kay became Arthur's squire, and then went on to serve as one of the knights of the Round Table.

A WELSH LORD, AN 'ENCHANTER KNIGHT'

Welsh folklore celebrated Sir Kay – known as Cai Hir ('Kay the Tall') – as a leading warrior with a hot temper. Some writers identify him as the 5th-century Welsh Lord of Caer Gai, who had this nickname.

The folk tales collected in the *Mabinogion* told of his great feats of bravery and chivalry. In the 11th-century tale *Cuhlwch and Olwen*, for example, Cai, Bedwyr and Gwalchmei (Kay, Bedivere and Gawain) were chosen among six champions to ride out with Culhwch from Arthur's court in Cornwall, on the quests Culhwch was set by the giant Ysbaddaden before he could marry Ysbaddaden's daughter Olwen. In the course of these adventures, Kay killed a giant named Wrnach and defeated Dillus the Bearded, making a dog's lead from his hair. Arthur made fun of his defeat of Dillus, and the two knights were briefly estranged.

In the 13th-century Welsh collection the *Triads of the Island of Britain*, Kay was celebrated as one of the three great enchanter knights of Britain. He was said to have the ability to grow as tall as a great oak, to hold his breath for nine days and nights under water and to go without sleep for the same period. He possessed a magical sword, capable of delivering wounds that would never heal, and had such bodily heat that his companions

▲ *Kay's character varied in different accounts, but he was loyal to the last. Arthur avenged Kay's murder before his own death.*

could warm themselves on his skin when the weather was cold in the wet forest – indeed when it rained, anything that Kay held would remain dry because his hand was so hot.

A CELTIC SAINT

Breton legend gave Sir Kay a further career as a hermit, churchman and saint. According to this tradition, he stood down as a knight of the Round Table in order to become the Bishop of Glastonbury. Later he went to Brittany and established a monastery there at Cléder, where a shrine was kept for centuries in honour of St Ké. He only returned to the English court in its last days when he tried without success to make peace in Arthur's war with Mordred. He also persuaded Guinevere to enter a nunnery.

A BUFFOON AT CAMELOT

In Geoffrey of Monmouth's *History of the Kings of Britain* (c.1135–9), Sir Kay was identified as the Count of Anjou and was said to serve as King Arthur's steward. Together with Sir Bedivere he rode out with the king to defeat the giant of Mont St Michel in Normandy. In the works of Chrétien de Troyes, however, Sir Kay was

presented as a boastful and incompetent
fool, a somewhat humorous figure who
made fun of truly heroic knights such as
Sir Lancelot or Sir Gawain, and who himself proved incapable of great deeds. In
Chrétien's poem *Lancelot, le Chevalier de la
Charrette* (*Lancelot, the Knight of the Cart*),
Sir Kay persuaded Arthur to allow him to
attempt the rescue of Guinevere when she
was taken captive by Sir Meleagant. He
failed, and ended up in prison, setting the
scene for Sir Lancelot's triumph. In the
tournament held at Le Hem, Picardy, in
1278 and described in the poem *Le Roman
du Hem*, the participating noblemen took
the roles of Arthurian knights and one
played Sir Kay as boastful buffoon.

SIR KAY THE MURDERER

From Chrétien de Troyes' time onwards,
Sir Kay was often presented as a fool and
braggart, but he was only once a villain –
in the early 13th-century French romance
Perlesvaus. In this narrative, Kay killed
Arthur's son Sir Loholt in an attempt to
take the credit for Sir Loholt's slaying of a
giant, but was found out when Sir Loholt's
head arrived at court in a box that would
only open to his murderer. Banished from
Camelot, he sided with Arthur's enemies
Sir Meliant and Brian of the Isles.

SIR KAY'S DEATH

The main tradition held that Sir Kay died
as a loyal knight in King Arthur's service.
According to Geoffrey of Monmouth, Sir
Kay was killed while fighting the fictional

Roman emperor Lucius Tiberius in France,
and the French prose romances likewise
suggested that he met his end in Arthur's
war in France against the Romans. Welsh
sources reported that Sir Kay was slain by
one of Arthur's enemies, Gwyddawg, and
that Arthur, enraged at the death of his
foster brother, avenged the murder.

▲ *Kay breaks his sword at a tournament.
He was diminished by being transformed
from the enchanter of the Welsh sources to a
middling knight in the Arthurian romances.*

▼ *According to Chrétien de Troyes, Lancelot
succeeded where Kay had failed in rescuing
Guinevere from Meleagant's castle.*

THE MARRIED KNIGHT ERRANT

SIR EREC'S CONFLICT BETWEEN MARRIED LIFE AND CHIVALRY

Sir Geraint, also known as Erec, was one of the first knights in Arthurian romance to embark as a knight errant on a journey of chivalric encounters. These marvellous adventures included combats against magical foes, visits to spellbound castles and intense jousts with unknown knights, events that inspired jousts of war and stately *pas d'armes* tournaments in the 14th and 15th centuries. By tradition Sir Geraint, variously said to be a Welsh knight or a king of Dumnonia (roughly Devon and Somerset), was famous for his great prowess in tournaments. He even won the hand of his wife, Lady Enid, at a tournament.

EREC AND ENIDE

As Sir Erec, Geraint was the hero of the first romance written by the great French poet Chrétien de Troyes, *Érec et Enide* (*c*.1170). This 7,000-line poem in Old French, called a 'tale of adventures' by its author, predates all other Arthurian romances – save perhaps the Welsh tale *Culhwch and Olwen*, which although it survives only in 14th-century manuscripts has been dated in its original form (now lost) to the 11th century. Chrétien's romance described the conflict experienced by Sir Erec between married love and the call of chivalry.

SHAMED BY SIR YDER

At the start of the story, Sir Erec – who was not wearing armour – attended on Queen Guinevere while the other knights of the Round Table rode through the forest hunting a stag. Guinevere and Sir Erec were approached by a knight named Sir Yder, accompanied by a dwarf, who treated Sir Erec discourteously before riding off. Guinevere, feeling slighted by the insult to her serving man, ordered Sir Erec to follow him and avenge the slight.

On this adventure Sir Erec rode to a far-off town where he met the Lady Enid, whose father was the archetype of a poor knight, a warrior blessed with honour and prowess but who had lost his title and worldly wealth; Sir Erec fought in the knight's old and rusty armour at a great tournament, where he defeated Sir Yder, who was competing in disguise as the 'Sparrow Hawk Knight', and made him beg for Guinevere's forgiveness. Sir Erec married Lady Enid.

MARRIAGE PROBLEMS

Sir Erec and Lady Enid settled into a happy marriage. However, Lady Enid became distressed to hear rumours accusing Sir Erec of losing some of his knightly stature because of his attachment to her and their marriage. His companions felt he was becoming soft, and failing in his duties because he was neglecting the life

◀ *Lady Enid leads the way on Sir Geraint's rather unusual chivalric quest. At the end of their adventure, they settled at Camelot.*

▲ *English poet Alfred, Lord Tennyson made Lady Enid and Sir Geraint the subject of one of his first four Arthurian poems, published as Idylls of the King in 1859. He celebrated their faithfulness in marriage.*

▶ *On their travels there is a marital power struggle between Erec (Geraint) and Enid, which is happily resolved at the end of their journey, with each taking their natural place in the partnership.*

CELTIC ORIGINS

The same story was told in the Welsh romance *Geraint mab Erbin* (*Geraint, Son of Erbin*), which survives in a 14th-century manuscript associated with the *Mabinogion*. Some historians argue that Chrétien's poem and the Welsh romance were both based on a common Celtic original, others that the Welsh poem was derived from Chrétien's work. Geraint was a well-known figure in Welsh and Celtic folklore and romance, where he appeared as King of Dumnonia (a Celtic kingdom in south-west England that included Devon and Somerset). In some versions he was said to have died fighting alongside King Arthur against the Saxons at the Battle of Llongborth; his death in this battle (perhaps in *c*.500) was lamented in the poem *Elegy for Geraint*, which celebrated

the speed and strength of Geraint's horses and named Arthur as 'emperor'. Other Welsh sources identified Sir Geraint as one of three great 'seafaring knights' in Britain. In Cornish legend Geraint was buried on Carne Beacon close to the village of Veryan in the Roseland Peninsula, Cornwall, and was celebrated as the patron saint of the village of Gerrans, near Falmouth.

of tournaments and chivalric sports in order to spend time with his wife. Erec found Enid weeping over these rumours, and he suspected that she no longer loved him, and even that she had been unfaithful to him, and at once ordered her to prepare for a journey in his company.

They set out on a series of adventures during which he was able to prove again his prowess as a knight and she was able to demonstrate her continuing love for him. He treated her roughly and ordered her to be silent throughout the quest, but she often disobeyed his command in order to save him from dangers. At the end, after he had fought no fewer than three giants, they returned to their original home in King Arthur's court and settled back into a life of great domestic happiness.

JOUSTERS AS KNIGHTS ERRANT

At Sandricourt in September 1493 Louis de Hédouville organised an Arthurian *pas d'armes* set in a series of locations taken from romance narratives: one part of the entertainment took place at a 'dangerous barrier', another at a 'dark crossing of ways', another in a 'thorny field', another in a 'forest wilderness'. The tournament featured ten defenders taking on all-comers. The defenders were reported to have taken up their positions 'like knights errant in search of adventures'.

▼ *The Arthurian legends were rich in mysterious settings of the kind used for the Sandricourt tournament. On one of his quests, Sir Lancelot rode into a magic wood.*

THE HOLY KNIGHT

SIR PERCEVAL

Sir Perceval was a knight marked by a profound – almost childlike – innocence. Raised away from courtly civilization, in the forest, he left his home to prove himself a knight and, after achieving great feats of chivalry at Camelot, became one of the knights of the Round Table. Set aside from the other knights by his innocence, he embarked on a sacred journey in search of the Holy Grail, the cup or dish used by Christ at the Last Supper before his crucifixion, said to be imbued with miraculous power.

The narrative of Perceval and the Grail quest first appeared in the late 12th century in Chrétien de Troyes' poem *Perceval, ou Le Conte du Graal* (*Perceval, or the Story of the Grail*), written in 1181–91. Chrétien wrote the poem towards the end of his life, and it was unfinished, ending after only 9,000 lines. But such was its popularity that four later authors wrote further sections – known as the 'Four Continuations' – that altogether added an extra 54,000 lines to the poem.

▼ *The Welsh romances that fed into the Perceval story weighed the qualities of courtliness and worldliness a knight might need to acquire during his rise to greatness.*

THE KNIGHT WITHOUT COURTESY

According to Chrétien's version, Perceval was raised in the forests of Wales by his mother, who had fled civilization following the death of her husband. When some knights rode by, Perceval was awestruck by their splendid appearance, and decided to become a knight himself. Ignoring his mother's pleas to remain, he rode to King Arthur's court, where he was knighted.

Sir Perceval was taunted by the foolish Sir Kay, then set out on a series of adventures, determined to make his name. He rescued a princess named Blanchefleur from a besieged castle, and received instructions in the ways of knighthood from Sir Gornemant. He quickly picked up the necessary physical skills, but because of his lack of a courtly education he was wanting in sophistication and the chivalric quality of courtesy; Sir Gornemant ordered him not to ask so many questions.

▲ *In some versions of his legend, Perceval married a maiden he had rescued, and fathered two sons; in others, he was devoted purely to the quest for the Grail.*

FIRST GLIMPSE OF THE GRAIL

This instruction had major consequences later in the adventures, when Sir Perceval reached the castle of two ailing kings set amid a wasteland. There were two kings, father and son, both crippled by being injured from the waist down; the elder was confined to the castle while the younger was able to come and go, well enough to visit the castle grounds.

Sir Perceval saw a mysterious procession in which young women and men passed before the younger king and his guests, carrying first a bleeding lance, then a pair of candelabras and finally a mysterious vessel (the Holy Grail) containing one wafer for the Christian Mass, said to be the only food that sustained the elder

CHRÉTIEN DE TROYES

The French poet Chrétien de Troyes was the author of five Arthurian romances. After *Erec and Enid* in c.1170, he wrote *Cligès*, in c.1176; *Lancelot ou Le Chevalier à la Charrette* (*Lancelot, or the Knight of the Cart*), and *Yvain, ou Le Chevalier au Lion* (*Yvain, or the Knight of the Lion*), both in 1176–81; and *Perceval, ou Le Conte du Graal* (*Perceval, or the Story of the Grail*), in 1181–91. He was one of the great poets of the medieval age, but we know very little about his life.

As his name indicates, he was from or was associated with the town of Troyes in north-eastern France. He served at the court of Marie de Champagne, daughter of Eleanor of Aquitaine, in the years 1160-72, and may have been herald-at-arms there. In his later years he was associated with Count Philip of Flanders, to whom he dedicated the Perceval poem. He also wrote four poems based on the *Metamorphoses* of Roman poet Ovid (1st century AD) but only one, *Philomela*, has survived.

king. Because of Sir Gornemant's warning, Sir Perceval did not ask what the procession meant, or what the Grail was; and it later emerged that if he had asked, the old king would have been healed. Back at Arthur's court, Perceval pledged to make his way back to the mysterious castle and find the Grail and its meaning.

THE STORY CONTINUED

Chrétien's poem continued with a section describing the adventures of Sir Gawain, in this context King Arthur's best knight, but it did not complete Sir Perceval's narrative. However, in the last of the Four Continuations the story was brought to a conclusion: Sir Perceval achieved his quest, the Grail King died and Perceval was crowned king in his stead, then after a rule of peace and prosperity lasting

seven years, Perceval returned to the woods, living as a hermit until he died. The poet suggested that on his death he took the Holy Grail with him to Heaven.

There were many other versions of the story. In later material, Sir Perceval was secondary to Sir Galahad in the Grail quest, but still retained a key role: with Sir Bors, he accompanied Sir Galahad in the final stages of the sacred quest, reaching the castle and achieving completion.

PERCEVAL WITHOUT THE GRAIL

The Welsh romance *Peredur ab Efrawg* (*Peredur, son of York*), which survives in two 14th-century manuscripts, told much of the same story about a knight raised in the woods and embarking on a long series of adventures in which he learned how to be a knight, but it left out the matter concerning the Holy Grail. It is possible that the Welsh romance and Chrétien shared a common Celtic or Breton source. There were various possible historical prototypes for Peredur – including a Welsh king of Gwynedd mentioned by Geoffrey of Monmouth and the Welsh Triads as fighting in the Battle of Arfderydd in AD573.

The Welsh romance told the same story as Chrétien up to Perceval's stay at King Arthur's court and his shaming by the boorish Sir Kay (here called Cei). Then, embarking on his adventures, Perceval met two uncles. The first trained him in knighthood, just as Sir Gornemant did in the other account, while the second was the equivalent of the crippled king: he also showed Sir Perceval a mysterious procession of objects, but instead of the Holy Grail he revealed a man's decapitated head on a platter. After an encounter with the Nine Witches of Gloucester, meeting his destined love, Angharad Golden-Hand, and many more adventures, Sir Perceval discovered that the decapitated head was that of his cousin and took vengeance upon his killers. The romance ended with celebrations of Sir Perceval's heroism. A Middle English romance, the 14th-century *Sir Perceval of Galles*, also omitted the Grail material from Percival's adventures.

▼ *Pre-Raphaelite painter Arthur Hacker makes the innocent Sir Perceval completely oblivious to temptations of the flesh – and even gives him a halo.*

A MYSTICAL JOURNEY

SIR PERCEVAL AND THE SPIRITUAL QUALITIES OF KNIGHTHOOD

Chrétien de Troyes' poem *Perceval, or the Story of the Grail* (*c*.1181–91) was the direct inspiration for the masterpiece *Parzival*, written *c*.1200–10 by German poet Wolfram von Eschenbach. *Parzival* and other later versions of the Grail legend, such as those in the 13th-century Prose *Lancelot* and Sir Thomas Malory's *Le Morte d'Arthur*, developed the spiritual and mystical elements of the narrative and presented Sir Perceval either as himself the purest embodiment of Christian chivalry, or as one of the great examples of religious knighthood alongside Sir Galahad.

ORIGINS OF THE HOLY GRAIL

In Chrétien de Troyes' poem the spiritual element of the Holy Grail was not well developed, for Chrétien did not explain clearly what the sacred object was. It is probable that the mysterious vessel derived from Celtic folklore about magical cups and cauldrons. Examples include the legend of Bran the Blessed, who possessed a cauldron that had the power to

▼ *Sir Galahad achieves a vision of the Holy Grail while Sir Bors and Sir Perceval look on. This is one of six tapestry designs on the Grail quest created by artist Edward Burne-Jones for Stanmore Hall.*

bring the dead back to life, and Welsh tales in which Arthur and his knights made a voyage in search of a magical cauldron – in one case searching in Ireland, in another looking in the Celtic spirit world.

The Grail may also have been intended as a Christian symbol from the beginning. At around the time that Chrétien wrote his Grail poem, the Church was promoting the ceremonial and mystical aspects of the sacrament of the Mass or Holy Communion – which certainly had its origins in the time of Christ, and was practised by the early Church in the first centuries AD, but was being celebrated with new ceremony in the 12th century – and this probably lay behind the development of the Christian interpretation of the Grail as the cup or plate that was used by Christ in the Last Supper with his disciples before the crucifixion.

In the late 12th-century verse romance *Joseph d'Arimathie* (*c*.1191–1202) – written just after Chrétien's Grail poem – French poet Robert de Boron described how Christ gave the cup from the Last Supper to Joseph (in the Christian Gospels, a wealthy man who allowed his prepared tomb to be used for the burial of Christ after the crucifixion), and how Joseph used the vessel to catch some of

the 'holy blood' from Christ's body. After Christ's resurrection, Joseph received instruction in the mysteries associated with the cup, and later travelled to Europe where he established a line of 'Grail-keepers' to look after the vessel.

SIR PERCEVAL'S CHIVALRIC AND SPIRITUAL EDUCATION

In *Parzival*, Sir Perceval was educated first in the ways of chivalry and of courtly love. He gradually overlaid his country upbringing with chivalric sophistication – symbolized by his winning a superb suit of red armour in a tournament outside the gates of Nantes, then riding off wearing the armour with his simple country clothes beneath.

Later, after his failure to ask the necessary question at the Grail castle, he went through a prolonged spiritual education, passing through guilt and despair, discovering a deep humility and learning from a holy man named Trevrizent whom he met on Good Friday, the day of Christ's crucifixion. So prepared, he was ready to meet and fight his half-brother Feirefiz (the pagan son of Perceval's father by an early marriage to a Moorish queen in Africa, explained at the beginning of Wolfram von Eschenbach's poem). The

▲ *On the Grail quest, Sir Perceval, Sir Bors and Sir Galahad encountered Perceval's sister Amide, who nobly sacrificed herself to cure a lady of leprosy.*

▲ *The Grail was carried and guarded by angels and ethereal beings. This Pre-Raphaelite portrait of one of the damsels of the Grail is by DG Rossetti.*

two knights fought without knowing each other's true identity, and Sir Perceval's sword broke, so that he was at the mercy of his opponent, but he was spared by the noble pagan and, making friends, they discovered that they were also brothers. They then proceeded together on the search for the Grail, and finally Sir Perceval was sufficiently prepared to ask the required question of the crippled king and complete the quest.

SIR PERCEVAL'S WIFE AND SONS
According to Wolfram von Eschenbach's version, Sir Perceval married the maiden he rescued from the besieged castle (Lady Blanchefleur according to Chrétien; Lady Condwiramurs according to Wolfram) and had two sons with her, Kardeiz and Lohengrin. In a version of the medieval legend of the 'Knight of the Swan', Lohengrin was also a Grail knight and was sent in a boat pulled by a swan, to rescue a maiden who was not permitted to ask

his name. In Wolfram's poem, Sir Perceval was reunited with Lady Condwiramurs at the conclusion of his quest.

In other later versions of the Grail romance, however, Sir Perceval was presented as a virgin whose quest for the Grail ended in his death. The Grail quests replaced the adventures of knights within the courtly love convention – where the knight was seeking to do great deeds in order to win fame and the acclaim of his lady – with a spiritual search for salvation or to gain some mystical knowledge and experience of God.

SYMBOLISM OF THE FISHER KING
The older and younger crippled kings in their castle, not named by Chrétien de Troyes, were called Titurel and Anfortas in *Parzival*. In many other versions they were called the Wounded King and the Fisher King: while the older king was confined to the interior of the castle, the younger one went fishing in the water near the castle. The character of the Fisher King would seem to be based both on Celtic keepers of magic cauldrons such as Bran the Blessed and on the idea of a guardian of the Grail, developed by Robert de Boron

in his *Joseph d'Arimathie*. In Robert's romance Joseph's brother-in-law, Bron, was said to be the 'Rich Fisher' and was the first keeper of the Grail. It is possible that the name 'Fisher King' derived from a pun in French, where the words for fisher and sinner are virtually identical. There is also a link to Christ sending his disciples to be 'fishers of men'.

In the Prose *Lancelot* (the part of the Arthurian romance tradition known as the Vulgate Cycle), the two kings are called Pellam and Pelles: the second brought about the birth of the perfect knight, Sir Galahad, by tricking Sir Lancelot into sleeping with Pelles's daughter Elaine. In the still later part of the tradition called the Post-Vulgate Cycle, Sir Pellam received his wound because he fell into sin; he was injured by Arthurian knight Sir Balin, using the spear that was used to pierce Christ's side at the crucifixion. The blow that injured Sir Pellam was called 'the dolorous stroke'.

THE FLAWED KNIGHT

SIR LANCELOT

Sir Lancelot was King Arthur's greatest and most trusted knight, blessed with unmatched chivalric prowess but undone by his love for Queen Guinevere. By entering into an adulterous relationship with Guinevere, he failed his king and set in motion the events that brought about Arthur's death and the end of the golden age of Camelot.

In his earlier appearances in the Arthurian cycle, Lancelot's love for Guinevere was celebrated within the conventions of courtly love, but as the story was developed in the Prose *Lancelot*, his adultery was presented as his undoing – both as a chivalric figure and as a religious knight. In the Grail romances, Lancelot was unable to achieve success in the quest

▼ *Lancelot fell unconscious at the sight of the Grail. He was unable to complete the quest because his love for Guinevere, and subsequent betrayal of his king, gave his knightly character a fatal flaw.*

because of his illicit love for the queen, but much of his extraordinary potential was realized in his son, Sir Galahad.

THE STORY OF LANCELOT

The story, as developed by the time of the 13th century Prose *Lancelot*, told that after his father King Ban of Benoic lost his kingdom and died of a broken heart as a result, Lancelot was carried off as a boy by a water-spirit, the Lady of the Lake, who brought him up in her own kingdom. In the version told in the 12th-century German poem *Lanzelet*, this was in a magical land, where no other men were permitted, but in the Prose *Lancelot* many other fine knights lived there, including Lancelot's cousins Lionel and Bors.

When Lancelot came of age he left, bound for King Arthur's court, without having been told his name or royal background; in the *Lanzelet* he was at this stage entirely untrained in knightly pursuits, and could not even handle a horse, but in

▲ *The Lady of Shalott, heroine of a work by 19th-century poet Alfred, Lord Tennyson, was based on Elaine of Astolat, who in the Arthurian legends fell hopelessly in love with Sir Lancelot.*

the Prose *Lancelot* he had benefited from a good chivalric training.

In the Prose *Lancelot*, from the moment of his arrival at court Lancelot was in love with Queen Guinevere. He rescued her from the castle of Sir Meleagant (as told in Chrétien de Troyes' poem). He recovered his father's kingdom, taken previously by the wicked Sir Claudas, but chose to live principally at King Arthur's court. At the castle of the Fisher King, he was tricked by the king into sleeping with his daughter Elaine and fathered the perfect knight, Sir Galahad. But Queen Guinevere, discovering the fact, was furious and drove him into madness and exile from Camelot.

He took part in the Grail quest, but – tainted by his sin with Guinevere – was unable to reach the end of the quest: he passed out at a mere glimpse of the Grail and remained unconscious for a length of time said to match the number of days on which he had sinned against Arthur with

▶ *One of the darker sides of the legend of the quest for the Grail was that it emptied Camelot of its knights, left Arthur's court open to attack and corruption, and caused individual self-doubt and failure.*

Guinevere. Subsequently, recovered and forgiven by Guinevere, he returned to Camelot, but then – after his love affair was betrayed to the king – he and Guinevere were discovered together by Arthur, who condemned the queen to death. Lancelot escaped and returned in time to save Guinevere, but in the battle kinsmen of Gawain were killed, sparking a long and bitter struggle between Gawain's kinsmen and Lancelot.

Finally, when Arthur travelled to France to defeat the Romans, the king was betrayed by Mordred. Lancelot took no part in this revolt, but his earlier treachery had destroyed the unity of the Round Table. Lancelot had to look on as Arthur

SIR HUGH DE MORVILLE

Sir Hugh de Morville, the English knight who supposedly gave Ulrich von Zatzikhoven the Anglo-Norman source for the romance *Lanzelet*, served King Richard I of England in the 1190s before standing hostage for the king. He may well be the same Sir Hugh de Morville who served Richard's father King Henry II and was one of the four knights who assassinated Thomas Becket in 1170 in Canterbury Cathedral after misunderstanding the king's forlorn complaint 'Who will rid me of this meddlesome priest?' as a command. The assassin Sir Hugh de Morville was disinherited by the king of his holdings as Lord of Westmoreland and sent to obtain forgiveness from Pope Alexander III (r. 1159–81). The pope told the four knights to travel to the Holy Land, and so perhaps Sir Hugh was on the Third Crusade with Richard I in 1189–92.

was killed in battle, Guinevere also died and the golden age of Camelot came to an end. He ended his life in a hermitage.

THE COURTLY LOVER

Lancelot first appeared in the Arthurian stories in the work of Chrétien de Troyes. Chrétien mentioned him in his poem *Erec et Enide* (c.1170) and made him the principal character of the poem *Lancelot, le Chevalier de la Charrette* (*Lancelot, the Knight of the Cart*), where he rescued Queen Guinevere after she had been taken captive by the wicked knight Sir Meleagant. The poem was the first to mention Lancelot's illicit love for Queen Guinevere; it was also the first to mention Arthur holding court at Camelot – although in this its first appearance, it is a minor court, less important than the king's main court at Caerleon.

Before the end of the 12th century the Swiss cleric Ulrich von Zatzikhoven developed the knight's character in his romance *Lanzelet* (c.1194), the first Arthurian work to describe Lancelot's upbringing by the Lady of the Lake. The poet wrote that his work was a translation of an Anglo-Norman work brought to Germany by the Crusader knight Sir Hugh de Morville, who stood hostage for King Richard I of England when he was captured by Holy Roman Emperor Henry VI. *Lanzelet* made

no mention of the knight's love for and adultery with Guinevere, and described his love for a princess named Iblis. It is possible that the original source legend about Lancelot was similar to that given in *Lanzelet*, and did not include the adulterous love, which would then have been added by Chrétien de Troyes, perhaps influenced by the Celtic legend of Tristan and Iseult. (Chrétien claimed that he had written a poem based on the Tristan story, but if he did it has been lost.)

A COURTLY INVENTION

Lancelot's relations with Guinevere as described by Chrétien in *The Knight of the Cart* were only comparable with those of Tristan and Iseult in the most general terms. As lovers Lancelot and Guinevere followed the conventions of courtly love whereas Tristan and Iseult's affair had far more of the magic associated with Celtic and Breton folklore. Chrétien wrote *The Knight of the Cart* for Marie de Champagne, a great patron of courtly love poems. Lancelot did not appear in earlier Arthurian material, such as Geoffrey of Monmouth's *History of the Kings of Britain*, in which Guinevere did have a lover, but he was the villain Mordred. Lancelot's story appears to have been invented with no antecedent in the Celtic legends that fed into so much of the Arthurian cycle.

THE PERFECT KNIGHT

SIR GALAHAD

In the later Grail romances Sir Galahad, son of Sir Lancelot, was the perfection of chivalry and the only knight capable of completing the Grail quest. These profoundly religious romances contrasted the religious inspiration of Sir Galahad's chivalry, based on spiritual fervour, with the courtly inspiration of Sir Lancelot's knightly achievements, which were done to impress his lady, Queen Guinevere.

Sir Galahad first appeared in Arthurian narratives in the early 13th-century *Queste del Saint Graal* ('Search for the Holy Grail'), part of the Prose *Lancelot* (also known as the Vulgate Cycle). His story was developed in the later romances of the Post-Vulgate Cycle and in *Le Morte d'Arthur* of Sir Thomas Malory.

▼ *The spear Sir Galahad carried on his sacred quest was said to be the holy lance that pierced Christ's side.*

SIR GALAHAD'S STORY

The Grail story as presented in the *Queste del Saint Graal* revealed the influence of Cistercian monks and of the mystical writings of the Cistercian St Bernard (1090–1153), founder of the great abbey of Clairvaux in France. The Cistercian ideal demanded sexual virginity for the leading heroes of the Grail narrative. As we have seen, Sir Perceval was no longer described as finding married love with Lady Blanchefleur, but was a virgin. Likewise, Sir Galahad possessed absolute purity, and was also a virgin. The stages by which Galahad rose to understanding and full vision of the Grail matched those of a mystic's movement towards realization of God, as described by St Bernard. The *Queste del Saint Graal* appears to have been written by a Cistercian clerk.

Sir Galahad was born after his father, Sir Lancelot, was tricked by magic into believing that Elaine, daughter of the Fisher King, was his beloved, Guinevere. Upon learning the truth Sir Lancelot returned at once to King Arthur's court, and when Galahad was born he was given to his great-aunt, who was an abbess. He had a profoundly religious upbringing in a nunnery. The great Merlin prophesied that Galahad would be braver even than Sir Lancelot and was the knight destined for success in the Holy Grail quest. The story stated, without giving details, that through his mother's side Sir Galahad was a descendant of the biblical King David.

Galahad was later brought to King Arthur's court at Camelot by a hermit and knighted by his father. Not knowing what he was doing, he sat down in the Siege Perilous – a magical empty seat at the Round Table that would kill any knight except the one capable of succeeding in the Grail quest. King Arthur, having

knights – guided by Sir Perceval's sister – set sail across the sea, where they came to a second ship and boarded it to find the Holy Grail once more, covered and set upon a silver table.

Bors, Perceval and Galahad then sailed on to the city of Sarras, where, Christ-like, Sir Galahad healed a cripple and made him walk. The three knights were thrown in jail by the local king, but in time the king died and Sir Galahad succeeded him; then at a celebration of the Mass Sir Galahad was taken aside and shown the glorious mysteries of the Grail by a man who revealed himself to be Joseph of Arimathea. Afterwards Sir Galahad bade his companions farewell and died, and Sir Bors and Sir Perceval saw their friend's soul carried up to heaven. The Grail was taken with him.

▼ *Sir Galahad was one of several Arthurian knights raised in obscurity but destined to prove their greatness at court and on quests.*

▲ Sir Galahad, fighting here incognito with Sir Lancelot, had the military prowess of a great knight as well as a religious seeker's determination and drive.

witnessed the proof of Galahad's special status, gave him another test – to draw the sword from the stone. Galahad also passed this test and Arthur proclaimed him the foremost knight of all and welcomed him to the company of the Round Table. They then had a vision of the Holy Grail and Sir Galahad, Sir Bors and Sir Perceval were chosen as the best knights to pursue the quest, for Galahad had such remarkable purity of character and motive that he lived without sin.

The assembled company then retired to a meadow close to Camelot where they fought a great tournament, in which Sir Galahad, even on his first day as a knight, outdid all the other knights of the Round Table except for his father, Sir Lancelot, and Sir Perceval.

SIR GALAHAD'S SHIELD

A pure knight needed the purest weapons, hallowed by sacred history. Sir Galahad embarked on the quest carrying a shield – white as snow, with a red cross at its centre reputedly drawn in blood by Joseph of Arimathea. This shield, a red cross on a white background, was the one carried by the Knights Templar. Sir Galahad later acquired the sword of David.

In one version of the conclusion of the Grail quest, he travelled with Sir Bors and Sir Perceval to the castle of the Fisher King, where they discovered the Holy Grail. Galahad used the spear (which was identified as the spear used to pierce Christ's side as he hung on the cross) to cure the Fisher King.

Some versions ended at this point, with Sir Galahad being granted a vision of the Holy Grail and then being raised to heaven. Others provided further adventures overseas in the city of Sarras in the Middle East. According to this version, the

A KNIGHT STRONG AS THE SUN

SIR GAWAIN

The character of Sir Gawain, King Arthur's nephew, changed with the development of the Arthurian legends. In early literature he was a trusted knight and exemplary warrior, but by the time of Sir Thomas Malory he was a treacherous lord known for his rough treatment of women.

From the beginning Gawain was associated with women: altogether, in the various legends told of him, he had no fewer than 21 lovers. He was also the hero of a story in which he stepped forward to marry an ugly lady for whom Arthur had promised to find a husband, in return for help that saved his life, and she turned out to be a great beauty cast under a spell.

The magic of folklore attended Gawain, and some of his feats may be distantly connected to folktales about the Irish hero Cúchulainn; although possessed of extraordinary strength, he was flawed as a chivalric figure, because he did not live up either to the ideal of courtly knight or to the ideal of the religious-mystical knight.

Sir Gawain's character is a case study in a knight's maturing understanding of the meaning of chivalry: moving from celebration of feats of physical strength and

▼ *In a scene based on the English poem* Sir Gawain and the Green Knight, *Gawain is tempted by the wife of his host Sir Bercilak.*

▲ *Gawain was renowned for his martial ability. In 13th-century romances he was often the only knight able to match a new hero, freshly arrived at court, in combat.*

martial endeavour, to praise for courtesy and the ability to thrive, as Sir Lancelot did, within the convention of courtly love, to reverence for humility and purity as embodied by Sir Galahad.

THE HISTORICAL GAWAIN

Sir Gawain's legend appears to have grown up around the life of a late 5th-century Welsh king, Gawain Gwalltafwyn. In the Arthurian narratives, however, he had Scottish roots, as the son of King Lot of Orkney and Lothian. His connection to Arthur was through his mother Morgause, Arthur's half-sister. Gawain's brothers were Sir Agravain, Sir Gaheris, Sir Gareth and Sir Mordred. In some accounts, but not in the early Welsh Arthurian legends, Sir Mordred was the product of Arthur's incestuous liaison with his half-sister.

A CELTIC SUN GOD?

In Malory and in a number of the romances, Sir Gawain's strength grew greater and less in the course of the day –

often it was said that he was three times stronger at noon than in the evening. For this reason, it has been suggested that he was based on a Celtic sun god. In early Welsh versions of the Arthurian legends, Gawain was known as Gwalchmei. He appeared with Cai and Bedwyr (Sir Kay and Sir Bedivere) in the 11th-century *Culhwch and Olwen*, where he was King Arthur's nephew and one of his foremost knights, who was selected to travel with Culhwch on his quest.

In the following century Geoffrey of Monmouth's *History of the Kings of Britain* presented Sir Gawain as one of the leading warriors of Arthur's court, who served as the ambassador to Rome. William of Malmesbury described Sir Gawain as an enduring foe for the Anglo-Saxons, although he was finally driven from the kingdom by the brother of the semi-legendary Anglo-Saxon king, Hengest. William also recorded that Gawain's grave had been discovered in south-west Wales.

WORLDLY KNIGHT

In the romances of Chrétien de Troyes, Gawain was one of the most prominent of Arthur's knights, but was often compared unfavourably with Sir Lancelot or Sir

Perceval. With the development of the Grail theme, Gawain was increasingly presented as lacking in the necessary spiritual qualities for the mystical quest – brave and forceful he might be, but too reliant also on his own strength and unable to understand the significance of the Grail.

HATRED FOR SIR LANCELOT

In the romances of the Vulgate Cycle (c.1210 onwards) Gawain played an important role in the end of the Round Table fellowship. He refused to take part when his brothers Agravain and Mordred exposed the secret love of Sir Lancelot and Queen Guinevere to King Arthur, but after Arthur had condemned his wife to death and Sir Lancelot returned to rescue Guinevere, a battle broke out in which all the brothers save Mordred were killed. Gawain's respectful friendship with Sir Lancelot became an implacable hatred that was the bitter backdrop for the final days of Camelot. In this version Gawain lost his life fighting against Mordred and before he died wrote to Lancelot asking for his forgiveness.

Sir Gawain's character had been transformed into a villain and even a murderer by the time of the Prose *Tristan* and the Post-Vulgate Cycle romances (both written c.1240). In his *Le Morte d'Arthur* (c.1450–70) Malory reproduced the largely negative image of Sir Gawain presented in the French romances.

ENDURING ENGLISH POPULARITY

Yet more positive images of Sir Gawain survived and endured: the English poem *Sir Gawain and the Green Knight* (c.1375) presented Gawain as a brave and loyal knight. His popularity endured: the story of his encounter with the Green Knight was retold in a rhyming romance of c.1500, and we know from a description by courtier Robert Laneham that a minstrel performed a Gawain romance as part of the festivities laid on at Kenilworth Castle in 1575 for Queen Elizabeth I.

The story of *Sir Gawain and the Green Knight* was based on an old folkloric nar-

▲ *Sir Gawain and Sir Yvain failed in the Grail quest. In one story Gawain saw the chalice but allowed himself to be distracted by the beauty of the maiden carrying it.*

rative of a beheading game, which was told of heroes including Cúchulainn. At Camelot when the court was celebrating New Year's Day a knight dressed in green armour arrived unannounced and proposed a game: he would allow anyone to strike him with an axe if the person agreed to the Green Knight returning the blow in one year's time. Sir Gawain took up the challenge and decapitated the knight. But after receiving this blow the knight stood and picked up his own head; before leaving, he instructed Sir Gawain to meet him at the Green Chapel in one year's time.

One year later, searching for the Green Chapel, Sir Gawain came to a fine castle and was welcomed by its lord Sir Bercilak and his ravishing wife. Sir Bercilak embarked on a hunt and proposed a deal with Sir Gawain: he would give Sir Gawain whatever game he caught while Gawain would give the lord whatever he gained during the day. When he was gone, the lady of the castle visited Sir Gawain's chamber to try to seduce him, but he resisted her advances, only allowing her to give him one kiss; in the evening, he gave the kiss to the lord. On the second day, the same thing happened, but the

lady gave two kisses; Sir Gawain later passed these on to Sir Bercilak. On the third day the lady gave him three kisses and a green girdle that she said would keep him safe from physical harm; in the evening he gave the three kisses to Sir Bercilak but withheld the girdle.

The following day being New Year's Day, Sir Gawain met with the Green Knight at the Green Chapel, wearing the girdle. The Green Knight swung his great axe three times, only injuring Gawain slightly on the third swing. He revealed himself to be Sir Bercilak, and said that he would not have hurt Sir Gawain at all had he been honest about the girdle; they had, he said, been taking part in a game arranged by the sorceress Morgan le Fay. Sir Gawain returned to Camelot wearing the green girdle as a sign of his shame at having been outwitted, but King Arthur on hearing the tale announced that all the knights of Camelot should henceforth wear a green sash in honour of Gawain.

A VILLAIN AT CAMELOT

SIR MORDRED AND OTHER KNIGHTS

The Arthurian court of legend had a large supporting cast of lesser knights. The principal of these must be the traitor Sir Mordred, the antithesis of chivalry. Others included Sir Bedivere, one of the king's earliest companions, and the paragon of purity Sir Bors the Younger, who played an important role in the quest for the Holy Grail.

ARTHUR'S NEMESIS

Sir Mordred was King Arthur's nemesis, the traitor son who rebelled against his king, bringing about the Battle of Camlann at which Arthur was fatally wounded and in which Sir Mordred himself lost his life. In some versions of the legend, King Arthur and Sir Mordred were the last two warriors left alive at the end of the Battle of Camlann and settled their dispute in single combat: Arthur killed Sir Mordred, but not before he had been fatally wounded himself.

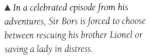

▼ *Mordred was the worst of rebels – a son (and/or nephew) who turned against his father or uncle. At the Battle of Camlann he fought Arthur in single combat.*

Sir Mordred was either Arthur's illegitimate son by his half-sister Morgause, or (in earlier traditions) Arthur's nephew and the legitimate son of Morgause with her husband King Lot of Orkney. The theme of Mordred's birth as a result of Arthur's incest was introduced in the 13th-century Prose *Lancelot* (the Vulgate Cycle). The

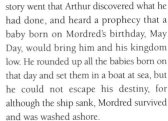

▲ *In a celebrated episode from his adventures, Sir Bors is forced to choose between rescuing his brother Lionel or saving a lady in distress.*

story went that Arthur discovered what he had done, and heard a prophecy that a baby born on Mordred's birthday, May Day, would bring him and his kingdom low. He rounded up all the babies born on that day and set them in a boat at sea, but he could not escape his destiny, for although the ship sank, Mordred survived and was washed ashore.

Sir Mordred first appeared as Sir Medraut in the 10th-century *Annales Cambriae* ('Annals of Wales'), where he was said to have died at the Battle of Camlann, with Arthur. In various Welsh legends, Sir Medraut was a raucous and violent man – in one story he rode to Arthur's court at Kelliwic in Cornwall, consumed all the drink and food, pulled Guinevere from her throne and beat her. In Geoffrey of Monmouth's account, he was a traitor, who rebelled when Arthur had to leave his kingdom to fight the

▲ Fatally wounded in the Battle of Camlann against his rebel son, Mordred, Arthur fell into the sleep of death. On the Isle of Avalon attendants guard his passing.

father's kingdom and raised with their cousin Lancelot by the Lady of the Lake.

Sir Bors was often tempted by maidens to abandon his vows of chastity. In one episode, he was approached by a fair lady who threatened to kill herself if he would not sleep with her; he refused, and the lady and her maidens were revealed to be demons. He did father one son, Sir Elyan the White, when he was tricked with a magic ring into making love to Lady Claire, the beautiful daughter of King Brandegoris of Estangore. Sir Bors the Younger survived the collapse of Camelot. According to legend he embarked on a Crusade, and was killed fighting in the Holy Land.

Romans in France and this set the tone for his role in the whole body of Arthurian literature. He was often described seducing or even raping noble ladies, and fighting their husbands.

SIR BEDIVERE THE STRONG

One of King Arthur's unfailingly loyal knights, Sir Bedivere was celebrated for his strength. His Welsh name, Bedwyr Bedrydant, meant Bedivere of the Immaculate Sinews, and it was said that although he had only one hand, he could still fight more swiftly and skilfully than any other warrior.

With Sir Kay and Sir Gawain, he was among the earliest known knights of King Arthur's court – listed, as we have seen, in the 11th-century Welsh tale *Culhwch and Olwen*. He was usually associated with Sir Kay, and fought with him and King Arthur in defeating the Giant of Mont St Michel in Brittany. In Geoffrey of Monmouth's account, Sir Bedivere was King Arthur's head butler and also Duke of Normandy.

BEDIVERE AND EXCALIBUR

Sir Bedivere was also the knight charged with returning the sword Excalibur to the Lady of the Lake as Arthur lay dying (see box). The story suggested that Sir Bedivere, with a very human response, found it difficult to cast so precious a

weapon into the water, and tried to trick his lord in order to keep the sword: he twice returned to the king's bedside and reported that he had thrown the sword away into the water as instructed, and when Arthur asked what had happened Sir Bedivere reported that it had slipped into the water and disappeared; Arthur knew he was lying and scolded him. The third time, when Bedivere at last threw it in, the hand of a mysterious lady emerged from the water, caught it and drew it under. Subsequently, following Arthur's death, Sir Bedivere retired to a hermitage, where he spent the rest of his life.

SIR BORS THE YOUNGER

The antithesis of Sir Mordred was Sir Bors the Younger, who was celebrated for his purity of character. He was even able to see the Holy Grail. He was the only knight to return to Camelot after the Grail quest.

Sir Bors was called the Younger because his father, another Bors, also had a part in the Arthurian legend. Sir Bors the Elder was king of Gaunnes (Gaul) and uncle to Sir Lancelot. Bors the Younger and his brother Lionel were exiled from their

CHAPTER TWENTY

KNIGHTS IN HISTORY

In November 1095 at the Council of Clermont in France, Pope Urban II issued the call to arms to Christian knights that resulted in the First Crusade. To stir up enthusiasm for a war against Muslims in the Holy Land, he held up the example of the great Frankish king Charlemagne and his knights, whose military encounters in Spain and southern France with Islamic warriors from the Iberian Peninsula and northern Africa were already celebrated, in works such as the epic Anglo-Norman poem the *Chanson de Roland* (*Song of Roland*), as great feats of war against Muslims. Urban's speech, which had such momentous consequences, is an indication of how literary tales of chivalry were intertwined with the historical deeds of knights.

The *Song of Roland* and other *chansons de geste* – songs celebrating the great figures and heroic exploits in the era of Charlemagne – were the first flowering in a long tradition of poetry and romances that wove colourful legends of chivalry around the past adventures of knights. These works, whose accounts of chivalric deeds were strongly influenced by legend, presented exemplary images of knighthood that were held up by Urban and others as an inspiration for the knights of their day. In addition, the accounts in the poems and romances were to some extent determined by the prevailing culture – in particular, they often filled a need for 'crusading propaganda', showing knights fighting heroically for Christ and their Muslim foes acting with dishonesty and cowardice.

▲ *An imagined joust between Richard I and a blue-skinned General Saladin.*

◀ *Charlemagne was said to have 12 paladins or leading knights – just as Christ had 12 disciples. This ceiling fresco of the great king is from the Palace of Justice in Paris, France.*

CHRISTIAN KNIGHTS IN BATTLE

ROLAND, CHARLEMAGNE'S FIRST KNIGHT

The *Song of Roland* is the earliest surviving example of the Anglo-Norman and French *chansons de geste* ('songs of heroic deeds'), epic poems that celebrated feats of arms performed by knights in the service of Charlemagne and other Frankish kings. It is the oldest surviving epic poem in French and because of its quality as well as its antiquity enjoys a pre-eminent place in medieval literature. Traditionally the poem was seen as a French work, but recent scholars have established that it belongs in the Anglo-Norman tradition.

The poem survives in a number of manuscripts, the oldest of which dates to *c.*1130–70, but it was composed by the time of the First Crusade and perhaps even earlier: according to the 12th-century Anglo-Norman poet Wace, at the

Battle of Hastings in 1066 Duke William of Normandy's minstrel performed the poem before the battle. This claim (made in his *Roman de Rou, c.*1160) and Pope Urban II's reference to Charlemagne and his knights at Clermont in 1095, indicate that the *Song of Roland* and perhaps other chansons about Charlemagne in the late 11th century already enjoyed wide currency as celebrations of Christian knights at war. Although no chansons survive from before the mid-12th century the poems were probably passed down orally and may have been developed 100 or even 200 years before they were written down.

CHARLEMAGNE AND MARSILIUN

The *Song of Roland* tells the story of the downfall and death of Charlemagne's favourite knight. The emperor was 36

when he led a short and largely unsuccessful campaign in Spain in AD778. In the poem, however, his army brought the whole of Muslim Spain under Christian control, save only the city of Saragossa; Charlemagne, moreover, was said to be 200 years old, a grizzled veteran of wars fought in God's name.

Marsiliun, the Muslim king of Saragossa, sent a message to Charlemagne saying that he would come to the French king's court at Aix for the festival of Michaelmas, would accept the Christian faith, and give Charlemagne hostages. His plan was to trick Charlemagne into returning to France, and he had no intention of honouring his promise: he would be happy to lose the hostages if it meant that Charlemagne was no longer threatening his city. Charlemagne accepted the offer.

THE TREACHERY OF GANELON

Charlemagne sent a message of acceptance through Roland's stepfather, Ganelon, who was jealous of Roland and plotted to bring about his downfall. Ganelon proposed a deal to Marsiliun: he would arrange for Roland and his friend Oliver to be in charge of the small rear section of Charlemagne's army, and Marsiliun could lie in wait for them in the mountains and defeat them. If he killed Roland, nothing would upset Charlemagne more.

Ganelon arranged it as he promised. Charlemagne was troubled by bad dreams, and was concerned that his beloved Roland would be vulnerable in the weak rear section of the army, so he made him promise to summon help with his horn if he needed it. The Muslim army attacked

◀ *Even the great must die. In this illustration from* The Mirror of History *by the 13th-century Dominican friar Vincent of Beauvais, the Battle of Roncesvalles rages while Roland's body is stretched out in death beside his sword.*

fiercely. Oliver urged Roland to blow the horn, but Roland refused, saying that a call for help would be shameful.

PASSAGES OF ARMS ON THE BATTLEFIELD

The poem presents the encounter between the armies as a series of individual combats between knights: in the first attack 11 Christian knights, including Roland, were victorious, while only one Muslim warrior, Margarit of Seville, triumphed. However, in the second attack, most of the Christian knights were laid low. Then Roland sounded his horn. Far ahead, beyond the Pyrenees in France, Charlemagne heard the call and ordered the front section of the army to mount and return to the pass.

But it was too late. On the battlefield only 60 Frankish knights were left alive. Oliver was mortally injured in one encounter, and having lost his sight, mistakenly attacked Roland with his great sword Halteclere. Roland identified himself and absolved Oliver, for he could see that he was dying. One by one the Christian knights died. Roland made sure

▼ *This image of Roland sounding his horn to summon the help of Charlemagne and the rest of the army is from a 13th-century German edition of the poem.*

that none of the Muslims could get their hands on his famous sword Durandel by arranging his body on top of it as he prepared for death. He died unconquered in spirit, asking God for forgiveness with his final breath.

AFTER THE BATTLE

Charlemagne and the Franks defeated the remaining Muslim forces. They marched home to France, carrying the bodies of Roland, Oliver and Archbishop Turpin, and buried them at Blaye, near Bordeaux. In Aix Charlemagne ordered the execution of the traitor Ganelon.

At the end of the poem, Charlemagne was called once more to holy war: the Archangel Gabriel visited the king in his bedchamber and demanded that he take his army to the aid of a certain King Vivien besieged by pagans in the city of Imphe. Charlemagne was deeply reluctant to agree to the angel's demands, and tore his beard, bemoaning his fate, but he knew that it was his duty to fight for Christianity and to turn back the infidels.

THE HISTORICAL BATTLE OF RONCESVALLES

We know nothing for sure about the Battle of Roncesvalles. Charlemagne certainly led a military campaign in Spain in 778, but the famous battle in the Pyrenees might never have taken place. If it did happen, it was probably a minor skirmish that was developed in legend and literature as a major chivalric event.

The earliest reference to Charlemagne's 778 campaign in Spain was broadly contemporary with the events, in the Royal Annals of his reign, but made no reference to a battle at Roncesvalles. However, when around a quarter of a century later the annals were revised, an account of an attack on the rear of his army in the Pyrenees was added.

Einhard's biography of Charlemagne, the *Vita Karoli Magni* (*Life of Charlemagne*), written in c.817–30, described the events as a minor defeat but named Hroudland, or Roland, as one of those killed. By c.840,

▲ *In northern Europe Roland became a symbol of the independence of cities from the nobility. Statues of the hero were raised in many squares – as here in Riga, Latvia.*

when a biography of Charlemagne's son Louis was written, the author not only mentioned the battle but also commented that the names of the men who died at Roncesvalles were so well known that they need not be mentioned; clearly the legend of the conflict and its aftermath was firmly established by this point.

If the battle did occur, we do not know whether Charlemagne was attacked by Basques or Muslims or by a combined army of both. In Spain, Charlemagne's troops had razed the city of Pamplona before heading northward through the Pyrenees, bound for France; perhaps the Basques wanted revenge for this act, and so launched a raid. Some accounts, on the other hand, suggested that Charlemagne had taken the emir of Barcelona hostage, and it may be that Spanish Muslims attacked the Frankish army in an attempt to avenge this act.

IN SEARCH OF GLORY

WILLIAM OF ORANGE, KNIGHT OF CHARLEMAGNE

One cycle of *chansons de geste* told of the heroic deeds of William of Orange, a knight in the service of the great Charlemagne. The poems celebrated in particular his battles against the Saracens in southern France.

THREE CYCLES OF CHANSONS

Chansons de geste were traditionally grouped in three cycles, according to a classification proposed by the trouvère Bertrand de Bar-sur-Aube in the first lines of his chanson *Girart de Vienne* in *c.*1180. The first cycle was the *Geste du roi*, songs principally about Charlemagne, including the *Song of Roland*. The second was the *Geste de Garin de Monglane*, a group of chansons mainly about William of Orange. The third cycle was the *Geste de Doon de Mayence*, about rebellions against the king's authority.

WILLIAM OF GELLONE

There were 24 chansons in the *Geste de Garin de Monglane* cycle, dating from the 12th–15th century. The cycle was named after the primarily legendary warrior Garin, and the hero of the poems was his great-grandson William – who was based on a combination of historical figures.

The main model was William (or Guihelm) of Gellone. As one of Charles Martel's grandsons, he was cousin to Charlemagne; under the king's patronage he was made count of Toulouse from AD790 to 811, and he took Charlemagne's son Louis the Pious into his household for his chivalric education. William was an obdurate opponent of the Muslim 'Saracens' of Spain on their incursions into southern France. In 793 he won a great victory over a Muslim army at the Roman city of Orange in southern France – this was celebrated in the 12th-century chanson *La Prise d'Orange* (*The Taking of Orange*) and his achievement won him his nickname as 'William of Orange'.

He fought the Saracens again at Villedaigne, and was defeated. This defeat, renamed the Battle of Aliscans and cast in heroic-elegiac light in the manner of the *Song of Roland*, became the subject of a whole series of treatments in the cycle of poems – including *La Chanson de Guillaume*, *Aliscans*, and *La Chevalerie Vivien* (see below).

Despite the upset at Villedaigne, William's manoeuvres drove the Islamic army to retreat to Spain; in the same campaign, however, another branch of the Saracen forces established a garrison at Narbonne. In 803 William campaigned in northern Spain and helped in the capture of Barcelona from the Muslims.

In 806, like many heroes of chivalric literature, he retired from life in the field to live as a monk in a monastery that he had founded at Gellone near Lodève. He made a gift to the monastery of a relic said

▲ *William of Orange and other paladins of Charlemagne were steadfast opponents of Islam in France and Spain. This illustration shows Turks and Moors regaining territory during the long struggle.*

to be a piece of Christ's cross, which Charlemagne had reputedly been given by the patriarch of Jerusalem and had passed on to William. He died in the monastery in 812 or 814, and was later sainted. The monastery became a major pilgrimage site for religious travellers bound for Santiago de Compostela.

WILLIAM OF PROVENCE

Another model for William was the 10th-century nobleman William I, Count of Provence, who decisively defeated Saracen raiders from Fraxinetum at the Battle of Tourtour in 973. The Saracens at Fraxinetum were pirate-raiders from

▲ *Louis I the Pious, son of Charlemagne, features often in the background to the chansons of Garin de Monglane.*

around the Mediterranean, who had been making inroads into southern France and northern Italy; the war of 973 began after the raiders took captive the abbot of the monastery of Cluny and demanded a ransom. William went on to take the Saracen base at Fraxinetum and drove the raiders right out of southern France. He was hailed as 'the Liberator' and 'Father of the Country'. Like William of Gellone, he subsequently retired from military life to become a monk.

THE BATTLE OF ALISCANS AND ITS AFTERMATH

In the poems William was celebrated as the paragon of feudal warriors, a loyal supporter of Louis the Pious. He took as his wife a Saracen sorceress, Orable, who converted to Christianity and accepted the name Guibourc.

The central episode in the William of Orange poems celebrated a chivalric defeat at the Battle of Aliscans (thought to be based on the Battle of Villedaigne, which was actually fought alongside the river Orbieux in south-western France but in the poem was relocated to an old Roman cemetery near Arles, farther east). The episode concerned William's beloved

nephew Vivien, who – like Roland – failed to summon his uncle's help in battle against a great Saracen army until it was too late; William rode on to the battlefield with a great army, but was himself defeated and then had to go home alone, with all his great knights cut down. This was described in *La Chanson de Guillaume* (*The Song of William*).

Another chanson, *Aliscans*, described how William had his revenge for this defeat, with the help of Guibourc's brother, a huge kitchen servant named Rainoart who fought with a wooden yoke used for bearing buckets of water. The chanson *La Chevalerie Vivien* explained Vivien's defeat by revealing that he had taken a vow never to retreat by even a single pace in battle, and had deliberately provoked an attack at Aliscans by killing an entire boatload of Saracen raiders. The battle was thought a fitting subject for chivalric literature for many years – the great 12–13th century German poet Wolfram von Eschenbach, author of *Parzival*, did his own version in the poem *Willehalm*.

YOUTHFUL EXPLOITS AND INHERITANCE TROUBLES

Two poems, *Les Enfances Guillaume* and *Les Enfances Vivien*, described the youthful exploits of the men who became these great knights. It was a convention to describe the youthful achievements of

knights either in a separate *enfances* poem or in a section of a longer work. Another chanson, *Les Narbonnais*, relates the *enfances* of all seven sons of William's father Aymeri of Narbonne. This chanson is interesting for casting light on the reality of land inheritance difficulties: Aymeri passed his land to his youngest son (rather than his oldest, as he would have done in reality) and the other six had either to conquer territories for themselves or to find paid employment at the court of the great Charlemagne. The poem ended with the six older sons riding in to drive off a besieging Saracen army at Narbonne.

AYMERI OF NARBONNE

One part of the cycle was based on the adventures of William's father, Aymeri of Narbonne. The poem *Aymeri de Narbonne* recounted how he captured Narbonne from the Saracens and was given feudal rights there as seigneur by Charlemagne. It also details his marriage to Ermenjart, sister of the king of the Lombards, and their many children – the fifth of his daughters was named as Blanchefleur and was said to be the wife of Charlemagne's son Louis the Pious.

▼ *Louis the Pious fought alongside William of Orange in one of his campaigns against Spanish Islam, leading an army to attack the city of Barcelona in 803.*

REBEL LORDS

CHANSONS DE GESTE CELEBRATING KNIGHTS IN REVOLT

The third main cycle of *chansons de geste*, the *Geste de Doon de Mayence*, celebrated the campaigns of feudal lords against royal authority. The main heroes of the poems were Ogier the Dane, the four sons of Duke Aymon, and Duke Huon of Bordeaux.

The cycle took its name from Doon de Mayence, whose character was probably developed late in the series to provide a heroic ancestor for the other lords. The chanson devoted to Doon de Mayence described his childhood and *enfances* ('youthful exploits'), then gave an account of the lord's rebel fighting in Saxony, which probably had a basis in history. There was also a tantalizing reference in the *Chronicle of Fredegar*, a history of the Franks for the years AD584–641, to a revolt by warriors of Mayence against King Sigebert III of Austrasia, in his war against Duke Radulph of Thuringia in 640.

In the poems the lords all rebelled against Charlemagne, but his name was used in place of that of other less celebrated kings, both earlier (such as Sigebert), and later (such as his son Louis the Pious, and Louis's successors).

▼ *In this illustration from Renaud of Montauban, Charlemagne is seen receiving the homage of his knights after battle.*

OGIER THE DANE

In the chanson *La Chevalerie Ogier de Danemarche*, Ogier was a Danish prince who had a son killed by Charlot, one of Charlemagne's sons, and rose in revolt. He killed Charlot and was only just stopped from killing the king himself. He then fought Charlemagne for seven years, but finally made peace in order to join the Frankish king in a war against the Saracens. In this conflict he killed a giant named Brehus.

Historians believe that Ogier was probably based on a Danish king, Godfred, who fought against Charlemagne's expansion in the north of Germany at the start of the 9th century. In Danish folklore Ogier became a major figure, with a stature like that of King Arthur; he is said to be sleeping in his castle at Kronborg, ready to return and fight when his nation needs him.

THE COLOURFUL ADVENTURES OF RENAUD OF MONTAUBAN

One of the most popular poems of the cycle was *Les Quatre Fils Aymon* (*The Four Sons of Aymon*), also known as *Renaud of*

▲ *In the chanson* Les Quatre Fils Aymon, *Maugis used his sorcerer's powers to overcome a serpent and win the enchanted horse Bayard.*

Montauban. It survives in a manuscript from the late 12th century, but it is possible that older versions have been lost. It described the rebellion of the four sons of Duke Aymon of Bordeaux – Aalard, Guichard, Renaud and Richard – which began when they accidentally killed Charlemagne's nephew Bertolai at the great king's court at Aachen and had to flee for their lives.

At first they took refuge in the Ardennes, described in the poem as an enchanted forest, where they built a great fortress named Montessor. Charlemagne, driven by his desire to avenge his nephew, tracked the rebels down and captured Montessor. The four lords escaped once more and lived for seven years as bandits in the countryside.

They were joined by their cousin Maugis, who was a sorcerer. Renaud then came to the aid of King Yon of Gascony in driving back an invasion by a Saracen army, and was rewarded with the hand in marriage of Yon's sister Clarisse. He built another fortress, Montauban.

Charlemagne arrived at Montauban in the company of the great Roland himself. Then Renaud, with the help of Maugis, disguised himself and on his great horse Bayard managed to outrun Roland in a horse race before seizing Charlemagne's crown and fleeing.

The horse Bayard was an important character in the poem, and enjoyed a prolonged popularity in other chivalric legends and poems. The horse had the power to change its size according to the size of its rider, and could carry all four sons of Aymon at once.

Many further adventures ensued with the brothers always following the code of chivalry, no matter how difficult things were; at one point they were so short of food and drink that they had to drink Bayard's blood to survive. Eventually, they made peace with Charlemagne. Under the terms of the agreement, Renaud travelled with Maugis to the Holy Land and helped the crusaders to capture Jerusalem; Charlemagne took possession of Bayard and ordered that the animal be thrown into a river with a millstone around its neck. But Bayard survived and went on to be reunited with Renaud.

Then Renaud returned to France, before in traditional manner renouncing the military life to live as a religious hermit. He found time to travel to Cologne and helped to build the superb cathedral there (the Gothic cathedral was begun in 1248 on the site of an earlier Christian building that had been burned down). However, Renaud was killed in a quarrel with other stonemasons.

REBELS AGAINST AUTHORITY

The character of Charlemagne in *Les Quatre Fils Aymon* was treacherous and committed to seeking vengeance for wrongs done, and the poet made a good deal of the king being outwitted by the sorcerer Maugis. But throughout all the adventures, feudal authority was upheld.

Of course revolts against feudal rule were by no means uncommon, even within ruling families. King Henry II of England, for instance, faced two revolts by his own sons and his queen, Eleanor of Aquitaine. In the first in 1173, he emerged victorious, but the second in 1189 proved to be the end of him. Tradition has it that it was the discovery of the involvement of his favourite youngest son, the future King John of England, that broke Henry's heart and sent him to his deathbed. He died, breathing these bitter words at his last: 'Shame, shame upon a vanquished king.'

DUKE HUON OF BORDEAUX

Colourful legend and the romance of the Orient, doubtless as reported by crusaders, entirely swamped historical fact in the late 12th-century chanson about Duke Huon of Bordeaux. Duke Huon was another lord who reputedly killed Charlemagne's troublesome son, Charlot, which led Charlemagne to set Huon a romantic quest: he must find his way to the court

▼ *Maugis and Queen Isanne, surprised in her bedroom by intruders in an illustration from the chanson* Maugis d'Aigremont.

of Sultan Gaudys, the admiral of Babylon, and there decapitate the Sultan's most celebrated guest, plant three kisses on the Sultan's daughter, and pluck hairs from the sultan's beard and four teeth from his mouth as trophies.

Huon set out with several knights in his company. He went first to Jerusalem, and prayed before Christ's tomb, then travelled in the company of a French penitent named Gerames through an enchanted forest ruled by Oberon, King of the Fairies. Later adventures included killing the giant Angolafer before they arrived at Babylon, which was presented as a city on the river Nile, in Egypt.

Huon succeeded in his first two tasks, then was cast in to a dungeon. The sultan allowed him out to fight and defeat another giant, Agrapart, brother of Angolafer, then laid on a banquet. This descended into a full-scale battle between the Sultan's Muslim knights and Duke Huon's Christian knights, who were helped in their hour of need by Oberon and a fairy host. Huon retuned to France, where Oberon reconciled him with Charlemagne. On Oberon's death, Huon succeeded him as king of the fairies.

GERMAN KNIGHT AT COURT

SIEGFRIED AND THE *NIBELUNGENLIED*

The dragon-slaying warrior Siegfried, fearless hero of the German epic poem the *Nibelungenlied* (*Song of the Nibelungs*) of c.1200, was primarily based on a mythical character from German and Norse oral legend and folklore. In the *Nibelungenlied*, this ancient legend was overlaid with historical material, and the Siegfried of the poem is thought to have been based on famous figures from the era of the Frankish kings and earlier.

HISTORICAL BACKGROUND

The destruction of the Nibelungs (or Burgundians) described in the poem may be based on the defeat of the Burgundian kingdom by the Roman general Flavius

▼ *Siegfried's great reputation as a warrior, and his many heroic feats, including the slaying of a dragon, persuaded Princess Kriemhild to accept him as her suitor and, ultimately, her husband.*

Aetius and an army of mercenary Huns at Worms in AD436 when approximately 20,000 Burgundians were reputedly slaughtered. There are other relevant historical events; one is the marriage of Attila, King of the Huns, to Ildikó, a Burgundian princess, in the middle of the 5th century. Another possible influence for the tale is the feud that arose between the Merovingian queens Brunhilda and Fredegunde in the 6th century, which was so fierce that each woman persuaded her husband to go to war against the other.

One possible model for Siegfried was a Merovingian king of the Franks of around AD600. Another much earlier archetype could be Arminius, leader of the Germanic Cherusci tribe from the northern Rhine, who in AD9 fought in scale armour as he led a coalition of Germanic tribes to a famous victory over three Roman legions in the Battle of Teutoburg Forest, a victory whose fame rang down the ages.

▲ *Known as Etzel in the* Nibelungenlied, *Attila, King of the Huns from 434 to 453, is referred to as Atli in the Icelandic sagas.*

ANCIENT LEGENDS IN A COURTLY SETTING

The *Nibelungenlied* recast the Germanic-Norse folklore and historical elements within the setting of Christian knighthood and the conventions of courtly love, in much the same way that Welsh legends about King Arthur were reinvented for a courtly audience in the works of Chrétien de Troyes and others. However, although Siegfried, while he was courting Kriemhild, behaved in accordance with the courtly love conventions, the poem also displayed violent emotions and an emphasis on revenge that was more at home in older legends and folklore than in courtly love literature.

SIEGFRIED IN THE *NIBELUNGENLIED*

Siegfried, a German prince from Xanten on the lower Rhine, arrived at Worms to woo Kriemhild, the Burgundian princess and sister of King Gunther. Kriemhild,

however, was resolved not to wed after she had a violent dream, which her mother interpreted as meaning that any man she married would meet a bloody end. A retainer of King Gunther, named Hagen, related Siegfried's many great feats including the killing of a dragon and his winning of a great treasure from brothers Schilbung and Nibelung. With King Gunther's permission, Siegfried led the Burgundian army in a war against the Danes and Saxons, and his heroism in battle helped to soften Kriemhild's feelings for him.

Then news arrived that a queen of wondrous beauty and martial strength named Brunhilde had offered to wed the knight who was capable of defeating her in conflict. King Gunther decided to send Siegfried, but used magic to make him invisible; while Siegfried performed acts of martial valour, Gunther would go through the motions and take the credit for Siegfried's victory. Siegfried's reward would be the hand of Lady Kriemhild in marriage. The plan worked: Brunhilde accepted Gunther as her husband, and Kriemhild wed Siegfried. But later, after a quarrel between the two wives, Kriemhild revealed the trick to Brunhilde.

Hagen then allied himself with Brunhilde to seek revenge and to protect Gunther's honour. From Kriemhild, he learned of Siegfried's only weak spot by pretending that he needed to know so that he could cover the great warrior in battle.

▲ *The water spirits of the Danube prophesy the defeat of Gunther's army to Hagen on his way to the court of Etzel.*

(After his slaughter of the dragon in his youth, Siegfried had bathed in the animal's blood and ever afterwards was invulnerable in battle – save in one tiny spot on his back, which without his knowing had been covered with a leaf from a linden tree while he was bathing.) Hagen put the knowledge to wicked use, and killed Siegfried by striking him with a spear in the vulnerable part of his back as he was leaning over a river during a hunting trip.

Siegfried was buried with great ceremony and Kriemhild, distraught with grief and brought low by mourning, lived on

in Worms. She began to distribute the treasure of her dead husband, but Hagen stole it and hid it in the river Rhine.

The remainder of the poem described Kriemhild's violent revenge against the Burgundians who had murdered her husband and stolen her fortune. She married Etzel (based on Attila, King of the Huns), hoping he would help her get revenge. Some years later, at her insistence, Etzel invited King Gunther and Hagen to his court and in a mass battle Gunther was defeated and killed while Kriemhild herself killed Hagen with Siegfried's own sword. Kriemhild was then killed by the aged knight Hildebrand, who was horrified by the violence she had unleashed.

Hildebrand, whose name meant 'battle sword', was the brother in arms of Dietrich von Bern, an archetype of the just ruler and a legendary incarnation of the historical 5th-century King of the Ostrogoths, Theodoric the Great. According to the *Nibelungenlied*, Dietrich and Hildebrand were living in exile at Etzel's court at the time, and fought with great heroism in the battle between kings Etzel and Gunther and their retainers.

◄ *The grief of Kriemhild upon the death of her love Siegfried soon turned to vengeful fury in the* Nibelungenlied. *She achieved terrible revenge with the help of her second husband Etzel – Attila, King of the Huns.*

EL CID

THE LIFE AND LEGEND OF DON RODRIGO DIAZ DE VIVAR

Legends grew up about the chivalric feats of Spanish knight Don Rodrigo Diaz de Vivar even before he died in 1099. He was Spain's greatest general of the 11th century, who fought both for the Spanish crown and for the Moors or Saracens. In his own lifetime he was known as El Campeador ('the Champion') and El Cid (derived from the Arabic title *assid*, meaning 'lord'). The heroic legend and stirring historical facts of his life inspired many ballads and chronicles about El Cid, as well as the magnificent 12th-century poem, *Cantar de Mio Cid* (*Song of My Cid*).

BIRTH AND RISE TO FAME

Don Rodrigo was born at Bivar, near Burgos, in 1043 and had his chivalric education at the court of King Ferdinand I of Castile and Leon, where he rose to become commander of the royal army by the age of 22 under Ferdinand's eldest son, King Sancho II. However, when Sancho died in 1072 and was succeeded by his brother

▼ *In a celebrated incident the Cid, on behalf of the parliament of Castile, made King Alfonso VI swear that he had no part in the death of the Cid's brother Sancho II.*

Alfonso, Don Rodrigo lost the position to Count Garcia Ordonez, who became a great rival. Nevertheless he remained at court and married Alfonso's niece Jimena, and they had a son and two daughters.

After Don Rodrigo took Count Ordonez captive in 1079, King Alfonso cast him into exile in 1081. Don Rodrigo then entered the service of al-Mu'tamin, Moorish king of Saragossa in north-eastern Spain. He fought for al-Mu'tamin, and his successor al-Musta'in II, for almost ten years, winning many victories against fellow Moors and Spanish Christian kings.

PRINCE OF VALENCIA

After being briefly recalled by Alfonso, Don Rodrigo fought on his own account to take control of the Moorish kingdom of Valencia in 1090–94. He ruled the city, nominally under Alfonso VI but in reality in his own right, governing both Muslims and Christians. He turned the city mosque into a cathedral and appointed a French bishop named Jerome. As a statement of his princely status, he was able to wed his daughters, Cristina and Maria, to, respectively, Ramiro, Lord of Monzón and Ramón Berenguer II, Count of Barcelona.

▲ *El Cid was a Christian knight equally at home in the service of Islamic kings. Castile lost a great servant when it exiled him.*

However, Valencia was not a Christian city for long. Soon after the Cid's death in 1099, the city was besieged by Almoravids (a fresh wave of Muslims who had invaded Spain in 1086). King Alfonso VI tried to save the city, but decided he could not hold it, and the city was evacuated and burned. The Cid's body was taken for burial at the monastery of San Pedro near Burgos in Castile. The Almoravids took control of the ruins of Valencia and the rebuilt city remained Muslim until 1238.

THE CID'S FIRST VICTORY

Legends about Don Rodrigo told how he first achieved notice as a great knight by defending the honour of his father, Diego Laynez: with a single blow of his sword, he defeated the knight, Don Gomez, who

▶ *El Cid defeats Don Gomez at Callaforra, avenging an insult to his father Diego Laynez. This illustration is from a 1344 manuscript of the* Chronicle of Spain.

had slighted Diego. Gomez's daughter, Ximena, married the Cid because she was so enamoured of his strength and virtue.

The legend then described a number of campaigns against the Moors, fought in the service of 'King Ferrando' (Ferdinand I), and the declaration by Ferrando – who had heard the Moors call Rodrigo 'Cid' – that the warrior should be called 'El Cid'. Subsequently, Holy Roman Emperor Henry III, with the support of Pope Victor II, demanded tribute from Ferrando, who refused. In the ensuing war the Cid beat Remon, Count of Savoy, and a French army, then went to Rome to oversee the chastened pope signing a guarantee that a Holy Roman Emperor could never demand tribute from a Spanish king.

GREAT CHIVALRY

According to legend, following Ferrando's death, while in exile, the Cid performed countless feats of great chivalry and Christian love. In one tale he was riding to Santiago de Compostela to worship at the shrine of Spain's patron saint, St James, and he picked up a leper from the roadside and gave him a ride on his great horse

▼ *A statue in Burgos shows the Cid mounted on his trusty horse, Bavieca, and brandishing his magnificent sword, Tizona.*

Bavieca. Later at the inn, he shared his table and bed with the leper, trusting God to protect him from infection. In the night he woke to find the leper transformed into Lazarus – the dead man brought back to life by Christ in the Gospels. Lazarus predicted a glorious career for the knight.

Many episodes in the ballads and chronicles and the *Song of My Cid* described the Cid's military feats in battle against the Moors, emphasizing his tactical intelligence, his magnanimity in victory, his fairness in dividing the spoils of victory among his men, his piety in diverting riches to the support of churches and monasteries, and his personal physical prowess as a knight.

Like other knights of legend, he had a magnificent sword and horse, themselves celebrated in stories. According to the *Song of My Cid*, the Cid did not acquire his horse, Bavieca, until late in his career, when he captured it from a king of Seville who had tried to take Valencia. Bavieca was unquestioningly loyal and obedient, and by tradition never accepted another

rider after the Cid's death. When the horse died it was buried opposite the monastery of San Pedro. His sword was called Tizona.

LEGENDS OF THE CID'S DEATH

The legend of the Cid's death told that the great knight, forewarned in a dream by St Peter that he was to be called to heaven, instructed his leading comrades how to fight off an impending Moorish siege of Valencia and arranged for his body to lead into battle as if he were alive. In the battle that followed it was said that 70,000 angel knights came to the aid of the Cid's men, including one who carried a flaming sword and a bloody cross. The Christians drove their foes into the sea, where their blood turned the waves red.

Afterwards, the Cid's body was again strapped to his trusty Bavieca and led back to the monastery of San Pedro de Cardena. There it was placed on an ivory throne, with the sword Tizona in its hand, and reputedly sat there for ten years. A sweet smell arose from the body – an indication that the Cid was a saint.

DEFENDER OF JERUSALEM

LEGENDS ABOUT CRUSADER KNIGHT GODFREY OF BOUILLON

Fantastical legends grew up around the achievements of the knights who retook Jerusalem on the First Crusade (1096–99), notably Godfrey of Bouillon, one of the key figures of that episode. Godfrey, second son of Eustace, Count of Boulogne, was one of the first knights to scale the walls of the city in July 1099; he refused to be declared king, taking instead the title 'Defender of the Holy Sepulchre'.

Godfrey was the hero of a 14th-century romance narrative that reworked a cycle of 11th-century *chansons de geste*, known as the Crusade cycle, and combined them with the medieval legend of the 'Knight of the Swan', telling of a sleeping knight in a swan-drawn boat who appeared to defend a lady's honour on condition that she did not ask his name. In the Arthur tradition presented by Wolfram von Eschenbach in his *Parzival*, the Swan Knight was Sir Lohengrin, son of Sir Perceval, but in the Godfrey tradition the Swan Knight was the grandfather of the crusader knight.

▼ *Sir Percival's horse is killed, from the Queste del Saint Graal, c.1380-85. In some chansons the figure of Percival is said to be the grandson of Godfrey.*

THE SONG OF ANTIOCH

The reworked group of Crusade chansons (not named in the categorization of songs by trouvère Bertrand de Bar-sur-Aube) included the *Chanson d'Antioche* (*Song of Antioch*), which survives in a version dating from *c.*1180, and was based on an early poem believed to have been written during the First Crusade. This original poem was reputedly composed by Richard le Pèlerin ('Richard the Pilgrim'), a poet who travelled with the crusaders and is said to have begun the poem during the siege of Antioch. The chanson contained many hyperbolic descriptions and great lists of knights' names.

The late 12th-century version of the poem was written by Graindor de Douai, author of the other two reworked poems in the cycle – the *Chanson de Jérusalem* (*Song of Jerusalem*) and the *Chanson de Chêtifs* (*Song of the Prisoners* – a reference to Christian knights held by Muslims in the Holy Land). All chansons featured Godfrey of Bouillon as a central figure.

The 14th-century Godfrey of Bouillon narrative began with an account of the birth of the Swan Knight and proceeded to describe how that knight came to the

▲ *In the French version of the legend of Lohengrin, the Knight of the Swan was named Elias and married Beatrix of Bouillon, grandmother of Godfrey.*

rescue of the duchess of Bouillon by winning a duel against her persecutor, Regnier of Saxony. He then married the Duchess's

▼ *This 19th-century depiction of Godfrey, his brother Baldwin and their men crossing into Anatolia in 1097 captures the sense of exaltation among the crusaders.*

daughter and they had a daughter named Ida, but his wife asked his true name and so the Swan Knight had to leave – afterwards it emerged that the name was Elias. Then Sir Pons and Sir Gerart, kinsmen of Sir Elias, went on crusade to Jerusalem where they met Cornumarant, Muslim king of the city.

GODFREY THE CRUSADER

Many years afterwards, Ida's three sons – Eustace, Godfrey and Baldwin – went through their chivalric education and emerged as great knights. In Jerusalem, King Cornumarant's mother had a vision in which she saw Godfrey and his kin arriving in their full glory as crusaders – and also later knights' famous conflicts with Saladin at the time of the Third Crusade. As a result, Cornumarant made a voyage to Europe to visit Godfrey, and met a whole host of great figures of the Crusades on his travels: Robert Curthose; Tancred, Prince of Galilee; Bohemond of Antioch; Adhemar of Le Puy; Raymond of Toulouse and Hugh of Vermandois. Cornumarant's plan was to assassinate Godfrey of Bouillon and so make it impossible for his mother's troubling prophecy to come true, but faced with the knight in

▼ *Unstained amid carnage, Godfrey leads the way into the Holy City of Jerusalem.*

all his glory the travelling king was unable to do the deed. In fact his presence and mention of the city of Jerusalem had the unlooked-for result of planting the idea of making a crusade in Godfrey's mind.

The next stage of the narrative was the reworked *Chanson d'Antioche*. It described Pope Urban II's preaching of the crusade, the planning and preparations among the crusaders, their farewells to those staying behind, the journey to Constantinople and then the successful siege of Antioch, which lasted for eight months.

The narrative proceeded to describe the adventures of Christian *chétifs* ('prisoners') in the company of Corbaran, the deposed king of Antioch, on his return to his homeland. It included a section in which the prisoners performed the familiar knightly feat of killing a dragon, and then one of their number, Sir Arpin of Bourges, went to the aid of King Corbaran's son in various escapades; finally the captives were released and joined the other crusaders at the walls of Jerusalem.

▲ *In July 1099 Godfrey and the crusaders marched in procession around Jerusalem (in emulation of the Israelite leader Joshua at Jericho) believing the city would then fall.*

The crusader army, led by Godfrey, survived several assaults by the Saracens; in this version, Bohemond of Taranto was fighting with the crusaders rather than looking after his own interests, at Antioch (as the historical Bohemond was doing during the siege of Jerusalem). The narrative described how the crusaders tried repeatedly to take the Holy City without success before their prayers were answered and the city fell.

The story described how even in their moment of raucous triumph Godfrey and the other leaders of the crusader army remembered their proper humility and declined to be named king in Christ's city, but God sent them a sign indicating that Godfrey should be given the honour. After the capture of Jerusalem, the narrative ended with the death of Cornumarant.

GERMAN CRUSADER

EMPEROR FREDERICK I 'BARBAROSSA'

Frederick I, nicknamed 'Barbarossa' (meaning 'red beard'), was the Holy Roman Emperor from 1152 until his death in 1190. He went on two crusades, fighting with distinction alongside his uncle, Conrad III of Germany, on the Second Crusade (1145–49), and at the end of his life leading an army of 15,000 men on the Third Crusade (1189–92). He died attempting to cross the river Saleph in Cilicia (now part of Turkey) en route to the Holy Land.

THE SLEEPING KING

Frederick Barbarossa was hailed as one of the greatest of German rulers. His deeds were celebrated in the Latin chronicle *Gesta Friderici I Imperatoris* (*Deeds of the Emperor Frederick I*), written by the Cistercian monk and bishop Otto von Friesing. Legends swiftly grew up around Frederick's name, most notably to the

▲ *Frederick became embroiled in a long power struggle in Italy with Pope Alexander III. Following defeat in the Battle of Legnano, he made peace with Alexander and his allies in the Treaty of Venice (1177).*

▼ *Because of his opposition to the papacy and efforts to impose authority in Germany Frederick was glorified in the 19th century as a symbol of German pride and unity.*

effect that he did not truly die, but can be found asleep in a cave in the Kyffhäuser mountain in central Germany, and will ride forth to save Germany in her hour of greatest need.

According to this legend, his red beard has grown through the table before which he sits with his eyes half-closed. He stirs periodically to send a boy out to see if ravens are still flying around the mountain, for the prophecy has established that when the ravens stop flying Germany will desperately need his help.

AUTHORITY IN GERMANY

As Holy Roman Emperor, Frederick set out to restore the empire to the greatness it had enjoyed in the time of its founding father Charlemagne, and also in the 10th century under Otto I. At the start of his reign, he sent out an order for peace in Germany and gave a number of concessions to the princes of his territory to

achieve this. He acted vigorously and effectively throughout his reign to defuse disputes and maintain his authority. He sought to emphasize his reign's continuity with that of Charlemagne, and organized a great celebration of the canonization of the former king of the Franks at Aachen in 1165.

CAMPAIGNS IN ITALY

Frederick led six expeditions into Italy to enforce his imperial rights there. On the first he was crowned Holy Roman Emperor by Pope Adrian IV (r. 1154–59), but he later fell out with the papacy and was excommunicated in 1160. On his fourth trip in 1167 he won a great military victory over a mighty papal army in the Battle of Monte Porzio near Tusculum (in modern Lazio, central Italy). Victory opened the way for Frederick to depose the pope, Alexander III (r. 1159–81), and appoint his own candidate, Paschal III, but an outbreak of plague in the imperial army ended the campaign and sent Frederick back to Germany.

THE EMPEROR WHO CHEATED DEATH

On the fifth Italian expedition, with an army of 8,000 knights, he suffered a heavy defeat fighting the pro-papal Lombard League at the Battle of Legnano. In the heat of the battle, Frederick's guard and standard bearer were killed and the emperor himself was thrown from his horse and left for dead. The army panicked and fled, and knights brought the news to Frederick's wife, Beatrice, in Pavia

▼ *A monument on the Kyffhauser mountain features this 6.5m (22ft) sandstone statue of Barbarossa apparently awaking from sleep, ready to come to Germany's aid.*

that her lord had been killed. For three days, his death was mourned, but he then appeared unannounced in Pavia, having recovered from his wound sufficiently to make his own way back home from the field of battle.

THE THIRD CRUSADE

Frederick made peace with the pope before embarking on the Third Crusade. He took the cross at Mainz Cathedral on 27 March 1188, and raised a vast German army, including 3,000 knights. They set out to follow the land rather than the sea route to the Holy Land since the army was too large to go by ship.

They travelled through Hungary and Serbia and reached Constantinople in 1189. They moved on into Anatolia and in May 1190 captured Iconium (now Konya in Turkey, at that time the capital of the Sultanate of Rum). The news of the army's approach caused consternation among Muslim leaders in the Holy Land, including Saladin. The Muslims began to gather their own army in readiness for a great conflict.

▲ *A 12th-century chronicle illustration shows Frederick, enthroned, with his two sons, Emperor Henry VI and Duke Frederick V of Swabia.*

However, on 10 June 1190 Frederick fell from his horse while crossing the river Saleph and died – either because the shock of the cold water gave him a heart attack or because he was impeded so badly by his armour that he drowned in the river, although the water was said to be only waist-deep. The death of their leader caused much of the army to panic and many abandoned the crusade and headed for home.

The command devolved on his son, Frederick of Swabia, who led the remnant of the army to Antioch. His aim was to bury his father in Jerusalem, but efforts to preserve the corpse using vinegar were not successful. Barbarossa's flesh was removed from his bones by boiling at Antioch, and buried there, while the bones were carried on by the army. Further reduced by fever, the army made its way to Tyre, where Frederick's bones were buried, and then to Acre. The crusade was carried on by Philip II of France and Richard I of England, who had travelled with their armies separately from Barbarossa.

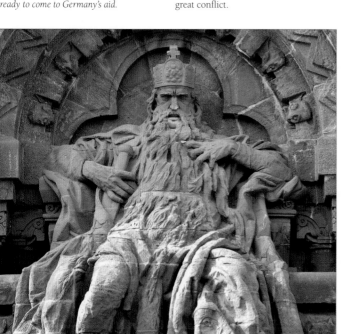

THE ROMANCE OF COEUR DE LION
COLOURFUL LEGENDS ABOUT KING RICHARD I OF ENGLAND

The legend of King Richard I of England was growing even before his death in 1199, and was firmly established by c.1250, when the Anglo-Norman romance of *Richard Coeur de Lion* was written. Before the end of the 13th century this was expanded into an English poem that celebrated Richard as the perfect embodiment of chivalric virtue. At this time, the romance suggests, chivalry was thought to be epitomized by a taste for combating Saracens and a love of court poetry. The Richard of the legend was also marked by a superhuman bravery.

The romance gave Richard a marvellous origin, which was typical of literature of the period but curious perhaps given that Richard's true parents, King Henry II and Eleanor of Aquitaine, hardly needed improving upon. In the poem King Henry was said to have married the fairy daughter of the pagan king of Antioch, and they had three children: Richard, John and a daughter, Topias.

▼ *Richard and the Muslim general Saladin met in the course of the Third Crusade. An image from the English* Luttrell Psalter *(1340s) represents them jousting. Richard's face is hidden by his helmet. Both ride horses wearing elaborate caparisons.*

One day the mother fled, because her fairy nature meant that she could not sit piously through a church Communion service. She ran from the church, carrying Topias and John, but dropped John, whose leg was broken. Richard became king and in his very first act declared a tournament, at which much bravery was displayed. He chose the two most chivalrous performers, Sir Thomas Multon and Sir Fulk Doyly, to be his close companions. (In reality, as we have seen, Richard was not a keen tourneyer, but his reign was associated with the fighting of tournaments throughout England because he introduced a system of licensing for the holding of such events.)

A TASTE FOR SARACEN BLOOD

Later parts of the romance made much of Richard's enthusiasm for killing Saracens on crusade, and described how he not only struck the fiercest warriors down but also cooked them and ate their flesh with relish. They also described an imaginary duel between Richard and the great Saracen general Saladin.

Richard was warned in a dream sent from heaven that Saladin was planning an elaborate trick: with apparent generosity, Saladin had provided his adversary with

▲ *Philip II of France receives a messenger and takes the cross with Richard I prior to the Third Crusade.*

a fine horse to ride for the encounter in the lists, but in truth the horse was the son of the distinguished mare that Saladin himself was to ride. When the mare whinnied, Richard's horse would kneel in an attempt to drink its mother's milk, putting Richard at the mercy of the Saracen leader. Richard matched his opponent's cunning and took the precaution of filling his horse's ears with wax, so that when Saladin's mare whinnied it had no effect. He defeated Saladin in the encounter, but allowed him to escape with his life.

HOW RICHARD GOT THE NAME 'LIONHEART'

The 13th-century English *Coeur de Lion* gave a colourful account of how Richard came by his *nom de guerre*. It told how before the king ever went on crusade, when he was returning from a reconnaissance mission to the Holy Land, he was imprisoned by a certain King Modard of Germany. Richard proved a troublesome prisoner, for he killed Modard's son and made love to his daughter while in captivity, and in his rage Modard arranged for a starving lion to be released into the English king's cell.

Marked above all else by his bravery, Richard showed no fear as the lion came for him, its mouth wide open. With lightning speed, he reached down the creature's throat and tore its heart out. Then he broke out of his prison and marched into the great hall of the castle, where the king was sitting at dinner with his retainers and his fair daughter. Richard waved the bloody heart under the king's nose, then dipped it in some salt and ate it raw with apparent delight – and, as the poet noted, without bread. In awe of his captive, King Modard declared that he should be called 'Richard Lion Heart'.

▼ *Richard I's faithful minstrel Blondel hears his master's voice emanating from the dungeon of an Austrian castle where the king is held captive.*

▲ *Richard's legend emphasized his noble qualities. On his deathbed, he pardoned Bertrand de Gurdun, the young man who had fatally injured him.*

RICHARD AND BLONDEL

An often-repeated part of the legend was based on events after the crusade, during Richard's disastrous return to Europe when, after being shipwrecked near Venice, he was captured and jailed first by Duke Leopold of Austria, and then by Holy Roman Emperor Henry VI.

At the time when Richard was in Duke Leopold's dungeon, the romance said, no one at the English court knew what had become of him and Richard's favourite minstrel, Blondel, set out to search for his king. The poet wandered across all the countries of Europe and eventually arrived in Austria where he heard from a local that a great lord was imprisoned in Duke Leopold's castle. Suspecting that it might be Richard, he managed to get employment there as a musician. But he was not able to find out whether the prisoner was Richard. For many months he worked there without success, but one day he was in the garden and Richard, happening to look out of the window of his dungeon, saw him. Richard sang aloud the first verse

of a song they had composed together, and which nobody else knew, and Blondel, hearing the song, knew for sure that his lord was confined within. Shortly afterwards he left the castle and returned to England and reported to all where their king was imprisoned.

Blondel's legend grew up around the reputation of a French trouvère named Blondel of Nesle (a place near Amiens, northern France). Blondel, who reputedly got his name because he had long blond hair, was the composer of 25 songs. He was either Jean, Lord of Nesle, who like Richard fought on the Third Crusade; or his son, also Jean, who succeeded his father and fought on both the Fourth Crusade and the Albigensian Crusade. We do not know whether there was actually a connection between the historical 'Blondel' and King Richard.

A later version of the romance has a slightly different account of the Blondel legend. It suggested that the minstrel went around Europe while singing the first verse of the song that only he and Richard knew outside places where he suspected Richard might be incarcerated. Finally, when he hit upon the right place by chance, he heard Richard's voice replying from within, singing the second verse.

ADVENTURES IN LOVE AND ON CRUSADE

THE COURTLY REPUTATION OF BONIFACE OF MONTFERRAT

Boniface, Marquess of Montferrat in north-western Italy, presided over one of the most highly regarded courts of chivalry in Europe. His chivalric exploits were celebrated in song by his court poet and friend, the troubadour Raimbaut de Vaqueiras. Boniface fought against the Lombard League in Italy and Sicily, and led the Fourth Crusade in 1201–04.

Raimbaut declared that Boniface's knightly virtues were so great that they must have been bequeathed by the great figures of chivalric legend, an indication of the way in which the great figures of chivalry past and imagined were not only inspiring examples, but almost presiding deities of knighthood. Alexander the Great had given Boniface his generosity, while he had got his daring and bravery from Roland and the other 12 knights of Charlemagne. His courtesy and his charm

▼ *In the early part of the Fourth Crusade, the crusader army attacked and captured the city of Zara in Dalmatia (now Croatia).*

with the women of the court he must have got from Berart de Montdidier (who was the subject of a now lost epic poem).

PROTECTOR OF LADIES

Boniface's achievements as a young man in the 1170s, as described in Raimbaut's *Epic Letter*, were the very stuff of courtly chivalry. In one adventure, he rescued Saldina de Mar, a prominent young woman from Genoa, who had been seized by Albert of Malaspina and taken to his most inaccessible retreat. Boniface and Raimbaut rode in at suppertime and took possession of the young woman, then carried her off to her lover Ponset d'Aguilar, who was, according to the poem, expiring in his bed for love of the young lady.

The *Epic Letter* also described Boniface's rescue of the wealthy young woman Jacopina of Ventimiglia from her wicked uncle, Count Otto, who was plotting to take her money and dispatch her to Sardinia. On hearing the news that Count Otto was plotting against Jacopina, the

▲ *A near-contemporary Byzantine mosaic represents Boniface's crusader army capturing Constantinople in 1204. The mosaic is from a church in Ravenna, Italy.*

chivalrous Boniface sighed deeply, for he remembered the kiss that the lady had given him when she had asked him to protect her against her scheming uncle. He and Raimbaut, along with three other knights – Bertaldo, Guiot and Hugonet del Far – rode by night to her rescue and plucked her to safety from the quayside only moments before she was to be sent into exile.

CHIVALRIC ADVENTURES

According to the poem, they then had many adventures in her company as they rode across country, with enemy knights in pursuit. They had to go into hiding when knights rode out from Pisa to encounter them, for they were extravagantly outnumbered, and went without food or water for two days. Then they had a dramatic encounter with a group of 12 brigands at Belhestar Pass, during which Raimbaut was wounded in the neck but then was rescued by Bertaldo and Hugonet del Far.

That night, at last, they were welcomed into a comfortable home, and their host Sir Aicio was so entranced by the virtue, good looks and good standing of Boniface,

▲ *In 1840 French romantic painter Eugène Delacroix painted this celebrated canvas of the crusaders' capture of Constantinople on the Fourth Crusade. The attack on the city was the culmination of centuries of ill-feeling between crusaders and Byzantines.*

that, according to the poem, he wanted to give his beautiful daughter, Aigleta, to the knight as a bride. However, Boniface did not wish to enter into this arrangement, although he did subsequently arrange a marriage for both Jacopina and Aigleta, and he ensured that Jacopina's inheritance was restored to her.

Raimbaut declared that with Boniface he had worked through many dramas of courtly love. His lord had arranged at least 100 marriages for ladies who would have otherwise pined away, tying them to the most noble barons, marquises and counts; and, Raimbaut claimed, he had never given in to the temptation to lie with a single one of those needy ladies.

PROWESS IN BATTLE

These adventures were recalled in the later part of the *Epic Letter*. The earlier sections praised Boniface's exceptional prowess as a warrior and recalled the many exploits patron and poet had shared in the field – charging and unseating foes, jousting both on bridges and in river-fords, attacking castles and clambering over sheer walls, and braving many a danger.

In 1191–93 Boniface and Raimbaut fought in Italy, on the side of the Cremona League against the League of Milan. Then in 1194 they joined in Holy Roman Emperor Henry VI's campaign to Sicily, where at the Battle of Messina, Raimbaut came to the rescue of Boniface, according to his writings, defending his lord with his shield against a storm of javelins, swords, daggers, knives and crossbow bolts. For this timely act of bravery, Boniface rewarded his loyal friend and court poet with a knighthood.

In the *Epic Letter* Raimbaut celebrated an incident in Italy in which Boniface, with only ten companions at his side, was pursued by 400 knights but did not take flight; instead he turned on his pursuers and struck them so hard that they were overcome with fear. The poem also praised Boniface's part in the Fourth Crusade, although this was not in truth a heroic endeavour – and diverted to the sacking of Constantinople, capital of the Byzantine Empire. Raimbaut summoned a vision of this event as a great chivalric encounter, the emperor of Constantinople fleeing from the crusader army, like a thief, with 'his heart down in his heels' and the Christian army as swift as hawks chasing herons, as fierce as wolves chasing sheep.

▼ *In 1201 Boniface was elected to lead the Fourth Crusade following the death of Count Theobald of Champagne, the original leader, from a mysterious malady.*

SCOTLAND'S GREATEST KNIGHT

SIR WILLIAM WALLACE

Sir William Wallace is celebrated as probably the greatest chivalric figure in Scottish history, heroic leader of resistance to the English invasion of Scotland, victor against all odds at the Battle of Stirling Bridge in 1297. His feats of chivalry inspired an oral tradition of tales about him that were collected together in the ballad *The Acts and Deeds of Sir William Wallace, Knight of Elderslie*, written in c.1470 by a poet called Henry the Minstrel or Blind Harry, and other works in the 16th century including the *History of William Wallace*.

Traditionally Wallace was said to have humble origins that were contrasted with the noble family of his contemporary

▼ *A bronze statue of William Wallace stands in a niche to the right of the gatehouse at Edinburgh Castle. It is matched by a statue of another great Scottish warrior, Robert the Bruce.*

Robert the Bruce. Modern research, however, suggests that Wallace's father was a minor noble, Ayrshire knight Sir David Wallace, a landholder as vassal to James Stewart, 5th High Steward of Scotland. The name 'knight of Elderslie' referred to Elderslie, near Paisley in Renfrewshire, which was once thought to be his place of birth, in c.1270.

GUERRILLA FIGHTER

Wallace first emerged as a guerrilla fighter combating the rule of King Edward I of England, who in 1296 sacked Berwick-upon-Tweed, defeated a Scottish army at the Battle of Dunbar, forced the Scottish king John Balliol to abdicate and, in an act of extreme provocation, removed the Scottish coronation stone, the Stone of Scone, to London.

In May 1297 Wallace led a company of 30 men in an attack on Lanark in which its English sheriff, William Heselrig, was killed. Wallace went on to attack and defeat a series of English garrisons that lay between the rivers Forth and Tay. Blind Harry's ballad invented a background story to add colour to these events. According to his version, Wallace's father and brother were killed after a fight with some English soldiers, and the attack on the sheriff of Lanark was an act of revenge for the Englishman's mistreatment of Wallace's young wife Marion.

Blind Harry also introduced a scene in which Edward I put 360 Scots barons to death at Ayr by sending them on horseback through a doorway, where a noose wrenched them from the saddle and hanged them. In Harry's account, these murders later provoked Wallace to kill the entire garrison by locking the gates and setting the city on fire. He then, according to Blind Harry, led his men to Selkirk Forest to hide, and subsequently – after a tip-off about English movements – they took refuge in the Highlands.

▲ *Sir William Wallace's story, as celebrated by the minstrel Blind Harry, was based more on legend than fact. Blind Harry's ballad was the basis for the 1995 historical movie Braveheart.*

THE BATTLE OF STIRLING BRIDGE

William Wallace's finest hour was on 11 September 1297 when, despite being vastly outnumbered, a Scottish army under his command defeated English forces under John de Warenne, Earl of Surrey, in the Battle of Stirling Bridge. The Scottish force took up position on flat ground to the north of a very narrow bridge across the river Forth and were able to pick off the vanguard of the English army after it had crossed the river, while the rest of the English army was stuck on the south side of the water – the bridge was so narrow that only two knights could cross at a time.

The weight of men made the bridge collapse, meaning that many Englishmen – hampered by weapons and armour – drowned in the river. According to Blind

Harry's version, the bridge was deliberately destroyed, brought down by a Scottish freedom fighter hiding beneath it. More than a hundred English knights were killed, including King Edward's treasurer in Scotland, Sir Hugh de Cressingham. The traditional accounts told that his skin was tanned and used to make belts and sporrans by the Scots, amid wild celebrations – including a new sword belt for William Wallace. After the battle Wallace was knighted, probably by Robert the Bruce himself, and was declared guardian of Scotland and leader of its armies.

THE BATTLE OF FALKIRK

In the aftermath of the battle Wallace raided Northumberland and Cumberland – Scotland was almost entirely clear of English forces at this point. Yet in the following summer Edward I invaded and defeated Wallace at the Battle of Falkirk on 22 July 1298, when the English king's cavalry and archers were far too much for Wallace's spearmen. One account of the battle reports that after the defeat, in flight from the battlefield, Wallace gained some consolation by overcoming and killing the

▼ *This 67m (220ft) sandstone Victorian Gothic monument near Stirling celebrates the career of Sir William Wallace and in particular his victory at Stirling Bridge.*

English knight Sir Brian de Jay, who was master of the English Templars. However, Wallace's reputation was ruined by the defeat and shortly afterwards he resigned as guardian of Scotland.

ESCAPE TO FRANCE?

Wallace disappeared from public view until his capture near Glasgow by the English on 5 August 1305. He may have carried on the battle against the English as a guerrilla fighter. According to tradition, however, he escaped to France – reputedly

▲ *A highly idealized and sentimental Victorian view of the trial of William Wallace at Westminster.*

he hid in the hold of a ship belonging to the pirate Richard Longoville, who was known as the 'Red Reiver' because of the red sails on his ships. Once at sea, Wallace was said to have burst from the hold, overpowered Longoville and forced him to carry Wallace and his men to France. He was also said to have travelled to Rome to ask the pope for aid against the English.

A TERRIBLE DEATH

After his capture Wallace was taken to London, where he was tried for treason – reputedly wearing a garland of oak leaves to signify that he was 'king of the outlaws'. He denied that he could have committed treason since he did not accept Edward I as his king, and was loyal only to King John Balliol of Scotland. After the trial, which inevitably found him guilty, Wallace was stripped naked and dragged by his heels through London to Smithfield, where he was hanged, drawn and quartered. His severed head was displayed on London Bridge and the four parts of his body put up in Aberdeen, Berwick, Newcastle and Stirling.

DEFENDER OF FRENCH CHIVALRY

MARSHAL DE BOUCICAUT

Jean le Meingre, known as Boucicaut, was a leading French knight of the 14th and 15th centuries, a major figure of the Hundred Years War, who also fought on crusades against the pagan Lithuanians in Prussia and against the Moors in Spain. He was famed for his skill in the saddle and defeated many of the greatest English knights of the day in the lists during the celebrated Jousts of St Inglevert in 1390. He also founded a chivalric order devoted to maintaining and defending the ideals of courtly love.

Boucicaut's feats were celebrated in a biography *Le livre des faits du Jean le Meingre, dit Boucicaut* (*An account of the deeds of Jean le Meingre, also known as Boucicaut*). The romanticized account combined real events with conventional stages in the life of a hero. It was written in 1408, while its subject was still alive, indicating the status he had achieved as an exemplar of chivalry.

▲ *Marshal de Boucicaut's final acts of chivalry were performed on the battlefield at Agincourt on 25 October 1415. He spent his last years as an English prisoner.*

LIFE AS A SQUIRE AND FIRST MILITARY ENCOUNTERS

Boucicaut began his chivalric education as a page at the court of King Charles VI of France. He had his first taste of military action at the age of just 12, when he rode out on campaign in the company of Louis II, Duke of Bourbon, in Normandy. He was knighted by the duke at the age of 16 in November 1382 and the next day fought in the Battle of Roosebeke in the County of Flanders (now in Belgium). He distinguished himself as the Duke of Bourbon's army defeated a Flemish force led by Philip van Artevelde.

Boucicaut's romanticized biography states that he was well in advance of other young people in his skill at the chivalric

pastimes, and that he grew up at a distance from others, with a natural reserve and haughtiness that his biographer deemed appropriate for a knight.

Two years later, in 1384, Boucicaut served alongside the knights of the Teutonic Order on their crusade against the pagan Lithuanians. Reputedly he was hungry to find opportunities to prove himself as a knight, and frustrated by a lack of warfare in France. Subsequently, he fought against the Moors in Spain, and afterwards travelled widely, as far as the Holy Land.

THE JOUSTS AT ST INGLEVERT

In 1390 Boucicaut and two other knights, Reginald de Roye and the Lord de Sempy, issued a challenge to fight all comers in a tournament at St Inglevert, near Boulogne, northern France. A year's truce was in place in the long war between England and France, and the challenge had the backing of King Charles VI of France, who made a grant of 6,000 francs to the defenders.

The French knights pledged that they would hold the lists for 30 days from 20 May. The challengers had to indicate on the day before they intended to fight whether they were to compete *à outrance* ('to the uttermost', with a sharpened lance) or *à plaisance* (in a joust of peace, 'for the pleasure', with a blunted lance). They were to do this by touching either a shield of war or a shield of peace put up by the defenders on a spruce tree beside the lists and giving their name, country and the name of their family to the nearby herald. Letters publicizing the challenge were sent far and wide, and as many as 100 knights and squires came from England, with around 40 from other countries.

There were 39 jousts in all, held on the 21–24 May, most fought *à outrance* but none resulting in death or serious injuries. The chronicle report of the event said that the jousting was of a very high standard, with several knights being knocked from their horses, many more losing helmets,

▼ *Boucicaut was a loyal servant of his country and the French king Charles VI, seen here at court receiving English envoys.*

and a large number of lances broken. King Charles VI reportedly attended the event incognito. There was no more jousting after 24 May although the three French knights 'held the lists' as promised in their challenge until 20 June. They were afterwards received as heroes in France.

MARSHAL OF FRANCE

On Christmas Day 1391, principally because of his great service as a crusader against heathens in Prussia and Livonia, Boucicaut was made Marshal of France by King Charles VI in a ceremony at the Cathedral of St Martin in Tours. In 1396 Boucicaut then took part in the Crusade of Nicopolis, as part of an army from France, the Holy Roman Empire, Hungary, Poland, England and other countries against the Ottoman Empire. This campaign ended in a major defeat at the Battle of Nicopolis in which the French general Jean de Vienne was killed and several knights, including Boucicaut, were taken prisoner. He was later ransomed.

THE ENTERPRISE OF THE GREEN SHIELD OF THE WHITE LADY

Back in Europe, in 1399 Boucicaut founded the chivalric order of the *Emprise de l'Escu Vert à la Dame Blanche*

▲ *Boucicaut was one of the three illustrious French knights who jousted against all challengers at St Inglevert in May 1390.*

('Enterprise of the Green Shield of the White Lady'). It had 12 knights as members, sworn for a period of five years to protect women who suffered oppression, particularly widows. Like the other main chivalric orders, the Green Shield of the White Lady had strong associations with tourneying – the order's members pledged to provide opponents in the lists for those who were required by a vow to a lady to perform a specific deed in a tournament but who could not find any competitors.

In 1401 King Charles VI appointed Boucicaut as the governor of Genoa, which had come under French control in 1396. Boucicaut had some success in conflicts against Venice and Cyprus, but the appointment proved short-lived, for the Genoese rid themselves of French control in 1409, while Boucicaut himself was absent on other business.

DEFEAT AT AGINCOURT

Boucicaut fought in the Battle of Agincourt in 1415, where he commanded the French vanguard. Following the English victory he was taken prisoner, and he died in Yorkshire in 1421 after spending his final years in captivity. His body was returned to France and buried in Tours.

THE EAGLE OF BRITTANY

BERTRAND DU GUESCLIN

Breton knight Bertrand du Guesclin, one of the great war captains of his age and a principal commander on the French side in the Hundred Years War, was another warrior celebrated in near-contemporary chivalric biographies. Known as a skilled general, who used guerrilla tactics to great effect against the English army, du Guesclin was famed above all for his impressive feats of arms. He was hailed as 'the Eagle of Brittany'.

Du Guesclin achieved legendary status in his lifetime, and was celebrated shortly after his death in 1380 in the *Chronique de Bertrand du Guesclin (Chronicle of Bertrand du Guesclin)*, a poem written by Cuvelier. He rose from relatively humble origins among the minor nobility of Brittany to become the Constable of France between

▼ *Du Guesclin's chivalric qualities earned him his elevation to the rarefied position of Constable of France by Charles V in 1370.*

1370 and 1380, and the biographical poem emphasized the point that through deeds of arms it was feasible for squires to attain greatness from humble beginnings.

POOR PROSPECTS

Cuvelier's account emphasized that early in life the future knight's prospects looked poor. His parents were put off by his unattractive, swarthy looks and his aggressive manner, and although he was their eldest son (of ten children) they treated him like a mere servant. However, a passing nun predicted great things for the young man and caused the parents to think again. Then he ran away from home and lived for a while as a leader of warring gangs of village boys.

THE UNKNOWN KNIGHT

We know little of du Guesclin's early career. Cuvelier made up a story that he distinguished himself, aged 17, as an

▲ *Bertrand du Guesclin rose to high office, but was renowned for his simple warrior qualities – generosity and great energy.*

unknown knight at a tournament in 1337 at Rennes. The story recounted how du Guesclin arrived on a carthorse at the tournament, at which his father was competing. With such inadequate equipment, the young man was laughed out of the lists, but he managed to borrow armour and a horse from one of his cousins. He entered the tournament lists with the visor of his helmet closed, so that no one could recognize him, and defeated 12 knights, knocking every one of them from their horses. When his own father challenged him (not knowing who he was) du Guesclin refused to fight. He then jousted on until a Norman knight rode up to him and raised his visor with the tip of his lance: all were astounded at the disclosure, and his father was delighted to see the young man's true identity.

In the 1340s du Guesclin appears to have fought as a 'robber knight' from a base in Paimpont forest, near Rennes, harassing English forces. One story recounted how he took the castle of Grand Fougeray with a clever ruse: he disguised some of his companions as woodcutters, and sent them to the castle gates carrying stacks of wood. The English garrison let them in, then the 'woodcutters' flung down their wood and so blocked the gates open, allowing support troops to enter and take the castle.

KNIGHTING AND EARLY SUCCESSES

In fact du Guesclin was not a squire who leaped to glory – he was already 34 years old when he was knighted on the battlefield while serving under Marshal Arnoul d'Audrehem. He received the honour after distinguishing himself in a minor engagement in 1354 while repelling a raid by the English knight Sir Hugh Calveley. In 1356–57 he defended Rennes during a siege set by Henry of Grosmont, 1st Duke of Lancaster (one of the founder members of the Order of the Garter). Although du Guesclin was eventually forced to pay 100,000 crowns to the English army, the

▼ It was a dark day for France when the 'Eagle of Brittany' succumbed to dysentery on campaign in the Languedoc. The castle that he captured in his last military action is visible in the background.

▲ Du Guesclin (left) lowers his lance to avoid fighting his father in the celebrated – and apocryphal – story of how he entered the lists as an unknown knight and defeated no fewer than 12 established knights.

staunch resistance went a long way to restoring French spirits after the utter humiliation of the Battle of Poitiers.

In 1364 du Guesclin won a resounding victory over the army of King Charles II of Navarre at the Battle of Cocherel. The conflict was part of a disputed claim over the Duchy of Burgundy, and du Guesclin's triumph forced Charles II to abandon his claim to the duchy and make peace with King Charles V of France.

TWO DEFEATS, TWO RANSOMS

However, later that same year du Guesclin suffered a major defeat at the Battle of Auray, which was part of the Breton War of Succession between John de Montfort (supported by the English) and Charles de Blois (supported by the French). Du Guesclin was captured and subsequently ransomed for 40,000 gold francs by the king. Then in 1367 he was fighting in Spain in support of Henry of Trastamara against King Pedro of Castile when he was defeated by Edward the Black Prince in the Battle of Najera (Navarette) and again

captured. On this occasion du Guesclin was allowed to name his own ransom – and set a seemingly unpayable amount, reputedly 100,000 francs. Such was his reputation, and his value to the French cause, that the money was raised by the king and du Guesclin was returned to France.

COMMANDER OF FRANCE

The Hundred Years War against England was renewed in 1369 and du Guesclin retook Poitou and Saintonge from English control. He achieved his country's highest military honour when he was made Constable of France in 1370. He went on to regain large areas of France from the English during the 1370s, using the tactic of avoiding pitched battles until the French were in a sufficiently advantageous position to win.

Bertrand du Guesclin died in 1380 due to dysentery while on campaign in the Languedoc. His life ended, appropriately enough, in a military success – he had just taken the castle of Châteauneuf de Randon from its English garrison. Accounts of his death tell how the captain of the garrison brought the keys and laid them on du Guesclin's body. Such was his stature that he was buried in the tomb of the French kings in the Saint-Denis Basilica, Paris.

HERO IN THE LISTS

JACQUES DE LALAING

The 15th-century knight Jacques de Lalaing was one of the greatest tourneyers of his day. He achieved such renown during his life that he became the subject of two contemporary biographies: the *Chronique de Jacques de Lalaing* (*Chronicle of Jacques de Lalaing*) and the *Livre des faits de Jacques de Lalaing* (*Book Recording the Deeds of Jacques de Lalaing*).

Jacques was born to a noble family from Wallonia (Belgium), and received his chivalric education as an associate of the Duke of Cleves at the court of Burgundy. He won notice in his teens and early 20s in the tiltyard. In 1443, according to the biographies, he excelled during a daring raid carried out by the Duke of Burgundy on the city of Luxembourg. The raiding party used ladders to scale the city walls at night and were at large in the streets before dawn. The city's residents burst from their houses fully armed and heavily armoured but Jacques accomplished many astonishing feats of chivalry with sword and lance, which added to his reputation.

FAME AT NANCY

In 1445, the biographies continue, Jacques amazed onlookers with his performance in a tournament at Nancy held in the presence of the kings of France, Aragon and Sicily. He won four jousts on the first day, even beating an experienced knight from the Auvergne whom he hit so hard on the helmet with his lance that sparks flew and the knight was knocked unconscious.

Jacques was treated as a hero that night and received many gifts from admirers. On the next day he defeated no fewer than eight more knights, but through all this he showed humility and noble bearing.

It was the normal practice in these chivalrous biographies for chroniclers to praise the achievement of their subjects very highly, and exaggerate them, sometimes combining actual events from the life history with exemplary events from a

typical knight's life. However, in the case of Jacques de Lalaing, although many of the events described were extraordinary we know that they were true. The principal author of the *Livre des faits de Jacques de Lalaing* was Jean le Fèvre de St Remy, who served as herald to the Order of the Golden Fleece. His balanced account of Jacques's life does not gloss over the times when the knight almost met his match.

'FEATS OF ARMS'

In the same year, 1445, Jacques embarked upon his 'feats of arms' – prearranged encounters with other knights fought in full armour with weapons of war but according to agreed rules – either a fixed

▲ *In the tournament at Nancy, Jacques struck one opponent from his saddle so hard that he landed a full 7m (24ft) away.*

number of courses on horseback and on foot, or until one of the combatants was knocked to the ground. The first meeting was in Antwerp with Jean de Boniface, an Italian knight who was on a tour seeking opportunities to prove his chivalric worth. The agreed terms were for jousting until one of the knights broke six lances, then fighting on foot using first spears, then poleaxes, swords or daggers. The fight would end when one knight surrendered, or touched the ground with his hand, knee or any part of his body.

Before the contest commenced, Jacques was knighted by the Duke of Burgundy. As was appropriate Jacques then proved himself worthy of the honour: he disarmed de Boniface by knocking the poleaxe out of his hands, then forced him backwards with his own weapon. The Duke of Burgundy, who was refereeing, brought the contest to an end.

IN CASTILE AND SCOTLAND

In 1446–47 Jacques went on tour seeking glory, in the course of which he defeated a champion in Castile. In 1449 with his uncle Simon de Lalaing and a Breton squire named Herve de Meriadec, Jacques fought in a 'combat of six' against three Scottish knights at Stirling, before the king of Scotland. In fierce combat Jacques and his compatriots acquitted themselves well.

Later that year in Bruges he defeated an English squire, Thomas Que, when he came as close to defeat as he ever would after his hand was badly cut by the spike of the English squire's poleaxe. Yet, in great pain and with blood flowing, Jacques fought on and threw Que to the ground.

▼ *In a long career in the lists Jacques saw off many challengers, but neither he or nor any knight could withstand siege cannon, one of which ended his life at Poucques.*

▲ *In many of Jacques's 'feats of arms', jousting was followed by fighting on foot.*

'PASSAGE OF THE FOUNTAIN OF WEEPING'

Jacques then announced a challenge to all-comers to defeat him in a passage of arms. He was to erect a pavilion on the first day of every month from 1 November 1449 to 30 September 1450 and accept challenges to fight, either on horseback with lances, or on foot, either with poleaxes or with swords. The pavilion was hung with three shields, representing the three types of combat: challengers approached the pavilion and touched the appropriate shield. It was next to a fountain with a statue of a weeping woman and Jacques's challenge was called the 'Passage of the Fountain of Weeping'. He remained undefeated throughout the entire year, fighting 11 knights and squires. He entered some of the conflicts without armour on his right leg, and in one he fought without an armoured gauntlet on his right hand.

Afterwards Jacques made a pilgrimage to Rome. When he returned to the court of Burgundy he received a hero's welcome. In 1451 he was admitted to the chivalric brotherhood of the Order of the Golden Fleece, founded by Philip the Good, Duke of Burgundy, in 1430.

Jacques was killed by cannon fire while fighting for the duke of Burgundy at the siege of Poucques on 3 July 1453 during a campaign against Ghent. Jacques was just 32 years old at the time of his death, which was given added poignancy by the sense that – as with 'the English Achilles', Sir John Talbot, killed by gunfire at Castillion just two weeks later on 17 July 1453 – modern weaponry had dispatched a great knight, one who understood the traditional ways of chivalry and fought according to them.

THE 'ENGLISH ACHILLES'

SIR JOHN TALBOT

John Talbot, 1st Earl of Shrewsbury, was probably the most daring English commander of the Hundred Years War, so feared by the French for the ferocity of his lightning campaigns in 1427–53 that he was called the 'English Achilles' in reference to the Greek warrior who vanquished Hector before the walls of Troy. Talbot was a prolific knight who won no fewer than 40 battles and minor encounters in France, where his speciality was in surprising the enemy and conducting very aggressive attacks. In a manner typical of the age in which he lived, he combined ruthlessness on the battlefield, and a liking for making trouble off it, with a deep respect for the chivalric tradition and a staunch Christian faith.

NO LOVER OF PEACE

Sir John was a soldier from his youth, and according to some accounts fought aged around 16 in the royal army at the Battle

▼ *King Henry VI of England, proclaimed as King of France following the death of the French king, Charles VI, invests Sir John Talbot as Constable of France in 1436.*

SIR JOHN TALBOT

Born: 1384

Died: 17 July 1453

Knighted: unknown; made a Knight of the Order of the Garter *c.*1424

Famous for: the ferocity and speed of attacks on French campaigns

Greatest achievement: routing the French forces at Ry, 1436 – despite commanding a far inferior force

---

of Shrewsbury in 1403 between King Henry IV of England and a rebel force under 'Hotspur' – Sir Henry Percy. Certainly by the following year he was serving the king in the wars against Welsh rebels, and he fought in Wales for five years until 1409.

In 1414–19 Talbot was Lieutenant of Ireland, and by this stage had already gained a reputation for ferocious raiding tactics, which he used against Gaelic chieftains. One local chronicler noted of him that 'from the time of King Herod there has never been a more wicked soldier here'. In Ireland and back in England he

was a troublemaker, quarrelling fiercely with rival lords, and at one stage being thrown into the Tower of London.

KNIGHT OF THE GARTER

Talbot served Henry V briefly in France then after the king's death in 1422 was made a Knight of the Garter in 1424 by Henry VI. In 1427 he began a long period of military service in France, during which he truly made his name.

But his start was not propitious: in 1428–29 he took part in the siege of Orléans, and was unable to prevent its relief by Joan of Arc, then in June 1429 he was captured at Patay and held in prison for four years. He was released only after the French knight keeping him captive was himself captured by the English.

FAMOUS VICTORIES IN FRANCE

Thereafter Talbot went from strength to strength. In 1434–35 he defended Paris against the French army, then in autumn 1435 he withdrew to Rouen to defend Normandy. Probably his most famous hour came in January 1436 when, with only a small force at his disposal and with Rouen under threat, he launched a surprise attack that completely wrong-footed a much larger French army at Ry. In 1436 he was appointed Constable of France. Another of his celebrated feats was the retaking of Pontoise in February 1437 when his army attacked across the winter ice at dawn on Ash Wednesday, and totally surprised a garrison that was still in recovery after the celebrations of Shrove Tuesday (Mardi Gras).

In 1439 Talbot won another victory with a small force against a 6,000-strong army under Constable Richemont. His swift manoeuvres were often an attempt to bring the enemy to battle. In 1441, for example, he chased a French army back and forth four times across the rivers Oise and Seine trying to force a pitched battle.

LAST OF THE GREAT KNIGHTS?

The way in which he met his end on 17 July 1453 enhanced his reputation. He was leading an attempt to relieve the town of Castillon, which was under French siege, and in characteristic fashion attempted to catch the French off guard with a swift attack. However, the French army was entrenched in a strong defensive position and had substantial artillery at its disposal. The English attack came to nothing and Talbot was shot when he attempted to rally his men. He was celebrated thereafter as one of a dying breed of great knights, and his death seemed to symbolize the collision between an old way of making war and the sheer destructive force of artillery guns.

For all that he was a troublesome man and could be utterly ruthless, Talbot had many notable chivalric qualities. Throughout his long career he was extremely loyal to the royal house of Lancaster, and as a military general he was admired for his spirited raiding and his bravery in battle. He had a genuine inter-

▲ *Talbot died at Castillon in 1453. The attack he launched there, in the face of the French artillery, was rash – and resulted in his death. Following this defeat England lost nearly all its French possessions.*

▼ The adventures imagined for questing knights could be quite exotic. In an image from a 'book of romances' given to Sir John by Margaret of Anjou c.1445, knights encounter some rather puny elephants.

est in the traditions of chivalry, and he compiled a collection of poems and handbooks that he gave to Margaret of Anjou when she married King Henry VI of England in 1445. He was a Knight of the Garter from 1424 to 1445, and quarrelled with fellow knight Sir John Falstoff whom

he accused of having disgraced the order when he fled from the field of battle at Patay. Talbot established a collection of ornaments with Garter decorations for use on St George's Day at the Church of the Sepulchre in Rouen. He went on pilgrimage to Rome in 1450.

Initially Talbot was buried at Castillon, where the French expressed their admiration for his chivalric life by building a chapel in his honour. (It was destroyed during the French Revolution, but a memorial continues to mark the place where he died.) On his death a French chronicler hailed him as one who had been a thorn in the side of the French for many years. Sir John had an enduring reputation for chivalry in England and is a significant character in Shakespeare's play *King Henry VI Part 2* (c.1590–91).

CHAPTER TWENTY-ONE

KNIGHTLY LOVERS AT COURT

The French churchman and courtier Andreas Capellanus (meaning 'chaplain') attempted to codify the rules of engagement between knights and their ladies at court in *De Amore* (*About Love* or *The Art of Courtly Love*), written in *c*.1190. It was traditionally believed that the book described 'courtly love' as practised at the court of Eleanor of Aquitaine at Poitiers in *c*.1170, and was written for her daughter Marie de Champagne, but modern historians have cast doubt on this. Andreas argued that true love could not exist between a husband and a wife since it must be secret, difficult if not impossible to act on, and unconsummated. In this form it ennobled both the lover and the beloved and inspired the lover to great deeds of chivalry. The social system and romantic conventions in *De Amore* had been developed throughout the 12th century by the troubadours of Provence. One pioneer was Eleanor's grandfather William IX of Aquitaine, said to be a fine knight, a composer of songs, a deceiver of women and one of the world's most courtly men. The rarefied society of the knights and ladies who accepted the conventions of courtly love was at odds with the simple military ethos of the knights of Charlemagne as celebrated in *chansons de geste*. While Charlemagne's noble paladins expressed themselves primarily through physical deeds, religious ardour and plain emotions, the primary concerns for those committed to courtly love were affairs of the heart and distinctions of status.

▲ *Knights in romantic tales would fight in single combat for the right to woo a lady.*

◄ *Sir Lancelot steals his first kiss with Queen Guinevere. Their affair was typical of courtly love, pursued in secret and in defiance of marriage vows, but unlike many romantic attachments it was consummated, with tragic results.*

GAMES OF LOVE
HOW KNIGHTS PROVED THEIR DEVOTION

The interactions between ladies and their knights, in gardens or at tournaments, or even when knights departed on quests to prove their love, often resembled games. They were played for a high stake – the lady's love.

The 13th-century French poet and author of romances Jean Renart produced a striking vignette of highly refined courtly love in his narrative poem *Le Lai de l'Ombre* (*The Lay of the Shadow*) in *c.*1220. The poem concerns an educated knight, skilful in chivalric pastimes such as chess and hawking, who courted a married lady.

▼ *Jean de Saintré kneels before the lady, the Dame de Belles-Cousines, who is giving him an education in courtly love. Jean is a fictional knight, hero of a book (c.1450) by the Provençal author Antoine de la Sale.*

In the manner of courtly love, he had been captivated by her beauty from afar, and having been struck by love, he could apply himself to nothing, and dreamt longingly of his lady.

The poem presented the encounter between the two lovers almost like a chess match, with each attempting to outwit the other within the rules of the game of love, exhibiting detachment from their feelings. The knight approached his lady in a garden by a well, determined to win her over, and she welcomed him. Her first counter-argument to his statement of love was two-pronged: since he was courteous it was impossible that he should be without a true love already, and because he was so skilful in love he was no doubt an old hand at deluding ladies with stories of false devotion. He replied by saying that

her welcome showed that she was pleased to see him, but she responded that her friendliness was only social politeness.

She criticized him for being like many knights in misinterpreting social politeness as the sign of passion. He should not have aimed so high as to attempt to win her, she said. In reply he likened himself to Sir Tristan, describing how that knight had set sail without a mast, trusting in good fortune to bring him to Iseult. She replied and pointed out that she had a husband already who was a paragon of gallantry and chivalry.

The knight said that he was plunged in suffering and implied that it was her Christian duty to relieve it, likening her relieving his pangs of love to going on a crusade. He said he was ready to die for love of her. This gambit seemed to plunge her into deep thought.

Then he slipped a ring from her finger and put his own ring in its place, before quickly departing. Noticing too late what he had done, she recalled him. She said to him that if he loved her he would take it back because all lovers were bound by convention to do their lady's bidding. At this point it seemed that she had caught him. Then he looked down to where her face was reflected in the waters of the well and said he would give the ring to the one person he loved best after his lady; he then cast it on to her reflection saying that since she would not accept his gift or his love he would give it to her shadow. She was charmed by the courtesy of this gesture and accepted his offer of love.

COURTS OF LOVE

The intricate arguments in *Le Lai de l'Ombre* suggested that a third party might sometimes have been needed to judge the victor in the games of courtly love. Indeed, Andreas Capellanus's *De Amore* contained a number of judgements passed by great ladies on lovers at 'courts of love'. These

▲ *Skilful chess playing was one of the prescribed qualities of an educated knight who would make a suitable courtly suitor.*

courts were, in theory, like courts of law, but with ladies as their judges making their decisions according to the rules of courtly love.

The ladies mentioned by Andreas as judges included Eleanor of Aquitaine, Marie de Champagne and Ermengarde, Viscountess of Narbonne. In the 19th century, when the term 'courtly love' was first used, historians suggested that these courts of love actually sat and handed down judgements, but modern historians have been unable to find evidence that the courts existed beyond the references to them in poems. The latest thinking is that the courts mentioned in the poems were a poetic image for the meetings held by ladies, knights and poets at which they enjoyed poetry and debated the niceties of courtly love.

WILLIAM IX OF AQUITAINE

Troubadour poet William of Aquitaine was a man of extremely colourful character and behaviour who was twice excommunicated, yet he was also one of the leaders of the crusade of 1101. Duke of Aquitaine and Gascony, and Count of Poitou, William was the first known troubadour poet, writing poems concerned with love in the vernacular Provençal language. Eleven of his poems survive under the name Count of Poitou. He was outspoken, and happy to court controversy. One of his poems described a convent in which the nuns should be selected for their beauty – or their ability as whores.

The first time he was excommunicated, for failure to pay Church taxes, he confronted the bishop of Poitiers at sword point, but did not persuade him to withdraw the anathema. The second time he was excommunicated was for kidnapping the Viscountess Dangereuse, the wife of his vassal Aimery I of Rochefoucauld (although she appeared to have been willingly taken). William installed her in his castle despite the fact that he was himself married. His wife retired to a monastery at Fontevrault, and the viscountess lived openly with William – he even carried her image on his shield.

As a knight he was less than exemplary: he was reckless in battle and lost many encounters while on the 1101 crusade. He subsequently fought in Spain, again without much success. His enduring fame rests more on his poetry and on the influence he had over his granddaughter, Eleanor of Aquitaine, who became one of the great courtly patrons.

▼ *In the 13th-century French poem of courtly love, the* Roman de la Rose *(Romance of the Rose), the garden is the arena for romance. The poem was composed in two halves: the first, by Guillaume de Lorris in c.1230; and the second, by Jean de Meung, in c.1280.*

IN A LADY'S SERVICE

A KNIGHT'S DUTIES IN LOVE

Knights believed that the love they felt for a lady was a spur to acts of great chivalry. As love of Christ and faith in God had driven knights of the First Crusade to overcome seemingly impossible odds and regain possession of Jerusalem, so more secular-minded chivalric successors from the mid-12th century onwards drew inspiration from the lady they admired at court.

A SPUR TO ACTS OF DARING

In c.1130 in his *History of the Kings of Britain*, Geoffrey of Monmouth noted during a description of a bohort or peaceful tournament held at the court of King Arthur, that 'the ladies refused to grant their love to any warlike man who had not proven his bravery three times in battle'. He added that, as a result, in order to win the love of fair ladies the knights of the Round Table were 'ever more daring'.

LADY BECOMES LORD

French troubadour Bernart de Ventadorn (c.1130–90) compared the ties between a lover and his lady to those of the feudal relationship between a knight and his suzerain (feudal superior). This became a common image in the poems of courtly love. As the knight conventionally went through a long training, first as page, then as squire and finally as knight, so a lover would have to emerge from the ranks of hopeful admirers to be accepted as a devoted suitor and, in cases of high achievement, might finally become the lady's lover.

The knight offered service to the lady, as in a feudal relationship, and she offered protection to the knight, just as a feudal lord would. From this idea developed the custom of knights wearing a lady's 'favour' – usually a scarf or cloth – in tournaments or during a campaign. From the lady's love, or at least her interest, the knight drew strength.

To win the love of his lady the knight had to impress her. All his chivalric traits – bravery, courtesy, generosity, prowess and loyalty – were used to this end in order to generate his worth in her eyes.

A DISTANT TARGET

Within the conventions of courtly love some knights declared their love for and devotion to ladies they had not even met. Just hearing tales of a lady's beauty and the perfection of her bearing and manners was enough in some cases to convince a knight to dedicate himself to her service. Even if she were close at hand, the lady was often elevated far above the knight who devoted himself to her. She could prove a very hard mistress to please – in many cases the greatest deeds of devotion were not enough to win her favour.

OBEDIENCE EVEN UNTO SHAME

The knight had also to be obedient to his lady. In chivalric literature knights were sometimes ordered by their lady to do

◄ *For honour, and to win the admiration of his lady, a knight throws himself lustily into the jousting at a country* pas d'armes.

what must almost have been unthinkable – to fight deliberately badly at tournaments and bring shame on themselves. In the Old French romance *Perlesvaus* (*c*.1210) Sir Gawain was told by his lady to identify himself among the other identically armoured knights in the lists by losing repeatedly. He was obedient. When a knight approached to fight, Gawain fled on horseback and spent the rest of the tournament hiding behind King Arthur. (In a colourful image the romance said that Gawain was clinging as closely to Arthur as a magpie clings to a bush when it is trying to escape falcons that are intent on seizing it.)

Gawain lost a great deal of honour in the escapade, for Arthur was greatly ashamed of his knight and the other knights commented openly that Gawain did not serve his great reputation. But he was sustained by the knowledge that he had done it out of motives of the purest chivalry – to prove that his love for his lady was stronger even than his concern for his standing at court.

JOURNEYS OF DEVOTION

It was a duty for newly made knights to seek opportunities to prove themselves worthy of their new condition. This was

▼ *As part of his adventures in* Chrétien de Troyes's Knight of the Cart, *Sir Lancelot beheads Sir Meleagant, who had abducted Guinevere, and presents the head to her.*

▲ *A devoted knight returns at the end of a quest in this romantic painting from 1921 by Sir Frank Bernard Dicksee.*

one reason why knights were often made at the start of a campaign or just prior to a battle, because the knighting was a spur to acts of chivalry. In the same way, within the conventions of courtly love, a knight who had just won a lady's attention or love was expected to find ways of proving himself worthy of her. This often involved embarking on a career of knight errantry, travelling away from the lady and seeking adventures to win her love.

THE CHURCH AND COURTLY LOVE

The Catholic Church condemned the conventions and culture of courtly love. The official Church position was that marriage was a sacrament of the Christian Church and that within it sex was acceptable only as a means of procreation – ideally, Christians of the period were expected to be celibate. The poets of courtly love, on the other hand, praised romantic love, often between knights and married ladies, emphasized the power of sexual attraction and implied that acts of adultery were understandable when passions ran so high. One response of the Church in the 12th century was to begin to promote the cult of the Virgin Mary, Mother of Christ, as a focus for some of the passionate devotion that was otherwise directed along secular channels in love affairs and courtly love attachments.

KNIGHTS ERRANT
TOURS OF CHIVALRY

A familiar figure in the medieval romances, a knight errant was a knight who embarked on a long journey of adventures, often to prove his worth to his chosen lady, in order to win or justify her love. The journey generally involved marvellous adventures such as encounters with giants or rogue knights.

THE FIRST KNIGHT ERRANT

The first knight known as a knight errant in chivalric literature was Sir Gawain in the late 14th-century English poem *Sir Gawain and the Green Knight*. Challenged to attend the Green Knight's chapel after a year had passed, Sir Gawain embarked on a long journey with many adventures. When he reached the castle of Sir Bercilak (who turned out to be the Green Knight), he was greeted as a 'knyght erraunt'.

▼ *The slaying of a dragon was one among the many feats of strength performed by Sir Yvain, with his companion the Lion.*

However, many knights undertook a life of adventures of the kind we now call 'knight errantry' long before the Gawain poem was written. The convention had its roots both in the extravagant adventures of folklore – such as the Welsh legends which contain the earliest accounts of Arthurian knights – and in the tourneying trips embarked upon by knights as early as the 11th or 12th centuries. On these tours knights would travel to different tournaments seeking sport, renown and wealth through taking ransoms.

A FRANKISH KNIGHT AT THE CROSSROADS

An anecdote told of a Frankish knight during the First Crusade indicates that when knights embarked upon these trips seeking adventures they expected contests on their travels as well as at more formal tournaments. The story, told by Anna Comnena, daughter of Byzantine emperor Alexius Comnenus, tells of a Frankish

▲ *A lady attends to her knight as he prepares to embark on the quest to which she has commanded him.*

knight who sat on the imperial throne of Byzantium in the presence of her father, and was reprimanded for his lack of respect. He responded with defiant pride, declaring himself a noble Frank, saying that back in the French countryside there was a well-known place for issuing and answering challenges to combat to prove one's worth as a knight. The spot was at a crossroads near an old shrine and any knight could wait there, ready to fight, until another warrior came who was brave enough to compete and determine who was the most chivalrous. The knight in Anna Comnena's story said he was so famous that, although he had often waited there, no one had ever challenged him.

THE KNIGHT WITH THE LION

For some knights the voyage as a knight errant became an end in itself, and undermined the relationship with the lady. The Arthurian knight Sir Yvain, for example,

stayed away so long on his journey of adventures that he clean forgot his lady at court – his wife, Lady Laudine – and for a while she banned him from returning.

Sir Yvain was based on Owain, an Arthurian knight in Welsh legend, where he was married to the sister of Iseult and in some versions was said to be the son of a goddess named Modron (a version of the witch Morgan le Fay). His story was given prominence by French poet Chrétien de Troyes in his poem *Yvain, the Knight of the Lion* (c.1170). In this account, Sir Yvain travelled into a magical forest to challenge a knight called Sir Esclados, who had defeated and humiliated Yvain's cousin, Sir Calogrenant. Sir Yvain killed Sir Esclados, then won the love of his widow, Lady Laudine, whom he married.

Back at court, Sir Gawain persuaded Sir Yvain to embark on a voyage of adventures and Lady Laudine allowed him to go on condition that he return within a year. When he forgot about her and she banned him from returning, Sir Yvain went mad with grief but at last recovered sufficiently to attempt to win her love back. He saved a lion from a serpent, and it became his companion, travelling with him as a symbol of his chivalric virtue: he became known as the 'Knight of the Lion'. Finally, impressed by his achievement, Lady Laudine permitted Sir Yvain to return.

As we saw in Chapter Five, this story was used as the basis for the staging of an Arthurian tournament held at Le Hem, Picardy, in 1278 by the lords of Bazentin and Longueval, when Robert II, Count of Artois, appeared as Sir Yvain with a live lion in his company. The stories of knight errantry were frequently the inspiration for theatrical enactments at tournaments, and there were many other examples of travelling knights in the Arthurian tales, notably in the story of Sir Lancelot.

SIR AMADIS OF GAUL

Another celebrated knight errant in the Arthurian tradition was the Portuguese hero Sir Amadis of Gaul, whose tale of wandering adventures dated from the

early 14th century. It was published in 1508 and became a great bestseller in Spain and Portugal in the 16th century.

Sir Amadis was said to be the son of Queen Elisena of England and King Perion of Gaul, and was abandoned on a barge in England. He had a chivalric upbringing from a knight named Sir Gandales in Scotland, then was knighted by King Perion and went through many adventures in an enchanted land. His lady, Oriana, became jealous of him and sent a letter denouncing him, which plunged him into madness from which he recovered only when Oriana's maid was sent to save him.

▲ *The forest – and in particular areas near water – was the haunt of female spirits. Warriors often encountered temptations of love on their trips of knight errantry.*

After fighting in support of Lady Oriana's father, King Lisuarte, he travelled for ten years as the 'Knight of the Green Sword' and ventured as far away as Constantinople where he defeated a great giant. Throughout his adventures Sir Amadis showed himself courteous and sensitive, and devoutly Christian, as well as unbeatable in battle and unafraid to spill blood.

THE GLORIES OF CHIVALRIC LOVE

ULRICH VON LICHTENSTEIN, JAUFRÉ RUDEL, LORD OF BLAYE AND SIR WILLIAM MARMION

The knights errant described in courtly romances had many imitators in the medieval era. The 13th-century Austrian knight and Minnesänger Ulrich von Lichtenstein described how he embarked on a long journey of adventure and fought in many tournaments to prove his love to his lady. The reputed feats of 12th-century French knight and troubadour Jaufré Rudel, Lord of Blaye, and those of the 14th-century English knight Sir William Marmion make intriguing comparisons.

JOURNEY IN A LADY'S SERVICE

Ulrich von Lichtenstein was a leading noble from the Duchy of Styria (now southern Austria), who served Margrave Heinrich of Istria as page and squire and was knighted in 1222 (in his early 20s) by Duke Leopold VI of Austria. He was also a notable poet, and portrayed himself as a chivalric knight and courtly lover par excellence in his 1255 poem *Frauendienst* (*Service of the Lady*).

According to the poem, Ulrich travelled from Venice to Vienna in 1226 disguised as the Roman goddess of love, Venus, to win honour for his lady. Every knight he met he challenged to a joust in his lady's name. In the course of his travels he broke no fewer than 307 lances and was undefeated in a single joust. But his lady remained unimpressed, and demanded further deeds to prove his devotion. He then planned a second quest in honour of a different lady, and disguised as King Arthur, but he never managed to embark on this quest.

In his poem he declared that a knight who, with courage in his heart, won the praise of his lady thereby also won great honour. He also declared that the knight should banish fear entirely, because the smallest trace of cowardice would make him unworthy of his lady's attentions, and he should also be willing to die rather than fail in order to win her acclaim.

JAUFRÉ RUDEL AND LOVE FROM AFAR

Jaufré Rudel, Lord of Blaye (near modern Bordeaux in western France), was a knight and troubadour of great renown in the mid-12th century about whom a colourful fictionalized biography was created.

In his poems he specialized in the convention of knights loving from afar ladies they may never have met. One of the few references to him outside his surviving songs – in a poem by the 12th-century troubadour Marcabru – suggests that he was *oltra mar* ('beyond the sea' – that is, on crusade). Rudel probably died while travelling on the Second Crusade, which took place between 1145 and 1149.

The legend of his life told that he took the cross and went on crusade because he was inflamed with a desire to glimpse and honour Countess Hodierna of Tripoli, whose beauty and dignity were praised lavishly by travel-weary pilgrims coming back from the Holy Land. He declared her to be his *amour de loin* ('distant love') and pledged his devotion to her before he departed; but during the voyage he fell terribly ill and when he reached Tripoli he was close to death. The countess, hearing of his devotion and his serious illness, descended from her castle to see him, and held the knight in her arms. In that instant he died in an ecstasy of fulfilled desire blended with a deep sense of his own unworthiness.

◄ *Knights could not really have jousted in the rounded area represented in this illustration from the 15th century. The knight on the left wears a fine heraldic swan on the top of his helmet.*

THE EXAMPLE OF SIR WILLIAM MARMION

In the 14th-century border wars fought between England and Scotland, Sir William Marmion rode to almost certain death to satisfy his lady's desire for renown. In c.1320 the Scots had the upper hand in the border conflict, and the castle of Norham in Northumberland was the scene of almost constant fighting between its English garrison and Scottish raiders. Around this time Sir William Marmion was feasting at Lincoln when his lady sent him a gilt-crested war helmet with the message that he should seek out the most dangerous place in the land to win her acclaim by wearing it in battle. He took counsel with his fellow knights at the feast and all agreed the best place to go would be Norham, so he travelled there with the splendid helmet in his possession.

Only four days after his arrival, a great raiding party numbering 160 brave-hearted warriors marched to the castle. The castle constable, Sir Thomas de Gray, called on Sir William and persuaded him that this was his chance to attain glory: 'Sir knight,' he declared, 'you have come to make your helmet famous … Climb on your horse, behold your enemies, use your glittering spurs to launch a charge into their midst.' The constable said that he would prepare to fight but would hold back until Sir William had had his chance to prove his worth.

▼ *By 1823, when JMW Turner painted this view of Norham Castle in Northumberland, the scene of Sir William Marmion's heroics was a romantic ruin.*

▲ *A knight takes leave of his noble wife. His exploits on campaign or his adventures win honour both for himself and for his lady.*

Then, wearing magnificent armour that shone with gold and silver, and with his bright helmet sparkling in the sunlight, Sir William rode out alone to take on the raiders. He put up a noble fight, but was so outnumbered that he was injured in the face, dragged from his horse and was at risk of death. At this point Sir Thomas and the knights of the garrison rode out and drove all the raiders back in disarray; they helped Sir William remount and at his side they chased the raiders far into the countryside. William Marmion's chivalric feat is told in the chronicle *Scalacronica* written in c.1355 by Sir Thomas Gray, son of the Sir Thomas in the narrative.

ORLANDO IN LOVE

THE ROMANCES OF ITALY

A new cycle of romance epics in 15th-and 16th-century Italy cast a fresh light on the adventures of Roland, Oliver and other paragons of chivalry at the court of Charlemagne. Matteo Maria Boiardo's poem *Orlando Innamorato* (*Orlando in Love*) and Lodovico Ariosto's *Orlando Furioso* (*Orlando Maddened*) combined the military feats of Charlemagne's knights with narratives of courtly love that were developed in the Arthurian romances.

LOVE SEEN THROUGH A KNIGHT'S EYES

Matteo Maria Boiardo was a knight and a lyric poet. He served as captain of Modena in 1480–82 and of Reggio in 1487–94. He wrote a highly personal collection of love poems, describing his passion for Antonia Caprara and published in 1499 as *Amorum libri tres* (*Three Books on Love*). His

▼ *Orlando learns the terrible news that Angelica has eloped with the Saracen knight Medoro to Cathay (China). The scene is from Lodovico Ariosto's* Orlando Furioso.

Orlando Innamorato was the first poem to combine elements from the Carolingian and Arthurian romances. Boiardo also added classical influences, for he was a poet during the Italian Renaissance and translated many classical works by authors including Herodotus, Xenophon and Apuleius.

Boiardo's epic, which was left unfinished at his death, described the quests of Orlando (Roland) and many other knights to win the love of the beautiful pagan princess Angelica, daughter of Galafrone, the king of Cathay (China), and her love for Orlando's cousin Ranaldo. (Ranaldo was previously encountered in the *Doon de Mayence* cycle of *chansons de geste* as the hero Renaud de Montauban.) These quests, which included a full complement of bruising encounters, amid celebrations of great icons of the chivalric tradition such as the horse Bayard, with magical spells and exotic characters, were set against the background of Charlemagne in Paris coming under attack from a great Moorish army. In *Orlando Innamorato* the

virtues of religious faith, military honour and love of one's country are celebrated above all others.

LOVESTRUCK AT THE TOURNAMENT

Orlando Innamorato began with an account of a great tournament held in Paris by Charlemagne. The beautiful Angelica and her brother and champion Argalia arrived, declaring that whoever could defeat Argalia could have the hand in marriage of Angelica.

Orlando fell in love with Angelica at first sight, despite the fact that the beautiful Lady Alda (in this version of events, his wife) was at his side. Argalia proved to be invincible since he wore magic armour; he and his sister had really come to lay low the great champions of Charlemagne in preparation for an invasion by an army of Moors led by Agramante, Emperor of Africa. Argalia was also drawn by the fame of the Frankish knights: he wanted above all to capture Orlando's famous sword (here known as Durindan) and Ranaldo's horse Bayard.

After the first two jousts, in which Argalia triumphed, he and Angelica withdrew into a magical forest called the Forest of Arden. The leading knights of the court followed. Ranaldo drank from a magical stream whose waters made a knight hate his lady: thereafter he loathed Angelica. She, on the other hand, drank water from a stream that made those who did so fall in love, and seeing Ranaldo asleep nearby she fell in love with him. He woke, saw her, looked on her with hatred and rode away. She fell asleep on the ground.

Orlando found Angelica and was watching her when he was challenged by a passing knight – a typical event in the romances and tales of knight errantry, and one that made them popular as themes for enactment at tournaments of the age of chivalry. The knight, named Feraguto,

▲ *Sir Roger, a knight in* Orlando Furioso, *rescues Lady Angelica while mounted on a hippogriff – a legendary creature that is half horse and half griffin.*

fought with Orlando until they were interrupted by Feraguto's sister Fiordespina, who told him he had to return to Spain to defend his homeland against attack by an Asian king.

FIGHT IN AN ENCHANTED GLADE

Many more adventures followed. Orlando spent a period in an enchanted garden where he forgot his love of Angelica, his loyalty to Charlemagne and even his own love of honour, but he escaped and then at Angelica's castle at Albraca (believed to be Bukhara in Uzbekistan) he fought a Tartar emperor, Agricane, who was

another rival for Angelica's love. Their epic battle, in a magical forest, went on all day and through the night by moonlight until dawn. When finally Orlando prevailed, his rival declared his desire to become a Christian and begged to be baptized. Orlando consented to his wish and baptized him at a fountain in the wood.

ORLANDO DRIVEN TO MADNESS

The wanderings of Ranaldo, Orlando and Angelica eventually led them back to France, where Charlemagne was still being besieged by a pagan army. The poem was left unfinished at Boiardo's death but a continuation was written by Lodovico Ariosto in his poem *Orlando Furioso*, published in 1516.

Ariosto was a knight and courtier who, after briefly serving as commander of the

citadel of Canossa, was in the service of Cardinal Ippolito d'Este and later became governor of the province of Garfagnana in the Apennines. His poem was also set against the backdrop of a war between Christians commanded by Charlemagne, and Saracens led by Agramante near Paris. Ariosto's poem described how Orlando was driven into madness and despair by his unrequited love for Angelica, while a pagan champion named Ruggiero (who was a descendant of the ancient paragon of chivalry, Hector of Troy) devoted himself to the Christian maiden Bradamante. She was Ranaldo's sister and rode in white armour as the 'Virgin Knight'. The plot involving them was a tribute to the poet's patrons, the Este family, who were traditionally said to be descended from these two lovers.

WHEN A CHRISTIAN LOVED A PAGAN

IF KNIGHTS OF ONE FAITH LOVED LADIES OF ANOTHER

Tales of love between Christians and pagans, such as that between the pagan warrior Ruggiero and the Christian maiden Bradamante in *Orlando Furioso*, were a common theme in the courtly romances. Another great Italian epic poem, *Jerusalem Delivered* by Torquato Tasso, cast the historical figure of Tancred de Hauteville, who was a hero of the First Crusade, as the central figure of a romance, and invented a love affair for him with a Muslim warrior maiden named Clorinda. Such difficult inter-faith romances allowed for enchanting adventures in exotic locations as well as celebration of the ultimate triumph of the 'true faith' – it was an essential conclusion, as in *Orlando Furioso*, for the pagan to renounce his or her faith and seek baptism in Christianity.

◀ *Cherubs look joyfully on as Tancred baptizes the Muslim maiden, Clorinda, in the climax of* Jerusalem Delivered.

A TALE TOLD BY CRUSADERS

A very popular version of this narrative was *Floire et Blancheflor*, a 12th-century French metrical romance that told of the undying love between Floire, warrior son of a Saracen king, and Blancheflor, the daughter of a Christian countess. The story is believed to have come originally from a Greco-Byzantine source, and was perhaps brought back to Europe from the Holy Land by crusader knights returning from a campaign.

The oldest known version of the tale was a French one of *c.*1160, and after 1200 it appeared for about 150 years in a variety of vernacular versions across Europe. An English romance version, *Floris and Blanchefleur*, of *c.*1250, was extremely well received. In the 14th century Giovanni Boccaccio told a version of the same story in his *Decameron* (*c.*1350).

PILGRIMS UNDER ATTACK

The original French version began with a Frankish knight travelling on the well-worn pilgrim path to the shrine of St James at Santiago de Compostela in north-west Spain. In his company was his daughter, recently widowed, and pregnant by her dead husband. The Frankish knight was killed in an attack by Fenix, King of Muslim Spain, and the daughter was taken into captivity. At Fenix's court – supposedly at Naples – the daughter gave birth, on Palm Sunday, to a girl, Blanchefleur, while on the same day Fenix's wife gave birth to a son, Floris.

The two children were raised together and when the time was ripe they fell in love. Fenix, wanting to prevent his son from marrying a Christian, sent Lady Blanchefleur away to Cairo (called Babylon in the poem), telling his son that his love

▲ *For veteran crusaders and pilgrims, stories of Christianity and Islam at odds in love were an intriguing recasting of the war of the faiths fought out in the Holy Land.*

Sir Floris's father King Fenix had died, and Floris and Lady Blanchefleur therefore returned to Spain. Sir Floris converted to Christianity and ruled justly with his Christian bride. He even persuaded the people of his kingdom to convert to Christianity as well.

The English version of the story emphasized the chastity of the lovers. When discovered by the emir they told him that they had not consummated their love and he tested their claim by making Lady Blanchefleur bathe her hands in magical water that would discolour if she were not a virgin. She passed the test and as a result, in honour of their chaste self-control, the emir set them both free.

AUCASSIN AND NICOLETTE

Another popular tale of love across the religious divide was that of *Aucassin et Nicolette*, an early-13th-century French *chantefable* (a story intended for singing at court, proceeding through alternating segments of sung verses and recited sections of prose). It told of the love between Aucassin (a Christian knight and the son of the count of Beaucaire) and a Saracen maiden in captivity, Nicolette. It is thought to have been based on the same Greco-Byzantine original as *Floire et Blancheflor*.

Nicolette, daughter of the king of Carthage, was stolen as a young girl by slave traders and ended up as a servant of Sir Garin, Count of Beaucaire, near Arles in Provence. Sir Garin's son Sir Aucassin saw the slave girl and began to fantasize about her. He had been a very promising knight, a strong young man of great prowess, but now he began to abandon the military arts of war and just drifted about, dreaming of Nicolette.

The situation became so bad that when the town was besieged, Sir Aucassin refused to help his father in the fight, declaring that he wanted only to ponder on his love for Nicolette. Then his father was furious and sent Nicolette away, although he did not tell Sir Aucassin. Eventually Sir Aucassin said he would fight for the defence of his city if he could

▲ *The forest, the place where Aucassin and Nicolette (and other lovers of romance) were reunited, is presented as a place untouched by the laws of the world.*

was dead. Sir Floris's grief was so extravagant that King Fenix, fearing his son might die, told him the truth. Sir Floris immediately travelled to Cairo to find her.

He found her incarcerated in a 'tower of maidens' kept for the pleasure of the emir, or ruler, of Cairo. Each year the emir selected a new virgin from the tower to be his wife, and killed the previous one. Floris played chess against the tower watchman, and managed to get himself smuggled into the tower by hiding inside a basket of flowers. There he encountered Lady Blanchefleur, and the couple were blissfully reunited. However, the emir grew suspicious and, visiting the tower, he caught Floris and Lady Blanchefleur together. His impulse was to kill them, but he restrained himself and asked his advisers, who were impressed by the intense love that the couple had for each other and asked that he spare them.

Floris was knighted by the emir, upon which he married Lady Blanchefleur; meanwhile, Blanchefleur's friend Lady Claris married the emir, who repented of the wickedness he had formerly shown and promised to kill no more brides. Shortly afterwards, the news arrived that

see Nicolette one more time. His father agreed, without admitting that he had sent her away, and Sir Aucassin spearheaded the garrison of the town to a great victory over the besieging army.

Then Sir Garin admitted what he had done to Nicolette. Sir Aucassin was overcome with distress. He went for a ride in the magical forest nearby, and discovered Nicolette there. They were together for a while, but later travelled to a distant land, and became separated again. Nicolette returned to her father in Carthage and Aucassin travelled sadly home.

The final stage of the drama began when Nicolette set forth from her home disguised as a minstrel, with her face darkened by berry juice, determined to track her lord down. She came to France and performed a song before Sir Aucassin, who did not recognize her. The song, about a lady called Nicolette, moved Sir Aucassin to tears, and he offered the minstrel a vast amount of money to travel to Carthage in order to persuade the lady to return. Then, seeing that her beloved lord was still deeply devoted to her, Lady Nicolette revealed her true identity and the lovers were joyfully reunited.

INTO THE OTHERWORLD

KNIGHTS AND THEIR FAIRY LOVERS

It was a common theme in courtly romances for knights to enter into a mysterious 'Otherworld', where they could became lovers of fairy noblewomen. They could generally come and go from this Otherworld without harm, although there was often an element of danger attached to their dealings with ladies and lords of that often menacing world.

LANVAL AND HIS LADY

In the intriguing 12th-century lay, or narrative song, *Lanval*, a knight of King Arthur had been reduced to poverty because the king was failing to support him, but he found a lover and a patroness in the fairy world. The poem was one of

12 Anglo-Norman lays written by a woman poet known to history as Marie de France (see box). The poems explored and glorified the themes of courtly love.

The song of *Lanval* described how one day Sir Lanval was wandering in the meadow near King Arthur's court when he was waylaid by two lovely fairy maidens – one was carrying water in a golden bowl, while the other held a towel. They took him to the fabulously wealthy home of their beautiful mistress. This Otherworld home was an elegant pavilion, topped with a golden eagle, and was found nearby as if beyond an invisible barrier in the meadow. The lady became Sir Lanval's lover and said she would appear

> **MARIE DE FRANCE**
> The author of the lay *Lanval* is known as Marie de France on the basis of a line in the epilogue to a collection of fables she wrote. Marie, whose poems were known in the 12th century, is the oldest known woman poet in French literature. Her delightful and very well-composed songs were almost certainly an influence on the work of later trouvères. Marie may have been Marie de Champagne, daughter of Eleanor of Aquitaine, but since there is some evidence that her poems were written in England, it is more likely that she was Marie, the Abbess of Shaftesbury, half-sister of King Henry II of England, or Marie the Countess of Boulogne, daughter of King Stephen of England, or Marie de Meulan, daughter of a great French lord, who was married to Hugh Talbot. She dedicated the lays to 'a noble king', thought to be Henry II or his son, Henry the Young King.

to him whenever he wished and make him as rich as he could want on one condition: that he must not tell another person of her existence. If he did, she would abandon him forever.

Sir Lanval happily accepted her terms. He enjoyed the comfort of eating and dressing well, and of being able to exhibit the chivalric virtue of *largesse* at court. He became known for his generosity: he would ransom prisoners, pay for jugglers and *jongleurs* and feed those without a patron of their own. His lady was happy

◄ *The Isle of Avalon, where Arthur is said to lie asleep, ready to come to the aid of England in her hour of greatest need, is part of the Otherworld realm. Ladies of that land attend him in his deathly sleep.*

for him to do as he pleased, as long as he did not break the one condition of their relationship – its secrecy.

However, one day Queen Guinevere approached Sir Lanval and attempted to seduce him. He rejected her advances, and she declared that he clearly did not like women. He retaliated rashly, declaring that he had a lady of his own who was fairer by far than Queen Guinevere.

Guinevere then accused Sir Lanval of trying to seduce her and denounced him for saying that a chambermaid was more beautiful than she was. Sir Lanval was called before the king in a full court with jury to answer for his actions. The jury declared that if Lanval could produce his mistress and prove that she was more beautiful than Guinevere he should go free. Lanval's heart sank as he realized that he had broken the terms of his agreement with his fairy mistress and that he could never expect her to help him again.

However, at the final moment the fairy mistress appeared before the court to prove that her knight had spoken the truth. She explained that even though he

▼ *In 'La Belle Dame Sans Merci', English poet John Keats wrote of a beautiful fairy lady who captivated a knight-at-arms and robbed him of all his energy and purpose.*

had broken their agreement, she did not want harm to come to him. All present, even King Arthur, were captivated by the beauty of this fairy lady, and they agreed that she was more beautiful even than Queen Guinevere.

As the lady was leaving, Sir Lanval leapt on the back of her white horse and rode away with her into the mists of magic. The poet said that Sir Lanval was never seen again, for she carried him off to the Isle of Avalon, the fabled final resting place of King Arthur himself.

Encounters with fairy women and the Otherworld were common in the Celtic folklore that fed into both the Arthurian romance tradition and into the Breton lays. The story of Sir Lanval, for example, may have had a common folkloric source with the story of Sir Yvain (as described in Chrétien de Troyes's *Yvain, the Knight of the Lion*), for Yvain also met a lady associated with water, and broke a promise to her.

SIR GUINGAMOR

Another Breton lay told the story of Sir Guingamor, with many similar themes to that of Sir Lanval (it was once thought to be another work of Marie de France, but modern historians think this unlikely). In

▲ *Knights who had encounters with ladies of the fairy realm risked losing control of their destiny. Here King Arthur himself lies in a daze before the queen of the fairies.*

this story, the knight was approached by the Queen of Brittany, who tried to seduce him, but he resisted her advances and so she taunted him, daring him to go on the hunt for the white boar – a task that had already cost the lives of ten knights. Like any good knight, Sir Guingamor could not resist the challenge to his prowess and his reputation, and departed on the quest with the king's horse and dogs.

While on the hunt he found a green marble palace and beyond it a beautiful maiden bathing in a pool. She promised him help if he stayed as her lover for three days; he did so and afterwards was able to catch the boar. His fairy lover allowed him to return to his home but warned him that he could not eat anything while there. When he returned to Brittany he found that three centuries had passed. Forgetting his instruction not to eat, he bit into a wild apple, and immediately became extremely weak. He was led back to the Otherworld and installed in the green marble palace by two beautiful maidens.

BRAVE KNIGHTS AND PHANTOM LADIES

LEGENDS OF MELUSINE AND THE HOUSE OF LUSIGNAN

A phantom lady, probably originally a water spirit from Celtic folklore, appeared repeatedly in the foundation myths of a number of noble and royal houses in medieval Europe. She was said to be the mother of crusader knight Guy de Lusignan, King Consort of Jerusalem.

The lady was half-woman, half-serpent, and could live among human society as long as she could keep her true nature secret. She therefore placed a prohibition on her noble lover ever seeing her bathe – in some versions of the tale, she revealed her true nature only on a Saturday or a Sunday, when she grew a scaly lower half. The most celebrated version of her tale was told by 15th-century French trouvère Jean d'Arras.

▼ *In a fateful moment, Count Raymond gives in to the temptation to spy on his fairy wife, and discovers her secret.*

▲ *It was believed that the fairy Melusine was a true ancestor of one of the most powerful families in medieval Europe, the family of de Lusignan. Here she is pictured as part of a genealogical family tree.*

According to this version, a Scottish king named Alynas met a beautiful lady named Pressyne in the forest when he was out hunting. He was captivated by her beauty and begged her to marry him, and she agreed on condition that he would not try to look at her when she was bathing. They lived together for some time, and Lady Pressyne gave birth to three girls, Melusine, Melior and Palatyne – but when King Alynas broke his promise not to spy on her, she left and fled to the Isle of Avalon with her daughters.

Melusine was later told of her father's actions, and she tried to punish him by locking him inside a mountain. For this she was herself punished, by being cursed to be a serpent from the waist down one day every week.

Years later Raymond de Lusignan was tracking a boar in the magical forests of France with his father. He had a chance to

Melusine escapes Raymond in the shape of a dragon, but returns secretly during the night to nurse her children.

kill the beast, but his sword deflected off the creature's thick hide and killed the old man. In a panic Raymond fled through the forest until he came to a musical bubbling stream, beside which he met the three beautiful daughters of Lady Pressyne. He asked Melusine to marry him and she agreed, promising she would create a wonderful castle beside the forest stream for them to live in. Her only condition was that he should not try to see her on a Saturday, but on that one day a week he should leave her to her private ablutions.

Lady Melusine was as good as her word. She magically created a great fortress and lived there with Raymond for many years. Her 11 sons, including Guy de Lusignan, were all strong and skilled in the arts of war, and they brought great fame on their father's house through their exploits fighting for the cross on crusade. But all, like their mother, had a secret flaw.

One day, stung by gossip in the town, Raymond broke his promise not to spy on Melusine on a Saturday. He looked through the keyhole to see her bathing and discovered that she had a serpent's tail. He was shocked but decided to keep

the matter secret – however, one day they quarrelled over a sin committed by one of their sons and Raymond forgot his good sense and denounced his wife as a serpent. That day she changed into a dragon and left, deserting her two youngest children.

Lady Melusine never returned during the day. Her ghostly form could afterwards be seen at night suckling the two infants she had abandoned, but in the morning she would be gone. She was also said to materialize at the Lusignan castle when a count of the family was about to die.

Lady Melusine was also claimed as an ancestor by Holy Roman Emperor Henry VII and also by the royal house of Luxembourg. A similar fairy lady was proposed, as we have seen, as the ancestor of King Richard I of England in the romance of his life. Like many other fairy ladies she could not remain in the church when the Mass was being said, and fled when the Host (the Body of Christ) was raised up.

PARTONOPE AND MELIOR

A later 12th-century romance version of the tradition told how a French knight named Sir Partonope won back the hand of Melusine's sister, Lady Melior, through his prowess in the lists. The story had a traditional beginning – Sir Partonope was caught up by fairy magic while out on a

hunt for a boar and was transported to a magical castle where he was seduced in darkness by Lady Melior, whom he was not permitted to see.

Sir Partonope begged this phantom lady to be his wife and she agreed on condition that he would never try to look on her. After spending a full year with her in the fairy Otherworld, Sir Partonope had to return to France to help fight against an invasion by the Vikings, and afterwards he was tricked by his mother into marrying an earthly woman.

Later Sir Partonope came to his senses, rejected this new woman and tried to return to Lady Melior. His mother persuaded him to take a lantern in order to get at least a glimpse of his phantom love. When the light from the lantern fell on Lady Melior, he was banished and returned to France.

There he wandered, distraught, until deep in the forests he met Lady Melior's sister (here called Lady Urrake), who announced that a grand tournament was to be held nearby and that the knight who broke the most spears in the lists would have the honour of winning the hand of Lady Melior. She helped him and in the lists he proved his worth, winning the tournament and the most precious prize: his fairy wife's love.

CHAPTER TWENTY-TWO

SAINTS AND OUTLAWS

The ideal of knighthood as represented in the image of the *miles Christi*, soldier of Christ, called for a saintly devotion to duty in protecting and defending the weak. The ideal found expression in the rule of life proposed for members of religious brotherhoods such as the Knights Templar, which called for taking vows of poverty and chastity, as well in the chivalric literature in the image of the saintly Sir Galahad, the purest of King Arthur's knights. In 1128 the Council of Troyes approved the rule for the Knights Templar that had been submitted by the order's co-founder, French knight Hugues de Payens. The Council's preamble, probably written by monastic reformer Bernard of Clairvaux, contrasted the new order of knighthood with secular knights, who were roundly condemned for failing to carry out their God-given duties, which were 'to defend poor men, widows, orphans and the Church'; far from doing this, the Council said, these knights were in competition among themselves to 'rape, despoil and murder'. The celebration of violence for religious ends embodied in the image of the soldier of Christ was supported by a vision of saints as chivalric warriors. Yet many knights did not live up to the ideal, and chivalric legends and romance also celebrated knights such as Robert le Diable, Guy of Warwick or Fulk Fitzwarin who fought from beyond the law, but were praised for their martial prowess and energy alongside the perfection of chivalry expressed in warrior saints such as St George.

▲ *Crusader knights fight in a battle.*

◄ *Medieval Christians interpreted the story of St George slaying the dragon as the victory of Christian chivalry over bestial sin and false religions.*

THE IDEAL CHRISTIAN KNIGHT

ST GEORGE

St George was venerated as an exemplar of Christian chivalry in the Middle Ages. His image as the perfect holy warrior partly had its origins in the celebration of his deeds by the Eastern Orthodox Church, where he was shown as a soldier in iconography from the 7th century onwards. Crusaders would have seen and been influenced by this iconography.

George was a Christian martyr of the 3rd century, who was traditionally said to have met his end in Lydda (now Lod in Israel). We know nothing for sure about his life, but his story was developed by the 6th century and was known in western Europe by at least the 8th century. The knights who returned from the First Crusade greatly popularized his name and his chivalrous deeds.

MARTYRED BY DIOCLETIAN

According to his hagiography, he was the son of an officer in the Roman army from Cappadocia (an ancient region now part of Turkey) and a mother from Lydda, who

▼ *When George refused to persecute Christians, and declared his own faith in Christ, the Roman authorities executed him before the walls of Nicodemia.*

were both Christians. George was a superb soldier and rose through the ranks to become a member of the personal bodyguard of Emperor Diocletian.

In 303, according to the story, the emperor ordered a wave of persecution of Christians, but George revealed himself to be a Christian and refused to take part. He was savagely tortured. One of his terrible punishments was being tied to a wheel of swords. Finally he was beheaded at Nicodemia on 23 April 303. So nobly did he die, dedicating his soul to Christ, that his example convinced the Empress Alexandra and a pagan priest named Athanasius to turn to Christianity, for which they too were executed – in one account more than 1,000 Roman soldiers also converted and were put to death. George's body was taken to his mother's birthplace, Lydda, for burial.

A church built there during the reign of the first Christian emperor, Constantine I, was supposedly dedicated to George and housed his remains. It became a significant pilgrimage site. This building was destroyed in 1010, then the crusaders rebuilt it and dedicated it to St George. During the Third Crusade the army of the great Islamic general Saladin destroyed the holy building once more. It was finally rebuilt a second time in the 19th century.

GEORGE AND THE DRAGON

The celebrated story of St George and the dragon was originally told in the East, and was brought back to the West with the returning crusaders. In Europe it was recast within the conventions of medieval chivalric life – George was represented on a white charger, and killing the dragon with a lance like any knight at a tournament or in a crusader battle charge. The story was part of the very popular *Legenda Sanctorum* (*Saints' Readings*) – better known as *Legenda Aurea* (*Golden Legend*) – a collection of saints' lives written in *c.*1260 by Jacobus de Voragine, the archbishop of Genoa, which ensured its widespread dissemination.

The story told that the citizens of 'Silene' (perhaps Cyrene in Libya) or, in some sources, of George's hometown Lydda, were terrorized by a dragon that had taken up residence at the spring (or lake) where they drew their water. In order to get water, they had to entice the dragon away from the spring by offering animals and a young virgin, chosen by lots from the townspeople.

One day the victim chosen by chance was the princess, and although the king offered all his wealth in return for his daughter's life, the people refused to draw the lots again. She was sent out to the dragon but George arrived on his charger just as she was about to be given up to the beast. The princess tried to send him away, but George remained and made the sign of the cross before himself, as any good Christian warrior would before combat.

▲ *George represents the Church and all the knights who support it as he rescues innocence in the form of the princess. This fresco of c.1350 is from Verona, Italy.*

▼ *George's cult was strong in the Eastern Orthodox Church. An artist of the Novgorod School painted this icon in c.1150.*

Then George charged at the dragon with couched lance and wounded the beast severely. He called for the princess to throw him her girdle and he put this around the dragon's neck. The dragon came meekly along behind them to the town, where the people, upon seeing it, were very frightened; but George killed it as they watched. The citizens were so grateful to their saviour that they turned their backs on the pagan faith and converted to Christianity. In all the medieval romance accounts, St George's lance was called Ascalon after the city of Ashkelon (now in Israel), which was the scene of the concluding triumphant conflict of the First Crusade, when – fresh from their capture of Jerusalem – the crusaders defeated a relief army that had been sent by Fatimids of Egypt, in the Battle of Ascalon on 12 August 1099.

The dragon-slaying story is ancient and may have had its origin among the Indo-European tribes who spread out from the central Asian steppes to places as diverse as India, Greece and western Europe. It is found in myths from the ancient Near East (told by the Hittites), ancient India and ancient Greece.

PATRON SAINT

By the 14th century, St George was effectively the patron saint of knighthood. In 1348 King Edward III of England designated St George as the patron of his new knightly brotherhood, the Order of the Garter, and during Edward's reign George became recognized as the patron saint of England, replacing St Edmund in the role. During the reign of King Henry V of England (1413–22), St George's Day (23 April) was celebrated as a national holiday. George is also the patron of a very wide range of other countries including Greece, Montenegro, Georgia, Russia and Palestine, and of cities including Beirut and Moscow.

PATRON SAINTS AT WAR

SAINTS AS CHIVALRIC WARRIORS

◄ *St James the Greater (far left) is the patron saint of Spain. Here he is shown with St Jude and St Simon the Zealot. All three were among Christ's twelve apostles.*

request, because he declared himself unworthy to be crucified on a cross that was identical to the kind used to kill his Lord. According to Scottish legend, St Andrew's relics had been brought with God's guidance from Constantinople to the town of St Andrews in Scotland. A story told that a Pictish king named Ongus (probably Oengus mac Fergus of the Picts, 729–761) had seen a cloud in the shape of St Andrew's cross when fighting the English, and declared that the saint was overseeing the battle and leading the Scottish warriors on to victory.

LEGENDS OF ST GEORGE

There was a well-established tradition of legends and romance stories that presented the saints as chivalric warriors. The English prose romance *The Famous History of the Seven Champions of Christendom* (1596) celebrated the legendary achievements of the patron saints of England, Wales, Ireland, Scotland, Italy, France and

▼ *Weak from hunger but strong in their faith, the crusaders defeated a large army at Antioch. They attributed the unlikely victory to the saints who fought with them.*

At the Battle of Antioch in June 1098 the crusaders reported that they saw St George, St Demetrius and St Maurice fighting alongside them. (St Demetrius and St Maurice were, like George, both martyrs killed during the persecution of Christians in the Roman Empire.) The conflict at Antioch came at a time of heightened religious perceptions. Just before the clash, a monk named Peter Bartholomew claimed to have had a vision of St Andrew, reporting that the Holy Lance used to pierce Christ's side on the Cross was buried in Antioch, and after a search, the Lance was supposedly found. St Andrew then appeared once more and urged the crusaders to fast for five days in order to ensure victory.

The Battle of Antioch was quickly won and the saints, particularly St George,

became associated with the success of the First Crusade. While fighting in Palestine during the Third Crusade of 1189–92 King Richard I of England put the English army under the protection of St George. About the same time, the banner of St George (the red cross on a white background) became the accepted garb for English soldiers.

ST ANDREW AND SCOTTISH TRADITIONS

St Andrew had become established as the patron saint of Scotland in around the 10th century. In the Bible, Andrew was a fisherman on the Sea of Galilee and the brother of Simon Peter, the first pope; he was martyred on a diagonally shaped cross (of the kind shown on the flag of Scotland; known as a saltire in heraldry) at his own

▲ *St Andrew, patron saint of Scotland, had many martial associations. According to St John's Gospel, St Andrew was originally a disciple of John the Baptist.*

Spain. It was written towards the close of the age of chivalry by English romance author Richard Johnson, who drew on a centuries-old popular tradition of tales about saints fighting as brave knights against great armies full of heathens and riding to the rescue of courtly maidens.

Johnson's romance claimed that St George was the son of the High Steward of England and was born after his mother dreamed that she was about to give birth to a dragon. He came into the world with a red cross on his hand and an image of a dragon on his chest.

Like many a knight of romance before him, he was raised by a fairy lady in the wilderness of the woods. When George came of age, the lady presented him with his chivalric equipment: a suit of armour made of steel from Libya that reflected the light of heaven, a horse named Bayard (like that of the Carolingian hero Renaud of Montauban) and a sword named Ascalon, supposedly made by the ancient Greek Cyclops.

The lady then showed George an enchanted castle in the forest where she had imprisoned the other patron saints of Europe: St Denis of France, St James of Spain, St Anthony of Italy, St Andrew of Scotland, St Patrick of Ireland, and St David of Wales. St George turned against the lady and imprisoned her in rock. Then he set the saints free and they embarked upon a series of adventures.

St George himself travelled to Egypt, where he killed a silver-scaled dragon and so saved King Ptolemy's daughter Lady Sabra, who was its next intended victim. Lady Sabra fell in love with St George, which enraged her suitor, King Almidor of Morocco.

King Almidor plotted against St George and sent him to the sultan of Persia with a letter. Without realizing, George was carrying his own death warrant, for the letter said he should be put to death as an enemy of Islam. He was thrown in jail, but on the day of his execution overawed his captor in the style of Richard I: two lions were sent into his cell and he plunged his hands into the animals' chests and tore their hearts out. He was spared execution, but imprisoned for seven years.

▼ *According to one tradition, St George went on to marry the princess he had saved from the dragon.*

UNDONE BY SORCERY

Finally George escaped and was reunited with the other seven patron saints. He sent the other six saints to Persia to defeat the sultan and his Saracen army. They did so in a five-day battle, but then they all fell victim to the tricks of a sorcerer who summoned up a glittering pavilion and a harem of beautiful maidens to entice the saints. The six champions, although saints, fell victim to this temptation and followed the maidens into the pavilion.

At this point St George arrived and he alone of all the saints was able to see through the sorcerer's spell. He pulled down the pavilion and set the other six champions free from enchantment for a second time. A final battle against the pagan forces of Persia followed, which ended in the death of 200,000 enemies of the Christian faith.

St George then enacted the pattern of the Crusades: a religious war led to political gains. He became ruler of Persia and parcelled out the lands he had gained among the other patron saints. Afterwards, all seven patron saints marched home to Europe. They made many converts to Christianity on their journey back.

HOLY WARRIOR

NORMAN KNIGHT ROBERT GUISCARD

The Norman knight and adventurer Robert Guiscard won a great name as a holy warrior in the mid-11th century, fighting on behalf of the papacy in Italy and Sicily against the Byzantine Greeks and Saracens. So great was his reputation that he was celebrated by the Italian poet Dante Alighieri in *La Divina Commedia* (*The Divine Comedy*) of c.1310–14, as one of the greatest Christian warriors, and was granted the right to abide in the 'Heaven of Mars', a place reserved for those who had achieved feats of undying fame in the service of the faith (see box).

◀ Byzantine Emperor Alexius II Comnenus 1169–83 (r. 1180–83), son of Emperor John Comnenus and Empress Irene, depicted in a mosaic in Hagia Sophia.

SOLDIER OF FORTUNE

Robert was the sixth son of Norman lord Tancred of Hauteville, and came to Italy in 1047 to seek his fortune. His older brothers William Iron-Arm, Drogo and Humphrey were already established in south-eastern Italy, where they fought for the Lombard princes against the Greeks of the Byzantine Empire. According to the traditional tale Robert left Normandy with just five knights and thirty footsoldiers in his company. Initially when he reached Italy he received no help from his older brothers and made his own way as leader of a robber gang, stealing from travellers and the Byzantine postal couriers and even pillaging monasteries.

STRONG BUT WILY

We know from an account by Byzantine princess Anna Comnena (1083–1153) that Robert was a man who had an exceptionally imposing physical presence. She wrote that he was taller than all his peers, broad-shouldered, red-faced with flaxen hair and with a powerful shout that was capable of making men flee. His eyes, she reported, burned with an indomitable spirit: he would be second to no one. (At the end of his career, Robert was a fierce

▲ Pope Gregory VII relied on Guiscard and on Norman military might in his struggle against Holy Roman Emperor Henry IV.

opponent of Anna Comnena's father, the Byzantine emperor Alexius Comnenus.)

Robert was also cunning – the name Guiscard was a form of the Old French *viscart*, meaning 'wily' or 'clever as a fox'. His feats were celebrated in *The Deeds of Robert Guiscard*, written by Norman chronicler William of Apulia in 1096–99.

FIERCE IN BATTLE

Robert first made his name fighting against the papal army at the Battle of Civitate in southern Italy, 1053, at a time when the papacy was trying to drive the Normans out of Italy. According to William of Apulia's account, Robert was knocked from his horse and remounted in the heat of battle no fewer than three times. Given the weight of the armour he would have worn and the chaos of the battlefield, this was an extraordinarily difficult feat and would have demanded enormous strength and fortitude.

ALLY OF THE PAPACY

Subsequently the papacy made allies of the Normans and in 1059 Pope Nicholas II (r. 1059–61) invested Guiscard as duke of Apulia, Calabria and Sicily. Guiscard pronounced himself to be a feudal vassal of the pope in these lands, but it would

▲ *Guiscard was one of the leaders of the Norman army that defeated the forces of Pope Leo IX at the Battle of Civitate.*

take a series of conquests over the following 20 years to make these titles a reality: Calabria was mostly held by the Byzantine Greeks, while Sicily was largely in Muslim hands.

Guiscard and his brother Roger took the Byzantine bases in Calabria at Cariati, Rossano, Geraco and Reggio in 1059–60. Then they returned to their base in Apulia to drive back a Byzantine army before invading Sicily. They gradually acquired control of the island.

Back on mainland Italy, in 1068–71 Guiscard besieged Bari, the capital of the Byzantine Empire in Italy. His victory there on 16 April 1071 drove the Byzantines out of southern Italy entirely. Then in 1072 he captured Palermo, making him master of Sicily as well.

THE LORD OF SOUTHERN ITALY

Guiscard made it his business to consolidate all these victories and the areas he had seized. He faced a number of revolts by Norman lords whom he had installed as vassals in his conquered lands, but put them all down in succession in 1073. His power had grown to such an extent that Pope Gregory VII excommunicated him for aggression against papal territories, but by the end of the 1070s they had been

reconciled. Guiscard controlled all of southern Italy save the independent Norman principality of Capua and the city of Naples.

ATTACK ON THE BYZANTINE EMPIRE

Beginning in 1081, Guiscard (although now aged 64) set out to make himself master of the Byzantine Empire. That year he occupied Corfu and then defeated the Byzantine emperor, Alexius, in the Battle of Dyrrhachium near Durazzo in October. The clash between Guiscard and Alexius, revered as among the greatest warriors of their day, soon achieved legendary status.

He might well have succeeded in achieving his ambition of becoming Byzantine emperor, but after taking Durazzo, with the way to Constantinople

open to him, he was recalled to Italy to save Pope Gregory VII. The pope was besieged in Castel Sant'Angelo in Rome by Holy Roman Emperor Henry IV, who had formed an alliance with Alexius.

Guiscard succeeded in lifting the siege and took the pope to safety. He resumed his Byzantine campaigns in 1084. He captured Corfu but he died of fever, along with 500 of his countrymen, on the Ionian island of Kefalonia on 17 July 1085.

After his death Guiscard was celebrated for having saved the ecclesiastical reforms of Pope Gregory VII in the face of the opposition of Henry IV, and as the founder of the Norman kingdom in Italy. He was typical of the younger son who was forced by the feudal system to make his own way in life, and achieved greatness by chivalric endeavour and strength of purpose.

WARRIORS OF THE FAITH IN THE HEAVEN OF MARS

The Heaven of Mars was the fifth of nine heavens encountered by the poet Dante, as described in perhaps the greatest of all works of medieval literature, *La Divina Commedia* (*The Divine Comedy*). The heaven was said to be for martyrs, confessors and soldiers. Biblical warriors Joshua and Judas Maccabeus also appeared to the poet in this heaven,

▼ *Beatrice leads the poet Dante through heaven in* The Divine Comedy. *The pair (left) view the eight holy warriors (right).*

among 'warriors of the faith', as did Charlemagne; Roland; William of Orange, another knight of Charlemagne, celebrated in romance; Renard, a Saracen knight reputedly converted by William; and the famous crusader Godfrey of Bouillon. Dante also praised Guiscard in the section of the poem dealing with Hell, where he described a devastated landscape with spirits reaching as far as the horizon as the image of what Robert Guiscard's enemies would look like after he had dealt with them using the full force of his martial vigour.

OUTLAW KNIGHTS

HEREWARD THE WAKE AND EDRIC OF SHREWSBURY

Alongside stories about the chivalric achievements of saints and biblical warriors, of the paladins of Charlemagne, of King Arthur's followers and of crusader knights, there was a medieval tradition of romance tales about outlaw knights. In England this tradition had its roots in popular narratives about Saxon and British warriors who fought the Norman invasion in the 11th century.

Prominent among these Saxon and British opponents of the Normans were Hereward and Edric. Hereward was a nobleman from Lincolnshire who led resistance to King William I of England from a base at Ely, deep in the treacherous fens, but finally succumbed to the power of the Norman war machine. He was the subject of a vigorous popular tradition, notably celebrated in the 15th-century *Gesta Herewardi* (*Deeds of Hereward*) by 'Ingulph of Crowland', Benedictine abbot at Croyland Abbey, Lincolnshire.

LINCOLNSHIRE LANDOWNER

Hereward appeared in the historical record as a landowner in Lincolnshire listed in the Domesday Survey. The *Anglo-Saxon Chronicle* named him as the leader of an

▼ *The Hereward tradition celebrated fierce native resistance to the Normans. His byname is believed to mean 'the Watchful'.*

▲ *Some accounts claim that Hereward was the son of Leofric, Earl of Mercia, and his wife Godiva, who famously rode naked in the streets of Coventry to persuade her husband to lift a toll imposed on his tenants.*

assault in 1070 on Peterborough Abbey, launched to protest the appointment of a Norman abbot named Turold. Afterwards, the *Chronicle* states, he retreated to Ely, and withstood Norman attacks for a year, then escaped when the rebel stronghold fell.

COURTLY ADVENTURES

The legends cast Hereward as a figure from courtly romance. They told that he was a wild character, who caused so much trouble to his noble father that he was banished from his estate. He then went on a series of romance adventures: tracking and killing a bear in Scotland; rescuing a lady from a giant in Cornwall; fighting in Ireland; then being shipwrecked in Flanders, where after a brief imprisonment he met his wife, Lady Tulfrida, and found a marvellous horse named Swallow.

A KNIGHT IN FLANDERS

It is likely that these adventures had some historical foundation: Hereward appears to have rebelled against King Edward the Confessor, unhappy at the monarch's close connections with the Normans, and was banished from England. In exile he found employment as a mercenary knight in the service of Baldwin V, Count of Flanders. He would have learned chivalry during this sojourn in Flanders.

According to the legend, Hereward returned to England in 1068 only to discover that his father's lands had been seized by the Normans, who had also killed his younger brother and stuck the dead man's decapitated head above the gateway to the family home. In that moment, Hereward dedicated his life to fighting the Normans. He killed the men responsible for his brother's death and gathered rebels around him at Ely. There on an island amid the marshes of fenland, they were besieged by the might of the Norman army, which was led by King William himself.

▶ *William defeats the Anglo-Saxon King Harold, and Norman rule begins in England, in this illumination, c.1280–1300.*

ASSAULT ON ELY

The Normans first tried to attack head-on, building a wooden causeway for their troops across the marshlands. But the causeway collapsed into the mud and many knights lost their lives and valuable equipment in the marshland. Then the Normans tried to bring the rebels down with magic: William employed a witch, who promised to cast a spell that would disarm the Saxons.

Hereward was determined to find out what the Normans were planning, and visited the besiegers' camp disguised as a wandering potter. There he heard the witch discussing her plans. He was not well disguised, however, and was almost discovered, and after getting into a fight in the kitchens he escaped. Just before he disappeared back into the safety of the fenland, he humiliated one of the finest Norman knights by disarming him and

sending him back to his companions with the news that they had missed the opportunity to capture Hereward himself.

Hereward and the rebels set a fire in the marshland that foiled the Normans' next attack. The blaze scattered the besiegers in all directions and the witch broke her neck in the ensuing panic. Eventually the Normans succeeded in reaching their island after the monks of the abbey of Ely showed the attackers a safe way across the marshes, but Hereward and his men, forewarned, took to their boats and vanished into the mists.

One version of the legend suggested that because of his great skill as a warrior Hereward was pardoned by William, and his lands were restored, but another suggested that he was finally tracked down and killed by the Normans.

WILD EDRIC

Another staunch opposer of William I was celebrated in legend as 'Wild Edric'. Edric was a Mercian aristocrat, believed to have been Earl of Shrewsbury, known by a

Latin name, Edric Sylvaticus ('Edric of the Woods') – because he primarily waged guerrilla warfare from the wilderness of the forests. Edric fought the Normans on the English–Welsh borders in c.1067–70. The *Anglo-Saxon Chronicle* reported that with a group of Welsh allies he attacked the Norman garrison at Hereford in 1067. He was also said to have been defeated by King William at Shrewsbury in 1069. In common with many of the local thegns, he had his land seized by force and then simply given to Norman lords; it was handed to either Ranulph de Mortimer or William FitzOsbern.

In the tales of Wild Edric he was said to have become lost while out hunting in the forests and to have taken a fairy bride. Like many other knights, he was deprived of his Otherworldly lady by failing to keep to an agreement – in this case not to speak of her origins. In Shropshire, Edric was celebrated as a warrior-leader in time of need, said to live in local lead-mines and be ready to ride forth at some future date when his country needed him sorely.

THE WILD HUNT

Both Hereward and Edric were said to ride in the Wild Hunt, a stampede of hunters, horses and dogs thought to be fairies or spirits of the dead, which was seen hurtling through the forests or sometimes the sky. Seeing the Wild Hunt was said to presage a disaster. In various traditions across Europe, the great figures of chivalry were said to be seen riding at the head of the Hunt: they included Charlemagne, with Roland carrying his standard; King Arthur; and Dietrich of Berne, the Germanic hero-king based on the 6th-century King Thedoric the Great of the Ostrogoths. Another leader of the Hunt was 'Herne the Hunter' who, according to the legend, was a huntsman in Windsor Park who had saved King Richard II's life then went mad and killed himself.

THE SCOURGE OF THE VIKINGS
SIR GUY OF WARWICK

Hero of English and French romances from the 13th to the 17th centuries, the legendary Guy of Warwick was celebrated as a native English opponent of Viking invaders, a knight errant, a vanquisher of fantastic monsters and paragon of Christian chivalry who rode to the Holy Land and defeated countless Saracens before finally retiring as a religious hermit. His story, probably written for the Norman earls of Warwick, is a good example of the 'ancestral romances' that were produced to glorify the origins of noble houses in the Middle Ages.

The oldest version of Sir Guy's story was probably in a 12th-century French tale. It was then reworked in English and Anglo-Norman versions. The oldest surviving manuscript is the 13th-century Anglo-Norman work *Gui de Warewic*; the oldest English version dates to *c*.1300. The central event in Guy's legend was the defeat in single combat of a mighty Danish warrior named Colbrand, a victory that was said to have saved King Athelstan of England when his capital Winchester was besieged by a Viking army led by kings Anlaf and Gonelaph. This may have had a historical foundation in the invasion of

▼ *The popularity of the Guy of Warwick tales derives in large part from their hero's successes in fighting Danish invaders.*

southern England by Danish troops in 993, although Winchester was actually saved from capture following payment of a bribe rather than victory by any English champion in single combat.

PARAGON OF CHIVALRY

The versions of Guy of Warwick's romance that survive probably contain additions by monastic scribes, for they include a wealth of religious elements. The legend of Guy remained extremely popular for centuries. In the 16th century his reputation as a great Christian knight was so high that he was included in contemporary lists of the 'Nine Worthies'.

According to the legend of his life, Guy was the son of the steward in the service of the earl of Warwick, and he was in love with the earl's daughter, Lady Felice. He was raised to knighthood, and to prove himself worthy of her love embarked on a career of knight errantry. He fought in numerous tournaments in France and Germany; then he freed the daughter of the emperor of Germany after she had been kidnapped; killed a dragon; he then went to Constantinople and fought against great armies of Saracens. He defeated the Saracens' champion Coldran in single combat, then killed the king of Tyre and the sultan of Constantinople. On his return to Warwick he was greeted as a

▲ *King Athelstan kneels before the warrior-turned-mendicant Guy. Athelstan was the first king to rule all of England.*

great Christian knight, a humbler of the enemies of the Christian faith, and Lady Felice finally agreed to become his wife.

PENITENT KNIGHT

However, almost immediately after the wedding, Sir Guy had a vision of Christ, who told him to undertake a penitential journey. Therefore Sir Guy embarked on a pilgrimage to the Holy Land. Perhaps mindful of the fate of Lady Laudine, wife of the Arthurian knight Sir Yvain, who was forgotten by his knight while he was away on a journey of knight errantry, Lady Felice gave Sir Guy a ring to wear, saying that each time he looked on it he should remember her. He wore the ring during his pilgrimage, on which he had many more extraordinary adventures, including conflicts with great giants.

Returning to Warwick once more, he defeated the Dun Cow, a vast cow that was terrorizing the countryside, as well as a boar in Windsor Park and a serpent in Northumberland. After these exploits, he

▲ *The lords and earls of Warwick are commemorated in this chronicle roll, written c.1477–85 by John Rous, priest at the chapel established at Guy's Cliffe.*

fought the Danish champion, Colbrand, who was holding Winchester under siege. The events were said to have taken place in 9th-century England, during the reign of King Athelstan. According to local Winchester tradition the battle against Colbrand took place by the walls of the Benedictine Abbey of Hyde, just outside

THE ANCESTRAL ROMANCE

Sir Guy's legends are examples of the 'ancestral romance': stories that celebrate the establishment of a noble house, or a branch of a family – in this case the earls of Warwick. These poems turn into legendary form the family's past elevation to greatness – as in this legend through the rise by way of martial exploits from humble origins to being fit to enter the established nobility as an equal of Lady Felice. Another of this type of ancestral romance is the Lusignan legend that built family history on the folklore about the water-spirit Melusine.

the city walls. (Hyde Abbey was demolished by Henry VIII in the mid-16th century Dissolution of the Monasteries.)

LIFE AS A HERMIT

Guy's victory over Colbrand won him King Athelstan's devotion. Afterwards, the knight returned to Warwick, but in disguise in order to hide himself away in a hermitage, to spend his last days in prayer and penitence after a life of violence in which he had spilled a great deal of blood. Each day he attended the house of his wife, Lady Felice, disguised in rags, in order to beg for alms. Finally as the appointed day of his death drew near, and he came to know for certain that he was to be called from his life on earth, he sent Lady Felice the ring so that at last she knew what had happened to her husband. She joined him at his hermitage and they were united for the last few days of Sir Guy's life.

GUY'S CLIFFE

The memory of Sir Guy was proudly celebrated in Warwick. Local legend claimed to have established the scene of his later hermitage to be a cliff in rocks above the River Avon just outside the town – a place afterwards called Guy's Cliffe. In 1394 a tower was added to Warwick Castle and

named in his honour, and supposed relics of his life, including his sword and pot, were collected there. A chantry (chapel) was established at Guy's Cliffe, complete with a statue of Guy, in 1423 by Richard de Beauchamp, 13th Earl of Warwick. A country house was built on the site in the 18th century, but it is now a ruin.

▼ *Christ commanded Guy to make penance for his many acts of violence by travelling to the Holy Land. This image is from the Athelstan Psalter (c.950) from Winchester.*

ROBBER KNIGHTS

EUSTACE THE MONK AND ROBERT LE DIABLE

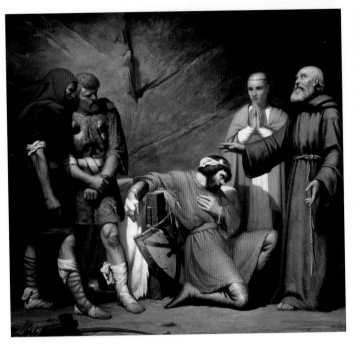

◀ *The tale of Norman knight Robert the Devil – perhaps based on the life of Duke Robert II of Normandy – was popular in later centuries. This scene is from an 1831 opera about Robert by Giacomo Meyerbeer.*

while he was there. It also stated that he became a Benedictine monk in France before embarking on his life of crime and mercenary exploits, and he only left the religious life in order to avenge the death of his father.

The romance told a number of stories in which Eustace put his powers of black magic to the service of his pleasure or in order to enact his revenge. One such tale recounts the time when, after an abbot of a monastery refused to feed him, Eustace brought a pig's carcass to life in the shape of a hideous old woman and made her fly around the refectory driving the monks mad with fear and leaving the way clear for Eustace to seat himself at the high table and enjoy the food on offer.

▼ *The romance of the wicked knight Robert the Devil was still very popular in the 16th century. This is the title page to* The Terrible and Marvellous Life of Robert the Devil, *published in 1563.*

Some knights of legend and romance were celebrated as anti-heroes for their wicked deeds pursued with great energy. One such story was that of Eustace the Monk, which told of an outlaw knight who was versed in black magic, switched sides at his convenience and accumulated a fortune as a naval mercenary. Similar tales were told in the legend of Robert the Devil, but in his case the wickedness had a purpose, for it led him eventually to take heed of his conscience and he ended his life a glowing example of Christian penitence and religious chivalry.

EUSTACE THE MONK

The romance of Eustace the Monk was written in the mid-13th century by a poet from Picardy. It was based on the exploits of a nobleman's son from Boulogne. According to the historical record, this Eustace was the seneschal of Renaud de Dammartin, Count of Boulogne, but in around 1204 Eustace was accused of being dishonest, declared an outlaw and had his lands confiscated.

He fled into the deep forest, then became a naval mercenary in the English Channel. He worked for King John of England in 1205–12, commanding a fleet of 30 ships and leading raids along the Normandy coast. With the king's backing he seized the Channel Island of Sark as his base. In 1212, however, he switched sides and began to raid English ports. In 1215 he supported the revolt by rebel barons against King John's rule and he lost his life in 1217 when, while carrying supplies by sea to the rebels in England, he was intercepted by an English fleet and decapitated.

The romance of Eustace followed the facts of this life story quite closely, adding that early in life Eustace had travelled to Toledo in Spain and studied black magic

THE WICKEDNESS OF
ROBERT THE DEVIL

The legend of Robert the Devil told the story of a French knight, the son of the Devil, cursed to only use his strength in battle for immoral ends. He sought forgiveness and found salvation by riding out as an unknown knight to save Europe three times from Saracen attack. His name and story were connected to those of King William I of England's father Robert II, Duke of Normandy, also known as 'Robert the Devil'.

Duke Robert II of Normandy won a reputation for wickedness, and the nickname 'the Devil', by poisoning his own elder brother Richard in order to win power for himself in Normandy. Both Robert's children – William and Adelaide of Normandy – were illegitimate; they were the offspring of Robert's mistress, Herleva of Falaise.

Towards the end of his life, Robert made William his heir in Normandy and departed on pilgrimage to the Holy Land. According to the account in the *Gesta Normanorum Ducum* (*Deeds of the Norman Dukes*), written by a monk named William of Jumièges in *c*.1060, Robert succeeded in reaching Jerusalem but died on the return journey at Nicaea (modern Iznik, Turkey) in July 1035.

The oldest known version of the legend of Robert the Devil was written in Latin by a Dominican friar named Stephen of Bourbon in *c*.1250. It was rewritten as a 13th-century French metrical romance and was also the subject of a 14th-century miracle play. In the late 15th century, it achieved great popularity as a printed romance, first in French and later in English and Spanish.

THE DEVIL'S CHILD

According to the legend, Robert's mother was unable to have a child and turned to the Devil to help her become pregnant. From his earliest youth Robert was a chivalric prodigy, superb in the saddle, unbeatable in the lists, feared by knights who saw him at large in the countryside.

But because of his father, he was incapable of putting his strength to good use. He was so troubled by his wickedness that he went to the pope to ask for help, and the pope sent him to a hermit who possessed such extraordinary saintliness that he had won dominion even over the evil works of the devil. The hermit told Robert to put himself through a demanding series of penances designed to defeat his self-will. He had to take a vow of silence, get food from the mouth of a dog and endeavour to bring about situations in which he would be ridiculed and humiliated. Robert gladly did these things and at last found peace in his soul.

▼ *Nicaea, where Duke Robert II died, was an important city from classical times, and in 1097 was the scene of the first major action of the First Crusade.*

THE UNKNOWN KNIGHT

However, at this point the city of Rome came under threat from a great Saracen army and memories of Robert's fierceness in battle were still fresh enough to make men call upon him to come to the aid of the Christian city. At first he did not want to go back to life in the saddle, but an angel of God descended to convince him that it was necessary. He rode out as an unidentified knight, without heraldic device on his shield or helmet, and three times he single-handedly drove off the besieging Saracen army.

Finally Robert had succeeded in saving his soul. In variant endings of the legend he was either rewarded with the hand in marriage of the Holy Roman Emperor's fair daughter, or he retired to a hermitage, where he lived out his last days in peace and great holiness.

KNIGHTS OF THE FOREST

FULK FITZWARIN AND ROBIN HOOD

Some knights of legend and romance fought as outlaws because they had been wrongly dispossessed, and were only trying to regain their rightful inheritance. One such outlaw was the Shropshire knight turned forest raider Fulk Fitzwarin.

THE HISTORICAL FULK FITZWARINS

The deeds of Fulk Fitzwarin were celebrated in an English verse romance that is now lost but which was summarized in French, Latin and English versions that do survive. The romance accounts were based on the life of a landowner of that name who lost his property at Whittington, Shropshire, following a lawsuit in 1200. He then spent three years as an outlaw in the forests before being granted a royal pardon in 1203. Then he lived as a knight until 1215, when he joined the barons' revolt against King John. In this period he lost his property again, but regained it after John's death in 1216 and then he spent his remaining years on his estate until he died in the mid-1250s. This life history may combine those of two knights called Fulk Fitzwarin, father and son.

The romance described how Fulk had been raised at the royal court at Windsor Castle following the death of his father, and in this period had quarrelled violently with the future King John over a game of chess. John was losing, it was said, so he turned the board over, scattering the pieces, and hit Fulk in the mouth; Fulk simply hit him back, so John ran to his father King Henry to complain, but Henry told his son off for telling tales. John did not forget this childhood humiliation.

FOREST OUTLAW

In 1200 John got his revenge by dispossessing Fulk of his lands at Whittington and giving them to a rival lord. Fulk swore that he would not serve such a king and with his brothers took to the forests of

▲ *Far from the safety of court or castle, hunting with a few retainers, kings and great lords were vulnerable to attack. King John was ambushed by Fulk Fitzwarin.*

Shropshire. There he made his living by robbing King John's wagon trains and his soldiers. In true romance style, he next had an overseas adventure, spending a period as a pirate in the English Channel, rescuing the daughter of the king of Orkney and saving the duke of Carthage from a dragon.

On his return to England he and his brothers heard that King John was holding court at Windsor Castle and travelled to Windsor Forest. One day when King John rode out hunting, Fulk disguised himself as a charcoal burner and led the king into a trap, where his brothers and supporters were waiting. They surrounded the royal party and made the king promise to become Fulk Fitzwarin's friend once more. But John was dishonest, and as

soon as he had been released he sent Sir James de Normandy out with an armed force to capture Fulk.

IN SIR JAMES'S ARMOUR

In the forest, Fulk was warned that the knight and his men were coming, and he laid another trap. He captured Sir James and then exchanged suits of armour and horses with him. Fulk rode into the castle at Windsor, pretending to be Sir James, and presented the real Sir James to the king as 'the prisoner Fulk Fitzwarin'. Fulk got away with the trick and rode off on a fresh horse provided by King John, before the king had lifted the visor of the prisoner's helmet and discovered that his leading knight had been humiliated by the forest outlaw.

Subsequently there was another great battle in the forest during which Fulk was injured and his brother William was taken captive. Fulk escaped on a horse with the Earl of Chester, rode hard to the coast and managed to make his escape to Spain. He enjoyed further adventures, this time on the Barbary Coast of Africa, before he returned to England to free his brother from the Tower of London. Subsequently he captured King John once more while the king was out hunting, and finally he was able to force him to make peace. Fulk was no longer an outlaw and his castle and lands were restored to him.

ROBIN HOOD

Another great figure of English legend and folklore, Robin Hood, made his living as an outlaw in the forests and was often celebrated as a scourge of King John. In the earliest ballads Robin was just a humble yeoman, but from the 16th century, when his stories were printed, he was presented like Fulk Fitzwarin as a noble knight deprived of his rightful lands. Some versions of the tale also identified him as a crusader knight who returned from his service in the Holy Land to discover that

▲ *Emerging from the forest, Robin and other outlaws have the danger and force that were associated with the teeming natural world, outside the order of a town.*

▼ *One great figure of chivalry hosts another, as Robin Hood and his merry men entertain Richard Coeur de Lion in the forest. Robin lost some of his original menace when he was transformed in legend from an anarchic robber to a supporter of the crusader king.*

his lands had been seized by the corrupt officials of the usurping King John.

There was probably never a single historical figure on which the legends of Robin Hood are based, for the name first appeared in the 13th century as a general one for outlaws. By the following century, popular rhymes were celebrating the feats of a particular legendary outlaw of this name. The tradition of Robin Hood was based on the deeds of actual outlaws such as Hereward the Wake, Eustace the Monk and Fulk Fitzwarin.

In the 15th and 16th centuries Robin Hood was incorporated into May Day festivities, with people dressing as characters from the ballads, a practice that was popular at the court of King Henry VIII. In the early ballads the events were said to take place in the reign of King Edward (without specifying exactly which one), but in the 16th century the stories were relocated to the 1190s, when King John's corruption blighted the lives of the people of England.

PART SIX

DECLINE AND LEGACY OF KNIGHTHOOD

The 14th-century English poet Geoffrey Chaucer, in the Prologue to The Canterbury Tales, drew a portrait of 'a true and perfect gentle knight'. Chaucer served as a squire for that great royal patron of chivalry, King Edward III of England, and fought in 1359–60 in France, where he was captured close to Rheims and had to be ransomed as a prisoner. Chaucer emphasized key qualities of the chivalric code in his knight, who from the first day that he rode out as a knight had 'loved chivalrie, trouthe and honour, fredom and curtesie'. He had, the poet wrote, ridden far and wide 'in his lords werre' (in service of his lord), both in Christendom and 'hethynesse' (heathen lands). He jousted three times 'for oure feith' (in support of Christianity) in 'Tramyssene' (Tlemcen, Algeria) and each time killed his opponent. He was a distinguished knight, who remained humble and modest – and had 'no vileynye ne sayde' (never spoken rudely) to anyone. But Chaucer's knight was soon to face new and well-nigh insurmountable challenges. Beginning in the 14th century, the increasing use of artillery guns and the rise of professional soldiers changed the face of warfare and made the knight outmoded on the field of battle; these developments were coupled with the effects of long-term social changes that brought an end to the feudal societies in which knights had emerged and prospered.

▲ Richard II of England became known for arrogance and an arbitrary style of government, which in retrospect can be seen to have undermined some of the central principles of chivalry.

► Geoffrey Chaucer reading the 'Legend of Custance' to Edward III and his Court, at the Palace of Sheen, on the anniversary of the Black Prince's 45th birthday.

TIMELINE OF DECLINE AND LEGACY

1139 Pope Innocent II condemns 'the deadly art, which God hates, or crossbowmen and archers', adding that they 'must not be used against Christian knights on pain of anathema'.

1213 Under England's oldest known military contract Lord Robert of Berkeley meets a debt of 500 marks to King John by agreeing to provide military service in a company of ten knights.

1248 The Islamic Moors use cannon to defend Seville, Spain. They are ahead of western armies in the use of artillery guns.

c.1260 Islamic armies use hand guns in battle against the Mongols.

1262 The Moors use artillery to defend Niebla, Spain.

1281 Italian armies include *scopettieri* (carriers of hand guns).

1292 The prestige of knighthood is declining. In England, gentlemen with an annual income of £40 or more are required to accept the obligations of being a knight.

1303 The Catalan Company, whose knights serve King Peter III of Aragon, are among the first paid 'mercenary' knights.

1326 The city of Florence acquires two wheeled cannon for its defences. This is the first reference to military artillery in western armies.

▼ *By the mid-14th century longbows and crossbows were dominating the battlefield.*

▲ *Sir John Hawkwood began life as the son of an English tanner, was knighted for his service to the king during the Hundred Years War, and found fame and fortune as company captain of the* condottieri *of Pisa.*

1335 Italian Giovanni Boccaccio bases *Filostrato* on the story of Troilus from Benoit de Sainte-Maure's *Romance of Troy*.

1342 The Moors use cannon to devastating effect at Algeciras during a siege.

1346 At the Battle of Crécy the artillery gun is used for the first time in a battle in the field. The English longbowmen also prove very effective in attacking knights.

1348 In the Order of the Garter, founded by King Edward III and the Black Prince this year, knights swear loyalty to the king rather than to Christ and the brotherhood, as they had in the old religious brotherhoods. The creation of new, 'secular' brotherhoods is a significant change.

1363 English knight Sir John Hawkwood, a leading figure in the army of King Edward III of England, joins the White Company of *condottieri* fighting for the Italian city-state of Pisa. He is elected company captain within a year.

1380 Breton knight Bertrand du Guesclin dies of dysentery in the Languedoc. He is buried in the tomb of the kings of France in the Saint-Denis Basilica, Paris.

c.1380 Heavy cannon called bombards are developed.

c.1390 Englishman Geoffrey Chaucer derives his poem *Troilus and Criseyde* from Boccaccio's *Filostrato*.

1394 After a very lucrative career as a leader of *condottieri*, Sir John Hawkwood dies in Florence.

1396 Military artillery play a key role in the defence of Constantinople against the Ottoman Turks.

1408 An account of the deeds of Jean le Meingre, also known as Boucicaut, a romanticized biography of the French knight who is an exemplar of chivalry, is written while its subject is still alive.

1415 English longbowmen prove a lethal weapon at the battle of Agincourt.

1421 After bring captured by the English at the Battle of Agincourt, Jean le Meingre (Boucicaut) dies in captivity in Yorkshire.

1422–61 Under King Charles VII 'the Victorious' in France, the army contains 1,500 cavalrymen serving for fixed pay rather than under any feudal obligation.

c.1430 Portuguese explorations of Africa and the Atlantic arranged and financed by Prince Henry 'the Navigator' of Portugal are driven by crusading rhetoric.

1449 Mons Meg, made for King James II of Scotland, is a bombard capable of firing shots weighing 396lb (180kg).

3 July 1453 French knight Jacques de Lalaing, a great chivalric figure, is killed by cannon fire at the siege of Poucques.

17 July 1453 Another knight falls to artillery; Sir John Talbot, the knight dubbed 'the English Achilles', is killed by gunfire at Castillion. Such is his reputation as a chivalric figure that the French build a chapel in his honour.

1453 In capturing Constantinople, the Ottoman Turks use 68 cannon.

c.1470 The ballad *The Acts and Deeds of Sir William Wallace, Knight of Elderslie* by 'Henry the minstrel' or 'Blind Harry' celebrates the deeds of 13th-century Scottish knight Sir William Wallace.

1508 The Portuguese romance of Sir

Amadis of Gaulis is published and is a bestseller in Spain and Portugal.

1521 After heroically defending Mézières against Holy Roman Emperor Charles V, French knight Pierre de Terrail is admitted to the chivalric Order of St Michael, given his own command and a unit of 100 cavalry – he is the first non-royal to achieve this latter distinction.

1524 A French knight called Pierre de Terrail – dubbed in his time as *le chevalier sans peur and sans reproche* ('the fearless and blameless knight') dies after being struck by a ball fired by an early gun at the River Sesia, Italy.

1525 After defeat in the Battle of Pavia, King Francis I of France declares 'All is lost save honour'. The idea of winning and maintaining honour was a key focus for chivalric action.

1528 Italian courtier and diplomat Baldassare Castiglione's handbook *The Courtier* is published in Venice. It teaches how to be a Renaissance gentleman, describing life at the court of Duke Guidobaldo da Montefeltro of Urbino in the early 1500s. The book's appearance is emblematic of a social shift in which the gentleman replaces the knight as an ideal.

1559 King Henry II of France is fatally injured jousting in the Place des Vosges, Paris, during a tournament held to celebrate the marriage of his daughter to King Philip II of Spain. A piece of his opponent's shattered lance enters the king's visor and drives through his brain.

7 October 1571 After the Christian 'Holy League' summoned by Pope Pius V defeats the Ottoman Empire's fleet in the naval Battle of Lepanto, the Church declares the day the Feast Day of St Mary of Victory.

1575 A minstrel performs a romance about Arthurian knight Sir Gawain as part of the celebrations at Kenilworth Castle for Queen Elizabeth I of England.

1579–90 On 17 November each year for 11 years Elizabeth I marks the anniversary of her accession to the throne in 1558 with a tournament: the 'Accession Day Tilt' at Whitehall Palace.

1588 Troops in the Italian Army are offered crusading privileges to fight Protestant England in the Armada.

1596 Richard Johnson writes the English prose romance *The Famous History of the Seven Champions of Christendom*, celebrating the legendary feats of the patron saints of England, Wales, Ireland, Scotland, Italy, France and Spain.

1602 William Shakespeare's tragic play *Troilus and Cressida* is based in part on Chaucer's *Troilus and Criseyde*, which in turn drew its inspiration via Italian poet Boccaccio from Benoit de Sainte-Maure's *Romance of Troy* of c.1160.

1687 A second Holy League summoned Pope Innocent XI defeats the Ottomans at the second Battle of Mohacs (Hungary).

1839 The 13th Earl of Eglington seeks to revive the chivalric tournament with jousting at Eglington Castle in Ayrshire.

6 June 1944 The word 'crusade' remains resonant of shared struggle and fierce commitment to a cause: US President Franklin D Roosevelt's prayer to mark the launch of the Allied forces' D-Day campaign in Normandy calls the struggle against Germany 'our united crusade'.

1958 TH White's *The Once and Future King* retells stories from the Arthurian tradition.

1960 White's book is the inspiration for the Broadway musical *Camelot!* by Alan Jay Lerner and Frederick Loewe.

1963 After the assassination of US President John F Kennedy the promise of his administration is likened to the fall of Camelot. The name of Arthur's court has come to be used to describe any golden age doomed to end before its time.

1981 onwards The continuing appeal of Arthurian legend is reflected by the movies such as *Excalibur* (1981, directed by John Boorman), *First Knight* (1995, directed by Jerry Zucker), *King Arthur* (2004, directed by Antoine Fuqua) and *Tristan and Isolde* (2006, directed by Ridley Scott).

2001 *A Knight's Tale* a movie directed by Brian Helgeland stars Heath Ledger masquerading as a knight, and features the historical figure of Chaucer.

2005 The success of the movie *Kingdom of Heaven* set during the build up to the taking of Jerusalem by Saladin in 1187, reflects the continuing interest in and resonance of crusading.

2009–10 New angles for examining the tales of Camelot include BBC TV's drama series *Merlin*, featuring a young Arthur.

▼ *Crusaders defend Jerusalem in the movie Kingdom of Heaven, 2005.*

CHAPTER TWENTY-THREE

THE END OF AN ERA

The Battle of Crécy in 1346 saw the first appearance on a battlefield of a new weapon that was severely to undermine the power of the mounted knight – the artillery gun. As the French advanced, their Genoese crossbowmen unleashed an assault on the English, who fought back with their longbowmen and a volley of fire from cannon. The Genoese fled, but the French continued their advance. Italian chronicler Giovanni Villani reported that at the battle's end 'the entire plain was strewn with men brought low by arrows and cannon balls'. Crécy was still a high point in the age of chivalry but the social, political and military changes that were to make chivalry outmoded can be traced back to this date.

Social and political conditions were becoming significantly different from those that had brought knighthood into being – the feudal system was eroding, and the nature of war was altering as kings needed armies for long-distance campaigns. Knights were becoming a minority in armies, and were generally fighting for a fee rather than as a feudal duty to their lord. The rise of the bowmen, the use of infantry and the appearance of artillery made knights less effective as a fighting force. At the same time, the ideal of an international chivalric brotherhood had been deflated as the Crusades petered out in disillusionment and failure. Knights were increasingly grouped in secular brotherhoods, devoted to the service of an earthly rather than heavenly sovereign. These changes played out over the following 250 years, with the result that by the 17th century knights had become something of an anachronism.

▲ *Cannon are depicted in a scene from a siege in 1400.*

◄ *The cannon at the Battle of Crécy marked a change in the character of warfare.*

THE CHANGING FACE OF WARFARE
THE RISE OF INFANTRY AND THE LONGBOW

Changes in military tactics and the evolving nature of warfare reduced the importance of knights riding into battle as cavalry. The increasing use of disciplined infantry lines, and the effectiveness of bowmen against a cavalry charge, increasingly meant that knights were no longer masters of the field of battle in their traditional role.

ARCHERS VERSUS KNIGHTS

It was once proudly declared by English historians that their country's famous victories over much larger French armies in the Hundred Years War were built on the heroic achievement of yeoman archers. However, this traditional view is now seen as rather outmoded and partisan. The more modern view, while arguing that the longbowmen were not decisive in battle, nevertheless accepts that they played a crucial role – the archers blunted the force

▼ *The Battle of Agincourt began with an exchange of arrows and crossbow bolts before the French cavalry made the first charge. The English archers then unleashed a storm of arrows, driving the French knights back into their own footsoldiers.*

of the charge made by the enemy knights, who were then turned back by the lines of infantry. These infantry lines played the decisive role. They included knights who had dismounted to fight on foot.

THE POWER OF THE LONGBOW

It is easy to see why the longbowmen played such an important part. The arrows unleashed by English bowmen in the army of King Edward III at Crécy in 1346,

▲ *Crossbowmen operate their powerful weapons during a siege of Wartburg Castle, Germany, in the early 14th century.*

or that of Henry V at Agincourt in 1415, could knock knights out of the saddle and rip into a horse's flank, sending the beast crashing to the ground and spilling the rider on to the mud. The archers used yew bows of 1.5–1.8m (5–6ft) in length, strung with hemp. Ordinary arrows were of aspen wood with a conventional tip, but the archers also used heavier ash-and-oak arrows capable of piercing a knight's armour – these were 83cm (33in) long with a very narrow 'bodkin' point. The archers sometimes used arrows with 5cm (2in)-wide barbed heads designed to dig into the side of the enemy horse.

The archers' extraordinary effectiveness in battle derived principally from their ability to fire as many as 15 arrows a minute, one every four seconds, to create a volley. They used a high trajectory so that the arrows rained down on the enemy from above in a deadly storm. They also drove sharp angled stakes into the ground, pointing at the enemy, and stood among them as they fired. As the remnants of the

▲ *In the armies of Europe, mounted and unmounted crossbowmen, often mixed with javeliners and archers, occupied a central position in battle formations.*

enemy cavalry charge came upon them, they withdrew backwards, still firing, and the enemy horses and their riders impaled themselves on the stakes.

THE DEVELOPMENT OF THE CROSSBOW

Bowmen in medieval armies used the crossbow as well as the longbow. The crossbow had a bigger range and better penetrative effect against armour than the longbow. The weapons came into widespread use in Europe as early as the 10th and 11th centuries when crossbows were frequently used in sieges by specialist mercenaries from Genoa (northern Italy) or Gascony (south-west France).

The first crossbows were made mainly of yew wood and horn, and fired a bolt, or 'quarrel', around 30cm (12in) long with a pointed steel head. They had a range of about 275m (900ft) but were difficult to load, and as the weapons were made more powerful they were usually fitted with a windlass to bend the bow. Crossbow bolts were very effective against chain mail – and, as discussed earlier, the desire to provide some protection against the bolt was

▶ *Duelling with hand-axes at tournaments gave knights the necessary practice in fighting on foot.*

one of the key incentives for those who sought to improve knights' armour. In the 15th century even more powerful steel crossbows were developed, with a range of up to 450m (1,500ft). They used a square-headed bolt that was strong enough to crack plate armour.

VULNERABLE TO CHANGE

Knights were not well equipped to cope with changes in military technology. As a class they were conservative – while knights dismounted to fight on foot with the infantry, no member of the chivalric class would have considered becoming an archer. Bows were the weapons of the lower classes: crossbows were initially the weapons of specialist Italian mercenaries, while the archers who won great victories for English armies were peasants. Moreover, the bow was considered to be

an unchivalric weapon because it encouraged fighting from a safe distance rather than in a face-to-face trial involving strength and prowess. Knights considered that using a bow was a sign of cowardice. The early 12th-century *chanson de geste* about the Burgundian chief Girart de Roussillon declares: 'May curses descend upon the first man who fought as an archer, for through fear he did not dare enter the fray.'

THE DECLINE OF KNIGHTHOOD

Military changes did not suddenly do away with knights in an instant. Both longbowmen and crossbowmen were a long-term problem for knights, dating back almost to the first years of chivalry. As early as 1139, Pope Innocent II had condemned 'the deadly art, which God hates, of crossbowmen and archers, must not be used against Christian knights on pain of anathema'; the effect of longbowmen was demonstrated in King Edward I of England's campaigns in Wales in the late 13th century, but knights continued to be an effective force long after that. The changes in military technology, the tactics of warfare, and the subsequent undermining of the role of knights, were slow and gradual – over centuries. In addition, these military evolutions are difficult to separate from the parallel social, political and cultural changes that were also contributing to the decline of the knight.

THE CANNON AND THE MUSKET

THE FIRST GUNS IN BATTLE

One key aspect of the military changes that undermined the importance of knights in battle was the introduction of the gun. Many of the early guns were difficult and dangerous to use, and they were often inaccurate, but they could be deadly even against full plate armour. Their introduction changed the balance of power on the battlefield, serving to weaken the strength of mounted knights and the use of cavalry as an offensive force.

THE ORIGINS OF GUNS

Gunpowder was probably invented in China, although some scholars argue that Arabs or even the peoples of ancient India were the first to develop the substance. One of the earliest guns was invented by Arabs in 1304: it was a tube of bamboo strengthened with iron, that fired an arrow using the explosive power of an early form of gunpowder called black powder. Gunpowder came to Europe in the mid-13th century – the English Franciscan philosopher Roger Bacon (c.1214–94) described its military uses – but guns of any sort were not widely used in battle until the 14th century.

▼ *John of Gaunt, Duke of Lancaster, used cannon during an assault on the town of Brest, France, in 1373.*

EARLY USE OF CANNON

Cannon were wheeled guns that fired iron balls or stones. The earliest reference to their manufacture is from 1326, when the city of Florence acquired two of the guns for defence. The first use of cannon in open battle was at Crécy in 1346.

There was a very wide range of heavy guns, with a wonderful variety of names including veuglaires, vasili, sclopi, pots-de-fer, crapaudines and serpentines. Very heavy cannon called bombards were developed in c.1380. Like many early guns they were inefficient and dangerous.

▲ *Firing produced a strong recoil, which was absorbed into the ground at the rear of the gun and through the wooden support.*

A later example of the bombard was Mons Meg, made for King James II of Scotland in 1449. It could fire shots weighing 180kg (396lb), and was one of the biggest types of bombard ever made.

Because heavy guns of this sort were so difficult to move about, they were mostly deployed in sieges, where they could have devastating effects on both stone and human flesh. They only came into serious use towards the close of the Hundred Years War (1337–1453). However, there are surprisingly few reports of knights being killed by cannon fire – one victim was Jacques de Lalaing, a knight from Wallonia, Belgium, who was killed in this way at the siege of Poucques in 1453 while serving the Duke of Burgundy in putting down a revolt by the people of Ghent. (De Lalaing's exploits were recorded by the celebrated Burgundian chronicler and herald Jean Le Fevre, a veteran of Agincourt, where he fought on the English side, and a member of the Order of the Golden Fleece.)

▲ *Gunners were vulnerable to attack while operating these early hand-held guns, which were very difficult to load, light and control.*

GUNS IN ISLAMIC ARMIES

The development of firearms and heavy artillery proceeded apace in the armies of Islam. The Moors in Spain used a form of cannon for defending the cities of Seville (1248) and Niebia (1262) under siege. Moorish artillery experts served in the armies of the kings of Spain in the mid-14th century. At the siege of Algeciras in 1342, Moorish defenders used cannon to great effect against the Christian besiegers. (The earls of Derby and Salisbury took part in this siege and may well have helped promote the cannon in England.)

The Ottoman Turks were on the receiving end of cannon fire when they were repelled by Byzantine guns during the siege of Constantinople in 1396. They had their revenge when they used 68 Hungarian cannon including 13 huge guns, each with a bore of more than 90cm (35in) and firing projectiles weighing 320kg (700lb), in their capture of Constantinople in 1453.

HAND-HELD GUNS

The first hand-held guns were developed in the 13th century. Called hand *gonnes*, or hand cannon, they were used in Islamic armies fighting the Mongols in *c.*1260 and appear to have been in use in Europe in 1281 when Italian *scopettieri* ('carriers of guns') were listed as fighting alongside crossbowmen. Early hand-operated guns of the 13th and 14th centuries looked like small cannon attached to wooden poles. The infantryman held the barrel under his arm and ignited the powder – hoping that the whole thing did not explode in his face. The early hand-guns were slow to load and difficult to aim, but if a gunner scored a direct hit he could kill a fully armoured knight outright.

More accurate hand-guns such as the arquebus, or hackbut, were developed in the 15th and 16th centuries. They used round balls as missiles, which could kill a knight in plate armour at short range, but at long range would only dent his armour. (New plate armour of this period was tested by firing an arquebus at its breast-plate and the dent from the ball would be made into a feature of the suit by surrounding it with engraving.) The arquebus was replaced by the matchlock musket in the late 16th century. This gun was as much as 2m (7ft) long and fired 4.5kg (10lb) shot, but could not be used in wet weather. During the 17th century the musket became the main weapon used by infantrymen, replacing the pike.

THE RISE OF GUNS

Knights despised gunners as much as they did bowmen, and in the early days Church authorities denounced them as the work of the devil. In practical terms guns had disadvantages: they were slow to load, of limited accuracy, the larger ones were difficult to transport and manoeuvre and, most of all, in bad weather they often could not be fired at all. But their advantages were that their missiles were more effective than arrows against plate armour, the guns were relatively cheap to produce and use in large numbers, and they could

be fired by troops with little or no training – in stark contrast to the longbow, which was so difficult to use properly that the archers needed to be members of an elite force, trained from childhood and even given a special diet.

CANNON AND NEW DEFENCES

The use of cannon in battle and sieges led to the development of new types of fortifications that were better able to withstand bombardment with cannonballs. The traditional medieval ring-shaped or square fortifications with perpendicular stone walls proved to be very vulnerable to cannon. In the mid-1400s in Italy the trace italienne, or star-shaped fort, was developed: this was a low-lying fortification, made from brick and earth since these materials, unlike stone, would not shatter when hit by a cannonball. It was designed in a star shape to give defenders the opportunity to provide covering fire from several different angles.

The first trace italienne fortifications were designed by the Florentine architect Antonio di Pietro Averlino (1400–69), also known as Filarete, in his *Trattato di architettura* ('Treatise on Architecture') of 1465. That great Renaissance man Michelangelo then put the theory into practice when he designed the earthwork fortifications for Florence. The style soon became widely popular, and was found outside Italy from the 1530s onwards.

▼ *The earliest cannon had to be moved into position by hand; the first wheeled gun carriages were developed in the 1400s.*

PAID TO FIGHT

THE RISE OF PROFESSIONAL SOLDIERS

The knight's military role was also undermined by the use of professional soldiers in armies. Beginning in the late 13th century, rulers in Europe had to force knighthood on wealthy landowners whose birth and wealth made them eligible to become a knight. This was a startling change from the situation in the previous two centuries, when achieving a knighthood was the crowning glory of many a life.

In England in 1292, for example, those gentlemen with an annual income of £40 per year or more were required to accept knighthood and its obligations. A principal reason why this kind of law was necessary is that the cost of equipping oneself as a knight, always high, had risen to such a level that many were unwilling to meet it. The recently developed plate armour was made by Italian and German specialists and was extremely expensive. Heavier armour meant that stronger horses needed to be bred: these, too, were very expensive, and a knight needed to take several with him on campaign because the horse, as we have seen, was a favourite target for the archers and was often killed beneath its rider during battle.

THE USE OF MERCENARIES

There was already a substantial history of paid soldiers and of mercenaries serving in armies. Mercenaries were skilled professionals who hired themselves out to the highest payer – such as the Genoese crossbowmen who were working in this way as early as the 11th century. From the time of King Henry I of England (r. 1100–35) onwards, there were some paid soldiers in otherwise feudal armies. Kings would accept *scutage* (payment) in lieu of feudal military service, and then use the money to pay soldiers.

The oldest surviving military contract in England is from 1213: Lord Robert of Berkeley agreed to provide military service, in company of ten knights, to meet a debt to King John of 500 marks. King Philip IV of France (r. 1285–1314) had a considerable proportion of his army in paid service, including cavalry known as gendarmes (from the French: *gens d'armes*, meaning 'men at arms').

The Hundred Years War (1337–1453) saw many paid soldiers in service on both sides. They were generally infantry or bowmen rather than knights, although King Charles VII of France had 1,500 cavalry serving for fixed pay. In this period Swiss mercenary infantrymen won a wide reputation for their discipline and effectiveness fighting with halberds (long spears with axe-like heads), with which they were able to haul a knight down from his horse. These men were available for hire, and their wearing of uniforms and marching to military music were widely influential. Under the influence of the Swiss, the first state infantry regiments were formed in France in the 1450s. This was part of a general movement in the 15th century towards the establishment of professional standing armies.

CONDOTTIERI

The same period saw the heyday of Italian mercenary bands of knights hired by competing Italian city-states. The leaders of these mercenary bands were called *condottieri*, from the Italian *condotta* for the 'contract' by which they tied themselves

▼ *Condottiere Guidoricchio da Fogliano was commander of the mercenary army of Siena, Italy in 1328, and he is commemorated in the famous fresco believed to be by Simone Martini.*

SIR JOHN HAWKWOOD

Leading *condottiere* Sir John Hawkwood came from humble origins as the son of a tanner in Essex, England. He achieved fame fighting in the army of King Edward III of England during the Hundred Years War, and was reputedly knighted for his battlefield prowess by the king or the Black Prince. In 1363, during a break in English–French hostilities, he entered the White Company of Italian *condottieri* in the service of Pisa and was elected their captain within a year. He used his own force of longbowmen, and equipped his knights with lighter armour that made his troops more mobile. In *condottieri* fashion, by 1369 he was fighting for a new paymaster, Perugia, against papal troops and within a few years was fighting for the pope against Florence. He became immensely wealthy, with estates near Florence. Chivalry was a foreign concept to him: he would threaten his employers with desertion in order to get more money out of them. He died in Florence in 1394.

◄ *Sir John Hawkwood was known as 'Giovanni Acuto' in Italy. He married Donnina, illegitimate daughter of his then paymaster the Duke of Milan, in 1377.*

to a particular city or nobleman. The bands consisted principally of armoured knights fighting with traditional medieval weapons. The *condottieri* were famous for their ruthlessness and lack of chivalry: they would negotiate hard, driving their fee as high as they could, and were not above switching sides (even in the middle of a battle) if offered more money.

The first of these mercenary bands were non-Italians. The knights of the Catalan Company formed in 1303 had originally been in the service of King Peter III of Aragon, the Grand Company of *c*.1350 principally contained Hungarians and Germans. The English knight Sir John Hawkwood (see box) led the White Company in the wars of northern Italy for much of the second half of the 14th century.

▶ *Erasmo of Narni was a leading Italian mercenary knight in the late 14th century. His fame was such that the armour in which he fought was preserved for posterity, and Donatello immortalized him in stone.*

In the 15th century the *condottieri* were mostly made up of Italians, and were often noblemen fallen on hard times. Knights in these bands could make a great deal of money in a short period. Towards the close of the century, the *condottieri* bands were mostly overwhelmed by the heavy artillery of the army of King Charles VIII of France, who invaded northern Italy to enforce his rather threadbare claim to the kingdom of Naples.

Probably the most famous *condottiere* was Erasmo di Narni, better known by his nickname Gattamelata ('Honeyed Cat'). He served Florence, Venice and the papacy and eventually became dictator of Padua in 1457. His renown was such that an equestrian statue of him by Donatello was erected in 1445–50, the first such statue since the days of the Roman Empire.

Another celebrated *condottiere* of the 16th century was Giovanni de' Medici (known as Giovanni delle Bande Nere – 'Giovanni of the Black Bands') who led a company of highly skilled Italian mercenaries during the Italian Wars. He initially fought for Pope Leo X in 1516–21 before switching sides in 1522 and joining the forces of Francis I of France. He then briefly went into the service of the Holy Roman Emperor, Charles V, before returning to French service. Giovanni was fighting in the army of Francis I when he was severely wounded at the Battle of Pavia in 1525. He died in 1526 after injuries sustained while fighting in the League of Cognac war. His name probably came from the black bands of mourning on his banner after the death of Pope Leo X in 1521.

THE LAST DAYS OF CHIVALRY

KNIGHTHOOD AS RANK AND TITLE

By the 15th and 16th centuries both the feudal system and the chivalric tradition had undergone profound changes. The age of chivalry was coming to an end.

DECLINE OF FEUDALISM

The rise of towns in the late Middle Ages had undermined the relationship between a feudal lord and his bonded vassals, replacing it with the one between the king and his subjects or between an elected representative body and a citizen. Because of the increasing importance of merchants, and the trade that made them rich, money was becoming more important than land.

Military changes, as we have seen, played their part in a decline of feudalism. The mounted warrior lost status on the battlefield. The supreme symbol of feudal power, the castle, lost its image of impregnability with the advent of more and more effective siege weaponry and guns. Military architects began to build low-lying fortifications from earth and brick such as the trace italienne in place of traditional defences.

▲ *King from the age of 10, Richard II of England became known for arrogance and arbitrary government that encouraged plotting and factions at court and undermined the workings of chivalry.*

CHIVALRIC SHIFT

At the same time there were changes in the philosophical, religious and cultural tradition of chivalry, which had grown up around knighthood and come to sustain it. Despite the erosion of the feudal system, knighthood retained its romance, but it began to function in a different context.

The rise of national feeling had profound effects. The religious brotherhoods of chivalry, in which knights' primary duty was religious, through swearing loyalty to Christ and the brotherhood, were replaced by secular brotherhoods of chivalry such as England's Order of the Garter or the Order of the Star in France, in which knights swore loyalty to their king. The traditional chivalric ideal of an international elite of knights, all equal in their brotherhood, was replaced by bodies of

knights tied to the service of their sovereign, conscious of national difference. Increasingly, distinctions of rank were made among knights, who once had been members of an equal brotherhood in which a humble warrior could be knighted on the battlefield for his prowess and become the equal of a prince.

Another contributing change was religious. The rise of Protestantism was associated with patriotism and national feeling and contributed to the undermining of the ideal of the international Christian brotherhood of knights. The humanistic philosophy of the Renaissance ran counter to the religious ardour that had sustained chivalry and driven knights to the Holy Land in the service of Christ.

PAGEANTS

Tournaments had once fulfilled a necessary role as martial training grounds, and provided an arena in which a man of relatively humble birth such as William

▼ *Baldassare Castiglione (1478–1529), author of* The Courtier, *ushered in a new concern with courtly etiquette among the nobility. When in Rome, he befriended the artist Raphael, who painted this portrait.*

Marshal could win sufficient honour to raise himself to the level of the upper nobility and of royalty. In the transformed world of the 15th and 16th centuries, tournaments were lavish affairs dominated by demonstrations of etiquette as much as prowess. Fighting became less important.

In the 13th and 14th centuries, lesser noblemen held their own tournaments, but the extravagant events of the next two centuries emphasized the pre-eminence of a prince or his near equivalents among the nobility. Tournaments increasingly became pageants, laid on by royal patrons, in order to demonstrate their own magnificence before their leading subjects. Chivalry stopped being a way of life and became an entertainment.

During this period, the chivalric romance that had embodied and sustained the philosophy of chivalry began to fade as a living literary form. Authors under the growing influence of Renaissance ideas turned to classical models. Tournaments abandoned the model of King Arthur and his knights and based their pageants on the warriors of the classical world.

COURTESY AND THE GENTLEMAN

The handbooks on chivalry that had once been so popular gave way to handbooks on courtesy. These books taught not how to be a knight but how to be a gentleman. An early example was *Il Cortegiano* (*The*

Courtier), written between 1513 and 1518 by the Italian courtier and diplomat Baldassare Castiglione. Presented in the form of discussions by courtiers at the Court of Urbino in 1507, the book considers how to act gracefully, with seeming effortlessness; the modesty and qualities that should mark a lady at court; how a courtier should avoid flattery in dealings with his prince; and what forms humour and honourable love should take.

◄ *Edward III confers the Order of the Garter on Edward the Black Prince. The creation of secular bodies of knights was at odds with the spirit of devotion that inspired the members of religious brotherhoods such as the Knights Templar and Hospitaller.*

The idealism of chivalric literature was notably absent in *The Courtier* and similar books on courtesy, which placed more emphasis on presentation, appearance and reputation than on virtues such as humility and bravery, so important in chivalry. In addition, the passion of courtly love was banished; a courtier was expected to show his prince the adoration and committed service that a knight showed his lady.

The gentleman replaced the knight as an ideal. He was a figure of society rather than a warrior. The key to being a gentleman was 'gentle birth': usually it was sufficient to show this status going back for three generations. The knight was a mounted warrior in origin with public status, but the gentleman had no such necessary function. By the end of the 16th century, the word 'knight' had become a title, and indication of social rank.

▼ *Flemish-born artist Marcus Gheeraerts the Elder engraved the procession of the Knights of the Garter in 1576, capturing the spirit of exclusiveness and refinement that was beginning to inform the brotherhood.*

THE ENDURING ROMANCE OF KNIGHTHOOD

REVIVALS OF CHIVALRY

Knighthood retained its romance throughout the long erosion of the feudal system and the decline of chivalric life. In the 16th and 17th centuries, and even later, princes and noblemen looked back with great enthusiasm on the glories of the age of chivalry. Occasionally, even into the 19th century, wealthy lords attempted to revive tournaments and other displays of knighthood.

TUDOR TOURNAMENTS

In England the monarchs of the late Tudor era were already looking back on the golden age of chivalry. Knighthood held a powerful appeal for them – particularly for King Henry VIII, who was a keen patron of and participant in tournaments. Henry designed some of his own armour for competing in tournaments and had an armoury established at Greenwich, near

▼ At the Field of the Cloth of Gold in 1520, kings Francis I and Henry VIII erected grand temporary buildings and tournament lists that made the area resemble a city.

London. He established tiltyards for holding tournaments at Greenwich, adjacent to Whitehall Palace (in Westminster) and at Hampton Court Palace (now part of south-west London).

Henry was matched in his devotion to tournaments by King Francis I of France, and their diplomatic meeting near Calais on 7–24 June 1520 was celebrated with an extraordinarily lavish show of the arts of chivalry. In line with the 15th-century *pas d'armes* ('passage of arms') that the kings were emulating, the event was extravagantly stage-managed.

The two kings and their retinues, numbering 5,000, camped in an array of tents and pavilions decorated with cloth of gold (a fabric made with gold thread and silk) – and for this reason the event became popularly known as the Field of the Cloth of Gold. Henry's camp took the form of a temporary palace – mainly built of canvas and painted cloth over timber frames – measuring 10,000sq m (108,000sq ft). Outside Henry's tent was a gilded fountain spouting claret, spiced wine and water.

Each king had a company of seven knights, supplemented by those who had arrived in response to proclamation of the event and who chose to fight on one side or the other. The kings jousted one against the other, and against the opposing team's knights. Upwards of 300 spears were broken, and one French knight was killed. After the jousting there was a form of tournament, but the knights fought in pairs rather than in an old-fashioned mêlée. There were also contests in archery and the two kings reputedly wrestled for a few throws. The kings and the knights dressed in great splendour in an attempt to revive the glories of the age of chivalry.

ACCESSION DAY TILTS

Henry's daughter, Elizabeth, continued the chivalric revival. On 17 November each year from 1570 until 1590 she celebrated the anniversary of her accession to the throne in 1558 with an 'Accession Day Tilt' at Whitehall Palace. The events were part of a deliberate official mythologizing of Elizabeth as a reigning goddess, and

▲ *Elizabeth I of England shared her father's enthusiasm for the age of chivalry and carried on his revival of tournament events.*

aimed also to replace some of the colour and popular entertainment of Catholic feast days, held no more under the Protestant Elizabeth. Her champion, Henry Lee, was one of her favourites, and he rode in her name in the tiltyard established by Henry VIII in the royal palace at Whitehall while the queen and her ladies, situated in a raised palace window, looked down on the chivalric exploits beneath them like ladies at one of the medieval tournaments.

Even in the beginning of the Stuart era in the early 17th century, the enthusiasm for the age of chivalry endured, and King James I's son Henry, Prince of Wales, was a keen jouster. But he died aged just 18 of typhoid fever in 1612. Thereafter, courtly interest in the chivalric tradition in England was focused on the court masques of Ben Jonson and Inigo Jones.

THE CARROUSEL

Events fashioned like tournaments continued to be held in continental Europe. The jousting and tourneying shrank to near disappearing point, while centre stage was given to displays of horsemanship in events called 'carrousels'. The knights in these extravaganzas often wore imitation

armour. The purpose was to make a show of the magnificence of the sponsor of the event. In time, these gave way to military parades, which fulfilled the same purpose.

INTO THE VICTORIAN ERA

Grand revivals of chivalric tournaments occurred as late as 1839, when the 13th Earl of Eglington held a tournament with jousting at Eglington Castle in Ayrshire. A great crowd of noble guests, enthused by the 19th-century revival of interest in chivalry and medieval life, wore medieval costumes and watched as knights paid homage to Lady Georgiana Sheridan, the Duke of Somerset's wife, in her guise as the event's 'Queen of Beauty'. However, the event was effectively rained off by a Scottish storm that made a mud bath of

▲ *Archibald Montgomerie, 13th Earl of Eglington, had an authentic-looking suit of armour made for his tournament of 1839.*

the lists. Two years in the planning, the event cost no less than £40,000 – the knightly way of life never did come cheap.

THE IDEAL KNIGHT

Right through to the 21st century, the knight has kept much of his lustre as a composite of nobleman and warrior, an idealized expression of personal honour, respectful devotion and religious fervour. His continued appeal is due as much to the knight's role in chivalric literature, with its enduringly popular narratives and affecting elegiac tone, as it is to his historical achievements.

THE LEGACY OF CRUSADING

AND THE MODERN ERA

On 7 October 1571 in the naval battle of Lepanto in the Ionian Sea, the ships of the Christian 'Holy League' commanded by Don John of Austria inflicted a heavy defeat on the fleet of the Ottoman Empire. The Holy League was an alliance of the papal states, Spain, Venice, Genoa, the Duchy of Savoy and the Knights of Malta (as the Knights Hospitaller were by then known). The league was formed by Pope Pius V (ruled 1566–72) to try to wrest control of the Mediterranean from the Ottomans – seemingly all-powerful in the region – after Sultan Selim II (reigned 1566–74) had invaded Cyprus in 1570.

The victory was celebrated as a great triumph for Christendom. The day of the battle, 7 October, was named the feast day of *Santa Maria della Vittoria* (Saint Mary of Victory) by the Catholic Church; in his

▲ *Religious or national war? Pope Sixtus V gave King Philip II of Spain's war against Queen Elizabeth I of England in 1588 the status of a crusade in support of true faith.*

▼ *No longer an invincible force? Christian ships drive the Ottoman fleet to destruction at the celebrated Battle of Lepanto, 1571.*

novel *Don Quixote* (first published 1605), Spanish author Cervantes wrote that Lepanto 'revealed to all the nations of the world the error under which they had been labouring in believing that the Turks were invincible at sea'. For all that, the

victory proved to have little or no long-term strategic effect, for Selim went on to conquer Cyprus in 1571 and in 1574 he drove the Spanish out of Tunisia, where they had made conquests at the start of the century. Nevertheless, Lepanto was important in that it gave a great boost to Christian morale in their long struggle against the Ottomans, which already by that date stretched back more than 200 years to the crusade of 1366, led by Venice, against Sultan Murad I.

The crusading spirit thus remained resolutely alive through the 16th century, and even survived well into the 17th. As late as the 1680s, Pope Innocent XI (ruled 1676–89) formed a new Holy League after the Ottomans besieged Vienna in 1683. The new League included the Holy Roman Empire, Poland, Muscovite Russia and the Venetian Republic and its campaign, culminating in a great victory at the second Battle of Mohacs (Hungary) in 1687, had definite crusading overtones.

▲ *The beautiful Alhambra palace and fort was the residence of the Granada's Moorish kings in Spain. Via the Islamic courts of Spain, classical learning passed to Christian Europe and helped power the Renaissance.*

AUTHORITY TO CALL WARS

Historians generally identify Lepanto as the last major encounter with the Ottomans explicitly preached and financed (through taxes and the sale of indulgences) as a crusade. Yet all authorities agree that it is impossible to pinpoint a single end date for the era of the crusades. Crusading died gradually away, as the authority for calling and organizing wars passed from the pope and the Catholic Church to kings, princes and other heads of state.

The Protestant Reformation played an important part in this process. Beginning in the 16th century, the Reformation split the Church and undermined crusading. Protestants did not accept the basic premises of crusading – that the pope had the authority to call a war or that Jerusalem needed liberating. German theologian Martin Luther declared that there was no call to free Jerusalem from Muslim control – what did the city contain but an empty tomb?

Protestants, in fact, became the object of crusades. In 1588 Spanish forces were offered crusading privileges to fight in the Spanish Armada against Queen Elizabeth I of England – the crusade in this instance being the war waged by Catholic Spain against Protestant England. In this atmosphere, Francis Bacon, the Elizabethan-Jacobean philosopher and statesman was scathing of crusades and crusaders, writing that the wars were 'the rendezvous of cracked brains that wore their feather in their head instead of their hat'.

EFFECTS OF THE CRUSADES

It is clear that the crusades formed a highly significant period in the long and bloody history of the Holy Land. They contributed to the region's legacy of religiously motivated violence, a legacy whose effects are still tragically felt today. They also have a powerful resonance in the long history of distrust and hatred between some Christians and some Muslims.

Certain historians argue that the crusades decisively changed the course of history in the East. According to this argument, crusader attacks on the Byzantine Empire and, in particular, the capture and sacking of Constantinople in 1203 by the armies of the Fourth Crusade, weakened the empire to such an extent that it was

▼ *As in many crusading conflicts before, the Christian victors at Lepanto attributed their triumph to the intervention of the saints, in this case saints Peter and Paul, in battle.*

unable to resist the later onslaught of the Mamluks of Egypt and the Ottoman Turks – far from strengthening the position of Christianity in the East, the crusades catastrophically undermined it.

Others hold that this argument, which characterizes the Mamluks and Turks as a tide from the East that might have been stopped and driven back by a stronger Constantinople, is mistaken. These historians point out that the Byzantine Empire would probably have been too weak to withstand the Mamluks and Ottomans even without the events of 1203 and that crusader activity resulted in enduring Christian possessions in the East (such as Cyprus) that proved to be important bases for the struggle against the Ottomans.

In Europe, meanwhile, the crusades had a significant effect. Crusading endeavours brought both the Iberian Peninsula and the Baltic region within Christendom, in the first place by reconquering land from the Moors and, in the second, by defeating pagan tribes. The crusades also contributed significantly to the growth in wealth and power of the maritime republics of what is now Italy – cities such as Venice and Genoa, whose merchants carried armies and pilgrims to the East and grew rich on the trade in exotic goods, such as spices, sugar and oranges, that they carried back to Europe from the Holy Land and ports in the Byzantine

achievements and endeavours were swept away by the Mamluks in the 13th century. The one truly enduring legacy was cultural, in focusing the attention of Christian Europe on the Holy Land, in encouraging the demonization of non-Christians and in contributing to the creation of a legacy of religious violence in the region.

CONTACT BETWEEN WEST AND EAST

One important side effect of the crusades, evidenced by the success of the trade carried on by Venetian, Genoan and other ships, was the establishment of increased contact between Europe and the East. Many now familiar foodstuffs – including spices (such as pepper, ginger, cloves and cinnamon) and fruits (such as dates, figs and oranges), as well as rice, almonds and cane sugar, according to some accounts – first came to Europe as a result of this trade. Returning traders, pilgrims and crusaders also introduced to European homes glass mirrors of the kind used in Constantinople and rugs and carpets like those found in the castles of Outremer.

Empire. It is no accident that it was in the city-states of Italy, made wealthy by trade, that the European Renaissance began.

By comparison, the crusades had a less permanent effect in the Holy Land and region. While the remains of buildings erected by crusaders, military brotherhoods and settlers of Outremer can still be seen in places, by and large their other

▲ *Venice grew rich on goods from the East – including the loot brought back after the sacking of Constantinople by the soldiers of the Fourth Crusade in 1204.*

▼ *Latterday crusade? A 19th-century painting imagines Christopher Columbus's landfall in the Americas as the coming of a Christian army driven by faith.*

▲ *The Monument to the Discoveries in Lisbon celebrates Henry the Navigator and other Portuguese who contributed to the explorations of the 15th–16th centuries.*

Some accounts claim that the game of chess, which originated in India and spread to the Persian Empire, was popularized in Europe by crusaders, travellers and traders returning from Outremer. Contact between Europeans and Arabs was made not only in the Byzantine Empire and the Holy Land but also in the Iberian Peninsula – itself, as we have seen, a crusade venue.

ANCIENT WISDOM

Contact with Arabs and Moors was, moreover, the route by which a great deal of classical philosophy and science made its way into Europe, where it powered the Renaissance of the 14th–17th centuries. Prior to the crusading era, when Muslim Arabs overran the lands of the Middle East in the 7th and 8th centuries, they found manuscripts and books from the days of ancient Greece and Rome; they were careful to preserve this knowledge, translating many volumes from Greek into Arabic.

Europeans came into contact with this knowledge in the Iberian Peninsula and via the Greek scholars of the Byzantine Empire; many of these Greeks fled to

Europe to escape the Ottoman conquest of Constantinople in 1453. One of these was the theologian and collector Cardinal Basilius Bessarion (1403–72), who had been Latin Patriarch of Constantinople: he brought a priceless collection of books to Italy and gave them to the republic of Venice. They today form the core part of the well-known Library of St Mark's.

CASTLES AND CITIES

The crusades also had an effect on the military and sacred architecture of Europe. The monastic military brotherhoods, such as the Knights Hospitaller and the Knights Templar, were great builders. The Templars, as we have seen, built a great number of churches, many round in form as a homage to the *Templum Solomonis* (Temple of Solomon) in Jerusalem, their original headquarters. The brotherhoods also developed the concentric design in castles – the fortress had two sets of walls, a taller set within, around the 'inner bailey', and a lower outer set, around the 'outer bailey'.

We know that the future King Edward I of England was profoundly impressed by Krak des Chevaliers, the Knights' Hospitaller concentric castle near Homs in Syria, which he inspected while travelling on the Ninth Crusade (1271–72) and later, in association with his builder Master

James of St Georges, used the design in his Welsh fortresses, such as Beaumaris Castle in North Wales.

The crusade era also saw the rise of cities. Just as the maritime cities of Italy thrived, so throughout Europe the spread of towns and cities was driven by trade. In addition, kings such as Richard I of England sold off rights of self-government to municipal boroughs as a way of raising money for their wars. Some historians also suggest that the repeated failures of the crusading armies served to undermine feudalism and contributed to its decline as a form of social organization.

CRUSADING'S NEW FRONTIER

In the 15th and 16th centuries, the exploration of Africa and the Americas was in part informed and inspired by crusading ideology. Portuguese explorations of Africa and the Atlantic, organized and financed by Prince Henry the Navigator, were explicitly driven by crusading ideals – Henry was intrigued by the story of Prester John (the legendary Christian king, believed by many of Henry's contemporaries to reside in the East or in Africa and to be preparing a great war against Islam), and one reason for Henry's exploration of Africa was to seek help in the conquest of Muslim powers in the Holy Land.

The adventurer Christopher Columbus was sponsored in his voyages to the West Indies and central and southern America by Ferdinand and Isabella of Spain, who approved his exploration in 1492 immediately after their conquest of Granada. Columbus later declared that the wealth discovered in central America could fund a new crusade to the Holy Land. The Conquistadores who swept into Mexico and Guatemala, were driven by a desire for gold and land, but also by a fervour for religious conversion informed by the Reconquista. The energy, spirit of adventure and religious devotion that had sustained centuries of crusading fed into these voyages of discovery across the great oceans and thus made an enduring mark in the countries of the 'New World'.

INDEX

▼ *King Arthur's homecoming.*

▲ *Lancelot and Guinevere.*

▼ Medieval heraldic devices.

▲ *The keep of Saladin's castle.*

▲ *Philip I and Tancred (right).*

▲ *The formidable citadel of Aleppo.*

▲ *German crusaders capture Beirut in 1197.*

PICTURE ACKNOWLEDGEMENTS

The Publishers would like to thank the following agencies for permission to produce their images.

AKG: pp3tl, 3bm, 3br, 4tl, 4bl, 8t, 8b, 10t, 10t, 11b, 12b, 14b, 17, 21, 31, 33, 34b, 56b, 39t, 39b, 40, 52b, 60br, 61t, 62b, 63t, 63b, 65tr, 65b, 69t, 77t, 80, 83b, 75t, 89, 91, 95b, 97b, 101t, 101b, 102, 103, 130t, 135b, 136, 150t, 151b, 153t, 157t, 159t, 161br, 161, 168, 173t, 179, 183tr, 188b, 190, 193t, 194, 196b, 197b, 198b, 200t, 202b, 203b, 204t, 205l, 205t, 218b, 218t, 219t, 223t, 224, 225b, 227t, 231t, 236, 246b, 247t, 248t, 251b, 254, 258b, 259b, 261b, 265, 266t, 271t, 274t, 277, 279t, 279r, 287bl, 287br, 294br, 297bl, 298b, 298t, 299tl, 299b, 319t, 319b, 321lb. 342b, 346t, 348, 349b, 349t, 350, 354t, 359, 362, 368t, 370t, 372, 373b, 378t,   391t, 398t, 404t, 408, 409tl, 409b, 413tr, 418b, 418b, 418t, 422, 423 & 438, 433b, 434t, 436b, 436t, 436b, 437t, 437b, 438t, 442b, 445t, 445b, 446b, 446t, 447t, 451, 455b, 457b, 458t, 463, 467t, 468b, 469, 472, 473, 474b, 476t, 477t, 477b, 479, 485t.495t, 498b.

ANCIENT ART AND ARCHITECTURE: pp112t, 130b, 139b, 174t, 220t, 239b, 261b, 297br, 305.

ART ARCHIVE: pp1, 2, 5 & 16, 12t, 15b, 16, 19, 20, 22t, 22b, 23t, 23b, 24t, 24b, 25t, 25b, 26, 27, 27b, 28, 29l, 29r, 30t, 30b, 31b, 32, 36, 37t, 37b, 38t, 43t, 44t, 45t, 45b, 49t, 49b, 50t, 50br, 51, 54b, 57, 58, 60br, 61bl, 61br, 62t, 65tl, 66, 67t, 69b, 76t, 83tl, 83tr, 84, 86b, 88, 95t, 97t, 99b, 104, 107t, 118t, 119b, 120b, 120b, 120t, 121tr, 122b, 123b 128, 129b, 132b, 132t, 135t, 146, 149t, 151t, 162, 174b, 175tr, 175b, 195, 203t, 208, 209, 211, 216b, 217t, 217b, 219b, 221t, 238b, 239b, 243b, 250b, 251b, 253b, 256b, 256t, 257tr, 257b, 261t, 262b, 270, 273t, 278b, 279bl, 280t, 284t, 285b, 286, 289t, 293t, 295tr, 300t, 304tr, 304br, 304br, 306b, 316b, 316t, 318t, 318b, 320t, 324b, 325t, 325b, 326t, 327t, 327b, 358, 360t, 360b, 361t, 361b, 363, 364, 365b, 365t, 367, 368b, 370b, 371, 372t, 373t, 380t, 380b, 381t, 382t, 382b, 491, 492t, 492b, 493t, 493b, 494t, 494t, 495b, 497t, 498t, 328, 329, 332, 333 & 257t, 335, 336b, 337tr, 338t & 459, 338b, 341t, 342t, 343t, 343b, 344t, 346b, 351, 352, 353t, 353b, 354b, 355t, 355bl, 355br, 356b, 357b, 389, 392t, 393t, 393b, 394t, 395, 396t, 396b, 398b, 398b, 405b, 410t, 421b, 425b, 439b, 439t, 433t, 440t, 450, 453 & 460, 454, 455t, 461t, 461b, 465t, 470, 475t, 481t, 484.

BRIDGEMAN ART LIBRARY: pp10b, 11, 13t, 13b, 14b, 14t, 15t, 18, 34bl, 34t, 35, 42b, 43b, 46t, 47t, 47b, 48t, 48b, 50bl, 52t, 53t, 53b, 54t, 54, 56t, 56b, 64b, 64t, 67b, 68, 70b, 71b, 72, 73t, 74& 5, 76b, 78t, 79t, 81tl, 81tr & 75, 81b, 82, 85b, 86t, 87, 90 & 5, 94, 96t, 98t, 98b, 99t, 102b, 105bl, 106b, 106t, 108t, 108b, 109b, 114, 116t, 117t, 117b, 118b, 119t, 121tl, 122t, 123b, 124b, 124b, 125t, 126, 127, 129tl, 129tr, 130, 132b, 133t, 134b, 134t, 137t, 138, 139t, 140t, 140b, 141t, 142, 144, 145t, 145b, 147t, 147b, 148t, 148b, 149t, 152t, 153b, 154, 155t, 157b, 158, 159bl, 160b, 160t, 166b, 169t, 169b, 170, 171t, 172b, 173, 175tr, 176t, 176b, 177t, 177b, 178, 180, 181t, 183b, 184b, 185t, 186, 187tl, 187b, 187tr, 188t, 189t, 189b, 191t, 191b, 192t, 192b, 196t, 197t, 199t, 199b, 200b, 201b, 202t, 204b, 207, 210, 214, 215t, 215b, 220b, 221t, 222b, 223b, 225t, 226, 227b, 228b, 229t, 229b, 230, 231b, 232b, 233t, 233b, 234, 235t, 236, 238t, 240, 241, 242, 243t, 244t, 244b, 245, 246t, 247b, 249b, 249t, 249b, 250t, 252, 253tl, 257tl, 258tl, 258t, 259t, 260t, 263t, 263b, 264t, 266b, 267, 268t, 268b, 269t, 269b, 271b, 272t, 272b, 273b, 274b, 275, 276, 278t, 280b, 282, 283, 284b, 285tl, 285tr, 287t, 288, 289b, 290bl, 290t, 290br, 291b, 291t, 292b, 293b, 294bl, 294t, 296bl, 294t, 296t, 296t, 297t, 300b, 301t, 301b, 302t, 302b, 303t, 304bl, 304t, 305t, 305b, 307, 308t, 308b, 309b, 310b, 311t, 311b, 312b, 312t, 313t, 313b, 314t, 314b, 315, 317t, 320b, 322b, 322t, 323, 324t, 326b, 334, 335t, 336tr, 337tr, 339, 340t, 340b, 341b, 341t, 344b, 345, 347t, 347b, 356t, 366, 369t, 374b, 375t, 376, 377t, 377b, 381b, 383t, 383b, 388, 390, 391b, 392b, 393t, 394b, 397t, 397b, 399, 400, 402t, 403, 405t, 406, 407b, 409tr, 410b, 411b,412, 413tl, 414b, 414t, 416, 417t, 417b, 419, 420t, 420b, 421t, 424, 426, 427t, 427b, 428t, 428b, 429, 431t, 431b, 432b, 432t, 434b, 435t, 435b, 439t, 439b, 440b, 441t, 442t, 443t, 444, 447b, 448t, 449t, 451b, 452, 456, 457t, 458b, 459, 462, 464, 465tl, 466, 467b, 468t, 473b, 474t, 475b, 476b, 478t, 478b, 480b, 480t, 481b, 482t, 482b, 483 & 471, 482t, 485b, 490, 496t, 497b, 499t, 499b, 500, 501tr, 501tl, 502t, 502b, 503b, 504t, 504b.

ISTOCK: pp35, 59, 71t, 78, 96, 100, 105, 166t, 167, 171, 181b, 235b, 264b, 295tl, 317b, 374, 375, 337, 402, 443. 503t, 505.